CONNECT FEATURES

Interactive Applications

Interactive Applications offer a variety of automatically graded exercises that require students to **apply** key concepts. Whether the assignment includes a *click and drag*, *video case*, or *decision generator*, these applications provide instant feedback and progress tracking for students and detailed results for the instructor.

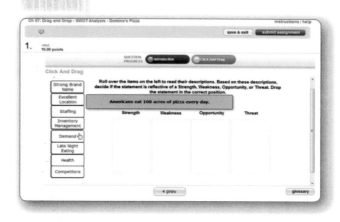

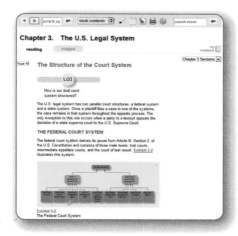

eBook

Connect includes a media-rich eBook that allows you to share your notes with your students. Your students can insert and review their own notes, highlight the text, search for specific information, and interact with media resources. Using an eBook with Connect gives your students a complete digital solution that allows them to access their materials from any computer.

Tegrity

Make your classes available anytime, anywhere. With simple, one-click recording, students can search for a word or phrase and be taken to the exact place in your lecture that they need to review.

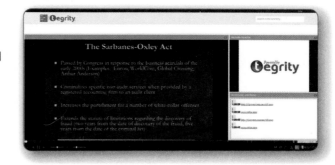

Connect Insight

The first and only analytics tool of its kind, Connect Insight is a series of visual data displays, each of which is framed by an intuitive question and provides at-a-glance information regarding how an instructor's class is performing. Connect Insight is available through Connect titles.

EASY TO USE

Learning Management System Integration

McGraw-Hill Campus is a one-stop teaching and learning experience available to use with any learning management system. McGraw-Hill Campus provides single sign-on to faculty and students for all McGraw-Hill material and technology from within the school website. McGraw-Hill Campus also allows instructors instant access to all supplements and teaching materials for all McGraw-Hill products.

Blackboard users also benefit from McGraw-Hill's industry-leading integration, providing single sign-on to access all Connect assignments and automatic feeding of assignment results to the Blackboard grade book.

The **Best** of **Both Worlds**

POWERFUL REPORTING

Connect generates comprehensive reports and graphs that provide instructors with an instant view of the performance of individual students, a specific section, or multiple sections. Since all content is mapped to learning objectives, Connect reporting is ideal for accreditation or other administrative documentation.

The Legal and Regulatory Environment of **BUSINESS**

Seventeenth Edition

Marisa Anne **PAGNATTARO**
Josiah Meigs Distinguished Teaching Professor of Legal Studies,
University of Georgia

Daniel R. **CAHOY**
Professor of Business Law and Dean's Faculty Fellow,
Pennsylvania State University

Julie Manning **MAGID**
Associate Professor of Business Law,
Indiana University

O. Lee **REED**
Emeritus Professor of Legal Studies, University of Georgia

Peter J. **SHEDD**
University Professor Emeritus of Legal Studies, University of Georgia

Mc Graw Hill Education

THE LEGAL AND REGULATORY ENVIRONMENT OF BUSINESS, SEVENTEENTH EDITION

Published by McGraw-Hill Education, 2 Penn Plaza, New York, NY 10121. Copyright © 2016 by McGraw-Hill Education. All rights reserved. Printed in the United States of America. Previous editions © 2013, 2010, and 2008. No part of this publication may be reproduced or distributed in any form or by any means, or stored in a database or retrieval system, without the prior written consent of McGraw-Hill Education, including, but not limited to, in any network or other electronic storage or transmission, or broadcast for distance learning.

Some ancillaries, including electronic and print components, may not be available to customers outside the United States.

This book is printed on acid-free paper.

2 3 4 5 6 7 8 9 0 DOW/DOW 1 0 9 8 7 6 5

ISBN   978-0-07-802385-9
MHID   0-07-802385-8

Senior Vice President, Products & Markets: *Kurt L. Strand*
Vice President, Content Design & Delivery: *Kimberly Meriwether David*
Managing Director: *Marty Lange*
Director: *Tim Vertovek*
Director, Product Development: *Rose Koos*
Brand Manager: *Kathleen Klehr*
Product Developer: *Jaroslaw Szymanski*
Marketing Manager: *Michelle Nolte*
Director, Digital Content Development: *Patricia Plumb*
Director, Content Design & Delivery: *Linda Avenarius*
Executive Program Manager: *Faye M. Herrig*
Content Project Managers: *Jessica Portz, Brian Nacik, Sandra Schnee*
Buyer: *Susan K. Culbertson*
Design: *Studio Montage, St. Louis, MO*
Content Licensing Specialists: *Shawntel Schmitt, Rita Hingtgen*
Cover Image: *Nikada/Getty Images*
Compositor: *Laserwords Private Limited*
Typeface: *10.5/12 Sabon Roman*
Printer: *R. R. Donnelley*

All credits appearing on page or at the end of the book are considered to be an extension of the copyright page.

Library of Congress Cataloging-in-Publication Data
The legal and regulatory environment of business / Marisa Anne Pagnattaro, Josiah Meigs Distinguished Teaching Professor of Legal Studies, University of Georgia, Daniel R. Cahoy, Associate Professor of Business Law, Pennsylvania State University, Julie Manning Magid, Associate Professor of Business Law, O. Lee Reed, Emeritus Professor of Legal Studies, University of Georgia, Peter J. Shedd, University Professor Emeritus of Legal Studies, University of Georgia.—Seventeenth edition.
     pages cm
  ISBN 978-0-07-802385-9 (alk. paper)
  1. Trade regulation—United States. 2. Commercial law—United States. 3. Industrial laws and legislation—United States. I. Pagnattaro, Marisa Anne, 1961- author.
KF1600.C6 2015
346.7307—dc23

                                    2014037061

The Internet addresses listed in the text were accurate at the time of publication. The inclusion of a website does not indicate an endorsement by the authors or McGraw-Hill Education, and McGraw-Hill Education does not guarantee the accuracy of the information presented at these sites.

www.mhhe.com

Marisa Anne **PAGNATTARO**

Marisa Anne Pagnattaro is Josiah Meigs Distinguished Teaching Professor of Legal Studies in the Terry College of Business at the University of Georgia. She received her Ph.D. in English at the University of Georgia, her J.D. from New York Law School, and her B.A. from Colgate University. Prior to joining the Georgia faculty, Dr. Pagnattaro was a litigation attorney with Kilpatrick & Cody (now known as Kilpatrick Townsend) in Atlanta. Dr. Pagnattaro is the recipient of numerous teaching awards, including the Richard B. Russell Undergraduate Teaching Award and Terry College of Business Excellence in Teaching Award. She also won the Academy of Legal Studies in Business Charles M. Hewett Master Teacher Competition in 2010. She is the author of many scholarly articles on national and international employment law issues, as well as labor issues related to international trade and the protection of trade secrets in China. She is an active member of the Academy of Legal Studies in Business and is a former Editor in Chief of the *American Business Law Journal*.

Daniel R. **CAHOY**

Dan Cahoy is a Professor of Business Law and Dean's Faculty Fellow in the Smeal College of Business at the Pennsylvania State University. He is a registered patent attorney, with a J.D. from the University of New Hampshire School of Law and a B.A. from the University of Iowa. Prior to joining Penn State, Professor Cahoy was a litigator at an intellectual property firm in New York City, where he specialized in pharmaceutical and biotechnology cases. He is the author of numerous scholarly articles on technology law, regulatory policy, and sustainability, and he received a Fulbright Scholarship in 2009 to serve as the Visiting Chair in International Humanitarian Law at the University of Ottawa. He is a former Editor in Chief of the *American Business Law Journal* and is an elected member of the Executive Committee of the Academy of Legal Studies in Business.

Julie Manning **MAGID**

Julie Manning Magid is an Associate Professor of Business Law and a Kelley Venture Fellow in the Kelley School of Business at Indiana University. She received her J.D. from the University of Michigan Law School and her A.B. from Georgetown University. Prior to joining the Kelley School faculty, Professor Magid was a litigation attorney specializing in employment and business litigation. Professor Magid is recognized for her teaching in the undergraduate,

graduate, specialized graduate, and online teaching environments, with numerous teaching awards, including the Kelley School of Business MBA Teaching Excellence Award and the Schuyler F. Otteson Undergraduate Teaching Excellence Award. Her teaching received international recognition from the Academy of Legal Studies in Business as the overall winner of the Charles M. Hewitt Master Teacher Award. Professor Magid is the author of numerous scholarly articles and book chapters focused on public policy related to health care, gender, innovation, and privacy. She is a Life Sciences Research Fellow with the Center for the Business of Life Science and a member of the Editorial Board of the *American Business Law Journal*.

O. Lee **REED**

Lee Reed retired in 2010 as the Scherer Chair in Public Affairs and Josiah Meigs Distinguished Teaching Professor in the Terry College of Business at the University of Georgia. He continues to be active at UGA as Emeritus Professor of Legal Studies in Business. He received his Doctor of Law degree at the University of Chicago and a B.A. degree at Birmingham-Southern College. Professor Reed holds a J.D. degree from the University of Chicago. A former president of the Academy in Legal Studies in Business, he has received five national research awards for his scholarly articles and is former Editor in Chief of the *American Business Law Journal*. He has also testified before the Federal Trade Commission and has twice written invited introductions for *The Advertising Law Anthology*. Professor Reed is a frequent speaker to trade and scholarly groups on the fundamental importance of the rule of law and property to the private market system.

Peter J. **SHEDD**

Peter Shedd is the University Professor Emeritus of Legal Studies in the Terry College of Business at the University of Georgia where he received his B.B.A. and J.D. degrees. He also has been a Visiting Professor in the Ross School of Business at the University of Michigan and the Warrington College of Business at the University of Florida. Professor Shedd has extensive experience as a teacher, researcher, administrator, and author of business-related texts. His teaching of undergraduate and MBA courses has earned Professor Shedd numerous teaching awards including being named a Josiah Meigs Distinguished Teaching Professor. Professor Shedd is an active member of the Academy of Legal Studies in Business and its Southeastern Regional. He served as national president during 1999–2000. Professor Shedd is a member of the State Bar of Georgia and is an experienced arbitrator and mediator.

This seventeenth edition continues the long, rich tradition of our commitment to presenting timely examples and cases that underscore the relevance of the law for business. We are passionate about helping students understand the importance of the legal and regulatory environment of business. Our goal is to make this text accessible, and we hope that they will embrace the study of the law with enthusiasm. In this preface, we strive to highlight themes, additions, and pedagogical devices—including important electronic features—that are key to this edition.

The Seventeenth Edition: Themes and New Additions

With each new edition, we endeavor to maintain the reputation of this text as being the most up-to-date on the latest important developments in the law for business. As we prepare each new edition, we consider the events that affect the business environment and discuss how to incorporate them into the text. Because of the ongoing fallout from the 2008 financial crisis, we continue to highlight the regulatory responses in this edition. Other additions to the seventeenth edition include the Affordable Care Act, focusing on *National Federation of Independent Business v. Sebelius* as the lead case, an elaborated discussion about fraud, and a new section on privacy. We also added a number of recent federal cases and Supreme Court decisions from the 2013–2014 term.

Each chapter includes a range of relevant examples and case opinions, with key points noted for each case. Sidebars within each chapter provide students and instructors with opportunities to learn about topics that illustrate the principles discussed within the text. Marginal comments also reinforce key themes and points of emphasis. We hope that that this layering of the law with examples reinforces each student's understanding of the law for business.

We believe that this text is well suited for both legal environment and business law classes. The fundamental message we wish our readers to grasp is that the law is at the core of the private market. The law determines ownership and protects owners. Based on this knowledge, individuals can make informed decisions about how the law can be strategically used to protect their rights.

Overall, it is important for our readers—primarily business students—to appreciate the crucial role of the law for business and to consider how it can be used for strategic advantage in the market.

Organization of the Seventeenth Edition

This edition consists of 22 chapters, divided into four parts. Part One introduces students to the legal foundations for business. The first chapter in this section underscores the importance of the legal environment of business to appreciate the role of law as the foundation for business in the private market system. This section also includes a chapter on ethics, as well as three chapters pertaining to dispute resolution: courts, litigation, and alternative dispute resolution. Lastly, this first part includes a chapter on the U.S. Constitution (including the Commerce Clause) and its fundamental role in the legal system for business.

Part Two consists of basic legal principles, incorporating eight chapters: property, contract formation, contractual performance, torts, intellectual property, international law, criminal law, and corporate governance/business organizations. These chapters are designed to help students learn basic legal principles, as well as how to identify them in business contexts.

Part Three details the regulatory landscape for business. Five chapters cover essential regulatory aspects of business: the regulatory process, anti-trust, financial and securities regulation, privacy and consumer protection, and environmental regulation.

The final section, Part Four, contains three chapters pertaining to the employer–employee relationship: discrimination, employment laws (including agency), and the labor–management relationship.

Taken together, these chapters should provide students with a comprehensive, yet accessible, sense of the laws and regulations crucial for companies doing business in the United States.

Authorship Team

One of the strengths of this text is its continuity of authorship and the coordination among the authorship team. Marisa Pagnattaro, who joined the team on the fourteenth edition, has undertaken the lead role on this edition. Dan Cahoy, who began on the sixteenth edition, has played a significant role in shaping this edition. Lee Reed joined the team in 1977 on the fourth edition. His legal philosophy continues to influence the text. Peter Shedd, who has long been, and continues to be, a steward of the text, joined the book as a co-author on the eighth edition in 1990. We are all very pleased to welcome Julie Manning Magid to the seventeenth edition. Her legal expertise and demonstrated teaching excellence enrich this edition.

Pedagogy

This seventeenth edition continues the reputation of our prior editions for having many valuable teaching elements. The following list highlights the various pedagogical tools in this edition:

- **Learning Objectives**—each chapter begins with a list that guides the students reading, studying, and learning. These learning objectives were designed with AACSB guidelines in mind.
- **Marginalia**—in the margins, each chapter includes notes, points of emphasis, definitions, quotes, and recommendations about what to do and what to avoid. These notations emphasize key points throughout each chapter.

- **Sidebars**—examples or further descriptions are separated from the text into boxes labeled "sidebars." As in the courtroom setting, when a judge calls for a conversation with the lawyers away from the jury, these boxes are sidebars to the overall discussion. Through these sidebars, we believe you will find the text is brought to life with business-related examples.

- **Cases**—except for the first two chapters, chapters include edited portions of actual court decisions. These cases contain the parties' arguments and the judge's decision of the issues. We have deleted most of the procedural aspects, citations, and footnotes. In addition to the edited cases, some of the sidebars contain references to cases that further illustrate points in the text.

- At the end of each case, **Key Points** are set forth to help students focus on the main points of each case.

- **Concept Summaries**—at appropriate points in each chapter, a summary of the preceding material appears. Through these summaries, complex and lengthy presentations are easily reviewable by the reader.

- **Key Terms**—a list of critical words or phrases is found at the end of each chapter. These terms are boldfaced in the text, and definitions are repeated in the glossary.

- **Review Questions and Problems**—following the text of each chapter is a series of questions and problems. These are tied to the various sections of each chapter and serve as an overview of the material covered.

- **Business Discussions**—the last item in each chapter is a factual situation designed to stimulate conversation among students causing them to review the material within the chapter.

Acknowledgments

We are all very proud to congratulate Jere Morehead on becoming the University of Georgia's 22nd president. He undertook this role in 2013, having previously served as senior vice president for academic affairs and provost. Recognized as a Josiah Meigs Distinguished Teaching Professor, he has always been a dedicated member of the faculty, committed to excellence in student learning. He was part of the authorship team for the tenth through sixteenth editions of this text. Although he is not part of the authorship team on this edition, his valuable contributions over seven editions and his support for the authorship team continue to endure in this edition.

We also want to thank a number of people who contributed to the seventeenth edition. We greatly appreciate the efforts of our team at McGraw-Hill: Tim Vertovec, Kathleen Klehr, Jarek Szymanski and Jessica Portz. This is their first edition working on this text, and we greatly appreciate their support of the authorship team and the development of crucial new electronic features of the text. We are also grateful to all of the regional sales team representatives for their enthusiastic marketing support.

The following colleagues gave of their time and provided insight during the review process. For their expert comments and suggestions, we are most grateful.

Perry Binder	Georgia State University
Marsha Cooper	California State University, Long Beach
Mark Edison	North Central College
Howard Ellis	Millersville University of Pennsylvania
Ken Ginsberg	Hodges University
Earl Clayton Hipp, Jr.	Wake Forest University
Johndavid Kerr	Harris-Stowe State University
Michael Koval	Salisbury University
Sharlene McEvoy	Fairfield University
Michael Monhollon	Hardin-Simmons University
Nancy Oretskin	New Mexico State University
David Orozco	Florida State University
Susan O'Sullivan-Gavin	Rider University
Debra Strauss	Fairfield University
Byron Stuckey	Dallas Baptist University
Lee Usnick	University of Houston, Downtown

Finally, we thank all of the professors and students who have used or are using our text. Your feedback continues to be important. Please feel free to share your thoughts with us. Your feedback also may be sent to The McGraw-Hill Companies.

Marisa Anne PAGNATTARO
Daniel R. CAHOY
Julie Manning MAGID
O. Lee REED
Peter J. SHEDD

This seventeenth continues the reputation of our prior editions for having many valuable teaching elements. In an effort to provide even more guidance and relevance for students, this edition introduces margin notes and comments and sidebars.

learning *objectives*

New to this edition are Learning Objectives at the beginning of each chapter. These objectives will act as a helpful road map of each chapter, narrowing the focus of each topic for both instructor and students. You will also find these Learning Objectives tagged for every test bank question to ensure that key points from each chapter are covered in every quiz and exam.

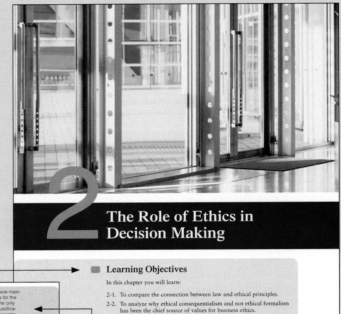

2 The Role of Ethics in Decision Making

Learning Objectives

In this chapter you will learn:

2-1. To compare the connection between law and ethical principles.

2-2. To analyze why ethical consequentialism and not ethical formalism has been the chief source of values for business ethics.

2-3. To generate an individual framework for ethical values in business.

2-4. To evaluate the obstacles and rewards of ethical business practice in our property-based legal system.

---

plant's profitability, yet the home office does not appreciate the difficulties under which the plant is operating. In such a situation the overemphasis on profit can easily lead to the manager's taking ethical and legal shortcuts to ensure profit.

An example of such shortcuts involved Columbia/HCA Healthcare Corporation, one of the major national hospital chains. Following a government investigation, many units of the company were accused of enhancing profits by improperly billing Medicare for laboratory tests and home health care services. It was also alleged that managers were "upcoding," or exaggerating patient illness, in order to get greater reimbursements from the Medicare system. Several managers were criminally indicted and convicted. The company's CEO resigned. To settle charges, the company agreed to pay the federal government $745 million to resolve fraud allegations. As part of its response, the company also stationed ethics and compliance officers in nearly every hospital, in part to prevent managers from "looking good" by producing profits through improper billings.

Does the emphasis on profit in a property-based private market mean that *only* profit must be considered in business decision making? For an example of a nation where not only profit is important in business, see Sidebar 2.8.

> "I do not believe maximizing profits for the investors is the only acceptable justification for all corporate actions. The investors are not the only people who matter. Corporations can exist for purposes other than simply maximizing profits."
>
> **–John Mackey, CEO, Whole Foods Market**

Don't forget that a nation is just a large group. This means that "culture matters" in the implementation (or not) of moral values.

sidebar 2.8

The Swedish Example of *Lagom*

The Swedes have a strong property-based private market, but the business emphasis in Sweden is not solely on profit making. Instead, the Swedes have a strong ethic of *lagom*, which means "not too much, not too little, but just enough."

As a result, the pay of corporate chief executive officers (CEOs) is only a small fraction of what it is in the United States and the average take-home pay of employees (excluding CEOs) varies from highest to lowest by a ratio of only 3 to 1. Sweden provides universal health care, public nursing homes, and subsidized child care and parental leave-taking during a child's first year. When Swedish companies go overseas, they treat employees there with much of the same ethic as in Sweden.

Lagom means that there are few wealthy Swedes, and Sweden's social welfare system of "just enough" depends on a tax rate of approximately twice that in the United States. Note also that Sweden is a small, homogenous country whose citizens share a common ethical culture that is often not found in larger nations.

Source: Susan Wennemyer, "Sweden: The Kindness Economy," *Business Ethics*, Fall 2003.

The Effect of the Group The social critic Ambrose Bierce once remarked that the corporation is "an ingenious device for obtaining individual profit without individual responsibility." He was referring to the fact that individuals in large groups such as the corporation feel less responsibility for what happens in the group than they do for what happens in their individual lives. They may also act differently, and to some extent less ethically, in a group.

That individuals will do unethical things as part of a mob which they would never do alone is widely recognized, and the same pattern can be observed in corporate behavior. Within corporations it becomes easy for a researcher not to pass on lately discovered concerns about the possible

marginalia

In the margins, each chapter includes notes, points of emphasis, definitions, quotes, and recommendations about what to do and what to avoid.

sidebars

Examples or further descriptions are separated from the text into boxes labeled Sidebars. As in the courtroom setting, when a judge calls for a conversation with the lawyers away from the jury, these boxes are sidebars to the overall discussion. Through these side-bars, the text is explained in more detail or is brought to life with a business-related example.

sidebar 2.5

Ethical Norms and Values for Marketers

PREAMBLE
The American Marketing Association commits itself to promoting the highest standard of professional ethical norms and values for its members. Norms are established standards of conduct that are expected and maintained by society and/or professional organizations. Values represent the collective conception of what people find desirable, important and morally proper. Values serve as the criteria for evaluating the actions of others. . . .

ETHICAL VALUES
Honesty—to be truthful and forthright in our dealings with customers and stakeholders.

- We will tell the truth in all situations and at all times.
- We will offer products of value that do what we claim in our communications.
- We will stand behind our products if they fail to deliver their claimed benefits.
- We will honor our explicit and implicit commitments and promises.

Responsibility—to accept the consequences of our marketing decisions and strategies.

- We will make strenuous efforts to serve the needs of our customers.
- We will avoid using coercion with all stakeholders.
- We will acknowledge the social obligations to stakeholders that come with increased marketing and economic power.
- We will recognize our special commitments to economically vulnerable segments of the market such as children, the elderly and others who may be substantially disadvantaged.

Fairness—to try to balance justly the needs of the buyer with the interests of the seller.

- We will represent our products in a clear way in selling, advertising and other forms of communication; this includes the avoidance of false, misleading and deceptive promotion.
- We will reject manipulations and sales tactics that harm customer trust.
- We will not engage in price fixing, predatory pricing, price gouging or "bait-and-switch" tactics.

- We will not knowingly participate in material conflicts of interest.

Respect—to acknowledge the basic human dignity of all stakeholders.

- We will value individual differences even as we avoid stereotyping customers or depicting demographic groups (e.g., gender, race, sexual orientation) in a negative or dehumanizing way in our promotions.
- We will listen to the needs of our customers and make all reasonable efforts to monitor and improve their satisfaction on an ongoing basis.
- We will make a special effort to understand suppliers, intermediaries and distributors from other cultures.
- We will appropriately acknowledge the contributions of others, such as consultants, employees and coworkers, to our marketing endeavors.

Openness—to create transparency in our marketing operations.

- We will strive to communicate clearly with all our constituencies.
- We will accept constructive criticism from our customers and other stakeholders.
- We will explain significant product or service risks, component substitutions or other foreseeable eventualities that could affect customers or their perception of the purchase decision.
- We will fully disclose list prices and terms of financing as well as available price deals and adjustments.

Citizenship—to fulfill the economic, legal, philanthropic and societal responsibilities that serve stakeholders in a strategic manner.

- We will strive to protect the natural environment in the execution of marketing campaigns.
- We will give back to the community through volunteerism and charitable donations.
- We will work to contribute to the overall betterment of marketing and its reputation.
- We will encourage supply chain members to ensure that trade is fair for all participants, including producers in developing countries.

---

concept *summary*

At appropriate points in each chapter, a summary of the preceding material appears. Through these summaries, complex and lengthy presentations are easily reviewable by the reader.

Conflicts of Interest Often embodied in business codes of ethics, avoiding conflicts of interest is a final ethical value flowing from the law, especially from agency law. A conflict of interest occurs when one attempts to "serve two masters," and no agent or employee of one principal can secretly work for another whose interest competes with that of the first principal. That is why a real estate agent may not represent both the seller and the buyer in a real estate transaction without permission from both parties.

Sometimes when corporations "go public" or otherwise sell new stock issues, they will give employees of their customers or suppliers the option of buying a number of the new stock shares at a special fixed price. If the market value of the stock rises, exercise of the stock options can be quite valuable to these employees as they resell the stock at market price. Is it a conflict of interest for employees of other companies to accept these stock options? Does it impair their objective judgment about continuing to do business with the corporation that has given them such a gift? Compaq Computer Corporation, Cisco Systems, and AT&T specifically forbid employees from accepting stock options from their suppliers or customers.

Conflicts of interest also arise in public service. For instance, it is a conflict of interest for a judge or administrative regulator to make a decision involving a company in which he or she owns stock. Note that in this instance the conflict of interest does not involve "serving two masters." The conflict arises because of the ownership interests that will make it difficult for the judge or regulator to make an unbiased decision. In terms of formalism and consequentialism, how do you evaluate the prohibition against conflicts of interest?

concept *summary*

Ethical Values from Legal Regulation

- Respect the liberty and rights of others.
- Act in good faith.
- Exercise due care.
- Honor confidentiality.
- Avoid conflicts of interest.

PROFESSIONAL CODES OF ETHICS

Another important source of business ethics comes from the historic tradition of the professional codes of ethics. Professions such as law and medicine have long traditions of codes of ethical conduct. Other professions, and more recently business and industry in general, have developed and adopted codes of ethical conduct. Here we use portions of professional codes to demonstrate sources of ethical values that come from the development of group standards for ethical conduct.

We begin with selected excerpts from codes of conduct for two professions: marketing and accounting. These codes are the Ethical Norms and Values for Marketers from the American Marketing Association, shown in Sidebar 2.5, and the American Institute of Certified Public Accountants Code

cases

Except for the first two chapters, chapters include edited portions of actual court decisions. These cases illustrate the parties' arguments and the judge's decision of the issues. We have deleted most of the procedural aspects, citations, and footnotes. An alternative to these edited cases appears in some sidebars; there a case may be explained in our own language.

case **4.1**

MAYER v. BELICHICK
605 F.3d 223 (3rd Cir.)

Season ticket-holder brought action against the New England Patriots and league, alleging various causes of action arising out of the team's alleged practice of surreptitiously videotaping the signals of opposing teams.

COWEN, Circuit Judge

Plaintiff Carl J. Mayer appeals from the order of the United States District Court for the District of New Jersey granting the respective motions to dismiss filed by Defendants Bill Belichick and the New England Football League ("NFL"). We will affirm.

1. This highly unusual case was filed by a disappointed football fan and season ticket-holder in response to the so-called "Spygate" scandal. This scandal arose when it was discovered that the Patriots were surreptitiously videotaping the signals of their opponents. Mayer, a New Jersey resident and New York Jets season ticket-holder, initially filed his complaint on September 7, 2007. He named as Defendants the Patriots, headquartered in Massachusetts, as well as the team's head coach, Belichick, a Massachusetts resident. Mayer eventually filed an amended complaint on August 19, 2008, which added the NFL, with its headquarters in New York, as a Defendant. . . .

2. The core of this action is that the Defendants, during a game with the New York Jets on September 9, 2007, instructed an agent of the Defendants to surreptitiously videotape the New York Jets coaches and players on the field with the purpose of illegally recording, capturing and stealing the New York Jets signals and visual coaching instructions. The Defendants were in fact subsequently found by the National Football League ("NFL") to have improperly engaged in such conduct.

3. Plaintiffs contend that in purchasing tickets to watch the New York Jets that, as a matter of contract, the tickets imply that each game will be played in accordance with NFL rules and regulations as well as all applicable federal and state laws. . . .

At their most fundamental level, the various claims raised here arose out of the repeated and surreptitious violations of a specific NFL rule. This rule provides

that " 'no video recording devices of any kind are permitted to be in use in the coaches' booth, on the field, or in the locker room during the game' " and that "all video for coaching purposes must be shot from locations 'enclosed on all sides with a roof overhead.' " . . .

On September 9, 2007, the Jets and the Patriots played the season opener in Giants Stadium, East Rutherford, New Jersey. Mayer possessed tickets and parking passes to this game, and the Patriots ultimately won, 38-14. ESPN.com then reported that the NFL was investigating accusations that an employee of the Patriots was actually videotaping the signals given by Jets coaches at this game. . . .

On September 13, 2007, "the NFL found the Defendants guilty of violating all applicable NFL rules by engaging in a surreptitious videotaping program." . . .

Mayer ultimately alleged nine separate counts in his amended complaint. He asserted, in order, the following causes of action against the Patriots and Belichick: (1) tortious interference with contractual relations; (2) common law fraud; (3) violations of the New Jersey Deceptive Business Practices Act; (4) violations of New Jersey's racketeering statute, (5) violations of the Racketeer Influenced and Corrupt Organizations Act ("RICO"); (6) the infringement of the rights of ticket-holders as third-party beneficiaries; (7) breach of implied contract or quasi-contract; and (8) violations of the New Jersey Consumer Fraud Act ("NJCFA"). Finally, he advanced a breach of contract claim against the NFL on account of its destruction of the videotapes. . . . After they were served with the amended complaint, the Patriots and Belichick filed a motion to dismiss for failure to state a claim pursuant to Federal Rule of Civil Procedure 12(b)(6). The NFL subsequently filed its own motion to dismiss as well. . . .

The District Court, while noting that Mayer alleged numerous theories of liability in this case, appropriately turned to the following dispositive question: namely, whether or not he stated an actionable injury (or, in other words, a legally protected right or interest) arising out of the alleged "dishonest" videotaping program undertaken by the Patriots and the NFL team's head coach. . . . we ultimately conclude that the District Court was correct to hold that Mayer failed to set forth a legally cognizable right, interest, or injury here. . . .

[continued]

Significantly, our ruling also does not leave Mayer and other ticket-holders without any recourse. Instead, fans could speak out against the Patriots, their coach, and the NFL itself. They could even go so far as to refuse to purchase tickets or NFL-related merchandise. . . .

However, the one thing they *cannot* do is bring a legal action in a court of law.

For the foregoing reasons, we will affirm the District Court's order dismissing Mayer's amended complaint in its entirety.

KEY POINTS

- To maintain a lawsuit, a plaintiff must have standing or a legally cognizable claim.
- The Third Circuit found that, because the plaintiff did not have a legally protected right arising out of the alleged "dishonest" videotaping program, he did not state an actionable injury.
- Accordingly, defendant's motions to dismiss were granted.

a lawsuit. A plaintiff must have a legally cognizable claim to maintain a lawsuit. The case reinforces the rule that the courts are careful to avoid overstepping their constitutional role and will only rule on actual cases or controversies.

PERSONAL JURISDICTION

Power to hear a case means a court must have authority not only over the subject matter of the case but also over the parties to the case. This latter authority is called **personal jurisdiction.** Personal jurisdiction over the plaintiff is obtained when the plaintiff files the suit. Such action indicates voluntary submission to the court's power.

Personal jurisdiction over the defendant usually is obtained by the service of a **summons,** or notice to appear in court, although in some cases it is obtained by the publication of notice and mailing a summons to the last known address. This delivery of notice is referred to as *service of process.* Service of a summons on the defendant usually is valid if it is served upon any member of the household above a specified age and if another copy addressed to the defendant is mailed to the home.

For many years, a summons could not be properly served beyond the borders of the state in which it was issued. However, states now have what are called **long-arm statutes,** which provide for the service of process beyond their boundaries. Such statutes are valid and constitutional if they provide a defendant with due process of law. Under the Fifth Amendment to the Constitution, no person shall "be deprived of life, liberty, or property without due process of law." The Fourteenth Amendment provides that states must also guarantee due process protection. Due process requires that if a defendant is not present within the state where the lawsuit is filed, he or she must have certain minimum contacts with the state so that

No case can proceed forward without the existence of both subject matter and personal jurisdiction.

key *points*

At the end of each edited case, key points can be found. These key points help students gasp the essential elements and relevance of each case.

91

review *questions and problems*

Following the text of each chapter is a series of questions and problems. These are tied to the sections of each chapter and serve as an overview of the material covered.

---

concept *summary*

Judicial Review

1. Judicial review allows the courts to review actions taken by legislative and executive branches of government.

2. The philosophy of judicial restraint is sometimes referred to as strict constructionism or a conservative approach.

3. Supporters of judicial activism believe the courts are the appropriate body to bring about social, political, and economic change.

4. The Supreme Court is deeply divided between these two competing views of judicial decision making.

Key Terms

Appeal 67
Appellate court 66
Courts of appeal 67
Diversity of citizenship 69
Federal question cases 68
Federal Rules of Civil
   Procedure 69

Judicial activism 74
Judicial restraint 74
Judicial review 73
Petit jury 63
Small-claims court 67
Subject matter jurisdiction 66
Supreme court 67

Trial court 66
Writ of *certiorari* 67

Review Questions and Problems

Personnel

1. *Judges and Justices*
   What are the essential responsibilities of a trial judge?

2. *Jurors*
   Why have several states eliminated the requirement of unanimity in jury trials?

3. *Lawyers*
   Name the three critical roles a lawyer serves in society. Why have many lawyers and their business clients had such conflict in recent years?

Organization of the Court System

4. *Subject Matter Jurisdiction*
   Mark, a citizen of Georgia, was crossing a street in Atlanta when he was struck by a car driven by David, a citizen of New York visiting Atlanta. The car was owned by David's employer, a Delaware corporation that has its principal place of business in Atlanta, Georgia. Mark sues both David and the corporation in federal district court in Atlanta alleging damages in the amount of $500,000. Does the court have subject matter jurisdiction? Why or why not?

5. *State Courts*
   What role do reviewing or appellate courts play in the judicial process? How do they differ from trial courts?

6. *Federal Courts*
   XYZ makes and markets a product that it believes will help control weight by blocking the human body's digestion of starch. The Food and Drug Administration (FDA) has classified the product as a drug and orders it removed from the market until it can evaluate its use through testing. XYZ disputes the FDA's action and seeks to bring suit in the federal courts. Will the federal courts have jurisdiction to hear the case? Why or why not?

7. *Decisions by the U.S. Supreme Court*
   Susan files a petition for certiorari in the U.S. Supreme Court following an adverse decision in the Illinois Supreme Court on a claim arising under a breach of contract. What chance does Susan have of the Supreme Court granting the petition? What special circumstances would she need to show?

The Power of Judicial Review

8. *Judicial Restraint*
   Define the power of judicial review. How do advocates of judicial restraint exercise that power?

9. *Judicial Activism*
   Define judicial activism. Compare and contrast judicial restraint and judicial activism.

10. *A Sample U.S. Supreme Court Case*
    Why are concurring and dissenting opinions important?

11. *The Nature of the Judicial Process*
    What are the forces that Justice Cardozo says shape the judicial process? How is the law made? In light of the liberal versus conservative divisions in the courts, are Cardozo's observations still relevant?

business *discussion*

1. You have spent the past four weeks away from work serving as a juror in a case deciding whether a pharmaceutical company should be held liable for the heart attack of a woman who took its painkiller, Oxxy-1. The lengthy case has taken a toll on your professional career, and you have many unanswered questions as jury deliberations begin.

- Where does your duty lie in serving on a jury?
- Are you protected against adverse employment action by your firm for missing work to serve on a jury?
- How do you reconcile the woman's prior heart palpitations from years ago with her recent attack? Was her heart already compromised before she began taking the painkiller Oxxy-1?
- Why didn't the pharmaceutical company withdraw the painkiller from the market at the first sign of a problem?

2. You are the president of a large corporation which is in the business of manufacturing, among other things, chemical products used to eradicate termites. You have just reviewed a confidential report, prepared by one of your top scientists, questioning the effectiveness of the product and the claims your business has been making to homeowners, pesticide treatment firms, and the general public. You have heard rumors that a lawsuit will be filed shortly against your corporation claiming that this product is ineffective.

  Who should you turn to for advice?
  Should you destroy the report?
  In which court can a lawsuit be filed?
  If you lose the lawsuit at trial, can you appeal?

---

expanded *business discussions*

The last item in each chapter are scenarios designed to stimulate conversation among students allowing them to review and apply the material within the chapter.

Instructor's Resource Manual

This manual consists of the teaching outline section, transparency masters, a case brief supplement, and video guide. The teaching outline section makes up the bulk of this Instructor's Manual, which is organized by text chapter. This section corresponds with the headings in the text, and typically includes suggestions on points of emphasis, answers to the case questions that appear within each chapter of the text, cases for discussion, and additional matters for discussion. Each chapter of this manual also includes a list of references that might be useful secondary sources of information; and suggested answers to all case questions and responses to the end-of-chapter review questions. The Case Brief section of the Instructor's Manual contains a brief of each edited case found in the text. For ease of use, the briefs are numbered by chapter in the order they appear in the text. There is a reference to the page in the text where the edited case appears. The tear-out format of this supplement allows instructors to remove any material and incorporate it into their lecture notes.

Test Bank

Instructors can test students' mastery of concepts as the instructors create exams with the use of this Test Bank. Organized by chapter, the Test Bank contains multiple choice, true/false, and essay questions. Many of the questions have been modified to correspond with the text's revision. Answers immediately follow each question, along with page references and corresponding Learning Objectives.

EZ Test

McGraw-Hill's flexible and easy-to-use electronic testing program allows instructors to create tests from book-specific items. It accommodates a wide range of question types, and instructors may add their own questions. Multiple versions of the test can be created, and any test can be exported for use with online course management systems. EZ Test Online allows you to administer EZ Test-created exams and quizzes online. The test bank includes true/false, multiple choice, and essay questions, with answers, page references, and level coding.

PowerPoint Presentation

The PowerPoint Presentation provides detailed lecture outlines for discussing key points and figures from the book.

Online Learning Center
www.mhhe.com/reed17e

The Online Learning Center (OLC) is a website that follows the text chapter by chapter. OLC content is designed to reinforce and build on the text content. As students read the book, they can go online to take self-grading quizzes and read chapter review material.

You Be the Judge Online

This interactive product features case videos that showcase courtroom arguments of business law cases. These case videos give students the opportunity to watch profile interviews of the plaintiff and defendant, read background information, hear each case, review the evidence, make their decisions, and then access an actual, unscripted judge's decision and reasoning. There are also instructor's notes available with each video to help prepare you for classroom discussion.

McGraw-Hill *Connect®* Business Law.   Less Managing. More Teaching. Greater Learning.

McGraw-Hill *Connect Business Law* is an online assignment and assessment solution that connects students with the tools and resources they'll need to achieve success.

McGraw-Hill *Connect Business Law* helps prepare students for their future by enabling faster learning, more efficient studying, and higher retention of knowledge.

McGraw-Hill *Connect Business Law* Features.   *Connect Business Law* offers a number of powerful tools and features to make managing assignments easier, so faculty can spend more time teaching. With *Connect Business Law,* students can engage with their coursework anytime and anywhere, making the learning process more accessible and efficient. *Connect Business Law* offers you the features described below.

Simple Assignment Management.   With *Connect Business Law,* creating assignments is easier than ever, so you can spend more time teaching and less time managing. The assignment management function enables you to:

- Create and deliver assignments easily with selectable end-of-chapter questions and test bank items.
- Streamline lesson planning, student progress reporting, and assignment grading to make classroom management more efficient than ever.
- Go paperless with the eBook and online submission and grading of student assignments.

Smart Grading.   When it comes to studying, time is precious. *Connect Business Law* helps students learn more efficiently by providing feedback and practice material when they need it, where they need it. When it comes to teaching, your time also is precious. The grading function enables you to:

- Have assignments scored automatically, giving students immediate feedback on their work and side-by-side comparisons with correct answers.
- Access and review each response; manually change grades, or leave comments for students to review.
- Reinforce classroom concepts with practice tests and instant quizzes.

Instructor Library.   The *Connect Business Law* Instructor Library is your repository for additional resources to improve student engagement in and out of class. You can select and use any asset that enhances your lecture. The *Connect Business Law* Instructor Library includes:

- Instructor's Manual
- PowerPoint Slides
- Test Bank
- eBook

Student Study Center.   The *Connect Business Law* Student Study Center is the place for students to access additional resources. The Student Study Center:

- Offers students quick access to lectures, practice materials, eBooks, and more.
- Provides instant practice material and study questions, easily accessible on the go.
- Gives students access to the Personalized Learning Plan described below.

Student Progress Tracking.   *Connect Business Law* keeps instructors informed about how each student, section, and class is performing, allowing for more productive use of lecture and office hours. The progress-tracking function enables you to:

- View scored work immediately and track individual or group performance with assignment and grade reports.
- Access an instant view of student or class performance relative to Learning Objectives.
- Collect data and generate reports required by many accreditation organizations, such as AACSB.

Lecture Capture.   Increase the attention paid to lecture discussion by decreasing the attention paid to note taking. For an additional charge Lecture Capture offers new ways for students to focus on the in-class discussion, knowing they can revisit important topics later. Lecture Capture enables you to:

- Record and distribute your lecture with a click of button.
- Record and index PowerPoint presentations and anything shown on your computer so it is easily searchable, frame by frame.
- Offer access to lectures anytime and anywhere by computer, iPod, or mobile device.
- Increase intent listening and class participation by easing students' concerns about note-taking. Lecture Capture will make it more likely you will see students' faces, not the tops of their heads.

McGraw-Hill *Connect Business Law*

McGraw-Hill reinvents the textbook learning experience for the modern student with *Connect Business Law*. *Connect Business Law* provides the following:

- An integrated eBook, allowing for anytime, anywhere access to the textbook.
- Dynamic links between the problems or questions you assign to your students and the location in the eBook where that problem or question is covered.
- A powerful search function to pinpoint and connect key concepts in a snap.

In short, *Connect Business Law* offers you and your students powerful tools and features that optimize your time and energies, enabling you to focus on course content, teaching, and student learning. *Connect Business Law* also offers a wealth of content resources for both instructors and students. This state-of-the-art, thoroughly tested system supports you in preparing students for the world that awaits.

For more information about Connect, go to **www.mcgrawhillconnect.com,** or contact your local McGraw-Hill sales representative.

Tegrity Campus: Lectures 24/7

Tegrity Campus is a service that makes class time available 24/7 by automatically capturing every lecture in a searchable format for students to review when they study and complete assignments. With a simple one-click start-and-stop process, you capture all computer screens and corresponding audio. Students can replay any part of any class with easy-to-use browser-based viewing on a PC or Mac.

Educators know that the more students can see, hear, and experience class resources, the better they learn. In fact, studies prove it. With Tegrity Campus, students quickly recall key moments by using Tegrity Campus's unique search feature. This search helps students efficiently find what they need, when they need it, across an entire semester of class recordings. Help turn all your students' study time into learning moments immediately supported by your lecture.

To learn more about Tegrity watch a two-minute Flash demo at **http://tegritycampus.mhhe.com.**

Assurance of Learning Ready

Many educational institutions today are focused on the notion of *assurance of learning,* an important element of some accreditation standards. *The Legal and Regulatory Environment of Business 17e* is designed specifically to support your assurance of learning initiatives with a simple, yet powerful solution.

Each test bank question for *The Legal and Regulatory Environment of Business 17e* maps to a specific chapter learning outcome/objective listed in the text. You can use our test bank software, EZ Test and EZ Test Online, or in *Connect Business Law* to easily query for learning outcomes/objectives that directly relate to the learning objectives for your course. You can then use the reporting features of EZ Test to aggregate student results in similar fashion, making the collection and presentation of assurance of learning data simple and easy.

AACSB Statement

The McGraw-Hill Companies is a proud corporate member of AACSB International. Understanding the importance and value of AACSB accreditation, *The Legal and Regulatory Environment of Business 17e* recognizes the curricula guidelines detailed in the AACSB standards for business accreditation by connecting selected questions in the text and the test bank to the six general knowledge and skill guidelines in the AACSB standards.

The statements contained in *The Legal and Regulatory Environment of Business 17e* are provided only as a guide for the users of this textbook. The AACSB leaves content coverage and assessment within the purview of individual schools, the mission of the school, and the faculty. While *The Legal and Regulatory Environment of Business 17e* and the teaching package make no claim of any specific AACSB qualification or evaluation, we have within *The Legal and Regulatory Environment of Business 17e* labeled selected questions according to the six general knowledge and skills areas.

McGraw-Hill Customer Care Contact Information

At McGraw-Hill, we understand that getting the most from new technology can be challenging. That's why our services don't stop after you purchase our products. You can e-mail our Product Specialists 24 hours a day to get product-training online. Or you can search our knowledge bank of Frequently Asked Questions on our support website. For Customer Support, call **800-331-5094,** e-mail **hmsupport@mcgraw-hill.com**, or visit **www.mhhe.com/support.** One of our Technical Support Analysts will be able to assist you in a timely fashion.

Craft your teaching resources to match the way you teach! With McGraw-Hill *Create™*,  **www.mcgrawhillcreate.com**, you can easily rearrange chapters, combine material from other content sources, and quickly upload content you have written like your course syllabus or teaching notes. Find the content you need in Create by searching through thousands of leading McGraw-Hill textbooks. Arrange your book to fit your teaching style. Create even allows you to personalize your book's appearance by selecting the cover and adding your name, school, and course information. Order a Create book and you'll receive a complimentary print review copy in 3–5 business days or a complimentary electronic review copy (eComp) via e-mail in about one hour. Go to **www.mcgrawhillcreate.com** today and register. Experience how McGraw-Hill Create empowers you to teach *your* students *your* way.

McGraw-Hill Higher Education and Blackboard Have Teamed Up

What does this mean for you?

1. Your life, simplified. Now you and your students can access McGraw-Hill's Connect and Create right from within your Blackboard course—all with one single sign-on. Say goodbye to the days of logging in to multiple applications.

2. Deep integration of content and tools. Not only do you get single sign-on with Connect and Create, you also get deep integration of McGraw-Hill content and content engines right in Blackboard. Whether you're choosing a book for your course or building Connect assignments, all the tools you need are right where you want them—inside of Blackboard.

3. Seamless grade books. Are your tired of keeping multiple grade books and manually synchronizing grades into Blackboard? We thought so. When a student completes an integrated Connect assignment, the grade for that assignment automatically (and instantly) feeds your Blackboard grade center.

4. A solution for everyone. Whether your institution is already using Blackboard or you just want tor try Blackboard on your own, we have a solution for you. McGraw-hill and Blackboard can now offer you easy access to industry leading technology and content, whether your campus hosts it, or we do. Be sure to ask your local McGraw-Hill representative for details.

The **Best** of **Both Worlds**

brief table of *contents*

Part TWO   Basic Legal Principles   183

7   The Property System   186

Introduction to the Property-Based Legal System   188

Rationale for the Property System   190

THE PROBLEM OF LIMITED RESOURCES   190

PROPERTY AND PROSPERITY   191

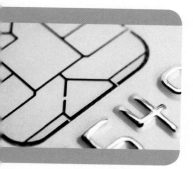

Part FOUR   The Employer–Employee Relationship   613

Part ONE

Introduction: Legal Foundations for Business

In the twenty-first century, business managers who understand how to handle legal challenges will be in a position to use law to their strategic advantage. As President John Adams said that the United States is a nation "of law." Certainly, law is all around us. The news media are full of stories about law, and many of our most popular television programs concern lawyers, courts, and law enforcement. Law surrounds how we buy and sell things, when we can drive a car and vote, and who we can see for many licensed services. Law taxes and punishes us as well as grants rights and privileges. Marriage and divorce apply rules of law, and even birth and death have legal significance. The conduct of modern business is hardly possible without the support of law, and everything you own is yours because of law. Part One of this book helps you understand the legal foundations for business.

Chapter 1 emphasizes the importance of understanding the fundamental role of law for business. The chapter explains that there are understandable organizing principles to the legal system, and it asserts that these principles—law, the rule of law, and property— provide a necessary foundation for successful modern business. Chapter 1 also covers the concepts of jurisprudence, explains the sources of law, sets out various classifications of law,

identifies legal sanctions, and introduces the concept of corporate governance. A good part of what you do in this course is to learn a legal vocabulary. Even more important, you must then learn to apply it. Chapter 1 gets this important process under way.

Chapter 2 emphasizes that the social basis of legal rules in a democracy are the traditional values, morals, and ethics of society. In a democracy, law is a very significant expression of society's moral beliefs and concerns. Law often prohibits behavior that we consider morally wrong and permits or tolerates customary behaviors. In business, ethical issues frequently concern property relationships between employees and employers, between management and business owners, and between businesses and society. Chapter 2 looks at two ethical systems: formalism and consequentialism. It then examines various sources of values for business ethics, including legal regulation, professional and organizational codes of ethics, and individual values. It also suggests an approach to individual ethics in business organizations.

The next three chapters address dispute resolution, by explaining the U.S. court system, as well as the process of litigation and alternative dispute resolution mechanisms. Learning about the court system and ways to resolve disputes will help you understand how business can use the law strategically. Also, as you read law-related news, these basic concepts are fundamental to grasp how and why a company resolves disputes.

Chapter 3 explains the court system, identifying key players: judges, jurors, and lawyers. Each plays a distinct and important role. This chapter also sets forth the organization of the state and federal court systems, including the appellate courts. This chapter also includes a guided reading of the text's first court opinion, the U.S. Supreme Court case *National Federation of Independent Business v. Sebelius,* which decided the constitutionality of the Patient Protection and Affordable Care Act.

Chapter 4 focuses on how civil cases move through the court system in a process known as *litigation.* This chapter describes how the filing of a complaint commences cases and then explains all of the other pleadings that can be filed, as well as all of the pretrial discovery procedures and motions. The chapter concludes with information about the stages of a trial and any posttrial appeals.

There are many drawbacks to litigation, and Chapter 5 illustrates alternative ways to resolve disputes. This chapter explains different negotiating techniques to settle disputes. It also demonstrates the key differences between mediation and arbitration. Although both use a neutral third party to assist in resolving the dispute, they have significantly different features, which are important to know before agreeing to resolve a dispute.

Chapter 6, the final chapter in Part One, discusses the U.S. Constitution and constitutional guarantees relevant to business, including First Amendment protections, due process, and equal protection. This chapter also explains the significance of the Commerce Clause. Decisions involving the Commerce Clause have played a major role in defining how business works in the United States. This clause has a rich history of empowering the federal government's authority to regulate business. As such, understanding the role of administrative agencies in carrying out that will is critical.

Taken together, these chapters introduce readers to the legal foundations for business. The following section makes suggestions about the best way to read and study *The Legal and Regulatory Environment of Business.*

How to Study This Textbook

To read this textbook we highly recommend a certain method called Survey, Question, Read, Recite, Review (SQ3R). SQ3R is much more effective than simply starting at the beginning of a chapter and reading straight through to the end. But it should not take much longer than reading straight through.

If you are allowing two hours for the reading of a chapter, first take no more than five or six minutes and "survey" the chapter. Flip through the chapter and look at all of the main headings and subheadings of the sections, perhaps also looking at the first sentences of several paragraphs in each section. In surveying you are not trying to learn or even understand the material but rather to get an idea of what the chapter is about.

After surveying the material, develop a "question" for each section as you read. If the section heading says "Why Nations Are Economically Weak or Strong," turn the heading into a question, like "Why are some nations economically weak and others economically strong?" Then "read" the section with the purpose of answering your question. When you finish reading, "recite" aloud or silently to yourself the answer to the question.

The last "R" refers to "review." Spend the last 10 minutes of your study time reviewing the chapter. A good way to do this is to go back to your questions and answer them again. If you will study by this method, we guarantee more effective results than if you simply read the chapter straight through. We have included a longer explanation of SQ3R as Appendix 1 in the back of the book, along with an explanation of the case briefing system, which you may need beginning with Chapter 3. •

1

Law as a Foundation for Business

Learning Objectives

In this chapter you will learn:

1-1. To understand that laws and regulations are fundamental foundations for business.

1-2. To explain that "property" in the law refers not to something that is owned but to the right of ownership itself, which gives incentive for wealth creation.

1-3. To analyze why *stare decisis* is different in common law nations than in civil law nations.

1-4. To classify what legal sources lawyers turn to in answering legal questions from their clients and the hierarchy of those sources.

Introduction

An understanding of the importance of the legal environment of business is essential to appreciate the role of law as the foundation for business practice in a private market system. Learning about the law is essential to understanding how the law can be used for strategic advantage and to developing sustainable business practices. This text and its accompanying electronic features are designed with a number of objectives in mind, including creating a learning environment in which you will gain:

- The legal vocabulary to communicate with lawyers and business colleagues about areas of the law in a sophisticated manner.

- The ability to identify legal issues potentially relevant to a particular business situation.

- The judgment to make sound business decisions to prevent legal disputes.

- The knowledge to determine legal issues that require advice from counsel.
- The foundation to act as a sophisticated consumer of legal services.

As you read this book, consider the impact of the law on business. This chapter provides a basic overview of the law, helping you understand the common classifications and sources of law. Many examples are provided throughout the chapters to underscore the relevance of the law for business.

sidebar 1.1

JPMorgan Chase & Co.'s Massive Legal Liability

If there was ever a question about the toll that wrongdoing can take on a company, it was addressed by Jamie Dimon, CEO of JPMorgan Chase & Co. In a 30-page letter to shareholders in 2014, Dimon addressed the ramifications of the bank's legal cases with multiple government agencies, stating that the previous year was "the most painful, difficult, and nerve wracking experience that I have ever dealt with professionally." At that time, the company had already spent more than $20 billion to settle a range of cases.

JPMorgan is in the process of adding more than 13,000 employees to handle regulatory compliance and risk control, including approximately 8,000 employees whose primary responsibility is to combat money laundering. The company is spending $2 billion to comply with new rules and regulations.

In the same letter to shareholders, Dimon acknowledged that the company was too self-assured when they saw regulators investigating their competitors and that they need to be "better listeners and do a better job at examining critiques of others so [they] can learn from other people's mistakes, too."

Source: David Henry, "JPMorgan's Dimon Calls Settling Legal Issues 'Nerve Wracking,'" *Reuters* (April 9, 2014).

LO 1-1 WHY LAW AND REGULATIONS ARE FUNDAMENTAL FOUNDATIONS FOR BUSINESS

In the twenty-first century, it is crucial for companies doing business in the United States to be aware of the legal and regulatory landscape. As vividly evidenced by the experience of JPMorgan Chase & Co. in Sidebar 1.1, companies must take steps to ensure that they are in full compliance with the law to avoid a range of civil and criminal liability. By studying the legal and regulatory environment of business, you will gain an understanding of basic legal vocabulary and gain the ability to identify problematic situations that could result in liability. Moreover, whether you are involved in contract negotiations, the development of intellectual property, or dealing with employees, learning the fundamentals of the law will not only help you make informed decisions, but also to know when to call an attorney for advice.

In fact, because of the positive role lawyers can play, they are increasingly being asked to join corporate boards. In 2000, only 24 percent of U.S. companies had lawyer directors on their boards, but by 2009, 43 percent did. A recent study demonstrated that having lawyer-directors resulted in an average 9.5 percent increase in firm value. Without question, lawyers on boards can help companies navigate a myriad of issues and help manage risk.[1]

"Privatization without necessary institutional infrastructure [such as law] in the transition countries led to asset stripping rather than wealth creation."

—**Joseph E. Stiglitz, economist**

[1] See Lubormi Litov, Simone Sepe and Charles Whitehead, "Lawyers and Fools: Lawyer Directors in Public Corporations," http://papers.ssrn.com/sol3/papers.cfm?abstract_id=2218855 (January 14, 2014).

Law, the Rule of Law, and Property

Three concepts establish a necessary framework for the most effectively functioning market in the modern nation: law, the rule of law, and property. Note how they connect to each other.

LAW

In the last 10,000 years, human society has moved from roving bands of hunter-gatherers to large modern nations with populations in the hundreds of millions. The social forces that hold together societies range from custom and religion to law and economic ties. In the modern nation, however, the most significant of the social forces is **law** because law can glue together diverse peoples of different backgrounds into very large, organized groups. Law is known by everyone as being intended to tell members of society what they can or cannot do. Strangers to a society may not understand or appreciate complex and subtle customs of behavior, but they can observe the formal laws governing what kinds of activities are permitted and prohibited in society. Lawyers, judges, and other trained interpreters of the rules can help them in this process.

A simple definition of law follows:

- Law is made up of rules.
- These rules are laid down by the state and backed up by enforcement.

Law is a formal social force, meaning that laws come from the state and are usually written down and accessible so those who need to understand and obey them can. To maintain order in society, adequate enforcement institutions such as courts and the police are a necessary part of the legal system. As countries such as China are finding out, written laws mean little unless they can be promptly and fairly enforced. Without adequate enforcement, resources can be taken from those who have them, and agreements can be disregarded. The certainty and trust necessary to make complex, long-term business arrangements are absent. People must spend much of their time guarding their resources rather than developing them.

The first known written set of laws was the Code of Hammurabi, named after the Babylonian king of the eighteenth century BC.

THE RULE OF LAW

In a modern nation, law is important to implement either the commands of a dictator or the will of the people in a democracy. However, only in democracies is there true concern for the rule of law, which goes beyond merely thinking of law as governmental commands backed up by force. Under the **rule of law,** laws that are made are *generally* and *equally* applicable. They apply to all or most members of society and they apply to various groups in the same way.

Under the rule of law, law applies to lawmakers as well as to the rest of society. Thus, lawmakers have an incentive to make laws that benefit everyone. Rule-of-law nations adopt laws supporting the private market because it is in everyone's interest, including the lawmakers'.

In today's international business environment, more and more voices are calling for the rule of law. The secretary-general of the United Nations says that "without confidence based on the rule of law; without trust and transparency—there could be no well-functioning markets." The managing director of the

"Without the rule of law, major economic institutions such as corporations, banks, and labor unions would not function, and the government's many involvements in the economy—regulatory mechanisms, tax systems, customs structure, monetary policy, and the like—would be unfair, inefficient, and opaque."

–ThomasCarothers, Director, Democracy and Rule of Law Project, Carnegie Endowment for International Peace

> "While economic growth can occur in the short run with autocratic regimes, long-run economic growth entails the development of the rule of law."
>
> **–Douglas C. North, acceptance speech for the Nobel Prize in Economics, 1993**

International Monetary Fund asserts that "high quality" economic growth depends "in particular on the rule of law" which is a "lodestar for all countries." Observes the managing director of JPMorgan Chase: "An environment in which courts cannot be relied upon to adhere to the rule of law is an environment in which businesses will be reluctant to invest and in which development will be stunted." He calls the rule of law "a cornerstone of free trade."

Unfortunately, the rule of law is an ideal rather than a complete fact in even the most democratic nation. Special interest groups attempt to persuade lawmakers to benefit these groups at the expense of others. And it is not always clear what it means to apply laws generally and equally. Still, in a democracy well-educated voters who understand the importance of the rule of law can hold to account lawmakers who excessively favor special interests. Judges also play a vital role in maintaining the rule of law. (See Sidebar 1.2.)

Almost all wealthy countries embrace the rule of law; for example, most European countries. Article 6 of the Treaty on European Union, called the Maastricht Treaty, says the EU is "founded" on "the rule of law." There are no countries with strong, diverse economies that do not have the rule of law. As former President Eisenhower warned, "The clearest way to show what the rule of law means to us in everyday life is to recall what has happened when there is no rule of law."

sidebar 1.2

The Chief Justice and the Rule of Law

Before someone can become a justice of the U.S. Supreme Court, the president must nominate and the U.S. Senate must confirm that person. The Senate must also confirm the president's choice to be chief justice. During the confirmation, the senators always ask questions about the rule of law. Here is how Chief Justice John Roberts responded to a confirmation question about the rule of law.

> Somebody asked me . . . , "Are you going to be on the side of the little guy," he said. And you obviously want to give an

immediate answer, but, as you reflect on it, if the Constitution says that the little guy should win, the little guy's going to win in court before me. But if the Constitution says that the big guy should win, well, then the big guy's going to win, because my obligation is to the Constitution.

Compare Chief Justice Roberts' statement to a similar observation made by former Chief Justice Warren E. Burger: "Judges rule on the basis of law, and not public opinion, and they should be totally indifferent to the pressures of the times."

LO 1-2   PROPERTY

Property is a legal right that allows you to exclude others from your resources.

The third concept necessary for a successful private market in the modern nation is **property**. In a dictionary, property has two common meanings: (1) something that is owned, and (2) ownership. We will be using the word in its second definition as "**ownership**." In law the word "property" (or "ownership") means the right to turn to public authorities like the police or the courts to help you keep others from interfering with what you own. Property is a legal fence that keeps others out without your permission. It allows you to exclude others from something without your permission.

Three types of ownership fences are

- Public property, which applies to public resources owned by the government (or "state") like roads, public buildings, public lands, and monuments.
- Private property, which applies to resources that you own as an individual.
- Common property, which applies to resources like land that more than one individual owns jointly.

So important is the right of private property that in this book we often just refer to private property as "property." We will specifically say "public property" or "common property" if we mean those applications of exclusionary right.

It is through the law of property that individuals and business organizations can possess, use, and transfer their private resources. The enforcement of the property right under the rule of law gives people incentive to develop the resources they own and a property-based legal system that enables such control by allowing people to exclude others from interfering with what their efforts produce. The exclusionary right of property provides a basis for the private market and modern business. Scholars have traced the economic flourishing of Western civilization during the last several hundred years to the increasing recognition of the right of property in the nations of the West.

Do remember that the property right gives a major incentive to develop resources.

PROPERTY IN ITS BROADEST SENSE

Property can be thought of as the central concept underlying Western legal systems. (See Figure 1.1.) Most of the topics discussed in this book relate to the exclusionary right of property. Contract law enables an owner to exchange resources (Chapters 8 and 9), especially at a future date. Tort law compensates owners whose resources are wrongfully harmed by the actions of others (Chapter 10). Criminal law punishes those who harm an owner's resources in particular ways, for example, by theft (Chapter 13). The law of corporate governance and business organizations identifies how individuals can own and use private resources in groups (Chapter 14).

Property is the central concept of Western legal systems.

Regulatory law both protects ownership and sets limits on private resource use (Chapter 15). Antitrust law forbids owners from monopolizing classes of resources and sets rules for how businesses can compete to acquire ownership in new resources (Chapter 16). Securities laws regulate the transfer of ownership in certain profit-making opportunities (Chapter 17). Environmental law controls how owners can use their resources when creating pollution (Chapter 19). Even labor laws and antidiscrimination laws involve property in the sense they protect the employees' right to exclude employers from interfering with certain self-ownership interests of the employees (Chapters 20, 21, and 22). Finally, a theme of the entire book, corporate governance, specifically concerns the law protecting the owners of a business organization from the managers who run it for them. Generally speaking, corporate governance also refers to any law regulating and limiting private owners' productive resources and their use.

To say that you have a "right" means that legally you can keep others from interfering with that right. To be able to exclude others is the essence of property.

In its broadest sense, property includes an ownership of individual constitutional and human rights in ourselves that excludes the state from interfering with these rights. Today, we usually call our relationship to these rights

Figure 1.1 *The wheel of property.*

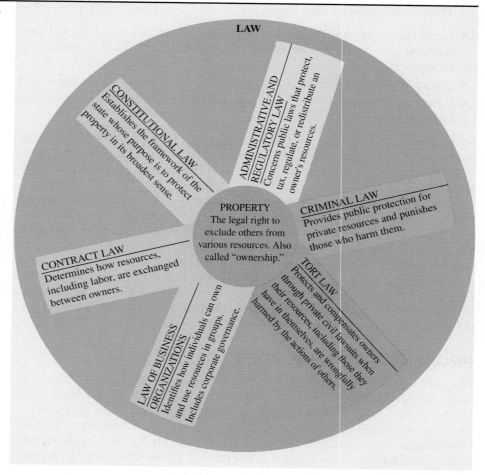

LAW

CONSTITUTIONAL LAW
Establishes the framework of the state whose purpose is to protect property in its broadest sense.

ADMINISTRATIVE AND REGULATORY LAW
Concerns public laws that protect, tax, regulate, or redistribute an owner's resources.

PROPERTY
The legal right to exclude others from various resources. Also called "ownership."

CRIMINAL LAW
Provides public protection for private resources and punishes those who harm them.

CONTRACT LAW
Determines how resources, including labor, are exchanged between owners.

TORT LAW
Protects and compensates owners through private civil lawsuits when their resources, including those they have in themselves, are wrongfully harmed by the actions of others.

LAW OF BUSINESS ORGANIZATIONS
Identifies how individuals can own and use resources in groups. Includes corporate governance.

"liberty," but liberty and property in this sense have almost identical meanings. John Locke, the seventeenth-century English philosopher who greatly influenced the framers of the Constitution, asserted that private property begins with the right we have in ourselves and in our efforts and actions. He said that an individual is the "proprietor [owner] of his own person, and the actions or labour of it" and that this is "the great foundation of property." Later, James Madison wrote that property "in its larger and juster meaning . . . embraces everything to which a man may attach value and have a right . . . . [A] man has property in his opinions and free communication of them. . . . In a word, as a man is said to have a right to his property, he may be equally said to have a property in his rights." For Madison and other constitutional framers, property protected not only physical resources like land but also human rights like freedom of speech, freedom of religion, and freedom from unreasonable intrusion by the government. The individual's very relationship to society was defined by the word *property*. Scholars have pointed out that the modern understanding of human rights began with the concept of property.

sidebar 1.3

Russia's Property Problems

When the former Soviet Union collapsed, many observers thought that the new private market would promptly improve Russia's economy. However, that economy went into a serious decline from which it has been slow to recover. Why? Most now consider that Russia's lack of the rule of law and the law of property accounts for its poor economy.

The government still controls over half of the resources in Russia. Much of what private control of resources exists in Russia has been gotten through force, fraud, and corruption. One study in Moscow found that small business owners must pay over $30,000 a year in bribes to corrupt officials and extortionists.

Developing property law in Russia often does not allow a single individual to control all the ways that land can be used. When disputes over agreements arise, businesses cannot depend on the courts to resolve issues justly and impartially. Recently, the Russian economy has been strengthened by the sale of oil to wealthy countries, but per person income in Russia remains low. In comparison, per person income in the United States is still approximately 3 times that in Russia.

Generally and equally applied property rights, their transfer by contract, and the support of adequate enforcement institutions like courts will provide a necessary basis to move the Russian economy toward prosperity.

JURISPRUDENCE

Over the centuries, several ideas have developed that help explain the origin of law and its justification. We call these ideas (or philosophies) of law **jurisprudence.** Briefly, the main types or "schools" of jurisprudence include the following:

- Natural law. Going back to Aristotle and other ancient philosophers, natural law theory asserts that law contains universal moral principles. These principles are observable in nature, and we can determine them through human reason. John Locke, the British philosopher whose writing influenced the framers of the U.S. Constitution, thought that "property" was part of natural law. Merely human laws that contradict the principles of natural law are improper. Compare natural law to "formalism," discussed in Chapter 2.

- Positive law. Positive law jurisprudence believes that law is simply the commands of the state backed up by force and punishments. It is contrary to the philosophy of natural law. Eighteenth-century philosopher Jeremy Bentham ridiculed the idea of natural law as "nonsense upon stilts." Compare positive law to "consequentialism," discussed in Chapter 2.

- Historical school. The historical school of jurisprudence emphasizes that contemporary law should focus on legal principles that have withstood the test of time in a nation. The historical school believes that law reflects the cultural traditions of a people and recognizes that different nations may have different traditions and, consequently, different laws. Friedrich Savigny, a prominent German legal philosopher, helped develop this jurisprudence.

- Sociological jurisprudence. Sociological jurisprudence supports the idea that law can and should change to meet new developments in society. From this point of view, the Second Amendment to the U.S. Constitution, which asserts the right to "bear arms," or weapons, should not be

Jurisprudence
is the philosophy of law.

"True law is right reason in agreement with nature; it is of universal application, unchanging and everlasting. . . ."

—Cicero, Roman historian

The definition of law at the beginning of this chapter is taken from positive law jurisprudence.

interpreted today to allow citizens to own and carry lightweight fully automatic rifles that can fire hundreds of rounds a minute. When the Second Amendment was written, a highly trained person carrying a 25-pound rifle could fire only about two rounds a minute.

- Legal realism. Legal realism tries to go beyond just the words of law to examine what police, administrators, prosecutors, and judges are actually doing as they enforce, interpret, and apply laws. When Supreme Court Justice Oliver Wendell Holmes Jr. said that "law is what officials do about it," he reflected the jurisprudence of legal realism. For instance, the posted speed limit around the Atlanta perimeter highway, Interstate 285, is 55 mph. However, almost no one drives within the posted speed limit and traffic police rarely ticket drivers until they go faster than 75 mph. In terms of legal realism, what is the actual speed limit on Atlanta's perimeter highway?

Several of these types of jurisprudence overlap. For instance, sociological jurisprudence and legal realism are types of legal positivism. Jurisprudence may also certainly influence the actual rules of law, but jurisprudence is a philosophy about law rather than the law itself. However, complicating matters is that the word *jurisprudence* also refers to the general body of law interpretations by judges as different from legislation passed by legislators.

Classifications of Law

Even when you understand jurisprudence and grasp the significance of our property-based legal system to the private marketplace, you still have much left to know about the legal and regulatory environment of business. In large part, learning about law demands an extensive vocabulary of legal terms and concepts. It will be useful in organizing this vocabulary to examine several major classifications of law.

COMMON LAW AND CIVIL LAW

LO 1-3

Common law
emphasizes the role of judges in determining the meaning of laws.

The world has two major legal systems: common law and civil law. The United Kingdom, the United States, Canada, Jamaica, India, Nigeria, New Zealand, and a few other countries—all colonized by England—follow the common law. The **common law** legal system emphasizes the role of judges in determining the meaning of laws and how they apply. It arose beginning in the eleventh and twelfth centuries as the English monarch appointed royal judges to ride circuits around the English countryside and to resolve disputes in the name of the king (or queen). As there was little formal law to apply to many disputes, the decisions handed down by the judges literally made the law.

By the time the English legislature (Parliament) emerged, a huge body of written judicial decisions was "common" to all of England. The role of judges in making and interpreting law was in place. English colonists then brought the common law to what became the United States and various other countries. The common law continues its development even today, and so significant is the role of judges in the United States that they determine the meaning of the Constitution and can declare void the legislation of Congress and the acts of the president.

The world's nations not colonized by England generally observe civil law legal systems. The **civil law** relies more on legislation than judicial decisions to determine what the law is. Like common law courts, courts in civil law nations decide the facts in a disputed case (for example, who did what, who committed a crime or breached a contract), but civil law courts do not make law nor do their judges think themselves obligated to follow prior judicial decisions, called *precedents,* as they do in common law nations, although they do refer to "settled" cases. Essentially, judges play a much more important role in determining law and its meaning in common law nations than in civil law nations. Only Louisiana among the U.S. states, follows a partial civil law system. This is due to Louisiana's historical ties with France, a civil law nation.

Civil law relies more on legislation than judicial decisions for law.

PUBLIC AND PRIVATE LAW

Another way of classifying the law is to divide it into matters of public law and matters of private law. **Public law** includes those matters that involve the regulation of society as opposed to individuals interacting. In each of these matters, a government official represents society, or "the people," and the official is responsible for seeking justice to achieve the ends of society. The main types of public law include:

Public law includes constitutional law, administrative law, and criminal law.

- **Constitutional law,** which involves the interpretation and application of either the federal or state constitutions.
- **Administrative law,** which covers the legal principles that apply to government agencies, bureaus, boards, or commissions.
- **Criminal law,** which specifies various offenses against the proper order of the state.

Special areas of property concern land, goods, copyrights, patents, and trademarks.

Private law covers those legal problems and issues that concern your private resource relationships with other people. Private law traditionally includes:

- **Property law,** which involves the recognition of exclusive right in both tangible (physically touchable) and intangible resources. Special areas of property law concern land, goods, copyrights, trademarks, patents, and trade secrets.
- **Contract law,** which covers the rules of how owners transfer resources by exchanging them. Contracts often involve enforceable promises to exchange resources in the future.
- **Tort law,** which establishes rules for compensation when an owner's legal boundaries are wrongfully crossed by another. Tort law often but not always requires actual injury to the owner's resources.

CIVIL LAW AND CRIMINAL LAW

Another means of classifying the law is to divide it into civil law and criminal law. For administrative purposes, courts usually separate criminal actions from all other lawsuits. *Civil* cases may include suits for breach of contract or tort cases, such as suits for personal injuries. Typically, they involve a request for damages or other appropriate relief that does not involve punishment of the wrongdoer. *Criminal* cases involve a representative of government attempting to prove the wrong committed against society and seeking to have the wrongdoer punished by the court system.

Don't confuse our reference to *civil* (or noncriminal) lawsuits with a *civil* law legal system, which is one emphasizing the importance of the legislature in determining the meaning of laws.

sidebar 1.4

Bank of America's Ongoing Post–Financial Crisis Legal Woes

By early 2014, Bank of America had spent more than $50 billion to resolve legal issues related to the 2008 financial crisis. Although some shareholders thought that the company's legal liability was waning, the bank set aside $6 billion more for additional potential costs resulting from litigation associated with post–financial crisis litigation. One ongoing concern is the investigation commenced by the Justice Department into "whether the bank sold shoddy residential-mortgage securities." A key aspect of the Justice Department's probe is how other financial settlements relate to acts by Countrywide Financial Corp., the subprime mortgage lender purchased by the bank. In addition to potential fines and settlements, Bank of America faces substantial legal costs, which can be difficult to assess.

Source: Christina Rexrode and Devlin Barrett, "Bank of America Swings to Loss on Legal Charge, Lower Mortgage Originations," *The Wall Street Journal* (April 17, 2014).

SUBSTANTIVE LAW AND PROCEDURAL LAW

That a plaintiff must prove the defendant failed to use reasonable care in order to establish the tort of negligence is an example of substantive law.

Another important classification or distinction in law is between substance and procedure. **Substantive law** defines the legal relationship of people with other people or between them and the state. Thus, the rules of law governing the creation or enforcement of a contractual promise are substantive in nature. **Procedural law** deals with the method and means by which substantive law is made and administered. The time allowed for one party to sue another and the rules of law governing the process of the lawsuit are examples of procedural laws. Thus, substantive rules of law define rights and duties, while procedural rules of law provide the machinery for enforcing those rights and duties.

Judicial procedures involve the conduct of lawsuits and appeals and the enforcement of judgments. The rules for conducting civil trials are different from those for criminal trials. For example, each party may call the other party to the witness stand for cross-examination in a civil trial, but the defendant may not be required to testify in a criminal case. Procedural problems sometimes arise concerning papers filed in lawsuits, the admission of evidence, and various other techniques involved in trying the case. They are the rules of the game. In Chapter 4 , you will study these procedural aspects of law in greater depth.

LO 1-4   Sources of Law

In the following sections, consider that you have a dry cleaning business and have gone to a lawyer to ask what the law says about your emitting certain chemical cleaning pollutants into the air. What sources of law will the lawyer have to be familiar with in order to answer your questions? The following sources form a hierarchy of law, which means that if a lower source of law conflicts with a higher source of law, it is legally void; that is, the higher source trumps, or prevails over, the lower.

FEDERAL LAW

Federal law is a very important source of law. It includes the U.S. Constitution, which is the supreme law of the nation. Any law, federal or state, that conflicts with the **Constitution** is said to be void and has no legal effect. In consulting sources of law, your attorney will look closely indeed to determine how the Constitution affects any other rules of law that adversely affect you. Chapter 6 examines more closely how the U.S. Constitution in particular applies to business practice.

Next in the hierarchy of federal law comes the **legislation** passed by Congress, also called "**acts**" or "**statutes**" (collections of legislation, often on the same subject, are **codes**). The Clean Air Act discussed in Chapter 19 is an example of such legislation that will be very important in answering the legal questions you have. Federal legislation that is constitutional prevails over all other sources of law. Finally, in federal law your attorney will also have to look at administrative law, specifically, administrative law that regulates business. Administrative law or regulation is made by agencies of the federal government like the Environmental Protection Agency. To answer your legal questions, the Environmental Protection Agency's regulation will be the most important regulatory law of the 15 independent regulatory agencies of the federal government. Chapter 15 will tell you more about administrative regulation in general.

STATE LAW

All federal law prevails over all state law in the hierarchy of our sources of law. But state law will still be very important in answering your legal questions about dry cleaning and putting certain pollutants into the air. At the state level, the hierarchy of law sources begins with the state constitution, followed by the statutes or acts adopted by the state legislature, like its commercial code you will study the **Uniform Commercial Code** or **UCC** in Chapter 8. Then there is also the regulatory law of the state administrative agencies. Even lower in the hierarchy of law at the state level is the law in the counties and cities called **ordinances.** Counties and cities also sometimes have administrative agencies that help plan local development, such as zoning boards that specify where businesses and housing can be located.

JUDICIAL DECISIONS OR CASE LAW

Finally, your attorney must consult the decisions of judges as a source of law. Even after considering constitutional language, reading legislation, and referring to administrative regulation, your attorney must still know the judicial decisions, called *case law,* that apply to your legal problem. These decisions interpret the relevant constitutional, legislative, and regulatory laws. As previously discussed, judges also make and interpret the common law.

When judges, especially judges who decide appeals from trial courts, make decisions on legal issues, they write their decisions, or **opinions,** setting out reasons. These case opinions are collected and published in book volumes known as "reporters," and these opinions now become **precedents** for future cases involving similar facts and legal issues. To locate prior precedents, it is helpful to know the **citation** for the case where a precedent is found. For example, a case opinion cited as 675 F.3d 23 (2014) can be located on page 23 of volume 675 of the *Federal Reporter*, third edition, a case decided in 2014. Knowing a case citation, you can easily locate the case in a library or through computer databases.

The extensive reliance of our legal system on judicial case law has both advantages and disadvantages. It is useful to summarize these.

> "The American Constitution is the most wonderful work ever struck off at a given time by the brain and purpose of man."
>
> **–William Gladstone, four-time prime minister of Great Britain in the 1800s**

Do remember that there are court systems in all 50 states plus a federal system. According to the U.S. Department of State, more than 31,000 judges nationwide make numerous decisions every year, adding to the volume of case law.

Advantages **Stare decisis** is the doctrine of prior precedents. The Latin meaning of these words is "let the prior decision stand." Under *stare decisis,* judges in current cases follow whenever possible the interpretation of law determined by judges in prior cases. This doctrine arose from the desire for certainty and predictability in the law. One important advantage of *stare decisis* was people became secure in their right of property. They then became willing to invest resources in fixed locations for factories and other immovable valuables because they were certain the state would not seize these resources for its own use. Case law helps specify in great detail the boundaries of our property-based legal system, and it protects what is "proper" to people from the interference of others.

Disadvantages Several disadvantages of case law are also important to know. Keep in mind, however, that we do not believe these disadvantages destroy the benefits of certainty, predictability, and stability provided by case law and *stare decisis.* Disadvantages of case law include:

- Volume of cases. Even with computers, searching through hundreds of thousands of cases and then identifying and reading the significant ones is often a very great task. At the very least, it is both time consuming for the attorney and expensive for the client.
- Conflicting precedents. Sometimes in searching prior cases, attorneys find cases in which judicial decisions conflict with each other. Conflicting precedents do not create confidence in the certainty of law.
- Dicta. Increasing the difficulty of determining how to follow prior precedent is the distinction between the **holding** in a prior case and mere **dicta.** The holdings in prior cases are precisely what was necessary to the decision reached. Dicta are whatever else the court said. Judges in future cases are not so likely to follow the dicta in prior cases as they are the holdings.
- Rejection of precedent. Because of *stare decisis,* courts usually hesitate to reject the precedents of prior cases, but sometimes they do. They may think that prior cases were wrongly decided, or they may think that times have changed. In constitutional law the idea that courts should understand the meaning of the Constitution relative to the times in which they interpret it is known as **constitutional relativity. Originalism** is the opposite of constitutional relativity. It stands for the idea that courts should interpret the Constitution only according to the intentions of those who wrote it.
- Conflicts of law. A buyer in Georgia orders equipment by telephone from a seller's representative in Illinois. The buyer directs the seller to ship the equipment to New York. When the equipment breaks down while being used in Pennsylvania, the buyer sues the seller in Ohio where the seller is incorporated. What state's law applies? Courts resolve such problems by applying **conflicts of law** rules, but even these rules may vary from state to state. A better solution is for the buyer and seller to specify in the contract which state's law will apply in case of a dispute. In a tort case, the usual conflicts of law rule applies the law of the state where the injury occurred, no matter where the injury occurred. If a contract specifies no particular state's law for the parties to a dispute to follow, a court interpreting the contract will usually apply the law of the state where the contract was made.

A baseball fan is hurt by a foul ball and sues the baseball team's owner. The court writes, "Whether a fan is injured by a foul ball or an accidentally thrown bat, the result is the same. The fan cannot recover damages against the team because the fan assumes the risk." The comment about "thrown bat" is dicta because the case involved only a foul ball. Bats are heavier and more dangerous than balls, and a judge in a future case may not feel obligated to follow the dicta in this case concerning bats.

Do make sure to include a provision for the payment of attorney's fees in any contract loaning money or extending credit to someone.

Regarding case law, you should note that courts are the institution in our legal system that interpret the meaning of the law, whether that law is the U.S. Constitution, legislation, administrative law, or the common law. Because there are an infinite number of possible cases, each a little bit different on its facts, the power of courts to interpret meaning is very important. Consider the Second Amendment to the Constitution: It says that "the right to bear arms shall not be infringed." What do these words mean? Do they apply constitutionally only to protect seven-foot muskets weighing 20 pounds that a well-trained person could only fire twice a minute? Do they apply constitutionally to protect possession of semiautomatic pistols that an eight-year-old child can fire 20 times a minute? Do they apply to protect ownership of machine guns that can be fired hundreds of times a minute? Now are you beginning to understand the powerful role that courts play in interpreting the meaning not only of the Constitution but of all laws in our legal system?

SOURCES OF LAW HIERARCHY IN REVIEW

So your lawyer has to know many sources of law and how they interact in order to answer your question about the pollutants from your cleaning business. It is mistaken to think that lawyers know all of the law that applies to every legal question that you may ask them. However, they should know how to go about answering your questions, including the fact that some questions may not have answers that can be known in advance and that require formal dispute resolution, that is, they require that a judge, or perhaps an arbitrator, decide them.

The hierarchy of the sources of law, however, is well understood. That hierarchy is as follows. Remember that each higher source of law voids, or prevails, over every lower source of law in the hierarchy, except that in many instances there will be no conflict between higher and lower sources of law and in other instances it may not be clear whether or not a higher source of law (such as a constitutional right of speech) conflicts with a lower source of law (such as a law regulating advertising expression).

Hierarchy of sources of law from highest to lowest:

- U.S. Constitution and Amendments.
- Statutes (also called "acts" or "legislation") of Congress.
- Federal administration regulation.
- State constitutions (apply only in individual states).
- State statutes (apply only in individual states).
- State administrative regulation (applies only in individual states).
- Local ordinances (apply only in cities, towns, and other such areas).
- Case law (court cases, as they interpret all of the other sources, may or may not void sources lower than the source being interpreted).

LEGAL SANCTIONS

The enforcement of the law is vital to the rule of law and a "proper" legal system. Law enforcement officials and the courts use several methods to encourage or to force compliance with the obedience to the law. These methods, often called **sanctions,** may be used against a person who has failed to comply with the law. The sanctions are in effect a form of punishment for violating the law. Sanctions also have a preventive function. The threat of sanctions usually results in compliance with the requirements of law.

Because punishment is used to secure obedience to the law, the Fourteenth Amendment to the Constitution of the United States provides in part: "No State shall . . . deprive any person of life, liberty or property without due process of law." This provision recognizes that the law is enforced by taking a person's life, freedom, or the resources that he or she owns. The taking of an owner's resources may be (1) for the benefit of society generally, as when land is taken through eminent domain; (2) to punish someone, as with a traffic fine; or (3) for the benefit of another person, as an award of damages. The right of an individual to take another person's resources (especially money) because that person has failed to meet the requirements of the law (e.g., the breach of a contract) is known as a **remedy.** As you study the following sections, identify the remedies available to those seeking through the courts what belongs to another, and keep in mind how important that adequately and fairly enforced sanctions are to a property-based legal system and how nations lacking adequate enforcement sanctions tend to be poor even when they claim to believe in private property.

SANCTIONS FOR CRIMINAL CONDUCT

A *crime* is a public wrong against society. Criminal cases are brought by the government on behalf of the people. The people are represented by a state's attorney or U.S. attorney or other public official. When a person is convicted of a crime, one of the following punishments may be imposed:

- Death.
- Imprisonment.
- Fine.
- Removal from office.
- Disqualification from holding any office and from voting.

Among the purposes of such punishments are to protect the public and to deter persons from wrongful conduct.

SANCTIONS FOR BREACH OF CONTRACT

Legally enforceable agreements, called *contracts* (see Chapter 8), are vitally important to business because they allow buyers and sellers to exchange resources and shape their agreements any legal way they wish. When one party to a contract fails to do what he or she agreed to do, a **breach of contract** occurs. The usual remedy for a breach is a suit for dollar damages. These damages, called **compensatory damages,** are awarded to make the victim of the breach "whole" in the economic sense. Such damages compensate the party for all losses that are the direct and foreseeable result of the breach of contract. The objective is that the party be in as good a position as he or she would have been in had the contract been performed. Damages do not make most parties totally "whole," however, because they do not as a general rule include attorney's fees. Unless the contract or some special law provides to the contrary, parties to the contract litigation pay their own attorneys.

In addition to compensatory damages, breach-of-contract cases may award consequential damages when the breaching party knew or had reason to know that special circumstances existed that would cause the other party to suffer additional losses if the contract were breached.

There are other remedies available for a breach of contract. If a breach by one party is serious enough, the other party may be permitted to rescind

Do remember that the law divides crimes into misdemeanors and felonies.

Compensatory damages awarded for breach of contract attempt to make a plaintiff "whole," as though in an economic sense the defendant had not breached the contract.

or cancel the contract. In some circumstances, the remedy of an injured party may be a decree of **specific performance**—an order by the court commanding the other party actually to perform a bargain as agreed. The single largest number of lawsuits today, especially in the federal courts, involves one business suing another business for breach of contract.

SANCTIONS FOR TORTIOUS CONDUCT

A **tort** is a civil wrong other than a breach of contract. Torts involve improper crossing of property boundaries, usually causing injury to our person or other things we own. The boundaries may be physical as when someone trespasses across the boundaries of another's land. Boundaries may also be behavioral as when someone acts unreasonably and injures another.

> Tort law helps protect property boundaries by providing *compensation* when someone wrongfully crosses such boundaries.

The law divides torts into the following three categories:

- **Intentional torts.** These torts all require the plaintiff (the person who initiates a lawsuit) to prove the defendant intended to cross the boundaries protecting the plaintiff. Intentional torts include assault (intentionally placing someone in apprehension of his physical safety), battery (intentionally making offensive, unconsented to physical contact with someone), conversion (intentionally depriving someone of goods owned), and trespass (intentionally crossing someone else's land boundaries without permission).
- **Negligence.** This tort requires the plaintiff to show that the defendant injured what was proper to the plaintiff through unreasonable behavior.
- **Strict liability.** Strict liability torts usually require the plaintiff to prove only that the defendant has injured something proper to the plaintiff. Injury caused by an ultrahazardous activity like blasting is an example.

> **Punitive damages** are a civil punishment for intentional or extremely negligent wrongdoing. Their purpose is to deter others from such conduct in the future.

In law, the sanction (or remedy) for tortious conduct is money damages. The damages compensate injured plaintiffs for medical expenses, lost wages or earning power, pain and suffering, and damages to other owned goods and land. **Punitive damages**—also called **exemplary damages**—are also appropriate when the tort is intentional or the unreasonable conduct is extremely severe.

SANCTIONS FOR VIOLATING STATUTES AND REGULATIONS

Statutes at both the federal and state levels of government impose a variety of sanctions for violating the statutes or regulations of administrative agencies adopted to accomplish statutory purposes. These sanctions are often similar to those imposed for criminal conduct, breach of contract, or tortious conduct. Many statutes, for example, impose a fine for a violation and authorized damages to injured parties as well. Although common law did not make a defendant pay a plaintiff's attorney fees, many statutes do require so in various circumstances.

You should keep in mind that the sanctions imposed for violating statutes or administrative agency regulations are an important part of enforcing the property-based legal system. These laws help define boundaries and protect us from the boundary infringements of others. Regulations often set boundaries of what it is proper for businesses to do in producing and selling goods and competing with other producers in the market. Many of the chapters in this book examine the boundaries set by various business regulations.

concept *summary*

1. Persons and businesses convicted of criminal conduct may be fined, imprisoned, or both.
2. A party who breaches a contract may be required to pay as compensatory damages to the other party the sum of money required to make the victim whole. In addition, special circumstances may justify consequential damages.
3. A tort victim is entitled to collect as damages the amount of money necessary to compensate the injured party for the total harm caused by the intentional or negligent conduct of the wrongdoer.
4. Punitive damages may be awarded in the case of intentional torts.
5. Statutes and regulations issued by government agencies often authorize sanctions similar to those used in the criminal law, contracts, and torts. They usually go further by using a multiplier for damages and award attorney's fees as well.

A Property-Based Legal System and Corporate Governance

Under the rule of law in a property-based legal system, all persons have an equal right to their resources. Property problems arise when one person harms another's resources or takes them without permission or authorization. When a stranger takes your car without permission, we call this "theft," and it is easy to appreciate how it violates your right of property under the rule of law. However, more complex property problems can arise.

Corporations are businesses chartered by the state to do business as legal persons.

Much, if not most, business in the United States is transacted through large corporate business organizations. A **corporation** is a business chartered by the state to do business as a legal person in a certain form of organization. Chapter 11 will explain to you the details of corporate legal ownership but, briefly, a corporation is owned by *shareholders* who have *stock* in the business. They vote to elect the *board of directors* who legally run the business but who often hire *managers* to be in charge of day-to-day business operations. In large corporations, few shareholders sit on the board of directors or are managers of these businesses, and thus ownership is usually separate from resource control.

THE SPECIFIC SENSE OF CORPORATE GOVERNANCE

Corporate governance defines the legal relationship between corporate agents like managers or boards of directors and the shareholder owners of the corporation.

Because of the separation of ownership and control, corporate governance is very important. **Corporate governance** refers to the legal rules that structure, empower, and regulate the *agents* (primarily the board of directors and managers) of corporations and define their relationship to the owners (shareholders). Specifically, *corporate governance rules protect the property interest that the owners have in corporations.*

Because of the complexity of modern corporations, there are sometimes breakdowns in corporate governance. Managers like the president, vice presidents, or chief financial officer of a corporation can abuse their control of its resources to benefit themselves in ways that impair or even destroy the corporation's value to the shareholders. For example, often these top managers have salaries, bonuses, or stock options that are tied to the corporation's profitability or stock price. If they manipulate the corporation's profit by puffing up assets or concealing debts, they may be able to raise their incomes by millions of dollars even as they mislead the owners about the true value of the corporation and risk corporate collapse when the true situation is disclosed. Other examples of corporate misgovernance include managers' engaging in insider trading of stock, running up stock prices in order to exercise stock options, and taking advantage of business opportunities that rightfully belong to the corporation and its shareholders.

Corporate governance can fail even when corporate managers do nothing illegal. An economically painful recession began in 2008 in part because lenders at large banks allowed and encouraged risky loans that loan applicants could not repay unless the market value of their homes went up substantially. Millions of homeowners borrowed under these conditions. When the market value of housing did not increase and borrowers could not repay their loans, the entire banking system came close to collapse.

Businesses depend on credit, and when they could not borrow money from banks because of the near collapse, many businesses either failed or had to lay off employees. Much harm was done to investors and others because those in control of the banks took risks they should not have. Why did they take these risks? That the risky loans they generated led to large salary increases, personal bonuses, stock options, and resale commissions and profits on packaged loans was a significant reason. Bank executives and managers chose to ignore the risk that the housing market might stop its rapid increase in value. After all, the risk was being taken not with their personal money, but with the money of the bank's shareholders and investors. As Nobel laureate Paul Krugman wrote, "[I]t was mainly about gambling with other people's money. The financial industry took big, risky bets with borrowed funds—bets that paid high returns until they went bad—but was able to borrow cheaply because investors didn't understand how fragile the industry was."

THE GENERAL SENSE OF CORPORATE GOVERNANCE

In a general sense, corporate governance also applies to the legal relationships that businesses have with each other, with their customers, and with society. The economic collapse of 2008 illustrates the need for corporate governance in this general sense. As previously explained, a major factor in the collapse was the risky homeowner lending practice of banks, added to by the risky practices of other financial institutions that repackaged, sold, and resold hundreds of billions of dollars of poor-quality housing loans that were inadequately secured. As long as housing prices were rising, many people made a great deal of money, but when the housing bubble burst and prices began to decline, economic collapse occurred, affecting not only the financial institutions but also the entire economy because credit was too expensive or unavailable. It has been suggested that lack of adequate corporate governance has allowed the risky lending practices that ultimately have led to the biggest recession since the Great Depression of the 1930s. A number of the chapters that follow discuss the general corporate governance that has followed this recession.

In a broad general sense, corporate governance includes the legal property relations that large businesses have with each other, with their customers, and with society.

Key Terms

Act 15
Administrative law 13
Breach of contract 18
Citation 15
Civil law 13
Codes 15
Common law 12
Compensatory damages 18
Conflicts of law 16
Constitution 14
Constitutional law 13
Constitutional relativity 16
Contract law 13
Corporate governance 20
Corporation 20
Criminal law 13

Dicta 16
Exemplary damages 19
Holding 16
Intentional torts 19
Jurisprudence 11
Law 7
Legislation 15
Negligence 19
Opinion 15
Ordinances 15
Originalism 16
Ownership 8
Precedent 15
Private law 13
Procedural law 14
Property 8

Property law 13
Public law 13
Punitive damages 19
Remedy 18
Rule of law 7
Sanctions 17
Specific performance 19
Stare decisis 16
Statute 15
Strict liability 19
Substantive law 14
Tort 19
Tort law 13
Uniform Commercial Code
   (UCC) 15

Review Questions and Problems

Introduction

1. *Why Nations Are Economically Weak or Strong*

   (a) Identify several reasons put forth to explain why nations are prosperous or poor.

   (b) What does this section say is the foundation of the private market and prosperity?

Law, the Rule of Law, and Property

2. *Law*

   (a) Define law. Compare and contrast law and custom.

   (b) What role do the courts and police play in the legal system?

3. *The Rule of Law*

   (a) Define the rule of law. How does the rule of law differ from law as the commands of the state?

   (b) Explain why the rule of law is "an ideal rather than a complete fact."

4. *Property*

   (a) What is property? How does property differ from "resources"?

   (b) Why is property important to society? To private enterprise?

5. *Property in Its Broadest Sense*

   (a) Explain why property can be thought of as the central concept underlying Western legal systems.

   (b) What does James Madison mean when he says we have property in our opinions "and free communication of them"?

6. *Jurisprudence*

   (a) Define jurisprudence and name four schools of jurisprudence.

   (b) Describe the main difference between the jurisprudences of natural law and sociological jurisprudence.

Classifications of Law

7. *Common Law and Civil Law*

   (a) What is "common law"? Why is the United States a "common law country"?

   (b) What is the primary distinction between common law and civil law legal systems?

8. *Public and Private Law*

   (a) What is public law? Give three examples of public law.

   (b) Explain private law. Give three examples.

9. *Civil Law and Criminal Law*

   (a) What is the difference between civil law and criminal law?

   (b) Explain the two ways that the words *civil law* are used in this chapter.

10. *Substantive Law and Procedural Law*

   (a) Define substantive law and procedural law.

   (b) Is contract law substantive law or procedural law? How about a rule specifying that a defendant has 30 days to respond to a complaint?

Sources of Law

11. *Federal Law*

   (a) Explain what it means to say that constitutions are the "highest laws of the nation."

   (b) Explain the important distinctions between state and federal constitutions.

12. *State Law*

   (a) Give two additional terms for legislation.

   (b) Why is uniformity of law important to business? How can legislators achieve uniformity of the laws affecting business? What is the most significant uniform law affecting business?

   (c) For what purposes do administrative agencies exist?

13. *Judicial Decisions or Case Law*

   (a) Define *stare decisis*. What are its advantages? Disadvantages?

   (b) What is the distinction between a precedent and dicta in judicial decisions, and how does this distinction relate to stare decisis?

   (c) Alex was on a coast-to-coast trip by automobile. While passing through Ohio, Alex had a flat tire. It was fixed by Sam's Turnpike Service Station, and later, while Alex was driving in Indiana, the tire came off and Alex was injured. Alex was hospitalized in Indiana, so he sued Sam in Indiana for the injuries. What rules of substantive law will the Indiana court use to determine if Sam is at fault? Explain.

14. *Sources of Law Hierarchy in Review*

   (a) Explain the relationship of case law to the other sources of law.

15. *Legal Sanctions*

   (a) Why are legal sanctions important in a property-based legal system?

   (b) What is the difference between a sanction and a remedy?

16. *Sanctions for Criminal Conduct*

   (a) What are the sanctions for criminal conduct.

   (b) Name three purposes of criminal sanctions.

17. *Sanctions for Breach of Contract*

   (a) What is the purpose of compensatory damages?

   (b) What is specific performance of a contract?

18. *Sanctions for Tortious Conduct*

   (a) What are the two premises of tort liability?

   (b) When are punitive damages appropriate in a tort case?

19. *Sanctions for Violating Statutes and Regulations*

   (a) What types of sanctions are used for the violation of statutes and regulations?

   (b) What is an injunction?

A Property-Based Legal System and Corporate Governance

20. *The Specific Sense of Corporate Governance*

   (a) What is the "specific" sense of corporate governance?

   (b) Why might some managers try to artificially raise or "puff up" the market price of their stocks? Describe several ways they could do this.

21. *The General Sense of Corporate Governance*

   (a) What is the "general" sense of corporate governance?

   (b) Discuss how effective corporate governance contributes to the creation of economic wealth.

business *discussions*

1. As the vice president of finance for a company producing and selling electronic switchboards, you are considering foreign investment to build a plant to assemble electronic components. A source in China advises you that a town near Shenzhen may be an excellent location for a new plant. Chinese are well educated and willing to work for reasonable wages. Projected construction costs are acceptable. Both rail lines and airports are nearby, and the current Chinese government seems politically stable. The town even has a technical college that will be an excellent source for skilled employees. The plant will ship most of the finished electronic components back to the United States.

   Do you know everything you need to make an investment decision?
   If not, what else do you need to know about investment in foreign countries?
   What does it mean to say that law is the foundation of the private enterprise system?

2. Three years ago the Darden Corporation bought a thousand acres of land that borders the Potowac River in Washam County. While waiting on development opportunities, Darden cut timber to help repay the mortgage loan it took out to buy the land. On March 2, the Washam County Commission proposed an ordinance to establish a 250-foot-wide greenway along the south side of the Potowac that will effectively ban both development and timbering on nearly 80 acres of Darden's land. The same day in an unrelated accident a Darden truck ran over a hunter who was hunting without permission on the company's land. Darden immediately contacted an attorney in Washam City.

   • What is law?
   • What does it mean to say that Darden has "property" in the land? That the hunter has "property" in himself?
   • What sources of law will the attorney have to understand in order to advise Darden about the proposed greenway? The company's potential responsibility to the hunter?

2

The Role of Ethics in Decision Making

◼ Learning Objectives

In this chapter you will learn:

2-1. To compare the connection between law and ethical principles.

2-2. To analyze why ethical consequentialism and not ethical formalism has been the chief source of values for business ethics.

2-3. To generate an individual framework for ethical values in business.

2-4. To evaluate the obstacles and rewards of ethical business practice in our property-based legal system.

Is ethics winning in business? A *Wall Street Journal* article posed this question in a report concerning research that found improving ethical behavior in business. For instance, the 2013 National Business Ethics Survey, conducted by the Ethics Resource Center, found the lowest number of people observing misconduct in their workplaces than at any time in the survey's history. Also, the percentage of people who felt pressured to compromise ethical standards fell substantially from earlier surveys.

If ethics is making a comeback in business, perhaps businesses learned lessons from the economic collapse and recession of 2008. The Financial Crisis Inquiry Report concluded that a "systemic breakdown in accountability and ethics" was one of the major factors that led to the worst financial market disruption since the Great Depression.

In pursuit of profits and personal reward, bankers and traders at leading financial institutions turned a collective blind eye to what might happen in their businesses if the bubble of steadily rising house prices burst and borrowers could not repay loans conditioned on ever-rising home values. Bank stockholders, which included large pension funds, lost hundreds of billions of dollars. Banks could not extend enough credit to enable many businesses to buy inventory and meet payrolls. Businesses laid off millions of workers who then could not buy goods and services, and the economy began a downward spiral.

By 2011, according to the Financial Crisis Inquiry Report, about four million families had lost their homes to foreclosure and another half million had slipped into the foreclosure process or were seriously behind on their mortgage loan payments. Some $11 trillion in household wealth had vanished, with retirement accounts and life savings swept away. Millions of workers lost their jobs during the recession, and even as the economy began to recover, they had difficulty finding new work.

In our interconnected economy, an individual's conduct affects many others, making a discussion of the moral sense especially significant to a book on the legal and regulatory environment of business. Justice Oliver Wendell Holmes wrote, "The law is the witness and external deposit of our moral life. Its history is the history of the moral development of the race." Ethical (or moral) values underlie much law, including the law of how business operates and is regulated, making it important for business students to know about the nature of ethics, sources of ethics, and problems of achieving an ethical business organization. This chapter introduces the study of business ethics by examining the current concern over business ethics. It explores the relationship of morality and ethics and then of ethics and law. Two principal approaches to ethics are presented: formalism and consequentialism.

Next, the chapter looks at ethical values for business decision making. It examines trends and looks at four sources of ethical values:

- Legal regulation.
- Professional codes of ethics.
- Codes of ethics from business organizations.
- Individual values.

The chapter also considers the problems faced in achieving an ethical business organization. When in groups, people often decide and act differently from the way they act as individuals. This fact has special significance for ethics in business corporations. The chapter examines how the profit motive and business bureaucracy put pressure on ethical decision making and how ethical reform must begin with the top leadership of business organizations. The importance of open communication to the ethical life of a business organization is emphasized, and several strategies for implementing corporate ethics are presented.

Contemporary Business Ethics

U.S. customs agents caught the president of Ann Taylor, a large chain store, trying to avoid paying duty on $125,000 worth of wristwatches for his personal collection. A substantial civil penalty was proposed. At an Ann Taylor board of directors meeting, one director told the president: "This calls into question your integrity." The president resigned from the company.

More than ever before, business ethics are of concern to the business community and to society. In the 1980s few corporations hired people as ethics officers. Today over 20% of big companies have ethics officers whose job is to develop ethics policies, listen to complaints of ethics violations, and investigate ethics abuses. The increase in the number of organizations with a chief ethics and compliance officer (CECO) is tied to increases in regulations following several high-profile business ethics failings. Congress agreed with President George W. Bush's statement that "the business pages of American newspapers should not read like a scandal sheet" when it overwhelming passed the Sarbanes-Oxley Act (SOX) in 2002. SOX established "higher standards for corporate responsibility and governance." SOX, along with new listing requirements by stock exchanges, governance standards, and new accounting rules has created a new operating environment for business. Often, businesses navigate the ethics and compliance requirements through its CECO, an executive who operates across business functions to hold the organization accountable for high ethical standards.

Importantly, there is evidence that higher accountability standards are working. The 2014 National Business Ethics Survey found a widespread decline in observed misconduct in the workplace such as conflicts of interest, abusive or intimidating behavior, and lying to employees. This continues a trend in declining ethical misconduct reported in the 2009 survey. The Ethics Resource Center, which sponsors the survey, concludes that less unethical conduct may reflect less risk-taking during the slow economic recovery following the recession of 2008 but more likely it reflects a change in business perspective, noting that, "that businesses' continuing and growing commitment to strong ethics and compliance programs is bearing fruit and that ethical performance is becoming a new norm in many workplaces."

ETHICS AND SOCIETY

On April 29, 2014, Adam Silver, still new to the job as NBA Commissioner, banned Los Angeles Clippers owner Donald Sterling from association with the NBA for life and fined him $2.5 million following public release of a recording in which the longest-tenured NBA owner made repeated racist comments. Commissioner Silver announced the decisive punishment for violation of NBA rules that all owners agree to follow. Commissioner Silver stated in reference to the racist statements that were universally condemned by players and defended by none, "Sentiments of this kind are contrary to the principles of inclusion and respect that form the foundation of our diverse multicultural and multiethnic league." During the 33 years that Donald Sterling owned an NBA team, society had changed. As society changes, shared values emerge that strengthen ethical foundations.

Changing Normative Values Ours is a diverse society formed from many ethnic backgrounds, races, and religions. When a business decision maker, such as Donald Sterling, does not share common values with society,

When asked "which of the following statements about ethics was most often transmitted by those of your professors who discussed ethical or moral issues?" 73% of college students chose "what is right and wrong depends on differences in individual values and cultural diversity."

Source: National Association of Scholars

the entire business organization is affected, as the NBA was in this context. Diversity fosters concern over values, and as America becomes increasingly pluralistic, changes in traditional norms create challenges in establishing shared values. Rather than a threat to ethics, however, the inevitable changes in societal norms create the opportunity to focus on foundational principles that bind all members of the society.

Economic Interdependence Increasing economic interdependence promotes concerns about business ethics. Not even farm families are self-sustaining. Each of us depends on business and industry for our every necessity—food, clothing, shelter, and energy. The marketplace dominates all aspects of life, and how the marketplace is conducted concerns us. The decisions people in business make have a significant impact on us. When there is a labor-management dispute in the coal industry, our source of electricity is threatened. When manufacturers conspire to raise prices, the cost of our goods goes up. The sale of dangerous pesticides or impure drugs threatens our health. A management decision to close a plant may threaten our jobs.

The 2008 recession also illustrates economic interdependence. As credit from the banks dried up, the adverse economic effects spiraled throughout the economy. A serious ethical problem arises from economic interdependence and the modern corporation, which is the structure of most large businesses in this country. The problem is that the corporate leaders are not the real owners of corporations. The stockholders are, and although corporate executives and managers may own some stock, they seldom own significant percentages of very large companies. The ethical problem that can arise is that the executives and managers who control what the stockholders own are sometimes able to manipulate corporate actions for their own benefit, actions that have unacceptable risks to the owners and others. Executives, managers, and other employees are sometime able to take actions that if successful benefit themselves greatly, but if unsuccessful impact many others harmfully.

The watchdog group, Citizen Works, documented the dips in stock prices that businesses experience following a corporate scandal.

Source: Citizen Works

News Media and the Internet Extensive coverage of business decisions and their impact on society makes us more aware than ever of failures of business ethics. The news media and the Internet make it increasingly difficult to hide the questionable behavior of large organizations. From the coverage of stock market manipulations to accounts of Enron's and Arthur Andersen's collapse, the news media and Internet heighten public attention and concern. The ethical issues that surround nearly every significant business decision are easier to see than they once were. As a result of greater visibility, more individuals can comment on the fairness, justice, and values reflected by actions, or inactions, of business executives. Changes in the law and workplace can improve the ethical processes that affect us all in our economically interdependent world.

Refer now to Sidebar 2.1. By the time they are in high school, students may have formed values that are not appropriate for ethical business practice. These statistics highlight the importance of ethical education to create a foundation for future business practices.

sidebar 2.1

High School Dishonesty Predicts Dishonesty in the Workplace

According to the Josephson Institute of Ethics: "The hole in the moral ozone seems to be getting bigger—each new generation is more likely to lie and cheat than the preceding one." A 2008 report of the Institute showed that during the year, 64% of students answering a survey cheated on an exam, 42% lied to save money, and 30% stole something from a store. Fifty-one percent answered that lying and cheating are necessary to succeed. The Institute further found that regardless of age people who believe lying and cheating are a necessary part of success are three times more likely to lie to a customer in the workplace and to inflate insurance claims. They are also twice as likely to inflate an expense claim and to lie to their bosses.

Compare these findings with a 2006 study of cheating published in Academy of Management Learning & Education. It found that of MBA students 56% cheated regularly, more than in any other graduate program.

ETHICS AND GOVERNMENT

These changes in society have been accompanied by changes in the role of government. When business fails to make ethical decisions, when it fails to live up to society's expectations for ethical behavior, government may step in. As noted in a prior section, and detailed throughout the chapters of this book, government regulates business when there are ethical failures such as those that preceded the Sarbanes-Oxley Act of 2002 when business scandals dominated headlines.

Business leaders have incentive to promote corporate integrity, and thereby to limit further governmental regulation. They recognize that by encouraging ethical conduct and self-regulation within business organizations, they will prevent outside standards from being imposed on them through public law. As a consequence, both business and industry have, in recent decades, developed codes of ethics. Such efforts by professions and businesses to set standards of behavior are evidence of the increasing tendency toward self-regulation. Self-regulation can mean more than helping a business stay out of trouble. Companies that are perceived as ethical and acting in a responsible manner can attract loyal customers, employees, and investors.

Federal law also encourages self-regulation. Federal sentencing guidelines reduce criminal fines for legal violations in companies that have taken specific steps to self-police ethical/legal conduct. See Chapter 13. In an increasingly international business environment, it is worth noting that outside the United States, governments value compliance programs. For example, in Italy, businesses may defend against charges of corrupt practices with evidence of a compliance program. See Chapter 12.

A study conducted by establishing an "ethics index" of companies with high rankings in corporate citizenship, governance, social responsibility, and sustainability practices showed an average five-year investment return of 102% compared to 26% for the S&P500.

Source: Corpedia

The Nature of Ethics

In 1759 Adam Smith wrote, "However selfish man believes himself to be, there is no doubt that there are some elements in his nature which lead him to concern himself about the fortune of others, in such a way that their happiness is necessary for him, although he obtains nothing from it except the pleasure of seeing it." With this statement the author of *The Wealth of Nations*, perhaps the most famous book on economic theory ever written, recognized a moral element in human nature that goes beyond self-interest.

What is it that makes us care about the fortunes of others? The next sections examine the nature of ethics. What is morality? What are ethics? How are morality and ethics similar? How do ethics relate to law? What are the major ethical systems? How do these systems apply to business decision making? When you have finished reading these sections, come back to these questions and see if you can answer them.

ETHICS AND MORALITY

Morality is the collection of values that guides our behavior.

In 2011, Gil Meche, a 32-year-old right-handed pitcher for the Kansas City Royals, had a baseball contract that called for a $12 million salary. The previous season he had hurt his arm, but under the terms of his contract, all he had to do was show up for spring training to earn his salary, even if he could not pitch well or needed surgery. Instead of collecting his $12 million salary as he was legally entitled to do, he retired, which meant that he would not be paid at all. Gil said, "Honestly, I didn't feel like I deserved the salary. Retiring is the right thing to do." This statement shows the pitcher's **morality**, which is the collection of values that guides human behavior.

In society at large, the sharing of moral values promotes social cooperation and is a significant means of social control. Shared moral values lead us to accept and trust others. Shared values allow us to recognize when there is proper behavior in others and where limits to behavior rightfully belong. Shared moral values create social harmony.

"If we are to go forward, we must go back and rediscover those precious values—that all reality hinges on moral foundations. . . ."

–Martin Luther King Jr.

The sharing of values in business life is as important as it is in other aspects of our lives. Today many businesses try to foster shared moral values in employees. It is right to strive for quality in products and service. It is wrong to discriminate against or harass a person because of race, gender, or religion. One of the successes of many Japanese companies has been to instill shared moral values in their employees.

Internationally, businesses often face problems when they do business with nations with different moral values. What is wrong in the United States may be right somewhere else and vice versa. Is it right to bribe customs officials so that your company's goods can enter a country? Is it wrong for a woman to appear in public without her face covered? Is it right to eat meat and consume alcohol? Is it wrong to talk business on Sunday? On Saturday? On Friday evening? To succeed in international operations, businesses must be sensitive to differences in moral values.

"If you don't have integrity, you have nothing. You can't buy it. You can have all the money in the world, but if you are not a moral and ethical person, you really have nothing."

–Henry Kravis, co-founder KKR equity firm

If morals involve what is right and wrong, **ethics** is a systematic statement of right and wrong together with a philosophical system that both justifies and necessitates rules of conduct. In the Judeo-Christian tradition, for example, private ownership of land and goods is highly valued. It is wrong to take something that does not belong to you—hence the rule "Thou shalt not steal."

Ethics involves a rational method for examining our moral lives, not only for recognizing what is right and wrong but also for understanding why we think something is right or wrong. "The unexamined life is not worth living," said the Greek philosopher Socrates. In other words, ethical self-examination is necessary for a meaningful human life.

The end result of ethical examination is what philosophers call **the good.** The concept of the good is central to the study of morality. *The good* may be defined as those moral goals and objectives we choose to pursue. It serves to define who we are. Thus, *leading a good life* means more than *having the good life.* It means more than material possessions and luxury. It means pursuing intangibles, being concerned, as Adam Smith put it, about the fortunes of others. That many in contemporary society do not achieve the good is evident. Too often, we confuse a good time with a good life.

In summary, morality involves what we mean by our values of right and wrong. Ethics is a formal system for deciding what is right and wrong and for justifying moral decisions. In everyday language, the terms *morality* and *ethics* are often used interchangeably. This chapter will also sometimes use the two words to mean the same thing.

ETHICS AND LAW

LO 2-1

Chief Justice Earl Warren once remarked: "In civilized life, law floats in a sea of ethics." Ethics and law have similar or complementary purposes. Both consist of rules to guide conduct and foster social cooperation. Both deal with what is right and wrong. Society's ethical values may become law through legislation or court decisions, and obedience to law is often viewed as being ethically correct. That society's ethical values often become law is the subject of Sidebar 2.2.

However, there are also differences between ethics and law. Unlike ethical systems, the legal system is an institution of the state. The state enforces legal rules through civil and criminal sanctions, like monetary damage awards, fines, and imprisonment. Many ethical values (regarding the treatment of animals, for example) are not enforced by the state, and many laws (regarding traffic violations, for example) do not address ethical concerns.

sidebar 2.2

Price Gouging after Hurricane Katrina

In 2005, Hurricane Katrina crippled many oil rigs in the Gulf of Mexico and temporarily put out of commission several oil refineries along the coast. The devastation caused a shortage of gasoline.

Responding to reduced supply and constant or increased demand, the price of gasoline shot up, doubling or in some instances tripling in price. Economists urge that retail price increases help ensure that those drivers who need and want gasoline the most will be able to get it during times of shortage. Price increases reduce unimportant driving and promote conservation.

However, many people see soaring prices during times of emergency as unethical. Almost half the states have passed laws prohibiting too rapid rises of retail prices during times of declared emergency. Throughout the South, there were numerous fines imposed for illegal "price gouging" after Katrina. And when following the hurricane the oil companies reported record profits, there was an outpouring of public criticism. Do you think it should be illegal to profit during times of public emergency?

Another difference between ethics and law concerns motivation. Although values found in ethics may be imposed on an individual (by the family, the company, or the law), the motivation to observe moral rules comes from within. On the other hand, even though the values found in law may also be personal ethical values of an individual, the motivation to observe the law comes from outside the individual in the form of state sanctions. As Justice Oliver Wendell Holmes explained:

> You can see very plainly that a bad man has as much reason as a good one for wishing to avoid an encounter with the public force, and therefore you can see the practical importance of the distinction between morality and law. A man who cares nothing for an ethical rule which is believed and practiced by his neighbors is likely nevertheless to care a good deal to avoid being made to pay money, and will want to keep out of jail if he can.

Ethical systems also involve a broader-based commitment to proper behavior than does the law. Law sets only the minimum standards acceptable to a society. As a former chief executive officer of Procter & Gamble points out: "Ethical behavior is based on more than meeting minimum legal requirements. It invariably involves a higher, moral standard."

Ultimately, the commitment to ethical values is superior to mere observance of the law in ensuring responsible business behavior. Legal rules can never be specific enough to regulate all business actions that may have socially undesirable or even dangerous consequences. And lawmakers often do not have the information to know whether specific conduct threatens employees, consumers, or the public generally. They may also lack the consensus to act quickly, or to act at all, in the face of potentially harmful business actions. However, a commitment to acceptable business ethics will usually ensure responsible business behavior.

Ethical values are ultimately superior to law in ensuring responsible business behavior.

Two Systems of Ethics

Two principal systems of ethics dominate thinking about morality in Western civilization. They are formalism and consequentialism. Although these two systems are not mutually exclusive in the outcomes of their moral analyses, they begin from different assumptions. Most people adopt elements of both systems in making ethical choices. *It is very important to appreciate how these systems have influenced your own values and moral beliefs even though until now you may have been unaware of it.*

FORMALISM

Formalism is an approach to ethics that affirms an absolute morality. A particular act is in itself right or wrong, always and in every situation. For example, lying is wrong. There are no justifications for it, and its wrongness does not depend on the situation in which the lie is told. Formalism is primarily a duty-based view of ethics. To be ethical, you have a **duty,** or moral obligation, not to lie. You have a duty to keep promises. You have a duty not to divulge confidences.

Do remember that formalism says certain behaviors are always wrong.

For the formalist (one who expresses the ethics of formalism), the ethical focus is on the worth of the individual. Individuals have rights, and these rights should not be infringed, even at the expense of society as a whole, because they have an intrinsic moral value to them. The Bill of Rights illustrates this view of the rights of individuals. When the First Amendment states "Congress shall make no law . . . abridging the freedom of speech," it takes the formalist approach.

Kant and Formalism

For the formalist thinker Immanuel Kant (1724–1804), to be ethical requires that you act with a good intent. To have a good intent, you have to act in ways that are ethically consistent. This emphasis on consistency Kant called the **categorical imperative.** You have a moral duty to act in the way you believe everyone should act. You should never act in a certain way unless you are willing to have everyone else act in the same way. You cannot make an exception for your own action. You cannot say, "I can lie (cheat) (steal) (cause injury), but others should not do this to me (to my family) (to my friends)." Kant said that to make an exception for your own behavior is immoral and unethical. Note the similarities between Kant's categorical imperative and the Golden Rule: "Do to others as you would have others do to you."

Formalist thinking raises many questions for business ethics. Are you treating your employees with respect for their rights as individuals, or are you treating them only as units of production to make a profit? If you are willing to lie about your ability to meet a production schedule in order to get a new customer, are you willing to have the customer lie to you about his or her ability to pay? If you pass on information that was told to you in confidence, are you willing to have your confidences passed on? Can business function with widespread lying, cheating, and stealing and without respect for the rights of individuals?

In his novel *The Turquoise Lament,* John D. MacDonald puts words into the mouth of his Travis McGee character that illustrate well a formalist approach:

> Integrity is not a conditional word. It doesn't blow in the wind or change in the weather. It is your inner image of yourself, and if you look in there and see a man who won't cheat, then you know he never will. Integrity is not a search for the rewards for integrity.

Table 2.1 illustrates other examples of a formalist approach to ethics.

Categorical imperative (Kant) says that you have a moral duty to act in the way you believe everyone should act.

> "Two things fill the mind with ever new and increasing wonder and awe—the starry heavens above me and the moral laws within me."
>
> **—Immanuel Kant, philosopher**

table 2.1 Examples of Ethical Formalism

Statement	Source
"We hold these truths to be self-evident."	Declaration of Independence
"Thou shalt not steal."	The Ten Commandments
"A sale made because of deception is wrong. . . . The end doesn't justify the means."	Caterpillar Code of Ethics
"There are fundamental values that cross cultures, and companies must uphold them."	Thomas Donaldson, business ethics scholar
"Openness in communications is deemed fundamental."	Business Roundtable
The moral sense is "the sense of what is inherently right and wrong. . . ."	Barbara Tuchman, historian

The Social Contract The social contract theory of Harvard philosopher John Rawls furnishes an important recent example of how formalism has influenced thinking about business and personal ethics. This theory is based not on duty but on contract (agreement).

Social contract theory concerns itself with how to construct a just society given the many inequalities of wealth, knowledge, and social status. Rawls suggests a simple first step in determining the ethical values on which a just society can be built. We should assume that we do not know our age, gender, race, intelligence, strength, wealth, or social status. This step is vital because it keeps us from being self-interested in the ethical values we consider. For example, not knowing our sex or race, will we agree that it is ethical to discriminate in employment compensation based on sex or race? Not knowing our wealth, will we agree that owning property is a fair prerequisite to being able to vote? Not knowing our age or work status, will we agree that it is just for a company to have mandatory retirement of its officers at age 65? Freeing ourselves of self-knowledge, Rawls argues, improves our ability to evaluate the terms of a fair agreement (contract) under which we enter society or join an organization like a corporation.

Rawls's "veil of igno-rance" means to think ethically you must lose the assumption that what you personally need or want is neces-sarily morally correct.

Placing himself behind a veil of self-ignorance, Rawls proposes two ethical principles. First, everyone is entitled to certain equal basic rights, including liberty, freedom of association, and personal security. Second, although there may be social and economic inequalities, these inequalities must be based on what a person does, not on who a person is, and everyone must have an equal opportunity for achievement. Since there are natural differences of intelligence and strength and persistent social differences of wealth, class, and status, defining "equal opportunity" is crucial to this second ethical principle. Rawls insists that individuals in a just society have the right to an equal place at the starting line. This is as true within a corporation as it is within a country.

Because of its emphasis on individual rights and self-worth, social contract theory has its origin in formalism. It provides a powerful process for ethical business decision making. Social contract theory is especially valuable in international business. In this arena, in the absence of much law, businesses from various cultures must agree as to the terms under which international business is to take place.

LO 2-2

CONSEQUENTIALISM

The second principal system of ethics is consequentialism. **Consequentialism** concerns itself with the moral consequences of actions rather than with the morality of the actions themselves. For the consequentialist, lying itself is not unethical. It is the consequences, or end results of lying, that must be evaluated for their ethical implications. It is the loss of trust or harm done by lying that is unethical.

If formalism focuses on individual rights, consequentialism focuses on the common good. The ethics of actions are measured by how they promote the common good. If actions increase the common good, they are ethical. If actions cause overall harm to society, they are unethical.

Modern economic theory reflects utilitarianism.

The dominant form of consequentialism is **utilitarianism.** Utilitarianism judges actions by *usefulness,* by whether they serve to increase the common good. For utilitarians, the end justifies the means. But to judge the utility of a particular action, it is necessary to consider alternative courses of action. Only after you consider all reasonable courses of action can you know whether a particular one has the greatest utility.

The International Franchising Association (IFA) adopted a new code of ethics. Officers of the association indicated that an important reason for adopting the new code was to head off government regulation of franchising through self-policing. The code states that when a franchiser is going to make a decision about adding a new franchise outlet into an area where a franchisee already owns an existing outlet, it should weigh "the positive or negative effect of the new outlet on the existing outlet." Another factor to be considered is "the benefit or detriment to the franchise system as a whole in operating the new outlet." The motivation of the IFA in adopting the new ethics code and the quoted language of the code suggest a consequentialist ethical view. Table 2.2 gives other examples of consequentialism.

Although business ethics reflect elements of both formalism and consequentialism, they focus more heavily on the latter. Business leaders feel a need to justify what they do in terms of whether or not it produces dividends for their shareholders. Their primary goal or end is to produce a profit. This orientation reflects consequentialism.

The many statements of business leaders that ethics are "good for business" illustrate this point. These statements imply that certain values are important because their end result is useful in increasing productivity and profit rather than because the values are intrinsically good. The way business managers evaluate alternative courses of action through cost-benefit analysis is a form of consequentialism.

One approach to business ethics, called "values-based management," also illustrates consequentialism. The emphasis of this approach teaches ethical values to employees that enhance the profitability of the company. Examples include why it is wrong to use company computers for personal entertainment during work hours and why it is unethical to use company long-distance phone service to contact friends and relatives. Sidebar 2.3 explores one of these examples.

In the book *Moral Intelligence: Enhancing Business Performance & Leadership Success* (2004), Doug Lennick and Fred Kiel use research to show that the best performing companies are led by those who can effectively promote moral principles throughout their organizations.

table 2.2 Examples of Ethical Consequentialism

Statement	Source
"There is no doubt that ethics pays off at the bottom line."	CEO, Procter & Gamble
"Loss of confidence in an organization is the single greatest cost of unethical behavior."	CEO, KPMG
"The strongest argument for raising the ethics bar boils down to self-interest."	CEO, KPMG
"Cost-benefit analysis (used by various governmental agencies and in business and finance)."	Economic theory, finance theory, and policy studies
"The greatest happiness of the greatest number is the foundation of morals and legislation."	Jeremy Bentham (1748–1832), English social philosopher

---

sidebar 2.3

Virtual Morality

Computers and the ease with which employees can use them for personal as well as employment reasons raise many ethical issues, which some have begun terming *virtual morality.* Is it wrong to use the Internet from work for holiday shopping? To help one's children with schoolwork? To send personal e-mail to a friend on the other side of the country? To hunt for a new job? Some businesses prohibit all personal use of company computers. Others, such as Boeing Company, permit personal use of computers during working hours, but limit such use to "reasonable duration and frequency." Even then such use should not cause "embarrassment to the company."

From the perspective of values-based management, it is easy to see that keeping employees from wrongful computer use may improve the profitability of the employer. On the other hand, improper use of what another owns raises individual moral issues as well. Similarly, if an employer has purchased the time and effort of an employee, is it morally right for the employee to use those resources for personal reasons?

Increasingly, employers are monitoring how employees use their computers. Currently over a third of large U.S. companies use software to monitor employee e-mails and website visits.

The Protestant Ethic   In part, the current focus on consequentialism in business ethics is due to the decline in business life of what has been described as the **Protestant ethic.** With the Protestant Reformation of the sixteenth century came a new emphasis on the importance of the individual. Instead of relying on the intercession of a church hierarchy to achieve grace, each person, Protestants asserted, had the means to address God personally. Thus religion provided the impetus to hard work and achievement. Human desire and indulgence, said Protestants, should be bent to God's will through self-denial, rational planning, and productivity. The Protestant ethic was rooted in a formalist approach: honesty and keeping promises were intrinsically good.

> The absolute moral values of the Protestant ethic declined. Hard work and planning become justified by the consequentialist results they produce.

The Protestant ethic was a boon to capitalism. The quest for economic independence fueled commercial growth, which fueled industrial growth, which created our modern consumer society. Along the way, however, the religious basis of the Protestant ethic was eroded by rising wealth and the encouragement of mass consumption. The part of the ethic that supported hard work, success, and rational planning continued, but without the original absolute moral values. The Protestant ethic became transformed into an organizational ethic that supports the modern bureaucratic managerial system. The sociologist Robert Jackall identifies this system as having "administrative hierarchies, standardized work procedures, regularized timetables, uniform policies, and centralized control." The goal of this system is to produce profit. Business actions are justified by their usefulness in accomplishing the goal. The religious formalism of the Protestant ethic has become a type of utilitarian consequentialism.

COMPARING THE TWO ETHICAL SYSTEMS

Formalists and consequentialists can arrive at the same conclusion for an ethical course of action, but they use a different evaluation process. Figure 2.1 illustrates how this might happen. Take as an example a company's decision

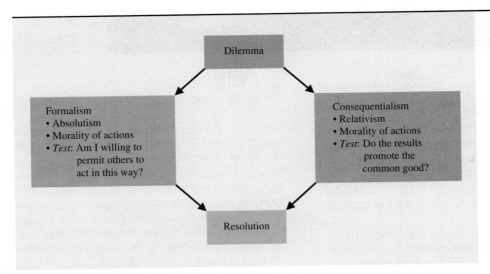

Figure 2.1
A common result.

whether or not to secretly monitor its employees' use of the e-mail system. The company suspects that some employees are using the system for personal business and to spread damaging rumors about the company and its executives. How would formalists and consequentialists approach this decision?

Formalists might say that secret monitoring treats employees only as a means to the end of increasing organizational efficiency and does not respect their self-worth as individuals. The monitoring also does not respect their dignity and their privacy. Formalists might conclude that secret monitoring is unethical. Explaining the problem to the employees and asking for their consent to monitor would be a more ethical action to take.

For a consequentialist, the act of secret monitoring itself is ethically neither right nor wrong. It is the end result that is ethically important. Secret monitoring and the punishment of wrongdoers are useful in improving productivity, which is an appropriate company goal and beneficial to society at large. To that extent, secret monitoring is ethically acceptable. But the punishment of wrongdoers will likely reveal to all employees that their e-mail has been secretly monitored. This breach of trust can lower employee morale and lessen employee loyalty to the company. Overall productivity may fall. In the examination of alternative solutions to the problem, a more beneficial overall solution, and thus a more ethical one, might be to explain the problem to the employees and ask for their consent to monitor all e-mail messages.

This example of the thinking processes of formalists and consequentialists does not exhaust all of the possible approaches that these groups might take to the e-mail problem. It does emphasize the fact that both formalist and consequentialist thinking can lead to the same business decision.

One of the most complex problems of contemporary business ethics concerns the promotion and sale of tobacco products. Cigarette smoking alone kills hundreds of thousands of people every year in the United States. Bring to bear your new knowledge about ethics by evaluating the tobacco facts presented in Sidebar 2.4. No one ever said that ethical evaluation would be easy.

In 2005 someone discovered that Sony BMG had secretly inserted a spyware program in several million CDs. The spyware installed itself when buyers ran the CDs on their computers. What are the ethics of this business decision?

sidebar 2.4

Tobacco Facts

Consider the ethical significance of the following facts:

Tobacco products have been consumed in the United States since at least the early 1600s.

Hundreds of thousands of people are involved in the growing, manufacturing, distributing, and selling of tobacco products.

In the first 20 years of tobacco litigation, juries did not award plaintiffs a single penny against tobacco companies.

Scientists and doctors accept that tobacco consumption is an important contributing factor in cancer and heart disease. Excess consumption of fatty foods and lack of exercise are also contributing factors to these diseases.

Some 435,000 people in the United States, or 1% of all cigarette smokers, die prematurely every year due to tobacco consumption.

Health-related tobacco disease costs more than $75 billion annually in spending for medical care.

The average age of beginning tobacco consumption is around 16.

Almost no one begins tobacco consumption past age 21. Three thousand new teenagers begin tobacco consumption every day.

Tobacco companies spend billions of dollars annually in advertising and marketing tobacco sales. A main strategy of tobacco promotion is to associate glamour, excitement, sex, and desirable life images with tobacco consumption. Another strategy is to get young people to sample cigarettes and other tobacco products.

The law requires that health warnings accompany the advertising and sale of tobacco products.

The nicotine in tobacco is considered addictive. However, millions have stopped tobacco consumption.

Primary sources: Federal Trade Commission Cigarette Report (2007); Centers for Disease Control; *The New York Times.*

Sources of Values for Business Ethics

There are at least four sources of values for business ethics. The sections that follow identify them as:

- Legal regulation.
- Professional codes of ethics.
- Organizational codes of ethics.
- Individual values.

LEGAL REGULATION

Don't forget that respect for law itself can help change moral values. Anti-discrimination laws have helped convince many people that discrimination based on race, gender, and religion is morally wrong.

Insider trading, bribery, fraudulent practices, and conflicts of interest are often cited as examples of ethical failures. But these practices are illegal as well. That the unethical may be illegal and vice versa is often confusing to students.

The way to understand the ethical-legal relationship is to realize that in our society ethical values frequently become law and that legal regulation can reflect society's ethical values. For example, society's ethical commitment to equal opportunity became law in the Civil Rights Act of 1964, which prohibits employment discrimination based on "race, sex, color, religion, and national origin."

At the same time, the very existence of legal regulation can influence society's view of what is ethical. In 1964, when the Civil Rights Act was passed, few people were concerned about sex discrimination in employment. Opponents of the bill inserted the prohibition against sex discrimination in hopes of preventing its passage. Obviously, these legislators believed that sex discrimination in employment was acceptable and that many others agreed with them. Despite their efforts, however, the Civil Rights Act passed, and over the years, as legal battles involving sex discrimination in employment were fought, Americans' moral sense of the importance of equal employment opportunity regardless of sex caught up with the law. Today a great majority of Americans believe women should not be discriminated against in employment simply because they are women and that such discrimination is wrong. To a significant extent, the law itself contributed to the change in values.

Legal regulation is, then, a significant source of values for business ethics. In fact, many business and professional organizations look to the law when drawing up their codes of ethical conduct. At least five major ethical rules can be drawn from the law. These include:

- Respect for the liberty and rights of others.
- The importance of acting in good faith.
- The importance of exercising due care.
- The importance of honoring confidentiality.
- Avoidance of conflicts of interest.

The following sections elaborate these concepts. These values derived from legal regulation are appropriate for use in ethical business decision making even when decisions do not involve legal issues.

Liberty and Rights

First, the law requires respect for the liberty and rights of others. We see this requirement in legislation protecting the right of privacy, promoting equal employment opportunity, and guaranteeing freedom of expression and due process of law. In one form or another, these legal rights often appear in ethical codes. Do you think that the concern for individual rights represents formalism or consequentialism?

Remember from Chapter 1 that respect for individual rights is historically connected to the legal concept of private property. To have exclusive legal rights over what you say (freedom of speech), for example, is quite similar to having exclusive rights to an area of land or a piece of machinery. The philosopher John Locke, who influenced the framers of the U.S. Constitution, even referred to "lives, liberties, and estates which I call by the general name *property*."

Good Faith

The law requires that good faith be demonstrated in various economic and other transactions. An example comes from the Uniform Commercial Code, adopted in 49 of the 50 states. It requires that all sales of goods must be carried out in *good faith,* which means "honesty in intent" and "honesty in fact."

The reverse of good faith is *bad faith,* which can be understood as dishonesty in intent. In cases involving a bad faith withholding of amounts due under insurance policies, some courts and juries have severely punished defendant insurance companies with large punitive damage awards. Acting with an honest intent is the key to understanding good faith. Is looking at the intent of parties to a business contract evidence of formalism or consequentialism?

> "At this moment, America's highest economic need is higher ethical standards— standards enforced by strict laws and upheld by responsible business leaders."
>
> **—President George W. Bush**

As legal principles, both liberty and property involve keeping others from interfering with what is *yours.*

Constitutional law also involves many balancing tests. Do these tests illustrate formalism or consequentialism?

Due Care   Another ethical value reflecting legal rules requires the exercise of *due care* in our behavior. This value comes from the law of torts, which Justice Oliver Wendell Holmes said "abounds in moral phraseology." Due care derives from society's expectations about how fair and reasonable actions are. Due care promotes the common good. In negligence law, failure to exercise due (or reasonable) care is the principal element that triggers liability against the defendant. Courts have examined due care in negligence cases in terms of a balancing test. The likelihood that the defendant's conduct will cause harmful consequences, taken with the seriousness of the harmful consequences, is balanced against the effort required to avoid the harmful consequences. The balancing test is central to the concept of due care.

Consider the following problem of due care. Bridgestone/Firestone became aware that certain of its tires were showing defects at much higher rates than what might be thought of as normal. Still, the tires operated perfectly on hundreds of thousands of vehicles. Was the company ethically required to warn the public about the tires? To recall the tires? A very small fraction of all tires showed defects. What level of defect is acceptable without warning those who use a product? Ford Explorer sport utility vehicles used the Firestone tire, and Ford decided to recall and replace the tires in Saudi Arabia. But Ford did not notify U.S. safety authorities or the public about what it was doing overseas, even though the same tires were on Ford Explorers in the United States. Was Ford acting ethically? What would you need to know in order to decide?

Chapter 13 further discusses the Federal Sentencing Guidelines.

Another form of the requirement to exercise due care comes from the Federal Guidelines for Sentencing for Criminal Convictions, which focus specifically on corporate white-collar crime. In determining what punishment a company should receive for the illegal business acts of its employees, the guidelines look at whether the company has "an effective program to prevent and detect violations of the law." An effective program is measured by whether "the organization exercised due diligence in seeking to prevent and detect criminal conduct by its employees and other agents." *Due diligence* is another way of saying "due care."

As with the determination of due care in negligence law, the determination of due diligence in sentencing guidelines requires use of a balancing test. Considering the significance of the balancing test to the exercise of due care (or due diligence), do you think that formalist or consequentialist values are reflected?

Confidentiality   Honoring confidentiality is the fourth major ethical value emerging from the law and legal regulation. The legal requirement of honoring confidentiality appears in agency law generally and in the professional-client relationship in particular. For a CPA to share with unauthorized third parties what has been learned during a client's audit is professional malpractice. Likewise, it is malpractice for an attorney, physician, real estate broker, or any professional agent to tell others what a client (principal) has related in confidence.

Many people consider it a type of conflict of interest for accounting firms to both advise their clients on general financial matters and to audit them when audits may uncover financial wrongdoing.

In addition to not telling others of a confidence, an agent must in many instances not act on the confidence related by a principal. The securities laws make it a crime for agents like the officers and managers of a corporation to buy and sell corporate stock on information only they know. (See Chapter 17.) Many "insider trading" scandals have occurred because corporate agents illegally traded on confidential information they learned from their positions in the corporation.

The legal requirement of honoring confidences contains both formalist and consequentialist ethical values. Can you identify these values?

Conflicts of Interest Often embodied in business codes of ethics, avoiding conflicts of interest is a final ethical value flowing from the law, especially from agency law. A conflict of interest occurs when one attempts to "serve two masters," and no agent or employee of one principal can secretly work for another whose interest competes with that of the first principal. That is why a real estate agent may not represent both the seller and the buyer in a real estate transaction without permission from both parties.

Sometimes when corporations "go public" or otherwise sell new stock issues, they will give employees of their customers or suppliers the option of buying a number of the new stock shares at a special fixed price. If the market value of the stock rises, exercise of the stock options can be quite valuable to these employees as they resell the stock at market price. Is it a conflict of interest for employees of other companies to accept these stock options? Does it impair their objective judgment about continuing to do business with the corporation that has given them such a gift? Compaq Computer Corporation, Cisco Systems, and AT&T specifically forbid employees from accepting stock options from their suppliers or customers.

Conflicts of interest also arise in public service. For instance, it is a conflict of interest for a judge or administrative regulator to make a decision involving a company in which he or she owns stock. Note that in this instance the conflict of interest does not involve "serving two masters." The conflict arises because of the ownership interests that will make it difficult for the judge or regulator to make an unbiased decision. In terms of formalism and consequentialism, how do you evaluate the prohibition against conflicts of interest?

concept *summary*

Ethical Values from Legal Regulation

- Respect the liberty and rights of others.
- Act in good faith.
- Exercise due care.
- Honor confidentiality.
- Avoid conflicts of interest.

PROFESSIONAL CODES OF ETHICS

Another important source of business ethics comes from the historic tradition of the professional codes of ethics. Professions such as law and medicine have long traditions of codes of ethical conduct. Other professions, and more recently business and industry in general, have developed and adopted codes of ethical conduct. Here we use portions of professional codes to demonstrate sources of ethical values that come from the development of group standards for ethical conduct.

We begin with selected excerpts from codes of conduct for two professions: marketing and accounting. These codes are the Ethical Norms and Values for Marketers from the American Marketing Association, shown in Sidebar 2.5, and the American Institute of Certified Public Accountants Code

sidebar 2.5

Ethical Norms and Values for Marketers

PREAMBLE

The American Marketing Association commits itself to promoting the highest standard of professional ethical norms and values for its members. Norms are established standards of conduct that are expected and maintained by society and/or professional organizations. Values represent the collective conception of what people find desirable, important and morally proper. Values serve as the criteria for evaluating the actions of others. . . .

ETHICAL VALUES

Honesty—to be truthful and forthright in our dealings with customers and stakeholders.

- We will tell the truth in all situations and at all times.
- We will offer products of value that do what we claim in our communications.
- We will stand behind our products if they fail to deliver their claimed benefits.
- We will honor our explicit and implicit commitments and promises.

Responsibility—to accept the consequences of our marketing decisions and strategies.

- We will make strenuous efforts to serve the needs of our customers.
- We will avoid using coercion with all stakeholders.
- We will acknowledge the social obligations to stakeholders that come with increased marketing and economic power.
- We will recognize our special commitments to economically vulnerable segments of the market such as children, the elderly and others who may be substantially disadvantaged.

Fairness—to try to balance justly the needs of the buyer with the interests of the seller.

- We will represent our products in a clear way in selling, advertising and other forms of communication; this includes the avoidance of false, misleading and deceptive promotion.
- We will reject manipulations and sales tactics that harm customer trust.
- We will not engage in price fixing, predatory pricing, price gouging or "bait-and-switch" tactics.

- We will not knowingly participate in material conflicts of interest.

Respect—to acknowledge the basic human dignity of all stakeholders.

- We will value individual differences even as we avoid stereotyping customers or depicting demographic groups (e.g., gender, race, sexual orientation) in a negative or dehumanizing way in our promotions.
- We will listen to the needs of our customers and make all reasonable efforts to monitor and improve their satisfaction on an ongoing basis.
- We will make a special effort to understand suppliers, intermediaries and distributors from other cultures.
- We will appropriately acknowledge the contributions of others, such as consultants, employees and coworkers, to our marketing endeavors.

Openness—to create transparency in our marketing operations.

- We will strive to communicate clearly with all our constituencies.
- We will accept constructive criticism from our customers and other stakeholders.
- We will explain significant product or service risks, component substitutions or other foreseeable eventualities that could affect customers or their perception of the purchase decision.
- We will fully disclose list prices and terms of financing as well as available price deals and adjustments.

Citizenship—to fulfill the economic, legal, philanthropic and societal responsibilities that serve stakeholders in a strategic manner.

- We will strive to protect the natural environment in the execution of marketing campaigns.
- We will give back to the community through volunteerism and charitable donations.
- We will work to contribute to the overall betterment of marketing and its reputation.
- We will encourage supply chain members to ensure that trade is fair for all participants, including producers in developing countries.

sidebar 2.6

American Institute of Certified Public Accountants Code of Professional Conduct

These Principles of the Code of Professional Conduct of the American Institute of Certified Public Accountants express the profession's recognition of its responsibilities to the public, to clients, and to colleagues. They guide members in the performance of their professional responsibilities and express the basic tenets of ethical and professional conduct. The Principles call for an unswerving commitment to honorable behavior, even at the sacrifice of personal advantage.

In carrying out their responsibilities as professionals, members should exercise sensitive professional and moral judgments in all their activities.

As professionals, certified public accountants perform an essential role in society. Consistent with that role, members of the American Institute of Certified Public Accountants have responsibilities to all those who use their professional services. Members also have a continuing responsibility to cooperate with each other to improve the art of accounting, maintain the public's confidence, and carry out the profession's special responsibilities for self-governance. The collective efforts of all members are required to maintain and enhance the traditions of the profession.

Members should accept the obligation to act in a way that will serve the public interest, honor the public interest, and demonstrate commitment to professionalism.

A distinguishing mark of a profession is acceptance of its responsibility to the public. The accounting profession's public consists of clients, credit grantors, governments, employers, investors, the business and financial community, and others who rely on the objectivity and integrity of certified public accountants to maintain the orderly functioning of commerce. This reliance imposes a public interest responsibility on certified public accountants. The public interest is defined as the collective well-being of the community of people and institutions the profession serves.

In discharging their professional responsibilities, members may encounter conflicting pressures from among each of those groups. In resolving those conflicts, members should act with integrity, guided by the precept that when members fulfill their responsibility to the public, clients' and employers' interests are best served.

---

of Professional Conduct, which appears in Sidebar 2.6. Understand that what follows are only excerpts from these codes, which in full may run several pages.

So important are ethics to the conduct of accounting that when Arthur Andersen, once one of the world's oldest and largest accounting firms, was implicated in a cover-up of why the energy firm Enron collapsed, the entire accounting firm went out of business. Enron had contributed only a small percentage of the worldwide business of Arthur Andersen.

From these excerpts, the ethical values expressed in the codes of ethics for marketers and accountants may seem overly general in nature. But each code has pages of rules that apply to specific situations arising in the marketer-client and accountant-client relationship. As the state does not enforce these codes, it is not proper to call them law. Yet the professional organizations that have adopted these codes employ specific sanctions to back them up. Because the state will likely regulate these professions if they do not do so themselves, it is appropriate to term their ethical codes **self-regulation.**

ORGANIZATIONAL CODES OF ETHICS

There are few industrywide codes of ethics, so many businesses have adopted ethical codes at the individual organization level. Nearly all large corporations now have their own codes of business ethics, often called codes of conduct. These codes are obviously an important source of business ethics.

The Business Roundtable, a national group of senior business leaders, has identified a general list of topics that organizational codes of business ethics should cover. These include:

- Fundamental honesty and adherence to the law.
- Product safety and quality.
- Health and safety in the workplace.
- Conflicts of interest.
- Fairness in selling/marketing practices.
- Financial reporting.
- Supplier relationships.
- Pricing, billing, and contracting.
- Trading in securities/using inside information.
- Payments to obtain business/Foreign Corrupt Practices Act.
- Acquiring and using information about others.
- Security.
- Political activities.
- Protection of the environment.
- Intellectual property/proprietary information

Some companies provide only general ethics guidelines to employees. Other companies provide very specific and detailed ethics rules.

Different Approaches to Ethical Codes Individual companies take different approaches to ethical codes. The Hertz Corporation developed a Standards of Business Conduct document that outlines ethics and compliance obligations for all Hertz employees, officers, and directors. The document begins with a clear statement of Hertz's motivation for promoting business ethics: "Simply stated, acting ethically is good for business. Indeed, it is a competitive advantage as it protects our brand and reputation in the marketplace." The Standards of Business Conduct is Hertz's guide for ethical decision-making and corporate contacts when more guidance is needed.

Boeing Corporation has a short code of conduct (see Sidebar 2.7).

Other companies spell out their expectations for employees' behavior in considerable detail. For instance, the Martin Marietta Corporation Code of Ethics and Standard of Conduct is 17 pages long and covers a wide variety of company activities and practices.

Many codes of business ethics contain both general statements of shared ethical values and more specific applied examples of these values. General statements of shared values remind employees what their companies stand for and at the same time serve to encourage ethical behavior in situations not covered by specific ethical guides. The applied examples address specific types of business conduct like those listed above by the Business Roundtable.

A majority of organizational codes of business ethics provide sanctions for their violation, up to and including employee termination. As with professional codes of conduct, it is appropriate to call these organizational codes self-regulation. Whether companies pursue ethical self-regulation with enthusiasm and commitment or the codes are mere window dressing to satisfy the government and the general public is an important issue in determining the value of these codes.

sidebar 2.7

Boeing Code of Conduct

The Boeing Code of Conduct outlines expected behaviors for all Boeing employees. Boeing will conduct its business fairly, impartially, in an ethical and proper manner, and in full compliance with all applicable laws and regulations. In conducting its business, integrity must underlie all company relationships, including those with customers, suppliers, communities and among employees. The highest standards of ethical business conduct are required of Boeing employees in the performance of their company responsibilities. Employees will not engage in conduct or activity that may raise questions as to the company's honesty, impartiality, reputation or otherwise cause embarrassment to the company.

Employees will ensure that:

- They do not engage in any activity that might create a conflict of interest for the company or for themselves individually.

- They do not take advantage of their Boeing position to seek personal gain through the inappropriate use of Boeing or non-public information or abuse of their position. This includes not engaging in insider trading.

- They will follow all restrictions on use and disclosure of information. This includes following all requirements for protecting Boeing information and ensuring that non-Boeing proprietary information is used and disclosed only as authorized by the owner of the information or as otherwise permitted by law.

- They observe that fair dealing is the foundation for all of our transactions and interactions.

- They will protect all company, customer and supplier assets and use them only for appropriate company approved activities.

- Without exception, they will comply with all applicable laws, rules and regulations.

- They will promptly report any illegal or unethical conduct to management or other appropriate authorities (i.e., Ethics, Law, Security, EEO).

Every employee has the responsibility to ask questions, seek guidance and report suspected violations of this Code of Conduct. Retaliation against employees who come forward to raise genuine concerns will not be tolerated.

Although many businesses have codes of ethics, effective implementation and enforcement of those codes is far more important than the creation of a code. The decision by General Motors not to recall the Chevrolet Cobalt after discovery of faulty ignition switches has renewed debate about when executive compensation policies should require forfeiture of past bonuses, or "claw back" of compensation. For more than 10 years, apparently, General Motors was aware of the problem with the ignition switch that is linked to 13 deaths. A 90-cent part would have fixed the defect. GM's ability to recover bonuses, similar to the majority of compensation policies in corporate America, is limited to issues related to accounting violations. The disastrous decision to not fix the Cobalt's ignition switches recently renewed the debate regarding whether past pay of executives should be recoverable when unethical conduct is discovered, utilizing personal bank accounts as a way to enforce ethical codes.

INDIVIDUAL VALUES

LO 2-3

The ultimate source of ethical values for business decision making comes from the individual. Others can tell you what is right or wrong. They can sanction you for failing to live up to their expectations. But only you can make your behavior ethical. Only you can intend your actions to be honest and fair or to serve the common good.

How to act ethically in every business situation is beyond the scope of this chapter, or that of any book, for that matter. Business life is just too complex. There is no way to create enough rules to cover all possible ethically significant situations, even if they could be identified in advance. However, there are five questions that you can ask yourself that will help you explore your ethical values before making personal or business decisions about what to do.

Do remember that a "good life" means more than having material possessions and a good time. It means being concerned about others.

1. **Have I thought about whether the action I may take is right or wrong?** John Smale, former CEO of Procter & Gamble, has said that "there is an ethical dimension to most complex business problems." If this is so, then you should consider whether any decision you propose to make to solve such a problem is ethical or not. The philosopher Hannah Arendt explained that evil often comes from a kind of thoughtlessness. Plato wrote that immoral behavior often flows from ignorance. A major goal of this chapter is to encourage you to think about the ethical implications of what you decide and what you do. It is the first step in leading a good life.

2. **Will I be proud to tell of my action to my family? To my employer? To the news media?** An excellent way to uncover whether there are ethical difficulties with a possible decision is to consider how proud you would be to share it with others. Before reaching an important business decision, consider how you would feel about telling your decision to your family, your employer, and the public through the news media. The less proud you are to share your decision with others, the more likely your decision is to be unethical. As Stephen Butler, former CEO of KPMG, said, "An essential part of an ethics process is identifying issues that would mortify a chief executive if he were to read about them on the front page of the newspaper."

3. **Am I willing for everyone to act as I am thinking of acting?** With this question you encompass a major principle of ethical formalism. If you consider suggesting to a co-worker that it would be advantageous for him or her to develop a sexual relationship with you, are you willing to have your superior suggest this relationship to you? Or to your friends or a member of your family? Trying to convince yourself that it is acceptable for you to do something but not acceptable for others in your situation to do it is virtually always immoral.

Numerous commentators have asserted that "harm" to the interests of others is the major limitation on both liberty and the use of an owner's resources.

4. **Will my decision cause harm to others or to the environment?** Asking this question exposes a significant principle of ethical consequentialism: promotion of the common good. Promoting the common good within your business organization is important, but it is even more important to consider whether your decision is good for society.

   You can approach this issue of the common good by asking whether your decision will cause harm. If the decision will cause no harm and will advance your business interests, it will also usually advance the good of society by increasing productivity, efficiency, or innovation.

   Many business decisions, however, do cause harm to others or to the environment. It is difficult to construct an interstate highway without workers being injured and trees being cut. The point of asking yourself the question about potential harm is so you can weigh the harm against the increase in the common good and so you can evaluate whether an alternative course of action might bring about the same increase in the common good with less harm.

Recall that ethical formalists maintain that harm to some individual rights is never justified by an increase in organizational or common good. But as ethical decision making in business often involves a mixed approach, including both formalism and consequentialism, it is appropriate for you to evaluate potential business decisions by weighing harms against benefits to the common good.

5. **Will my actions violate the law?** Both formalists and consequentialists believe that you have an ethical duty to obey the law except in very limited instances. The law provides only minimum standards for behavior, but they are standards that should be observed. Thus, to be ethical, you should always consider whether any business decision you make will require illegal actions.

   Sometimes it is not clear whether proposed actions will violate the law. Then you should consult with legal counsel. Many regulatory agencies will also give legal advice about whether actions you are considering are legal or not.

   When you are convinced that a law itself is morally wrong, you may be justified in disobeying it. Even then, to be ethical, you should be willing to make public your disobedience and to accept the consequences for it. Both Mohandas Gandhi and Martin Luther King Jr. deliberately disobeyed laws they thought were morally wrong, and they changed society by doing so. Ultimately they changed both laws and ethics. But they made their disobedience to these laws public, and they willingly accepted punishment for violating them. Dr. King wrote: "I submit that an individual who breaks a law that conscience tells him is unjust, and who willingly accepts the penalty of imprisonment in order to arouse the conscience of the community over its injustice, is in reality expressing the highest respect for the law."

To be ethical and violate a law, you should be willing to accept the consequences for it.

Leading an ethical business life may be difficult at times. You will make mistakes. You will be tempted. It is unlikely that you will be perfect. But if you want to be ethical and will work hard toward achieving your goal, you will be rewarded. As with achieving other challenging business objectives, there will be satisfaction in ethical business decision making.

concept *summary*

Self-Examination for Self-Regulation

- Have I thought about whether the action I may take is right or wrong?
- Will I be proud to tell of my action to my family? To my employer? To the news media?
- Am I willing for everyone to act as I am thinking of acting?
- Will my decision cause harm to others or to the environment?
- Will my actions violate the law?

In business as well as in personal life, the key to ethical decision making is wanting to be ethical and having the will to be ethical. If you do not want to be ethical, no code of conduct can make you ethical. Potential harm you may cause to individuals and to society will best be deterred by the threat of legal punishment and the sanctions of professional and corporate codes. You may never get caught, lose your job, or go to jail. But, as Mortimer Adler observed, you will lack "much that is needed for the good life."

Achieving an Ethical Business Corporation

The primary reason that corporations dominate the business landscape is that their ownership is divisible into small shares that make them easily sellable.

The dominant form of organization in modern business is the corporation. Currently, the top 100 manufacturing corporations produce more than two-thirds of the nation's entire manufacturing output. In 1840 the largest manufacturing firm in the United States, the Springfield Armory, employed only 250 workers. Today, many corporations have tens of thousands of employees. Some have hundreds of thousands. In substantial part, the development of the corporate form of business organization made possible this growth in business size.

Ethical problems, however, arise in corporate life that are not present in one's individual experience. In a study published of Harvard MBAs during their first five years following graduation, 29 of 30 reported that business pressures had forced them to violate their own ethical standards. The next sections focus on the ethical problems of an individual in the corporation and suggest several ways of dealing with them.

LO 2-4   THE OBSTACLES

Some may contend that the corporation by its very nature, with its dependence on a competitive edge and on profit and its limited liability, is so constituted as to make ethical behavior unlikely. That is not true, but there are certain obstacles to ethical corporate behavior that deserve serious consideration.

"The cult of short-term stockholder value has been corrupting."

–John S. Reed, former chair of the New York Stock Exchange

The Emphasis on Profit   The primary goal of the modern business corporation is to produce a profit. Management demands it, the board of directors demands it, and shareholders demand it. Making a profit motivates our entire economic system, and it promotes the common good by providing incentive for job creation and the efficient fulfillment of social needs for goods and services.

Unfortunately, with the decline of the Protestant ethic, emphasis on corporate profit alone sometimes conflicts with ethical responsibility. How a profit is made becomes less important than that it is made. Various business scandals illustrate this point.

In many corporations the responsibility for profit making is decentralized. The home office expects a plant in another state to meet certain profit goals, but the home office does not know much about the particular operations of that plant. Meeting profit goals places enormous pressure on the local plant manager. The manager's career advancement depends on the plant's profitability, yet the home office does not appreciate the difficulties under which the plant is operating. In such a situation the overemphasis on profit can easily lead to the manager's taking ethical and legal shortcuts to ensure profit.

An example of such shortcuts involved Columbia/HCA Healthcare Corporation, one of the major national hospital chains. Following a government investigation, many units of the company were accused of enhancing profits by improperly billing Medicare for laboratory tests and home health care services. It was also alleged that managers were "upcoding," or exaggerating patient illness, in order to get greater reimbursements from the Medicare system. Several managers were criminally indicted and convicted. The company's CEO resigned. To settle charges, the company agreed to pay the federal government $745 million to resolve fraud allegations. As part of its response, the company also stationed ethics and compliance officers in nearly every hospital, in part to prevent managers from "looking good" by producing profits through improper billings.

Does the emphasis on profit in a property-based private market mean that *only* profit must be considered in business decision making? For an example of a nation where not only profit is important in business, see Sidebar 2.8.

> "I do not believe maximizing profits for the investors is the only acceptable justification for all corporate actions. The investors are not the only people who matter. Corporations can exist for purposes other than simply maximizing profits."
>
> **—John Mackey, CEO, Whole Foods Market**

Don't forget that a nation is just a large group. This means that "culture matters" in the implementation (or not) of moral values.

---

sidebar 2.8

The Swedish Example of *Lagom*

The Swedes have a strong property-based private market, but the business emphasis in Sweden is not solely on profit making. Instead, the Swedes have a strong ethic of *lagom,* which means "not too much, not too little, but just enough."

As a result, the pay of corporate chief executive officers (CEOs) is only a small fraction of what it is in the United States and the average take-home pay of employees (excluding CEOs) varies from highest to lowest by a ratio of only 3 to 1. Sweden provides universal health care, public nursing homes, and subsidized child care

and parental leave-taking during a child's first year. When Swedish companies go overseas, they treat employees there with much of the same ethic as in Sweden.

Lagom means that there are few wealthy Swedes, and Sweden's social welfare system of "just enough" depends on a tax rate of approximately twice that in the United States. Note also that Sweden is a small, homogenous country whose citizens share a common ethical culture that is often not found in larger nations.

Source: Susan Wennemyer, "Sweden: The Kindness Economy," *Business Ethics,* Fall 2003.

The Effect of the Group The social critic Ambrose Bierce once remarked that the corporation is "an ingenious device for obtaining individual profit without individual responsibility." He was referring to the fact that individuals in large groups such as the corporation feel less responsibility for what happens in the group than they do for what happens in their individual lives. They may also act differently, and to some extent less ethically, in a group.

That individuals will do unethical things as part of a mob which they would never do alone is widely recognized, and the same pattern can be observed in corporate behavior. Within corporations it becomes easy for a researcher not to pass on lately discovered concerns about the possible

> "Study after study confirms it: the vast majority of people act based on the circumstances in their environment and the standards set by their leaders and peers, even if it means compromising their personal moral ideals. 'Good' people do bad things if they are put in an environment that doesn't value values, if pressured to believe that they don't have any choice but to get the job done—whatever it takes."
>
> **–Ethics Resource Center (2008)**

(yet not certain) side effects of a new skin lotion that upper management is so enthusiastic about. In corporate life it is not difficult to overlook the unethical behavior of a superior when many fellow employees are also overlooking it. And of course, "I did it because everyone else did it" is a common rationalization in groups of all kinds. "Just following orders" is a similar rationalization.

That individuals in groups may feel a diminished sense of responsibility for decisions made and actions taken invites ethical compromise. Coupled with an overemphasis on profit, the group effect increases the difficulty of achieving an ethical business corporation.

The Control of Resources by Nonowners

In the modern corporation, the owners (or *shareholders*) are often not in possession and control of corporate resources. Top management of many corporations effectively possess and control vast resources that they do not own. This produces the problems of corporate governance mentioned in Chapter 1. Managerial agents like the president and vice presidents of a large corporation have ethical and legal duties to manage the corporate resources for the benefit of their owners. But because they control corporate resources, it may be easy to manipulate the resources in their own interest and difficult for others to find out that they have done so. In other words, managers may be in an ideal position to infringe on the property interest of the corporate owners.

Sometimes, managers embezzle corporate money or abuse expense accounts. At other times they misrepresent the financial condition of the corporation in order to exercise stock options, obtain huge bonuses, or prop up loans they have secured with company stock. Because the very nature of corporate structure gives managers the opportunity to abuse and misappropriate corporate resources owned ultimately by the shareholders, ethical business practice is made more important yet more difficult. Consider Sidebar 2.9.

sidebar 2.9

Failure and Collapse

In the financial collapse and recession of 2008, many financial institutions were paying executives enormous sums of money. Lehman Brothers Holdings Inc., an investment bank, paid its CEO, Richard Fuld, a reported $480 million in salary and bonuses between 2000 and 2008. During this period, Lehman Brothers had leveraged its assets more than 30 to 1, meaning that it had debts of over 30 times the value of its assets, and it bought and sold extremely high-risk, mortgage-based securities. However, when the housing market declined and these securities turned out to have little value, Lehman Brothers fell, helping to start a series of worldwide financial collapses. Consider the ethical implications, both to shareholders and society, of business agents like Richard Fuld taking risks with money they do not own in return for the possibility of enormous personal returns.

Consider also that the executives of Lehman Brothers were telling investors, right up until the time of their collapse, that the company was in good financial shape. Are such statements unethical, illegal? In 2002, Bernard J. Ebbers, the chief executive officer of WorldCom, characterized investors's concerns as mostly "unfounded nonsense" and said that "bankruptcy or a credit default is not a concern" and that "it has been 10 years since WorldCom has been so well positioned from an operating perspective." Immediately following these statements, the company's stock rose in market value. However, five months later WorldCom filed for bankruptcy. Mr. Ebbers was arrested and in 2005 a court sentenced him to 25 years in prison.

THE STEPS

Despite the obstacles that sometimes stand in the way of ethical corporate behavior, certain steps can be taken to promote business ethics in corporate life.

Involvement of Top Management To encourage corporate ethics, it is not enough merely to adopt a code of conduct. For the code to change behavior, corporate employees must believe that the values expressed by the code represent the values of the corporation's top management. Top management must act as a role model for values it wishes corporate employees to share.

The sociologist Robert Jackall attributes the importance of a corporation's top management in encouraging business ethics to the bureaucratic system for career advancement. Each employee owes loyalty to his or her immediate corporate superior. As a practical matter, career advancement for the employee is generally tied to career advancement for the superior. In turn, that supervisor has a corporate superior to whom loyalty is owed, and so on up the corporate bureaucratic hierarchy.

Beyond a certain level in corporate bureaucracy, argues Jackall, social indicators about how well an employee "fits in" to the company management are as important as merit performance in securing further career advancement. For this reason, corporate employees tend to be very sensitive to the values of top corporate management and take these values as their own. Due to the interlocking system of loyalties that run between employment levels of the corporate hierarchy, top management's values filter down quite effectively to lower-level employees.

The values adopted by lower-level employees, however, will be top management's *real* values. So if the corporation has a code of conduct that expresses excellent ethical values, but top management shows that it expects profit at any cost, then the values adopted by lower-level employees will likely relate to profit at any cost rather than to values appearing in the code of conduct.

Top management must really believe in the ethical values expressed in codes of conduct for these values to take hold throughout the corporation. But if they do believe them and will communicate this belief through the corporation, there is an excellent chance that these values will be adopted within the corporate group. As Stephen Butler, former CEO of KPMG, says, "I really believe that corporate ethics are essential for a successful business today, and the CEOs of corporate America are the only ones who can institutionalize them."

Unfortunately, some top management support for business ethics may be merely for show. One survey concluded that 59% of the largest British companies offered no training to lower management on the meaning and use of their corporate codes of conduct. These findings are similar to those conducted by the U.S.-based Ethics & Compliance Officers Association, where an even larger percentage of companies offered no guidance on the meaning and use of ethical codes.

> "Ethics . . . is a responsibility given to every employee in the company, but it must be led by top leadership.
>
> **–Ira A. Lipman, chairman, Guardsmark LLC**

Openness in Communication For ethical corporate values to make their most significant impact on decision making, corporate employees must be willing to talk with each other about ethical issues. "Openness in communication is deemed fundamental," states the Business Roundtable. Openness promotes trust, and without trust even the best-drafted code of ethics will likely fall short of achieving an ethical business corporation.

The complexity of information required to evaluate the implications of many business decisions requires openness in communication.

Beyond helping establish trust, openness in communication is necessary for ethical corporate decision making because of the complexity of information required to evaluate the implications of many business decisions. Without open discussion of these implications among employees and between employees and their superiors, ethical decision making is severely hindered. Information crucial to making an ethical decision may be lacking.

For example, consider the complexity of a firm's decision to sell in other countries a pesticide that is banned for sale in the United States. Evaluating the ethical implications of the sale (assuming there are no legal ones) will demand considerable information. To make a fully informed decision the firm must know:

- What the effects of the pesticide on humans and the environment are.
- Why the pesticide was banned in the United States.
- Why the pesticide is useful in other countries.
- Whether in spite of its ban for use in the United States there may be good reasons to use the pesticide in other countries.
- Whether there are alternatives to its use in other countries.

The sharing of information about the implications of this pesticide sale will greatly assist the making of an ethical decision about its use. Openness in communication among employees on these implications will be vital in reaching an ethically informed corporate decision about this complex matter.

How is openness in communication on ethical issues promoted within the corporation? There is no single answer. For top management to provide a good role model of concern for speaking out on ethical issues is certainly a right beginning. Another possibility is for employees to meet periodically in small groups to consider either real or hypothetical ethical problems. In general, a shared corporate commitment to the ideal of ethical decision making is important to openness in communication.

Consideration of All Stakeholders

Consideration of All Stakeholders Large corporations affect the interests of many different groups in society, which are called "stakeholders" because they have something at risk when the company acts and thus have a "stake" in it. Investor-owners, employees, the board of directors, and managers typically have a stake in the actions of large corporations, but so do customers, suppliers, financial creditors like banks, and the community in which a company is located. If a company pollutes as a by-product of production, society itself may have a stake in what actions a corporation takes.

Stakeholder theory holds that ethical corporate behavior requires that directors and managers take into account everyone whose interests the corporation impacts, called "stakeholders."

The consequentialist ethics known as **stakeholder theory** maintains that ethical corporate behavior depends on managers who recognize and take into account the various stakeholders whose interests the corporation impacts. Stakeholder theory includes but goes beyond the responsibilities of corporate governance, which focuses on the *legal* responsibilities of managers to society and to the investor-owners of the corporation. Stakeholder theory suggests that through its managers, an ethical corporation

- Considers the concerns of all proper stakeholders and weighs their interests when making decisions.
- Allows stakeholders to communicate with decision makers and informs them about risks to their interests that may arise from corporate action.

- Adopts communication methods that are appropriate to the sophistication levels of various stakeholders.
- Realizes the interdependence of all stakeholders and demonstrates fairness toward both voluntary stakeholders (e.g., employees) and involuntary stakeholders (e.g., the community).
- Works actively and cooperatively to reduce the risk of corporate harm to all stakeholders and to compensate them when harm occurs.
- Avoids risks to stakeholders which, if explained, would be clearly unacceptable.
- Acknowledges the potential conflict between managerial self-interest and the ethical responsibility of managers to other stakeholders, and promotes open procedures that allow managers to monitor their own ethical performance.

Stakeholder theory is part of the ethics sometimes also called "corporate social responsibility."

For an example of what can happen to a large business when ethical values collapse at the top, see Sidebar 2.10.

---

sidebar 2.10

The Demise of Arthur Andersen

For much of the last century, the firm of Arthur Andersen was one of the largest and most influential accounting firms in the world. Yet in 2002 it collapsed following the firm's criminal prosecution for obstruction of justice in shredding the documents of Enron, one of its clients known for massive corporate governance problems. In the end, three of the five largest bankruptcies ever recorded involved Arthur Andersen clients with financial accounting problems.

In her book *Final Accounting: Ambition, Greed and the Fall of Arthur Andersen,* business ethicist and former Harvard professor Barbara Ley Toffler recounts what led to the demise of the accounting firm. Although the firm employed thousands of honest accountants, its top management cut ethical and legal corners in the auditing of some of its biggest clients, clients from whom the firm also collected millions of dollars in financial consulting fees. Within a business culture that encouraged loyalty, conformity, and obedience to the leadership of its senior partners, the conflicts of interest between impartial accounting and partisan consulting set the stage for the final corruption leading to the fall of the firm.

Companies attract investors (and lenders) who depend on the reputation of the accountants who audit the companies' books for accurate financial information about the companies. When almost all their clients abandoned them after their prosecution, Arthur Andersen fell. The firm's demise illustrates Robert Jackall's emphasis on the importance of top management on the ethical values within business organizations.

THE REWARDS

Of the world's 100 largest economies, 49 of them are countries and 51 are companies. General Motors has greater annual sales than the gross national products of Denmark, Thailand, Turkey, South Africa, or Saudi Arabia. Walmart's economy is larger than that of Poland, Ukraine, Portugal, Israel, or Greece. Because of the size and influence of modern corporations, business ethics take on special significance. Although there are unique problems with promoting ethical corporate decision making, the rewards for making the attempt are important both to business and society.

Walmart also has over one million employees.

The Spanish journal *Boletín Círculo* makes four observations about business ethics. A paraphrase of these observations provides a good way to highlight a chapter on ethics and self-regulation:

1. Profits and business ethics are not contradictory. Some of the most profitable businesses have also historically been the most ethical.

2. An ethical organizational life is a basic business asset that should be accepted and encouraged. The reverse is also true. Unethical behavior is a business liability.

3. Ethics are of continuing concern to the business community. They require ongoing reevaluation. Businesses must always be ethically sensitive to changes in society.

4. Business ethics reflect business leadership. Top firms can and should exercise leadership in business ethics.

> Legal regulation lacks flexibility and is inadequately informed to be the only social guide for business decision making.

Business plays a vital role in serving society, and we cannot isolate the impact of important business decisions from their social consequences. For businesses merely to observe the law is not sufficiently responsible. Legal regulation lacks flexibility and is inadequately informed to be the only social guide for business decision making. Ethics belong in business decision making. A business that does not act ethically severs itself from society, from the good, and ultimately from its own source of support.

In reading the next chapters on the regulatory environment, consider how passage of much of the regulation was preceded by breaches of business ethics. If ethical self-regulation does not guide business behavior, legal regulation often follows quickly.

CAN A BUSINESS HAVE A CONSCIENCE?

This chapter has emphasized the importance of creating and sustaining shared values within a business so that integrity guides decision making throughout the organization and each member of the organization is accountable for high ethical standards. Is it possible to take that to the next level? Can the business itself exercise religious values and morality? The courts are considering that question in light of a controversial provision of the Affordable Care Act.

The "personhood" rights of a corporation have long been recognized in the law. For example, the Supreme Court ruled in the *Citizens United v. Federal Election Committee* case of 2010 that corporations had the right to express political views and that the law attempting to ban political contributions by corporations was, therefore, a violation of the U.S. Constitution. In addition to political speech, what else can businesses express? Moral views?

The Affordable Care Act includes a provision that businesses' health care insurance plans offered to employees must include coverage for a wide range of contraceptives. Several corporations filed a lawsuit on the basis that the coverage of contraceptives violates the businesses' religious conscience. If a corporation is a "person" with free expression rights, does it likewise have freedom of religion? One of the businesses answering that question in the affirmative is Hobby Lobby because its owners believe the business is an extension of their religious lives and that it would be a violation of conscience to pay for others' contraception through its business.

This issue of business ethics has many implications. Certainly, laws that force individuals' to violate a religious value are problematic. But what are the parameters of business and religious expression? Hobby Lobby, for example, does not sell shot glasses because the owners' religious values include an aversion to alcohol. From another perspective, should employees risk termination for partaking in legal behavior that may violate their employer's religious code, such as having a child out of wedlock or drinking alcohol? If the business has a conscience, does it have greater weight and validity than the individual consciences of its employees? See Sidebar 2.11 for another example of a business representing its business owners' religious beliefs. See Chapter 6 for a discussion of the legal issues in *Citizens United* and the *Hobby Lobby* case.

---

sidebar 2.11

Same-Sex Marriage Debate and "Kiss-Ins"

The president and CEO of restaurant chain Chick-fil-A, Dan Cathy, regretted speaking out on same-sex marriage following a media firestorm that erupted after he affirmed his personal support for traditional marriage in the summer of 2012. The chain was founded by Dan Cathy's father and operates with Christian values, such as keeping its stores closed on Sundays to give all employees a day to rest, spend time with family and friends, and attend worship services if they so choose.

When same-sex marriage initiatives were on four state ballots in 2012, Dan Cathy responded to a question and affirmed his opposition to same-sex marriage. Supporters of Mr. Cathy's beliefs lined up for hours to eat at the stores, while opponents held highly publicized "kiss-ins" outside the stores. Throughout the United States, media covered the developments.

Two years later, Mr. Cathy stated that he had made a mistake in "making the company a symbol in the marriage debate" and "alienating market segments." "Consumers want to do business with brands that they can interface with, that they can relate with and it's probably very wise from our standpoint to make sure that we present our brand in a compelling way that the consumer can relate to."

Although his personal views on same-sex marriage have not changed, Mr. Cathy states, "I know others feel very different from that and I respect their opinion and I hope that they would be respectful of mine."

Source: *Atlanta Journal-Constitution*

Key Terms

Categorical imperative 35
Consequentialism 36
Duty 34
Ethics 32

Formalism 34
Morality 32
Protestant ethic 38
Self-regulation 45

Social contract theory 36
Stakeholder theory 54
The good 33
Utilitarianism 36

Review Questions and Problems

Contemporary Business Ethics

1. *Ethics and Society*
   Describe the reasons for the rising concern over business ethics.

2. *Ethics and Government*
   How has government action in recent years encouraged increased business attention to ethical matters?

The Nature of Ethics

3. *Ethics and Morality*

Compare and contrast ethics and morality. What do philosophers call the end result of ethical examination?

4. *Ethics and Law*

A marketing consultant to your firm comments that being ethical in business means nothing more than obeying the law. Discuss.

Two Systems of Ethics

5. *Formalism*

As amended in 1988, the Foreign Corrupt Practices Act prohibits bribery as a practice for U.S. companies to use in obtaining business in other countries. In passing the act, Congress expressed the concern that bribery was inherently wrong. Which major system of ethical thought does this concern suggest? Explain.

6. *Consequentialism*

A headline from *The Wall Street Journal* read "U.S. Companies Pay Increasing Attention to Destroying Files." The article discussed how many companies are routinely shredding files in the ordinary course of business to prevent future plaintiffs from obtaining the files and finding incriminating evidence. Is this practice unethical? Evaluate.

7. *Comparing the Two Ethical Systems*

(a) Is it ethical to advertise tobacco products in association with a desirable, exciting, or sophisticated lifestyle?

(b) Is it ethical to advertise these products in association with a cartoon character that is appealing to young people?

Sources of Values for Business Ethics

8. *Legal Regulation*

Explain how, in our society, ethical values frequently become law and how legal regulation can promote change in ethical values. Describe several common ethical values that are found in law.

9. *Professional Codes of Ethics*

Discuss why lawyers are sometimes viewed as being unethical. Is the average lawyer more or less ethical than the average business manager?

10. *Organizational Codes of Ethics*

A study of one major company's code of ethics by the Business Roundtable found that the lower the level of employees on the corporate ladder, the greater their hostility and cynicism toward codes of business ethics.

(a) Why might this be true?

(b) What can top business management do to change this view?

11. *Individual Values*

In addition to the five questions listed in the text, can you think of questions to ask yourself to help explore your ethical values before making a business (or personal) decision?

Achieving an Ethical Business Corporation

12. *The Obstacles*

(a) A *Newsweek* article on business ethics concludes, "Even in today's complex world, knowing what's right is comparatively easy. It's doing what's right that's hard." Explain why this statement may be true in modern corporate decision making.

(b) In 2010, average CEO pay was 319 times higher than the average employee's pay, according to the Institute for Policy Studies. In 1980, CEO pay was only 42 times higher. Discuss possible reasons for this tremendous increase in CEO pay and analyze the ethical implications.

13. *The Steps*

Another article from *The Wall Street Journal* carries the headline "Tipsters Telephoning Ethics Hot Lines Can End Up Sabotaging Their Own Jobs." Discuss why whistle-blowing is unpopular within the corporation. Apply to your discussion what sociologist Robert Jackall said about a subordinate's loyalty to supervisors within the corporation. Is whistle-blowing an appropriate subject for corporate ethics codes?

14. *The Rewards*

Why are formal legal rules alone not an adequate ethical system for business?

business *discussions*

1. As the chief executive officer of a Silicon Valley software company, you become aware that your chief competitor is working on a new computer program that will revolutionize interactive voice-based applications. You know that if you can find out about several key functions relating to your competitor's program, your own programmers can duplicate the function of the program without actually copying its code.

Is it ethical for you to hire away from your competitor a secretary who may have overheard something that will be useful to you?

Is it ethical for you to send an attractive employee to a bar where your competitor's programmers hang out in the hope of getting the information you want?

Is it ethical for you to have someone hunt up and read everything published by your competitor's programmers in case they may have let slip something that will help you?

2. The research director of PharmCo, a midsize pharmaceutical company, tells top management of an important new discovery. After years of effort, one of the company's research teams has discovered a drug that will reverse pattern baldness, the leading cause of male hair loss. The potential for profit from such a drug is enormous, but the director cautions that two of the eight principal researchers on the team believe that the drug may also increase the possibility of potentially fatal cerebral aneurysms in a very tiny percentage of users.

- If follow-up animal studies of the new drug do not show significant side effects, would it be ethical for the company to tell the two researchers to keep quiet about their concerns?
- Is it ethical to put animals at risk in order to test the drug's safety?

Many poor men in the world will be unable to afford the new drug if PharmCo sets the price too high.

- Is it morally right for PharmCo to maximize its profit even if it means that many men will have to remain bald?
- Does your answer change if the drug cures rheumatoid arthritis? AIDS?

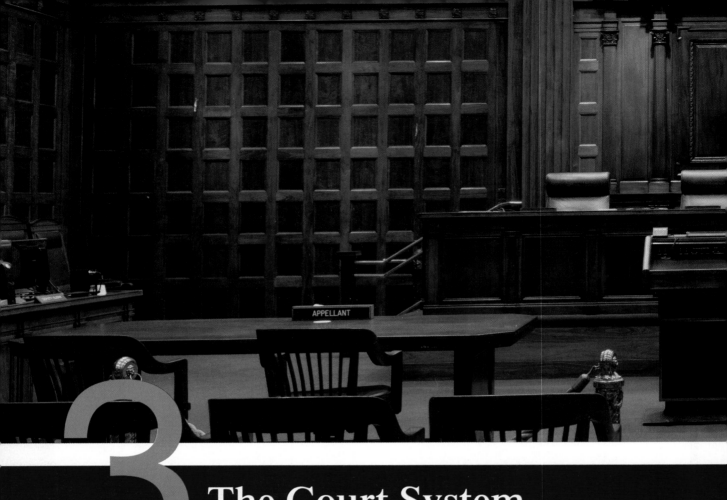

3 The Court System

Learning Objectives

In this chapter you will learn:

3-1. To recognize the role of key personnel associated with the courts.

3-2. To know the organization of the state and federal court systems.

3-3. To understand the power of judicial review and the philosophies of judicial restraint and judicial activism.

3-4. To appreciate and contrast the background and judicial alignment of the justices of the U.S. Supreme Court.

3-5. To analyze a sample case from the U.S. Supreme Court, including the majority, concurring, and dissenting opinions.

A viable court system is crucial to maintaining the rule of law. This chapter deals with the court system and the court's authority to decide disputes between parties. First, it examines the personnel who operate our courts, including the role of judges, jurors, and lawyers in a case. It next explores the organizational structure of both the state and federal courts and the differences between trial courts and appellate courts. Finally, the chapter examines the U.S. Supreme Court and the concept of judicial review and the role of courts in interpreting the Constitution, state and federal legislation, and the making of common law in the process of deciding cases (*stare decisis*).

By the time you have completed this chapter, you should have an understanding of the court system and a greater sensitivity for how the courts apply the law. You will understand the importance of every citizen willingly serving on a

Managers often are involved in the litigation process as either parties or witnesses in a case.

jury and receiving the cooperation of employers and the protection of the government for doing so. You will appreciate the difficult questions jurors must answer and the complex cases juries must decide. Finally, you will appreciate the difficulty that arises in resolving legal disputes. See Sidebar 3.1 about the costs associated with legal representation.

---

sidebar 3.1

The Soaring Cost of Legal Representation

When a lawsuit is filed, how much does it cost to defend a company and its executives? How much can it cost to defend against a criminal prosecution? In some cases, the mere investigation may run into tens of millions of dollars. Massive legal expenses are a major concern for both executives and shareholders. Defense costs can bankrupt a small business. In an accounting fraud investigation, Qwest Communications spent $75 million on legal fees in one year. Tyco International spent about $50 million to defend and investigate its practices. In 2011, it is estimated that Galleon Group LLC co-founder Raj Rajaratnam spent as much as $40 million unsuccessfully defending an insider trading criminal action. His legal bills were about two-thirds of the amount he allegedly made from the trades.

LO 3-1

Personnel

Before we look at the court system, you should have some background and understanding of the individuals who operate our court system. Judges apply the law to the facts, jurors find or determine the facts from conflicting evidence, and the facts as found by the jury are given great deference. In the process of representing clients, lawyers present evidence to the jury and argue the law to the court. Collectively, these persons conduct the search for truth. The court system is the way we enforce our laws in a property-based legal system. Without the courts, our legal system could not operate.

JUDGES AND JUSTICES

"Facts are stubborn things; and whatever may be our wishes, our inclinations, or the dictates of our passion, they cannot alter the state of facts and evidence."

—John Adams

The individuals who operate our courts are called judges or magistrates. In some appellate courts, such as the U.S. Supreme Court, members of the court are called justices. In this discussion, we will refer to trial court persons as judges and reviewing court persons as justices.

In all cases, the function of the trial judge is to determine the applicable rules of law to be used to decide the case. Such rules may be procedural or substantive. In cases tried without a jury, the judge is also responsible for finding the facts. In cases tried before a jury, the function of the jury is to decide questions of fact. The judge still is responsible for deciding questions of law.

Most cases are resolved before trial and even fewer cases lead to an appeal.

Trial judges are the main link between the law and the citizens it serves. The trial judge renders decisions that deal directly with people in conflict. These judges have the primary duty to observe and to apply constitutional limitations and guarantees. They bear the burden of upholding the dignity of the courts and maintaining respect for the law.

Justices do more than simply decide an appeal—they often give reasons for their decisions. These reasoned decisions become precedent and a part of our body of law that may affect society as a whole, as well as the litigants. So in deciding cases, justices must consider not only the result between the parties but also the total effect of the decision on the law. In this sense, their role is similar to that of legislators. When reviewing appeals, justices are essentially concerned with issues of *law;* issues of *fact* normally are resolved at the trial court level.

For these reasons, the personal characteristics required for a justice or appellate judge are somewhat different from those for a trial judge. The manner of performing duties and the methods used also vary between trial and reviewing courts. A trial judge who has observed the witnesses is able to use knowledge gained from participation as an essential ingredient in his or her decisions. A justice must spend most of the time studying the briefs, the record of proceedings, and the law in reaching decisions.

The judiciary, because of the power of judicial review, has perhaps the most extensive power of any branch of government. This issue will be extensively examined later in the chapter. Lower court judges' decisions may be reviewed by a reviewing court, but they have personal immunity from legal actions against them based on their judicial acts.

> Judges and justices often sacrifice considerable financial opportunities by giving up the practice of law in the prime of their careers.

JURORS

It is important to understand the role of the jury as a fact-finding body. Since litigation may involve both questions of law and questions of fact, the deference given to the decisions of a jury is very important. Trial by jury is a cherished right guaranteed by the Bill of Rights. The Sixth and Seventh Amendments to the Constitution guarantee the right of trial by jury in both criminal and civil cases. The **petit jury** is the trial jury that returns a verdict in both situations.

Although juries are used in only a very small percentage of all cases, they remain critical to the administration of justice. In civil cases the right to trial by a jury is preserved in suits at common law when the amount in controversy exceeds $20. State constitutions have similar provisions guaranteeing the right of trial by jury in state courts.

> Rule 48 of the Federal Rules of Civil Procedure states that the "court shall seat a jury of not fewer than six and not more than twelve members." Local rules allow district courts to set the number of jurors consistent with this rule.

Historically, a jury consisted of 12 persons. Today many states and some federal courts have rules of procedure that provide for smaller juries in both criminal and civil cases. Such provisions are acceptable since the federal law does not specify the *number* of jurors—only the *types* of cases that may be brought to trial before a jury at common law. Several studies have found no discernible difference between results reached by a six-person jury and those reached by a 12-person jury. As a result, many cases are tried before six-person juries today.

In most states, a jury's decision must be unanimous because many believe that the truth is more nearly to be found and justice rendered if the jury acts only on one common conscience. However, there is growing evidence that the requirement of unanimity is taking its toll on the administration of justice in the United States. Holdout jurors contribute to mistrials and many cases are routinely deadlocked by margins of 11–1 or 10–2. Many states have eliminated the requirement of unanimity in their courts in civil cases and two states have done so in criminal cases. Several legal commentators have argued

> The quality of a jury depends upon the ability to get competent and dedicated citizens to serve.

that unanimous jury verdicts are not constitutionally mandated and should be eliminated to help restore public confidence in our jury system.

Thanks to a series of sensationalized trials, the jury system has been subject to much criticism. Many argue that jurors are not qualified to distinguish fact from fiction, that they vote their prejudices, and that their emotions are too easily swayed by skilled trial lawyers who may work with jury consultants and have other technical support to present a case to a jury (Sidebar 3.2). However, most members of the bench and bar feel the right to be tried by a jury of one's peers in criminal cases is the most effective method of discovering the truth and giving the accused his or her "day in court."

sidebar 3.2

Jury Consultants and Technical Support: Other Key Parties in Litigation

Both before and during a civil trial, jury consultants and technical support services are often a key aspect of litigation. The following list provides a sense of the ways in which they offer trial support:

- Coaching attorneys
- Conducting community attitude surveys

- Providing focus groups
- Developing *voir dire* to elicit attitudes and experiences
- Creating a theme for the case
- Preparing sophisticated demonstrative exhibits, including timelines
- Helping with media management for high-profile cases

Jurors normally do not give reasons for their decisions, although some special verdicts may require juries to answer a series of questions. Actually, it would be almost impossible for the jury to agree on the reasons for its verdict. A jury may agree as to the result but disagree on some of the facts, and different jurors may have different ideas or understandings of the testimony.

Many individuals attempt to avoid jury duty. Some lose money because of time away from a job or profession. Others feel great stress in having to help make important decisions affecting the lives of many people. Because so many potential jurors seek relief from jury duty, many trials often end up with more jurors who are unemployed or retired than should be the case. Today, there is a strong trend toward requiring jury duty of all citizens, irrespective of any hardship that such service may entail. Courts often refuse to accept excuses because jury duty is a responsibility of all citizens in a free society.

One of the most difficult issues facing the judicial system is the right to a trial by jury in very complex and complicated cases that frequently take a long time to try. For example, many antitrust cases involve economic issues that baffle economists, and such cases may last for several months or even years. The average juror may not comprehend the meaning of much of the evidence, let alone remember it when it is time to make a decision. As a practical matter, many persons cannot serve on a jury for several weeks or months. How does a free and democratic society deliver a trial by jury of one's peers, if busy people are excused from jury service? For these and other reasons, some experts recommend that the right to a trial by jury be abolished in very complex and time-consuming cases.

"I do not assert that the jury trial is an infallible mode of ascertaining truth. Like everything human, it has its imperfection. I only say, that it is the best protection for innocence and the surest mode of punishing guilt that has yet been discovered."

—Jeremiah Black, defense attorney in *Ex Parte Milligan*, 71 U.S. 2 (1886)

Many of the largest jury verdicts involve medical malpractice, products liability, fraud, or breach of contract. Juries have been increasingly generous to plaintiffs who suffer death or serious physical injury. Many plaintiffs' lawyers now contend that million dollar awards—once the standard for measuring a successful case—are no longer indicative of a major victory.

LAWYERS

Our court system is an adversarial one. Although private parties may represent themselves without a lawyer, as a practical matter, lawyers are required in most cases. Since knowledge of court procedures and substantive law is required as a bare minimum in most cases, lawyers serve as the representative advocates in our court system. They present the evidence, the points of law, and the arguments that are weighed by juries and judges in making their decisions.

A lawyer's first duty is to the administration of justice. As an officer of the court, he or she should see that proceedings are conducted in a dignified and orderly manner and that issues are tried on their merits only. The practice of law should not be a game or a battle of wits, but a means to promote justice. The lawyer's duties to each client require the highest degree of fidelity, loyalty, and integrity.

A lawyer serves in three capacities: counselor, advocate, and public servant. As a counselor, a lawyer by the very nature of the profession knows his or her client's most important secrets and affairs. A lawyer is often actively involved in the personal decisions of clients, ranging from their business affairs and family matters such as divorce to their alleged violations of the criminal law. These relationships dictate that a lawyer meet the highest standards of professional and ethical conduct.

Obviously, if a lawyer is to give competent advice, he or she must know to the fullest extent possible all the facts involved in any legal problem presented by the client. To encourage full disclosure by a client, the rules of evidence provide that confidential communications to a lawyer are privileged. The law does not permit a lawyer to reveal such facts and testify against a client, even if called to do so at a trial. This is the attorney-client privilege, and it may extend to communications made to the lawyer's employees in certain cases. This is especially important today because law firms frequently use paralegals (legal assistants) to gather facts and assist attorneys.

Lawyers can be sanctioned for unethical conduct and some have gone to jail for illegal conduct.

Lawyers may have many clients and often handle complex and complicated cases. The American Bar Association reported over 1.2 million licensed lawyers in the United States in 2011.

concept *summary*

Personnel

1. Trial judges determine the applicable law and, in cases without a jury, they also are responsible for finding the facts.
2. Appellate courts act as reviewing courts and generally are concerned with issues of law.
3. The petit jury is the trial jury that returns a verdict.
4. The nation's top 10 jury verdicts include 3 over $500 million.
5. Lawyers serve three roles: counselor, advocate, and public servant.

LO 3-2 # Organization of the Court System

There are two major court systems in the United States: the federal courts and the 50 state courts. The federal court system and those in most states contain three levels—trial courts, courts of appeals, and supreme courts. Lawsuits begin at the **trial court** level, and the results may be reviewed at one or more of the other two **appellate court** levels. Critical to every lawsuit is the question of subject matter jurisdiction.

SUBJECT MATTER JURISDICTION

Jurisdiction refers to the power of a court, at the state or federal level, to hear a case. For any court to hear and decide a case at any level, it must have **subject matter jurisdiction,** which is the power over the issues involved in the case. Some state trial courts have what is called general jurisdiction, or the power to hear any type of case. Other state courts have only limited jurisdiction, or the power to hear only certain types of cases. Jurisdiction may be limited as to subject matter, amount in controversy, or area in which the parties live.

Courts of different scope and subject matter jurisdiction help create order and efficiency.

Courts, especially those of limited jurisdiction, may be named according to the subject matter with which they deal. Probate courts deal with wills and the estates of deceased persons, juvenile courts with juvenile crime and dependent children, criminal and police courts with violators of state laws and municipal ordinances, and traffic courts with traffic violations.

Even trial courts (courts of general jurisdiction) cannot attempt to resolve every dispute or controversy that may arise. Some issues are simply nonjusticiable. For example, courts would not attempt to referee a football or basketball game. They would not hear a case to decide how English or math should be taught in the public schools. Moreover, courts do not accept cases involving trivial matters.

STATE COURTS

Currently, 39 states elect judges at some level.

State court systems are created, and their operations are governed, from three sources. First, state constitutions provide the general framework for the court system. Second, the state legislature, pursuant to constitutional authority, enacts statutes that add body to the framework. This legislation provides for various courts, establishes their jurisdiction, and regulates the tenure, selection, and duties of judges. Other legislation may establish the general rules of procedure to be used by these courts. Each court sets forth its own rules of procedure within the statutory bounds. These rules are detailed and may specify, for example, the times when various documents must be filed with the court clerk.

Trial Courts Depending upon the particular state, a general trial court can take on any number of names: the *superior court,* the *circuit court,* or the *district court.* In the trial courts, parties file their lawsuits or complaints seeking to protect their property rights or redress a wrongdoing. The complaint describes the parties (John Doe versus Sally Smith), the facts and law giving rise to a cause of action, the authority of the court to decide the case, and the relief requested from the court. (See Chapter 4 for a more complete explanation of the litigation process including a sample complaint.) The trial court is responsible for determining both the facts and the law in the case.

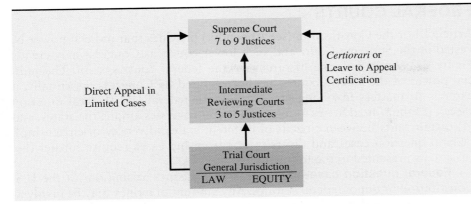

Figure 3.1 *Typical state court system.*

Appellate Courts   The parties to litigation are entitled as a matter of right to a review of their case by a higher court, or an **appeal,** if the requirements of procedural law are followed in seeking the review. In some states there is only one appellate court, which is usually called the supreme court of the state. In more populous states, there often are two levels of reviewing courts—an intermediate level and a court of final resort. In states with two levels of review, the intermediate courts are usually called the **courts of appeal,** and the highest court is again called the **supreme court.** In states with two levels of reviewing courts, most appeals are taken to the lower of the two courts, and the highest court of the state will review only very important cases. Intermediate courts of review typically consist of three to five judges. A state supreme court typically has seven to nine judges.

Reviewing courts review are essentially concerned with questions of law. Although a party is entitled to one trial and one appeal, he or she may obtain a second review if the higher reviewing court, in the exercise of its discretion, agrees to such a review. The procedure for requesting a second review is called in some states a *petition for leave to appeal* and in others a petition for a **writ of certiorari.** The process for requesting a review is explained more fully later in this chapter. Deciding such requests is a major function of the highest court in each state. As a practical matter, less than 5% of all such requests are granted. See Figure 3.1 for an overview of a typical state court system.

95% to 98% of all complaints are settled or fully resolved at the trial court level. Very few cases, by comparison, are appealed.

sidebar 3.3

Small-Claims Courts

One court of limited jurisdiction, falling below the trial court, is especially important to the business community. This court, usually known as **small-claims court,** handles much of the litigation between businesses and its customers. Small-claims courts are used by businesses to collect accounts and by customers to settle disputes with the business community that are relatively minor from a financial perspective. Such suits are often quite important from the standpoint of principle.

Landlord-tenant disputes are an example of controversies decided in these courts. Small-claims courts have low court costs and simplified procedures. The informality of the proceedings speeds up the flow of cases. The services of a lawyer are not usually required, and some states do not allow lawyers to participate in these proceedings. Lawsuits filed in small-claims courts usually are subject to a dollar limitation, such as a maximum of $25,000, often ranging from $500 to $5,000.

FEDERAL COURTS

Article III of the Constitution (see Appendix) provides that judicial power be vested in the Supreme Court and such lower courts as Congress may create. Figure 3.2 shows you the hierarchy of the federal court system. The judicial power of the federal courts has been limited by Congress. Essentially, it extends to matters involving (1) questions of federal law (federal question cases), (2) the United States as a party, (3) controversies among the states, and (4) certain suits between citizens of different states (diversity of citizenship). Federal question cases and diversity of citizenship cases require further discussion as presented in the following paragraphs.

Federal courts have subject matter jurisdiction over federal question cases and diversity of citizenship cases.

Federal question cases may be based on issues arising out of the U.S. Constitution or out of federal statutes. Any amount of money may be involved in such a case, and it need not be a suit for damages. For example, a suit to enjoin a violation of a constitutional right can be filed in a federal court as a federal question case. These civil actions may involve matters based on federal laws such as those dealing with patents, copyrights, trademarks, taxes, or employment discrimination. The rights guaranteed by the Bill of Rights of the Constitution also may be the basis for a federal question case.

Figure 3.2 *The federal court system.*

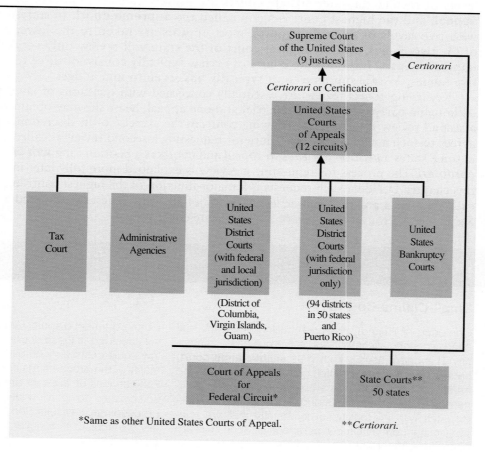

Diversity of citizenship requires that all plaintiffs be citizens of different states from all defendants. If a case involves a party on one side that is a citizen of the same state as a party on the other, there will then be no diversity of citizenship and thus no federal jurisdiction. Courts have held that it is the citizenship of the party in the case that determines whether diversity of citizenship exists. For example, diversity jurisdiction is based on the citizenship of all members of a partnership.

The fact that business corporations, which are considered persons before the law, are frequently incorporated in one state and have their principal place of business in another state also causes problems in determining when diversity of citizenship exists. For purposes of diversity jurisdiction, a corporation is a citizen of the state of incorporation and also a citizen of the state in which it has its principal place of business. Thus, a Delaware corporation with its principal place of business in Illinois is a citizen of both Delaware and Illinois for purposes of diversity. If any party on the other side of a lawsuit with such a corporation is a citizen of either Illinois or Delaware, there is then no diversity and no federal jurisdiction.

In diversity of citizenship cases, the federal courts have a jurisdictional amount of more than $75,000. If a case involves multiple plaintiffs with separate and distinct claims, *each* claim must satisfy the jurisdictional amount. Thus, in a class-action suit, the claim of each plaintiff must be greater than the $75,000 jurisdictional amount.

One of the reasons Congress provides for diversity of citizenship jurisdiction is to guard against state court bias against the nonresident party in a lawsuit. Since the biggest increase in federal lawsuits in recent years has been over businesses suing one another in contract disputes, diversity jurisdiction preserves the sense of fairness in such situations when one of the parties is out of state.

District Courts The federal district courts are the trial courts of the federal judicial system. There is at least one such court in every state and the District of Columbia. These courts have subject matter jurisdiction over all the cases mentioned above. These courts have the authority to review lawsuits, receive evidence, evaluate testimony, impanel juries, and resolve disputes. Most significant federal litigation begins in this court. The **Federal Rules of Civil Procedure** provide the details concerning procedures to be followed in federal court litigation. These rules are strictly enforced by the courts and must be followed by the parties in every lawsuit.

An adverse decision from a federal district court in Atlanta may be appealed to the Eleventh Circuit Court of Appeals.

Appellate Courts Under its constitutional authorization, Congress has created 12 U.S. Courts of Appeal plus a special Court of Appeals for the Federal Circuit as intermediate appellate courts in the federal system. This special reviewing court, located in Washington, D.C., hears appeals from special courts such as the U.S. Claims Court and Contract Appeals as well as from administrative decisions such as those made by the Patent and Trademark Office. Other courts, such as the Court of Appeals for Armed Forces, have been created to handle special subject matter. Figure 3.3 illustrates the location of the Courts of Appeals.

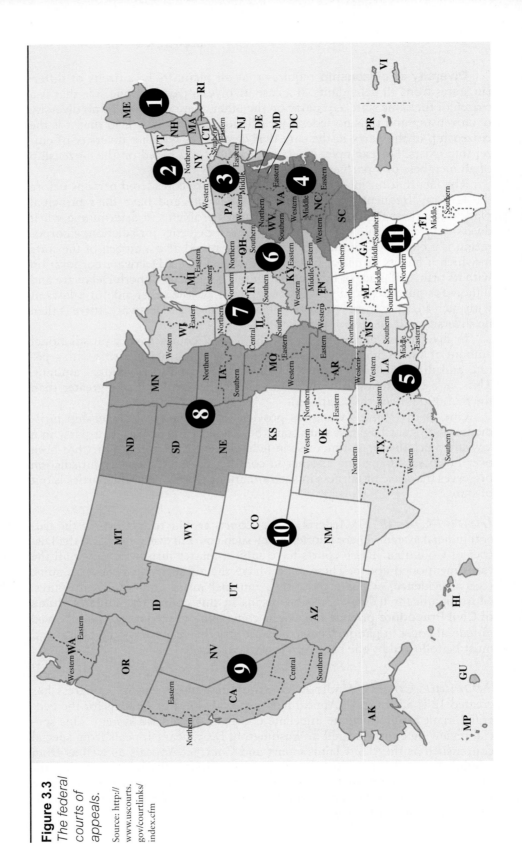

Figure 3.3
The federal courts of appeals.

Source: http://
www.uscourts.
gov/courtlinks/
index.cfm

sidebar 3.4

Circuit Scorecard

The following chart illustrates the number of cases granted certiorari by the U.S. Supreme Court and their disposition for the 2013–2014 term:

CIRCUIT	NUMBER OF CASES	%	DECIDED	% AFF'D	% REV'D
CA1	4	5%	4	25%	75%
CA2	5	7%	5	60%	40%
CA3	2	3%	2	0%	100%
CA4	2	3%	2	50%	50%
CA5	7	9%	7	14%	86%
CA6	11	15%	11	18%	82%
CA7	4	5%	4	75%	25%
CA8	2	3%	2	0%	100%
CA9	12	16%	12	8%	92%
CA10	4	5%	4	50%	50%
CA11	3	4%	3	33%	67%
CA DC	4	5%	4	50%	50%
CA Fed	6	8%	6	17%	83%
State	8	11%	8	25%	75%
Dist. Ct	1	1%	1	0%	100%
Original	—	—			

Source: SCOTUSblog Stat Pack, October Term 2013, http://sblog.s3.amazonaws.com/wp-content/uploads/2014/07/SCOTUSblog_scorecard_OT13.pdf (Julu 3, 2014).

DECISIONS BY THE U.S. SUPREME COURT

In addition to the court of appeals, the federal court system provides for a Supreme Court. Because the litigants are entitled to only one review, or appeal, a subsequent review by the U.S. Supreme Court must be obtained through a petition for a *writ of certiorari* to the Supreme Court. Sidebar 3.4 provides an overview of the number of cases granted certiorari and their disposition.

A petition for a *writ of certiorari* is a request by the losing party in the court of appeals for permission to file an appeal with the U.S. Supreme Court. In such situations, the Supreme Court has discretion as to whether or not it will grant the petition and allow another review. This review is not a matter of right. *Writs of certiorari* are granted primarily in cases of substantial federal importance or where there is an obvious conflict between decisions of two or more U.S. Circuit Courts of Appeal in an important area of the law that needs clarification. Pursuant to the U.S. Constitution (Art. III. Sec. 2), the Supreme Court also has original jurisdiction over a small range of cases, including those affecting ambassadors and in which the state is a party. The

Four U.S. Supreme Court justices must vote yes to grant a petition for a *writ of certiorari.*

Supreme Court's decision becomes the law of the land and reconciles the division of opinion between the lower courts.

When the U.S. Supreme Court reviews petitions for a *writ of certiorari,* the writ is granted if four of the nine justices vote to take the case. The Supreme Court spends a great deal of time and effort in deciding which cases it will hear. It is able to pick and choose those issues with which it will be involved and to control its caseload. The Supreme Court normally resolves cases involving major constitutional issues or interpretation of federal law. Sidebar 3.5 illustrates the very slim odds of the U.S. Supreme Court hearing a case.

sidebar 3.5

Very Slim Odds

Every year, thousands of petitions are filed in the U.S. Supreme Court by parties seeking review of adverse decisions by federal circuit courts of appeal or state supreme courts. The Supreme Court grants only a fraction of the petitions filed. During the 2001–02 term, the Supreme Court agreed to hear 88 cases; then, during the 2004–05 term, that number fell to 80 cases. Of the 8,517 petitions filed in the Court's 2005–06 term, 78 were granted argument (0.9%). For the 2013–14 term, 71 merits opinions are expected. For ongoing updates, see the Stat Pack compiled by SCOTUS, Supreme Court of the United States blog: www .scotusblog.com/.

Sources: David Thompson & Melanie Wachtell, "An Analysis of Supreme Court Petition Procedures," 16:2 *George Mason Law Review,* 240 (2009); and Kedar Bhatia, Update, October Term 2013, SCOTUS Stat Pack and Key Takeaways, www.scotusblog.com/2014/04/updated-october-term-2013-stat-pack/ (April 11, 2014).

Supreme Court case reviews have been steadily declining in recent years.

The Supreme Court is far more likely to review and reverse a decision rendered by the Ninth Circuit Court of Appeals—treating it, as one commentator noted, like a wayward child. Many commentators attribute the difference to the judicial activism of the Ninth Circuit, which often is at odds with the philosophy of judicial restraint found in the Supreme Court in recent years. In contrast, decisions rendered by the Fourth Circuit Court of Appeals tend to be far more conservative or consistent with the philosophy of judicial restraint. A more thorough discussion of these two philosophies will follow later in this chapter.

The federal district courts and the courts of appeal cannot review, retry, or correct judicial errors charged against a state court. Final judgments or decrees rendered by the highest court of a state are reviewed only by the Supreme Court of the United States. State cases reviewed by the U.S. Supreme Court must concern a federal question involving the validity of state action on the grounds that the statute under review is repugnant to the Constitution, treaties, or laws of the United States. If the case does not involve a federal question, the decision of the highest state court is not subject to review by the Supreme Court of the United States. Sidebar 3.6 elaborates on the role of the reviewing court.

sidebar 3.6

The Role of the Reviewing Court

Since reviewing courts create case law or precedent in the process of deciding cases, most final decisions of reviewing courts are published in order to make the precedent of each case available for inclusion into the total body of law. The opinions usually include the procedures which have been followed, the facts of the case, the law applicable to the facts, the decision of the court, and the reasons for the decision. Opinions may be written in the name of the author of the opinion or they may be written *per curiam*—by the court without identifying the author.

It is not surprising that the decisions of a reviewing court often are not unanimous. Some Supreme Court decisions are closely divided and 5–4 or 6–3 decisions in cases involving highly controversial issues are quite common. Recent examples of controversial issues

include the Patient Protection and Affordable Care Act (see Case 3.1), election campaign financing, affirmative action in the college admissions process, and gay marriage. Presidential appointments to the Supreme Court are evaluated, in part, on their potential effect on the court alignment as perceived in the close decisions of the past.

The written opinions in the cases in this textbook reflect the majority opinion of the reviewing court and as such they reflect the current status of the law. Dissenting opinions of the court also make a contribution to our jurisprudence and to the public debate on important social and public policy issues. Dissents often provide the foundation for changes in public policy and they often provide guidance to legislative bodies on issues under consideration.

concept *summary*

Organization of the Court System

1. The court system—both at the federal and state level—operates on three levels: the trial court, the court of appeals, and the supreme court.
2. Trial courts focus on the law and facts while reviewing courts focus only on the law.
3. The parties to litigation are entitled as a matter of right to one review of their case by a higher court.
4. Subject matter jurisdiction must exist for a court to hear a case.
5. Federal courts typically obtain jurisdiction upon diversity of citizenship or federal questions.
6. The highest legal authority in the United States is the U.S. Supreme Court.
7. Parties seek permission to bring their case to the Supreme Court through a petition for a *writ of certiorari.*

The Power of Judicial Review

LO 3-3

In the United States the most significant power of the courts, or "judiciary," is **judicial review,** which is the power to review laws passed by the legislative body and to declare them to be unconstitutional and void. It also allows the courts to review actions taken by the executive branch and to declare them unconstitutional. Although the Constitution does not expressly provide that

Judicial review is the ultimate power to invalidate actions by the president or the Congress.

the judiciary shall be the overseer of the government, the net effect of this power is to make it so. Chief Justice John Marshall in *Marbury v. Madison*, 5 U.S. 137 (1803), announced the power of judicial review using in part the following language and reasoning:

> It is a proposition too plain to be contested, that the constitution controls any legislative act repugnant to it; or, that the legislature may not alter the constitution by an ordinary act. . . .
>
> It is emphatically the province and duty of the judicial department to say what the law is. Those who apply the rule to particular cases, must of necessity expound and interpret that rule. If two laws conflict with each other, the courts must decide on the operation of each. So, if a law be in opposition to the constitution; if both the law and the constitution apply to a particular case, so that the court must either decide that case, conformably to the law, disregarding the constitution; or conformably to the constitution, disregarding the law; the court must determine which of these conflicting rules governs the case: this is of the very essence of judicial duty. If then, the courts are to regard the constitution, and the constitution is superior to any ordinary act of the legislature, the constitution, and not such ordinary act, must govern the case to which they both apply.

In practice, the U.S. Supreme Court rarely exercises its extraordinary powers and has developed carefully crafted rules as self-imposed limits on its authority as individual jurists.

LO 3-4

The terms judicial restraint and judicial activism are not exclusive to particular judges. Many judges may share aspects of both in their judicial philosophy.

As individual jurists exercise the power of judicial review, they do so with varying political attitudes and philosophies. Some judges believe that judicial power should be used very sparingly, although others are willing to use it more often. Those who believe that the power should not be used except in unusual cases are said to believe in **judicial restraint**. Those who think that the power should be used whenever the needs of society justify its use believe in **judicial activism**. All members of the judiciary believe in judicial restraint and all are activists to some extent. Often a jurist may be an activist in one area of the law and a firm believer in judicial restraint in another. Both judicial restraint and judicial activism describe attitudes or tendencies by matters of degree. Both terms are also used to describe general attitudes toward the exercise of the power of judicial review.

Traditionally, judicial restraint has been associated with conservative judges often appointed by Republican presidents. Judicial activism primarily is linked to liberal judges generally appointed by Democratic presidents. The tension between these philosophies can lead to divided confirmation hearings before the U.S. Senate where less attention often is paid to a nominee's qualifications than to his or her political views. It is important to remember, however, that conservative judges may take activist positions. Court decisions should be analyzed on their merits with an open mind. Sidebar 3.7 describes the process of becoming a Supreme Court justice. Sidebar 3.8 highlights the first five years of the Roberts court.

JUDICIAL RESTRAINT

The philosophy of judicial restraint developed naturally from the recognition that, in exercising the power of judicial review, the courts are overseeing coequal branches of government. When the power of judicial review is used to set aside decisions by the other branches of government, the courts are wielding great power. A commitment to the constitutional system dictates that this almost unlimited power be exercised with great restraint.

sidebar 3.7

Choosing a Supreme Court Justice

In the federal system, the U.S. Constitution gives the president the power to appoint federal judges, including Supreme Court justices, subject to the advice and consent of the U.S. Senate. In practical terms, this means a majority of the U.S. Senate must vote to confirm the president's nominee. Typically, after the president announces his nominee, interest groups on both sides search out information, including past decisions, about the candidate.

The nominee is questioned by the Senate Judiciary Committee, which also hears testimony from others about the nominee's qualifications and judicial philosophy. If the Judiciary Committee approves the nominee, the nomination is forwarded to the entire Senate for debate before a vote is taken. The confirmation process can take months and is often subject to conflict between Republican and Democratic senators and the White House.

sidebar 3.8

The First Five Years of the Roberts Court

An analysis of the first five years of the U.S. Supreme Court led by Chief Justice John G. Roberts, Jr. (2005–2010) illustrates the conservative nature of the court:

- The Court issued conservative decisions 58% of the time, with the number at 65% at the end of the 2009 term.
- Chief Justice Roberts and Justices Scalia, Alito, and Thomas are considered to be among the most conservative justices on the court since 1937.
- Although the number of laws deemed unconstitutional and precedents revered is consistent with

the rate of other courts, the "ideological direction of the court's activism has undergone a marked change toward conservative results."

Here are the results of a 2009 survey asking "Is the U.S. Supreme Court too conservative, too liberal, or about right?"

22% Too Conservative   29% Too Liberal   47% About Right

Source: Adam Liptak, "The Most Conservative Court in Decades," *The New York Times* (July 25, 2010). The article cites Nathaniel Persily (Columbia Law School) and Stephen Ansolabehere (Harvard University) for the survey.

Those who believe in judicial restraint think that many constitutional issues are too important to be decided by courts unless absolutely necessary and are to be avoided if there is another legal basis for a decision. They believe the proper use of judicial power demands that courts refrain from determining the constitutionality of an act of Congress unless it is absolutely necessary to a decision of a case. This modest view of the role of the judiciary is based on the belief that litigation is not the appropriate technique for bringing about social, political, and economic change.

The philosophy of judicial restraint is sometimes referred to as *strict constructionism,* or *judicial abstention.* Strict constructionists believe that the Constitution should be interpreted in light of what the Founding Fathers intended. They place great weight on the debates of the Constitutional Convention and the language of the Constitution. Those who promote judicial abstention hold that courts should decide only those matters they must to

Followers of judicial restraint favor a very limited role for the courts in our system of government.

resolve actual cases and controversies before them. Courts should abstain from deciding issues whenever possible, and doubts about the constitutionality of legislation should be resolved in favor of the statute. Cases should be decided on the facts if possible and on the narrowest possible grounds.

Those who believe in judicial restraint believe that social, political, and economic change in society should result from the political process rather than from court action.

Judges who identify with judicial restraint give great deference to the political process. They believe that the courts, especially the federal courts, ought to defer to the actions of the states and of the coordinate branches of government unless these actions are clearly unconstitutional. They allow the states and the federal legislative and executive branches wide latitude in finding solutions to the nation's problems.

Judicial restraint jurists have a deep commitment to precedent. They overrule cases only when the prior decision is clearly wrong. They try to refrain from writing their personal convictions into the law. They do not view the role of the lawyer and the practice of law as that of social reform. To them, reform is the function of the political process.

Followers of judicial restraint often take a pragmatic approach to litigation. Whenever possible, decisions are based on the facts rather than a principle of law. Reviewing courts exercising judicial restraint tend to accept the trial court decisions unless they are clearly wrong on the facts or the law. If there is any reasonable basis for the lower court decision, it will not be reversed. Such courts often engage in a balancing approach to their decisions. They weigh competing interests. For example, justices who adhere to judicial restraint often weigh the rights of the person accused of crime with the interests of the victim and of society in determining the extent of the rights of the accused in criminal cases.

Throughout most of our history, judicial restraint has been the dominant philosophy.

JUDICIAL ACTIVISM

Followers of judicial activism favor a more expansive role for the courts in our system of government.

Those who believe in the philosophy of judicial activism believe that courts have a major role to play in correcting wrongs in our society. To them, courts must provide leadership in bringing about social, political, and economic change because the political system is often too slow or unable to bring about those changes necessary to improve society. Activists tend to be innovative and less dependent on precedent for their decisions. They are value oriented and policy directed. Activist jurists believe that constitutional issues must be decided within the context of contemporary society and that the meaning of the Constitution is relative to the times in which it is being interpreted. Activists believe that the courts, and especially the Supreme Court, sit as a continuing constitutional convention to meet the needs of today.

Although dissenting opinions are not usually included in this textbook, they remain an important part of the judicial process and may become the law of the land in the future as the composition of the Supreme Court changes over time.

During the 1950s and 1960s, there was an activist majority on the Supreme Court. This activist majority brought about substantial changes in the law, especially in such areas as civil rights, reapportionment, and the criminal law. For example, the activist court of this period ordered desegregation of public schools and gave us the one-man, one-vote concept in the distributing of legislative bodies. Earl Warren, chief justice during that period, used to request that lawyers appearing before the Court address themselves to the effect of their clients' positions on society. "Tell me why your position is 'right' and that of your opponent is 'wrong' from the standpoint of society" was a common request to lawyers arguing cases before him.

Activist courts tend to be more result conscious and to place less reliance on precedent. Activists also believe that justices must examine for themselves the great issues facing society and then decide these issues in light of contemporary standards. Otherwise, they believe we are governed by the dead or by people who are not aware of all of the complexities of today's problems.

Sidebar 3.9 provides insight into the general alignment of the justices. It is important to understand, however, that this overall perspective does not translate into predicatbility. It is often fascinating to analyze each justice's position as set forth in concurring and dissenting opinions.

sidebar 3.9

Typical Alignment of Justices

LEFT	SWING	RIGHT
Ginsburg		Roberts
Bryer		Scalia
Sotomayor		Thomas
Kagan		Alito
	Kennedy	

Mirroring societal trends, the Supreme Court's divided decisions are often peppered with angry words about each other. Justices use phrases like "scanty and equivocal evidence" and "analytical confusion" and words such as "unrealistic" and "indefensible" in response. The importance of the issues and the close division of the Court contributes to the tension found in many divided opinions. Sidebar 3.10 offers another perspective on the differences found on the Supreme Court.

A SAMPLE U.S. SUPREME COURT CASE

We present the following case at the outset of this edition as an example of how the Supreme Court influences critically important areas of the law. Case 3.1, *National Federation of Independent Business v. Sebelius*, involves legal challenges to the Patient Protection and Affordable Care Act ("Affordable Care Act"). Passed by Congress in 2010, this heath care reform is a defining legislative achievement of President Obama's presidency. As you read the case, you will see that this 5–4 decision upheld the individual mandate requiring all Americans (who are not exempt for religious or other reasons) and who can afford health insurance coverage to obtain coverage or be subject to a penalty. The Supreme Court also substantially limited the Affordable Care Act's expansion of Medicaid.

Because of the magnitude of the Affordable Care Act, both in terms of the law itself and the ramifications for federal regulation of commerce, the Supreme Court heard three days of oral argument. Chief Justice Roberts wrote the majority opinion. This complicated decision also includes a concurring opinion by Justice Ginsburg and a dissenting opinion by Justices Scalia, Kennedy, Thomas, and Alito, as well as an additional dissenting opinion by Justice Thomas. Selections from all four opinions are included in Case 3.1 to illustrate the lively nature of the Justices' positions.

Overall, the decision has resulted in many more Americans covered by health care insurance. According to the White House, by April 2014, more than eight million people selected health care plans through exchanges set up under the Affordable Care Act. Another five million people also gained health care coverage through the Medicaid expansion.

 case **3.1**

NATIONAL FEDERATION OF INDEPENDENT BUSINESS V. SEBELIUS
567 U.S. __, 132 S. Ct. 2566 (2012)

According to the Syllabus (the summary appearing before the beginning of the majority opinion, which is added to help readers understand the facts and case) of the case, Congress passed the Patient Protection and Affordable Care Act (Affordable Care Act) in 2010 to increase the number of Americans covered by health insurance and decrease the cost of health care. A key provision requires most Americans to maintain "minimum essential" health care coverage. If non-exempt individuals fail to do so, they must make a "shared responsibility payment" (penalty) to the Internal Revenue Service.

Another key provision was the Medicaid expansion, increasing the number of individuals the states must cover beyond existing coverage for pregnant women, children, needy families, the blind, the elderly, and the disabled. The Affordable Care Act increased federal funding to cover the states' costs; however, if a state decided not to comply with the new expanded coverage, it could lose all of its federal Medicaid funding.

Twenty-six states, several individuals, and the National Federation of Independent Business brought suit in federal district court challenging the constitutionality of the individual mandate and the Medicaid expansion. The U.S. District Court for the Northern District of Florida granted summary judgment to the defendants on the claim that the Affordable Care Act's expansion of Medicaid was unconstitutional concluded that the individual mandate provision exceeded congressional authority and was not severable. Accordingly, the entire Affordable Care Act was declared invalid. The Eleventh Circuit Court of Appeals reversed the determination of nonseverability, upheld the Medicaid expansion as a valid exercise of Congress's spending power, but concluded that Congress lacked the authority to enact the individual mandate.

The Supreme Court was asked to determine if Congress has the power to enact the challenged provisions.

CHIEF JUSTICE ROBERTS delivered the opinion of the Court.

Today we resolve constitutional challenges to two provisions of the Patient Protection and Affordable Care Act of 2010: the individual mandate, which requires individuals to purchase a health insurance policy providing a minimum level of coverage; and the Medicaid expansion, which gives funds to the States on the condition that they provide health care to all citizens whose income falls below a certain threshold. We do not consider whether the Act embodies sound policies. That judgment is entrusted to the Nation's elected leaders. We ask only whether Congress has the power under the Constitution to enact the challenged provisions. . . .

The Government claims that Congress has power under the Commerce and Necessary and Proper Clauses to enact this solution [the individual mandate]. The Government contends that the individual

mandate is within Congress's power because the failure to purchase insurance "has a substantial and deleterious effect on interstate commerce" by creating the cost-shifting problem. . . . The individual mandate, however, does not regulate existing commercial activity. It instead compels individuals to *become* active in commerce by purchasing a product, on the ground that their failure to do so affects interstate commerce.

Construing the Commerce Clause to permit Congress to regulate individuals precisely *because* they are doing nothing would open a new and potentially vast domain of congressional authority. . . . The Government argues that the individual mandate can be sustained as a sort of exception to this rule because health insurance is a unique product. According to the Government, upholding the individual mandate would not justify mandatory purchases of items such as cars or broccoli because, as the Government puts it, "[h]ealth insurance is not purchased for its own sake like a car or broccoli; it is a means of financing health-care consumption and covering universal risks." But cars and broccoli are no more purchased for their "own sake" than health insurance. They are purchased to cover the need for transportation and food. . . . The individual mandate forces individuals into commerce precisely because they elected to refrain from commercial activity. Such a law cannot be sustained under a clause authorizing Congress to "regulate activity."

The government next claims that Congress has the power under the Necessary and Proper Clause to enact the individual mandate because the mandate is an "integral part of a comprehensive scheme of economic regulation"–the guaranteed-is-sue and community-rating insurance reforms. . . . Just as the individual mandate cannot be sustained as a law regulating the substantial effects of the failure to purchase health insurance, neither can it be upheld as a "necessary and proper" component of the insurance reforms. The commerce power thus does not authorize the mandate. . . .

That is not the end of the matter. Because the Commerce Clause does not support the individual mandate, it is necessary to turn to the Government's second argument: that the mandate may be upheld as within Congress's enumerated power to "lay and collect taxes." . . . The Affordable Care Act's requirement that certain individuals pay a financial penalty for not obtaining health insurance may be reasonably characterized as a tax. Because the Constitution permits such a tax, it is not our role to forbid it, or to pass upon its wisdom or fairness. . . .

The States also contend that the Medicaid expansion exceeds Congress's authority under the Spending Clause. They claim that Congress is coercing the States to adopt the changes it wants by threatening to withhold all of a State's Medicaid grants, unless the State accepts the new expanded funding and complies with the conditions that come with it. . . . The legitimacy of Congress's exercise of the spending power "rests on whether the voluntarily and knowingly accepts the terms of the 'contract.'" Respecting this limitation is critical to ensuring that Spending Clause legislation does not undermine the status of the States as independent sovereigns in our federal system. . . . Permitting the Federal Government to force the States to implement a federal program would threaten the political accountability key to our federal system. . . .

[The States] argue that the Medicaid expansion is far from the typical case. They object the Congress has "crossed the line distinguishing encouragement from coercion," in the way it has structured the funding: Instead of simply refusing to grant the new funds to States that will not accept the new conditions, Congress has also threatened to withhold those States' existing Medicaid funds. . . . Given the nature of the threat and the programs at issue here, we must agree. We have upheld Congress's authority to condition the receipt of funds on the States' complying with restrictions on the use of those funds, because that is the means by which Congress ensures that the funds are spent according to its view of the "general Welfare." Conditions that do not here govern the use of the funds, however, cannot be justified on that basis. . . .

The Affordable Care Act is constitutional in part and unconstitutional in part. The individual mandate . . . is within Congress's power to tax. As for the Medicaid expansion, that portion of the Affordable Care Act violates the Constitution by threatening existing Medicare funding. . . . Congress may offer States grants and require States to comply with accompanying conditions, but the States must have a genuine choice whether to accept the offer. The States are given no such choice in this case . . . The remedy for that constitutional violation is to preclude the Federal Government from imposing such a sanction. That remedy does not require striking down other portions of the Affordable Care Act.

GINSBURG, J., CONCURRING: *Although Justice Ginsburg joined most of the majority opinion, she filed a concurring opinion explaining the legal basis for her concurrence.*

Unlike THE CHIEF JUSTICE, I would hold, alternatively, that the Commerce Clause authorizes Congress to enact the minimum coverage provision. I would also hold that the Spending Clause permits the Medicaid expansion exactly as Congress enacted it. . . . In the Social Security Act, Congress installed a federal system to provide monthly benefits to retired wage earners and, eventually, to their survivors. Beyond question, Congress could have adopted a similar scheme for health care. Congress chose, instead, to preserve a central role for private insurers and state governments. According to THE CHIEF JUSTICE, the Commerce Clause does not permit that preservation. This rigid reading of the Clause makes scant sense and is stunningly retrogressive.

SCALIA, J., KENNEDY, J., THOMAS, J., and ALITO, J., DISSENTING: This case is difficult in one respect: it presents two questions of first impression. . . . The case is easy and straightforward, however, in another respect. What is absolutely clear, affirmed by the text of the 1789 Constitution, by the Tenth Amendment ratified in 1791, and by innumerable cases of ours in the 220 years since, is that there are structural limits upon federal power—upon what it can prescribe with respect to private conduct, and upon what it can impose upon the sovereign States . . . That clear principle carries the day here.

The values that should have determined our course today are caution, minimalism, and the understanding that the Federal Government is one of limited powers. But the Court's ruling undermines those values at every turn. In the name of restraint, it overreaches. In the name of constitutional avoidance, it creates new constitutional questions. In the name of cooperative federalism, it undermines state sovereignty . . . we would find the Act invalid in tis entirety.

THOMAS, J., DISSENTING: I write separately to say a word about the Commerce Clause . . . I adhere to my view that "the very notion of a 'substantial effects' test under the Commerce Clause is inconsistent with the original understanding of Congress' powers and with this Court's early Commerce Clause cases." As I have explained, the Court's continued use of that test "has encouraged the Federal Government to persist in its view that the Commerce Clause has virtually no limits." The Government's unprecedented claim in this suit that it may regulate not only economic activity but also *inactivity* that substantially affects interstate commerce is a case in point.

KEY POINTS

- The Supreme Court upheld the individual mandate as it was enacted pursuant to its Constitutional power to tax. As such, most Americans are now required to purchase and maintain health care insurance with minimum essential coverage or to pay a penalty.
- Because Congress exceeded its authority by attempting to coerce states into participating in the Medicaid expansion, the Supreme Court held that the provision in the Affordable Care Act that would have allowed the federal government to withhold all Medicaid finds from states not participating in the mandated expansion of Medicaid coverage is unconstitutional.
- All other portions of the Affordable Care Act were left in force.

THE NATURE OF THE JUDICIAL PROCESS

In deciding cases and in examining the powers discussed in the prior sections, courts are often faced with several alternatives. They may decide the case by use of existing statutes and precedents and demonstrate a deep commitment to the common law system. They may also refuse to apply existing case law or declare a statute to be void as unconstitutional. If there is no statute or case law, the court may decide the case and create law in the process. However, case law as a basis for deciding controversies often provides only the point of departure from which the difficult labor of the court begins. The court must examine and compare cases cited as authority to it so it can determine not only which is correct, but also whether the principles should continue to be followed. In reaching its decision, the court must consider whether the ruling will provide justice in the particular case and whether it will establish sound precedent for future cases.

The foregoing alternatives raise several questions: Why do courts reach one conclusion rather than another in any given case? What formula, if any, is used in deciding cases and in determining the direction of the law? What forces tend to influence judicial decisions when the public interest is involved?

There is no simple answer to these questions. Many people assume that logic is the basic tool of the judicial decision. But Justice Oliver Wendell Holmes stated, "the life of the law has not been logic; it has been experience."[1] Others argue that courts merely reflect the attitudes of the times and simply follow the more popular course in decisions where the public is involved.

Justice Benjamin Cardozo, in a series of lectures on the judicial process,[2] discussed the sources of information judges utilize in deciding cases. He stated that if the answer were not clearly established by statute or by unquestioned precedent, the problem was twofold: "He [the judge] must first extract from the precedents the underlying principle, the *ratio decidendi;* he must then determine the path or direction along which the principle is to work and

---

[1]Holmes, *The Common Law* 1 (1938).
[2]Cardozo, *The Nature of the Judicial Process* (1921). *Excerpts are used by permission from the Yale University Press.*

sidebar 3.11

U.S. Supreme Court Justices

 John Roberts, Chief Justice of the United States (born 1955). He received his B.A. from Harvard College and his J.D. from Harvard Law School. President George W. Bush nominated him as chief justice, and he took office in 2005.

 Anthony Kennedy, Associate Justice (born 1936). He received his B.A. from Stanford University and the London School of Economics, and his LL.B. from Harvard Law School. President Reagan nominated him as an associate justice of the Supreme Court, and he took office in 1983.

 Antonin Scalia, Associate Justice (born 1936). He received his A.B. from Georgetown University and the University of Fribourg, Switzerland, and his LL.B. from Harvard Law School. President Reagan nominated him as an associate justice of the Supreme Court, and he took office in 1986.

 Clarence Thomas, Associate Justice (born 1948). He attended Conception Seminary and received an A.B., cum laude, from Holy Cross College, and a J.D. from Yale Law School. President George H. W. Bush nominated him as an associate justice of the Supreme Court, and he took office in 1991.

 Ruth Bader Ginsburg, Associate Justice (born 1933). She received her B.A. from Cornell University, attended Harvard Law School, and received her LL.B. from Columbia Law School. President Clinton nominated her as an associate justice of the Supreme Court, and she took office in 1993.

 Stephen Breyer, Associate Justice (born 1938). He received an A.B. from Stanford University, a B.A. from Magdalen College, Oxford, and an LL.B. from Harvard Law School, magna cum laude. President Clinton nominated him as an associate justice of the Supreme Court, and he took office in 1994.

 Samuel Alito, Associate Justice (born 1950). He received his A.B. from Princeton University and his J.D. from Yale Law School. President George W. Bush nominated him as associate justice, and he took office in 2006.

 Sonia Sotomayor, Associate Justice (born 1954). She received her B.A. from Princeton University, summa cum laude, and a J.D. from Yale Law School. President Obama nominated her as an associate justice of the Supreme Court, and she took office in 2009.

 Elena Kagan, Associate Justice (born 1960). She received her A.B. from Princeton University, summa cum laude, an M. Phil from Oxford University, and her J.D. from Harvard Law School, graduating magna cum laude. President Obama nominated her as an associate justice of the Supreme Court, and she took office in 2010.

develop, if it is not to wither or die." The first part of the problem is separating legal principles from dicta so that the actual precedent is clear.

In Cardozo's judgment, the rule of analogy also was entitled to certain presumptions and should be followed if possible. He believed that the judge who molds the law by the method of philosophy is satisfying humanity's deep-seated desire for certainty. History, in indicating the direction of precedent, often illuminates the path of logic and plays an important part in decisions in areas such as real property. Custom or trade practice has supplied much of the direction of the law in the area of business. All judicial decisions are at least in part directed by the judge's viewpoint on the welfare of society. The end served by law must dictate the administration of justice, and ethical considerations, if ignored, will ultimately overturn a principle of law.

Noting the psychological aspects of judges' decisions, Cardozo observed that it is the subconscious forces that keep judges consistent with one another. He recognized that all persons, including judges, have a philosophy that gives coherence and direction to their thought and actions whether they admit it or not.

> All their lives, forces which they do not recognize and cannot name, have been tugging at them—inherited instincts, traditional beliefs, acquired conviction; and the resultant is an outlook on life, a conception of social needs, . . . which when reasons are nicely balanced, must determine where choice shall fall. In this mental background every problem finds its setting. We may try to see things as objectively as we please. None the less, we can never see them with any eyes except our own. To that test they are all brought—a form of pleading or an act of parliament, the wrongs of paupers or the rights of princes, a village ordinance or a nation's charter.

Sidebar 3.12 contains excerpts from Cardozo's famous book, *The Nature of the Judicial Process.*

---

sidebar 3.12

THE NATURE OF THE JUDICIAL PROCESS (1921)

Benjamin N. Cardozo

. . . My analysis of the judicial process comes then to this, and little more: logic, and history, and custom, and utility, and the accepted standards of right conduct are the forces which singly or in combination shape the progress of the law. Which of these forces shall dominate in any case must depend largely upon the comparative importance or value of the social interests that will be thereby promoted or impaired. One of the most fundamental social interests is that law shall be uniform and impartial. There must be nothing in its action that savors of prejudice or favor or even arbitrary whim for fitfulness. Therefore in the main there shall be adherence to precedent. There shall be symmetrical development, consistently with history or custom when history or custom has been the motive force, or the chief one, in giving shape to existing rules, and with logic or philosophy when the motive power has been theirs. But symmetrical development may be bought at too high a price. Uniformity ceases to be a good when it becomes uniformity of oppression. The social interest served by symmetry or certainty must then be balanced against the social interest served by equity and fairness or other elements of social welfare. . . .

If you ask how he is to know when one interest outweighs another, I can only answer that he must get his knowledge just as the legislator gets it, from experience and study and reflection; in brief, from life itself. Here, indeed, is the point of contact between the legislator's work and his. The choice of methods, the appraisement of values, must in the end be guided by like considerations for the one as for the other. Each indeed is legislating within the limits of his competence. No doubt the limits for the judge are narrower. He legislates only between gaps. He fills the open spaces in the law. How far he can go without traveling beyond the walls of the interstices cannot be staked out for him upon a chart. . . . Nonetheless, within the confines of these open spaces and those of precedent and tradition, choice moves with a freedom which stamps its action as creative. The law which is the resulting product is not found, but made. The process, being legislative, demands the legislator's wisdom. . . .

concept *summary*

Judicial Review

1. Judicial review allows the courts to review actions taken by legislative and executive branches of government.
2. The philosophy of judicial restraint is sometimes referred to as strict constructionism or a conservative approach.
3. Supporters of judicial activism believe the courts are the appropriate body to bring about social, political, and economic change.
4. The Supreme Court is deeply divided between these two competing views of judicial decision making.

Key Terms

Appeal 67
Appellate court 66
Courts of appeal 67
Diversity of citizenship 69
Federal question cases 68
Federal Rules of Civil
  Procedure 69

Judicial activism 74
Judicial restraint 74
Judicial review 73
Petit jury 63
Small-claims court 67
Subject matter jurisdiction 66
Supreme court 67

Trial court 66
Writ of certiorari 67

Review Questions and Problems

Personnel

1. *Judges and Justices*

   What are the essential responsibilities of a trial judge?
2. *Jurors*

   Why have several states eliminated the requirement of unanimity in jury trials?
3. *Lawyers*

   Name the three critical roles a lawyer serves in society. Why have many lawyers and their business clients had such conflict in recent years?

Organization of the Court System

4. *Subject Matter Jurisdiction*

   Mark, a citizen of Georgia, was crossing a street in Atlanta when he was struck by a car driven by David, a citizen of New York visiting Atlanta. The car was owned by David's employer, a Delaware corporation that has its principal place of business in Atlanta, Georgia. Mark sues both David and the corporation in federal district court in Atlanta alleging damages in the amount of $500,000. Does the court have subject matter jurisdiction? Why or why not?
5. *State Courts*

   What role do reviewing or appellate courts play in the judicial process? How do they differ from trial courts?

6. *Federal Courts*

   XYZ makes and markets a product that it believes will help control weight by blocking the human body's digestion of starch. The Food and Drug Administration (FDA) has classified the product as a drug and orders it removed from the market until it can evaluate its use through testing. XYZ disputes the FDA's action and seeks to bring suit in the federal courts. Will the federal courts have jurisdiction to hear the case? Why or why not?

7. *Decisions by the U.S. Supreme Court*

   Susan files a petition for certiorari in the U.S. Supreme Court following an adverse decision in the Illinois Supreme Court on a claim arising under a breach of contract. What chance does Susan have of the Supreme Court granting the petition? What special circumstances would she need to show?

The Power of Judicial Review

8. *Judicial Restraint*

   Define the power of judicial review. How do advocates of judicial restraint exercise that power?

9. *Judicial Activism*

   Define judicial activism. Compare and contrast judicial restraint and judicial activism.

10. *A Sample U.S. Supreme Court Case*

    Why are concurring and dissenting opinions important?

11. *The Nature of the Judicial Process*

    What are the forces that Justice Cardozo says shape the judicial process? How is the law made? In light of the liberal versus conservative divisions in the courts, are Cardozo's observations still relevant?

business *discussion*

1. You have spent the past four weeks away from work serving as a juror in a case deciding whether a pharmaceutical company should be held liable for the heart attack of a woman who took its painkiller, Oxxy-1. The lengthy case has taken a toll on your professional career, and you have many unanswered questions as jury deliberations begin.

- Where does your duty lie in serving on a jury?
- Are you protected against adverse employment action by your firm for missing work to serve on a jury?
- How do you reconcile the woman's prior heart palpitations from years ago with her recent attack? Was her heart already compromised before she began taking the painkiller Oxxy-1?
- Why didn't the pharmaceutical company withdraw the painkiller from the market at the first sign of a problem?

2. You are the president of a large corporation which is in the business of manufacturing, among other things, chemical products used to eradicate termites. You have just reviewed a confidential report, prepared by one of your top scientists, questioning the effectiveness of the product and the claims your business has been making to homeowners, pesticide treatment firms, and the general public. You have heard rumors that a lawsuit will be filed shortly against your corporation claiming that this product is ineffective.

Who should you turn to for advice?
Should you destroy the report?
In which court can a lawsuit be filed?
If you lose the lawsuit at trial, can you appeal?

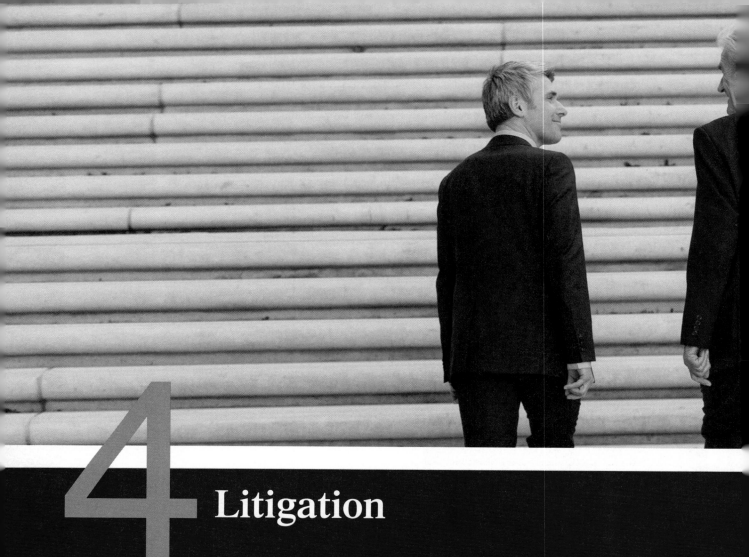

4 Litigation

Learning Objectives

In this chapter you will learn:

4-1. To understand the litigation process and the parties to a case.

4-2. To discuss how issues such as standing, personal jurisdiction, and class actions can affect litigation.

4-3. To understand how pretrial procedures, including pleadings, discovery, and motions affect litigation.

4-4. To recognize the major steps in a civil trial.

4-5. To appreciate posttrial issues, such as appeals and enforcement.

The court system and the litigation process help the business community resolve actual disputes under the rule of law. An impartial enforcement and dispute resolution process is essential to any system that preserves private property interests. In order to conduct business and enforce rights, we need a process to resolve disputes. Effective business leaders should develop an appreciation and understanding of the litigation process. Lawsuits and the threat of lawsuits impact every business regardless of size. By the time you have completed this chapter, you should have acquired a knowledge base regarding litigation and greater sensitivity to how a lawsuit is an immense drain of time, money, and energy on everyone involved in the case.

In this chapter, you will study the parties to litigation and the barriers presented to the resolution of a case in court. You will study a lawsuit

The complaint formally starts the lawsuit. However, parties often have already attempted to informally or formally resolve their dispute through negotiation and alternative dispute resolution, which you will learn about in Chapter 5.

itself—from pretrial procedures to the trial. Finally, you will learn about the process for resolving appeals and, ultimately, the enforcement of a final judgment.

A sample complaint, is contained in Appendix II. The complaint sets out the parties, jurisdiction, venue, facts, and legal causes and remedies just like a real case. You should study it carefully before reading this chapter and refer back to it often to help you understand this chapter better. Another important consideration is the cost of litigation. See Sidebar 4.1 for an example of the high cost of litigation and the importance of having effective strategies to handle legal issues and disputes.

Litigation—An Overview

To fully understand the litigation process, you need to be familiar with the terminology used to describe the parties who are adversaries in lawsuits. The next section reviews a variety of relevant terms. Following that, the legal concepts of when a party has the right to file a lawsuit, when a court has power over the parties, and when one person might sue on behalf of a much larger number of other persons are discussed.

The first of these issues is generally described as *standing to sue.* If a plaintiff has standing to sue, the court next must determine if it has *personal jurisdiction* over the defendant. The third problem area relates to *class-action suits,* which involve one or more individuals suing on behalf of all who may have the same grounds for suit. These concepts are discussed in more detail throughout the chapter.

---

sidebar 4.1

The High Cost of Litigation

Litigation can be very expensive. By April 2014, Bank of America had spent more than $50 billion to resolve legal issues connected to the financial crisis. It also set aside an additional $6 billion for additional potential costs related to these legal issues.

In addition to paying settlements and judgment, the cost of legal representation can be high. If you are a plaintiff, your lawyer may be paid on a contingency basis—that is, if you prevail, your lawyer receives a percentage of the settlement or judgment. In most other circumstances, however, attorneys bill by the hour. The hourly rate for top attorneys in the U.S. can run as much

as $1,250 for highly specialized advice about legal issues related to mergers and acquisitions, bankruptcy, China trade and investment, high-end litigation, and capital markets. Although most attorneys do not command these rates, the costs of litigating a dispute can add up very quickly and should be taken into consideration as part of your overall strategy for handling a dispute.

Sources: Christina Rexrode and Devlin Barrett, "Bank of America Swings to Loss on Legal Charge, Lower Mortgage Originations," *The Wall Street Journal* (April 17, 2014); and Vanessa O'Connell, "Big Law's $1,000-Plus an Hour Club," *The Wall Street Journal* (February 23, 2011).

The sample complaint keeps things very simple. However, in many complex cases there may be several plaintiffs and defendants and multiple claims.

PARTIES

The party who files a civil action is called the **plaintiff.** The party sued is known as the **defendant.** The term *defendant* also is used to describe the person against whom a criminal charge is filed by the prosecuting state or federal government. When a defendant wants to sue the plaintiff, the defendant files a **counterclaim.** Most jurisdictions use the terms **counterplaintiff** and **counterdefendant** to describe the parties to the counterclaim. Thus, the defendant becomes a counterplaintiff and the plaintiff becomes a counterdefendant when a counterclaim is filed.

In most state jurisdictions and in federal courts, the law allows all persons to join in one lawsuit as plaintiffs if the causes of action arise out of the same transaction or series of transactions and involve common questions of law or fact. In addition, plaintiffs may join as defendants all persons who are to a complete determination or resolution of the questions involved.

In addition, if a defendant alleges that there cannot be a complete determination of a controversy without the presence of other parties, he or she may bring in new third parties as **third-party defendants.** This procedure usually is followed when there is someone who may have liability to a defendant if the defendant has liability to the plaintiff. For example, assume Never-Fail Inc. supplies brake shoes to the Ready-to-Go Mechanics Corporation. Ready-to-Go worked on your brakes, and thereafter you were injured when your car failed to stop at an intersection. After you filed a lawsuit against Ready-to-Go, it could bring Never-Fail Inc. into the case as a third-party defendant. In essence, Ready-to-Go is arguing that if it is liable to you, then Never-Fail is liable to Ready-to-Go since the cause of the accident easily could be faulty brake shoes.

STANDING TO SUE

LO 4-2

A court's power to resolve a controversy is limited by the subject matter involved in the case. The plaintiff must show the court that it has subject matter jurisdiction to hear the case. Moreover, a plaintiff must establish that he or she is entitled to have the court decide the dispute, that is, he or she has **standing to sue.**

To establish the required standing, a plaintiff must allege two things. First, the plaintiff must allege that the litigation involves a case or controversy. Courts are not free to litigate matters that have no connection to the law. For example, one business cannot maintain a suit against another business just because the two are competitors. There must be some allegation of a wrong that would create a dispute between plaintiff and defendant.

Second, the plaintiff must allege a personal stake in the resolution of the controversy. This element of standing prevents any individual from asserting the rights of the general public or of a group of which he or she is not a member. For instance, only a shareholder of one of the two companies involved in a merger could sue to stop the combination of these companies, despite the fact that such a merger may have a substantial adverse impact on competition in general.

In essence, through the standing-to-sue requirements, courts are able to insist that there be an adversarial relationship between plaintiff and defendant. This adversarial relationship helps present the issues to be litigated in sharper focus. To establish standing, plaintiffs must assert their personal legal positions and not those of third parties. Without the requirements of standing, courts would be faced with abstract legal questions of potentially wide public significance, questions generally best left to legislative bodies or administrative agencies.

It is very important to note that standing to sue does not depend upon the merits of the plaintiff's contention that particular conduct is illegal. The presence of standing is determined by the nature and source of the plaintiff's allegations. Standing is determined at the outset of the litigation, not by the outcome. Case 4.1 illustrates the critical nature of standing in winning

In the sample complaint, the plaintiff satisfies standing by alleging facts demonstrating that the defendant has committed two legal wrongs causing a serious property loss to the plaintiff.

In environmental harm cases, standing often is satisfied by showing the plaintiff uses the affected area and its aesthetic and recreational value has been lessened by the pollution.

MAYER v. BELICHICK
605 F.3d 223 (3rd Cir.)

Season ticket-holder brought action against the New England Patriots and league, alleging various causes of action arising out of the team's alleged practice of surreptitiously videotaping the signals of opposing teams.

COWEN, Circuit Judge

Plaintiff Carl J. Mayer appeals from the order of the United States District Court for the District of New Jersey granting the respective motions to dismiss filed by Defendants Bill Belichick and the New England Patriots ("Patriots") as well as by Defendant National Football League ("NFL"). We will affirm.

1. This highly unusual case was filed by a disappointed football fan and season ticket-holder in response to the so-called "Spygate" scandal. This scandal arose when it was discovered that the Patriots were surreptitiously videotaping the signals of their opponents. Mayer, a New Jersey resident and New York Jets season ticket-holder, initially filed his complaint on September 7, 2007. He named as Defendants the Patriots, headquartered in Massachusetts, as well as the team's head coach, Belichick, a Massachusetts resident. Mayer eventually filed an amended complaint on August 19, 2008, which added the NFL, with its headquarters in New York, as a Defendant. . . .

2. The core of this action is that the Defendants, during a game with the New York Jets on September 9, 2007, instructed an agent of the Defendants to surreptitiously videotape the New York Jets coaches and players on the field with the purpose of illegally recording, capturing and stealing the New York Jets signals and visual coaching instructions. The Defendants were in fact subsequently found by the National Football League ("NFL") to have improperly engaged in such conduct.

3. Plaintiffs contend that in purchasing tickets to watch the New York Jets that, as a matter of contract, the tickets imply that each game will be played in accordance with NFL rules and regulations as well as all applicable federal and state laws. . . .

At their most fundamental level, the various claims alleged here arose out of the repeated and surreptitious violations of a specific NFL rule. This rule provides that " 'no video recording devices of any kind are permitted to be in use in the coaches' booth, on the field, or in the locker room during the game'" and that "all video for coaching purposes must be shot from locations 'enclosed on all sides with a roof overhead.'" . . .

On September 9, 2007, the Jets and the Patriots played the season opener in Giants Stadium, East Rutherford, New Jersey. Mayer possessed tickets and parking passes to this game, and the Patriots ultimately won, 38-14. ESPN.com then reported that the NFL was investigating accusations that an employee of the Patriots was actually videotaping the signals given by Jets coaches at this game. . . .

On September 13, 2007, "the NFL found the Defendants guilty of violating all applicable NFL rules by engaging in a surreptitious videotaping program." . . .

Mayer ultimately alleged nine separate counts in his amended complaint. He asserted, in order, the following causes of action against the Patriots and Belichick: (1) tortious interference with contractual relations; (2) common law fraud; (3) violations of the New Jersey Deceptive Business Practices Act; (4) violations of New Jersey's racketeering statute; (5) violations of the Racketeer Influenced and Corrupt Organizations Act ("RICO"); (6) the infringement of the rights of ticket-holders as third-party beneficiaries; (7) breach of implied contract or quasi-contract; and (8) violations of the New Jersey Consumer Fraud Act ("NJCFA"). Finally, he advanced a breach of contract claim against the NFL on account of its destruction of the videotapes. . . . After they were served with the amended complaint, the Patriots and Belichick filed a motion to dismiss for failure to state a claim pursuant to Federal Rule of Civil Procedure 12(b)(6). The NFL subsequently filed its own motion to dismiss as well. . . .

The District Court, while noting that Mayer alleged numerous theories of liability in this case, appropriately turned to the following dispositive question: namely, whether or not he stated an actionable injury (or, in other words, a legally protected right or interest) arising out of the alleged "dishonest" videotaping program undertaken by the Patriots and the NFL team's head coach. . . . we ultimately conclude that the District Court was correct to hold that Mayer failed to set forth a legally cognizable right, interest, or injury here. . . .

Significantly, our ruling also does not leave Mayer and other ticket-holders without any recourse. Instead, fans could speak out against the Patriots, their coach, and the NFL itself. In fact, they could even go so far as to refuse to purchase tickets or NFL-related merchandise. . . .

However, the one thing they *cannot* do is bring a legal action in a court of law.

For the foregoing reasons, we will affirm the District Court's order dismissing Mayer's amended complaint in its entirety.

KEY POINTS

- To maintain a lawsuit, a plaintiff must have standing or a legally cognizable claim.
- The Third Circuit found that, because the plaintiff did not have a legally protected right arising out of the alleged "dishonest" videotaping program, he did not state an actionable injury.
- Accordingly, defendant's motions to dismiss were granted.

a lawsuit. A plaintiff must have a legally cognizable claim to maintain a lawsuit. The case reinforces the rule that the courts are careful to avoid overstepping their constitutional role and will only rule on actual cases or controversies.

PERSONAL JURISDICTION

Power to hear a case means a court must have authority not only over the subject matter of the case but also over the parties to the case. This latter authority is called **personal jurisdiction.** Personal jurisdiction over the plaintiff is obtained when the plaintiff files the suit. Such action indicates voluntary submission to the court's power.

Personal jurisdiction over the defendant usually is obtained by the service of a **summons,** or notice to appear in court, although in some cases it is obtained by the publication of notice and mailing a summons to the last known address. This delivery of notice is referred to as *service of process.* Service of a summons on the defendant usually is valid if it is served upon any member of the household above a specified age and if another copy addressed to the defendant is mailed to the home.

For many years, a summons could not be properly served beyond the borders of the state in which it was issued. However, states now have what are called **long-arm statutes,** which provide for the service of process beyond their boundaries. Such statutes are valid and constitutional if they provide a defendant with due process of law. Under the Fifth Amendment to the Constitution, no person shall "be deprived of life, liberty, or property without due process of law." The Fourteenth Amendment provides that states must also guarantee due process protection. Due process requires that if a defendant is not present within the state where the lawsuit is filed, he or she must have certain minimum contacts with the state so that

No case can proceed forward without the existence of both subject matter and personal jurisdiction.

maintenance of the suit does not offend "traditional notions of fair play and substantial justice."

The typical long-arm statute allows a court to obtain jurisdiction over a defendant even though the process is served beyond its borders if the defendant:

1. Has committed a tort within the state.
2. Owns property within the state that is the subject matter of the lawsuit.
3. Has entered into a contract within the state or transacted the business that is the subject matter of the lawsuit within the state.

Long-arm statutes do not authorize out-of-state service of process in all cases. Personal jurisdiction is obtained under long-arm statutes only when requiring an out-of-state defendant to appear and defend does not violate due process. Sidebar 4.2 details a classic case on personal jurisdiction and the importance of establishing minimum contacts. See Sidebar 4.3 for an example of establishing personal jurisdiction over an individual.

---

sidebar 4.2

Personal Jurisdiction: Minimum Contacts

The *World-Wide Volkswagen* case is the leading case on the constitutional limits associated with personal jurisdiction on out-of-state defendants. In this case, the plaintiff filed a products liability lawsuit in Oklahoma to recover for personal injuries sustained in an automobile accident in that state. The defendants were the German manufacturer of the automobile, the importer of the car, the wholesale distributor, and the retail dealership. The wholesaler and retailer were located in New York State, and they challenged personal jurisdiction because they did not do business in Oklahoma and had no ties or contacts to the state. The court held in favor of the defendants, under the due process clause of the Fourteenth Amendment to the U.S. Constitution, because these defendants had not "purposefully availed" themselves of the privilege of conducting business in Oklahoma. The plaintiff should have sued these defendants in New York State. The manufacturer and importer were proper defendants in Oklahoma since they envisioned that the cars they made and imported had contacts with all states, including Oklahoma.

Source: *World-Wide Volkswagen v. Woodson*, 100 S.Ct. 559 (1980).

In the context of the Internet, courts have held that there are sufficient minimum contacts with the state when the website is targeted to the state or knowingly conducts business within the state.

In criminal suits, the crime must have been committed within the state for the court to have jurisdiction over the case. Jurisdiction over the person of the defendant is obtained by arrest. In the event of arrest in a state other than that in which the crime was committed, the prisoner must be transported back to the state where the crime occurred. This is done by the governor of the state of arrest voluntarily turning the prisoner over to the governor of the requesting state. The process of requesting and transporting the prisoner from one state to another is called **extradition.**

Regardless of the type of case, a defendant may decide not to object to a court's exercise of personal jurisdiction. In other words, a defendant may agree to submit to a court's authority even though personal jurisdiction may not be obtained under the rules discussed in this section. A defendant may waive or forgo any objection to a court's exercise of personal jurisdiction.

sidebar 4.3

Where Does Mark Zuckerberg Reside?

 Claiming that he is entitled to 84 percent of Facebook, Paul Ceglia sued Mark Zuckerberg in state court in Buffalo, New York. Zuckerberg's lawyers removed the case to federal court on diversity grounds: Zuckerberg resides in California, Facebook Inc. is a Delaware corporation, and Ceglia resides in New York.

Arguing that Zuckerberg should be considered domiciled in New York because he represented in a 2004 lawsuit that he lived in New York, Ceglia moved the court to reconsider the move.

U.S. District Judge Richard Arcana sided with Zuckerberg, ruling that after moving to California in 2004, and as owner, founder, and CEO of a multi-billion-dollar company with over 1,600 employees within "walking distance" of his current residence in California, Zuckerberg is domiciled in California. Judge Arcana flatly rejected Ceglia's arguments, stating "It is simply incomprehensible to believe that Zuckerberg intends to abandon his life, friends, and daily management of his multi-billion-dollar company to return to New York and live near his parents."

Source: Ceglia v. Zuckerberg, Decision and Order (W.D. N.Y. March. 28, 2011), available at http://nyctlitigation.foxrothschild.com/WDNY%20 Facebook%20Ruling.pdf.

CLASS-ACTION SUITS

A **class-action suit** is one in which one or more plaintiffs file suit on their own behalf and on behalf of all other persons who may have a similar claim. For example, all sellers of real estate through brokers were certified as a class in an antitrust suit against the brokers. All persons suing a drug company, alleging injuries from a product, constituted a class for a tort action. Class-action suits may also be filed on behalf of all shareholders of a named corporation. The number of people constituting a class is frequently quite large. Class-action suits are popular because they often involve matters in which no one member of the class would have a sufficient financial interest to warrant litigation. However, the combined interest of all members of the class not only makes litigation feasible, it quite often makes it very profitable for the lawyer who brings the suit. In addition, such litigation avoids a multiplicity of suits involving the same issue, especially when the issues are complex and the cost of preparation and defense is very substantial.

At the federal level, the Supreme Court discourages class-action suits. Federal cases require that members of the class be given notice of the lawsuit; actual notice and not merely notice by newspaper publication is usually required. This notice must be given to all members of the class whose names and addresses can be found through reasonable efforts. In addition, those plaintiffs seeking to bring the class-action suit must pay all court costs of the action, including the cost of compiling the names and addresses of those in the class. If the trial court denies the plaintiff a right to represent the class, that decision cannot be appealed until there is a final decision in the lawsuit itself. Denial of class-action status making it impractical to continue the litigation does not give grounds for an immediate appeal.

One legal commentator has described the class-action suit as the law's version of a nuclear weapon—it is so destructive no side wants to set it off. A plaintiff's threat to aggregate thousands of individual claims is so powerful that it can destroy a defendants business. However, if the class action fails, the plaintiff wins nothing and loses the investment in the litigation. Simple cost-benefit analysis leads the litigants to settle a class-action suit.

If a class-action suit is in federal court because of diversity of citizenship, only one member of the class must meet the jurisdictional amount of $75,000. Sidebar 4.4 explains the Supreme Court's rationale for this rule.

---

sidebar 4.4

Class-Actions in Federal Court

In the case of *Exxon Mobil Corp. v. Allapattah Service,* 125 S. Ct. 2611 (2005), the Court considered a class-action case filed by Exxon dealers against Exxon Corporation. The Court found that it could consider the claims of class members who had not met the $75,000 minimum amount in controversy requirement in diversity cases. "Once a court has original jurisdiction over some claims in the action, it may exercise supplemental jurisdiction over additional claims that are part of the same case or controversy. . . . [The law] confers supplemental jurisdiction over all claims, including those that do not independently satisfy the amount-in-controversy requirement."

Don't assume that class-action suits can be easily settled.

In the past, the federal courts routinely approved class-action settlements provided there was some benefit to the class and a release of all class members' claims. Typically, large attorneys' fees were included in the settlements. However, in recent years, the federal courts have begun carefully examining class-action settlements and have developed a much higher standard for approving settlements. A tougher standard is especially important where settlements have been proposed because of the risk that the class representatives and their lawyers could sacrifice the interests of the class in order to financially benefit themselves. Class-action suits in federal courts may be settled on a classwide basis only if the settlement's terms are fair and equitable and only if all the class certification requirements for trial have also been met. Sidebar 4.5 offers examples of high-profile class-action lawsuits.

"Justice is the great interest of man on earth. It is the ligament which holds civilized beings and civilized nations together."

–Daniel Webster

Some attorneys have found a way around the costs of litigation and continue to file class-action lawsuits. The practice of consumers' and plaintiffs' lawyers of combining a single grievance into a lawsuit on behalf of every possible litigant is quite common in state courts. Numerous state class-action statutes allow consumers and others to file suit in state courts on behalf of all citizens of that state. So although the Supreme Court has attempted to reduce class-action cases, it is apparent that public companies are still subject to this type of claim.

sidebar 4.5

Major Class-Action Lawsuits

As this sidebar illustrates, class-action lawsuits can result in substantial awards and settlements.

Master Tobacco Settlement Agreement (1998)	$206 billion over 25 years
Enron Inc. (2006)	$7.2 billion
World Com Inc. (2005)	$6.2 billion
Exxon Mobil Corp. (1994–2001)	$5 billion punitive damages award, later reduced to $500 million
Breast Implant Litigation (1994)	$3.4 billion
Tyco International Ltd. (2005–2007)	$3.2 billion
Cendant Corp. (2000)	$3.1 billion
AOL Time Warner (2005)	$2.5 billion
Nortel Networks (2006)	$2.4 billion

Source: *Holding Corporations Accountable: LawInfo's Top 10 Class Action Lawsuits* (April 2010).

concept *summary*

Litigation—An Overview

1. The party who files a civil action is called the plaintiff and the party sued is known as the defendant.
2. To establish standing to sue, a plaintiff must establish that a case or controversy exists and that he or she has a personal stake in the resolution of the case.
3. Long-arm statutes are constrained or limited by the requirement the defendant has sufficient minimum contacts with the state.
4. Many requirements must be met to bring a class-action suit, particularly in a federal court.

Pretrial Procedures

LO 4-3

How does a lawsuit begin, and how are issues presented to a court? How does a court decide whether it is the proper place for the lawsuit to be tried? To what extent do the parties in a civil lawsuit learn of the opposing party's legal arguments and factual presentations? How can one party test the validity of the other party's claims prior to trial? And what are the protections against one party harassing another by filing improper or unwarranted lawsuits? The following sections provide the answers to these questions. See Figure 4.1 for a graphic representation.

Figure 4.1
Pretrial procedure

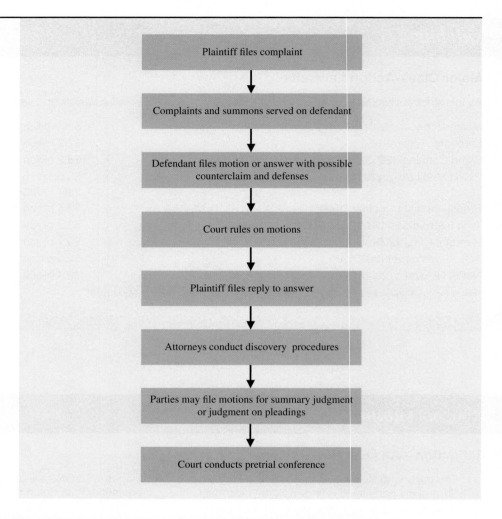

Plaintiff files complaint

↓

Complaints and summons served on defendant

↓

Defendant files motion or answer with possible counterclaim and defenses

↓

Court rules on motions

↓

Plaintiff files reply to answer

↓

Attorneys conduct discovery procedures

↓

Parties may file motions for summary judgment or judgment on pleadings

↓

Court conducts pretrial conference

---

sidebar 4.6

Understanding the Sample Complaint

The sample complaint sets out the parties (plaintiff and defendant) and also explains how the court has subject-matter jurisdiction over the case (discussed earlier in Chapter 3). The sample complaint also explains how the parties can be served. In criminal cases, by contrast, the government files the case as the prosecutor and the defendant is the party charged with a crime. See Appendix II.

PLEADINGS

Do review the sample complaint in Appendix II referenced in Sidebar 4.6.

The legal documents that are filed with a court to begin the litigation process are called **pleadings.** Through the contents of the pleadings, the issues to be resolved are brought into sharper focus. Lawsuits begin by a plaintiff filing a pleading, called a **complaint,** with the court clerk. The complaint contains allegations by the plaintiff and a statement or request of the relief sought. The clerk issues the summons, and a court official (usually a sheriff or marshal) delivers the summons and a copy of the complaint to the defendant.

The summons provides the date by which the defendant must respond to the complaint. This response usually takes the form of a written pleading, called an **answer.** The defendant's answer will either admit or deny each allegation of the plaintiff's complaint and may contain affirmative defenses that will defeat the plaintiff's claim. The answer may also contain causes of action the defendant has against the plaintiff. These statements are called *counterclaims*. If the defendant does not respond in any way, the court may enter an order of **default** and grant the plaintiff the relief sought by the complaint.

After receiving an answer that contains one or more counterclaims, the plaintiff files a reply that specifically admits or denies each allegation of the defendant's counterclaims. The factual issues of a lawsuit are thus formed by one party making an allegation and the other party either admitting it or denying it. In this way, pleadings give notice of each party's contentions and serve to set the boundary lines of the litigation.

The complaint and the answer provide the framework for the lawsuit.

STEPS IN DISCOVERY

Lawsuits are often high drama in the movies and on television. Inevitably, in these dramatized courtroom scenes, some element of surprise is the turning point, thereby ensuring a favorable outcome for the popular client or lawyer. In reality, civil litigation seldom concludes with a surprise witness or new piece of evidence. The reason the surprises do not occur is the process of **discovery.**

Purpose Discovery procedures are designed to take the "sporting aspect" out of litigation and ensure that the results of lawsuits are based on the merits of the controversy and not on the ability, skill, or cunning of counsel. Historically, an attorney who had a weak case on the facts or law could win a lawsuit through a surprise witness at the trial. Today, the law is such that verdicts should not be based on the skill of counsel but on the relative merits of the controversy.

Discovery practice is designed to ensure that each side is fully aware of all the facts involved in the case and of the intentions of the parties. Discovery aids trial preparation by permitting the parties to learn how a witness will answer questions prior to actual questioning at the trial. Discovery provides a "dress rehearsal" for the trial. Even more important, discovery narrows the issues disputed by the parties. In this way, discovery encourages the settlement of the lawsuit, thereby avoiding the actual trial.

Do take advantage of the discovery process to learn as much as you can about the strengths and weaknesses of the case.

Methods During the discovery phase of litigation, clients and lawyers need to work very closely together. Several methods of discovery can be utilized, or it might be decided that some methods will not produce new information and thus will be skipped. It is only through the aid of a client that a lawyer can gain the confidence that the discovery is complete and that the case is ready to go to trial.

Typically, the least expensive method of discovery is to present a series of written questions to the opposing parties. These questions, called **interrogatories,** must be answered by the party receiving them. It is fairly common for plaintiff and defendant to attach a series of interrogatories to

The plaintiff's lawyer often will want to have a trial without delay as opposed to the defendant's lawyer who will have a greater incentive to extend the case through discovery and other pretrial procedures.

their respective pleadings. A common interrogatory is "Please furnish the names and addresses of all persons known to you that witnessed the occurrence which is the subject matter of this lawsuit."

After answers to the interrogatories are received, either party might ask the other to produce specific documents, called **request for production of documents,** that are important to the lawsuit's outcome. For example, a buyer of merchandise who is suing the seller can request that this defendant produce the original sales contract that contains certain warranties covering the merchandise. Sidebar 4.7 addresses issues related to discovery and massive electronic data.

In a personal injury action, the defendant can require the plaintiff to submit to a physical examination by the defendant's expert physician. Although the plaintiff may object to the specific doctor, a general objection to the physical examination is not permissible.

The most expensive method of discovery is also the most revealing with regard to preparing for the trial. To conduct discovery to the greatest extent possible, the lawyers will want to take **depositions** of all potential witnesses. In a deposition, the lawyer orally asks questions of the possible witness and an oral response is given. All the spoken words are recorded by a court reporter, and a written transcript is prepared. In this way, a permanent record of the anticipated testimony is created. With depositions, lawyers seldom need to ask a question during a trial to which they do not already know the answer.

Finally, after some or all of these methods of discovery are used, either party may request the other to admit that certain issues presented in the pleadings are no longer in dispute. The **request for an admission** narrows some issues and makes settlement more likely.

> Depositions of all potential witnesses can be very expensive and burdensome. Lawyers advise their witnesses to answer truthfully but not volunteer information in a deposition.

sidebar 4.7

Discovery and Massive Client Data: Are Clouds the Answer?

One of the most formidable challenges in discovery is handling massive electronic data. A glaring example of this is illustrated by the Viacom copyright infringement lawsuit against YouTube. In that case, the judge ordered 12 terabytes of data to be produced. How much data? According to one estimate, "One terabyte equals 50,000 trees, and 10 terabytes would be the equivalent of all the printed collections of the Library of Congress."

Cloud computing, or using a network of remote servers hosted on the Internet (as opposed to keeping data on local servers or personal computers) to store, manage, and process data may simplify the process of e-discovery. Data generated by cloud computing, however, is not without risks. Here are some ways to protect data stored offsite:

- Always remember that data created or stored offsite is vulnerable to loss of control and privacy concerns.
- When working with a cloud service provider (CSP), ask plenty of questions about its policies and practices for protecting data, including liability for any security breaches.
- Ensure that data remains in a form compatible with your in-house computer applications.
- Retain control over the production of data to third parties to prevent your CSP from producing information without providing you with advance notice.
- Consider additional backups of data, perhaps including physical copies of critical documents.

Source: Joe Dysart, "As Bulging Client Data Heads for the Cloud, Law Firms Ready for a Storm," *ABA Journal* (April 1, 2011).

SCOPE OF DISCOVERY

The discovery procedures are intended to be used freely by the parties to litigation without the court's direct supervision. At times, a question about the scope of what is discoverable arises, and the party objecting to discovery seeks the judge's opinion. In this setting, a ruling must be given. Generally, judges provide a very broad or liberal interpretation of the degree of discoverable information. The usual rule is that as long as the information sought in discovery will lead to evidence admissible during the trial, the information is discoverable and an objection is overruled. If a party fails to produce relevant, requested evidence, the party seeking the information may file a motion to compel discovery, asking the court to order production of the material. See Sidebar 4.8 for a discussion about the costs of discovery.

Discovery imposes a tremendous burden on the judicial system because judges must be diverted from other important matters, such as hearing criminal cases or conducting trials, to resolve heated discovery disputes. Rule 37 of the Federal Rules of Civil Procedure provides that "a party, upon reasonable notice to the other parties and all persons affected thereby, may apply for an order compelling disclosure or discovery."

Parties can become very aggressive during the discovery process causing significant damage to the litigation process. The key for both sides is to act in a reasonable and prudent manner. The plaintiff should only ask for things needed to prepare for trial, and the defendant should be open and responsive to reasonable requests for discoverable information. In the end, the plaintiff and the defendant can do themselves great harm by acting otherwise. One of the faults with the litigation process is the tendency for both sides to stake out extreme positions and engage in a strategy of open warfare leading up to trial. Since many cases are settled without a trial, the best chance of that taking place quickly, and thereby avoiding greater lawyer expense, is for the parties to act in a moderate and reasonable manner during the discovery process. Moreover, as illustrated in Sidebar 4.9, if there is pending or imminent litigation, litigation holds should be issued to preserve data.

Don't try to impede the discovery process. Such efforts often backfire, and you could be sanctioned.

sidebar 4.8

Costs of Discovery

Although the use of discovery is essential to our system of litigation, it also carries significant costs. In a recent survey of 1,000 judges, abusive discovery was rated highest among the reasons for the high cost of litigation. Discovery imposes several costs on the litigant. These burdens include the time spent searching for and compiling relevant documents; the time, expense, and aggravation of preparing for and attending depositions; the costs of copying and shipping documents; and the attorneys' fees generated in interpreting discovery requests, drafting responses to interrogatories and coordinating responses to production requests, advising the client as to which documents should be disclosed and which ones withheld, and determining whether certain information is privileged. The party seeking discovery also bears costs, including attorneys' fees generated in drafting discovery requests and reviewing the opponent's objections and responses. Both parties incur costs related to the delay discovery imposes on reaching the merits of the case. Many companies want to be very aggressive in discovery.

sidebar 4.9

Litigation Holds and E-Discovery

When there is pending or imminent litigation, your company should issue a "litigation hold" to preserve all relevant data from being destroyed, altered, or mutilated. The litigation hold applies to all documents, including electronic ones.

What are the best ways to identify and produce all electronic documents that may be used to support claims and defenses? Here are best practices suggestions to streamline the process:

- Select an individual to take the lead in preserving all documents.

- Identify all custodians of information (including former employees) and both hard copies of documents and electronic material.
- Notify all custodians about the pending litigation.
- Create a chart or content map of all categories of documents and custodians.
- Remind all custodians to suspend routine destruction policies and to preserve all documents.

MOTIONS

During the pretrial phase of litigation, either plaintiff or defendant or both may attempt to convince the court that there are no questions about the factual setting of the dispute. An argument is presented that there are only questions of law for the judge to resolve. For example, the parties may be in complete agreement that the plaintiff has not been paid by the defendant for the merchandise that was delivered by the plaintiff and received by the defendant. The dispute between these parties is simply whether, under the stated facts, the defendant must pay the plaintiff. This dispute presents only an issue of law, not of fact.

Motion practice is a critical part of the litigation process.

When a question of law is at issue, the parties can seek a pretrial determination of their rights by filing a **motion** with the court. These motions can be made at any point in the litigation process. First, the defendant may, instead of filing an answer, file a *motion to dismiss for failure to state a cause of action.* By this pleading the defendant, in effect, says to the court, "Even if everything the plaintiff says in his complaint is true, he is not entitled to the relief he seeks." For example, the defendant in the case involving the nonpayment for merchandise can argue the plaintiff failed to allege that the defendant ordered the goods. By federal law, merchandise sent unsolicited does not have to be paid for even when it is kept. In essence, the defendant, in the motion to dismiss, argues that the plaintiff failed to plead an essential element of a valid claim.

In addition, a defendant may move to dismiss a suit for reasons that as a matter of law prevent the plaintiff from winning his or her suit. Such matters as a lack of jurisdiction of the court to hear the suit, or expiration of the time limit during which the defendant is subject to suit, may be raised by such a motion. This argument is usually referred to as the **statute of limitations.** Each state has prescribed a time limit after which a suit cannot be filed. For example, if the plaintiff fails to sue within the stated period, the defendant is not liable for the nonpayment of the merchandise.

The rules of procedure in the federal court system and in most of the state systems provide for motions for a **judgment on the pleadings,** which asks the judge to decide the case based solely on the complaint and the answer. If in the example involving the nonpayment for the merchandise the complaint does contain all the elements needed to state a claim and if the defendant offers no explanation or excuse for nonpayment in the answer, the judge can enter a judgment that the defendant must pay the plaintiff a specified amount. Through this motion, a time-consuming but unnecessary trial can be avoided.

A motion for **summary judgment** seeks a similar conclusion to the litigation prior to trial. However, the party filing this motion is asking the judge to base a decision not only on the pleadings but also on other evidence. Such evidence usually is presented in the form of sworn statements called **affidavits.** The judge also may conduct a hearing and allow the lawyers to argue the merits of the motion for summary judgment. If there are no material disputed issues of fact, the judge will decide the legal issues raised by the case and enter a judgment in favor of one party over the other. Even if the motion for summary judgment is not granted in full, its use often narrows the issues for trial. Figure 4.2 presents typical motions.

Many cases settle after a ruling on the motion for summary judgment.

Figure 4.2 *Typical Pretrial Motions*

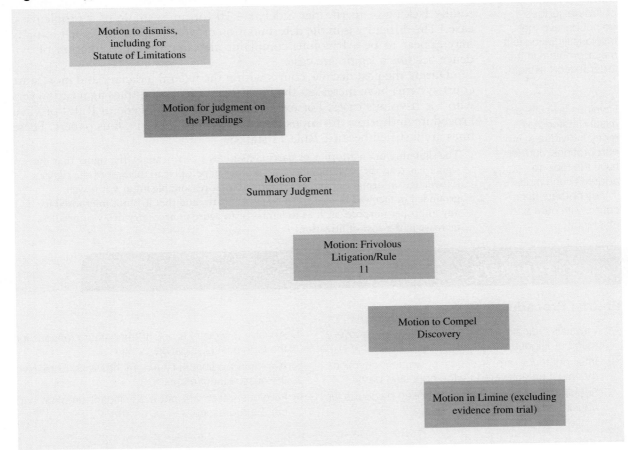

Motion to dismiss, including for Statute of Limitations

Motion for judgment on the Pleadings

Motion for Summary Judgment

Motion: Frivolous Litigation/Rule 11

Motion to Compel Discovery

Motion in Limine (excluding evidence from trial)

sidebar 4.10

Frivolous Lawsuits against Ringling Brothers

 The Humane Society of the United States and other animal-rights groups agreed to pay Feld Entertainment, the producers of Ringling Bros and Barnum & Bailey Circus, a combined $15.75 million to settle allegations by the company that the groups and their attorneys bribed a former circus employee to fabricate allegations that Asian elephants were abused in Feld circus productions.

The settlement follows a 14-year legal battle in which a federal judge levied an unprecedented penalty for making "frivolous," "vexatious," and "groundless" claims against Feld. After learning that the animal groups paid the former Feld elephant cleaner and feeder nearly $200,000, Feld brought a RICO action against the animal-rights groups. To date, Feld has recovered $25 million in the litigation, recouping all of the money it has spent on legal fees.

Source: Jacob Gershman, "Animal Rights Groups Pay Circus Producer Millions to Settle Suit," *The Wall Street Journal* (May 15, 2014).

A recent study by the Federal Judicial Center found that the overwhelming majority of federal judges do not believe that frivolous litigation is a major problem in the federal court system.

Frivolous lawsuits are misunderstood by many individuals and corporations. Judges have the tools to address such matters if they operate their courts with care and efficiency.

FRIVOLOUS CASES

Either on a motion by a party or on their own initiative, judges may terminate the litigation process if there is a finding that the lawsuit is frivolous, that is, totally lacking in merit. (See Sidebar 4.10 for an example of a problematic case.) The difficulty is in the determination of what is frivolous. What initially may appear to be a frivolous complaint may upon the presentation of evidence become a legitimate case.

During the past decade, courts within the federal judiciary and most state court systems have increased the frequency of assessing fines against lawyers who file frivolous cases. For example, Rule 11 of the Federal Rules of Civil Procedure authorizes the imposition of fines for filing frivolous papers. These fines are justified because Rule 11 states:

> The signature of an attorney or party constitutes a certificate by the signer that the signer has read the pleading, motion, or other paper; that to the best of the signer's knowledge, information, and belief formed after reasonable inquiry it is well grounded in fact and is warranted by existing law, and that it is not interposed for any improper purpose, such as to harass or to cause unnecessary delay or needless increase in the cost of litigation.

concept *summary*

Pretrial Procedures

1. Lawsuits typically are won and lost at the discovery stage of litigation.
2. Interrogatories are a series of written questions that must be answered by the opposing party.
3. Substantial penalties can be imposed by courts for abusing the discovery process.
4. Abusive discovery is one of the primary reasons for the high cost of litigation.
5. A motion for summary judgment seeks to resolve the case without a trial.
6. Frivolous cases are not a significant problem and can be redressed.

Most states have a rule similar to Federal Rule 11. The courts have upheld fines against lawyers and clients who sign frivolous documents. These holdings make it essential that businesspeople have thorough discussions with their lawyers about litigation strategies.

The Trial

If efforts to resolve a case through pretrial motions or negotiations have been unsuccessful, the case will proceed to trial. A trial normally involves the presentation of evidence to a jury to determine the actual facts in dispute. After the evidence is presented, the judge explains the applicable law to the jury. The jury is asked to deliberate and render a verdict and the trial court must then decide whether to enter a judgment based on the jury's verdict.

> "I consider trial by jury as the only anchor yet devised by man, by which a government can be held to the principles of its constitution."
>
> **—Thomas Jefferson**

---

sidebar 4.11

The Intersection of the Internet and Juries

 Google, Facebook, and Twitter are adding a new dimension to jury selection and dynamics. Here are a few examples:

- Some lawyers might search the Internet for personal information about jurors. Social media sites may provide lawyers with information not typically revealed in *voir dire.*
- Information on social networking sites such as Facebook can offer clues about a potential juror's sympathy or the lack thereof to a client.
- Likewise, jurors should not send a "friend" request to a witness or other person involved in the trial.

- Jurors need to be advised that commenting about an ongoing trial is not allowed. The Judicial Conference of the U.S. is recommending that federal judges explicitly tell jurors that "You may not communicate with anyone about the case on your cell phone, through e-mail, BlackBerry, iPhone, text messaging, or on Twitter, through any blog or website, through any Internet chat room, or by way of any other social networking websites including Facebook, My Space, LinkedIn, and YouTube." reasonable? Did the court properly respond or overreact?

JURY SELECTION

LO 4-4

As the case is called, the first order of business is to select a jury. Prior to the calling of the case, the court clerk will have summoned prospective jurors. Their names are drawn at random from lists of eligible citizens, and the number of jurors required is selected or called into the jury box to conduct the *voir dire* examination. **Voir dire** literally means to speak the truth. This examination allows the court and often the attorneys for each party to examine each potential juror as to his or her qualifications and ability to be fair and impartial. A party to a lawsuit is entitled to fair and impartial jurors in both civil and criminal cases. Prospective jurors are sworn to give truthful answers to the questions on *voir dire.*

Do remember that most civil cases are settled or resolved prior to trial.

Peremptory challenge means no cause or reason needs to be given to excuse a prospective juror. It can be traced at least as far back as fourteenth-century England.

Either party in the lawsuit may challenge or excuse a prospective juror for a specific reason or cause. For example, if a prospective juror is related to one of the parties or to a witness or the juror admits bias favoring one side, that person may be excused as a juror because of the specific reason. In addition to the excuses for cause, the plaintiff and defendant are given a certain number of challenges, known as **peremptory challenges,** for which no cause or reason need be given to excuse a prospective juror. The number of peremptory challenges varies from court system to court system and on the type of case being tried. The number also may vary between the parties. For instance, in a criminal case, the defendant may have twelve peremptory challenges, and the government may have only six. The process of *voir dire* examination continues until all the peremptory challenges are exhausted and a full jury panel is selected.

On the basis of a series of U.S. Supreme Court decisions, beginning with *Batson v. Kentucky,* 476 U.S. 79 (1986), outlawing racial discrimination in jury selection, the jury has become increasingly more representative of the racial diversity in the United States. *Batson* represented a major development in Supreme Court jurisprudence allowing lawyer misconduct in a single case to establish discriminatory motive in making peremptory strikes. The Court banned gender discrimination in jury selection in the case of *J.E.B. v. Alabama Ex Rel. T.B.,* 511 U.S. 127 (1994) (see Sidebar 4.12).

The peremptory challenge, the method by which attorneys have traditionally been able to disqualify prospective jurors without having to state any reason, occupies an increasingly uneasy position in the law today as more questions are raised by each passing decision. See Sidebar 4.13 for issues related to religion and peremptory challenges.

sidebar 4.12

The Jury and Constitutional Limits on Peremptory Challenges

J.E.B. v. Alabama Ex Rel T.B., 511 U.S. 127 (1994), was the Supreme Court's initial expansion of the protections of the Fourteenth Amendment in the jury selection context. In a paternity suit, the state used nine of its ten preemptory challenges to remove males from the jury. As a result, the trial court empanelled in all-female jury. After the jury found the defendant to be the father of the child in question and the court ordered him to pay child support, the defendant appealed on the basis of the Equal Protection Clause of the Fourteenth Amendment.

The Supreme Court held that the Equal Protection Clause prohibits discrimination on the basis of gender in the jury selection process. The state maintained its reason for the gender-based peremptory challenges was stereotypes of the genders that indicated men were more sympathetic to the man in a paternity action. The Court held this reason was based on actions that the Fourteenth Amendment was aimed at eliminating. By relying on those stereotypes when it made the peremptory challenges, the state ratified and reinforced prejudicial views of the abilities of men and women. The Supreme Court reversed the trial court's determination and remanded for a new trial with a new jury.

WAL-MART STORES, INC. v. DUKES
564 U.S. __ (2011)

Respondents, current or former employees of petitioner Wal-Mart, sought judgment against the company for injunctive and declaratory relief, punitive damages, and backpay, on behalf of themselves and a nationwide class of some 1.5 million female employees, because of Wal-Mart's alleged discrimination against women in violation of Title VII of the Civil Rights Act of 1964. They claim that local managers exercise their discretion over pay and promotions disproportionately in favor of men, which has an unlawful disparate impact on female employees; and that Wal-Mart's refusal to cabin its managers' authority amounts to disparate treatment. The District Court certified the class.

The Ninth Circuit substantially affirmed.

Justice Ginsburg filed a dissenting opinion on the "common question" issue under Rule 23(a)(2). She emphasized that the majority opinion "disqualifies the class at the starting gate" because it puts too much burden on the plaintiffs to show how their individual claims are sufficiently similar to form a class action. She was joined by Justices Breyer, Sotomayor, and Kagan.

SCALIA, J.: We are presented with one of the most expansive class actions ever. . . . We consider whether the certification of the plaintiff class was consistent with Federal Rules of Civil Procedure 23(a) and (b)(2). Petitioner Wal-Mart is the Nation's largest private employer. . . . In all, Wal-Mart operates approximately 3,400 stores and employs more than one million people.

Pay and promotion decisions at Wal-Mart are generally committed to local managers' broad discretion, which is exercised "in a largely subjective manner." . . . Local store managers may increase the wages of hourly employees (within limits) with only limited corporate oversight. As for salaried employees, such as store managers and their deputies, higher corporate authorities have discretion to set their pay within preestablished ranges.

Promotions work in a similar fashion. Wal-Mart permits store managers to apply their own subjective criteria when selecting candidates as "support managers," which is the first step on the path to management. Admission to Wal-Mart's management training program, however, does require that a candidate meet certain objective criteria, including an above-average performance rating, at least one year's tenure in the applicant's current position, and a willingness to relocate. But except for those requirements, regional and district managers have discretion to use their own judgment when selecting candidates for management training. Promotion to higher office—*e.g.*, assistant manager, co-manager, or store manager—is similarly at the discretion of the employee's superiors after prescribed objective factors are satisfied.

The named plaintiffs in this lawsuit, representing the 1.5 million members of the certified class, are three current or former Wal-Mart employees who allege that the company discriminated against them on the basis of their sex by denying them equal pay or promotions, in violation of Title VII of the Civil Rights Act of 1964, 78 Stat. 253, as amended. . . .

[The plaintiffs/respondents] do not allege that Wal-Mart has any express corporate policy against the advancement of women. Rather, they claim that their local managers' discretion over pay and promotions is exercised disproportionately in favor of men, leading to an unlawful disparate impact on female employees, see 42 U. S. C. §2000e–2(k). And, respondents say, because Wal-Mart is aware of this effect, its refusal to cabin its managers' authority amounts to disparate treatment, see §2000e–2(a). . . . Importantly for our purposes, respondents claim that the discrimination to which they have been subjected is common to *all* Wal-Mart's female employees. The basic theory of their case is that a strong and uniform "corporate culture" permits bias against women to infect, perhaps subconsciously, the discretionary decision making of each one of Wal-Mart's thousands of managers—thereby making every woman at the company the victim of one common discriminatory practice.

Class certification is governed by Federal Rule of Civil Procedure 23. Under Rule 23(a), the party seeking certification must demonstrate, first, that:

(1) the class is so numerous that joinder of all members is impracticable,

(2) there are questions of law or fact common to the class,

(3) the claims or defenses of the representative parties are typical of the claims or defenses of the class, and

(4) the representative parties will fairly and adequately protect the interests of the class . . .

The crux of this case is commonality—the rule requiring a plaintiff to show that "there are questions of law or fact common to the class." . . . Quite obviously, the mere claim by employees of the same company that they have suffered a Title VII injury, or even a disparate impact Title VII injury, gives no cause to believe that all their claims can productively be litigated at once. Their claims must depend upon a common contention. . . .

In this case, proof of commonality necessarily overlaps with respondents' merits contention that Wal-Mart engages in a *pattern or practice* of discrimination . . . Here respondents wish to sue about literally millions of employment decisions at once. Without some glue holding the alleged *reasons* for all those decisions together, it will be impossible to say that examination of all the class members' claims for relief will produce a common answer to the crucial question *why was I disfavored*. . . .

The first manner of bridging the gap [use of a biased testing procedure] obviously has no application here; Wal-Mart has no testing procedure or other companywide evaluation method that can be charged with bias. The whole point of permitting discretionary decision making is to avoid evaluating employees under a common standard.

The second manner of bridging the gap requires "significant proof" that Wal-Mart "operated under a general policy of discrimination." That is entirely absent here. Wal-Mart's announced policy forbids sex discrimination, see App. 1567a–1596a, and as the District Court recognized the company imposes penalties for denials of equal employment opportunity . . . Respondents have not identified a common mode of exercising discretion

that pervades the entire company . . . Respondents attempt to make that showing by means of statistical and anecdotal evidence, but their evidence falls well short [The Court was not persuaded by regression analyses submitted by a statistician and labor economist]. . . .

Even if they are taken at face value, these studies are insufficient to establish that respondents' theory can be proved on a classwide basis. . . . There is another, more fundamental respect in which respondents' statistical proof fails. Even if it established (as it does not) a pay or promotion pattern that differs from the nationwide figures or the regional figures in *all* of Wal-Mart's 3,400 stores, that would still not demonstrate that commonality of issue exists. Some managers will claim that the availability of women, or qualified women, or interested women, in their stores' area does not mirror the national or regional statistics. And almost all of them will claim to have been applying some sex-neutral, performance-based criteria—whose nature and effects will differ from store to store. . . .

In sum, we agree with Chief Judge Kozinski that the members of the class: "held a multitude of different jobs, at different levels of Wal-Mart's hierarchy, for variable lengths of time, in 3,400 stores, sprinkled across 50 states, with a kaleidoscope of supervisors (male and female), subject to a variety of regional policies that all differed. . . . Some thrived while others did poorly. They have little in common but their sex and this lawsuit." . . .

The judgment of the Court of Appeals is *Reversed.*

KEY POINTS

- "Commonality," which requires a plaintiff to show that there are "questions of law or fact common to the class," is an essential element to establish a class action.
- Because the plaintiffs were unable to demonstrate commonality, class certification was denied.
- Even though class certification was denied, women in the potential class can still bring claims if they can demonstrate discrimination.

Given all of the criticism raised about juries today, particularly their ability to decide celebrity criminal cases or complex civil cases, we are likely to see further court decisions clarifying the use of peremptory challenges. Several legal commentators have suggested following the example of England and eliminating the use of peremptory challenges altogether. These commentators argue that there would be fewer problems and more just results if the first 12 prospective jurors who walked through the courtroom door were seated. By taking this action, the cost spent on hiring jury selection experts or litigating the use of peremptory challenges would be eliminated.

sidebar 4.13

Religion and Peremptory Challenges

The next big question in jury selection is whether peremptory strikes based on religion violate the Equal Protection Clause. Lower courts are divided on this issue. One distinguishing factor between religion as opposed to race and gender is that religion is not visible from a juror's appearance. The Supreme Court of Minnesota, in *State v. Davis,* 504 N.W.2d 767 (Min. 1993), held that *Batson* protection does not extend to religious affiliation. It reasoned that such protection of religion was not necessary because "the use of the peremptory strike to discriminate purposefully on the basis of religion does not appear to be common and flagrant . . . there is no indication that irrational religious bias so pervades the peremptory challenge as to determine the integrity of the jury system." The Second Circuit, however, in *United States v. Brown,* 352 7.3d 654 (2nd Cir. 2003), held that a peremptory strike based on a person's religious affiliation was a *Batson* violation.

OTHER STEPS DURING A TRIAL

After selecting jurors to hear the case, the attorneys make their opening statements. An opening statement is not evidence; it familiarizes the jury with the essential facts that each side expects to prove. So that the jury may understand the overall picture of the case and the relevancy of each bit of evidence as presented, the lawyers inform the jury of the facts they expect to prove and of the witnesses they expect to call to make such proof.

After the opening statements, the trial continues with the plaintiff introducing evidence to establish the truth of the allegations made in the complaint. Evidence is normally presented in open court by the examination of witnesses and production of documents and other exhibits. After the plaintiff has presented his or her evidence, the defendant may make a motion for a **directed verdict.** Under rule 50 of the Federal Rules, this motion is called a Judgment as a Matter of Law. The court can only direct a verdict for one party if the evidence, taken in the light most favorable to the other party, establishes as a matter of law that the party making the motion is entitled to a verdict. Just as a plaintiff must *allege* certain facts or have the complaint dismissed by motion to dismiss, he or she must have some *proof* of each essential allegation or lose the case on a motion for a directed verdict.

Defendants typically make a motion for a directed verdict after the plaintiff has presented his or her case.

After the parties have completed the presentation of all the evidence, the lawyers have an opportunity to summarize the evidence. Unlike the opening statements, which involved simply a preview of what was to come, the lawyers in closing argument try to convince the jury (or judge if no jury is used) of what the case's outcome should be.

Following the closing arguments, the judge acquaints the jury with the law applicable to the case. These are the **jury instructions.** As the function of the jury is to find the facts and the function of the court is to determine the applicable law, the purpose of jury instructions is to bring the facts and the law together in an orderly manner that will result in a decision. A typical jury instruction might be:

Don't underestimate the importance of jury instructions given at the close of the case.

> The plaintiff in his complaint has alleged that he was injured as the proximate cause of the negligence of the defendant. If you find from the evidence that the

defendant was guilty of negligence, which proximately caused plaintiff's injuries, then your verdict should be for the plaintiff.

In this instruction, the court is in effect saying that the plaintiff must prove that the defendant was at fault. Thus, the jury is instructed as to the result to be returned if the jurors have found certain facts to be true. At the conclusion of the jury instructions, the judge informs the jurors to begin their deliberations and to return to the courtroom when they have reached a decision. See Figure 4.3 for a list of the steps in a trial.

---

sidebar 4.14

Technology in the Courtroom: The "OpenCourt" Project

U.S. Supreme Court justices may continue to be skeptical about television cameras in the courtroom, but that is not the case in state court in Quincy, Massachusetts. The proceedings in the Quincy District Court are streamed live over the Internet. In a grand experiment, the courtroom now welcomes laptops, iPads, and smartphones.

The court will also permit live blogging and communicating via Twitter and Facebook. As judges across the country grapple with how to use digital technology, this is one attempt to "bring the courts and what goes on in the courts closer to the people so they will understand how the law and the justice system work in this country." Court officials are optimistic that the pilot project will help establish effective guidelines for courts.

Sources: "OMG, Tweets, Facebook Welcome in Mass. Courtroom," *ABC News/Technology* (May 2, 2011); and http://opencourt.us/.

BURDEN OF PROOF

The term **burden of proof** has two meanings depending on the context in which it is used. It may describe the burden or responsibility that a person has to come forward with evidence on a particular issue. The party alleging the existence of certain facts usually has the burden of coming forward with evidence to establish those facts.

Burden of proof may also describe the responsibility a person has to be persuasive as to a specific fact. This is known as the *burden of persuasion*. The party with this burden must convince the trier of fact on the issue involved. If a party with the burden of persuasion fails to meet this burden, that party loses the lawsuit. Thus, the burden of persuasion is a legal device used to help determine the rights of the litigating parties.

The burden of proof used in a case often can determine the outcome for one side or the other.

Criminal Cases   The extent of proof required to satisfy the burden of persuasion varies, depending upon the issue and the type of case. There are three distinct levels of proof recognized by the law. For criminal cases, the burden of proof is described as **beyond a reasonable doubt.** This means that the prosecution in a criminal case has the burden of convincing the trier of fact, usually a jury, that the defendant is guilty of the crime charged and that the jury has no reasonable doubt about the defendant's guilt. This burden of proof does not require evidence beyond any doubt, only beyond a reasonable doubt. A reasonable doubt is one that a reasonable person viewing the evidence might reasonably entertain. This standard is not used in civil cases.

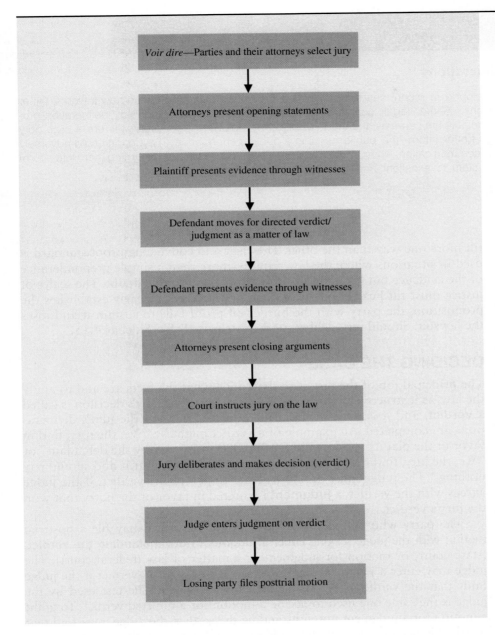

Figure 4.3
Trial steps

Voir dire—Parties and their attorneys select jury

Attorneys present opening statements

Plaintiff presents evidence through witnesses

Defendant moves for directed verdict/ judgment as a matter of law

Defendant presents evidence through witnesses

Attorneys present closing arguments

Court instructs jury on the law

Jury deliberates and makes decision (verdict)

Judge enters judgment on verdict

Losing party files posttrial motion

Civil Cases In civil cases, the party with the burden of proof is subject to one of two standards: the **preponderance of evidence** standard or the **clear and convincing proof** standard. The preponderance of evidence standard is used most frequently. It requires that a party convince the jury by a preponderance of evidence that the facts are as he or she contends. Preponderance of evidence is achieved when there is greater weight of evidence in support of the proposition than there is against it. The scales of justice, in other words,

Preponderance of the evidence standard is typically used in contract and tort cases.

sidebar 4.15

Televising Jury Deliberations

A raging debate has developed in recent years over televising jury deliberations. Some legal scholars believe that jurors are oblivious to the cameras and that the televised proceedings better inform the public in the modern age of mass communication. They argue that the American jury system is excellent and that we should not be ashamed to see how it works. Other scholars think that televising the jury deliberation process is a terrible idea because it will turn a civic duty into a public performance. They fear it could adversely impact the jury deliberations by turning them into a form of reality television. What do you think?

tilt more one way than the other. The clear and convincing proof standard is used in situations where the law requires more than a simple preponderance of the evidence but less than proof beyond a reasonable doubt. The scales of justice must tilt heavily one way. Unless the evidence clearly establishes the proposition, the party with the burden of proof fails to sustain it and loses the lawsuit. Should jury deliberations be televised? See Sidebar 4.15.

DECIDING THE CASE

The principal job of the jury is to determine what the facts are and to apply the law, as instructed by the judge, to these facts. The jury's decision is called a **verdict,** and it is announced in the courtroom when the jury's deliberations are completed. An example of a verdict might be "We, the jury, find in favor of the plaintiff and award $1,000,000 to be paid by the defendant" or "We, the jury, find the defendant is not liable to the plaintiff and should pay nothing." The judge must decide whether to accept the verdict. If the judge agrees with the verdict, a **judgment** is entered in favor of the party that won the jury's verdict.

> Judges do not like to admit to making mistakes during the trial.

The party who is dissatisfied with the jury's verdict may file a posttrial motion with the judge seeking either a **judgment notwithstanding the verdict,** (state court) or motion for judgment as a matter of law (federal court). The judge may enter a judgment opposite to that of the jury's verdict if the judge finds that the verdict is erroneous as a matter of law. The test used by the judge is the same one used to decide a motion for a directed verdict. To grant a motion for a judgment notwithstanding the verdict, the judge must find that reasonable persons viewing the evidence would not reach the verdict the jury returned. Because jurors are presumed to be reasonable, this motion is not frequently granted.

The party who receives the adverse judgment may file a motion for a new trial. This motion may be granted if the judge is convinced that a legal mistake was made during the trial. Because a judge is not usually inclined to acknowledge that mistakes have been made, a motion for a new trial is usually denied. It is from the ruling on this motion that the losing party appeals.

concept *summary*

The Trial

1. Peremptory challenges may not be based upon race or gender discrimination.
2. A direct verdict or judgment as a matter of law may be granted when the evidence establishes, as a matter of law, that the moving party is entitled to a verdict.
3. Jury instructions are used to acquaint the jury with the law applicable to the case.
4. In most civil cases, the preponderance standard is used to evaluate the case.
5. A judgment notwithstanding the verdict may be entered if the verdict is erroneous as a matter of law.

Posttrial Issues

LO 4-5

Even after the trial, a number of issues may still exist. First among these is this one: How can a disappointed litigant obtain a review of the trial judge's legal rulings? If the trial court's judgment is final, what can the victorious party do to collect the dollar damages awarded? Finally, can the same subject matter be relitigated? These questions are the subject of the final three sections of this chapter.

When the result at the trial court level is appealed, the party appealing is usually referred to as the **appellant,** and the successful party in the trial court is called the **appellee.** Most jurisdictions, in publishing decisions of reviewing courts, list the appellant first and the appellee second, even though the appellant may have been the defendant in the trial court. As a result, the names used in a case are somewhat misleading. When a petition for certiorari is filed to the Supreme Court, the party initiating the petition is the **petitioner** and the other party is known as the **respondent.**

Losing parties have the right to appeal the case to a higher court.

APPEALS

Each state prescribes its own appellate procedure and determines the jurisdiction of its various reviewing courts. Although having knowledge of the procedure used in an appeal is essentially a responsibility for the lawyer,

table 4.1 Litigating Parties

Action Filed	Party Filing the Action	Party against Whom the Action Is Filed
Civil case	Plaintiff	Defendant
Criminal case	State or federal government as represented by a prosecutor	Defendant
Appeal	Appellant	Appellee
Petition for a writ of certiorari	Petitioner	Respondent

sidebar 4.16

Qualcomm and Posttrial Sanctions

The 2008 Qualcomm versus Broadcom case should send shock waves far outside of the state of California. Following the completion of a trial, the trial court referred six attorneys to the State Bar of California for investigation of possible ethical lapses. The lawyers for Qualcomm called a witness to testify. During cross-examination by Broadcom's lawyers, the witness revealed receiving multiple e-mails that had not been produced during discovery. The case ended, and the jury found for Broadcom. However, the court retained jurisdiction to address the discovery misconduct. Several months after the adverse verdict, lawyers for Qualcomm advised the court that Qualcomm had located thousands of other unproduced e-mails that appeared to be inconsistent with certain arguments made on Qualcomm's behalf during the case. The documents were located by searching the e-mail archives of less than two dozen key Qualcomm employees, searches that had not earlier been undertaken.

The court found that Qualcomm's failure to conduct basic searches at any time prior to trial amounted to an intentional withholding of documents. The court rejected Qualcomm's assertion that its legal counsel should have given more guidance on the scope of searches that should have been performed. Qualcomm was responsible for its own failings and for the failings of its chosen counsel.

The case likely would not have been brought, or would have been quickly dismissed, if Qualcomm had produced the documents that made Broadcom's defense effective. So the court imposed a discovery sanction of over $8.5 million—the full amount of Broadcom's legal fees. The court rejected the possibility that Qualcomm had hoodwinked its lawyers. The lawyers should have seen through Qualcomm's failures to conduct basic searches, whether that failure was intentional or negligent. The court noted that the lawyers ignored obvious signs that Qualcomm's production was incomplete.

This decision significantly affected the professional reputations of the attorneys involved. Update: In April 2010, the court held that although there was "an incredible breakdown in communication," there was insufficient evidence of bad faith on the part of the attorneys to support any sanctions for misconduct.

Sources: Jerold S. Solovy and Robert L. Byman, "Qualcomm Case Sends Tremors Nationwide," *The National Law Journal* (January 31, 2008); and Elizabeth S. Conan, "Qualcomm: Scandal and Professional Reputation," *ABA GPSolo Magazine* (October/November 2010).

> Courts of appeal are looking to see if harmful errors were made by the trial court.

understanding certain aspects of this procedure may assist you in understanding our judicial system.

Appellate Procedures

Courts of appeal deal with the record of the proceedings in lower court. All the pleadings, testimony, and motions are reduced to a written record, which is filed with the court of review. The court of appeal studies the issues, testimony, and proceedings to determine whether prejudicial errors occurred or whether the lower court reached an erroneous result. In addition to the record from the trial, each party files a **brief.** The briefs contain a short description of the case; a factual summary; legal points and authorities; and arguments for reversing or affirming the lower court decision.

> Oral argument is used less frequently today with courts often relying on written briefs.

In addition to the brief, the reviewing court is often given the benefit of **oral argument** in deciding the case. The attorneys are given a specified amount of time to explain orally to the court their position in the case. This also gives the court of review an opportunity to question the attorneys about various aspects of the case.

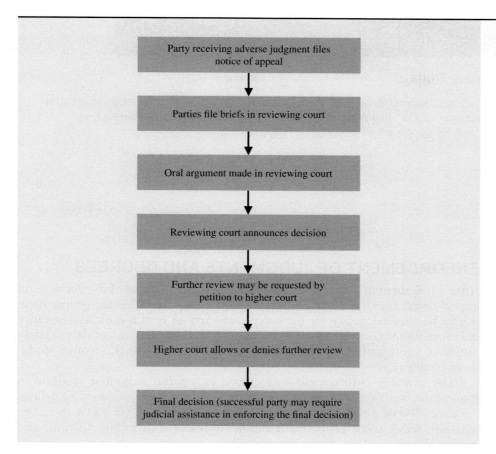

Figure 4.4
Appellate review

After oral argument, an initial vote of the judges' or justices' impressions is usually taken. The case is assigned to one judge or justice to prepare an opinion. Each judge or justice has a staff of clerks assisting in the preparation of opinions. After the opinion is prepared, it is circulated among the other members of the court. If a majority approve the opinion, it is adopted. Those who disagree may prepare a dissenting opinion. If the review is conducted by an intermediate appellate court, the losing party may petition the highest court in the system for a *writ of certiorari*. See Figure 4.4 for an overview of appellate review.

Deference to Trial Courts

Courts of appeal are essentially concerned with questions of law. However, a reviewing court may be asked to grant a new trial on the ground that the decision in the lower court is contrary to the manifest weight of the evidence found in the record. In the federal courts and in many states, appellate courts are not allowed to disturb factual findings unless they are clearly erroneous. This limitation recognizes the unique opportunity afforded the trial judge in evaluating the credibility of witnesses and weighing the evidence. Determining the weight and credibility of the evidence is the special function of the trial court. An appellate court cannot substitute its interpretation of the evidence for that of the trial court simply because it construes the facts or resolves the ambiguities differently. Sidebar 4.17 lists what is necessary to appeal an evidentiary ruling.

Great deference is given to the trial court in reviewing appeals.

Appealing an Evidentiary Ruling

Judges are required to make split-second rulings on the admissibility of evidence during trial. Lawyers, in order to preserve an argument for appeal, must show the following:

1. An objection is made
2. In a timely manner
3. Challenging the evidence on specific grounds
4. The lower court's ruling was wrong and
5. The error harmed your client.

ENFORCEMENT OF JUDGMENTS AND DECREES

After a judgment in a court has become final, either because of the decision on appeal or because the losing party has failed to appeal within the proper time, it may become necessary for the successful party to obtain judicial assistance in enforcing the court decision. For example, the loser (judgment debtor) may not have voluntarily paid the amount of the judgment to the winner (judgment creditor).

An adverse judgment can lead to the partial loss of wages to satisfy the creditor.

The primary enforcement mechanism is for the judgment creditor to request the court's assistance to have the **execution** of the judgment or decree. An execution of a judgment occurs when a court official, such as a sheriff or marshal, seizes some property of the debtor, sells it at public auction, and applies the proceeds to the creditor's claim.

Another form of execution is **garnishment.** This method of enforcement involves having a portion of the debtor's wages paid to the court, which in turn pays the creditor.

Sidebar 4.18 details a situation in which a new trial was ordered following a finding that a party failed to produce key document in the litigation.

Discovery of Misconduct Causes Lockheed to Lose Its $37 Million Verdict

Federal District Judge Charles A. Pannell, Jr. vacated a $37.3 million trade secrets verdict and dismissed a motion for more than $16 million in attorneys' fees in favor of Lockheed Martin Corp. and ordered a new trial. Why? The court found that Lockheed failed to produce a defendant's competitor documents critical to the litigation. The documents at issue are internal corporate e-mails that may have contradicted the testimony of witnesses.

Defendant L-3 Communications Integrated Systems argued that Lockheed intentionally withheld evidence critical to L-3's defense, which "undoubtedly changed the outcome of the trial." The parties later settled.

Sources: R. Robin McDonald, "Lockheed Withheld Discovery Documents in Trade Secrets Case, Court Records Show," *Fulton County Daily Report* (May 19, 2010); and "Discovery Failure Sinks Lockheed's $37 Million Win," *Fulton County Daily Report* (April 6, 2010).

RES JUDICATA

Once a decision of the court has become final, it is said to be ***res judicata*** (the thing has been decided), meaning that a final decision is conclusive on all issues between the parties, whether raised in the litigation or not. *Res judicata* means either that the case has been finally decided on appeal or that the time for appeal has expired and a cause of action finally determined by a competent court cannot be litigated by the parties in a new proceeding by the same court or in any other court. *Res judicata* prevents successive suits involving the same factual setting between the same parties and brings disputes to a conclusion. A matter once litigated and legally determined is conclusive between the parties in all subsequent proceedings.

---

sidebar 4.19

How Do You Prevent a Lawsuit in Your Firm?

- Make sure supervisors and managers have access to legal counsel and use it before small issues explode into major disputes.
- Encourage teambuilding and development of cooperative relationships in the workplace.
- Develop internal mechanisms for resolving disputes.
- Perform regular audits to ensure compliance with legal rules and best practices.
- Require legal analysis of major decisions under consideration.

Key Terms

Review Questions and Problems

Litigation—An Overview

1. *Parties*

   A building contractor is sued by homeowners alleging that their homes were poorly constructed resulting in several defects. The contractor adds to the lawsuit a building supplier that it claims provided faulty support beams. How can the contractor add the building supplier as a party to the lawsuit? What is this procedure called and how does it work?

2. *Standing to Sue*

   A group of environmentalists filed a lawsuit challenging commercial fishing in Glacier Bay National Park and sued the secretary of the interior and the National Park Service in order to prevent more commercial fishing.

   (a) What must the environmentalists show in order to satisfy the requirement of standing to sue in this case?

   (b) At what point should the issue of standing be decided by the court during the course of litigation?

3. *Personal Jurisdiction*

   Smith, a resident of Michigan, was in Florida for a business meeting where he was served with a divorce petition filed by his wife, who had moved to Florida recently. Smith objected to the Florida court's exercise of personal jurisdiction. What is the basis of Smith's objection? Should he prevail? Why or why not?

4. *Class-Action Suits*

   How have the federal courts discouraged class-action lawsuits? What are the key requirements for federal courts to permit class-action suits?

Pretrial Procedures

5. *Pleadings*

   Describe the purpose of a complaint and an answer in civil litigation. What is the function of the pleading stage in a lawsuit?

6. *Steps in Discovery*

   (a) Why do surprises rarely occur at trial?

   (b) What are some of the key devices a litigant can use in discovery?

7. *Scope of Discovery*

   How do abusive discovery practices raise the cost of litigation?

8. *Motions*

   Under what circumstances may a court grant a motion for summary judgment?

9. *Frivolous Cases*

   Federal Rule 11 sanctions are available against both lawyers and their clients to curb frivolous litigation. Under what circumstances may sanctions be imposed?

The Trial

10. *Jury Selection*

    In light of recent court decisions restricting the use of peremptory challenges, should they be eliminated from litigation altogether? Would the elimination of peremptory challenges improve the efficiency of the trial process?

11. *Other Steps during a Trial*

    What is the purpose of jury instructions?

12. *Burden of Proof*

There are three distinct levels of proof required by law depending upon the kind of case involved. Describe them and when they are used.

13. *Deciding the Case*

Under what circumstances should a judge enter a judgment notwithstanding the verdict?

Posttrial Issues

14. *Appeals*

What normally is contained in an appellate brief? An oral argument?

15. *Enforcement of Judgments and Decrees*

How does the court enforce judgments?

16. *Res Judicata*

Why is the notion of *res judicata* critical in civil litigation?

business *discussions*

1. You are the manager of a used car firm known as Reliant Motor Company. Your lawyer has called to tell you that John Doe, a customer you have been dealing with for several months, has filed a lawsuit against the firm. The customer claims the vehicle he purchased is a lemon and no longer even operates. You knew the vehicle was not in the best of condition at the time of sale, but you believe the buyer caused most of the problems by taking the vehicle "off road" several times. You are not looking forward to discovery or trial in this case. You have several questions.

How does discovery work?
Can you be required to testify twice in a deposition and at trial?
Should you shred all documents you have about this case? You know that some of the documents will not put the firm in the best light.

You wonder what will happen at trial. Will it be like what you have seen on TV or in the movies?

2. You are the owner of a small firm that manufactures lawn mowers. While using one of your products, a person suffers severe injury and now is suing, claiming that your product was negligently designed because it did not adequately protect the user. You have no experience with the legal system. You learn that lawyers charge as much as $250 per hour and must be paid whether they win or lose their cases. You are surprised at what must happen before a trial can occur to determine who is at fault. First, your lawyer may move to dismiss the case on jurisdictional grounds. If that fails, both sides will take costly depositions of likely witnesses. You will have to turn over reams of internal documents related to the design of your mower. Each side also will have to pay several hundred dollars per hour for experts as the lawyers prepare the case. These experts will have to be paid again when they testify at trial. As the time for the trial approaches, each side will spend money trying to discern the most sympathetic type of jury. Years after the lawsuit was first filed, the parties will be sitting in the courtroom waiting for jury selection to begin. More money will have been spent defending this case than the plaintiff was seeking when the lawsuit was first filed. Many questions come to mind:

- Should you have settled the case at the beginning?
- Has your attorney been getting rich at your expense?
- Is discovery more of a burden than a help?

5

Alternative Dispute Resolution

■ Learning Objectives

In this chapter you will learn:

5-1. To understand why disputing parties seek alternatives to the litigation process as methods to revolve their differences.

5-2. To appreciate the importance of effective negotiation and to recognize the basic methods of negotiation.

5-3. To evaluate the various forms of ADR systems so that efficient choices can be made as to the means of resolving disputes.

5-4. To explain the differences between arbitration and mediation and to know when each is the most appropriate method of ADR.

5-5. To comprehend why courts have a very limited role in reviewing the actions of arbitrators and mediators.

From the preceding chapter, you should appreciate that the litigation process within the court system imposes tremendous costs in terms of time, money, emotional stress, and harmony in relationships. This fact is a major reason why you probably have very little personal experience with litigation. It also is the reason most businesses try to avoid litigation and use it as a means of last resort to resolve disputes.

One way to confirm how seldom we litigate is to examine some data. Ask yourself, have I ever had a conflict with someone? Maybe a better question is, does a day go by without me experiencing one or more conflicts? We constantly and consistently deal with conflicts, and even disputes, without filing a lawsuit to resolve our problems.

However, sometimes lawsuits are necessary. Even after beginning the litigation process, most parties reach some type of resolution before the case is presented to a jury for a verdict and judgment. The general rule, usually cited, is 95 percent or more of the lawsuits filed settle prior to the completion of the litigation process.

The litigation process provides individuals and businesses with a formal method to enforce agreements. It can be said that business cannot be conducted without the existence of the court system to protect property interests. A more accurate statement probably is we transact business, personally and professionally, in a way that hopefully avoids the need to use litigation as our dispute resolution system.

In this chapter, you will study a variety of alternatives to litigation. Prior to reviewing more formal alternative dispute resolution (ADR) systems, we take a look at the distinction between conflicts and disputes and how negotiation is a skill we each use all the time.

Conflicts and Negotiation

In answer to one of the earlier questions, a day does not go by without encountering conflicts at home, on the road, and at work. Only a day of total isolation might be the exception. Even then the lonely person likely experiences internal conflicts over how best to utilize this time alone.

In the following sections, the distinction between a conflict and a dispute helps emphasize the importance of how people negotiate.

LO 5-1

Conflict is ubiquitous and can be productive.

Conflict + Claim that is rejected = Dispute

CONFLICTS AND DISPUTES

Conflict exists whenever there are two or more points of view. Even in productive relationships, involving amicable co-workers or happily married couples, conflict is always present. Conflicts are not negative; indeed, conflict can stimulate significant thoughts and produce great discoveries. So, why do we shy away from conflict? Why do most of us perceive conflict as bad and try to avoid it?

The answer likely lies in the fact that conflict leads to disputes. A **dispute** arises when one party makes a claim that another party denies. For example, two co-workers may have a conflict because they both think they need to use a copy machine right now. This conflict escalates when one person asks the other to move aside and the request is refused. These parties now are in dispute as to who gets to use the copier first. In essence, the process of both workers claiming a right to the machine likely causes the dispute to become more emotional and thus uncomfortable for both involved.

Does this example prove disputes are bad and conflicts should be left alone? Not necessarily. Suppose one worker simply stood in line and waited for the other to finish. The worker doing the copying may not know about the frustration and angst that exists inside the co-worker. On the other hand, the worker waiting may be expressing impatience through comments or sighs without ever asking or claiming to go ahead. The worker making the copies may feel this pressure and become upset by what is perceived as rudeness or a lack of respect. Leaving the conflict unresolved may cause larger problems among those co-workers later. Thus, it may be more beneficial to everyone involved to have the conflict become a dispute so the parties can more easily express their emotions. Such expressions may lead to an earlier resolution between these co-workers.

STYLES AND METHODS OF NEGOTIATION

LO 5-2

All of us instinctively engage in some form of negotiation. Even as evidence of a conflict is exhibited (through comments or sighs or groans), the parties are negotiating. **Negotiation** is the process used to persuade or coerce someone to do what you want them to do. All of us negotiate all the time with ourselves, our family members, our co-workers, and even with strangers.

The issue to focus on is not *when* do I negotiate but *how* do I negotiate. Think again about the co-workers and the copy machine. The actual request (or claim) to make copies first is the beginning of a negotiation. How the other worker responds to this request likely will set a tone for the negotiation process. An examination of how this tone is set can be viewed through the illustration in Sidebar 5.1.

"When do we negotiate? Always!"

–Dialogue from the movie *The Devil's Advocate*

sidebar 5.1

Negotiation Styles

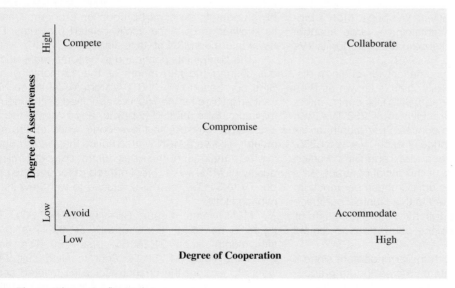

Source: Thomas-Kilmann Conflict Mode Instrument

Can you imagine the conversation between these two co-workers that illustrates each style listed? Avoiding could be seen through the person at the copier ignoring the request by pretending not to hear. Accommodating occurs if the request to go first is granted. Competing comes into play if the worker at the copier turns around and tells the co-worker who requested priority to stand in line and be patient. Collaborating might exist if the worker making the copies agrees to use another copier or explains to the co-worker how another machine is available to use. Compromising is the hardest to demonstrate even though it is a common response in a negotiation. Perhaps a compromise occurs in this example if these two co-workers get into a discussion/argument and a third worker takes over the use of the copier such that neither of the disputing parties gets the work done.

Understanding the styles used in negotiations is not enough. Analyses of negotiation processes also need to focus on the methods used by the negotiators. The next two sections examine two of the most studied methods of negotiations. To help illustrate these methods, consider the factual situation in Sidebar 5.2.

sidebar 5.2

A Business Dispute

Mickey Shears and Naomi Hamilton operate a business that manufactures large (40+ inches) flat-screen 3-D televisions. The business name is M&N TVs Inc. The principal market for M&N televisions has been buyers for home use. M&N's reputation is based on assembling a high-quality TV for a relatively low price. M&N's biggest problem has been maintaining a large enough, qualified sales force while keeping the price for its TVs below the market average.

William Dalton operates a nationwide chain of discount department stores. This chain is known as Bill's Discount Centers. One year ago, Bill's Discount Centers agreed to buy from M&N a minimum of 250 TVs (with specifications stated in the contract) per month for six months. The agreed-upon price of each TV was $1,250.

The relationship between M&N and Bill's worked very well. In the fifth month of this initial contract, Bill's agreed to increase its minimum purchase per month to 750 TVs, and Bill's committed to this monthly purchase for a 12-month period to begin after the sixth month of the original contract. The price per TV was to remain at $1,250.

M&N was delighted with the arrangement since it allowed M&N to concentrate on increasing its production capacity while reducing the costs of maintaining a large active sales force.

Unlike the success of its initial relationship with M&N, Bill's began receiving complaints from its customers about the lack of quality of M&N's TVs. These complaints were traced by Bill's customer service representatives to the newer TVs that M&N was assembling under its expanded production program. Despite its knowledge of these quality-related problems, Bill's never informed M&N of its findings.

The complaints continued to become more numerous. During the fifth month of the 12-month period, Bill's purchased only 350 TVs from M&N. When M&N sent an invoice for the 750 TVs specified as the monthly minimum, Bill's refused to pay for any TVs over the 350 actually purchased. In the second week of the sixth month, Bill's sent M&N written notice that it was canceling the remainder of the sales contract due to declining quality of M&N's TVs. M&N offered to reduce the price per TV to $1,050, but Bill's refused to withdraw its termination letter.

M&N wants to sue Bill's for $7,062,500. This figure is based on the shortfalls of 400 TVs in the fifth month times $1,250/TV plus 750 TVs times 7 months times $1,250/TV. Prior to filing suit, M&N wants to explore the chances for a negotiated settlement in the hope of salvaging a constructive relationship with Bill's.

POSITIONAL NEGOTIATION

Most people instinctively use a negotiation method called **positional bargaining.** Typically, these parties begin in a competitive style by stating their respective expectations. For example, in a sales transaction, the seller starts with as high an asking price as is considered reasonable. Likewise, the buyer begins with the lowest reasonable price. The gap between these two opening prices provides room for give and take. If the negotiation remains focused on the sales price, all the parties do is change their respective positions on the acceptable price. This process of exchange moves the parties toward the middle of the gap.

In the factual situation in Sidebar 5.2, Bill's is saying that it owes nothing to M&N. On the other side, M&N is demanding payment of more than $7 million. The difference between these two positions is so wide that it may be difficult to bring these parties into agreement.

Even if Bill's was willing to buy some TVs at a revised price and even if M&N agreed to a reduced quantity or selling price, the issue of quality is not being addressed. Does Bill's gain any market advantage in selling an inferior product, albeit at a lower price, to its customers? Clearly not.

If the positions on quantity and price are the only items open for negotiation, Bill's and M&N are unlikely to reach a satisfactory compromise. Hence, the chances of a negotiated settlement through positional bargaining are minimal. This result occurs because positional bargaining does not focus on the underlying conflicts.

There is another method of negotiation that might help these parties. This alternative is discussed in the next section.

Positional Bargaining

PRINCIPLED NEGOTIATION

A better approach to negotiating among disputing parties has been described as **principled, interest-based negotiations** in the book *Getting to Yes* by Roger Fisher, William Ury, and Bruce Patton.[1] These authors present seven elements that should become the focus of negotiators. The elements will vary in importance depending on the factual situation in dispute and on the parties' individual perspectives. However, concentrating on these elements can help remove some of the barriers created by positional negotiation. A quick focus on these elements illustrates how M&N and Bill's can be more productive in their negotiation efforts.

The Seven Elements of Interest-Based Negotiation:
   Communication
   Relationship
   Interests
   Options
   Legitimacy
   Alternatives
   Commitment

Communication First, as expressed in the factual situation above, Bill's has not openly explained to M&N the nature of its dissatisfaction. Sharing customer complaints, either in general or with specificity, might help M&N locate a production operations problem. Likewise, M&N does not appear to be informing Bill's of any difficulties it faced as it expanded production capacities. Clear communication between these parties may assist them in becoming joint problem solvers. Without this exchange of information, these parties are likely to continue blaming each another. To change from a "game" of blaming, effective negotiators put significant energy into listening to the other party. Communication involves a balance of talking and listening.

"If negotiation is half talking and half listening, the more important half is listening."

–Roger Fisher

Relationship Second, these parties would likely benefit by discussing how each could benefit by continuing their relationship of customer and supplier. Can they solve the current problem and maintain, if not enhance,

[1] *Penquin Books, 3d ed., 2011.*

their future business opportunities together? Maintaining, or even enhancing, the relationship may be possible if these parties focus on effective communications.

Interests   Third, have M&N and Bill's communicated their real interests to each other? Perhaps these interests are not mutually exclusive. For example, Bill's might want to expand its offerings in TV technology to customers. M&N might want to dissolve its sales force and concentrate on production of a variety of TVs. These interests, once communicated, may help the parties realize that a continuing relationship is in their mutual best interests.

Options   Fourth, M&N and Bill's should brainstorm possible options or solutions to their dispute. This exploration process is best done with the parties agreeing that an option mentioned is not necessarily a proposal for compromise. One attractive option might be for Bill's to agree to buy all the TVs M&N can produce and for Bill's to market these TVs under its own name. Rather than severing their business relationship, M&N could become the exclusive supplier of store-brand TVs. The renaming of these products also can help overcome the "quality problems" customers associate with M&N's TVs.

Legitimacy   Fifth, legitimacy involves the application of accepted standards to the topic negotiated—rather than having the parties state unsupported propositions. Bill's probably will not be impressed by M&N stating it will improve the quality of its TVs. Instead the parties should focus on how quality can be improved and how customers will accept the improvements. Production engineers may help address the former issue while specific test marketing plans may assist in legitimizing the latter.

Alternatives   Sixth, alternatives are outcomes that are possible without the agreement of the other party. In essence, alternatives are the thing that parties to a negotiation can do away from the bargaining table. If the parties understand their alternatives to negotiating a settlement and understand the unattractive nature of these alternatives, the desire to negotiate, instead of litigating, is enhanced. M&N, for example, may perceive that bankruptcy is a very likely result if this dispute is not resolved. Bill's, on the other hand, may believe that another supplier is readily available. The desirable result of any negotiation is to agree on an outcome that is better than both parties' alternatives.

Commitment   Seventh, any successful negotiation must conclude with the parties making realistic commitments that can be put into practice. Perhaps an initial commitment that assists the overall process of negotiation is to have the parties agree that they will continue to meet and focus on these seven elements. Hopefully, the conclusion of the negotiation will be an agreement between the parties that avoids the expense (dollars, time, and emotions) of litigation. If that commitment is not a settlement, then it might be an agreement to utilize one of the following ADR systems.

Alternative Dispute Resolution (ADR) Systems

Negotiations occur in everything we do. Thus, even as we present the following material on formal and informal alternative dispute resolution (ADR) systems, remember the negotiation processes still govern the success or failure of such ADR systems.

It is important to remember several things at the outset of this discussion. First, litigation does not preclude the use of ADR techniques. Indeed, it is very common for disputes to be arbitrated, mediated, or settled through negotiations during the pretrial process discussed in the preceding chapter.

Second, disputing parties do not have to begin a lawsuit to use any form of ADR. In the rest of this chapter, you will study how ADR systems relate to formal litigation and how they are utilized independently from the litigation process.

Third, ADR systems used by disputing parties may be part of a contractual relationship between these parties. For example, even before any problem arises, it is an effective dispute resolution tool to have the parties' contract specify a preferred ADR system. Disputing parties also may agree to use an ADR technique after the dispute arises even if they did not foresee the possibility of needing to use a dispute resolution system at the time of their original agreement.

Fourth, effective use of ADR systems can save disputing parties many of the costs associated with litigation. Especially important is the preservation of an ongoing business relationship. The ability to keep doing business often is destroyed through litigation. ADR systems, when used appropriately, help ensure the productive relationships needed for successful business transactions.

RANGE OF OPTIONS

Figure 5.1 illustrates an array of ADR systems. These are arranged along a spectrum of high cost (in dollars, time, emotions, and relationships) to lowest cost. Although any given factual situation may cause the items on this

Figure 5.1
Scale of dispute resolution systems

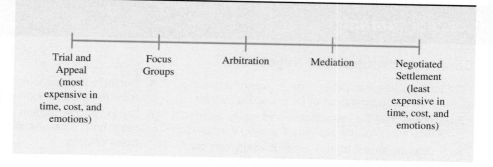

spectrum to shift places, this figure presents a generally accepted view of dispute resolution systems.

The next two sections briefly address why settlement is attractive and how lawyers utilize focus groups. Arbitration and mediation are discussed in more detail since they are the most popular ADR systems used by businesses and people attempting to resolve disputes.

SETTLEMENTS

It is universally acknowledged that both parties to litigation are losers. The winning party in a lawsuit is a loser to the extent of the attorney's fees—which are often substantial. The fact that the loser usually also has to pay court costs is an added incentive to settlement without litigation.

There are also personal reasons to settle controversies. The desire to resolve differences is instinctive for many Americans. Most of us dislike trouble, and many fear going to court. The opinions of others are often a motivating force in encouraging amicable settlements.

Businesses tend to settle disputes with customers for two additional reasons. First, it is simply not good business from a goodwill and public relations standpoint to sue a customer. Second, juries are frequently sympathetic to individuals who have suits against large corporations or defendants who are covered by insurance. Juries often decide close questions of liability, as well as size of the verdict, against business organizations because of their presumed ability to pay. As a result, businesses settle many disputes even though they might possibly prevail in litigation.

Table 5.1 provides a summary of cases recently settled. The size of these settlements represents evidence that companies want to avoid the litigation process even when the settlement costs are high.

FOCUS GROUPS

Recognizing that a jury's function is to determine the facts, attorneys frequently use **focus groups** in significant cases. The attorneys assemble a group of citizens and present their evidence. This group then deliberates and makes findings. This dress rehearsal gives attorneys insight into possible jury reaction to the evidence and points up weaknesses in the case. Sometimes issues are tested without introducing evidence. Lawyers argue the case on the basis of assumed facts to the mock jury for a few hours, and this jury returns a verdict.

The verdicts often cause plaintiffs to take a more realistic view of the damages to which they think they are entitled. This "reality test" helps disputing

The Department of Justice reports 98 percent of tort cases filed in the U.S. District Courts settled prior to either a bench or jury trial. http://bjs. ojp.usdoj.gov/content/ glance/tables/ torttrialtab.cfm

table 5.1 Samples of Recent Major Settlements

Company	Product or Action	Settlement
British Petroleum (BP)	Gulf Oil Spill (Deepwater Horizon explosion)	$20 billion distributed among thousands of claimants
Bank of America	Securities fraud claims	$9.5 billion
Merck	Vioxx linked to heart attacks and strokes	$4.85 billion to 47,000 possible claimants
GlaxoSmithKline	Off-label promotion	$3 billion
Citicorp	Conspiring with Enron executives to misstate Enron's financial condition	$1.66 billion to Enron Creditors Recovery Corporation
JPMorgan Chase Mortgage Lending	Practices	$13 billion to the Justice Dept.
Pfizer	Off-label promotion	$2.3 billion
Eli Lilly	Failure to disclose information about side effects of Zyprexa	$1.2 billion to 31,000 possible claimants
Pfizer Claims	Failure to disclose accurate information about Bextra	$669 million under False Act; $331 million for state Medicaid programs
Novartis	Gender bias in pay	$175 million to 5,600 current and former female sales representatives

parties to engage in more meaningful negotiations. Through such negotiations, these parties often settle their dispute without having to go through the formal process of either a trial or an arbitration.

Arbitration

LO 5-3

LO 5-4

To avoid the various expenses of litigation, disputing parties sometimes agree to have a third party decide the merits of the dispute. This formal ADR system is called **arbitration.** The decision maker, who should be disinterested in any financial impact of the decision and neutral regarding the issues presented in the dispute, is known as an **arbitrator.** The distinctive characteristic of this form of ADR is the arbitrator's decision on the merits. In essence, the arbitrator takes the place of the jury and judge in the litigation process.

Over the past 80 years, arbitration has played an increasingly important role in resolving business disputes. Historically, arbitration has been the most commonly used ADR system. The primary reason for the use of arbitration is the laudable goal of providing a relatively quick and inexpensive resolution of disputes. Arbitration not only helps the parties avoid the expense of litigation but also provides a means of avoiding the formalities of the courtroom. Formal pleadings, for example, and other procedural steps such as discovery and the rules of evidence are usually not used in an arbitration hearing.

Arbitration also serves to help ease congested court dockets. A primary function of arbitration is to serve as a substitute for and not a prelude to litigation. It is a private proceeding with no public record available to the press

Arbitrators are authorized to make decisions that are binding on the parties, thereby resolving the dispute.

and others. Thus, by keeping their dispute private, adversaries may be more likely to preserve their business relationship.

Arbitration also has the advantage of submitting many disputes to experts for solutions. For example, if the issue involves whether a building has been properly constructed, the matter could be submitted to an architect for resolution. If it involves a technical accounting problem, it could be submitted to a certified public accountant. The Securities and Exchange Commission (SEC) has approved an arrangement whereby investors with complaints against securities dealers must submit them for arbitration to arbitrators assigned by the various stock exchanges and the Financial Industry Regulatory Authority. These arbitrators are selected because they possess the special knowledge required to determine if a customer of a brokerage house has a legitimate complaint.

Arbitration is of special importance in labor relations, where it provides the grievance procedures under collective bargaining contracts. Arbitration is a means for industrial self-government, a system of private law for all problems that may arise in the workplace.

Sidebar 5.3 illustrates the growing importance and widespread use of arbitration as an alternative dispute resolution system.

---

sidebar 5.3

Examples of Contracts with Arbitration Clauses

Stockbroker and client
Commodities broker and customer
Brokerage firm and employee
Attorney[1] and client
Union-management collective bargaining agreements

Owner-contractor and contractor-subcontractor
Insurance company and insured
Public carrier and shipper of goods

[1]Most bar associations require lawyers to arbitrate disputes with clients.

Submission is the process of beginning an arbitration proceeding.

The parties authorize an arbitrator to make a decision that binds these parties and resolves their dispute. The act of referring a matter to arbitration is called **submission.** Submission to arbitration often occurs when the disputing parties agree to use this form of ADR. Such an agreement by the parties is a submission to **voluntary arbitration.** Generally, an agreement to submit an issue to arbitration is irrevocable, and a party that thinks the process is not going well cannot withdraw from the arbitration and resort to litigation. Another form of a submission occurs when a statute or court requires parties to arbitrate. This type of submission results in a **mandatory arbitration.**

After the submission, a hearing is conducted by the arbitrator or arbitrators. Both parties are allowed to present evidence and to argue their own points of view. Then a decision, known as an **award,** is handed down. In most states the arbitrator's award must be in writing. The award is valid as long as it settles the entire controversy and states which party is to pay the other a sum of money.

Sidebar 5.4 discusses trends in the use and popularity of arbitration. It will be interesting, throughout your business careers, to see how arbitration is utilized when compared to other ADR systems.

sidebar 5.4

Trends in Arbitration

Throughout the second half of the twentieth century, businesses increasingly included arbitration clauses in various types of contracts. Most common among these examples have been business-to-business contracts (e.g., customer-supplier), employment contracts, and securities broker-investor contracts. Beginning in 2007, pressures mounted to provide employees and investors with options to either pursue arbitration or to litigate.

Advocates for litigation cite studies showing that arbitration in securities brokerage cases tends to favor the brokerage firm. To counter this perceived bias, the Financial Industry Regulatory Authority, FINRA, administers arbitrations involving investors. FINRA recently completed a pilot project allowing investors to use non-industry experts as arbitrators. This process, known as an all-public panel of arbitrators, has been submitted to the SEC for final approval. "'Giving each individual investor the option of an all-public panel will enhance confidence in and increase the perception of fairness in the FINRA arbitration process,' said Richard Ketchum, FINRA's chief executive officer. FINRA spokeswoman Nancy Condon said 23

of the pilot cases went through to a ruling, with the rest reaching settlements. Among 17 cases heard by all-public panels, investors were awarded damages 71% of the time."[1]

This argument in favor of litigation is contradicted by statistics and polls about efficiency. "A poll . . . finds that most Americans do not want their day in court. Rather they prefer cheaper and faster methods of settling arguments. When asked how they'd like to settle a dispute with a company, 82% chose arbitration, which avoids the time and expense of going to court. Only 15% opted for litigation. Americans are not confident that a lawsuit will produce a fair result, but a solid majority looks favorably on mediation and arbitration."[2] The 2010 law providing reforms of financial institutions and services empowers the Bureau of Consumer Financial Protection to protect consumers by restricting and even prohibiting arbitration clauses. In the years ahead, the trend may be toward mediation clauses, rather than arbitration clauses, in contracts.

[1]Joseph A. Giannone, "FINRA Arbitration Change Seen Aiding Investors," *Reuters* September 28, 2010.

[2]Editorial, *The Wall Street Journal*, April 5, 2008.

SUBMISSIONS

Submission by contract occurs if the parties enter into an agreement to arbitrate an existing dispute. The arbitration agreement is the submission in this case. In addition, the parties may contractually agree to submit to arbitration all issues that may arise in the future. Submission in these circumstances occurs when a demand to arbitrate is served on the other party.

Most state statutes authorizing voluntary arbitration require the agreement to arbitrate to be in writing. Since the goal of arbitration is to obtain a quick resolution of disputes, most statutes require submission within a stated time period, usually six months, after the dispute arises.

In the absence of a statute, the rights and duties of the parties to a submission are described and limited by their agreement. Parties that have contracted to arbitrate are not required to arbitrate any matters other than those they contractually agree to arbitrate. Sidebar 5.5 contains an example of an agreement to arbitrate.

---

sidebar 5.5

Sample Arbitration Clause

All disputes, claims, or controversies arising from or relating to this contract shall be resolved by binding arbitration by one arbitrator selected by the parties from an American Arbitration Association list of qualified arbitrators. This arbitration contract is made pursuant to a transaction in interstate commerce, and it shall be governed by the Federal Arbitration Act.

The parties voluntarily and knowingly waive any right they have to a jury trial. The parties agree and understand the arbitrator shall have all powers provided by the law and this contract. These powers shall include all legal and equitable remedies, including, but not limited to, money damages, declaratory relief, and injunctive relief.

The issues submitted to arbitration, as framed in the submission, may be questions of fact, questions of law, or mixed questions of fact and law. They may include the interpretation of the arbitration agreement. Sometimes a dispute arises as to whether the parties have agreed to submit an issue to arbitration. In such a case, one party refuses to arbitrate and the other files suit to compel arbitration. The court hearing the case decides the issue of arbitrability but does not decide the basic issue between the parties. The U.S. Supreme Court explained these distinct roles of the court and the arbitrator in a case summarized in Sidebar 5.6.

---

sidebar 5.6

To Arbitrate or Litigate

The communication workers union, as the bargaining agent of employees working for AT&T Tech. Inc. negotiated a contract that contained an arbitration clause covering disputes that might arise. Another provision of the contract allowed management to make decisions regarding hiring, placement, and termination of employees. Exercising its authority, management laid off 79 employees due to a lack of work. The union challenged this action by claiming there was no lack of work justifying the layoffs. The union sought to have this dispute arbitrated; however, management refused to arbitrate claiming its authority to terminate employees was clear. The union filed suit and asked the court to compel arbitration.

Does a judge or an arbitrator decide what issues should be submitted to arbitration?

The question of whether the parties agreed to arbitrate is decided by a judge, not an arbitrator. However, in deciding what issues can be arbitrated, a judge is not to rule on the merits of the underlying claim. Judges should presume arbitration is appropriate; thus, any doubt should be resolved in favor of arbitration over litigation.[1] Later, the Supreme Court discussed "gateway issues" and whether an arbitrator or judge decides such matters. The Court ruled the application of a statute of limitations should be decided by the arbitrator.[2] However, the Court has held that a judge must determine the ratification date of a collective bargaining agreement.[3]

[1]*AT&T Tech., Inc. v. Communications Workers*, 106 S. Ct. 1414 (1986).
[2]*Howsam v. Dean Witter Reynolds, Inc.*, 123 S. Ct. 588 (2002).
[3]*Granite Rock Company v. International Brotherhood of Teamsters*, 130 S. Ct. 2847 (2010).

ARBITRATORS

Arbitrators generally are chosen by the disputing parties. A provision in the agreement to arbitrate or in the statute that requires the arbitration describes how the arbitrator is selected. Of concern in the selection process are the expertise of the arbitrator and the number of arbitrators to be chosen.

Expertise   One reason arbitration is frequently preferable to litigation is the use of an expert to resolve the dispute. Appraisers can be used to decide disputes about the value of real estate, medical doctors can be used to decide health care disputes, and academicians can be used to decide issues within their area of expertise.

This use of experts is especially important in labor-management relations. Arbitration is the technique used in collective-bargaining contracts to settle grievances of employees against their employers. Arbitration is able to resolve disputes arising out of labor contracts without resorting to judicial intervention. It is quick and efficient and minimizes disruption in the workplace. Labor arbitration has attracted a large number of experts—both lawyers and academicians.

Arbitration provides for decision making by experts with experience in the particular industry and with knowledge of the customs and practices of the particular work site. Parties expect the arbitrator to look beyond strictly legal criteria to other factors that bear on the proper resolution of a dispute. These factors may include the impact of a particular result on productivity, its consequences to morale, and whether tensions will be heightened or diminished. The ablest judge usually does not bring the same experience and competence to bear upon the determination of a grievance, because the judge cannot be as informed as the expert arbitrator.

Number Chosen   Another issue relates to the number of arbitrators to hear a dispute. It is common to use one arbitrator who is considered objective and impartial. Any person the disputing parties agree upon can be an arbitrator. There are no licensing requirements an arbitrator must satisfy. However, an arbitrator often is chosen from a list of qualified arbitrators provided by the arbitration service. The disputing parties are not limited to the list unless they have agreed to make their selection from this list.

It is also common to have a panel of three arbitrators. In such cases, each party selects an arbitrator and the two so selected choose a third. It is not surprising that when this procedure is used, allegations of bias are often made by the losing party. Courts generally do not allow such allegations to form a basis for overturning a panel's award unless there is evidence of overt corruption or misconduct in the arbitration proceedings. Since such evidence usually is difficult to obtain, allegations of bias normally do not impact the results of arbitration.

Authority over Certain Matters   What arbitrators have authority to decide has been a topic of controversy and litigation. Case 5.1 attempts to clarify whose responsibility it is to decide preliminary matters prior to the actual arbitration. You should read this case as clarification of the cases discussed in Sidebar 5.6.

For information about available arbitrators and their expertise, examine the following websites:

- *American Arbitration Association* www.adr.org
- *JAMS* www.jamsadr .com/professionals
- *National Arbitration Forum* www.arb-forum .com
- *Arbitrator.com* (listing by states) www .arbitrator.com

"Although arbitration does not guarantee well-reasoned decisions or moderate damage awards, the conventional wisdom is that arbitrators tend to be both more predictable in decision-making and reasonable in awarding damages than juries."

Robert M. Shea at www.mbbp.com/ resources/employment/ pdfs/arbitration.pdf

The number of arbitrators is based on the agreement of the parties.

case 5.1

RENT-A-CENTER, WEST, INC., v. ANTONIO JACKSON
130 S. Ct. 2772 (2010)

Antonio Jackson works for Rent-A-Center. As a condition of this employment, Jackson signed a Mutual Agreement to Arbitrate Claims (Agreement). This Agreement provides that all disputes arising out of Jackson's employment will be submitted to arbitration. The Agreement specifically states that claims for discrimination and claims for violations of any federal law would be arbitrated, not litigated. Furthermore, the Agreement provided that the "Arbitrator, and not any federal, state, or local court or agency, shall have exclusive authority to resolve any dispute relating to the interpretation, applicability, enforceability or formation of this Agreement including, but not limited to any claim that all or any part of this Agreement is void or voidable." On February 1, 2007, Jackson filed a federal lawsuit claiming that Rent-A-Center had discriminated against Jackson based on his race.

Rent-A-Center filed a motion to dismiss or stay the lawsuit and to compel arbitration. Jackson responded, claiming that the Agreement to arbitrate is unconscionable under Nevada law and is unenforceable. Rent-A-Center argued that the issue of unconscionability and unenforceability are matters for the arbitrator, not the courts, to decide. The District Judge agreed with Rent-A-Center and compelled arbitration. The Ninth Circuit Court of Appeals reversed, deciding that the threshold question of unconscionability is for the court to decide. Upon Rent-A-Center's petition, the Supreme Court granted certiorari.

SCALIA, J.: . . . The [Federal Arbitration Act] FAA reflects the fundamental principle that arbitration is a matter of contract. Section 2, the primary substantive provision of the Act, provides:

> "A written provision in . . . a contract evidencing a transaction involving commerce to settle by arbitration a controversy thereafter arising out of such contract . . . shall be valid, irrevocable, and enforceable, save upon such grounds as exist at law or in equity for the revocation of any contract."

The FAA thereby places arbitration agreements on an equal footing with other contracts and requires courts to enforce them according to their terms. Like other contracts, however, they may be invalidated by generally applicable contract defenses, such as fraud, duress, or unconscionability.

The Act also establishes procedures by which federal courts implement §2's substantive rule. Under §3, a party may apply to a federal court for a stay of the trial of an action "upon any issue referable to arbitration under an agreement in writing for such arbitration." Under §4, a party "aggrieved" by the failure of another party "to arbitrate under a written agreement for arbitration" may petition a federal court "for an order directing that such arbitration proceed in the manner provided for in such agreement." The court "shall" order arbitration "upon being satisfied that the making of the agreement for arbitration or the failure to comply therewith is not in issue."

The Agreement here contains multiple written provisions to settle by arbitration a controversy. Two are relevant to our discussion. First, the section titled "Claims Covered By The Agreement" provides for arbitration of all "past, present or future" disputes arising out of Jackson's employment with Rent-A-Center. Second, the section titled "Arbitration Procedures" provides that "[t]he Arbitrator . . . shall have exclusive authority to resolve any dispute relating to the . . . enforceability . . . of this Agreement including, but not limited to any claim that all or any part of this Agreement is void or voidable." The current controversy between the parties is whether the Agreement is unconscionable. It is the second provision, which delegates resolution of that controversy to the arbitrator, that Rent-A-Center seeks to enforce. Adopting the terminology used by the parties, we will refer to it as the delegation provision.

The delegation provision is an agreement to arbitrate threshold issues concerning the arbitration agreement. We have recognized that parties can agree to arbitrate "gateway" questions of "arbitrability," such as whether the parties have agreed to arbitrate or whether their agreement covers a particular controversy. . . . An agreement to arbitrate a gateway issue is simply an additional, antecedent agreement the party seeking arbitration asks the federal court to enforce, and the FAA operates on this additional arbitration agreement just as it does on any other. The additional agreement is valid under §2 "save upon such grounds as exist at law or in equity for the revocation of any contract," and federal courts can enforce the agreement by staying federal litigation under §3 and compelling arbitration under §4. The question before us, then, is whether the delegation provision is valid under §2.

There are two types of validity challenges under §2: One type challenges specifically the validity of the agreement to arbitrate, and the other challenges the contract as a whole, either on a ground that directly affects the entire agreement (*e.g.,* the agreement was fraudulently induced), or on the ground that the illegality of one of the contract's provisions renders the whole contract invalid. In a line of cases neither party has asked us to overrule, we held that only the first type of challenge is relevant to a court's determination whether the arbitration agreement at issue is enforceable. . . .

If a party challenges the validity under §2 of the precise agreement to arbitrate at issue, the federal court must consider the challenge before ordering compliance with that agreement under §4. . . . [I]f the claim had been fraud in the inducement of the arbitration clause itself, then the court would have considered it. . . . In some cases the claimed basis of invalidity for the contract as a whole will be much easier to establish than the same basis as applied only to the severable agreement to arbitrate. Thus, in an employment contract many elements of alleged unconscionability applicable to the entire contract (outrageously low wages, for example) would not affect the agreement to arbitrate alone. But even where that is not the case, . . . we nonetheless require the basis of challenge to be directed specifically to the agreement to arbitrate before the court will intervene.

Here, the written provision to settle by arbitration a controversy, that Rent-A-Center asks us to enforce is the delegation provision—the provision that gave the arbitrator "exclusive authority to resolve any dispute relating to the . . . enforceability . . . of this Agreement." . . . [U]nless Jackson challenged the delegation provision specifically, we must treat it as valid under §2, and must enforce it under §3 and 4, leaving any challenge to the validity of the Agreement as a whole for the arbitrator.

The District Court correctly concluded that Jackson challenged only the validity of the contract as a whole. Nowhere in his opposition to Rent-A-Center's motion to compel arbitration did he even mention the delegation provision. . . .

Jackson's appeal to the Ninth Circuit confirms that he did not contest the validity of the delegation provision in particular. His brief noted the existence of the delegation provision, but his unconscionability arguments made no mention of it. . . . At oral argument, counsel stated: "There are certain elements of the arbitration agreement that are unconscionable and, under Nevada law, which would render the *entire arbitration agreement* unconscionable." . . .

We reverse the judgment of the Court of Appeals for the Ninth Circuit.

Reversed.

KEY POINTS

- Jackson filed his race discrimination lawsuit in federal court instead of arbitrating his claim because he claimed that the agreement to arbitrate was unconscionable and unenforceable under Nevada law. He took the position that this was an issue for the court to decide.
- Rent-A-Center took the position that Jackson was required to arbitrate any claims arising out of the contract, including the issue of unconscionability and unenforceability.
- The Supreme Court held that because Jackson challenged the contract as a whole, as opposed to just the delegation provision (i.e., the provision that delegates resolution of the controversy to an arbitrator), the matter should be resolved by an arbitrator.

AWARDS

Generally an arbitrator's award does not need to set forth findings of fact, conclusions of law, or the reasons for the award. However, a disclosure of findings and the reasons must be given if the applicable statute, arbitration agreement, or submission so requires. When the arbitrator does provide the

An **award** is the decision by an arbitrator.

basis for decision in the form of an opinion or letter, that document becomes a part of the award.

Because the parties themselves, by virtue of the submission, frame the issues to be resolved and define the scope of the arbitrator's powers, the parties are generally bound by the resulting award. A court will make every reasonable presumption in favor of the arbitration award and the arbitrator's acts and proceedings. The U.S. Supreme Court favors a broad scope of the arbitrators' authority. Restrictions on this authority will be allowed only when the disputing parties clearly state such limits.

An arbitrator's award is final on all issues submitted, and it will be enforced by the courts as if it were a judgment of the court. As is discussed later, awards are not subject to judicial review on the merits of the decision. Only when fraud or other clearly inappropriate action by the arbitrator can be shown is a court willing to reverse the award granted in a voluntary arbitration proceeding.

After the award is made by the arbitrator, it is usually filed with the clerk of an appropriate court. If no objections are filed within a statutory period, it becomes final and enforceable, like a judgment.

THE FEDERAL ARBITRATION ACT

The Federal Arbitration Act encourages disputing businesses to utilize arbitration.

The important role and positive perception of arbitration among businesses today probably would not exist without the Federal Arbitration Act (FAA). Prior to the enactment of the FAA, our common law system preferred litigation over arbitration as a means of resolving disputes. In 1925, congressional enactment of the FAA began to change this presumed way of dispute resolution. However, it was not until after the revision and reenactment of the FAA in 1947 that courts began to encourage disputing parties to use arbitration instead of litigation. Clearly, the FAA changed public policy perceptions of arbitration and how states can regulate its use. These two impacts of the FAA are discussed now.

Impact on Policy   The FAA covers any arbitration clause in a contract that involves interstate commerce. Under it, courts are "rigorously" to enforce arbitration agreements. A court assumes arbitration was intended unless it can say with positive assurance that the arbitration clause was not intended to include the particular dispute. The federal policy clearly favors arbitration of commercial disputes. The FAA provides that arbitration agreements "shall be valid, irrevocable, and enforceable, save upon such grounds as exist at law or in equity for the revocation of any contract."

As illustrated by Case 5.2 and Sidebar 5.8, the U.S. Supreme Court, through its decisions, gives strong support to the use of arbitration.

An interesting question remains following the decision in Case 5.2. What if the EEOC had decided to pursue the claim of age discrimination on behalf of Pyett? Sidebar 5.7 describes a case in which the Supreme Court concludes other federal laws provide the EEOC the right to litigate even though an employee signed an arbitration clause.

State laws cannot prevent arbitration of disputes if the parties are engaged in or impact interstate commerce.

Impact on State Laws   The federal policy favoring arbitration frequently conflicts with state laws favoring litigation as the means to resolve a dispute.

14 PENN PLAZA LLC. v. PYETT
129 S. Ct. 1456 (2009)

The Service Employees International Union is the exclusive bargaining representative of its members. These members are building cleaners, porters, and doorpersons working in New York City. The union has a collective bargaining agreement (CBA) with the Realty Advisory Board on Labor Relations Inc. (RAB), a multiemployer bargaining association for the New York City real estate industry.

The CBA contains a commitment to non-discrimination based on race, creed, color, age, disability, national origin, sex, union membership, or any other characteristic protected by law. The CBA further states that all claims of discrimination shall be subject to arbitration procedures specified in the CBA as the sole and exclusive remedy for such violations.

14 Penn Plaza LLC is a member of the RAB. As an owner of an office building, 14 Penn Plaza hired unionized workers as night lobby watchmen. Later, 14 Penn Plaza, with the union's consent, employed licensed security guards to staff the lobby and entrances of its building. This hiring resulted in the night lobby watchmen being reassigned as night porters and cleaners. These latter jobs paid less than the watchmen positions. These union members, including Mr. Pyett, filed a complaint with the Equal Employment Opportunity Commission (EEOC) on the grounds of age discrimination by 14 Penn Plaza, their employer. The EEOC did not find a violation but granted the employees/union members the right to sue their employer.

A lawsuit alleging age discrimination was filed, and 14 Penn Plaza sought to have the case dismissed. A motion to compel arbitration, as required under the CBA, was denied by the District Court for the Southern District of New York. On appeal, the Second Circuit affirmed this decision stating that a CBA cannot deny an employee's opportunity to litigate federal statutory protected right. The Supreme Court granted certiorari to review that decision.

THOMAS, J.: The question presented by this case is whether a provision in a collective-bargaining agreement that clearly and unmistakably requires union members to arbitrate claims arising under the Age Discrimination in Employment Act of 1967 (ADEA) is enforceable. The United States Court of Appeals for the Second Circuit held that this Court's decision in *Alexander v. Gardner-Denver Co.*, 415 U. S. 36 (1974), forbids enforcement of such arbitration

provisions. We disagree and reverse the judgment of the Court of Appeals. . . .

In this instance, the Union and the RAB, negotiating on behalf of 14 Penn Plaza, collectively bargained in good faith and agreed that employment-related discrimination claims, including claims brought under the ADEA, would be resolved in arbitration. This freely negotiated term between the Union and the RAB easily qualifies as a condition of employment that is subject to mandatory bargaining. . . . The decision to fashion a CBA to require arbitration of employment-discrimination claims is no different from the many other decisions made by parties in designing grievance machinery.

Respondents, however, contend that the arbitration clause here is outside the permissible scope of the collective-bargaining process because it affects the employees' individual, non-economic statutory rights. We disagree. Parties generally favor arbitration precisely because of the economics of dispute resolution. As in any contractual negotiation, a union may agree to the inclusion of an arbitration provision in a collective-bargaining agreement in return for other concessions from the employer. Courts generally may not interfere in this bargained-for exchange. Judicial nullification of contractual concessions . . . is contrary to what the Court has recognized as one of the fundamental policies of the National Labor Relations Act—freedom of contract.

As a result, the CBA's arbitration provision must be honored unless the ADEA itself removes this particular class of grievances from the NLRA's broad sweep. It does not. This Court has squarely held that the ADEA does not preclude arbitration of claims brought under the statute. . . .

Gardner-Denver mistakenly suggested that certain features of arbitration made it a forum well suited to the resolution of contractual disputes, but a comparatively inappropriate forum for the final resolution of rights created by Title VII. . . .

These misconceptions have been corrected. For example, the Court has recognized that arbitral tribunals are readily capable of handling the factual and legal complexities of antitrust claims, notwithstanding the absence of judicial instruction and supervision and that there is no reason to assume at the outset that arbitrators will not follow the law. An arbitrator's capacity to resolve complex questions of fact and law extends with equal force to discrimination claims brought under the ADEA. Moreover, the recognition that arbitration procedures are more streamlined than federal litigation is not a basis for finding the forum somehow inadequate; the relative informality of arbitration is one of the chief reasons that parties select arbitration. Parties trade the procedures and opportunity for review of the courtroom for the simplicity, informality, and expedition of arbitration. In any event, it is unlikely that age discrimination claims require more extensive discovery than other claims that we have found to be arbitrable, such as RICO and antitrust claims. . . .

We hold that a collective-bargaining agreement that clearly and unmistakably requires union members to arbitrate ADEA claims is enforceable as a matter of federal law. The judgment of the Court of Appeals is reversed, and the case is remanded for further proceedings consistent with this opinion.

Reversed and remanded.

KEY POINTS

- Members of the Service Workers International Union filed a lawsuit alleging age discrimination under the Age Discrimination in Employment Act of 1967 (ADEA).
- The defendant, a member of the Realty Advisory Board on Labor Relations Inc. (RAB), asserted that the union members were required to arbitrate their claims pursuant to a collective bargaining agreement with RAB.
- The Supreme Court held that the provision in the collective bargaining agreement that "clearly and unmistakably" required union members to arbitrate claims under the ADEA is enforceable.

sidebar 5.7

Do Agreements to Arbitrate Limit the EEOC's Remedies?

The Equal Employment Opportunity Commission (EEOC) has authority to bring enforcement actions against employers whenever the EEOC believes illegal discrimination has occurred. An employee of Waffle House was discharged from employment because he had a seizure at work. This employee did not pursue the contractual remedy of arbitration; however, he did file a complaint with the EEOC. His complaint alleged Waffle House fired him because of his disability. After investigating the factual situation, the EEOC filed a lawsuit against Waffle House in federal district court. Waffle House sought to have the suit dismissed since the remedy provided by the employment contract was arbitration, and the employee did not seek arbitration. Waffle House argues that the EEOC takes the place of the employee and therefore cannot avoid the requirement of arbitration.

The Supreme Court reviews the legislative history of the EEOC by examining the Civil Rights Act of 1964, the Equal Employment Opportunity Act of 1972, and the Civil Rights Act of 1991. The Court finds that the EEOC can be a plaintiff in its own right and not simply a representative of an aggrieved employee. Due to the authority given to the EEOC, it can pursue court-ordered victim-specific relief, such as backpay, reinstatement, and damages for violations involving discrimination without first resorting to arbitration. The power of the EEOC to avoid agreed-upon arbitration does not extend to nongovernmental third parties. Investors in tax-sheltered organizations may not sue tax advisors to these organizations when the tax shelter fails. Instead, these investors are subject to the arbitration agreement that exists in the contract between the organizations and the tax advisors. When third parties, like these investors, benefit from the contracts of other parties, the third parties are bound by the original parties' agreement to arbitrate.

Sources: *Arthur Andersen LLP v. Carlisle*, 129 S. Ct. 1896 (2009); *Equal Employment Opportunity Commission v. Waffle House, Inc.*, 122 S. Ct. 754 (2002).

Sometimes a state law specifically provides that designated matters are not to be submitted to arbitration. Are these state laws constitutional when applied to businesses engaged in interstate commerce? The Commerce Clause and the Supremacy Clause of the U.S. Constitution are often used to set aside such state laws that deny arbitration of certain disputes.

---

sidebar 5.8

Strict Enforcement of a Class Action Waiver in an Arbitration Agreement

The Supreme Court continued to strictly enforce the terms of arbitration agreements in a case involving American Express's arbitration agreement with merchants. In *American Express, Co. v. Italian Colors Restaurant* [133 S.Ct. 2304 (2013)], the Supreme Court held that a contractual waiver of class arbitration is enforceable under the Federal Arbitration Act, even if the cost of proving an individual claim in arbitration exceeds the potential recovery. Unless there is specific legislation to the contrary or evidence (such as unconscionability under state law) that could establish grounds for revocation of the contract, class-action waivers are "ironclad."

Source: David Garcia and Leo Caseria, "Opinion Analysis: A Class Action Waiver in an Arbitration Agreement Will Be Strictly Enforced under the Federal Arbitration Act," SCOTUSblog (June 21, 2013), www.scotusblog .com/2013/06/opinion-analysis-a-class-action-waiver-in-an-arbitration-agreement-will-be-strictly-enforced-under-the-federal-arbitration-act/.

STATUTORILY MANDATED ARBITRATION

Another reason why arbitration has become more widespread during the last few decades is that legislation may require disputing parties to submit to arbitration. A growing number of states have adopted statutes that require mandatory arbitration for certain types of disputes. Those whose disputes fall within the boundaries of the mandatory arbitration statute must submit the dispute to arbitration prior to being allowed to litigate. On the basis of studies showing that a dispute requiring three days for resolution before a 12-person jury takes only two to four hours for resolution by an arbitrator, the mandatory arbitration statute is clearly a viable alternative for controlling court congestion.

The arbitrators in the mandatory arbitration process are retired judges and practicing lawyers, usually experienced trial attorneys. A list of eligible arbitrators is maintained by court officials in charge of the mandatory process. Although the parties may agree on using only one arbitrator, mandatory arbitration cases are usually presented to a panel of three. Arbitrators are paid a per-diem fee. The parties involved in the arbitration are responsible for paying these costs.

Types of Cases Mandatory arbitration statutes cover only a few types of cases. A typical statute might apply the procedure to claims exclusively for money of a small amount, such as those for less than $15,000, not including interest and costs. Some statutes require arbitration of specific subject matter, like issues arising out of divorces. In addition, arbitration is required only in those cases in which a party has demanded a jury trial, as it can be assumed that a judge hearing a case is basically as efficient as an arbitrator.

Procedures Mandatory arbitration, while requiring substantially less time than litigation, does not necessarily provide speedy justice. The usual

Do check with your state and local courts to determine which cases are subject to mandatory arbitration.

procedure for a claim filed in court that is covered by the mandatory arbitration law is to place the claim in the arbitration track at time of filing. At this time the date and time of hearing are assigned, typically eight months from the date of filing.

Discovery procedures may be used prior to the hearing on arbitration. Since no discovery is permitted after the hearing without permission of the court, an early and thorough degree of preparation is necessary to achieve a full hearing on the merits of the controversy. This preparation also prevents the hearing from being used as an opportunity to discover the adversary's case en route to an eventual trial. Most discovery is by interrogatories rather than by deposition.

The arbitrators have the power to determine the admissibility of evidence and to decide the law and the facts of the case. Rulings on objections to evidence or on other issues that arise during the hearing are made by the arbitrators. States have different rules relating to the admissibility of evidence. In most states the established rules of evidence must be followed by the arbitrators. Several jurisdictions, however, do not require hearings to be conducted according to the established rules of evidence. New Jersey law, for example, provides: "The arbitrator shall admit all relevant evidence and shall not be bound by the rules of evidence." Other states leave to the discretion of the arbitrator the extent to which the rules of evidence apply.

VOLUNTARY/CONTRACT-BASED ARBITRATION

Although the statutes that mandate arbitration of certain types of disputes clearly have increased the use of this ADR method, the larger growth in the number of arbitration cases comes from disputing parties agreeing to arbitrate, not litigate.

These agreements to voluntarily arbitrate come in two basic forms. One is known as the **predispute arbitration clause.** Such clauses commonly appear in business contracts. In essence, the contracting parties show good judgment in understanding conflicts exist, conflicts give rise to disputes, and disputes are better resolved through arbitration rather than by litigating.

Don't rely on getting a party to sign a postdispute arbitration agreement; relying on a predispute arbitration clause is smarter.

People often view a contract as the beginning of a productive business relationship. They do not want to lessen the forthcoming opportunities with any expectation that problems might occur. And they view including an arbitration clause in the contract as an indication that bad things will happen. These people may need to utilize a **postdispute arbitration agreement.** Such agreements arise when parties already in dispute decide that arbitration is better than litigation.

On the basis of your study of this chapter, we trust you understand why a predispute arbitration is the wiser and ultimately more efficient approach to ADR than the postdispute agreement. An obvious disadvantage to relying on the latter approach is that disputing parties may not be able to find the common ground to agree to arbitrate.

To encourage businesspeople to use voluntary arbitration, the goal of an efficient and affordable alternative to litigation must be achieved. When arbitration is as expensive and time-consuming as litigation, the attractiveness of the ADR system declines. Sidebar 5.9 discusses how the Supreme Court interprets arbitration agreements that limit claims to single parties, thereby prohibiting class action arbitrations.

sidebar 5.9 Arbitration Agreements

Single Claims v. Class Actions

When a party with a complaint suffers a small amount of damages, it is not feasible to litigate. The same might be said of arbitration, even though this process is intended to be simpler and less expensive than a lawsuit. To increase the chance of a satisfactory result, a party claiming a wrong with little damages would like to create a class action involving similarly situated parties.

This was the situation after the Concepcions enrolled for cellular phone service with AT&T. As a part of the subscription for this service through AT&T, the Concepcions signed a voluntary arbitration agreement indicating they would arbitrate any dispute with AT&T. This arbitration clause clearly stated the process would be limited to only the Concepcions' dispute.

As a party of the contract with AT&T, the Concepcions were told they would receive two "free" phones. Instead of getting the phones free of all charges, the Concepcions were billed for the sales tax on the retail value of these phones. The total amount of this tax was $30.22. When the Concepcions discovered this charge, they filed a class-action suit in federal district court claiming they and other customers had been defrauded. AT&T sought to have this action dismissed, claiming the Concepcions' dispute had to be arbitrated.

The impact of AT&T's argument would be to prohibit class-action litigation and even class-action arbitration. The Concepcions sought to have the arbitration agreement declared invalid, arguing it was unconscionable under California law to deny them the right to bring this class action. Even though the District Court and Ninth Circuit Court of Appeals ruled for the Concepcions, holding the prohibition of class actions was unconscionable, the U.S. Supreme Court reversed and upheld the arbitration agreement.[1] The Court's majority found that the Federal Arbitration Act preempts the California law on unconscionability as it applies to this situation. The Court's decision upheld the belief that arbitration is preferred over litigation.

The impact of this decision and a previous one[2] by the Court appears to be that consumers will have to negotiate to preserve the right to arbitrate class-action claims. If the arbitration agreement clearly states that the parties limit the arbitration to their personal claims, such class actions will be prohibited.

[1]*AT&T Mobility LLC v. Concepcion*, 131 S. Ct. 1740 (2011).
[2]*Stolt-Nielsen SA v. AnimalFeeds Int'l Corp.*, 130 S.Ct. 1758 (2010).

JUDICIAL REVIEW   LO 5-5

The arbitration process is less time consuming and less costly than litigation only if the parties are limited in seeking judicial review of the arbitrators' awards. From this perspective, voluntary arbitration is a more effective alternative to litigation than mandatory arbitration. The following subsections discuss the extent of judicial review of awards depending on the type of arbitration.

Review of Voluntary/Contract-Based Arbitration Awards

Generally, the award resulting from the voluntary arbitration procedure is final. The arbitrator's findings on questions of both fact and law are conclusive. The judicial review of an arbitrator's award is quite restricted and is more limited than the appellate review of a trial court's decision.

Arbitration clauses are liberally interpreted when the issue contested is the scope of the clause. If the scope of an arbitration clause is debatable or reasonably in doubt, the clause is construed in favor of arbitration.

The fact that the arbitrator made erroneous rulings during the hearing, or reached erroneous findings of fact from the evidence, is no ground for setting aside the award because the parties have agreed that he or she should be the judge of the facts. An erroneous view of the law no matter how egregious is binding because the parties have agreed to accept the arbitrator's view of the law. Error of law renders the award void only when it requires the parties to commit a crime or otherwise to violate a positive mandate of the law. Courts do not interfere with an award by examining the merits of the controversy, the sufficiency of the evidence supporting the award, or the reasoning supporting the decision. Were it otherwise, arbitration would fail in its chief purpose: to preclude the need for litigation. Instead of being a substitute for litigation, arbitration would merely be the beginning of litigation. Broad judicial review on the merits would render arbitration wasteful and superfluous.

Judicial review can correct fraudulent or arbitrary actions by an arbitrator. Further, courts of review are sometimes called upon to set aside an award when the decision is allegedly against public policy. In such cases, the reviewing court must establish that an arbitration award is contrary to the public policy which arises from laws and legal precedents. A reviewing court cannot reject an award simply because that court bases public policy on general considerations of presumed public interests. In essence, the scope of review by courts of an arbitrator's award in a voluntary/contract-based arbitration is extremely limited, as discussed in Sidebar 5.10.

sidebar 5.10

Judicial Review of Arbitrator's Award

Can a judge reject an arbitrator's factual findings and award and substitute a decision by that judge? This is the issue that the Supreme Court resolved in a case involving major league baseball. Steve Garvey sought damages of $3,000,000 after his contract with the San Diego Padres was not extended because of the team's alleged collusion with other teams. This collusion was supposedly in violation of the Major League Baseball Players Association collective bargaining agreement with the various Major League baseball clubs.

Garvey's claim was submitted to arbitration, and the arbitrator denied the claim stating that Garvey had failed to establish proof of the fact that his contract was not extended because of collusion. Garvey sought

review at the district court level, and that judge denied Garvey's motion to set aside the arbitrator's award. Garvey appealed to the Ninth Circuit Court of Appeals. This court of appeals reversed the district court's decision, vacated the arbitrator's award, and decided the case on the basis of record established by the arbitrator.

The Supreme Court reversed the decision of the court of appeals. It held when a court finds that the arbitrator made a mistake, that court should vacate the award and remand the matter to the arbitrator for further arbitration proceedings. The court should not resolve the merits of the parties' dispute.

Source: *Major League Baseball Players Association v. Garvey,* 121 S. Ct. 1724 (2001).

Review of Statutorily Mandated Arbitration Although a party may voluntarily consent to almost any restriction upon or deprivation of a right, a similar restriction or deprivation, when compelled by government, must be in accord with procedural and substantive due process of law. Therefore, statutorily mandated arbitration requires a higher level of judicial review of the award.

Laws providing for mandatory arbitration are subject to numerous constitutional challenges. Many courts have generally held that mandatory arbitration statutes that effectively close the courts to the litigants by compelling them to resort to arbitrators for a final and binding determination are void as against public policy and are unconstitutional in that they:

1. Deprive one of property and liberty of contract without due process of law.
2. Violate the litigant's Seventh Amendment right to a jury trial and/or the state's constitutional access to courts' provisions.
3. Result in the unconstitutional delegation of legislative or judicial power in violation of state constitutional separation-of-powers provisions.

Mandatory arbitration may be constitutional, however, if fair procedures are provided by the legislature and ultimate judicial review is available. Courts throughout the United States have uniformly upheld mandatory arbitration statutory schemes as against the constitutional challenges previously mentioned where a dissatisfied party can reject the arbitrator's award and seek a ***de novo* judicial review** of that award. *De novo* review means that the court tries the issues anew as if no arbitration occurred.

De novo hearings may be possible following a mandatory arbitration.

In mandatory arbitrations, a record of proceedings is required. Also, findings of fact and conclusions of law are essential if there is to be enough judicial review to satisfy due process. Judicial review of mandatory arbitration requires a *de novo* review of the interpretation and application of the law by the arbitrators.

The right to reject the award and to proceed to trial is the sole remedy of a party dissatisfied with the award. In a sense, the award is an intermediate step in resolving the dispute if the trial itself is desired. The right to reject the award exists without regard to the basis for the rejection. Many jurisdictions authorize fee and cost sanctions to be imposed on parties who fail to improve their positions at the trial as compared to the arbitration. Hopefully the quality of the arbitrators, the integrity of the proceedings, and the fairness of the awards will keep the number of rejections to a minimum.

The failure of a party to be present, either in person or by counsel, at an arbitration constitutes a waiver of the right to reject the award and seek *de novo* judicial review. In essence, a party's lack of participation operates as a consent to the entry by the court of a judgment on the award. Since the procedure of mandatory-court-annexed arbitration is an integral part of the judicial process of dispute resolution, its process must be utilized either to resolve the dispute or as the obligatory step prior to resolution by trial. To allow any party to ignore the arbitration would permit a mockery of this deliberate attempt to achieve an expeditious and less costly resolution of private controversies.

Review under the Federal Arbitration Act

When the arbitration is pursuant to state statute, that statute determines what, if any, grounds are available to challenge an award in court. In cases that involve interstate commerce issues, the provisions of the Federal Arbitration Act control.

Section 10 of the Federal Arbitration Act provides that an arbitration award may be vacated or set aside on any one of four grounds:

(a) Where the award was procured by corruption, fraud, or other undue means.

(b) Where the arbitrators were obviously partial or corrupt.

(c) Where the arbitrators were guilty of misconduct in refusing to post-pone the hearing, upon sufficient cause shown, or in refusing to hear evidence pertinent and material to the controversy or by engaging in any other misbehavior by which the rights of any party have been prejudiced.

(d) Where the arbitrators exceeded their powers or so imperfectly executed them that a mutual, final, and definite award upon the subject matter submitted was not made.

As set in subsection (a), the Federal Arbitration Act provides that an award can be vacated if it can be proved that it was procured by "corruption, fraud, or other undue means." "Undue means" goes beyond the merely inappropriate or inadequate nature of the evidence and refers to some aspect of the arbitrator's decision or decision-making process that was unfair and beyond the normal process contemplated by the arbitration act. The courts tend to interpret "undue means" in conjunction with the terms "corruption" and "fraud" which precede it, and thus, "undue means" requires some type of bad faith in the procurement of the award.

The grounds for over-turning an arbitrator's award are very limited; being disappointed with an award is not a basis for changing the award.

When the disputing parties each choose an arbitrator and these arbitrators choose a third to make up a three-person panel, the disputing parties may be inclined to charge that the arbitrator chosen by the parties is partial or corrupt. Under subsection (b), the use of "partial or corrupt" in the FAA means that an arbitrator lacks the ability to consider evidence and to reach a fair conclusion.

Subsection (c) covers arbitral misconduct. The concept of arbitral "misconduct" does not lend itself to a precise definition. Among the actions found to constitute such misconduct on the part of an arbitrator that justify vacating an arbitration award are the following:

1. Participation in communications with a party or a witness without the knowledge or consent of the other party.
2. Receipt of evidence as to a material fact without notice to a party.
3. Holding hearings or conducting deliberations in the absence of a member of an arbitration panel or rendering an award without consulting a panel member.
4. Undertaking an independent investigation into a material matter after the close of hearings and without notice to the parties.
5. Accepting gifts or other hospitality from a party during the proceedings.

An award may likewise be set aside on the basis of procedural error if an arbitrator denies a reasonable request for postponement of a hearing or commits an egregious evidentiary error, such as refusing to hear material evidence or precluding a party's efforts to develop a full record.

Finally, subsection (d), involving the question of whether the arbitrators exceeded their power, relates to the arbitrability of the underlying dispute. An arbitrator exceeds powers and authority when attempting to solve an issue that is not arbitrable because it is outside the scope of the arbitration agreement. Conversely, if the issues presented to the arbitrators are within the scope of the arbitration agreement, subsection (d) does not require the court to review the merits of every construction of the contract.

Sidebar 5.11 describes how parties to an arbitration cannot grant courts greater authority to review an arbitrator's award than described in the Federal Arbitration Act.

---

sidebar 5.11

Standard of Review of Arbitrator's Decision—Can Parties Expand the Statute?

A complicated factual situation involving whether Mattel Inc. as a tenant is liable to its landlord, Hall Street Associates, for the cost of an environmental cleanup forms the issue of whether parties can expand the scope of the Federal Arbitration Act. To resolve the lawsuit filed in federal district court over whether Mattel has to pay for the cost of cleaning up a manufacturing site, these parties agreed to arbitrate this dispute. These parties' agreement to arbitrate gave the U.S. District Court for the District of Oregon the authority to "vacate, modify or correct any award; (i) where the arbitrator's findings of fact are not supported by substantial evidence, or (ii) where the arbitrator's conclusions of law are erroneous."

Following arbitration resulting in a finding favoring Mattel (finding it was not liable to pay for the environmental cleanup), Hall Street Associates asked the district court judge to vacate or modify the arbitrator's findings and conclusions. The judge did vacate the arbitrator's award. The Ninth Circuit reversed the judge's order, and the Supreme Court granted certiorari. The Supreme Court states, "Under the terms of section 9, a court must confirm an arbitration award unless it is vacated, modified, or corrected as prescribed in sections 10 and 11. Section 10 lists grounds for vacating an award, while section 11 names those for modifying or correcting one."

The Justices decide that parties, even under the jurisdiction of a district court, cannot expand this quoted language. The parties cannot set a standard of review of an arbitrator's award that is different from the Federal Arbitration Act. The arbitrator's decision favoring Mattel must be reviewed in such a way as to confirm to the limits of the statute.

Source: Hall Street Associates, LLC v. Mattel, Inc., 128 S. Ct. 1396 (2008).

---

concept *summary*

Voluntary versus Mandatory Arbitration

	VOLUNTARY	MANDATORY ARBITRATION
Submission	Based on parties' agreement after dispute arises or on contract clause before dispute arises.	Required by statute.
Procedures	Since process is not tied to a court, it is quick, informal, often with no discovery, and not bound by rules of evidence.	The procedure is associated with a court's supervision; discovery usually is done, and many states require arbitrators to follow the formal rules of evidence.
Review of award	The award is final with no judicial review, unless a party can prove that the arbitrator engaged in fraudulent, arbitrary, or other inappropriate actions.	The court will conduct a *de novo* hearing as if the arbitration process had not occurred.

LO 5-3

LO 5-4

Mediation

As the preceding sections document, arbitration has played a significant role in ADR, particularly throughout the last half of the twentieth century. More recently, individuals and businesses have been utilizing the process of mediation as a preferred means of ADR. **Mediation** is the process by which a third person, called a **mediator,** attempts to assist disputing parties in resolving their differences. A mediator cannot impose a binding solution on the parties. However, as an unbiased and disinterested third party, a mediator is often able to help the parties bring about an understanding of a dispute and thus avoid litigation of it. Typically, mediators utilize the principles of interest-based negotiations, discussed earlier in this chapter.

Parties in a mediation are the decision makers; mediators provide a procedure of facilitated negotiation; and the parties are responsible for finding a solution to the dispute.

The process of mediation may be utilized by the disputing parties as a result of their agreement to mediate. This agreement may have been made as a part of a contract before a dispute arose. On the other hand, parties to a dispute may agree that mediation should be attempted as an alternative to litigating their controversy.

"Mediation has emerged as the primary ADR process in federal courts."

ADR and Settlement in Federal District Courts

A trial judge can require the disputing parties to submit to the mediation process before a complaint can be litigated formally. There is a growing movement in this court-annexed mediation as one means of controlling the heavy caseload faced by courts. Rules related to court-annexed mediation are local in nature; thus, there are wide variations as to the type of cases that courts require to be mediated. Generally, cases involving domestic-relations issues (such as divorce and child custody) and cases involving a dollar amount in dispute below a stated threshold level are examples of those that are subject to court-annexed mediation.

Mediation often allows disputing parties to preserve or reestablish relationships.

The number of mediations have increased for three primary reasons. First, and perhaps most important, the disputing parties retain control over when to settle and when to continue disputing. This fact allows an effective mediation procedure to help parties address the conflicts that cause the dispute to erupt. An arbitrator's award may benefit one party while punishing another; however, the award likely does not assist the parties in developing a constructive, ongoing business relationship. Since mediation typically focuses on getting the parties to negotiate through an interest-based method, existing and potential conflicts can be handled productively. Sidebar 5.12 attempts to capture this point.

sidebar 5.12

Bill's and M&N Revisited

Earlier in this chapter, you were introduced to the business transactions and resulting disputes between Bill's Discount Centers and M&N TV Inc. Let's suppose these parties litigated or arbitrated the dispute involving the quality of M&N's TVs and the reduced purchases, over time, by Bill's. What would be the likely result? The court's judgment or arbitrator's award probably would take the form of a dollar amount in favor of one party or the other. Would such a judgment or award address the underlying concerns of the parties, thereby helping them continue to do business? Probably not!

To achieve some creative result, like the one suggested earlier, the parties will have to negotiate. The mediation form of ADR is the process that focuses on the parties negotiating.

The second reason mediation is growing in popularity relates to the cost savings compared to litigation and even arbitration. Since there is no presentation of evidence in a mediation, the active role of lawyers is reduced. The resulting savings in time and money can be quite substantial. In mediations, parties are actively engaged in negotiation, which allows these parties to be more efficient with their time.

A third reason businesses are relying more and more on mediation is found in the reduction of the legal system governing the process.

PROCEDURES

Despite the fact that mediations are informal and controlled by the disputing parties, the odds for a successful mediation occurring increase greatly when the mediator follows some basic procedures. Sidebar 5.13 summarizes the typical steps of the mediation process, and a more complete description follows.

"The good news today is that there are many different ways to resolve disputes. Within a generation, the default method has moved from litigation to mediation."

www.adrtoolbox.com/ decision-resources/ adr-decision-tree/

---

sidebar 5.13

Steps in the Mediation Process

1. Mediator's introduction and explanation of mediation.
2. Parties' opening statements.
3. Parties' exchange (or dialogue or negotiation).
4. Brainstorming possible options (or solutions).
5. The agreement (written and signed).
6. Private sessions or caucuses. (These are optional at the mediator's discretion.)

First, the mediator usually makes an opening statement. During this statement, mediators should explain the procedures to which they are asking the parties to agree. In essence, the mediator explains much of what you are reading in this section. Also, any "rules"—such as the common courtesy of not interrupting the party speaking—are specified.

Second, all parties are allowed to make a statement about their views of this dispute. These statements are made in the presence of each other and the mediator. A party's attorney may be the spokesperson; however, it often is more enlightening when the parties speak for themselves.

Third, the mediator attempts to get the parties talking to one another in what some refer to as the dialogue or exchange phase of mediation. Through an exchange based on open communication, the parties "clear the air" and hopefully begin to shift their focus from "the wrongs done in the past" to "how can business be conducted in the future."

Fourth, once the parties concentrate on how to work together or how best to end a relationship, the mutual generation of possible solutions should occur. Brainstorming options that resolve the dispute becomes the purpose of this stage of the mediation process. Skillful mediators assist parties in evaluating the possible solutions. Through productive questioning (some call this reality testing) by the mediator, parties should be able to make informed choices as to the best solution. At this point, the parties hopefully are ready to make a realistic commitment to resolve their dispute and conflict.

Sometimes, the mediator may decide that the process will be more productive if the parties and their attorneys meet with the mediator outside the presence of the other disputant. This private meeting is called a **caucus**. After each side caucuses with the mediator, the mediator may call the parties back together for continued discussions, or the mediator may begin to act as a shuttle diplomat, moving back and forth between the parties who are in separate rooms. Especially during these caucuses, the mediator must win the trust and confidence of each party to the dispute.

Through the good judgment and experience of the mediator, the differences between the parties hopefully will be resolved and a common agreement can be produced. The final step to a successful mediation is the writing of the agreement and the signing of the agreement by the parties.

ADVANTAGES/DISADVANTAGES

The basic advantage of mediation over litigation and arbitration is that the disputing parties retain full control over the resolution (or lack thereof) of their controversy. Through retaining this control, the parties can decide how much time and effort to put into the mediation process. The fact that mediation is party driven and does not involve even an informal presentation of evidence makes the process much more efficient than other ADR systems. If parties are making progress toward a settlement, the mediation can be continued and perhaps expanded to involve a possible agreement on other potential disputes. When the mediation is not aiding the parties, any of them can stop the process by simply stating that they will not participate further.

This same aspect of the parties controlling the mediation process may be viewed as a disadvantage rather than as an advantage when compared to other ADR systems. Even in the court-annexed mediations, a party usually satisfies the court's order to mediate by simply showing up. Generally, there is no enforcement mechanism that ensures the parties will mediate in good faith.

An additional disadvantage relates to the selection of the neutral mediator. The parties must be able to agree at least on who will be their mediator. The parties can avoid the need to agree on a mediator by allowing the person or organization that administers the mediation program to select the mediator. If the disputing parties cannot "get together" to select a mediator, the mediation process cannot begin.

Finally, the requirements for training as a mediator are not universally defined. Furthermore, licensing requirements are nonexistent at present. Therefore, anyone can serve as a mediator. The disputing party should be aware of the experience (or lack thereof) of the party chosen as their mediator. The Federal Mediation and Conciliation Service, the American Arbitration Association, and other similar organizations are valuable sources of credible mediators.

A **caucus** in mediation occurs when the mediator meets privately with one party without the other party.

"Mediators must have the facility to listen to what the negotiators are saying and to hear priorities and demands that may not be articulated explicitly. When they start making progress, more tradeoffs follow pretty quickly, once you can break the ice."

—Jerome Lefkowitz, a labor lawyer, on the end of the New York City Transit strike in December 2005 (Source: Sewell Chan and Steven Greenhouse, "From Back-Channel Contacts, Blueprint for a Deal," *The New York Times*, December 23, 2005)

Do weigh the benefits and detriments of the mediation process. Remember, some disputes can involve issues that need to be litigated for society's gain.

LACK OF JUDICIAL INVOLVEMENT

There is no need for judicial review of the mediation process. If mediation is successful, it is the parties' agreement that resolves the dispute. If the parties are not pleased with the mediation, they are free to end their voluntary involvement. A court-mandated mediation either will result in the parties settling their differences and dismissing the lawsuit or will result in no agreement being reached, which likely means the litigation process continues.

LO 5-5

In essence, mediations do not involve the legal issues found in the arbitration process. Typically, the conduct of the mediator is not subject to judicial review. Furthermore, mediators usually have the disputing parties sign a consent to mediate that states the mediator cannot be subpoenaed or otherwise be made to testify in any judicial hearing.

COMBINATION OF ADR SYSTEMS

LO 5-4

The benefit of flexibility related to mediation allows parties to utilize this process in conjunction with other dispute resolution systems. For example, in the middle of heated litigation, parties can agree to mediate just one issue. The resolution of one issue may help the litigation of the remaining issues proceed in a more efficient manner.

One of the more popular variations has given rise to what some people are calling an additional ADR technique. This variation involves the mediation of a dispute. The parties resolve all the matters of contention that they can and they agree to arbitrate the unresolved matters. This variation has become known as **Med-Arb.** The opportunities to use mediation in beneficial ways are limited only by the creativity of the parties involved.

Some laws encourage the parties to be creative in utilizing ADR systems. For example, the Magnuson-Moss Warranty Act provides that if a business adopts an informal dispute resolution system to handle complaints about its product warranties, then a customer cannot sue the manufacturer or seller for breach of warranty without first going through the informal procedures. This law does not deny consumers the right to sue, nor does it compel a compromise solution. It simply allows a manufacturer to require mediation, for instance, before the complaining consumer can litigate.

Key Terms

Arbitration 127
Arbitrator 127
Award 128
Caucus 146
Conflict 120
De novo judicial review 141
Dispute 120
Focus groups 126

Mandatory arbitration 128
Med-Arb 147
Mediation 144
Mediator 144
Negotiation 121
Positional bargaining 122
Postdispute arbitration agreement 138

Predispute arbitration clause 138
Principled, interest-based negotiations 123
Submission 128
Voluntary arbitration 128

Review Questions and Problems

Conflicts and Negotiation

1. *Conflicts and Disputes*

   What are the distinguishing characteristics of a conflict versus a dispute? Think about recent conflicts that did and did not become a dispute. Think about a recent dispute and describe how you handled it.

2. *Styles and Methods of Negotiation*

   List the five instinctive responses used in negotiation and describe how each of these applies to you.

3. *Positional Negotiation*

   In business disputes, what two items are most likely to dominate a position-based negotiation?

4. *Principled Negotiation*

   (a) Summarize the seven elements of principled, interest-based negotiations.

   (b) How does focusing on these elements assist the negotiation process?

Alternative Dispute Resolution (ADR) Systems

5. *Range of Options*

   What are the various items along the spectrum of ADR systems between litigation and negotiated settlements?

6. *Settlements*

   Why do businesses have incentives to settle disputes rather than relying on jury verdicts in the litigation process?

7. *Focus Groups*

   What is the benefit to lawyers and parties of conducting a focus group?

Arbitration

8. *Submissions*

   (a) What is th e purpose of a submission in an arbitration?

   (b) What is the proper role of the courts in determining whether a submission to arbitrate is valid?

9. *Arbitrators*

   As a client of a brokerage firm, Howsam invested in four limited partnerships. These investments were made between 1986 and 1994. The client agreement signed by Howsam required all disputes with the brokerage firm to be arbitrated. When she lost money on her investments, Howsam filed for arbitration, claiming the firm misrepresented the investments in the limited partnerships. The arbitration agreement has a six-year statute of limitations. The brokerage firm filed a lawsuit seeking to have the arbitration submission enjoined, since the statute of limitations had run out. Who—a judge or an arbitrator—makes the decision concerning the application of a statute of limitations to an arbitration proceeding? Why?

10. *Awards*

    Generally, what does an arbitrator have to include in the award to make it valid?

11. *The Federal Arbitration Act*

    (a) A dispute arose between partners. The partnership agreement provided that if the parties were unable to agree on any matter, it would be submitted to arbitration. One partner filed suit asking a court to appoint a receiver for the business. The other insisted on arbitration. How will the dispute be resolved? Why?

    (b) What impact does the FAA have on state laws that prefer the litigation process to arbitration?

12. *Statutorily Mandated Arbitration*

(a) What is meant by the phrase *statutorily mandated arbitration?*

(b) Is arbitration required in all cases? Why or why not?

13. *Voluntary/Contract-Based Arbitration*

The contract arising from Randolph's purchase and financing of a mobile home contained an arbitration clause covering all disputes that might arise. When a dispute arose, Randolph filed a lawsuit in federal court alleging violations of the Truth-in-Lending Act and the Equal Credit Opportunity Act. Randolph claimed the arbitration agreement was unenforceable, since it did not specify what Randolph might have to pay associated with an arbitration proceeding. Is an arbitration agreement that doesn't specify anything about costs enforceable? Why?

14. *Judicial Review*

(a) Explain why there are different standards of review of arbitration awards depending on whether the arbitration is voluntary or statutorily mandated.

(b) Barbara and Cole Inc. disputed the amount of money due as "minimum royalties" under a mineral lease. They submitted the dispute to arbitration, and the arbitrators awarded Barbara $37,214.67. The court held that there was no substantial evidence in the record to support an award of less than the minimum royalty of $75,000 and directed entry of a judgment for that amount. Was it proper for the court to increase the award? Why or why not?

Mediation

15. *Procedures*

What steps usually are followed to provide an effective and efficient mediation? Explain.

16. *Advantages/Disadvantages*

(a) How is mediation fundamentally different from an arbitration?

(b) What are some of the advantages and disadvantages of the mediation process?

17. *Lack of Judicial Involvement*

What is the nature of mediation that reduces the degree of judicial supervision?

18. *Combination of ADR Systems*

Describe how mediation can be used in conjunction with arbitration.

business *discussions*

1. Your employer, Let's-Get-It-Done, has a history of multiple employee disputes. These disputes range from claims of illegal discrimination to general complaints of worker dissatisfaction with supervisors. You have been assigned the task of changing the organization's culture. Since litigation is the typical method of resolving company disputes, you are considering alternatives to litigation.

> What are possible alternative dispute resolution systems (ADRs)?
> Should employees be required to sign a contract that an ADR method will be used before any lawsuit is filed against the organization?

2. As the vice president for sales of a company that manufactures and sells commercial carpet, you notice an alarming increase in the number of customers filing complaints with your company service representatives. Of particular importance is the number of complaints that involve claims in excess of $10,000. Because these large dollar amounts can lead to lawsuits being filed, you want to investigate what is causing the increase in complaints and how your company can be processing these complaints to avoid burdensome litigation.

> What steps should you take to discover, in the most accurate and efficient manner, the reasons customers are filing complaints?
> What is the distinction between mediation and arbitration?
> Should your company's sales contracts include a clause that requires the parties to attempt resolution of dispute by mediation? By arbitration? By some other mechanisms?
> If your company's sales contracts did include a dispute resolution (other than litigation) clause, when can the courts still be used?

3. After working as a consultant for the "We Can Help You" firm for seven years, you recently received a promotion to manager. In this new role, you report to a partner and are responsible for various consulting teams. You now create these teams in collaboration with the partner. These teams typically consist of four to seven consultants with a senior consultant serving as the team leader. Teams are organized or adjusted as the client demands dictate. As a new manager, you are becoming increasingly aware of conflicts among team members and disputes between the teams and clients.

> What is the difference between a conflict and a dispute?
> What steps should you take to discover, in an accurate and efficient manner, the reasons conflicts and disputes exist?
> Should your consulting firm's contracts with employees contain a dispute resolution clause? What about the firm's consulting agreement with clients? If so, what system of dispute resolution should be included?

6 The Constitution

Learning Objectives

In this chapter you will learn:

6-1. To appreciate how the structure of the U.S. Constitution provides the framework for our federal government.

6-2. To understand the importance of the supremacy clause and the contracts clause for business.

6-3. To understand the power of the federal government to regulate business.

6-4. To recognize the major amendments to the U.S. Constitution.

6-5. To analyze the basic protections created by the First, Second, and Fourteenth Amendments.

The U.S. Constitution provides the legal framework of our federal government and the authority it has to regulate business activities. Reading the Constitution and its amendments in Appendix III will give you an appreciation for the thoughtfulness of this document. Although it is relatively short, it evidences an enormous degree of forethought. The original document was drafted in 1787 as an alternative to the Articles of Confederation. Today, the U.S. Constitution is upheld as a cherished document of democracy. However, the Constitution was an experiment in government since the states, under the Articles of Confederation, were not acting as a nation.

In some ways, the genius of the Constitution is in its simplicity. In other ways, the Constitution is hailed for the way it balances the complexity of government. There are seven articles in the original Constitution. The first three articles establish the

The Constitution creates the Congress, the presidency and vice presidency, and the Supreme Court.

legislative, executive, and judicial branches, respectively. A key aspect of Article I is the Commerce Clause, the constitutional provision that gives the power to the government to regulate business. In the twenty-first century, examples of expansion of government regulation include the Sarbanes-Oxley Act, economic recovery legislation, and financial and health care reforms. Article IV ensures one nation versus individual states will provide the framework for citizenship and commercial activities. This article contains the full faith and credit clause and the privileges and immunities clause. Article V provides the process governing the amendment of the Constitution. Article VI describes how this Constitution will be the supreme law of the land. This article also clarifies that federal laws take priority when there is a conflicting state or local law.

Finally, Article VII states the Constitution will become effective upon ratification of the states. This ratification occurred in 1789. Two years later, in 1791, the first ten amendments also were ratified. These amendments, known as the Bill of Rights, provide clear statements of individuals' freedoms and protections from government action. Some of the key provisions of the Bill of Rights related directly to business are discussed in this chapter. Other provisions from these amendments are found in Chapter 13 on criminal law.

Do understand that an amendment must be ratified by 38 states through legislative action or by a constitutional convention. The U.S. has never held a convention for the purposes of amending the Constitution.

There have been a total of 27 amendments to the Constitution; thus, only 17 amendments have been approved since 1791. Twelve of these 17 amendments relate to how the federal government operates or who has the right to vote. This leaves five amendments, beyond the Bill of Rights, that substantially impact the government and the rights of individuals. Of these five, one amendment operates to cancel out or repeal another. The Eighteenth Amendment made the manufacture and sale of alcohol illegal. This is known as the Prohibition amendment. The Twenty-first Amendment repealed Prohibition and the Eighteenth Amendment. Table 6.1 highlights the first fourteen amendments to the Constitution.

It can be argued that only three amendments influence social policy. The Thirteenth Amendment abolished slavery. The Fourteenth Amendment

table 6.1 First Fourteen Amendments to the U.S. Constitution

I.	Freedom of Speech, Press, Religion and Petition (1791)
II.	Right to Keep and Bear Arms (1791)
III.	Conditions for the Quarters of Soldiers (1791)
IV.	Right of Search and Seizure (1791)
V.	Provisions Regarding Prosecution (1791)
VI.	Right to a Speedy Trial, Witnesses, etc. (1791)
VII.	Right to a Trial By Jury (1791)
VIII.	Excessive Bail and Cruel Punishment (1791)
IX.	Rule of Construction of the Constitution (1791)
X.	Rights of States (1791)
XI.	State Sovereign Immunity (1798)
XII.	Electoral College (1804)
XIII.	Abolishment of Slavery and Involuntary Servitude (1865)
XIV.	Due Process and Equal Protection (1868)

provides protection to citizens against the actions of the states. This amendment contains three important clauses—privileges and immunities, due process, and equal protection. The Sixteenth Amendment authorizes the federal income tax.

Basic Concepts

The Constitution contains many concepts that frame how the federal government operates and interacts with state and local governments. Three of these are of great significance to the creation of a strong centralized, federal government. They are the separation of powers concept, the supremacy clause, the commerce clause, and the contract clause. Each is discussed in the following sections.

SEPARATION OF POWERS

LO 6-1

Historians describe the success of "the constitutional experiment" as founded in the division of powers. The concept of checks and balances among the three branches of the federal government is well known. A lesser emphasized separation of powers is that between the federal government and governments at the state and local levels.

This **separation of powers** between levels of government is known as **federalism**. This concept recognizes that each level of government has a separate and distinct role to play. The federal government recognizes that it was created by the states and that states have some sovereignty. The Tenth Amendment reserves some powers to the states and to the people. Congress may not impair the ability of state government to function in the federal system. Likewise, state government may not limit the federal government's exercise of powers. Federalism, the separation of powers between the federal and state/local governments, is an important topic facing the Supreme Court every year.

SUPREMACY CLAUSE

LO 6-2

In allocating power between federal and state levels of government, the Constitution, in Article VI, makes it clear that the Constitution is supreme under all laws and that federal law is supreme over a state law or local ordinance. Under the **supremacy clause**, courts may be called upon to decide if a state law is invalid because it conflicts with a federal law. They must construe or interpret the two laws to see if they are in conflict. A conflict exists if the state statute would prevent or interfere with the accomplishment and execution of the full purposes and objectives of Congress.

It is immaterial that a state did not intend to frustrate the federal law if the state law in fact does so. For example, an Arizona statute provided for the suspension of licenses of drivers who could not satisfy judgments arising out of auto accidents, even if the driver was bankrupt. The statute was declared unconstitutional since it was in conflict with the federal law on bankruptcy. The purpose of the Bankruptcy Act is to give debtors new opportunity unhampered by the pressure and discouragement of preexisting debt. The challenged

When various laws are not consistent, the order of priority is (1) U.S. Constitution, (2) U.S. laws, (3) state and local laws.

state statute hampers the accomplishment and execution of the full purposes and objectives of the Bankruptcy Act enacted by Congress.

Preemption   Sometimes a federal law is said to preempt an area of law. If a federal law preempts a subject, then any state law that attempts to regulate the same activity is unconstitutional under the supremacy clause. The concept of **preemption** applies not only to federal statutes but also to the rules and regulations of federal administrative agencies. Sidebar 6.1 lists several examples of business-related cases in which the courts have found federal preemption of areas involving business regulations. The federal laws in this list are covered throughout this book. When you study these laws, remember the constitutional issues related to preemption. This concept helps explain the vast authority of the federal government.

In an important decision for business, the U.S. Supreme Court ruled that the state of Michigan cannot regulate the mortgage lending subsidiary of a major national bank.[1] This ruling reaffirms that the federal Office of the Comptroller of the Currency (OCC) has greater authority than a state to regulate banks and associated activities. In 2011, the U.S. Supreme Court upheld an Arizona law that penalizes employers who knowingly hire unauthorized foreign workers. In *Chamber of Commerce v. Whiting,* the Court ruled that federal immigration law does not preempt the Arizona statute. For more about this Arizona law, see Chapter 21 employment laws.

sidebar 6.1

Examples of State Laws Preempted by Federal Law

STATE OR LOCAL LAW PREEMPTED BY	FEDERAL LAW
A city conditions renewal of taxicab franchise on settlement of a labor dispute.	National Labor Relations Act
Municipal zoning ordinance governs size, location, and appearance of satellite dish antennas.	Federal Communications Commission Regulation
A state statute permits indirect purchasers to collect damages for overcharges resulting from price-fixing conspiracies.	Sherman Antitrust Act
A state law authorizes a tort claim by workers that a union has breached its duty to ensure a safe workplace.	Labor-Management Relations Act (Landrum-Griffin)
A state law prohibits repeat violators of labor laws from doing business with the state.	National Labor Relations Act
A state nuisance law purports to cover out-of-state sources of water pollution.	Clean Water Act
State criminal prosecution for aggravated battery is filed against corporate officials because of unsafe workplace conditions.	Occupational Safety and Health Act
State statute prohibits use of the direct molding process to duplicate unpatented boat hulls or knowing sale of hulls so duplicated.	Patent Law

[1]*Watters v. Wachovia Bank NA, 127 S.Ct. 1559 (2007).*

Federal Government's Authority to Regulate Business—The Commerce Clause

LO 6-3

The **commerce clause** can be found in Article 1, Section 8, of the United States Constitution. This clause declares "The Congress shall have Power . . . to regulate Commerce with foreign Nations, and among the several States, and with the Indian Tribes." The commerce clause gives rise to the federal government's power to regulate business activity.

This simple-sounding clause requires analysis in the following four areas:

- Regulation of foreign commerce
- Regulation of interstate commerce
- Impact on interstate commerce
- Possible limitations on federal regulatory authority

The next four sections focus on these areas and the impact on businesses and businesspeople.

REGULATION OF FOREIGN COMMERCE

The first part of the commerce clause grants the federal government power to regulate foreign commerce. The power to regulate foreign commerce is vested exclusively in the federal government, and it extends to all aspects of foreign trade. In other words, the power to regulate foreign commerce is total. The federal government can prohibit foreign commerce entirely. In recent years, for example, the federal government has imposed trade embargoes on countries such as Iran, North Korea, and Libya. It can also allow commerce with restrictions.

That the federal power to regulate foreign commerce is exclusive means state and local governments may not regulate such commerce. State and local governments sometimes attempt directly or indirectly to regulate imports or exports to some degree. Such attempts generally are unconstitutional. However, a state may regulate activities that relate to foreign commerce if such activities are conducted entirely within the state's boundaries. For example, the U.S. Supreme Court has upheld a state tax on the leases of cargo containers used in international trade. This decision was based on the tax being fairly apportioned to the use of the cargo containers within the state. Hence, the Court concluded that the state tax did not violate the foreign commerce clause.[2]

REGULATION OF INTERSTATE COMMERCE

Among the most significant early decisions by the United States Supreme Court was one involving the meaning of "Commerce among the several States." As a result of Robert Fulton achieving success with the steam engine, he and Robert Livingston, his father-in-law, were granted by the New York legislature the exclusive right to operate steamboats in New York waters. This monopoly right was operated by Aaron Ogden.

Several potential competitors to this monopoly operated steam-powered ferries that transported people from the New Jersey shores to the harbors in

---

[2]*Itel Containers In't Corp. v. Huddleston*, 113 S. Ct. 1095 (1993).

New York. Among the more aggressive competitors was Thomas Gibbons, who hired Cornelius Vanderbilt to run steamboats between New Jersey and New York. Mr. Ogden filed a lawsuit against Mr. Gibbons alleging the latter was violating the legal monopoly granted by the State of New York. This lawsuit eventually ended up before the relatively new United States Supreme Court.

In 1824, Chief Justice John Marshall announced what has been called one of the Court's landmark decisions when he concluded that the Commerce Clause prohibits one state from interfering with commerce that crosses state lines. In short, the case of *Gibbons v. Ogden*[3] stands for the proposition that states cannot impede interstate commerce.

IMPACT ON INTERSTATE COMMERCE

Do appreciate the significant grant of power given to the federal government through the commerce clause.

It has been clear since the early 1800s that Congress has the power to regulate commerce that passes across state lines. Less clear has been the federal government's power to regulate business activities that are not engaged in interstate commerce. While there was little litigation during the rest of the nineteenth century on this issue, the first half of the twentieth century created a clearer picture. In a series of judicial decisions, the power of the federal government expanded through interpretation to include not only persons *engaged* in interstate commerce but also activities *affecting* interstate commerce.

The power of Congress over commerce is very broad; it extends to all commerce, be it great or small. Labeling an activity a "local" or "intrastate" activity does not prevent Congress from regulating it under the commerce clause. The power of Congress to regulate commerce "among the several states" extends to those intrastate activities that affect interstate commerce as to make regulation of them appropriate. Regulation is appropriate if it aids interstate commerce. Even activity that is purely intrastate in character may be regulated by Congress, when the activity, combined with like conduct by others similarly situated, substantially affects commerce among states. As a result of various Supreme Court decisions, it is hard to imagine a factual situation involving business transactions that the federal government cannot regulate.

LIMITATION ON FEDERAL AUTHORITY

The scope of the federal government's power to regulate commerce has become so broad that the focus, in the early twenty-first century, turns to whether there is any limitation on this authority. This topic requires examination from two perspectives. First, does the commerce clause contain any unstated restriction on the federal government? Second, are there areas of regulation of commerce that require the federal government to defer to the states or local governments?

CONTRACT CLAUSE

Article I, Section 10, of the Constitution says, "No State shall . . . pass any . . . Law impairing the Obligation of contracts." This is the **contract clause**. It does not apply to the federal government, which does in fact frequently enact laws and adopt regulations that affect existing contracts. For example, the

[3] *22 U.S. 1 (1824).*

Department of Agriculture from time to time embargoes grain sales to foreign countries, usually as a result of problems in foreign affairs. Prohibitions of sales of electronic equipment to certain nations are upheld if the federal government prohibits such sales.

Under the contract clause, states cannot enact laws that impact rights and duties under existing contracts. Suppose your company has a contract to provide natural gas to customers for stated minimum costs. A state or local government cannot impose new lower minimum prices on these existing contracts. The new minimum prices would be applicable only to newly created contracts.

The limitation on state action impairing contracts has not been given a literal application. As a result of judicial interpretation, some state laws that affect existing contracts have been approved, especially when the law is passed to deal with a specific emergency situation. On the other hand, this constitutional provision does generally limit alternatives available to state government and prevents the enactment of legislation that changes existing contract rights.

The contract clause regulates state and local government; it does not restrict the federal govenrnment's power to impact contractual relationships.

Amendments and Basic Protections

LO 6-4

The original seven constitutional articles created basic, fundamental concepts or principles of a centralized government. However, the language of the original Constitution was criticized for not restricting the newly formed federal government in some important ways. The first ten amendments, known as the Bill of Rights, establish a variety of important protections. Oftentimes we do not think of the protections in a business context. Instead, we think of them as the personal rights of individuals living in a free society. Indeed, many of the basic protections are referred to as freedoms. As you read this chapter keep in mind how constitutional protections relate to economic opportunity and business activities.

As you study the impact of these basic protections keep four important aspects in mind. First, basic constitutional rights are not absolute. Second, the extent of any limitation on a basic constitutional guarantee depends upon the nature of the competing public policy. Cases involving the Bill of Rights almost always require courts to strike a balance either between some goal or policy of society and the constitutional protection involved or between competing constitutional guarantees. For example, such cases may involve conflict between the goal of protecting an individual's or business's reputation and the right of another to speak freely about the reputation. The courts are continually weighing the extent of constitutional protections.

Do remember constitutional rights are not absolute.

Third, constitutional guarantees exist in order to remove certain issues from the political process and the ballot box. They exist to protect the minority from the majority. Freedom of expression (press and speech) protects the unpopular idea or viewpoint. Freedom of assembly allows groups with ideologies foreign to most of us to meet and express their philosophy.

Finally, constitutional rights vary from time to time and may be narrowly interpreted during emergencies such as war or civil strife. Even during peacetime, constitutional principles are constantly reapplied and reexamined.

The next four sections cover topics arising from the Bill of Rights. Then the provisions of the Fourteenth Amendment that extend constitutional protections by restricting the authority of state and local governments are examined.

LO 6-5   ## FIRST AMENDMENT PROTECTIONS

Freedom of Religion The First Amendment states that Congress shall make no law "respecting an establishment of religion" (the **establishment clause**) "or prohibiting the free exercise thereof" (the **free exercise clause**). These clauses guarantee freedom of religion through the separation of church and state. Sidebar 6.2 details characteristics generally attributed to churches.

Most business-related freedom of religion cases involve the free exercise clause. The Supreme Court has held that the denial of unemployment benefits to a worker who refused a position because the job would have required him to work on Sunday violated the free exercise clause of the First Amendment. The constitution requires that the owner of the business either allow the person to have Sunday off or allow the state to pay unemployment compensation and increase the business's taxes. Most businesses are likely to face this issue in employment discrimination claims brought under Title VII. These issues appear in detail in Chapter 20.

Freedom of religion has been used to challenge legislation requiring the closing of business establishments on Sunday. Although the motive for such legislation may be, in part, religious, there are also economic reasons for such legislation. As a result, if a law is based on economic considerations, it

sidebar 6.2

How Does the IRS Define "Churches"?

The term *church* is found, but not specifically defined, in the Internal Revenue Code. Certain characteristics are generally attributed to churches. These attributes of a church have been developed by the IRS and by court decisions. They include:

Distinct legal existence
Recognized creed and form of worship
Definite and distinct ecclesiastical government
Formal code of doctrine and discipline
Distinct religious history
Membership not associated with any other church or denomination
Organization of ordained ministers
Ordained ministers selected after completing prescribed courses of study
Literature of its own

Established places of worship
Regular congregations
Regular religious services
Sunday schools for the religious instruction of the young
Schools for the preparation of its members

The IRS generally uses a combination of these characteristics, together with other facts and circumstances, to determine whether an organization is considered a church for federal tax purposes.

Source: www.irs.gov/charities/churches/article/0,,id=155746,00.html.

sidebar 6.3

Business and the Religious Freedom Restoration Act

In *Burwell v. Hobby Lobby Stores, Inc.*, 573 US. __ (2104), the Supreme Court considered whether the Religious Freedom Restoration Act:

permits the United States Department of Health and Human Services (HHS) to demand that three closely held corporations provide health-insurance coverage for methods of contraception that violate the sincerely held religious beliefs of the companies' owners.

The contraception methods at issue are drugs or devices that may operate after the fertilization of an egg.

In this 5–4 case, Justice Alito wrote the majority opinion, holding that as applied to closely held corporations, the regulations promulgated by HHS under the Affordable Care Act requiring employers to provide their female employees with no-cost access to contraception violate the RFRA. In other words, closely held companies can invoke religious objections to avoid covering four specific kinds of contraception in their health care plans. The decision prompted spirited dissenting opinions by Justices Ginsburg, Sotomayor, Breyer, and Kagen.

may be upheld if its classifications are reasonable and in the public interest. See Sidebar 6.3 for information about the Supreme Court decision in *Burwell* v. Hobby Lobby Stores, Inc. regarding religious objections to certain forms of contraception.

Freedom of Speech Freedom of speech, sometimes referred to as freedom of expression, covers both verbal and written communications. This protection relates to governmental action that restricts our ability to express ourselves. The Amendment protection does not apply to private action. Whether a restriction is imposed by the government or a private company is critical to understand. The First Amendment does not apply to action by private companies.

Free speech also covers conduct or actions considered **symbolic speech.** Although freedom of speech is not absolute, it is as close to being absolute as any constitutional guarantee. It exists to protect the minority from the majority. It means freedom to express ideas antagonistic to those of the majority. Freedom of speech exists for thoughts many of us hate and for ideas that may be foreign to us. It means freedom to express the unorthodox, and it recognizes that there is no such thing as a false idea.

Not all speech, however, is protected. "Fighting words," or speech inciting a hostile reaction, is unprotected. In *Chaplinsky v. State of New Hampshire* (1942), the Court held words that "inflict injury or tend to incite an immediate breach of the peace" are not subject to First Amendment protection. The Court held "that such utterances are no essential part of any exposition of ideas, and are of such slight social value as a step to truth that any benefit may be derived from them is clearly outweighed by the social interest in order and morality." Similarly, in *Brandenburg v. Ohio*, the Court held that to be unprotected, such speech must be an "incitement to imminent lawless action."

Obscenity is also unprotected speech. To determine if speech is legally obscene, the following test should be applied from the perspective of the "average person, applying contemporary community standards":*

- Whether the work, taken as a whole, appeals to the prurient interest in sex
- Whether the work depicts or describes, in a patently offensive way, sexual conduct specifically defined by applicable state law
- Whether the work, taken as a whole, lacks serious literary, artistic, political, or scientific value (*Miller v. California*, 413 U.S. 15 (1973))

This test for obscenity evolved in the twentieth century as the result of a number of challenges to laws and ordinances prohibiting a range of speech in books, records, films, and pamphlets. Well-known literary works by writers such as James Joyce, D.H. Lawrence, Allen Ginsberg, and Henry Miller formed the basis of obscenity prosecutions. With the exception of child pornography, very little material is prohibited in the U.S. as legally obscene. See Sidebar 6.4 for examples of art exhibits challenged as obscene.

The Federal Communications Commission (FCC) has the power to restrict certain speech. It prohibits legally obscene broadcasts at all times, and it is a violation of FCC rules to air "indecent programming or profane language" between 6 A.M. and 10 P.M. on broadcast radio and television. The FCC defines "indecency" as "language or material that, in context, depicts or describes, in terms patently offensive as measured by contemporary community standards for the broadcast medium, sexual or excretory organs or activities." Although this material does not rise to the level of being legally obscene, its broadcast may be restricted during the day when children may be in the audience. Sidebar 6.5 contains examples of high-profile FCC actions.

sidebar 6.4

Art and Obscenity

Art exhibits can also be subject to obscenity challenges. One notorious trial involved the photography exhibit *Robert Mapplethorpe: The Perfect Moment* in Cincinnati. Of the approximately 175 photographs in the exhibit, seven portraits were at issue, primarily depicting sadomasochistic acts. The Contemporary Arts Center and its director, Dennis Barrie, were indicted for displaying obscene material. The openly homosexual nature of Mapplethorpe's work generated negative public attention. Ultimately, Barrie and the museum were acquitted at trial.

Another high-profile action involved an exhibit at the Brooklyn Museum, *Sensation: Young British Artists from the Saatchi Collection.* Then-mayor Rudolph Giuliani threatened to cut off city funding for the museum if it did not remove a number of works from the exhibit. One work at issue, Chris Ofili's painting "The Holy Virgin Mary," uses elephant dung and cut-outs from pornographic magazines. Viewed as "Catholic-bashing" and an attack on religion, the mayor wanted it removed from the exhibit. The Brooklyn Museum refused to remove the piece. After New York City stopped funding the museum, the director filed a First Amendment lawsuit. Many actors, artists, and writers spoke out in support of the museum. A federal judge subsequently ordered New York City to restore the denied funding and to refrain from continuing its ejection action.

Both cases are viewed as reaffirming First Amendment protection of art.

sidebar 6.5

The FCC Is Not Amused

 During the 2004 Super Bowl, MTV, a Viacom subsidiary, produced the half-time show, featuring Janet Jackson and Justin Timberlake. According to the FCC decision, the "joint performance by Ms. Jackson and Mr. Timberlake culminated in Mr. Timberlake pulling off part of Ms. Jackson's bustier and exposing her bare breast." The FCC was not persuaded by CBS's argument that "the exposure . . . was unexpected and the duration of the exposure was for only 19/32 of a second." The FCC found that "the nudity here was designed to pander to, titillate and shock the viewing audience." The FCC fined CBS $550,000 for violating indecency rules.

After several tame Super Bowl half-time shows, another controversy erupted in 2012 after singer M.I.A. was seen on live TV flipping her middle finger and mouthing "I don't give a s**t" at a cameramen during her appearance with Madonna and Nicki Minaj. The FCC levied a $1.5 million fine and the NFL filed an arbitration action against M.I.A., claiming that she made an "offensive gesture" that was "in flagrant disregard for the values that form the cornerstone of the NFL brand and the Super Bowl."

Other FCC fines:

- Clear Channel Communications $755,000 for graphic drug and sex talk on a "Bubba the Love Sponge" radio program
- Clear Channel $175 million for indecency complaints against Howard Stern and other radio personalities

For more examples of FCC actions, see http://transition.fcc.gov/eb/oip/Actions.html.

The issue of freedom of speech arises in many other business situations. Sidebar 6.6 discusses several situations that arise when considering the protection of picketing and the limitation of free speech. Case 6.1 and Case 6.2 illustrate the scope of the First Amendment to protect speech.

sidebar 6.6

Picketing as Free Speech

Cases involving picketing, for example, especially with unions, often are concerned with the issue of free speech. The right to picket peacefully for a lawful purpose is well recognized. A state or local law that prohibits all picketing would be unconstitutional since the act of picketing, itself, is a valuable form of communication. However, a state law that limits picketing or other First Amendment freedoms may be constitutional if:

- The regulation is within the constitutional power of government.
- It furthers an important or substantial governmental interest.
- It is unrelated to suppression of free expression.
- The incidental restriction on First Amendment freedoms is no greater than is essential to further the government's interest.

Under these principles, laws that prevent pickets from obstructing traffic and those designed to prevent violence would be constitutional. For example, a Texas statute that prohibits "mass picketing," defined as picketing by more than two persons within 50 feet of any entrance or of one another, does not violate the First Amendment. The Supreme Court has held that a city ordinance prohibiting picketing in front of an individual residence was constitutional. The law was enacted to prevent picketing of the homes of doctors who perform abortions.

Courts may limit the number of pickets to preserve order and promote safety, but they will not deny pickets the right to express opinions in a picket line. For example, a court order preventing a client from picketing her lawyer was held to be a violation of the First Amendment. Freedom of speech even extends to boycotts of a business for a valid public purpose such as the elimination of discrimination.

SNYDER v. PHELPS
131 S.CT. 1207 (2011)

Father of deceased military service member brought action against fundamentalist church and its members, stemming from defendants' anti-homosexual demonstration near service member's funeral, and asserting claims for intentional infliction of emotional distress (IIED), invasion of privacy by intrusion upon seclusion, and civil conspiracy. A jury awarded Snyder $2.9 million in compensatory damages and $8 million in punitive damages. Following jury's verdict for father, the United States District Court for the District of Maryland remitted aggregate punitive damages award to $2.1 million, but otherwise denied post-trial motions. Defendants appealed. The United States Court of Appeals for the Fourth Circuit reversed, concluding that Westboro's statements were entitled to First Amendment protection. The U.S. Supreme Court granted certiori.

ROBERTS, C.J., A jury held members of the Westboro Baptist Church liable for millions of dollars in damages for picketing near a soldier's funeral service. The picket signs reflected the church's view that the United States is overly tolerant of sin and that God kills American soldiers as punishment. The question presented is whether the First Amendment shields the church members from tort liability for their speech in this case. . . .

Fred Phelps founded the Westboro Baptist Church in Topeka, Kansas, in 1955. The church's congregation believes that God hates and punishes the United States for its tolerance of homosexuality, particularly in America's military. The church frequently communicates its views by picketing, often at military funerals. In the more than 20 years that the members of Westboro Baptist have publicized their message, they have picketed nearly 600 funerals. Brief for Rutherford Institute as *Amicus Curiae* 7, n. 14. Marine Lance Corporal Matthew Snyder was killed in Iraq in the line of duty. Lance Corporal Snyder's father selected the Catholic church in the Snyders' hometown of Westminster, Maryland, as the site for his son's funeral. Local newspapers provided notice of the time and location of the service. Phelps became aware of Matthew Snyder's funeral and decided to travel to Maryland with six other Westboro Baptist parishioners (two of his daughters and four of his grandchildren) to picket. On the day of the memorial service, the Westboro congregation members picketed on public land adjacent to public streets near the Maryland State House, the United States Naval Academy, and Matthew Snyder's funeral. The Westboro picketers carried signs that were largely the same at all three locations . . . The church had notified the authorities in advance of its intent to picket at the time of the funeral, and the picketers complied with police instructions in staging their demonstration. . . . Although Snyder testified that he could see the tops of the picket signs as he drove to the funeral, he did not see what was written on the signs until later that night, while watching a news broadcast covering the event . . . .

Whether the First Amendment prohibits holding Westboro liable for its speech in this case turns largely on whether that speech is of public or private concern, as determined by all the circumstances of the case. "[S]peech on 'matters of public concern' . . . is 'at the heart of the First Amendment's protection.'" . . .

Speech deals with matters of public concern when it can "be fairly considered as relating to any matter of political, social, or other concern to the community," . . .

Deciding whether speech is of public or private concern requires us to examine the "'content, form, and context'" of that speech, "'as revealed by the whole record.'" . . .

The "content" of Westboro's signs plainly relates to broad issues of interest to society at large, rather than matters of "purely private concern." . . .

The placards read "God Hates the USA/Thank God for 9/11," "America is Doomed," "Don't Pray for the USA," "Thank God for IEDs," "Fag Troops," "Semper Fi Fags," "God Hates Fags," "Maryland Taliban," "Fags Doom Nations," "Not Blessed Just Cursed," "Thank God for Dead Soldiers," "Pope in Hell," "Priests Rape Boys," "You're Going to Hell," and "God Hates You." App. 3781–3787. While these messages may fall short of refined social or political commentary, the issues they highlight—the political and moral conduct of the United States and its citizens, the fate of our Nation, homosexuality in the military, and scandals involving the Catholic clergy—are matters of public import. The signs certainly convey Westboro's position on those issues, in a manner designed, unlike the private speech in *Dun & Bradstreet*, to reach as broad a public audience as possible. And even if a few of the signs—such as "You're Going to Hell" and "God Hates You"—were viewed as containing messages related to Matthew Snyder or the Snyders specifically, that would not change the fact that the overall thrust and dominant theme of Westboro's demonstration spoke to broader public issues.

. . . Given that Westboro's speech was at a public place on a matter of public concern, that speech is entitled to "special protection" under the First Amendment. Such speech cannot be restricted simply because it is upsetting or arouses contempt. "If there is a bedrock principle underlying the First Amendment, it is that the government may not prohibit the expression of an idea simply because society finds the idea itself offensive or disagreeable." . . .

Snyder argues that even assuming Westboro's speech is entitled to First Amendment protection generally, the church is not immunized from liability for intrusion upon seclusion because Snyder was a member of a captive audience at his son's funeral. . . . As a general matter, we have applied the captive audience doctrine only sparingly to protect unwilling listeners from protected speech. . . .

Here, Westboro stayed well away from the memorial service. Snyder could see no more than the tops of the signs when driving to the funeral. And there is no indication that the picketing in any way interfered with the funeral service itself. We decline to expand the captive audience doctrine to the circumstances presented here. Because we find that the First Amendment bars Snyder from recovery for intentional infliction of emotional distress or intrusion upon seclusion—the alleged unlawful activity Westboro conspired to accomplish-we must likewise hold that Snyder cannot

recover for civil conspiracy based on those torts . . . Our holding today is narrow. . . .

Speech is powerful. It can stir people to action, move them to tears of both joy and sorrow, and—as it did here—inflict great pain. On the facts before us, we cannot react to that pain by punishing the speaker. As a Nation we have chosen a different course to protect even hurtful speech on public issues to ensure that we do not stifle public debate. That choice requires that we shield Westboro from tort liability for its picketing in this case. The judgment of the United States Court of Appeals for the Fourth Circuit is affirmed.

It is so ordered.

Justice ALITO, dissenting.

Our profound national commitment to free and open debate is not a license for the vicious verbal assault that occurred in this case. Petitioner Albert Snyder is not a public figure. He is simply a parent whose son, Marine Lance Corporal Matthew Snyder, was killed in Iraq. Mr. Snyder wanted what is surely the right of any parent who experiences such an incalculable loss: to bury his son in peace. But respondents, members of the Westboro Baptist Church, deprived him of that elementary right. They first issued a press release and thus turned Matthew's funeral into a tumultuous media event. They then appeared at the church, approached as closely as they could without trespassing, and launched a malevolent verbal attack on Matthew and his family at a time of acute emotional vulnerability. As a result, Albert Snyder suffered severe and lasting emotional injury . . . The Court now holds that the First Amendment protected respondents' right to brutalize Mr. Snyder. I cannot agree.

KEY POINTS

- The Supreme Court held that the First Amendment protected the picketing because it pertained to a matter of "public concern." Although many may consider the messages problematic, the Court found that they address a range of issues, including political and moral conduct, which pertain to broad public issues.

- The Court declined to expand the captive audience doctrine to a situation such as this one, in which the protesters stayed in the authorized location, away from the memorial service, and there were no facts that suggested that the picketing disrupted the funeral service.

- This decision underscores a level of protection afforded to the First Amendment. In his dissenting opinion, Justice Alito expresses a very different stance.

In some free-speech cases, an individual whose own speech or conduct may not be prohibited is nevertheless permitted to challenge a statute limiting speech because it also threatens other people not before the court. The person is allowed to challenge the statute because others who may desire to engage in legally protected expression may refrain from doing so. They may fear the risk of prosecution, or they may not want to risk having a law declared to be only partially invalid. This is known as the **overbreadth doctrine**. It means that the legislators have gone too far in seeking to achieve a goal.

For example, an airport authority resolution declared the central terminal area "not open for First Amendment activities." The resolution was unconstitutional under the First Amendment overbreadth doctrine. The resolution reached the "universe of expressive activity" and in effect created a "First-Amendment-Free Zone" at the airport. Nearly every person who entered the airport would violate the resolution, since it bars all First Amendment activities, including talking and reading.

As you can see, the freedom of speech is cherished as a fundamental right of citizenship. While this right's importance provides significant protection, it sometimes can contradict other critical interests, such as the right of privacy. Sidebar 6.7 highlights the balance that courts often seek to find.

> The overbreadth doctrine was used by the courts to declare certain versions of child pornography laws unconstitutional. Governmental restrictions on expression must be narrowly drafted.

---

sidebar 6.7

Free Speech versus an Individual's Right of Privacy

Through wiretapping and electronic surveillance statutes, the federal government and most states make it illegal to intercept and record oral, wire, and electronic conversations. A more complicated issue arises when an illegally obtained conversation involving public issues is broadcast or published by someone who is not involved in the illegal activity. For example, does the free speech clause protect a radio commentator who broadcasts a cell phone conversation when that conversation is illegally recorded but when the commentator is not the party who illegally taped the conversation?

The U.S. Supreme Court holds it would be most unusual to hold "speech by a law-abiding possessor of information can be suppressed in order to deter conduct by a non-law-abiding third party." When the recorded conversation involves public issues (such as the pay of public school teachers), the publication of this public information is protected compared to the interest of individuals to have their conversation remain private.

Source: *Bartnicki v. Vopper*, 121 S. Ct. 1753 (2001).

Commercial Speech   Historically, **commercial speech** was not protected by the First Amendment. However, in the 1970s the Supreme Court began to recognize that free commercial speech was essential to the public's right to know. Therefore, today, freedom of speech protects corporations as well as individuals. The public interests served by freedom of expression protect the listener as well as the speaker. Freedom of expression includes freedom of information or the rights of the public to be informed. Since corporations may add to the public's knowledge and information, they also have the right to free speech.

Freedom of speech for corporations may not be as extensive as the right of an individual. However, a government cannot limit commercial speech without a compelling state interest expressed to justify the restriction. State regulatory commissions often seek to limit the activities of public utilities. Such attempts usually run afoul of the First Amendment. Sidebar 6.8 is an interesting example of the FDA's failed attempt to require graphic warnings on cigarette.

---

sidebar 6.8

The Controversy Over Cigarette Warning Labels

The Food and Drug Administration (FDA) sought to require very graphic labels and warnings on all cigarette packages. R.J. Reynolds and other tobacco companies opposed the labels, which included photos of a man exhaling smoke through a hole in his throat, a mouth with cancerous sores, and diseased lungs juxtaposed with healthy lungs. Under the proposal, the word and image warnings would have covered half of the cigarette packaging and 20% of cigarette advertising.

After a federal judge ruled in favor of the tobacco companies and the U.S. Court of Appeals for the District of Columbia panel affirmed the ruling, the FDA backed off of the proposal. It is now working on new warning labels consistent with the requirements of the Tobacco Control Act.

Source: Steve Almasy, "FDA Changes Course on Graphic Warning Labels for Cigarettes," *CNN* (March 20, 2013).

---

 case **6.2**

BROWN v. ENTERTAINMENT MERCHANTS ASSOCIATION
564 U.S. _____ (2011)

Respondents, representing the video-game and software industries, filed a pre-enforcement challenge to a California law that restricts the sale or rental of violent video games to minors. The Federal District Court concluded that the Act violated the First Amendment and permanently enjoined its enforcement. The Ninth Circuit affirmed. In a 7–2 decision, the Supreme Court affirmed the Ninth Circuit decision. Justice Scalia delivered the opinion of the Court in which Justices Kennedy, Ginsburg, Sotomayor and Kagan joined. Justice Alito filed a concurring opinion in which Chief Justice Roberts joined. Justices Thomas and Breyer filed dissenting opinions.

SCALIA, J.: We consider whether a California law imposing restrictions on violent video games comports with the First Amendment.

I California Assembly Bill 1179 (2005), Cal. Civ. Code Ann. §§1746–1746.5 (West 2009) (Act), prohibits the sale or rental of "violent video games" to minors, and requires their packaging to be labeled "18." The Act covers games "in which the range of options available to a player includes killing, maiming, dismembering, or sexually assaulting an image of a human being, if those acts are depicted" in a manner that "[a] reasonable person, considering the game as a whole, would find appeals to a deviant or morbid interest of minors," that is "patently offensive to prevailing standards in the community as to what is suitable for minors," and that "causes the game, as a whole, to lack serious literary, artistic, political, or scientific value for minors." §1746(d)(1)(A). Violation of the Act is punishable by a civil fine of up to $1,000. §1746.3.

Respondents, representing the video-game and software industries, brought a preenforcement challenge to the Act in the United States District Court for the Northern District of California. That court concluded that the Act violated the First Amendment and permanently enjoined its enforcement. The Court of Appeals affirmed, and we granted certiorari.

California correctly acknowledges that video games qualify for First Amendment protection. The Free Speech Clause exists principally to protect discourse on public matters, but we have long recognized that it is difficult to distinguish politics from entertainment, and dangerous to try. "Everyone is familiar with instances of propaganda through fiction. What is one man's amusement, teaches another's doctrine." *Winters* v. *New York,* 333 U. S. 507, 510 (1948). Like the protected books, plays, and movies that preceded them, video games communicate ideas—and even social messages—through many familiar literary devices (such as characters, dialogue, plot, and music) and through features distinctive to the medium (such as the player's interaction with the virtual world). That suffices to confer First Amendment protection. Under our Constitution, "esthetic and moral judgments about art and literature . . . are for the individual to make, not for the Government to decree, even with the mandate or approval of a majority." *United States* v. *Playboy Entertainment Group, Inc.,* 529 U. S. 803, 818 (2000). And whatever the challenges of applying the Constitution to ever-advancing technology, "the basic principles of freedom of speech and the press, like the First Amendment's command, do not vary" when a new and different medium for communication appears.

. . .

Last Term, in *Stevens,* we held that new categories of unprotected speech may not be added to the list by a legislature that concludes certain speech is too harmful to be tolerated. *Stevens* concerned a federal statute purporting to criminalize the creation, sale, or possession of certain depictions of animal cruelty. See 18 U. S. C. §48 (amended 2010). The statute covered depictions "in which a living animal is intentionally maimed, mutilated, tortured, wounded, or killed" if that harm to the animal was illegal where the "the creation, sale, or possession t[ook] place," §48(c)(1). A saving clause largely borrowed from our obscenity jurisprudence, see *Miller* v. *California,* 413 U. S. 15, 24 (1973), exempted depictions with "serious religious, political, scientific, educational, journalistic, historical, or artistic value," §48(b). We held that statute to be an impermissible content-based restriction on speech. There was no American tradition of forbidding the *depiction of* animal cruelty—though States have long had laws against *committing* it.

. . .

That holding controls this case. As in Stevens, California has tried to make violent-speech regulation look like obscenity regulation by appending a saving clause required for the latter. That does not suffice. Our cases have been clear that the obscenity exception to the First Amendment does not cover whatever a legislature finds shocking, but only depictions of "sexual conduct" . . . Because speech about violence is not obscene, it is of no consequence that California's statute mimics the New York statute regulating obscenity-for-minors that we upheld in *Ginsberg* v. *New York,* 390 U. S. 629 (1968). That case approved a prohibition on the sale to minors of *sexual* material that would be obscene from the perspective of a child . . .

The California Act is something else entirely. It does not adjust the boundaries of an existing category of unprotected speech to ensure that a definition designed for adults is not uncritically applied to children. California does not argue that it is empowered to prohibit selling offensively violent works *to adults*—and it is wise not to, since that is but a hair's breadth from the argument rejected in *Stevens.* Instead, it wishes to create a wholly new category of content-based regulation that is permissible only for speech directed at children. That is unprecedented and mistaken . . .

California's argument would fare better if there were a longstanding tradition in this country of specially restricting children's access to depictions of violence, but there is none. Certainly the *books* we give children to read—or read to them when they are younger—contain no shortage of gore. Grimm's Fairy Tales, for example, are grim indeed. As her just deserts for trying to poison Snow White, the wicked queen is made to dance in red hot slippers "till she fell dead on the floor, a sad example of envy and jealousy." The Complete Brothers Grimm Fairy Tales 198 (2006 ed.). Cinderella's evil stepsisters have their eyes pecked out by doves. *Id.,* at 95. And Hansel and Gretel (children!) kill their captor by baking her in an oven. *Id.,* at 54.

High-school reading lists are full of similar fare [citing *The Odyssey of Homer,* the *Inferno* and *Lord of the Flies*] . . . California claims that video games present special problems because they are "interactive," in that the player participates in the violent action on screen and determines its outcome. The latter feature is nothing new: Since at least the publication of The Adventures of You: Sugarcane Island in 1969, young readers of choose-your-own adventure stories have been able to make decisions that determine the plot by following instructions about which page to turn to . . .

Because the Act imposes a restriction on the content of protected speech, it is invalid unless California can demonstrate that it passes strict scrutiny—that is, unless it is justified by a compelling government interest and is narrowly drawn to serve that interest . . .

California cannot meet that standard . . . The State's evidence is not compelling . . . [The studies relied on by California] do not prove that violent video games *cause* minors to *act* aggressively (which would at least be a beginning) . . . California cannot show that the Act's restrictions meet a substantial need of parents who wish to restrict their children's access to violent video games but cannot do so. The video-game industry has in place a voluntary rating system designed to inform consumers about the content of games. . . . California's legislation straddles the fence between (1) addressing a serious social problem and (2) helping concerned parents control their children. Both ends are legitimate, but when they affect First Amendment rights they must be pursued by means that are neither seriously under inclusive nor seriously over inclusive . . . Legislation such as this, which is neither fish nor fowl, cannot survive strict scrutiny.

Affirmed.

KEY POINTS

- The Court was asked to determine the constitutionality of a California law prohibiting the sale or rental of violent video games to minors and requiring their packaging to be labeled "18."
- The Court held that the law did not meet the requirements of strict scrutiny. Although the law may have had worthwhile intentions, California did not demonstrate a compelling interest that is narrowly drawn to serve that interest. As such, the law was deemed unconstitutional.
- Should the First Amendment protect violent speech? If not, where should the line be drawn?

Freedom of the Press

The publishing business is the only organized private business given explicit constitutional protection. The First Amendment states that "Congress shall make no law . . . abridging the freedom of . . . the press." This guarantee essentially authorizes a private business to provide organized scrutiny of government.

Freedom of the press is not absolute. The press is not free to print anything it wants without liability. Rather, freedom of the press is usually construed to prohibit **prior restraints** on publications. If the press publishes that which is illegal or libelous, it has liability for doing so. This liability may be either criminal or civil for damages. See Sidebar 6.9 about how WikiLeaks is presenting challenges to this doctrine.

A major area of litigation involving freedom of the press involves **defamation.** The tort theory known as **libel** is used to recover damages as a result of printed defamation of character. Libel cases compensate individuals for harm inflicted by defamatory printed falsehoods. Defamation is discussed in full detail in Chapter 10 in the context of torts.

Second Amendment: The Right to Possess Guns

Unlike the extensive litigation that defines the meaning of the First Amendment, there have been very few Supreme Court opinions involving the Second Amendment. The language of this amendment is as follows: "A well regulated Militia, being necessary to the security for a free State, the right of the people to keep and bear Arms, shall not be infringed."

Do realize that the concept of prohibiting prior restraints means a community must allow a performance to occur; the community can charge the actors with violating a local ordinance if the performance is inappropriate.

sidebar 6.9

WikiLeaks, Edward Snowden, and Freedom of the Press

According to its website,

> Wikileaks is a non-profit media organization dedicated to bringing important news and information to the public. We provide an innovative, secure and anonymous way for independent sources around the world to leak information to our journalists. We publish material of ethical, political and historical significance while keeping the identity of our sources anonymous, thus providing a universal way for the revealing of suppressed and censored injustices.

WikiLeaks is challenging the bounds of freedom of the press. Its release of thousands of confidential messages about controversial subjects, such as the wars in Iraq and Afghanistan, as well as thousands of U.S. Embassy diplomatic cables, sparked international debate. Similarly, Edward Snowden, disclosed information about U.S. intelligence activities, including the NSA's widespread warrantless surveillance of domestic and international communications. Snowden is charged with violations of the Espionage Act.

What are the implications for traditional media outlets? Under U.S. law, even if government documents are illegally obtained, news organizations may publish the material. The most famous case on this point is *New York Times v. United States,* 403 U.S. 713 (1971), upholding the right to publish the Pentagon Papers (about U.S. involvement in Vietnam), which were classified at the time.

Sources: Christina Wells, "Edward Snowden, the Espionage Act and First Amendment Concerns," JURIST—Forum (July 25, 2013); WikiLeaks, http://www.wikileaks.ch/; and Alan Greenblatt, "WikiLeaks Fallout: Unease Over Web Press Freedoms," *NPR* (December 8, 2010).

Guns are big business. According to industry reports, the U.S. fire-arms industry consists of 200 companies with annual revenue of $2 billion.

In 2008, the U.S. Supreme Court addressed the meaning of the Second Amendment as it applies to the maintenance of a militia versus an individual's right to possess and use guns in their homes.[4] By a 5–4 margin, the Court ruled that the Second Amendment is not limited by its introductory phrase. The Court struck down, as unconstitutional, the District of Columbia's ban on handguns and its requirement that other guns, such as rifles, be kept unloaded or disassembled, or subject to a trigger-locking mechanism. The Court's majority concluded individuals in the District of Columbia can possess handguns in their homes and can have their guns loaded and ready for use in self-defense.

Even as this opinion was announced, commentators speculate that this decision will lead to increases in litigation under the Second Amendment. Regulation of guns by states and cities will be challenged since this Supreme Court opinion is very narrow even as it strikes down, as unconstitutional, a very broad restriction. The Supreme Court's majority opinion simply affirms the right to possess guns, including handguns, in one's home and to have them ready for use in self-defense. Left unanswered are many questions. For example, can individuals carry guns, especially concealed handguns, in public places like restaurants, parks, transit systems, and even airports? These and other issues related to the language of the Second Amendment should become a significant part of future constitutional cases. Two years after the Heller case, the Court considered a challenge to Chicago's gun laws. See Sidebar 6.10 for details about this case.

[4]*District of Columbia v. Heller, 554 U.S. 570 (2008).*

sidebar 6.10

The Second Amendment After the *Heller* Case

In *District of Columbia v. Heller* (554. U.S. 570 (2008), the U.S. Supreme Court held that the Second Amendment protects the right to keep and bear arms for the purpose of self-defense, and it struck down a Washington, D.C., law that banned the possession of handguns in the home. This decision led to a challenge of Chicago and Oak Park, IL, laws effectively banning handgun possession by almost all private citizens. In a 5–4 decision, the Court held that the Second Amendment is fully applicable to the States. In other words, the right to keep and bear arms recognized in the Heller case applies to the States. Justices Stevens, Ginsburg, Breyer, and Sotomayor dissented, contending that the Heller decision remains incorrect, that "the Framers did not write the Second Amendment in order to protect a private right of armed self-defense."

Source: *McDonald v. City of Chicago*, 561 U.S. _____ , 130 S. Ct. 3020 (2010).

The Fifth Amendment: Takings Clause Zoning and many regulatory limitations on property protect some owners from being harmed by other owners. Eminent domain, however, is quite different. This important concept specifically exists to limit the exclusive right of property in order to serve the common good by allowing the government to take away property-protected resources from owners.

Eminent Domain and the Common Good Jeremy Bentham, a philosopher who lived a century after John Locke, thought that Locke's ideas about property being a natural right from God were "nonsense upon stilts." He called the right of property the "noblest triumph" but believed that property served only the common good, which he defined as the "greatest happiness for the greatest number." This definition is similar to the one expressed earlier that the common good reflects the maximum conditions for providing what people need and want. It assumes only that satisfying what people need and want makes them happy.

The takings clause of the Fifth Amendment to the Constitution allows the government to take specific resources (usually but not always land) away from private owners for "public use" upon the payment of "just compensation." The clause recognizes the existence and importance of private ownership, but allows the government to "condemn" and take specific private resources for money under the power called **eminent domain.**

Three significant questions of interpretation arise:

- What constitutes a "taking"?
- What is a "public use"?
- What is "just compensation"?

As to the first question, it is clear that when the government builds a public road through private land, it has *taken* the land and must pay compensation. But what if the government merely limits specific uses of the land, perhaps for environmental purposes? Does it have to pay compensation? The cases have been unclear, but they seem to say that as long as some economic use has been left to the landowner, no taking has occurred. One way to determine

Eminent domain means the government can take private property for public use upon paying just compensation.

whether regulation is a taking is to see if it is necessary to protect an established property right of others that concerns safety, health, or other general welfare. The courts do not consider such regulation a taking. It is merely determining the location of boundaries, often boundaries of use.

Over the years public use *has come to mean* public purpose.

Public Use   The easiest way to define *public use* is to say it is a use *by* the public. A public road, a public park, a public building, a public sewage treatment plant or landfill—taking a private owner's land for any of these uses is a public use. What about the government's taking a right to string power wires across your land, then selling it to a private electric company that charges you for electricity? Is that a public use?

Courts have certainly allowed the government to take private property right for use by electric and other private utility companies. These companies benefit the public greatly. Over the years public use has come to mean *public purpose*, that is, any *purpose* that benefits the public, whether the public uses the resource or not.

What about the government's taking of land in order to sell it for private development in order to stimulate employment and increase the public tax base? Is employment stimulation and increased tax revenue a public use, or at least a public purpose? Consider Case 6.3.

 case 6.3

KELO v. CITY OF NEW LONDON, CONNECTICUT
125 S.Ct. 2655 (2005)

In 2000, the city of New London, Connecticut, approved a development plan that was projected to create in excess of 1,000 jobs, increase tax and other revenues, and revitalize an economically distressed community. In assembling the land needed for this project, the city's development agency, the New London Development Corporation (NLDC), purchased property from willing sellers and initiated condemnation proceedings against the plaintiffs for the remainder of the land. The plaintiffs are nine landowners of property within the area where the new development was planned.

The trial court prohibited NLDC from taking part of the land but on appeal the Supreme Court of Connecticut reversed, allowing the NLDC to take all of the land. The U. S. Supreme Court granted Ms. Kelo's petition for a writ of certiorari to decide the question of whether a city's decision to take property for the purpose of economic development satisfies the "public use" requirement of the Fifth Amendment.

STEVENS, J: . . . Two polar propositions are perfectly clear. On the one hand, it has long been accepted that

the sovereign may not take the property of *A* for the sole purpose of transferring it to another private property *B*, even though *A* is paid just compensation. On the other hand, it is equally clear that a State may transfer property from one private party to another if future "use by the public" is the purpose of the taking; the condemnation of land for a railroad with common-carrier duties is a familiar example. Neither of these propositions, however, determines the disposition of this case.

The disposition of this case therefore turns on the question whether the City's development plan serves a "public purpose." Without exception, our cases have defined that concept broadly, reflecting our longstanding policy of deference to legislative judgments in this field.

In *Berman v. Parker*, 348 U.S. 26 (1954), this Court upheld a redevelopment plan targeting a blighted area of Washington, D.C., in which most of the housing for the area's 5,000 inhabitants was beyond repair. Under the plan, the area would be condemned and part of it utilized for the construction of streets, schools, and other public facilities. The remainder of the land would be leased or sold to private parties for the purpose of redevelopment, including the construction of low-cost housing.

The owner of a department store located in the area challenged the condemnation, pointing out that his store was not itself blighted and arguing that the creation of a "better balanced, more attractive community" was not a valid public use. Writing for a unanimous Court, Justice Douglas refused to evaluate this claim in isolation, deferring instead to the legislative and agency judgment that the area "must be planned as a whole" for the plan to be successful. The Court explained that "community redevelopment programs need not, by force of the Constitution, be on a piecemeal basis—lot by lot, building by building." The public use underlying the taking was unequivocally affirmed:

> We do not sit to determine whether a particular housing project is or is not desirable. The concept of the public welfare is broad and inclusive. . . . The values it represents are spiritual as well as physical, aesthetic as well as monetary. It is within the power of the legislature to determine that the community should be beautiful as well as healthy, spacious as well as clean, well-balanced as well as carefully patrolled.

Viewed as a whole, our jurisprudence has recognized that the needs of society have varied between different parts of the Nation, just as they have evolved over time in response to changed circumstances. . . . For more than a century, our public use jurisprudence has wisely eschewed rigid formulas and intrusive scrutiny in favor of affording legislatures broad latitude in determining what public needs justify the use of the takings power. . . .

The City has carefully formulated an economic development plan that it believes will provide appreciable benefits to the community, including but by no means limited to new jobs and increased tax revenue. . . . To effectuate this plan, the City has invoked a state statute that specifically authorizes the use of eminent domain to promote economic development. . . . Because that plan unquestionably serves a public purpose, the takings challenged here satisfy the public use requirement of the Fifth Amendment.

To avoid this result, petitioners urge us to adopt a new bright-line rule that economic development does not qualify as a public use. Putting aside the unpersuasive suggestion that the City's plan will provide only purely economic benefits, neither precedent nor logic supports petitioners' proposal. Promoting economic development is a traditional and long accepted function of government. There is, moreover, no principled way of distinguishing economic development from the other public purposes that we have recognized. . . . It would be

incongruous to hold that the City's interest in the economic benefits to be derived from the development has less of a public character than any of those other interests. Clearly, there is no basis for exempting economic development from our traditionally broad understanding of public purpose.

Petitioners contend that using eminent domain for economic development impermissibly blurs the boundary between public and private takings. Again, our cases foreclose this objection. Quite simply, the government's pursuit of a public purpose will often benefit individual private parties. . . . The owner of the department store in *Berman* objected to "taking from one businessman for the benefit of another businessman," referring to the fact that under the redevelopment plan land would be leased or sold to private developers for redevelopment. Our rejection of that contention has particular relevance to the instant case: The public end may be as well or better served through an agency of private enterprise than through a department of government—or so the Congress might conclude. We cannot say that public ownership is the sole method of promoting the public purposes of community redevelopment projects. . . .

It is further argued that without a bright-line rule nothing would stop a city from transferring citizen *A*'s property to citizen *B* for the sole reason that citizen *B* will put the property to a more productive use and thus pay more taxes. Such a one-to-one transfer of property, executed outside the confines of an integrated development plan, is not presented in this case. While such an unusual exercise of government power would certainly raise a suspicion that a private purpose was afoot, the hypothetical cases posted by petitioners can be confronted if and when they arise. They do not warrant the crafting of an artificial restriction on the concept of public use. . . .

Just as we decline to second-guess the City's considered judgments about the efficacy of its development plan, we also decline to second-guess the City's determinations as to what lands it needs to acquire in order to effectuate the project. It is not for the courts to oversee the choice of the boundary line nor to sit in review on the size of a particular project area. Once the question of the public purpose has been decided, the amount and character of land to be taken for the project and the need for a particular tract to complete the integrated plan rests in the discretion of the legislative branch. . . .

The judgment of the Supreme Court of Connecticut is affirmed.

It is so ordered.

DISSENT: THOMAS, J.: Long ago, William Blackstone wrote that "the law of the land . . . postpone[s] even public necessity to the sacred and inviolable rights of private property." The Framers embodied that principle in the Constitution, allowing the government to take property not for "public necessity," but instead for "public use." Defying this understanding, the Court replaces the Public Use Clause with a "'[P]ublic [P]urpose'" Clause, a restriction that is satisfied, the Court instructs, so long as the purpose is "legitimate" and the means "not irrational." This deferential shift in phraseology enables the Court to hold, against all common sense, that a costly urban-renewal project whose stated purpose is a value promise of new jobs and increased tax revenue, but which is also suspiciously agreeable to the Pfizer Corporation, is for a "public use."

I cannot agree. If such "economic development" takings are for a "public use," any taking is, and the Court has erased the Public Use Clause from our Constitution. I do not believe that this Court can eliminate liberties expressly enumerated in the Constitution. Regrettably, however, the Court's error runs deeper than this. Today's decision is simply the latest in a string of our cases construing the Public Use Clause to be a virtual nullity, without the slightest nod to its original meaning. In my view, the Public Use Clause, originally understood, is a meaningful limit on the government's eminent domain power. Our cases have strayed from the Clause's original meaning, and I would reconsider them.

The Fifth Amendment provides: "No person shall. . . .be deprived of life, liberty, or property, without due process of law; *nor shall private property be taken for public use without just compensation.*" (Emphasis added.)

In my view, it is "imperative that the Court maintain absolute fidelity to" the Clause's express limit on the power of the government over the individual, no less than with every other liberty expressly enumerated in the Fifth Amendment or the Bill of Rights more generally. . . .

The most natural reading of the Clause is that it allows the government to take property only if the government owns, or the public has a legal right to use, the property, as opposed to taking it for any public purpose or necessity whatsoever. . . .

More fundamentally, *Berman* erred by equating the eminent domain power with the police power of States. . . . The question whether the State can take property using the power of eminent domain is therefore distinct from the question whether it can regulate property pursuant to the police power. . . .

The consequences of today's decision are not difficult to predict, and promise to be harmful. So-called "urban renewal" programs provide some compensation for the properties they take, but no compensation is possible for the subjective value of these lands to the individuals displaced and the indignity inflicted by uprooting them from their homes. Allowing the government to take property solely for public purposes is bad enough, but extending the concept of public purpose to encompass any economically beneficial goal guarantees that these losses will fall disproportionately on poor communities. Those communities are not only systematically less likely to put their lands to the highest and best social use, but are also the least politically powerful. . . .

I would reverse the judgment of the Connecticut Supreme Court.

KEY POINTS

- The Supreme Court considered the scope of the "public use" requirement in connection with the taking of private property. The specific consideration was whether a city's development plan serves a "public purpose."

- The Court concluded that the city of New London designed its plan to provide significant benefits to the community, including new jobs and increased tax revenue.

- Accordingly, the Court held that the public use requirement of the takings clause was satisfied because the development plan serves a public purpose.

- In his dissenting opinion, Justice Thomas declined to view "economic development" takings as a "public use" and expressed concern about the ramifications of the Majority opinion.

A national uproar arose after the 2005 Supreme Court case *Kelo v. New London*, Connecticut, over whether private property interest should *ever* be taken and turned over for private development. In that case, the Court held that the city's decision to take property for the purpose of economic development satisfied the "public use" requirement of the Fifth Amendment. Note that state and local governments have been taking private land and turning it over in this way for many years. The *Kelo* case merely represents the first time the Supreme Court has squarely decided the issue. The Supreme Court did not require that state governments take anyone's land for private development. It merely decided that it was a constitutional public use to do so under the given circumstances. Under pressure from voters, a number of states have passed laws preventing the units of government from taking private land for private development purposes.

> A number of states have passed laws preventing the units of government (cities and counties) from taking private land for private development purposes.

Just Compensation   The government can only take what belongs to private owners upon payment of "just compensation." The courts have generally defined just compensation in terms of market value. In most instances the government offers compensation to an owner, a negotiation follows, and an amount is agreed upon as a just compensation. However, courts have ruled that due process requires that an owner can go to court and have a jury determine a just compensation if the owner cannot agree with the government's offer.

Do you understand now how eminent domain illustrates that property right is limited by the common good? *Public use* means basically the same thing as *common good*. When the state decides to take an owner's resources, it is determining that the right of property in these resources no longer serves the common good and that the greater common good requires that the resources be taken. Even so, the owner who has lost a property interest through eminent domain must receive just compensation.

> *Public use* means basically the same thing as *common good*. These terms are also similar to *general welfare*.

The Fourteenth Amendment: Equal Protection and Due Process of Law   The Fourteenth Amendment to the Constitution states, "No state shall make or enforce any law which shall abridge the privileges or immunities of citizens of the United States; nor shall any state deprive any person of life, liberty or property, without due process of law, nor deny to any person within its jurisdiction the equal protection of the laws." Two of this amendment's provisions are of very special importance to businesspeople— the **due process clause** and the **equal protection clause.**

Prior to reading about these clauses, look again at the language quoted in the preceding paragraph. It is critical to understand that the first ten amendments describe individual protections against action by the federal government. The Fourteenth Amendment explicitly clarifies that certain restrictions also apply to state (and local) governments.

> The Fourteenth Amendment restricts actions by state and local governments.

DUE PROCESS OF LAW

The term *due process of law* as used in the Fourteenth Amendment probably arises in more litigation than any other constitutional phrase. It cannot be narrowly defined. The term describes fundamental principles of liberty and justice. Simply stated, due process means "fundamental fairness and decency." It means that *government* may not act in a manner that is arbitrary, capricious, or unreasonable. The clause does not prevent private individuals or corporations, including public utilities, from acting in an arbitrary or unreasonable manner. The due process clause applies only to governmental bodies; it does not apply to the actions of individuals or businesses.

Procedural due process cases involve whether proper notice has been given and a proper hearing has been conducted. Such cases frequently involve procedures established by statute. However, many cases involve procedures that are not created by statute. For example, the due process clause has been used to challenge the procedure used in the dismissal of a student from a public university.

In essence, the due process clause can be invoked anytime procedures of government are questioned in litigation. For example, in recent years, the Supreme Court has used the due process clause as its justification for defining the limits for a jury awarding punitive damages to a plaintiff in a civil lawsuit.

Incorporation Doctrine The due process clause has played a unique role in constitutional development—one that was probably not anticipated at the time of its ratification. This significant role has been to make most of the provisions of the Bill of Rights applicable to the states. The first phrase of the First Amendment begins: "Congress shall make no law." How then are state and local governments prohibited from making such a law? Jurists have used the due process clause of the Fourteenth Amendment to "incorporate" or "carry over" the Bill of Rights and make these constitutional provisions applicable to the states. Starting in 1925, the Supreme Court began applying various portions of the first eight amendments to the states using the due process clause of the Fourteenth Amendment as the reason for this incorporation and application.

The concept of incorporation through the due process clause has made the protections of the Bill of Rights applicable to individuals subject to state and local regulations.

The role of the due process doctrine goes well beyond incorporation. For example, the Fifth Amendment contains a due process clause applicable to the federal government. The Fourteenth Amendment contains a due process clause applicable to state and local governments. Due process essentially means the same thing under both amendments. Through the due process clause, all of the constitutionally guaranteed freedoms we discuss in this chapter and in Chapter 13 have been incorporated into the Fourteenth Amendment and are applicable to the state government's regulation of our personal and professional lives.

EQUAL PROTECTION

The Fourteenth Amendment's equal protection language is also involved in a great deal of constitutional litigation. No law treats all persons equally; laws draw lines and treat people differently. Therefore, almost any state or local law imaginable can be challenged under the equal protection clause. It is obvious that the equal protection clause does not always deny states the power to treat different persons in different ways. Yet the equal protection clause embodies the ethical idea that law should not treat people differently without a satisfactory reason. In deciding cases using that clause to challenge state and local laws, courts use three distinct approaches. One is the traditional, or **minimum rationality,** approach, and a second is called the **strict scrutiny** approach. Some cases are analyzed as falling in between these approaches. Courts in these cases use the **quasi-strict scrutiny** approach.

As a practical matter, if the traditional (minimum rationality) approach is used, the challenged law and its classifications are usually found *not* to be a violation of equal protection. On the other hand, if the strict scrutiny test is used, the classifications are usually found to be unconstitutional under the equal protection clause.

Do understand the role of each test under the equal protection clause.

Minimum Rationality Under the minimum rationality approach, a law creating different classifications will survive an equal protection challenge if it has a *rational* connection to a *permissible* state end. A permissible state end is one not prohibited by another provision of the Constitution. It qualifies as a legitimate goal of government. The classification must have a reasonable basis (not wholly arbitrary), and the courts will assume any statement of facts that can be used to justify the classification. These laws often involve economic issues or social legislation such as welfare laws.

Such laws are presumed to be constitutional because courts recognize that the legislature must draw lines creating distinctions and that such tasks cannot be avoided. Only when no rational basis for the classification exists is it unconstitutional under the equal protection clause. For example, a state law restricting advertising to company-owned trucks was held valid when the rational-basis test was applied to it because it is reasonable to assume less advertising on trucks provides for safer roads. Therefore, under this state law, a trucking company could not use the sides of its trucks to carry other companies' ads. Sidebar 6.11 provides an additional case example of the rational-basis test.

Strict Scrutiny Under the strict scrutiny test, a classification will be a denial of equal protection unless the classification is necessary to achieve a *compelling* state purpose. It is not enough that a classification be permissible to achieve any state interest; it must be a compelling state objective. To withstand constitutional challenge when this test is used, the law must serve

---

sidebar 6.11

Economic Regulations and the Rational-Basis Test

The state of Iowa taxes revenues from slot machines on riverboats at a maximum rate of 20 percent. Iowa provides a maximum tax rate of 36 percent on revenues from slot machines at racetracks. A group of racetracks and an association of dog owners filed a lawsuit to have these different tax rates declared unconstitutional under the equal protection clause.

The U.S. Supreme Court wrote that these tax rates are subject to the rational-basis test under the equal protection analysis, stating:

> The Equal Protection Clause is satisfied so long as there is a plausible policy reason for the classification, the legislative

facts on which the classification is apparently based rationally may have been considered to be true by the governmental decisionmaker, and the relationship of the classification to its goal is not so attenuated as to render the distinction arbitrary or irrational.

The Court finds that the Iowa legislators could rationally support riverboats by providing a lower tax on slot machines. This action does not unconstitutionally harm the racetracks since this case simply involves an economic decision of the legislature.

Source: *Fitzgerald v. Racing Association of Central Iowa*, 123 S. Ct. 2156 (2003).

important governmental objectives and the classification must be substantially related to achieving these objectives.

The strict scrutiny test is used if the classification involves either a suspect class or a fundamental constitutional right. A suspect class is one that has such disabilities, has been subjected to such a history of purposeful unequal treatment, or has been placed in such a position of political powerlessness that it commands extraordinary protection from the political process of the majority. For example, classifications directed at race, national origin, and legitimacy of birth are clearly suspect. As a result, the judiciary strictly scrutinizes laws directed at them. Unless the state can prove that its statutory classifications have a compelling state interest as a basis, the classifications will be considered a denial of equal protection. Classifications that are subject to strict judicial scrutiny are presumed to be unconstitutional. The state must convince the court that the classification is fair, reasonable, and necessary to accomplish the objective of legislation that is compelling to a state interest.

sidebar 6.12

Same-Sex Marriage and the Constitution

Two major cases represent significant victories for gay rights:

United States v. Windsor, 570 U.S. __ (2013) held the federal Defense of Marriage Act (DOMA) is unconstitutional as a depravation of the equal liberty of persons that is protected by the Fifth Amendment to the Constitution. DOMA defined "marriage" and "spouse" as excluding same-sex partners. Writing for the majority, Justice Kennedy stated, "[t]he federal statute is invalid, for no legitimate purpose overcomes

the purpose and effect to disparage and injure those whom the State, by its marriage laws, sought to protect in personhood and dignity."

In *Hollingsworth v. Perry*, 570 U.S. __ (2013), although the Supreme Court ruled that the opponents of same-sex marriage lacked standing to appeal a lower court ruling, the result of the case is to leave in place the California trial court decision that held Proposition 8 unconstitutional and reinstated same-sex marriage in California.

Strict judicial scrutiny is applied to a second group of cases involving classifications directed at fundamental rights. If a classification unduly burdens or penalizes the exercise of a constitutional right, it will be stricken unless it is found to be necessary to support a compelling state interest. Among such rights are the right to vote, the right to travel, and the right to appeal. Doubts about such laws result in their being stricken by the courts as a denial of equal protection. Two cases involving same-sex marriage and the Constitution are discussed in Sidebar 6.12.

One reason gender has not been moved to the strict scrutiny analysis is cases involving gender discrimination are so infrequent; states understand that unequal protection on the basis of gender is unacceptable.

Quasi-Strict Scrutiny Some cases actually fall between the minimum rationality and strict scrutiny approaches. These cases use what is sometimes called quasi-strict scrutiny tests because the classifications are only partially suspect or the rights involved are not quite fundamental. For example, classifications directed at gender are partially suspect. In cases involving classifications based on gender, the courts have taken this position between the two tests or at least have modified the strict scrutiny approach. Such classifications are unconstitutional unless they are *substantially* related to an *important* government objective. This modified version of strict scrutiny has resulted in holdings that find laws to be valid as well as unconstitutional.

Equal protection cases run the whole spectrum of legislative attempts to solve society's problems. For example, courts have used the equal protection clause to require the integration of public schools. In addition, the meaning and application of the equal protection clause have been central issues in cases involving:

- Apportionment of legislative bodies.
- Racial segregation in the sale and rental of real estate.
- Laws distinguishing between the rights of legitimates and illegitimates.
- The makeup of juries.
- Voting requirements.
- Welfare residency requirements.
- Rights of aliens.

Sidebar 6.13 summarizes the legal approaches courts use when analyzing equal protection cases.

The equal protection clause is the means to the end, or goal, of equality of opportunity. As such, it may be utilized by anyone claiming unequal treatment in any case. At the same time the clause will not prevent states from remedying the effect of past discrimination.

sidebar 6.13

Analysis of Equal Protection

	MINIMUM RATIONALITY	QUASI-STRICT SCRUTINY	STRICT SCRUTINY
Classifications Must Be	Rationally connected to a permissible or legitimate government objective	Substantially related to an important government interest	Necessary to a compelling state interest
	Presumed Valid	*Quasi-Suspect Classes*	*Suspect Classes*
Examples	Height	Gender	Race
	Weight		National origin
	Age		Legitimacy
	Testing		*Fundamental Rights*
	School desegregation		To vote
	Veteran's preference		To travel
	Marriage		To appeal

Key Terms

Commercial speech 166
Commerce clause 157
Contract clause 158
Defamation 169
Due process clause 175
Eminent domain 171
Equal protection clause 175
Establishment clause 160

Federalism 155
Free exercise clause 160
Libel 169
Minimum rationality 176
Obscenity 162
Overbreadth doctrine 166
Preemption 156
Prior restraints 169

Procedural due process 175
Quasi-strict scrutiny 176
Separation of powers 155
Strict scrutiny 176
Supremacy clause 155
Symbolic speech 161

Review Questions and Problems

Basic Concepts

1. *Separation of Powers*

   Describe the two concepts that (a) balance power within the federal government and (b) provide distinctions in the role of the federal, state, and local governments.

2. *Supremacy Clause*

   In 1916, the federal government passed a law that allows national banks to sell insurance in towns with a population of less than 5,000. In 1974, Florida passed a law prohibiting insurance agents from associating with financial institutions that are owned by or affiliated with a bank holding company. A bank located in a small Florida town is affiliated with a national bank. This bank wants to sell insurance through licensed insurance agents. Can the bank successfully challenge the Florida prohibition as being preempted by the federal law? Explain your reasoning.

3. *Commerce Clause*

   (a) What is the legal analysis used by the courts to grant the federal government broad authority to regulate business activity?

   (b) Why is it necessary to find the limits of the federal government's authority to regulate commerce?

4. *Contract Clause*

   (a) Does this provision of the Constitution apply to the federal government, state government, or both? Explain.

   (b) Does this provision of the Constitution apply to present contractual relationships, future ones, or both? Explain.

Amendments and Basic Protections

5. *Freedom of Religion*

   Explain the purposes of and distinction between the establishment clause and the free exercise clause.

6. *Freedom of Speech*

   Silvia, an attorney in Florida, also was a licensed certified public accountant (CPA) and a certified financial planner (CFP). Silvia placed an ad in the yellow pages listing her credentials, including the CPA and CFP designations. The Florida Board of Accountancy reprimanded Silvia for using both the CPA and CFP credentials in an ad essentially emphasizing her legal work. Silvia challenged the board's right to issue this reprimand. What is the legal basis for Silvia's challenge? Explain.

7. *Freedom of the Press*

   (a) A promoter of theatrical productions applied to a municipal board (charged with managing a city-leased theater) for a license to stage the play *Hair*. Relying on outside reports that because of nudity the production would not be in the best interests of the community, the board rejected the application. The promoter sought a court order permitting it to use the auditorium. Why should the court allow the production to proceed?

(b) What are the distinctions in how the law treats public persons versus private persons with respect to defamation?

8. *Right to Possess Guns*

The Supreme Court recently interpreted the Second Amendment for the first time in decades. Based on that decision, can individuals have guns in their homes for self-defense or is the right to possess guns limited only to members of a governmental-approved militia unit?

9. *Due Process of Law*

Explain what is meant by the Incorporation Doctrine and how it was used to expand the impact of the due process clause.

10. *Equal Protection*

There are three levels of judicial scrutiny under this clause. Describe what these levels are and when they are applicable.

business *discussions*

1. Other retail businesses in the mall in which your sports shoes shop is located have decided to open on Sundays from 12 noon to 6 P.M. You decide to follow suit, but two of your employees refuse to go along, saying it is against their religious beliefs to work on the Sabbath. You terminate their employment. They apply for unemployment compensation, and contend their unemployed status is your fault. If the state grants them benefits, you will be penalized since your unemployment compensation taxes will go up.

Should you contest their claim?

What would be the result if the employees refuse to work on Sunday because of their desire to play golf on that day?

2. The Mayor of the City of New York took issue with a number of works in a Brooklyn Museum temporary exhibit titled "Sensation: Young British Artists from the Saatchi Collection." Especially troubling to him was a painting by Nigerian artist Chris Ofili, entitled "The Holy Virgin Mary." In that work, Ofili depicted Mary with African features, and attached a clump of elephant dung as well as photographs of female genitalia to his work. The Mayor termed Ofili's painting "sick" and "disgusting." He insisted that a city-supported museum had no right to display the exhibit.

Could the mayor prohibit the work from appearing in the show?

Why or why not? Explain your answer using the appropriate legal standard.

Part TWO

Basic Legal Principles

A complex, modern economy cannot function well without the private market, often called the *free market*. This market, which is guided by the "invisible hand" of competition, requires the rules of a legal system to achieve the maximum conditions for production and distribution. Part Two introduces the principal areas of law that set the rules for the private market.

Chapter 7 introduces you to the concept of property. It explains how ownership is acquired and details different common applications of ownership. Chapter 7 broadly defines "property" to include the ownership of security interests and describes the rules for mortgages and secured transactions. The chapter concludes by describing limitations on property that promote the common good.

Contracts are the binding agreements under which owners buy and sell goods and services. Chapter 8 examines contract terminology and the rules of contract formation. It discusses common mistakes that may result in unenforceable contracts. Chapter 9 covers the performance of contracts and remedies for their breach. It concludes with a discussion of third-party contract rights.

Torts are legal wrongs other than breaches of contract. In business, the law of torts sets boundaries for how business owners and managers can use what they own in the private market by defining when that use wrongfully injures

others. Chapter 10 discusses these concepts and also provides liability rules of "damages" or compensation for wrongful injuries.

Chapter 11 examines the important application of the exclusionary right of property in the areas of trade secrets, patents, trademarks, and copyrights. The nations that lead the world in producing new products and services all have strong protection of intellectual property. Chapter 11 explores the incentive goal of intellectual property rights and describes the rules for gaining protection in each of its forms.

Chapter 12 considers business at an international level. It looks at the sources of international law, the various methods of transacting business internationally, different types of risks involved in international trade, and how businesses resolve disputes at the international level. Note that the concepts of property and the rule-based exchange of privately owned resources are almost as important internationally as they are nationally.

Tort law and criminal law have much in common, and torts are also often (but not always) crimes. But tort law mostly concerns private enforcement of compensation for behavior that injures what belongs to others, whereas criminal law involves the government's punishment of wrongful acts through fines and/or imprisonment. Chapter 13 examines criminal law issues relevant to business and addresses constitutional issues of criminal law like search and seizure, the protection against self-incrimination, and the famous "Miranda rights." It focuses on various specific business-related crimes such as endangering workers, obstruction of justice, Internet crime, and, particularly, fraud.

This section concludes with Chapter 14 on business organizations. This chapter explains the laws that set boundaries within which private owners can join their resources into business organizations called *corporations, partnerships, limited liability companies,* and *limited liability partnerships.* These organizations are the driving force behind modern business production. •

rights," and say that if you have "property," you have the right to *possess* some resource, to *control* it, *to use* it in various ways, to *transfer* it, to *gain income* from it, and so forth. Rather than regarding property as a bundle of rights, we regard it as a single right—the right to exclude. If you can legally exclude others from some resource, whether it is a physical resource or various uses of something physical, you have a private property in that resource. The legal system will protect you and allow you to exclude others from interfering with that resource.

Exactly what resources can or cannot be the objects of property protection is very important in society. For instance, in every state you can own a piece of land, but in most states, you cannot own the use of that land to grow marijuana or own the marijuana that you grow on the land. Those are not private resources that are protected by the exclusive legal fence of property. Likewise, under federal law, you cannot own as a resource bald eagle feathers for sale. The same thing is true of prescription drugs, which you cannot sell or even give away so that another person will have property in them. Which resources society protects by the private property fence are determined in our legal system by tradition, decisions of courts, legislation, and regulation. In our legal system, many resources can be privately owned, and property is the foundation of the "free" market (see Sidebar 7.1), but be very clear that people cannot privately own every resource, especially not every resource of use.

sidebar 7.1

Property as the Foundation of the Private Market

People are often very sloppy in the way they use words. For instance, we talk about the "free" market when what we really mean is the "private" market—that is, *the private property market*. What we call the free market is really a market in the resources people privately own that others want and need. Economists know that we can have a market in things we do not own, but we would not want to live in a system where society did not legally define and protect private property in the resources that people want and need. In a market system without private property, the transfer of goods and services would be way too costly, since everyone could take what everyone else held. Each person would have to protect what he or she held all the time to keep it from being taken by others.

We often do not think about the importance of our legal system, but in parts of the world that are poor, there is inadequate enforcement of the law establishing private property. The market is "free," but it does not produce goods and services nearly so well as a system where the law enforces private property fences adequately. People in truly free markets have to spend most of their time guarding what they possess and have very little time to produce more than they can consume and to transfer it to others, which is what business is all about. Business is truly based on law, the law of private property, and the modern private market arises out of which resources society legally protects by the private property fence.

Property law does not function well when it is not adequately enforced. Honest police are needed to deter robbery and theft. Impartial courts are required to settle disputes over who owns what and whether X has wrongfully injured Y's resources. Property becomes not just an exclusionary right but also an entire system, and it is upon this property system of law that business depends.

This chapter explores the benefits of the property system and many of the rules that apply the property fence to different kinds of resources. It concludes with an examination of how various principles of property protect the common good. As you read the chapter, you should note that the various rules you study are not themselves "property," which is the principle of the legally exclusive private fence. The rules you study simply describe different ways of applying the fence. You should finish this chapter with a deeper knowledge of the central significance of property law to business. Quite simply, property is the necessary foundation for private enterprise and the market in the modern nation.

Rationale for the Property System

Arguably, the most significant issue for any society is how it orders the relationships among people concerning limited and valued resources, resources needed to survive and flourish. As long as people need or want more resources than they have available to them, society will order how people relate to each other in acquiring and possessing these resources. Such resources include land, food, raw materials, manufactured products, and even some types of information. Importantly, limited resources also include useful applications of the physical world and the human effort necessary for these applications. In other words, limited resources include the uses of physical raw materials and of yourself.

THE PROBLEM OF LIMITED RESOURCES

In Western political theory, the state comes into being in response to the problem of limited resources. Through law, the state establishes a framework for handling the problem. At least two basic legal frameworks exist. In one framework the state itself, represented by a ruler or legislature, makes the major decisions about the production and distribution of resources. The state takes ownership of resources or acquires them through taxation. It also may direct people in how, when, and where to work, thus assuming rights over the resources people have in themselves, their efforts, and talents. Distribution of resources occurs through state planning.

Communism is one system providing such a framework. The state requires that its citizens produce according to their abilities and share according to the needs of everyone else. The communist state expects people to want to do this, but it legally coerces them when necessary.

A second legal framework that orders how people relate to each other concerning scarce resources is private property. Private property, which we will just call "property," is a system of law under which the state recognizes and enforces an individual's rights to acquire, possess, use, and transfer scarce resources. (As for property other than private property, see Sidebar 7.2) In the property system, the state does not plan what people should have nor does it acquire and redistribute resources to them. Rather, the people themselves determine how resources are distributed through voluntary exchange, usually for money that they use to acquire other resources they need or want. The role of the state is to recognize legally when people have exclusive property rights in scarce resources and to allow them to enforce their rights through legal institutions like courts.

sidebar 7.2

The Three Faces of Property

Legal scholars divide the word "property" into three main usages: private, public, and common. *Private property* protects private persons and allows them to exclude others, including in most instances the state, from interfering with resources that are acquired without force, theft, or fraud. *Public property* refers to the state's right under various circumstances to exclude people from state monuments, buildings, equipment, land, and other public resources.

Common property has two meanings. First, it refers to the right we all have to common resources like the air,

rivers, or oceans. However, this meaning is appropriate only to the extent we can legally exclude others from interfering with our usage of these resources, for example, as when anyone who uses a river can sue to prevent or stop its illegal pollution. Second, "common property" sometimes refers to the private ownership by two or more people of a specific resource such as a piece of land.

For studying the legal and regulatory environment of business, private property is most important. It provides the foundation for the conduct of the modern market, and it is often just called "property."

All nations recognize some applications of private property. Even the most communist society may allow individuals some right as to how they use their productive efforts, and it usually allows them exclusive control over limited personal possessions and food consumption. On the other hand, societies founded on private property law always have legal limitations on how owners can use their resources, prohibiting harm to others and recognizing both some state taxation and regulation over property. The difference in the two frameworks is a matter of degree, and most societies have mixed frameworks for dealing with the reality of limited resources.

However, if the goal of society is to produce more of what people need and want (i.e., to increase the total amount of limited resources), one of the legal frameworks is superior to the other. The available evidence suggests that a property system produces more for a society than a state planning system. And if "freedom" is measured as individual autonomy and the absence of state coercion, then a property system also makes people more free.

For the property system to function most effectively in promoting prosperity, it should be applied according to the rule of law, which means it should be applied generally and equally to everyone. All members of society must have an equal guarantee of exclusive rights to their resources. The following section discusses more specifically how property promotes prosperity.

What does it mean to say that all nations recognize private property?

PROPERTY AND PROSPERITY

Property is central to the legal environment of business. It is also central to society's achievement of prosperity. In fact, property creates some of the maximum conditions known for producing and sustaining prosperity. Since property refers to a particular system of laws, rather than to useful resources, it is fair to conclude that certain laws are a major contributing factor to prosperity. Let us examine how property helps generate prosperity.

First, property powerfully promotes *incentive*. By allowing people to keep and benefit from what they produce, property motivates effort in a

Private property establishes maximum conditions for wealth creation through promoting incentive.

way that Chapter 1 suggested is very natural to human beings. Whether the activity is growing crops, manufacturing cars, or starting a new business, people will generally expend more effort when they have a protected property in what they produce than when they do not. Likewise, they are willing to produce more when they do not have to spend much of their time defending their homes or other acquisitions from those who may desire to take them. Under conditions where others are likely to take through force, theft, fraud, or even government mandate what people have or produce, there comes a point at which people will simply not work as hard, take as many risks, nor innovate as much. We may debate where that point is (e.g., how much people can be taxed before they slow their efforts), but the fact that property and incentive bear a direct relationship seems beyond debate.

Next, property helps generate prosperity by establishing the conditions necessary for *capital formation,* which refers to that quality of resources that produces new or different resources. For example, property enables people to borrow money at reasonable cost. In the United States most entrepreneurs start businesses by capitalizing the resource they have in their houses. They borrow money, and in a **mortgage** agreement put up their houses to secure the loans. (See the subsequent discussion of security interests in property.)

> Private property also promotes capital formation.

Lenders are willing to loan money at affordable rates primarily because property law guarantees (1) that a borrower's house is on an identifiable piece of land recognized by the state, (2) that the state recognizes a borrower's claim to the house, and (3) that the state permits lenders to enforce the mortgage agreement through the courts and sell a borrower's house to satisfy the loan if the borrower fails to repay it. The law of property enables entrepreneurs to change the form of their resources from houses to money, so they can start a business. This type of capital formation may seem curiously obvious to business students

sidebar 7.3

The Mystery of Capital

In the book *The Mystery of Capital,* Peruvian economist Hernando de Soto asserts that the reason "why capitalism triumphs in the West but fails everywhere else" is because of the secure system of property law that exists in Western nations. Not new technology, hard work, a superior culture, better management techniques, nor "exploitation" account principally for prosperity in the West, but rather the willingness of lenders in an adequate property system to risk their money to entrepreneurs with business ideas. De Soto's research team estimates that in less-developed countries there exists $9 trillion of "dead capital"—resources that

people possess which they cannot capitalize because the laws in their countries do not adequately guarantee property in these resources, and affordable collateral-secured loans are unavailable. Without the legal recognition of property, many resources may also be difficult to sell since a buyer cannot be sure that the state will recognize and protect a seller's right to transfer the resources. This problem is especially acute with the sale of land and buildings. The lack of an adequate property law system may not account totally for poverty in less-developed countries, but it is arguably the most important contributing factor.

in the United States. However, as Sidebar 7.3 discusses, it is virtually unavailable in the poorer nations of the world due to the absence of adequate property law.

Of course, the relationship of capital formation to property law means more than just mortgages or other collateral-secured loans. Large-scale businesses are capitalized by investors who buy ownership shares. For instance, corporations capitalize by selling stock shares, which are legally recognized property interests in a corporation. This method of capitalization is feasible only because the law recognizes stockholders' property interests in corporations (see Chapter 14). Likewise, securities markets (i.e., markets for stocks, bonds, and other ownership interests in businesses) are not possible without law enforcing the property interests in what these markets sell. Securities markets are vital to capital formation and prosperity in modern nations. Both corporate stock shares and securities markets enable businesses to change a property interest in future profit potential into the money necessary for business operation.

A final contribution property makes to prosperity is to make resources easily divisible. *Divisibility* also relates to capital formation and refers to how property permits resources to be broken into parts and used in many ways while the owner still retains a property interest in each part. Under property law, an owner of a single piece of land can sell part of it outright (change it into money), sell another part of it on credit and hold a mortgage to ensure payment, lease part of it to tenants who pay rent, incorporate part of it and sell shares to investors, and secure a loan against part of it in order to start an Internet business. In each of these transactions regarding the single piece of land, the owner retains identifiable and protected property interests. Each transaction is made practically possible because the law of property enables resources to be subdivided as an owner may find advantageous.

This feature of property facilitates the development of resources, which creates new wealth and causes prosperity. The next section further elaborates the divisibility of property.

Defining Property in the Legal System

LO 7-2

The preceding section asserted that the easy divisibility of property contributes to prosperity, and it gave several examples of how property can be divided. This section introduces the two basic legal divisions of property: real property and personal property. It describes how tangible property is defined in physical world and how interests in property are delineated with respect to other people.

TWO BASIC DIVISIONS OF PROPERTY

Real property law applies ownership to land and interests in land such as mining rights or leases (figure 7.1). Because of the historical importance of land, real property rules are very formal. As Chapter 8 on contracts discusses, agreements transferring interests in land ownership should be written, and many special rules apply to the registration and taxation of land ownership. Land ownership is also known as *real estate* or *realty*.

Real property law applies to land and interests in land. All other resources are protected by **personal property** law.

Figure 7.1 *Divisions of property.*

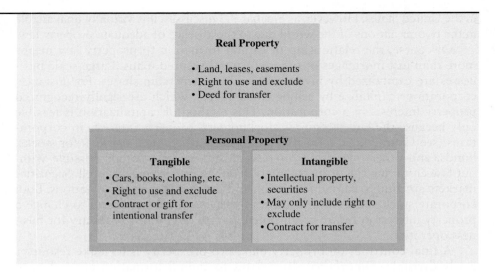

Personal property applies to movable resources, those things that people do not annex to the land. The law divides personal property into rules applying to tangible and intangible resources. **Tangible property** applies to things one can touch, that is, to physical things. Computers, cars, and carrots are such touchable things. The sale of tangible things, also known as "goods," is controlled by the Uniform Commercial Code, a type of contract law explained in Chapter 8. Intangible property applies to nonphysical things, particularly various types of valuable information. Intellectual property—patents, copyrights, trademarks and trade secrets—is an important form of intangible property. The rules relating to intellectual property are discussed in Chapter 11. Securities are another important form of intangible property, and they are discussed in Chapter 17. Real property rules and personal property rules are often different, as are rules applying personal property to tangible or intangible things.

PROPERTY BOUNDARIES IN THE PHYSICAL WORLD

We think of physical property as a three-dimensional object that can be possessed and protected. In the legal system, it is important to define exactly what the boundaries of this three-dimensional object are so that we know when another interferes with the property owner's rights. For example, if we determine that you own a field that extends to the edge of a public road, someone who drives onto your field from that road without permission has committed a *trespass* (a tort explained in more detail in Chapter 10). If the federal government claims part of your field for military equipment storage, it has exercised its *eminent domain* powers (explained in more detail in Chapter 6) and owes just compensation. If someone steals a tractor that you have parked on your field (or anywhere else), they have committed the tort of *conversion* (Chapter 10) and the crime of *larceny* (Chapter 13). To enforce your rights against any of these wrongdoers, we must first know what you own. As you read on, keep in mind that, as described in Sidebar 7.4, the task of defining intangible property can present even more complications.

sidebar 7.4

Additional Complexity in Defining Intangible Property

Because the same issues regarding interference (infringement) exist with intangible property, the law must define the boundaries of those rights as well. In the case of intellectual property and securities, the law first sets forth the rights associated with ownership. For example, the owner of a copyright in a song possesses the right to exclude others from copying the author's original expression in that song. Second, the law provides a structure for identifying the specific property actually controlled by the intangible property owner. For example, a patent owner has rights over an invention that is specifically defined in the patent claims. The patent is infringed if someone makes, uses, or sells something that replicates the invention in the claims.

One aspect of some intangible rights that can be more complex than tangible property is the tendency for society (the courts and the legislature) to revise the rules for what can be owned. That creates a measure of uncertainty that does not exist in tangible property. Cases like *Coastal Oil v. Garza*, described in Case 7.1, in which land ownership is reinterpreted, are relatively rare. But, as Chapter 11 details cases reinterpreting intellectual property subject matter have been quite frequent.

The physical dimensions of tangible personal property are generally easy to define. We understand what it means to own a car or a smartphone and realize immediately when someone interferes with it. Real property is more complex. Because land is not fully contained when owned, or transported when sold, law rather than intuition must define the physical boundaries. States can differ in their specific land rules, but the following are general concepts that are applicable in most jurisdictions.

Defining Land At the outset, it is important to understand that land ownership consists of more than the surface of the property. In English common law, as famously articulated by Lord Coke more than 300 years ago, ownership in land was understood to extend from the surface to the heavens and back down to the center of the earth. When the practical use of land was limited to near the surface, it was possible to present ownership in such grand terms without impacting societal interests. However, with the advent of aircraft as well as subsurface drilling for minerals, oil, gas, and water, it has become necessary to place reasonable limits on a landowner's rights.

Air Rights The owner of real property also possesses the air above the land to the extent that the owner can occupy or use it in connection with the land. This means that although you cannot exclude a jetliner from flying overhead, you can prevent a neighbor's deck or tree from extending over the surface of your land. Importantly, you do not need to touch the surface of the land to infringe or trespass on another's air rights. It may be possible to sell your air rights to another for development. Additionally, some municipalities allow landowners to forego development on their own land and transfer the air development right to for use on another piece of property. New York City has a well-established system for trading or transferring air development rights.[1]

[1] New York State, *Transfer of Development Rights*, James A. Coon Local Govt. Technical Series (Rev. 2010).

Subsurface Rights A landowner may also owns the liquids, gases and minerals beneath the land. Like air rights, an owner may be able to separate subsurface rights and sell them. An energy company could have the right to extract coal under the land while allowing another owner the right to occupy the surface. In many cases, the subsurface owner has the right to utilize some part of the surface of the land to extract minerals.

Subsurface rights have additional complications in that many below-ground substances are not stationary. Liquids, like oil and water, and gases, like natural gas, can flow from one parcel to another. Should the owner of an adjacent property be permitted to drill and extract fluids and gasses that flow from underneath another's property? States that apply the so-called rule of capture say yes. The strict rule of capture may be limited by additional rules that preserve the rights of adjoining owners.

A current topic of interest in subsurface rights involves the extraction of natural gas through a process called hydraulic fracturing. Is such gas extraction—which involves pumping water and solids (proppants) into the ground under high pressure to fracture and release trapped gas—the same as capturing a natural flow? The court in Case 7.1 was compelled to address that very question.

 case **7.1**

COASTAL OIL & GAS CORP. v. GARZA ENERGY TRUST ET AL.
268 S.W.3d 1 (Tex. 2008)

Collective owners of a 748-acre tract of land in Texas (referred to below as Salinas) sued Coastal Oil for infringing on their property rights by removing natural gas from beneath their land, which was known as Share 13. Although Salinas already leased Share 13 gas to Coastal, Salinas alleged that Coastal was not extracting the gas fast enough. Rather, they argued that Coastal was drilling on neighboring land that it owned and extracting gas from beneath Share 13 through hydraulic fracturing. Salinas claimed that Coastal was drilling on the neighboring land instead of Salinas's land to avoid paying Salinas a royalty on the gas. According to Salinas, this constituted a trespass because it removed gas that would otherwise remain after Coastal's lease of Salinas's land ended. The court had to determine whether Coastal's acts were protected by the "rule of capture."

NATHAN L. HECHT.: We begin with Salinas's contention that the incursion of hydraulic fracturing fluid and proppants into another's land two miles below the

surface constitutes a trespass for which the minerals owner can recover damages equal to the value of the royalty on the gas thereby drained from the land. . . .

Had Coastal caused something like proppants to be deposited on the surface of Share 13, it would be liable for trespass, and from the ancient common law maxim that land ownership extends to the sky above and the earth's center below, one might extrapolate that the same rule should apply two miles below the surface. But that maxim—*cujus est solum ejus est usque ad coelum et ad inferos*—"has no place in the modern world." Wheeling an airplane across the surface of one's property without permission is a trespass; flying the plane through the airspace two miles above the property is not. Lord Coke, who pronounced the maxim, did not consider the possibility of airplanes. But neither did he imagine oil wells. The law of trespass need no more be the same two miles below the surface than two miles above.

We have not previously decided whether subsurface fracing can give rise to an action for trespass. . . .

We need not decide the broader issue here. In this case, actionable trespass requires injury, and Salinas's only claim of injury—that Coastal's fracing made it possible for gas to flow from beneath Share 13 to the Share 12 wells—is precluded by the rule of capture. That rule gives a mineral rights owner title to the oil and gas produced from a lawful well bottomed on the property, even if the oil and gas flowed to the well from beneath another owner's tract. The rule of capture is a cornerstone of the oil and gas industry and is fundamental both to property rights and to state regulation. Salinas does not claim that the Coastal Fee No. 1 violates any statute or regulation. Thus, the gas he claims to have lost simply does not belong to him. He does not claim that the hydraulic fracturing operation damaged his wells or the Vicksburg T formation beneath his property. In sum, Salinas does not claim damages that are recoverable.

Salinas argues that the rule of capture does not apply because hydraulic fracturing is unnatural. The point of this argument is not clear. If by "unnatural" Salinas means due to human intervention, the simple answer is that such activity is the very basis for the rule, not a reason to suspend its application. Nothing is more unnatural in that sense than the drilling of wells, without which there would be no need for the rule at all. If by "unnatural" Salinas means unusual, the facts are that hydraulic fracturing has long been commonplace throughout the industry and is necessary for commercial production in the Vicksburg T and many other formations. And if by "unnatural" Salinas means unfair, the law affords him ample relief. He may use hydraulic fracturing to stimulate production from his own wells and drain the gas to his own property—which his operator, Coastal, has successfully done already—and he may sue Coastal for not doing so sooner—which he has also done, in this case, though unsuccessfully, as it now turns out.

Salinas argues that stimulating production through hydraulic fracturing that extends beyond one's property is no different from drilling a deviated or slant well—a well that departs from the vertical significantly—bottomed on another's property, which is unlawful. Both produce oil and gas situated beneath another's property. But the rule of capture determines title to gas that drains from property owned by one person onto property owned by another. It says nothing about the ownership of gas that has remained in place. The gas produced through a deviated well does not migrate to the wellbore from another's property; it is already on another's property. The rule of capture is justified because a landowner can protect himself from drainage by drilling his own well, thereby avoiding the uncertainties of determining how gas is migrating through a reservoir. It is a rule of expedience. One cannot protect against drainage from a deviated well by drilling his own well; the deviated well will continue to produce his gas. Nor is there any uncertainty that a deviated well is producing another owner's gas. The justifications for the rule of capture do not support applying the rule to a deviated well.

We are not persuaded by Salinas's arguments. Rather, we find four reasons not to change the rule of capture to allow one property owner to sue another for oil and gas drained by hydraulic fracturing that extends beyond lease lines.

First, the law already affords the owner who claims drainage full recourse. This is the justification for the rule of capture, and it applies regardless of whether the drainage is due to fracing. If the drained owner has no well, he can drill one to offset drainage from his property. If the minerals are leased and the lessee has not drilled a well, the owner can sue the lessee for violation of the implied covenant in the lease to protect against drainage. If an offset well will not adequately protect against drainage, the owner (or his operator) may offer to pool, and if the offer is rejected, he may apply to the [regulatory] Commission for forced pooling. . . .

Second, allowing recovery for the value of gas drained by hydraulic fracturing usurps to courts and juries the lawful and preferable authority of the [regulatory] Commission to regulate oil and gas production. Such recovery assumes that the gas belongs to the owner of the minerals in the drained property, contrary to the rule of capture. While a mineral rights owner has a real interest in oil and gas in place, "this right does not extend to *specific* oil and gas beneath the property"; ownership must be "considered in connection with the law of capture, which is recognized as a property right" as well. The minerals owner is entitled, not to the molecules actually residing below the surface, but to "a fair chance to recover the oil and gas in or under his land, *or* their equivalents in kind." . . .

Third, determining the value of oil and gas drained by hydraulic fracturing is the kind of issue the litigation process is least equipped to handle. One difficulty is that the material facts are hidden below miles of rock, making it difficult to ascertain what might have happened. Such difficulty in proof is one of the justifications for the rule of capture. But there is an even greater difficulty with litigating recovery for drainage resulting from fracing, and it is that trial judges and juries cannot take into account social policies, industry operations, and the greater good which are all tremendously important in deciding whether fracing should or should not be against the law. While this Court may

[continued]

consider such matters in fashioning the common law, we should not alter the rule of capture on which an industry and its regulation have relied for decades to create new and uncertain possibilities for liability with no more evidence of necessity and appropriateness than this case presents. . . .

Fourth, the law of capture should not be changed to apply differently to hydraulic fracturing because no one in the industry appears to want or need the change. . . .

Accordingly, we hold that damages for drainage by hydraulic fracturing are precluded by the rule of capture. It should go without saying that the rule of capture cannot be used to shield misconduct that is illegal, malicious, reckless, or intended to harm another without commercial justification, should such a case ever arise. But that certainly did not occur in this case, and no instance of it has been cited to us.

KEY POINTS

- The court refused to hold Coastal liable for a technical trespass under Salinas's land. It determined that the nature of subsurface rights required a showing of some injury.
- Salinas leased the right to drill on Share 13. The court argued that any losses from gas captured from neighboring land could be addressed by increased drilling on one's own land.

Fixtures on Land A particular kind of interest in land is the **fixture**. A fixture is an object of personal property that has become an object of real property (1) by physical annexation (attachment) to the land or its buildings or (2) because its use has become closely associated with the use to which the land is put. Unless sellers and buyers agree differently when they sell land, the fixtures go with the land to the buyers. Manufacturing equipment is a fixture when it is sold along with a manufacturing plant. Carpeting is a fixture if it is nailed down or glued to the floor. Not being attached to the land, rugs are usually not fixtures. To prevent misunderstandings in land sales, sellers and buyers should identify which things are fixtures and stay with the buyers and which things remain protected under personal property and go with the sellers.

LO 7-3

Interests in Property with Respect to Others and Time

TYPES OF OWNERSHIP

The law allows division of resource ownership into various types, or degrees. This division is another indication of how sensitive property law is in allowing owners to do exactly what they need and want with their resources: Not all states still use the common law terms that follow, but all states recognize the various aspects of ownership that the terms represent. *These terms usually apply to land ownership, but ownership of movable and intangible things can be held practically in the same way.*

Fee simple.

The bundle of rights and powers of land ownership are called an **estate. Fee simple** represents the maximum estate allowed under law, the owner having the fullest legal rights and powers to possess, use, and transfer the land. The fee simple *absolute* estate has no limitations or conditions attached. The fee simple *defeasible* may have a condition attached to its conveyance (transfer). For example, a seller may convey land to a buyer "as long as it is used for agricultural purposes." If the new owner (buyer) develops the land for other than agricultural purposes, the ownership goes back to the original owner (seller).

Life estate.

A **life estate** grants an ownership in land for the lifetime of a specified person. "To Brodie Davis for her life" grants such an estate. Upon Brodie Davis's death the land reverts to the original grantor who is said to keep a *reversion* interest in the land. If the land goes to someone other than the grantor upon Brodie Davis's death, that person has a *remainder* interest. Reversion and remainder property interests are also called *future* interests as opposed to the life estate, which is a *present* interest. Subject to any attached conditions, all of these estates can be capitalized or transferred. For example, it is possible to borrow upon or sell a future interest.

> Having a **life estate** means that the property fence only protects your interest in something for your lifetime.

Leasehold estate.

A **leasehold estate** is simply the property right granted to tenants by a landlord. Although it is not common to think of tenants as "owners," they do in a meaningful way have an estate or property. Tenants have a qualified possession, use, and transfer of the land, qualified in that they cannot *waste* the land, which means do something that substantially reduces the value of the land. For an apartment tenant to rip up carpeting and knock holes in the walls would be a waste of the interest in the land. The landlord could terminate the lease and sue the tenant.

> When you lease an apartment for a year, what is it that you own?

Unless prohibited by the lease, the rights owned by tenants can be capitalized by transfer to someone else. Thus, unless prohibited, a tenant who is paying $3,000 per month under a two-year lease of an office can sell the balance of time remaining on the lease at $5,000 per month. Many leases, however, do require that a tenant obtain approval from a landlord, or even of the other tenants, before transferring lease rights.

A landlord may lease land for a *definite duration* of time like two years, or for an *indefinite duration* with rent payable at periodic intervals like monthly, or simply *at will*, which means "for as long as both shall agree." State law generally specifies that the landlord and tenant must give each other written notice of 30 days or 60 days in order to terminate a lease that does not run for a definite duration.

Concurrent ownership.

Both personal and real property interests can have concurrent owners. That is, more than one person can own the same thing. The ownership is undivided, meaning that no concurrent owner owns a specific piece of the resources that are owned. The shareholders of a corporation are concurrent owners as are the partners of a partnership. In fact, concurrent ownership greatly facilitates almost all forms of modern private enterprise.

The surviving tenant in a joint tenancy with right of survivorship becomes the sole owner of the entire resource, usually interests in land.

Other forms of concurrent ownership include the **joint tenancy** and the **tenancy in common.** In both of these forms of ownership, the property interest is undivided, but the tenants in common can own different shares of the resource (e.g., two-thirds and one-third), whereas the joint tenants must have equal ownership shares (e.g., one-half and one-half). On the other hand, joint tenants, but not tenants in common, can have the *right of survivorship*. This right means that if one of the joint tenants dies, the remaining tenant becomes the sole owner of the entire resource. To create a joint tenancy requires special words, such as "convey to X and Y as joint tenants, and not as tenants in common, together with the right of survivorship."

The owners themselves, or the creditors, of a joint tenancy or tenancy in common can usually force the separation of these concurrent ownerships under the doctrine of *partition*.

Specialty Applications of Property

The following sections discuss specialty applications of property. Generally, the private legal fence of property allows an owner to exclude others from interfering with (1) the possession of an object or resource, (2) the transfer of the object or interest by gift or through exchange with other owners, and (3) all uses of the object that do not harm other owners in what belongs to them. However, a number of specialty applications are quite narrow and one or more of the three general property characteristics may be lacking. In fact, many scholars do not recognize some of the specialty applications discussed here to apply to property at all. However, we note that all of these specialty applications involve some object or interest that is legally exclusive in some important fashion, leading us to believe these applications deserve the name "property."

EASEMENTS

An **easement** is often a right to cross over land.

An **easement** places a particular use of land behind the exclusive legal fence. Usually, this use involves the right of passage across the land, for example, when a timbering company has purchased the right to bring its harvest of trees out across an owner's land. Once the easement has been acquired, the timbering company can exclude others, especially the titleholder of the land, from interfering with passage of its trucks across the land. An easement can also be reserved in a deed, for example, when Martina sells a piece of her land to George and the deed reserves an easement for George to cross over Martina's remaining land. Easements can also involve such uses as the laying of water pipes or the stringing of power wires across land.

An easement can be acquired in various ways. For instance, it can be bought directly from a titleholder, or reserved in a deed as part of the purchase and sale of land. At common law owners of land also had a *natural easement* (also called easement by necessity) to get from their land to the nearest public road. A *negative easement* means that an adjoining landowner cannot do anything that would cause your land to cave in or collapse, such as digging a ditch that would cause the land on your side to collapse. Finally, an *easement by prescription* arises when one person has used another's land, such as by crossing it openly, wrongfully, and continuously for a period of years (frequently 20), and once an easement by prescription arises, a title-holder of the land can no longer prevent a person from continuing to use the land by crossing it. The titleholder cannot now use the land in such a way to prevent the easement holder from crossing it, and the easement holder can legally exclude a titleholder from trying to prevent passage.

Statutes in many states set standards for easements and their acquisition. The easements mentioned here merely give you a general idea about these specialty applications of property.

BAILMENTS

In many common situations, an owner puts an object protected by personal property into the intentional possession of another person with the under-standing that the other person must return the object at some point or other-wise dispose of it. This property arrangement is known as a **bailment,** with the owner known as the **bailor** and the possessor of the object known as the **bailee.** Bailments arise when you store something in a warehouse, rent furni-ture from the rental store, lease a piece of equipment, loan your lawnmower to a neighbor, or store your car in a friend's garage while you are on vacation. Can you figure out in each instance who is the bailor and who is the bailee? Bailments fall into three categories:

- For the sole benefit of the bailor.
- For the sole benefit of the bailee.
- For the mutual benefit of both parties.

Can you explain the three different types of bailments?

Think about the examples mentioned above. Do you understand that storing your car in a friend's garage while you are on vacation is a bailment for the sole benefit of the bailor and that the furniture and equipment rentals are mutual benefit bailments? The loan of your mower to your neighbor to mow the grass is a bailment for the sole benefit of the bailee. Consider the following situation: You go to a business meeting at a hotel, removing your expensive leather coat, and hanging it on a hanger in a small room provided by the hotel. The coat turns up missing. Is the hotel responsible as a bailee? Would the situation have been different if the hotel had someone taking care of coats? The answers depend on whether or not the hotel has taken *inten-tional* possession of the coat, and it is likely that merely by providing a coat hanger, the hotel is not taking intentional possession of the coat. But if a hotel employee hangs up the coat for you, the hotel becomes a bailee.

In the business world, most bailments are of mutual benefit to both par-ties. Although the bailee has an absolute duty to return the object to the bailor (or to dispose of it as the bailor directs), and becomes liable to the bailor for failing to do so correctly, an issue often arises when something happens to the object while it is in the bailee's possession and control. What if someone steals it? What if a natural disaster, called "an act of God," destroys it, or it is damaged in an accident? To understand the potential liability from these events, you have to understand the legal duty the bailee is under. In a mutual benefit bailment, such as a rental arrangement, the bailee is under a duty to use "reasonable care" in taking care of the object in possession, but if an Act of God destroys or damages the object, the bailee is not likely liable to the bailor. However, see Sidebar 7.5.

sidebar 7.5

Follow Instructions or Else

Roger, a graduate student, leases a car from Acme Car Dealership in Texas. The lease contract contains a clause that limits Roger's driving to the United States. However, Roger drives the car over the border down to Mexico City where an earthquake causes a building to collapse on the car after Roger parks it on the street. Although in mutual benefit bailments such as this one, the bailee is not often responsible to the bailor for acts of God, in this instance by using a car in a way specifically prohibited by the bailor, Roger becomes liable to the car dealership in spite of the fact his fault did not cause the damage to the car. When a bailee uses an object in a way not authorized or prohibited by the bailor, the bailee becomes absolutely liable as an "insurer" for anything that happens to it.

Another example of this liability might arise when a bailee returns an object improperly. For example, imagine a woman purchases expensive jewelry on approval from a jewelry store promising the manager to return the jewelry to him personally if she did not wish to keep it. Several days later there is a knock on her door and a man dressed in a store uniform asks if she wishes to return the jewelry. The woman returns the jewelry to the man, who turns out to be a thief in a stolen uniform. The store will likely be able to recover the price from the woman because the bailee became absolutely liable for loss when she returned the jewelry improperly.

When your roommate borrows your car and returns it with a dent in it, the law makes your roommate liable unless she can prove she has met the duty of extremely high care.

In a bailment for the sole benefit of a bailor, the bailee owes only a slight duty of care while the object is in the bailee's possession, but in a bailment for the sole benefit of the bailee, such as where the bailee has borrowed the object, the bailee owes a very high duty of care, one that is greater than merely what is "reasonable." These duties of care become important when the parties are negotiating a settlement, or when a judge is instructing a jury about the bailee's responsibility to the bailor. Many times it may be difficult for a bailor who sues a bailee to prove why the object in the bailee's possession has been damaged and how the bailee has breached the duty of care. Therefore, the law presumes that the bailee has breached the duty of care when the bailee cannot return the object to the bailor in proper condition, placing the burden of proof on the bailee to prove that he or she has met the duty of care.

Case 7.2 illustrates the bailee's liability for failing to return some pieces of sculpture in the proper condition.

 ### case 7.2

SEMOON v. THE WOOSTER SCHOOL CORP.
2010 Conn. Super. LEXIS 1816

OZALIS, JUDGE: ... The plaintiff, Suk Semoon, commenced this action against the defendants, the Wooster School Corporation (the Wooster School) and the Wooster Community Art Center (WCAC). This case arises out of the alleged loan by the plaintiff of seven pieces of sculpture to the defendant WCAC which allegedly was controlled and operated by the defendant Wooster School.

The plaintiff has alleged . . . that the defendants Wooster School and WCAC in September 2001 willingly took possession of seven of the plaintiff's outdoor sculptures and displayed them in plain view on its campus. The plaintiff further alleges that when she asked for the return of the seven sculptures, she was advised that three were missing and one had been damaged. The plaintiff alleges that the defendants Wooster School and WCAC failed to redeliver all of the seven sculptures to her at her request . . . and are therefore liable for the full value of the missing/damaged sculptures. . . .

In order to prove a bailment, the plaintiff must prove that she delivered the seven sculptures to the defendants. In this action, there is no dispute as to this issue and in fact the parties stipulated that the seven sculptures were delivered to the defendant WCAC. It is also undisputed in this action that . . . the director of the defendant WCAC accepted the delivery of the sculptures and intended to and did use them as an outdoor sculpture garden to enhance the landscape of the defendants' facilities. It is clear, based on the evidence at trial, that the director had authority to accept the sculptures on behalf of the defendants. It is also undisputed that the plaintiff in 2006 asked for the return of all seven sculptures, but only three were fully returned. The court finds that a mutual benefit bailment did in fact exist between the parties as the loan of the sculptures benefited the defendants and the plaintiff as well, as she had a place to exhibit her artwork and contribute to the community.

"Once a bailment has been established and the bailee is unable to redeliver the subject of the bailment in an undamaged condition a presumption arises that the damage to or loss of the bailed property was the result of the bailee's negligence [failure to use reasonable care]." . . . "This presumption prevails unless and until the bailee proves the actual circumstances involved in the damaging of the property.

If these circumstances are proved, then the burden is upon the bailor [the plaintiff here who put her artwork in the hands of the defendants] to satisfy the court that the bailee's conduct in the matter constituted negligence. . . . The circumstances which a bailee must prove must be something more than those indicating the immediate cause of damage. The proof must go so far as to establish what, if any, human conduct materially contributed to that immediate cause. . . . The bailee must prove something more if he is to overcome the presumption. The bailee must prove the actual circumstances connected with the origin of the damage, and these include the precautions taken to prevent the loss." "Whether the bailee has proved the actual circumstances of the loss and overcome the presumption of negligence in that the bailee has taken reasonable precautions under the circumstances is a question of fact for the trier [the judge]."

This court agrees with the plaintiff that the defendants . . . have put forth no evidence as to the actual circumstances surrounding the loss of sculptures one, two and three. Accordingly, the court finds that the presumption arises that the loss of sculptures one, two and three was due to the defendants' negligence. With respect to the destruction of sculpture seven, the defendants Wooster School and WCAC have put forth no evidence that it took any efforts, let alone reasonable efforts, to secure or protect this sculpture from being destroyed or damaged during construction. The court finds that the defendants' actions were woefully inadequate in protecting this sculpture from the construction that was occurring and that the loss that occurred was due to the defendants' negligence.

For the reasons set forth above, the court finds that the plaintiff has met her burden of proof as to the breach of bailment contract and judgment shall enter in favor of the plaintiff in the amount of $26,100.

KEY POINTS

- The court determines that the bailment is one of mutual benefit because both parties gained from the transaction. The school received the cultural enhancement of the sculpture, and the artist received the exposure.
- In a mutual benefit context, the bailee owes reasonable care to the bailor. A presumption arises against the bailee if the property is damaged in its care.

The bailor also has duties to the bailee. In a mutual benefit bailment, the bailor must pay the bailee for storing or otherwise keeping possession of something, such as when the bailee is a warehouse. According to the type of bailment, the bailor also warrants or guarantees that she has no knowledge of defects in the objects bailed or no knowledge of defects that could have been discovered through reasonable inspection. In a number of states, courts have made merchants in mutual benefit bailments liable for any defect in a bailed object that causes personal injury.

You should read the terms of a bailment contract very carefully.

Many states have laws that apply to particular kinds of bailments, such as those involving common carriers, warehouses, and innkeepers (hotels). In particular, these bailees are often able to limit their potential liability to bailors for damage to the bailed objects, for example, by inserting contractual terms that limit compensation to a certain value. Common carriers, which include airlines, railroads, and public trucking companies, carry packages for the public. Common carriers are also not responsible for acts of God or of public enemies, the acts of the bailor in failing to package properly, defects in the packaged object itself, or acts of the public authority (such as the stopping of a truck carrying produce at a state border because of concern about plant disease).

In legal terms, a bailee is usually not considered to have "property" regarding the bailed object. However, the bailee has both possession and control over the object and can exclude the rest of the world, including the bailee in some instances, from interfering with this possession and control. For this reason, we are treating bailments as a specialty application of property, although they are often a very narrow one.

LO 7-4   Acquiring Resources in a Property System

How do you come to own resources in a property system? In other words, how does the right of property to something attach to a specific person? Although you can acquire resources in many ways, including by force (called "robbery"), theft (various forms of stealing), and fraud (intentionally lying and harming others to get what belongs to them), there are only five basic legal ways to become an owner of something in a property system. As you read what follows, consider that **ownership** means the same thing as "property." Both terms refer to the legal right that makes resources exclusive, that makes resources "mine," instead of "yours," or "no one's."

ACQUIRING RESOURCES THROUGH EXCHANGE

The most common way of coming to have a property in something is through exchanging resources. For example, when you buy a car, or buy a company, you exchange one form of resources you own (money) for another form of resources (car or company). You are now the legal owner of the car or company. Resources have been switched but property (or ownership) remains. Likewise, when you exchange your services for a paycheck, you become the owner of the paycheck and the money it represents. The employer becomes the owner of your services and what they produce.

Contract rules control the way owners make agreements to exchange resources in the property-based legal system.

The rules under which people exchange resources in a property system are called the rules of **contract**. Contract rules are the subject of Chapters 8 and 9, but you should understand now that contract rules make agreements to exchange resources between owners legally binding and enforceable. In particular, the rules of contract make it possible for owners to commit legally to future exchange of resources. These rules also make it possible for one owner to sue another if agreements to exchange resources in the future are broken by one of the owners. Further, contract rules allow lawsuits against those who have not adequately performed their agreements. If owner A agrees to sell goods to owner B in 30 days and then does not deliver them, owner B may sue owner A for damages. Likewise, owner B may sue owner A if owner A does deliver the goods, but they turn out to be defective. In addition to damages, contract rules may specify other remedies for contract breach.

It is difficult to overemphasize the importance of contract rules in the property system. Professor Philip Nichols of the Wharton School asserts that observing legally enforceable contracts is the single most significant indicator that a country's economy is ready for international trade. If the right of property is the foundation for the modern private market, the rules of contract are perhaps the keystone of that foundation.

ACQUIRING RESOURCES THROUGH POSSESSION

Sometimes you can become an owner of something merely through possession, that is, by physically holding and controlling it. The **rule of first possession** is that the first person to reduce previously unowned things to possession becomes their owner. In Sylacauga, Alabama, a meteorite crashed through the roof of a rented house in 1954 and struck the tenant on the leg, the only recorded instance in history when a meteorite has struck a person. Initially, both the owner of the house and the tenant (owner of the lease) claimed the meteorite, but because the tenant was the first person to reduce it to possession, she acquired the right of property to it.

> The **rule of first possession** is that the first person to reduce previously unowned things to possession becomes their owner.

Similar to the rule of first possession, is the rule that when someone has *abandoned* what they own, the first person to reduce it to possession owns it. The law determines whether or not someone has abandoned what they previously owned by measuring *intent*, whether the previous owner intended to abandon something. The law measures intent by the circumstances of the situation. If it looks like someone meant to abandon something, we say they intended to do it. When it is not clear who is the first person to reduce previously unowned or abandoned resources to possession, lawsuits may follow. See Sidebar 7.6.

Lost Items   Things that are *lost* also can acquire a new owner through possession. The finder of a lost item becomes its owner by reducing it to possession and following a statutory procedure, which may require the finder to turn the item over to the police and to advertise it in a local paper for a period of time to allow the original owner to claim it. But at the end of the specified statutory period the finder becomes the new owner.

The law distinguishes things that have been lost from things that have simply been mislaid. Things that have been lost go to the first person who subsequently reduces them to possession, but things that have been *mislaid* go to the person who owns the premises where the item was mislaid. A $100 bill on the table in the library has been mislaid, but if it is on the floor it has been lost. The difference in the way the law treats these two situations is based on an assumption that the original owner will know where to come back and reclaim mislaid things.

> Can you distinguish between things that are lost and things that are merely mislaid?

sidebar 7.6

Barry Bonds' Home-Run Ball

When Barry Bonds blasted his record-setting 73rd home run ball into the stands of PacBell Park on October 7, 2001, ownership of the ball was abandoned. Unlike in football, where a ball that goes into the stands must be returned, Major League Baseball—the association of team owners—deliberately abandons the balls and allows fans to keep them. But who had the right of property in the record-setting ball—Alex Popov who initially appeared to catch it before a wild crowd of fans knocked him to the ground, or Patrick Hayashi who shortly afterward saw the ball rolling free, grabbed it, and stuck it in his pocket?

Popov sued Hayashi, arguing that he was the owner because he had caught and first possessed the ball, which had an estimated value of $1 million. After trial, Judge Kevin McCarthy recognized that the principle of first possession applied to the ball, but did Popov or Hayashi first possess it? The facts were not clear as to whether Popov caught or dropped the ball. The judge stated, "An award

of the ball to Mr. Popov would be unfair to Mr. Hayashi. It would be premised on the assumption that Mr. Popov would have caught the ball. That assumption is not supported by the facts. An award of the ball to Mr. Hayashi would unfairly penalize Mr. Popov. It would be based on the assumption that Mr. Popov would have dropped the ball. That conclusion is also unsupported by the facts."

With the facts unclear, Judge McCarthy ruled that it was fairest to divide the ownership of the ball. "The court therefore declares that both plaintiff and defendant have an equal and undivided interest in the ball. . . . In order to effectuate this ruling, the ball must be sold and the proceeds divided equally between the parties." Rather than appeal, Popov and Hayashi agreed they would sell the ball and divide the proceeds. For additional insight, you can read the court's decision at *Popov v. Hayashi*, No. 400545, 2002 WL 31833731 (Cal. Super. Ct. Dec. 18, 2002).

Adverse Possession   Another form of ownership through possession arises through **adverse possession.** Adverse possession gives you ownership of land (and it only applies to land) under state statute when the possession is as follows:

- Open and notorious. The possessor must occupy the land in such a way as to put the true owner of the land on notice.
- Actual and exclusive. The possessor must physically occupy the land. However, the building of a fence around the land or construction of a building on it constitutes physical occupation.
- Continuous. Possession must not be interrupted.
- Wrongful. The possessor must not have the owner's permission to be on the land, for example, under a lease.
- For a prescribed period of time. Most states specify an adverse possession of between 10 and 20 years before the possessor becomes the new owner.

Adverse possession encourages land use and prevents an absent owner from claiming rights many years down the road. The rule may be applied to a part of a person's property. For example, if a landowner builds a wall extending five feet over a neighbor's property, the landowner can eventually gain ownership over the five feet, but not the rest of the property. As described in Sidebar 7.7, adverse possession has even been proposed as a means for dealing with vacant, foreclosed properties.

Perhaps the most common way to destroy a claim of adverse possession is to sue for trespass. But the easiest way may be to simply give permission to occupy for a period of time.

sidebar 7.7

Curing Blight through Adverse Possession?

As a result of the financial crisis in 2008 and beyond, many homeowners fell behind in mortgage payments. Some abandoned their property or were foreclosed upon. The result has been many vacant homes in distressed areas where new buyers are scarce. Such homes reduce property values and create dangerous conditions. One solution may be to encourage individuals to occupy the homes and attempt to eventually gain ownership through adverse possession. The required period of possession would seem to be an impediment to this scheme. However, in areas in which the true owners seem uninterested in reclaiming the property, it may end up serving as a viable urban renewal mechanism.

Source: Catharine Skipp and Damien Cave, "At Legal Fringe, Empty Houses Go to the Needy," *New York Times*, November 8, 2010, p. A1.

The Homestead Act of 1862 illustrates the historical significance of ownership through possession. This act allowed those who lived on certain public land to obtain legal ownership of it by possessing it for five years and making certain improvements. Upward of a half million settlers possessed and then gained title to the 160-acre homesteads under the act.

In parts of the world today, governments are granting ownership of land to "squatters" who possess it without legal right. Studies show that this is one of the best ways to distribute land in poor nations. Squatters become owners and can then capitalize land by selling it or borrowing money and putting up the land as collateral.

Some have criticized the "squatter-to-owner" process because many of the new owners sell their land. However, the process enables poor squatters to raise money for the first time. It is also less violent than a situation where squatting alone occurs, and squatters may have to defend their possession by force. Further, it is more efficient than for the government to specify that the land cannot change ownership. In U.S. history there were numerous instances in which legal title was given to settlers who at first possessed land by squatting. Many of them, too, sold their land after receiving legal title to it.

> Peruvian economist Hernando de Soto believes that nations can strengthen their economies through the "squatter-to-owner" process.

ACQUIRING RESOURCES THROUGH CONFUSION

Ownership through **confusion** arises when *fungible* goods (i.e., goods that are identical) are mixed together. The common example involves grain in a silo when two or more batches of separately owned grain are mixed together. If the confusion occurs by honest mistake or agreement, the owners of the originally separate goods now own a proportional share of the confused goods. Careful records of who owned what grain must be kept since lacking evidence, a court in the case of dispute will assume that everyone claiming the confused mass owns an equal share. If a court determines that the confusion was intentionally wrongful, perhaps done by someone willfully attempting to defraud another, the court will grant ownership of the entire confused mass to the innocent party.

The doctrine of confusion also illustrates the importance of *boundaries* to the concept of property (see earlier discussion), and it explains one

> Be aware that disputes arise concerning not only boundary problems involving physical location but also boundaries of permissible uses of things.

determination of ownership when resource boundaries are not certain. Problems of where boundaries lie are common, however, to various types of resources. Boundaries to the ownership of the water in a creek that crosses your land may be measured by a certain volume of water per minute. Landowners upstream may legally not be able to divert that flow.

ACQUIRING RESOURCES THROUGH ACCESSION

When the owner of an old airplane engine has it restored and has an airplane built around it, the owner of the engine now owns the entire airplane through the doctrine of **accession,** which refers to something "added." Normally, this is not a problem, but suppose a thief steals the engine, repairs it, and builds it into an airplane. A court will likely grant ownership of the entire airplane to the engine's owner.

However, if the builder *accidentally* picked up someone else's engine and builds it into an airplane, a court will probably give ownership of the airplane to the builder, requiring only that the builder adequately compensate the engine's original owner. An exception gives ownership of the entire airplane to the engine's owner if the engine is substantially more valuable than the additions to it. The court may even require the engine's owner to pay for the valuable additions.

The law of accession also explains that when you apply your efforts or ingenuity to any raw materials you own and change their nature into finished products, you own the finished products. Generally, because you own your efforts, you own what they produce, whether it is an airplane, a paycheck (through exchange), or a work of art. Much of the property foundation of the modern private market arises from the right to exclude others legally from what you own and what you add to that.

The philosopher John Locke, whose ideas were very important to the framers of the U.S. Constitution, said that the principle of property was justified when someone contributed labor to a previously unowned natural resource. In other words, if people own themselves and their work efforts and transform something previously unowned into something new by their work, they also own the new thing. This view and the rule of accession have strong similarities.

Can you explain how Locke used the concept of **accession** *to justify how people come to own previously unowned things?*

ACQUIRING RESOURCES THROUGH GIFT

Receiving a **gift** is also a way of acquiring ownership. In the making of a gift, no mutual exchange of resources occurs. Instead, a *donor* who owns something gives it to a *donee,* who becomes the new owner. The rules of gifts specify that the gift does not generally take place until the donor (1) *intends* to make the gift and (2) *delivers* the gift by physical transfer to the donee. Note that in some instances, a *constructive delivery,* like turning over the keys to a car or the deed to land, constitutes an adequate delivery.

A particular kind of gift is a *testamentary gift,* or one that is made through a will. The rules of such a gift pass ownership not by delivery but upon the death of the donor (called a "testator") and the proving of a valid will that specifies the gift. Some people believe that the purpose of a property system is to stimulate efforts to generate further wealth which benefits society. They argue that permitting people to pass property to vast fortunes through testamentary gifts does not give incentive to those who receive such gifts.

In your opinion, what justifies people being able to pass large wealth on to their children through testamentary gifts?

TITLE AND PROPERTY REGISTRATION

Ownership is frequently referred to by the term **title**. Thus, someone who owns something has title to it. When an owner transfers ownership, the owner is said to "pass title." For specific types of resources the law requires that the title be represented by a physical document registered with the state. The title to an automobile is one example of such an ownership document that must be registered with the state. Many states also require the registration of boat titles.

A **deed** is the document of title that transfers ownership of land. The deed contains a precise legal description of the land that specifies the exact location and boundaries according to a mapping or surveying system. Without this description, few buyers or lenders would be willing to risk their money on the land. The fact that exact, accepted boundaries identify land ownership provides the basis for much capital formation.

Even knowing the precise location of the land does not always ensure that there are no problems with the ownership. A lender may have a mortgage claim against the land, or the grantor of a deed may have conveyed the land to more than one person. There are two protections against these problems. First, the kind of deed the buyer receives from the seller can protect the buyer. A *warranty deed* promises the grantee (usually, the buyer) that the grantor (seller) has good ownership and the full power to convey it. The buyer can sue the seller if someone else claims the land. A *special warranty deed* specifies that certain legal claims against the land, like mortgages, exist but guarantees that no other claims exist. A *quitclaim deed* makes no guarantees other than that the grantor surrenders all claim against the land. Several other types of deeds may apply in certain states.

Second, buyers and lenders are protected by registration statutes. The law enables buyers to register their deeds to land and lenders to register their mortgage claims against land. Potential buyers or other lenders are thus put on notice regarding the land, and the legal owner or claimant is legally and publicly identified. By going to the county courthouse or other place of record, you can often trace the ownership history of a piece of land for 200 years or more.

> Land, automobiles, and in many states, boats, require a registration of ownership called title.

> What does it mean to say that a quitclaim deed does not convey ownership?

Property and Security Interests

LO 7-5

In a property-based legal system resources can be highly divisible. Importantly, they are divisible both in specific type and by time. Sellers can transfer resources to buyers now and depend upon getting paid for these resources later. That is a subject of contract law, which begins in the next chapter. The following sections, however, deal with how sellers can increase their confidence in the risky business of transferring goods, rendering services, and making loans by securing particular types of property interests in something usually possessed by the buyer. These property interests are usually conditional and end when a buyer-debtor fulfills some condition, frequently repayment of what is owed. The two principal types of **security interests** are mortgages and secured transactions under Article 9 of the Uniform Commercial Code.

Many scholars do not appreciate that these security interests are in fact property applications because these interests are not physical objects. But they involve a legal fence that protects the holder of the security interest from the general claims of all other persons, and if the buyer-debtor (from here on, just *debtor*) fails to comply with the condition, the seller-creditor (from here on, just

> How is a security interest a property arrangement?

creditor or *secured party*) can usually seize (and/or sell) the object of the security interest to help satisfy the obligation of repayment. Identifying security interests as applications of property helps explain why we say that property, the concept of the private fence, is the central concept of capitalism and private markets.

SECURITY INTERESTS IN LAND

Security interests in land and the structures on the land include mortgages, deeds of trust, and land sales contracts. As observed at the beginning of this chapter, the major way that small business owners raise money to begin their businesses is through mortgaging their homes. They borrow money from a bank or financial institution and in return give that creditor a security interest called a *mortgage* on their homes and the land associated with their homes. In recent years it has also become quite common for homeowners in their capacity as consumers to take out a mortgage on their homes in order to access the value of their homes for purchases they wish to make.

Similar to mortgages are **deeds of trust.** Under the deed of trust, a borrower signs a *note,* which shows the borrower's debt to the lender, and then signs a deed of trust, which grants the lender a security interest in the building and land put up to secure the loan. The deed is held by a third party called a *trustee* who holds full legal ownership to the land. Under this arrangement the debtor will obtain legal ownership, or *title,* only when the deed has been repaid.

Unimproved land and farmland are often sold through land sales contracts. Under a **land sales contract,** the owner of land sells it by contract subject to the condition that the seller retains title to the land until the buyer pays the purchase price. Until that time, the buyer has the legal right to possess and use the land and is responsible for paying taxes and insurance.

Recording Statutes   Generally, mortgages and deeds of trust must be registered in a recording office in the county where the land is located. Recording gives notice of the security interest to potential buyers of the land and to potential lenders who will then consider that fact in determining whether or not to buy the land or to loan money. That potential buyers or lenders become aware of the mortgage is important since the land is subject to satisfy the mortgagee's debt whether or not the land is sold or a subsequent mortgage is taken out on the land.

If **mortgagees** (the creditors) fail to record mortgages, new buyers of the lands who are unaware of mortgages will take the lands free and clear of the mortgages, although the debts will still be owed by the **mortgagors** (debtors). Likewise, a creditor who registers a subsequent mortgage on land, being unfamiliar with the unrecorded first mortgage, will have priority over the first mortgage.

Foreclosure, Deficiency, and Redemption   Almost all states regulate how mortgagees can exercise their property interest when the obligation owed to them is not satisfied. **Foreclosure** is the term used for the exercise of the secured property interest, and foreclosure usually means that the creditor must go through the court system to ensure that procedures are properly followed before debtors lose their homes and land. Foreclosure as it relates to land sales contracts is generally simpler and less expensive to exercise than foreclosure of mortgages and deeds of trust. Foreclosure means that the court will order the land sold to satisfy the debt owed, usually by auction to the highest bidder, with any excess after payment of what is owed to the secured creditor going to the debtor.

You should appreciate that the property represented by these types of security interests is separate from the loan obligation owed by the debtor-mortgagor. In many states, if foreclosure and auction do not produce enough money to satisfy the debt owed by the mortgagor, the creditor-mortgagee can still sue the debtor for the balance owed, called a **deficiency.** Some states, however, have passed statutes, called *antideficiency judgment statutes,* that prevent mortgagees from obtaining anything else from mortgagors once the land has been foreclosed and auctioned. These statutes generally only apply to protect homeowners.

Before the actual foreclosure, most states permit a **right of redemption,** which allows the mortgagor to get back the land upon payment of the full amount of the debt, including all interest and costs. Even after foreclosure some states have a statutory period of redemption, usually six months or one year after foreclosure, in which the mortgagor can redeem the land from a new buyer. If a first mortgagor fails to redeem, most states permit second mortgage holders to redeem the land.

In 2008, following a collapse of the mortgage due to poor lending practices, the right of redemption did not prevent many homeowners from losing their homes. See Sidebar 7.8.

> The **right of redemption** allows a mortgagor, before foreclosure, to get back the land upon payment of the full amount of the debt. Statutory redemption allows a mortgagor to regain ownership of the land upon payment of all interest and costs for a period of time after foreclosure.

sidebar 7.8

Financial Collapse and Recession

In 2008, a financial collapse and recession occurred, caused in major part by lenders offering "subprime mortgages" to borrowers. These subprime mortgages had little to do with the mortgage rules discussed here, but related to the eagerness of borrowers to obtain homes that they could not afford to buy, and the willingness of lenders to take risks by loaning to these borrowers, by obtaining mortgages based on poor credit worthiness, and then by turning around and reselling the mortgages loans as investments in complex financial packages called "derivatives." Repayment of these subprime mortgage loans, however, depended on housing prices continuing to increase rapidly so the loans could be renegotiated and become affordable. When prices stopped going up and loans could not be renegotiated and repaid, millions of homeowners were unable to meet their loan payments, the housing market collapsed, the derivatives market was devastated, many financial institutions went into bankruptcy, credit became difficult to obtain, businesses had to lay off millions of workers, and a very serious recession followed.

SECURED TRANSACTIONS

Article 9 of the Uniform Commercial Code is the principal set of laws controlling security interests in objects of personal property. Article 9 contains the law of **secured transactions.** This law is highly complicated and technical, and what follows merely introduces you to some of the concepts found in Article 9. A secured transaction involves a creditor who has sold something on credit or made a loan to a debtor who agrees to give the creditor a security interest in a valuable object, called **collateral.**

> Article 9 of the Uniform Commercial Code covers the law of secured transactions.

Explain to yourself how **attachment** takes place.

Secured transaction law applies to a variety of things, including consumer goods (which are not bought for business purposes), farm products, inventory, equipment, stocks, bonds, negotiable instruments (orders or promises to pay in a certain form, such as checks), valuable documents such as those transferring goods, accounts receivable (money owed, but not in a certain form like negotiable instruments), and "general intangibles" like interests in patents, trademarks, and copyrights. A security interest in any of these things arises when it attaches. **Attachment** takes place when (1) a secured party has given value, (2) the debtor owns the collateral, and (3) a security agreement is given. This agreement must be in writing, signed by the debtor, and contain a reasonable description of the collateral. The collateral may include not only things currently owned by the debtor but also *after-acquired property* that the debtor acquires in the future. Proceeds realized from the sale of the collateral can also be covered by the security interest.

Perfection   As soon as the security interest attaches it is effective against the debtor, but to be effective against third parties, such as other creditors and people to whom the collateral may be sold or transferred, the secured party must *perfect* the security interest. **Perfection** arises when a security interest has attached and the creditor has taken all proper steps required by Article 9. A creditor perfects a security interest differently according to the type of collateral.

Be able to discuss all the different ways that **perfection** can take place.

The general way of perfecting a security interest under Article 9 is to file a **financing statement.** The form of the financing statement differs from state to state, but the statement should contain the names and addresses of the creditor and debtor, a reasonable description of the collateral, and the signature of the debtor. Financing statements expire five years after the date of filing unless a maturity date is stated and are usually filed in the county where the collateral is located or with an office of the state government, depending on the state and the type of collateral. Financing statements are appropriate to perfect any type of collateral except negotiable ones, which can always be transferred free of a secured creditor's claim unless they are kept in the creditor's possession.

A **PMSI** secures the purchase price of goods bought for personal or household use.

Some types of security interests are perfected by attachment alone, for example, a **purchase money security interest (PMSI)** in consumer goods, meaning a security interest that secures the purchase price of goods bought for personal or household use. Such security interests perfect as soon as they properly attach. Similarly, there is a temporary 21-day perfection in negotiable instruments or documents as soon as they attach, which allows the creditor time to take possession of these valuables. An automatic 10-day perfection in proceeds realized from the sale of collateral also exists even if the perfected security interest in the original collateral did not mention proceeds.

PRIORITY PROBLEMS AND EXAMPLES

Consider the following problems and examples that illustrate the complexity of determining the outcomes of several different situations involving secured creditors. Are you sure you want to be a business attorney?

1. A secured creditor with an attached security interest has priority over a creditor without a security interest. However, a secured creditor does not have priority over a purchaser who gives value for collateral and takes it before a security interest is perfected.

2. John loans Carl $5,000 and attaches a security interest in Carl's printing machinery. John's security interest takes priority against a judgment creditor who tries to seize the machinery to satisfy a damage award. An attached security interest wins over an unattached creditor's claim, but if neither a creditor's claim nor a security interest has attached, the first to attach has priority.

3. A perfected security interest has priority over one that is not perfected but merely attached. If John loans Carl $5,000 on April 5 and attaches a security interest in the printing machinery on that day, John will lose priority to the bank that has filed a financing statement perfecting a security interest in the same machinery on April 15.

4. In the same situation, if John perfects his security interest on April 18, he still loses to the bank. Generally, when two creditors each have a perfected security interest, the creditor to perfect first has priority over the other, and the times the security interests attached are not important.

5. However, an exception to the rule in (3) occurs in that a PMSI in non-inventory collateral, such as a printing machine for a print shop, which is received on August 1, takes priority over a bank's perfected financing statement in "all equipment presently owned or after acquired" that is perfected in the printing shop's equipment on July 9, *but only if the August 1 creditor perfects within a statutory period defined by state law, frequently 20 days.*

6. Likewise, if a publishing company sells books to a retail bookstore on credit, and has a PMSI in the books sold, which will go into the inventory of the bookstore, the publishing company will have priority over a secured creditor like a bank that has previously filed a financing statement on the bookstore's "present inventory and after-acquired inventory," but *only if the publishing company has perfected its interest in the inventory at the time the bookstore receives the books.* Also, the publisher must check financing statements covering the bookstore's inventory, which are a matter of public record, and inform previously perfected security interests of the publisher's PMSI, and must describe the new inventory to them.

7. Print shop B that buys a piece of printing machinery from print shop A in another town will find that the machinery is still subject to the security interest held by a bank that has filed a proper financing statement on the machinery prior to B's purchase. However, a **buyer in the ordinary course of business** will have priority over a perfected security interest, meaning that if the seller of the printing machinery is a manufacturer of that machinery and is selling *in the ordinary course of business,* a buyer would take the machinery free and clear of a bank's previously perfected security interest. Note that in this latter instance the bank does continue to have a security interest for a period of time in the proceeds realized from the sale of the machinery that will have priority over a judgment creditor or a trustee in bankruptcy.

8. Susan sells her computer to Greg for his personal use and a computer store holding a PMSI in the computer attempts to repossess it from Greg. The rule is that if Greg had no knowledge of the security

Generally, a creditor with an attached security interest has priority over a creditor without a security interest, a creditor with a perfected security interest has priority over one whose security interest has not been perfected, and when two creditors have perfected security interests the one whose interest was perfected first has priority.

A **buyer in the ordinary course of business** has priority over a perfected security interest.

interest he takes the computer free and clear of the computer store's perfected interest.

9. Artisan's liens and mechanic's liens usually have priority over even perfected Article 9 security interests. See Sidebar 7.9.

A secured creditor can
repossess collateral
only if the repossession
is peaceful.

After a debtor has defaulted, which usually means it has failed to repay the credit that the secured creditor extended, the secured creditor may peacefully repossess the collateral without going to court unless the debtor orally protests the repossession, in which case the secured party will have to obtain a court order to repossess. Following repossession, the secured creditor can dispose of the collateral in any "commercially reasonable" fashion, such as sale or lease, and must return to the debtor any excess money realized over the amount owed. The secured party can also propose to keep the collateral in complete satisfaction of the debt.

---

sidebar 7.9

Artisan's Liens and Mechanic's Liens

You take your car to the garage for a new transmission but when the work is complete, the credit card company refuses to extend additional credit, asserting that your limit has been reached. You are unable to pay the garage for its materials and labor. The garage can legally refuse to release your car until you have paid it. This is because the garage has an **artisan's lien** on your car, a narrow property interest that arises when someone who contributes parts and/or services to an object of personal property is not paid. This lien has priority over even an Article 9 perfected security interest held by the bank that loaned you the money to buy the car. This result is so because the garage has added value to the car by its parts and labor, and if the garage has to sell the car, it can only realize the value of the parts and labor it added. An artisan's lien is *possessory,* meaning that generally the lien has

priority only as long as the creditor keeps possession of the collateral.

A **mechanic's lien** arises when someone contributes materials and/or services to real estate, usually a building, and is not paid. Unlike the artisan's lien, this lien is not possessory and has priority only if it is perfected by the filing of a written notice, usually in the county where the real estate is found. This lien also has priority over an Article 9 perfected security interest when a fixture, an object of personal property like a carpet, is incorporated into real estate by becoming a physical part of it. The carpet can be subject to a perfected security interest that will follow the carpet's incorporation into the real estate if the owner of the real estate receives the required notice. However, a mechanic's lien that adds value to the real estate has priority over a perfected security interest in a fixture.

LO 7-6   # Limitations on Property and the Common Good

As discussed earlier, private property serves the common good or general welfare of the nation. However, private property also has limits, and these limits tell us that an individual private property right is always subject at some point to the rights of others.

PROPERTY, THE USE OF RESOURCES, AND THE EQUAL RIGHTS OF OTHERS

In law, property is not a *thing*. It is an owner's *right* to exclude others from resources. One of the most important resources is the use owners can make of another resource, for example, a piece of land. Owners can build a house, a shopping mall, or a skyscraper on their land. Or farm it. Or leave it unoccupied. They can take their money and open a computer store with it, or save it for retirement, or invest it in the stock market. All of these ways of using resources come within the legal guarantee of property. Implied in the exclusive rights to private resources is the legal protection to use them in many ways. This quality helps make the marketplace dynamic and responsive to needs and wants.

In an important and meaningful sense, owners also have a property in using their efforts. They have an exclusive right to direct their resource in themselves any way they wish. They can use it to pursue any line of employment, or they can leave the job market and do volunteer work for Meals on Wheels. Or go back to school for an MBA. Or retire on their savings and garden, travel, or watch football.

Explain what it means to say that you have a property in your efforts. How is such a property related to *liberty*?

Having a property right to direct the resources of one's efforts and to be able to exclude others from the further resources one acquires with these efforts is closely related to other concepts like "freedom" and "liberty." The American colonists and the framers of the Constitution certainly thought so. John Dickinson, who helped draft the Constitution, observed that Americans "cannot be happy, without freedom; nor free, without security of property; nor so secure, unless the sole power to dispose of it be lodged within themselves." Revolutionary War diplomat Arthur Lee wrote, "The right of property is the guardian of every other right, and to deprive people of this, is in fact to deprive them of their liberty." In 1768 a colonial American observed, "Liberty and Property are not only join'd in common discourse, but are in their own natures so nearly ally'd [allied], that we cannot be said to possess the one without the other." The early Americans firmly believed that they had a property not only in their material possessions but also in liberty, speech, and other rights. In summary, they had an exclusive right to use freely their resource in themselves and the resources produced by their efforts.

Generally speaking, owners are prohibited from using their resources in ways that harm or injure the resources of other owners. See also Sidebar 7.10. As James Madison explained, the concept of property "leaves to everyone else a like advantage." Under the rule of law, a property system protects the equal right of all to their resources, including the resources they have in themselves. Tort law (Chapter 10), criminal law (Chapter 13), and much of the regulatory law discussed throughout this book attempt to prevent owners from using their resources to injure the resources that belong to others.

Two limits on land use that protect the equal right of all landowners is especially relevant to this chapter. They involve the law of nuisance and zoning.

sidebar 7.10

The Property System and Corporate Governance

Chapter 1 explained why the issues of corporate governance are property issues. The explanation bears reemphasizing.

The property system allows us to enjoy exclusive resources. It protects our resources from the harm of others, but at the same time it limits us from harming the resources of others. Corporate governance illustrates how this property system functions.

In the *specific* sense, corporate governance laws protect the investment resources of corporate owners, or shareholders. These laws define the authority and responsibility of the board of directors, who are elected by the shareholders. The laws also regulate the managers appointed by the board.

In the *broad* sense, corporate governance also includes those laws that protect the resources of others from harm by the corporation. Such laws include antitrust laws, employment discrimination and employee protection laws, environmental protection laws, and a great many antifraud laws.

Sometimes the law does not protect the boundary between what is *mine* and what is *yours*. Sometimes there is disagreement about where proper boundaries lie. Sometimes we have failures of corporate governance. But under a system that permits private resource ownership, corporate governance issues are property issues.

NUISANCE AND ZONING

The law limits certain uses of one's land through the doctrine of nuisance. What constitutes a nuisance is somewhat vague, but in most jurisdictions the common law cases have been put in statutory form. Several common elements exist in the law of nuisance in most states. To begin with, there are two types of nuisance: public and private.

A **public nuisance** is one arising from some use of land that causes inconvenience or damage to the public. For example, discharging industrial waste from one's land that kills the fish in a river constitutes a public nuisance since fishing rights are publicly held. Public nuisance claims may be brought only by a public official, not private individuals, unless the latter have suffered some special damage to their property as a result of the public nuisance. Note that many public nuisances can also violate various regulatory laws, such as environmental laws (see Chapter 19). Sidebar 7.11 describes the public nuisance created as a byproduct of an otherwise desirable good.

Any unreasonable use of one's property so as to cause substantial interference with the enjoyment or use of another's land establishes a common law **private nuisance.** The unreasonableness of the interference is measured by a balancing process in which the character, extent, and duration of harm to the plaintiff is weighed against the social utility of the defendant's activity and its appropriateness to its location. Since society needs industrial activity as well as natural tranquility, people must put up with a certain amount of smoke, dust, noise, and polluted water if they live in concentrated areas of industry. But what may be an appropriate industrial use of land in a congested urban area may be a private nuisance if it occurs in a rural or residential location.

Once the plaintiff establishes a substantial and unreasonable interference with the use or enjoyment of his or her property, the court must decide what remedy the plaintiff is entitled to. The court may award damages if

A **private nuisance** is an *unreasonable* use of one's property so as to cause substantial interference with the enjoyment or use of another's land.

sidebar 7.11

Hot Sauce or Fresh Air?

The Huy Fong Foods factory in Irwindale, California, makes a very popular hot sauce called Sriracha. The sauce, which has Thai origins, is made from red chili peppers and a combination of more neutral ingredients like vinegar and sugar. Huy Fong Foods' Irwindale factory is very successful and contributes to the community in terms of employment and tax revenue.

Unfortunately, the factory also contributes a strong odor. In October 2013, several Irwindale residents complained of sore throats, nosebleeds, and burning eyes that were allegedly due to Sriracha manufacture. The city council considered the complaints and, in April 2014, declared the factory a "public nuisance." This move gave the city the power to shut down the plant pending a trial on the issue.

The Huy Fong Foods case presents a classic property rights problem. Should Irwindale residents have the power to shut down a factory—i.e., eliminate its value as a property asset—because of its impact on the community's enjoyment of their land (a property rule)? Or should the factory be required to compensate for proven injuries while being permitted to make its own decision on the economics of staying in business (a liability rule)?

Source: Jenn Harris, "Irwindale Declares Sriacha Factory a Public Nuisance," *Los Angeles Times*, April 10, 2014.

the plaintiff has suffered economic loss, but when damages are inadequate the court may also order the defendant to do something, like correct the problem, or else cease the nuisance-creating activity. In determining whether to issue an injunction, the court will take into consideration (1) the relative economic hardship that will be placed upon the parties if such relief is grante and (2) the public interest in the continuation of the defendant's activity. This balancing of interests required by nuisance law can bring about some unusual remedies.

In Case 7.3, the court requires the defendants to move their house.

Can you see now how nuisance law attempts to balance the equal right of all in the property system? It does so by preventing landowners from *unreasonably* interfering with other publicly and privately owned resources. Determining what is unreasonable is an ongoing and controversial process in a property-based legal system. You should understand now that property boundaries of use are not infinite and may be ambiguous until a court order legislature sets them.

Through their exercise of the police powers, states and local governments protect the public health, safety, morals, and general welfare. It is under the police powers that a major governmental regulation of land use takes place: zoning. **Zoning ordinances** are generally laws that divide counties or municipalities into use districts designated residential, commercial, or industrial. Zoning limits the use to which land can be put to that specified. For instance, industrial facilities cannot be built in residential districts. Zoning may also specify the height, size, number, and location of buildings that can be built on land. Restricting buildings in a commercial district to no more than eight stories in height is an example. Zoning may additionally impose aesthetic requirements concerning color and exterior design. Zoning boards (or commissions), which are generally agencies of local governments, enforce the zoning ordinances. Owners should always check to determine how zoning limits land use.

Do you agree with the principle of **zoning ordinances** or not?

COOK v. SULLIVAN
829 A.2d 1059 (N.H. Sup. Ct. 2003)

DALIANIS, J: . . . The defendants, John and Diane Sullivan, appeal a decision of the Superior Court finding that they created a nuisance on the plaintiffs' property by filling in wetlands and constructing a home on their property.

Since 1946, the plaintiffs [the Cooks] have owned property on Lake Winnipesaukee in Moultonboro. Over the years, they have built various structures on the property, including a main house, a garage, and a guest house. In 1996, the defendants purchased adjoining property.

At the time of the purchase, the defendants [Sullivans] . . . had a three-bedroom modular house placed on their property. In the course of construction, the defendants used large quantities of fill in the area where they were building the house. In 1997, the plaintiffs began experiencing increased wetness, which they claim lasted for extended periods of time, on their property. Specifically, the plaintiffs claimed, among other things, that, since the construction, standing water accumulated in their garage and underneath the house, and that the water has interfered with their ability to use their property as they had in the past. They also claimed that this condition persisted each summer from 1997 to 2001.

In 1999, the plaintiffs complained to the defendants, who attempted to remedy the problem by removing some fill along the parties' common boundary line, digging a drainage ditch and moving a wall. The plaintiffs, however, claimed that the condition of their land did not change [and they sued].

The trial court ruled that the defendants' construction activities constituted a nuisance that damaged the plaintiffs' property, and that the remedy was to remove the fill and foundation from the jurisdictional wetlands, which would necessarily require the defendants' house to be moved. . . . [T]his appeal followed.

A private nuisance exists when an activity substantially and unreasonably interferes with the use and enjoyment of another's property. "To constitute a nuisance, the defendants' activities must cause harm that exceeds the customary interferences with land that a land user suffers in an organized society, and be an appreciable and tangible interference with a property interest." In determining whether an act interfering with the use and enjoyment is so unreasonable and substantial as to amount to a nuisance and warrant an injunction, a court must balance the gravity of the harm to the plaintiff against the utility of the defendant's conduct, both to himself and to the community. It is the plaintiffs' burden to prove the existence of a nuisance by a preponderance of the evidence.

The evidence supports the trial court's finding of nuisance. At trial, witnesses testified that large portions of the defendants' lot were swampy and had pools of standing water prior to construction. The plaintiffs' expert, Randall Shuey, a certified soil scientist, testified that he conducted extensive testing of the defendants' property subsequent to their construction and stated that the defendants' activities had had caused subsurface waters to divert to the plaintiffs' property.

Further, the plaintiffs testified that their property was substantially wetter after the defendants built their house. The defendants assert that there was insufficient evidence to support this finding, or that the wetness problems continued to exist at the time of final hearing, because the plaintiffs' property was wet before construction. While there was evidence that portions of the plaintiffs' property were wet prior to the defendants' construction, numerous witnesses testified that the water levels increased following the defendants' construction. This testimony was corroborated by Shuey's statement that the defendants' construction altered the elevation of the defendants' land as well as the flow of subsurface waters, causing increased wetness on the plaintiffs' property. While there was evidence introduced of flooding in 1998, Shuey stated that, while having a short-term effect, the flooding did not cause the prolonged wetness the plaintiffs experienced in later years. Moreover, the plaintiffs testified that this condition on their property repeated each spring and early summer from 1997 to 2001.

The plaintiffs also illustrated various problems associated with the increased wetness. For example, they testified that following the construction, there was standing water on their property, both on a large portion of the lawn, including the backyard between the house and the garage, and under the garage and chalet. They explained that because of the increased wetness, they were forced to move dog pens that they traditionally kept in the lower part of their property, and that they could no longer hang a clothesline or stack firewood in the backyard, or use the backyard for recreational activities. Plaintiffs testified that they had trouble mowing the lawn because of the water. The plaintiffs also explained that they could no longer store things directly on their garage floor due to standing water in the spring and early summer months. Further, they testified that there was a strong, musty odor in the house after water began collecting under the foundation, which prevented them from using the house during those months when the windows are closed.

Given the evidence in the record, we cannot hold that the trial court erred in finding that the defendants' construction created a nuisance resulting in damages to the plaintiffs' property.

Having concluded that there was sufficient evidence to support the trial court's findings that the defendants' activities constitute a nuisance, we now must determine whether the remedy was appropriate. In evaluating the appropriateness of injunctive relief, the court utilizes the same balancing test that is used to first identify whether a nuisance exists, "although the scales must weigh more heavily in the [plaintiff's] favor because of the extraordinary nature of this form of relief." The propriety of affording relief in a particular case rests in the sound discretion of the trial court. . . . We will uphold a trial court's order unless its decision constitutes an unsustainable exercise of discretion. If the defendants' activity can be carried on without causing unreasonable interference to the plaintiffs, then they should not be required to remove their house. On the other hand, an order requiring such removal is justified if there is no other way to abate the private nuisance.

The defendants challenge the ordered remedy, arguing that the trial court neglected to balance the hardships between the parties and that there was insufficient evidence to support its decision.

With regard to remedying the nuisance, Shuey stated specifically that "the only way to guarantee that we're not going to have any additional impacts on the property, or to restore it to what it was previously, is to move that house and all that fill out of the jurisdictional area, out of the jurisdictional wetlands." He also stated that this could be accomplished by moving the defendants' house and foundation back forty or fifty feet on the property.

The defendants did propose a less stringent remedy to the trial court, which involved removing fill within twenty feet of the plaintiffs' boundary and constructing a ditch near the boundary for water discharge. Shuey testified, however, that he could not guarantee that the plaintiffs' property would be restored to its condition prior to the defendants' construction. The defendants did not offer any expert testimony at trial in support of their proposed remedy nor did they offer any other alternate remedies.

The record reflects that the trial court took the hardships of both parties into consideration when deciding the remedy. For example, the trial court explained in its final verdict that it was prepared to decide what remedy "would be equitable and fair under all the circumstances." Further, the court told the parties during trial that it was considering the equities of both parties when considering the appropriate remedy. Moreover, the court adopted the unusual procedure of viewing the property both before and after it took testimony and reviewed the exhibits. Having considered the evidence before the trial court, we agree that the gravity of harm to the plaintiffs resulting from the defendants' nuisance is significant enough to support the trial court's remedy.

Consequently, we find sufficient evidentiary support for the trial court's remedy and uphold its decision. *Affirmed.*

KEY POINTS

- The Sullivans transformed their property to support a new house, but this had the effect of unreasonably and substantially harming the Cooks' property. They did not internalize the costs of their behavior.
- The water that flooded the Cooks' property did not necessarily flow from the Sullivans' property. If it had, the water might have constituted a trespass rather than a nuisance.
- If the Sullivans had provided the court with another option other than moving their house, the balance of hardships might have come out differently.

An owner can ask a zoning board for a *variance* to allow use of land in a way not permitted under a zoning ordinance. The board is likely to grant a variance only when the owner can prove that the ordinance prevents a reasonable economic return on the land as zoned. Zoning ordinances allow uses of land that existed prior to passage of the ordinances. Such uses are called "nonconforming" uses.

Like nuisance law, zoning regulations are highly controversial because they involve limits on how owners can use their land. The purpose of zoning laws may be to protect the right of all to their lands, but not everyone is going to agree with the limits that zoning laws establish.

PROPERTY LIMITATIONS AND THE COMMON GOOD

The fact that there are limitations property illustrates that this exclusive right serves the common good. The property-related concepts of duration limitations and taxation illustrate that when society believes that property no longer promotes the general public welfare, owners lose the resources it protects.

The **rule against perpetuities** serves the common good by preventing dead owners from indefinitely limiting the new productive ways that resources can be used.

Duration Limitations on Property   Do not believe for a minute that when you own something you own it forever. For instance the Constitution grants patents and copyrights—only for "limited Times." The reasoning behind the limitation is to ensure that inventions and creative expressions enter the public domain so as to serve the common good as quickly as possible after allowing for the profit necessary to encourage people to create new things in the first place.

Patents and copyrights, however, are not the only property concept that limits the duration of an owner's exercise of exclusive right over resources. The **rule against perpetuities** limits all exercise of property over resources to a duration of "lives in being plus twenty-one years." The rule prevents an owner from controlling resources through many future generations by setting up *trust* arrangements, under which trustees are legally required to carry out the wishes of the owner for extended duration. As it is, a trust may not extend the control of an owner beyond twenty-one years of the death of someone who is alive at the time of the owner's death.

Taxation   The justification for property may be the common good. And the common good may consist primarily of setting conditions for the maximum private production of what people need and want. However, the government provides other resources that people need and want, including public roads, public education, law enforcement, a judicial system, defense of the nation, and public assistance for the poor. These services are also a part of the general welfare (or common good) of the nation, and they are expensive. Some people believe that in the common good the government should provide even more public services such as more public health care. The taxes to support these services limit the right of private property and suggest that property's claim to promoting the common good is not absolute.

Federal taxation is a specified power of Congress, contained in Article 1, Section 8 of the Constitution: "The Congress shall have the Power to lay and collect Taxes . . . to . . . provide for the common Defense and general Welfare of the United States. . . ." Because the Supreme Court ruled that Article 1, Section 8, did not authorize indirect taxes, like the progressive income tax, the Constitution was amended in 1913 by the Sixteenth Amendment, which permits such taxes.

According to the Congressional Budget Office, the top 1% of federal income taxpayers pay more dollars of tax than the bottom 60% of taxpayers do. On the other hand, poorer taxpayers pay a higher percentage of their incomes in state and local sales taxes than do wealthier taxpayers. The fairness of the tax system and the adequacy of public services are frequent issues around election time. One thing is certain, however: These issues intertwine with perceptions of the common good, which in turn connects with the exclusive right called property. They illustrate that property, which promotes the common good, is also limited by it.

> The CBO also reports that the top 20% of taxpayers pay 60% of all federal income tax.

The wealth produced by the property system must actually reach people in order to produce the greatest happiness for the greatest number. Exclusive right is not an ethical or moral end in itself. Although there can be much debate about its extent, taxation of wealth generated by the incentives of the property system is part of what contributes to the common good.

> Can property exist both as an individual right and for the common good? Discuss.

PROPERTY: A CONCLUSION AND COMMENT

This chapter has introduced the law of property as it orders society's limited resources. Although many chapter sections have explained the rules making up property law, the chapter has also focused on the general importance of the legal property system to private enterprise and society. The key to the most rapid increase of total wealth—the greatest expansion of limited resources—is a property system that applies generally and equally to everyone's resources.

In the modern nation, property law founds the marketplace by establishing an essential framework for the voluntary and certain exchange of identifiable private resources. There is strong reason to think that a prime determinant of wealth in the world today is the presence or absence of an adequate property system under the rule of law. Thus, it is significant that business students appreciate the fundamental role of law in business and the necessity for a strong legal system even when they oppose the wisdom of specific rules or regulations.

Although effective property law may be the foundation for society's material flourishing and the liberty of the individual, it also has another side to it. Property law permits the accumulation of unequal exclusive resources, and as James Madison wrote in *The Federalist:* "The most common and durable source of factions has been the various and unequal distribution of property." A property system functions best when there is a large middle class with adequate resources, or at least a well-educated populace that understands the benefits of property. Otherwise, in a democracy the temptation is great to redistribute resources through taxation, and at some point the motivation to produce additional limited resources diminishes.

> Why does a property system function best when there is a large middle class with adequate resources?

The major issues of poverty and prosperity in the new millennium involve the understanding of property law's effects on society. To deal knowledgeably with the legal environment of business, students must grasp how law founds the private marketplace for the common good.

Chapters 8 and 9 introduce you to the rules of *contract* law. As you read these chapters, keep in mind the important connection between property and contract. The rules of contract law concern the legally binding promises by which owners exchange resources in our property-based legal system. When you sign a contract to buy a new 3-D television set, you promise to exchange the ownership of money for the ownership of the television set.

Key Terms

Accession 208
Adverse possession 206
Artisan's lien 214
Attachment 212
Bailee 201
Bailment 201
Bailor 201
Buyer in the ordinary course of business 213
Collateral 211
Confusion 207
Contract 204
Deed 209
Deeds of trust 210
Deficiency 211
Easement 200
Estate 199

Fee simple 199
Financing statement 212
Fixture 198
Foreclosure 210
Gift 208
Intangible personal property 193
Joint tenancy 200
Land sales contract 210
Leasehold estate 199
Life estate 199
Mechanic's lien 214
Mortgage 192
Mortgagees 210
Mortgagors 210
Ownership 204
Perfection 212

Personal property 193
Private nuisance 216
Property 188
Public nuisance 216
Purchase money security interest (PMSI) 212
Real property 193
Right of redemption 211
Rule against perpetuities 220
Rule of first possession 205
Secured transactions 211
Security interest 209
Tangible personal property 193
Tenancy in common 200
Title 209
Zoning ordinance 217

Review Questions and Problems

The Property System

1. *The Problem of Limited Resources*

   The Soviet Constitution guaranteed the citizens' private property. Why then was the former Soviet Union so poor?

2. *Property and Prosperity*

   (a) How does property help generate prosperity? Discuss.

   (b) Explain the importance of the visibility of resources to the wealth of nations.

Defining Property in the Legal System

3. *Two Basic Divisions of Property*

   (a) Explain the two basic divisions of property.

   (b) Martin sold his house to Cheryl. Later, when he tried to take the beautiful chandelier in the dining room, which had belonged to his grandparents, with him, Cheryl objected. What is the issue here? Legally, who is likely to win this dispute? Discuss.

Property Boundaries in the Physical World

4. *Defining Land*

   (a) Real estate is no longer defined as extending from the center of the earth to the heavens. Explain how modern property law imposes more limits.

   (b) If David tosses a ball across Laura's yard, but it does not touch the surface of her yard, has it infringed (trespassed) on her property?

   (c) If WaterCo drills a horizontal well next to (but not over) Lee's property line and drains water from under Lee's land, has WaterCo interfered with Lee's rights? Consider the application of the rule of capture.

   (d) Property law distinguishes between land (real property) and personal property. Decide whether the following are land or personal property and explain why.

      i. A porch light

      ii. A lamp next to a bed

      iii. A song about a porch light

Interests in Property with Respect to Others and Time"

5. *Types of Ownership*

   (a) What does it mean to have a fee simple defeasible estate?

   (b) What is the difference between a remainder interest and a reversion?

   (c) Arla and Jack own a house as joint tenants with right of survivorship. What is the legal significance of this?

6. *Easements*

   (a) In what way is an easement protected by a property fence?

   (b) Explain an easement by prescription.

7. *Bailments*

   (a) Is a lease of a mowing tractor a bailment? Explain.

   (b) A warehouse contract requires that your equipment be stored in "warehouse 314." For its own convenience the warehouseman moves your equipment to warehouse 212, and your equipment is destroyed by a tornado that sweeps through town. Is the warehouse liable to you for the value of the equipment? What if the equipment had been destroyed in warehouse 314? Would your answer be different? Because of these types of problems, what sort of arrangements do bailors and bailees often make regarding bailed goods?

   (c) How are common carriers different from other sorts of bailees?

Acquiring Resources in a Property System

8. *Acquiring Resources through Exchange*

   (a) How does the law of contracts fit into our property-based legal system?

   (b) Explain why more resources are exchanged by contracts than by any other method.

9. *Acquiring Resources through Possession*

   (a) Along a winding dirt road, Lee finds an old, rusty car with no license plates. Looking through the car, which is unlocked, he finds a valuable diamond ring. Later, the original buyer of the ring comes forward and admits that he has dumped the old car along the road, but wants his ring back. Who is legally entitled to the ring? Explain.

   (b) The owner of Downtown Condos discovers that Schuyler Skyscraper actually extends 6 inches on to land belonging to Downtown. Discuss the legal ramifications.

10. *Acquiring Resources through Confusion*

   (a) What are fungible goods? Give an example.

   (b) Discuss why boundaries of use are sometimes difficult to determine.

11. *Acquiring Resources through Accession*

   (a) Explain what it means to acquire ownership by accession.

   (b) Discuss why to John Locke a doctrine similar to accession justifies who owns what.

12. *Acquiring Resources through Gift*

   (a) In terms of a gift, explain *delivery* and constructive *delivery*.

   (b) What is a testamentary gift?

13. *Title and Property Registration*

   (a) Name three kinds of deeds to land and explain what they mean.

   (b) Why is it important to register a deed? Discuss.

Property and Security Interests

14. *Security Interests in Land*

   (a) Name three types of security interests in land and explain them.

   (b) Discuss why recording mortgages and deeds of trust is so important. Why is recording less important in the case of the land sales contract?

15. *Secured Transactions*

   (a) Describe the requirements for attachment of a security interest under UCC, Article 9.

   (b) Describe four different instances that demonstrate perfection of a security interest.

16. *Priority Problems*

   Roger sells his expensive mowing tractor to his neighbor Zan. Shortly after Zan takes possession, someone representing the lawn equipment company tells Zan that the store holds a purchase money security interest (PMSI) in the tractor. Does the store have priority regarding the mower, meaning does the security interest continue on the mower following Zan's purchase of it?

Limitations on Property and the Common Good

17. *Property, the Use of Resources, and the Equal Right of Others*

   Discuss why it is important to have a property right in the uses of things.

18. *Nuisance and Zoning*

   (a) Distinguish a public nuisance from a private nuisance. What does nuisance have to do with the common good? Discuss.

   (b) What is the "coming to the nuisance" doctrine?

19. *Property Limitations and the Common Good*

   What is the rule against perpetuities? What does it have to do with the common good?

20. *Taxation*

   Why is taxation of private property legal?

21. *Property: A Conclusion and Comment*

   (a) What does James Madison think is the problem with a private property system, a system he nevertheless supported?

   (b) Suppose you say to your roommate, "I have as much property as Bill Gates," although more accurately in terms of law you should say, "I have the *same* property as Bill Gates." What do you mean by this statement? Answer by explaining the basic confusion about the term "property."

business *discussions*

1. While you are attending a business conference in South America, someone approaches you and says, "A private property system might work well in your country, but it will never work in mine. There are only a few wealthy families in my country who own almost everything. Our only hope for the people is for the government to confiscate their lands and administer our resources through socialism."

What do you say to this person in light of what you have read in this chapter?

What strategy might you suggest regarding getting more private land into the hands of the poor in that country?

2. Richard Epstein, a University of Chicago law professor, said in his book *Takings* that the principles of nuisance illustrate more clearly than any other doctrine how our property-based legal system functions.

What did he mean by this statement? Discuss.

Explain what it means to say that property is the central concept in our legal system.

8

Contract Formation

Learning Objectives

In this chapter you will learn:

8-1. To describe the rationale and legal basis for contracts.

8-2. To classify contracts and understand the terminology used to describe contracts.

8-3. To describe the requirements needed to create an enforceable contract.

8-4. To identify instances in which mutual agreement cannot exist.

8-5. To know when a contract must be in writing.

GREEMENT

whose

(her

The average person's day is filled with agreements. Consider these activities:

- Updating a social networking page while adhering to the use rules.
- Promising to meet a friend for lunch.
- Purchasing a cup of coffee.
- Committing to work with a colleague on a group assignment.
- Downloading an app to a cell phone.

Do all of these interactions create *contracts*? Would we expect a court to enforce them? What are the consequences if one party refuses to follow through with his or her promise?

Contracts involve
promises that are
enforceable, with pre-
dictable *consequences*
for performance
failures.

These and many other issues related to contracts are important because they are fundamental to the business environment. At the outset, understanding the basic definition of a contract is essential. Simply stated, a contract is a legally enforceable **promise** or an exchange of promises. Although this chapter and the next contain many important details of contract classifications, terminology, formation, and performance, it is important to remember that the heart of this topic is a promise or commitment to do or not to do something.

Every day, millions of contracts are created and performed by both businesspeople and consumers. Without contracts and the court systems to enforce contracts, buyers and sellers would not be able to account for future risks or have confidence in exchanging valuable property interests. In fact, it is fair to say that no other area of the law has been as important as contracts in supporting private enterprise. As you read and study this chapter and the next, keep in mind the fundamental role that contracts have in making business possible.

There are also nonlegal business considerations in every contract. If your company tries to avoid a deal that a customer believes was settled, you risk losing that customer's future business. Moreover, a company that uses contracts aggressively to trap customers in agreements that are unexpected or unfair risks negative publicity that can undermine a good reputation for products or services. In so many ways, your business acumen is enhanced when you know the rules of contract law.

In this chapter, you will study the following topics:

- The legal foundation of contracts.
- When communications become a contract.
- What parties have to do when changes to a contract occur.
- Who has the capacity to create contracts.
- The necessary format of a contract.
- When fraud or mistake prevent enforcement of a contract.

Chapter 9 continues with an examination of the performance and breach of contracts.

Basic Concepts

When was the last time you entered into a contract? You might be thinking of your most recent computer purchase or apartment lease. But, in fact, we enter into a contract when doing something as mundane as buying a meal or a snack from a vending machine. Most people contract daily for a great variety of goods and services. The rules of contract law underlie the private enterprise system at every turn.

LO 8-1   ### CONTRACT LAW IN PRIVATE ENTERPRISE

A contract need not be a formal, written document, and those who make such an agreement do not have to use the word *contract* or recognize that they have made a legally enforceable promise. The rules of contract law still apply. If the expectations of the parties to a contract are not met, these rules affect legal negotiations and may result in a lawsuit. For instance, contract law says that a restaurant makes an implied "promise" that its food is fit to eat (see Sidebar 8.3 later in the chapter). Should the restaurant serve a meal that gives the buyer food poisoning, it could be liable for the injury caused by breaking its promise.

Contract law enables private agreements to be legally enforceable. Enforceability of agreements is desirable because it gives people the certainty they need to rely on promises contained in agreements. For instance, a shirt manufacturer in Los Angeles must know that it can rely on the promise of a store in Boston to pay for a thousand specially manufactured shirts. The manufacturer is more likely to agree to sew the shirts if it can enforce payment from the buyer, if necessary, under the law of contracts. In an important sense, then, the law of contracts is vital for our private enterprise economy. It helps make buyers and sellers willing to do business together.

Contract law provides enormous flexibility and precision in business dealings. It provides flexibility in that you can agree (or require agreement) to literally anything that is not illegal or against public policy. It gives precision in that with careful thinking you can make another agree to exactly the requirements that accomplish even a very complex business purpose. Sidebar 8.1 provides an example of the precise use of contractual language to accomplish a business purpose.

sidebar 8.1

The Confidentiality Agreement

Many companies require employees to sign contractual confidentiality agreements. In these agreements, employees promise not to disclose certain things they learn during their employment. Confidentiality agreements are very useful in keeping employees or ex-employees from disclosing a company's research discoveries, marketing plans, customer lists, and other sensitive information.

Confidentiality agreements are important to firms in any industry where internal secrets provide a competitive advantage. This can include producers of cutting-edge, high-technology products like smartphones, but it can also impact providers of more commonplace and traditional items, like baked goods. The knowledge held by individual employees, encompassing sales techniques, corporate strategy, and even secret formulas, can be among a firm's most valuable assets. Contracts are an important way of ensuring the information does not fall into the hands of a competitor.

For example, when an executive for a company that produces well-known brands of English muffins, pastries, and other baked goods decided to move to a competitor, the company invoked the executive's contractual promise to maintain confidentiality. It argued that it was impossible for the executive to work for the competitor and not disclose proprietary information on new product plans, customer identities, and product formulas, among other things. The court agreed and issued a preliminary injunction preventing the employee from beginning work.

Source: Bimbo Bakeries v. Chris Botticella, 613 F.3d 102 (3d Cir. 2010).

SOURCES OF CONTRACT LAW

Most of the contract law outlined in this chapter is common law. Recall from Chapter 1 that common law comes from judges' decisions. Through common law, the courts have developed principles controlling contract formation, performance, breach, and remedies. This judge-made law affects many types of contracts, including real property, service, employment, and general business contracts.

Another source of contract law is legislation. Various states have enacted common law rules in statutes. In some cases, legislatures have replaced common law rules with different statutory requirements. Perhaps the most important example of state-based legislation impacting contract law is the **Uniform Commercial Code (UCC)**. Article 2 of the UCC covers the sale of **goods.** Goods are tangible, movable items of personal property. The UCC applies to individuals as well as firms. Every state has adopted some version of Article 2 of the UCC, thereby making state contract law relatively uniform in the area of goods contracts. Throughout this chapter and the next, you will study both the common law principles of contracts, which governs most other contracts, and the UCC. Remember the distinction between these two primary sources of contract law.

LO 8-2　# Contractual Classifications and Terminology

We use a number of terms to help classify different types of contracts. Learning these terms will greatly help you understand contract law. This section introduces the following contractual terminology:

- Bilateral and unilateral contracts
- Express and implied-in-fact contracts
- Implied-in-law or quasi-contracts
- Enforcement terminology
- Performance terminology

BILATERAL AND UNILATERAL CONTRACTS

Bilateral contracts involve a promise-for-promise exchange.

Contracts involve either an exchange of promises by the parties or a promise conditioned on the performance of an act. A **bilateral contract** is an agreement containing mutual promises. For example, suppose Paul promises to sell his laptop computer to Pearl in exchange for her promise to pay $1,000 to Paul for the equipment. When Pearl makes her promise in response to Paul's, a bilateral contract is formed. This relationship is depicted in Figure 8.1. Notice that a bilateral contract involves two promises, two rights, and two duties.

Unilateral contracts exist when a promise is made in exchange for performance.

While a bilateral contract involves a promise for a promise, a **unilateral contract** is an agreement with only one promise, and only one party is committed to perform. The maker of such a promise seeks an action rather than a promise in return. If that action does not occur, there is no breach. Suppose Pat tells Alex, "If you sell 100 units this year, I will pay you a bonus of $1,000." Here, Alex is not committed to perform, but if he does, Pat is bound to pay the promised amount. In Figure 8.2, notice that there is only one promise, one duty, and one right.

Most business contracts take the bilateral form. Indeed, courts presume a bilateral nature of an agreement whenever there is doubt about the form.

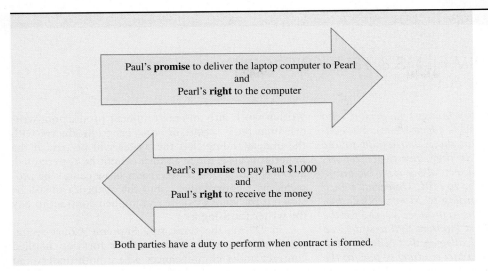

Figure 8.1 *Bilateral contract.*

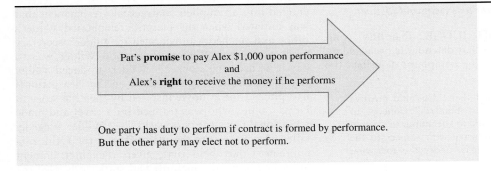

Figure 8.2 *Unilateral contract.*

Nevertheless, the party making a promise can control the application of many concepts of contract law by understanding the distinction between bilateral and unilateral contracts.

EXPRESS AND IMPLIED-IN-FACT CONTRACTS

Many contracts arise from interactions in which parties actually discuss the promised terms of their agreement. These are called **express contracts.** A negotiated purchase of land for construction of a manufacturing plant is an example of an express contract. There are also **implied-in-fact contracts,** which arise from the conduct of the parties rather than from words. For instance, asking a person such as an accountant for professional advice *implies* a promise to pay the going rate for this advice even though you do not make an *express* promise to pay for it. Case 8.1 involves a court's attempt to determine the existence of an implied-in-fact contract in the context of the entertainment industry.

MONTZ v. PILGRIM FILMS & TELEVISION, INC.
649 F.3d 975 (9th Cir. 2011)

Larry Montz was a parapsychologist (a person who studies paranormal or psychic phenomena). He conceived of a reality television show that would follow paranormal investigators as they investigate reports from different locations. Montz, along with his publicist, Smoller, pitched the idea to NBC Universal, which indicated no interest. According to Montz, NBC then partnered with Pilgrim Films to produce a series for the Sci-Fi Channel called Ghost Hunters that was derived from Montz's idea. He sued, alleging that NBC and Pilgrim breached an implied-in-fact contract to pay for the use of the reality show concept. The defendants argued that Montz's allegation was actually an improper attempt to control an idea that would be unprotectable under copyright law. The court had to determine whether the contract claim was clear and distinct.

SCHROEDER, CIRCUIT JUDGE.: Plaintiffs' complaint specifically alleged that defendants breached an implied-in-fact contract. The complaint described the terms of the agreement:

> Plaintiffs communicated their ideas and creative concepts for the "Ghost Hunters" Concept to the Defendants, pursuant to the standard custom and practice in the industry with respect to the exchange of creative ideas, under the following terms:
>
> a. that Plaintiffs' disclosure of their ideas and concepts was strictly confidential;
> b. that the Defendants would not disclose, divulge or exploit the Plaintiffs' ideas and concepts without compensation and without obtaining the Plaintiffs' consent; and
> c. that, by accepting the Plaintiffs' disclosure of its concept, the Defendants accepted and agreed to abide by the foregoing terms.

The complaint further alleged that plaintiffs presented the concept on the express condition that they made the presentation as an offer to partner with the defendants and that plaintiffs justifiably expected to receive a share of the profits derived from any use of the idea. . . .

Writers in the Hollywood film industry often submit scripts to producers, or set up meetings with them, in the hope of selling them scripts and concepts for movies. The practice has carried over into television. Since the writer is looking for someone to turn the written work into an entertainment production, writers often pitch scripts or concepts to producers with the understanding that the writer will be paid if the material is used. Since an idea cannot be copyrighted, a concept for a film or television show cannot be protected by a copyright. . . . But the concept can still be stolen if the studio violates an implied contract to pay the writer for using it.

In *Desny*, the California Supreme Court recognized [that] a writer and producer form an implied contract under circumstances where both understand that the writer is disclosing his idea on the condition that he will be compensated if it is used. . . . There, defendant Billy Wilder, famed director of *Sunset Boulevard* and *Witness for the Prosecution*, allegedly entered into an implied contractual arrangement that was initiated when the plaintiff telephoned Wilder's office and pitched a movie idea to Wilder's secretary who, along with Wilder, understood Wilder was to pay if he used the story. . . . Wilder produced a film, *Ace in the Hole*, allegedly based on the idea plaintiff had pitched for a movie inspired by the "life story of Floyd Collins who was trapped [in a cave] and made sensational news for two weeks." . . . Wilder allegedly failed to compensate the plaintiff, and the California Supreme Court held that, given the entertainment industry norms, the plaintiff had sufficiently pled the breach of an implied contract to pay for use of his idea. The issue here is whether copyright law now preempts such claims. . . .

The Copyright Act of 1976 expressly preempts state claims where the plaintiff's work "come[s] within the subject matter of copyright" and the state law grants "legal or equitable rights that are equivalent to any of the exclusive rights within the general scope of copyright." . . .

[T]he major focus of litigation has been on the second prong of the preemption test: whether the asserted state right is equivalent to any of the exclusive rights within the general scope of copyright. . . . To survive preemption, a state cause of action must assert rights that are qualitatively different from the rights protected by copyright. In [a similar case], we held that the rights created under California law emanating from *Desny* were qualitatively different from the rights protected by federal copyright law because a *Desny* claim includes an added element: an agreement to pay for use of the disclosed ideas. . . . Contract claims generally survive preemption because they require proof of such an extra element. . . . The extra element, the implied agreement of payment for use of a concept, is a personal one, between the parties. . . .

This approach not only accords with the Copyright Act's preemption guidelines, but it also recognizes the gap that would otherwise exist between state contract law and copyright law in the entertainment industry. The *Desny* innovation serves to give some protection for those who wish to find an outlet for creative concepts and ideas but with the understanding that they are not being given away for free. Without such legal protection, potentially valuable creative sources would be left with very little protection in a dog-eat-dog business. *See* Woody Allen, CRIMES AND MISDEMEANORS (Orion Pictures 1989) ("Show business is worse than dog-eat-dog. It's dog-doesn't-return-other-dog's-phone-calls."). Thus we were correct when we observed that "[c]ontract law, whether through express or implied-in-fact contracts, is the most significant remaining state-law protection for literary or artistic ideas." *Benay*, 607 F.3d at 629. . . .

Plaintiffs' claim for breach of confidence also survives copyright preemption. The claim protects the duty of trust or confidential relationship between the parties, an extra element that makes it qualitatively different from a copyright claim. . . .

Defendants argue that the complaint fails to allege sufficient facts to make out a claim for breach of implied contract. They assert that it lacks any allegation (1) that Montz and Smoller disclosed their idea for sale, (2) that they expected to be reasonably compensated for the idea, and (3) that defendants knew the conditions on which it was offered. Yet the complaint makes all three allegations. . . .

Defendants similarly argue that Montz and Smoller failed to allege sufficient facts to make out their claim for breach of confidence. They argue that there is no allegation (1) that plaintiffs disclosed "confidential and novel information," and (2) that defendants knew it was supposed to be kept confidential. . . . But the complaint clearly contains these allegations as well.

The judgment of the district court is reversed and the matter remanded for further proceedings on plaintiffs' remaining claims.

KEY POINTS

- Enforcing implied-in-fact agreements is an important means of ensuring that one party does not get the benefit of a contract without compensating to the other party.
- Implied-in-fact agreements must contain the same elements as express contracts, including acceptance and consideration.
- When an agreement concerns an expressive idea like a story, picture or writing, courts must differentiate a copyright claim (covered in Chapter 11) from a contract claim.

"As a result of cases like *Montz*, some firms are wary of accepting unsolicited product ideas unless a clearly defined contractual relationship exists (see Sidebar 8.2).

In most business contracts, conflicts and disputes can be avoided if the parties take time to express clearly the terms of the agreement. However, businesspeople can get in a hurry to complete the contract arrangements so they can begin doing business. For example in a typical customer-supplier relationship, a written contract may omit specific terms of delivery. These terms will be implied by the courts to ensure the contractual relationship is ongoing. Details about delivery terms, as an aspect of performing contractual promises, are presented in chapter 9. In addition, as described in Sidebar 8.3, the law automatically adds terms to certain types of contracts unless specifically excluded by the parties. For now, you should understand courts will try to fill in the gaps the parties fail to expressly state.

A typical rule of thumb—parties expressing the detail of contractual commitments is better than leaving terms unstated.

sidebar 8.2

Unsolicited Ideas

A common concern for businesses is the creation of an unintended contractual obligation on receipt of an unsolicited idea. For example, imagine that an inventor develops a new idea for an improved toothbrush design and submits it to a firm that manufactures dental care products. But suppose that firm already has a similar idea in development. If the firm eventually markets the improved toothbrush design, it may appear that the idea was taken from the inventor without compensation.

In such a case, it is easy to see how the inventor could perceive a breach of an implied-in-fact contract—acceptance of an idea with the understanding by both parties that compensation is owed if the idea is used—and sue on that basis.

Some businesses address this problem by refusing to accept external idea submissions. Although they may miss out on a few business opportunities, they avoid costly litigation over allegedly stolen ideas.

sidebar 8.3

Implied Warranties

Some contracts contain additional, implied warranties (promises) that are dictated by statute. For example, the Uniform Commercial Code states that the following warranties are implied in in contracts for the sale of goods:
- *Merchantability*—if the seller is a merchant, the goods will be of fair average quality and conform to any labeling (U.C.C. § 2-314).
- *Fitness for a Particular Purpose*—the goods are suitable for the buyer's purpose if the seller is aware of it (U.C.C. § 2-315).

These promises are made even if the parties do not explicitly state them (or even know of them). However, warranties can be disclaimed in writing if the parties so choose. Other types of contracts contain warranties as well. For example, many states dictate that residential leases include an implied warranty of habitability, which means that a dwelling have a minimum level of livability.

IMPLIED-IN-LAW OR QUASI-CONTRACTS

When one party is unjustly enriched at the expense of another, the law may imply a duty on the first party to pay the second even though there is no contract between the two parties. The doctrine that requires this result is based on an **implied-in-law contract**. Since there really is no actual contractual agreement, the phrase **quasi-contract** is also used.

Quasi-contracts are a judicial remedy to prevent one party from receiving unjust enrichment.

If a debtor overpays a creditor $5,000, the debtor can force the creditor to return that amount by suing under quasi-contract. It would be an unjust enrichment to allow the creditor to keep the $5,000. Likewise, when John has paid taxes on land, thinking that he owns it, and Mary comes along with a superior title (ownership) to the land and has John evicted, the remedy of quasi-contract requires that Mary reimburse John for the taxes paid.

It is important to understand that the remedy of quasi-contract generally applies only when no actual contract exists to cover the dispute. But note that quasi-contract is not an answer to every such situation. Over the years, courts have come to apply quasi-contract in a fairly limited number of cases based on unjust enrichment. More often, it is applied when parties clearly intended a contract, but that contract is not valid or is unenforceable for some reason (such as a lack of capacity). After an exchange has taken place, it would be unjust for a court to leave the parties without a remedy.

CONTRACTUAL ENFORCEMENT TERMINOLOGY

Terms used in contract law related to the enforceability of agreements include *enforceable, unenforceable, valid, void,* and *voidable.*

The ultimate purpose of a contract is the creation of an agreement that courts will order parties to perform or to pay consequences for the failure of performance. When courts uphold the validity of such promises, the resulting agreement is an **enforceable contract.** If a nonperforming party has a justifiable reason for noncompliance with a promise, the result is an **unenforceable contract.** In essence, in this latter situation, a defense exists that denies the legal enforcement of an agreement.

When an agreement is enforceable because all the essential requirements (discussed later in the chapter) are present, courts refer to a **valid contract.** At the other end of the spectrum, a **void contract** is one that appears to be an agreement but lacks an essential requirement for validity and enforceability. The most typical example of a void contract is an apparent agreement that has an illegal purpose. For example, a business contract that involves the shipment of contraband is void and unenforceable. As described in the legality section in more detail, courts usually refuse to hear arguments of parties to a void contract. Courts simply leave these parties where they are regardless of whether the illegal agreement has been partially or fully performed. Thus, in states where gambling is illegal, a bet on a football game is void. Courts will not enforce the betting agreement and do not care if the losing party has or has not paid off the bet.

A **voidable contract** is an agreement when at least one party has the right to withdraw from the promise made without incurring any legal liability. That party has the power to end the enforcement of a voidable contract. In some cases, a contract is voidable by both parties and either one can withdraw. An interesting aspect of voidable contracts involves the fact that these agreements are enforceable in court until a party with the legal right to do so decides to void the contract, thereby making the agreement unenforceable. Typically this middle ground situation arises when a party to the contract lacks capacity or is disadvantaged by specific situations.

> **Valid contracts** are enforceable; **void contracts** are unenforceable; **voidable contracts** are enforceable until a party with the right to do so elects to void the agreement.

CONTRACTUAL PERFORMANCE TERMINOLOGY

In addition to issues related to enforcing contracts in court, the topic of parties performing their commitments is vital to contract law. The key terms related to performance are *executed* and *executory.* An **executed contract** is one in which the parties have performed their promises. When the parties have not yet performed their agreement, it is called an **executory contract.**

Since most business contracts are bilateral in nature involving an exchange of promises by the parties, most contracts are executory at some time. For example, if you promise your new employer to begin working next month and that employer promises to pay you at the end of the first month's work, this employment contract is executory from both parties' perspective.

Contracts cover a multitude of situations and these performance terms may be more or less relevant. Suppose you take a grocery item to the cashier and pay for it. The resulting contract is executed at the time of its creation. In fact, there probably was no exchange of spoken promises. The exchange of money for the item results in the performance being the proof of the contract.

In more complicated business transactions, the performance or lack thereof by one party becomes very important in determining the rights and duties under the contracts. A supplier of raw materials may ship its product and await the buyer's payment. The seller's performance is executed while the buyer's performance remains executory. How these terms impact enforceability issues is a part of the discussion in Chapter 9.

LO 8-3   Contract Formation

How a contract is formed is one of the most important issues to understand about contract law. Many agreements are void, and thus unenforceable, because they lack some essential element of contract formation.

The following sections focus on the essential elements and how they come together to form contracts (see Figure 8.3). Before an agreement can become a legally binding contract, someone must make a specific promise to another and also a specific demand of that person. This is the offer. The other person must accept the terms of the offer in the proper way. Both parties must give consideration to the other. Consideration is the promise to give, or the actual giving, of a requested benefit or the incurring of a legal detriment (i.e., doing something one does not have to). Both parties must be of legal age and sound mind, and the purpose of the agreement cannot be illegal or against public policy.

Figure 8.3 *Contract Elements and Defenses*

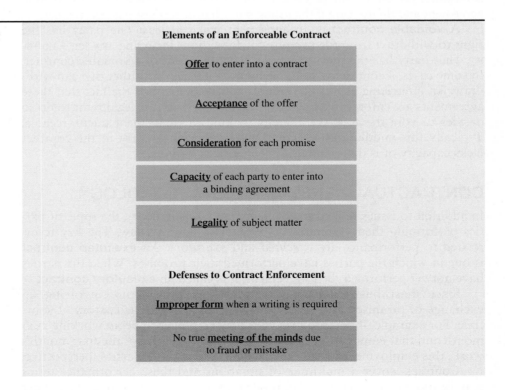

Elements of an Enforceable Contract

Offer to enter into a contract

Acceptance of the offer

Consideration for each promise

Capacity of each party to enter into a binding agreement

Legality of subject matter

Defenses to Contract Enforcement

Improper form when a writing is required

No true **meeting of the minds** due to fraud or mistake

OFFER TO CONTRACT

An **offer** contains a specific promise and a specific demand. "I will pay $15,000 for the electrical transformer" promises $15,000 and demands a specific product in return. An *offeror* (person making the offer) must intend to make the offer by making a commitment to the offeree (the person to whom the offer is made). Many issues about an offer can and do arise. For example, is the language of the offer clear enough to conclude that a valid contract can result? What if a person makes a statement ("I'll give you $100 for a ride to the mall"), intending it as a joke. Is this an offer? Courts answer this question by measuring intent from a reasonable person's perspective in the position of the offeree. This standard is known as the objective, rather than the subjective, intent of the offeror.

When does the language used in negotiation become an offer? Suppose a seller asks a potential buyer, "Would you be willing to pay $1,500 for this?" Is this an offer or an invitation to continue negotiating? The answers to these questions relate to the specificity of the language used to state a commitment or willingness to be bound. An offer is much more likely to exist when a seller says, "I will sell this to you for $1,500."

Definite Terms Under the common law of contracts, contractual terms must be definite and specific. An offer to purchase a house at a "reasonable price" cannot be the basis for a contract because of **indefiniteness.** Most advertisements, catalog, and web page price quotes are considered too indefinite to form the basis for a contract unless they are specific about the quantity of goods being offered, as well as the intended offeree. Otherwise, the retailer would be required to have sufficient stock to supply all readers of the advertisement or face multiple contract breaches.

Sidebar 8.4 presents an interesting case that emphasizes the importance of determining whether or not a definite offer exists.

---

sidebar 8.4

Is There a Definite Offer?

Many websites, including those for social networking services, have privacy policies that are separate from the so-called "terms of service" or "terms of use." Although it is generally acknowledged that the terms of service are an attempt to contractually set the conditions for website access, the effect of additional privacy policies is less clear. Is a website operator contractually bound to adhere to its promises to respect privacy? Or are such policies merely an aspirational expression without legal effect?

Interestingly, courts have issued inconsistent rulings in this area. In some cases, they have found that privacy policies are a part of the terms-of-service contract, and that a failure to adhere to the promises constitutes a breach. In other cases, courts have found that the policies are insufficiently definite to provide a basis for fashioning a remedy.

Even in cases where courts find a sufficiently definite offer as well as the intent to contract, damages resulting from any breach must be shown. Without any established monetary loss, the breach of contract claim may fail.

Source: Richard Raysman and Peter Brown, "Contractual Nature of Online Policies Remains Unsettled," *New York Law Journal,* August 10, 2010.

Do be very thoughtful in the choice of spoken words; decide whether you are ready to make an offer or want to continue discussions about possible arrangements.

Under the UCC, contracts for the sale of goods can leave open nonquantity terms to be decided at a future time (§2-305). For example, an agreement for the sale of 500 hats will bind the parties even though they leave open the price to be decided on delivery in six months. Note that this rule applies only to sales of goods. It does not apply to sales of real estate or services.

Termination of Offer   Offers create a legal power in the offeree to bind the offeror in a contract. However, that legal power does not last forever. When an offer *terminates,* the offeree's legal power to bind the offeror ends.

Offers can terminate due to an explicit act of one of the parties. This means that either the offeror or offeree has done something *before the acceptance* to destroy the offer. The following acts terminate offers:

- **Revocation**—when the offeror retracts the offer before the acceptance.
- **Rejection**—when the offeree rejects the offer.
- **Counteroffer**—when the offeree makes a counterproposal. Due to the mirror image rule described later, a counteroffer has the effect of rejecting the original offer and sending back a new offer for a different contract (but note the UCC flexibilities on additional terms, also described later).
- **Lapse of time**—when the offeree fails to accept by a deadline defined in the offer or after a reasonable period of time.

Even if the parties do not act to terminate the offer, there are circumstances in which contract law automatically dictates that an offer has expired. Again, they must occur *before the acceptance.* Termination by operation of law occurs in the following situations:

- **Subject matter destruction**—when the object of the contract is destroyed or legally eliminated.
- **Offeror death or insanity**—when the offeror no longer has the capacity to make the offer.
- **Subject matter illegality**—when a change in the law renders the agreement illegal, acceptance is no longer possible.

ACCEPTANCE OF OFFER

Acceptance of an offer is necessary to create a valid, enforceable contract. An offer to enter into a bilateral contract is accepted by the offeree's making the required promise. When Toni offers Aaron certain vinyl flooring for $2,500 to be delivered by November 30 on 90-day credit terms, and Aaron accepts, Aaron is promising to pay $2,500 on 90-day credit terms.

Unilateral contracts are accepted by performing a requested act, not by making a promise. A company's offer of a $2,500 reward for information leading to the conviction of anyone vandalizing company property is not accepted by promising to provide the information. Only the act of providing information accepts such an offer.

The language of the offer determines whether acceptance should be a promise resulting in a bilateral contract or an act resulting in a unilateral contract. The rights and duties of the contracting party can turn on the form of the acceptance.

Other issues relating to the importance of acceptance in the formation of a valid contract are discussed under the following headings.

Don't change the terms of the offer in an acceptance unless you want to create a counteroffer.

Mirror Image Rule For an acceptance to create a binding contract, standard contract law requires that the acceptance must "mirror" the offer, that is, must match it exactly. This is the **mirror image rule.** If the acceptance changes the terms of the offer or adds new terms, it is not really an acceptance. It is a *counteroffer,* and negotiations continue.

UCC Battle of the Forms Section 2-207 of the UCC changes the mirror image rule for contracts involving the sale of goods. In general, an expression of acceptance or a written confirmation is treated as an acceptance even if such communication adds or changes terms in the offer. If at least one party to the contract is a non-merchant, the new or revised terms are considered proposals for additions to the contract. When the contract is between two merchants, the additional terms become a part of the contract unless one of the following takes place:

1. The offer expressly limits acceptance to the original terms.
2. The proposed terms materially (importantly) alter the contract.
3. The offeror rejects the proposed terms.

This provision of the UCC most often comes into play when merchants exchange form documents such as purchase orders and invoices with different terms. Courts must decide which terms are included in the final contract. This "battle of the forms" is depicted in Case 8.2.

Between merchants means both parties to a contract do business in the goods being bought and sold.

 case **8.2**

GOTTLIEB & CO., INC. v. ALPS SOUTH CORPORATION
985 So. 2d 1 (Fla. App. 2007).

Gottlieb was in the business of supplying specialty knitted fabrics to manufacturers. Alps was a manufacturer of medical devices such as prosthetic limbs. Alps purchased Gottlieb's fabric for use as a liner in certain devices. In its finished goods form provided in response to Alps order, Gottlieb limited its liability to exclude consequential damages.

During the course of the parties' relationship, Gottlieb substituted the yarn used in making the fabric. This resulted in complaints from Alps' customers and caused Alps to suffer severe economic loss. To obtain compensation, Alps requested consequential damages from Gottlieb related to the customer complaints. Gottlieb claimed that its finished goods form excluded such liability. The court was required to determine whether the limitation on consequential damages became part of the parties' final contract.

CASANUEVA, JUDGE.: This dispute arises from the common, but risky, commercial practice where the seller and buyer negotiate a contract involving goods by exchanging each others' standardized forms. The transactions of this type involved here are governed by section 2-207 of the U.C.C., codified in section 672.207, Florida Statutes (2000).

Here, Gottlieb first contends that the trial court erred by failing to enforce the limitation of liabilities clause found on the back of its finished goods contract. The clause in contention reads:

> Buyer shall not in any event be entitled to, and seller shall not be liable for indirect or consequential damages of any nature, including, without being limited to, loss of profit, promotional or manufacturing expenses, injury to reputation or loss of customer.

The Battle of the Forms

"[T]he rules of engagement for the 'battle of the forms' are set out in the Uniform Commercial Code ('U.C.C'), s. 2-207." *Bayway Ref. Co. v. Oxygenated Mktg. & Trading*, 215 F.3d 219, 223 (2d Cir. 2000). The same rules of engagement apply in Florida and are codified in section 672.207. Subsections (1) and (2) of the statute are intended, according to the Florida Code Comments provided with the 1965 Enactment, to end the battle by eliminating the uncertainty that often results from the exchange of conflicting purchase order forms and acknowledgement and acceptance forms. The battle lines are frequently created where, as here, "the seller's form contains terms different from or additional to those set forth in the buyer's form." . . . Despite the differences in the forms, the parties proceed with the commercial transactions and fight the battle after the transaction concludes. . . .

These statutory provisions allow the formation of a contract where an acceptance contains additional or different terms than the original offer. While such an acceptance ordinarily would not meet the strict requirements of the common law mirror image rule, the U.C.C. provides a more flexible approach. Under section 672.207(2), additional terms included in an acceptance are construed as proposals for addition to the contract. . . . Between merchants, the terms become part of the contract unless they fall into an exception. . . . Within the context of section 672.207(2), the parties do not dispute that they are merchants, that Gottlieb's offer did not expressly limit acceptance to its terms, and that Alps did not object to the additional terms within a reasonable amount of time. The remaining issue is whether the limitation of damages clause, as an additional term, materially altered the contract. If the additional term materially alters the contract, it is excluded. . . .

Surprise or Hardship

Having determined [that Alps] bears the burden of proof, we next address the nature of proof that a party must offer to meet its burden. Unfortunately, the law in this area is not yet clearly developed. For example, Official Comment 4 to U.C.C. § 2-207 offers examples of "typical clauses which would normally 'materially alter' the contract" and that would "result in surprise or hardship if incorporated without express awareness by the other party."

. . . Alps must prove "that, under the circumstances, it cannot be presumed that a reasonable merchant would have consented to the additional term." *See Bayway Refining*, 215 F.3d at 224. The finished goods contract at issue was the sixth in a series between the two parties and each contract included the limitation of liability term. Each proposed contract contained the terms, which were visible on its face. The sole evidence presented at trial to establish surprise was that Alps had not read the contract before the dispute arose. Florida law has never excused a party from a contract simply because it failed to read the contract terms. . . . The record in this case does not allow a conclusion that Gottlieb's limitation of liability clause was an unreasonable surprise to Alps.

The record is similarly lacking with respect to hardship as a result of surprise. . . . Gottlieb never represented that, in the event of a breach, it would reimburse Alps for any or all consequential damages it sustained resulting from the breach. Instead, the evidence showed that Alps previously had returned a sample of nonconforming fabric to Gottlieb with a letter insisting on conforming goods. This letter did not mention or make claim for additional costs or damages resulting from Gottlieb's prior breach of performance. The evidence shows that Alps never informed Gottlieb of any consequences other than discontinuing their relationship. Alps did not inform Gottlieb of the specific manner in which the subject fabric would be used or what product would be crafted. Thus, Gottlieb could not foresee the *greater extent* of its potential liability, should a subsequent breach occur. Because Alps neglected to inform Gottlieb of the larger consequences of the breach, we conclude that Alps cannot maintain that incorporating the limitation of liability clause would result in a severe economic hardship. Thus, Alps failed to carry the burden of proof on hardship.

For these reasons, we conclude that the trial court erred by not enforcing the limitation of consequential damages clause. The award of consequential damages must be stricken.

Finally, we note that enforcing of the clause at issue only bars consequential damages. The limitation in this clause does not exclude other damages available under the law. . . .

We hold that the trial court erred in awarding Alps consequential damages. We reverse and remand with instructions to strike the consequential damages and lost profits awards and order the circuit court to hold a hearing on the limited question of damages only. As outlined above, these damages include incidental and certain benefit-of-the-bargain (direct) damages stemming from Gottlieb's undisputed breach.

Reversed and remanded with instructions.

KEY POINTS

- The court found that Gottlieb's term (the consequential damages limitation) was included in the contract even though it appeared only on Gottlieb's forms and was not specifically discussed by the parties.
- Alps' failure to read Gottlieb's forms was irrelevant, according to the court. This is generally true as a contract law principle.
- If Alps foresaw the likelihood of certain outcomes, like consequential damages from customer complaints, it should have addressed it with Gottlieb.

Silence Not Acceptance In general, an offeree's failure to reject an offer does not imply acceptance. Another way to say this is that silence alone is not acceptance. The offeree has no usual duty to reply to the offer even if the offer states that the offeror will treat silence as acceptance. Note, however, that an *action,* such as using an Internet search engine after having the opportunity to review contractual terms of use, may constitute acceptance.

There are major exceptions to this rule. For instance, parties may have a contract that specifies that future shipments of goods be made automatically unless the offeree expressly rejects them.

A related doctrine looks at the parties' prior *course of dealing*—the way they have done business in the past. Silence may well imply acceptance if the parties previously dealt with each other by having the buyer take shipments from the seller unless the buyer notified the seller in advance not to ship.

Finally, in an implied-in-fact contract, both the offer and the acceptance may be made without explicit language. Additionally, the UCC says that a contract may arise from the *conduct* of a buyer and seller of goods. Emphasis is placed on how the parties act rather than on a formal offer and acceptance of terms.

Mailbox Rule When does the acceptance become legally binding on the offeror? Unless the offeror specifies a particular time, the acceptance usually binds the parties *when the offeree dispatches it*. Since the offeree frequently mails the acceptance, the acceptance becomes binding when it is "deposited" with the postal service—hence the **mailbox rule,** also called the **deposited acceptance rule.**

The importance of the mailbox rule is that the offeror cannot revoke the offer once the offeree has accepted it. An added significance is that an offeror's revocation is not effective until the offeree actually receives it. Thus, a deposited acceptance creates a binding contract even though a revocation is also in the mail.

Sidebar 8.5 highlights the relevance of the mailbox rule in modern business transactions.

As this section and the prior one illustrate, understanding the nature of the parties' mutual assent to a contract can become complex. Despite the variety of rules associated with offers and acceptances, the purpose of these essential contractual elements remains simple: determining if the parties made a binding agreement and defining its terms.

Don't rely on the other party's silence as evidence of acceptance. It can mislead you concerning the existence of a contract.

sidebar 8.5

Is the Mailbox Rule Still Relevant?

Many modern contracts are not accepted though the U.S. Mail or other physical delivery service, but rather through an electronic means like e-mail, fax, or a web page. Is the mailbox rule relevant in any of these situations? In general, the answer is yes. In any case where the contracting parties are not interacting simultaneously, the mailbox rule applies. While the time between an offeree's acceptance and the offeror's receipt is extremely short, the exact point at which acceptance occurs is still governed by the mailbox rule. Although this will often have little impact in electronic transactions, there may be cases where it is important.

Two states employ a modified mailbox rule when the transaction involves computer information, like software. Under the Uniform Commercial Information Transactions Act (UCITA), which only Maryland and Virginia have adopted, acceptance of such contracts is valid only when received.

Source: Valerie Watnick, *The Electronic Formation of Contracts and the Common Law "Mailbox Rule."* 56 Baylor L. Rev. 175 (2004).

CONSIDERATION

Not all promises are enforceable through legal action. There must be some incentive or inducement for a person's promise or it is not binding. The legal mechanism for evaluating the existence of this incentive is **consideration,** the receipt of a legal benefit or the suffering of a legal detriment. Courts will not enforce contractual promises unless they are supported by consideration.

> To be valid, a contract must involve the exchange of consideration between the parties.

Before Laura can enforce a promise made by David, Laura must have given consideration that induced David to make the promise. In a bilateral contract, each party promises something to the other. The binding promises are the consideration. In a unilateral contract, the consideration of one party is a promise; the consideration of the other party is performance of an act. When it is not clear whether there is consideration to support a promise, a court will often examine a transaction as a whole.

Consideration need not be money, though a promise to pay a certain amount is one type of consideration. Valid consideration can include any promise to do something one has no obligation to do, refrain from doing something one has the right to do, or in the case of a unilateral contract, a performance when there is no obligation to do so. That is the definition of a legal detriment. The amount of the consideration is generally irrelevant. An important part of consideration is that it must be *bargained for.* In other words, the consideration must be contemporaneous and a part of both parties' understanding of the contract terms.

Agreement Not to Sue

> The phrase "paid in full" placed on a check offered in settlement of a disputed amount acts as an accord and satisfaction if the check is cashed or deposited.

When reasonable grounds for a lawsuit exist, an agreement not to sue is consideration to support a promise. If Maria is at fault in an automobile accident with Peter, and Peter accepts $100 from Maria as full compensation for his damages on the spot, Peter has been given compensation. He has promised to surrender his legal right to sue Maria.

Likewise, suppose that a consulting firm bills a client $5,000 for 50 hours of work at $100 per hour. The client disputes the bill and contends that the consulting firm worked only 25 hours and should get only $2,500. If the two parties compromise the bill at $3,500 for 35 hours, this agreement binds them both. Each has surrendered the right to have a court determine exactly what amount is owed. Such an agreement and the payment of the $3,500 to resolve a dispute over the amount owed is an **accord and satisfaction.**

Occasionally, parties will try to avoid consideration by drafting one-sided contracts that obligate one party but allow the other party to escape performance. Such clever drafting may backfire. A court may determine that a one-sided contract is *illusory* because one party is not truly bound. Case 8.3 is an example of a contract that initially appears to include consideration by both parties but, on closer examination, obligates only one.

 case **8.3**

VASSILKOVSKA v. WOODFIELD NISSAN, INC.
830 N.E.2d 619 (III. App. 2005)

Nadejda Vassilkovska purchased used car from Woodfield Nissan. In an agreement separate from the purchase contract, Vassilkovska promised to arbitrate any claim against Woodfield instead of suing in court. Woodfield promised to arbitrate claims against Vassilkovska as well, but excluded several different types of claims from the agreement. In fact, the excluded claims were the only circumstances in which Woodfield would ever be likely to sue a customer. Subsequently, Vassilkovska sued Woodfield for misrepresenting the price of the car in a financing agreement. Woodfield argued that Vassilkovska was required to arbitrate the claim. The court had to address whether the arbitration agreement was valid.

JUSTICE GARCIA DELIVERED THE OPINION OF THE COURT.: An agreement to arbitrate is treated like any other contract. . . . However, without a contract to arbitrate, there can be no forced arbitration. . . .

The plaintiff contends that the Arbitration Agreement is not a contract at all because any promise to arbitrate by Woodfield was illusory and, therefore, the Arbitration Agreement is unenforceable because of the absence of the essential requirement of consideration to make out an enforceable contract. . . .

Woodfield asserts that the parties' Arbitration Agreement was supported by consideration and argues its retention of certain rights does not invalidate that consideration.

The plaintiff, on the other hand, contends that Woodfield's promise to arbitrate was "illusory" and there was no consideration because Woodfield "made sure that as to every conceivable right that it might

want to press, the arbitration provision did not stand as a bar to [Woodfield's] going to court."

We agree with the plaintiff. A legally enforceable contract is an exchange, and the elements of a contract include offer, acceptance, and consideration. . . . "It is a basic tenet of contract law that in order for a promise to be enforceable against the promisor, the promisee must have given some consideration for the promise." *Gibson,* 121 F.3d at 1130. Consideration is defined as a bargained-for exchange, whereby the promisor, here, the plaintiff, receives some benefit, or the promisee, here, Woodfield, suffers detriment. . . . Thus, in order for the plaintiff's agreement to arbitrate, rather than to litigate, any claim against Woodfield, there must be some detriment to Woodfield, or some benefit to the plaintiff, that was bargained for in exchange for the plaintiff's promise to arbitrate all disputes. Clearly, what is required is consideration, as with any contract . . . .

. . . Woodfield cannot point to its own promise to arbitrate in order to make enforceable the plaintiff's promise to do likewise. . . . The Arbitration Agreement contains no promise on Woodfield's part to submit claims to arbitration. . . . In fact, the Arbitration Agreement, by virtue of the exceptions outlined in it, leaves no claim that Woodfield would be required to submit to arbitration. . . . The language of the Arbitration Agreement makes clear that its purpose is to force the plaintiff to arbitrate any claim she may assert against Woodfield, while excluding Woodfield from that same promise. There is nothing in the Arbitration Agreement to suggest that Woodfield was required to forgo a judicial forum in favor of arbitration. Therefore, we conclude that the Arbitration Agreement itself did not contain consideration for the plaintiff's promise in the form of a promise by Woodfield to submit disputes to arbitration. . . .

We further note that Woodfield is correct in asserting that, often, consideration for one party's promise to arbitrate is the other party's promise to do the same. A *mutual* promise to arbitrate would be sufficient consideration to support an independent arbitration agreement. . . . Mutuality of obligation is required only to the extent that both parties to an agreement are bound or neither is bound; that is, if the requirement of consideration has been met, mutuality of obligation is not essential. The converse, of course, is where there is no consideration independent of the mutuality of obligation, then both parties to an agreement are bound or neither is bound. If there is no consideration and no mutuality of obligation, then neither party is bound.

Although both parties signed the Arbitration Agreement in which they "waived all rights to pursue any legal action in a court of law," Woodfield exempted itself from arbitration by specifically securing its right to seek assistance in a court of law for a host of issues, primarily those dealing with the recoupment of money from the plaintiff. Specifically, Woodfield retained the right to pursue the following claims: (1) the plaintiff's failure to pay according to the purchase contract; (2) a check not being honored by the plaintiff's bank; (3) the plaintiff's failure to provide good title on a trade-in vehicle; (4) the plaintiff's misrepresentation concerning the loan amount due on any trade-in vehicle; (5) any claim relating to possession, repossession, or replevin of the automobile; and (6) any action to enforce any retail installment contract executed by the purchaser. Thus, the plaintiff, as purchaser, waives any right to sue Woodfield in a court of law, but Woodfield, as seller, retains the right to sue the plaintiff for a laundry list of reasons. . . .

Accordingly, we hold that where the agreement to arbitrate is itself a separate document, purporting to bind each party to the arbitration agreement, but subsequently creates a total exclusion of one party's obligation to arbitrate, the obligation to arbitrate is illusory and unenforceable. . . . At the time the Arbitration Agreement in this case was signed, there was no consideration on the part of Woodfield to support the plaintiff's promise to arbitrate and "waive any and all rights to pursue any legal action in a court of law."

While we agree with Woodfield that "parties do not have to agree to identical obligations to nonetheless have a valid and enforceable arbitration agreement," in this case, Woodfield's promise to arbitrate was an empty one because Woodfield completely exempted issues that could arise from its sale of the automobile to the plaintiff. Effectively, in its Arbitration Agreement with the plaintiff, Woodfield enumerated all the reasons it would have to sue the plaintiff and, thus, exempted itself from the parties' Arbitration Agreement. What claims, other than those related to the purchase of the plaintiff's vehicle, would Woodfield pursue? We can think of no specific claim, and Woodfield was unable to provide us with a specific example, either in its brief or during questioning in oral argument, of a claim that it would be compelled to submit to arbitration pursuant to the Arbitration Agreement. . . .

We find that the Arbitration Agreement, as a separate and distinct contract between the parties, lacked consideration from Woodfield as it exempted itself from arbitrating all conceivable claims against the plaintiff. It is Woodfield that, by virtue of excluding every conceivable claim it may have had against the plaintiff from the arbitration process, has made the Arbitration Agreement a nullity, which, in effect, goes against Illinois's public policy favoring arbitration. . . .

We therefore affirm the trial court's denial of Woodfield's motion to dismiss and compel arbitration.

KEY POINTS

- Contracts require consideration for both promises. Care must be taken in limiting one's obligations, particularly if the result is no legal detriment at all.
- The amount of consideration is generally not an issue, but it must be more substantial than simply an acknowledgement or statement.

Preexisting Obligation A party to an agreement does not give consideration by promising to do something that he or she is already obligated to do. For example, suppose a warehouse owner contracts to have certain repairs done for $20,000. In the middle of construction, the building contractor demands an additional $5,000 to complete the work. The owner agrees, but when the work is finished, he gives the contractor only $20,000. If the contractor sues, he will lose. The owner's promise to pay an extra $5,000 is not supported by consideration. The contractor is under a *preexisting obligation* to do the work for which the owner promises an additional $5,000. If the contractor promises to do something he was not already obligated to do, there would be consideration to support the promise of the additional $5,000. Promising to modify the repair plans illustrates such new consideration.

Sidebar 8.6 discusses how the UCC changes the legal requirement of consideration.

Many contractual modifications are not enforceable because there is a lack of consideration. If Gerald agrees to paint your house for $2,000 and halfway through the job insists on receiving another $1,000, what consideration would you receive if you agree to pay the additional amount?

sidebar 8.6

Consideration Not Necessary

The preexisting obligation rule does not apply to a sale-of-goods contract. The UCC states that parties to a sale-of-goods contract may make binding modifications to it without both parties giving new consideration. If a buyer of more than $500 of supplies agrees to pay your company an additional $500 over and above the amount already promised, this buyer is bound, although your company gives only the consideration (supplies) that it is already obligated to give (§2-209(1)).

Under the UCC, the rules of consideration also do not apply to a **firm offer.** A firm offer exists when a merchant offering goods promises in writing that the offer will not be revoked for a period not to exceed three months. This promise binds the merchant, although the offeree buyer gives no consideration to support it (§2-205).

Prior Consideration Prior consideration is no consideration; performance made before the parties discuss their agreement does not count. For instance, after many years of working at Acme Co., Bigman retires as vice president for financial planning. The company's board of directors votes him a new car every year "for services rendered." One year later, the board rescinds this vote. If Bigman sues for breach of contract, he will lose. He gave no consideration to support the board's promise. The past years of service were not "bargained for" by the company's board when it took its vote. The board merely promised to give an unenforceable gift to Bigman.

Promise to Make a Gift The promise to give something to another—in other words, a promise to make a gift—is not binding *as a contract* because no bargained-for consideration supports the promise. In some cases, insignificant consideration in return for a great one may raise concerns that the exchange is actually a gift. For example, a promise of $1 might be made in return for a promise to convey 40 acres of land. In such situations, a court must decide whether the party promising to convey the land really bargained for the $1 or merely promised to make a gift. Note that a true gift can be enforceable as a property transfer (not a contract), but it requires delivery of the item. Moreover, even a promise to make a gift may be enforceable under a non-contract theory called promissory estoppel (as described later).

Option Contract In contracts that are not between merchants selling goods, a promise to keep an offer open for a certain time period must be supported by the offeree's consideration. Such agreement to not revoke an offer is called an **option**. A typical use of options is found in real estate transactions. A seller of land may promise to let a prospective buyer have two weeks to study the deal and accept the offer at a specific price. The buyer must provide some consideration (usually a small sum of money) to the seller, or the seller's offer is not an enforceable option because it can be revoked.

Promissory estoppel often is used to prevent a party who has made a unilateral offer from withdrawing the offer after the requested work has begun.

Promissory Estoppel An important exception to the rule requiring consideration to support a promise is the doctrine of **promissory estoppel** (also known as "detrimental reliance"). This doctrine arises when a promisee justifiably relies on a promisor's promise to his or her economic injury. The promisor must know that the promisee is likely to rely on the promise.

Promissory estoppel may be used when the facts of a business relationship do not meet the requirements of an express or implied contract. For example, a pledge to a charity elicits no consideration from the other party and is not enforceable as a contract. Similarly, an oral promise to pay a another's student loan if that person enrolls in graduate school is not enforceable under the statute of frauds. But a court may enforce these promises based on the doctrine of promissory estoppel.

The extent to which promissory estoppel can create liability for an employer that withdraws a job offer is another common issue. As courts may consider reliance on an at-will job offer to be unjustified, plaintiffs are likely to experience difficulty recovering under this theory.

CAPACITY OF PARTIES TO CONTRACT

Capacity refers to a person's ability to be bound by a contract. Courts have traditionally held the following three classes of persons to lack capacity to be bound by contractual promises:

- Minors (also called "infants")
- Intoxicated persons
- Mentally incompetent persons

Don't enter into contracts with minors without considering their lack of capacity; they have the power to affirm or void the agreement.

Minors In most states, a *minor* is anyone under age 18. Minors usually cannot be legally bound to contractual promises unless those promises involve *necessaries of life* such as food, clothing, shelter, medical care, and—in some states—education. Even for necessaries, minors often cannot be sued for the contract price, only for a reasonable value. However, in a number of states, courts will hold a minor who has misrepresented his or her age liable for contractual promises.

A contract into which a minor has entered is voidable at the election of the minor. The minor can *disaffirm* the contract and legally recover any consideration given to the other party, even if the minor cannot return the consideration he or she received. On the other hand, the adult is bound by the contract unless the minor elects to disaffirm it.

The minor may disaffirm a contract anytime before reaching the age of majority (usually 18) and for a reasonable time after reaching majority. If the minor fails to disaffirm within a reasonable time after reaching majority, the minor is said to *ratify* the contract. In addition, a minor can explicitly ratify a contract and forego disaffirmance, but only after reaching the age of majority. Upon ratification, the minor loses the right to disaffirm.

Intoxicated and Mentally Incompetent Persons Except when a court has judged an adult to be mentally incompetent, that adult does not lose capacity to contract simply because of intoxication or mental impairment. In most cases involving adult capacity to contract, courts measure capacity by whether the adult was capable of understanding the nature and purpose of the contract. Obviously, the more complex a contractual transaction gets, the more likely a court is to decide that an intoxicated or mentally impaired person lacks capacity to contract and has the right to disaffirm the contract. In such factual situations, the contracts are voidable by the intoxicated or mentally impaired person.

Traditionally, the descriptive phrase *mentally impaired* applies to adults with a history of medically documented disabilities. With the aging of the population, the number of cases involving elderly citizens claiming contractual incapacity grows. These cases will develop additional nuances in the law of capacity to contract. Practical business advice is to be aware when contracting with an elderly person. It may be best to insist that a friend or family member assist (if not cosign with) an older contracting party. Take steps to ensure you will not be accused of taking advantage of the elderly.

Beware of signs that an elderly person may have difficulty understanding the nature of the contractual agreement.

LAWFUL PURPOSE

A basic requirement of a valid contract is *legality of purpose.* A "contract" to murder someone is obviously not enforceable in a court of law. Contracts that require commission of a crime or tort or violate accepted standards of behavior (*public policy*) are void. Courts will generally take no action on a void contract, and they will leave the parties to a contract where they have put themselves. Sidebar 8.7 gives a common example of a contract with legality issues.

There are several exceptions to the general rule that courts will take no action on an illegal contract. A contract may have both legal and illegal provisions to it. In such a case, courts will often enforce the legal provisions and refuse to enforce the illegal ones. For instance, a contract providing services or leasing goods sometimes contains a provision excusing the service provider or lessor from liability for negligently caused injury. Courts usually will not enforce this provision but will enforce the rest of the contract.

Often, courts will allow an innocent party to recover payment made to a party who knows (or should know) that a contract is illegal. For example, courts will allow recovery of a payment for professional services made by an innocent person to a person who is unlicensed to provide such services.

In some cases courts may allow a person to recover compensation under quasi-contract for services performed on an illegal contract. Recovery may be allowed when an otherwise qualified professional lets his or her license expire and provides services to a client before renewing the license.

sidebar 8.7

Unconscionable Contracts

Contracts that courts find "unconscionable" are unenforceable as illegal. In such cases, it is often said that terms or circumstances that are so unfair that they shock the conscience of the court should not be enforced against the innocent party. One common type of unconscionability involves adhesion contracts. Adhesion contracts are those that are drafted by one party and presented to the other without a substantial opportunity for revision. They include many standard form contracts. In general, adhesion contracts are often enforceable. But, in some cases, a court may find that the lack of negotiation renders such a contract unconscionable, particularly when it contains terms that are severe or detrimental to the non-drafting party.

Contracts involving a sale of goods under the UCC may be found unconscionable when a difference in bargaining power or education leads a merchant to take unreasonable advantage of a consumer (§2-302).

In 2011, the U.S. Supreme Court addressed the issue of unconscionability in the context of a wireless carrier contract that compelled customers to arbitrate disputes rather than sue in a class action. California, the state in which the contract was signed, has a law that makes such clauses unenforceable. The Supreme Court held that federal law facilitating arbitration, the Federal Arbitration Act (FAA), preempted the California law. If state contract law regarding unconscionability were permitted to apply so broadly, the Court reasoned, it would frustrate the purpose of the FAA.

Source: *AT & T Mobility LLC v. Concepcion*, 131 S. Ct. 1740 (2011).

Contracts That Restrain Trade   Contracts that restrain trade often are illegal and void. They include contracts to monopolize, to fix prices between competitors, and to divide up markets. Chapter 16 on antitrust law discusses these contracts and their illegality.

Other contracts that restrain trade are important to the efficient operation of business. **Covenants not to compete** are important in protecting employers from having the employees they train leave them and compete against them. They also protect the buyer of a business from having the seller set up a competing business.

However, some covenants not to compete are illegal. Courts will declare such agreements illegal unless they have a valid business purpose, such as to protect the goodwill a business buyer purchases from the seller of the business. Covenants not to compete must also be "reasonable as to time and space." If they restrain competition for too long or in an area too large, the courts will declare them unreasonable and void them as being illegal. Four or five years is generally as long a time as the courts are willing to find reasonable, and even then the length of time must be justified. As to space, the courts will void covenants not to compete any time the area restrained exceeds the area in which the restraining business operates.

LO 8-4   When a "Meeting of the Minds" Is Lacking

In addition to the basic elements described earlier, we also require that the parties to a contract have a mutual understanding of the essential terms and underlying facts. This is often referred to as a "meeting of the minds." On the other hand, if it is clear that the parties had fundamentally different beliefs about the contract, it may be voidable. In most cases, a mutual understanding is assumed unless evidence to the contrary exists. A party usually raises the lack of mutual agreement as a defense to enforcement.

FRAUD OR INNOCENT MISREPRESENTATION

Contracts based on fraud or misrepresentation are important examples of agreements in which a mutual understanding is lacking. **Fraud** involves an intentional misstatement of fact that induces another to enter into a contract to which they would not otherwise agree. The specific elements that must be demonstrated to establish fraud are (1) a **misrepresentation** of fact (as opposed to an opinion), (2) an intent to deceive, (3) justified reliance on the misstatement by the innocent party, and (4) injury resulting from the reliance. You will note that fraud is also described in Chapter 10. Here, it specifically functions as a tort that acts as a barrier to formation of a legitimate contract.

Intent is one of the most important elements of fraud. For example, if a person selling a ring with a glass stone states that it is a diamond ring instead, the misstatement must be a knowing lie to constitute fraud. But also note that the innocent party must reasonably believe that lie. If the stone in a ring is obviously glass, then the purchaser did not justifiably rely on the deception.

Fraud can be explicit as described earlier. It can also arise from a deceptive act by a party, such as tampering with the odometer on a car. In general, silence does not constitute fraud. However, failing to disclose a material fact that creates a dangerous condition may rise to that level. For example, if a seller removes the airbag from a car and does not inform the buyer, fraud may be found.

A party who is injured due to another's fraud generally has the option to avoid the contract and seek return of any consideration conveyed. In addition, the injured party may enforce the contract and sue for damages resulting from the fraud. It may also be possible to seek punitive damages based on the fraud.

When a party misrepresents a material fact without intent to mislead, harm still occurs. However, this "innocent" misrepresentation simply makes the contract voidable by the innocent party. Heightened remedies such as punitive damages are inappropriate without the intent to deceive. Due to the difficulties an individual may experience in establishing all of the elements of fraud or innocent misrepresentation, the government may step in (see Sidebar 8.8).

sidebar 8.8

Deceptive Advertising and the FTC

In many cases in which a merchant misrepresents something about its product, it may be difficult to establish the intent necessary to bring a fraud case. A consumer may have insufficient incentive to sue. If the misrepresentation is widespread—such as though a national advertisement—the Federal Trade Commission (FTC) may act to address the harm. The FTC has the power to prevent deceptive acts or practices that involve a misrepresentation or omission that is likely to mislead consumers and is material to the decision to purchase a product. The agency can bring an enforcement action without the need to demonstrate intent to deceive. If deceptive advertising is found, the agency can impose civil penalties, consumer compensation, and corrective advertising. State consumer protection agencies may have similar powers. Government regulation of deceptive advertising can be an important complement to consumer fraud cases.

Source: FTC Policy Statement on Deception, 103 F.T.C. 110, 174 (1984).

MISTAKE

What happens when each party misunderstands something very basic and material about a contract? Although no tortious act has occurred, such a situation goes right to the heart of whether there has been voluntary consent to a single set of terms. If it is clear that there has been a **mutual mistake** as to a material fact relating to the contract, **rescission** by either party is appropriate. The test of materiality is whether the parties would have contracted had they been aware of the mistake. If they would not have contracted, the mistaken fact is material. In addition, the mistake must be one of fact as opposed to value. When parties misconstrue only the value of their transaction but fully appreciate the subject matter, the contract is not voidable.

Significantly, the both parties must be mistaken in their understanding. For example, if both a seller and buyer believe they have made an agreement concerning an original Picasso painting, but it turns out to be the work of another artist, both should have the right to avoid the contract. On the other hand, if only one party is mistaken about some aspect of the contract (a **unilateral mistake**) no remedy is generally available. We do not want to impose the costs of one party's mistake on the other party who acted with complete knowledge. For example, suppose that Royal Carpet Co. bids $8.70 per yard for certain carpet material instead of $7.80 per yard as it had intended. If the seller accepts Royal Carpet's bid, a contract results even though there was a unilateral mistake.

DURESS OR UNDUE INFLUENCE

Other examples of contracts in which a mutual agreement is lacking include those induced by **duress** or **undue influence**. Duress means force or threat of force. The force may be physical or, in some instances, economic. However, duress cannot be based on one's assertion of legitimate business consequences; it must rise to the level of a tort. For example, if a seller informs a buyer that his or her offer is so advantageous the buyer's business will suffer if the buyer does not form a contract, no duress has occurred. Similarly, threatening to sue unless the parties reach a settlement is also not duress.

Undue influence occurs when one is taken advantage of unfairly through a contract by a party who misuses a position of relationship or legal confidence. Contracts voidable because of undue influence often arise when persons weakened by age or illness are persuaded to enter into a disadvantageous contract. Someone who has a special relationship of power and trust over the other party, such as a psychiatrist or lawyer, may also exert undue influence.

LO 8-5   Contract Form

Knowing what elements must exist to form a valid contract is only the beginning of understanding the use of contracts in business transactions. Among the other important topics is whether contracts have to be in writing and signed by the parties. The following sections examine the formality of contracts.

ORAL CONTRACTS

Because of the importance of contracts in our personal and professional lives, many people believe a contract must be written and signed to be valid. Typically, this impression is wrong. Oral contracts generally are as enforceable as written ones. Many of our everyday transactions involve informal contracts.

This does not mean we should ignore reasons for greater formality. When contracts are of significant importance or the dollars involved are larger than typical day-to-day transactions or it is important to have a record of the precise agreement, writing and signing a contract is best. In certain situations, the law requires contracts to be in a written, signed format. The next two sections discuss this requirement and explain the types of agreements that must be in writing. The impact of oral changes to written contracts is examined later, in Chapter 9.

> Oral contracts generally are valid and enforceable. Certain types of contracts must be evidenced by a writing that is signed by the party to be bound.

STATUTE OF FRAUDS

The law requiring that certain contracts be in writing is known as the statute of frauds. Note, however, that this rule does not address fraud in the formation of a contract. Rather, it is designed to prevent potential deception or fraud from oral contracts. The original English statute was adopted in 1677, and today, every state has its own statute of frauds. The role of these statutes requiring certain written contracts is to minimize confusion in court whenever a party claims a contract is breached. If courts have to decide the validity of an oral agreement, parties can make allegations that contradict one another. One party says to the judge, "We have a contract." The other party says, "We never finalized a contract" or "the terms are different." Judges can have difficulty knowing whom to believe. Written contracts reduce the potential for confusion, fraud, and deceit. If the required writing is not met, the parties are left with an unenforceable contract. The statute of frauds requires certain types of business-related contracts to be in writing. Sidebar 8.9 provides a list of these agreements.

---

sidebar 8.9

Types of Contracts Required to Be Evidenced by a Signed Writing

- Contracts involving an interest in land.
- Collateral contracts to pay the debt of another person.
- Contracts that cannot be performed within one year from the date of the agreement.
- Contracts for the sale of goods of $500 or more.

In some states, the statute of frauds requires that the actual contract between the parties must be in writing. However, most states merely require that the contract be evidenced by writing and be signed by the party against whom enforcement is being sought. This requirement means that the party being sued must have signed a note, memorandum, or another written form short of a formal contract that describes with reasonable certainty the terms of the oral agreement. In sales of goods between merchants, the writing may

> Exchange of e-mail messages may satisfy the requirement of a writing.

not need to be signed by the party being sued. Despite these rules, the best practice is to have contracts carefully written and signed. Written documentation will save time and expense if a dispute arises. Chapter 9 provides more detail about how written contracts get interpreted.

Sale of an Interest in Land

Sales of interests in land are common contracts covered by the statute of frauds. Although "sales of interests in land" covers a contract to sell land, it includes much more. Interests in land include contracts for mortgages, mining rights, and easements (rights to use another's land, such as the right to cross it with electric power wires). However, a contract to insure land or to erect a building is not an interest in land.

Collateral Promise to Pay Another's Debt

A collateral promise is a secondary or conditional promise. Such a commitment arises when one person, a business shareholder for example, promises to repay the loan of the corporation if and only when that organization does not make payments. This collateral promise usually arises at a time different from the original obligation. Suppose the corporation borrows money from a bank and later finds it is having trouble making payments on time. To avoid the bank's calling the entire loan in default, the shareholder may promise to pay if the corporation does not. This promise by the shareholder is of a collateral nature and must be in writing to be enforced by the bank.

Remember the difference between guaranteeing a person's performance and agreeing to become liable if a person fails to perform.

To avoid this situation of a collateral promise, banks often require a small business organization to have someone guarantee the performance of its contracts. If a shareholder makes an original promise to be responsible for the corporation's performance, this commitment is not collateral and does not have to be in writing. In essence, in such situations the corporation and the shareholder are considered equally obligated to perform the contract. There is no conditional promise by the shareholder. Although such original promises often are in writing, the law does not require a written agreement.

If it is possible, even if unlikely, to perform a contract within one year, an oral contract involving that performance is enforceable.

Cannot Be Performed within One Year

The statute of frauds applies to a contract the parties cannot perform within one year after its making. Courts usually interpret the one-year requirement to mean that the contract must specify a period of performance longer than one year. Thus, an oral contract for services that lasts 20 months or a lease of longer than one year are generally not enforceable. But an oral contract for services to be completed "by" a date 20 months away is enforceable. The difference is that the latter contract can be performed within one year, even if it actually takes longer than that to perform it.

As interpreted by the courts, the statute of frauds applies only to executor contracts that the parties' cannot perform within a year. Once one of the parties has completed his or her performance for the other, that party can enforce an oral multiyear contract.

Sale of Goods of $500 or More

Under the UCC, the statute of frauds covers sales of goods of $500 or more. Modifications to such are also included and must be in writing. While this provision appears arbitrary with respect to the $500 amount, its purpose is clear. Contracts involving the sale and purchase of goods that are less than $500 usually are performed quickly.

There is very little room for disputes about terms or performance that arise. As the dollar amount increases, the need for a written agreement also increases. This is particularly true if the contract will remain executory (not performed) for an extended period of time.

As you think about this requirement in sale of goods transactions, ponder a typical transaction. Assume you go into a electronics store and buy a new laptop computer for $1,500. You probably do not sign a written contract before completing the purchase. The reason is there is no need for a written contract. The agreement to buy and the actual sale occur almost simultaneously—at least in very quick order. Suppose, instead of going to the store, you go online to order a laptop. The online transaction contains information telling you the laptop will be prepared and shipped within three weeks. The paperwork generated through the website likely will include a contract for you to sign electronically. This writing is needed to satisfy the statute of frauds (see Sidebar 8.10). The written agreement governs the parties' relationship until the contract is performed—you pay and the manufacturer delivers the laptop.

Other Contracts In addition to the basic contracts covered by the statute of frauds, other contracts must be in writing in various states. Most states require insurance policies to be written. Several states require written estimates in contracts for automobile repair.

---

sidebar 8.10

Are Electronic Contracts Considered Writings?

When one imagines a "written" contract, one usually has in mind terms printed on paper with handwritten signatures at the end. However, many business transactions that formerly took place face-to-face or through the mail now occur electronically. Is it possible for an electronic exchange to constitute a writing, and if so, can it be signed? The trend in the courts has been to answer in the affirmative: electronic contracts are generally as enforceable as paper contracts. A signature need not be the stylized, handwritten letters of one's name, but merely an indication that a party intends to be bound to the contract. A typed name or even a check-box will usually suffice.

Recent legislation supports the enforceability of electronic contracts. The federal Electronic Signatures in Global and National Commerce Act (ESIGN) ensures that contracts and other documents are not considered invalid solely because they are in electronic form. States have passed similar laws, such as the Uniform Electronic Transactions Act (UETA), which complements ESIGN in guaranteeing that electronic contracts satisfy the writing requirement. Therefore, consider the impact of sending that e-mail message, fax or even text message; a written contract may be the result.

Source: Jay M. Zitter, *Construction and Application of Electronic Signatures in Global and National Commerce Act (E-Sign Act)*, 29 A.L.R. Fed. 2d 519 (2008).

EXCEPTIONS TO THE WRITING REQUIREMENT

In addition to understanding that the statute of frauds requires certain types of contracts to be in writing, it is important to know there are exceptions to the writing requirement. If an agreement is orally stated, parties may be able to convince a judge that a contract does exist. If such proof can be established in a way that convinces the judge the contract was agreed upon, there is little chance of fraud. Under certain circumstances, oral contracts are enforceable.

Such exceptions fall into the following categories:

- Part performance
- Rules involving goods
- Judicial admissions

The part performance exception sometimes is called promissory estoppel.

Part Performance
The doctrine of part performance creates an exception to the requirement that sales of interests in land must be in writing. When a buyer of land has made valuable improvements in it, or when the buyer is in possession of it and has paid part of the purchase price, even an oral contract to sell is enforceable. The courts will enforce an oral agreement involving land title if the part performance clearly establishes the intent of the parties as buyer and seller. If a court can envision the parties in some other relationship, such as landlord and tenant, the part performance is not sufficient to substitute for a written agreement.

Rules Involving Goods
The UCC creates a number of situations that allow the enforcement of oral agreements involving the sale of goods. In essence, the law strives to facilitate transactions involving goods as long as the parties cannot deceive the judge who is asked to determine a contract's validity. Sidebar 8.11 lists exceptions to the writing requirement for transactions involving the sale of goods.

---

sidebar 8.11

Exceptions to Statute-of-Frauds Requirement That Sale-of-Goods Contracts Be in Writing

- Contract for goods specially manufactured for the buyer on which the seller had begun performance.
- Contract for goods for which payment has been made and accepted or that have been received and accepted.
- Contract for goods in which the party being sued admits in court or pleadings that the contract has been made.

- Contract for goods between merchants in which the merchant sued has received a written notice from the other merchant confirming the contract and in which merchant sued does not object to the confirmation within 10 days.

Source: UCC §2–201.

The first exception is known as the specifically manufactured goods rule. If a buyer places an oral order for more than $500 worth of goods that are made especially for this buyer, the seller who has started production on this special order can enforce this agreement to avoid undue hardship.

Since the seller would not be able to resell this special goods to other buyers, courts enforce the oral contact. A written confirmation between merchants is another example of how the law facilitates business transactions. A merchant can avoid the impact of this provision by simply noting its objection to any written confirmation within ten days of receiving it.

Judicial Admissions If one party sues another party for failing to perform promises that are made orally, the defendant might argue the contract cannot be enforced since it must be in writing under the statute of frauds. This defense asks the judge to dismiss the lawsuit. Based on the historical background of the statute of frauds, a judge does not want the burden of deciding which party is telling the truth about the existence or nonexistence of an oral contract. However, if the defendant admits in court or in documents filed in court that an oral contract does exist, the judge does not have to guess about the contract's existence.

This judicial admissions exception is most important when the acknowledged oral contract is for the sale of goods. The UCC explicitly recognizes this exception [2-201(3)(b)]. Does this exception apply when the oral contract involves the sale of an interest in land, a collateral promise to pay another's debt, or performances that cannot be completed in one year? The answer is mixed among the states. Courts in a number of states permit the plaintiff to ask the defendant to admit the oral contract exists. If there is a judicial admission, the statute of fraud-based defense disappears. The judge proceeds to decide whether the oral contract is valid and enforceable.

Key Terms

Acceptance 238
Accord and satisfaction 243
Bilateral contract 230
Capacity 246
Consideration 242
Counteroffer 238
Covenants not to compete 248
Deposited acceptance rule 241
Duress 250
Enforceable contract 235
Executed contract 235
Executory contract 235
Express contract 231
Firm offer 245
Fraud 249

Goods 230
Implied-in-fact contract 231
Implied-in-law contract 234
Indefiniteness 237
Lapse of time 238
Mailbox rule 241
Mirror image rule 239
Misrepresentation 249
Mutual mistake 250
Offer 237
Offeror death or insanity 238
Option 246
Promise 228
Promissory estoppel 246
Quasi-contract 234

Rejection 238
Rescission 250
Revocation 238
Subject matter destruction 238
Subject matter illegality 238
Undue influence 250
Unenforceable contract 235
Uniform Commercial Code (UCC) 230
Unilateral contract 230
Unilateral mistake 250
Valid contract 235
Void contract 235
Voidable contract 235

Review Questions and Problems

Basic Concepts

1. *Contract Law in Private Enterprise*

   Discuss the importance of contract law to the private market system. How does contract law provide flexibility and precision in business dealings?

2. *Sources of Contract Law*

   (a) What is meant by the common law of contracts?

   (b) What is the UCC?

Contractual Classifications and Terminology

3. *Bilateral and Unilateral Contracts*

   (a) What is the distinction between a bilateral and a unilateral contract?

   (b) Which type is more common in business?

4. *Express and Implied-in-Fact Contracts*

   (a) Using an instance in which you bought or sold something in the last week describe the terms of an express contract that might arise between the supplier and the seller.

   (b) When would an implied-in-fact contract arise between a seller and a buyer?

5. *Implied-in-Law or Quasi-Contracts*

   Why are courts willing to apply contractual principles when the parties fail to create contractual relationships?

6. *Contractual Enforcement Terminology*

   How can someone reasonably say that a voidable contract is both enforceable and unenforceable?

7. *Contractual Performance Terminology*

   Pat hires a tailor to make a suit. The tailor completes all the sewing and now waits for Pat to pick up the suit and pay for it. Is this contractual agreement executed or executory? Explain.

Contract Formation

8. *Offer to Contract*

   Condor Equipment Company offers to sell a dough cutting machine to Snappy Jack Biscuits Inc. The offer states: "This offer expires Friday noon." On Thursday morning, the sales manager for Condor calls the president of Snappy Jack and explains that the machine has been sold to another purchaser. Discuss whether Condor has legally revoked its offer to Snappy Jack.

9. *Acceptance of Offer*

   Fielding Bros. offers to ship six furnaces to Central City Heating and Cooling Co. for $4,500 cash. Central City accepts on the condition that Fielding give 120 days' credit. Has a contract resulted? Explain.

10. *Consideration*

    Jefferson and Goldberg enter a contract for the sale of five acres of land at $10,000 per acre. Later, Goldberg, the buyer, asks if Jefferson will agree to modify the contract to $9,000 per acre.

    (a) Jefferson agrees. Is Jefferson's promise binding on him?

    (b) Would your answer be different if five used cars were being sold instead of five acres of land?

11. *Capacity of Parties to Contract*

    Describe the circumstances under which an adult lacks the capacity to contract.

12. *Lawful Purpose*

    Hunt signs an equipment lease contract with Edwards Rental. The contract contains a clause stating: "Lessor disclaims all liability arising from injuries caused by use of this equipment."

Because the equipment has been improperly serviced by Edwards Rental, Hunt is injured while using it. If Hunt sues, will the disclaimer clause likely be enforced? Explain.

13. *When a Meeting of the Minds Is Lacking*

    Chatter is a social networking service that promises to keep its user's data private. However, Chatter sells its data to a data broker who then sells it online. A Chatter user experiences a career impact from the disclosure. State whether this situation involves fraud, or innocent misrepresentation, and explain your answer.

14. *Laura advertises a used car for $20,000. David asks why it is so expensive and Laura states that it is only two years old. David agrees to purchase the car for $20,000. But when he arrives home, he discovers the book value of the car is only $12,000. May David avoid the contract under the doctrine of mutual mistake?*

Contract Form

15. *Written versus Oral Contracts*

    (a) In general, are oral contracts as valid and enforceable as written ones?

    (b) Why should contracting parties consider reducing their agreement to writing?

16. *Statute of Frauds*

    (a) Explain the purpose of requiring certain types of contracts to be in writing.

    (b) List four types of contracts covered by the traditional statute of frauds.

17. *Exceptions to the Writing Requirement*

    Elegante Haberdashery telephones an order to Nordic Mills for 500 men's shirts at $15 each. Each shirt will carry the Elegante label and have the Elegante trademark over the pocket. After the shirts are manufactured, Elegante refuses to accept delivery of them and raises the statute of frauds as a defense. Discuss whether this defense applies to these facts.

business *discussion*

You are the Marketing Manager for We-Can-Furnish-It Office Supply Company. In your role, you work with your company's sales staff. This staff is divided between personnel who travel to make face-to-face calls and those who answer the phones and accept orders during these conversations. In addition to the sales staff, you also are responsible for the technicians who ensure online orders can be placed and filled.

The transactions with customers range from supplying an entire office building with furniture and everything that allows an office to function to delivering small amounts of basic office supplies. As you study the documentation, including purchase order forms and confirmation statements, of these various transactions, you wonder about the answers to the following questions:

When does the negotiation end and a binding contract exist?
If there is conflicting language in the buyer's purchase order and the seller's confirmation, which language controls?
How can you determine when a contract has been performed fully?

9

Contractual Performance and Breach

Learning Objectives

In this chapter you will learn:

9-1. To understand how courts interpret contracts.

9-2. To identify when contract performance duties arise.

9-3. To understand how contractual duties are discharged.

9-4. To understand that nonperformance of contracts results in a breach unless performance is excused.

9-5. To evaluate the consequences of a breach of contract.

9-6. To understand how contracts can benefit third parties.

In the preceding chapter, you studied the basics of contract terminology and classifications. You learned about the essential elements and form required to create a valid, enforceable contract. Finally, you read about how contracts impact third parties.

In this chapter, your study of contracts continues as you learn about the performance of contracts and the consequences of breach. In addition, you will learn the basic principles of agency authority related to contracts and other legal contexts. These topics are of critical importance to businesspeople. After studying this chapter, you should have answers to the following questions:

- Are there rules that businesspeople should know that determine what contract language means?

- How do parties (and courts) decide if promises in a contract have been fully performed?
- What happens if a contract is not fully performed?
- Can someone besides the contracting parties enforce the agreement?

LO 9-1   # Interpretation of Contracts

If each party is satisfied with the other's performance under a contract, interpretation of the contract is generally not an issue. But when there is disagreement about what a term means or whether additional promises were made, interpretation often becomes necessary. How do we decide who is right?

One of the most important interpretation principles is that courts decide what a contract means. The meaning of a contract is a *question of law*, which means that a judge makes the final determination. However, depending on the circumstances and issues, that determination may require factual information from the parties or other witnesses. To guide their interpretation, courts use established rules designed to reduce ambiguity in a predictable manner. Understanding these rules can ensure that a contract is not interpreted differently than you predict.

RULES OF INTERPRETATION

In the interpretation of contract terms, handwriting is the best evidence of intention.

HANDWRITTEN terms

|
control
|

TYPED terms

|
control
↓

Pre-Printed terms/forms

Common words are given their usual meaning. "A rose is a rose is a rose" wrote Gertrude Stein, and a court will interpret this common word to refer to a flower. If the meaning of the word is clear on the face of the contract, courts will usually reject a party's attempt to reinterpret it later. However, if there is evidence that a word has a particular *trade usage,* courts will give it that meaning. In a contract in the wine trade, the term *rose* would not refer to a flower at all but to a type of wine.

Many businesses today use printed form contracts. Sometimes the parties to one of these printed contracts type or handwrite additional terms. What happens when the typed or handwritten terms contradict the printed terms? What if the printed terms of a contract state "no warranties," but the parties have written in a 90-day warranty? In such a case, courts interpret handwritten terms to control typed terms and typed terms to control printed ones. The written warranty will be enforced since the writing is the best evidence of the parties' true intention.

Another rule is that when only one of the parties drafts (writes) a contract, courts will interpret ambiguous or vague terms against the party that drafts them. Courts often apply this rule to the adhesion contracts (discussed in Sidebar 8.7 in Chapter 8) as well as insurance contracts and interpret the contract to give the non-drafting party the benefit of the doubt when deciding the meaning of a confusing term or phrase.

Sidebar 9.1 illustrates how the interpretation of contractual language can have a major impact on the parties' businesses.

Macy's v. Martha Stewart and J.C. Penney: What Is a Stand-Alone Store?

Martha Stewart is a famous figure in the United States, known nationally for her expertise in home design. Through her company, Martha Stewart Living Omnimedia (MSLO), she has sold Martha Stewart–branded products in various stores over the years. In 2006, MSLO contracted with Macy's to sell Martha Stewart–branded products in its stores. The agreement was exclusive, meaning that certain product categories would be sold only in Macy's stores. Because Martha Stewart was considering opening her own stand-alone stores, the parties carved out an exception for "MSLO Stores," which allowed her to sell the same categories there. But at the time of the contract, no such stores existed.

In 2011, MSLO and JCPenney announced a deal to sell Martha Stewart–branded products in Penney's stores. The products comprised the same categories in the Macy's contract. The catch was that MSLO products would be sold in a Martha Stewart store *inside* Penney's—in other words, a "store-within-a-store."

When Macy's objected, MSLO and Penney's argued that their arrangement fell within the contract exception for MSLO stores. Millions of dollars of product sales hinged on the interpretation of this exception. Macy's sued MSLO for breach of contract.

Before the court ruled on the proper interpretation of the contract, JCPenney agreed to stop selling the disputed product categories under Martha Stewart's brand. The move appeared to be a concession that the store-within-a-store idea was not reasonably interpreted as a stand-alone store. Eventually, MSLO settled with Macy's in 2014, and JCPenney and Macy's set out to finalize their own settlement.

This case demonstrates the importance of using clear language in contracts. It also highlights the danger in counting on a court to support a technical interpretation down the road, after the parties have made investments.

Source: Elizabeth A. Harris, "Martha Stewart Living and Macy's Settle Dispute and Keep Partnership," *New York Times*, January 2, 2014, p. B3.

THE PAROL EVIDENCE RULE

Like the statute of frauds, the **parol evidence rule** influences the form of contracts. This rule states that parties to a complete and final written contract cannot introduce oral evidence in court that changes the intended meaning of the written terms.

The parol evidence rule applies only to evidence of oral agreements made at the time of or prior to the written contract. It does not apply to oral modifications coming after the parties have made the written contract (although the statute of frauds may apply).

Suppose that Chris Consumer wants to testify in court that a merchant of an Ultima washing machine gave him an oral six-month warranty on the machine, even though the $450 written contract specified "no warranties." If the warranty was made after Chris signed the contract, he may testify about its existence. Otherwise, the parol evidence rule prevents him from testifying about an oral agreement that changes the terms of the written contract.

An exception to the parol evidence rule allows evidence of oral agreement that merely explains the meaning of written terms without changing the terms. Also, oral evidence that changes the meaning of written terms can be given if necessary to prevent fraud.

The parol evidence rule prohibits testimony about the oral negotiation that results in a written contract; thus, read the contract before signing.

Performance

The fundamental reason any of us enter into a contract is to assure the performance of the promise made or to secure the performance of the action desired. What we want is the other party's **duty of performance.** In turn, they want this same duty to be performed by us. An extremely high percentage of contracts are performed in such a way that makes the contracting parties happy. Thus, the most simple (and realistic) statement concerning performance of contracts is that it typically happens. When the parties perform, the obligations of the contract are discharged. A party to a contract is **discharged** when that party is relieved from all further responsibility of performance.

However, not all contractual obligations are fully performed. When less than full performance occurs, a number of legal issues arise. For example, a complete lack of performance results in a breach of the contract. As summarized in Figure 9.1, less than full performance results in issues about the level of performance and excuses for nonperformance. As you study this figure and read the next sections, keep in mind that contracting parties ultimately arrive at one of two conclusions: (1) they are discharged from the obligation to perform or (2) they are liable for breaching the contract.

CONDITIONS OF PERFORMANCE

As an employee, you usually have a responsibility to work for a certain amount of time (equivalent to a pay period) before your employer is obligated to pay you. You are entitled to be paid before working the next period. The performance of work is a condition to be paid, and receiving your pay is a condition for you to continue working.

Parties typically put conditions in their contracts to clarify when performance is due. While conditions reflect the creativity of the contracting parties, classifications of conditions usually take three forms.

If something must take place in the future, before a party has a duty to perform, it is a **condition precedent.** For example, a building developer may contract to buy certain land "when the city annexes it." The annexation is a condition precedent to the developer's duty to purchase the land. Parties should think through their business environment and state clearly the conditions governing their performance. For example, in a supplier-customer contract, the parties should state whether payment by the customer is a condition precedent for the seller to deliver or is delivery by the seller a condition precedent for payment. Failure to satisfy a condition precedent excuses performance even if the condition is a minor part of the transaction. Case 9.1 illustrates this point.

A **condition subsequent** excuses contractual performance if some future event takes place. A marine insurance policy might terminate coverage for any shipping losses "if war is declared." This is a condition subsequent. Another typical example of this type of condition is the requirement that an insured motorist or homeowner must notify the insurance company of a claim (from a car accident or homeowner's loss) within a short time period (five days perhaps) of the claim arising from the accident of the loss. Failure to provide this notice relieves the insurance company of its duty to provide coverage.

The distinction between conditions precedent and conditions subsequent can appear quite subtle. The key difference is found in the timing of the duty to perform. A contracting party has no duty to perform prior to

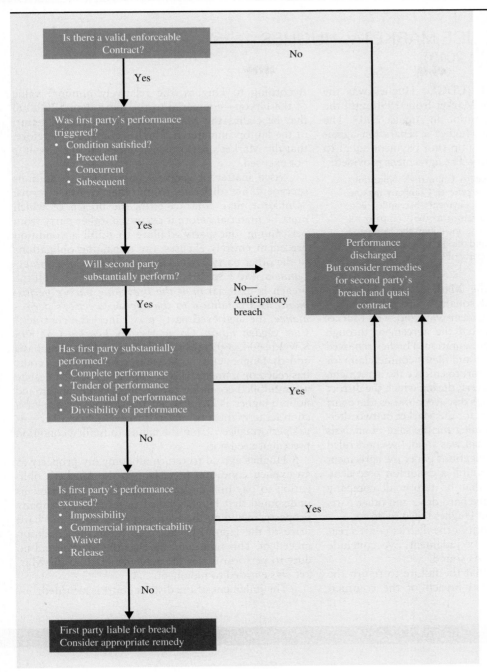

Figure 9.1
Contractual performance flow chart.

a condition precedent being satisfied. Once the condition precedent is met, the duty to perform is owed. The failure to meet a condition subsequent relieves the other contracting party from having to perform the duties previously promised.

ST. LOUIS PRODUCE MARKET v. HUGHES
735 F.3d 829 (8th Cir. 2013)

COLLOTON, CIRCUIT JUDGE.: Hughes was the property manager for the Market from 1990 until the Market eliminated his position in August 2009. The Market drafted and sent Hughes a separation agreement that granted him a lump sum payment equal to fourteen weeks of his salary. The agreement provided:

> As a condition precedent to Company's obligations under this Agreement and prior to Company making any additional separation payments hereunder, Former Employee agrees to return to the Company all Company-owned property, including the company camera, company tools, and the like, and certify that he has returned all such property of Company in writing.

. . .

In October 2009, the Market sued Hughes in Missouri state court and sought a declaratory judgment that the signed agreement was void. The Market claimed that Hughes secured the agreement through fraud or negligent misrepresentation. Hughes removed the case to the district court and filed a counterclaim for breach of contract in an effort to enforce the agreement.

After protracted discovery, during which the district court sanctioned Hughes for discovery abuses, the court granted summary judgment for the Market on two alternative grounds. First, assuming for the sake of analysis that the separation agreement was valid, the court ruled that the Market had no obligations under the agreement because Hughes failed to fulfill a condition precedent. The agreement required that he return all company property, which included the hard drive and other parts to his company laptop, and Hughes failed to do so. . . .

Hughes challenges both of the district court's reasons for granting summary judgment. We conclude that the court's decision was sound.

Hughes first argues that the failure to return the laptop was not a material breach of the contract. According to Hughes, the relatively minimal value of the laptop—compared to the more than $200,000 that he claims the Market owes him—makes return of the laptop immaterial. Hughes contends, therefore, that the Market's performance under the agreement is not excused.

As a matter of general contract law, conditions precedent are different from other contract terms: "Unlike a mere contract term, the breach of which must be material before it excuses another party from performing, one party's failure to fulfill a condition precedent entirely excuses any remaining obligations of the other party." *AIG Centennial Ins. Co. v. Fraley-Landers*, 450 F.3d 761, 763 (8th Cir. 2006). . . . "If the breach is material *or if the breaching party's performance is a condition to the aggrieved party's performance*, the aggrieved party may cancel the contract." *Curt Ogden Equip. Co. v. Murphy Leasing Co.*, 895 S.W.2d 604, 609 (Mo. Ct. App. 1995) (emphasis added). Hughes cites no Missouri case in which a court has relied on immateriality to enforce a contract despite an unfulfilled condition precedent, and we have found none. Hughes is correct that one party's *breach* of a contract term must be material to excuse the other party's performance . . . but the failure to fulfill a condition precedent need not.

Hughes agreed to return all company property as an explicit condition precedent to the Market's obligation to pay him under the agreement. Because it is undisputed that Hughes failed to return all company property, including the battery, power cord, and hard drive of the laptop, he failed to fulfill the condition precedent. This failure means that the Market had no duty to perform under the agreement . . . so the Market was entitled to judgment. . . .

The judgment of the district court is affirmed.

KEY POINTS

- The failure of a condition precedent can excuse a party's performance, even if it is minor. Similarly, the existence of a minor condition subsequent can cut off a party's obligation to perform.
- Parties often use conditions to ensure that a transaction occurs under favorable and anticipated circumstances.
- Parties should carefully consider whether conditions are necessary and understand that they may, at times, provide hold-up power to one side.

What happens if the parties do not have **express conditions** governing performance specified in their contract? Courts may be asked whether **implied conditions** can be read into the parties' obligations to perform. When courts decide the conditions of performance, a common decision can be the parties have a simultaneous duty to perform. In essence, there is a **concurrent condition** of performance. In a contract for the transfer of title to land, the buyer and seller usually expect to meet at a closing event and perform their obligations concurrently. The buyer provides the necessary funds to cover the purchase price while, at the same time, the seller signs and delivers the legal documents transferring ownership.

Most of our everyday purchases involve implied concurrent conditions of performance. While shopping you take items to a cashier and expect to pay and take the items with you. Your contractual duty to pay and the store's contractual duty to deliver are exchanged simultaneously. As business contracts often involve more complicated transactions, issues related to performance require further examination.

PAYMENT, DELIVERY, SERVICES TENDERED IN GOODS CONTRACTS

The preceding sections' content on conditions allows us to examine more fully the order of performance by the parties. Performance often is based on one or more conditions occurring or being satisfied. For example, in a typical contract involving the delivery of goods by a seller and payment of money by a buyer, what is the required order of performance? In essence, who goes first? The best way to answer these questions is to have the contracting parties provide specific guidance in the contract. When the parties fail to provide this level of detail, the law states the buyer's payment is a condition that must be satisfied before the seller has the duty to deliver (§2-511(1)).

Delivery is a legal term referring to the transfer of possession from the seller to the buyer. The buyer and seller may presume to know implicitly how and when the goods will be delivered. Sidebar 9.2 illustrates how the UCC serves as a gap-filler, thereby not leaving the terms of delivery of goods to the parties' uncertain presumptions.

The UCC provides valuable guidance to performance issues in contracts for the sales of goods. However, when a contract involves the performance of services, the parties to the contract should take time to provide specific conditions. If their agreement lacks specificity, reasonableness needs to govern the relationship and performance. For example, let's assume your manufacturing company hires software consultants to oversee the installation and implementation of new programs that hopefully will enhance your overall efficiency. The contract specifies the date for the completion of this work by the consultants; however, the contract does not provide a beginning date. Reasonable standards should govern your company and these consultants. Hopefully, effective negotiation will overcome the lack of direction in the contract. The concept of tendering performance may help. To **tender performance** means to offer to perform. When the consultants offer to send a team to your plant next week, they are tendering performance. A reasonable response is to permit this work to begin by allowing the consultants access to your facility. Once work begins, the contract's provisions on when payment is owed will govern your performance.

One party's tender of performance may satisfy a required condition leading to the other party's duty to perform.

sidebar 9.2

Terms of Delivery in the UCC

Suppose your company sells office equipment to a buyer. Further suppose that the contract carefully describes the equipment and the purchase price. However, the contract provides no specific guidance as to when or where the equipment is to be delivered.

The UCC permits and encourages the enforceability of this contract by providing a series of gap-filling provisions. In essence, if the parties fail to write clear instructions on delivery of the equipment, the UCC controls.

The seller's obligation is to tender delivery of the goods, and the buyer's duty is to accept and pay for them (§2-301). The phrase *tender of delivery* means the seller must make the goods available to the buyer. If, as in our example, the contract makes no statement about delivery, the presumption is the buyer must make arrangements to pick up the goods at the location the seller designates (§2-503(1)).

Many buyers may not want to assume the burden of picking up the goods at the seller's location. Thus, it is common for the buyer and seller to agree the goods will be shipped to the buyer. If the contract does not provide additional details, how does the seller satisfy its obligation to ship the goods? The UCC states the seller satisfies its obligation to ship goods once they are transferred to the shipper for transportation (§2-504). If the goods are damaged in transit, the liability rests on the buyer, not the seller.

To avoid the assumption of risk, experienced buyers may insist on what is called a destination contract. This contract requires the seller to get the goods shipped and delivered to a specific place of business designated by the buyer. The risk of loss for damage to the goods remains with the seller until the goods safely arrive at the buyer's destination (§2-310(1)(b)).

LO 9-3   # SUBSTANTIAL PERFORMANCE

Beyond the order of performance as determined through conditions, the degree or amount of performance can become an issue. A party to a contract may not always perfectly perform the duties owed. The more complex a contract is, the more difficult it is for a party to complete every aspect of performance. Courts generally recognize three levels of performance. These levels are summarized in Sidebar 9.3.

---

sidebar 9.3

Levels of Performance

1. *Complete Performance* recognizes that a contracting party has fulfilled every duty required by the contract. Payment of money, for example, is a contractual duty of performance that a party can perform completely. A party that performs completely is entitled to a complete performance by the other party and may sue to enforce this right.

2. *Material Breach* is a level of performance below what is reasonably acceptable. A party that has materially breached a contract cannot sue the other party for performance and is liable for damages arising from the breach.

3. *Substantial Performance* represents a less-than-complete performance. However, the work done is sufficient to avoid the claim of a breach. A party who substantially performs may be entitled to a partial recovery under the contract.

Substantial performance is a middle ground between full performance and a breach due to nonperformance. Substantial performance is much more than some performance. It is even greater than significant performance. A very typical example when substantial performance is applicable occurs in service-oriented contracts. The consultants in the software installation/implementation contract should recover for work performed even if the entire contract is not completed on time.

Likewise, a construction contractor who gets a home built but has not finished all the landscaping and finishing details by the due date is not denied a financial recovery. This builder can recover under the contract but remains liable for any damages to the homeowner for delays. It would be unfair, from the legal perspective, to allow the homeowner to refuse to pay the builder because a deadline is missed.

> Substantial performance is close to, but less than, full performance. Some or even significant performance may not satisfy the requirement of substantial performance.

DIVISIBILITY OF PERFORMANCE

Up to this point, we have assumed a contract specified aspects of performance by one party followed by the next party's performance. Alternatively, a contract may call for both parties to perform concurrently. It is possible, and indeed quite common, for a contract to be divided into segments or installments. An employment contract is a good example. One party (the employee) performs services for a period of time followed by the other party (the employer) paying the wages that are due. This pattern of recurring conditions precedent allows the employment contract to be divided into parts. This contract is considered to be divisible, typically into segments timed as pay periods.

Many contracts that at first glance appear divisible actually are not. While our consulting contract example may look to be divided into monthly or quarterly periods, the manufacturer would have a good argument that it wants the installation and implementation of the software complete. A portion of the work is not what is desired. The contract calls for all the work to be done. Thus, this contract is not divisible. Similarly most construction contracts are viewed as a whole and not as divisible into installments. The fact that the contract may call for payment to be forthcoming following certain benchmarks are met does not make the contract divisible.

> The divisibility or entirety of a contract helps determine when performance of duties should occur.

With respect to performance, the benefit of divisibility is to view the duty to perform as a series of smaller contracts. This may reduce the amount of disputes (numbers of them and the dollar figures involved) that arise due to nonperformance of the contract.

Excuses for Nonperformance

> **LO 9-4**

Generally speaking, in contracts the party who refuses to perform a promise can expect to be sued for breaching the agreement. However, even beyond the special situations related to performance presented in the previous sections, the law may provide for nonperforming with a valid excuse. If such an excuse for nonperformance exists, there can be no legitimate claim of a breach. In other words, a legitimate excuse for nonperformance can result in a party being discharged from contractual performance.

> Remember, a discharge relieves a party from the obligation to perform contractual promises.

IMPOSSIBILITY OF PERFORMANCE

Impossibility of performance is less likely to occur compared to impracticability.

A party's nonperformance is excused because of **impossibility of performance.** If the subject matter of the contract is destroyed, the contract becomes impossible to perform. When a contract exists for the sale of a building, and the building burns, the seller is discharged from performance. Likewise, when there is a contract for personal services, and the party promising the services becomes ill or dies, the party receives discharge from performances. The party that promises performance that becomes illegal is also discharged because of impossibility of performance.

Mere increased difficulty or reduced profitability, however, does not constitute impossibility of performance. Moreover, the impossibility must be objective and apply to any party in a similar circumstance. Case 9.2 provides a good example of a court's assessment of the alleged impossibility of a party's performance due to financial hardship.

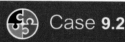 Case **9.2**

EAST CAPITOL VIEW COMMUNITY DEVELOPMENT CORP. v. ROBINSON
941 A.2d 1036 (D.C. App. 2008).

WASHINGTON, CHIEF JUDGE.: East Capitol hired Denean Robinson pursuant to a written employment contract for a one-year term. Before the end of that term, however, East Capitol informed her that her employment would be terminated early for lack of funding. Although the employment contract stated that Robinson's "continued employment with [East Capitol] will be contingent on successfully achieving all performance goals and outcomes," there was no language stating that a lack of funding could excuse appellant from prematurely terminating appellee's contract. Robinson filed suit against appellant for breach of contract. . . . The jury returned a verdict in favor of appellee. This appeal followed. . . .

Appellant contends that the trial court erred in failing to instruct the jury on the impossibility of performance defense. In essence, appellant argues that it was entitled to an impossibility of performance instruction because "the central issue in the case was whether appellant had an excuse for terminating the contract with appellee because its [g]rant funding had been cancelled and it was no longer able to pay her salary." . . . Accordingly, in order to receive an impossibility of performance instruction, East Capitol must demonstrate that there was record evidence that could at least support such a defense. . . .

A party's obligation to perform under a contract may be excused if performance is rendered impossible

. . . To establish impossibility or commercial impracticability, "a party must show (1) the unexpected occurrence of an intervening act; (2) the risk of the unexpected occurrence was not allocated by agreement or custom; and (3) the occurrence made performance impractical." *National Ass'n of Postmasters of the United States v. Hyatt Regency Washington*, 894 A.2d 471, 477 n.5 (D.C. 2006). . . .

The doctrine of impossibility relieves nonperformance only in extreme circumstances. . . . The party asserting the defense of impossibility bears the burden of proving "a real impossibility and not a mere inconvenience or unexpected difficulty." . . . Moreover, courts will generally only excuse non-performance where performance is objectively impossible—that is, the contract is incapable of performance by anyone—rather than instances where the party subjectively claims the inability to perform. . . . Indeed, "[i]t is generally well settled that subjective impossibility, that is, impossibility which is personal to the promisor and does not inhere in the nature of the act to be performed, does not excuse nonperformance of the contractual obligation." . . .

Under this analysis, a party's alleged financial inability to perform a contract that it voluntarily entered would rarely, if ever, excuse non-performance . . . Although this court has not directly ruled on whether financial inability to meet a contractual obligation excuses non-performance, most, if not all, other jurisdictions that have addressed this issue agree that it does not. . . . Indeed, even insolvency is unlikely to excuse performance: "In short, it must be deemed an implied term of every contract that the promisor will not permit himself, through insolvency or acts of bankruptcy, to be disabled from making performance." *Central Trust Co. v. Chicago Auditorium Ass'n*, 240 U.S. 581, 591, 36 S. Ct. 412, 60 L. Ed. 811 (1916). . . .

Nor does the promisor's reliance on some third party for the ability to perform convert financial inability to perform into an objective impossibility. "[T]he rationale is that a party generally assumes the risk of his own inability to perform his duty. Even if a party contracts to render a performance that depends on some act by a third party, he is not ordinarily discharged because of a failure by that party because this is also a risk that is commonly understood to be on the obligor." RESTATEMENT (SECOND) OF CONTRACTS § 261 cmt. e; . . . Thus, the anticipation of funding from one source does not alter the party's duty to perform. . . .

Of course, parties may contractually reallocate risk to the other party. However, in this case, there is no evidence that appellant assigned the risk of its financial instability to the appellant. . . . Though appellant maintained that the revocation of funding deprived the corporation of sufficient assets to continue paying its employees, it failed to include such a possibility as a condition precedent in the employment agreement. Indeed, while appellant specifically included language warning appellee that her continued employment was contingent upon successful performance, it failed to address funding in any way. . . . The agreement does not mention the source of the salary, let alone warn appellee that her continued employment was contingent upon continued grant funding.

Robinson's employment contract was objectively capable of performance, and East Capitol did nothing to reallocate the risk of its own inability to pay. As East Capitol was not entitled to a defense of impossibility, the trial court's decision to withhold the impossibility defense jury instruction was not error. Accordingly, the judgment of the trial court is

Affirmed

KEY POINTS

- Courts are reluctant to excuse performance due to impossibility or impracticability.
- The court specifically distinguishes between objective impossibility and personal impossibility. Only the former excuses performance.
- Contracting parties have the ability to allocate known risks in the contract. For that reason, impossibility must be an unexpected occurrence.

COMMERCIAL IMPRACTICABILITY

Under the UCC a party to a sale-of-goods contract receives discharge from performance because of **commercial impracticability** (§2–615). The *impracticability* standard is not as difficult to meet as the *impossibility* standard. What constitutes impracticability of performance depends upon the circumstances of the situation. For instance, a manufacturer may be discharged from an obligation to make goods for a buyer when the manufacturer's major source of raw materials is unexpectedly interrupted. But if the raw materials are reasonably available from another supplier, the manufacturer may not receive discharge because of impracticability.

WAIVER OR RELEASE

A party may be excused from not performing contractual obligations by the other party to the agreement. When a party intentionally relinquishes a right to enforce the contract, a **waiver** occurs. When a party announces the other party does not have to perform as promised, a **release** exists. The distinction between a waiver and a release is not important when examining the resulting discharge of the contract. Nonperformance of the contract is forgiven and there is no liability for a breach of contract.

To gain some clarity regarding these closely related terms, focus on the timing of the nonperformance. Waivers generally occur after a contracting party fails to perform. In this situation, nonperformance by one party may cause the other party to waiver its right to enforce the contract. The waiver typically is unilateral. The nonbreaching party grants the waiver. A landlord may waive the right to collect a late payment fee when the rent is only two days overdue.

Releases usually occur before a contracting party fails to perform. A release often takes the form of a negotiated contract. The release is bargained for and is supported by consideration. A borrower may seek the lender's release to avoid having to make an interim payment. This borrower may have to agree to pay the entire debt before its original due date to get the lender's release from the interim payment.

LO 9-5

Breach of Contract

A party that does not live up to the obligation of contractual performance is said to breach the contract. There are several remedies or solutions available for a breach of contract. One party may, of course, attempt to reach a voluntary, negotiated settlement with the other party. The parties may also agree to arbitration, as outlined in Chapter 5, and have a neutral third party decide a fair outcome. In many cases, however, a court's intercession is required to determine the appropriate remedy. Options include the following:

You contract with P to paint your house for $2,000. P does not complete the job, and you hire R and pay $3,000. You are entitled to $1,000 from P as compensatory damages.

- Damages awards, including compensatory, consequential, and liquidated damages
- Equitable remedies including specific performance, injunction, and rescission

Figure 9.2 provides a summary of these remedies for breach of contract. Note that the choice of one remedy may exclude others. For example, if one chooses rescission, one cannot also make a claim for damages.

Awarding money damages is the more common way courts provide remedies to nonbreaching parties. The theory behind such an award rests in putting the damaged person in the same financial position as if the contract was fully performed. Usually compensatory damages suffice to achieve this objective of making a party whole. Compensatory damages may be calculated in a variety of ways, depending on the losses the defendant suffered:

- Contract price—if a defendant fails to pay for goods or services provided.
- Lost profits—if a defendant fails to pay but plaintiff makes a replacement sale for a lower price.
- Difference in market price versus contract price—if a/defendant fails to deliver product or service and it must be secured from a higher-priced source.

Occasionally courts will add consequential damages to create a fair outcome. Such damages reflect the downstream impact of the breach, such as having to close your restaurant because a new refrigerator does not arrive. Consequential damages are awarded only if the consequence was foreseeable.

Figure 9.2 *Remedies for breach of contract.*

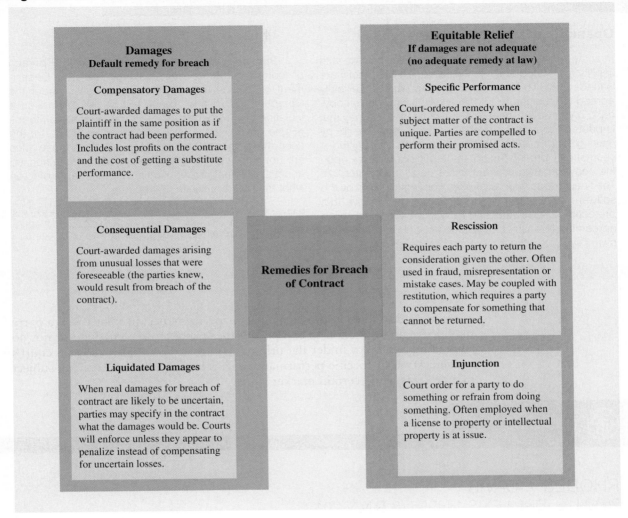

Damages
Default remedy for breach

Compensatory Damages

Court-awarded damages to put the plaintiff in the same position as if the contract had been performed. Includes lost profits on the contract and the cost of getting a substitute performance.

Consequential Damages

Court-awarded damages arising from unusual losses that were foreseeable (the parties knew, would result from breach of the contract).

Remedies for Breach of Contract

Liquidated Damages

When real damages for breach of contract are likely to be uncertain, parties may specify in the contract what the damages would be. Courts will enforce unless they appear to penalize instead of compensating for uncertain losses.

Equitable Relief
If damages are not adequate
(no adequate remedy at law)

Specific Performance

Court-ordered remedy when subject matter of the contract is unique. Parties are compelled to perform their promised acts.

Rescission

Requires each party to return the consideration given the other. Often used in fraud, misrepresentation or mistake cases. May be coupled with restitution, which requires a party to compensate for something that cannot be returned.

Injunction

Court order for a party to do something or refrain from doing something. Often employed when a license to property or intellectual property is at issue.

Liquidated, or agreed-upon, damages can simplify disputes when a breach occurs. However, it is important to understand that liquidated damages cannot constitute a penalty for breach; they must be a reasonable attempt to assess actual damages in the face of uncertainty when the contract is formed.

The victim of a contract breach must **mitigate** damages when possible. Mitigating damages requires the victim to take reasonable steps to reduce them. For example, when a tenant breaches a house lease by moving away before the lease expires, the landlord must mitigate damages by attempting to rent the house to another willing and suitable tenant if such a person is available.

At times, money damages are not satisfactory as a remedy. Instead, the nonbreaching party might desire either a return of the value given, which involves the equitable remedy of rescission or restitution. Or a party might request an order that the breaching party specifically perform the contractual

Mitigation is the purposeful reduction of damages; it usually is the responsibility of the nonbreaching party.

sidebar 9.4

Opening the Door to Related Liability

In some cases, a breach of contract may coincide with liability for related actions. For example, when software is loaded onto your computer, you have almost certainly agreed to an electronic license for the program's copyright. If you violate the terms of that license in a way that impacts a copyright owner's exclusive rights—e.g., by making more copies of the software than permitted—you not only breach the contract, but also infringe upon the copyright (discussed in more detail in Chapter 11). The license was your relief from copyright claims by the software owner, and by breaching it you remove that protection. On the other hand, if you breach your license agreement in a way that has no impact on a copyright owner's rights, infringement may not be an issue.

The liability for actions associated with a breach of contract can be quite severe. The U.S. Department of Justice (DOJ) has brought cases under the Computer Fraud and Abuse Act based in part on a violation of a website's terms of use. In general, terms of use grant access to a website in exchange for the user agreeing to follow certain rules. When those rules are not followed, the user is engaged in unauthorized access. Criminal prosecution may result depending on what the user does with that access.

Sources: *MDY Indus., LLC v. Blizzard Entertainment, Inc.*, 629 F.3d 928 (9th Cir. 2010); Nick Akerman, "When a Breach of Contract Is Evidence of Computer Fraud," *The National Law Journal*, November 29, 2010.

---

promise made, which is known as specific performance. In some cases, a party may desire an injunction to compel another party to do something or not do something agreed to under the original contract. Case 9.3 involves a court's consideration of specific performance as a remedy in a case involving subject matter that has no certain market value.

 case **9.3**

RHODES v. DAVIS
2012 U.S. Dist. LEXIS 144955 (S.D.N.Y. 2012)

GEORGE B. DANIELS, DISTRICT JUDGE.: Plaintiff Neil Rhodes and Defendant Gary Davis are co-owners of Alarm Specialists, Inc. ("ASI"). Each holds a fifty percent interest in ASI and fifty percent of the membership interests in OTR Realty, LLC ("OTR"), an affiliated real estate company. In an attempt to resolve a prior dispute before this Court . . . the parties entered into a Stipulation of Discontinuance ("Stipulation"), under which they agreed that Defendant would buy out Plaintiff's ownership interest in ASI for $2,500,000 on or before October 1, 2009 with a down payment of $250,000 by September 5, 2008. Although the down payment was timely made, the closing date passed without any sale, and Plaintiff

subsequently brought a second action for damages stemming from Defendant's breach of contract. . . .

. . .

Ultimately, both parties agree that specific performance is the proper remedy in this case. . . .

Specific performance is an extraordinary remedy to be invoked only after remedies at law have been determined to be "incomplete and inadequate to accomplish substantial justice." . . . New York courts have consistently held specific performance to be appropriate in cases involving stock transfer agreements in closely held corporations, finding that the market value of such stock is difficult to ascertain for the purposes of calculating damages. . . .

Both parties ultimately agree in their briefs to this Court that specific performance is an appropriate remedy with respect to Defendant's breach of contract. ASI is a closely held corporation, and Plaintiff and Defendant are ASI's only shareholders. Due to the inherent difficulty in assessing the market value of ASI's stock and the lack of a market that would allow Plaintiff to sell his shares at a price comparable to what Defendant agreed to pay, substantial justice is not achieved without specific performance. . . .

Under well-established principles of New York law, "when parties set down their agreement in a clear, complete, document, their writing should . . . be enforced according to its terms." . . . Where the terms of the agreement contain no ambiguities, the Court limits its review to the four corners of the contract. . . . Here, the Stipulation was an unambiguous and enforceable contract containing the complete terms of their agreement. . . . Thus, specific performance limited to the explicit terms of the Stipulation itself is appropriate.

Judge Robinson previously determined that Defendant breached the Stipulation between the parties by insisting on terms not contained in the Stipulation. Judge Robinson granted partial summary judgment to Plaintiff on this issue. Under ¶2 of the Stipulation, Defendant agreed to buy out Plaintiff's shares in ASI for the purchase price of $2,500,000 by the closing date of October 1, 2008 with a down payment of $250,000 by September 5, 2008. Defendant did make a timely down payment but failed to make the rest of payment. Thus, with regard to specific performance in adherence to the original terms of the Stipulation, Plaintiff is entitled to the payment of the original purchase price less Defendant's $250,000 down payment, for a total sum of $2,250,000.

Pursuant to UCC § 2-709, Plaintiff is also entitled to an award of prejudgment interest at the statutory rate of 9% per year from the date of Defendant's breach on October 1, 2008, until the date of final judgment. . . .

Both parties respectively argue that they each should be awarded attorneys' fees for legal expenses incurred throughout the course of their ongoing litigation. . . . The Stipulation addresses the issue of attorneys' fees in the event of a breach. . . .

The plain language of the Stipulation awards attorneys' fees to the non-breaching party. As Judge Robinson previously found that Defendant was liable for breaching the Stipulation, Plaintiff is entitled to reasonable attorneys' fees arising out of this litigation in an amount to be determined at a Magistrate Judge's Inquest.

KEY POINTS

- When a contract involves unique subject matter, courts may award specific performance because there is no market equivalent.
- Rhodes and Davis had a good understanding of their value for the transaction, and there was no reason for the court to substitute its own reasoning.

Efficient Breach Should you always perform your contractual obligations if at all possible? Scholars have long debated whether performance of contractual duties should be predicated on more than economic benefit. One school of thought suggests that if one monetarily compensates the nonbreaching party according to the contract terms, nothing more is required. You may be able to breach, fully compensate the nonbreaching party, and still end up better off. That scenario is termed an efficient breach, because all parties end up either indifferent or in a better position than if the contract was performed. But another view argues that one is morally obligated to carry through on one's promises.

Mortgage contracts provide a current context for considering the issue of efficient breach. This is discussed in Sidebar 9.5.

sidebar 9.5

Walking Away from a Mortgage

In essence, a mortgage is a contract. In such an arrangement, a bank or other lender (mortgagee) has provided the funds for purchasing property (a home) in exchange for the homeowner's (mortgagor) agreement to make payments with interest. Property is pledged as security for the loan. In a "title" state, the lender actually holds the deed until the mortgage is paid, but in a "lien" state, the lender merely has a right to obtain title if payments are not made. In either case, the failure to make payments on a mortgage—a breach of contract—can result in a "foreclosure" wherein the lender takes ownership of the property. In some states, the mortgagor has no further obligation after the mortgagee forecloses.

In a strong economy, when home prices rise, making payments on a mortgage seems like a good economic arrangement for all involved. However, in a bad economy, home prices may fall so quickly that a mortgagee's payments will cover only the inflated portion of the loan for many years. Such a mortgage is said to be "underwater," with the property being worth far less than the amount owed to the lender. When this happens, a homeowner may be inclined to simply walk away from the mortgage, permitting the lender to take over the property and recoup only a part of the amount loaned. To many, this makes economic sense, at least from the perspective of the homeowner. But is it morally wrong?

Consider whether it is acceptable to walk away from a mortgage that is substantially underwater. What would be the impact on the housing market if many people did this? Try to imagine arguments for both sides.

LO 9-6   Third Parties' Rights

Parties usually negotiate and enter into contracts for personal or organizational reasons. The purpose of the contractual agreement is to gain a direct benefit. Despite this common practice, sometimes third parties become involved in the performance of the contract. This occurrence could be anticipated by the original contracting parties, or it could arise due to the occurrence of unforeseen circumstances. Regardless of the factual situations, third parties and contract rights provide the focus of the concluding part of this chapter. The next two sections discuss third-party beneficiaries and assignments. The final section examines how a novation impacts the liability of the original contracting parties.

BENEFICIARIES

One or more of the original parties to a contract may intend for their agreement to benefit a third party. Such parties are called **third-party beneficiaries.** In general, persons who are not parties to a contract have no rights to sue to enforce the contract or to get damages for breach of contract. However, a third-party beneficiary can sue if the parties to the contract *intended* to benefit that person.

Intended third-party beneficiaries fall into two distinct categories; however, any intended beneficiary has rights to enforce the contract to gain the intended benefit. The first category involves a *creditor beneficiary*. Suppose Carl owes Terry $10,000 for work Terry already has performed. Also assume Carl does work for Chris and contracts to have Chris pay Terry. Terry is a creditor beneficiary of the Carl–Chris contract and can sue Chris for the payment owed.

When the performance under a contract is meant as a gift to a third party, that person is a *donee beneficiary*. Donee beneficiaries can sue the party who owes them a performance under a breached contract, but they cannot sue the party who contracted to make them a gift. The beneficiary of a life insurance policy is usually a donee beneficiary.

An *incidental beneficiary* is a third party who unintentionally benefits from a contract. The incidental beneficiary has no rights under a contract. If merchant A contracts to have security service patrol her property—a contract that will likely also protect the other merchants on the block—and if one evening when the service fails to show up merchant B on the block is burglarized, B cannot sue the security service for breach of contract. B is only an incidental beneficiary of the contract between A and the service.

> You are a donee beneficiary if a parent buys a car for you. If the seller does not deliver the car, you can sue.

ASSIGNMENT OF CONTRACTS

Contracts often are thought as involving only two parties—the offeror and the offeree. In business, such a view is overly simplistic. Contracts may involve many original parties and sometimes third parties who are not a part of the negotiation resulting in the original contract. This section discusses how these third parties become involved in the contract's performance through the process of assignment.

Electronics, Inc., sells 250 radios on credit at $20 apiece to Radio Land Retail. Electronics then sells its rights under the contract to Manufacturers' Credit Co. When payment is due, can Manufacturers' Credit legally collect the $5,000 owed to Electronics by Radio Land? This transaction is controlled by the law of **assignment**, which is a transfer (generally a sale) of rights under a contract. Figure 8.3 shows the transaction and introduces important terminology.

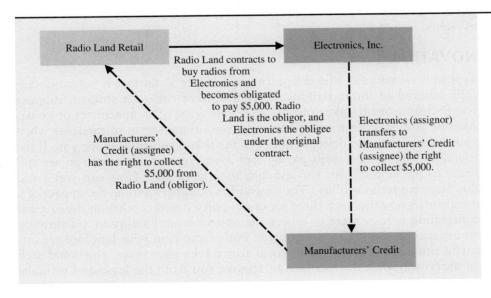

Figure 9.3
Assignment.

As Figure 8.3 illustrates, in an assignment one of the original contracting parties becomes an **assignor** and assigns rights or duties or both to a third party, known as the **assignee.** If the assignment is properly structured, the assignee can enforce the original contract. When an assignor assigns rights, an implied warranty is made that the rights are valid and enforceable. If the assignee is unable to enforce the rights against the obligor because of illegality, incapacity, or breach of contract, the assignee can sue the assignor for breach of the implied warranty. However, if the obligor simply refuses to perform for the assignee, the assignee's legal claim is against the obligor, not the assignor.

Notice of Assignment When an assignment is made, an assignee should notify the obligor immediately. Otherwise, the obligor may perform for the obligee-assignor. If Radio Land pays Electronics before being notified by Manufacturers' Credit of the assignment, Radio Land cannot be held liable to Manufacturers' Credit.

A dishonest or careless assignor may assign the same contract rights to two different assignees. Notification of the obligor is especially important in this situation. In most states, the law says that the first assignee to notify the obligor has priority no matter which assignee receives the first assignment of rights.

Contracts That Cannot Be Assigned Although most contracts can be assigned, certain ones cannot. An assignment that increases the burden of performance to the obligor cannot be assigned. For instance, a right to have goods shipped to the buyer's place of business cannot be assigned by an Atlanta buyer to a Miami buyer if a New York seller has to ship the goods to Miami instead of Atlanta. Similarly, a *requirements contract* to supply a retail buyer with all the radios needed cannot be assigned because it depends upon the buyer's personal situation.

Most states regulate the assignment of wages. They limit the amount of wages a wage earner can assign to protect wage earners and their families.

A party to a contract cannot assign (delegate) performance of duties under a contract when performance depends on the character, skill, or training of that party. Otherwise, duties under a contract can be assigned as well as rights.

NOVATIONS

Typically, an assignor who delegates duties under a contract is not automatically relieved of future liability. In your current role as a student, suppose you find someone to take your place on your lease of an apartment or house. Assume you have six months left under the original term of the lease when you assign rights and delegate duties to the friend substituting for you. If the friend moves out and stops paying rent after only two months, you are still liable to the landlord for the last four months of rent. How can you avoid this lingering responsibility? The answer lies in understanding the impact of a novation. A **novation** is a three (or more) party contract wherein the original contracting parties agree to relieve the obligor from liability by substituting an assignee in the place of this party. For example, in your landlord-tenant-friend situation, when you have your friend take your place, you could seek an agreement with the landlord to remove you from the lease and to make your friend liable for the remainder of the lease period. This arrangement is a novation. Such agreements usually are found in business contracts when an organization is acquired through purchase or merger transactions.

Practical Perspective on Contracts

Before concluding your study of contracts, the point made at the beginning of Chapter 8 should be reemphasized. Understanding contracts is critical because they are the key to transacting business. Having an appreciation for contract law may make you a more effective negotiator in some instances. However, as your career advances and you get involved in more complicated business transactions, you will work closely with lawyers to create contractual documentation. Sidebar 9.6 offers some concluding guidance on how to maintain a balanced relationship with your lawyer. Remember, your goal should always be to create contracts that enhance your business activities.

---

sidebar 9.6

Suggestions for Businessperson/Lawyer Relationship on the Drafting of Contracts

- Contracts are business documents; they should be in writing whenever possible.
- Use plain English.
- Tell story of relationship; provide timeline of obligations.
- Avoid legalese (whereas; party of the first part, etc.); be careful with "and," "or," "before," "on," "after," "each," "every," etc.

- There should be a flow from section to section.
- Create clear definitions, if necessary.
- Proofread carefully.
- Ask questions about language or issues you do not understand.
- Consistently redraft to update.

Key Terms

Review Questions and Problems

Interpretation of Contracts

1. *Rules of Interpretation*

   Gus contracts to buy a used car from Cars Galore Inc. The printed contract specifies "no warranties." But Gus and the sales manager of Cars handwrite into the contract a 90-day guarantee on the transmission. If the transmission fails after 60 days, is there a warranty protecting Gus? Explain.

2. *The Parol Evidence Rule*

   Caryn negotiates to buy 50 washers and 50 dryers from the "We-Clean-It Company." These machines are going into laundromats that Caryn operates with her family. Because these machines will be heavily used, Caryn got the company to agree to a one-year warranty instead of the standard 90-day warranty. Following the negotiation, Caryn signs a written contract. Only later, Caryn realizes there is no warranty provision in the written contract. What should Caryn do to be able to enforce the original extended warranty agreement?

Performance

3. *Conditions of Performance*

   (a) Why are conditions important in understanding how and when contracts are performed?

   (b) List the three types of conditions that are most common in contractual performance.

4. *Payment, Delivery, Services Tendered*

   (a) Explain the role of tender of performance.

   (b) What is the impact of one party tendering its performance?

5. *Substantial Performance*

   Ace Contracting constructs an office building for Realty Enterprises. Realty's tenants quickly find a number of minor problems with the plumbing and insulation of the new building. When Realty contacts Ace about bringing its work up to standard, Ace promises to correct the problems, but never does.

   (a) Can Realty rescind the contract?

   (b) What are Realty's legal remedies?

6. *Divisibility of Performance*

   Why is an employment contract usually viewed as being divisible while a construction contract is not considered divisible?

Excuses for Nonperformance

7. *Impossibility of Performance*

   To be a legitimate excuse for nonperformance, impossibility must be real and absolute. What are three examples of factual situations involving real impossibility of performance?

8. *Commercial Impracticability*

   A tripling of prices by an illegal cartel of uranium producers caused Westinghouse Electric Corp. to default on uranium delivery contracts to a number of utility companies. The companies sued and Westinghouse settled. If the case had gone to trial, what defense might Westinghouse have raised to excuse its nonperformance under the contracts?

9. *Waiver or Release*

   What do waivers and releases have in common?

Breach

10. *Damages*

    (a) How are damages different than equitable remedies?

    (b) If David breaches his agreement to pay $5000 to Laura for her car, and she later sells the car to Ellysa for $4000, what is the measure of Laura's damages from David's breach.

    (c) Explain one's duty to mitigate contract damages.

11. *Efficient Breach*

    It is legitimate (fair or moral) for one party to breach his or her agreement with another to take advantage of a better opportunity, so long as the non-breaching party can be fully compensated? In other words, does the law create a duty to keep our promises beyond economic consequences?

Third Parties' Rights

12. *Beneficiaries*

    What is the distinction between an intended and an incidental beneficiary?

13. *Assignment of Contracts*

    Franchetti Rifle Distributors assigns a $20,000 claim against Top Gun, Inc., to the Zenith Collection Agency. When Zenith sues Top Gun, Top Gun asserts that it rejected a shipment of rifles from Franchetti out of which the claim arose because they had defective trigger guards. Explain whether Top Gun can properly assert its defense against plaintiff Zenith.

14. *Novations*

    Explain the purpose of a novation and who must be party to it.

business *discussions*

As a new sales representative for Misco Equipment Corporation, you take a customer out to dinner. Before dinner is over, you have shaken hands on a deal to sell the customer nearly a half-million dollars' worth of industrial equipment. In writing up the formal contract the next morning, you discover that you misfigured the equipment's price. Your error could cost Misco $60,000. You telephone your customer and explain the situation.

Is the "deal" you made an enforceable contract?
Does the mistake you made permit you to get out of an enforceable contract?
What do you think will happen in this situation?

10

Torts Affecting Business

Learning Objectives

In this chapter you will learn:

10-1. To categorize torts into three main types and to compare what actions create legal responsibility in the three tort categories.

10-2. To explain the elements of negligence and to relate these elements to the development of negligence law.

10-3. To analyze damages awarded in tort litigation and to understand why tort damage awards generate controversy.

The word **tort** means "wrong." Legally, a tort is a civil wrong other than a breach of contract. Unlike contract law, the basis for the wrong is not an agreement between the parties involved, but an obligation imposed by common law and legislation. Tort law sets limits on how people can act and use their resources so they do not violate the right others have to their resources. If a person is injured or suffers a monetary loss based on the wrongful actions of another, tort law establishes a way for that person who has suffered a loss to receive compensation, known as "damages."

Legal wrongs inflicted on the resources of others may be crimes as well as torts (see Chapter 13), but the law of tort itself is civil rather than criminal. The usual remedy for a tort is dollar damages. Behavior that constitutes a tort is called *tortious* behavior. One who commits a tort is a *tortfeasor.*

Torts are divided into intentional torts, negligence, and strict liability.

This chapter divides torts into three main categories: intentional torts, negligence torts, and strict liability torts. Intentional torts involve deliberate actions that cause injury. Negligence torts involve injury following a failure to use reasonable care. Strict liability torts impose legal responsibility for injury even though a liable party neither intentionally nor negligently causes the injury.

Important to torts are the concepts of duty and causation. One is not liable for another's injury unless he or she has a *duty* toward the person injured. And, of course, there is usually no liability for injury unless one has *caused* the injury. We explain these concepts under the discussion of negligence, where they are most relevant.

This chapter also covers the topic of damages. The topic concerns the business community because large damage awards, frequently against businesses, have received a great deal of attention in recent years.

LO 10-1 Intentional Torts

Intent is the desire to bring about certain results.

An important element in the following torts is *intent,* as we are dealing with intentional torts. **Intent** is usually defined as the desire to bring about certain results. But in some circumstances the meaning is even broader, including not only desired results but also results that are "substantially likely" to result from an action. Recently, employers who knowingly exposed employees to toxic substances without warning them of the dangers have been sued for committing the intentional tort of battery. The employers did not desire their employees' injuries, but these injuries were "substantially likely" to result from the failure to warn.

The following sections explain the basic types of intentional torts. Sidebar 10.1 lists these torts.

sidebar 10.1

Types of Intentional Torts

- Assault and battery
- Intentional infliction of mental distress
- Invasion of privacy
- False imprisonment and malicious prosecution
- Trespass
- Conversion
- Defamation
- Fraud
- Interference with business relations

ASSAULT AND BATTERY

An **assault** is the placing of another in immediate apprehension for his or her physical safety. "Apprehension" has a broader meaning than "fear." It includes the expectation that one is about to be physically injured. The person who intentionally creates such apprehension in another is guilty of the tort of assault. Many times a battery follows an assault. A **battery** is an illegal touching of another. As used here, "illegal" means that the touching is done without justification and without the consent of the person touched.

Hitting someone with a wrench causes physical injury, but as the following case illustrates, the "touching" that constitutes part of a battery need not cause physical injury.

A store manager who threatens an unpleasant customer with a wrench, for example, is guilty of assault. Actually hitting the customer with the wrench would constitute battery.

 case **10.1**

HARPER v. WINSTON COUNTY
892 So.2d 346 (Ala. Sup. Ct. 2004)

Sandra Wright, the revenue commissioner of Winston County, Alabama, fired her employee, Sherry Harper. Harper sued, claiming among other things that Wright had committed an assault and battery in grabbing her and jerking her arm in trying to force her to go to Wright's office. Before trial, the court granted summary judgment in favor of Wright. The plaintiff, Harper, appealed, and the case reached the Alabama Supreme Court.

SEE, J: . . . Harper argues that the trial court erred in entering a summary judgment in favor of Wright, on Harper's assault and battery claim, because, she claims, she presented substantial evidence in support of her claim. Harper argues that Wright admits that she intentionally grabbed Harper's arm and, she asserts, Wright's grabbing of her arm was offensive. Harper states: "[Wright] jerked my arm and tried to pull me back." She argues that Alabama law does not require that Wright strike or hit her in order for a battery to occur. In response, Wright argues that she merely "took a hold of [Harper's] hand." Wright states that she did not touch Harper in an offensive manner and that she was only trying to coax Harper into stepping into her office so that they could continue their conversation away from the view of the customers and the employees of the Department. The trial court stated in its summary-judgment order that "the undisputed evidence from Sandra Wright clearly points out that the touching was not in any way harmful or offensive, but was instead done in an attempt to bring [Harper] under control."

The plaintiff in an action alleging assault and battery must prove "(1) that the defendant touched the plaintiff; (2) that the defendant intended to touch the plaintiff; and (3) that the touching was conducted in a harmful or offensive manner." In *Atmore Community Hospital,* the plaintiff presented evidence indicating that the defendant "touched her waist, rubbed against her when passing her in the hall, poked her in the armpits near the breast area, and touched her leg." The plaintiff also presented evidence indicating that "each of these touchings was intentional, was conducted with sexual overtones, and was unwelcome." We held that these factual assertions constituted substantial evidence that the defendant had committed a battery.

In *Surrency,* we stated that an actual injury to the body is not a necessary element for an assault-and-battery claim. We also stated that when the evidence as to whether a battery in fact occurred is conflicting, the question whether a battery did occur is for the jury. Quoting *Singer Sewing Machine Co.,* this Court stated:

> "To what acts will constitute a battery in a case like this, the rule is well stated by Mr. Cooley in his work on Torts. He says: 'A successful assault becomes a battery. A battery consists in an injury actually done to the person of another in an angry or revengeful or rude or insolent manner, as by spitting in the face, or in any way touching him in anger, or violently jostling him out of the way, or in doing any intentional violence to the person of another.' *The wrong here consists, not in the touching, so much as in the manner or spirit in which it is done, and the question of bodily pain is important only as affecting damages. Thus, to lay hands on another in a hostile manner is a battery, although no damage follows;* but to touch another, merely to attract his attention, is no battery and not unlawful. And to push gently against one, in the endeavor to make way through a crowd, is no battery; but to do so rudely and insolently is and may justify damages proportioned to the rudeness. . . ."

Alabama courts have recognized that privilege can be a defense to a plaintiff's claim that the defendant battered her. This Court has held that when a merchant suspects a customer of shoplifting, it is reasonable for the merchant's employee to use reasonable force to ensure that the suspected shoplifter is detained.

In this case, there is no question that Wright intended to touch Harper's arm; it is the "manner or spirit" in which Wright touched Harper's arm that is in dispute. Harper testified at the June 13, 2000, hearing that Wright forcefully grabbed her arm. Wright testified that she reached for Harper's arm in an attempt to lead her into her office so they could continue their discussion away from the public area. In *Surrency,* we noted that "to touch another, merely to attract his attention, is no battery and not unlawful. While it is certainly conceivable that this type of touching is all that occurred in this case, Harper presents substantial evidence to the contrary. Harper testified at her hearing that Wright "jerked" her arm. In her response to Wright's motion for a summary judgment, Harper states that Wright's touch greatly offended her and that this fact is evidenced by the fact that she filed her complaint with the Winston County Commission on May 9, 2000. In her complaint, Harper states that "[Wright] grabbed my arm and tried to force me to go with her." Reviewing the facts in the light most favorable to Harper, as this Court is required to do on an appeal from a summary judgment, we conclude that the question whether a battery occurred in this case—specifically, whether Wright touched Harper in a harmful or offensive manner—is a question of fact for the jury to decide.

We reverse the summary judgment in favor of Wright on Harper's assault-and-battery claim; and we remand this case to the trial court for proceedings consistent with this opinion.

KEY POINTS

- Harper was not physically injured, but she still can claim battery if she was touched in an offensive or hostile way, like being "grabbed" and "pulled."
- The trial court ruled that Wright was touching merely to gain control of Harper. However, there is no legal exception for offensive touching to gain control of an employee, like there may be for a merchant detaining a shoplifter.
- The appeals court ruling in favor of Harper does not mean that she prevailed on her battery claim. The case can go back to a trial court so that Harper has an opportunity to prove her claim of battery at trial.

INTENTIONAL INFLICTION OF MENTAL DISTRESS

This tort usually requires the plaintiff to prove not only mental distress but also physical symptoms.

Intentional **infliction of mental distress** is a battery to the emotions. It arises from outrageous, intentional conduct that carries a strong probability of causing mental distress to the person at whom it is directed. Usually, one who sues on the basis of an intentional infliction of mental distress must prove that the defendant's outrageous behavior caused not only mental distress but also physical symptoms, such as headaches or sleeplessness.

The most common cases of intentional infliction of mental distress (also called *emotional distress*) have concerned employees who have been discriminated against or fired. Many such cases, however, do not involve the type of outrageous conduct necessary for the mental distress tort.

In the business world, other examples of infliction of mental distress come about from the efforts of creditors to extract payment from their debtors. Frequent, abusive, threatening phone calls by creditors might provide the basis for a claim of intentional infliction of mental distress. As torts go, this one is of fairly recent origin. It is a judge-made tort, which furnishes a good example of how the courts are increasingly sensitive to the range of injuries for which compensation is appropriate. In some states, courts have established liability for carelessly inflicted mental distress, such as the distress of a mother who sees her child negligently run down by a delivery truck.

INVASION OF PRIVACY

The tort of **invasion of privacy** is one that is still in the early stages of legal development. As the statutes and court cases recognize it, the tort at present comprises three principal invasions of personal interest. An invasion of any one of these areas of interest is sufficient to trigger liability.

Most commonly, liability will be imposed on a defendant who appropriates the plaintiff's name or likeness for his or her own use. Many advertisers and marketers have been required to pay damages to individuals when pictures of them have been used without authorization to promote products, or when their names and identities have been used without permission for promotional purposes. In one recent case, EA Sports ended its popular NCAA College Football video game series and settled a lawsuit filed by former and current student-athletes for using their images in the video games without compensating them. Before using anyone's picture or name, an advertiser must obtain a proper release from that person to avoid possible liability.

> That you can recover damages for misappropriation of likeness illustrates that you own your name and likeness in certain respects.

A second invasion of privacy is the defendant's intrusion upon the plaintiff's physical solitude. Illegal searches or invasions of home or possessions, illegal wiretapping, and persistent and unwanted telephoning can provide the basis for this invasion-of-privacy tort. In one case, a woman even recovered damages against a photographer who entered her sickroom and snapped a picture of her. Employers who enter their employees' homes without permission have also been sued successfully for invasions of privacy. If the invasion of privacy continues, it may be enjoined by the court. Jacqueline Kennedy Onassis sought and obtained an injunction that forbade a certain photographer from getting too close to her and her children. Under this tort, the invasion of physical solitude must be highly objectionable to a reasonable person.

Social media is often a factor in recent invasion of privacy claims. The case below considers whether an individual has an expectation of privacy in a posting to social media.

 case **10.2**

EHLING v. MONMOUTH-OCEAN HOSPITAL SERVICE CORP.
872 F.Supp. 2d 369 (D. N. J. 2012)

Monmouth-Ocean Hospital (MONOC) provides emergency medical services, and employed Deborah Ehling as a registered nurse and paramedic. Ehling maintained a Facebook account for social networking. Ehling did not invite any members of MONOC management to be her Facebook "friend" and without that "friend" invitation, the postings on her Facebook "wall" were not accessible. Many non-management co-workers, however, were invited by Ehling to be Facebook friends. The plaintiff, Ehling, claims that MONOC supervisors accessed her Facebook wall that included a posting regarding a shooting at the Holocaust Museum

in Washington D.C. that stated: "An 88 yr old sociopath white supremacist opened fire in the Wash D.C. Holocaust Museum this morning and killed an innocent guard (leaving children). Other guards opened fire. The 88 yr old was shot. He survived. I blame the D.C. paramedics. I want to say 2 things to the DC medics 1. WHAT WERE YOU THINKING? and 2. This was your opportunity to really make a difference!" MONOC sent letters regarding Ehling's Facebook post to the New Jersey Board of Nursing and Department of Health stating concern that the posting showed a disregard for patient safety. Ehling filed a lawsuit for common law invasion of privacy and MONOC asked the court to dismiss the claim.

MARTINI, J: Under New Jersey law, to state a claim for intrusion upon one's seclusion or private affairs, a plaintiff must allege sufficient facts to demonstrate that (1) her solitude, seclusion, or private affairs were intentionally infringed upon, and that (2) this infringement would highly offend a reasonable person. . . . "[E]xpectations of privacy are established by general social norms" and must be objectively reasonable—a plaintiff's subjective belief that something is private is irrelevant.

Privacy in social networking is an emerging, but underdeveloped, area of case law. . . . There appears to be some consistency in the case law on the two ends of the privacy spectrum. On one end of the spectrum, there are cases holding that there is *no* reasonable expectation of privacy for material posted to an unprotected website that anyone can view. . . . On the other end of the spectrum, there are cases holding that there is a reasonable expectation of privacy for individual, password-protected online communications. . . .

Courts, however, have not yet developed a coherent approach to communications falling between these two extremes. Although most courts hold that a communication is not necessarily public just because it is accessible to a number of people, courts differ dramatically in how far they think this theory extends. . . . What is clear is that privacy determinations are made on a case-by-case basis, in light of all the facts presented.

In this case, Plaintiff argues that she had a reasonable expectation of privacy in her Facebook posting because her comment was disclosed to a limited number of people who she had individually invited to view a restricted access webpage. Defendants argue that Plaintiff cannot have a reasonable expectation of privacy because the comment was disclosed to dozens, if not hundreds, of people. The Amended Complaint and underlying documents do not indicate how many Facebook friends Plaintiff had at the time the comment was made; thus, there is no indication of how many people could permissibly view Plaintiff's posting.

The Court finds that Plaintiff has stated a plausible claim for invasion of privacy, especially given the open-ended nature of the case law. Plaintiff may have had a reasonable expectation that her Facebook posting would remain private, considering that she actively took steps to protect her Facebook page from public viewing. More importantly, however, reasonableness (and offensiveness) are highly fact-sensitive inquiries. As such, these issues are not properly resolved on a motion to dismiss.

Accordingly, the motion to dismiss . . . is denied.

KEY POINTS

- The social norms around privacy change and are dependent on what is objectively reasonable, not what a plaintiff alone thinks is reasonable or what he or she may believe is private.

- There is generally no expectation of privacy on unprotected websites that are publicly accessible but password-protected online communication may have a reasonable expectation of privacy. In between those two extremes, however, there is not a clear legal consensus.

- Courts determine what is reasonable privacy based on the facts of each case. Disclosure to one or more people does not mean that a plaintiff has forfeited privacy rights, but where to draw the line is very specific to the circumstances of each case.

Don't forget that the First Amendment protects you when you publish even highly personal truthful information about public officials and public figures.

The third invasion of personal interest that gives rise to the invasion-of-privacy tort is the defendant's public disclosure of highly objectionable, private information about the plaintiff. A showing of such facts can be the basis for a cause of action, even if the information is true. Thus, publishing in a newspaper that the plaintiff does not pay his or her debts has been ruled to create liability for the defendant creditor. Communicating the same facts to a credit-reporting agency or the plaintiff's employer usually does not impose liability, however. In these cases, there has been no disclosure to the public in general. Also, the news media are protected under the First Amendment when they publish information about public officials and other public figures.

FALSE IMPRISONMENT AND MALICIOUS PROSECUTION

Shoplifting accounts for some $18 billion a year in business losses, almost 1% of retail sales. Claims of **false imprisonment** stem most frequently in business from instances of shoplifting. This tort is the intentional unjustified confinement of a nonconsenting person. Although most states have statutes that permit merchants or their employees to detain customers suspected of shoplifting, this detention must be a reasonable one. The unnecessary use of force, lack of reasonable suspicion of shoplifting, or an unreasonable length of confinement can cause the merchant to lose the statutory privilege. The improperly detained customer is then able to sue for false imprisonment. Allegations of battery are also usually made if the customer has been touched. Not all false imprisonment lawsuits arise because of shoplifting. In one instance a KPMG employee sued for false imprisonment alleging that his manager blocked a door with a chair during a performance review and caused the employee to have to remain in the room against his will.

> One false imprisonment lawsuit arose when a tow-truck operator towed a car with the driver still in it.

The tort of **malicious prosecution** is often called *false arrest*. Malicious prosecution arises from causing someone to be arrested criminally without proper grounds. It occurs, for instance, when the arrest is accomplished simply to harass someone. A former bank teller at Bank of America reached a $600,000 settlement with the bank in a malicious prosecution case. When two incidents of money missing from bank vaults occurred, the corporate security officer had the teller arrested although several other bank employees had access to the vaults. The security officer misled investigators and provided only evidence incriminating the teller, who was found not guilty at trial.

TRESPASS

To enter another's land without consent or to remain there after being asked to leave constitutes the tort of **trespass**. A variation on the trespass tort arises when something (such as particles of pollution) is placed on another's land without consent. Although the usual civil action for trespass asks for an injunction to restrain the trespasser, the action may also ask for damages.

Union pickets walking on company property (in most instances), customers refusing to leave a store after being asked to do so, and unauthorized persons entering restricted areas are all examples of trespass. Note that trespass is often a crime as well as a tort. Intentional wrongdoing is frequently criminal.

Trespass concerns the crossing of an owner's boundaries. Today, trespass usually refers to violating the physical boundaries of an owner's land, but in legal history trespass was the legal remedy for direct injuries caused by another to one's person as well. The famous British constitutional historian Frederick Maitland wrote, "Trespass is the fertile mother of actions." By this he meant that many of our modern day causes of action in tort—like battery—come from trespass. In an important sense, we own ourselves and various things we have acquired, and those who violate our boundaries become liable to compensate us.

CONVERSION

Conversion is the wrongful exercise of dominion (power) and control over the personal (nonland) resources that belong to another. Conversion deprives owners of their lawful right to exclude others from such resources. The deprivation may be either temporary or permanent, but it must constitute a serious invasion of the owner's legal right. Abraham Lincoln once convinced an Illinois court that a defendant's action in riding the plaintiff's horse for 15 miles was not sufficiently serious to be a conversion since the defendant had returned the horse in good condition. The plaintiff had left the horse with the defendant to be stabled and fed.

In one case a student drove a rental car into Mexico although the lease specifically prohibited cross-border driving. When an earthquake destroyed the car while it was parked in Mexico City, the rental company successfully sued the student for conversion.

Conversion often arises in business situations. Stealing something from an employer is conversion, as is purchasing—even innocently—something that has been stolen. Failing to return something properly acquired at the designated time, delivering something to the wrong party, and destruction or alteration of what belongs to another are all conversions when a deprivation of ownership is serious or long-lived. Even if you intend to return something, if you have converted it you are absolutely liable for any damage done to it. A warehouse operator who improperly transfers stored goods from a designated to a nondesignated warehouse is absolutely liable when a tornado destroys the goods or when a thief steals them.

DEFAMATION

Defamation is the publication of untrue statements about another that hold up that individual's character or reputation to contempt and ridicule. "Publication" means that the untruth must be made known to third parties. If defamation is oral, it is called **slander.** Written defamation, or defamation published over radio or television, is termed **libel.**

Is it defamation of character to say that someone is gay or lesbian? How about that someone is of a different race than is correct? Is calling someone a "communist" defamatory?

False accusations of dishonesty or inability to pay debts frequently bring on defamation suits in business relationships. Sometimes, such accusations arise during the course of a takeover attempt by one company of another through an offering to buy stock. In a recent instance, the chairman of one company called the chairman of a rival business "lying, deceitful, and treacherous" and charged that he "violated the standards by which decent men do business." If untrue, these remarks provide a good example of defamation of character. At one major university, a former business professor received a multi-million-dollar settlement following allegations made by university administrators that he had vandalized the new business school. The allegations cost him a deanship at another university. Punitive or punishment damages, as well as actual damages, may be assessed in defamation cases.

Individuals are not the only ones who can sue for defamation. A corporation can also sue for defamation if untrue remarks discredit the way the corporation conducts its business. Untruthfully implying that a company's entire management is dishonest or incompetent defames the corporation.

In 2008, publisher Judith Reagan and her employer News Corporation settled her $100 million lawsuit against News Corporation for defaming her by saying it had fired her because she had made anti-Semitic remarks.

Nearly one-third of all defamation suits are currently brought by employees against present and former employers. Often these suits arise when employers give job references on former employees who have been discharged for dishonesty. As a result, many employers will now not give job references or will do no more than verify that former employees did work for them.

There are two basic defenses to a claim of defamation. One defense is that the statements made were true. *Truth* is an absolute defense. The second defense is that the statement arose from *privileged communications*. For example, statements made by legislators, judges, attorneys, and those involved in lawsuits are privileged under many circumstances.

Defamation and the First Amendment Because of the First Amendment, special rules regarding defamation apply to the news media. These media are not liable for the defamatory untruths they print about public officials and public figures unless plaintiffs can prove that the untruths were published with "malice" (evil intent, that is, the deliberate intent to injure) or with "reckless disregard for the truth." Public figures are those who have consciously brought themselves to public attention. See Sidebar 10.2.

---

sidebar 10.2

Football Coaches as Public Figures

The U.S. Supreme Court issued the "public official" standard requiring defamation plaintiffs to prove "malice" or "reckless disregard for the truth" in *New York Times v. Sullivan,* 376 U.S. 254 (1964), a case involving criticism of an Alabama police commissioner. The Court extended essentially the same standard to defamation cases against "public figures" in *Curtis Publishing Co. v. Butts,* 388 U.S. 130 (1967). The facts of this case are interesting.

The *Saturday Evening Post,* one of the nation's leading feature story magazines for many years, published a story about the University of Georgia's athletic director and former football coach Wallace ("Wally") Butts and the University of Alabama's football coach Paul ("Bear") Bryant. The *Post* alleged that in a telephone conversation overheard accidentally by an Atlanta insurance salesman, Butts told Bryant how to beat Georgia in an upcoming game. "Before the University of Georgia played the University of Alabama. . . , Wally Butts . . . gave to Bear Bryant Georgia's plays, defensive patterns, all the significant secrets Georgia's football team possessed." The article continued, "The Georgia players, their moves analyzed and forecast like those of rats in a maze, took a frightful physical beating." Georgia lost the game, and Alabama went on to win the national championship.

Although the conversation between the two coaches may really have involved only a routine request to exchange game films, Butts ended up being forced to resign as athletic director. Both he and Bryant sued the *Post* for defamation. The coaches won their lawsuit, which was appealed to the Supreme Court.

The Court determined that the two coaches were "public figures" and that the First Amendment protected comment about them in much the same way it protected comment about public officials. However, the Court also concluded that the coaches had met their heavy burden of proof. It affirmed the judgment against the *Post.*

Plaintiffs' verdicts in media defamation cases are often overturned by trial or appellate judges. In one instance a Houston investment firm, now defunct, sued *The Wall Street Journal,* claiming that a story published by the newspaper caused the firm to go out of business. Following a huge jury verdict, the trial judge threw out $200 million in damages, ruling that the firm had not proved the newspaper published certain statements with knowledge of their falsity or with reckless disregard for the truth.

Plaintiffs' verdicts in defamation cases are often overturned by appellate courts. Because of the constitutional protection given to speech and the media, appellate judges reexamine trial evidence very closely to determine whether the necessary elements of defamation had been proven.

FRAUD

According to a survey by the Association of Certified Fraud Examiners, U.S. companies lose an average of 6% of their profit to fraud.

Business managers must be alert to the intentional tort of **fraud**, also known as *deceit*. A fraud is an intentional misrepresentation of a material fact that is justifiably relied upon by someone to his or her injury. An intentional misrepresentation means a lie. The lie must be of a material fact—an important one. The victim of the fraud must justifiably rely on the misrepresentation and must suffer some injury, usually a loss of money or other resource one owns.

Fraud applies in many different situations. Business frauds often involve the intentional misrepresentation of property or financial status. Lying about assets or liabilities in order to get credit or a loan is a fraud. Likewise, intentionally misrepresenting that land is free from hazardous waste when the seller knows that toxic chemicals are buried on the land constitutes fraud.

You can also prove fraud by giving evidence that another has harmed you by failing to disclose a material (important) hidden fact. The fraud of failure to disclose arises when the defendant is under a legal duty to disclose a fact, such as when a defendant seller knows that the foundations of a house are weakened by termites and must disclose this to the buyer.

Likewise, a defendant who has intentionally concealed an important fact and has induced reliance on it to the plaintiff's injury is liable for fraud. Following the financial collapse that began in 2007, hundreds of plaintiffs filed fraud lawsuits against banks, other financial institutions, and various of their executives based on concealment. In one such case, the former chief executive of Countrywide Financial agreed to pay $67.5 million to settle a fraud case brought by the Securities and Exchange Commission. The alleged fraud was the intentional concealment of the risks of subprime mortgages from investors in the then-largest national mortgage lender. Note that not only the common law but also many statutes regulating the financial industry provide for causes of action based on fraud.

In another concealment case, New York State filed a lawsuit based on fraud against Guidant Corporation. The complaint alleged that heart defibrillators manufactured by the company were defective and that the implanted devices had already failed in 28 patients. Further, the complaint asserted that Guidant had known of the defect for several years and concealed this information while continuing to sell the defibrillators. Said New York's former attorney general, "Concealment of negative facts that might influence a consumer to purchase another manufacturer's product is the essence of fraud."

Fraud is a broad term that is used in many different areas of the law. Fraud is not only a tort but a crime as well. Do you understand the difference between torts and crimes? (See Sidebar 10.3.)

sidebar 10.3

Tort or Crime? or Both?

Some torts are crimes and some are not. How do we make sense out of this? Crimes, which you will study in Chapter 13, generally require *intent* (also called *willfulness*). The prosecutor has to prove that the defendant intended to cross the proper boundaries established by law. These crossings injure or harm what belongs to people and the state punishes such harm, often through imprisonment or other limitations on personal freedom such as probation. But people also deserve compensation because of the injury. That is where tort law comes in.

The most serious torts like assault, battery, conversion, and fraud, which are also frequently crimes, are all intentional. Accidental boundary crossings are usually not criminal unless they are extremely reckless, but when they injure what belongs to an owner, the owner can still get compensation through tort law, for example, through proof of unreasonable and careless boundary crossing called *negligence* (discussed later in this chapter). Likewise, certain other accidental boundary crossings that cause injury, like the sale of a defective product, result in the person crossing the legal fence being held *strictly liable,* that is, liable even in the absence of unreasonable behavior in the crossing. However, because these torts are unintentional, they are usually not crimes as well.

Since torts are civil and crimes are, well, criminal in nature, they have different burdens of proof, as explained in Chapter 4. The judge instructs the jury that the plaintiff must prove the tort by a preponderance of the evidence but instructs the jury in a criminal case that the prosecutor must prove the victim's intentional injury by the defendant beyond a reasonable doubt. The burdens of proof are different because to deprive criminal defendants of their freedom is considered much more serious than merely to deprive them civilly of their money. And burdens of proof exist in both civil and criminal cases because to punish a criminal defendant to protect the proper order of the state or to compensate a civil plaintiff for a wrongful boundary crossing involves the taking of something that was previously proper to defendants, whether it is their freedom, their money, or some other resource belonging to them.

Do you understand better now why the same trespass across a legal fence can be both a tort and a crime?

INTERFERENCE WITH BUSINESS RELATIONS

Specific claims under tort are made when intentional acts cause interference with existing business relations or potential business relations. The same basic facts of a case can give rise to a number of different tort claims. See Sidebar 10.4.

Injurious Falsehood   **Injurious falsehood,** sometimes called *trade disparagement,* is a common business tort. It consists of the publication of untrue statements that disparage the business owner's product or its quality. General disparagement of the plaintiff's business may also provide basis for liability. As a cause of action, injurious falsehood is similar to defamation of character. It differs, however, in that it usually applies to a product or business rather than character or reputation. The requirements of proof are also somewhat different. Defamatory remarks are presumed false unless the defendant can prove their truth. But in disparagement cases the plaintiff must establish the falsity of the defendant's statements. The plaintiff must also show actual damages arising from the untrue statements.

As an example of injurious falsehood, consider the potential harm to Procter & Gamble of the assertions that associated its former logo of moon and stars with satanism. The company threatened to sue a number of individuals. In another instance Warnaco sued Calvin Klein, alleging that Klein

> **Do** remember that you can be sued for making statements about a competitor's product that the competitor considers false.

sidebar 10.4

One Set of Facts But Several Tort Claims?

When you consider the examples used to illustrate intentional torts in this section, the facts may suggest a claim based on another tort described in this chapter. Oftentimes, the same set of facts alleging tortious behavior potentially includes several claims that fall under the legal concept of tort. For example, in *Hayne vs. Innocence Project*, 2011 U.S. Dist. LEXIS 5586 (S.D. Miss. 2011), a doctor sued The Innocence Project, a not-for-profit organization that works to exonerate those wrongfully convicted. The Innocence Project had sent a letter to the state medical licensing board asking for the doctor's license to be revoked because, "by providing false and misleading autopsy reports and testimony in criminal prosecutions which carry a death sentence, [he] has played a critical role in improperly sending an unknown number of people to death row or prison for life." The doctor, a pathologist who had testified at numerous trials, was a "public figure," and claimed the letter sent to the licensing board constituted defamation, false light invasion of privacy, intentional infliction of emotional distress, and injurious falsehood. The parties settled the lawsuit.

A different set of facts in *Greico v. Sean & Co. L.P.,* 9 Pa. D. & C.5th 477 (2009) brought claims of trespass, conversion, and fraud against owners building a new Tractor Supply Company store. The Tractor Supply Company wanted trees and other vegetation removed from adjoining property so that the signs for the store could be seen from the major road. Negotiations with property owners resulted in a general agreement to remove certain trees with the property owners supervising. When the property owners were out of town, however, contractors for the store removed a significant amount of vegetation from the adjoining property. The court determined that, given the vague nature of the agreement between the parties, there was no contract claim but the property owners could proceed with the tort claims.

It is important to understand the specific elements of each tort to determine what claim is appropriate given a certain set of facts, but it is possible the facts meet the elements of more than one tort claim.

had made publicly disparaging remarks about how Warnaco made Calvin Klein clothing under license. The lawsuit alleged that Klein "falsely accused [Warnaco] of effectively 'counterfeiting' Calvin Klein apparel."

Intentional Interference with Contractual Relations

A second type of business tort is **intentional interference with contractual relations.** Probably the most common example of this tort involves one company raiding another for employees. If employees are under contract to an employer for a period of time, another employer cannot induce them to break their contracts. In a variation on this tort, the brokerage firm PaineWebber Group sued Morgan Stanley Dean Witter & Company over PaineWebber's merger agreement with J. C. Bradford & Company. PaineWebber claimed that Morgan Stanley pursued "a carefully planned, broad-based campaign to raid Bradford personnel and interfere with the merger agreement between PaineWebber and Bradford."

Don't induce the employees of another company to come to work for you when they are under contract to work for a period of time.

One of the most famous tort cases in history involved interference with a contract of merger. In that case a jury awarded Pennzoil over $10 billion against Texaco for persuading Getty Oil to breach an agreement of merger with Pennzoil. After Texaco filed for bankruptcy, Pennzoil accepted a settlement of around $3 billion.

Negligence

The second major area of tort liability involves unreasonable behavior that causes injury. This area of tort is called **negligence.** In the United States more lawsuits allege negligence than any other single cause of action.

Negligence takes place when one who has a duty to act reasonably instead acts carelessly and causes injury to another. Actually, five separate elements make up negligence, and the following sections discuss these elements. Sidebar 10.5 also summarizes them. In business, negligence can occur when employees cause injury to customers or others; when those invited to a business are injured because the business fails to protect them; when products are not carefully manufactured; when services, such as accounting services, are not carefully provided; and in many other situations.

---

sidebar 10.5

Elements of Negligence

Existence of a duty of care owed by the defendant to the plaintiff

Unreasonable behavior by the defendant that breaches the duty

Causation in fact

Proximate causation

An actual injury

DUTY OF CARE

A critical element of the negligence tort is **duty.** Without a duty to another person, one does not owe that person reasonable care. Accidental injuries occur daily for which people other than the victim have no responsibility, legally or otherwise.

Duty usually arises out of a person's conduct or activity. A person doing something has a duty to use reasonable care and skill around others to avoid injuring them. Whether one is driving a car or manufacturing a product, she or he has a duty not to injure others by unreasonable conduct.

Usually, a person has no duty to avoid injuring others through *nonconduct.* There is no general duty requiring a sunbather at the beach to warn a would-be surfer that a great white shark is lurking offshore, even if the sunbather has seen the fin. There is moral responsibility but no legal duty present.

When there is a special relationship between persons, the situation changes. A person in a special relationship to another may have a duty to avoid unreasonable nonconduct. A business renting surfboards at the beach would probably be liable for renting a board to a customer who was attacked by a shark if it knew the shark was nearby and failed to warn the customer. The special business relationship between the two parties creates a duty to take action and makes the business liable for its unreasonable nonconduct.

> A person doing something has a legal duty to act reasonably to avoid injuring others.

In recent years, negligence cases against businesses for nonconduct have grown dramatically. Most of these cases have involved failure to protect customers from crimes. The National Crime Prevention Institute estimates that such cases have increased tenfold since the mid-1970s.

One famous case involved the Tailhook scandal. A group of male naval aviators was sexually groping female guests as they walked down the hallway at a Hilton hotel. (Remember that an unconsented-to touching is an intentional tort.) One of the females who was sexually touched sued the Hilton hotel for negligence in knowing of the aviators' behavior and failing to protect her. A jury awarded her a total of $6.7 million against Hilton.

The extent of a business's duty to protect customers is still evolving. Note that in Case 10.3 the New Hampshire Supreme Court says that the defendant restaurant has no special relationship to the plaintiff, but still rules that it may have a duty to protect restaurant customers.

 case **10.3**

IANNELLI v. BURGER KING CORP.
200 N. H. Lexis 42 (N. H. Sup. Ct. 2000)

MCHUGH, J.: The plaintiffs, Nicholas and Jodiann Iannelli, individually and on behalf of their three children, brought a negligence action against the defendant, Burger King Corporation, for injuries sustained as a result of an assault at the defendant's restaurant. During the late afternoon or early evening hours of December 26, 1995, the Iannelli family went to the defendant's restaurant for the first time. Upon entering the restaurant, the Iannellis became aware of a group of teenagers consisting of five males and two females, whom they alleged were rowdy, obnoxious, loud, abusive, and using foul language. Some in the group claimed they were "hammered." Initially this group was near the ordering counter talking to an employee whom they appeared to know. The Iannellis alleged that one of the group almost bumped into Nicholas. When that fact was pointed out, the teenager exclaimed, "I don't give an F. That's his F'ing problem."

Nicholas asked his wife and children to sit down in the dining area as he ordered the food. While waiting for the food to be prepared, Nicholas joined his family at their table. The teenagers also moved into the dining area to another table. The obnoxious behavior and foul language allegedly continued. One of the Iannelli children became nervous. Nicholas then walked over to the group intending to ask them to stop swearing. As Nicholas stood two or three feet from the closest of the group, he said, "Guys, hey listen, I have three kids." Whereupon, allegedly unprovoked, one or more of the

group assaulted Nicholas by hitting him, knocking him to the ground and striking him in the head with a chair.

The plaintiffs argue that a commercial enterprise such as a restaurant has a general duty to exercise reasonable care toward its patrons, which may include a duty to safeguard against assault when circumstances provide warning signs that the safety of its patrons may be at risk. The most instructive case, given the issues presented, is *Walls v. Oxford Management Co.* In *Walls*, a tenant of an apartment complex alleged that the owner's negligent maintenance of its property allowed her to be subjected to a sexual assault in the parking lot. We held that as a general principle landlords have no duty to protect tenants from criminal attacks. In as much as landlords and tenants have a special relationship that does not exist between a commercial establishment and its guests, it follows that the same general principle of law extends to restaurants and their patrons. We recognized in *Walls*, however, that particular circumstances can give rise to such a duty. These circumstances include when the opportunity for criminal misconduct is brought about by the actions or inactions of the owner or where overriding foreseeability of such criminal activity exists.

Viewing the evidence in the light most favorable to the plaintiffs, we must decide whether the behavior of the rowdy youths could have created an unreasonable risk of injury to restaurant patrons that was foreseeable to the defendant. If the risk of injury was reasonably foreseeable, then a duty existed. We hold that the teenagers' unruly behavior could reasonably have been anticipated to escalate into acts that would expose patrons to an unreasonable risk of injury. The exact occurrence or precise injuries need not have been foreseen.

Viewed in a light most favorable to the plaintiffs, the evidence could support a finding that the teenagers' obnoxious behavior in the restaurant was open and notorious. Because the group was engaging in a conversation at times with a restaurant employee, it could be found that the defendant was aware of the teenagers' conduct. The near physical contact between one teenager and Nicholas Iannelli at the counter and the indifference expressed by the group member thereafter could be deemed sufficient warning to the restaurant manager of misconduct such that it was incumbent upon him to take affirmative action to reduce the risk of injury. The plaintiffs allege that at least one other restaurant patron expressed disgust with the group's actions prior to the assault. The manager could have warned the group about their behavior or summoned the police if his warnings were not heeded.

In summary, the trial court's ruling that as a matter of law the defendant owed no duty to the plaintiffs to protect them from the assault was error. While as a general principle no such duty exists, here it could be found that the teenagers' behavior in the restaurant created a foreseeable risk of harm that the defendant unreasonably failed to alleviate. Accordingly, we **reverse and remand.**

KEY POINTS

- A restaurant has a duty of reasonable care to those who are eating in the restaurant, but protecting them from assault does not normally fall within the duty owed to diners at a restaurant.
- When warning signs indicate that individuals eating in the restaurant may not be safe, the manager of the restaurant has a duty to take action to try to prevent injury. Warning signs in this case included obnoxious behavior by teenagers and one of them almost bumping into a child yet expressing indifference to the encounter.
- The court found that a duty to protect diners from assault might exist if restaurant employees become aware of the danger and do not take basic measures to prevent it.

Note that the duty to act reasonably also applies to professional providers, like doctors, lawyers, CPAs, architects, engineers, and others. In most negligence cases, however, the standard of reasonableness is that of a *reasonable person*. In negligence cases involving professionals, the negligence standard applied is that of the *reasonable professional*. The negligence of professionals is called *malpractice*.

As Sidebar 10.6 suggests, professional negligence is a controversial area of tort law.

UNREASONABLE BEHAVIOR—BREACH OF DUTY

At the core of negligence is the unreasonable behavior that breaches the duty of care that the defendant owes to the plaintiff. The problem is how do we separate reasonable behavior that causes accidental injury from unreasonable behavior that causes injury? Usually a jury determines this issue, but negligence is a mixed question of law and fact. Despite the trend for judges to let juries decide what the standard of reasonable care is, judges also continue to be involved in the definition of negligence. A well-known definition

A train rounds a bend but cannot stop in time to avoid running over an intoxicated person who has fallen asleep on the track. A jury is not likely to find the railroad's behavior "unreasonable."

295

sidebar 10.6

Medical Malpractice Crisis

Few people would disagree that physicians are extremely unhappy about the rapidly growing insurance premiums they have to pay. Some physicians have gone on strike; others have left the practice of medicine. The exact causes of the situation, however, are difficult to determine. Consider the following and make your own evaluation.

- Studies suggest between 44,000 and 98,000 people die annually from medical errors.
- A study in the *New England Journal of Medicine* found that 9 out of 10 patients who suffer disability from medical errors go uncompensated.
- In 2004 total payments for medical malpractice claims fell 8.9% nationally.
- As of 2005, 27 states have capped malpractice awards.
- In 2004 malpractice insurance costs for various medical specialties rose between 6.9% and 24.9%.

Question: what would be the impact on the cost of malpractice insurance if physicians had patients sign arbitration clauses before providing service in all but emergency cases? These clauses might provide that disputes with a physician be resolved before an arbitration board appointed by the state medical association. These clauses are currently not widely used and are specifically prohibited by several states. But under the Federal Arbitration Act, the state prohibitions are likely preempted by the federal law because medical practice has a substantial impact on interstate commerce. The Supreme Court has already ruled that law practice has such an impact, so it is likely that medical practice does as well.

Sources: *BusinessWeek; The New York Times;* Department of Health and Human Services.

by Judge Learned Hand states that negligence is determined by "the likelihood that the defendant's conduct will injure others, taken with the seriousness of the injury if it happens, and balanced against the interest which he must sacrifice to avoid the risk."

Examples of Negligence

Failure to exercise reasonable care can cost a company substantial sums. In one instance the licensed owner of a National Car Rental agency in Indianapolis was ordered to pay $5.5 million to a man who slipped on the floor and broke his hip. To save overtime pay the rental agency had had its floors mopped during, instead of after, normal working hours. Unaware that someone was mopping the floors behind him, the plaintiff had stepped backward, slipped, and fallen on the wet floor.

In another case arising from unreasonable behavior, Wal-Mart Stores agreed to pay two young girls a settlement of up to $16 million. A store employee had sold the girls' father a shotgun used to kill their mother in spite of the fact that a federal form filled out by the buyer indicated that he was under a restraining order. Federal law bars those under restraining orders from purchasing guns.

Even before the terrorist attacks of 9/11, New York's World Trade Center (WTC) had been bombed. In 2005 a Manhattan jury determined that the Port Authority of New York was negligent in the earlier attack, which involved a blast from a truck filled with explosives that terrorists had driven into the public parking lot under the WTC. Six people died and over a thousand were injured. Is it an example of litigation gone wild to hold the Port Authority liable for a terrorist act? Consider that before the bombing a report commissioned by the Port Authority, which controlled the WTC parking, had specifically warned against such a bombing and recommended: "Eliminate all public parking at the World Trade Center." Citing potential loss of revenue, the Port Authority had declined to follow the report's recommendation.

Willful and Wanton Negligence A special type of aggravated negligence is **willful and wanton negligence.** Although this does not reveal intent, it does show an extreme lack of due care. Negligent injuries inflicted by drunk drivers show willful and wanton negligence. The significance of this type of negligence is that the injured plaintiff can recover punitive damages as well as actual damages. For example, following the *Exxon Valdez* oil spill in Alaska, commercial fishers sued Exxon for damage to their livelihoods. A jury awarded substantial actual and punitive damages when it found that Exxon was willful and wanton in allowing the ship captain to be in charge of the ship when they knew he was an alcoholic.

> Willful and wanton negligence allows an injured plaintiff to recover punitive as well as actual damages.

In 2005 a New Jersey state court awarded a 2-year-old boy $105 million for an accident that left him permanently paralyzed from the neck down. A drunken Giants football fan had caused the accident. Before driving, the fan consumed at least 12 beers sold to him by a Giants Stadium concessionaire. The award for willful and wanton negligence against the concessionaire is the largest ever for the careless sale of alcohol. The award included $30 million in compensatory and $75 million in punitive damages.

Because employers are also liable for the intentional torts of employees in advancing the interests of their employers (see Chapter 21), employers face punitive damage awards in those instances even when they are also liable for simple negligence, or have not acted negligently at all. (See Sidebar 10.7.)

---

sidebar 10.7

Strip Search Hoax Costs McDonald's $6.1 Million

The caller identified himself as a police officer and told the McDonald's assistant manager that Louise Ogburn had stolen the purse of a customer who had recently left the restaurant and should be searched. For more than an hour the assistant manager and other McDonald employees detained, searched, and even committed sexual battery against Ogburn at the instruction of the caller. However, the caller was not a police officer and the call was a hoax.

Ogburn sued McDonald's and the jury awarded her a million dollars in actual damages for pain and suffering and $5 million in punitive damages against the company. To understand why McDonald's is liable, you have to understand that numerous instances of such hoaxes were known to the company involving various fast-food restaurants, yet the jury found that the company had not reasonably trained its employees such calls might be hoaxes.

If McDonald's negligence were extreme, that is, willful and wanton, that would justify the $5 million punitive damage award, but McDonald's is also liable for the intentional torts of its employees that justify awarding punitive damages. In this case the employees committed such intentional torts as false imprisonment and battery in the course of Ogburn's detention. Such detention advanced the interests of McDonald's in dealing with dishonest employees and made the intentional acts accompanying Ogburn's treatment the company's responsibility when they turned out to be wrongful.

CAUSATION IN FACT

Before a person is liable to another for negligent injury, the person's failure to use reasonable care must actually have "caused" the injury. This observation is not so obvious as it first appears. A motorist stops by the roadside to change a tire. Another motorist drives past carelessly and sideswipes the first as he changes the tire. What caused the accident? Was it the inattention of the second motorist or the fact that the first motorist had a flat tire? Did the argument the second motorist had with her boss before getting in the car cause the accident, or was it the decision of the first motorist to visit one more client that afternoon? In a real sense, all these things caused the accident. Chains of causation stretch out infinitely.

Still, in a negligence suit the plaintiff must prove that the defendant actually caused the injury. The courts term this **cause in fact**. In light of the many possible ways to attribute accident causation, how do courts determine if a plaintiff's lack of care, in fact, caused a certain injury? They do so very practically. Courts leave questions of cause in fact almost entirely to juries as long as the evidence reveals that a defendant's alleged carelessness could have been a substantial, material factor in bringing about an injury. Juries then make judgments about whether a defendant's behavior in fact caused the harm.

A particular problem of causation arises where the carelessness of two or more tortfeasors contributes to cause the plaintiff's injury, as when two persons are wrestling over control of the car which strikes the plaintiff. Tort law handles such cases by making each tortfeasor *jointly and severally* liable for the entire judgment. The plaintiff can recover only the amount of the judgment, but she or he may recover it entirely from either of the tortfeasors or get a portion of the judgment from each.

Approximately 40 states have limited joint and several liability in certain cases, for example, medical injury cases. In these states and types of cases, multiple defendants are each liable usually only for that portion of the damages juries believe they actually caused.

Many states are currently modifying the common law of torts regarding rules like that of joint and several liability.

PROXIMATE CAUSATION

It is not enough that a plaintiff suing for negligence prove that the defendant caused an injury in fact. The plaintiff also must establish proximate causation. **Proximate cause** is, perhaps, more accurately termed *legal cause*. It represents the proposition that those engaged in activity are legally liable only for the *foreseeable* risk that they cause.

Defining proximate causation in terms of foreseeable risk creates further problems about the meaning of the word *foreseeable*. In its application, foreseeability has come to mean that the plaintiff must have been one whom the defendant could reasonably expect to be injured by a negligent act. For example, it is reasonable to expect, thus foreseeable, that a collapsing hotel walkway should injure those on or under it. But many courts would rule as unforeseeable that someone a block away, startled upon hearing the loud crash of the walkway, should trip and stumble into the path of an oncoming car. The court would likely dismiss that person's complaint against the hotel as failing to show proximate causation.

Another application of proximate cause doctrine requires the injury to be caused *directly* by the defendant's negligence. Causes of injury that intervene

British Petroleum promised $20 billion to pay for claims arising from its oil spill in the Gulf. The payout by claims adjusters has been very slow. Part of the problem relates to proximate causation. How do claimants prove, for instance, that a falloff in business miles inland is directly caused by the oil spill instead of poor business practice, or for some other reason?

between the defendant's negligence and the plaintiff's injury can destroy the necessary proximate causation. Some courts, for instance, would hold that it is not foreseeable that an owner's negligence in leaving keys in a parked car should result in an intoxicated thief who steals the car, crashing and injuring another motorist. These courts would dismiss for lack of proximate cause a case brought by the motorist against the car's owner. For one of the most famous tort cases in history, see Sidebar 10.8.

sidebar 10.8

Explosion on the Long Island Railroad

Helen Palsgraf stood on the loading platform on the Long Island Railroad. Thirty feet away, two station guards were pushing a man onto a departing train when one guard dislodged an unmarked package held by the man. The package, which contained fireworks, fell to the ground with a loud explosion.

The explosion caused a heavy scale to fall on Helen Palsgraf, injuring her. She sued the railroad for the negligence of its guard and won at trial and in the appellate court. Three justices of the Court of Appeals (New York's supreme court) agreed with the lower courts: "The act [of the guard] was negligent. For its proximate consequences the defendant is liable."

However, four justices of the Court of Appeals decided that proximate causation was "foreign to the case before us." The majority ruled that what the guard did could not be considered negligence at all in relation to the plaintiff Palsgraf. The guard owed no duty to someone 30 feet away not to push a passenger— even carelessly—onto a train. The Court of Appeals reversed the damage award to the plaintiff.

The famous *Palsgraf* case illustrates the complexity of legal analysis. Question: Was it negligent for the passenger to carry fireworks in a crowded railroad station? Why didn't the plaintiff just recover damages from the passenger?

Source: *Palsgraf v. Long Island R.R.*, 162 N.E. 99 (1928).

DEFENSES TO NEGLIGENCE

There are two principal defenses to an allegation of negligence: contributory negligence and assumption of risk. Both these defenses are *affirmative defenses*, which means that the defendant must specifically raise these defenses to take advantage of them. When properly raised and proved, these defenses limit or bar the plaintiff's recovery against the defendant. The defenses are valid even though the defendant has actually been negligent.

Contributory Negligence As originally applied, the **contributory negligence** defense absolutely barred the plaintiff from recovery if the plaintiff's own fault contributed to the injury "in any degree, however slight." The trend today, however, in the great majority of states is to offset the harsh rule of contributory negligence with the doctrine of **comparative responsibility** (also called *comparative negligence* and *comparative fault*). Under comparative principles, the plaintiff's contributory negligence does not bar recovery. It merely compares the plaintiff's fault with the defendant's and reduces the damage award proportionally. For example, a jury determined damages at $3.1 million for an Atlanta plaintiff who was run over and dragged by a bus. But the jury then reduced the damage award by 20% ($620,000) on the basis that the plaintiff contributed to his own injury by failing reasonably to look out for his own safety in an area where buses come and go.

Adoption of the comparative negligence principle seems to lead to more frequent and larger awards for plaintiffs. This was the conclusion of a study by the Illinois Insurance Information Service for the year following that state's adoption of comparative negligence.

Assumption of Risk   If contributory negligence involves failure to use proper care for one's own safety, the **assumption-of-the-risk** defense arises from the plaintiff's knowing and willing undertaking of an activity made dangerous by the negligence of another. When professional hockey first came to this country, many spectators injured by flying hockey pucks sued and recovered for negligence. But as time went on and spectators came to realize that attending a hockey game meant that one might occasionally be exposed to flying hockey pucks, courts began to allow the defendant owners of hockey teams to assert that injured spectators had assumed the risk of injury from a speeding puck. It is important to a successful assumption-of-the-risk defense that the assumption was voluntary. Entering a hockey arena while knowing the risk of flying pucks is a voluntary assumption of the risk. However, that the injured person has really understood the risk is also significant to the assumption-of-the-risk defense. In one 2007 case, a University softball coach smacked his player in the face with a bat while demonstrating a batting grip to her. She required surgery for multiple fractures of her face and sued the coach and his employer, the university. The court denied the assumption-of-the-risk defense, asserting that it was up to the jury to determine whether the coach had acted negligently in hitting his player. The court observed that the player did not appreciate the risk of being hit by her coach with the bat.

Courts have often ruled that people who imperil themselves while attempting to rescue their own or others' property from a risk created by the defendant have not assumed the risk voluntarily. A plaintiff who is injured while attempting to save his possessions from a fire negligently caused by the defendant is not subject to the assumption-of-the-risk defense.

Assumption of the risk may be implied from the circumstances, or it can arise from an express agreement. Many businesses attempt to relieve themselves of potential liability by having employees or customers agree contractually not to sue for negligence, that is, to assume the risk. Some of these contractual agreements are legally enforceable, but many will be struck down by the courts as being against public policy, especially where a business possesses a vastly more powerful bargaining position than does its employee or customer.

Strict Liability in Tort

Strict liability is a catchall phrase for the legal responsibility for injury-causing behavior that is neither intentional nor negligent. There are various types of strict liability torts, some of which are more "strict" than others. What ties them together is that they all impose legal liability, regardless of the intent or fault of the defendant. The next sections discuss these torts and tort doctrines.

Contractual notices regarding assumption of the risk are more likely to be enforced if they prominently bring to attention the risk involved.

People injured by a baseball at a baseball game or a golf ball on the golf links also usually assume the risk. Does someone assume the risk of a racing car veering off a race track and going over a barrier and into the crowd?

STRICT PRODUCTS LIABILITY

A major type of strict tort liability is **strict products liability,** for the commercial sale of defective products. In most states any retail, wholesale, or manufacturing seller who sells an unreasonably dangerous defective product that causes injury to a user of the product is strictly liable. For example, if a forklift you are using at work malfunctions because of defective brakes and you run off the edge of the loading dock and are injured, you can sue the retailer, wholesaler, and manufacturer of the product for strict liability. The fact that the retailer and wholesaler may have been perfectly careful in selling the product does not matter. They are strictly liable.

Strict products liability applies only to "commercial" sellers, those who normally sell products like the one causing injury, or who place them in the stream of commerce. Included as commercial sellers are the retailer, wholesaler, and manufacturer of a product, but also included are suppliers of defective parts and companies that assemble a defective product. Not included as a commercial seller is your next door neighbor who sells you her defective lawnmower. The neighbor may be negligent, for instance, if she knew of the defect that caused you injury and forgot to warn you about it, but she cannot be held strictly liable.

An important concept in strict products liability is that of "defect." Strict liability only applies to the sale of unreasonably dangerous *defective* products. There are two kinds of defects. **Production defects** arise when products are not manufactured to a manufacturer's own standards. Defective brakes on a new car are a good example of a production defect. Another example involves the clam chowder in which a diner found a condom, which led in 2005 to a rapid settlement between the diner and a seafood restaurant chain. **Design defects** occur when a product is manufactured according to the manufacturer's standards, but the product injures a user due to its unsafe design. Lawsuits based on design defects are common but often very controversial. Recent such lawsuits have included one against Ford that claimed Ford should have designed its vans to have a heat-venting system so children accidentally locked in the vans would be safe. Lack of adequate warnings concerning inherently dangerous products can also be considered a design defect. American Home Products settled a wrongful death lawsuit for an estimated $10 million. The lawsuit alleged that the company had not adequately warned users of its diet drug about the risks of hypertension, which had been linked to diet-drug use.

In practice, strict products liability is useful in protecting those who suffer personal injury or property damage. It does not protect businesses that have economic losses due to defective products. For instance, a warehouse that loses profits because its defective forklift will not run cannot recover those lost profits under strict products liability. The warehouse would have to sue for breach of contract. However, if the forklift defect causes injury to a worker, the worker can successfully sue the forklift manufacturer for strict products liability.

Under strict products liability, contributory negligence is not a defense but assumption of the risk is. The assumption-of-the-risk defense helped protect tobacco manufacturers from health injury liability for many years. Misuse is another defense that defendants commonly raise in product liability cases. Removing safety guards from equipment is a common basis for the misuse defense. Defendants have also argued that if a product meets some federally required standard, it cannot be considered defective. Most courts, however, have ruled that federal standards only set a minimum requirement

Don't forget that strict products liability applies only against *commercial* sellers.

In one case, a jury found the defendant liable when its cleaning product warned users to "vent" rooms being cleaned but failed to say "vent to outside." Vapors from the product injured several people when it was used in a room with a closed circulation venting system.

Defenses available under strict product liability are different from defenses available for negligence.

for safe design and that meeting federal standards does not automatically keep a manufacturer from being sued for strict products liability.

In recent years many states have changed or modified the rules of product liability. See Sidebar 10.9. These changes to the rules of products liability (and modifications to the rules of medical malpractice) are often known generally as "tort reform." The federal government has also enacted tort reform that applies to product liability.

---

sidebar 10.9

Tort Reform

The rapid growth of products litigation during the past two decades has brought forth many calls for "tort reform." Numerous states have changed their laws to modify the tort doctrines discussed in this section and chapter. At the federal level, comprehensive tort reform has been strongly advocated although it has not passed as of this writing. Some of the tort reforms proposed or passed by the states include the following:

- Permitting only negligence actions against retailers and wholesalers unless the product manufacturer is insolvent.
- Eliminating strict liability recovery for defective product design.
- Barring products liability claims against sellers if products have been altered or modified by a user.

- Providing for the presumption of reasonableness defense in product design cases in which the product meets the **state-of-the-art;** that is, the prevailing industry standards at the time of product manufacture.
- Creating a **statute of repose** that would specify a period (such as 25 years) following product sale after which plaintiffs would lose their rights to bring suits for product-related injuries.
- Reducing or eliminating punitive damage awards in most product liability cases.

Importantly, note that not all, or even most, of these reforms have been adopted by every state.

Another important development in products liability is that in nearly every state product liability case based on design defects, failures to warn adequately and testing inadequacies are now decided according to "reasonableness" standards, making these product liability cases based on negligence standards. Consider Case 10.4 involving Ford Motor Company's failure to test a seatbelt sleeve.

---

 case 10.4

BRANHAM v. FORD MOTOR CO.
701 S.E.2d 5 (S.C. Sup. Ct. 2010)

Hale was driving several children to her house in her Ford Bronco. No one was wearing a seatbelt. Hale admittedly took her eyes off the road and turned to the backseat to ask the children to quiet down. When she took her eyes off the road, the Bronco veered towards *the shoulder of the road, and the rear right wheel left the roadway. She responded by overcorrecting to the left. Her overcorrection caused the Bronco to roll over. One of the children, Jesse Branham, was thrown from the vehicle, was severely injured, and sued Ford Motor*

Company and Hale. At trial, Branham did not seriously pursue the claim against Hale. The case against Ford was based on two product liability claims, one for failing to test the seatbelt sleeve, and the other a design defect claim related to the vehicle's tendency to rollover. Both of these claims were pursued in negligence and strict liability. The jury found both Ford and Hale responsible and awarded Branham $16 million in actual damages. Ford appealed to the South Carolina Supreme Court. The court found that the seatbelt sleeve claim should have been dismissed. It then turned to the "handling and stability" design defect claim in strict liability and negligence.

KITTREDGE, J.: We next address Ford's two-fold argument that: (1) Branham failed to prove a reasonable alternative design pursuant to the risk-utility test; and (2) South Carolina law requires a risk-utility test in design defect cases to the exclusion of the consumer expectations test. For a plaintiff to successfully advance a design defect claim, he must show that the design of the product caused it to be "unreasonably dangerous." In South Carolina, we have traditionally employed two tests to determine whether a product was unreasonably dangerous as a result of a design defect: (1) the consumer expectations test and (2) the risk-utility test.

In *Claytor v. General Motors Corp.*, this Court phrased the consumer expectations test as follows: "The test of whether a product is or is not defective is whether the product is unreasonably dangerous to the consumer or user given the conditions and circumstances that foreseeably attend use of the product." The *Claytor* Court articulated the risk-utility test in the following manner: "[N]umerous factors must be considered when determining whether a product is unreasonably dangerous, including the usefulness and desirability of the product, the cost involved for added safety, the likelihood and potential seriousness of injury, and the obviousness of danger." In *Bragg v. Hi-Ranger, Inc.*, our court of appeals phrased the risk-utility test as follows: "[A] product is unreasonably dangerous and defective if the danger associated with the use of the product outweighs the utility of the product."

Ford contends Branham failed to present evidence of a feasible alternative design. Implicit in Ford's argument is the contention that a product may only be shown to be defective and unreasonably dangerous by way of a risk-utility test, for by its very nature, the risk-utility test requires a showing of a reasonable alternative design. Branham counters, arguing that under *Claytor* he may prove a design defect by resort to the consumer expectations test or the risk-utility test. Branham also argues that regardless of which test is required, he has met both, including evidence of a feasible alternative design. We agree with Branham's contention that he produced evidence of a feasible alternative design. Branham additionally points out that the jury was charged on the consumer expectations test *and* the risk-utility test.

As discussed above, Branham challenged the design of the Ford Bronco II by pointing to the MacPherson suspension as a reasonable alternative design. A former Ford vice president, Thomas Feaheny, testified that the MacPherson suspension system would have significantly increased the handling and stability of the Bronco II, making it less prone to rollovers. Branham's expert, Dr. Richardson, also noted that the MacPherson suspension system would have enhanced vehicle stability by lowering the vehicle center of gravity. There was further evidence that the desired sport utility features of the Bronco II would not have been compromised by using the MacPherson suspension. Moreover, there is evidence that use of the MacPherson suspension would not have increased costs. Whether this evidence satisfies the risk-utility test is ultimately a jury question. But it is evidence of a feasible alternative design, sufficient to survive a directed verdict motion.

While the consumer expectations test fits well in manufacturing defect cases, we do agree with Ford that the test is ill-suited in design defect cases. We hold today that the exclusive test in a products liability design case is the risk-utility test with its requirement of showing a feasible alternative design. . . . Some form of a risk-utility test is employed by an overwhelming majority of the jurisdictions in this country. . . . States that exclusively employ the consumer expectations test are a decided minority. By our count 35 of the 46 states that recognize strict products liability use some form of risk-utility analysis in their approach to determine whether a product is defectively designed. Four states do not recognize strict liability at all. Those four states are Delaware, Massachusetts, North Carolina, and Virginia.

We believe that in design defect cases the risk-utility test provides the best means for analyzing whether a product is designed defectively. Unlike the consumer expectations test, the focus of a risk-utility test centers upon the alleged defectively designed product. The risk-utility test provides objective factors for a trier of fact to analyze when presented with a challenge to a manufacturer's design. Conversely, we find the consumer expectations test and its focus on the consumer ill-suited to determine whether a product's design is unreasonably dangerous.

As we observed in *Marchant v. Mitchell Distributing Co.*: "Most any product can be made more safe. Automobiles would be safer with disc brakes and steel-belted radial tires than with ordinary brakes and ordinary tires, but this does not mean that an automobile dealer would be held to have sold a defective product merely because the most safe equipment is not installed. By a like token, a bicycle is safer if equipped with lights and a bell, but the fact that one is not so equipped does not create the inference that the bicycle is defective and unreasonably dangerous. There is, of course, some danger incident to the use of any product."

In a product liability design defect action, the plaintiff must present evidence of a reasonable alternative design. The plaintiff will be required to point to a design flaw in the product and show how his alternative design would have prevented the product from being unreasonably dangerous. This presentation of an alternative design must include consideration of the costs, safety and functionality associated with the alternative design. On retrial, Branham's design defect claim will proceed under the risk-utility test and not the consumer expectations test.

[*Reversed and remanded*]

KEY POINTS

- The court reviewed the two major tests used by state courts to determine if a design defect made a product unreasonably dangerous: the consumer expectations test and the risk-utility test.
- Branham used expert testimony to show that Ford could have used the "McPherson suspension" system to significantly increase the Bronco II's handling and stability. This alternative suspension would not result in increased costs or compromised the sport utility features of the Bronco II.
- The court determined that, in South Carolina, the risk-utility test is now the standard for all product design defect cases because it focuses on the design of the product rather than the consumer of the product. In addition to using the risk-utility standard, the plaintiff must present evidence of a reasonable alternative design that considers the cost, safety, and functionality of the product.

ULTRAHAZARDOUS ACTIVITY

Some states have analyzed fireworks-related explosions that cause accidental injury by the standard of ultrahazardous activity.

In most states, the courts impose strict liability in tort for types of activities they call *ultrahazardous*. Transporting and using explosives and poisons fall under this category, as does keeping dangerous wild animals. Injuries caused from artificial storage of large quantities of liquid can also bring strict liability on the one who stores. For an example of the unusual dangers of ultrahazardous activity, see Sidebar 10.10.

OTHER STRICT LIABILITY TORTS

The majority of states impose strict liability upon tavern owners for injuries to third parties caused by their intoxicated patrons. The acts imposing this liability are called **dram shop acts**. Because of the public attention given in recent years to intoxicated drivers, there has been a tremendous increase in dram shop act cases.

sidebar 10.10

The Great Molasses Flood

The Purity Distilling Co. had filled the enormous steel tank on the Boston hillside with two million gallons of molasses to be turned into rum. Unusually warm weather caused the molasses to expand. On January 15, 1919, with sounds like gunfire as the restraining bolts sheared, the tank exploded. A wave of hot molasses 30-feet high raced down the street toward Boston Harbor, faster than people could run, engulfing entire buildings. Before it subsided, 150 people were injured and 21 drowned. "The dead," reported the *Boston Herald,* "were like candy statues."

It took months to clean up the harbor. It took six years to resolve the 125 lawsuits that followed. The artificial storage of large quantities of liquid can be a sticky matter indeed.

Source: Anthony V. Riccio, *Portrait of an Italian-American Neighborhood* (1998).

Common carriers, transportation companies licensed to serve the public, are also strictly liable for damage to goods being transported by them. Common carriers, however, can limit their liability in certain instances through contractual agreement, and they are not liable for (1) acts of God, such as natural catastrophes; (2) action of an alien enemy; (3) order of public authority, such as authorities of one state barring potentially diseased fruit shipments from another state from entering their state; (4) the inherent nature of the goods, such as perishable vegetables; and (5) misconduct of the shipper, such as improper packaging.

Damages

LO 10-3

One legal scholar concludes that "the crucial controversy in personal injury torts today" is in the area of damages. For dramatic examples of the size of recent awards, refer to Sidebar 10.11. Juries determine the size of damage awards in most cases, but judges also play a role in damages, especially in damage instructions to the jury and in deciding whether to approve substantial damage awards.

COMPENSATORY DAMAGES

Most damages awarded in tort cases compensate the plaintiff for injuries suffered. The purpose of damages is to make the plaintiff whole again, at least financially. There are three major types of loss that potentially follow tort injury and are called **compensatory damages.** They are:

- Past and future medical expenses.
- Past and future economic loss (including property damage and loss of earning power).
- Past and future pain and suffering.

sidebar 10.11

Highest Jury Tort Awards of 2010

EVENT CAUSING INJURY	JURY AWARD IN MILLIONS OF DOLLARS
1. Pharmaceutical products liability causing hepatitis C outbreak.	$505.1
2. Products liability for secondhand asbestos exposure to worker's laundry.	$208.8
3. Verdict against a cigarette company for providing deceased woman free cigarettes when she was a child.	$152
4. Products liability for design defect in a Ford Bronco rollover accident.	$132.5
5. Negligence verdict against a bus company to seven passengers injured or killed while riding in an unlicensed commercial van.	$124.5
6. Verdict against the world's largest law firm involving malpractice and intentional interference with business (contractual) relationships.	$103
7. Products liability against a cigarette company involving lung cancer death.	$90.8
8. Products liability for production defect of a carburetor in an airplane crash.	$89
9. Negligence in a natural gas explosion causing death at a plant.	$82.5
10. Cigarette products liability for lung cancer death.	$80

Note: Although virtually ignored in news media headlines, the damages in almost all of these large jury verdicts were reduced significantly. In some instances the judge reduced the damages as a matter of law. In other cases, appeals courts reduced damages or reversed the trial court. In many cases, however, the parties simply negotiated a reduced settlement to avoid the risk of an appeal that upheld or reversed the damages entirely. In reading about large jury verdicts, this final outcome is an important point for you to remember.

Compensatory damages may also be awarded for loss of limb, loss of consortium (the marriage relationship), and mental distress.

Calculation of damage awards creates significant problems. Juries frequently use state-adopted life expectancy tables and present-value discount tables to help them determine the amount of damages to award. But uncertainty about the life expectancy of injured plaintiffs and the impact of inflation often makes these tables misleading. Also, awarding damages for pain and suffering is an art rather than a science. These awards measure jury sympathy as much as they calculate compensation for any financial loss. The recent dramatic increases in the size of damage awards help underline the problems in their calculation. One result is that many individuals and businesses are underinsured for major tort liability.

Currently, compensatory damage awards for pain and suffering are very controversial. How do you compensate injured plaintiffs for something like pain which has no market value? Many plaintiffs suffer lifelong pain or the permanent loss of vision, hearing, or mobility. No amount of damages seems large enough to compensate them, yet no amount of damages, however high, will cause their pain and suffering to stop. In 2003, President Bush called for the limitation of tort damages for pain and suffering in a case to $250,000 per person. Do you agree or disagree?

PUNITIVE DAMAGES

Compensatory damages are not the only kind of damages. There are also **punitive damages.** By awarding punitive damages, courts or juries punish defendants for committing intentional torts and for negligent behavior considered "gross" or "willful and wanton." The key to the award of punitive damages is the defendant's motive. Usually the motive must be "malicious," "fraudulent," or "evil." Increasingly, punitive damages are also awarded for dangerously negligent conduct that shows a conscious disregard for the interests of others. These damages punish those who commit aggravated torts and act to deter future wrongdoing. Because they make an example out of the defendant, punitive damages are sometimes called *exemplary damages.*

Punitive or exemplary damages arise from intentional torts or extreme "willful and wanton" negligence.

Presently, there is much controversy about how appropriate it is to award punitive damages against corporations for their economic activities. Especially when companies fail to warn of known danger created by their activities, or when cost-benefit decisions are made at the risk of substantial human injury, courts are upholding substantial punitive damage awards against companies. Yet consider that these damages are a windfall to the injured plaintiff who has already received compensatory damages. And instead of directly punishing guilty management for wrongdoing, punitive damages may end up punishing shareholders by reducing their dividends.

Many court decisions also overlook a very important consideration about punitive damages. Most companies carry liability insurance policies that reimburse them for "all sums which the insured might become legally obligated to pay." This includes reimbursement for punitive damages. Instead of punishing guilty companies, punitive damages may punish other companies, which have to pay increased insurance premiums, and may punish consumers, who ultimately pay higher prices. As a matter of public policy, several states prohibit insurance from covering punitive damages, but the great majority of states permit such coverage. This fact severely undermines arguments for awarding punitive damages against companies for their economic activities.

"If you were to talk to foreign businesses about what scares them the most about the U.S. judicial process, they would say class actions and punitive damages."

–Carter G. Phillips, Sidney Austin Brown & Wood (law firm)

Consider also that an award of punitive damages greatly resembles a criminal fine. Yet the defendant who is subject to these criminal-type damages lacks the right to be indicted by a grand jury and cannot assert the right against self-incrimination. In addition, the defendant is subject to a lower standard of proof than in a criminal case. However, defendants in tort suits have challenged awards of punitive damages on a constitutional basis. See Sidebar 10.12.

Finally, note that almost no other country in the world except the United States permits civil juries to award punitive damages. For instance, in 2007 an Italian court refused to enforce a $1 million award against an Italian helmet maker whose defective helmet had caused the death of a 15-year-old motorcyclist in Alabama because the award contained punitive damages. However, a few courts in other countries have enforced U.S. punitive damage awards even though courts in their own countries cannot award them.

sidebar 10.12

Punitive Damage Guidelines

In 2003 the Supreme Court determined that $145 million in punitive damages in a case was unconstitutional. In *State Farm v. Campbell,* the Court decided that the large difference between punitive and compensatory damages violated due process. The Court suggested that a single-digit ratio of punitive to compensatory damages (9/1 or less) would be more constitutionally appropriate than a 145/1 ratio.

State Farm v. Campbell also reaffirmed general punitive damage guidelines from an earlier case. The Court stated, in evaluating the appropriateness of punitive damages, that courts should consider:

- "the responsibility of the defendant's conduct (how bad it was),
- the ratio of punitive to actual damages, and
- how the punitive damages compare with criminal or civil penalties for the same conduct."

Note that juries award punitive damages in only about 2% of litigated cases.

Key Terms

Assault 282
Assumption-of-the-risk 300
Battery 282
Cause in fact 298
Comparative
    responsibility 299
Compensatory damages 305
Contributory negligence 299
Conversion 288
Defamation 288
Design defect 301
Dram shop acts 304
Duty 293

False imprisonment 287
Fraud 290
Infliction of mental
    distress 284
Injurious falsehood 291
Intent 282
Intentional interference with
    contractual relations 292
Invasion of privacy 285
Libel 288
Malicious prosecution 287
Negligence 293
Production defects 301

Proximate cause 298
Punitive damages 307
Slander 288
State-of-the-art 302
Statute of repose 302
Strict liability 300
Strict products liability 301
Tort 281
Trespass 287
Willful and wanton
    negligence 297

Review Questions and Problems

Intentional Torts

1. *Assault and Battery*

    Under what theory can an employee sue her employer for merely touching her? Explain.

2. *Intentional Infliction of Mental Distress*

    In business the intentional infliction of mental distress tort has most often involved what type of situation?

3. *Invasion of Privacy*

    Explain the three principal invasions of personal interest that make up invasion of privacy.

4. *False Imprisonment and Malicious Prosecution*

    Explain the difference between false imprisonment and malicious prosecution. In what business situation does false imprisonment most frequently arise?

5. *Trespass*

In recent months, homeowners downwind from International Cement Company have had clouds of cement dust settle on their property. Trees, shrubbery, and flowers have all been killed. The paint on houses has also been affected. Explain what tort cause of action these homeowners might pursue against International Cement Company.

6. *Conversion*

Bartley signs a storage contract with Universal Warehouses. The contract specifies that Bartley's household goods will be stored at Universal's midtown storage facility while he is out of the country on business. Later, without contacting Bartley, Universal transfers his goods to a suburban warehouse. Two days after the move, a freak flood wipes out the suburban warehouse and Bartley's goods. Is Universal liable to Bartley? Explain.

7. *Defamation*

Acme Airlines attempts to get control of Free Fall Airways by making a public offer to buy its stock from shareholders. Free Fall's president, Joan, advises the shareholders in a letter that Acme's president, Richard, is "little better than a crook" and "can't even control his own company." Analyze the potential liability of Free Fall's president for these remarks.

8. *Fraud*

Fraud can be used to void a contract and as a basis for intentional tort. What is the advantage to a plaintiff of suing for the tort of fraud as opposed to using fraud merely as a contractual defense?

9. *Interference with Business Relations*

You are concerned because several of your employees have recently broken their employment contracts and left town. Investigation reveals that Sly and Company, your competitor in a nearby city, has paid bonuses to your former employees to persuade them to break their contracts. Discuss what legal steps you can take against Sly.

Negligence

10. *Duty of Care*

(a) Do you have a duty of care to warn a stranger on the street of the potential danger of broken glass ahead?

(b) Do you have a duty to warn an employee of similar danger at a place of employment? Explain.

11. *Unreasonable Behavior—Breach of Duty*

In litigation who usually determines if the defendant's behavior is unreasonable?

12. *Causation in Fact*

(a) What does it mean to say that "chains of causation stretch out endlessly"?

(b) What is the standard used by the judge in instructing the jury about causation?

13. *Proximate Causation*

Explain the difference between proximate causation and causation in fact.

14. *Defenses to Negligence*

A jury finds Lee, the defendant, liable in a tort case. It determines that José, the plaintiff, has suffered $200,000 in damages. The jury also finds that José's own fault contributed 25% to his injuries. Under a comparative negligence instruction, what amount of damages will the jury award the plaintiff?

Strict Liability in Tort

15. *Strict Products Liability*

While driving under the influence of alcohol, Joe runs off the road and wrecks his car. As the car turns over, the protruding door latch hits the ground and the door flies open. Joe, who is not wearing his seat belt, is thrown from the car and badly hurt. Joe sues the car manufacturer, asserting that the door latch was defectively designed. Discuss the legal issues raised by these facts.

16. *Ultrahazardous Activity*

Through no one's fault, a sludge dam of the Phillips Phosphate Company breaks. Millions of gallons of sludge run off into a nearby river that empties into Pico Bay. The fishing industry in the bay area is ruined. Is Phillips Phosphate Company liable to the fishing industry? Explain.

17. *Other Strict Liability Torts*

Explain when common carriers are not strictly liable for damage to transported goods.

Damages

18. *Compensatory Damages*

Explain the three types of loss that give rise to compensatory damages.

19. *Punitive Damages*

During a business lunch, Bob eats salad dressing that contains almond extract. He is very allergic to nuts and suffers a severe allergic reaction. There are complications and Bob becomes almost totally paralyzed. Because Bob had instructed the restaurant waiter and the chef that he might die if he ate any nuts, he sues the restaurant for negligence. Discuss the types of damages Bob may recover.

business *discussions*

1. You own University Heights Apartments, a business that rents primarily to students. One evening, your tenant Sharon is attacked by an intruder who forces the lock on the sliding glass door of her ground-floor apartment. Sharon's screams attract the attention of Darryl, your resident manager, who comes to Sharon's aid. Together, he and Sharon drive the intruder off, but not before they both are badly cut by the intruder.

   Is the intruder liable for what he has done?
   Do you have legal responsibilities to Sharon and Darryl?
   What should you consider doing at your apartments?

2. You manufacture trunk locks and your major account is a large car company. When an important piece of your equipment unexpectedly breaks, you contact Mayfair Inc., the only manufacturer of such equipment, and contract to replace it. The Mayfair sales representative assures you orally and in writing that the prepaid equipment will arrive by October 1, in time for you to complete your production for the car company. Instead, there is a union strike in the Mayfair trucking division, and the equipment does not arrive until December 1.

   By December 1 the car company has made an agreement with another lock manufacturer. You threaten to sue Mayfair for their failure to deliver on time, but Mayfair reminds you of a contract term that relieves them of contractual liability because of "labor difficulties." Then you learn from a former secretary to the Mayfair sales representative that Mayfair knew that its trucking division was likely to strike. In fact the sales representative and the sales vice president had discussed whether or not to tell you of this fact and decided not to out of concern that you would not place your order.

   Has Mayfair done anything legally wrong?
   Is your legal remedy against Mayfair limited to breach of contract?
   Will you be able to get damages from Mayfair other than a refund of your prepayment? Explain.

11

Intellectual Property

Learning Objectives

In this chapter you will learn:

11-1. To recognize why intellectual property is important to our economy and explain how it creates incentives for investment.

11-2. To identify the type of information that is protected by trade secret law and characterize circumstances that constitute misappropriation.

11-3. To list the requirements for a valid patent and recognize important issues in the enforcement of patents.

11-4. To categorize source indicators as trademark types and to differentiate between trademark dilution and infringement.

11-5. To define copyright protection and fair use limitations.

11-6. To describe the basic elements of the international system for protecting intellectual property rights.

In reading the previous chapters, you should have come to understand that the essence of "property" is a certain system of law. **Property** establishes a relationship of legal exclusion between an owner and other people regarding limited resources. It makes a particular resource like a new discovery legally "proper" to the owner rather than someone else.

The concept of ownership is easiest to understand in the context of something physical. You can readily intuit what it means to own a plot of land surrounded by a fence or an automobile, and laws that protect such ownership seem natural. Of course, it is a mistake to think that you can always know the exact boundaries of what is legally proper to you. Your property includes the legal uses of what you own, and the full extent of these uses is frequently unclear. By using what you own, you will at some point collide with the equal right of others to what they own. It is the job of both common law and statutory tort law to determine when you cross the boundary separating your proper use from wrongful injury to what belongs legally to others.

If defining boundaries is a daunting task in the tangible world, consider how much more difficult it is for the intangible. Should individuals or firms be permitted to own information as if it were property? If so, how do we determine the limits? These are important questions, because when property boundaries are unknown or difficult to determine and to enforce, much concern arises about the property system.

The decision to permit the ownership of information is not theoretical. Modern businesses count on the advantage of controlling inventions, expressions, marks, designs and business secrets like marketing plans or a list of customers. The different kinds of intangible, mostly knowledge-based assets that businesses may possess include the following:

- Employee skills and talents
- Production designs, inventions, and technologies
- Processes and methods of business operation
- Reports, manuals, and databases
- Customer lists and data about preferences and purchasing habits
- Relationships with suppliers and brand identity
- Software
- New product or service research
- Marketing plans

To provide the necessary control, we apply property law to such information through rights like trade secrets, patents, trademarks, and copyrights. Today, intellectual property represents protection of some of the most valuable resources that businesses have. However, against this backdrop of economic significance, we continue to explore the proper boundaries of information ownership.

sidebar 11.1

The Increasing Importance of Intellectual Property

Knowledge assets are among the most valuable resources of modern businesses. How to make things, how to do things, where to get things, how to sell things, how to buy things, and how to manage people are all vitally important to a firm, no matter what the industry. To some extent, knowledge assets can be protected by property, and property enables businesses to capture or realize the value of these assets.

Although it is impossible to know the exact value of all of the intellectual property owned by a firm at any given time, there is a general consensus that it constitutes an ever-greater percentage of firm assets. In fact, the value of some firms may consist almost entirely of information assets.

Consider the ride-sharing companies Uber or Lyft. As services that connect private drivers with passengers, they own no vehicles or rental locations. Most of the value in the companies is derived from information such as the implementation of the business model, the customer interface, and driver information. And that value—which was estimated in the billions of dollars for both companies in 2014—is substantial. If such valuable information cannot be excluded from other companies, the competitive advantage may disappear.

Source: Serena Saitto, "Uber in Funding Talks for More Than $10 Billion Value," Bloomberg.com, May 16, 2014.

The information economy, in which some successful businesses never produce a single physical product, has increased the importance of intangible information. In addition, the business community has become more aware of the advantages of intellectual property ownership. Firms are seeking portfolios that are striking in their breadth and diversity. Sports teams and universities vigorously protect trademarks. Social networking services like Facebook even own patents. In the modern business world, it is critical to understand the basics of intellectual property just to compete.

This chapter begins by considering the justification for intellectual property. It then explores the importance of knowledge assets to businesses, followed by the major forms of intellectual property: trade secrets, patents, trademarks, and copyrights. It concludes by reviewing the international legal environment and examining how intellectual property serves the common good.

THE JUSTIFICATION FOR INTELLECTUAL PROPERTY   `LO 11-1`

The justification for **intellectual property** is the same as for the private property system generally. Property relationships are believed to be more productive in allocating scarce resources and producing new ones than legal relationships that merely divide resources equally.

Abraham Lincoln said that intellectual property couples "the fuel of interest with the fire of genius." He was referring to how an exclusive right to what you acquire and produce gives incentive to create new things, new ways of doing things, and new invention generally. As the only U.S. president to own a patent (no. 6,469), Lincoln may have been particularly well suited to comment on the topic. But the sentiment in the U.S. extends back to the framers of the U.S. Constitution, who made sure that Congress could protect intellectual property. Article 1, Section 8, of the Constitution grants Congress the power "[t]o promote the Progress of Science and useful Arts, by securing for limited Times to Authors and Inventors the exclusive Right to their respective Writings and Discoveries." Note that the justification for "securing" an "exclusive Right" is "[t]o promote the Progress of Science [knowledge and creativity] and the useful Arts [inventions]." The Constitution recognizes that exclusive property boundaries promote, or give incentive to, the business production of what people need and want. However, the Constitution also ensures that after "limited Times" defined by Congress, the resources of new expression and invention, which were formerly exclusive to "Authors and Inventors," will be freely available to everyone.

INTELLECTUAL PROPERTY AND COMPETITION

The basic economic system of intellectual property is grounded in the idea of incentives. We give firms and individuals the ability to secure property rights if they produce certain types of information. Those property rights provide exclusivity that can lead to market advantages such as the ability to charge premium prices or utilize customer recognition. The possibility of economic return on investment encourages firms and individuals to create more information than they otherwise would. For some types of intellectual property, information is disclosed to the public in exchange for exclusive rights, which supports, follow-on research efforts.

Conversely, without intellectual property, the pace of creative research and development (R&D) in business would slow dramatically. R&D is

"The American view, as enshrined in the Constitution and reflected in over two hundred years of practice, is that inventors should be able to patent their inventions and creators should be able to copyright their works. That view is also informed by a sense of balance, of the importance of matching incentives for innovation with mechanisms to assure access and dissemination as well."

—Remarks by U.S. Trade Representative Michael Froman at the Center for American Progress, February 18, 2014

expensive. If businesses have to finance R&D and then compete against others who quickly copy the resulting new invention, the businesses paying for R&D will be at a competitive disadvantage.

Countering the benefits of intellectual property protection are certain costs. Property rights in information reduce competition (at least temporarily) that could otherwise increase availability and keep prices low for consumers. Intellectual property systems presume that the long-term benefits of increased information and investment are greater than the short-term costs.

Is intellectual property protection necessary for the production of *all* information? Intuitively, you know this is not true. An artist may paint simply to express herself without any notion of making a profit or excluding others from the work. A university scientist may investigate the mechanism of disease for the notoriety of discovery and the desire to benefit humanity. A blogger may write a post solely for the satisfaction of knowing that it will be shared widely and many people will read it. It is fair to say that intellectual property is believed to *incrementally increase* the production of information and investment over that which would normally occur. Society obtains this benefit in exchange for allowing some information to be controlled through property. The great debate regarding our intellectual property laws is whether they are truly calibrated to provide a net benefit to society.

---

sidebar 11.2

The Open Source Alternative

You may have heard of information products like software being distributed under an open source model. This means that the information is shared freely, and individuals and firms are able to build upon it outside of the strict control of the creator. Open source models of information development have been particularly successful in networked communities as exist across the Internet. Some believe that it is a better alternative than intellectual property or contract for producing certain types of information.

Note that open source products are not necessarily divorced from intellectual property rights. For example, open source software is often accompanied by a license that sets certain use limitations. The purpose of the license may be to ensure continued open access and to prevent unauthorized commercialization, which is usually not a property-centric goal. Yet, these open access provisions may be enforced through intellectual property. Failure to adhere to the terms constitutes infringement.

Source: Yochai Benkler, "Coase's Penguin, or, Linux and the Nature of the Firm," 112 *Yale Law Journal* 369 (2002).

CAPTURING INTELLECTUAL PROPERTY

The protections of property often do not apply automatically to intangible knowledge resources all information you or your business create. Depending on the type of information, you may be required to undertake certain steps to protect the time, effort, and money spent in developing knowledge in order to transform it into valuable intangible assets. Some intellectual property forms have very strict deadlines for asserting rights or other formal requirements. The failure to follow the rules may mean that information that could have been captured is instead dedicated to the public domain, meaning that anyone can use it. In general, once information is in the public domain, an intellectual property right cannot be applied to recapture it. Firms that do not have an intellectual property strategy in place risk losing valuable assets.

The sections that follow describe the forms of property that protect knowledge-based intangible business resources. Some general principles are conveyed, that can guide you in finding more detailed information. This chapter concludes by examining the right of property and the common good.

Trade Secrets

One of the most common ways of asserting property in knowledge-based intangible business resources is through the trade secret. Trade secret law developed in the common law industrial revolutions of the 1800s. Before this time, the relationship of confidence and trust between skilled artisans (craftspersons) and their apprentices (as well as the guild system) protected what the artisans knew from harmful competition by their former apprentices. But the 1800s brought large factories to the economy. The employees of these factories were not apprentices and at first were free to take their employers' knowledge, leave employment, and compete against their former employers. Trade secret law arose to protect the employers' valuable knowledge. It also facilitated economic development by making employers willing to hire employees who might come into contact with the employers' knowledge.

A **trade secret** is any form of knowledge or information that has economic value from not being generally known to others, or readily ascertainable by proper means and has been the subject of reasonable efforts by the owner to maintain secrecy. To violate another's trade secret rights, one must misappropriate the information. This is an important distinction from intellectual property rights that make one liable simply for unauthorized use. The majority of states have adopted the Uniform Trade Secrets Act (UTSA), but some states continue to rely on common law protection. In large part, the elements are the same. A successful trade secret case consists of two primary elements: (1) establishing that a trade secret exists and (2) demonstrating misappropriation.

ESTABLISHING THE EXISTENCE OF A TRADE SECRET

As described above, businesses may possess many different forms of valuable knowledge. It may be financial, technical, scientific, economic, or engineering knowledge. When a business has spent time, effort, or money in employee training, preparing materials, making plans, or developing relationships with customers and suppliers, the business may wish to keep competitors away from this knowledge. However, not all of this knowledge is protected by the law of trade secrets. To protect information as a trade secret, the information must actually be secret, and the business must take *reasonable measures* to keep it so.

A first step in protecting trade secrets is to identify confidential knowledge-based resources. It is useful for all businesses to conduct a *trade secret audit*, which simply identifies all the valuable forms of information possessed by the business, including formulas, plans, reports, manuals, research, and

> "More than ever before, information is what gives businesses their competitive edge, and they want to make sure that inside dope on products and services doesn't walk out the door."
>
> **—*BusinessWeek*, November 12, 2007, p. 76**

LO 11-2

Trade secret audits help you identify the valuable information that a business produces.

knowledge of customers and suppliers. Note that trade secrets do not have to be unique; two businesses may have trade secret property in substantially the same knowledge. For example, they may each have customer lists that overlap with many of the same names. As long as there are actual or potential competitors who are not aware of all the customer names, the knowledge still has economic value.

Having identified potential trade secrets, a business must next work to preserve secrecy. Reasonable measures include physically locking away written material, securing computer-stored knowledge with protective "firewalls" and encryption to keep hackers from obtaining access, and imposing confidentiality restrictions on those who have contact with the firm. Some companies maintain two different computer systems in order to protect proprietary (owned) knowledge, one connected to the Internet and one networked only internally. Employees use the internal network to send messages about matters that are not for public consumption. To protect trade secrets from outsiders, companies often also carefully regulate who can visit the business and what areas of the business visitors can see. Visitors are sometimes required to sign agreements not to disclose to the public what they see and learn in a company they visit.

Prospective business partners, customers, suppliers, and repair technicians—may also have access to knowledge that a company values and protects. These parties may also be asked to sign nondisclosure agreements (NDAs). As long as a company takes such reasonable measures to prevent the public dissemination of trade secrets, it does not lose its property in knowledge-based resources merely because customers, suppliers, repair technicians, or even visitors come into contact with the secrets.

Establishing the existence of a trade secret is a critical step in controlling valuable knowledge resources. The failure to maintain secrecy, or to prove that the knowledge was secret in the first place, can mean that competitors may be able to access it. Case 11.1 is an illustration of how broad the concept of a trade secret can be.

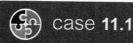 case 11.1

AL MINOR & ASSOCIATES, INC. v. MARTIN
881 N.E.2d 850 (Ohio, 2008)

O'DONNELL, J.: . . . .AMA is an actuarial firm that designs and administers retirement plans and that employs several "pension analysts" who work with approximately 500 clients. Al Minor Jr., who founded AMA in 1983 and serves as its president and sole shareholder, developed AMA's clientele, for which the firm maintains a confidential list.

In 1998, AMA hired Martin as a pension analyst but did not require him to sign either an employment contract or a noncompete agreement. In 2002, while still employed by AMA, Martin organized his own company, Martin Consultants, L.L.C., with the purpose of providing the same type of services as AMA. In 2003, he resigned from AMA and, without taking any documents containing confidential client information, successfully solicited 15 AMA clients with information from his memory.

After learning of Martin's competing business, AMA filed the instant action against him for monetary and injunctive relief, claiming that he had violated Ohio's Trade Secrets Act by using confidential client information to solicit those clients. . . .

In this court, Martin asserts that a client list memorized by a former employee cannot be the basis of a trade secret violation. . . .

In 1937, this court acknowledged that "[t]he authorities are quite uniform that disclosures of trade secrets by an employee secured by him in the course of confidential employment will be restrained by the process of injunction, and in numerous instances attempts to use for himself or for a new employer information relative to the trade or business in which he had been engaged, such as lists of customers regarded as confidential, have been restrained." *Curry v. Marquart* 11 N.E.2d 868. (1937).

In 1994, the General Assembly enacted UTSA . . . which [in part R.C. 1333.61(D)] defines a "trade secret" as follows:

[I]nformation, including the whole or any portion or phase of any scientific or technical information, design, process, procedure, formula, pattern, compilation, program, device, method, technique, or improvement, or any business information or plans, financial information, or listing of names, addresses, or telephone numbers, that satisfies both of the following:

> "(1) It derives independent economic value, actual or potential, from not being generally known to, and not being readily ascertainable by proper means by, other persons who can obtain economic value from its disclosure or use."
>
> "(2) It is the subject of efforts that are reasonable under the circumstances to maintain its secrecy."

Furthermore, in *The Plain Dealer v. Ohio Dept. of Ins.* 687 N.E.2d 661 (1997), we established a six-factor test for determining whether information constitutes a trade secret pursuant to R.C. 1333.61(D): "(1) The extent to which the information is known outside the business; (2) the extent to which it is known to those inside the business, i.e., by the employees; (3) the precautions taken by the holder of the trade secret to guard the secrecy of the information; (4) the savings effected and the value to the holder in having the information as against competitors; (5) the amount of effort or money expended in obtaining and developing the information; and (6) the amount of time and expense it would take for others to acquire and duplicate the information." . . .

Neither R.C. 1333.61(D) nor any other provision of the UTSA suggests that for purposes of trade secret protection, the General Assembly intended to distinguish between information that has been reduced to some tangible form and information that has been memorized. R.C. 1333.61(D) refers only to "information," including "any business information or plans, financial information, or listing of names, addresses, or telephone numbers," and the statute makes no mention of writings or other physical forms that such information might take. Furthermore, nothing in our six-factor test . . . indicates that the determination whether a client list constitutes a trade secret depends on whether it was capable of being memorized or had been memorized. . . .

In addition, more than 40 other states have adopted the Uniform Trade Secrets Act in substantially similar form, and the majority position is that memorized information can be the basis for a trade secret violation . . . .

We recognize that the protection of trade secrets involves a balancing of public policies, and as stated in *E.I. duPont de Nemours & Co. v. Am. Potash & Chem. Corp,* 200 A.2d 428. (1964), "Among the substantial and conflicting policies at play . . . are the protection of employers' rights in their trade secrets . . . versus the right of the individual to exploit his talents." However, by adopting the Uniform Trade Secrets Act, with the express purpose "to make uniform the law with respect to their subject among states," the General Assembly has determined that public policy in Ohio, as in the majority of other jurisdictions, favors the protection of trade secrets, whether memorized or reduced to some tangible form. . . .

Based on the foregoing, we conclude that the determination of whether a client list constitutes a trade secret pursuant to R.C. 1333.61(D) does not depend on whether it has been memorized by a former employee. Information that constitutes a trade secret pursuant to R.C. 1333.61(D) does not lose its character as a trade secret if it has been memorized. It is the information that is protected by the UTSA, regardless of the manner, mode, or form in which it is stored—whether on paper, in a computer, in one's memory, or in any other medium.

Every employee will of course have memories casually retained from the ordinary course of employment. The Uniform Trade Secrets Act does not apply to the use of memorized information that is not a trade secret pursuant to R.C. 1333.61(D).

Moreover, we recognize that no conflict exists between the appellate court's decision in this case and the decision of the Cuyahoga County Court of Appeals in *Greenwald*, because the latter case predated the legislature's adoption of the UTSA.

In this case, AMA's client list constituted a trade secret pursuant to R.C. 1333.61(D), and the fact that Martin had memorized that client list before leaving AMA does not change its status as a trade secret or remove it from the protection of the UTSA. For these reasons, we affirm the judgment of the court of appeals.

Judgment accordingly.

KEY POINTS

- A client list can serve as a trade secret because it provides value to the owner.
- The court found that even information that was memorized and not written down can be subject to trade secret protection.
- It is important to understand that all information used within a company is not necessarily a trade secret.

DEMONSTRATING MISAPPROPRIATION

To be liable in a trade secret case, a defendant must have misappropriated the information in question. **Misappropriation** obviously occurs when one improperly acquires secret information through burglary, espionage, or computer hacking. However, misappropriation also occurs when one discloses information that one had a duty to keep secret, even if the original acquisition was proper. Such a duty may arise from an employment relationship or a contractual agreement. Additionally, if one acquires a secret from another who has a duty to maintain secrecy, and one knows of that duty, misappropriation has occurred. On the other hand, innocently acquiring a secret from another without knowledge of their theft is generally not misappropriation.

Importantly, independent creation does *not* constitute misappropriation. If, through your own effort, you are able to recreate the same information that another considers to be a trade secret, no misappropriation has occurred. In addition, reverse engineering a secret by looking at a product and figuring out how it works or how it is formulated is not misappropriation. An exception to this principle would be if one contractually agreed to keep the information secret. For example, it is common in the software industry to make users promise not to decompile (take apart) purchased software to figure out how the code works.

The fact that secrets can get out through normal product marketing is an important limitation on trade secret rights. For that reason, as discussed below, a patent may provide better protection for a valuable invention embodied in a product, assuming the stringent requirements can be met. But if the valuable information relates to processes or techniques that will not be disclosed when a product or service is sold, trade secret rights may be a viable, relatively inexpensive, and long-lived option.

Employee Mobility and Trade Secrets

Businesses have to take reasonable measures to protect trade secrets even from employees. Employees may leave an employer and use the knowledge they have gained to compete against their former employer, or they may go to work for their former employer's competitors.

Increasingly, employers require employees to sign confidentiality contracts promising not to disclose what they learn in confidence in the workplace. This promise, however, applies only to knowledge that is unknown

Do remember that contractual confidentiality agreements and noncompete agreements have a role in trade secret protection but are not always required.

publicly and amounts to trade secrets. Additionally, not all states presume that former employees are likely to disclose confidential information in a new position. This creates difficulty in establishing misappropriation. As an additional measure of protection, employers frequently request that employees agree not to compete against them if the employees leave their employment.

The law states that employers can enforce agreements (or contractual "covenants") not to compete only when there is a "valid business purpose" for the contract. Generally, this means that employers are protecting trade secrets, or, at least protecting their investment in the training of their employees, which itself can be a trade secret. However, laws of unfair competition limit the extent to which employers can prevent employees from competing against them.

CIVIL ENFORCEMENT OF TRADE SECRETS

The owner of a trade secret may go into court and get an injunction to prevent others—often former employees—from divulging or using a trade secret. An **injunction** is an order by a judge either to do something or to refrain from doing something. In the case of trade secrets, the injunction orders those who have *misappropriated* the trade secret to refrain from using it or telling others about it. In rare instances, the injunction may also order that one delay in taking a new job.

The wrongful taking of any kind of intellectual property is called *misappropriation* or *infringement*.

Trade secret owners can also obtain damages against those who misappropriate trade secrets. In 2011, a California jury awarded St. Jude Medical Inc. $2.3 billion in a dispute against a former employee and rival medical device company, Nervicon. The employee allegedly left St. Jude with documents related to a crystal oscillator, and used the document to help Nervicon create the same device.

CRIMINAL ENFORCEMENT OF TRADE SECRETS

In addition to civil enforcement of trade secret boundaries, criminal prosecution can also result from misappropriation of trade secrets. Although various state laws make intentional trade secret misappropriation a crime, most criminal prosecutions today take place under the federal **Economic Espionage Act** (EEA). The act makes it a crime to steal (intentionally misappropriate) trade secrets and provides for fines and up to ten years' imprisonment for individuals and up to a $5 million fine for organizations. Only the federal government can bring a case under the EEA. The Coca-Cola case in Sidebar 11.3 is an example of an EEA criminal prosecution.

Although one provision of the EEA makes one liable for standard trade secret misappropriation, another provision addresses misappropriation to benefit a foreign government—true espionage. Penalties are enhanced in this case. There is a great deal of concern that foreign governments may be spying on U.S. companies to make their domestic industries more competitive. In recent years, the U.S. government has promised to crack down on such acts. For example, in 2014, Attorney General Eric Holder announced indictments of five Chinese military hackers for stealing "information from American entities that would be useful to their competitors in China,

sidebar 11.3

Soda Secrets

The Coca-Cola Company considers the formula for its namesake drink, also known as Coke, to be a valuable secret. Even though it was created over 100 years ago, the company refuses to disclose the original formula and continues to undertake measures to maintain its secrecy. Through various reformulations, the basic recipe remains confidential according to the company.

However, is it possible to discern the formula for Coca-Cola from a purchased bottle? Science provides the means for characterizing the various elements of chemical compounds, and one would assume that such techniques could be applied to a soft drink to learn its composition. Absent a contract, patent, or employee relationship, this type of reverse engineering does not violate the law. In fact, over the years, several people have claimed to be in possession of the secret formula for Coca-Cola through disclosure or reverse engineering, including the host of the radio program

This American Life in 2011. Without a confirmation from the Coca-Cola Company, it is difficult to know for certain how accurate such claims are.

Regardless of whether the actual formula for Coca-Cola is known outside the company, it is certainly true that Coca-Cola can possess protectable trade secrets on newer products. In 2007, a jury convicted a former Coca-Cola secretary for conspiring with others to steal secrets for products in development and sell them to rival Pepsi for $1.5 million. She was sentenced to eight years in prison. The scheme came to light when Pepsi informed the FBI that it received an offer to obtain Coca-Cola's product secrets.

Sources: Robbie Brow & Kim Severson, "Recipe for Coke? One More to Add to the File," *The New York Times*, February 19, 2011; "Ex-Secretary Gets 8-Year Term in Coca-Cola Secrets Case," The Associated Press, May 24, 2007.

including state-owned enterprises (SOEs)." Of course, it is not always easy to prosecute those who commit espionage from abroad due to jurisdictional issues. Even if prosecution is remote, indictments can serve as a political statement as well as a legal tool.

sidebar 11.4

Federal Government Intellectual Property Enforcement

Although private parties carry out much enforcement of state and federal intellectual property laws, governments also play an important role. In particular, the federal government prosecutes criminal cases involving copyright infringement (referred to as piracy in some cases), trademark infringement (also known as counterfeiting in some cases), and trade secret misappropriation. In 2008, the Prioritizing Resources and Organization for Intellectual Property Act (PRO IP Act) became law, creating a new position for coordinating federal agency intellectual property enforcement known as the Intellectual

Property Enforcement Coordinator (IPEC). Agencies that enforce the nations intellectual property laws include the Department of Justice, through its Computer Crime and Intellectual Property Section (CCIPS), the Federal Bureau of Investigation (FBI), and Customs and Border Protection, as well as many others. CCIPS conducts the actual prosecution of intellectual property cases, and a significant amount of information on its work and the relevant laws can be found at www.cybercrime.gov.

Source: PRO IP Act, Pub. L. No. 110-403 (2008).

Patent Law

LO 11-3

Patents have existed for hundreds of years as property rights. Historically, a patent was any legal monopoly openly issued by the government, and it was not necessarily associated with a new idea. However, there is evidence of patents being associated with invention at least as early as the 1400s. The Venetian Patent Act of 1474 is generally considered to be the world's first patent statute for the purpose of rewarding new ideas. Many of its basic principles for protecting inventions are present in modern patent law.

Today, a **patent** is firmly associated with an inventive act, and conveys a right to exclude others from making, using, selling, or importing the covered invention. The U.S. Constitution authorizes Congress to create patents, and Congress has passed numerous laws providing for exclusive patent rights as a form of property. Since colonial times, the United States has been a world leader in establishing patent law, and many of the constitutional framers were interested in technology and new invention. For example, during the Constitutional Convention in Philadelphia, the framers apparently took time off one afternoon to watch a newly invented steamboat cruising on the Delaware River. George Washington signed the first U.S. patent statute into law in 1790, and none other than Thomas Jefferson served on the three-member board that reviewed applications and issued patents.

OBTAINING A PATENT

A patent is an exclusive right created by statute and conveyed by the U.S. Patent and Trademark Office (PTO) for a limited period of time. This property applies to inventions, which are new applications of information.

Don't forget that patents last for only a limited period of time.

Patent Type It is important to understand that there are actually three types of patents granted by the PTO, each with their own distinct subject matter (see Figure 11.1). An easy way to remember the distinction between a **utility patent** and a design patent is that the former applies to useful, functional inventions. Such inventions are what most of us think of when we see

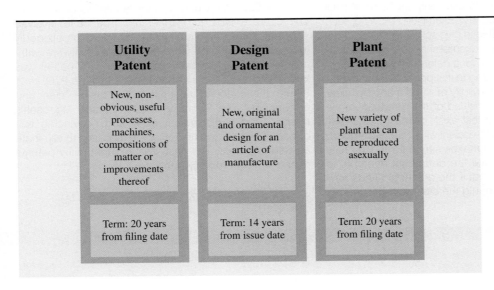

Figure 11.1 *Types of Patents.*

Utility Patent	Design Patent	Plant Patent
New, non-obvious, useful processes, machines, compositions of matter or improvements thereof	New, original and ornamental design for an article of manufacture	New variety of plant that can be reproduced asexually
Term: 20 years from filing date	Term: 14 years from issue date	Term: 20 years from filing date

the word "patent." On the other hand, design patents apply to the appearance of an article of manufacture, unrelated to its function. They cover subject matter more similar to copyrights (discussed later in this chapter). **Plant patents** apply to new varieties of asexually reproduced plants. However, note that many inventions related to plants may also be protected as utility patents. For example, one or more utility patent rights often cover genetically modified plants. Therefore, just because the subject matter is a plant, the relevant property right is not necessarily a plant patent.

> In 2013, the U.S. Patent and Trademark Office granted a record 302,948 patents. This was nearly a 10% increase over the previous year and more than double the number issued in 1997.

To obtain a patent, an inventor must pay a filing fee and file an application with the PTO. In the case of a utility patent the application must, in words and drawings, (1) explain how to make and use the basic invention; (2) show why the invention is different from *prior art,* that is, from all previous and related inventions or state of knowledge; and (3) precisely detail the subject matter that the inventor regards as the invention (called *claims*). The PTO assigns a *patent examiner* to consider the application, and there is usually a great deal of communication between the examiner and the applicant over the adequacy of the application's explanations, the scope of the proposed patent (exactly what the patent applies to), and whether the invention even qualifies for a patent. The applicant can amend the application, and the process can take several years from start to finish.

In 2011, President Obama signed into law the *America Invents Act,* the first substantial revision to U.S. patent law since 1999. Among the law's many changes is the eventual switch from a first-to-invent system to a first-inventor-to-file system. This means that, in a contest between two inventors claiming the same patentable idea, the first to get to the patent office will win. On the other hand, the law increases the ability of companies to keep

sidebar 11.5

Should Utility Patents Always Be Presumed Valid?

As noted above, utility patents issue only after a substantial analysis by a professional PTO Examiner. Following such scrutiny, it seems reasonable to give some degree of credit to the process. Patent law accomplishes this by establishing a higher burden of proof for a defendant who wishes to challenge a patent. According to this principle, courts have determined that proof of invalidity must be made by "clear and convincing evidence" instead of the "preponderance of the evidence" standard that exists in most civil cases. This makes it more likely that a patent will be upheld in court.

An increased burden makes sense if the PTO fully considered every issue that the defendant attempts to raise in court. However, what if the defendant finds new evidence of invalidity? Should the clear and convincing standard still apply?

The Supreme Court considered this issue in *Microsoft Corp. v. i4i LTD. Partnership.* The case involved software code patented by i4i that Microsoft allegedly incorporated into its word processing software without permission. Microsoft argued that i4i's patent was invalid based on facts not considered by the PTO, even though these facts did not rise to the level of "clear and convincing." The Supreme Court rejected Microsoft's position and decided that clear and convincing evidence of invalidity is necessary in all cases to eliminate an issued patent. The case ensures that utility patents remain strong property rights.

Source: *Microsoft Corp. v. i4i LTD. Partnership,* 131 S.Ct. 2238 (June 9, 2011).

some internal processes secret and avoid infringing another's patent through "prior user rights."

Another provision in the law that has had unintended effects is a change that makes it harder to join several defendants together in a single case (joinder). This has contributed to a significant rise in patent litigations in the years after the AIA was passed, while the number of defendants sued has not changed that much.

PATENTABLE SUBJECT MATTER

After the PTO issues a patent, the patent owner may choose to maintain its exclusivity in the invention. Alternatively, the patentee may license others to use the invention. However, if another infringes the patent by making, using, selling, or importing the invention without permission, the patent owner may have to defend its property. When the patent owner threatens a lawsuit, it is common for the alleged infringer to respond by attacking the validity of the patent. Validity can be challenged in court or the PTO. If the patent is found invalid, the alleged infringer will win. A finding that a patent is completely invalid in one case is very significant, as it renders the patent invalid against all future defendants, essentially eliminating it.

> A *process* is a way of doing something through a series of operations.

Attacking the "subject matter" of a patent is one common way of testing the validity of a patent. Although not unlimited, the subject matter for a potential patent is quite broad. This is particularly true for utility patents. In *Diamond v. Chakrabarty*, 447 U.S. 303 (1980), the Supreme Court ruled that a scientist could cover with a utility patent a genetically modified bacterium that ate hydrocarbons found in oil spills. The Court said, "Congress is free to amend §101 [the subject matter section of the general patent law] so as to exclude from patent protection organisms produced by genetic engineering. . . . Or it may choose to craft a statute specifically designed for such living things. But until Congress takes such action, the language of §101 fairly embraces the respondent's invention." In an example of such congressional action, the 2011 revisions to the patent act explicitly preclude patents covering humans.

The courts have carved out categories of subject matter that cannot be patented because they do not represent true inventions. One of the most important is the prohibition against patenting natural phenomena. One cannot simply find a new plant growing in a field and file a patent on it. On the other hand, a chemical compound that is extracted from the plant and isolated from other components may be patentable. Determining what can be said to exist in nature is the focus of the Supreme Court's recent inquiry into the patentability of DNA in Case 11.2.

One of the most controversial areas of potentially patentable subject matter concerns "processes." What is a process? Is a computer program a process? Are ways of doing business a process? Mere abstract ideas are not a patentable process. Nor are mathematical algorithms or formulas like $E = mc^2$ that express truths about the universe. Historically, business methods like double-entry bookkeeping were considered unpatentable, but they are after all processes, methods for doing things.

ASSOCIATION FOR MOLECULAR PATHOLOGY v. MYRIAD GENETICS, INC.
133 S. Ct. 2107 (2013)

Myriad Genetics, Inc. (Myriad) produced a true research breakthrough when it identified the location and sequence of two genes related to breast and ovarian cancer. Genes are segments of DNA that can be transcribed into certain amino acids and proteins in cells. Mutations in the genes that Myriad discovered, known as BRCA1 and BRCA2, significantly increase the chance of developing cancer. Myriad filed for patents on the full genes and smaller segments. The effect of the patents was to give Myriad the right to exclude others from isolating BRCA1 and BRCA2 from the human body. That would preclude the use of isolated genes in test kits useful for detecting breast and ovarian cancer.

The Association for Molecular Pathology (AMP), and various other public interest groups, objected to Myriad's patent claims on the basis that they claimed ownership over a natural phenomenon (DNA). AMP asked the Court to declare the claims invalid.

NOTE: *The following is the part of the opinion that addresses naturally occurring DNA. The Court also determined that Myriad's claims to a form of DNA that is based on naturally occurring segments but is shorter and does not exist in the body (cDNA) is patentable.*

JUSTICE Thomas delivered the opinion of the Court.

Section 101 of the Patent Act provides:

"Whoever invents or discovers any new and useful . . . composition of matter, or any new and useful improvement thereof, may obtain a patent therefor, subject to the conditions and requirements of this title."

We have "long held that this provision contains an important implicit exception[:] Laws of nature, natural phenomena, and abstract ideas are not patentable." *Mayo Collaborative Services v. Prometheus Laboratories, Inc.*, 132 S. Ct. 1289 (2012). Rather, "they are the basic tools of scientific and technological work" that lie beyond the domain of patent protection. *Id.* . . . As the Court has explained, without this exception, there would be considerable danger that the grant of patents would "tie up" the use of such tools and thereby "inhibit future innovation premised upon them." *Id.* . . . This would be at odds with the very point of patents, which exist to promote creation. *Diamond v. Chakrabarty*, 447 U.S. 303 (1980).

The rule against patents on naturally occurring things is not without limits, however, for "all inventions at some level embody, use, reflect, rest upon, or apply laws of nature, natural phenomena, or abstract ideas," and "too broad an interpretation of this exclusionary principle could eviscerate patent law." *Mayo*, 132 S. Ct. 1289. As we have recognized before, patent protection strikes a delicate balance between creating "incentives that lead to creation, invention, and discovery" and "imped[ing] the flow of information that might permit, indeed spur, invention." *Id.* . . . We must apply this well-established standard to determine whether Myriad's patents claim any "new and useful . . . composition of matter," §101, or instead claim naturally occurring phenomena.

It is undisputed that Myriad did not create or alter any of the genetic information encoded in the BRCA1 and BRCA2 genes. The location and order of the nucleotides existed in nature before Myriad found them. Nor did Myriad create or alter the genetic structure of DNA. Instead, Myriad's principal contribution was uncovering the precise location and genetic sequence of the BRCA1 and BRCA2 genes within chromosomes 17 and 13. The question is whether this renders the genes patentable.

Myriad recognizes that our decision in *Chakrabarty* is central to this inquiry. . . . In this case, by contrast, Myriad did not create anything. To be sure, it found an important and useful gene, but separating that gene from its surrounding genetic material is not an act of invention.

Groundbreaking, innovative, or even brilliant discovery does not by itself satisfy the §101 inquiry. . . .

Indeed, Myriad's patent descriptions highlight the problem with its claims. . . . Many of Myriad's patent descriptions simply detail the "iterative process" of discovery by which Myriad narrowed the possible locations for the gene sequences that it sought. , , ,. Myriad seeks to import these extensive research efforts into the §101 patent-eligibility inquiry. . . . But extensive effort alone is insufficient to satisfy the demands of §101.

Nor are Myriad's claims saved by the fact that isolating DNA from the human genome severs chemical bonds and thereby creates a nonnaturally occurring molecule. Myriad's claims are simply not expressed in terms of chemical composition, nor do they rely in any way on the chemical changes that result from the isolation of a particular section of DNA. Instead, the claims understandably focus on the genetic information encoded in the BRCA1 and BRCA2 genes. If the patents depended upon the creation of a unique molecule, then a would-be infringer could arguably avoid at least Myriad's patent claims on entire genes (such as claims 1 and 2 of the' 282 patent) by isolating a DNA sequence that included both the BRCA1 and BRCA2 genes and one additional nucleotide pair. Such a molecule would not be chemically identical to the molecule "invented" by Myriad. But Myriad obviously would resist that outcome because its claim is concerned primarily with the information contained in the genetic *sequence,* not with the specific chemical composition of a particular molecule. . . .

It is important to note what is *not* implicated by this decision. First, there are no method claims before this Court. Had Myriad created an innovative method of manipulating genes while searching for the BRCA1 and BRCA2 genes, it could possibly have sought a method patent. But the processes used by Myriad to isolate DNA were well understood by geneticists at the time of Myriad's patents "were well understood, widely used, and fairly uniform insofar as any scientist engaged in the search for a gene would likely have utilized a similar approach," . . . and are not at issue in this case.

Similarly, this case does not involve patents on new *applications* of knowledge about the BRCA1 and BRCA2 genes. Judge Bryson aptly noted that, "[a]s the first party with knowledge of the [BRCA1 and BRCA2] sequences, Myriad was in an excellent position to claim applications of that knowledge. Many of its unchallenged claims are limited to such applications." . . .

Nor do we consider the patentability of DNA in which the order of the naturally occurring nucleotides has been altered. Scientific alteration of the genetic code presents a different inquiry, and we express no opinion about the application of §101 to such endeavors. We merely hold that genes and the information they encode are not patent eligible under §101 simply because they have been isolated from the surrounding genetic material.

KEY POINTS

- The Court determined that naturally occurring sequences of DNA isolated from the human body are not patent eligible. However, nonnaturally occurring or manufactured DNA sequences can be patented.
- The Court's decision retroactively affects existing patent claims covering natural DNA—they are now invalid.
- Patent law is intended to reward invention, not investment *per se.*

Many of the Supreme Court's opinions on patentable subject matter refer to the idea of idea or concept "preemption." Would an inventor's patent go beyond protecting something she invented and lock down an entire field of discovery? If so, it is likely that the patent claims have overstepped the Court's limits on appropriate subject matter.

NOVELTY, NONOBVIOUSNESS, AND UTILITY

To be patentable, it is not enough for something to be appropriate subject matter. An invention must also have certain characteristics. Namely, it must be novel, nonobvious, and useful. An alleged infringer can always defend against an infringement lawsuit by proving that the patent is invalid because the invention is previously known, obvious, or lacks utility.

Perhaps the most common way of challenging a patent's validity is to claim that the invention is obvious to someone with knowledge in the field.

sidebar 11.6

Is Software Patentable? Maybe.

Where does software fall in the subject matter inquiry? At base, software is nothing more than computer code that instructs an electronic device to do something. That sounds like a mathematical algorithm that should be unpatentable. On the other hand, software is often more complex and creative than a traditional formula. It transforms how certain problems are solved and information is produced. Traditional patents rules are an imperfect fit.

Another problem with software is that patentees tend to claim it by the functions it performs rather than the code that an inventor first developed. This means that a software patent might cover dozens of different programs that accomplish the same task.

The resolution to these issues is important because software patents already exist and are important to many segments of the economy. The Supreme Court considered the patentability of a software claim in the recent case of *Alice Corp. Pty. Ltd. v. CLS Bank International,* 134 S.Ct. 2347 (2014). Alice Corporation owned several patents covering schemes to manage financial risk. CLS Bank argued that the patents were invalid and filed suit. The Supreme Court agreed with CLS Bank and articulated a general test for future cases. First, one must determine if the claims cover an abstract concept. If so, the second step is to determine if they contain "an 'inventive concept' sufficient to 'transform' the claimed abstract idea into a patent-eligible application." After *Alice,* some software will fail to meet this test, but it appears that software can still be patent-eligible in some form.

The characteristic of novelty indicates that something is new and different from the prior art (the previous state of knowledge in the field). The test is met when no single piece of prior art meets all of the elements of an invention's claims. However, under patent law, even if an invention is otherwise new, it fails the novelty test if it has been described in a publication, sold, or put to public use more than one year before a patent application on it is filed (the one-year grace period). This limitation exists even if it is the inventor who undertakes such actions. The 2011 revisions to the law apply the one-year grace period only to an inventor's publication, use or sale. Activity by others before a patent is filed precludes patentability, even within a year. While this may seem harsh, note that many countries have no grace period at all.

Nonobviousness refers to the ability of an invention to produce surprising or unexpected results; that is, results not anticipated by prior art. The nonobviousness standard is measured in relation to someone who has ordinary skill in the prior art. For instance, to be patentable, a computer hardware invention would need to be nonobvious to an ordinary computer engineer. Importantly, obviousness is assessed as of the date of the application as opposed to later in the litigation. Courts are careful to avoid "highlight" bias, which is the tendency to see any invention as obvious after it is revealed and its significance is known.

Patent litigation over the obviousness of an invention is typically very subjective, with each side producing experts who disagree. Ultimately it is up to the court to determine the state of knowledge existing when the inventor filed the application and whether the invention is nonobvious. See Sidebar 11.7.

sidebar 11.7

The Determination of Obviousness

A problem of the patent system is that a single manufactured item like an automobile may have hundreds of patents applying to various parts. Any time an improvement is made on a part by manufacturer X, there is always the possibility that a current patent holder Y will sue claiming infringement. X often responds that Y's patent claim is invalid because it was obvious. If Y's patent claim is obvious, then the fact that X based its new improvement on technology covered by Y's claim is not patent infringement because the patent is invalid.

The Supreme Court faced this situation in *KSR International Co. v. Teleflex, Inc.,* 127 S. Ct. 1727 (2007), a case involving Teleflex's accusation that KSR infringed its patent by adding a new electronic sensor to an adjustable automobile accelerator pedal. Teleflex believed it had a patent that covered the use of electronic sensors along with adjustable automobile accelerator pedals, a combination that did not exist in the prior art. KSR responded by asserting that the patent claim was invalid because the technology of attaching the electronic sensor to the pedal was obvious. In its decision favoring KSR, the Supreme Court rejected a prior decision by the U.S. Court of Appeals for the Federal Circuit, which deals with patents. That prior case decided that a patent claim is only proved obvious when some

specific reference like a journal article prior to the patent in question teaches, suggests, or motivates one of ordinary skill to create the claimed invention (in this case suggesting the attaching of the electronic sensor to an adjustable automobile accelerator pedal prior to the Teleflex patent).

Instead, the Supreme Court observed that a variety of factors could lead a court to conclude legally that a patent was invalid for obviousness. Importantly, the Court said, "We build and create by bringing to the tangible and palpable reality around us new works based on instinct, simple logic, ordinary inferences, extraordinary ideas, and sometimes even genius. These advances, once part of our shared knowledge, define a new threshold for which innovation starts once more. And as progress beginning from higher levels of achievement is expected in the normal course, the results of ordinary innovation are not the subject of exclusive rights under the patent laws. Were it otherwise patents might stifle, rather than promote, the progress of useful arts."

What the Supreme Court has done is to make it somewhat easier to challenge the validity of patents by arguing that patent claims are obvious and that new improvements in technology or designs do not violate patents in the old technology or designs.

Except for patents issued on designs or plants, an invention to be valid must have utility, that is, it must do something useful. Suppose that Acme Laboratory scientists invent a new chemical compound. Until the compound has a use, say, ridding pets of fleas, Acme will be unable to get a utility patent on it. Generally speaking, establishing utility is not difficult. Any utility is sufficient, even if it is not the use that is eventually commercialized by the patentee. One major category of patent claims that lack utility are those that do not work. An inoperable invention, by definition, is not useful.

PATENT ENFORCEMENT

As the U.S. Constitution specifies, the property represented by patents runs for limited duration. Statutes limit utility patents and plant patents to 20 years from the filing date, and design patents to 14 years from the issue date. When a patent expires, the invention is in the public domain, and others may use it without limitation. Remember that at this point, it is easy to use the invention since the patent application explains exactly how the invention works, including drawings of its construction. The explicit purpose of

When a patent expires, the patent is in the *public domain,* and others may use it without limitation.

Figure 11.2
Overlapping Intellectual Property Rights.

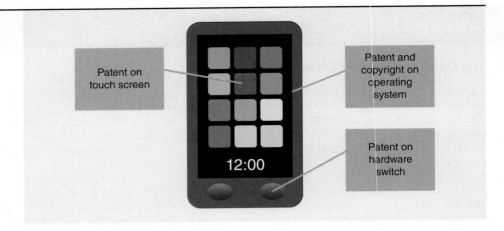

patent law is to make inventions public following the limited period of legal property right. For the duration of a patent, the owner can sue those who infringe on it. If successful, the owner can get an injunction prohibiting future infringement, damages, including triple damages for willful infringement.

Complicating the business environment for patents is the fact that inventions can cover methods and articles that can overlap. Simply owning a patent is not a license to produce a product or service. A fundamental concept in patent law is that patents only convey the right to exclude others from making, using, selling, and importing the invention. They do not include the right to use the invention. At first glance, the latter point may seem counterintuitive. Can you really own a patent and have no right to make a product that is covered by it? The answer, surprisingly, is yes, and the key to understanding it is to realize that multiple intellectual property rights can cover the same article. There is often more than one patent to a product.

Consider an average smartphone. Imagine that you own a patent that covers touch screen technology, enabling you to open programs and type by placing your fingers on the screen. Now, imagine that another firm owns a patent on technology that allows a phone to switch between hardware buttons and a touch screen. Add another firm that has a patent and perhaps a copyright that cover the phone's operating system (see Figure 11.2). Even though you own a patent that covers part of a smartphone, you cannot produce the smartphone with the characteristics above without using the rights of others. In reality, of course, cell phones are covered by hundreds of patents as well as other rights. Many licenses are required to produce a single phone. This situation of overlapping patents exists to varying degrees with other products.

PATENT TROLLS AND THE LITIGATION THREAT

As described above, patents may overlap to cover a single product, and in some fields the number overlapping rights can be quite large. In addition, it can be hard to know whether the functional descriptions of some patent claims apply to one's products or business. This makes it difficult to identify and license all of the patents one might infringe. The ambiguity provides an opportunity for investment firms to purchase patent rights and threaten to

The consequences of patent infringement can be high, with recent cases involving jury awards of over $1 billion. Such awards are often reduced on appeal, but still amount to millions in damages.

Some non-practicing patent entities have quite large portfolios, raising concerns on their impact on the marketplace. For example, a company called Intellectual Ventures claims to own more than 70,000 patents.

sue existing companies. Because the damages (from trial or settlement) can be great and the risk to the patent owners relatively small, an early, quick settlement is the most common result. Essentially, it is easier and cheaper for most businesses to simply pay the patent owner to go away. Out of the belief that such non-practicing patent owners are nothing more than a self-appointed toll-taker on a bridge, they have been widely referred to as "**patent trolls.**" The pejorative term suggests that non-producing patent owners do not contribute as much to the innovation environment compared to the costs imposed by their enforcement.

As a counter to the patent troll rhetoric, one might consider the fact that non-practicing entities are exercising a legitimate right under their property grants. Patents do not require their owners to actually make and sell a product. This concept is similar to land property, wherein one may own a plot land but decide not to build anything. However, the overlapping nature of intellectual property sets the stage for greater conflict than with non-producing landowners.

Judges have some ability to reduce trolling incentives by forcing the losing party to pay the winning side's costs ("fee-shifting"). A troll who has no real case will be less likely to make a threat under these circumstances. In 2014, the Supreme Court held that a court may permit fee-shifting in cases that are exceptional in terms of their baseless nature or plaintiff's bad faith (*Octane Fitness, LLC v. Icon Health & Fitness, Inc.*, 134 S.Ct. 1749). This is an easier standard for the defendant to meet. At least two aspects of the 2011 reforms to patent law may reduce troll behavior. The new law prevents patent owners from suing multiple parties merely because they infringe the same patent, a change that makes litigation more expensive for trolls. Going forward, patent owners must show a common set of facts or a case arising out of the same occurrence to join multiple parties in a suit. Additionally, business method patents, as described above, are subject to a new review proceeding if litigated. Legislation to further address patent trolls was introduced in Congress in 2014 and supported by President Obama, but it was eventually placed on hold.

In addition to measures in the federal courts and legislature, state governments have taken action against patent trolls under their consumer protection laws. A troll that makes vague and unsupported assertions of infringement in letters sent to individuals may be considered to be acting in bad faith and subject to fines.

Trademark Law

LO 11-4

For thousands of years, people have used marks on what they produce to represent the origin of goods and services. Pottery from ancient Greece, Rome and China often bears the mark of its maker. The same is true for ancient building materials like brick and tile. Today, we generally call such marks **trademarks** and when they indicate a specific producer, the law protects them against use by others.

Trademarks are a form of intellectual property. Like patents you can register them with the PTO, and also like patents, trademarks are some of the most valuable properties that businesses own. McDonald's golden arches, the Nike "swoosh," Coca-Cola, Apple, Facebook, Amazon.com, Exxon, Kleenex,

> "In most [industries], the cost of invention is low; or just being first confers a durable competitive advantage because consumers associate the inventing company's brand name with the product itself; or just being first gives the first company in the market a head start in reducing its costs as it becomes more experienced at producing and marketing the product; or the product will be superseded soon anyway, so there's no point to a patent monopoly that will last 20 years; or some or all of these factors are present. Most industries could get along fine without patent protection."
>
> **–Judge Richard A. Posner, "Why There Are Too Many Patents in America," *The Atlantic*, July 12, 2012**

According to a 2013 study by *Interbrand*, the five most valuable brands belong to Apple, Google, Coca-Cola, IBM, and Microsoft.

the Olympic rings, Rolex, Levi's—the list of famous trademarks is almost endless, but always recognizable.

Although registration systems exist at the federal and state level, it is important to understand that trademark rights come from *use* of the mark in association with goods or services. One can have rights in an unregistered trademark, and even sue for infringement. You cannot presume that, simply because a mark is unregistered, it is open for use in your field. However, this is not to say that registration is irrelevant. Particularly at the federal level under the Lanham Act, registration conveys important advantages. Therefore, it is advisable for a business to pursue a federal trademark registration for its source indicating marks whenever possible.

Recognizability or *distinctiveness* is the function of trademarks. In a world cluttered with stimulation, information, and advertising, trademarks pierce through the clutter and let people know that the goods or services represented are "the real thing"—that they come from one source. They are an information property, exclusively distinguishing the reputation and goodwill of a particular business from that of all other businesses. Trademarks protect both businesses and consumers from confusion regarding who makes or provides what. As one recent Federal Court of Appeals case observed:

> Trademarks are designed to inform potential buyers who makes the goods on sale. Knowledge of origin may convey information about a product's attributes and quality, and consistent attribution of origin is vital when vendors reputations matter. Without a way to know who makes what reputations cannot be created and evaluated, and the process of competition will be less effective. *Top Tobacco, L.P. v. North Atlantic Operating Co.*, 509 F. 3d 380, 381 (7th Cir. 2007).

Trademark infringement, which may involve intentional use of the owner's mark or an accidental design of one's own mark too similarly to another's, is a major business problem, especially in the Digital Age when often the only point of contact people have with a goods or service provider is a computer or smartphone screen.

TYPES OF TRADEMARKS

Although state law protects trademarks, this chapter focuses on the federal protection given trademarks by the Lanham Act of 1946. The Lanham Act protects the following marks used to represent a product, service, or organization:

- Trademark—any mark, word, picture, or design that attaches to goods to indicate their source.
- Service mark—a mark associated with a service, for example, LinkedIn.
- Certification mark—a mark used by someone other than the owner to certify the quality, point of origin, or other characteristics of goods or services, for example, the Good Housekeeping Seal of Approval.
- Collective mark—a mark representing membership in a certain organization or association, for example, the National Football League logo.

For convenience, all of these marks will be referred to as trademarks. The law generally treats them the same.

sidebar 11.8

Brands vs. Trademarks

In a marketing class you may have heard the term "brand" used quite frequently. However, in law, the term "trademark" is used. Do these terms have the same meaning, and are they completely interchangeable?

The terms have a long history of association. Branding as a means of marking animals to designate ownership could be considered the original form of trademark. And its modern use related to marking products is derived by analogy to this ancient practice. The term "brand" actually comes from the Anglo-Saxon verb that means "to burn."

In the modern business context, a mark, symbol, or picture that someone refers to as a brand would also qualify in almost all cases as a trademark. A brand is a marketing concept that invokes a corporate strategy to capture a family of products or services in a readily identifiable manner. A trademark is the legal designation given to a mark that serves as a source identifier. It may not be as broad as a brand. Consider, for example, the different models of cars sold under the Ford brand. Each model name likely qualifies as a trademark itself, but may not be considered a separate brand. It is probably fair to say that most brands are trademarks, but not all trademarks are brands.

Source: Sidney A. Diamond, "The Historical Development of Trademarks," 65 *Trademark Reporter* 265 (1975).

Trade Dress Similar to trademarks, and also protected by the Lanham Act, is trade dress. **Trade dress** refers to a color or shape associated with a product or service. The red color scheme of Coca-Cola when associated with the general design of Coca-Cola labeling constitutes trade dress. Trade dress protection prevents Coca-Cola competitors from designing a shape that resembles a "Coca-Cola" bottle and attaching the characteristic Coke red to the design in such a way as to confuse potential Coke customers about what they are getting. Trade dress also includes distinctive store decorating motifs (e.g., McDonald's) or package shapes and colors.

An important trade dress case is *Two Pesos, Inc. v. Taco Cabana, Inc.,* 505 U.S. 763 (1992). In that case the Supreme Court defined trade dress as "the total image and overall appearance" of a business. The Court upheld a decision that Two Pesos had violated Taco Cabana's trade dress. The Court stated that "trade dress [in this case] may include the shape and general appearance of the exterior of the restaurant, the identifying sign, the interior kitchen floor plan, the décor, the menu, the equipment used to serve food, the servers' uniforms and other features reflecting on the total image of the restaurant." The law protects trade dress from being copied as long as it is distinctive. If it is distinctive and registered, the law protects it even without proof that the public has come to identify the trade dress with a specific source.

The distinctive "wasp-shaped" Coca-Cola bottle is part of its trade dress.

TRADEMARK REGISTRATION

If one wishes to register a trademark with the PTO, one must use the mark in interstate commerce. Posting the trademark on an Internet website in association with a product or service meets this qualification. Alternatively, an intent-to-use application may be filed, followed by an amended application when actual use begins.

To be registerable, a trademark must be distinctive. The PTO will deny registration in the following circumstances:

- If the mark is the same or similar to a mark currently used on similar related goods, for example, a computer company's cherry mark that resembles the apple mark of Apple Inc.
- If the mark contains certain prohibited or reserved names or designs, including the U.S. flag, other governmental symbols, immoral names or symbols, the names or likenesses of living persons without their consent, and the names or likenesses of deceased American presidents without the permission of their spouses.
- If the mark merely describes a product or service, for example, "Fast Food" for a restaurant franchise.
- If the mark is **generic** and represents a product or service, for example, "cell phone" for a wireless communication company.

Note that a mark that is descriptive or generic in one context may be unique and distinctive in another. "Apple" appears to be an arbitrary term in the context of consumer electronics because it easily distinguishes the source of one company's products and services from another's. However, it would not be registerable for a fruit stand that sells apples.

---

sidebar 11.9

"Washington Redskins" Is a Disparaging Name

Under Section 2a of the Lanham Act, the U.S. Patent and Trademark Office (PTO) will refuse to register a trademark that will "disparage . . . persons, living or dead, institutions, beliefs, or national symbols, or bring them into contempt, or disrepute." This prohibition certainly includes racial slurs. Recently, the PTO has had the opportunity to consider whether a registration for the name of the NLF football team known as the Washington Redskins falls into the disparaging category and should be canceled.

The PTO's scrutiny of the name had its genesis in a 1999 action to cancel the Redskins registration brought by Native Americans in *Harjo v. Pro-Football Inc*. The case was ultimately decided against the plaintiffs due to their delay in bringing the case. However, another action, *Blackhorse v. Pro-Football Inc.,* was filed in 2006 involving younger plaintiffs who did not face the same delay issues as *Harjo*. In the course of the proceeding, the PTO considered a voluminous record that included

documents and expert testimony. The issue the PTO had to decide was whether the name was disparaging when the registrations were first filed between 1967 and 1990. In June 2014, the PTO ruled that Redskins marks were in fact disparaging in that time period. Accordingly, the agency canceled six of the team's trademark registrations.

It is important to understand that, even though the PTO has canceled certain registrations related to the Redskins mark, the team is not required to stop using the name. This is because trademark rights are derived from use, not registration. It may even sue those who use the name without authorization. Of course, team owner Daniel Snyder is free to change the name on his own.

Sources: *Amanda Blackhorse v. Pro-Football Inc.*, Cancellation No. 92046185, 2014 WL 2757516 (Trademark Tr. & App. Bd., June 18, 2014); Ken Belson and Nick Corasaniti, "Redskins Trademark: A Primer on the Cancellation," *New York Times*, June 18, 2014.

As part of the trademark application process, the PTO places a proposed mark in the *Official Gazette,* which gives existing mark owners notice and allows them to object that the proposed mark is similar to their own. If existing mark owners object to the proposed mark's registration, the PTO holds a hearing to resolve the objection and, possibly, to deny registration. Finally, if the PTO determines the mark acceptable, it registers the mark on the *Principal Register.* This registration provides notice of official trademark registration status. All of the documents relating to registration and the application back and forth are available online at www.uspto.gov. Given the easy access to such an electronic record, it is worth investigating anyone's claim that they have an exclusive registration for a particular trademark.

Unlike a patent, which specifies a limited property duration, the trademark enjoys a potentially unlimited protection period. But after six years the trademark owner must notify the PTO that the trademark is still in use. Currently, every ten years the owner must renew the trademark registration.

The attempt to register certain descriptive terms, or a person's name, presents a special problem. Generally, the PTO will not accept a person's name or a descriptive term for protection on the *Principal Register.* However, there is a process by which a name or descriptive term can achieve full trademark status and protection. If it is listed on the PTO's *Supplemental Register* for five years *and* acquires a secondary meaning, it can then be transferred to the *Principal Register* for full protection.

Secondary meaning refers to a public meaning that is different from its meaning as a person's name or as a descriptive term, a public meaning that makes the name or term distinctive. In the public mind, "Ford" now refers to an automobile rather than a person, "Levis" means jeans rather than a family, and "Disney" refers to a specific entertainment company rather than its founder.

TRADEMARK ENFORCEMENT

Trademark law protects the trademark's owner from having the mark used in an unauthorized way. Using a mark that is confusingly similar to the trademark owner's mark violates the law. The standard for liability is proof that a defendant's use has created a "likelihood of confusion" with the plaintiff's trademark. To make this determination, courts use a multi-factored test that considers elements such as the defendant's intent and proof of actual consumer confusion. The law establishes both civil and criminal trademark violation.

Civil violation of a trademark (or a patent) is termed **infringement.** The violator infringes on the trademark's property right through an unintentional or a willful unauthorized use, misappropriating the goodwill and reputation that the trademark represents and confusing the public about the identity of the user. Remedies for civil infringement include a variety of damages, injunctions prohibiting future infringement, and orders to destroy infringing products in anyone's possession.

Case 11.3 illustrates the application of the **likelihood of confusion** in the context of a case wherein parties with strong marks in different areas may be in conflict when selling products in the same stores.

KRAFT FOODS GROUP BRANDS LLC. v. CRACKER BARREL OLD COUNTRY STORE, INC.
735 F.3d 735 (7th Cir. 2013)

POSNER, *Circuit Judge.* Kraft is a well-known manufacturer of food products sold in grocery stores. Its products include a wide variety of packaged cheeses, a number of them sold under the trademarked "Cracker Barrel" label. Kraft has been selling cheese in grocery stores under that name for more than half a century. Thousands of grocery stores carry Kraft cheeses bearing that label. Kraft does not sell any non-cheese products under the name Cracker Barrel.

[Cracker Barrel Old Country Store (CBOCS)] is a well-known chain of low-price restaurants (it opened its first restaurant in 1969), 620 in number at last count, many of them just off major highways. Upon learning recently that CBOCS planned to sell a variety of food products (not including cheese, however), such as packaged hams, in grocery stores under its logo, "Cracker Barrel Old Country Store" (the last three words are in smaller type in the logo), Kraft filed this suit. It claims that many consumers will be confused by the similarity of the logos and think that food products so labeled are Kraft products, with the result that if they are dissatisfied with a CBOCS product they will blame Kraft.

Kraft acknowledges that a trademark does not entitle its owner to prevent all other uses of similar or even identical marks. . . . And likewise identical marks used on similar products sold through different types of sales outlet might cause no confusion—indeed Kraft does not question CBOCS's right to sell the food products at issue under the name Cracker Barrel in CBOCS's restaurants, in CBOCS's small "country stores" that adjoin the restaurants, or by mail order or on the Web. It objects only to their sale in grocery stores. . . .

Below, copied from CBOCS's website, is a picture of the logo that appeared on CBOCS food products shipped to grocery stores.

Up close at least, it looks different from the label "Cracker Barrel" that appears on Kraft's cheeses. Yet even if a Cracker Barrel cheese and a CBOCS ham (or other food products) were displayed side by side in a grocery store, which would make a shopper likely to notice the difference between the labels, the words "Cracker Barrel" on both labels—and in much larger type than "Old Country Store" on CBOCS's label—might lead the shopper to think them both Kraft products.

Most consumers of Cracker Barrel cheese must know that it's a Kraft product, for the name "Kraft" typically though not invariably appears on the label, as in the [above] picture. . . .

Kraft is concerned with the potential for confusion of shoppers at the 16,000 or so grocery stores (or similar retail entities) that sell Cracker Barrel cheeses, if the stores also carry CBOCS food products under the CBOCS logo (not only ham but also delicatessen meats, bacon, sausages, jerky, meat glazes, baking mixes, coating mixes, oatmeal, grits, and gravies—all are sold by CBOCS). Were Cracker Barrel cheeses and Cracker Barrel meats exhibited side by side on the shelf, the difference in the appearance of the logos of the two brands might as we said lead some consumers to think they were made by different companies—but might lead others to think the opposite, since different products of the same manufacturer are often exhibited together. If on the other hand the Kraft cheeses and CBOCS food products are at different locations in the store, some consumers might forget the difference between the logos and think all the products Kraft products. . . . Even savvy consumers might be fooled, because they know that producers often vary the appearance of their trademarks.

It's not the fact that the parties' trade names are so similar that is decisive, nor even the fact that the products are similar (low-cost packaged food items). It is those similarities coupled with the fact that, if CBOCS

prevails in this suit, similar products with confusingly similar trade names will be sold through the same distribution channel—grocery stores, and often the same grocery—advertised together. (In the brief period before the preliminary injunction was issued, in which CBOCS hams were sold in grocery stores, an online ad for Cracker Barrel Sliced Spiral Ham by a coupons firm provided a link to a coupon for Kraft's Cracker Barrel cheeses.) The competing products would also be likely to appear in the same store circulars. Such similarities and overlap would increase the likelihood of consumer confusion detrimental to Kraft. . . .

Still another reason to expect confusion is that both Cracker Barrel cheeses and most meat products that CBOCS has licensed for sale to grocery stores are inexpensive—under $5. Generally only very cost-conscious consumers are apt to scrutinize carefully the labels of the less expensive items sold in a grocery store. Familiarity is likely to have made the name Cracker Barrel salient to grocery shoppers, and so any product bearing that name might be attributed to Kraft even if close scrutiny of the label would suggest that the product might well have a different origin.

If a significant number of consumers confused the names and thought CBOCS's products were made by Kraft, Kraft could be badly hurt. A trademark's value is the saving in search costs made possible by the information that the trademark conveys about the quality of the trademark owner's brand. The brand's reputation for quality depends on the owner's expenditures on product quality and quality control, service, advertising, and so on. Once the reputation is created, the firm will obtain greater profits because repeat purchases and word-of-mouth endorsements will add to sales and because consumers will be willing to pay a higher price in exchange for a savings in search costs and an assurance of consistent quality. These benefits depend on the firm's ability to maintain that consistent quality. When a brand's quality is inconsistent, consumers learn that the trademark does not enable them to predict their future consumption experiences from their past ones. The trademark does not then reduce their search costs. They become unwilling to pay more for the branded than for the unbranded good, and so the firm no longer earns a sufficient return on its expenditures on promoting the trademark to justify them.

The particular danger for Kraft of CBOCS's being allowed to sell food products through the same outlets under a trade name confusingly similar to Kraft's "Cracker Barrel" trade name is that if CBOCS's products are inferior in any respect to what the consumer expects—if a consumer has a bad experience with a CBOCS product and blames Kraft, thinking it the producer—Kraft's sales of Cracker Barrel cheeses are likely to decline; for a consumer who thinks Kraft makes bad hams may decide it probably makes bad cheeses as well. . . .

So the grant of the preliminary injunction must be affirmed.

KEY POINTS

- Both Kraft and Cracker Barrel restaurants have legitimate trademarks. Their use in the same location is what creates the problem.
- Even though Kraft and Cracker Barrel may not use identical marks on identical products, a likelihood of confusion can still exist, according to the court.
- The court suggests that sophisticated consumers for luxury products would look more closely at labels.

Trademark owners must be vigilant in protecting their marks because if a trademark becomes **generic,** if it loses its distinctiveness, it also loses its status as a protected trademark. A trademark becomes generic when, through the owner's actions or another's inappropriate use, the mark becomes synonymous in the consumers' mind with the name of the goods or services. Due to concern that its famous trademark not become generic, Coca-Cola seeks to prevent trademark infringement by employees at soda fountains who without

Don't forget that **generic** marks cannot be protected as trademarks.

table 11.1 Trademarks Lost due to Generic Use

The following generic terms were once trademarks:

Aspirin	Lite beer
Cellophane	Refrigerator
Cola	Thermos
Escalator	Zipper

To ensure that its well-known trademark not be lost to generic use, the Xerox Corporation spent millions of dollars advertising to the public that *xerox* is a registered trademark and that the term should not be used as a verb (to "xerox" a copy) or as a noun (a "xerox").

Note that a term that is generic in one country may be protectable in another. For example, the term "aspirin" is a protected trademark of Bayer AG in many countries, including Canada.

---

comment give customers other colas when asked for a "Coke." Employers are warned to advise employees to specify that another cola will be substituted if Coke is not available.

As Table 11.1 illustrates, a number of trademarks have been lost because the public came to think of them as generic terms.

To win a trademark infringement lawsuit, a defendant will usually present one of three basic defenses: (1) the mark is not distinctive, (2) there is little chance of the public being confused by use of a term trademarked by someone else, or (3) the use is a "fair use." In arguing the first defense, the defendant maintains that the mark is descriptive or generic and that the PTO should not have protected it in the first instance. Alternatively, the defendant argues that the mark has become generic since its first use and that it now stands for a class of items. Note that a court can declare a mark invalid even if the PTO accepted registration.

The use of trademarked names in this textbook is a "fair use."

The second defense argues that there is little chance of public confusion over two uses of the same mark. For example, the public is not likely confused between the Ford automobile and the Ford Modeling Agency. But the confusion defense does not always work. In 2010, a federal district court awarded the owners of the Rolls-Royce trademark $2 million against a defendant calling itself "Rolls-Royce USA" for willful infringement in the context of clothing such as t-shirts. Despite the fact that the trademark owners primarily manufacture airplane engines and automobiles, not clothing, confusion was established.

The third defense raised in trademark infringement lawsuits is that of fair use. *Fair use* of a registered trademark is allowed by the Lanham Act and relates to a discussion, criticism, or parody of the trademark, the product, or its owner, for example, in the news media, on the Internet, or in a textbook. The courts have been explicit that the use of a rival's trademark in comparative advertising is also a fair use. You can legally advertise the results of a study that show your product to be superior to a competitor's, even if you mention the competitor's trademarked product by name.

Criminal trademark penalties apply to those who manufacture or traffic in *counterfeit* trademarked products such as imitation "Rolex" watches or "Levi" jeans. What makes counterfeiting criminal is the deliberate intent to pass off, or *palm off,* fake products as real by attaching an unauthorized trademark.

Trademarks and the Internet   The Internet creates a combination of old and new trademark issues. One new issue concerns the relationship between a website domain name registered with the Internet Corporation for Assigned Names and Numbers (ICANN) and a trademark registered with the PTO. There have been numerous instances in which people attempt to register domain names containing well-known trademarks that did not belong to them. Generally, it is a violation of trademark law to use another's registered mark in your domain name. Further, the Anticyber-squatting Consumer Protection Act of 1999 provides a remedy of statutory damages and transfer of a trademark domain name to its owner if it was registered in "bad faith." As an alternative to litigation, a trademark owner can pursue an arbitration against an improper domain name registrant. ICANN, an international organization that administers the Internet's addressing system, has a formal dispute resolution policy. ICANN has the authority to cancel or transfer the registration of the losing party.

> "The International Chamber of Commerce estimates that the value of counterfeit and pirated products worldwide is about $600 billion, and projects that figure to double by 2015."
>
> **–Elizabeth Holmes in *the Wall Street Journal,* June 30, 2011**

TRADEMARK DILUTION

In 1995, Congress passed the Federal Trademark Dilution Act. This law prohibits you from using a mark the same as or similar to another's "famous" trademark so as to dilute its significance, reputation, and goodwill. Even if an owner of a famous trademark cannot prove that the public is confused by another's use of a similar mark (called a "junior" mark), the owner of the "senior" famous trademark can still get an injunction prohibiting further use of the junior mark on the basis of **trademark dilution**. The court also has discretion to award the owner the infringer's profits, actual damages, and attorney's fees if the infringer "willfully intended to trade on the owner's reputation or to cause dilution of the famous mark."

> Remember: only the owners of famous marks can prevail under the Federal Trademark Dilution Act.

There are two types of dilution that are recognized under federal law: blurring and tarnishment. **Blurring** occurs when firm uses another trademark in a way that blurs the distinctiveness of a famous mark. For example, even if a reasonable person would know the company behind "Google Lawn Service" was different than the search engine giant, Google would have a good argument that permitting the lawn service use would blur or reduce its trademark's power. **Tarnishment** occurs when a firm uses a trademark in a way that creates a negative impression about the famous company. For example, Ben & Jerry's sued a distributer of adult films who wished to use the name "Ben & Cherry's." Even if no one would believe an actual connection existed, the ice cream company's reputation for family fun could be tarnished.

Because allowing companies to pursue dilution cases in the absence of consumer confusion could create significant speech issues, dilution is limited to famous marks. Additionally, federal law specifically carves out exceptions for non-commercial speech, news reporting, comparative advertising and parody.

In 2006, Congress passed the Trademark Dilution Revision Act, which established that dilution exists when a defendant creates a "likelihood of dilution." The law was designed, in part, to overrule an earlier Supreme Court decision, *Moseley v. V. Secret Catalogue, Inc.,* which set a higher standard of actual dilution. Thus, it is now slightly easier to win a dilution case.

LO 11-5 Copyright Law

Like patent, **copyright** gives those who have this property a monopoly over the right to exclude others from copying and marketing for a limited period of time. Unlike patent, copyright deals with original *expression* rather than invention. The importance of copyright began with the development of the printing press in the early 1400s, but the first copyright law was the Statute of Anne, enacted in England in 1710. In the United States, copyright is authorized in the Constitution, and Congress has revised copyright several times. Until the late 1800s, however, the United States did not recognize foreign copyright laws as they protected the works of foreign authors. As a result, U.S. publishers felt free to publish the works of foreign authors without permission or the payment of fees called *royalties.*

Today the United States has joined most other countries in international agreements, such as the Berne Convention, in protecting the copyright of other nations, but once again copyright has come to a turning point in the road. Digital technology makes it ever easier to copy not only printed material, but music, movies, and software as well. No longer is a large business necessary to copy and distribute copyrighted materials illegally. Individuals can copy materials quickly and almost without cost and send them around the world in a blink of an eye. As you read the following sections on copyright law, keep in mind the new digital age you have entered.

COPYRIGHT OWNERSHIP

Copyright law grants property in certain creative expressions that keeps others from reproducing it without the owner's permission. The copyright attaches not to an idea or to facts but to the original *expression* of an idea or facts. Three criteria are necessary for copyright protection to occur:

- A work must be original. It must be created, not copied. Facts are not original, though collections of facts may be, depending on the selection and arrangement.
- The work must be fixed in a tangible medium of expression like a book, canvas, compact disk, hard drive, or flash memory.
- The work must show some creative expression. For example, the Supreme Court ruled in *Feist Publications, Inc. v. Rural Telephone Service Co.,* 499 U.S. 340 (1991) that the mere effort and alphabetic arrangement of names that went into a telephone directory's white pages was insufficiently creative to warrant a copyright.

Copyright laws protect authors rather than inventors. An author creates works of a literary, dramatic, musical, graphic, choreographic, audio, or visual nature. Ranging from printed material to photographs to records and motion pictures, these works receive automatic federal protection under the Copyright Act of 1976 from the moment the author creates them. Importantly, no registration is required to obtain a copyright under federal law. Additionally, notice—for example, a copyright symbol or the word "copyrighted"—is also *not* required. For that reason, businesses are often advised to assume that a work created by another is copyrighted, no matter if it appears freely available without notice.

Companies can be considered authors under copyright law. In fact, when an employee creates a work within the scope of their employment, the employer is automatically the owner and author. This type of work is called a "work-for-hire." It eliminates the need for companies to negotiate the rights to letters, documents, web pages, etc., that employees produce in the course of every day work.

The copyright allows the holder to control the reproduction, display, distribution, and performance of a protected work. The copyright runs for the author's lifetime, plus 70 additional years for an individual, and 95 years from publication or 120 years from creation for a work by a company. Congress has occasionally extended the term for copyrights in existence. The last time was in 1998 under the Copyright Term Extension Act, which added 20 years to the term.

COPYRIGHT ENFORCEMENT

Although copyright protection attaches at the moment a work is created, an action for copyright infringement cannot be begun unless the author has properly registered the work with the Copyright Office. To make a case of infringement, a copyright owner must establish that a defendant violated one of the owner's exclusive rights, which can be generally stated as: (1) reproduction; (2) creation of derivative works; (3) distribution; (4) performance, in the case of literary, musical, and audiovisual works; or (5) display, in the case of literary, musical, audiovisual, pictorial, or graphical works. Because there is no innocent infringement in copyright—your own expression cannot infringe, even if it is similar to another's—it is essential to prove that an infringer actually used the copyrighted work. Some cases may involve direct evidence of a defendant's copying. But most cases require circumstantial proof. We look to see if the defendant had *access* to the original work and then produced something that was *substantially similar*.

If successful, the copyright owner may be able to obtain an injunction to stop the defendant's infringement. An owner may request actual damages for any losses. Significantly, copyright law also allows a plaintiff to elect statutory damages as an alternative to actual damages. This is a certain amount set by the judge for each work infringed, regardless of any lost revenue. It is through this provision that copyright defendants may end up owing thousands of dollars for sharing a few movie files, even if a studio cannot prove that it lost theatre revenue. Although, as noted earlier, registration is optional until a lawsuit is considered, a copyright owner can obtain statutory damages only if the work is registered before a defendant's infringement.

There are also criminal penalties for willful copyright infringement. Large-scale copyright infringement is often referred to as **piracy**. In these criminal cases, illegally reproduced copies may be seized, fines may be imposed, and defendants may actually be sent to jail. Remember that only the U.S. government can pursue a case of criminal copyright infringement. Due to the number of instances each year, most litigation takes place in the civil courts.

COPYRIGHT FAIR USE

The Copyright Act specifies that a fair use of copyrighted materials is not an infringement of the owner's property. **Fair use** includes copying for "criticism, comment, news reporting, teaching (including multiple copies for classroom use), scholarship, or research." In determining whether a particular use is a fair one, a court will consider the following four factors:

- The purpose and character of the use, including whether such use is for commercial or nonprofit educational purposes
- The nature of the copyrighted work
- The amount and substantiality of the portion used in relation to the copyrighted work as a whole
- The effect of the use upon the potential market for the copyrighted work

The determination of a fair use in light of these factors is made on a case-by-case basis. In Case 11.4, the Supreme Court considers whether one song makes a fair use of a previous song's copyrighted lyrics. The fair use being considered concerns *parody,* a form of expression that criticizes by poking fun at something through exaggeration.

 case **11.4**

CAMPBELL v. ACUFF-ROSE MUSIC, INC.
510 U.S. 569 (1994)

The rap group 2 Live Crew recorded and sold a commercial parody of Roy Orbison's copyrighted song "Oh Pretty Woman." Acuff-Rose Music, Inc., the copyright holder, sued the 2 Live Crew members after nearly a quarter million copies of the recording had been sold. The case came before the Supreme Court after the court of appeals decided that 2 Live Crew's parody had taken too much of "Oh Pretty Woman" to be protected as a fair use.

SOUTER, J: It is uncontested here that 2 Live Crew's song would be an infringement of Acuff-Rose's rights in "Oh Pretty Woman," under the Copyright Act of 1976, but for a finding of fair use through parody. From the infancy of copyright protection, some opportunity for fair use of copyrighted materials has been thought necessary to fulfill copyright's very purpose, "to promote the Progress of Science and useful Arts. . . ." For as Justice Story explained, "in truth, in literature, in science and in art, there are, and can be, few, if any, things, which in an abstract sense, are strictly new and original throughout. Every book in literature, science

and art, borrows, and must necessarily borrow, and use much which was well known and used before."

The first factor in a fair use enquiry is "the purpose and character of the use, including whether such use is of a commercial nature or is for nonprofit educational purposes." The enquiry here may be guided by looking to whether the use is for criticism, or comment, or news reporting, and the like. The central purpose of this investigation is to see, in Justice Story's words, whether the new work merely "supersede[s] the objects" of the original creation, or instead adds something new, with a further purpose or different character, altering the first with new expression, meaning, or message; it asks, in other words, whether and to what extent the new work is "transformative." Although such transformative use is not absolutely necessary for a finding of fair use, the goal of copyright, to promote science and the arts, is generally furthered by the creation of transformative works. Such works thus lie at the heart of the fair use doctrine's guarantee of breathing space within the confines of copyright, and the more transformative the new work, the less will be the

[continued]

significance of other factors, like commercialism, that may weigh against a finding of fair use.

The second statutory factor, "the nature of the copyrighted work," calls for recognition that some works are closer to the core of intended copyright protection than others, with one consequence that fair use is more difficult to establish when the former works are copied. We agree with both the District Court and the Court of Appeals that the Orbison original's creative expression for public dissemination falls within the core of the copyright's protective purposes. This fact, however, is not much help in this case, or ever likely to help much in separating the fair use sheep from the infringing goats in a parody case, since parodies almost invariably copy publicly known, expressive works.

The third factor asks whether "the amount and substantiality of the portion used in relation to the copyrighted work as a whole" are reasonable in relation to the purpose of the copying. The District Court considered the song's parodic purpose in finding that 2 Live Crew had not helped themselves overmuch. The Court of Appeals disagreed, stating that "while it may not be inappropriate to find that no more was taken than necessary, the copying was qualitatively substantial. . . . We conclude that taking the heart of the original and making it the heart of a new work was to purloin a substantial portion of the essence of the original."

Suffice it to say here that, as to the lyrics, we fail to see how the copying can be excessive in relation to its parodic purpose, even if the portion taken is the original's "heart." As to the music, we express no opinion whether repetition of the bass riff is excessive copying, and we remand to permit evaluation of the amount taken, in light of the song's parodic purpose and character, its transformative elements, and considerations of the potential for market substitution sketched more fully below.

The fourth fair use factor is "the effect of the use upon the potential market for or value of the copyrighted work." It requires courts to consider not only the extent of market harm caused by the particular actions of the alleged infringer, but also "whether unrestricted and widespread conduct of the sort engaged in by the defendant . . . would result in a substantially adverse impact on the potential market" for the original. The enquiry "must take account not only of harm to the original but also of harm to the market for derivative works."

Although 2 Live Crew submitted uncontroverted affidavits on the question of market harm to the original, neither they, nor Acuff-Rose, introduced evidence or affidavits addressing the likely effect of 2 Live Crew's parodic rap song on the market for a nonparody, rap version of "Oh Pretty Woman." And while Acuff-Rose would have us find evidence of a rap market in the very facts that 2 Live Crew recorded a rap parody of "Oh Pretty Woman" and another rap group sought a license to record a rap derivative, there was no evidence that a potential rap market was harmed in any way by 2 Live Crew's parody, rap version.

It was error for the Court of Appeals to conclude that the commercial nature of 2 Live Crew's parody of "Pretty Woman" rendered it presumptively unfair. No such evidentiary presumption is available to address either the first factor, the character and purpose of the use, or the fourth, market harm, in determining whether a transformative use, such as parody, is a fair one. The court also erred in holding that 2 Live Crew had necessarily copied excessively from the Orbison original, considering the parodic purpose of the use. We therefore reverse the judgment of the Court of Appeals and remand the case for further proceedings consistent with this opinion.

Reversed and remanded.

COPYRIGHT IN THE DIGITAL AGE

Under copyright law it is illegal not only to make copies that violate the law but also to assist others in doing so. When copyright holders challenged certain programs that assisted file sharing of materials—mostly, copyrighted music—one case went to the Supreme Court. In *Metro-Goldwyn-Mayer Studios v. Grokster,* 125 S. Ct. 2764 (2005), the Court asserted: "We hold that one who distributes a device with the object of promoting its use to infringe copyright, as shown by clear expression or other affirmative steps taken to foster infringement, is liable for the resulting acts of infringement by third parties." In addition to inducing others to infringe, one can be liable for materially contributing to another's infringement with knowledge of the infringement. Obtaining financial benefit with the ability to supervise the infringement also makes one vicariously liable.

sidebar 11.10

Is Copyright Law Too Inflexible for the Modern World?

Much of the core of U.S. copyright law was written decades ago. The last major revision was the Copyright Act of 1976. Some argue that archaic statutes are ill equipped to deal with the modern world in which digital distribution is the norm and pieces of works are mixed and remixed to produce something new. Many people are surprised to find themselves in violation of the copyright law for activities that do not seem nefarious.

Harvard law professor Larry Lessig commented on this uncomfortable legal state in his book, *Remix: Making Art and Commerce Thrive in the Hybrid Economy.* Summed up during a related TED talk, Lessig stated:

> [I]f copyright law at its core regulates something called copies, then in the digital world the one fact we can't escape is that every single use of culture produces a copy. Every single use therefore requires permission; without permission, you are a trespasser. . . . Common sense here, though, has not yet revolted in response to this response that the law has offered to [remixing] forms of creativity. Instead, what we've seen is something much worse than a revolt. There's a growing extremism that comes from both sides in this debate, in response to this conflict between the law and the use of these technologies.

Resolving modern copyright conflicts will likely require better communication between rights holders and users. However, in some cases, it may be difficult to assess whether infringement is occurring in the first place. The recent Supreme Court decision in *American Broadcasting Companies, Inc. v. Aereo, Inc.* is a case in point. The dispute involved a company, Aereo, that intercepted broadcast television signals and transmitted them to customers over the Internet. Because each customer was assigned an individual antenna, Aereo argued that it simply provided equipment to customers who were responsible for initiating transmissions to their own devices. The Court disagreed, finding that Aereo's transmission of live programming to customers constituted an infringing public performance. Cases like this are complex because the relevant technology did not exist when the law was written. Future courts will face the same task of fitting decades-old law to new technology.

Sources: Larry Lessig, "Laws That Choke Creativity," TED2007, www.ted.com/talks/larry_lessig_says_the_law_is_strangling_creativity/transcript; *American Broadcasting Cos. Inc. v. Aereo, Inc.*, 134 S.Ct. 2498 (2014).

International piracy of copyrighted material is a major problem, but international enforcement efforts are improving slowly.

Criminal prosecutions and civil lawsuits for "file sharing" copyrighted material over the Internet continue. The motion picture and recording industries have been particularly active over the years in pursuing individuals for file sharing. Some excuse file sharing by saying that intellectual property does not diminish the way that tangible property does when someone misappropriates it. But consider this: property is a legal right to exclude, not a physical thing, and the object of a property copyright includes the reproduction of music for commercial profit. The holder of a copyright owns the right to exclude others from what is copyrighted, and the market resource is diminished for the copyright owner when file sharers misappropriate music. In the early years of this century, the volume of sales for copyrighted music has declined significantly, largely due to misappropriation.

Digital Millennium Copyright Act Because copyrighted property is easily misappropriated over the Internet, Congress passed a law in 1998 that prohibits certain activities leading to copyright violation. The **Digital Millennium Copyright Act** (DMCA) makes illegal the effort to get around (circumvent) devices used by copyright owners to keep their works from being infringed. In particular, the act prevents the production, marketing, or sales of a product or service designed to circumvent technological protections of computer software, videos, and compact disks. The act also prevents circumvention of access protections for such products.

A second part of the DMCA enlists the help of Internet service providers (ISPs) to curb infringement. The law provides a safe-harbor for ISPs, protecting them from liability (1) for illegal copies that pass temporarily through their systems and (2) for permanent illegal copies stored in their systems, for example, at a website, but *only if* the service provider removes the offending material upon request of a copyright owner. Finally, the act relieves service providers from liability for unintentionally linking to a website that contains infringing materials.

sidebar 11.11

Knowledge of Users' Infringing Activity

Internet service providers (ISPs), which include companies that provide Internet access as well as those that host content like videos, have protection against claims of contributory infringement so long as they act to address copyright owner claims. For hosting services, the DMCA requires content removal when a copyright owner provides notice. However, ISPs may be obligated to act even before a copyright owner notifies them. Under the act, actual knowledge of infringing works posted by users requires action. Additionally, knowledge of facts or circumstances from which infringement is apparent requires that an ISP remove the infringing content.

When do facts and circumstances make infringement apparent? Is a general knowledge that some users post infringing content enough? This question was addressed in the recent case *Viacom Intern. Inc. v. YouTube, Inc.,* 940 F.Supp.2d 110 (S.D.N.Y. 2013). Viacom contended that YouTube was aware of infringing activity on its service and did not work sufficiently to eliminate it. The court rejected that argument, finding that YouTube was protected by the DMCA's safe harbor provisions.

Violations of the DMCA permit civil remedies, including injunction, actual damages, and statutory damages. A court can assess triple damages against a repeat offender. Willful circumvention for financial gain can also result in up to ten years' imprisonment.

International Intellectual Property Rights

LO 11-6

To this point, this chapter has presented the basic rules of U.S. intellectual property rights. You may be aware that you can obtain similar rights in other countries. Is such protection automatic once you have protection in the United States? Is there an international system for protecting intellectual property? These are essential questions for any modern business. As commerce becomes global, the protection of intellectual property internationally is increasingly important.

There are in fact no fully international intellectual property rights, *per se.* Local or regional law controls the creation and ownership of patents, copyrights, trademark, and trade secrets. However, there are international standards that most industrialized nations have agreed to uphold. The most important source for standards is an international treaty known as the

Agreement on Trade-Related Aspects of Intellectual Property Rights **(TRIPS)**. This agreement was formed in 1994 as part of the treaty that created the World Trade Organization (WTO). The United States has been a member since the agreement's inception, and was a major force in drafting its provisions. TRIPS requires that member countries provide protection for all of the forms of intellectual property discussed in this chapter. In addition, it sets forth baseline rules for that protection in terms of subject matter, procedure, and enforcement. By virtue of the TRIPS agreement, businesses can count on being able to obtain similar protection for intellectual property in other countries. However, differences in the manner in which counties comply with TRIPS require that companies exercise due care in pursuing international rights.

In addition to substantive protection, international treaties exist that can facilitate filing for rights in several countries at the same time. In the context of patents, there is the Patent Cooperation Treaty (PCT), which allows an applicant to obtain a preliminary international examination and then pursue final rights in multiple countries at the same time. Similarly, trademark owners can pursue rights in several countries at the same time through the Madrid System for International Registration of Marks. Because members of the Berne Convention, described above, are not required to undertake any formalities to obtain copyright protection, no international filing system is necessary. Members agree to provide rights if similar rights are obtained in an author's home country.

In order to monitor and administer certain aspects of international intellectual property agreements, countries have provided authority to certain independent international organizations. The most important two organizations are the WTO and the World Intellectual Property Organization (WIPO). The WTO administers the TRIPS agreement, including the settlement of disputes concerning its interpretation. The WIPO administers the PCT and Madrid System in addition to many other international intellectual property treaties. Both organizations provide much useful information to businesses, and it is worth consulting their respective web resources before pursuing international protection.

A Conclusion about Intellectual Property

Intellectual property, like property itself, serves the common good. The U.S. Constitution points this out in Article 1, Section 8, by asserting that the purpose for Congress granting "to authors and inventors the exclusive right to their respective writings and discoveries" is to promote the progress of science and business, which society believes promotes the common good. The framers of the Constitution believed, as do modern economists, that property, including intellectual property, gives incentive for private production of goods and services, which benefits not only the owners providing goods and services, but also to the overall wealth of society.

A property system is only as effective as the mechanism for enforcing it. Without adequate enforcement, a property system cannot function for the common good, and enforcement relies upon more than laws and courts. It depends also on the attitudes of people toward legitimacy of the property. Without social recognition of the exclusive legal fences that are at the heart of the property system and without adequate enforcement of property, the system cannot provide the incentive necessary for private productive effort.

Increasingly, we live in a global society, and the information that is the resource of intellectual property moves easily across national borders. This means that the enforcement of intellectual property is something important to all nations that are part of the global trading system.

Key Terms

Blurring 339
Copyright 340
Digital Millennium Copyright
   Act 344
Economic Espionage Act 321
Fair use 342
Generic 334, 337
Infringement 335

Injunction 321
Intellectual property 315
likelihood of confusion 335
Misappropriation 320
Patent 323
patent trolls. 331
Piracy 341
Plant patents 324

Property 313
Tarnishment 339
Trade dress 333
Trade secret 317
Trademark 331
Trademark dilution 339
utility patent 323

Review Questions and Problems

1. *The Justification for Intellectual Property*
   (a) What is the purpose of patents and copyrights as identified in the Constitution?
   (b) Explain the claim that the pace of research and development of new products would slow if intellectual property right did not protect it.

2. *Intellectual Property and Competition*
   (a) Explain the balance between intellectual property's rights of exclusion and competition.
   (b) Articulate alternatives to intellectual property for encouraging information creation.

3. *Capturing Intellectual Property*
   Explain the assertion that businesses can lose rights if they do not diligently assess and pursue intellectual property protection.

Trade Secrets

4. *Trade Secret: Taking Reasonable Measures to Keep the Secret*
   (a) How do trade secrets differ from other applications of property?
   (b) Discuss several ways of preserving trade secrets.

5. *Demonstrating Misappropriation*
   What types of actions constitute misappropriation under trade secret law?

6. *Trade Secret: Civil Enforcement*
   What are the remedies available for the civil enforcement of trade secrets?

7. *Trade Secret: Criminal Enforcement*
   Why has criminal misappropriation of trade secrets become an issue of greater concern in recent years?

Patent Law

8. *Obtaining a Patent*
   Describe the process for obtaining a patent.

9. *Patentable Subject Matter*

   Through long, expensive research you determine that both a bowling ball and a feather fall at the rate of 32 feet per second in a vacuum. Can you patent this knowledge? Explain.

10. *Nonobviousness, Novelty, and Usefulness*

    (a) Imagine that you discover a long-ignored cure for headaches in an old U.S. medical journal from the 1800s, and you apply for a patent. Explain why a patent examiner would likely reject your application.

    (b) Discuss the patent requirement of nonobviousness.

11. *Patent Enforcement*

    Is it possible for two utility patents owned by different people to cover the same product? Explain.

12. *Current Issues in Patent Law*

    (a) Discuss the propriety of entities that acquire and assert patents but make no product.

    (b) You discover a specific human gene that determines male pattern baldness. Explain what it means to say that you can patent this gene.

Trademark Law

13. *Types of Trademarks*

    Name four types of marks that are often called "trademarks."

14. *Trademark Registration*

    (a) Can you register the name "Fast Food" as a trademark? Explain.

    (b) Under what conditions can you *not* register a mark?

15. *Trademark Enforcement*

    Do you ever "google" something on the Internet? Is the company Google in danger of losing its name as a trademark? Explain.

16. *Trademark Dilution*

    Articulate an example that would constitute trademark dilution, but not infringement. Can you come up with one that constitutes infringement but not dilution?

Copyright Law

17. *Copyright Ownership*

    (a) If you spend the time and effort necessary to alphabetize the names of the students at your school and list their e-mail addresses, can you copyright a printed version? Explain.

    (b) Explain the rights a company has to the works created by its employees.

18. *Copyright enforcement*

    Imagine that you are making a presentation to a class on the occurrence of product advertising in film. You display a short clip of a recent film to illustrate your point. Explain how one would argue that this use constitutes a "fair use" of the copyrighted material.

19. *Copyright in the Digital Age*

    Explain why digital copies of works create greater difficulties in controlling infringement.

20. *Digital Millennium Copyright Act*

    Are file-hosting sites like YouTube liable for infringing videos posted by their users?

1. Colonel Cars Inc. plans to introduce a new speaker complex in the steering wheels of its automobiles. It believes the change will revolutionize the drivers' music-listening enjoyment. The company is also preparing an advertising campaign around the improved listening experience. Both the new steering-wheel speakers and the ad campaign are carefully kept secrets. But Colonel Cars' vice president for marketing is hired by European Motor Works (EMW) to be the president of its international division. Before Colonel Cars can begin its advertising, EMW comes out with an ad campaign centered on—you guessed it—speakers in the steering wheels of its new model cars.

> Can a company have property in its marketing plans the way you can have property in your car?
>
> Can EMW use Colonel Cars' marketing plans without permission?

International Law

Learning Objectives

In this chapter you will learn:

12-1. To understand the legal risk inherent in international transactions, including the requirements of the Foreign Corrupt Practices Act.

12-2. To identify the basic sources of international law and major institutions.

12-3. To consider the importance of free trade agreements on the global economy.

12-4. To grasp the basic methods of transacting international business.

12-5. To realize the complexity of resolving international disputes.

The risks of engaging in global transactions are apparent in the news on a daily basis. From increased prosecutions for bribery to lawsuits involving global operations, the international marketplace is fraught with potential legal issues.

The collapse of Lehman Brothers during the fall of 2008, illustrates the interconnectedness of international business. Lehman's bankruptcy triggered a "cash crunch" around the world, precipitating losses and accelerating the demise of other businesses. The U.S. laws and regulations governing financial institutions immediately were subjected to international scrutiny. The global economy still is trying to recover from the aftermath of this financial disaster.

Law is fundamental to business in the United States and throughout the globe. As American businesses become increasingly global in a very competitive international marketplace, some understanding of legal issues in this context is essential. Throughout this text, the importance of *the rule of law* is emphasized. This concept is particularly important for companies doing business abroad. Property rights and contracts must be enforced to minimize risk in international transactions.

The United States enters into treaties and trade agreements to govern competition and the way goods and technology are sold from one country to the next. Every country is interested in developing rules that make its products and services more competitive in the global market. Nation-states and corporations alike are protected by a mutual respect for property and contractual rights.

The goal of American trade policy is to open markets throughout the world. The idea is to create new opportunities for business and also higher living standards. The United States is a party to many trade agreements and is continually negotiating new ones to further open markets to free trade. National economies rely on their ability to export products and services abroad to create jobs and economic growth at home. Companies likewise are continually looking for productive ways to expand their international business. Overall, however, the United States has a huge trade deficit because it buys more than it sells abroad. At the end of 2010, the trade deficit was $497.8 billion. For a chart of the top trading partners with the United States, see Figure 12.1.

This chapter discusses the risks of global trade, with increased emphasis on the pressure for bribes. It then provides a basic understanding about international law and organizations that affect trade, including major trade agreements. Next, it provides an overview of methods of transacting international business and concludes with ways of resolving international disputes. Overall, this chapter should help you understand the issues affecting business in the international landscape.

> "Travel is fatal to prejudice, bigotry, and narrow-mindedness . . . Broad, wholesome, charitable views of men and things cannot be acquired by vegetating in one little corner of the earth all one's lifetime."
>
> **– Mark Twain, American humorist (1857)**

Figure 12.1 *Top Ten Trading Partners with the United States.*

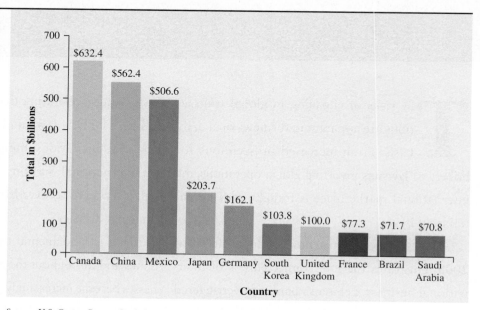

Source: U.S. Census Bureau Statistics, Year-to-Date Trade Totals (December 2013).

Risks Involved in International Trade

LO 12-1

Because international trade means dealing with different legal systems, cultures, and ways of doing business, there are a number of risks involved. For example, when a firm expands globally, a host of potential risks and concerns are raised, such as:

- What U.S. laws have an "extraterritorial" reach?
- Are property rights enforced?
- Will foreign courts uphold the validity of contracts?
- Is intellectual property protected or is it vulnerable to infringement?
- Are there export or import restrictions on the firm's products?
- Are there risks associated with political instability and/or war?
- What international trade agreements will affect the firm's expansion?
- What national laws (e.g., labor and environmental) affect the firm?
- How should language and cultural differences be bridged?

See Sidebar 12.1 as an example of problems that can arise with outsourcing manufacturing. This section addresses specific concerns about pressures for bribes, expropriation and nationalization, and export controls.

---

sidebar 12.1

Problems with Outsourcing in China: Mattel's Massive Toy Recall

  In 2007, Mattel, Inc., recalled over ten million toys manufactured in China. What was at issue? Lead paint and tiny magnets presented safety hazards for children. At least one U.S. child died and 19 others required surgery after swallowing magnets in the toys. The recall included some of Mattel's most popular toys, including Barbie, Dora, Thomas the Train, Polly Pocket, and *Cars* movie items. The over $33 billion U.S. toy industry heavily relies on manufacturing in China for approximately 80 percent of its toys.

 PRACTICAL CONSIDERATIONS FOR BUSINESS

Who is responsible?

What is the best way to address the problem?

Should there be tighter consumer standards?

How can companies better control outsourced manufacturing?

PRESSURES FOR BRIBES

Following widespread disclosure of scandalous payments by domestic firms to officials of foreign government, Congress enacted the **Foreign Corrupt Practices Act (FCPA)** in 1977. The law is designed to stop bribery of foreign officials and to prohibit U.S. citizens and companies from making payments to foreign officials whose duties are not "essentially ministerial or clerical" for the purpose of obtaining business. Since 2009, FCPA enforcement increased substantially. Any company trading on a U.S. stock exchange can be prosecuted for FCPA violations.

This statute has the following two principal requirements:

1. Financial records and accounts must be kept "which, in reasonable detail, accurately and fairly reflect the transactions and dispositions of assets" of the business.
2. The business must "devise and maintain a system of internal accounting controls sufficient to provide reasonable assurances" that transactions are being carried out in accordance with management's authorization.

These provisions are intended to correct the previously widespread practice of accounting for bribes as commission payments, payments for services, or other normal business expenses and then illegally deducting the payments on income tax returns.

Many legal observers criticized the FCPA for creating a significantly chilling effect on U.S. companies seeking business in many developing countries where under-the-table payments to government officials are an accepted practice. Indeed, many civil servants in other nations are expected to supplement their salaries in this manner. The U.S. prohibition of such payments is perceived as an attempt to impose U.S. standards of morality in other parts of the world, and it has caused resentment and discrimination against U.S. businesses. Moreover, the FCPA arguably puts U.S. firms at a competitive disadvantage with businesses in other countries that are not operating under similar constraints. See Sidebar 12.2 for a sample of how countries are ranked according how corrupt they are perceived.

sidebar 12.2

Turning Back the Tide of Corruption

An international group known as Transparency International generates the Corruption Perceptions Index annually. It ranks 175 countries and territories according to perception of corruption in the public sector. This global coalition against corruption measures perceptions as a reliable measure of the degree of corruption of a country. Here is a sampling of countries from the 2014 report:

Denmark #1
Canada #10
Germany #12

United States #17
Brazil #69
China #100
Mexico #103
Vietnam #119
Myanmar #156
North Korea and Somalia tied for #174
#1 = least corrupt #174 = most corrupt

Source: Transparency International Corruption Perceptions Index, www.transparency.org (2014).

As a result of intensive lobbying by the U.S. business community, Congress amended the FCPA in 1988 in an effort to eliminate ambiguity and uncertainty over what constitutes improper conduct. Although the law still

---

table 12.1 FCPA: Legal or Permissible Payments

The following payments are permissible under the FCPA:

"Facilitating," "expediting," or "grease" payments for "routine government action." Examples include obtaining permits, licenses, or other official documents; processing governmental papers (e.g., visas and work orders); providing police protection; loading and unloading cargo; and scheduling inspections associated with contract performance or transit of goods across country.

Any payments permitted under the written laws of the foreign country.

Travel expenses of a foreign official for the purpose of demonstrating a product or for performing a contractual obligation.

---

prohibits bribery and corruption, the amendments establish clearer standards for firms to follow in overseas operations. The amendments limit criminal liability for violations of accounting standards to those who "knowingly" circumvent accounting controls or falsify records of corporate payments and transactions. The amendments also clarify the level of detail required in such record keeping and should improve compliance by businesses and enforcement by the government. Moreover, under the new law otherwise prohibited payments to foreign officials may be defended if they were legal under the written laws of the host country or if they cover "reasonable and bona fide" expenses associated with the promotion of the product and the completion of the contract (see Table 12.1).

The FCPA also prohibits corrupt payments through intermediaries. It is unlawful to make a payment to a third party, while knowing that all or a portion of the payment will go directly or indirectly to a foreign official. The term *knowing* includes conscious disregard and deliberate indifference. Additionally, the antibribery provisions of the FCPA apply to foreign firms and persons who take action in furtherance of a corrupt payment while in the United States.

Criminal penalties may be imposed for violations of the FCPA: corporations and other business entities are subject to a fine of up to $2,000,000; officers, directors, stockholders, employees, and agents are subject to a fine of up to $100,000 and imprisonment for up to five years. Fines imposed on individuals may *not* be paid by their employer or principal. The attorney general or the SEC, as appropriate, may also bring a civil action for fines against any firm, as well as any officer, director, employee, or agent of a firm or stockholder acting on behalf of the firm who violates the antibribery provisions. The conduct that violates the antibribery provisions of the FCPA may also give rise to a private cause of action for treble damages under the Racketeer Influenced and Corrupt Organizations Act (RICO). For example, a RICO action could be brought by a competitor who alleges that the bribery caused the defendant to obtain a foreign contract. See Sidebar 12.3 for examples of successful FCPA prosecutions.

Payment of a bribe in violation of the FCPA can buy you jail time.

sidebar 12.3

FCPA Prosecutions: U.S. Government Success Stories

 Siemens AG paid a record-breaking $800 million for FCPA violations. The total consisted of a $450 million fine to the Department of Justice and $350 million in disgorgement of profits to the Securities and Exchange Commission. Siemens allegedly violated the FCPA by paying $1.36 billion in bribes around the world in connection with obtaining contracts. According to the prosecution, the corruption implicated all levels of management, including senior management, and involved elaborate payment schemes and off-book accounts to conceal payments. The Department of Justice described the level of corruption at Siemens as a "pattern of bribery" that was "unprecedented in scale and geographic reach."

Hewlett-Packard agreed to pay $108 million to settle charges that employees at subsidiaries bribed government officials in Poland, Russia, and Mexico to win and retain lucrative public contracts.

OTHER RECENT PROSECUTIONS

Daimler paid a $93.6 million fine and $91.4 million fine for disgorgement of profits. The company and its subsidiaries allegedly made hundreds of improper payments in at least 22 countries, including China and Russia.

Johnson & Johnson agreed to pay $70 million to settle civil and criminal bribery charges involving bribes paid to public doctors and public hospital administrators in Greece, Poland, and Romania.

Baker Hughes paid $44 million following accusations that the company used bribes to win an oil fields contract in Kazakhstan.

IBM agreed to pay $10 million to settle civil bribery charges involving payments by more than 100 employees of subsidiaries and joint ventures in Asia.

Tyson Foods Inc. paid $5.2 million in criminal and civil penalties to resolve FCPA allegations involving meat inspectors employed by the Mexican government.

INVESTIGATIONS CAN BE EXPENSIVE

Wal-mart reported in March 2014 that it spent $439 million in the last two years to investigate possible payment of foreign bribes. It projects investigation and compliance costs of $200 to $240 million for fiscal year 2015. The retailer is under investigation for bribery in Mexico, China, India, and Brazil.

OTHER INVESTIGATIONS

Investigations are ongoing into the hiring practices in Asia of JPMorgan Chase and Goldman for possible FCPA violations.

concept *summary*

Risks Involved in International Trade

1. The FCPA seeks to stop the bribery of foreign government officials.
2. Expropriation and nationalization are risks involved in international business.
3. Expert controls seek to balance national security interests against global trade.

EXPROPRIATION AND NATIONALIZATION

If a domestic firm is involved in a foreign country to the extent of locating assets there (whether through branches, subsidiaries, joint ventures, or otherwise), it may be subject to the ultimate legal and political risk of international business activity—expropriation. **Expropriation,** as used in the context of international law, is the seizure of foreign-owned property by a government. When the owners are not fairly compensated, the expropriation is also considered to be a *confiscation* of property. Usually, the expropriating government also assumes ownership of the property, so the process includes **nationalization** as well. In the United States, the counterpart of expropriation is called the *power of eminent domain.*

Creeping expropriation is a series of acts, such as taxes, regulation, or other changes in law that have an expropriatory effect, reducing or eliminating foreign investments.

This power of a government to take private property is regarded as inherent; yet it is subject to restraints upon its exercise. The U.S. Constitution (as well as the constitutions and laws of most nations) prohibits the government from seizing private property except for "public purposes" and upon the payment of "just compensation."

However, the extent of such protection varies widely. Treaties (or other agreements) between the United States and other countries provide additional protection against uncompensated takings of property. It is customary for international law to recognize the right of governments to expropriate the property of foreigners only when accompanied by "prompt, adequate, and effective compensation." This so-called modern traditional theory is accepted by most nations as the international standard and requires full compensation to the investor including fair market value as a going concern.

EXPORT CONTROLS

Another risk involved in doing business abroad is **export controls** placed on the sale of U.S. strategic products and technology abroad. Controlling the export of such items has been the cornerstone of Western policy since the conclusion of World War II. Most of the attention was focused on preventing the acquisition of technology by the former Soviet Union and its allies. However, since the end of the Cold War the policy rationale behind export controls has been drawn into question, with many Western countries contending they should be eliminated to increase trading opportunities with Russia, China, Eastern Europe, and the Middle East. Indeed, the Coordinating Committee for Multilateral Export Controls (COCOM), an organization created by the major Western nations (including the United States, Europe, and Japan) to control exports, came to an end in 1994.

Exports from the United States to countries such as Cuba, Iran, Libya, North Korea, Sudan, and Syria are restricted.

Query: Should the U.S. lift its trade embargo with Cuba? The EU agreed to lift its sanctions against Cuba in June 2008.

Since that time, a new organization supported by 33 countries, known as the Wassenaar Arrangement, has come into existence to help control the spread of both military and dual-use technology to unstable areas of the world. Participating nations seek, through their national policies, to ensure that transfer of conventional arms and strategic goods and technologies do not destabilize regional and international security. The 2002 plenary meeting of the Wassenaar Arrangement, held in Vienna, resulted in several significant initiatives to combat terrorism. The member countries agreed on several measures aimed at intensifying cooperation to prevent terrorist groups and individuals from acquiring arms and strategic goods and technologies.

The U.S. export control system currently is regulated by the Department of State and the Department of Commerce under authority provided by the Export Administration Act and the Arms Export Control Act. The Department of Defense also plays a key role in determining the technology to be controlled as does the U.S. Customs Service in the enforcement of the controls.

sidebar 12.4

Export Control Reform

The Comprehensive Iran Sanctions, Accountability, and Divestment Act of 2010 makes significant improvements for the nation's export enforcement authorities. This law harmonizes the different maximum export control criminal penalties under four different statutes. It also permanently restores the Department of Commerce's export enforcement authorities.

On November 9, 2010, the President signed Executive Order 13558, establishing an Export Enforcement Coordination Center (EECC) among the Departments of State, the Treasury, Defense, Justice, Commerce, Energy, and Homeland Security, as well as elements of the Intelligence Community. The Department of Homeland Security will administer the EECC. The EECC is designed to:

- Prevent conflicts in criminal and administrative enforcement operations and coordination of industry enforcement outreach activity.

- Provide a conduit between federal law enforcement agencies and the U.S. intelligence community.
- Serve as the primary point of contact between enforcement agencies and export licensing agencies for enforcement and licensing matters.
- Resolve interagency conflicts not settled in the field.
- Establish governmentwide statistical tracking capabilities for U.S. export enforcement activities.

The goal of this reform is to harmonize business practices and processes across the export enforcement agencies.

Source: www.export.gov/ecr/eg_main_027618.asp

Significant criminal and administrative sanctions may be imposed upon corporations and individuals convicted of violating the law.

According to the U.S. Export Control and Related Border Security Assistance (EXBS) Program, exporters should be aware of the following "red flags":

- *A customer* is reluctant to provide end-use/user information; is willing to pay cash for high-value shipments; has little background in the relevant business; declines normal warranty/service/installation; or orders products incompatible with the business.

- *A shipment* involves a private intermediary in a major weapons sale; shipments are directed to entities with no connection to the buyer; requests for packing are inconsistent with the normal mode of shipping; or circuitous or illogical routing.

- *The end-user* requests equipment inconsistent with inventory; spare parts in excess of projected needs; the end-use is at variance with standard practices; a middleman from a third country places the order; or the end-user refuses to state whether the goods are for domestic use, export, or re-export.

In 2000, the U.S. government extended the Export Administration Act and raised the penalties for violators. The export control agenda for the twenty-first century remains focused on maintaining national security and reducing the proliferation of weapons, while also facilitating U.S. competitiveness in the global economy.

The successful prosecution of two leading American aerospace companies, Hughes Electronics and Boeing Satellite Systems, illustrates the government's commitment to vigorous export control to prevent harmful proliferation of weapons. The companies paid a record $32 million in penalties to settle charges in connection with 123 alleged violations of export control laws regarding the transfer of rocket and satellite data to China.

However, the future of the U.S. system remains in doubt with many proposals pending in Congress to reform and limit the current export control system. Over the past several years, these controls have become an extremely controversial topic in the international business community. Export controls make successful business deals more difficult because foreign buyers may be reluctant to trade with a U.S. firm due to the red tape involved in obtaining governmental approval as compared with Europe or Japan.

---

sidebar 12.5

Twenty-First-Century Pirates

 Although it continues to be a problem, kidnapping is down from the record amount of attacks in 2011. In 2013, there were 264 actual and attempted attacks on ships, down 41 percent from 2011. Despite the fact that there are fewer attacks (largely due to fewer Somali attacks), Southeast Asia continues to be an increasingly dangerous area, particularly near Indonesia. The reason may be a result of overfishing and pollution, which is resulting in declining fish stocks. Unable to earn a living fishing, some fishermen may be turning to piracy. A study by One Earth Future estimates that maritime piracy costs between $7 and $12 billion a year.

Sources: "Pirates Seized Record 1,181 Hostages in 2010," *Report BBC News* (January 1, 2011); One Earth Future at www.oneearthfuture. org/; Lily Kuo, "Why Pirate Attacks Are Falling Everywhere in the World except for Southeast Asia" (April 23, 2014). Quartz http://qz.com/202157/why-pirate-attacks-are-falling-everywhere-in-the-world-except-for-southeast-asia/

International Law and Organizations

What is "international law"? Inasmuch as there is no "world government" or "world legislature," international law is not created the same way as domestic law. International law is found in a variety of sources, including U.S. domestic law, national laws of other countries, international agreements, treaties, and even in what is called "customary international law." Customary international law involves principles that are widely practiced and acknowledged by many civilized nations to be law.

In the landmark case of *The Paquette Habana* (1900), the U.S. Supreme Court held that "[i]nternational law is part of our law, and must be ascertained and administered by the courts of justice of appropriate jurisdiction as often as questions of right depending upon it are duly presented for their determination."

International organizations, such as the United Nations (UN), the World Trade Organization (WTO), and the European Union (EU), directly impact international business transactions. Agreements entered into by the United States, including the Convention on the International Sale of Goods, the North American Free Trade Agreement (NAFTA), and the Central America-Dominican Republic Free Trade Agreement (CAFTA-DR) also affect the global sale of goods. These agreements facilitate trade and minimize risk for business.

sidebar 12.6

What Are Corporate Codes of Conduct?

Corporate codes of conduct are policy statements adopted by companies to define ethical standards for their conduct. These are completely voluntary, often addressing topics such as follows:

- Forced labor
- Child labor
- Discrimination
- Health and safety of workers
- Freedom of association and collective bargaining
- Hours of work, wages, benefits, and overtime compensation
- Working conditions
- Environmental issues
- Monitoring and enforcement of the code of conduct

Recognizing that there are different legal and cultural environments around the world, companies often develop a code of conduct to establish a foundation for their standards in international business. Seeking to promote global corporate citizenship, the UN developed the Global Compact, a voluntary code of conduct supported by companies and organizations around the world. For a list of participants, see www.globalcompact.org. Many major corporations engaging in global operations, including Microsoft, GAP Inc., and Cisco Systems Inc., also have supplier or vendor codes of conduct. These codes allow companies to set standards for their suppliers and vendors consistent with the companies' mission and values.

LO 12-2   SOURCES OF INTERNATIONAL LAW

What are the principles or rules of international law that apply to a particular contract or dispute? Generally, international law is classified as either **public international law** or **private international law.** Public international law examines relationships between nations and uses rules that are binding on all countries in the international community. Private international law examines relationships created by commercial transactions and utilizes international agreements, as well as the laws of nations to resolve business disputes. Business managers are primarily concerned with private international law issues.

The ICJ's hearings are open to the public, unless one of the parties asks for the proceedings to be *in camera* or the Court so decides. The hearings take place in the Great Hall of Justice in the Peace Palace, in The Hague.

Public International Law   Article 38 of the Statute of the **International Court of Justice (ICJ)** is the traditional place for ascertaining what is public international law. However, in contrast to what you learned in Chapter 1 regarding U.S. cases, the decisions made by the ICJ, the World Court, do not create binding rules of law or precedent in future cases.

The ICJ is the judicial branch of the UN and sits at The Hague in the Netherlands. It consists of 15 judges representing all of the world's major legal systems. The judges are elected by the U.N. General Assembly and the Security Council after having been nominated by national groups, not governments. No more than one judge may be a national of any country.

The ICJ has not been a major force in settling disputes since it began functioning in 1946. The ICJ renders, on average, only one contested decision per year and one advisory opinion every two years. There has been widespread reluctance to resort to the ICJ as a forum for resolving international disputes for several reasons. First, only countries have access to the Court. Private parties or corporations may not directly present claims before the

Court. No device exists under U.S. law by which a firm or individual can compel the U.S. government to press a claim on its behalf before the ICJ. Furthermore, only countries that have submitted to the Court's jurisdiction may be parties, since there is no compulsory process for forcing a country to come before the Court. A country may choose to accept the Court's jurisdiction only when the use of the Court may suit its own interests. Moreover, the ICJ has no enforcement authority and must rely on diplomacy or economic sanctions against countries that breach international law. For these reasons, infractions of international law often are settled through diplomacy or arbitration, rather than by the presentation of formal charges to the ICJ.

Of course, deciding whether international law has been violated is often a very difficult question. Article 38 sets forth the following order of importance for determining what is international law in a given case:

> The Court, whose function is to decide in accordance with international law such disputes as are submitted to it, shall apply:
>
> a. *International Conventions*, whether general or particular, establishing rules expressly recognized by the contesting states;
>
> b. *International Custom*, as evidence of a general practice accepted as law;
>
> c. *The General Principles of Law* recognized by civilized nations;
>
> d. *Judicial Decisions and the Teachings of the Most Highly Qualified Publicists* of various nations, as subsidiary means for the determination of rules of law.

International Conventions are similar to legislation or statutes and represent formal agreements between nations. International Custom describes common legal practices followed by nations in working with each other over a long period of time. General Principles of Law may be found in national rules common to the countries in a dispute. Finally, Judicial Decisions and Teachings, although not binding, may be used for guidance in resolving a dispute. See Sidebar 12.7 for an example of an ICJ decision and the interplay with U.S. courts.

sidebar 12.7

Medellin v. Texas (2008): The U.S. Supreme Court and the International Court of Justice (ICJ)

What is the effect of an ICJ judgment in the United States? In a 6–3 ruling, the U.S. Supreme Court held that President Bush went too far when he decreed that the states must abide by a 2004 decision by the ICJ. The ICJ found that several dozen Mexican citizens sentenced to death in the United States had not been given the assistance of Mexican diplomats that they were entitled to under the Vienna Convention.

The case in question involved Jose Medellin, a onetime Houston gang member who took part in the rape and murder of two teenage girls. After he was arrested, and read his Miranda Rights, Medellin confessed to the crimes, including revealing particularly egregious details. The conviction was challenged because law enforcement authorities failed to inform him of his right under the Vienna Convention.

In the majority opinion, Chief Justice Roberts states that neither the defendant nor his supporters "have identified a single nation that treats ICJ judgments as binding in domestic courts." In response, Mexico has asked the ICJ to declare that the United States "must provide review and reconsideration of the convictions and sentences" consistent with its 2004 decision.

Do include choice of law and forum selection clauses in all international contracts.

Eight UN Millennium Development Goals:

1. Eradicate extreme poverty and hunger.
2. Achieve universal primary education.
3. Promote gender equality and empower women.
4. Reduce child mortality.
5. Improve maternal health.
6. Combat HIV/AIDS, malaria, and other diseases.
7. Ensure environmental sustainability.
8. Develop a global partnership for development.

Private International Law   Private international law is represented by the laws of individual nations and the multilateral agreements developed between nations to provide mutual understanding and some degree of continuity to international business transactions. Even in purely domestic business deals, the law is rarely predictable or certain. When different national laws, languages, practices, and cultures are added to the transaction, the situation can become very unstable for international business.

International law can be complicated and a single business transaction can involve several companies in different nations. For example, a contract dispute between a Chinese manufacturer, an American wholesaler, and a Canadian retailer could potentially involve the law of all three countries. Which law controls? The answer could affect the outcome of the case. Determining which nation's court may hear the case can be difficult. For this reason, most international contracts contain choice of law and forum provisions to eliminate this uncertainty.

INTERNATIONAL ORGANIZATIONS

Several international organizations play important roles in the development of political, economic, and legal rules for the conduct of international business. The two primary organizations are the UN and the WTO. Additionally, the EU plays an important role in international trade.

United Nations   Established after World War II, the **United Nations** has grown considerably from the 51 founding nations. Almost every country in the world is a member today. The Charter of the UN sets forth as its primary goal "to save succeeding generations from the scourge of war" and, to that end, authorizes "collective measures for the prevention and removal of threats to the peace, and for the suppression of acts of aggression or other breaches of the peace."

The General Assembly is composed of every nation represented in the UN and permits each country to cast one vote. The real power in the UN rests in the Security Council, which is composed of 15 member states. The Security Council has the power to authorize military action and to sever diplomatic relations with other nations. The five permanent members of the Council (United States, Russia, China, France, and United Kingdom) have veto power over any action proposed in the Council. France and Russia used the threat of a veto in 2003 to force the United States to go forward with the war in Iraq without clear United Nations' authority. Although the United States contended that its authority for war came from previously passed UN resolutions regarding Iraq, the U.S. government was disturbed by the veto threat. The failure of the UN to dictate the resolution of the U.S.-Iraq conflict created serious questions about the future authority and role of the UN in international conflicts.

A number of organizations affiliated with the UN have authority over activities that directly affect international business. The United Nations Commission on International Trade Law (UNCITRAL) was created in 1966 to develop standardized commercial practices and agreements. One of the documents drafted by the UNCITRAL is the Convention on the International Sale of Goods, which is discussed in more detail later in this chapter. The UNCITRAL has no authority to force any country to adopt any of the conventions or agreements that it proposes. The United Nations Conference on Trade and Development (UNCTAD) deals with international trade reform and the redistribution of income through trading with developing countries. The UNCTAD drafted both the Transfer of Technology Code and the Restrictive Business Practices Code, which are largely ignored by most nations.

At the Bretton Woods Conference of 1944, two important institutions were also created under the auspices of the United Nations. The **International Monetary Fund (IMF)** encourages international trade by maintaining stable foreign exchange rates and works closely with commercial banks to promote orderly exchange policies with members. The **World Bank** promotes economic development in poor countries by making loans to finance necessary development projects and programs.

For more information about current projects at the World Bank and IMF, see www.worldbank.org/ and www.imf.org/.

World Trade Organization Every nation has the right to establish its own trading policies and has its own national interests at stake when dealing with other nations. Ultimately, after years of economic conflict, many countries concluded that their own interests could be served best by liberalizing trade through reduced tariffs and free markets. The **General Agreement on Tariffs and Trade (GATT)** was originally signed by 23 countries after World War II and represented the determination of a war-weary world to open trade and end the protection of domestic industries. Since GATT was created in 1948, it has undergone eight major revisions, including the 1994 Uruguay Round, which culminated in the creation of the **World Trade Organization (WTO)** as an umbrella organization to regulate world trade. The 1994 agreement was signed by 125 countries.

The WTO is an international organization which, as its primary purpose, seeks to resolve trade disputes between member nations. The WTO administers the GATT but does not have the authority to regulate world trade in any manner it desires. The WTO expects nations to avoid unilateral trade wars and rely on GATT dispute settlement procedures to avert conflict. At the heart of the 1994 Uruguay Round are several enduring GATT principles:

1. Nondiscrimination (treating all member countries equally with respect to trade).
2. National treatment (countries not favoring their domestic products over imported products).
3. Elimination of trade barriers (reducing tariffs and other restrictions in foreign products).

Under the WTO, existing tariffs are reduced and the agreement extends GATT rules to new areas such as agricultural products and service industries. The WTO further restricts tariffs on textiles, apparel, and forest products. It also requires countries to upgrade their intellectual property laws to protect patents and copyrights and to guard against the piracy of items such as computer software and videotapes.

Another important aspect of the WTO is the **Agreement on Trade-Related Aspects of Intellectual Property Rights (TRIPS),** including trade in counterfeit goods. Recognizing that there are widely different standards for the

> "The human spirit is indomitable. Each individual matters. The seeds of policies and innovations planted today can influence tomorrow. And free men and women can move the world."
>
> **–Robert B. Zoellick, president of the World Bank Group (2008)**

protection of intellectual property, as well as a lack of a multilateral framework of rules for dealing with counterfeit goods, the WTO directly addressed this issue with TRIPS. This agreement discusses the applicability of GATT principles and those of relevant international property agreements in an effort to strengthen the protection of intellectual property in the international sphere.

The WTO has the power to hear disputes involving member states. The United States has been involved in a number of disputes. For example, the United States brought an action against the EU claiming that the Europeanwide restrictions on genetically modified food violate WTO rules. Additionally, the United States brought a successful challenge against Mexico; the WTO held that Mexico's beverage tax on soft drinks made with imported sweeteners is discriminatory. Under the beverage tax, soft drinks made with cane sugar are tax exempt. Because the beverage tax discriminates against U.S. products, it is contrary to WTO rules.

If a nation does not comply with a WTO ruling, the organization has the power to impose sanctions. Like any international institution, compliance by the most powerful trading nations is necessary to give the WTO credibility.

The WTO faces opposition from antiglobalization protesters. There are many reasons to support the WTO and the important role it plays in trade. Concerns, however, are raised by opponents who are concerned about human rights, environmental, and labor issues. Tensions between developed and developing nations are hindering negotiations to cut tariffs. Overall, the future of the WTO is uncertain. The cooperation of member states is critical to its success in liberalizing trade.

The marginal note reads: The WTO is the only global international trade organization dealing with the rules of trade between nations.

The European Union

The EU is an economic and political partnership among 28 democratic European countries. In 1957, six European countries, Belgium, France, Germany, Luxembourg, and the Netherlands signed the Treaty of Rome, creating the European Community. Six successive enlargements created the **European Union (EU),** as it is known today. See Table 12.2 for a complete list of states, accession dates, and those countries using the euro as legal tender. Negotiations are ongoing with Croatia, the Republic of Macedonia, and Turkey about possible membership in the EU.

Europe's mission in the twenty-first century is to:

- Provide peace, prosperity, and stability for its peoples.
- Overcome the divisions on the continent.
- Ensure that its people live in safety.
- Promote balanced economic and social development.
- Meet the challenges of globalization and preserve the diversity of the peoples of Europe.
- Uphold the values that Europeans share, such as sustainable development and a sound environment, respect for human rights, and the social market economy.

For more detailed information about these goals, see the official website of the EU at http://europa.eu.

The major institutions of the EU are the Council of Ministers, the Commission, the Parliament, and the Court of Justice. The Council is composed of one representative from each member state. The Council coordinates the

The marginal note reads: The aims of the EU are: "Peace, prosperity and freedom for its 495 million citizens—in a fairer, safer world."

table 12.2 Twenty-Eight European Union Member States

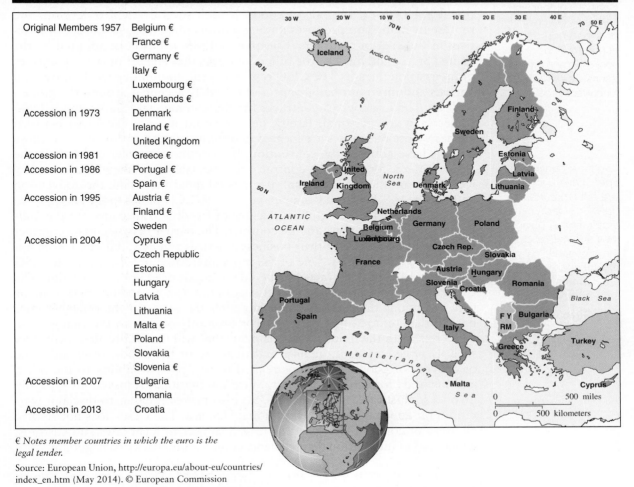

Original Members 1957	Belgium €
	France €
	Germany €
	Italy €
	Luxembourg €
	Netherlands €
Accession in 1973	Denmark
	Ireland €
	United Kingdom
Accession in 1981	Greece €
Accession in 1986	Portugal €
	Spain €
Accession in 1995	Austria €
	Finland €
	Sweden
Accession in 2004	Cyprus €
	Czech Republic
	Estonia
	Hungary
	Latvia
	Lithuania
	Malta €
	Poland
	Slovakia
	Slovenia €
Accession in 2007	Bulgaria
	Romania
Accession in 2013	Croatia

€ *Notes member countries in which the euro is the legal tender.*

Source: European Union, http://europa.eu/about-eu/countries/index_en.htm (May 2014). © European Commission

policies of the member states in a variety of areas from economics to foreign affairs. The Commission consists of individuals who represent the will and interests of the entire EU, rather than specific national concerns. Elected representatives from each member state compose the Parliament, which plays an active role in drafting legislation that has an impact on the daily lives of its citizens. The Parliament, for example, has addressed environmental protection, consumer rights, equal opportunities, transport, and the free movement of workers, capital, services, and goods. Parliament also has joint power with the Council over the annual budget of the EU. Finally, the Court of Justice decides the nature and parameters of EU law. Justices are appointed by the Council, and each member state has a justice seated on the Court.

MAJOR AGREEMENTS AFFECTING TRADE   LO 12-3

In addition to the international institutions discussed in this chapter, a number of international agreements also facilitate trade.

The U.S. Trade Representative is a Cabinet member who serves as the president's principal trade adviser, negotiator, and spokesperson on trade issues. See www.ustr.gov for current trade news.

"We must continue to open markets if we want our exports to grow. . . . Open markets create higher paying jobs and help support the prosperity of American workers, farmers, and entrepreneurs."

–Susan C.Schwab, U.S. Trade Representative (2008)

Convention on the International Sale of Goods   The **Convention on the International Sale of Goods (CISG)** outlines standard international practices for the sale of goods. It took several years to develop, and represents many compromises among nations that follow a variety of practices in the area of contracts. Effective in 1988, it has been adopted by the United States and most of the other countries that engage in large quantities of international trade. The CISG represents the cumulative work of over 60 nations and international groups and is widely accepted around the globe.

The CISG applies to contracts for the commercial sale of goods (consumer sales for personal, family, or household use are excluded) between parties whose businesses are located in different nations, provided that those nations have adopted the convention. If a commercial seller or buyer in the United States, for example, contracts for the sale of goods with a company located in another country that also has adopted the CISG, the convention and not the U.S. Uniform Commercial Code (UCC) applies to the transaction.

Under the CISG, a significant degree of freedom is provided for the individual parties in an international contract. The parties may negotiate contract terms as they deem fit for their business practices and may, if desired, even opt out of the CISG entirely. One of the most interesting provisions in the CISG includes a rule that contracts for the sale of goods need not be in writing. The CISG also provides that in contract negotiations an acceptance that contains new provisions that do not materially alter the terms of the offer becomes part of the contract, unless the offeror promptly objects to the change. The CISG sets forth the fundamental elements that will materially alter a contract such as price, payment, quality, and quantity of the goods, place and time of delivery of goods, provisions related to one party's liability to the other, and methods for settling disputes. Since international transactions typically involve sophisticated parties, the CISG also makes it easier to disclaim warranties on goods than under traditional U.S. law. The CISG does not resolve all areas of contract law; parties are still subject to local laws and customs, which makes international agreements complex and tricky to negotiate.

North American Free Trade Agreement   The passage of the **North American Free Trade Agreement (NAFTA)** in 1993 set in motion increased trade and foreign investment and opportunities for economic growth in the United States, Mexico, and Canada. Free trade is at the core of NAFTA, through the reduction and eventual elimination of tariffs and other barriers to business between these three countries. NAFTA also provides for a dispute settlement mechanism that makes it easier to resolve trade disputes between the three countries. Based upon concerns that cheap labor and poor environmental controls might cause U.S. firms to relocate to Mexico, side agreements also were reached to improve labor rights and environmental protection in Mexico. Since its enactment, NAFTA has expanded shipments of U.S. goods to Mexico and Canada, as well as Mexican and Canadian exports to the United States.

Central America-Dominican Republic Free Trade Agreement
Similar to NAFTA, the passage of the **Central America-Dominican Republic Free Trade Agreement (CAFTA-DR)** in 2005 opened up many opportunities for business in Central America. CAFTA-DR is a comprehensive trade agreement between Costa Rica, El Salvador, Guatemala, Honduras, Nicaragua, the Dominican

Republic, and the United States. This agreement is designed to eliminate the barriers on products trades between the member countries. Prior to CAFTA-DR, many exports of American goods to Central America faced high tariffs. This trade agreement is a step to create a fairer playing field for American exports.

Recent Free Trade Agreements The United States ratified trade agreements with South Korea, Panama, and Colombia in 2011. Negotiations are under way for the Transatlantic Trade and Investment Partnership, a trade agreement between the United States and the EU. The United States is also in the process of negotiating the Trans-Pacific Partnership Agreement with 11 nations: Australia, Brunei Darussalam, Canada, Chile, Japan, Malaysia, Mexico, New Zealand, Peru, Singapore, and Vietnam.

concept *summary*

International Law and Organizations

1. International law is classified as either public or private.
2. The ICJ is the traditional place for determining public international law.
3. The WTO regulates world trade for member nations.
4. The Convention on the International Sale of Goods governs international practices for the sale of goods.
5. The EU has evolved into the most important economic force in Europe.
6. The NAFTA has substantially expanded trade with Mexico and Canada.

sidebar 12.8

Philip Morris: Restrictions Affecting Their Global Business

With more and more anti-smoking laws in the United States and general public opposition to smoking, global markets are increasingly important to tobacco giant Philip Morris. What kinds of issues does it face abroad?

- Limits on cigarette advertising in Britain
- More detailed health warnings in South America
- Higher cigarette taxes in the Philippines and Mexico
- Prohibitions on store displays in Ireland and Norway
- The World Health Organization Framework Convention on Tobacco Control, a public health treaty ratified by 171 nations
- Mandatory health warnings that cover 80 percent of cigarette packages in Uruguay

Alleging that its tobacco regulations are excessive, Philip Morris sued the government of Uruguay. Philip Morris also brought an action against Brazil, arguing that the images the government wants to put on cigarette packages "vilify" tobacco companies.

The next smoking frontier to watch is the rise in vaping. Phillip Morris and other major tobacco companies are entering the e-cigarette market. There is a lot at stake in terms of regulation: Should the devices be regulated as a drug? As a tobacco product? Should flavorings be limited? Should advertising be restricted? Regulatory agencies in Australia, Brazil, Canada, the EU, and the United States are actively working on these issues.

Sources: Duff Wilson, "Cigarette Giants in Global Fight on Tighter Rules," *The New York Times* (November 13, 2010); World Health Organization Framework Convention on Tobacco Control, www.who.int/fctc/en/; Saundra Young, "FDA Proposes Crackdown on e-cigarettes," CNN (April 24, 2014).

Methods of Transacting International Business

A U.S. business that wants to engage in international trade is presented with an almost limitless array of possibilities. Choosing a method of doing business in foreign countries not only requires understanding the factors normally involved in selecting an organization and operating a business domestically but also demands an appreciation of the international trade perspective. Depending upon the country, type of export, and amount of export involved in a particular transaction, international trade may involve direct foreign sales, licensing agreements, franchise agreements, or direct foreign investment.

FOREIGN SALES

Do learn more about the traditions, culture, and etiquette of a host nation before you travel, including business card protocol.

The most common approach for a manufacturer to use when trying to enter foreign markets is to sell goods directly to buyers located in other countries. However, with foreign sales, increased uncertainty over the ability to enforce the buyer's promise to pay for goods often requires that more complex arrangements for payment be made than with the usual domestic sale. International sales involve many risky legal issues. Commonly, an **irrevocable letter of credit** is used to ensure payment. Transactions using such a letter involve, in addition to a seller and buyer, an *issuing bank* in the buyer's country. The buyer obtains a commitment from the bank to advance (pay) a specified amount (i.e., the price of the goods) upon receipt, from the carrier, of a **bill of lading,** stating that the goods have been shipped. The issuing bank's commitment to pay is given, not to the seller directly, but to a *confirming bank* located in the United States from which the seller obtains payment. The confirming bank forwards the bill of lading to the issuing bank in order to obtain reimbursement of the funds that have been paid to the seller. The issuing bank releases the bill of lading to the buyer after it has been paid, and with the bill of lading the buyer is able to obtain the goods from the carrier. Use of a letter of credit in the transaction thus reduces the uncertainties involved. The buyer need not pay the seller for goods prior to shipment, and the seller can obtain payment for the goods immediately upon shipment.

There is no room in documentary transactions for substantial performance. All of the duties and responsibilities of parties must be evaluated based upon the documents tendered, and these documents must comply *strictly* with the letter of credit.

LICENSES OR FRANCHISES

In appropriate circumstances, a domestic firm may choose to grant a foreign firm the means to produce and sell its product. The typical method for controlling these transfers of information is the **license** or **franchise** contract. In this manner, intangible property rights, such as patents, copyrights, trademarks, or manufacturing processes, are transferred in exchange for royalties in the foreign country. A licensing arrangement allows the international business to enter a foreign market without any direct foreign investment. Licensing often is used as a transitional technique for firms expanding international operations since the risks are greater than with foreign sales but considerably less than with direct foreign investment. Licensing and franchise agreements also must follow the local laws where they operate.

sidebar 12.9

Successful International Franchising Ventures

Each day, McDonald's serves an average of 70 million customers in over 100 countries.

Subway is one of the fastest growing franchises with over 42,949 restaurants in 108 countries.

Yum! Brands Inc. has more than 37,000 restaurants in more than 110 countries and territories. Their restaurant brands are KFC, Pizza Hut, Taco Bell and Long John Silver's.

Licensing technology or the sale of a product to a foreign firm is a way to expand the company's market without the need for substantial capital. The foreign firm may agree to this arrangement because it lacks sufficient research and development capability or the management skills or marketing strategies to promote the product alone. Of course, as with all international trade agreements, there is some level of risk. The licensor must take care to restrict the use of the product or technology to agreed-upon geographic areas and must take adequate steps to protect the confidential information that is licensed to the foreign firm so that third parties cannot exploit it.

DIRECT FOREIGN INVESTMENT

As a business increases its level of international trade, it may find that creation of a **foreign subsidiary** is necessary. Most countries will permit a foreign firm to conduct business only if a national (individual or firm) of the host country is designated as its legal representative. Since this designation may create difficulties in control and result in unnecessary expense, the usual practice for multinational corporations is to create a foreign subsidiary in the host country. The form of subsidiary most closely resembling a U.S. corporation is known as a *société anonyme (S.A.)* or, in German-speaking countries, an *Aktiengesellschaft (AG)*. Other forms of subsidiaries may also exist that have characteristics of limited liability of the owners and fewer formalities in their creation and operation.

Creation of a foreign subsidiary may pose considerable risk to the domestic parent firm by subjecting it to foreign laws and the jurisdiction of foreign courts. An industrial accident in Bhopal, India, where hundreds of people were killed and thousands injured as a result of toxic gas leaks from a chemical plant, resulted in lawsuits against both the Indian subsidiary corporation and Union Carbide, the parent firm in the United States. Union Carbide agreed to pay more than $450 million to settle outstanding claims and compensate the victims of the disaster.

In many instances, however, the only legal or political means a firm has to invest directly in a foreign country is to engage in a **joint venture** with an entity from that host country. A host country's participant may be a private enterprise or, especially in developing countries, a government agency or government-owned corporation. Many foreign countries favor joint ventures because they allow local individuals and firms to participate in the benefits of economic growth and decrease the risk of foreign domination of local industry. Many of the developing countries require that the local partner have majority equity control of the venture and also insist on joint ventures with government participation.

Chiquita Brands International: Payments to Death Squads for "Protection"

Chiquita Brands International pled guilty to doing business with the United Self-Defense Forces of Colombia (UAC), a right-wing paramilitary group in Colombia. Prosecutors said the banana company made $1.7 million in "protection payments" to this death squad, which is reportedly responsible for some of Colombia's worst massacres. In 2001, the U.S. State Department declared that UAC was an "international terrorist group," making it a violation of U.S. law to conduct business with the group. To settle the charges, Chiquita paid $25 million, arguing that it had no choice but to pay protection money to prevent the UAC from turning death squads loose on its banana workers.

Families of over 350 people thought to have been killed by UAC are suing Chiquita in U.S. federal court seeking $7.86 billion in civil damages. The families claim that Chiquita aided and abetted terrorism, war crimes, and crimes against humanity because of its financial support of UAC. In May 2011, the seven pending lawsuits were consolidated into one action involving allegations of over 4,000 killings of Colombian nationals. In June 2011, the federal judge in Florida overseeing the litigation denied Chiquita's motion to dismiss some of the claims brought under the ATCA and Torture Victim Protection Act. The judge rejected Chiquita's argument that the case should be dismissed because it could have foreign policy implications.

Colombia's attorney general has also threatened to seek extradition of eight Chiquita executives to face criminal prosecution.

LO 12-5

Resolving International Disputes

International law can be complicated, and a single business transaction may involve several companies in different nations. For example, a contract dispute between a Chinese manufacturer, an American wholesaler, and a Canadian retailer could potentially involve the law of all three countries. Which law controls? What jurisdiction has the power to resolve the dispute? The answers to these questions could affect the outcome of the case. As such, most international contracts contain choice of law and forum provisions to eliminate this uncertainty. This section addresses the limitations on suing foreign governments in the United States, issues raised when suing foreign firms in the United States, and international arbitration options.

ALIEN TORT STATUTE

The ATS is viewed by some as a way to hold U.S. companies responsible for their participation in human rights abuses abroad.

The **Alien Tort Statute (ATS),** enacted in 1789, grants jurisdiction to U.S. federal district courts over "any civil action by an alien for a tort only, committed in violation of the law of nations or a treaty of the United States." For nearly 200 years, the law lapsed into obscurity. In the last 20 years, however, it has been revived in a number of human rights contexts, including claims brought against U.S. global companies. An essential aspect of a successful claim under the ATS is to demonstrate that the acts committed violate the law of nations. This prompts many unanswered legal questions in the international labor context. What constitutes the "law of nations"? In general, the law of nations is embodied in international agreements, treaties, and conventions. ATS actions have been alleged against many

U.S. companies, including Bridgestone, Chevron, Del Monte, Drummond Company, DynCorp, ExxonMobil, Gap Inc., Texaco Inc., Unocal Corp., Walmart, and, most recently, Yahoo. Claims typically involve allegations of forced labor, but may also include other human rights abuses such as murder, rape, torture, unlawful detention, and kidnapping. It is not unusual for these cases to also allege that acts were committed by paramilitaries hired by the company.

The legal landscape shifted substantially, however, with the Supreme Court decision *Kiobel v. Royal Dutch Petroleum* (see Case 12.1). Pursuant to this case, it is not very difficult to litigate human rights claims using the ATS.

case 12.1

KIOBEL v. ROYAL DUTCH PETROLEUM, CO.
569 U.S. ___ (2013)

The petitioners, Nigerian nationals residing in the United States, filed suit in federal court under the Alien Tort Statute (AT) alleging that respondents (certain Dutch, British, and Nigerian corporations) aided and abetted the Nigerian government in committing violations of the law of nations in Nigeria.

The District Court dismissed several of the petitioners' claims, but on interlocutory appeal. The Second Circuit dismissed the entire complaint, reasoning that the law of nations does not recognize corporate liability.

The U.S. Supreme Court granted certiorari and ordered supplemental briefing on whether and under what circumstances courts may recognize a cause of action under the ATS, for violations of the law of nations occurring within the territory of a sovereign other than the United States.

ROBERTS, C.J.: The question presented is whether and under what circumstances courts may recognize a cause of action under the Alien Tort Statute, for violations of the law of nations occurring within the territory of a sovereign other than the United States. . . .

Throughout the 1990's, the complaint alleges, Nigerian military and police forces attacked Ogoni villages, beating, raping, killing, and arresting residents and destroying or looting property. Petitioners further allege that respondents aided and abetted these atrocities by, among other things, providing the Nigerian forces with food, transportation, and compensation, as well as by allowing the Nigerian military to use respondents' property as a staging ground for the attacks. . . .

According to petitioners, respondents violated the law of nations by aiding and abetting the Nigerian Government in committing (1) extrajudicial killings; (2) crimes against humanity; (3) torture and cruel treatment; (4) arbitrary arrest and detention; (5) violations of the rights to life, liberty, security, and association; (6) forced exile; and (7) property destruction. . . .

The question here is not whether petitioners have stated a proper claim under the ATS, but whether a claim may reach conduct occurring in a territory of a foreign sovereign. Respondents contend that the claims under the ATS do not, relying primarily on a canon of statutory interpretation knows as the presumption against extraterritorial application. The canon provides that "[w]hen a statute gives no clear indication of an extraterritorial application, it has none" . . . and reflects the "presumption that United States law governs domestically but does not rule the world." . . .

Indeed, the danger of unwarranted judicial interference in the conduct of foreign policy is magnified in the context of the ATS, because the question is not what Congress has done but instead what courts may do. This court in *Sosa* repeatedly stressed the need for judicial caution in considering which claims could be brought under the ATS, in light of foreign policy concerns. . . .

The question under *Sosa is* not whether a federal court has jurisdiction to entertain a cause of action provided by foreign or even international law. The question is instead whether the court has authority to recognize a cause of action under U.S. law to enforce a norm of international law. . . . In the end, nothing in the test of the ATS evinces the requisite clear intention of extraterritoriality. Nor does the historical background against which the ATS was enacted overcome the presumption against application to conduct in the territory of another sovereign. . . . This court has generally treated the high seas the same as foreign soil for purposes of the presumption against extraterritorial application. . . .

Finally, there is no indication that the ATS was passed to make the United States a uniquely hospitable forum for the enforcement of international norms. . . .

We therefore conclude that the presumption against extraterritoriality applies to claims under the ATS, and that nothing in the stature rebuts that presumption . . . and petitioners' case seeking relief for violations of the law of nations occurring outside the United States is barred. . . . On these facts, all the relevant conduct took place outside of the United States. And even where the claims touch and concern the territory of the United States, they must do so with sufficient force to displace the presumption against extraterritorial application. . . . Corporations are often present in many countries, and it would reach too far to say that more corporate presences suffices.

The judgment of the Court of Appeals is affirmed.

KEY POINTS

- In accordance with *Kiobel*, the ATS only applies to conduct within the United States or on the high seas. Arguably, however, if a substantial aspect of the "relevant conduct" occurs within the United States along with acts outside of the United States, a claim may be sustainable.
- The Supreme Court also found that there was nothing in the history of the ATS demonstrating the intention to make the United States a forum for the enforcement of international norms.

SUING FOREIGN GOVERNMENTS IN THE UNITED STATES

The doctrine of **sovereign immunity** provides that a foreign sovereign is immune from suit in the United States. Under the doctrine of sovereign immunity, the foreign sovereign claims to be immune from suit entirely based on its status as a state.

Until approximately 1952, this notion was absolute. From 1952 until 1976, U.S. courts adhered to a *restrictive theory* under which immunity existed with regard to sovereign or public acts but not with regard to private or commercial acts. In 1976, Congress enacted the **Foreign Sovereign Immunities Act (FSIA)**, which codifies this restrictive theory and rejects immunity for *commercial acts* carried on in the United States or having direct effects in this country.

The Supreme Court held that the doctrine should not be extended to foreign governments acting in a commercial capacity and "should not be extended to include the repudiation of a purely commercial obligation owed by a foreign sovereign or by one of its commercial instrumentalities." This interpretation recognizes that governments also may act in a private or commercial capacity and, when doing so, will be subjected to the same rules of law as are applicable to private individuals. A nationalization of assets, however, probably will be considered an act in the "public interest" and immune from suit under the FSIA.

Sovereignty is defined as the supreme, absolute, and uncontrollable power by which any state is governed.

SUING FOREIGN FIRMS IN THE UNITED STATES

As foreign products and technology are imported into the United States, disputes may arise over either the terms of contract or the performance of the goods. To sue a foreign firm in the United States, the Supreme Court held that the plaintiff must establish "minimum contacts" between the foreign defendant and the forum court. The plaintiff must demonstrate that exercise of personal jurisdiction over the defendant "does not offend traditional notions of fair play and substantial justice."

Once the plaintiff decides to sue in the United States, he or she also must comply with the terms of the Hague Service Convention when serving the foreign defendant notice of the lawsuit. The Hague Service Convention is a treaty that was formulated "to provide a simpler way to serve process abroad, to assure that defendants sued in foreign jurisdictions would receive actual and timely notice of suit, and to facilitate proof of service abroad." Many countries, including the United States, follow this convention. The primary requirement of the agreement is to require each nation to establish a central authority to process requests for service of documents from other countries. After the central authority receives the request in proper form, it must serve the documents by a method prescribed by the internal law of the receiving state or by a method designated by the requester and compatible with the law.

See Sidebar 12.11 for an example of the reach of U.S. law.

> Although punitive damages may be awarded in U.S. courts against a foreign company doing business in the United States, it may be difficult or impossible to enforce the award in the company's home country. Outside of the United States, very few countries allow punitive damage awards, which are viewed as a "peculiarity of American law."

---

sidebar 12.11

The Reach of U.S. Law: *Spector v. Norwegian Cruise Line, Ltd.* 545 U.S. 119 (2005)

Issue: Whether foreign-flagged cruise ships serving U.S. ports must comply with the public accommodations provisions in Title III of the Americans with Disabilities Act (ADA).

Key Facts: Disabled plaintiffs and their companions alleged that physical barriers on the Norwegian Cruise Line Ltd. (NCL) ships denied them access to various equipment, programs, and facilities on the ships. They sought injunctive relief requiring NCL to remove certain barriers that obstructed their access to the ships' facilities.

Procedural History: The district court found that foreign-flagged cruise ships *are* subject to the ADA. The Fifth Circuit Court of Appeals *reversed.*

Outcome: The U.S. Supreme Court reversed, holding that Title III of the ADA is applicable to foreign-flagged cruise ships in U.S. waters.

INTERNATIONAL ARBITRATION

International businesses now are focusing on the need for new methods of resolving international commercial disputes and, as a result, are frequently resorting to the use of arbitration. The advantages of arbitration in domestic transactions, previously discussed in Chapter 5, are more pronounced in international transactions where differences in languages and legal systems make litigation costs still more costly.

sidebar 12.12

Chevron and Texaco in Ecuador: $18 Billion Judgment

In February 2011, an Ecuadorian court in Lago Agrio rendered an $18 billion judgment against Chevron for alleged environmental damage. Chevron's subsidiary, Texaco Petroleum Co. (TexPet), conducted oil operations in Chevron. Chevron claims that TexPet fully remediated its share of environmental impacts arising from oil production and that any remaining environmental issues are the responsibility of Ecuador's state-owned oil company, Petroecuador.

Chevron is appealing the Ecuadorian verdict on the grounds that it "lacks scientific merit and that it ignores overwhelming evidence of fraud and corruption." Chevron also claims that it was not afforded due process in Ecuador.

SUBSEQUENT EVENTS

- Southern District of New York Judge Lewis Kaplan issued a preliminary injunction "enjoining and restraining" the plaintiffs from enforcing the ruling anywhere in the world.

- An International Tribunal from the Permanent Court of Arbitration in The Hague ordered Ecuador to suspend the enforcement or recognition of the judgment.

- Chevron filed a Racketeer Influenced and Corrupt Organizations Act (RICO) against Steven Donziger (the plaintiffs' lead U.S. lawyer), Ecuadorian lawyer Pablo Fajardo, environmental activist Luis Yanza, and three organizations, including Amazon Watch.

- In March 2014, Judge Kaplan found Donzinger liable under RICO. Chevron subsequently asked Judge Kaplan to order Donzinger to pay $32.3 million in legal fees incurred in connection with the RICO case.

The documentary *Crude* presents the controversial story of the environmental damage and the ensuing complicated litigation.

The United Nations Convention on the Recognition and Enforcement of Foreign Arbitral Awards of 1958 (New York Convention), adopted in more than 50 countries, encourages the use of arbitration in commercial agreements made by companies in the signatory countries. Under the New York Convention it is easier to compel arbitration, where previously agreed upon by the parties, and to enforce the arbitrator's award once a decision is reached.

Once the parties to an international transaction agree to arbitrate disputes between them, the U.S. courts are reluctant to disturb that agreement. In the case of *Mitsubishi Motors v. Soler Chrysler-Plymouth* (1985) the Supreme Court upheld an international agreement even where it required the parties to arbitrate all disputes, including federal antitrust claims. The Court decided that the international character of the undertaking required enforcement of the arbitration clause even as to the antitrust claims normally heard in a U.S. court.

There are many advantages to arbitrating international disputes. The arbitration process likely will be more streamlined and easier for the parties to understand than litigating the dispute in a foreign court. Moreover, the parties can avoid the unwanted publicity that often results in open court proceedings. Finally, the parties can agree, before the dispute even arises, on a neutral and objective third party to act as the arbitrator. Several organizations, such as the International Chamber of Commerce in Paris and the Court of International Arbitration in London, provide arbitration services for international disputes.

China International Economic and Trade Arbitration Commission
The China International Economic and Trade Arbitration Commission (CIETAC) is a permanent arbitration institution established to resolve economic and trade disputes arising in China. The parties must agree in writing to submit their dispute for arbitration. Here is a sample arbitration clause recommended by CIETAC:

> Any dispute arising from or in connection with this Contract shall be submitted to CIETAC for arbitration, which shall be conducted in accordance with the Commission's arbitration rules in effect at the time of applying for arbitration. The arbitral always is final and binding upon both parties.

Frequently, the parties will also stipulate the location of the arbitration; the language of the proceeding; the number of arbitrators; the nationality of the arbitrators; the method of selecting the arbitrators; and the law governing the contract. For more information, including a current list of arbitrators and their areas of expertise, see www.cietac.org.

The World Intellectual Property Organization: Arbitration and Mediation Center
The World Intellectual Property Organization (WIPO) Arbitration and Mediation Center hears cases involving domain name disputes and cybersquatting. The Uniform Domain Name Dispute Resolution Policy (UDRP) went into effect in 1999. Since that time, over 8,350 disputes involving 127 countries and some 16,000 domain names have been handled by the WIPO.

Many UDRP cases involve high-value, well-known brands. In fact, cases involving most of the 100 largest international brands by value have been heard by the WIPO. Well-known individuals, including Madonna, Julia Roberts, Eminem, Pamela Anderson, J K Rowling, Morgan Freeman, and Lance Armstrong have used the WIPO's services. For more information about WIPO cases, see www.wipo.int.

Key Terms

Agreement on Trade-Related Aspects of Intellectual Property Rights (TRIPS) 363
Alien Tort Statute (ATS) 370
Bill of lading 368
Central America-Dominican Republic Free Trade Agreement (CAFTA-DR) 366
Convention on the International Sale of Goods (CISG) 366
European Union (EU) 364
Export controls 357
Expropriation 357

Foreign Corrupt Practices Act (FCPA) 353
Foreign Sovereign Immunities Act (FSIA) 372
Foreign subsidiary 369
Franchise 368
General Agreement on Tariffs and Trade (GATT) 363
International Court of Justice (ICJ) 360
International Monetary Fund (IMF) 363
Irrevocable letter of credit 368

Joint venture 369
License 368
Nationalization 357
North American Free Trade Agreement (NAFTA) 366
Private international law 360
Public international law 360
Sovereign immunity 372
United Nations 362
World Bank 363
World Trade Organization (WTO) 362

Review Questions and Problems

Risks Involved in International Trade

1. *Pressures for Bribes*

   XYZ Company, a U.S. firm, is seeking to obtain business in Indonesia. XYZ learns that one of its major competitors, a German firm, is offering a key Indonesian governmental official a trip around the world for choosing their firm in the transaction. Can XYZ report this bribe to the Department of Justice and have the German firm prosecuted under the FCPA?

2. *Expropriation and Nationalization*

   Explain the "modern traditional theory" of compensation related to the taking of private property by a foreign government.

3. *Export Controls*

   (a) Why is the future of export controls in doubt?

   (b) What are some of the dangers associated with having an inadequate export control regime as nations combat terrorism?

International Law and Organizations

4. *Sources of International Law*

   (a) What are the essential differences between the ICJ and the U.S. Supreme Court?

   (b) How does the ICJ determine international law?

5. *International Organizations*

   (a) What are the three major principles of the WTO?

   (b) Has adherence to those principles improved international trade?

   (c) Describe the organization of the EU.

   (d) How is it similar to the structure of the government of the United States?

6. *Major Agreements Affecting Trade*

   (a) How does the CISG facilitate international sales of goods?

   (b) How do free trade agreements, such as NAFTA and CAFTA-DR, benefit U.S. businesses?

Methods of Transacting International Business

7. *Foreign Sales*

   BMW, a German buyer, opens an irrevocable letter of credit in favor of Goodyear, an American seller, for the purchase of tires on BMW automobiles. BMW confirms the letter of credit with Goodyear's bank in New York, JPMorgan Chase. How will the seller obtain payment?

8. *Licenses or Franchises*

   (a) How should a licensor protect its investment in a foreign country?

   (b) Is licensing a less risky approach for the seller than direct foreign investment?

9. *Direct Foreign Investment*

   What are the advantages and disadvantages of a joint venture with a foreign firm?

Resolving International Disputes

10. *Alien Tort Claims Act*

    Several citizens of Colombia filed an action in the United States against Super Bananas, a U.S. company that owns the banana plantation where the individuals worked. In their complaint, the plaintiffs allege that they were threatened, beaten, and tortured by Super Banana's security guards when they tried to unionize. Do they have an actionable claim under the ATCA?

11. *Suing Foreign Governments in the United States*

Belgium arrests an American citizen, while he is visiting Brussels, on suspicion that he is an international drug smuggler. After a thorough investigation, Belgium realizes that it has arrested the wrong person. Can the American citizen successfully sue Belgium in the United States for false arrest?

12. *Suing Foreign Firms in the United States*

What is the primary requirement of the Hague Service Convention and how does it help a plaintiff when filing a lawsuit?

13. *International Arbitration*

Why are arbitration clauses in international agreements favored by the courts and likely to be enforced when conflicts arise between the contracting parties?

business *discussions*

1. XYZ Company is a U.S. firm that makes communication software used in a variety of consumer goods manufactured and sold in the United States. XYZ recently learned that one of the manufacturing firms it supplies, ABC Company, is exporting finished goods to a country where U.S. goods and component parts are prohibited because of numerous conflicts with the U.S. government.

Does XYZ have any moral or legal responsibility in this case?

How should XYZ protect itself under these circumstances?

Should American business practices be impacted by conflicts between governments?

2. Hello-Hello is a U.S. telecommunications company with global operations. Sophia is an assistant vice president of Hello-Hello. She is dispatched to China to handle two situations. First, a shipment of 500 cases of cell phones is stalled in customs. She is assigned the task of getting the goods out of customs and into retail stores. Sophia learns through the grapevine that customs officials expect $5 (U.S.) per case to help "speed things along." Second, she is instructed by her boss to do "whatever is necessary" to secure cell tower permits from local officials in two outlying areas. A local agent suggests that she give him $500,000 in cash so they can get to know the officials better. When Sophia asks him what the money will be used for, he tells her that he wants to take them out to dinner, maybe on a weekend outing in the city, and that he generally needs "flexibility."

Should Sophia call the home office to ask for advice?

If her boss says to pay the money, should she do it?

What potential legal problems are presented by the payments?

13 Criminal Law and Business

Learning Objectives

In this chapter you will learn:

13-1. To recognize the basic terms and procedures relevant to criminal conduct.

13-2. To explain Fourth, Fifth, and Sixth Amendment rights.

13-3. To identify the elements of specific crimes.

13-4. To understand the far-reaching impact of criminal behavior as the same acts can give rise to both civil and criminal liability.

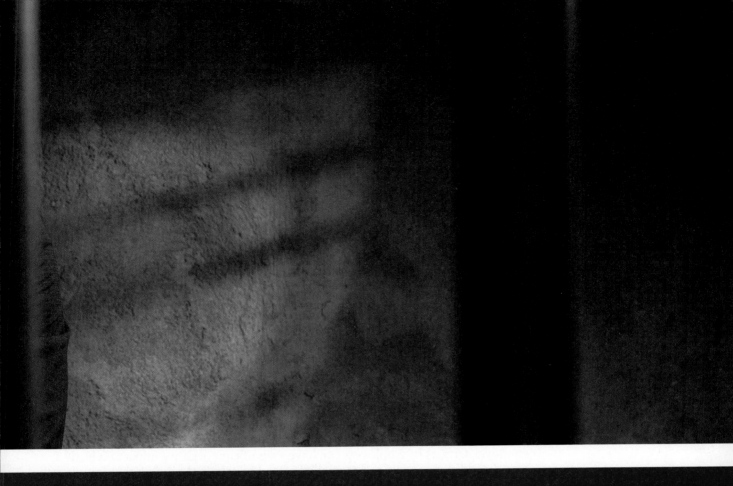

Ongoing government investigations of financial fraud and bribery of foreign officials is prompting many large law firms to increasing their capacity to handle white-collar defense.

Just as civil law protects an individual's property, criminal law punishes wrongdoers who affect the ownership of property. Crimes are wrongs against society, and the government has the power to impose punishment and fines on individuals and corporations convicted of crimes. Federal and state penal codes define criminal acts and omissions.

Criminal conduct is extremely destructive for business. In the most extreme cases, legal costs and settlements can cost billions of dollars. The worldwide crisis, which was estimated to cost over $20 trillion, resulted in millions of people losing investments, homes, and jobs. Similarly, the fall of Bernie Madoff, the energy firm Enron, and the telecommunications company WorldCom, illustrate the devastating effects of criminal wrongdoing. Documentaries, such as *"Inside Job"* and *Enron: The Smartest Guys in the Room,* detail some of these effects and the impact on business, employees, consumers, and investors.

Civil law allows individuals to bring actions for damages and criminal law allows society, or "the people," to punish wrongdoers. Some crimes, such as rape or murder, are said to be *malum in se* or inherently wrong. They are universally recognized as wrongful conduct that society must punish even where the victim is a single person.

A legislative body can, however, decide that it is in the interest of society to criminalize conduct that is not inherently wrongful. By passing laws declaring certain conduct to be criminal, legislative bodies purport to act in the interest of all society. An example of such a crime is price fixing among competitors. In 1890, price fixing was made illegal by the Sherman Antitrust Act when it became apparent that such behavior was an impediment to fair competition.

Crimes can involve acts of violence, such as arson, burglary, and robbery. Businesses are often the target of these crimes, which are frequently perpetrated by persons who have no connection to the business. The terrorist attack on the World Trade Center is an example of a crime of violence against the resident businesses and their employees. That crime also immediately impacted many of the businesses in New York City, as well as many international businesses, ultimately affecting the economies of countries throughout the world.

Many crimes against businesses do not involve acts of violence. Sometimes, employees of a business will commit nonviolent crimes against their employer. Crimes by employees can have a significant negative impact on business. In addition, society is financially harmed by criminal conduct that injures business. In the 1930s, Edwin H. Sullivan coined the term **white-collar crime** to apply to criminals of high socioeconomic status, such as corporate executives who commit fraud. Today, *white-collar crime* usually means any illegal offense that occurs in a business or professional setting. Such crimes are generally committed for personal financial gain. These crimes are not dependent on the threat of physical force or violence. They are committed to obtain money, property, or services; to avoid the payment or loss of money, property or services; or to achieve a personal or business advantage. White-collar crime costs business over $100 billion annually. See Table 13.1 for examples of white-collar crimes.

"More than 1 in 100 American adults are in prison."

—Pew Center on the States

table 13.1 Examples of White-Collar Crimes

Accounting fraud	Forgery	Obstruction of justice
Bankruptcy fraud	Income tax evasion	Price fixing
Bribery	Insider trading	Racketeering
Conspiracy	Kickbacks	Securities fraud
Counterfeiting	Larceny	Wire fraud
Embezzlement	Mail fraud	
False statements	Money laundering	

Employees may commit white-collar crime for personal gain or to harm the business. Other times, the criminal activity benefits the business and there is no intention to harm others, such as competitors or customers. White-collar crime takes many forms. Common examples include embezzling money, making electronic advances to fictitious employees, accepting kickbacks from suppliers in exchange for orders, rigging bids, selling trade secrets, falsifying inventories to conceal theft, and paying false invoices. White-collar crime affects the targeted companies as well as consumers who must pay higher prices to make up for the losses.

Although a corporation cannot be put in jail or in a prison, it can be fined and can face other criminal penalties. Ordering a company out of business is a type of "death sentence" for business. Individuals found guilty of a crime can be sent to jail or prison, ordered to pay fines, or excluded from certain types of work.

To raise awareness and combat the effects of criminal activity on business, most business schools include courses on business ethics. Most major corporations have ethical codes and extensive compliance programs. Despite these efforts, television and print media regularly depict executives in handcuffs, pictures that mark a surge in white-collar crime in recent years.

Many of the examples of criminal activity in this chapter are the result of greed replacing integrity. The purpose of this chapter is to help you understand what activity is criminal, the penalties that can result, and the effect on business. See Sidebar 13.1 for examples of successful prosecutions.

sidebar 13.1

Handcuffs and Jail Time

SUCCESSFUL PROSECUTIONS: A SAMPLE OF CONVICTIONS AND GUILTY PLEAS

- Phillip R. Bennett, former Refco Inc. CEO, having pled guilty to fraud (in connection with hiding hundreds of millions of dollars from investors who bought stock) could be sentenced to up to 315 years in prison under federal sentencing guidelines.

- Conrad Black, Hollinger International CEO and chairman, convicted for obstruction of justice and mail fraud, sentenced to 6½ years in prison.

- L. Dennis Kozlowski, former chief executive of Tyco International, convicted for grand larceny, conspiracy, falsifying business records, and securities fraud, $97 million in restitution, $70 million in fines, and 8⅓ to 25 years in prison.

- F. David Radler, COO of Hollinger International, guilty plea to a mail and wire fraud charge in exchange for 29-month prison sentence and a $250,000 fine.

- John J. Rigas, founder of Adelphia Communications, and his son, Timothy, convicted for looting the company of $2.3 billion in assets and misrepresenting the company's health to investors, respectively 15 and 20 years in prison. The Rigas family also agreed to forfeit 95 percent of their holdings (about $1.5 billion) to compensate investors.

- Richard Scrushy, founder and CEO of HealthSouth Corp., convicted for paying $500,000 to former Alabama Governor Don Siegelman's campaign for a state lottery in exchange for a seat on a state hospital regulatory board. Scrushy was sentenced to 6 years and 10 months in prison, ordered to pay $267,000 in restitution, 3 years' probation, and a fine of $150,000.

Terms and Procedures

LO 13-1 ## CLASSIFICATIONS OF CRIMINAL CONDUCT

There are several ways to classify criminal conduct. Some crimes are violations of federal law, some crimes violate state laws, and other crimes violate both federal and state laws. Although many crimes involve violence, nonviolent conduct may also be criminal.

Crimes are classified as **felonies** or **misdemeanors.** This classification is based on the punishment imposed if the person is convicted of the alleged crime. Felonies are punishable by fine or imprisonment in a penitentiary for a period of one year or more. Misdemeanors are punishable by a fine or jail sentence of less than one year.

Felony cases are commenced by a grand jury **indictment;** misdemeanor cases are usually commenced when the government files a charge called an **information.** Grand juries are different from petit juries. A grand jury determines if there is sufficient evidence to warrant a trial. A petit jury determines the guilt or innocence of the accused. The role of the grand jury is discussed in more detail later in this chapter.

BASIC CONCEPTS

Intent is an important element of many criminal laws. Many laws use either the term **willfully** or **knowingly** to define criminal intent. If an act is done willfully, it is committed voluntarily and purposefully with the specific intent to do something. A person does not act willfully if there is a good-faith misunderstanding of the requirements of the law. Similarly, if an act is done knowingly, it is voluntary and intentional, not because of mistake or accident.

Knowledge usually cannot be established by demonstrating that the accused was negligent, careless, or foolish; knowledge, however, can be inferred if the accused deliberately ignored the existence of a fact.

Some laws provide that reckless conduct is a crime even though the one doing the act does not intend to do harm. Reckless driving is an obvious example of such a crime. Reckless disregard for the truth is often the basis of white-collar criminal conduct.

Criminal cases are brought or prosecuted by public officials such as a U.S. attorney or a state's attorney (often called a *district attorney*) on behalf of the people. In the case of federal crimes, the United States brings an action against the individual defendant. Imagine your feelings if a case style read: "The United States v. you."

In a criminal case, the defendant has three possible pleas to enter: *guilty, not guilty,* or **nolo contendere.** The last plea, Latin for "no contest," allows sentencing just as if the defendant pleaded guilty or was found guilty. Pleading "nolo," as it is sometimes referred to, advantages the defendant by avoiding the cost of trial and avoiding the effect of a guilty plea or finding in a subsequent civil action. Criminal convictions may provide a basis for civil damage suits. This can be avoided by the nolo contendere plea. The high cost of white-collar crime is illustrated in Sidebar 13.2.

In 1973, Vice President Spiro Agnew made one of the most famous *nolo contendere* pleas (to tax evasion) on the condition that he resign from office.

sidebar 13.2

The Price of the $11 Billion Accounting Fraud at WorldCom

Bernard J. Ebbers, the former chief executive officer, president, and a director of WorldCom Inc., was convicted of securities fraud, conspiracy, and filing false documents with regulators. The acts at the heart of the case were fraudulent adjustments to WorldCom's books and records; false statements and misleading omissions in WorldCom's SEC filings and public statements; and fraud in connection with the purchase and sale of securities.

Federal prosecutors argued that Ebbers was motivated to commit fraud during a time when there was tremendous pressure on the company's share price.

Ebbers's personal fortune was largely based on WorldCom shares and he borrowed nearly $400 million using the shares as collateral.

Scott Sullivan, former WorldCom CFO, testified that Ebbers knew about the massive accounting fraud. Sullivan also testified that Ebbers intimidated him into committing fraud so that the company could meet Wall Street expectations.

Ebbers was sentenced to serve 25 years in prison. This $11 billion accounting scandal also resulted in nearly 17,000 employees losing their jobs.

Recommended Reading: Cynthia Cooper, *Extraordinary Circumstances: The Journey of a Corporate Whistleblower* (Wiley, 2008).

THE GRAND JURY

The Fifth Amendment to the U.S. Constitution provides that before anyone can be tried for a capital or otherwise infamous crime, there must be a presentment or an indictment by a grand jury. This protection prevents political trials and unjustified prosecutions by placing a group of citizens between prosecutors and persons accused of major crimes.

A grand jury normally consists of 23 citizens who live within the jurisdiction of the court that would try one accused of a crime. At least 16 persons must be present for the grand jury to hear evidence and vote on cases. For an indictment to be returned, a majority of the grand jury must find that a crime has been committed and that the evidence is sufficient to warrant the accused's standing trial. This determination is **probable cause.**

The grand jury does not attempt to determine if the accused is guilty, only that probable cause exists to believe the accused committed the crime. Since probable cause is the standard for grand jury action, it is not difficult to obtain an indictment. Even an indicted person, however, is entitled to the **presumption of innocence**—to be presumed innocent until found guilty by a petit jury.

Grand juries also serve as an investigative body and occupy a unique role in our criminal justice system. Law enforcement officials such as agents for the Federal Bureau of Investigation, U.S. Customs Service, U.S. Postal Service, and Secret Service often act as arms of federal grand juries investigating possible criminal activities. Persons who are the targets or subjects of investigations may be called before grand juries and may be questioned under oath about possible illegal conduct. In such cases, the persons subpoenaed to testify before the grand jury are entitled to invoke their Fifth Amendment privilege against compulsory self-incrimination and refuse to answer questions. Although they are entitled to have the benefit of legal advice, defense counsel is not allowed to accompany a witness before a grand jury. However, counsel may be outside the grand jury room and thus available for consultation whenever a witness desires it.

> It is a felony for prosecutors, court reporters, and grand jury members to leak testimony heard in grand jury proceedings.

After testifying before the grand jury in the *Valerie Plame case*, *New York Times* reporter Judith Miller broke her silence and spoke with reporters on the courthouse steps.

Grand jurors may also subpoena business records. Witnesses may be called and questioned about documents and records delivered in response to a subpoena. However, grand juries are not authorized to engage in arbitrary fishing expeditions and may not select targets of criminal probes out of malice.

Proper functioning of the grand jury system depends upon the secrecy of the proceedings. This secrecy protects the innocent accused from disclosure the accusations made against him or her before the grand jury. In judicial proceedings, however, transcripts of grand jury proceedings may be obtained if necessary to avoid possible injustice. For example, a defendant may use a grand jury transcript at a trial to impeach a witness, to refresh the witness's recollection, or to test his or her credibility. The disclosure of a grand jury transcript is appropriate only in those cases where the need for it outweighs the public interest in secrecy, and the burden of demonstrating this balance rests upon a private party seeking disclosure.

LO 13-2 Constitutional Issues

Before covering the elements of some of the more important business-related crimes, it is essential to understand the protections all individuals have under the U.S. Constitution. These protections are in the Bill of Rights, the first ten amendments to the Constitution. The Bill of Rights was Congress's response to concerns that the Constitution gave too much power to a central government at the expense of the individual citizen. Often referred to as "civil liberties," these rights protect individuals from the power of government, including individuals accused of crimes. The Bill of Rights also protects businesses from excessive regulation. As you study the Fourth, Fifth, and Sixth Amendments to the Constitution, pay particular attention to their impact on the regulatory process.

---

sidebar 13.3

The Fourth Amendment: Exigent Circumstances and Warrantless Searches

Key facts: Police officers followed a suspected drug dealer to an apartment complex. They smelled marijuana outside an apartment door, knocked loudly, and announced their presence. As soon as the officers began knocking, they heard noises coming from the apartment. The officers believed that the noises were consistent with the destruction of evidence. The police announced their intent to enter the apartment, kicked in the door, and found the defendant and drugs in plain view. The trial court denied the defendant's motion to suppress the evidence. He was convicted.

The law: "Exigent circumstances," including the need to prevent the destruction of evidence, permit police officers to conduct a search without first obtaining a warrant. Under the "police-created exigency" doctrine, exigent circumstances do not justify a warrantless search when the exigency is "created" or "manufactured" by the police.

The issue: Does this rule apply when police, by knocking on the door of a residence and announcing their presence, cause the occupants to attempt to destroy evidence?

Holding: Warrantless entry to prevent the destruction of evidence is allowed where the police do not create the exigency through an actual or threatened Fourth Amendment violation. In this case, the conduct of the police prior to their entry into the apartment was lawful and did not violate the Fourth Amendment.

Dissent by Justice Ginsburg: "The Court today arms the police with a way routinely to dishonor the Fourth Amendment's warrant requirement in drug cases. In lieu of presenting their evidence to a neutral magistrate, police officers may now knock, listen, then break the door down, never mind that they had ample time to obtain a warrant. I dissent from the Court's reduction of the Fourth Amendment's force."

Source: *Kentucky v. King,* 131 S. Ct. 1849 (2011).

THE FOURTH AMENDMENT: ILLEGAL SEARCH AND SEIZURE

The Fourth Amendment protects individuals and corporations from **unreasonable searches and seizures** by the government. It primarily protects persons from unwarranted intrusions on their privacy by requiring the police to obtain a court order called a **search warrant.** As a general rule, the search warrant must be obtained by the police prior to a search of a person, any premises, or other property such as the trunk of an automobile. Before a court issues a search warrant, the police must offer evidence that a crime has been committed and there is cause to believe that the intended search will assist in its investigation.

> The Fourth Amendment protects persons and corporations from unreasonable searches and seizures *by the government.*

To protect police officers, courts have held that officers making an arrest do not need a search warrant to search that person and the immediate area around that person for weapons. Officers are given far more latitude in searching an automobile than in searching a person, a home, or a building. The right to search for evidence also extends to the premises of persons not suspected of criminal conduct. Such premises may include offices of newspapers and attorneys. Electronic surveillance may not violate the Fourth Amendment if used pursuant to a court-authorized order. If "exigent circumstances" exist, in which police believe that evidence may be destroyed, they may conduct a search without a warrant. See Sidebar 13.3 for a recent case about this doctrine.

Fourth Amendment protection also extends to certain civil matters. For example, building inspectors do not have the right to inspect for building code violations without a warrant if the owner of the premises objects. The Securities and Exchange Commission (SEC) cannot use confidential reports obtained in the course of its routine operations to establish a violation of federal law. The Occupational Safety and Health Act (OSHA) inspectors must go to court and obtain a search warrant if an owner of a business objects to an inspection. To obtain this warrant, inspectors must show that the standards for conducting an inspection are satisfied; they do not need to show probable cause that a violation exists.

The protection of the Fourth Amendment provides an expectation of privacy. The Supreme Court has said that warrantless searches of junkyards are constitutional because operators of commercial premises in closely regulated industries have a reduced expectation of privacy. In pervasively regulated industries the privacy interests of the business are weakened and government interests in regulating particular businesses are heightened. Generally, a warrantless inspection of commercial premises may well be reasonable within the meaning of the Fourth Amendment, whereas a warrantless inspection of a private residence may be unconstitutional.

> The Fourth Amendment *does not* prohibit drug testing in most workplaces.

Many business operations do not have an **expectation of privacy.** For example, nursing homes that receive Medicaid funds are presumed to have voluntarily consented to warrantless searches. Random surveys for compliance with federal standards should be expected by businesses required to conform to the standards.

Today's increased security at airports and at border crossings does not violate the Fourth Amendment. Neither a warrant, probable cause, nor any level of suspicion is required to search vehicles, persons, or goods arriving in the United States. Presenting oneself at an airport checkpoint is an irrevocable consent to a warrantless search.

Employees of some businesses also do not have Fourth Amendment protection because of public policy. For example, alcohol and drug testing of railroad employees and airline pilots cannot be successfully challenged using the Fourth Amendment.

case 13.1

RILEY v. CALIFORNIA
573 U.S. __ (2014)

Petitioner Riley was stopped for a traffic violation, which eventually led to his arrest on weapons charges. An officer searching Riley in connection with the arrest seized a cell phone from Riley's pants pocket. The officer accessed information on the phone and, based in part on information found in the phone, Riley was charged in connection with a shooting that had occurred a few weeks earlier, and the prosecution also sought enhanced sentence based on Riley's alleged gang membership. Riley moved to suppress all evidence obtained from his cell phone. The trial court denied the motion. Riley was convicted and the California Court of Appeal affirmed the conviction. In the following opinion, the Supreme Court reversed and remanded the case. Justices Scalia, Kennedy, Thomas, Ginsburg, Breyer, Sotomayor, and Kagan joined the majority opinion. Justice Alito filed an opinion concurring in part and concurring in the judgment. Note that this decision also involved a second similar case.

ROBERTS, C.J.: These two cases raise a common question: whether the police may, without a warrant, search digital information on a cell phone seized from an individual who has been arrested. . . .

Petitioner David Riley was stopped by a police officer for driving with expired registration tags. In the course of the stop, the officer also learned that Riley's license had been suspended. . . . An officer searched Riley incident to the arrest and found items associated with the "Bloods" street gang. He also seized a cell phone from Riley's pants pocket. According to Riley's uncontradicted assertion, the phone was a "smart phone," a cell phone with a broad range of other functions based on advanced computing capability, large storage capacity, and Internet connectivity. The officer accessed information on the phone and noticed that some words (presumably in text messages or a contacts list) were preceded by the letters "CK"—a label

that, he believed stood for "Crip Killers," a slang terms for members of the Bloods gang.

At the police station about two hours after the arrest, a detective specializing in gangs further examined the contents of the phone . . . he "went through" Riley's phone "looking for evidence, because . . . gang members will often video themselves with guns or take pictures of themselves with guns." [Incriminating videos and photographs were found on the phone.]

Riley was ultimately charged, in connection with [an] earlier shooting, with firing at an occupied vehicle, assault with a semiautomatic firearm, and attempted murder. The State alleged that Riley had committed those crimes for the benefit of a criminal street gang, an aggravating factor that carries an enhanced sentence. . . .

Prior to trial, Riley moved to suppress all evidence that police obtained from his cell phone. He contended that the searches of the phone violated the Fourth Amendment, because they had been performed without a warrant and were not otherwise justified by exigent circumstances. The trial court rejected the argument . . . Riley was convicted and received an enhanced sentence of 15 years to life in prison. . . .

In 1914, this Court first acknowledged in dictum "the right on the part of the Government, always recognized under English and American law, to search the person of the accused when legally arrested to discover and seize the fruits or evidences of crime." Since that time, it has been well accepted that such a search constitutes an exception to the warrant requirement. Indeed, the label "exception" is something of a misnomer in this context, as warrantless searches incident to an arrest occur with far greater frequency than searches conducted pursuant to a warrant. . . .

These cases require us to decide how the search incident to arrest doctrine applies to modern cell phones, which are now such a pervasive and insistent part of daily life that the proverbial visitor from Mars might conclude that they were an important feature of human anatomy. . . . Cell phones place vast quantities of personal information literally in the hands of individuals. A search of information on a cell phone bears little resemblance to the type of brief physical search considered in [a previous case].

We therefore . . . hold that officers must generally secure a warrant before conducting such a search.

The United States asserts that a search of all data stored on a cell phone is "materially indistinguishable" from searches of physical items [such as a billfold, address book, or purse]. That is like saying a ride on horseback is materially indistinguishable from a flight to the moon. Both are ways of getting from point A to point B, but little else justifies lumping them together.

Modern cell phones, as a category, implicate privacy concerns far beyond those implicated by the search of a cigarette pack, a wallet, or a purse. . . . We cannot deny that our decision today will have an impact on the ability of law enforcement to combat crime. Cell phones have become important tools in facilitating coordination and communication among members of criminal enterprises, and can provide valuable incriminating information about dangerous criminals. Privacy comes at a cost.

Our holding, of course, is not that the information on a cell phone is immune from search; it is instead that a warrant is generally required before such a search, even when a cell phone is seized incident to arrest. We reverse the judgment of the California Court of Appeal and remand the case for further proceedings not inconsistent with this opinion.

KEY POINTS

- In general, the police must obtain a warrant to search a cell phone.
- In cases involving exigent circumstances, such as when there is an immediate risk to public safety or a risk of loss of evidence, police may be able to act without a warrant.
- The digital data stored in cell phones involve a more substantial privacy interest than other items that may be found in an arrestee's pockets.

sidebar 13.4

Know Your *Miranda* Rights

Despite challenges, the rights set forth in *Miranda v. Arizona* (1966) are still the law. If you are taken into custody, the law enforcement officer must read you your "Miranda Rights" and make sure that you understand them.

WARNING OF RIGHTS

1. You have the right to remain silent and refuse to answer questions. Do you understand?
2. Anything you do say may be used against you in a court of law. Do you understand?
3. You have the right to consult an attorney before speaking to the police and to have an attorney present during questioning now or in the future. Do you understand?
4. If you cannot afford an attorney, one will be appointed for you before any questioning if you wish. Do you understand?
5. If you decide to answer questions now without an attorney present you will still have the right to stop answering at any time until you talk to an attorney. Do you understand?
6. Knowing and understanding your rights as I have explained them to you, are you willing to answer my questions without an attorney present?

THE FIFTH AMENDMENT: PROTECTION AGAINST SELF-INCRIMINATION

"The Fifth Amendment" protects the accused from being compelled to testify against himself or herself. See Sidebar 13.4 for an elaboration of Miranda Rights.

The Fifth Amendment is best known for its protection against compulsory self-incrimination. When a person giving testimony pleads "the Fifth," he or she is exercising the right to this protection. The privilege against self-incrimination protects an accused from being compelled to testify against himself or herself. The Fifth Amendment does not protect the accused from being compelled to produce real or physical evidence. Fingerprints can be taken, as can voice samples and bodily fluids. In order to be testimonial and protected, an accused's communication must itself, explicitly or implicitly, relate to a factual assertion or disclosure information. Importantly, criminal suspects must speak up and make it clear that they are invoking their Miranda rights. See Sidebar 13.5; mere silence does not invoke Miranda protections.

Issues concerning the Fifth Amendment protection as it relates to a business may arise when a businessperson is called to testify about a business matter or is served with a subpoena requiring the production of records. A businessperson may not be called upon to testify against himself or herself in any governmental hearing such as a congressional proceeding. But the protection against compulsory self-incrimination does not protect a businessperson from having to produce, in court, records prepared in the ordinary course of business. Since the production of records does not compel oral testimony, the Fifth Amendment does not prevent the use of written evidence, including documents in the hands either of the accused or of someone else such as an accountant. Of course, corporate officials, union officials, and

---

sidebar 13.5

Fifth Amendment Rights: Mere Silence Does Not Invoke Miranda

Key facts: Police advised the murder suspect of his Fifth Amendment Miranda rights. They then interrogated him for several hours. During that time, the defendant did not say that he wanted to remain silent or that he did or did not want to speak with an attorney. He was largely silent, until he was asked "Do you pray to God to forgive you for shooting that boy down?" At that point, the defendant answered, "Yes." He refused to make a written confession and the interrogation ended about 15 minutes later. This statement was used at trial where he was convicted of first-degree murder.

The issue: Should this statement have been excluded at trial? Did the defendant waive his right to remain silent?

Holdings: In this 5-4 decision, the Court held: (1) defendant's silence was insufficient to invoke

his right to remain silent under *Miranda;* (2) the defendant waived his right to remain silent by responding to questions by the interrogating officer; (3) police are not required to obtain a waiver of a defendant's right to remain silent before commencing an interrogation.

Dissent by Justice Sotomayor: In her first major dissent, Justice Sotomayor said that the majority decision created a kind of paradox in which a "suspect who wished to guard his right to remain silent . . . must, counter intuitively, speak." As such, the majority "turns Miranda upside down" and bodes poorly for the fundamental principles that Miranda protects." (Justices Stevens, Ginsburg and Breyer joined the dissent.)

Source: *Berghuis v. Thompkins,* 130 S. Ct. 2250 (2010).

partners cannot be required to give oral testimony if such testimony may tend to incriminate them. However, these individuals must produce subpoenaed documents. Therefore, business records can be obtained even if they are incriminating.

Obviously a corporation or other collective entity cannot be called upon to testify; only individuals can do so. Therefore, the protection against compulsory self-incrimination does not apply to corporations, including professional corporations and partnerships. These collective entities have no Fifth Amendment right to refuse to submit their books and records in response to a subpoena. The only business protected by the Fifth Amendment privilege against compulsory self-incrimination is a sole proprietorship. A closely held corporation with only one shareholder is not protected.

THE FIFTH AMENDMENT: DOUBLE JEOPARDY

The Fifth Amendment provides in part that no "person [shall] be subject for the same offense to be twice put in jeopardy of life or limb." This language is known as the **double jeopardy** clause. Courts do not allow individuals to be tried twice by the same governmental entity for the same crime based on the same factual situation. If an illegal activity violates both federal and state laws, double jeopardy does not prohibit two trials, one in federal court and the other in the state court system. Although federal and state governmental prosecutors may cooperate resulting in only one conviction, the double jeopardy clause does not prevent two prosecutions. In its essence, this clause keeps a U.S. district attorney from having a second trial on the same facts if a defendant is found innocent or has the charges dismissed. The same prohibition of a second trial holds true for state prosecutors also. Note that in civil law, the doctrine of *res judicata* bars subsequent civil actions involving the same parties, claims, demands, or causes of action.

The same offense may give rise to both a criminal prosecution and a civil suit for damages.

THE SIXTH AMENDMENT: RIGHTS IN A CRIMINAL CASE

The Sixth Amendment, like the Fifth, provides multiple protections in criminal cases. Its protections give you the right:

- To a speedy and public trial.
- To a trial by jury.
- To be informed of the charge against you.
- To confront your accuser.
- To subpoena witnesses in your favor.
- To have the assistance of an attorney.

The American concept of a jury trial contemplates a jury drawn from a fair cross-section of the community. The jury guards against the exercise of arbitrary power by using the common sense judgment of the community as a hedge against the overzealous or mistaken prosecutor. The jury's perspective on facts is used in preference to the professional, or perhaps biased, response of a judge.

Community participation in administering criminal law is consistent with our democratic heritage, and it is also critical to public confidence in the

Consider: What is a "jury of one's peers"?

fairness of the criminal justice system. Therefore, a state may not restrict jury service only to special groups or exclude identifiable segments playing major roles in the community. Likewise, minorities may not be systematically excluded from jury duty. As discussed in Chapter 4, peremptory challenges during *voir dire* examination cannot be used to deny a defendant a jury of one's peers.

The right to a jury trial does not extend to state juvenile court delinquency proceedings because they are not criminal prosecutions. However, juveniles do have the right to counsel, to confront the witnesses against them, and to cross-examine them.

The right to an attorney exists in any cases where incarceration is a possible punishment. It exists at every stage of the proceeding, beginning with an investigation that centers on a person as the accused. There are many technical aspects to the Sixth Amendment, and numerous cases still arise concerning it. For example, a criminal defendant's right to counsel of his or her choice may be limited in certain situations by the attorney's prior representation of a corporation. By representing the corporation, an attorney may obtain potentially privileged information from employees who later become adverse witnesses against the corporation or individual officers in criminal prosecutions. These potential conflicts of interest also become very complicated when employees provide incriminating information to corporate counsel on the mistaken belief that he or she represents their interests as well as those of the corporation.

To further complicate the issue of representation, a 1994 U.S. Department of Justice rule allows government lawyers to contact workers who are not "high level" in a company without going through the company's legal department. Prosecutors may interview middle managers or line workers about company practices and try to persuade them to blow the whistle on upper management in criminal investigations. Normally, ethical rules would bar an attorney from directly contacting a person who is already represented by counsel. The Justice Department has rejected that rule in the context of corporate counsel primarily on the ground that it would frustrate the development of successful criminal investigations against corporations and corporate officials.

LO 13-3   Specific Crimes

Specific crimes relevant to business are discussed below. Such crimes may be prosecuted at the federal level and many states also have laws prohibiting these acts. Federal crimes are set forth in the U.S. Code. As illustrated by numerous media examples over the last ten years, these crimes are committed by individuals at all levels. Many crimes against business may also result in civil suits for money damages against a company. An individual convicted of a crime may face jail time and may also be required to pay money damages in a civil case.

FRAUD

As you learned earlier in the text, **fraud** can be a defense to a contract and can also form the basis of a civil tort action. The same fraudulent acts can also create criminal liability. The U.S. Code contains a number of provisions making it a crime to carry out a scheme to defraud. In general, whoever

sidebar 13.6

Madoff's Multi-Billion-Dollar Ponzi Scheme

Bernard L. Madoff surrounded himself with a formidable socialites and Wall Street power brokers. He was responsible for managing billions of dollars for individuals and foundations. Unfortunately, instead of investing the money, Madoff used the money to advance a massive Ponzi scheme. According to bankruptcy court filings, victims of Madoff's fraud include a wide range: Fairfield Greenwich Group ($7.5 billion); HSBC ($1 billion); Jewish Community Foundation of Los Angeles ($18 million); Elie Wiesel Foundation for Humanity ($15.2 million); Yeshiva University ($100 to 125 million); and Korea Teachers Pension ($9.1 million); as well as Zsa Zsa Gabor, Jeffrey Katzenberg, Larry King, John Malkovich, and Steven Spielberg (amounts unknown).

Despite concerns expressed to the Securities and Exchange Commission (SEC), Madoff was not caught until 2008, when his sons reported him to federal authorities. In 2009, Madoff pleaded guilty to 11 federal felonies, including securities fraud, wire fraud, mail fraud, money laundering, making false statements, perjury, and making false filings with the SEC. He was sentenced to 150 years in prison.

For more information about the guilty plea, see the March 2009 press release from the U.S. Attorney, Southern District of New York, at www.justice.gov/usao/nys/pressreleases/March09/madoffbernardpleapr.pdf. For detailed information about the Madoff case, see the New York Times focus and chronology of coverage, http://topics.nytimes.com/top/reference/timestopics/people/m/bernard_l_madoff/index.html?inline=nyt-per.

knowingly and willfully (1) falsifies, conceals, or covers up any trick, scheme, or device a material fact; (2) makes any materially false, fictitious, or fraudulent statement or representation; or (3) makes or uses any false writing or document knowing the same to contain any materially false, fictitious, or fraudulent statement or entry can face fines and/or imprisonment. There are many examples of fraud. After Hurricane Katrina, federal criminal investigations of fraud exceeded 1,000. The cases involved using debit cards meant for Katrina victims; claims submitted by individuals who did not live in affected areas; fraud by contractors submitting fake claims; and organized rings of criminals submitting multiple fake claims to maximize the amount of money they can fraudulently receive from the government.

Fraud is also actionable under state criminal codes. For example, in many states "theft by deception" is a crime. Theft by deception may occur when a person intentionally creates or reinforces an impression that is false; fails to correct an impression that is false and that the person does not believe to be true if there is a confidential or fiduciary relationship between the parties; preventing another from acquiring information that is relevant to a transaction; and failing to disclose a known lien or other legal impediment to property being transferred.

Federal law outlaws fraud in many specific contexts, including mail and wire transactions, securities transactions, health care, use of counterfeiting devices, and bankruptcy. A prosecutor must establish the presence of a **scheme to defraud**—a plan or program designed to take from a person the tangible right of honest services. In essence, a scheme involves a course of action to deceive others. See Sidebar 13.7 for examples of fraud schemes. Nearly all major white-collar criminal prosecutions involve some type of fraud.

sidebar 13.7

FBI (Federal Bureau of Investigation) Report: Common Fraud Schemes

Telemarketing Fraud. Use care when sending money to people you do not know personally and never give personal or financial information to unknown callers.

Advance Fee Scheme. This fraud occurs when the victim pays money to someone in anticipation of receiving something of greater value, then receives little or nothing in return.

Nigerian Letter or "419" Fraud. This fraud combines the threat of impersonation fraud with a variation of an advance fee scheme where the recipient has the "opportunity" to share a percentage of millions of dollars.

Impersonation/Identity Fraud. This fraud occurs when someone assumes your identity to perform a fraud or other criminal act.

Ponzi Schemes. These frauds are a kind of investment fraud where the operator promises high financial returns or dividends that are not available through traditional investments. Instead of investing the funds, the operator pays "dividends" to initial investors, then once he has a sufficient number of new investors, the operator flees with the remainder of the money.

Mail and Wire Fraud Various provisions of the U.S. Code make it illegal to use either the U.S. Postal Service or electronic means of interstate communication to carry out a scheme to defraud. These provisions provide significant criminal penalties for **mail** or **wire fraud.** The statutory penalties involve fines set by judges and up to 20 years in prison. If mail or wire fraud impacts a financial institution, the fine may be as high as $1 million and imprisonment may be up to 30 years. Each use of the mail or wire communication constitutes a separate violation. Thus, the criminal sanctions can be enormous.

"To mail" means a communication is sent or received through use of the U.S. Postal Service or any interstate carrier. A "wire transmission" includes the use of radio, television, telephone, Internet, or other wired form of communication. Prosecutors must prove the person accused of mail or wire fraud used the mail or wire communication. However, the government has substantial leeway in proving its case. Courts have held that the use of mail or wire communication can be proven by circumstantial evidence. For example, evidence of business custom and practice may establish that a mailing or wire communication occurred. The accused does not have to actually place a letter in the mail or send an e-mail message. Others may do so as long as the mailing is a part of the fraudulent scheme, the accused person does not have to be the party using the mail.

Legal Aspects of Mail and Wire Fraud A statement or representation is *false* or *fraudulent* if it is known to be untrue or is made with reckless indifference as to its truth or falsity. A statement or representation may also be *false* or *fraudulent* if it constitutes a half-truth or effectively conceals a material fact with intent to defraud. A *material fact* is a fact that would be important to a reasonable person in deciding whether to engage or not to engage in a particular transaction.

Intent to defraud means to act knowingly and with the specific intent to deceive someone, ordinarily for the purpose of causing some financial loss to another or bringing about some financial gain to oneself. In many fraud cases the defendant asserts a good-faith defense to the allegations of the indictment. **Good faith** is a complete defense because good faith on the part of a defendant is inconsistent with intent to defraud or willfulness, purposes essential to the charges. A person who expresses an opinion honestly held or a belief honestly entertained does not have fraudulent intent even though the opinion is erroneous or the belief is mistaken. Evidence that establishes only that a person made a mistake in judgment or an error in management or was careless does not establish fraudulent intent. Honest services is another important concept. In accordance with 18 U.S.C. Section 1346, the term "scheme or artifice to defraud" includes a scheme or artifice to deprive another of the intangible right to honest services. Case 13.2 addresses this scope of honest services, limiting it to only bribery and kickback schemes.

 case **13.2**

SKILLING v. UNITED STATES
130 S. Ct. 2896 (2010)

Defendant, the former chief executive officer of Enron Corporation, a bankrupt corporation, was convicted in the United States District Court for the Southern District of Texas, of conspiracy, securities fraud, making false representations to auditors, and insider trading, and he appealed. The United States Court of Appeals for the Fifth Circuit, affirmed defendant's convictions. Certiorari was granted.

GINSBURG, J.: In 2001, Enron Corporation, then the seventh highest-revenue-grossing company in America, crashed into bankruptcy. We consider in this opinion two questions arising from the prosecution of Jeffrey Skilling, a longtime Enron executive, for crimes committed before the corporation's collapse. First, did pretrial publicity and community prejudice prevent Skilling from obtaining a fair trial? Second, did the jury improperly convict Skilling of conspiracy to commit "honest-services" wire fraud, 18 U.S.C. §§371, 1343, 1346? Answering no to both questions, the Fifth Circuit affirmed Skilling's convictions. We conclude, in common with the Court of Appeals, that Skilling's fair-trial argument fails; Skilling, we hold, did not establish that a presumption of juror prejudice arose or that actual bias infected the jury that tried him. But we disagree with the Fifth Circuit's honest-services ruling. In proscribing fraudulent

deprivations of "the intangible right of honest services," §1346, Congress intended at least to reach schemes to defraud involving bribes and kickbacks. Construing the honest-services statute to extend beyond that core meaning, we conclude, would encounter a vagueness shoal. We therefore hold that §1346 covers only bribery and kickback schemes. Because Skilling's alleged misconduct entailed no bribe or kickback, it does not fall within §1346's proscription. We therefore affirm in part and vacate in part.

I

Founded in 1985, Enron Corporation grew from its headquarters in Houston, Texas, into one of the world's leading energy companies. Skilling launched his career there in 1990 when Kenneth Lay, the company's founder, hired him to head an Enron subsidiary. Skilling steadily rose through the corporation's ranks, serving as president and chief operating officer, and then, beginning in February 2001, as chief executive officer. Six months later, on August 14, 2001, Skilling resigned from Enron. Less than four months after Skilling's departure, Enron spiraled into bankruptcy. The company's stock, which had traded at $90 per share in August 2000, plummeted to pennies per share in late 2001. Attempting to comprehend what caused the corporation's collapse, the U.S. Department of Justice formed an Enron Task Force, comprising prosecutors and FBI agents from around the Nation. The Government's investigation uncovered an elaborate conspiracy to prop up Enron's short-run stock prices by overstating the company's financial wellbeing. In the years following Enron's bankruptcy, the Government prosecuted dozens of Enron employees who participated in the scheme. In time, the Government worked its way up the corporation's chain of command: On July 7, 2004, a grand jury indicted Skilling, Lay, and Richard Causey, Enron's former chief accounting officer. These three defendants, the indictment alleged, "engaged in a wide-ranging scheme to deceive the investing public, including Enron's shareholders, . . . about the true performance of Enron's businesses by: (a) manipulating Enron's publicly reported financial results; and (b) making public statements and representations about Enron's financial performance and results that were false and misleading." Skilling and his co-conspirators, the indictment continued, "enriched themselves as a result of the scheme through salary, bonuses, grants of stock and stock options, other profits, and prestige." . . .

In November 2004, Skilling moved to transfer the trial to another venue; he contended that hostility toward him in Houston, coupled with extensive pretrial publicity, had poisoned potential jurors. To support this assertion, Skilling, aided by media experts, submitted hundreds of news reports detailing Enron's downfall; he also presented affidavits from the experts he engaged portraying community attitudes in Houston in comparison to other potential venues. . . .

Pointing to "the community passion aroused by Enron's collapse and the vitriolic media treatment" aimed at him, Skilling argues that his trial "never should have proceeded in Houston." And even if it had been possible to select impartial jurors in Houston, "[t]he truncated voir dire . . . did almost nothing to weed out prejudices," he contends, so "[f]ar from rebutting the presumption of prejudice, the record below affirmatively confirmed it." . . . Important differences separate Skilling's prosecution from those in which we have presumed juror prejudice. . . .

First, we have emphasized in prior decisions the size and characteristics of the community in which the crime occurred. . . . Second, although news stories about Skilling were not kind, they contained no confession or other blatantly prejudicial information of the type readers or viewers could not reasonably be expected to shut from sight. . . . Third, unlike cases in which trial swiftly followed a widely reported crime [citation omitted] over four years elapsed between Enron's bankruptcy and Skilling's trial. Although reporters covered Enron-related news throughout this period, the decibel level of media attention diminished somewhat in the years following Enron's collapse. . . . Finally, and of prime significance, Skilling's jury acquitted him of nine insider-trading counts. Similarly, earlier instituted Enron-related prosecutions yielded no overwhelming victory for the Government. . . . Skilling's trial, in short, shares little in common with those in which we approved a presumption of juror prejudice. . . . Persuaded that no presumption arose, we conclude that the District Court, in declining to order a venue change, did not exceed constitutional limitations. . . .

We next consider whether Skilling's conspiracy conviction was premised on an improper theory of honest-services wire fraud. The honest-services statute, §1346, Skilling maintains, is unconstitutionally vague. Alternatively, he contends that his conduct does not fall within the statute's compass. . . . A prohibition on fraudulently depriving another of one's honest services by accepting bribes or kickbacks presents neither a fair-notice nor an arbitrary-prosecution problem. Skilling did not violate §1346, as the Court interprets the statute. The Government charged Skilling with conspiring to defraud Enron's shareholders by misrepresenting the company's fiscal health to his own profit, but the Government never alleged that he solicited or accepted side payments from a third party in exchange for making these misrepresentations. Because the indictment alleged three objects of the conspiracy—honest-services wire fraud, money-or-property wire fraud, and securities fraud—Skilling's conviction is flawed.

KEY PONITS

- The Supreme Court rejected Skilling's claim that he did not receive a fair trial because he did not establish that a presumption of juror prejudice against him arose or that any actual bias infected the jury in the case.

- The Court did, however, find in Skilling's favor on the issue of honest services. The Court concluded that 18 US.C. § 1346 covers only bribery and kickback schemes and does not extend to honest services. As such, it vacated that aspect of Skilling's conviction.

The burden of proof is not on the defendant to prove good faith or honesty, because he or she has no burden to prove anything. The government must establish beyond a reasonable doubt that the defendant acted with specific intent to defraud. The government does not have to prove actual reliance upon the defendant's misrepresentations. Proof of damage has no application to criminal liability for mail and wire fraud. By prohibiting the "scheme to defraud" rather than the completed fraud, the elements of reliance and damage would clearly be inconsistent with the statutes Congress enacted.

An example of wire fraud involves former Wal-Mart Stores Inc. Vice Chairman Thomas M. Coughlin. Mr. Coughlin pled guilty to wire fraud and tax evasion charges for using fraudulent expense reports. Wal-Mart alleged that he stole cash, gift cards, and equipment worth about $500,000. Coughlin is serving a home-confinement sentence of 27 months, plus 1,500 hours of community service. He also had to pay $400,000 in restitution. Coughlin was a company icon who worked closely with company founder Sam Walton.

Securities Fraud One of the most important federal laws defining criminal conduct is the Securities Exchange Act of 1934. This act and Rule 10(b)5 of the Securities and Exchange Commission cover fraud in the purchase or sale of a security. The details of this law are discussed in Chapter 17.

Many of the prosecutions stem from accounting fraud based on false financial statements. The defendants are typically corporate officers responsible for the financial statements furnished to the investing public. Sidebar 13.8 provides examples of identity theft, a common form of fraud.

> **Don't** be pressured to "change the numbers" to meet unrealistic corporate goals.

sidebar 13.8

Preventing Identity Theft

WHAT ARE THE MOST COMMON FORMS OF IDENTITY THEFT?

1. Dumpster Diving. Rummaging through trash looking for personal information.
2. Skimming. Stealing credit/debit card numbers using a special storage device when processing a card.
3. Phishing. Pretending to be financial institutions or companies to get individuals to reveal their personal information.
4. Changing Your Address. Diverting billing statements to other locations.
5. "Old-Fashioned" Stealing. Stealing wallets, purses, mail, credit cards, checks, tax information, and so forth.

WHAT CAN I DO TO DETER IDENTITY THIEVES?

1. Shred financial documents and paperwork before you discard them.
2. Protect your Social Security number.
3. Don't give out personal information over the phone, through the mail or Internet, unless you know the person.
4. Never click on links sent in unsolicited e-mails and protect your computer with firewalls, anti-spyware, and anti-virus software.
5. Keep all personal information in a secure location, away from roommates and others who may be in your home.

Source: www.ftc.gov/idtheft

Losses due to health care fraud are estimated to add $100 billion to the annual cost of health care in the United States.

Always review your medical bills. One expert estimates that "eight out of every ten" bills she reviews contain multiple errors.

Health Care Fraud Another important area of criminal law enforcement against businesses is the health care industry. The Department of Justice has specialized investigative units concentrating on health care fraud. The prosecution usually involves false claims under the False Claims Act. Prosecuting false claims results in the recoupment of millions of dollars for the federal government.

Examples of health care fraud include:

- Billing for services not actually performed.
- Falsifying a patient's diagnosis to justify tests, surgery, or other procedures that are not medically necessary.
- "Uncoding" or billing for a more costly procedure than the one actually performed.
- "Unbundling" or billing each stage of a procedure as if it were a separate procedure.
- Accepting kickbacks for patient referrals.
- Billing a patient more than the copay amount for services that were paid in full by a benefit plan under the terms of a managed care contract.

Health care fraud investigations are aided by information revealed by "whistleblower" suits brought under the False Claims Act. This act allows a citizen "relator" who successfully brings a lawsuit that recovers fraudulently obtained federal funds to keep a portion of the recovery as a bounty.

Counterfeiting Federal law outlaws the use of counterfeit access devices, including bank cards, plates, codes, account numbers, or other means of account to initiate a transfer of funds. The use of an *unauthorized access device,* such as a lost, stolen, expired, revoked, canceled, or fraudulently obtained bank card, is also prohibited. The counterfeit or unauthorized access device used must result in at least $1,000 being fraudulently obtained within a one-year period.

sidebar 13.9

False Claims Act and Whistleblower Lawsuits

In recent years, there has been a substantial escalation in False Claims Act (FCA) enforcement by the Department of Justice (DOJ), as well as *qui tam* lawsuits brought by whistleblowers on behalf of the United States.

In 2012, the DOJ recovered $5 billion in civil fraud judgments and settlements and $3.8 million in 2013. A record-breaking number of *qui tam* lawsuits were brought by whistleblowers in 2013: 752 complaints, an increase of 100 over 2012.

The U.S. Chamber of Commerce claims that the federal government is critical of the prosecutions and is pushing to reform the FCA. The Chamber of Commerce is pushing for concrete "incentives," including assurances that lower damages will be imposed to encourage companies to implement rigorous compliance programs and to report potential misconduct.

Sources: Jack W. Selden et al., "False Claims Act: 2013 Year in Review," *Lexicology* (January 14, 2014); U.S. Chamber Institute for Legal Reform, "Fixing the False Claims Act: The Case for Compliance-Focused Reforms" (October 2013).

Bankruptcy Fraud Bankruptcy proceedings are conducted in federal courts. To protect the interests of all parties to the proceedings, the U.S. Code makes certain conduct by the debtor and certain conduct by creditors and others a federal crime. These are **bankruptcy crimes.** First, it is a crime for the bankrupt debtor to falsify the information filed in the bankruptcy proceedings. Similarly, it is a crime for anyone to present a false claim in any bankruptcy proceeding.

Any person, including the debtor, in possession of property belonging to the estate of a debtor in bankruptcy is guilty of a felony if he or she conceals the property from the person charged with control of the property in the bankruptcy proceeding. The law requires that the act of concealment be fraudulent. An act is done fraudulently if done with intent to deceive or cheat any creditor, trustee, or bankruptcy judge. In this context, *conceal* means to secrete, falsify, mutilate, fraudulently transfer, withhold information or knowledge required by law to be made known, or take any action preventing discovery. Since the offense of **concealment** is a continuing one, the acts of concealment may have begun before as well as be committed after the bankruptcy proceeding began.

It is no defense that the concealment may have proved unsuccessful. Even though the property in question is recovered for the debtor's estate, the defendant may still be guilty of concealment. Similarly, it is no defense that there was no demand by any officer of the court or creditor for the property alleged to have been concealed.

The Criminal Investigation Unit of the IRS is actively involved in uncovering bankruptcy fraud. For examples of successful actions, see www.irs.gov/compliance/.

CONSPIRACY

It is a separate criminal offense for anyone to conspire or agree with someone else to do something that, if carried out, would be a criminal offense. A **conspiracy** is an agreement or a "kind of partnership" for criminal purposes in which each member becomes the agent or partner of every other member. A formal agreement is not required, and all members of the conspiracy need not plan all of the details of the scheme.

To convict a person of a conspiracy, it is not necessary for the government to prove the conspirators actually succeeded in accomplishing their intended crime. The evidence must show beyond a reasonable doubt that:

U.S. Federal prosecutors may bring an action against WikiLeaks founder Julian Assange for his role in the dissemination of classified government documents.

- Two or more persons, in some way or manner, came to a mutual understanding to try to accomplish a common and unlawful plan.
- The defendant willfully became a member of such conspiracy.
- During the existence of the conspiracy, one of the conspirators knowingly committed at least one of the overt acts described in the indictment.
- Such overt act was knowingly committed in an effort to carry out or accomplish some object of the conspiracy.

A person may be convicted of conspiracy even if he or she did not know all the details of the unlawful scheme. If a defendant has an understanding of the unlawful nature of a plan and knowingly and willfully joins in that plan on one occasion, that is sufficient evidence for conviction.

The essence of a conspiracy offense is the making of the agreement itself followed by the commission of any overt act. An **overt act** is any transaction or event knowingly committed by a conspirator in an effort to accomplish some object of the conspiracy. Standing alone, the act may be entirely innocent;

sidebar 13.10

Anatomy of a Prosecution: The Fall of Enron

The fall of Enron Corp. is one of this country's largest corporate scandals. According to the prosecution, Enron's founder, Kenneth Lay, and former CEO, Jeffrey Skilling, instigated a massive fraud before the company collapsed. The prosecution alleged that Lay and Skilling committed crimes "through accounting tricks, fiction, hocus-pocus, trickery, misleading statements, half-truths, omissions and outright lies."

The prosecution scorecard includes: Convictions:

Kenneth Lay—Found guilty on all six counts relating to fraud, including conspiracy to commit wire fraud, perpetrating wire and bank fraud, making false and misleading statements to employees, banks, securities analysts and corporate credit-rating agencies. Lay died unexpectedly before sentencing and his conviction was vacated under legal precedent.

Jeffrey Skilling—Found guilty of 19 of the 28 counts accusing him of insider trading, securities fraud and conspiracy. Sentenced to prison for 24 years and 4 months.

See Case 13.2 regarding Skilling's appeal to the U.S. Supreme Court.

Eighteen Guilty Pleas, including Enron Chief Financial Officer Andrew Fastow. Facing 98 counts, Fastow pleaded guilty to conspiracy to commit wire fraud and conspiracy to commit wire and securities fraud.

Fastow's "cooperation" with prosecutors significantly contributed to the successful criminal case against Lay and Skilling. Sentence: six years in prison.

Source: www.chron.com/news/specials/enron/. For additional information, see *Power Failure: The Inside Story of the Collapse of Enron* by Mimi Swartz with Enron whistleblower Sherron Watkins.

---

the context of the conspiracy makes it criminal. For example, driving a car to a bank to pick up a bank robber would constitute an overt act by the driver.

The law on conspiracies is often used to "drag in" defendants who did not actually participate in the commission of an offense. A person may become a coconspirator through participation in routine business meetings if the meetings are followed by illegal conduct. If illegal plans or conduct are in the planning process, it is imperative that persons not wishing to participate in the conspiracy disassociate themselves from the process immediately upon discovery of the illegal scheme.

Circumstantial evidence may prove a conspiracy. A person can be charged with conspiracy even if the individual becomes involved after the conspiracy is stopped and the criminal conduct does not occur. The fact that law enforcement discovers a plot to commit a crime and thwarts it does not prevent prosecution for a conspiracy. The threat of a conspiracy is a public danger beyond the commission of the crime because it is likely that the conspirators will commit more crimes.

Do be fully forthcoming with any investigation. Never be tempted into altering or destroying documents when an investigation or litigation is pending.

OBSTRUCTION OF JUSTICE

Obstruction of justice occurs when an individual commits an act with the intent to obstruct the legislative process or a judicial process. Obstruction of justice laws are designed to protect the integrity of legislative proceedings, judicial proceedings, and the proceedings before federal departments or agencies. The term *obstruction of justice* is interpreted broadly to encompass all steps and stages from the inception of an investigation to the conclusion of a trial.

Section 1505 of Title 18 of the U.S. Code provides

> Whoever, with intent to avoid, evade, prevent, or obstruct compliance, in whole or in part, with any civil investigative demand duly and properly made under the Antitrust Civil Process Act, willfully withholds, misrepresents, removes from any place, conceals, covers up, destroys, mutilates, alters, or by other means falsifies any documentary material, answers to written interrogatories, or oral testimony, which is the subject of such demand; or attempts to do so or solicits another to do so; or

> Whoever corruptly, or by threats or force, or by any threatening letter or communication influences, obstructs, or impedes or endeavors to influence, obstruct, or impede the due and proper administration of the law under which any pending proceeding is being had before any department or agency of the United States, or the due and proper exercise of the power of inquiry under which any inquiry or investigation is being had by either House, or any committee of either House or any joint committee of the Congress—Shall be fined under this title or imprisoned not more than five years, or both.

As you can see, this law is worded very broadly and can encompass a range of acts. The law was drafted with the recognition that there is an unlimited variety of methods by which the proper administration of justice might be impeded or thwarted by those who are criminally inclined. Any act made with the intent to obstruct the legislative process or judicial process may be a crime. Sidebar 13.11 contains examples of obstruction of justice.

---

sidebar 13.11

Think Before You Act: Examples of Obstruction of Justice

E-mailing a message to "clean up the files."

Changing records of phone conversations.

Shredding documents when an investigation or litigation is pending.

Exploiting a special relationship with a judge to obtain a favorable decision.

Testifying falsely before Congress.

EXAMPLES OF SUCCESSFUL PROSECUTIONS

- **I. Lewis "Scooter" Libby,** Vice President Dick Cheney's former Chief of Staff, convicted of perjury and obstruction of justice, 2½ years in prison.

- **Martha Stewart** convicted for obstruction of justice and lying to investigators, 5 months in prison, 5 months home confinement, 2 years probation.

- **Kenneth Branch,** former Boeing Co. manager, pleaded guilty to obstruction of justice stemming from an investigation into the theft of sensitive documents from competitor Lockheed Martin Corp. (during a battle for $1.99 billion in U.S. government contracts), 6 months home detention and a fine.

- **Barry Bonds,** baseball's home-run king, was found guilty of obstruction of justice for lying to a federal grand jury investigation into illegal steroid distribution.

FALSE STATEMENT TO A BANK

There is no requirement that the institution was influenced or misled.

Borrowers from banks are routinely required to furnish financial statements. These statements intend to supply information to the bank so it can make its decision on the loan request. Financial statements are relied upon by banks even though many of them are not certified as correct by a certified public accountant. It is a federal crime for anyone willfully to make a false statement to a federally insured financial institution. The purpose behind making such falsehoods a crime is to protect banks and attempt to ensure the accuracy of financial information. To prove the crime of a false statement to a bank, the prosecutor must prove beyond a reasonable doubt that the false statement or report was made with the intent to influence the action of the insured financial institution upon an application, advance, commitment, loan, or any change or extension thereof. An *insured bank* is one whose deposits are insured by the Federal Deposit Insurance Corporation. An insured credit union is one whose deposits are insured by the National Credit Union Administration.

A statement or report is *false* when made if it relates to a material fact and is untrue and is then known to be untrue by the person making it. A fact is *material* if it is important to the decision to be made by the officers or employees of the institution involved and has the capacity of influencing them in making that decision. It is not necessary, however, to prove that the institution involved was, in fact, influenced or misled. The gist of the offense is an attempt to influence such an institution by willfully making the false statement or report concerning the matter. The maximum penalty for a violation is two years' imprisonment and a $5,000 fine.

FALSE STATEMENT TO A FEDERAL AGENCY

The U.S. Code makes it a federal crime for anyone willfully and knowingly to make a false or fraudulent statement to a department or agency of the United States. The false statement must be related to a material matter, and the defendant must have acted willfully and with knowledge of the falsity. It is not necessary to show that the government agency was in fact deceived or misled. The issue of materiality is one of law for the courts. The maximum penalty is five years' imprisonment and a $10,000 fine.

"I truly hope people will learn from my mistakes."

—Olympic track star Marion Jones, sentenced to six months in prison for lying to investigators

A person may be guilty of a violation without proof that he or she had knowledge that the matter was within the jurisdiction of a federal agency. A businessperson may violate this law by making a false statement to another firm or person with knowledge that the information will be submitted to a government agency. Businesses must take care to avoid puffery or exaggerations in the context of any matter that may come within the jurisdiction of a federal agency.

Due to the sweeping nature of this statute, seven federal appellate courts recognized an **exculpatory no** exception for simple denials made in response to government questioning as part of a criminal investigation. This narrow exception protected an individual from prosecution for making a false statement when the person's statement simply denies criminal wrongdoing. The exculpatory no was permitted when a person, in response to governmental questioning, had to choose between three undesirable options: self-incrimination by telling the truth; remaining silent and raising greater suspicions; or denying guilt by making a false statement to the governmental official. Courts permitting this exception believed it balanced the need for protecting the basic functions of government

sidebar 13.12

Massey Energy Co. Explosion: Multiple Charges

Multiple charges followed a coal mine explosion that killed 29 Massey Energy Co. workers at its Upper Big Branch mine in West Virginia. A grand jury indicted Hughie Elbert Stover for:

- lying to investigators for the federal Mine Safety and Health Administration (MSHA) during their investigation of the explosion;
- lying to criminal investigators; and
- destroying evidence related to the blast.

According to the indictment, Stover told MSHA officials that there was a policy at the mine against providing advance notice of a safety inspection. To the contrary, Stover trained guards to alert employees by radio when an inspector was on the property. A 13-month independent investigation into the explosion concluded that the accident "could have been prevented" and "was the result of failures of basic safety systems identified and codified to protect the lives of minors." Additionally, federal and state regulators failed to correct the safety violations. More indictments and civil law suits may be forthcoming. Stover was ultimately convicted and sentenced to serve 36 months in prison. The prosecution sought a 25-year sentence.

Additionally, David Hughart, a former Massey Energy official, was sentenced to 42 months in jail after pleading guilty to conspiracy to impede the MSHA and conspiracy to violate mine health and safety laws. Gary May, the former superintendent of the Upper Branch Mine, pled guilty to a federal fraud charge and was sentenced to 21 months in prison. Former Massey Energy CEO Don Blankenship is also charged with conspiring to violate safety and health standards. His case was pending at the end of 2014.

Sources: For more information and the report, see "Report on the Upper Big Branch Mine Explosion," *The New York Times* (May 19, 2011), www.nytimes.com/interactive/2011/05/20/us/20110520_MINE_REPORT_DOC.html; Sandy Smith, "Another Massey Energy Official Sentenced on Federal Criminal Charges," *EHS Today* (September 13, 2013); John Raby, "Gary May, Former Upper Branch Mine Superintendent, Pleads Guilty to Federal Conspiracy Charges," *Huffington Post* (March 29, 2012); Walter Pavlo, "Former Massey Energy Security Chief Sentenced to 36 Months in Prison," *Forbes* (February 29, 2012).

agencies conducting investigations against the Fifth Amendment protection against self-incrimination.

In early 1998, the Supreme Court rejected the exculpatory no exception in the case of *Brogan v. United States*, 118 U.S. 805 (1998). The Court found the exception was not supported by the plain language of the statute and held that the Fifth Amendment does not confer a privilege to lie.

LARCENY

Larceny is the unlawful taking of personal property with the intent to deprive the rightful owner of it permanently. Larceny is commonly referred to as theft or stealing. Shoplifting by customers is a common form of larceny. Larceny by violence or threat such as with a gun is **robbery.** Breaking into a building with the intent to commit a felony is **burglary.** The most common felony in burglary cases is larceny.

Larceny by employees of a business is a common white-collar crime. If an employee appropriates funds of his employer to his or her own use, the employee is guilty of embezzlement. Embezzlement is often committed by highly trusted employees with access to cash or to the check-writing process. It is a crime easily committed when there is a lack of internal control over funds. Simple policies such as using cosigned checks, dividing check-writing duties from bank reconciliation duties, and requiring all employees to take vacations can often prevent embezzlement.

Embezzlement
occurs when a person entrusted with another's money or property fraudulently appropriates it.

Larceny by employees takes many forms. Use of company property such as vehicles or computers without permission is a form of larceny. Padding expense accounts and falsifying time records are also a taking of property and they are a sophisticated form of theft.

Money laundering is falsely reporting income that is obtained through criminal "dirty" activity as income obtained through a legitimate "clean" business enterprise.

Although larceny by rank-and-file employees is important, it pales to insignificance when compared to the larcenies committed by some corporate officers and directors. Larceny at the top-management level of some corporations in recent years has involved millions of dollars. In some cases, the stealing can only be described as looting the business just as if a mob broke into a store and stole its inventory.

Larceny by directors and officers usually has the appearance of being legal. The business may loan large sums to an officer at little or no interest. If there is no intent to repay the loan and no expectation of repayment, larceny as well as conspiracy to commit larceny has occurred. A company may purchase an airplane or yacht ostensibly for the business. If these are used only by the president for his personal enjoyment, larceny may have been committed. Likewise, if a company buys season tickets for the games of a local professional sports team and the tickets are used only by the officers, a form of larceny occurs. Technically, these examples could be stealing as well as tax fraud because the executive may not report receiving these benefits on his or her tax returns.

Company lawyers are not immune from prosecution for white-collar crimes. The general counsel for a company who helped cover up $600 million in looting of the corporation by company executives was given a $12 million bonus. He was indicted for grand larceny.

RACKETEER INFLUENCED AND CORRUPT ORGANIZATIONS ACT (RICO)

The most controversial of the federal criminal laws relating to business is the Racketeer Influenced and Corrupt Organizations Act, commonly known as **RICO**. This law imposes criminal and civil liability upon those businesspersons who engage in certain *prohibited activities* and who engage in interstate commerce. Specifically, liability extends to any person who:

- Uses or invests income from prohibited activities to acquire an interest in or to operate an enterprise.
- Acquires or maintains an interest in or control of an enterprise.
- Conducts or participates in the conduct of an enterprise while being employed by or associated with it.

Each prohibited activity is defined to include, as one necessary element, proof either of a **pattern of racketeering** *activity* or of *the collection of an unlawful debt*. **Racketeering** is defined in RICO to mean "any act or threat involving" specified state law crimes, any "act" indictable under various specified federal statutes, and certain federal "offenses." As to the term *pattern,* the statute says only that it "requires at least two acts of racketeering activity" within a ten-year period. It is not otherwise defined. See Table 13.2 for examples of racketeering activity.

The requirement of a pattern of racketeering activity is not the only issue created by the wording of the RICO statute. The law makes it unlawful for any

table 13.2 RICO: What Is "Racketeering Activity"?

Racketeering activity encompasses a range of criminal acts. Examples of crimes that may form the basis of a RICO prosecution:

- Acts or threats involving murder, kidnapping, gambling, arson, robbery, bribery (including sports bribery), extortion, dealing in obscene matter, or controlled substances.

- Counterfeiting.
- Mail and wire fraud.
- Financial institution fraud.
- Obstruction of justice.
- Tampering with a witness, victim, or informant.
- Trafficking in counterfeit goods.

person employed by or associated with any enterprise to conduct or participate in a violation. Thus, the law foresees two separate entities, a person and a distinct enterprise. An issue arises when a person incorporates and that person is the president and sole shareholder of the corporation. Courts have held in such cases that there are two separate entities and both may have RICO liability.

RICO allegations of fraud must be pled with particularity. A RICO plaintiff must describe the predicate acts of fraud with some specificity and state the time, place, and content of the alleged communications perpetrating the fraud. If there are multiple defendants, the allegations must put each defendant on notice of his alleged participation. Sidebar 13.13 provides examples of major RICO prosecutions.

Remember, RICO provides for both civil remedies and criminal penalties.

sidebar 13.13

Major RICO Prosecutions

- In January 2011, the FBI charged 127 individuals with RICO crimes, including murder, drug trafficking, extortion, gambling, loan-sharking, and prostitution. More than 800 federal and local law enforcement officials arrested the individuals in New York, New Jersey, and Rhode Island. Prosecutors targeted New York's five largest Mafia families: the **Gambinos, Genoveses, Bonannos, Luccheses,** and **Colombos.** In February 2012, ten of those charged pled guilty to various crimes. For detailed information, see FBI, "Four Gambino Crime Family Members and Associates Plead Guilty in Federal Court (February 17, 2012). http://www.fbi.gov/newyork/press-releases/2012/four-gambino-crime-family-members-and-associates-plead-guilty-in-manhattan-federal-court.

- In May 2011, RICO indictments were unsealed against 13 alleged leaders of the **Philadelphia mafia,** charging them with racketeering, extortion, loan-sharking,

and illegal gambling. See Patrick Walters, Reputed Mob Boss, 12 Others Arrested, ABC Action News (May 23, 2011), http://6abc.com/archive/8146349/.

- Well-known plaintiff's class action lawyer, **Melvyn I. Weiss,** faced a multi-count indictment, including RICO and money laundering charges. Prosecutors alleged that Weiss and other law partners at the firm obtained $251 million in attorney pay fees by paying $11 million in illegal kickbacks to lead plaintiffs. His sentence: 30 months in prison, forfeiture of $9.7 million in "ill-gotten gains," and a $250,000 fine. In Weiss's own words: "I deeply regret my conduct and apologize to all those who have been affected, including all of the wonderful and extremely talented lawyers and other employees of the firm, none of whom had any involvement in my wrongdoing." For in depth coverage, see the New York Times feature on Melvyn Weiss, http://topics.nytimes.com/top/reference/timestopics/people/w/melvyn_i_weiss/index.html.

A plaintiff in a civil action is, in effect, a private attorney general. In filing a complaint, the plaintiff must also allege that the defendant participated in the operation or management of the enterprise and played a part in directing the affairs of the enterprise. Mere employment in an organization is not sufficient to hold someone liable under RICO.

RICO provides drastic remedies. Conviction for a violation of RICO carries severe criminal penalties and forfeitures of illegal proceeds. Upon filing a RICO indictment, the government may seek a temporary restraining order to preserve all forfeitable assets until the trial is completed and judgment entered. A person in a private civil action found to have violated RICO is liable for treble, or triple, damages as well as for costs and attorneys' fees.

CYBER CRIME

One of the most significant trends in criminal law is a product of the rapid increase of the Internet. The Internet is a part of everyday business and, along with that fact, is the opportunity to use the Internet in connection with criminal activity. With billions of dollars flowing through cyberspace, it is not surprising that criminals are taking advantage of the system. Hackers commit crimes throughout the world that are very costly to business. Identity theft—when someone uses stolen information to create a new form of identity—is also a high-tech threat.

Federal law provides that a person who intentionally accesses a computer without authorization or exceeds authorized access to obtain classified, restricted, or protected data, or attempts to do so, is subject to criminal prosecution. Protected data includes financial and credit records, information from any department or agency of the United States, and information from any protected computer if the conduct involves an interstate or foreign communication.

Are you the victim of an Internet crime? Complaints may be filed with the Internet Crime Complaint Center, www.ic3.gov/. The center operates in partnership with the FBI.

Electronic theft is not limited to money. Employees have been caught issuing corporate stock to themselves. Trade secrets, personnel records, and customer lists have been stolen by hackers. Company plans are sometimes stolen and sold to competitors.

Most experts agree that cyber crime is more difficult to detect than crimes that preceded the Internet. Proof based on digital evidence about anonymous persons seldom leads to convictions. There has been an increase in law enforcement agents assigned to combat cyberspace thieves, and the training and their education in this area have improved. There are several companies in the security intelligence business that are attempting to help the business community install systems to prevent hacking.

Certain aspects of cyberspace crime should be recognized by managers and shareholders. Electronic crimes are most often committed by employees. Access to confidential information should be limited and carefully controlled. Losses from such crimes are easily hidden in cost of goods sold or in bad debt write-offs. They are usually kept secret for fear of encouraging other criminal acts. Investors typically have little or no knowledge of losses resulting from cyber crime. For examples of cyber crimes, see Sidebar 13.14.

ENDANGERING WORKERS

Most of the crimes committed by business are white-collar crimes. It is possible for corporate officials to be charged with crimes, such as assault and

sidebar 13.14

HACKED! Examples of Cyber Crimes

During 2013, the FBI notified more than 3,000 U.S. companies that their computer systems had been hacked. The cyber attacks included major retailers such as Target. During 2014, major high-profile security breaches involved JPMorgan Chase, Home Depot, and Sony Pictures. Other examples of cyber crimes include:

- A former Bank of America computer programmer was sentenced to 27 months in federal prison plus two years of supervised release and $419,310 in restitution for unauthorized access to the bank's protected computers.

- A college student was indicted for creating and disseminating counterfeit online coupons for consumer and electronic goods over the Internet. The alleged crimes cost retailers and manufacturers hundreds of thousands of dollars.

- A 20-year-old computer hacker from North Carolina was sentenced to 37 months without parole in federal prison for planning to hack into ATMs in the Houston area.

- A Georgia man pleaded guilty to trafficking in counterfeit credit cards and aggravated identity theft. According to court documents, special agents found more than 675,000 stolen credit card numbers and related information in his computers and e-mail accounts. The defendant admitted to obtaining the information either by hacking into business networks and downloading credit card databases or purchasing the information from others on the Internet in "carding forums."

For more examples and information, *see,* The U.S. Department of Justice, Computer Crime and Intellectual Property Section, www.cybercrime.gov/.

battery, reckless **endangerment of workers** if a worker is injured, or even accidental homicide if a worker is killed on the job. *In most cases,* when a worker is injured on the job, the appropriate remedy is through the workers' compensation system, which is discussed in Chapter 21. If a company is involved in an extremely dangerous process, such as handling dangerous chemicals, or does not have adequate safety precautions, criminal liability *may be imposed* if a worker is injured or killed.

Some states have specific statutes requiring employers to warn employees of life-threatening hazards in the workplace. In California, any corporation or person who is a manager is required to report any serious concealed danger in the workplace. Serious concealed danger encompasses products and practices that create a substantial probability of death, great bodily harm, or serious exposure to an employee. Failure to do so is a crime.

The Occupational Safety and Health Administration (OSHA) can also bring actions against businesses for violation of health and safety standards. If a business exposes workers to dangerous situations, such as exposing workers to dangerous falls and hazardous chemicals, OSHA has the power to impose money penalties for each violation.

AIDING AND ABETTING

The law recognizes that businesspeople accused of criminal behavior likely did not act alone. Such persons can be assisted by co-workers, subordinates, or individuals outside the business organization. If a person acts under the direction of someone accused of criminal activities, this person might be held responsible for

aiding and abetting in the commission of the crime. The charge of aiding and abetting is similar to the allegation of participating in a conspiracy. This individual accused of aiding and abetting did not necessarily commit the same criminal acts as others. For example, the accountant who assists the chief financial officer in embezzling funds likely is guilty of aiding and abetting in the actual theft. This accountant also may be guilty of conspiring to steal money.

Indictments often charge persons both with a conspiracy to commit a crime and with aiding and abetting others to do so. These allegations are used to indict persons only minimally involved with the actual substantive crime. To avoid going to trial, many will agree to testify against those more directly involved in return for lesser punishment or even immunity from prosecution. The value to the government of the conspiracy theory and the charge of aiding and abetting should not be underestimated. Corporate officials may be potentially liable for criminal acts committed without their direct involvement.

At the state level, a charge similar to the federal charge of aiding and abetting is that a person is an **accessory** to a crime. A person may be an accessory before the crime is committed. If the person is accused of being involved after the crime is committed, the charge is as an accessory after the fact. A person who assists a perpetrator of a crime in eluding the police would be such an accessory. *Accessories before the crime* assist in preparation for the crime, and they may be punished the same as the person who committed the crime. *Accessories after the fact* are usually subject to specific penalties for their actions as determined by the laws of the various states.

BRIBERY AND KICKBACKS

Bribery, or the offering, receiving, or soliciting of something of value for the purpose of influencing the action of an official in the discharge of his or her public or legal duties, is illegal in both the domestic and international contexts. Bribery of a public official is illegal under federal law, 18 U.S.C. Section

---

sidebar 13.15

Bribery Prosecutions

Examples of bribery include the following:

- New Orleans Mayor Ray Nagin was convicted on 20 of 21 corruption charges, including bribery for accepting bribes, free trips, and other gratuities from contractors in exchange for city contracts. He was sentenced to ten years in federal prison for his participation in the $500 scheme.

- Former Louisiana congressman William Jefferson who was sentenced to 13 years in prison after being convicted of 11 criminal counts, including bribery and racketeering. The scheme involved trying to enrich himself and relatives with bribes and payoffs involving business ventures in Africa.

- Two American businessmen who were charged with bribery in connection with obtaining multi-million-dollar contracts to supply the American military and their efforts to rebuild Iraq. The alleged bribes given to Army officers were in the form of airline tickets, spa vacations, and more than 1 million.

Sources: Cameron McWhirter, "New Orleans Ex-Mayor Ray Nagin Sentenced to Ten Years," Wall Street Journal (July 9, 2014); Jerry Markon, "Ex-Rep. Jefferson (D-La.) Gets 13 Yeas in Freezer Cash Case," Washington Post (Nov. 14, 2009); Jack Healy, "2 Americans Indicted in Iraq Contract Bribery," New York Times (May 30, 2011).

201. After accepting a bribe, a public official has a conflict of interest, which compromises his or her ability to act without undue influence.

It is also illegal for a sporting official to accept a bribe in exchange to "fix" a sporting event. Under 18 U.S.C. Section 224, the person accepting the bribe could be fined and/or imprisoned for up to five years. The FBI has a Sports Bribery Program to help college and professional sporting associations ensure the integrity of sporting events. They also investigate violations of federal statutes related to gambling and corruption in sports.

Kickbacks are payments made to a person who has facilitated a transaction. An example of a kickback is a building contractor giving money back to a government official in exchange for a building contract.

For an extended discussion of illegal bribery in the global context, *see* the **Foreign Corrupt Practices Act** in Chapter 12.

SENTENCING GUIDELINES

Historically, the fate of a person convicted of a crime depended heavily on the judge doing the sentencing. Because some judges were lenient and others were tough, the sentencing of criminals was sometimes referred to as "judicial roulette." To make the criminal system more just and to help ensure that similar crimes receive similar sentences, in the late 1980s a federal sentencing commission developed **sentencing guidelines** for federal crimes.

> "No punishment has ever possessed enough power of deterrence to prevent the commission of crimes."
> —**Hannah Arendt, political theorist**

These guidelines were the subject of much study, debate, and controversy. Many federal judges resented the loss of control during the sentencing phase of a case. Judges also criticized the complexity of the guidelines, which are hard to follow. Initially, the guidelines were mandatory. In accordance with a U.S. Supreme Court decision, the guidelines are now advisory, requiring a court to consider the guideline ranges, but permitting it to tailor the sentence in light of other concerns. Federal judges are now free to decide for themselves if the defendants deserve sentences longer or shorter than the ranges in the guidelines. If, however, an appeals court finds the sentence to be "unreasonable" under the facts of the case, the sentencing decision can be reversed. The Supreme Court, however, ruled in 2007 that sentences falling within the guidelines may be presumed "reasonable" by courts reviewing sentences on appeal.

Because corporations cannot be jailed, the sentencing commission has developed special guidelines for sentencing organizations convicted of federal crimes. The emphasis is on monetary penalties. It must be kept in mind, however, that in most criminal cases involving organizations, corporate officers can also be charged. As a result, the guidelines are designed so that the sanctions imposed upon organizations and their agents, taken together, will provide just punishment, adequate deterrence, and incentives for organizations to maintain internal mechanisms for preventing, detecting, and reporting criminal conduct. Punishment and deterrence are goals of the guidelines.

To illustrate how these guidelines would work, assume that a large corporation committed fraud in selling its product to the federal government. Perhaps the test results on the product were falsely reported. If a high official in the company and some middle managers knew that the test results were falsified and the company had a previous conviction of fraud within ten years, the fine would be $20 to $40 million. However, if the company received good points for cooperation with investigators and had an aggressive internal audit program to detect and prevent fraud, the fine would be only $4 to $8 million. In either case, the court would also order *restitution.* The court may also put the business on probation, preventing it from selling stock and paying dividends, or the court may otherwise be involved in major corporate decisions. This probation provision serves to get and keep the attention of senior management. Management in a company on probation must prevent violations of federal laws by its employees.

TRENDS

LO 13-4

One of the more significant trends is an increase in prosecution of white-collar criminals and legislative efforts to protect the public from fraud. To this end, the Sarbanes-Oxley Act (discussed in detail in Chapter 17) is causing companies to employ rigorous new accounting and compliance mechanisms. The goal is to renew investor confidence in the markets.

Another important trend is the government's effort to obtain proof of illegal activity by top corporate officials. Initiating an investigation that focuses on lower-mid-level managers, the government will obtain evidence that assists it in implicating higher-level executives. If wrongful conduct is found in the lower ranks, these employees are charged with conspiracy to violate a federal law. Prosecutors will then plea bargain with these defendants in exchange for testimony against persons higher on the organizational chart. This enables prosecutors to go after the real high-value target: top management. Although plea bargains typically require that prosecutors agree to drop or reduce charges, it is becoming increasingly more likely for prosecutors to insist on some jail time.

Prosecutors are also capitalizing on high-profile prosecutions. Where the stakes are high, prosecutors use the media to characterize white-collar criminals as "common street thugs." After an arrest, prosecutors may also seek millions of dollars in bail money and may object to the source of the funds if the money is the product of illegal activity. For example, a $5 million bond was required of Enron's chief financial officer. The size of the bond made it necessary for his parents to offer their home as security. Likewise, prosecutors may seek criminal penalties that include forfeiture of illegally obtained assets such as luxury homes, bank accounts, yachts, and automobiles. All of this is designed to deter similar conduct by other would be corporate felons.

Key Terms

Accessory 406
Aiding and abetting 406
Bankruptcy crimes 397
Burglary 401
Concealment 397
Conspiracy 397
Double jeopardy 389
Endangerment of workers 405

Exculpatory no 400
Expectation of privacy 385
Felonies 382
Foreign Corrupt Practices Act 407
Fraud 390
Good faith 393
Indictment 382

Information 382
Intent 382
Intent to defraud 393
Kickbacks 407
Knowingly 382
Larceny 401
Mail fraud 392
Misdemeanors 382

Nolo contendere 382
Obstruction of justice 398
Overt act 397
Pattern of racketeering 402
Presumption of innocence 383
Probable cause 383

Racketeering 402
RICO 402
Robbery 401
Scheme to defraud 391
Search warrant 385
Sentencing guidelines 407

Unreasonable search and
  seizure 385
White-collar crime 380
Willfully 382
Wire fraud 392

Review Questions and Problems

Terms and Procedures

1. *Classifications of Criminal Conduct*
   (a) Why is it important for business persons to have an understanding of the basic principles of criminal law and white-collar crime?
   (b) What is the difference between felonies and misdemeanors?

2. *Basic Concepts*
   Who are the parties to a criminal case?

3. *The Grand Jury*
   James was indicted by a federal grand jury. During the trial jury's deliberation one juror said, "I think James is guilty or else the grand jury would not have sent us the case." Another juror objected to this statement and said, "The action of the grand jury is irrelevant in our determination of guilt or innocence." Which juror is more accurate about the role of grand juries in our criminal justice system?

Constitutional Issues

4. *The Fourth Amendment: Illegal Search and Seizure*
   Burger's junkyard business consists of dismantling automobiles and selling their parts. A New York statute authorized warrantless inspections of automobile junkyards. Police officers entered his junkyard, conducted an inspection, and discovered stolen vehicles and parts. Burger, who was charged with possession of stolen property, moved to suppress the evidence obtained as a result of the inspection. He contends that the administrative inspection statute is unconstitutional when it authorizes warrantless searches. Is he correct? Why or why not?

5. *The Fifth Amendment: Protection against Self-Incrimination*
   Roberts was the president and sole shareholder of a corporation. A federal grand jury issued a subpoena to him in his capacity as president. The subpoena required Roberts to produce corporate records. Roberts moves to quash the subpoena on Fifth Amendment grounds.
   (a) Must Roberts deliver the records? Why or why not?
   (b) Could Roberts be required to testify about the documents? Why or why not?
   (c) If Roberts takes steps to dissolve the corporation, can he then avoid the subpoena? Why or why not?

6. *The Fifth Amendment: Double Jeopardy*
   Does the double jeopardy clause apply to civil penalties? Why or why not?

7. *The Sixth Amendment: Rights in a Criminal Case*
   What are the six constitutional rights provided in the Sixth Amendment?

Specific Crimes

8. *Fraud*
   Mary lost her billfold, which contained credit cards and an ATM access card. She had written her pin number on a piece of paper, which was also in the billfold. Al found the billfold. He used the credit cards and ATM card to obtain over $2,500 in goods, services, and cash. Is Al guilty of a federal offense?

9. *Conspiracy*

Allen, Mary, and Jon agreed to participate in a program to manipulate the values of securities. Allen made several telephone calls to securities brokers in which he delivered false information about a number of companies. Before any further actions were taken, Mary and Jonathan decided to withdraw as active participants in the program. Did Mary and Jon commit any crime? Why?

10. *Obstruction of Justice*

Quincy was a successful investment banker specializing in underwriting and merger advice. A federal grand jury was investigating the sales of initial public offerings, and Quincy knew that the grand jury had issued subpoenas seeking information about Quincy's deals. Quincy sent an e-mail to colleagues and encouraged them to "clean up" their files. What crimes, if any, did Quincy commit? If a colleague shredded files, what crimes may have been committed?

11. *False Statement to a Bank*

Your business is in need of additional working capital. You contact your bank about a loan. A line of credit of $500,000 is tentatively approved pending you furnish audited financial statements. You meet with your auditor who is also a personal friend. Suppose you ask your auditor to add $250,000 as an account receivable. In fact, this asset does not exist. The auditor certifies the financial statements with this phantom asset. You mail the audited financial statements to the bank. What crimes have you committed? What crimes did the auditor commit? What should have been the auditor's response to your request?

12. *False Statement to a Federal Agency*

Adam was hired by a defense contractor for a position that required a clearance for classified material. He failed to disclose a criminal conviction on a Department of Defense personnel security questionnaire, but admitted that he knew there was false information on the form which he signed.

(a) Did Adam willfully violate any federal law?

(b) If Adam didn't actually realize that the form would be submitted to a federal agency, is that a defense?

13. *Larceny*

Joe, a purchasing agent of ABC Company, entered into a contract to purchase software on behalf of ABC from a software company represented by Harry. The contract stated a price of $10,000 but the actual cost was $8,000. Joe and Harry split the $2,000. What crimes were committed?

14. *Racketeer Influenced and Corrupt Organizations Act (RICO)*

Don, a promoter of prize fights, formed a corporation. Don was the sole shareholder, sole director, and president of the corporation. Don was charged with a violation of RICO. Is the requirement of both a person and an enterprise met?

15. *Cyber Crime*

Why is cyber crime difficult to detect and to prosecute successfully?

16. *Endangering Workers*

Beth was killed when a trench collapsed. An investigation revealed that the trench was 27 feet deep and without adequate shoring, in violation of safety standards. Bob, the president of the firm, is charged with negligent homicide. Is a finding of guilt possible? Why or why not?

17. *Aiding and Abetting*

Susan, a partner in a CPA firm, prepares a federal income tax return knowing that it contains false information. Because the client wants the return prepared in this manner, Susan obtains the taxpayer's signature on the return and files it with the IRS. Has Susan aided and abetted in the commission of a crime? Why?

18. *Bribery and Kickbacks*

A pharmaceutical company tried to boost its sales by encouraging doctors to use its new drug, LDL Control, to treat high cholesterol. An important part of their sales pitch included paying for lavish dinners and weekend trips for the doctors and their families. The company also gave doctors expensive gifts if they prescribed a certain number of prescriptions of LDL Control each month. Is this an acceptable form of marketing or criminal behavior?

19. *Sentencing Guidelines*

The U.S. sentencing guidelines apply a mathematical formula to sentencing. How do the guidelines operate?

20. *Trends*

Describe three trends in criminal law that impact business organizations and businesspeople.

business *discussion*

A drug company applied for the approval of the Food and Drug Administration (FDA) to market a miracle drug that the company believed could cure some cancers. During the period that the application was under consideration the company's stock rose to $65 per share. The president of the company learned that the FDA application was about to be denied. You are a personal friend of the president, and he told you that he believed that the stock will start trading downward. You sell 4,000 shares of stock which you purchased for $10 per share. Your decision appears to be a good one since you made a profit of about $200,000. When questioned about the sale by an investigator from the Securities and Exchange Commission, you state that the sale was because of a preexisting arrangement to sell the shares when the price fell below $60 per share. Following the announcement that the FDA application was denied, the stock went to $7 per share.

Did you commit a crime when you sold the stock?
Did you commit a crime in your answer to the federal agent?
Were you part of an illegal conspiracy?

14

Business Organizations

Learning Objectives

In this chapter you will learn:

14-1. To describe the factors to consider when deciding on the form of organization.

14-2. To contrast the basic organizational forms that businesses select to conduct business.

14-3. To compare the hybrid organizational forms businesses may utilize to take advantage of attributes of various basic structures.

14-4. To understand the complexity of making a decision on the organizational form and recognize trends in managing organizations.

Have you ever thought about how businesses are organized? Why is one business a partnership and another a corporation? How do these businesses get transactions completed through someone other than the owner? There must be some legal principles at work because you know you do not have to deal with the owner of the clothing store when you make a purchase. A multinational company transacts business all over the world and its shareholders (owners) are not parties to its contracts.

Previous chapters discuss legal issues related to various business transactions. In this chapter, we focus on how these transactions are accomplished and the selection of which organizational form is best to complete such transactions. As you begin the study of this chapter, ask yourself, How does a company enter into a contract? How does an organization become liable to its customers, shareholders, or other parties. The answers to these questions depend on how the business is organized. In addition, to understand the material in this chapter, the material on agency in Chapter 21 is important. It provides a helpful foundation for the following.

In this chapter, you will examine the factors that should be considered when deciding the most appropriate organizational form. You also will review the various choices of organizations used to conduct business. Prior to this examination and review, a quick introduction to the forms of organizations is presented.

FORMS OF BUSINESS ORGANIZATIONS

People conduct business using a number of different organizational forms. The law recognizes three basic forms and several hybrid forms that contain attributes of two or more basic forms. These various forms are listed in Sidebar 14.1.

---

sidebar 14.1

Possible Forms of Business Organizations

The three basic forms include:

- Sole proprietorships
- Partnerships
- Corporations

The hybrid forms include:

- Limited partnerships
- S corporations
- Limited liability companies
- Limited liability partnerships

Two terms are important as they relate to the number of owners of a business organization. Some organizations are owned by only a few persons. Such organizations are said to be **closely held**. Family-owned and family-operated businesses are common examples of closely held organizations. Other businesses may be owned by hundreds, if not thousands, of persons. These organizations are **publicly held** ones. Examples of publicly held businesses include those whose stock is traded on a public exchange.

You should understand that the decision of selecting an appropriate organizational form usually is limited to those situations involving the few owners of a closely held business. When a business is publicly held by a large number of owners, the form of organization usually is a corporation. The reason for this corporate form being used is that shareholders can transfer their ownership without interfering with the organization's management.

The issue of which organizational form is best usually involves closely held businesses; publicly held businesses typically are corporations.

Factors to Consider When Selecting a Business's Organizational Form

Significant factors to consider in selecting the best organizational form for a particular business activity include:

- The cost of creating the organization.
- The continuity or stability of the organization.
- The control of decisions.
- The personal liability of the owners.
- The taxation of the organization's earnings and its distribution of profits to the owners.

In the following sections, each of these factors is defined so that you can more easily apply their meaning in the detailed sections on business structures.

CREATION

The word *creation* means the legal steps necessary to form a particular business organization. At times, a businessperson may be concerned with how much it will cost to have each form established. Usually, the cost of creation is not a major factor in considering which form of business organization a person will choose to operate a business. The most significant creation-related issues are how long it will take to create a particular organization and how much paperwork is involved.

The issues when considering methods of creating business organizations usually are time and money.

CONTINUITY

Another factor to consider when selecting the best organizational form for a business activity is the continuity of the organization. How does an organization's existence relate to its owners? By this question the meaning of the word *continuity* becomes associated with the stability or durability of the organization.

The crucial issue with this continuity factor is the method by which a business organization can be dissolved. A **dissolution** is any change in the ownership of an organization that changes the legal existence of the organization. In essence, the questions become: Is the organization easily dissolved? What impact does a dissolution of the organizational form have on the business activity of that organization?

The death, retirement, or withdrawal of an owner creates issues of whether an organization and its business will continue.

MANAGERIAL CONTROL

The factor of control concerns who is managing the business organization. Often this issue is of vital importance to the owners. The egos of businesspeople can cause them to insist on equal voices in management. As you study this factor under each organizational form, keep in mind the difficulties that can arise when a few strong-willed business owners disagree with one another. Usually when people are excited about getting started in a business

Don't assume you and your co-owners have to be equal in all aspects; voice in management can be decided among you.

opportunity, no one takes time to discuss methods of resolving potential deadlocks. The failure to consider how to overcome disputes involving managerial control can cause business activities to suffer and the organization to fail. Therefore, consideration of potential conflict and mechanisms to resolve disputes are essential to consider when selecting a form for a business venture.

LIABILITY

Do always examine how liability passes from the organization to the owner.

When considering the liability factor, you should ask yourself: To what degree is the owner of a business personally liable for the debts of the business organization? Additionally, you may ask: When is the owner liable under the law for harm caused by the business organization? Generally, businesspeople want to limit their personal liability. Although there are organizations that appear to accomplish this goal, you will see that such appearances might be misleading when actually conducting business transactions. For this reason, this liability factor is very important and deserves significant consideration as it relates to each of the organizational forms presented below.

TAXATION

Remember a single tax is not always better than a double tax.

This factor often is viewed as the most critical when selecting the form of business organization. At issue is: How is the income earned by the business taxed? How is the money distributed to the business owners taxed? Is it possible that owners may have to pay taxes on money that is attributed to them as income but which they have not actually received? The answers to these questions provide much needed guidance when deciding which form of organization is best suited for a business's operation.

People have stated that the double taxation of corporate income should be avoided by selecting a different form of organization. As you will see, there are specific advantages to creating the organizational forms that are "single taxed." However, advantages also exist when an organization is subject to the supposed "double tax."

LO 14-2 Selecting the Best Organizational Form

The next six sections apply the above factors to major organizational forms. Following these sections is a brief discussion on how to select the best organizational form for a particular business activity.

SOLE PROPRIETORSHIPS

When considering the relevant factors, the **sole proprietorship** has many virtues. However, the use of this business organization is very limited because multiple owners cannot create a proprietorship. Depending on the factual situation presented, greater continuity, less liability, and more flexible tax planning may be required than those afforded by the law of the sole proprietorship.

A sole proprietorship is the easiest and least expensive business organization to create. In essence, the proprietor obtains whatever business licenses

Figure 14.1 *Corporate Form Selection Factors.*

Form	Creation	Continuity	Control	Liability	Taxation
Sole Proprietorship	No formal documentation—business licenses only	So long as proprietor desires, but no transfer to others	Total control by proprietor	Personal obligation for all debts and liabilities	All business income subject to personal taxation
Partnership	Automatic based on business conduct; modified by agreement	Dissolved whenever one partner withdraws	Each partner has equal voice; modified by agreement	Personal obligation for all debts and liabilities; joint and several liability	All business income subject to personal taxation, divided equally
Corporation	Incorporators apply for state charter with articles of incorporation	Perpetual, so long as it can conduct business	Managed by officers, appointed by directors, who are elected by shareholders	Shareholder obligations limited to investment, absent other commitments	Corporate income taxed; shareholders taxed only on income distributed
Limited Partnership	Partnership agreement and certificate filed in public office where business is conducted	Dissolved when general partner withdraws	General partners have total control	Personal obligation for general partners; limited partners obligated for investment	All business income subject to personal taxation
S Corporation	Incorporators apply for state charter with articles of incorporation	Perpetual, so long as number of shareholder limited	Managed by officers, appointed by directors, who are elected by shareholders	Shareholder obligations limited to investment, absent other commitments	All business income subject to personal taxation
Limited Liability Company or Partnership	Organizers file articles of organization with state official	Dissolved when member withdraws, but may be continued by those remaining	Equal management by members unless manager designated	Members are agents, but liable only for investment	All business income subject to personal taxation

Source: Delaware Division of Corporations, Legal Business Structure Table, http://revenue.delaware.gov/services/
Business_Tax/business_structures_table.pdf

are necessary and begins operations. Legally, no formal documentation is needed. The ease of (perhaps the lack of) the steps used to create a proprietorship makes it an attractive alternative when beginning a new business venture. However, as the other factors might dictate, a business may shift away from the proprietorship form as it becomes more successful.

A proprietorship's continuity is tied directly to the will of the proprietor. In essence, the proprietor may dissolve his or her organization at any time by simply changing the organization or terminating the business activity.

The fact that the proprietorship's business activity may be more stable than the proprietor's willingness to remain actively involved in the business indicates that the sole proprietorship is a less desirable organizational form. Ownership of a sole proprietorship cannot be transferred.

The sole proprietor is in total control of his or her business's goals and operations. While the proprietor has complete responsibility for the business's success or failure, the owners of all other organizational forms usually share control to some degree. As long as this control issue is carefully thought out, there can be real value in having more than one voice in control of managing a business enterprise.

A sole proprietor is personally obligated for the debt of the proprietorship. Legally speaking, this owner has unlimited liability for the obligations of this type of business organization. The business organization's creditors can seek to hold the proprietor personally liable for 100% of the debts and legal obligations that the proprietorship cannot satisfy. The desire to avoid the potentially high risk of personal liability is an important reason why other organizational forms might be viewed as preferable to the proprietorship.

A sole proprietorship is not taxed as an organization. All the proprietorship's income subject to taxation is attributed to the proprietor. The initial appearance of this tax treatment may appear favorable because the business organization is not taxed. However, the individual proprietor must pay the applicable personal tax rate on the income earned by the proprietorship whether the proprietor actually receives any of the income from the organization or not. If the organization retains its profits for business expansion purposes instead of distributing this money to the proprietor, that owner still must pay taxes on the income made by the proprietorship.

A sole proprietorship may appear to have many advantages; sharing responsibility and liability with others are not among them.

PARTNERSHIPS

Whenever two or more people wish to own a business together, a partnership is a possible organizational form. In general, a **partnership** is an agreement between two or more persons to share a common interest in a commercial endeavor and to share profits and losses. The word *persons* in the previous sentence should be interpreted broadly enough to allow business organizations, as well as individuals, to form a partnership. For example, two or more individuals, an individual and a corporation, a partnership and a corporation, or any combination of these entities may agree to create a business organization called a partnership.

Due to the potentially complex relationships established through a partnership, factors to consider when studying the appropriateness of this organizational form are presented under subheadings that correspond to the factors presented above.

Creation When compared to other forms of business organizations (other than the sole proprietorship), a partnership is easily formed. The cost of forming a partnership is relatively minimal. In addition, the creation of a partnership is made easier since it does not need to get permission from each state in which it does business.

The key to a partnership's existence is satisfying the elements of its definition:

1. Two or more persons.
2. A common interest in business.
3. Sharing profits and losses.

If the parties conduct their affairs in such a way as to meet these definitional elements, a partnership exists regardless of whether the persons involved call themselves partners or not. Sidebar 14.2 presents issues related to the existence and naming of a partnership.

Don't operate a business with one or more co-owners without a carefully drafted partnership agreement; unresolved issues lead to major legal problems.

---

sidebar 14.2

Formation and Naming of a Partnership

Since the existence of a partnership is based on the partners' agreement, it is possible that this agreement is implied from the conduct or actions of the parties. Partners should never rely on implied agreements. Rather, their agreement should be explicitly stated among the parties and drafted into a formal document. The formal agreement is called the **articles of partnership.**

Since a partnership is created by agreement, the partners select the name of the partnership. This right of selection is subject to two limitations in many states. First, a partnership may not use any word in the name, such as "company," that would imply the existence of a corporation. Second, if the name is other than that of the

partners, the partners must give notice as to their actual identity under the state's **assumed-name statute.** Failure to comply with this disclosure requirement may result in the partnership being denied access to courts, or it may result in criminal actions being brought against those operating under the assumed name.

An example of these naming concepts could arise in the creation of a partnership to conduct business as a consulting firm. If the firm's name is a listing of your surname and those of your partners, your identities are clear via your firm's name. However, if you called your partnership "We are the Best Consulting," you and your partners would need to comply with any applicable assumed-name statute.

Continuity A general partnership is dissolved any time there is a change in the partners. For example, if a partner dies, retires, or otherwise withdraws from the organization, the partnership is dissolved. Likewise, if a person is added as a new partner, there is a technical dissolution of the organization. Therefore, it generally is said that the partnership organization is easily dissolved. Even if the partnership agreement provides that the partnership will continue for a stated number of years, any partner still retains the power to dissolve the organization. Although liability may be imposed on the former partner for wrongful dissolution in violation of the agreement, the partnership nevertheless is dissolved.

A dissolution does not necessarily destroy the business of a partnership. Dissolution is not the same thing as terminating an organization's business activity. Termination involves the winding up or liquidating of a business; dissolution simply means the legal form of organization no longer exists. Sidebar 14.3 addresses how parties might prevent dissolution from destroying a partnership's business success.

sidebar 14.3

Anticipating a Partnership's Dissolution—Buy and Sell Agreements

To prevent problems that may arise when a partner dies or withdraws from a partnership, the articles of partnership should include a **buy and sell agreement.** This agreement, which should be entered into when the business entity is created, provides for the amount and manner of compensation for the interest of the deceased or withdrawing owner.

Buy and sell agreements frequently use formulas to compute the value of the withdrawing partner's interest and provide for the time and method of payment. In the case of death, the liquidity needed is often provided by the cash proceeds from life insurance taken out on the life of the deceased and made payable to the business or to the surviving partners. Upon payment of the amount required by the buy and sell agreement to the estate of the deceased, the interest of the deceased ends, and all the surviving partners can continue the business, as members of a new partnership.

Don't rely on partners having an equal voice in managing the organization; negotiate how to share this managerial responsibility.

Managerial Control In a general partnership, unless the agreement provides to the contrary, each partner has an equal voice in the firm's affairs. Partners may agree to divide control in such a way as to make controlling partners and minority partners. The decision of who has what voice in management is of crucial importance to the chances of the business's success and to the welfare of the partners' relationship with each other. The possibility of a deadlock among partners is very real, especially when there are only a few partners and there are an even number of them. Care should be taken to design mechanisms to avoid or at least handle the disputes that will arise when partners share managerial control. A written partnership agreement should provide specific language governing issues of managerial control.

Liability All partners in a general partnership have unlimited liability for their organization's debts. These partners' personal assets, which are not associated with the partnership, may be claimed by the partnership's creditors. From a creditor's perspective, this personal liability of each partner extends to the organization's entire debt, not just to a pro rata share. These partners are **jointly and severally liable** for the partnership's obligations. For example, assume that a general partnership has three partners and that it owes a creditor $300,000. If it is necessary to collect the debt, this creditor can sue all three partners jointly for the $300,000. As an alternative, the creditor can sue any one partner or any combination of two for the entire $300,000. Among the partners, anyone who has to pay the creditor more than her or his pro rata share of the liability usually can seek contribution from the remaining partners.

Taxation Like proprietorships, partnerships are not a taxable entity. The fact that this type of organization pays no income tax does not mean that the profits of the partnership are free from income tax. A partnership files an information return that allocates to each partner his or her proportionate share of profits or losses from operations, dividend income, capital gains or losses, and other items that would affect the income tax owed by a partner.

Partners then report their share of such items on their individual income tax returns, irrespective of whether they have actually received the items.

This aspect of a partnership is an advantage to the partners if the organization suffers a net loss. The pro rata share of this loss is allocated to each partner, and it can be used to reduce these partners' personal taxable income. However, by this same reasoning, a partnership is a disadvantage if the organization retains any profits made by the organization for the purpose of expansion. Suppose a partnership with three equal partners has $30,000 in net income. If the partnership keeps this money, there still is a constructive distribution of $10,000 to each partner for tax purposes. Assuming that these partners are in a 28 percent personal income tax bracket, they each would have to pay $2,800 in taxes even though they actually received nothing from the partnership.

> A partnership does not pay taxes; this may be a benefit or detriment to the partners depending on whether the organization makes or loses money and whether it distributes or retains any profits made.

concept *summary*

Advantages and Disadvantages of Partnerships

The basic law relating to partnerships is found in the Uniform Partnership Act., a state law that can exist in slightly different forms in different states. As articulated in the act, the partnership form of organization generally has the following advantages:

1. A partnership is easily formed because it is based on a contract among persons.
2. Costs of formation are not significant.
3. Partnerships are not a tax-paying entity.
4. Each partner has an equal voice in management, unless there is a contrary agreement.
5. A partnership may operate in more than one state without obtaining a license to do business.
6. Partnerships generally are subject to less regulation and less governmental supervision than are corporations.

Offsetting these advantages, the following aspects of partnerships have been called disadvantages:

1. For practical reasons, only a limited number of people can be partners.
2. A partnership is dissolved anytime a partner ceases to be a partner, regardless of whether the reason is withdrawal or death.
3. Each partner's liability is unlimited, contrasted with the limited liability of a corporate shareholder.
4. Partners are taxed on their share of the partnership's profits, whether the profits are distributed or not. In other words, partners often are required to pay income tax on money they do not receive.

CORPORATIONS

The third basic organizational form that might be used to operate a business is the corporation. A **corporation** is an artificial, intangible entity created under the authority of a state's law. A corporation is known as a **domestic corporation** in the state in which it is incorporated. In all other states, this corporation is called a **foreign corporation**. A corporation created under the authority of a foreign country may be called an **alien corporation**, though it is generally treated the same as a foreign corporation under the law. As a creature of state legislative bodies, the corporation is much more complex to create and to operate than other forms of businesses. These legal complexities associated with the corporation are presented in a way that parallels the preceding section so that comparisons with partnerships can be easily made.

Do check the website of your state's authority responsible for issuing corporate charters. In most states, this authority is under the secretary of state.

Creation   A corporation is created by a state issuing a **charter** upon the application of individuals known as **incorporators.** In comparison with partnerships, corporations are more costly to form. Among the costs of incorporation are filing fees, license fees, franchise taxes, attorneys' fees, and the cost of supplies, such as minute books, corporate seals, and stock certificates. In addition to these costs of creation, there also are annual costs in continuing a corporation's operation. These recurring expenses include annual reporting fees and taxes, the cost of annual shareholders' meetings, and ongoing legal-related expenses. Sidebar 14.4 describes the process of incorporation.

---

sidebar 14.4

Steps in Creation of a Corporation

The formal application for a corporate charter is called the **articles of incorporation.** These articles must contain the proposed name of the corporation. So that persons dealing with a business will know that it is a corporation, the law requires that the corporate name include one of the following words or end with an abbreviation of them: "corporation," "company," "incorporated," or "limited." In addition, a corporate name must not be the same as, or deceptively similar to, the name of any domestic corporation or that of a foreign corporation authorized to do business in the state to which the application is made. The corporate name is an asset and an aspect of goodwill. As such, it is legally protected.

In addition to the proposed corporate name, the articles of incorporation usually will include the proposed corporation's period of duration, the purpose for which it is formed, the number of authorized shares, and information about the initial corporate officials.

Once drafted, these papers are sent to the appropriate state official (usually the secretary of state), who approves them and issues a corporate charter. Notice of this incorporation usually has to be advertised in the local newspaper in order to inform the public that a new corporation has been created. The initial board of directors then meets, adopts the corporate bylaws, and approves the sale of stock. At this point, the corporation becomes operational.

If a corporation wishes to conduct business in states other than the state of incorporation, that corporation must be licensed in these foreign states. The process of qualification usually requires payment of license fees and franchise taxes above and beyond those paid during the initial incorporation process. If a corporation fails to qualify in states where it is conducting business, the corporation may be denied access to the courts as a means of enforcing its contracts.

The separation of the corporate organization's existence from its owners' willingness to remain associated with it is viewed as a major advantage to the corporation's stability.

Continuity   In contrast to a partnership, a corporation usually is formed to have perpetual existence. The law treats a corporation's existence as distinct from its owners' status as shareholders. Thus, a shareholder's death or sale of her or his stock does not affect the organizational structure of a corporation. This ability to separate management from ownership is an often cited advantage of the corporation.

Although the sale of stock by a major shareholder or the shareholder's death has no legal impact on the organization's existence, this event may have a very real adverse impact on that corporation's ability to do business. The shareholder may have been the driving force behind the corporation's success. Without this shareholder, the corporation's business may fail.

Managerial Control In the corporate form of organization, the issue of control is complicated by three groups. First, the **shareholders** elect the members of the board of directors. These **directors** set the objectives or goals of the corporation, and they appoint the officers. These **officers**, such as the president, vice president, secretary, and treasurer, are charged with managing the daily operations of the corporation in an attempt to achieve the stated organizational objectives or goals. Thus, which one of these three groups really controls the corporation?

To answer this question effectively, you must realize that the issue of who controls a corporation varies depending on the size of the ownership base of the organization. In essence, matters of managerial control require us to examine the publicly held corporation as distinct from the closely held corporation.

sidebar 14.5

Why Are So Many Companies Incorporated in Delaware?

If you look for the state of incorporation for a large company, there is a good chance that you will discover it is Delaware. In fact, by the state's own estimate, more than 50 percent of publicly traded companies and 64 percent of Fortune 500 companies are incorporated in Delaware. You may find this surprising considering the state's relatively small population and geographic size. There must be a reason that so many companies choose Delaware.

Several factors have been suggested to explain Delaware's success as an incorporating forum. One of the most frequently cited is the state's stable legal environment. This includes Delaware's respected judiciary, and in particular the Court of Chancery, which is highly experienced in deciding issues related to the state General Corporation Law. Additionally, the legislature is generally believed to be supportive of business interests. There is no income tax for businesses that do not operate in Delaware (though there is a franchise tax). And the state Division of Corporations makes the process of incorporation simple and efficient.

Sources: Delaware Division of Corporations, http://corp.delaware.gov/; Theodore Eisenberg and Geoffrey Miller, "Ex Ante Choices of Law and Forum: An Empirical Analysis of Corporate Merger Agreements," *59 Vanderbilt Law Review* 1975 (2006).

Publicly Held Corporations In very large corporations, control by management (a combination of the directors and officers) is maintained with a very small percentage of stock ownership through the use of corporate records and funds to solicit proxies. Technically, a **proxy** is an agent appointed by a shareholder for the purpose of voting the shares. Management can, at corporate expense, solicit the right to vote the stock of shareholders unable to attend the meetings at which the directors of the company are elected. An outsider must either own sufficient stock to elect the directors or must solicit proxies at his or her own expense. The management of a large corporation usually can maintain control with only a small minority of actual stock ownership.

During the first years of this century, we have seen evidence of the negative aspects arising from a few shareholders, who also serve as officers and directors, controlling large, publicly held corporations. The lack of sufficient review and influence from those called "outside directors" contributed to corporate scandals that shocked the public confidence in business and the economy. You should appreciate that limiting the role of corporate governance to only a few people can lead to massive fraud. Despite legal requirements designed to increase the influence of corporate directors, all accounting records are not perfect.

Closely Held Corporations Unlike the situation with a large, publicly held corporation, one shareholder (or at least a small group of shareholders) may be able to control a closely held corporation. This can result because this individual (or the group) can own an actual majority of the issued shares. This majority can control the election of a board of directors. In fact, the shareholders with the largest amount of stock are often elected to this board of directors. The directors, in turn, elect officers, who again may be the shareholders with the largest interests. In a very real sense, those who own a majority of a closely held corporation can rule with near-absolute authority.

What are the rights of those who do not possess control in a closely held corporation—the so-called minority interest? To a large degree, the owners of the minority interest are subject to the decisions of the majority. The majority may pay themselves salaries that use up profits and may never declare a dividend. However, the minority interest is not without some rights, because the directors and officers stand in a fiduciary relation to the corporation and to the minority shareholders if the corporation is closely held. This relation imposes a duty on directors to act for the best interests of the corporation rather than for themselves individually.

If the majority is acting illegally or oppresses the rights of the minority shareholders, a lawsuit known as a **derivative suit** may be brought by a minority shareholder on behalf of the corporation. Such suits may seek to enjoin the unlawful activity or to collect damages for the corporation. For example, contracts made between the corporation and an interested director or officer may be challenged. If a suit is brought, the burden is on the director or officer (who may be the majority shareholder) to prove good faith and inherent fairness in such transactions.

The basic difficulty of owning a minority interest in a closely held corporation arises from the fact that there is no ready market for the stock should the shareholder desire to dispose of it. Of course, if there is a valid buy and sell agreement, then there is a market for the stock. Thus, as with partnerships, buy and sell agreements are absolutely essential in closely held corporations.

Liability The legal ability to separate a corporation's shareholders from its managers means that the owners are liable for the debts of the corporation only to the extent of those shareholders' investment in the cost of the stock. Thus, corporate shareholders are said to have **limited personal liability.**

The generalization that the investors in a corporation have limited liability but those in a partnership have unlimited liability is too broad and needs qualification. To be sure, someone investing in a company listed on the New York Stock Exchange will incur no risk greater than the investment, and the concept of limited liability certainly applies. However, if the company

Do realize that any minority ownership intere st in a corporation provides you with very little influence.

Your status as a shareholder in a closely held corporation probably limits your liability for torts; you likely forgo your limited liability for contracts by cosigning your corporation's contracts.

is a small, closely held corporation with limited assets and capital, it will be difficult for it to obtain credit on the strength of its own net worth. As a practical matter, shareholders will usually be required to add their own individual liability as security for borrowing. For example, if the XYZ Company seeks a loan at a local bank, the bank often will require the owners, X, Y, and Z, to personally guarantee repayment of the loan.

This is not to say that shareholders in closely held corporations do not have some degree of limited liability. Shareholders have limited liability for contractlike obligations that are imposed as a matter of law (such as taxes). Liability also is limited when the corporate obligation results from torts committed by company employees while doing company business.

Even in these situations, the mere fact of corporate existence does not guarantee the shareholders will have liability limited to their investment. When courts find that the corporate organization is being misused, the corporate entity can be disregarded. This has been called **piercing the corporate veil.** When this veil of protection has been pierced, the shareholders are treated like partners who have unlimited liability for their organization's debts.

The **alter-ego theory,** by which the corporate veil can be pierced, may also be used to impose personal liability upon corporate officers, directors, and stockholders. If the corporate entity is disregarded by these officials themselves, so that there is such a unity of ownership and interest that separateness of the corporation has ceased to exist, the alter-ego theory will be followed and the corporate veil will be pierced.

Simply alleging that a person is the sole owner of a corporation engaged in wrongful activity will not result in a piercing of the corporate veil. This conclusion is appropriate when the owner has respect for the existence of the organization. In Case 14.1, note the number of factors that must be considered before the corporate veil is pierced.

> The phrases *limited liability* and *unlimited liability* are overly simplistic; an understanding of a business owner's liability goes beyond these simple terms.

 case **14.1**

ALLI v. U.S.
83 Fed. Cl. 250 (2008)

This case involves Dr. Alli and his spouse, property owners who sued the U.S. Department of Housing and Urban Development (HUD) for failure to pay housing assistance for residents of three apartment complexes. The owners held the apartment complexes through a business organization called BSA Corporation. HUD counterclaimed that the Allis breached the agreement for housing assistance due to multiple health and safety violations. Moreover, HUD argued that the Allis were personally liable for the violations, which compelled HUD to pay for relocation of the affected residents.

Among other issues, the court was required to determine whether to strip away the liability protection of the Allis' corporation and "pierce the corporate veil."

The court investigated the extent to which the corporate form was merely used as a shield for illegal activity.

ALLEGRA, J.: In its counterclaims, defendant [HUD] has asserted three breach of contract claims—one each for Pingree, Riverside, and Collingwood—attributable to plaintiffs' failure to maintain the property in good repair and condition so as to provide decent, safe and sanitary housing. . . . For Collingwood, defendant seeks $90,646.40 for the cost of moving families to safe housing, $18,128.80 for foreclosures costs, and $1,112,173.45 for the cost to HUD of providing basic services, security, and repairs while acting as mortgagee-in-possession of Collingwood.

Defendant must carry the burden of proof on its counterclaims. . . . Based on the record, the court finds that defendant has done so, demonstrating that plaintiffs breached the HAP contracts in failing to maintain the properties in a safe, decent and sanitary state. . . .

The next question is who is liable for the damages caused by these breaches. Defendant asserts that the Allis should be "jointly and severally" liable for these damages. As to Collingwood, that means that the court must decide whether the corporate veil of BSA Corp. should be disregarded and liability imposed directly upon Dr. Alli and his wife. "The concept of 'piercing the corporate veil' is equitable in nature," the Federal Circuit has stated, and "courts will pierce the corporate veil 'to achieve justice, equity, to remedy or avoid fraud or wrongdoing, or to impose a just liability.' . . . Because BSA Corp. was incorporated under the laws of Michigan, the court applies that law in deciding whether the corporate veil should be pierced.

. . . Michigan courts often have employed the following tripartite formula:

> First, the corporate entity must be a mere instrumentality of another entity or individual. Second, the corporate entity must be used to commit a fraud or wrong. Third, there must have been an unjust loss or injury to the [party seeking to pierce the veil].

. . . In considering the first of these prongs—whether the corporation is a mere instrumentality—courts have examined, *inter alia,* the adequacy of the corporation's capitalization, the commingling of funds, the diversion of corporate assets for personal use, a failure to comply with the formalities of corporate organization, and domination and control over the corporation by another person or entity. . . .

In general, then, under Michigan law, when the notion of a corporation as a legal entity is used to defeat public convenience, justify a wrong, protect fraud or defend a crime, that notion may be set aside and the corporation treated as being one with its shareholders. . . . As the Sixth Circuit once commented:

> Michigan appears to follow the general rule that requires demonstration of patent abuse of the corporate form in order to pierce the corporate veil. There must be such a unity of interest and ownership that the separate personalities of the corporation and its owner cease to exist, and the circumstances must be such that adherence to the fiction of separate corporate existence would sanction a fraud or promote an injustice.

United States v. Cordova Chem. Co., 113 F.3d 572, 580 (6th Cir. 1997) (en banc), *vacated on other grounds, sub nom., United States v. Bestfoods,* 524 U.S. 51, 118 S. Ct. 1876, 141 L. Ed. 2d 43 (1998) . . .

Other cases emphasize that while there must be some misuse of the corporate form to trigger piercing, that misuse need not necessarily constitute fraud. . . .

In the case *sub judice,* the Allis were the sole owners of BSA Corp., which they purportedly hired to manage their properties and which purportedly owned Collingwood. Every indication is that this corporation was a mere instrumentality that the Allis relied upon when it served their purposes and ignored when it did not. They commingled their funds with those of the corporation—indeed, at trial and in his earlier deposition, Dr. Alli admitted that he and his wife provided interest-free loans to BSA Corp. and, at other times, deposited their personal funds into accounts supposedly controlled by the corporation. The Allis certainly treated the assets of the corporation as if their own—on June 30, 1992, for example, they entered into a deed of trust, as individuals, that encumbered the Collingwood property in exchange for two loans of $250,000 and $75,000, respectively. They provided no evidence to indicate that the proceeds from these loans were used to maintain or improve Collingwood—in fact, BSA Corp. never requested HUD's approval of the loans, as would have been required under the Collingwood regulatory agreement. Periodically, thereafter, the Allis took funds from the Collingwood project account to make payment on these loans and to pay for personal expenses. Accordingly, there is clear proof that BSA Corp. was a merely instrumentality here, disregarded when it served the Allis' purposes, thereby satisfying one of the requirements for piercing the corporate veil. . . .

The other requirements under Michigan law for piercing the corporate veil are satisfied here, as well. First, BSA Corp. certainly was wielded by the Allis to commit a wrong—the failure to maintain the buildings in question in safe, decent and sanitary condition, consistent with BSA Corp.'s contractual obligations. And this entire opinion is a testament to magnitude and seriousness of this wrong. Second, every indication is that the failure to pierce the veil of this thinly-capitalized corporation would lead the United States to suffer an unjust loss. Defendant is seeking well in excess of $1 million in its counterclaims, insofar as it relates to Collingwood, with the majority of those costs associated with HUD's taking over as mortgagee-in-possession. The record suggests that BSA Corp. lacks the funds to pay a judgment of even a fraction of that magnitude. Accordingly, the court concludes that the circumstances here are appropriate for allowing defendant to pierce the corporate veil and hold Dr. Alli and his wife personally liable for any damages arising under the Collingwood counterclaim. . . .

[continued]

KEY POINTS

- Dr. Alli and his wife claimed that the corporate structure shielded them from decisions made in the name of the corporation.
- The court concluded that Dr. Alli and his wife did not act as though the corporation was independent from their personal assets.
- The court also found that the corporate form had been used to commit a wrong by failing to adhere to obligations to keep BSA's properties in a decent and safe condition for tenants.

Taxation Corporations must pay income taxes on their earnings. Sidebar 14.6 sets forth these tax rates. The fact that there is a separate corporate income tax may work as an advantage. For example, if the corporation makes a profit that is to be retained by the corporation to support growth, no income is allocated to the shareholders. These shareholders will not have their personal taxable income increased, as would a partner in a similar situation. In addition, the corporate rate may be lower than the individual rates.

But corporations also have tax disadvantages. Suppose a corporation suffers a loss during a given tax year. The existence of the corporate tax works as a disadvantage, since this loss cannot be distributed to the shareholders in order to reduce their personal tax liability. Indeed, a net operating loss (NOL) to a corporation can be used only to offset corporate income earned in other years. And the allocation of such a loss can be carried back only for two years and carried forward for 20 years. Under the American Recovery and Reinvestment Act of 2009, small businesses can take advantage of additional years to carry back losses. (*Note:* There are many different rules concerning specialized carryover situations. The Internal Revenue Code should be examined prior to relying on the general rule just stated.)

> "Using allowed deductions and legal loopholes, large corporations enjoyed a 12.6 percent tax rate far below the 35 percent tax that is the statutory rate imposed by the federal government on corporate profits."
>
> **—Nelson D. Schwartz,** *New York Times*, **July 1, 2013 (reporting GAO study finding)**

sidebar 14.6

Corporate Tax Rates*

INCOME	TAX RATE
$0–$50,000	15%
$50,000–$75,000	25%
$75,000–$10,000,000	34%
over $10,000,000	35%

*In addition to these rates, there are excess taxes when corporate taxable income exceeds $100,000. These taxes increase again if corporate taxable income exceeds $15,000,000.
Source: 26 U.S.C. §11.

Perhaps a greater disadvantage of the corporate tax occurs when a profit is made and the corporation wishes to pay a dividend to its shareholders. The money used to pay this dividend will have been taxed at the corporate level. It is then taxed again because the shareholder must take the amount of the dividend into his or her own personal income. The existence of the second tax is potentially significant in selecting the best organizational form for a business. This situation has been called the **double tax** on corporate income. A similar situation of double taxation occurs when a corporation is dissolved and its assets are distributed to shareholders as capital gains. Yet, as the discussion next indicates, the double tax may not be as big a disadvantage as it appears at first.

Avoiding Double Taxation   Corporations have employed a variety of techniques for avoiding the double taxation of corporate income. First, reasonable salaries paid to corporate officials may be deducted in computing the taxable income of the business. Thus, in a closely held corporation in which all or most shareholders are officers or employees, this technique may avoid double taxation of substantial portions of income. As might be expected, the Internal Revenue Code disallows a deduction for excessive or unreasonable compensation and treats such payments as dividends. Therefore, the determination of the reasonableness of corporate salaries is often a tax problem in that form of organization.

Second, corporations provide expense accounts for many employees, including shareholder employees. These are used to purchase travel, food, and entertainment. When so used, the employee, to some extent, has compensation that is not taxed. In an attempt to close this tax loophole, the law limits deductions for business meals and entertainment to 50 percent of the cost. Meal expenses and entertainment are deductible only if the expenses are directly related to or associated with the active conduct of a trade or business. For a deduction, business must be discussed directly before, during, or directly after the meal. Additionally, meal expenses are not deductible to the extent the meal is lavish or extravagant. Thus, the use of the expense account to avoid taxation of corporate income is subject to numerous technical rules and limitations.

Third, the capital structure of the corporation may include both common stock and interest-bearing loans from shareholders. For example, assume that a company needs $100,000 cash to go into business. If $100,000 of stock is issued, no expense will be deducted. However, assume that $50,000 worth of stock is purchased by the owners and $50,000 is lent to the company by them at 10 percent interest. In this case, $5,000 interest each year is deductible as an expense of the company and thus subject to only one tax as interest income to the owners. Just as in the case of salaries, the Internal Revenue Code has a counteracting rule relating to corporations that are undercapitalized. If the corporation is undercapitalized, interest payments will be treated as dividends and disallowed as deductible expenses.

The fourth technique for avoiding double taxation, at least in part, is simply not to pay dividends and to accumulate the earnings. The Internal Revenue Service seeks to compel corporations to distribute those profits not needed for a business purpose, such as growth. When a corporation retains earnings in excess of $250,000, there is a presumption that these earnings are being accumulated to avoid a second tax on dividends. If the corporations cannot rebut this presumption, an additional tax is imposed.

Fifth, a corporation may elect to file under Subchapter S of the Internal Revenue Code. This election eliminates the corporate tax; this subject is discussed further later in the chapter.

Ways corporate shareholders might avoid paying two taxes on the business's income and dividend payments: Reasonable salaries. Reasonable expense accounts. Reasonable loans from shareholders. Reasonable accumulation of earnings. Subchapter S election.

concept *summary*

Advantages and Disadvantages of Corporations

The usual advantages of the corporate form of organization include the following:

1. This form is the best practical means of bringing together a large number of investors.
2. Control may be held by those with a minority of the investment.
3. Ownership may be divided into many unequal shares.
4. Shareholders' liabilities are limited to their investments.
5. The organization can have perpetual existence.
6. In addition to being owners, shareholders may be employees entitled to benefits such as workers' compensation.

Among the frequently cited disadvantages of the corporate organization are the following:

1. The cost of forming and maintaining a corporation, with its formal procedural requirements, is significant.
2. License fees and franchise taxes often are assessed against corporations but not partnerships.
3. A corporation must be qualified in all states where it is conducting local or intrastate business.
4. Generally, corporations are subject to more governmental regulation at all levels than are other forms of business.
5. Corporate income may be subject to double taxation.

LIMITED PARTNERSHIPS

A limited partnership basically has all the attributes of a partnership except that one or more of the partners are designated as **limited partners.** This type of partner is not personally responsible for the debts of the business organization. However, these limited partners are not permitted to be involved in the control or operations of the limited partnership. The management is left in the hands of one or more **general partners** who remain personally liable for the organization's debts.

LO 14-3

The attributes of a general partnership and a corporation that combine to make the limited partnership an attractive alternative form of business organization are discussed under the subheadings that follow.

Creation Like a general partnership, a limited partnership is created by agreement. However, as in the case of a corporation, state law requires that the contents of a certificate must be recorded in a public office so that everyone may be fully advised as to the details of the organization. This certificate contains, among other matters, the following information: the name of the partnership, the character of the business, its location, the name and place of residence of each member, those who are to be the general partners and those who are to be the limited partners, the length of time the partnership is to exist, the amount of cash or the agreed value of property to be contributed by each partner, and the share of profit or compensation each limited partner shall receive.

Limited partnerships are complex organizations that have been used to raise money for real estate investments and management of complex entities, such as professional sports teams.

The limited partnership certificate is required to be recorded in the county where the partnership has its principal place of business. An additional copy has to be filed in every community where the partnership conducts business or has an office. Whenever there is a change in the information contained in the filed certificate, a new certificate must be prepared and recorded. If an accurate certificate is not on record and the limited partnership continues its operation, the limited partners become liable as general partners. Substantial compliance with all the technical requirements of the limited partnership law is essential if the limited partners are to be assured of their limited liability.

The terms of the limited partnership agreement control the governance of the organization. These terms should be read carefully and understood by all general and limited partners before the agreement is signed. Failure of the parties to state their agreement clearly may result in a court's interpreting the limited partnership agreement.

Continuity The principles guiding partnerships also apply to limited partnerships if there is a change in the general partners. A limited partner may assign his or her interest to another without dissolving the limited partnership.

Managerial Control In a limited partnership, the general partners are in control. Limited partners have no right to participate in management. The impact of this relationship on the operations of a limited partnership is discussed in detail in the next subsection.

Liability The true nature of the limited partnership being a hybrid is in the area of owners' liability. Traditionally, the general partners in a limited partnership have unlimited liability. However, the limited partners are not personally liable for the partnership's debts. These limited partners' liability typically will not exceed the amount of their investments.

Under the Revised Uniform Limited Partnership Act (RULPA), a limited partner's surname may not be used in the partnership's name unless there is a general partner with the same name. If a limited partner's name is used in the firm's name, that partner will become personally liable to unsuspecting creditors.

Limited partners also may not participate in the management of the limited partnership. Under the RULPA, a limited partner who participates in the organization's management becomes liable as a general partner if a third party had knowledge of the limited partner's activities. Sidebar 14.7 lists actions by a limited partner that are not considered participation in management.

sidebar 14.7

Actions by Limited Partner

Limited partners do not lose the benefit of limited personal liability when performing the following:

- Acting as an agent or employee of the partnership.
- Consulting with or advising a general partner.
- Acting as a guarantor of the partnership's obligations.
- Inspecting and copying any of the partnership's financial records.
- Demanding true and full information about the partnership whenever circumstances render it just and reasonable.

- Receiving a share of the profits or other compensation by way of income.
- Approving or disapproving an amendment to the partnership's certificate.
- Voting on matters of fundamental importance such as dissolution, sale of assets, or change of the partnership's name.
- Having contribution returned upon dissolution.

S CORPORATIONS

Beginning in 1958, the federal government permitted shareholders of certain corporations to unanimously elect to have their organization treated like a partnership for income tax purposes. This election is made possible through the language of Subchapter S of the Internal Revenue Code. Today, organizations that are subject to this election often are referred to simply as **S corporations.**

The S corporation has all the legal characteristics of the corporation previously discussed in this chapter. The one exception to this similar treatment is that shareholders in the S corporation are responsible for accounting on their individual income tax returns for their respective shares of their organization's profits or losses. In essence, these shareholders can elect to have their business organization treated, for tax purposes, as if it were a partnership. Through this election, the shareholders avoid having a tax assessed on the corporate income itself. Even though the S corporation does not pay any taxes, like a partnership, it must file an information return with the Internal Revenue Service.

S corporations cannot have more than 100 shareholders, each of whom must elect to have the corporate income allocated to the shareholders annually in computing their income for tax purposes, whether actually paid out or not. Only individuals are eligible to elect under Subchapter S. Therefore, other forms of business organization, such as partnerships, limited partnerships, or corporations, cannot be shareholders in an S corporation.

Do remember the limitation on the number of shareholders in an S corporation reduces it as an option for many business ventures.

sidebar 14.8

Nonprofit Corporations

Depending on the purpose of your organization, you may find that creating a nonprofit corporation instead of one of the above forms is a better choice. A nonprofit corporation must file articles of incorporation with the state, it is run by a board of directors and has limited liability, just like a traditional corporation. However, a nonprofit does not return a profit to its owners. Rather, it must return any profits made to the organization to be used for future operations. Importantly, a nonprofit can have paid employees, the payment to whom is considered an expense. Many different types of businesses are run as nonprofits, including charities, religious organizations, museums, and even universities.

One critical attribute for many nonprofits is tax-exempt status. In addition to eliminating tax liability, such status permits donors to deduct contributions from their taxes. The U.S. Internal Revenue Service must approve exempt status, and many nonprofits file under section 501(c)(3) of the IRS code. Similar filings must be made with the relevant state. Yearly filings to the IRS are required, and organizations that do not comply or meet the exemption requirements may have their status revoked. In 2011, the IRS announced that it was revoking the tax-exempt status of 275,000 nonprofits, shrinking the sector by 17 percent. This action demonstrates the diligence that is required if a corporation is to effectively operate as a nonprofit.

Sources: National Council of Nonprofits, www.councilofnonprofits. org; IRS, Tax Information for Charitable Organizations, www.irs.gov/ Charities-&-Non-Profits/Charitable-Organizations; Stephanie Strom, "I.R.S. Ends Exemptions for 275,000 Nonprofits," *The New York Times,* June 8, 2011.

In addition to the limitations just stated, there are many technical rules of tax law involved in S corporations. However, as a rule of thumb, this method of organization has distinct advantages for a business operating at a loss because the loss is shared and immediately deductible on the returns of the shareholders. It is also advantageous for businesses capable of paying out net profits as earned. In the latter case, the corporate tax is avoided. If net profits must be retained in the business, Subchapter S tax treatment is disadvantageous because income tax is paid on earnings not received, and there is a danger of double taxation to the individual because undistributed earnings that have been taxed once are taxed again in the event of the death of a shareholder. Thus, the theoretical advantage of using an S corporation to avoid double taxation of corporate income must be carefully qualified.

LIMITED LIABILITY ORGANIZATIONS

The **limited liability company** is an increasingly popular organizational alternative. In 1977, Wyoming was the first state to pass a law permitting the creation of this type of business organization.

In 1988, the Internal Revenue Service ruled that limited liability companies (LLCs) would be treated as nontaxable entities, much like partnerships, for federal income tax purposes. Following this ruling, states rushed to pass legislation authorizing businesspeople to operate their businesses as LLCs. In essence, its owners have more flexibility than with the S corporation while not having to struggle with the complexities of the limited partnership.

A variation of the LLC is known as the **limited liability partnership**. This organization often is used by professionals, such as doctors, lawyers, and accountants. In the true sense of a hybrid, an LLC and an LLP have characteristics of both a partnership and a corporation.

> Over the last two decades, the growth of LLPs and LLCs has made these organizational forms very popular for closely held businesses.

The growing popularity of these forms of business organizations requires a careful examination of various factors. The focus of the following subheadings is on the LLC.

Creation   An LLC is created through filings much like those used when creating a corporation. **Articles of organization** are filed with a state official, usually the secretary of state. Instead of "incorporators," the term **organizers** is used. The name of any LLC must acknowledge the special nature of this organizational form by including the phrase "limited liability company," or "limited company," or some abbreviation, such as "LLC" or "LC." An LLC created in a state other than the one in which it is conducting business is called a foreign LLC. Like a foreign corporation, this LLC must apply to the state to be authorized to transact business legally. An LLC also must file annual reports with the states in which it operates.

Continuity   The owners of LLCs are called **members** rather than shareholders or partners. Membership in LLCs is not limited to individuals. Unlike in the S corporation, a business organization can be an owner in any LLC. The transferability of a member's interest is restricted in the fashion of a partner as opposed to the free transferability of a corporate shareholder.

Anytime a member dies or withdraws from the LLC, there is a dissolution of the business organization. However, the business of a dissolved LLC is not necessarily adversely impacted if the remaining members decide to continue business. Either as provided in the articles of organization or by agreement of the remaining members within 90 days of the withdrawing member's disassociation, the business of the LLC may be continued rather than wound up.

Managerial Control The managerial control of an LLC is vested in its members, unless the articles of organization provide for one or more **managers.** Regardless of whether members or managers control the LLC, a majority of these decision makers decide the direction of the organization (the fiduciary duties of LLC managers are addressed in Sidebar 14.9). In a few situations enumerated in the state law authorizing LLCs, unanimous consent of the members is required for the organization to make a binding decision. Similarly to partners in a partnership, members of LLCs make contributions of capital. They have equal rights to share in the LLC's profits and losses, unless these members have agreed otherwise. When a member is in the minority with respect to decisions being made on behalf of the LLC, that dissenting member may have rights very much like a dissenting shareholder in a corporation. These rights include bringing a derivative lawsuit against the controlling members of the LLC. Ultimately, a dissenting member has the right to sell the membership interest to the other members of the LLC.

sidebar 14.9

Fiduciary Duties in LLCs

It is a standard proposition that corporate officers and directors owe fiduciary duties of care and loyalty to shareholders. Do managers of limited liability companies owe similar duties to members? Surprisingly, this is an area of law that is still being developed. Some states treat LLC fiduciary duties similar to those owed in corporations, while others apply the rules for partnership. Fiduciary duties are clearly spelled out in some state statutes, while others are silent. In some cases, different duties are triggered in a "manager managed" LLC versus one that is "member managed." Delaware provides an especially strong mechanism for limiting fiduciary duties by permitting their contractual elimination in the LLC agreement. Courts are still working out what the above statutory language means in the context of this relatively new form of business organization. It is an important issue. In deciding what state is best for LLC organization and what language to include in the agreement, the desired nature of fiduciary duties should be considered.

Source: Sandra K. Miller, "What Fiduciary Duties Should Apply to the LLC Manager After More Than a Decade of Experimentation?" 32 *Journal of Corporate Law* 565 (2007).

Liability For liability purposes, members do act as agents of their LLC. However, they are not personally liable to third parties. Thus, these members have attributes of both partners and shareholders with respect to liability.

Taxation Finally, state laws and the IRS recognize LLCs as nontaxable entities. Although the LLC appears to have many advantages, do not forget that careful analysis is needed in every situation to determine whether this type of tax treatment is in the members' best interests.

 ## Operating the Organization

With an understanding of the various organizational forms and the factors businesspeople need to consider when deciding how to do business, we are ready to focus on making the decision as to which form of organization is most appropriate for conducting business. Following the next section, this chapter concludes with some thoughts on trends in operating business organizations.

MAKING THE DECISION

Don't assume there is an easy answer to which organizational form is best; careful analysis and consultation with experts help businesspeople make wise decisions in the selection process.

There usually is no absolutely right answer to the question, Which organizational form is best for a particular business's operation? Hopefully the preceding sections have presented you with some helpful background material to consider when this important decision is made.

The criteria used to select a form of organization needs to be reviewed periodically. This review should be done in consultation with close advisers such as attorneys, accountants, bankers, and insurers. These people weigh the factors and costs involved and then select the most suitable organizational form for the business's needs at that time. Because this selection process balances advantages against disadvantages, the decision often is to choose the least objectionable form of organization.

Today, the growth in limited liability partnerships and limited liability companies could lead you to think these are the best options for your business activities. While one of these forms may be best, a careful analysis will consider the various factors discussed in this chapter.

It is not unusual for the growth in a business to be reflected in changes in organizational forms as a part of a life cycle. For example, business activity could begin through the efforts of a sole proprietor. As the business grows and investors join the business, the organizational form could shift to a partnership or limited partnership (depending on the active or passive nature of the investor). An alternative to the partnership or limited partnership could be a limited liability organization. As the business matures and prepares to conduct a public offering of its stock, the corporate form becomes the most feasible organization.

TRENDS IN MANAGING THE ORGANIZATION

"The idea of a benefit corporation is to weave some social responsibility into the DNA of the company itself through its charter."

—Ben Schreckinger,
Boston Globe,
November 25, 2012

In the next chapter, you will study the Dodd-Frank Wall Street Reform and Consumer Protection Act (Dodd-Frank Act), which includes corporate governance reform among its many provisions. Subsequent chapters address other legal issues important to governance, such as competition laws and securities and financial regulations. Since control of business organizations is a major topic in this chapter, three important trends merit consideration here.

A first significant trend in corporate organization and control is the emergence of the **benefit corporation.** It combines aspects of non-profit and profit organizations in a way intended to permit the business to make a profit while pursuing explicit, socially oriented goals. First approved as a corporate form in Maryland in 2010, it has spread to about half the states, including Delaware, California, Illinois, Massachusetts, New Jersey, and New York. Variations with similar goals include California's flexible-purpose corporation and Washington's social-purpose corporation. Remember to distinguish a benefit corporation from a "B-Corp," which is a private certification rather than a legal business structure.

The impetus for creating the benefit corporation structure comes from the perception that traditional corporate forms place too much emphasis on profit maximization. This may conflict with business decisions that would yield less profit but achieve a social goal such as preserving the environment or enhancing employment opportunities in the community. In most states with the benefit corporation structure, firms identify the targeted public benefit in the articles of incorporation and subsequently provide reports to shareholders on progress in achieving the benefit. It may be possible to change an existing corporate structure to a benefit corporation.

Benefit corporations are not without criticism. Some note that traditional corporations are not legally or functionally precluded from offering essentially the same social benefits due to the flexibility in corporate governance.[1] Justice Alito made this point explicitly in *Burwell v. Hobby Lobby Stores, Inc.* (2014). Moreover, there may be less accountability to shareholders in a benefit corporation. To date, only a few hundred of these corporations have been formed in the various states, and it remains to be seen whether the movement will grow significantly in the future.

A second trend is the continued definition of the nature of corporate personhood. As described above, corporations are considered legal persons under the law. They undertake activities like individuals, such as buying and selling property. In addition, corporations incur liability for their actions, such as manufacturing defective products. The U.S. Code even explicitly states that, in interpreting U.S. law, "the words 'person' and 'whoever' include corporations, companies, associations, firms, partnerships, societies, and joint stock companies, as well as individuals" (1 U.S.C. §1). Thus, corporations and individuals reasonably have a largely equal claim to rights and protections under the law. For example, in *Citizens United v. Federal Election Commission,* 558 U.S. 310 (2010), the Supreme Court affirmed a corporation's speech protections under the Constitution's First Amendment by striking down a federal law that limited spending on political advertising. And in *Burwell v. Hobby Lobby Stores, Inc.* (2104), the Supreme Court was compelled to determine whether for-profit corporations are "persons" within the meaning of the Religious Freedom Restoration Act. The Court found that closely-held corporations (non-publicly traded) are indeed persons that have a right to the free exercise of religion (see Chapter 6 for an excerpt of this case).

To be sure, it is not always obvious when corporations should be treated identically to individuals. As detailed in Case 14.2, the U.S. Supreme Court considered whether corporations possess personal privacy rights as defined by the federal Freedom of Information Act.

[1] *Angus Loten,* "With New Law, Profits Take a Back Seat," Wall Street Journal online, *January 19, 2012.*

FEDERAL COMMUNICATIONS COMMISSION v. AT&T INC.
131 S. Ct. 1177 (2011)

AT&T voluntarily disclosed to the Federal Communications Commission (FCC) that it might have overcharged the government for telecommunications and information services related to a program designed to enhance access to schools and libraries. The FCC investigated, and AT&T provided various documents in response. AT&T eventually agreed to pay the government $500,000 to settle the case.

When a trade association representing some of AT&T's competitors requested the company's documents through a Freedom of Information Act (FOIA) request, AT&T objected on the basis that it would constitute a violation of personal privacy. However, the FOIA's "personal privacy" exemption to making records public had never been applied to corporations. Although corporations are considered legal persons, it was not clear under the statute that the broad legal definition of "person" applied here. Thus, the Court was required to determine when corporate "persons" have "personal privacy" rights protected by the FOIA.

ROBERTS, C.J.: The Freedom of Information Act requires federal agencies to make records and documents publicly available upon request, unless they fall within one of several statutory exemptions. One of those exemptions covers law enforcement records, the disclosure of which "could reasonably be expected to constitute an unwarranted invasion of personal privacy." . . . The question presented is whether corporations have "personal privacy" for the purposes of this exemption. . . .

AT&T relies on the argument that the word "personal" in [the FOIA exemption] incorporates the statutory definition of the word "person." . . . The Administrative Procedure Act defines "person" to include "an individual, partnership, corporation, association, or public or private organization other than an agency." . . . Because that definition applies here, the argument goes, "personal" must mean relating to those "person[s]": namely, corporations and other entities as well as individuals. This reading, we are told, is dictated by a "basic principle of grammar and usage." . . .

We disagree. Adjectives typically reflect the meaning of corresponding nouns, but not always. Sometimes they acquire distinct meanings of their own. The noun "crab" refers variously to a crustacean and a type of apple, while the related adjective "crabbed" can refer to handwriting that is "difficult to read,"; . . . "corny"

can mean "using familiar and stereotyped formulas believed to appeal to the unsophisticated," . . . which has little to do with "corn," . . .; and while "crank" is "a part of an axis bent at right angles," "cranky" can mean "given to fretful fussiness,". . . .

Even in cases such as these there may well be a link between the noun and the adjective. "Cranky" describes a person with a "wayward" or "capricious" temper . . . which might bear some relation to the distorted or crooked angular shape from which a "crank" takes its name. That is not the point. What is significant is that, in ordinary usage, a noun and its adjective form may have meanings as disparate as any two unrelated words. The FCC's argument that "personal" does not, in fact, derive from the English word "person," but instead developed along its own etymological path . . . simply highlights the shortcomings of AT&T's proposed rule.

"Person" is a defined term in the statute; "personal" is not. When a statute does not define a term, we typically "give the phrase its ordinary meaning." . . . "Personal" ordinarily refers to individuals. We do not usually speak of personal characteristics, personal effects, personal correspondence, personal influence, or personal tragedy as referring to corporations or other artificial entities. This is not to say that corporations do not have correspondence, influence, or tragedies of their own, only that we do not use the word "personal" to describe them.

Certainly, if the chief executive officer of a corporation approached the chief financial officer and said, "I have something personal to tell you," we would not assume the CEO was about to discuss company business. Responding to a request for information, an individual might say, "that's personal." A company spokesman, when asked for information about the company, would not. In fact, we often use the word "personal" to mean precisely the *opposite* of business-related: We speak of personal expenses and business expenses, personal life and work life, personal opinion and a company's view . . .

AT&T dismisses these definitions, correctly noting that "personal"—at its most basic level—simply means "[o]f or pertaining to a particular person.". . . . The company acknowledges that "in non-legal usage, where a 'person' is a human being, it is entirely unsurprising that the word 'personal' is used to refer to human beings.". . . But in a watered-down version

[continued]

of the "grammatical imperative" argument, AT&T contends that "person"—in common *legal* usage—is understood to include a corporation. "Personal" in the same context therefore can and should have the same scope, especially here in light of the statutory definition. . . .

The construction of statutory language often turns on context, . . . which certainly may include the definitions of related words. But here the context to which AT&T points does not dissuade us from the ordinary meaning of "personal." We have no doubt that "person," in a legal setting, often refers to artificial entities. The Dictionary Act makes that clear . . . But AT&T's effort to ascribe a corresponding legal meaning to "personal" again elides the difference between "person" and "personal." . . .

Regardless of whether "personal" can carry a special meaning in legal usage, "when interpreting a statute . . . we construe language . . . in light of the terms surrounding it." . . .

AT&T's argument treats the term "personal privacy" as simply the sum of its two words: the privacy of a person. Under that view, the defined meaning of the noun "person," or the asserted specialized legal meaning, takes on greater significance. But two words together may assume a more particular meaning than those words in isolation. We understand a golden cup to be a cup made of or resembling gold. A golden boy, on the other hand, is one who is charming, lucky,

and talented. A golden opportunity is one not to be missed. "Personal" in the phrase "personal privacy" conveys more than just "of a person." It suggests a type of privacy evocative of human concerns—not the sort usually associated with an entity like, say, AT&T. . . .

AT&T contends that this Court has recognized "privacy" interests of corporations in the Fourth Amendment and double jeopardy contexts, and that the term should be similarly construed here. . . . But this case does not call upon us to pass on the scope of a corporation's "privacy" interests as a matter of constitutional or common law. The discrete question before us is instead whether Congress used the term "personal privacy" to refer to the privacy of artificial persons in FOIA Exemption 7(C); the cases AT&T cites are too far afield to be of help here.

. . . AT&T has given us no sound reason in the statutory text or context to disregard the ordinary meaning of the phrase "personal privacy." . . .

We reject the argument that because "person" is defined for purposes of FOIA to include a corporation, the phrase "personal privacy" in Exemption 7(C) reaches corporations as well. The protection in FOIA against disclosure of law enforcement information on the ground that it would constitute an unwarranted invasion of personal privacy does not extend to corporations. We trust that AT&T will not take it personally.

KEY POINTS

- Even though a corporation is treated the same as an individual under most aspects of the law, there are some rights that only individuals can possess.
- The Court determined that corporations do not have personal privacy rights, at least in the way intended by Congress.

In third trend, criminal prosecutions for corporate wrongdoing may be declining due to the increased use of "deferred prosecution agreements" (DPAs) by the federal government. A DPA is used to encourage self-reporting and remediation of illegal acts before a criminal case is commenced. This alternative avoids some of the harsh consequences that can accompany prosecutions while still addressing the crime itself. The use of DPAs increased after the government's case against accounting firm Arthur Andersen in the early part of the last decade. The firm was initially convicted for its role in destroying documents related to its client, Enron. Its conviction was eventually overturned, and Arthur Andersen was severely damaged, unable to continue its operations as one of the country's largest accounting firms. If the government had used a DPA instead, many believe, the firm might still be around and the employees who had nothing to do with the alleged crime would not have suffered. DPAs have been used in many recent cases, including the U.S. government's prosecution of Credit Suisse for aiding client tax evasion, Toyota for concealing safety defects in automobiles, and JPMorgan Chase for failing to maintain anti-money laundering controls in the Bernard Madoff scandal.

Despite the advantages, there is some concern that the overuse of DPAs could lead to an overly lenient environment for addressing corporate malfeasance. Perhaps some companies will be perceived as "too big to jail." Coupled with the Supreme Court's recent narrowing of the federal "honest services" law to incidents of bribery and kickbacks in *Skilling v. U.S.*, 561 U.S. 358 (2010), the future may yield fewer corporate criminal cases.

We encourage you to use what you learn in this chapter to stay current in this area of operating and managing business organizations.

Key Terms

Alien corporation 421
Alter-ego theory 425
Articles of incorporation 422
Articles of organization 432
Articles of partnership 419
Assumed-name statute 419
Benefit corporation 434
Buy and sell agreement 420
Charter 422
Closely held 414
Corporation 421
Derivative suit 424
Directors 423
Dissolution 415
Domestic corporation 421
Double tax 428
Foreign corporation 421
General partner 429
Incorporator 422
Jointly and severally liable 420
Limited liability company 432
Limited liability partnership 432
Limited partner 429
Limited personal liability 424
Managers 433
Members 432
Officer 423
Organizer 432
Partnership 418
Piercing the corporate veil 425
Proxy 423
Publicly held 414
S corporation 431
Shareholder 423
Sole proprietorship 416

Review Questions and Problems

1. *Forms of Business Organizations*
   (a) What are the three traditional business organizations and the four hybrid forms?

Factors to Consider When Selecting a Business's Organizational Form

2. *Creation*
   Relative to other factors discussed in this chapter, how important is the factor of creation?

3. *Continuity*
   Why does dissolution of a business organization not necessarily impact that organization's business activities?

4. *Managerial Control*

   Why should business owners take time to discuss the control each will exert over the organization's activities?

5. *Liability*

   What is meant by the phrase liability of a business organization as compared to the liability of the owners?

6. *Taxation*

   Why is taxation an important element to consider when selecting the appropriate organization for your business activities?

Selecting the Best Organizational Form

7. *Sole Proprietorships*

   What are the limitations of the sole proprietorship?

8. *Partnerships*

   Terry is the senior partner in an accounting firm. One of Terry's partners performs an audit. The audited firm sues Terry, as the senior partner, for alleged errors in the audit. If Terry is found liable, can Terry sue to collect a pro rata share of this liability from the other partners? Why or why not?

9. *Corporations*

   (a) Who controls the closely held corporation? Explain.

   (b) Describe five techniques that a corporation might use to avoid the double taxation of corporate profits.

10. *Limited Partnerships*

    Laura and Gary have formed a limited partnership, with Gary agreeing to be the general partner. This partnership has purchased supplies from Sam. Sam has received a promissory note signed on behalf of the partnership as payment. If the partnership is unable to pay this note, can Sam hold Gary personally liable? Explain.

11. *S Corporations*

    (a) Although it is technically a corporation, the S corporation has the attributes of which business organization when considering the taxation factor?

    (b) What is the implication of this treatment if the S corporation has a profitable year but does not distribute dividends to its shareholders?

12. *Limited Liability Organizations*

    What is the advantage of this organizational form compared to the S corporation?

Operating the Organization

13. *Making the Decision*

    Albert and Barbara wish to enter into the business of manufacturing fine furniture. Which form of business organization would you recommend in each of the following situations? Explain each of your answers.

    (a) Barbara is a furniture expert, but she has no funds. Albert knows nothing about such production, but he is willing to contribute all the money needed to start the business.

    (b) The furniture-manufacturing process requires more capital than Albert or Barbara can raise together. However, they wish to maintain control of the business.

    (c) The production process can be very dangerous, and a large tort judgment against the business is foreseeable.

    (d) Sales will be nationwide.

    (e) A loss is expected for the first several years.

14. *Trends in Managing the Organization*

Detail three trends in the law related to corporate governance. Discuss whether you believe these trends, taken together, reflect an increase or decrease in legal risk associated with managing the organization.

business *discussions*

1. You and two of your college roommates have discussed plans to open a restaurant. You intend to attract college-age students who are health- and fitness-minded to your restaurant. You and your co-owners agree that each will invest equally in terms of time and money. However, in addition to contributions made by each of you, another $700,000 is essential for the restaurant to succeed.

What type of organization is best suited for this business activity?
Who will manage the restaurant during times that you and your co-owners are not present?
What liabilities do you and your co-owners face?

2. Three years following your graduation with a business degree, you and three classmates began operating a consulting business. Your firm specializes in offering support related to payroll-and account-management computer applications. So far, your firm has relied on the four of you as its only consultants. A potential major client requests that your firm make a proposal for a year-long project. This project would result in your firm hiring several additional consultants and support staff. Because of the length of time and financial commitment this project may take, you and your co-owners take time to address the following questions:

How would your firm conduct business on such a large scale?
How could you limit potential liability for and by various consultants?
Which form of business organization is best suited to meet the needs of your growing firm?

Part **THREE**

The Regulatory Landscape for Business

Part Three of this text focuses on some of the most important questions discussed in our society today. Can the government's regulatory powers protect and improve the lives of individuals and level the playing field for business competition yet still encourage businesses to thrive and innovate? It is a difficult balance of interests that requires an understanding of the complex regulatory environment. The next five chapters describe and discuss critical elements of business regulation.

Chapter 15 focuses on the regulatory process, highlighting the role of administrative agencies in the development of rules and promulgation of regulations to carry out the laws passed by Congress. Courts oversee the work of the administrative agencies as a check on the executive branch. The chapter also explores this important dynamic.

Chapter 16 illustrates why the Sherman Act and other antitrust laws remain important in the early years of the twenty-first century. The regulation of business activities to ensure a competitive environment is now over 100 years old—the Sherman Antitrust Act became law in 1890—yet it continues to be of critical significance. From the market dominance of Microsoft to Apple to Google, the regulatory environment attempts to find the right balance of restrictive and free market principles to ensure workable competition in international marketplaces.

We know the regulation of the securities industry began as an attempt to help the United States emerge from the Great Depression in the 1930s. One of the commonplace responses to economic troubles caused by business excesses has been further regulation of financial institutions and securities firms and exchanges. The accounting scandals involving Enron, WorldCom, and many other major companies produced the Congressional response called Sarbanes-Oxley. The more recent economic crises resulted in the Dodd-Frank Wall Street Reform and Consumer Protection Act of 2010. Chapter 17 provides details on the history that lead to securities regulations and financial reforms.

Another critically important area of regulations concerns how individuals are protected from various business activities that might produce harm. Chapter 18 examines privacy and important consumer laws. New in this edition is an expanded discussion of privacy. As technology and security become more pervasive parts of our lives, the impact on privacy increasingly is discussed. Protecting privacy is now as prominent a government regulatory issue as consumer protection. Consumer law regulates by establishing legal requirements that protect consumers and their resources from harmful trade practices. Chapter 18 focuses on the Federal Trade Commission's consumer protection authority, various laws protecting consumers in the extension of credit, limitations on debt collection, and the financial discharge of consumers in bankruptcy.

Finally, in this part of the text, we look at the laws designed to protect our physical environment. Chapter 19 examines the efforts of federal, state, and local governments to enact laws limiting pollution of air, water, and land. This chapter also provides examples of environmental laws that protect human health, endangered species, and other aspects of the environment. At this moment in time, some argue that our environmental laws have been so successful in creating a cleaner environment that there is little to gain from increased regulation. Others argue that businesspeople will sacrifice the environment's well being for all in return for increased profits for a few. Chapter 19 provides information so you can make your own judgment as to how businesspeople should act to ensure a safe future. •

15

The Regulatory Process

Learning Objectives:

In this chapter, you will learn:

15-1. To analyze the essential reasons for and requirements of administrative agencies.

15-2. To evaluate the role of courts in reviewing the actions of administrative agencies.

15-3. To understand the trade-offs involved in the regulatory processes.

From a historical perspective, there are many eras during which significant laws were passed. However, three periods stand out as involving major expansion of government regulation of business activities. First, the New Deal of the 1930s and 1940s included the creation of securities regulations, social security, minimum wages, and several labor laws. During the period of the Great Society in the 1960s and 1970s, the Civil Rights Act, Medicare, other employment laws, and environmental regulations were enacted. Since the turn to the twenty-first century, a third period of expansion has included the Sarbanes-Oxley Act, economic recovery legislation, health care, and financial reforms.

While it is beyond the scope of this text to explain whether a 30-year pattern exists and whether one of these eras is more significant than the others, it is clear we need to address several questions related to government regulation of business.

This chapter focuses on the regulatory process and the role of regulation in the legal system. You will be introduced to the regulatory process through administrative agencies at the federal, state, and local levels. In addition to learning about the reasons for and functions of agencies, the role of the courts in reviewing and enforcing administrative rules and regulations are examined.

LO 15-1 Regulatory Process—Administrative Agencies

Recall from the Constitution discussion in Chapter 6 that authority of the federal, state, and local governments to regulate our professional and personal lives is founded in the constitutional principles of the commerce clause and police powers. Typically, the actual regulatory activity is performed by administrative agencies. The term **administrative agencies** describes the boards, bureaus, commissions, and organizations that make up the governmental bureaucracy. Sidebar 15.1 lists several federal agencies and briefly describes their functions.

These agencies have either one or both types of regulatory authority. The first type is called **quasi-legislative** in that an agency can issue rules (regulations) that have the impact of laws. The second type is **quasi-judicial** in that agencies can make decisions like a court.

The direct day-to-day legal impact on business of the rules and regulations adopted and enforced by these agencies is probably greater than the impact of the courts or other branches of government. Administrative agencies create and enforce the majority of all laws constituting the legal environment of business. The administrative process at either the state or federal level regulates almost every business activity.

> The regulatory process involves agencies at all levels of government.

Although we focus on federal agencies in this chapter, keep in mind that state and local governments also have many agencies. For example, state workers' compensation boards hear cases involving industrial accidents and injuries to employees, and most local governments have zoning boards that make recommendations that impact business activities. State governments usually license and regulate intrastate transportation, and state boards usually set rates for local utilities supplying gas and electricity.

In the rest of this chapter, you will study the following:

- The reasons our governments have come to rely on administrative agencies
- The basic functions of administrative agencies
- The organization and workings of these agencies
- The limits of courts' review of agencies' actions

REASONS FOR AGENCIES

There are many reasons why administrative agencies are necessary. Almost every governmental agency exists because of a recognized problem in society and the expectation that the agency may be able to help solve the problem.

sidebar 15.1

Major Federal Agencies

NAME	FUNCTIONS
Consumer Product Safety Commission (CPSC)	Protects the public against unreasonable risks of injury associated with consumer products.
Environmental Protection Agency (EPA)	Administers all laws relating to the environment, including laws on water pollution, air pollution, solid wastes, pesticides, toxic substances, etc.
Federal Aviation Administration (FAA) (part of the Department of Transportation)	Regulates civil aviation to provide safe and efficient use of airspace.
Federal Communications Commission (FCC)	Regulates interstate and foreign communications by means of radio, television, wire, cable, and satellite.
Federal Energy Regulatory Commission (FERC)	Promotes dependable, affordable energy through sustained competitive markets.
Federal Reserve Board (FRB)	Regulates the availability and cost of money and credit; the nation's central bank.
Federal Trade Commission (FTC)	Protects the public from anticompetitive behavior and unfair and deceptive business practices.
Food and Drug Administration (FDA)	Administers laws to prohibit distribution of adulterated, misbranded, or unsafe food and drugs.
Equal Employment Opportunity Commission (EEOC)	Seeks to prevent discrimination in employment based on race, color, religion, sex, or national origin and other unlawful employment practices.
National Labor Relations Board (NLRB)	Conducts union certification elections and holds hearings on unfair labor practice complaints.
Occupational Safety and Health Administration (OSHA)	Ensures all workers a safe and healthy work environment.
Securities and Exchange Commission (SEC)	Enforces the federal securities laws that regulate sale of securities to the investing public.

This section contains a discussion of the reasons why agencies are the essential part of the regulatory process.

Administrative agencies are needed to provide specificity, expertise, protection, regulation, and services.

Providing Specificity Legislative branches often cannot legislate in sufficient detail to cover all aspects of many problems. Congress cannot possibly legislate in minute detail, and, as a consequence, it uses more and more general language in stating its regulatory aims and purposes. For example, Congress cannot enact a securities law that covers every possible issue that might arise. Therefore, it delegates to the Securities and Exchange Commission the power to make rules and regulations to fill in the gaps and create the necessary details to make securities laws workable. In many areas an agency develops detailed rules and regulations to carry out a legislative policy.

The Internal Revenue Service (IRS) implements federal tax policy.

Also courts cannot handle all disputes and controversies that may arise. For example, each year tens of thousands of industrial accidents cause injury or death to workers. If each of these industrial accidents results in traditional litigation, the courts simply will not have the time or the personnel to handle the multitude of cases. Therefore, workers' compensation boards decide such claims. Likewise, most cases involving alleged discrimination in employment are turned over to agencies for investigation and resolution.

Zoning and Planning Boards are local agencies that provide specificity, expertise, and protection.

Providing Expertise   A reason many agencies are created is to refer a problem or area to experts for solution and management. The Federal Reserve Board (FRB), the Nuclear Regulatory Commission (NRC), and the Food and Drug Administration (FDA) are examples of agencies with expertise beyond that of Congress or the executive branch. The development of sound policies and proper decisions in many areas requires expertise, and thus we tend to resort to administrative agencies for this expertise. Similarly, administrative agencies often provide needed continuity and consistency in the formulation, application, and enforcement of rules and regulations governing business.

Providing Protection   Many governmental agencies exist to protect the public, especially from the business community. Business often fails to regulate itself, and the lack of self-regulation is contrary to the public interest. For example, the failure of business to voluntarily refrain from polluting many streams and rivers as well as the air led to the creation of the Environmental Protection Agency (EPA). The sale of worthless securities to the investing public was a major reason for the creation of the Securities and Exchange Commission (SEC). The manufacture and sale of dangerous products led to the creation of the Consumer Product Safety Commission (CPSC). Americans tend to turn to a governmental agency for assistance whenever a business or business practice may injure significant numbers of the general public. A prevailing attitude exists that the government's duty is to protect the public from harm.

Providing Regulation   Agencies often replace competition with regulation. When a firm is given monopoly power, it loses its freedom of contract, and a governmental body is given the power to determine the provisions of its contracts. For example, electric utility companies are usually given a monopoly in the geographic area which they serve. A state agency such as a public service commission then has the power to set the rate structure for the utility. Similar agencies regulate transportation and banking because of the difference in bargaining power between the business and the public. Regulation is often a substitute for competition.

Providing Services   Many agencies arise simply out of necessity. If we are to have a mail service, a post office is necessary. Welfare programs require government personnel to administer them. Social Security programs necessitate that there be a federal agency to determine eligibility and pay benefits. The mere existence of most government programs automatically creates a new agency or expands the functions of an existing one.

The Affordable Care Act created and authorized dozens of new entities to implement the legislation, providing a recent example of how Congress relies on regulatory bodies to fulfill legislative mandates. A complex undertaking such as coordinating aspects of the health care law affects numerous existing agencies as well.

FUNCTIONS OF AGENCIES

Administrative agencies tend to possess functions of the other three branches of government, including:

- Rule making
- Adjudicating
- Advising
- Investigating

These functions do not concern all administrative agencies to the same degree. Some agencies are primarily adjudicating bodies, such as industrial commissions that rule on workers' compensation claims. Others are primarily supervisory, such as the SEC, which oversees the issue and sale of investment securities. To be sure, most agencies perform all these functions to some degree in carrying out their responsibilities. Figure 15.1 illustrates how these functions have been delegated to these agencies.

Rule Making Agencies exercise their quasi-legislative power by issuing rules and regulations that have the force and effect of law. Because of the vast volume of rules and regulations, many business organizations struggle to know all the legal requirements. By allowing time periods for public comments on proposed regulations, interested parties have an opportunity to be heard on the desirability and legality of the proposals.

The Federal Trade Commission and the Justice Department have guidelines to help determine which mergers are legal and which ones are likely to be challenged as illegal.

Rules and regulations may apply to a business practice irrespective of the industry involved, or they may apply only to an industry. For example, Occupational Safety and Health Administrative (OSHA) rules may cover anyone's workplace, or a rule may be drafted so that its coverage is limited to an industry such as drug manufacturing.

Guidelines are also issued by agencies to supplement rules. Guidelines are administrative interpretations of the statutes that an agency is responsible for

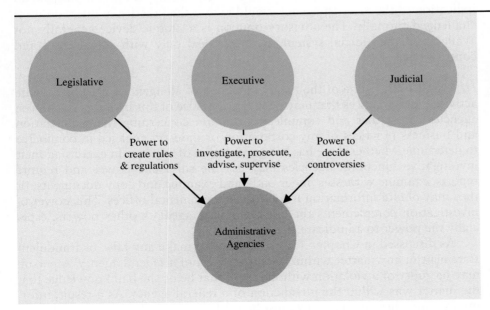

Figure 15.1
The powers of administrative agencies

enforcing. Often, guidelines help businesses determine whether certain practices may or may not be viewed as legal. While guidelines can be helpful in understanding an agency's policy, these guidelines do not have the same force of law as rules and regulations do.

Adjudicating   The quasi-judicial function involves both fact-finding and applying law to the facts. If violations of the law are found, sanctions, such as a fine or other penalty, may be imposed. In addition, an agency may order that a violator stop (cease) the objectionable activity and refrain (desist) from any further similar violations. This type of agency action is called a **cease and desist order.** Violations of a cease and desist order are punishable by fines, which can be as much as $10,000 per day.

Many cases before agencies are settled by agreement before a final decision, just as most lawsuits are settled. Such a settlement results in the issuance of a **consent order,** which requires that the organization or individual accused admit to the jurisdiction of the agency and waive all rights to seek a judicial review. There is no admission that the business has been guilty of a violation of the law, but there is an agreement not to engage in the business activities that were the subject of the complaint. A consent order saves considerable expense and has the same legal force and effect as a final cease and desist order issued after a full hearing.

Consent orders are settlement agreements in which a business or individual agrees to comply with all administrative rules.

Advising   The advisory function of an administrative agency may be accomplished by making reports to the president or to Congress. For example, an agency may propose new legislation to Congress, or it may inform the attorney general of the need for judicial action due to violations of the law. Agencies also report information to the general public that should be known in the public interest, and they publish advisory opinions. For example, a commission may give advice as to whether a firm's proposed course of action might violate any of the laws that commission administers. Advisory opinions are not as binding as formal rulings, but they do give a business an indication of the view an agency would take if the practice in question were challenged formally. The advisory opinion is a unique device generally not available in the judicial system, as courts deal only with actual cases and controversies.

"The Commodity Futures Trading Commission (CFTC) opened a record 419 investigations over the last year, into things as diverse as small-time Ponzi schemes and claims of market manipulation."

—Julie Creswell and Graham Bowley, "Once on Sleepy Beat, Regulator Is Suddenly Busy," *New York Times,* November 4, 2010

Investigating   One of the major functions of all agencies is to investigate activities and practices that may be illegal. Because of this investigative power, agencies can gather and compile information concerning the organization and business practices of any corporation or industry engaged in commerce to determine whether there has been a violation of any law. In exercising their investigative functions, agencies may use the subpoena power and require reports, examine witnesses under oath, and examine and copy documents, or they may obtain information from other governmental offices. This power of investigation complements the exercise of the agency's other powers, especially the power to adjudicate.

As discussed in Chapter 13, it is a crime to make any false or fraudulent statement in any matter within the jurisdiction of a federal agency. A person may be guilty of a violation without proof that he or she had knowledge that the matter was within the jurisdiction of a federal agency. As a result, information furnished to an agency must be truthful.

ORGANIZATION OF AGENCIES

Administrative agencies, boards, or commissions usually consist of five to seven members, one of whom is appointed as chair. Laws creating the regulatory body usually specify that no more than a simple majority of the members (three of the five or four of the seven) may belong to the same political party. Appointments at the federal level require Senate confirmation, and appointees are not permitted to engage in any other business or employment during their terms. They may be removed from office by the president only for inefficiency, neglect of duty, or malfeasance in office.

The following case highlights the constitutional requirements related to the appointment of administrative officials.

 case **15.1**

FREE ENTERPRISE FUND v. PUBLIC COMPANY ACCOUNTING OVERSIGHT BOARD
130 S. Ct. 3138 (2010)

As a part of the Sarbanes-Oxley Act, Congress created the Public Company Accounting Oversight Board (PCAOB or Board). This Board consists of five members who are appointed by the Securities and Exchange Commissioners. Board members serve 5-year, staggered terms and are not considered Government officers or employers. This allows the recruitment from the private sector since the Board members' salaries are not subject to governmental limitations. These members can be removed by the SEC Commissioners only "for good cause" if the Board member:

"(A) has willfully violated any provision of the Act, the rules of the Board, or the securities laws; (B) has willfully abused the authority of that member; or (C) without reasonable justification or excuse, has failed to enforce compliance with any such provision or rule, or any professional standard by any registered public accounting firm or any associated person thereof."

This arrangement concerning the appointment and potential removal of Board members makes the PCAOB a Government-created, Government-appointed entity with expansive powers to govern an entire industry (public accounting firms). It further makes the Board members insulated from the direct supervision of the SEC Commissioners.

Following the Board's release of a negative report about Beckstead and Watts LLP, a public accounting firm, this lawsuit was filed by that firm and The Free Enterprise Fund challenging the constitutionality of the Sarbanes-Oxley Act at least as far as the creation and operation of the PCAOB. The basis of

this challenge is the Board members are not subject to the appointed powers of the President of the United States. The United States Government joined the suit to defend the Sarbanes-Oxley Act and the PCAOB. The District Judge granted summary judgment in favor of the United States, and the D.C. Circuit Court of Appeals affirmed. Certiorari was granted to review the constitutional issue.

ROBERTS, C.J.: . . . We hold that the dual for-cause limitations on the removal of Board members contravene the Constitution's separation of powers.

The Constitution provides that "[t]he executive Power shall be vested in a President of the United States of America." Art. II, §1, cl. 1. As Madison stated on the floor of the First Congress, "if any power whatsoever is in its nature Executive, it is the power of appointing, overseeing, and controlling those who execute the laws."

The removal of executive officers was discussed extensively in Congress when the first executive departments were created. The view that "prevailed, as most consonant to the text of the Constitution" and "to the requisite responsibility and harmony in the Executive Department," was that the executive power included a power to oversee executive officers through removal; because that traditional executive power was not "expressly taken away, it remained with the President." . . .

The landmark case of *Myers* v. *United States* reaffirmed the principle that Article II confers on the President "the general administrative control of those executing the laws." It is *his* responsibility to take care that the laws be faithfully executed. The buck stops with the President, in Harry Truman's famous phrase. As we explained in *Myers,* the President therefore must have some "power of removing those for whom he cannot continue to be responsible." . . .

We have previously upheld limited restrictions on the President's removal power. In those cases, however, only one level of protected tenure separated the President from an officer exercising executive power. It was the President—or a subordinate he could remove at will—who decided whether the officer's conduct merited removal under the good-cause standard. The Act before us does something quite different. It not only protects Board members from removal except for good cause, but withdraws from the President any decision on whether that good cause exists. That decision is vested instead in other tenured officers—the Commissioners— none of whom is subject to the President's direct control. The result is a Board that is not accountable to the President, and a President who is not responsible for the Board. The added layer of tenure protection makes a difference. Without a layer of insulation between the Commission and the Board, the Commission could remove a Board member at any time, and therefore would be fully responsible for what the Board does. The President could then hold the Commission to account for its supervision of the Board, to the same extent that he may hold the Commission to account for everything else it does. A second level of tenure protection changes the nature of the President's review. Now the Commission cannot remove a Board member at will. The President therefore cannot hold the Commission fully accountable for the Board's conduct, to the same extent that he may hold the Commission accountable for everything else that it does. The Commissioners are not responsible for the Board's actions. They are only responsible for their own determination of whether the Act's rigorous good-cause standard is met. And even if the President disagrees with their determination, he is powerless to intervene—unless that determination is so unreasonable as to constitute inefficiency, neglect of duty, or malfeasance in office.

This novel structure does not merely add to the Board's independence, but transforms it. Neither the President, nor anyone directly responsible to him, nor even an officer whose conduct he may review only for good cause, has full control over the Board. The President is stripped of the power our precedents have preserved, and his ability to execute the laws—by holding his subordinates accountable for their conduct—is impaired.

That arrangement is contrary to Article II's vesting of the executive power in the President. Without the ability to oversee the Board, or to attribute the Board's failings to those whom he *can* oversee, the President is no longer the judge of the Board's conduct. He is

not the one who decides whether Board members are abusing their offices or neglecting their duties. He can neither ensure that the laws are faithfully executed, nor be held responsible for a Board member's breach of faith. This violates the basic principle that the President cannot delegate ultimate responsibility or the active obligation to supervise that goes with it, because Article II makes a single President responsible for the actions of the Executive Branch.

Indeed, if allowed to stand, this dispersion of responsibility could be multiplied. If Congress can shelter the bureaucracy behind two layers of good-cause tenure, why not a third? At oral argument, the Government was unwilling to concede that even *five* layers between the President and the Board would be too many. The officers of such an agency—safely encased within a Matryoshka doll of tenure protections— would be immune from Presidential oversight, even as they exercised power in the people's name.

Perhaps an individual President might find advantages in tying his own hands. But the separation of powers does not depend on the views of individual Presidents, nor on whether the encroached-upon branch approves the encroachment. The President can always choose to restrain himself in his dealings with subordinates. He cannot, however, choose to bind his successors by diminishing their powers, nor can he escape responsibility for his choices by pretending that they are not his own.

The diffusion of power carries with it a diffusion of accountability. The people do not vote for the Officers of the United States. They instead look to the President to guide the assistants or deputies . . . subject to his superintendence. Without a clear and effective chain of command, the public cannot determine on whom the blame or the punishment of a pernicious measure, or series of pernicious measures ought really to fall. That is why the Framers sought to ensure that those who are employed in the execution of the law will be in their proper situation, and the chain of dependence be preserved; the lowest officers, the middle grade, and the highest, will depend, as they ought, on the President, and the President on the community.

By granting the Board executive power without the Executive's oversight, this Act subverts the President's ability to ensure that the laws are faithfully executed— as well as the public's ability to pass judgment on his efforts. The Act's restrictions are incompatible with the Constitution's separation of powers. . . .

This case presents an even more serious threat to executive control than an "ordinary" dual for-cause standard. Congress enacted an unusually high standard that must be met before Board members may be removed. A Board member cannot be removed except for willful violations of the Act, Board rules, or the securities laws; willful abuse of authority; or unreasonable failure to enforce compliance—as determined in a formal Commission order, rendered on the record and after notice and an opportunity for a hearing. The Act does not even give the Commission power to fire Board members for violations of *other* laws that do not relate to the Act, the securities laws, or the Board's authority. The President might have less than full confidence in, say, a Board member who cheats on his taxes; but that discovery is not listed among the grounds for removal. . . .

The rigorous standard that must be met before a Board member may be removed was drawn from statutes concerning private organizations like the New York Stock Exchange. While we need not decide the question here, a removal standard appropriate for limiting Government control over private bodies may be inappropriate for officers wielding the executive power of the United States. . . .

Petitioners' complaint argued that the Board's "freedom from Presidential oversight and control" rendered it "and all power and authority exercised by it" in violation of Constitution. We reject such a broad holding. Instead, we agree with the Government that the unconstitutional tenure provisions are severable from the remainder of the statute. . . .

The Sarbanes-Oxley Act remains fully operative as a law with these tenure restrictions excised. . . .

It is so ordered.

KEY POINTS

- The president not only has the constitutional power to appoint individuals to help execute laws, but must necessarily, then, have the power to remove individuals from their positions.
- Individuals appointed to office must have accountability to the president. The PCAOB protected Board members from removal except when a good cause standard was met, but those officers who make the good cause determination were not in control of the president. The Court characterizes this as a "novel structure."
- The Court ruled the process of removal created by the Sarbanes-Oxley Act for the PCAOB unconstitutional.
- The entire Sarbanes-Oxley Act was not deemed unconstitutional; rather, the Court "severed" the unconstitutional PCOAB process and allowed the rest of the law to remain in force.

Regulatory agencies require staffs to carry out their duties. While each agency has its own distinctive organizational structure to meet its responsibilities, most agencies have persons performing certain functions common to all agencies. Because agencies have quasi-legislative and quasi-judicial functions as well as the usual executive ones, the organizational chart of an agency usually embraces the full range of governmental duties. Figure 15.2 shows an organizational chart outlining the general functions and duties of administrative agencies.

In General The chairperson is designated as such at the time of nomination by the president and is the presiding officer at agency meetings. The chairperson usually belongs to the same political party as the president and, while an equal in voting, is somewhat more important than the other agency members because of visibility and the power to appoint staff. For example, the chairman of the Federal Reserve Board is often in the news, while the other board members are relatively unknown.

The secretary is responsible for the minutes of agency meetings and is legal custodian of its records. The secretary usually signs orders and official correspondence and is responsible for publication of all actions in the *Federal*

Figure 15.2
Organizational chart of typical agency, board, or commission

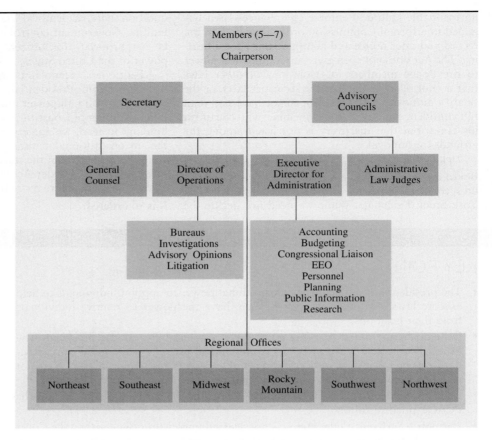

Register. The secretary also coordinates the activities of the agency with others involved in the regulatory process.

The office of **general counsel** is so important in many agencies that the appointment usually requires Senate approval. The general counsel is the chief law officer and legal adviser. He or she represents the agency in court and often makes the decision to file suit or pursue other remedies. The general counsel has significant impact on policy and is often as powerful as a commissioner or board member.

Advisory councils are persons not employed by the agency but interested in its mission. Persons serving on councils are usually selected because of their expertise. For example, the Consumer Product Safety Commission has an advisory council on poison prevention packaging and another on flammable fabrics. These councils provide for interaction between regulators and those being regulated.

The executive director for administration is the chief operating official of an agency and supervises usual administrative functions such as accounting, budgeting, and personnel. Research and planning are usually also supervised by the executive director. Since agencies spend a great deal of time lobbying with Congress, most of them have a legislative liaison, reporting to the executive director for administration.

The duties and suborganization of the director of operations vary greatly from agency to agency. These operating bureaus are assigned specific areas of

All the staff of an administrative agency are employees of the appointed commissioners or board members.

activity. For example, at the EPA, one group will be concerned with clean air and another with water problems.

Regional offices investigate alleged violations of the law. In addition, they usually have an educational function. Many regional offices have their own administrative law judges and special legal counsel.

Quasi-Judicial Staff **Administrative law judges** perform the adjudicative fact-finding functions. Like other types of judges, administrative law judges are protected from liability for damages based on their decisions. This protection is called **immunity.** Because these administrative law judges must exercise independent judgment on the evidence presented, they must be free from pressures possibly asserted by the parties.

These administrative law judges hear cases of alleged law violations and apply the law to the facts. The members of the agency board or commission hear only appeals from the decisions of the administrative law judges. The judges are organizationally separate from the rest of the agency so that the quasi-judicial function will be performed impartially. Administrative law judges use prior decisions or precedent. In addition, they must follow the procedural rules of the agency as well as its policy directives.

Historically, administrative law judges and all other personnel involved in a quasi-judicial hearing have been employees of the administrative agency bringing the complaint. Despite their best efforts to serve as neutral adjudicators, administrative law judges have been accused of being biased in favor of their employer (the agency). To reduce the likelihood of this accusation, several states have created an Office of Administrative Hearings. Such an office provides impartial administrative law judges for hearings involving all agencies in the state government. The movement toward this type of office is likely to continue due to the importance of citizens believing that they are treated fairly by governmental agencies.

Sidebar 15.2 presents an overview of the procedures typically followed in quasi-judicial matters.

Since even the administrative law judges work for the appointed agency leaders who hear appeals of the decision made, there is a clear appearance of bias that must be overcome to maintain the confidence of the parties regulated.

sidebar 15.2

Procedures Followed in Quasi-Judicial Proceedings

Quasi-judicial proceedings usually begin with a complaint filed by the agency. The complaint is often the result of an investigation of information received from a consumer or other person affected by business conduct that may be illegal. The complaint contains allegations of fact concerning the alleged illegal conduct. The business or individual accused of some illegality is called the respondent. After the formal complaint is served, the respondent files an answer to the charges and allegations. The case is then assigned to an administrative law judge. At the hearing, counsels for the agency and the respondent produce evidence to prove or disprove the allegations of fact in the complaint and answer. The judge rules on the admissibility of evidence, rules on motions made by counsel, and renders an initial decision that includes a statement of findings and conclusions, along with reasons for them, as to all material issues of fact and law. The ruling also includes an order the judge deems appropriate in view of the evidence in the record. This order becomes final if not challenged within 30 days after it is filed. On the appeal, the agency, board, or commission reviews the record of the initial decision and has all the powers it could have exercised if it had rendered that decision itself.

INFLUENCING AGENCY DECISIONS

The Food and Drug Administration (FDA) was a strong advocate for regulating tobacco. More recently, the FDA has been criticized for granting licenses for products like Vioxx without completing sufficient testing.

As discussed previously, agencies adopt rules and regulations. Due process of law requires that before a rule or regulation may be adopted by an agency, interested parties must be given notice of the proposed rules and an opportunity to express their views on them. Agencies give public notice of proposed rules and hold public hearings on them.

At public hearings, interested parties are allowed to present evidence in support of, or in opposition to, a proposed rule or regulation. As a result, the best means of influencing a quasi-legislative decision of an administrative agency is to participate in the adoption process.

Agencies are not politically responsible, in the sense that they are elected by the people. However, it is clear that they react, sometimes dramatically, to the force of public opinion. For example, the Securities and Exchange Commission (SEC) consistently garners media attention as it strives to investigate, adopt rules, and assess fines covering corporate scandals.

Citizens writing letters to agencies to obtain action or a change in policy may be effective. These are probably even more effective if directed to a member of Congress, who in turn asks the agency for an official response or explanation. At various times, an agency may find itself bombarded with official congressional inquiries into its activities. Investigations may result in either budget cutbacks or increases. Just the threat of such a proceeding is often sufficient to cause a review of administrative policy.

Checks and balances are supposed to keep agencies from becoming too political.

Furthermore, each branch of government has some control over the administrative process. The executive branch normally appoints the top officials of an agency with the advice and consent of the legislative branch. In addition, the executive branch makes budget recommendations to the legislature and has veto power over its statutes. The legislature can review and control administrative activity by abolishing the agency, enacting specific legislation contrary to rules adopted by the agency, more explicitly defining limitations on the agency's activities, providing additional procedural requirements for the agency's adjudications, or limiting appropriations of funds to the agency.

LO 15-2 ## Judicial Review of Agency Decisions

What alternatives are available to a person, business, or industry unhappy with either rules and regulations that have been adopted or with the quasi-judicial decisions? What are the powers of courts in reviewing decisions of administrative agencies? What chance does a party upset with an agency's decision have in obtaining a reversal of the decision? How much deference is given to an agency's decisions? Answers to these questions must be clearly understood to appreciate the role of administrative agencies in our system.

The following section discusses a requirement that must be satisfied by the parties challenging an agency's rule-making or adjudicating function. Then, you will see that the issues before a court reviewing an agency's decision vary depending on whether a quasi-legislative or quasi-judicial decision is being reviewed.

STANDING TO SUE

Any party seeking the judicial review of any administrative agency's decision must be able to prove *standing to sue*. To establish standing, the challenging party must address two issues.

Reviewability   First, is the action or decision of the agency subject to judicial review? Not all administrative decisions are reviewable. The Federal Administrative Procedure Act provides for judicial review except where "(1) statutes preclude judicial review or (2) agency action is committed to agency discretion by law." Few statutes actually preclude judicial review, and preclusion of judicial review by inference is rare. It is most likely to occur when an agency decides not to undertake action to enforce a statute. For example, prison inmates asked the Food and Drug Administration (FDA) to ban the use of lethal injections to carry out the death penalty. It refused to do so. The Supreme Court held that this decision of the FDA was not subject to judicial review.

Aggrieved Party   Second, is the plaintiff "an aggrieved party"? Generally the plaintiff must have been harmed by an administrative action or decision to have standing. This aspect of standing was discussed in Chapter 4. It is clear that persons who may suffer economic loss due to an agency's action have standing to sue. Recent decisions have expanded the group of persons with standing to sue to include those who have noneconomic interests, such as First Amendment rights.

Sidebar 15.3 summarizes the U.S. Supreme Court's explanation of why broad meaning should be given to the concept of standing to sue.

---

sidebar 15.3

Standing to Sue or Who May Challenge an Administrative Policy

The Administrative Procedures Act states:

> A person suffering legal wrong because of agency action, or adversely affected or aggrieved by agency action within the meaning of a relevant statute, is entitled to judicial review thereof.

Through United States Supreme Court cases, we know that a plaintiff must show a claim within the "zone of interest" protected by the statute under consideration. The plaintiff does not need to prove that the legislative body envisioned protecting this particular plaintiff.

An example of this broad nature of standing to sue is found in the decision of the Supreme Court allowing banks to challenge whether credit unions must limit membership to persons who have a common bond, such as employment with the same company.

Source: *National Credit Union Administration v. First National Bank & Trust Co.*, 118 S. Ct. 927 (1998).

REVIEW OF RULE MAKING

The rule-making function in the administrative process is essentially legislative in character. Legislatures usually create administrative agencies or quasi-legislative power to the agency. An administrative agency must propose rules and regulations within the confines of its grant of power from the legislature, or a court will find the proposal void.

However, once courts decide that an act of the legislature is constitutional or a rule of an agency is authorized, the courts will not inquire into its wisdom or effectiveness. An unwise or ineffectual law may be corrected by political action at the polls; an unwise rule or regulation adopted by an agency may be corrected by the legislature that gave the agency power to make the rule in the first place.

There are two basic issues in litigation challenging the validity of a rule made by an administrative agency. First, is the delegation valid? Second, has the agency exceeded its authority?

Do remember to ask two critical questions: Is the delegation valid? Has authority been exceeded?

Is Delegation Valid?   Delegation of quasi-legislative authority to administrative agencies is subject to two constitutional limitations:

- It must be definite.
- It must be limited.

First, delegation of authority must be definite or it will violate due process. Definiteness means that the delegation must be set forth with sufficient clarity so that all concerned, and especially reviewing courts, will be able to determine the extent of the agency's authority. Broad language has been held sufficiently definite to meet this test. For example, the term *unfair methods of competition* is sufficiently definite to meet the requirements of due process and validate the delegation of this authority to the Federal Trade Commission (FTC).

Second, the delegation of authority to an agency from the legislative or executive branch must have limitations. This delegation of authority must provide that the agency's power to act is limited to areas that are certain, even if these areas are not specifically defined. For example, the FTC regulates unfair methods of competition *in or affecting commerce*. Regulations or enforcement activities by the FTC that focus solely on intrastate business are void as being beyond the "limited" authority delegated to that agency. Also, procedural safeguards must exist to control arbitrary administrative action and any administrative abuse of discretionary power.

State and local agencies may regulate areas of business that are not subject to federal regulation.

Just as broad language has been approved as being sufficiently definite for a delegation to be valid under the due process clause since the 1930s, broad standards meet the limited-power test. Today, it is generally agreed that delegations of authority to make rules may involve very broad language. For example, the delegation of authority to make such rules as the "public interest, convenience and necessity may require" is a valid standard.

The general language used in delegating quasi-legislative authority usually involves grants of substantial discretion to an agency. It must be kept in mind that this delegation of discretion is to the agency and not to the judiciary. Therefore, courts cannot interfere with the discretion given to the agency and cannot substitute their judgment for that of the agency. In essence, there is a policy of deference by the judges to the decision of the administrators. This practice of deference further emphasizes why a businessperson's influence on the rule-making process is greater in the administrative process than through appellate procedures.

Sidebar 15.4 illustrates the Supreme Court's use of this philosophy of deference. It demonstrates the expansive discretion given to administrative agencies and how courts are not to substitute their judgment for that of the administrative process.

sidebar 15.4

Standard of Review of Agency Actions

The Federal Communications Commission (FCC) is charged with regulatory broadcasters. One of the controversial areas of FCC regulation concerns the censorship of indecent language in broadcasts. In a series of actions since 2003, the FCC has narrowed the permissible use of certain words. Even a one-time use of a word that inherently has a sexual connotation or a word that refers to excrement can be considered vulgar and censored as indecent.

Broadcasters challenged the FCC's penalty for broadcasting these words during the presentation portion of an awards show. The Second Circuit reversed the FCC finding the agency had not adequately reasoned its conclusion. While the Second Circuit did not

reach a final conclusion on the constitutional protection of the one-time use of certain words, it did question the FCC's conclusion.

The Supreme Court reversed the Second Circuit and reinstates the FCC's ruling and penalty. The Court relies on the long-held principle that judges should defer to the administrator's ruling unless the court finds the administrator's action was arbitrary or capricious. The Court concludes that the Second Circuit failed to apply this standard. Furthermore, the Court did not find the FCC acted in an improper manner, even though the FCC's ruling was controversial.

Source: *Federal Communications Commission v. Fox Television Stations, Inc.,* 129 S. Ct. 1800 (2009).

Authority Exceeded? Although it is highly unlikely that a court would hold a delegation invalid because of indefiniteness or lack of standards, from time to time courts do find that agencies exceed their authority. Courts will hold that an agency exceeds its authority if an analysis of legislative intent confirms the view that the agency has gone beyond that intent, however noble its purpose may be.

Case 15.2 presents a case that impacts all of us. Regardless of your personal views on smoking, the Supreme Court's analysis of the agency's authority to regulate cigarettes is quite interesting. Notice how the Court struggles with the dilemma present in this case and how the rules of **administrative law** assist in reaching a decision.

 case **15.2**

FOOD AND DRUG ADMINISTRATION v. BROWN & WILLIAMSON TOBACCO CORPORATION
120 S. Ct. 1291 (2000)

O'CONNOR, J.: This case involves one of the most troubling public health problems facing our Nation today: the thousands of premature deaths that occur each year because of tobacco use. In 1996, the Food and Drug Administration (FDA), after having expressly disavowed any such authority since its inception, asserted jurisdiction to regulate tobacco products. The FDA concluded that nicotine is a "drug" within the

meaning of the Food, Drug, and Cosmetic Act (FDCA or Act), and that cigarettes and smokeless tobacco are "combination products" that deliver nicotine to the body. Pursuant to this authority, it promulgated regulations intended to reduce tobacco consumption among children and adolescents. The agency believed that, because most tobacco consumers begin their use before reaching the age of 18, curbing tobacco use by minors could substantially reduce the prevalence of addiction in future generations and thus the incidence of tobacco-related death and disease.

Regardless of how serious the problem an administrative agency seeks to address, however, it may not exercise its authority in a manner that is inconsistent with the administrative structure that Congress enacted into law. And although agencies are generally entitled to deference in the interpretation of statutes that they administer, a reviewing court, as well as the agency, must give effect to the unambiguously expressed intent of Congress. In this case, we believe that Congress has clearly precluded the FDA from asserting jurisdiction to regulate tobacco products. Such authority is inconsistent with the intent that Congress has expressed in the FDCA's overall regulatory scheme and in the tobacco specific legislation that it has enacted subsequent to the FDCA. In light of this clear intent, the FDA's assertion of jurisdiction is impermissible.

The FDCA grants the FDA . . . the authority to regulate, among other items, "drugs" and "devices." The Act defines "drug" to include "articles (other than food) intended to affect the structure or any function of the body." It defines "device," in part, as "an instrument, apparatus, implement, machine, contrivance, . . . or other similar or related article, including any component, part, or accessory, which is . . . intended to affect the structure or any function of the body." The Act also grants the FDA the authority to regulate so-called "combination products," which "constitute a combination of a drug, device, or biologic product." The FDA has construed this provision as giving it the discretion to regulate combination products as drugs, as devices, or as both.

On August 11, 1995, the FDA published a proposed rule concerning the sale of cigarettes and smokeless tobacco to children and adolescents. . . . A public comment period followed, during which the FDA received over 700,000 submissions, more than "at any other time in its history on any other subject."

On August 28, 1996, the FDA issued a final rule entitled "Regulations Restricting the Sale and Distribution of Cigarettes and Smokeless Tobacco to Protect Children and Adolescents." The FDA determined that nicotine is a "drug" and that cigarettes and smokeless tobacco are "drug delivery devices," and therefore it had jurisdiction under the FDCA to regulate tobacco products. . . .

Based on these findings, the FDA promulgated regulations concerning tobacco products' promotion, labeling, and accessibility to children and adolescents. The access regulations prohibit the sale of cigarettes or smokeless tobacco to persons younger than 18; require retailers to verify through photo identification the age of all purchasers younger than 27; prohibit the sale of cigarettes in quantities smaller than 20; prohibit

the distribution of free samples; and prohibit sales through self-service displays and vending machines except in adult-only locations. The promotion regulations require that any print advertising appear in a black-and-white, text-only format unless the publication in which it appears is read almost exclusively by adults; prohibit outdoor advertising within 1,000 feet of any public playground or school; prohibit the distribution of any promotional items, such as T-shirts or hats, bearing the manufacturer's brand name; and prohibit a manufacturer from sponsoring any athletic, musical, artistic, or other social or cultural event using its brand name. . . .

Respondents, a group of tobacco manufacturers, retailers, and advertisers, filed suit . . . challenging the regulations. . . .

We granted the Government's petition for certiorari to determine whether the FDA has authority under the FDCA to regulate tobacco products. . . .

A threshold issue is the appropriate framework for analyzing the FDA's assertion of authority to regulate tobacco products. Because this case involves an administrative agency's construction of a statute that it administers, our analysis is governed by *Chevron U.S.A. Inc. v. Natural Resources Defense Council, Inc.*, 104 S. Ct. 2778 (1984). Under *Chevron*, a reviewing court must first ask "whether Congress has directly spoken to the precise question at issue." If Congress has done so, the inquiry is at an end; the court "must give effect to the unambiguously expressed intent of Congress." But if Congress has not specifically addressed the question, a reviewing court must respect the agency's construction of the statute so long as it is permissible. Such deference is justified because the responsibilities for assessing the wisdom of such policy choices and resolving the struggle between competing views of the public interest are not judicial ones, and because of the agency's greater familiarity with the ever-changing facts and circumstances surrounding the subjects regulated. . . .

Viewing the FDCA as a whole, it is evident that one of the Act's core objectives is to ensure that any product regulated by the FDA is "safe" and "effective" for its intended use. This essential purpose pervades the FDCA. . . .

In its rulemaking proceeding, the FDA quite exhaustively documented that "tobacco products are unsafe," "dangerous," and "cause great pain and suffering from illness." It found that the consumption of tobacco products "presents extraordinary health risks," and that "tobacco use is the single leading cause of preventable death in the United States." . . .

These findings logically imply that, if tobacco products were "devices" under the FDCA, the FDA would be required to remove them from the market. . . .

Congress, however, has foreclosed the removal of tobacco products from the market. A provision of the United States Code currently in force states that "the marketing of tobacco constitutes one of the greatest basic industries of the United States with ramifying activities which directly affect interstate and foreign commerce at every point, and stable conditions therein are necessary to the general welfare:" 7 U.S.C. §1311(a). More importantly, Congress has directly addressed the problem of tobacco and health through legislation on six occasions since 1965. . . . Congress stopped well short of ordering a ban. Instead, it has generally regulated the labeling and advertisement of tobacco products, expressly providing that it is the policy of Congress that "commerce and the national economy may be . . . protected to the maximum extent consistent with" consumers "being adequately informed about any adverse health effects." 15 U.S.C. §1331. Congress' decisions to regulate labeling and advertising and to adopt the express policy of protecting "commerce and the national economy . . . to the maximum extent" reveal its intent that tobacco products remain on the market. Indeed the collective premise of these statutes is that cigarettes and smokeless tobacco will continue to be sold in the United States. A ban of tobacco products by the FDA would therefore plainly contradict congressional policy. . . .

[O]ur inquiry into whether Congress has directly spoken to the precise question at issue is shaped, at least in some measure, by the nature of the question presented. Deference under *Chevron* to an agency's construction of a statute that it administers is premised on the theory that a statute's ambiguity constitutes an implicit delegation from Congress to the agency to fill in the statutory gaps. In extraordinary cases, however, there may be reason to hesitate before concluding that Congress has intended such an implicit delegation.

This is hardly an ordinary case. Contrary to its representations to Congress since 1914, the FDA has now asserted jurisdiction to regulate an industry constituting a significant portion of the American economy. In fact, the FDA contends that, were it to determine that tobacco products provide no "reasonable assurance of safety," it would have the authority to ban cigarettes and smokeless tobacco entirely. Owing to its unique place in American history and society, tobacco has its own unique political history. Congress, for better or for worse, has created a distinct regulatory scheme for tobacco products, squarely rejected proposals to give the FDA jurisdiction over tobacco, and repeatedly acted to preclude any agency from exercising significant policymaking authority in the area. Given this history and the breadth of the authority that the FDA has asserted, we are obliged to defer not to the agency's expansive construction of the statute, but to Congress' consistent judgment to deny the FDA this power. . . .

Nonetheless, no matter how important, conspicuous, and controversial the issue, and regardless of how likely the public is to hold the Executive Branch politically accountable, an administrative agency's power to regulate in the public interest must always be grounded in a valid grant of authority from Congress. . . . Reading the FDCA as a whole, as well as in conjunction with Congress' subsequent tobacco-specific legislation, it is plain that Congress has not given the FDA the authority that it seeks to exercise here. For these reasons, the judgment of the Court of Appeals for the Fourth Circuit is

Affirmed.

KEY POINTS

- Although a core objective of the FDCA is to ensure that products regulated by the FDA are safe for their intended use, Congress has established policies for balancing the economic and health implications of tobacco products with more specific legislative enactments.
- This is a relatively rare case in which the Court cannot give deference to an administrative agency's interpretation of the law it is responsible for administering. The Court noted that tobacco has a "unique political history."
- An administrative agency's ability to enforce laws through the executive branch must derive its authority from Congress. In this case, Congress has chosen to control tobacco products separately from other similar products within the FDA's purview.

In 2009, Congress passed and President Obama signed the Family Smoking Prevention and Tobacco Control Act. This legislation increased the FDA's authority beyond that discussed in the preceding case. However, the FDA still cannot totally ban nicotine.

REVIEW OF ADJUDICATIONS: PROCEDURAL ASPECTS

Judicial review of agencies' adjudications by its very nature is quite limited. Legislatures have delegated authority to agencies because of their expertise and knowledge, and courts usually exercise restraint and resolve doubtful issues in favor of an agency. For example, courts reviewing administrative interpretations of law do not always decide questions of law for themselves. It is not unusual for a court to accept an administrative interpretation of law as final if it is warranted in the record and has a rational basis in law. Administrative agencies are frequently called upon to interpret the statute governing an agency, and an agency's construction is persuasive to courts.

Administrative agencies develop their own rules of procedure unless mandated otherwise by an act of the legislature. These procedures are far less formal than judicial procedures, because one of the functions of the administrative process is to decide issues expeditiously. To proceed expeditiously usually means, for example, that administrative agencies are not restricted by the strict rules of evidence used by courts. Such agencies cannot ignore all rules, but they can use some leeway. They cannot, for example, refuse to permit any cross-examination or unduly limit it. Because an agency "is frequently the accuser, the prosecutor, the judge and the jury," it must remain alert to observe accepted standards of fairness. Reviewing courts are, therefore, alert to ensure that the true substance of a fair hearing is not denied to a party to an administrative hearing.

The principle that federal administrative agencies should be free to fashion their own rules of procedure and pursue methods of inquiry permitting them to discharge their duties grows out of the view that administrative agencies and administrators will be familiar with the industries they regulate. Thus, they will be in a better position than courts or legislative bodies to design procedural rules adapted to the peculiarities of the industry and the tasks of the agency involved.

In reviewing the procedures of administrative agencies, courts lack the authority to substitute their judgment or their own procedures for those of the agency. Judicial responsibility is limited to ensuring consistency with statutes and compliance with the demands of the Constitution for a fair hearing. The latter responsibility arises from the due process clause. Due process usually requires a hearing by an agency, but on occasion sanctions may be imposed prior to the hearing.

Two doctrines guide courts in the judicial review of agency adjudications:

- Exhaustion of remedies
- Primary jurisdiction

Exhaustion of Remedies   The doctrine of **exhaustion of remedies** is a court-created rule that limits when courts can review administrative decisions. Courts refuse to review administrative actions until a complaining party

Don't ignore what may appear to be a biased administrative hearing. Relying on courts to reverse the agency's decision is a bad plan.

Your school likely has an administrative process for handling students' grade appeals. You must follow this administrative procedure.

has exhausted all of the administrative remedies and procedures available to him or her for redress. Judicial review is available only for final actions by an agency. Preliminary orders such as a decision to file a complaint are not reviewable. Otherwise, the administrative system would be denied important opportunities to make a factual record, to exercise its discretion, or to apply its expertise in its decision making. Also, exhaustion allows an agency to discover and correct its own errors, and thus it helps to dispense with any reason for judicial review. Exhaustion clearly should be required in those cases involving an area of the agency's expertise or specialization; it should require no unusual expense. It should also be required when the administrative remedy is just as likely as the judicial one to provide appropriate relief. The doctrine of exhaustion of remedies avoids the premature interruption of the administrative process.

This doctrine is not an absolute principle. Courts do allow parties to litigate prior to exhausting administrative remedies. Sidebar 15.5 provides explanation for exceptions to this administrative requirement.

sidebar 15.5

Exceptions to Requirement of Exhaustion

When there is nothing to be gained from the exhaustion of administrative remedies and when the harm from the continued existence of the administrative ruling is great, the courts have not been reluctant to discard this doctrine. This is especially true when very fundamental constitutional guarantees such as freedom of speech or press are involved or when the administrative remedy is likely to be inadequate.

Also, probably no court would insist upon exhaustion when the agency is clearly acting beyond its jurisdiction (because its action is not authorized by statute or the statute authorizing it is unconstitutional) or where it would result in irreparable injury (such as great expense) to the petitioner. Finally, an exception to the doctrine is fraud. If an agency is acting fraudulently, immediate access to the court is appropriate.

Primary Jurisdiction A doctrine similar to exhaustion of remedies is known as **primary jurisdiction**. *Exhaustion* applies when a claim must go in the first instance to an administrative agency alone. *Primary jurisdiction* applies when a claim is originally filed in the courts. It comes into play whenever enforcement of the claim requires the resolution of issues that, under a regulatory scheme, have been placed within the special competence of an administrative body. In such a case, the judicial process is suspended pending referral of such issues to the administrative body for its views. Primary jurisdiction ensures uniformity and consistency in dealing with matters entrusted to an administrative body. The doctrine is invoked when referral to the agency is preferable because of its specialized knowledge or expertise in dealing with the matter in controversy. Statutes such as those guaranteeing equal employment opportunity that create a private remedy for dollar damages sometimes require the parties to resort to an administrative agency as a condition precedent to filing suit. Some of these are federal statutes that require referral to state agencies. In these cases, referral must occur, but the right to sue is not limited by the results of the administrative decision.

A judge hearing a case involving a dispute over licensing requirements for a nuclear power plant likely would refer this case to the Nuclear Regulatory Commission (NRC).

REVIEW OF FACTUAL DETERMINATIONS

When it reviews the findings of fact made by an administrative body, a court presumes them to be correct. A court of review examines the evidence by analyzing the record of the agency's proceedings. It upholds the agency's findings and conclusions on questions of fact if they are supported by substantial evidence in the record. In other words, the record must contain material evidence from which a reasonable person might reach the same conclusion as did the agency. If substantial evidence in support of the decision is present, the court will not disturb the agency's findings, even though the court itself might have reached a different conclusion on the basis of other conflicting evidence also in the record. For example, the determination of credibility of the witnesses who testify in quasi-judicial proceedings is for the agency to determine and not the courts.

Courts do not (1) reweigh the evidence, (2) make independent determinations of fact, or (3) substitute their view of the evidence for that of the agency. However, courts do determine if there is substantial evidence to support the action taken. But in their examination of the evidence, all that is required is evidence sufficient to convince a reasonable mind to a fair degree of certainty. Thus, substantial evidence is that which a reasonable mind might accept as adequate to support the conclusion.

For the courts to exercise their function of limited review, an agency must provide a record that sets forth the reasons and basis for its decision. If this record shows that the agency did not examine all relevant data and that it ignored issues before it, a court may set aside the agency's decision because such a decision is arbitrary and capricious. Agencies cannot assume their decisions. They must be based on evidence, and the record must support the decision.

concept *summary*

Judicial Review of Agency Decisions

1. Regardless of whether a party is challenging an agency's rule making or adjudication, that party must have standing to sue.

2. To establish standing to sue, the challenger must show the reviewing court that the agency's decision is subject to review and that the challenger is personally affected by the agency's decision.

3. When the decision challenged involves the agency's rule-making function, the court must determine if the agency's authority was validly delegated.

4. If the delegation of authority is definite and limited, the court will decide if the agency has exceeded its authority. If the answer is no, the agency's rule will be upheld.

5. When the decision challenged involves the agency's adjudicatory function, the law requires the challenger to exhaust the available administrative remedies and the court to determine whether an agency should have primary jurisdiction.

6. The factual findings of an agency are presumed to be correct.

7. Courts are not permitted to substitute their personal views for the agency's findings and conclusions if a reasonable person could reach the same result as the agency.

8. An agency's expertise is entitled to great deference and will not be reversed unless it is clearly erroneous.

After reading this section and the preceding ones, do you understand why it is important for businesses to take seriously the procedures within the administrative agency?

Criticism of Administrative Agencies

Administrative agencies and the regulatory process face many problems and much criticism. Sidebar 15.6 summarizes issues relating to the people involved, to the process followed, and to the substantive outcomes of agencies' rule-making and adjudicating authority.

At the heart of many of these problems and criticisms is the cost associated with the regulatory process.

---

sidebar 15.6

Criticisms of Administrative Process

RELATING TO PERSONNEL

1. Government has difficulty in hiring and retaining the best-qualified people. Salaries are often not competitive, and advancement is often slower than in the private sector. Also, some people are over-qualified for their positions.

2. The reward system usually does not make a significant distinction between excellent, mediocre, and poor performances. There are few incentives to improve productivity and job performance.

3. It is very difficult, if not impossible, to discharge unsatisfactory employees. Transfers of employees are easier to accomplish than discharges.

4. Personnel in many top positions are selected for political reasons. They often lack the necessary expertise to run an effective organization.

RELATING TO PROCEDURES

1. Delay in the decision-making process is quite common. There often is no reason to expedite decisions, and a huge backlog of cases is common in agencies such as EEOC.

2. The administrative process is overwhelmed with paperwork and with meetings.

3. Rules and regulations are often written in complex legal language—"legalese"—which laypeople cannot understand.

4. There is often a lack of enforcement procedures to follow up on actions taken to ensure compliance.

5. The administrative process can be dictatorial; there may be too much discretionary power, often unstructured and unchecked, placed in many bureaucratic hands. Formal as well as informal administrative action can amount to an abuse of power.

RELATING TO SUBSTANCE

1. There are so many agencies making rules and regulations directed at the business community that the rules and regulations often overlap and are in conflict.

2. Some agencies are accused of "sweetheart regulations," or favoring the industry or industries they regulate over the public interest. This may arise as a result of the "revolving door" relationship. Regulators are often persons who had former high executive positions in the industries they regulate. The reverse is also true: people in high-paying jobs in certain industries often were regulators of those very industries.

3. Many actions for illegal conduct end only with consent orders. A business accused of a violation agrees not to violate the law in the future without admitting any past violation. Such actions have little deterrent effect on others, and little or no punishment is imposed for illegal conduct.

4. The volume of rules adopted by agencies is beyond the ability of the business community to keep up with and comply with.

5. Enforcement of some laws varies over time.

THE COSTS TO BUSINESS

Regulation is a form of taxation. It directly increases the cost of government. But these direct costs of regulation are only a small fraction of the indirect costs. Regulation significantly adds to the cost of doing business, and these costs are passed on to the tax-paying, consuming public. The consumer, for whose protection many regulations are adopted, pays both the direct cost of regulation (in taxes) and the indirect cost (when purchasing products and services).

The existence of a governmental agency usually forces a business subject to the agency's jurisdiction to create a similar bureaucracy within its own organization to deal with the agency. For example, the existence of EEOC has caused most large corporations to designate affirmative action officers. These employees assist their companies in complying with the laws, rules, and regulations enforced by EEOC. Whenever a bureaucracy exists, firms dealing with it must have internal groups with responsibilities that are the mirror image of the agency.

Attempts to comply with administrative agencies can cause businesses to become more and more bureaucratic.

Other costs the public must absorb result from agency regulations that inhibit competition and innovation. Regulation may protect existing companies by creating a barrier to entry into a market. Regulation tends to protect "cozy competition" to the extent that, quite often, the parties that object the most to deregulation are the businesses being regulated.

Perhaps the most disturbing additional cost to the business community is the cost of paperwork. The burden of the paperwork involved in filing applications, returns, reports, and forms is overwhelming and a major cost of doing business.

Small businesses can be forced out of business by the regulatory process.

Federal administrative agencies are required to work with the Small Business Administration's Office of Advocacy as it attempts to lessen the burdens of regulation on small businesses. These requirements are spelled out in the Regulatory Flexibility Act and the Small Business Regulatory Enforcement Fairness Act.

THE COSTS TO SOCIETY

Historically, there was little or no cost-benefit analysis when new rules and regulations were proposed. Government has tended only to assess the benefits accruing from a cleaner environment, safer products, healthier working conditions, and so on, in deciding to embark upon vast new regulatory programs. The primary focus of policymaking by way of such social regulation has not been on balancing the costs of the programs with their potential benefits. The public, and especially consumers, has frequently been forced to pay for many things it did not want or need in the sense that the cost far exceeded the benefits.

At first glance, the application of cost-benefit analysis to the administrative process would seem to make sense. However, on closer examination, it is obvious that in many cases it is not possible to weigh the costs against the benefits of regulation.

How do you apply cost-benefit analysis to a rule dealing with human life? How much dollar benefit is to be assigned to a life in measuring it against the cost? Assume that a Department of Transportation rule requiring front- and side-impact air bags in all new automobiles sold adds a cost of $800 to each car. Assume also that it saves 50,000 lives per year. Is the cost worth the benefit? Your answer may depend on whether you are one of the 50,000.

Cost-benefit analysis becomes ethically awkward when there is an attempt to place a dollar value on things not usually bought and sold, such as life, health, or mobility.

A greater cost to each of us occurs when the regulatory process causes inefficiencies. The regulatory process can be so cumbersome that even the administrative agency involved becomes less effective. However, you must ask—what should you do to stay current and in compliance? As much as you may want to say, "Let's not worry about all the details," it is essential that your company know the rules and guidelines of relevant agencies. As this chapter describes, it is much easier to influence an agency's action than it is to convince a court you have been wronged by such action.

At the federal level, all agencies are required to publish guidelines and rules in their proposed and final versions. The place for such publications is the *Federal Register,* which appears daily. Reading the *Federal Register* is more than a full-time job. The volume of pages printed is beyond what anyone can manage day-after-day. Although it may take a staff, actions by federal administrative agencies can be followed. Unfortunately the same cannot be said for each state and all local administrative proposals and decisions. There simply is nothing like a state or local version of the *Federal Register.* To keep track of regulations of all levels requires personnel beyond that which businesses can afford. Reliance on local attorneys or trade organizations becomes an incomplete means of staying current. The cost of "keeping up" is balanced against the cost of being out of compliance. As with the issue of how to enhance efficiency in the regulatory process, there is no easy answer to staying fully informed of administrative actions at all governmental levels.

CONCLUSION

Perhaps from the time the U.S. Constitution was debated and adopted, people have complained "There is too much government." This feeling probably exists today anytime a governmental action interferes with a property interest we have.

How did we get to this situation? you might ask. The answer is rather complicated and subject to some controversy. What is clear is all levels of governments are larger and more complex in this first decade of the twenty-first century than even 25 years ago. Indeed, each generation of Americans has seen an increase in the government's influence.

Sidebar 15.7 presents a historical overview of the growth of the regulatory process and some corresponding administrative agencies.

The topics presented in Sidebar 15.7 are not exhaustive of important administrative agencies. In fact, a complete list of agencies would take up too much space. One federal government website lists 136 federal agencies. And there are countless state and local administrative agencies.

Some additional data provides further insight as to the growth of government. In colonial times, more than 90 percent of the people were engaged in some agricultural activity. The westward expansion continued this trend. In 1840, four out of every five adults were self-employed. Ask yourself: How much government protection/influence/interference did this society need? Today, over 90 percent of adults are employees. This shift in our economy has resulted in a larger role for government regulation.

"The total number of *Federal Register* pages per decade has increased from 170,325 in the 1960s, to 450,821 in the 1970s, to 529,233 in the 1980s, to 622,368 in the 1990s, to 713,920 in the 2000s (based on a four-year average)."

—"Reviving Regulatory Reform: Options for the President and Congress" by Marlo Lewis, Jr.

"Most regulations reviled by some are cherished by others, meaning that any effort to reduce regulation is a political process, not a question of housekeeping."

—Binyamin Appelbaum and Edward Wyatt, "Obama May Find Useless Regulations Are Scarcer Than Thought," *New York Times,* **January 21, 2011**

Do review the agencies found at www.whitehouse .gov/government/ independent-agencies. html.

sidebar 15.7

Trends in Regulations: Growth of Government in the Twentieth Century

As the 1800s ended and the 1900s began, a major concern of the federal government was the concentration of economic power into the hands of America's wealthiest. This concern led to the creation of antitrust laws. Although it was not the first federal administrative agency, the Federal Trade Commission (FTC), created in 1914 to prevent unfair methods of competition, started the growth of administrative agencies in the twentieth century. (*Note:* This topic is the subject matter of Chapter 16.)

The financial crash of the country's capital markets and the ensuing depression caused Congress to pass several laws attempting to restore economic order. Among some of the most important laws were the securities acts. These laws, passed in the 1930s, and subsequent laws intended to address the business scandals of the 1980s, 1990s, and early twenty-first century, make up the subject matter of Chapter 17. This chapter emphasizes the role of the Securities and Exchange Commission (SEC).

Throughout the first half of the twentieth century, Congress attempted to balance the bargaining power of business management and organized labor. These various laws and others impacting the employment relationship are the topics of Chapter 22. A key administrative agency studied in that chapter is the National Labor Relations Board (NLRB).

The second half of the twentieth century saw a focus on discriminatory practices and their negative impact on society and business. At the heart of regulating and preventing discrimination is the Equal Employment Opportunity Commission (EEOC). This agency and the related laws are described in Chapter 20.

Also, in the latter portion of the last century we saw a growing concern for protecting the environment. In the 1970s, Congress passed clean air and clean water legislation. To ensure businesses and individuals remain aware of their environmental impact, Congress created the Environmental Protection Agency (EPA). Chapter 19 discusses this area of the law.

Key Terms

Administrative agency 446
Administrative law 459
Administrative law judges 455
Cease and desist order 450

Consent order 450
Exhaustion of remedies 462
General counsel 454
Immunity 455

Primary jurisdiction 463
Quasi-judicial 446
Quasi-legislative 446

Review Questions and Problems

Regulatory Process—Administrative Agencies

1. *Reasons for Agencies*
   This chapter discusses five reasons for having administrative agencies. Give an example for each reason.

2. *Functions of Agencies*
   Describe the four possible functions of an administrative agency.

3. *Organization of Agencies*
   (a) Why is the position of general counsel of an administrative agency so important?
   (b) What is the purpose of the administrative law judges within administrative agencies?

4. *Influencing Agency Decisions*

Suppose that a company is interested in a newly proposed regulation on clean air by the Environmental Protection Agency. What should this company do to provide its input on this EPA regulation?

Judicial Review of Agency Decisions

5. *Standing to Sue*

What are the two issues that must be considered by courts to determine whether a person has standing to challenge an agency's decision?

6. *Review of Rule Making*

(a) Again there are two issues that must be addressed by courts when they review the rule-making (quasi-legislative) functions of agencies. What are these two issues? Explain each.

(b) A national bank sought permission from the comptroller of the currency to sell annuities. This permission was granted as "incidental to the business of banking." The Variable Annuity Life Insurance Company filed suit claiming the comptroller should not have granted this permission. What standard of review of this administrative decision should courts apply?

7. *Review of Adjudications: Procedural Aspects*

Plaintiffs purchased state lottery tickets and were winners along with 76 others. The state had advertised that $1,750,000 would be the prize, but it distributed only $744,471. Plaintiff sued the lottery director, alleging fraud in the conduct of the lottery. The state lottery law provides for administrative hearings upon complaints charging violations of the lottery law or of regulations thereunder. It also allows any party adversely affected by a final order of the administrative agency to seek judicial review. Must the plaintiffs exhaust their administrative remedies? Why or why not?

8. *Review of Factual Determinations*

What standard of review do courts use to decide whether to uphold the factual determinations made by an administrative agency?

Criticism of Administrative Agencies

9. *The Costs to Business*

Describe four types of costs that businesses must absorb due to the regulatory process.

10. *The Costs to Society*

Why has there been so little use of cost-benefit analysis when judging the merits of an agency's proposals and actions?

11. *Conclusion*

Why has the complaint against excessive government been consistent throughout the years?

1. Suppose it has been two years since your graduation. During the time you have worked for a large energy company. In your work, you have been exposed to the numerous ways your employer is investing in energy. These sources include oil, coal, natural gas, solar, wind, nuclear, and electrical plants.

Just last month, you were told you were being transferred to the CEO's office. Your first assignment is to work with the general counsel's staff to determine how your company is regulated and how all divisions are complying with the various, relevant laws and regulations. As you ponder this assignment, you ask yourself the following questions:

Is this company regulated only by the federal government, or are state and local regulations relevant?

How does the company and its divisions keep track of laws and regulations?

If an administrative agency begins an investigation of your company, should your company cooperate with or fight the agency's action?

2. You are chief executive officer of a toy manufacturing firm. Your firm has been inspected by officials at OSHA, the federal Occupational Safety and Health Administration, for alleged violations of workplace safety regulations. The evidence presented to the agency was confusing and conflicting. You feel strongly that the company should not be penalized. Nevertheless your firm has been ordered to pay a substantial fine, and an administrative law judge ordered you to make some very expensive modifications in its manufacturing processes.

Should you continue to seek review of your case before the agency's officials?

Should you appeal by filing a lawsuit to reverse the agency's decision?

If you are successful in court, under what circumstances can you recover your attorney's fees?

3. As a manager employed by Want-It-Now Rapid Delivery Service, you are responsible for pricing the services involving same-day deliveries. Among your primary concerns is the competitive aspects of your business. You have proposed contractual language that states "any package picked up after 10:00 a.m. will be considered as if it is picked up the next business day. Any package delivered before 10:00 p.m. on the day of pick up will be considered to have arrived on that business day. Under the language, a package received at 11:00 a.m. on Tuesday and delivered by 10:00 p.m. on Wednesday is considered, by you, to involve a "same-day delivery." The impact of this language is that a business day lasts for as long as 36 hours; thereby giving a customer the wrong impression of the phrase "same-day delivery."

The Federal Trade Commission (FTC), under its authority to protect the public from unfair or deceptive trade practices, has contacted your company asking questions about the plain meaning of "same-day delivery." In anticipation of a face-to-face meeting with an FTC investigator, you strive to answer these questions.

To what degree does the FTC have authority to question your business practices?

Are your clearly stated contractual provisions unfair or deceptive?

Should you cooperate with this investigator or seek a court order enjoining this investigation?

How do you challenge the FTC's action if a formal complaint is filed against your company?

16

Regulating Competition— Antitrust Laws

Learning Objectives

In this chapter, you will learn:

16-1. To understand the rationale for promoting a competitive business environment and the role of federal and state antitrust law in preserving competition.

16-2. To evaluate how the Sherman Act scrutinizes agreements that unreasonably restrain trade.

16-3. To analyze how the Sherman Act regulates monopolization in business markets.

16-4. To understand the penalties for violating the Sherman Act and important exceptions to liability.

16-5. To analyze how the Clayton Act expands the national policy to preserve competition in the marketplace.

16-6. To evaluate the powers of the Federal Trade Commission in conjunction with and independent from the Justice Department.

Why is it important to study antitrust laws? First, the application of antitrust policy can have significant implications for you and your company. Major fines and a prison sentence are not beyond the realm of possibilities. You need to know that antitrust laws apply equally to small, local businesses and to large, multinational corporations.

The U.S. Department of Justice has imposed more than $3 billion in fines related to antitrust violations since 2009. Moreover, the DOJ was successful in obtaining prison sentences for 78% of defendants in 2012, double the rate from the 1990s.[1] The United States is not the only country actively engaged in antitrust enforcement. During the same period, other countries' antitrust penalties reached similarly high totals.

These figures are intended to catch your attention and to emphasize the significant impact of the antitrust laws presented in this chapter. It is wise to take into account the consequences of anticompetitive behavior.

[1] *U.S. Department of Justice, Division Update, Spring 2013, www.justice.gov/atr/public/division-update/2013/criminal-program.html.*

LO 16-1

John Rockefeller gained control of the petroleum industry; Cornelius Vanderbilt controlled railroads; and Andrew Carnegie controlled the steel industry.

HISTORICAL DEVELOPMENT

The term *antitrust* is somewhat misleading. Trusts are a legal arrangement in which a fiduciary holds legal title to property for benefit of another. In the last part of the nineteenth century, businesspeople used the trust device extensively to gain monopolistic control of several industries. Through it, a group of corporations in the same type of business could unite to eliminate competition among themselves. The trust device allowed all or at least a majority of the stock of several companies to be transferred to a trustee. The trustee then was in a position to control the operations and policy-making of all the companies. The trust not only controlled production, but also dominated and divided the market and established price levels. The effect of these concentrations was to destroy the free market—"to restrain trade," as the Sherman Act would put it.

Because the purpose of the laws discussed in this chapter was to "bust" the trusts, these laws became known as the antitrust laws. Today the term is used to describe all laws that intend to promote and regulate competition and make our competitive economic system work. The goal is workable competition and all the benefits that are intended to flow from it.

During its first hundred years, the federal government's role in relation to commerce was that of promoter. The U.S. Constitution itself eliminates trade barriers among the states. In the early and mid-nineteenth century, through its sponsorship of internal improvements such as canals and roads and its support for railroads, the federal government facilitated trade and commerce. However, by the end of the nineteenth century business and industrial combinations were so powerful that reformers called on government to break these monopolies and restore healthy competition. The government responded by enacting the **Sherman Act** in 1890.

The goal of the Sherman Act is competition. Competition, these reformers pointed out, tends to keep private markets working in ways that are socially desirable. It encourages an efficient allocation of resources and stimulates efficiency and product innovation. A competitive system that allows easy entry to and withdrawal from the marketplace is consistent with individual freedom and economic opportunity. In 1958, Justice Hugo Black, in *Northern Pacific Ry. Co. v. United States* (356 U.S. 1), reflected on the purpose of the Sherman Act when he stated in part:

> The Sherman Act was designed to be a comprehensive charter of economic liberty aimed at preserving free and unfettered competition as the rule of trade. It rests on the premise that the unrestrained interaction of competitive forces will yield the best allocation of our economic resources, the lowest prices, the highest quality and the greatest material progress, while at the same time providing an environment conducive to the preservation of our democratic, political and social institutions.

The Sherman Act still provides the basic framework for the regulation of business and industry. It seeks to preserve competition by prohibiting two types of anticompetitive business behavior:

- Sherman Act, Section 1—contracts, combinations, and conspiracies that unreasonably restrain trade or commerce.
- Sherman Act, Section 2—monopolization or attempts to monopolize a market.

The Sherman Act is general in its terms and does not specifically set forth every act that would constitute a violation of the law. It does not define *trust*, *monopoly* or *restraint of trade*. It also does not make clear whether it applies to combinations of labor as well as capital.

In 1914, the Congress, recognizing that the Sherman Act needed to be more specific, enacted the **Clayton Act** as an amendment to the Sherman Act and later amended the Clayton Act (1936, 1950, and 1980) to clarify its provisions. The Clayton Act declares that certain enumerated practices in interstate commerce are illegal. These are practices that might adversely affect competition but were not clear violations under the Sherman Act.

In 1914, Congress also passed the **Federal Trade Commission Act.** This act created the Federal Trade Commission (FTC), an independent administrative agency charged with keeping competition free and fair. The FTC enforces the Clayton Act. In addition, it enforces Section 5 of the FTC Act, which prohibits unfair methods of competition and unfair or deceptive acts or practices.

The antitrust laws are enforced by the federal and state governments and by private parties. The federal government's basic enforcement procedures are utilized through the Department of Justice and the Federal Trade Commission (FTC). The Department of Justice alone has the power to bring criminal proceedings, but it shares its civil enforcement powers with the FTC.

State government also plays an important role in the enforcement of antitrust laws. A state attorney general may bring civil suits for damages under the Sherman Act as well as suits for an injunction. In addition, state legislators have enacted antitrust laws that cover both products and services. These laws cover intrastate activities and are designed to prevent loss of competition in local communities.

In addition to these governmental enforcers, private parties may bring civil suits seeking monetary damages or injunction as a means of enforcing the antitrust laws. The penalties that help protect the competitive nature of the marketplace are discussed later in the chapter.

The Sherman Act, Section 1—Agreements in Restraint of Trade

LO 16-2

Section 1 of the Sherman Act prohibits contracts, combinations, and conspiracies in **restraint of trade** or commerce. *Contracts* in restraint of trade usually result from verbal or written agreements; *combinations* usually result from conduct; *conspiracies* are usually established by agreement and followed up by some act carrying out the plan of the conspiracy.

Joint activities by two or more persons may constitute a violation of Section 1. The most common contract in restraint of trade is an agreement among competitors to charge the same price for their products (**price fixing**). Such agreements among producers to set prices in advance rather than allow prices to be set by the free market are obviously anticompetitive and in restraint of trade. Agreements relating to territories of operation also violate Section 1 of the Sherman Act. So does an attempt to extend the economic power of a patent or copyright to unrelated products or services.

As the courts deal with potential violations of Section 1 of the Sherman Act, they employ different analyses depending on the relationship of the parties. The most important division is in agreements between horizontal competitors versus agreements between parties in vertical relationships. Horizontal competitors

Section 1 of the Sherman Act states: "Every contract, combination, in the form of trust or otherwise, or conspiracy, in restraint of trade or commerce among the several States, or with foreign nations, is declared to be illegal."

are firms that could compete for the same customers in the same market. For example, imagine three supermarket chains in a town, each of which have different corporate owners (see Figure 16.1). They sell goods to the same population of consumers and are in direct competition. Agreements they make with each other to offer certain products or price goods at a certain level are **horizontal restraints**. Horizontal restraints face significantly more scrutiny under the Sherman Act and are much more likely to be deemed illegal

Parties in vertical relationships include manufacturers, distributors, and retailers that may enter into agreements concerning pricing, supply, or territory. For example, imagine a milk producer makes an agreement with a dairy distributor related to territory, or a diary distributor makes agreements with supermarkets on maximum price for goods (see Figure 16.2). These agreements are termed **vertical restraints**. Although such restraints *may* violate the Sherman Act, as discussed later, they may be permitted if the net impact is to benefit consumers.

Figure 16.1
Horizontal restraints.

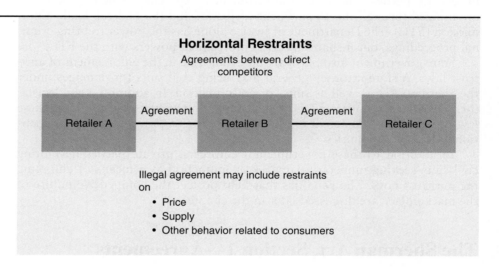

Figure 16.2
Vertical restraints.

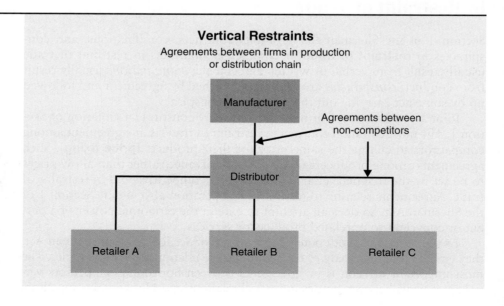

ANALYSIS IN ANTITRUST LAW

To analyze potential violations of the Sherman Act, two categories of analysis are used:

- The rule of reason.
- Per se illegality.

The first category consists of agreements and practices that are illegal only if they impose an unreasonable restraint upon competitors. The per se category consists of agreements or practices that are so plainly anticompetitive and so lacking in any redeeming values that they are conclusively presumed to be illegal without further examination under the rule of reason.

THE RULE OF REASON

Section 1 of the Sherman Act provides that "*every* contract, combination . . . or conspiracy in restraint of trade . . . is declared to be illegal." However, the United States Supreme Court has held that Congress did not really mean it when it used the word *every*. For example, if you and I enter into a contract whereby I agree to buy your car, this contract restrains trade. You cannot sell your car to another person without becoming liable to me for a breach of our contract. The Court felt that Congress did not intend our contract to be a violation of the Sherman Act.

The **rule of reason** was announced in *Standard Oil Co. v. United States*, 221 U.S. 1 (1911). The Supreme Court in that case held that contracts or conspiracies in restraint of trade were illegal only if they constituted *undue* or *unreasonable* restraints of trade and that only *unreasonable* attempts to monopolize were covered by the Sherman Act. As a result, acts that the statute prohibits may be removed from the coverage of the law by a finding that they are *reasonable*.

The *test of reasonableness* asks whether challenged contracts or acts are unreasonably restrictive of competitive conditions. Unreasonableness can be based on:

- The nature or character of the contracts.
- Surrounding circumstances giving rise to the inference or presumption that the contracts were intended to restrain trade and enhance prices.

Under either branch of the test, the inquiry is confined to a consideration of impact on competitive conditions. If an agreement promotes competition, it may be legal. If it suppresses or destroys competition, it is unreasonable and illegal.

Per Se Illegality Agreements falling within the per se category have such a pernicious effect on competition that elaborate inquiry as to the precise harm they may cause or a business excuse for them is unnecessary. They are **per se illegal**. The concept simplifies proof in these cases of clearly wrongful conduct. If the activity is deemed is illegal *per se*, proof of the activity is proof of a violation and proof that it is in restraint of trade. It is unreasonable as a matter of law.

Courts develop the distinction between rule of reason and per se illegality on a case-by-case basis. However, history tells us the horizontal restraints or agreements defined earlier are much more likely to satisfy the per se illegality standards. Courts hold that the sharing among competitors of product information, pricing policies, and territorial allocations is not going to increase competition. Indeed, the anticompetitive results of this sharing results in such arrangements being viewed as illegal per se. On the other hand, analysis of vertical agreements usually requires consideration of the rule of reason as opposed to being judged as per se illegal.

Sherman Act cases must satisfy an interstate commerce element. The facts must show that an allegedly illegal activity was either in interstate commerce or had a substantial effect on interstate commerce. The facts need not prove a change in the volume of interstate commerce but only that the activity had a substantial and adverse or not insubstantial effect on interstate commerce. As discussed in Chapter 15, the impact on interstate commerce often is readily apparent.

HORIZONTAL PRICE FIXING

Horizontal price fixing is an agreement between competitors to fix prices. The term *price fixing* means more than setting a price. For example, if partners in a firm set the price of their goods or service, they have engaged in a form of price fixing but not the type envisioned by the Sherman Act. The price fixing covered by the Sherman Act is that which threatens free competition.

It is no defense to a charge of price fixing that the prices fixed are fair or reasonable. It also is no defense that price fixing is engaged in by small competitors to allow them to compete with larger competitors. A common point that courts make in antitrust cases is the fact that antitrust law protects consumers, not competitors. The per se rule makes price fixing illegal whether the parties to it have control of the market or not, and whether or not they are trying to raise or lower the market price. It is just as illegal to fix a low price as it is to fix a high price. Maximum-price agreements are just as illegal as minimum-price agreements. In Case 16.1, the court had to determine whether Apple Inc.'s coordination of competitor restraints placed it in the role of a price fixer.

 case **16.1**

UNITED STATES OF AMERICA v. APPLE INC.
952 F. Supp. 2d 638 (S.D.N.Y. 2012)

The Plaintiffs have shown through compelling evidence that Apple violated Section 1 of the Sherman Act by conspiring with the Publisher Defendants to eliminate retail price competition and to raise e-book prices. There is overwhelming evidence that the Publisher Defendants joined with each other in a horizontal price-fixing conspiracy. Through that conspiracy, the Publisher Defendants raised the prices of many of their New Releases and NYT Bestsellers above the $9.99 price at which they had previously been sold through Amazon. They also raised the prices of many of their backlist e-books. The Plaintiffs have also shown that Apple was a knowing and active member of that conspiracy. Apple not only willingly joined the conspiracy, but also forcefully facilitated it.

There is little dispute that the Publisher Defendants conspired together to raise the prices of their e-books. They shared a common motivation: the elimination of the "wretched" $9.99 retail price that Amazon, the chief distributor of their e-books, chose for many of their New Releases, including NYT Bestsellers. They believed that this price point in the nascent but swiftly growing e-book market would, if left unchallenged, unalterably affect the consumer perception of the value of a book and severely undermine their more profitable physical book business. To protect their then-existing business model, the Publisher Defendants agreed to raise the prices of e-books by taking control of retail pricing. . . .

From late 2008 through 2009, the Publisher Defendants had collectively tried through a variety of means to pressure Amazon to raise the prices of their e-books. Their efforts proved futile. Then, through agency agreements that each Publisher Defendant executed with Apple over the course of just three days in January 2010, and with Amazon (and other e-retailers) in the weeks that followed, the Publisher Defendants simultaneously switched from a wholesale to an agency model for the distribution of their e-books. When the iPad went on sale and the iBookstore went live in early April 2010 (or shortly thereafter, in the case of Penguin), each of the Publisher Defendants used their new pricing authority to raise the prices of their e-books overnight and substantially.

This price-fixing conspiracy would not have succeeded without the active facilitation and encouragement of Apple. Before Apple even met with the Publisher Defendants in mid-December 2009, it was fully aware that the Publishers were adamantly opposed to Amazon's $9.99 price point and were actively searching for an effective means, including through collective action, to pressure Amazon to raise its prices. Inspired by the impending Launch of the revolutionary iPad, scheduled for January 27, Apple seized the moment.

Apple met with the Publishers in December 2009 and heard their unanimous condemnation of the $9.99 price point and desire to raise e-book prices. Volunteering that it was willing to price e-books as high as $14.99 in an e-bookstore, Apple won their rapt attention. Apple then presented a strategy—the agency Agreements—that would allow the Publishers to take control of and raise e-book retail prices in a matter of weeks. Knowing full well, however, that the Publisher Defendants wanted to raise e-book retail prices significantly above the $9.99 price point, even in some instances above the retail prices of the corresponding physical book, Apple placed pricing restrictions or caps on categories of e-books to ensure that the prices in its iBookstore were "realistic" and didn't embarrass Apple. In negotiating the caps for its pricing tiers, Apple understood that it was setting the new retail prices at which e-books would be sold.

Apple had several reasons for engaging as it did with the Publisher Defendants. It wanted to announce a well-stocked iBookstore in less than two months,

when it launched its iPad; it wanted to avoid competing with Amazon, an arch rival in the market, on the basis of price; and it wanted a guaranteed profit on any new business it entered. To accomplish these goals, Apple was willing to offer the Publisher Defendants a roadmap for raising retail e-book prices well above Amazon's $9.99 price point and urged the Publisher Defendants to use that roadmap to do so. In short, Apple convinced the Publisher Defendants that Apple shared their goal of raising e-book prices, and helped them to realize that goal.

Apple included the [most-favored-nations] MFN, or price parity provision, in its Agreements both to protect itself against any retail price competition and to ensure that it had no retail price competition. Apple fully understood and intended that the MFN would lead the Publisher Defendants inexorably to demand that Amazon switch to an agency relationship with each of them. As Apple's Cue reminded Macmillan's Sargent, this was no more than what the Publisher Defendants had already assured Apple that they wanted to, and would, do.

Because of the MFN, Apple concluded that it did not need to include as an explicit term in its Agreements a demand that a Publisher Defendant move all of its resellers to agency. The MFN was sufficient to force the change in model. The economics of the Agreements were, simply put, "terrible" for the Publishers. The Publisher Defendants already expected to lose revenue from their substitution of an agency model for the wholesale model of e-book distribution. Unless a Publisher Defendant followed through and transformed its relationships with Amazon and other resellers into an agency relationship, it would be in significantly worse terms financially as a result of its agency contract with Apple. As significantly, unless the Publisher Defendants joined forces and together forced Amazon onto the agency model, their expected loss of revenue would not be offset by the achievement of their ultimate goal: the protection of book value.

A chief stumbling block to raising e-book prices was the Publishers' fear that Amazon would retaliate against any Publisher who pressured it to raise prices. Each of them could also expect to lose substantial sales if they unilaterally raised the prices of their own e-books and none of their competitors followed suit. This is where Apple's participation in the conspiracy proved essential. It assured each Publisher Defendant that it would only move forward if a critical mass of the major publishing houses agreed to its agency terms. It promised each Publisher Defendant that it was getting identical terms in its Agreement in every material way. It kept each Publisher Defendant apprised of how many others had agreed to execute

Apple's Agreements. As Cue acknowledged at trial, "I just wanted to assure them that they weren't going to be alone, so that I would take the fear awa[y] of the Amazon retribution that they were all afraid of." As a result, the Publisher Defendants understood that each of them shared the same set of risks and rewards.

Working against its own internal deadline, Apple achieved for this industry in a matter of weeks what the Publisher Defendants had been unable to accomplish for months before Apple became their partner. In the words of Simon & Schuster's Reidy, Apple herded cats. Apple gave the Publishers a deadline and required them to examine with care but quickly how committed they were to challenging Amazon and altering the landscape of e-book pricing. And when it appeared a Publisher Defendant might be too scared to commit to this dramatic business change, Cue reminded that Publisher Defendant that Apple's entry into the market represented a once-in-a-lifetime opportunity to eliminate Amazon's control over pricing. As he warned Penguin just days before the Launch, "There is no one outside of us that can do this for you. If we miss this opportunity, it will likely never come again."

Without the collective action that Apple nurtured, it is unlikely any individual Publisher would have succeeded in unilaterally imposing an agency relationship on Amazon. Working together, and equipped with Apple's agency Agreements, Apple and the Publisher Defendants moved the largest publishers of trade e-books and their distributors from a wholesale to agency model, eliminated retail price competition, and raised e-book prices. . . .

In sum, the Plaintiffs have shown not just by a preponderance of the evidence . . . but through compelling direct and circumstantial evidence that Apple participated in and facilitated a horizontal price-fixing conspiracy. As a result, they have proven a *per se* violation of the Sherman Act. . . . If it were necessary to analyze this evidence under the rule of reason, however, the Plaintiffs would also prevail.

KEY POINTS

- The court found that Apple's agreements with various publishers restrained trade because they coordinated efforts to force Amazon to permit higher e-book prices. If not for the coordination, the individual firms' negotiations with Amazon would likely be legal.
- Ensuring the survival of competing publishers is not important under antitrust law.
- Although the agreements did not fix a particular price, they permitted competitors to work together to affect prices.

It is a defense to a charge of price fixing if two competitors enter into a joint venture and agree what the combined company will charge for its product. In *Texaco v. Dagher,*[2] the Court found that Texaco and Shell Oil were not fixing prices when they operated a joint venture to refine and sell gasoline.

Historically, the Sherman Act was thought to apply only to the sale of goods. Price fixing in the service sector was commonly engaged in by professional persons such as architects, lawyers, and physicians. Persons performing services argued they were not engaged in trade or commerce and thus they were not covered by the Sherman Act. They also contended there was a "learned profession" exception to the Sherman Act.

Courts have held lawyers, doctors, real estate agents, engineers, and dentists subject to antitrust laws.

In the mid-1970s, the Supreme Court rejected these arguments and held that the Sherman Act covers services, including those performed by the learned professions such as attorneys-at-law. Today, it is just as illegal to fix the price of services as it is to fix the price of goods.

[2]*547 U.S. 1 (2006).*

Some professional groups have attempted to avoid restrictions on price fixing through the use of ethical standards. Although such ethical standards are not illegal per se, they are nevertheless anticompetitive and a violation of the Sherman Act. Others have attempted to determine the price of services indirectly by using formulas and relative-value scales. For example, some medical organizations have determined that a given medical procedure would be allocated a relative value on a scale of 1 to 10. Open-heart surgery might be labeled a 9 and an appendectomy a 3. All members of the profession would then use these values in determining professional fees. Such attempts have been uniformly held to be illegal.

Table 16.1 lists examples of horizontal price-fixing cases. The companies and industries listed illustrate the far-reaching nature of the Sherman Act.

VERTICAL PRICE FIXING

Attempts by manufacturers to control the ultimate retail price for their products is known as **vertical price fixing** or **resale price maintenance.** Such efforts result in part from the desire to maintain a high-quality product image, the assumption being that a relatively high price suggests a relatively high quality. These efforts are also based on a desire to maintain adequate channels of distribution. If one retailer is selling a product at prices significantly below those

table 16.1 Examples of Horizontal Price-Fixing Cases

Business	Type of Case	Sherman Act Violation	Case Result
21 Airline Companies and 19 executives	Criminal	Fixed prices to passengers and for cargo	$1.7 billion
Archer Daniels Midland Company and others	Criminal and civil	Fixed prices on citric acid	$70 million fine and $35 million civil settlement
President of Pepsi-Cola Bottling Co.	Criminal	Agreed with Coca-Cola bottler to stop discounts to retailers	4 months in jail, $45,000 fine, 3 years' probation, community service
Southland Corp. and Borden Inc.	Criminal and civil	Rigged bids for dairy products sold to Florida school-milk programs	$8 million combined fine and $2.5 million in civil claims
American Institute of Architects	Civil, injunction	Discouraged competitive bidding, discount fees, and free services	Consent decree that practices would cease plus $50,000 in costs
Fireman's Fund Home Insurance Co., Liberty Mutual Insurance, and Travelers Corp.	Civil, class action, triple damages	Boycotted Minnesota law requiring workers' compensation rates to be established by competition	$34 million settlement
Delta, United, USAir, American, TWA, and Northwest Airlines	Civil	Use of computerized clearinghouse to fix airfares	$458 million settlement involving the issuance of coupons for future air travel

of other retailers, there is a strong likelihood that the other retailers will not continue to carry the product.

Although resale price-maintenance schemes can run afoul of the Sherman Act, it is possible for a manufacturer to control the resale price of its products. The primary method of legally controlling the retail price is for a manufacturer simply to announce its prices and refuse to deal with those who fail to comply. Under what is commonly referred to as the Colgate doctrine, the Supreme Court recognizes that such independent action by a manufacturer is not a per se violation of the Sherman Act. Resale price maintenance is legal only if there is no coercion or pressure other than the announced policy and its implementation.

Whether or not vertical price fixing harms competition or consumers has been a matter of debate among economists and politicians. There is a possibility that a vertical restraint imposed by a single manufacturer or wholesaler may stimulate interbrand competition as it reduces intrabrand competition. This debate led to the Supreme Court's decision in *Leegin Creative Leather Products, Inc. v. PSKS, Inc.*, which held that a luxury leather products firm's efforts to force retailers to maintain minimum prices in its products was not per se illegal. Overruling prior case law, the Court recognized many of the arguments in favor vertical price fixing and determined that a firm should be permitted to justify such conduct under the rule of reason.

The Supreme Court reached a similar conclusion when a manufacturer attempts to fix a maximum price that its distributors can charge.[3] It now appears the Court is comfortable limiting the per se illegality analysis to horizontal agreements among competitors. Vertical agreements involving pricing (high and low) and territorial arrangements within channels of distribution are analyzed under the rule of reason.

INDIRECT PRICE FIXING

The ingenuity of businesspersons produces numerous attempts to fix prices by indirect means. Such attempts to control prices take a variety of forms and appear in diverse circumstances. Some arise out of a desire to protect a channel of distribution or a marketing system. Others result from attempts to keep marginal competitors in business to avoid becoming a monopoly.

In one case, indirect price fixing took the form of an exchange of price information. Economic theory was used to support the assumption that prices would be more unstable and lower if the information had not been exchanged. This case established that conduct directed at price stabilization is per se anticompetitive. The warning to business and industry is clear: Cooperation and cozy relationships between competitors may be illegal.

TERRITORIAL AGREEMENTS

Territorial agreements restrain trade by allocating geographical areas among competitors. They may be either horizontal or vertical. Competing businesses may enter into a **horizontal territorial agreement** for the purpose of giving each an exclusive territory. For example, if all lawn care and landscaping companies in a county agree to allocate to each an exclusive territory, a

---

[3] *State Oil Company v. Khan, 118 S.Ct. 275 (1997).*

concept *summary*

Price Fixing

1. Horizontal price fixing in the sales of goods or services is illegal per se.
2. It is just as illegal for competitors to fix a low price as it is a high price.
3. Professionals and service providers cannot legally conspire to fix prices.
4. Ethical standards cannot be used to fix prices.
5. Attempts by manufacturers to control the ultimate sale of their product (vertical price fixing) is analyzed under the rule of reason.
6. The mere exchange of price information among competitors may constitute a Sherman Act violation.

horizontal arrangement would exist. This agreement is illegal per se under the Sherman Act. This is true even if the arrangement is made with a third party. For example, an agreement among competing cable television operators to divide the market in Houston, Texas, was found to be a per se violation even though the agreement required city council approval.

A **vertical territorial agreement** is one between a manufacturer and a dealer or distributor. It assigns the dealer or distributor an exclusive territory, and the manufacturer agrees not to sell to other dealers or distributors in that territory in exchange for an agreement by the dealer that it will not operate outside the area assigned. Such agreements are usually part of a franchise or license agreement. These vertical arrangements are not per se violations; they are subject to the rule of reason.

CONCERTED ACTIVITIES

Many antitrust cases involve agreements or conduct by competitors that have anticompetitive effects. Competitors sometimes attempt to share some activities or join together in the performance of a function. These are known as **concerted activities.** Case 16.2 discusses aspects of concerted activities in the

 case **16.2**

AMERICAN NEEDLE, INC. v. NATIONAL FOOTBALL LEAGUE
560 U.S. 183 (2010)

The National Football League (NFL) consists of 32 independently owned teams. In 1963, the existing NFL teams formed the National Football League Properties (NFLP) to develop, license, and market the intellectual property of each team and the league. Prior to 2000, the NFLP granted nonexclusive licenses to several vendors, including American Needle, Inc. American Needle manufactured

and sold apparel with the various teams' logos. Beginning in 2000, NFLP entered into a 10-year exclusive arrangement with Reebok International Ltd allowing Reebok to be the only licensee to manufacture and sell headwear associated with NFL teams. Due to this exclusive agreement with Reebok, the nonexclusive license previously awarded to American Needle was not renewed.

American Needle filed a lawsuit alleging the NFL, its 32 teams, the NFLP, and Reebok violated sections 1 and 2 of the Sherman Act.

The Supreme Court granted American Needle's petition for a writ of certiorari to address whether the NFL respondents are capable of engaging in a "contract, combination . . . or conspiracy" as defined in section 1 of the Sherman Act.

STEVENS, J.: . . . We have long held that concerted action under §1 does not turn simply on whether the parties involved are legally distinct entities. Instead, we have eschewed such formalistic distinctions in favor of a functional consideration of how the parties involved in the alleged anticompetitive conduct actually operate. As a result, we have repeatedly found instances in which members of a legally single entity violated §1 when the entity was controlled by a group of competitors and served, in essence, as a vehicle for ongoing concerted activity.

Conversely, there is not necessarily concerted action simply because more than one legally distinct entity is involved. Although, under a now-defunct doctrine known as the "intraenterprise conspiracy doctrine," we once treated cooperation between legally separate entities as necessarily covered by §1, we now embark on a more functional analysis. . . .

Because the inquiry is one of competitive reality, it is not determinative that two parties to an alleged §1 violation are legally distinct entities. Nor, however, is it determinative that two legally distinct entities have organized themselves under a single umbrella or into a structured joint venture. The question is whether the agreement joins together "independent centers of decisionmaking." If it does, the entities are capable of conspiring under §1, and the court must decide whether the restraint of trade is an unreasonable and therefore illegal one.

The NFL teams do not possess either the unitary decision making quality or the single aggregation of economic power characteristic of independent action. Each of the teams is a substantial, independently owned, and independently managed business. . . . The teams compete with one another, not only on the playing field, but to attract fans, for gate receipts and for contracts with managerial and playing personnel.

Directly relevant to this case, the teams compete in the market for intellectual property. To a firm making hats, the Saints and the Colts are two potentially competing suppliers of valuable trademarks. When each NFL team licenses its intellectual property, it is not pursuing the common interests of the whole league but is instead pursuing interests of each corporation itself; teams are acting as separate economic actors pursuing separate economic interests, and each team

therefore is a potential independent center of decision making. Decisions by NFL teams to license their separately owned trademarks collectively and to only one vendor are decisions that deprive the marketplace of independent centers of decision making, and therefore of actual or potential competition.

In defense, respondents argue that by forming NFLP, they have formed a single entity, akin to a merger, and market their NFL brands through a single outlet. But it is not dispositive that the teams have organized and own a legally separate entity that centralizes the management of their intellectual property. An ongoing §1 violation cannot evade §1 scrutiny simply by giving the ongoing violation a name and label. . . .

The NFL respondents may be similar in some sense to a single enterprise that owns several pieces of intellectual property and licenses them jointly, but they are not similar in the relevant functional sense. Although NFL teams have common interests such as promoting the NFL brand, they are still separate, profit-maximizing entities, and their interests in licensing team trademarks are not necessarily aligned.

Common interests in the NFL brand partially unite the economic interests of the parent firms, but the teams still have distinct, potentially competing interests.

It may be, as respondents argue, that NFLP has served as the single driver of the teams' promotional vehicle, pursuing the common interests of the whole. But illegal restraints often are in the common interests of the parties to the restraint, at the expense of those who are not parties. It is true, as respondents describe, that they have for some time marketed their trademarks jointly. But a history of concerted activity does not immunize conduct from §1 scrutiny. Absence of actual competition may simply be a manifestation of the anticompetitive agreement itself. . . .

The question whether NFLP decisions can constitute concerted activity covered by §1 is closer than whether decisions made directly by the 32 teams are covered by §1. This is so both because NFLP is a separate corporation with its own management and because the record indicates that most of the revenues generated by NFLP are shared by the teams on an equal basis. Nevertheless we think it clear that for the same reasons the 32 teams' conduct is covered by §1, NFLP's actions also are subject to §1, at least with regards to its marketing of property owned by the separate teams. NFLP's licensing decisions are made by the 32 potential competitors, and each of them actually owns its share of the jointly managed assets. Apart from their agreement to cooperate in exploiting those assets, including their decisions as the NFLP, there would be nothing to prevent each of the teams from making its own market decisions relating to purchases of apparel and headwear, to the sale of such items, and to the granting of licenses to use its trademarks.

We generally treat agreements within a single firm as independent action on the presumption that the components of the firm will act to maximize the firm's profits. But in rare cases, that presumption does not hold. Agreements made within a firm can constitute concerted action covered by §1 when the parties to the agreement act on interests separate from those of the firm itself, and the intrafirm agreements may simply be a formalistic shell for ongoing concerted action.

For that reason, decisions by the NFLP regarding the teams' separately owned intellectual property constitute concerted action. Thirty-two teams operating independently through the vehicle of the NFLP are not like the components of a single firm that act to maximize the firm's profits. The teams remain separately controlled, potential competitors with economic interests that are distinct from NFLP's financial well-being. Unlike typical decisions by corporate shareholders, NFLP licensing decisions effectively require the assent of more than a mere majority of shareholders. And each team's decision reflects not only an interest in NFLP's profits but also an interest in the team's individual profits. The 32 teams capture individual economic benefits separate and apart from NFLP profits as a result of the decisions they make for the NFLP. NFLP's decisions thus affect each team's profits from licensing its own intellectual property. . . . In making the relevant licensing decisions, NFLP is therefore an instrumentality of the teams. . . .

Football teams that need to cooperate are not trapped by antitrust law. . . . The fact that NFL teams share an interest in making the entire league successful and profitable, and that they must cooperate in the production and scheduling of games, provides a perfectly sensible justification for making a host of collective decisions. But the conduct at issue in this case is still concerted activity under the Sherman Act that is subject to §1 analysis.

When restraints on competition are essential if the product is to be available at all, *per se* rules of illegality are inapplicable, and instead the restraint must be judged according to the flexible Rule of Reason. In such instances, the agreement is likely to survive the Rule of Reason. . . .

Other features of the NFL may also save agreements amongst the teams. We have recognized, for example, that the interest in maintaining a competitive balance among athletic teams is legitimate and important. While that same interest applies to the teams in the NFL, it does not justify treating them as a single entity for §1 purposes when it comes to the marketing of the teams' individually owned intellectual property. It is, however, unquestionably an interest that may well justify a variety of collective decisions made by the teams. What role it properly plays in applying the Rule of Reason to the allegations in this case is a matter to be considered on remand.

Accordingly, the judgment of the Court of Appeals is reversed, and the case is remanded for further proceedings consistent with this opinion.

Reversed and remanded.

KEY POINTS

- The Court initially discusses the issue of whether National Football League Properties (NFLP) is an entity distinct from the individual teams. If the case involved coordination between the individual teams, the antitrust violation would be more clear.
- If the members of an association like the NFPL make decisions based on interests separate from the association, concerted action occurs.
- The court finds that the NFL and the NFLP are simply representations of the 32 teams. But agreements they make may, in some cases, be legal.

context of whether professional sports teams should be considered as separate entities, subject to antitrust laws, or as one body organized as a league. A league, acting on behalf of all teams, would be free from antitrust laws since it would not be acting in concert with others.

Concerted activities are often beneficial to society even though they reduce competition. For example, joint research efforts to find a cure for cancer or to find substitutes for gasoline would seem to provide significant benefits to society. A sharing of technology may be beneficial also. Joint efforts in other areas may reduce costs and improve efficiency, with direct benefit to the public.

Congress has recognized the need to encourage cooperation among competitors. For example, in 1984, the National Cooperative Research Act was enacted. In 1990, Congress created an exception to the Sherman Act so that television industry officials could discuss the development of joint guidelines to limit the depiction of violence on television.

Again, in 1993, Congress made it easier for U.S. companies to engage in joint production ventures. The National Cooperative Production Amendments Act does not protect joint production ventures from all possibilities of antitrust violations. Rather, this law provides protection to activities described in Sidebar 16.1. Despite these exceptions to the Sherman Act that permit specific joint activities, you should always remain aware that concerted activities among competitors can lead to the severe sanctions discussed later in this chapter.

sidebar 16.1

Basic Provisions of National Cooperative Production Amendment Act

- Joint production ventures will be subject to the rule of reason analysis rather than the per se illegality standard.
- A joint production venture must notify the Justice Department and the FTC of its plans to engage in joint activities.

- In a private civil antitrust action brought against the joint production venture, the plaintiff can be awarded only actual damages plus costs. The joint production venture will not be subject to triple damages.

LO 16-3

The Sherman Act, Section 2—Monopolization

Section 2 of the Sherman Act regulates **monopoly** and the attempts to monopolize any part of interstate or foreign commerce. The law establishes the means to break up existing monopolies and to prevent others from developing. It is directed at single firms and does not purport to cover shared monopolies or oligopolies.

Under Section 2 of the Sherman Act, it is a violation for a firm to monopolize, attempt to monopolize, or conspire to monopolize any part of interstate or foreign commerce. To establish a violation of the law, a plaintiff must prove that the defendant (1) had monopoly power and (2) willfully acquired or maintained that power. Attempts to monopolize cases require proof of intent to destroy competition or achieve monopoly power along with a dangerous probability that monopolization will occur. This is most difficult to prove, and as a result, there have been few cases concerning attempts to monopolize. A conspiracy to monopolize requires proof of specific intent to monopolize and at least one overt act to accomplish it. Proof of monopoly power or even that it was attainable is not required. This conspiracy theory is usually joined with the allegation of actual monopoly in most cases.Sidebar 16.2 provides an example of a monopolization case.

Importantly, simply having monopoly power is not illegal. Some monopolies are lawful. If monopoly power is "thrust upon" a firm or if it exists because of a patent or franchise, there is no violation of Section 2 if the firm does not engage in conduct that has the effect or purpose of protecting, enforcing, or extending the monopoly power. The power must have been either acquired or used in ways that go beyond normal, honest industrial business conduct for a violation to exist. To be illegal, the monopoly must have been *deliberatively* acquired or used. A firm is guilty of monopolization when it acquires or maintains monopoly power by a course of deliberate conduct that keeps other firms from entering the market or from expanding their share of it. Deliberativeness is not difficult to prove in most cases.

Conduct that proves deliberativeness may be anything in restraint of trade. For example, predatory conduct would prove deliberativeness. Predatory conduct is seeking to advance market share by injuring actual or potential competitors by means other than improved performance. It may be for the purpose of driving out competitors, for keeping them out, or for making them less effective. Pricing policies are frequently examined for proof of predatory conduct. **Predatory pricing** takes place when a firm sells at below cost in order to drive out competition. One must also prove that the low-price

A utility, such as a power company, usually substitutes regulatory requirements by a public service commission in return for its near-monopoly status.

sidebar 16.2

Example of Monopoly

The case of *Aspen Skiing Co. v. Aspen Highlands Skiing Corp, 572 U.S. 585 (1985).* provides an example of the kind of factual situation and legal analysis that leads to a finding of a §2 violation. In the early years of snow skiing in Aspen, three facilities were operated by three distinct companies. The two parties involved in this case were among these competitors. In addition to offering a daily ski-lift ticket for their own mountain, each competitor sold a multiday, interchangeable, all-Aspen ticket.

Aspen Skiing acquired the third facility and opened a fourth. Eventually, this company sold a multiday ticket that allowed its patrons access to only its facilities. As a result of this action, Aspen Highlands lost a significant share of its business. Ultimately, Aspen Highlands sued Aspen Skiing, alleging that the refusal to sell an all-Aspen ticket was an illegal attempt to monopolize the Aspen Skiing market.

Aspen Skiing argued that it was not in violation of §2 of the Sherman Act because nothing in this law required it to do business with a competitor. Even

though the trial judge agreed with this legal conclusion, the judge instructed the jury that it could find Aspen Skiing in violation of the Sherman Act unless that company persuaded the jury that its conduct was justified by any normal business purpose.

Apparently the jury was not convinced by Aspen Skiing's presentation. The jury rendered a verdict finding Aspen Skiing in violation of §2 and awarding Aspen Highlands actual damages of $2.5 million. This award was tripled to $7.5 million, and costs and attorneys' fees were added to this amount.

Aspen Skiing was unable to convince either the court of appeals or the United States Supreme Court to reverse this jury verdict. The Supreme Court was particularly influenced by the market studies that showed skiers wanted to have access to the Highlands facilities but refused to ski there due to the lack of an all-area ticket. The Court concluded that the jury was justified in finding that inappropriate motivations to monopolize were behind Aspen Skiing's decision to stop selling the all-area ticket.

scheme is likely to eventually produce a rise in prices sufficient to recoup the initial income loss. Profit-maximizing pricing; limit pricing, whereby the price is limited to levels that tend to discourage entry; and the practice of price discrimination all may tend to prove monopoly power and predatory conduct.

In *Weyerhauser Company v. Ross-Simons Hardwood Lumber Company,*[4] the U.S. Supreme Court ruled that alleged predatory conduct associated with low prices charged by a seller or high prices paid by a buyer has to meet the same standards. There must be proof the prices were intended to drive competitors out of business followed by the wrongdoer recouping these initial losses.

In Case 16.3, the court considers whether restrictive supply agreements were employed by a dominant company in order to maintain a monopoly or attempt to monopolize.

[4]127 S.Ct. 1069 (2007).

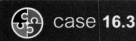
case **16.3**

KOLON INDUSTRIES INC. V. E.I. DUPONT DE NEMOURS & CO.
748 F.3d 160 (4th Cir. 2014)

DuPont invented para-aramid fiber in 1965, which is sells under the trademark Kevlar®. Such fibers are useful in making body armor, fiber optic cables, and other applications. Although once the exclusive supplier of para-aramid fiber in the United States, DuPont has shared the market with other companies since 1987 and now has about a 55% share. Kolon wished to break into the para-aramid fiber market in 2005 but had little success. The company alleged that DuPont's restrictive multi-year supply agreements with customers prevented competitors from gaining market share. According to Kolon, DuPont used its market dominance in concert with the restrictive agreements to maintain or attempt to maintain a monopoly in para-aramid fiber. As part of a broader litigation on other issues, the court was required to determine whether DuPont's activities violated Section 2 of the Sherman Act.

Diaz, Circuit Judge

Under § 2 of the Sherman Act, a defendant is liable for a monopolization claim when that defendant (1) possesses monopoly power and (2) willfully acquires or maintains that power. . . .

"Monopoly power is the power to control prices or exclude competition." *United States v. E.I. du Pont de Nemours & Co.*, 351 U.S. 377, 391(1956). . . . Although there is no fixed percentage market share that conclusively resolves whether monopoly power exists, the Supreme Court has never found a party with less

than 75% market share to have monopoly power. . . . And we have observed that "when monopolization has been found the defendant controlled 70–100% of the relevant market." *E.I. du Pont de Nemours & Co. v. Kolon Indus., Inc. (DuPont I)*, 637 F.3d 435, 450 (4th Cir. 2011).

Beyond percentage market share, "some courts have also focused on the durability of the defendant's market power, particularly with an eye toward other firms' (in)ability to enter the market." Id. at 451.

. . . the court observed, "Kolon's own expert takes the view that DuPont had a maximum market share of 59% during the relevant time period, and that DuPont's market share decreased to 55% during that three-year period rather than increased." Id.

This decline in DuPont's market share, combined with [another competitor's] corresponding ascendance and the fact that DuPont was charging lower prices in the United States than in Europe (which Kolon identified as a comparable market), led the court to its conclusion. "[T]he fact that there are significant entry barriers," the district court continued, "is insufficient to fill the factual gaps in Kolon's monopolization claim." Id. "DuPont clearly lacks the power to control prices and exclude competition," the court summarized, "otherwise, it would have been able to prevent the decrease in its market share and the rise of one of its major competitors." Id.

488

Even viewing all evidence in the light most favorable to Kolon, we agree with the district court that DuPont did not possess monopoly power in the U.S. para-aramid market during the relevant period between 2006 and 2009. First, although Kolon is correct that DuPont's market share of less than 60% during the relevant period does not necessarily foreclose a finding of monopoly power, it does weigh heavily against such a finding. Quite simply, this percentage falls significantly short of where we have previously drawn the line for monopoly power. . . .

Meanwhile, although Kolon is also correct that certain other factors do demonstrate DuPont's strength in the market (e.g., high barriers to entry, ability to price discriminate, high profit margins), a showing of DuPont's "market power" is not itself sufficient to prove that DuPont possesses "monopoly power." . . . Furthermore, this evidence falls short of showing DuPont's durability in the market. As the district court observed, uncontested facts demonstrate that DuPont has experienced a steady, decades-long loss in significant market share to Teijin.

Ultimately, in light of DuPont's reduced market share and lack of durable market power, the evidence cannot sustain a jury finding that DuPont had the "power to control prices or exclude competition" . . . or was "truly predominant in the market" during the relevant period." . . .

Even if Kolon had presented a triable issue on the monopoly-power element, Kolon also needed to show that DuPont willfully maintained that power. To violate this prong, a defendant must engage in conduct "to foreclose competition, to gain a competitive advantage, or to destroy a competitor." . . . On this element, Kolon's theory was—and is—that DuPont maintained its alleged monopoly power through the use of long-term, multi-year, exclusive supply agreements with certain U.S. para-aramid customers.

Although exclusive dealing agreements are not per se illegal, they "may be an improper means of acquiring or maintaining a monopoly." . . . The Supreme Court has held that an exclusive dealing arrangement does not violate antitrust laws unless its probable effect is to "foreclose competition in a substantial share of the line of commerce affected." *Tampa Elec. Co. v. Nashville Coal Co.*, 365 U.S. 320, 327 (1961). . . .

On appeal, Kolon again stresses its "critical bridge" theory. While it does not deny that DuPont had supply agreements with only 21 of the roughly 1,000 potential U.S. commercial para-aramid customers, Kolon contends that the district court's emphasis on those figures . . . was shortsighted. Pointing to evidence that DuPont perceived Kolon's market entry as a threat, Kolon argues that DuPont "strategically entered

into supply agreements with high-volume customers in the key commercially sustainable entry segments . . . that Kolon sought to enter." . . . Kolon submits that despite the relatively low number and short duration of DuPont's supply agreements, these agreements "choked off the 'critical bridge' to Kolon's entry into the U.S. market" because they foreclosed Kolon's access to the most important high-volume customers. . . .

While we acknowledge that a singular emphasis on the percentage of customers foreclosed cannot resolve the inquiry (as foreclosure of a few important customers could substantially foreclose access to a market), we agree with the district court that Kolon failed to show what "proportionate volume of commerce" in the entire relevant market was foreclosed by DuPont's supply agreements. . . . Likewise, although Kolon's "critical bridge" theory is certainly plausible, the evidence does not support its application here. . . .

We next review the district court's grant of summary judgment on Kolon's attempted monopolization claim. . . .

To prevail on an attempted monopolization claim under § 2, a claimant must show (1) a specific intent to monopolize a relevant market, (2) predatory or anticompetitive acts, and (3) a dangerous probability of successful monopolization. *Spectrum Sports, Inc. v. McQuillan*, 506 U.S. 447 (1993). . . .

But again, even viewing the evidence in the light most favorable to Kolon, the claim fails.

First, as discussed earlier, DuPont's alleged anticompetitive conduct—its customer supply agreements—did not have the probable effect of "foreclos[ing] competition in a substantial share of the line of commerce affected." . . . Nor, contrary to its suggestion, did Kolon show that the agreements were anticompetitive as without business justification or against DuPont's own interest. Rather, DuPont introduced unrebutted evidence that it entered the supply agreements as a competitive response to [a different competitor's] use of that same practice, and because customers requested them.

Second, Kolon has not raised a genuine issue that DuPont had a "dangerous probability" of successfully achieving monopoly power during the relevant period. As the district court observed, DuPont's market share had been in steady decline for 17 years, and DuPont has proven unable to control U.S. prices or exclude [another company] from entering the market. And even if declining market share does not preclude a finding of monopoly power, Kolon pointed to no affirmative evidence indicating a "dangerous probability" that DuPont would sooner or later regain its former market dominance.

Accordingly, we affirm the district court's grant of summary judgment to DuPont on Kolon's attempted monopolization claim.

[continued]

KEY POINTS

- The court found DuPont's market share of less than 70% important. Monopoly power generally requires more control.
- Exclusive dealing arrangements are not always illegal. They key question is whether they foreclose a substantial portion of the market.
- Actions that respond to competitors are less likely to violate the law than actions that are undertaken only to increase or maintain market power.

While the *Kolon* case describes what is not a monopoly, it is critically important to understand when a monopoly exists. Sidebar 16.3 describes the proof needed to document the existence of an illegal monopoly.

sidebar 16.3

Proving an Illegal Monopoly Exists

A firm violates Section 2 if it follows a course of conduct through which it obtained the power to control price or exclude competition. The mere possession of monopoly power is not a violation. There must be proof that the power resulted from a deliberate course of conduct or proof of intent to maintain the power by conduct. Proof of deliberateness is just as essential as is proof of the power to control price to exclude competition.

Section 2 cases require proof of market power—the power to affect the price of the firm's products in the market. Whether such power exists is usually determined by an analysis of the reaction of buyers to price changes by the alleged monopolist seller. Such cases require a definition of the relevant market and a study of the degree of concentration within the market. Barriers to entry are analyzed, and the greater the barriers, the greater the significance of market share. The legal issues in such cases require structural analysis.

In defining the relevant market, the courts examine both product market and geographic market. A relevant market is the smallest one wide enough so that products from outside the geographic area or from other producers in the same area cannot compete with those included in the defined relevant market. In other words, if prices are raised or supply is curtailed within a given area while demand remains constant, will products from other areas or other products from within the area enter

the market in enough quantity to force a lower price or increased supply?

Some monopoly cases involve products for which there are few or no substitutes. Other cases involve products for which there are numerous substitutes. For example, aluminum may be considered a product that is generally homogeneous. If a firm has 90% of the virgin aluminum market, a violation would be established. However, if a firm had 90% of the Danish coffee cake market, the decision is less clear, because numerous products compete with Danish coffee cakes as a breakfast product. The relevant product is often difficult to define because of differences in products, substitute products, product diversification, and even product clusters. . . .

Section 2 cases may involve a variety of proofs and many different forms of economic analysis. The degree of market concentration, barriers to entry, structural features such as market shares of other firms, profit levels, the extent to which prices respond to changes in supply and demand, whether or not a firm discriminates in price between its customers, and the absolute size of the firm are all factors usually considered by courts in monopoly cases. In addition, courts examine the conduct of the firm. How did it achieve its market share? Was it by internal growth or acquisition? Does the firm's current conduct tend to injure competition? These and other issues are important aspects in any finding of the existence of monopoly power.

490

Sherman Act Sanctions and Exceptions

LO 16-4

SANCTIONS

The Sherman Act as amended by the Clayton Act recognizes four separate legal sanctions:

1. Violations may be subject to criminal fines and imprisonment.
2. Violations may be enjoined by the courts.
3. Injured parties may collect **triple damages.**
4. Any property owned in violation of Section 1 of the Sherman Act that is being transported from one state to another is subject to a seizure by and forfeiture to the United States.

The first sanction is criminal punishment. Crimes under the Sherman Act are felonies. An individual found guilty may be fined up to $1 million and imprisoned up to 10 years. A corporation found guilty may be fined up to $100 million for each offense. These sanctions show congressional intent to keep the antitrust laws current. Figure 16.3 lists the fines the U.S. Justice Department imposed since 2003. The general trend of increasing severity illustrates the serious nature of antitrust violations.

The second sanction of the Sherman Act empowers courts to grant injunctions, at the request of the government or a private party, that will prevent and restrain violations or continued violations of its provisions. An injunction may prevent anticompetitive behavior, or it may even force a breakup of a corporation.

The injunction is frequently used when the success of a criminal prosecution is doubtful. It takes less proof to enjoin an activity (*preponderance of*

These financial penalties were updated in the Antitrust Criminal Penalty Enhancement and Reform Act of 2004.

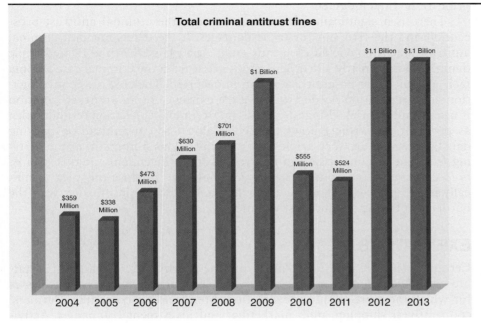

Total criminal antitrust fines

2004	$359 Million
2005	$338 Million
2006	$473 Million
2007	$630 Million
2008	$701 Million
2009	$1 Billion
2010	$555 Million
2011	$524 Million
2012	$1.1 Billion
2013	$1.1 Billion

Figure 16.3 *Criminal Antitrust Fines (2003–2013).*

Source: Antitrust Division, Department of Justice www.justice.gov/atr/public/criminal/264101.html.

the evidence) than it does to convict of a crime (*beyond a reasonable doubt*). There have been cases involving this remedy even after an acquittal in a criminal case. In effect, the court ordered the defendant not to do something it had been found innocent of doing.

Do realize that individuals or businesses harmed by an antitrust violation have the incentive of triple damages to act as an enforcer of the law.

The third sanction affords relief to persons, including governments, injured by another's violations of the Sherman Act. Section 4 of the Clayton Act authorizes such victims in a civil action to collect three times the damages they have suffered plus court costs and reasonable attorneys' fees. Normally, the objective of awarding money damages to individuals in a private lawsuit is to place them in the position they would have enjoyed, as nearly as this can be done with money, had their rights not been invaded. The triple-damage provisions of the antitrust laws, however, employ the remedy of damages to punish a defendant for a wrongful act in addition to compensating the plaintiff for actual injury. Today it is perhaps the most important sanction for an antitrust violation, because it allows one's competitors as well as injured members of the general public to enforce the law. Legislation also allows both federal and state governments to file a suit for triple damages.

Successful triple-damage suits may impose financial burdens on violators far in excess of any fine that could be imposed as a result of a criminal prosecution. This significant liability may be far in excess of the damages caused by any one defendant, because the liability of defendants is based on tort law and is said to be *joint and several*. For example, assume that 10 companies in an industry conspire to fix prices and that the total damages caused by the conspiracy equal $100 million. Also, assume that nine of the defendants settle out of court for $25 million. The remaining defendant, if the case is lost, would owe $275 million ($3 \times 100 - 25$). The Supreme Court has held that there is no right of contribution by the losing party against those that settled prior to the final judgment.

A firm that is indicted for violating the Sherman Act often will face civil actions as well. The firm may resolve the criminal case through a *nolo* plea so the civil plaintiffs do not benefit from a criminal conviction.

There is a significant relationship between the criminal antitrust prosecution and the civil suit for triple damages. If the defendant in a criminal antitrust suit is convicted or pleads guilty, the plaintiff in the related triple damages suit is greatly aided. This result arises from the criminal case's prima facie evidence that an antitrust violation occurred. The cost of the investigation and preparation needed to prove the existence of an antitrust violation is usually substantial. Using the defendant's criminal conviction or guilty plea as proof of the wrong allows the civil plaintiff to concentrate on proving damages, which are then tripled by the court. This automatic proof deriving from the criminal case can be avoided if the defendant enters a plea of *nolo contendere* (no contest) in the criminal case. Because this plea technically is interpreted as avoiding a conviction, the civil plaintiff is left with the burden of proving the antitrust violation.

LO 16-5   # EXEMPTIONS

Certain businesses may be exempt from the Sherman Act because of a statute or as the result of a judicial decision. Among activities and businesses for which there are statutory exemptions are insurance companies; farmers' cooperatives; shipping, milk marketing, and investment companies. Activities required by state law are exempt. In addition, normal activities of labor unions are exempt.

concept *summary*

Antitrust Sanctions

1. Four sanctions are recognized by the antitrust laws:
   a. Federal criminal penalties.
   b. Injunctions ordered by the courts.
   c. Triple damages payable to an injured party.
   d. Seizure and forfeiture of property owned in restraint of trade if such property is transported between states.

2. The federal criminal penalties are, for an individual, up to a $1,000,000 fine plus up to ten years in prison, and for a corporation, up to $100 million in fines.

3. An injunction may prevent anticompetitive behavior.

4. Under the triple-damage sanctions, a defendant cannot seek contribution from other wrongdoers.

5. To avoid the impact of a guilty plea or a conviction on a pending civil antitrust suit, the criminally accused defendant often pleads *nolo contendere* (no contest).

These exemptions are narrowly construed and do not mean that every activity of a firm is necessarily exempted simply because most activities are exempted. For example, an agreement between an insurance company and a pharmaceutical organization that regulates the price of prescription drugs given to policyholders of the insurance company is not exempt—it was not the business of insurance involved in this transaction. It is the business of insurance that is exempt and not the business of insurance companies. Likewise, a labor union would forfeit its exemption when it agrees with one set of employers to impose a certain wage scale on other employers' bargaining units. It is only the usual and legitimate union activity that is exempt. In Chapter 22, we discuss how a union must deal directly with the company involved in the labor dispute. Therefore, the arrangement in the example above is beyond the normal and proper activities of a union and not protected from antitrust claims.

In a 1943 case known as *Parker v. Brown,* the Supreme Court created a **state action exemption** to the Sherman Act. This state action exemption, referred to as the Parker v. Brown doctrine, is based on the reasoning that the Sherman Act does not apply to state government. When a state acts in its sovereign capacity, it is immune from federal antitrust scrutiny. For example, an unsuccessful candidate for admittance to the Arizona bar alleged a conspiracy by the bar examiners in violation of the Sherman Act. He contended that the grading scale was dictated by the number of new attorneys desired rather than by the level of competition and answers on the exam. The courts held that this activity was exempt from the Sherman Act. The grading of bar examinations is, in reality, conduct of the Arizona Supreme Court and thus exempt. Action by the courts is just as immune as actions by the legislature.

Another exemption from the Sherman Act extends to concerted efforts to lobby government officials, regardless of the anticompetitive purposes of the lobbying effort. The doctrine, known as the **Noerr-Pennington doctrine** is based on the First Amendment. For example, Budget Rent-A-Car filed suit against Hertz and National Rent-A-Car because the defendants lobbied officials at three state-owned airports to limit the number of car-rental operations.

> **Don't** rely on an exemption from antitrust laws to justify anticompetitive behavior.

sidebar 16.4

Antitrust vs. Securities Regulation

Buyers of newly issued securities filed an antitrust law-suit against underwriting firms for allegedly engaging in anticompetitive activities in marketing of the shares. The U.S. Supreme Court reviewed a series of cases that try to balance the role of securities laws and antitrust laws. The implied repeal of antitrust laws should be found only where there is a "plain repugnancy" between the anti-trust and securities regulations.

The Court ruled as follows:

"We believe" it fair to conclude that, where conduct at the core of the marketing of new securities is at issue; where

securities regulators proceed with great care to distinguish the encouraged and permissible from the forbidden; where the threat of antitrust lawsuits, through error or disincentive, could seriously alter underwriter conduct in unde-sirable ways, to allow an antitrust lawsuit would threaten serious harm to the efficient functioning of the securities markets.

Thus, the Supreme Court emphasizes that antitrust laws are not to be used to replace other regulations.

Source: *Credit Suisse Securities LLC v. Billing,* 127 S. Ct. 2383 (2007).

This lobbying was ruled exempt from the Sherman Act under the First Amendment right to petition government for a redress of grievances and recognition of the value of the free flow of information.

Sidebar 16.4 describes a recent Supreme Court case involving the issue of whether securities laws take priority over antitrust laws in practices related to the sale of securities in public offerings.

The Clayton Act

LO 16-6

INTRODUCTION

By 1914, it was obvious that the Sherman Act of 1890 had not accomplished its intended purpose. Practices that reduced competition were commonplace. In order to improve the antitrust laws, Congress in 1914 enacted the Clayton Act and the Federal Trade Commission Act. The Clayton Act is more specific than the Sherman Act in declaring certain enumerated practices in commerce illegal. These were practices that might adversely affect competition but were not themselves contracts, combinations, or conspiracies in restraint of trade; such practices did not go far enough to constitute actual monopolization or attempts to monopolize. Further, the enumerated practices did not have to actually injure competition to be wrongful; they were outlawed if their effect may substantially lessen competition or tends to create a monopoly. Thus, the burden of proving a violation was eased. The Clayton Act made it possible to attack in their incipiency many practices which, if continued, eventually could destroy competition or create a monopoly. The idea was to remedy these matters before full harm was done.

Note the lesser burden of the Clayton Act test.

Violations of the original Clayton Act were not crimes, and the act contained no sanction for forfeiture of property. However, it did provide that the Justice Department might obtain injunctions to prevent violations. Individuals or organizations injured by a violation could obtain injunctive relief on their own behalf. In addition, they were given the right to collect three times the damages suffered plus court costs and reasonable attorney's fees.

The following three sections of this chapter focus on three important provisions of the Clayton Act. As you study this material, ask yourself what business practices occur today that may violate the Clayton Act.

PRICE DISCRIMINATION

Section 2 of the Clayton Act as originally adopted in 1914 made it unlawful for a seller to discriminate in the price that is charged to different purchasers of commodities when the effect may be to lessen competition substantially or to tend to create a monopoly in any line of commerce. Discrimination in price on account of differences in the grade, quality, or quantity of the commodity sold, or that makes only due allowance for differences in the cost of selling or transportation was not illegal.

In the 1920s and early 1930s, various techniques such as large-volume purchases with quantity discounts were used by big retailers, especially chain stores, to obtain more favorable prices than those available to smaller competitors. In addition to obtaining quantity discounts, some large businesses created subsidiary corporations that received brokerage allowances as wholesalers. Another method used by big buyers to obtain price advantages was to demand and obtain larger promotional allowances than were given to smaller buyers. The prevalence of these practices led to the enactment in 1936 of the **Robinson-Patman amendment** to Section 2 of the Clayton Act. This statute attempted to eliminate the advantage that a large buyer could secure over a small buyer solely because of the larger buyer's quantity-purchasing ability.

The Robinson-Patman amendment attempts to ensure equality of price to all customers of a seller of commodities for resale. The law protects a single competitor who is victimized by price discrimination. It is a violation both to knowingly give and to receive the benefits of such discrimination. Therefore, the law applies to both sellers and buyers. It is just as illegal to receive the benefit of price discrimination as it is to give a lower price to one of two buyers.

The Robinson-Patman amendment extends only to transactions in interstate commerce; it does not extend to transactions that affect only intrastate commerce. In addition, the law is applicable only to the sale of goods; it does not cover contracts that involve the sale of services or the sale of advertising such as television time.

Price discrimination originally focused on the seller offering various prices to its customers. The Robinson-Patman amendment addresses the power of large buyers to demand favorable prices.

The Robinson-Patman amendment gives the Federal Trade Commission (FTC) jurisdiction and authority to regulate quantity discounts. It also prohibits certain hidden or indirect discriminations by sellers in favor of certain buyers. Section 2(c) prohibits an unearned brokerage commission related to a sale of goods. For example, it is unlawful to pay or to receive a commission or discount on sales or purchases except for actual services rendered. Section 2(d) outlaws granting promotional allowances or payments on goods bought for resale unless such allowances are available to all competing customers. For example, a manufacturer who gives a retailer a right to purchase three items for the price of two as part of a special promotion must give the same right to all competitors in the market. Section 2(e) prohibits giving promotional facilities or services on goods bought for resale unless they are made available to all competing customers.

The Robinson-Patman amendment makes it a crime for a seller to sell either at lower prices in one geographic area than elsewhere in the United States to eliminate competition or a competitor, or at unreasonably low prices to drive out a competitor. This conduct may also be termed predatory pricing, which is also a violation of Section 2 of the Sherman Act, as described earlier.

Importantly, the law recognizes certain exceptions or defenses:

- Sellers may select their own customers in good-faith transactions and not in restraint of trade.
- Price changes may be made in response to changing conditions, such as actual or imminent deterioration of perishable goods, obsolescence of seasonal goods, distress sales under court process, or sales in good faith in discontinuance of business in the goods concerned (**changing conditions defense**).
- Price differentials based on differences in the cost of manufacture, sale, or delivery of commodities are permitted (**cost justification defense**).
- A seller in good faith may meet the equally low price of a competitor (**good-faith meeting-of-competition defense**).

As you can see from the foregoing sections on the Sherman Act and the Clayton Act, different antitrust analyses are applied to pricing in different contexts. Figure 16.4 summarizes the analysis for the the most important categories.

Figure 16.4 *Analysis of pricing.*

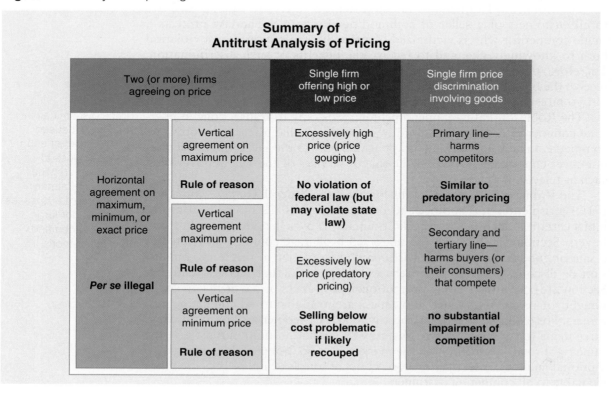

SPECIAL ARRANGEMENTS

Section 3 of the Clayton Act limits the use of certain types of contractual arrangements involving goods when the impact of these contracts may substantially lessen competition or tends to create a monopoly. These special arrangements include sales contracts that tie one product with another, contracts that contain reciprocal arrangements in which each party is a buyer and a seller, and provisions foreclosing buying or selling with others.

A **tying contract** is one in which a product is sold or leased only on the condition that the buyer or lessee purchase a different product or service from the seller or lessor. In order to face liability, the seller requiring the tying arrangement must have market power in one product or service that it seeks to extend through the tied product or service. A common form of tying arrangement is known as **full-line forcing.** In full-line forcing, the seller compels the buyer or lessee to take a complete product line from the seller. Under these arrangements, the buyer cannot purchase only one product of the line. A typical illegal agreement is one in which a clothing manufacturer requires a retailer to carry the manufacturer's full line of articles in order to sell a popular line of shirts. Another common factual situation relates to how a holder of a potential product using the patent protection to market that product and related, but unpatented, products. In addition to being addressed by the Clayton Act, courts have found tying arrangements to violate section 1 of the Sherman Act. The agreement in restraint of trade in the tying arrangement is between the buyer and the seller, though the buyer faces no liability. Sidebar 16.5 summarizes a recent Supreme Court decision discussing tying arrangements involving a patented and unpatented, but related, product.

---

sidebar 16.5

Tying Contracts, Patents, and Standard of Review

Trident Inc. is owned by Illinois Tool Works Inc. Trident manufactures and markets printing systems that consist of patented equipment and unpatented ink. In marketing its printing systems, Trident insists its buyers agree to purchase only Trident ink for use in its equipment.

Independent Ink Inc. produces an ink that is chemically similar to Trident's ink. Independent files an antitrust lawsuit against Trident claiming its tying contracts are per se illegal under Sections 1 and 2 of the Sherman Act and Section 3 of the Clayton Act.

The Supreme Court reviews the history of the patent misuse doctrine and its holdings that tying a patented product to an unpatented one creates a *per se* antitrust violation. The Court explains that Congress's changes to the patent law removes the patent misuse doctrine and that commentators have been critical of the Court's prior decisions allowing antitrust claims to limit the benefits of patents. The Court concludes:

> Congress, the antitrust enforcement agencies, and most economists have all reached the conclusion that a patent does not necessarily confer market power upon the patentee. Today, we reach the same conclusion, and therefore hold that, in all cases involving a tying arrangement, the plaintiff must prove that the defendant has market power in the tying product.

In essence, the Court now requires the plaintiff in antitrust claims to prove the defendant acted unreasonably in tying the patented and unpatented product. The anticompetitive nature of the tying arrangement will no longer be presumed.

Source: *Illinois Tool Works, Inc. v. Independent Ink, Inc.,* 126 S. Ct. 1281 (2006).

A **reciprocal dealing** arrangement exists when two parties face each other as both buyer and seller. One party offers to buy the other's goods but only if the second party buys other goods from the first party. For example, suppose that company A is a manufacturer of microprocessor chips for personal computers. Further assume that company B manufactures personal computers. A reciprocal dealing occurs if B agrees to buy processor chips only if A agrees to buy a specified number of B's computers for use in A's offices.

An **exclusive dealing** contract contains a provision that one party or the other (buyer or seller) will deal only with the other party. For example a seller of tomatoes agrees to sell only to Campbell Soup. A buyer of coal may agree to purchase only from a certain coal company. Such agreements tend to foreclose a portion of the market from competitors.

A similar arrangement is known as a **requirements contract.** In a requirements contract, a buyer agrees to purchase all of its needs of a given contract from the seller during a certain period of time. The buyer may be a manufacturer who needs the raw materials or parts agreed to be supplied, or it may be a retailer who needs goods for resale. In effect, the buyer is agreeing not to purchase any of the products from competitors of the seller.

Do be wary of the restrictive nature of franchise contracts.

Franchise contracts often require that the franchisee purchase all of its equipment and inventory from the franchiser as a condition of the agreement. These provisions are commonly inserted because of the value of the franchiser's trademark and the desire for quality control to protect it. For example, Baskin-Robbins ice cream may require its franchisees to purchase all of their ice cream from Baskin-Robbins. The legitimate purpose is to maintain the image of the franchise and the product. Customers expect the same ice cream from every retail operation. Such agreements, while anticompetitive, are legal because the legitimate purpose outweighs the anticompetitive aspects.

However, a franchiser is not able to license its trademark in such a manner that it can coerce franchisees to give up all alternate supply sources, because such agreements are unreasonable restraints of trade. The quality-control aspect is not present for items such as packaging materials and food items in which special ingredients or secret formulas are not involved; thus, the purpose of the "exclusive source of supply" proviso is only to limit competition. Franchise agreements are not per se violations; they are subject to the rule of reason.

Exclusive contracts and requirements contracts are less likely to harm competition than are tying contracts. Such contracts may add competition by eliminating uncertainties and the expense of repeated contracts. However, the courts tend to give per se violation treatment to exclusive contracts if they substantially affect commerce.

MERGERS AND ACQUISITIONS

To review Horizontal Merger Guidelines, see www.justice.gov/atr/public/guidelines/hmg-2010.html.

Section 7 of the Clayton Act makes certain mergers and acquisitions illegal. Specifically, a merger that will substantially lessen competition violates the law. Because issues of agreements and alleged monopolization can be involved, Sections 1 and 2 of the Sherman Act may be relevant to merger analysis as well.

Mergers are usually classified as horizontal, market extension, vertical, or conglomerate. A **horizontal merger** usually combines two businesses in the same field or industry. The acquired and acquiring companies have competed with each other, and the merger reduces the number of competitors and leads to greater concentration in the industry. A **market extension merger** describes an acquisition in which the acquiring company extends its markets. This market extension may be either in new products (**product extension**) or in new areas (**geographic extension**). For example, if a brewery that did not operate in New England acquired a New England brewery, it would have accomplished a geographic market extension merger.

A **vertical merger** brings together one company that is the customer of the other in one of the lines of commerce in which the other is a supplier. Such a combination ordinarily removes or has the potential to remove the merged customer from the market as far as other suppliers are concerned. It also may remove a source of supply if the acquiring company is a customer of the acquired one. A **conglomerate merger** is one in which the businesses involved neither compete nor are related as customer and supplier in any given line of commerce. Some analysts consider product extension and geographic extension mergers to be conglomerate ones with many characteristics of horizontal ones. In any event, there is a great deal of similarity in the legal principles applied to market extension and to conglomerate mergers.

Both the Department of Justice and the Federal Trade Commission (through its Section 5 powers) have the authority to challenge mergers. In general, one agency takes the lead in investigating. To determine the impact of a proposed merger, the investigating agency considers the change in market concentration before and after. Market concentration is measured using the **Herfindahl-Hirschman Index (HHI),** which squares the market share of each firm in the market and adds them together for a final number. For example, if there are five firms in the market, each with a 20% share, the final HHI is 2,000 points. If two of those firms merge, the HHI would rise to 2,800 points. According to the DOJ's and FTC's joint guidelines, an HHI in excess of 2,500 points is highly concentrated, and an increase by more than 200 points that results in highly concentrated markets is presumed to enhance market power.[5] In addition to market power, other factors are taken into account such as evidence from existing mergers, whether the merging firms substantially competed and whether a merging firm was disruptive in a positive way for consumers but will now be quieted.

The determination that a merger is illegal can have a devastating impact after the parties have already combined assets. Therefore, in 1976, the Hart-Scott-Rodino Antitrust Improvements Act was passed to facilitate early government evaluation by requiring **premerger notification**. Under the program, parties to a merger must notify the DOJ and FTC before consummating and wait 30 days for the agencies to conduct their review. The outcome of the review may be to permit the merger without opposition. However, if the merger is found to violate the Clayton Act, the DOJ or FTC may seek an injunction to prevent it. State antitrust enforcers may also join in the suit. Firms commonly find that they can sell off assets in a process called divestment to address the agencies' concerns and permit the merger to go forward.

[5]DOJ and FTC, Horizontal Merger Guidelines (August 19, 2010), www.justice.gov/atr/public/guidelines/hmg-2010.html#5c.

sidebar 16.6

American Airlines Merges with a Rival

The recent merger of American Airlines and US Airways Group Inc. provides an excellent example of the procedure and analysis described above. In February 2013, the two airlines announced plans to merge in a deal worth approximately $11 billion. After investigating the impact of the merger, the DOJ and six states filed a lawsuit to challenge it in August 2013. They contended that the merger would result in significantly increased market concentration for certain air travel routes. For example, the agencies stated that on the Charlotte–Dallas city pair, the post-merger HHI would increase by 4,648 points to a total of 9,319 points. Less dramatic increases would occur for other routes, but would still be very significant due to the already concentrated airline industry. The agencies argued that such extremely high concentration would result in passengers paying higher airfares and receiving less service.

In November 2013, the parties announced a settlement. In exchange for the DOJ and states permitting the merger to go forward, American Airlines and US Airways agreed to divest (sell to rivals) slots, gates, and ground facilities at airports around the country, particularly Reagan National and LaGuardia. In December 2013, the merger was finalized and the two companies are now one.

Sources: Complaint, *United States of America v. U.S. Airways*, 1:13-cv-01236 (D.D.C. Aug. 13, 2013), www.justice.gov/atr/cases/f299900/299968.pdf; *Justice Department Requires US Airways and American Airlines to Divest Facilities* (November 12, 2013), U.S. Department of Justice, www.justice.gov/opa/pr/2013/November/13-at-1202.html.

LO 16-7

The Federal Trade Commission Act—Unfair Competition

As previously noted, the Federal Trade Commission (FTC) enforces the Clayton Act. The FTC also enforces Section 5 of the Federal Trade Commission Act, which made "unfair methods of competition" in commerce unlawful. The Wheeler-Lea amendment in 1938 added that "unfair or deceptive acts or practices in commerce" are also unlawful under Section 5.

The FTC has broad, sweeping powers and a mandate to determine what methods, acts, or practices in commerce constitute unfair competition. The original Section 5 of the Federal Trade Commission Act outlawed unfair methods of competition in commerce and directed the FTC to prevent the use of such, but it offered no definition of the specific practices that were unfair. The term *unfair methods of competition* was designed by Congress as a flexible concept, the exact meaning of which could evolve on a case-by-case basis. It can apply to a variety of unrelated activities. It is generally up to the FTC to determine what business conduct is "unfair." Great deference is given to the FTC's opinion as to what constitutes a violation and to the remedies it proposes to correct anticompetitive behavior.

To decide whether challenged business conduct is "unfair" as a method of competition or as a commercial practice, the FTC asks three major questions if there is no deception or antitrust violation involved:

1. Does the conduct injure consumers significantly?
2. Does the conduct offend an established public policy? (Conduct may offend public policy even though not previously unlawful.)
3. Is the conduct oppressive, unscrupulous, immoral, or unethical?

Answering any one of these questions affirmatively could lead to a finding of unfairness. The Supreme Court has declared that the FTC can operate "like a court of equity" in considering "public values" to establish what is unfair under Section 5.

Business conduct in violation of any provision of the antitrust laws may also be ruled illegal under Section 5. However, the purpose of Section 5 was to establish that anticompetitive acts or practices that *fall short* of transgressing the Sherman or Clayton Act may be restrained by the FTC as being "unfair methods of competition." If a business practice is such that it is doubtful that the evidence is sufficient to prove a Sherman or Clayton Act violation, the FTC may nevertheless proceed and find the business practice is unfair.

The primary function of the FTC is to prevent illegal business practices rather than punish violations. It prevents wrongful actions by the use of cease and desist orders. To prevent unfair competition, the FTC issues trade regulation rules that deal with business practices in an industry plus FTC guidelines on particular practices.

The FTC also periodically issues trade practice rules and guides, sometimes referred to as industry guides. These rules are the FTC's informal opinion of legal requirements applicable to a particular industry's practices. Although compliance with the rules is voluntary, they provide the basis for the informal and simultaneous abandonment by industry members of practices thought to be unlawful. For example, the FTC has said the American Medical Association must allow doctors to advertise. FTC guidelines are administrative interpretations of the statutes the commission enforces, and they provide guidance to both FTC staff and businesspeople evaluating the legality of certain practices. Guidelines deal with specific practices and may cut across industry lines.

> Section 5 of the FTC Act arguably gives the FTC power beyond the sections of other antitrust laws.

INTERNATIONAL ANTITRUST ENFORCEMENT

The U.S. antirust laws described earlier also apply to companies outside the United States. So long as their activities have a substantial impact on U.S. commerce, foreign companies must comply with U.S. antitrust law. In recent years, the U.S. Department of Justice has concentrated much of its antitrust enforcement effort on international cartels. In recent years, more than 90% of the criminal fines imposed by the U.S. Antitrust Division relate to activities of foreign companies or international cartels.

Similarly, U.S. companies doing business in other countries must comply with those countries' antitrust laws. Perhaps the most important antitrust enforcement agency outside the United States is the European Commission, part of the European Union. The commission has authority under the Treaty on the Functioning of the European Union to investigate and regulate anticompetitive activity. Its enabling treaty is similar in many respects to U.S. law. The EU treaty specifically prevents price fixing, market divisions, and production controls. It also holds companies liable for monopolization, which is termed "abuse of a dominant position" in the EU. The commission also has the power to challenge mergers.

Fines for violating EU antitrust law can be as large as those in the United States. In 2012, the European Commission fined six electronics firms a total of 1.47 billion euros (nearly $2 billion) for fixing prices and dividing up the market in television and computer cathode-ray tubes. Intel was fined 1 billion euros (about $1.3 billion) in 2009 for abusing its dominant position in the CPU market. An additional controversial aspect of EU antitrust power is the fact that its decisions need not mirror those of the U.S. government. The EU may impose fines or require changes in business practices related to activities that do not violate U.S. law. In 2014, the European Commission and Google announced a settlement requiring Google to provide promotion space for rival advertisers when delivering results from a Google specialized search. This system will appear only in Europe.

Other countries have antitrust enforcement agencies as well. Global businesses must be aware of the extent to which various antitrust regimes complement or conflict.

Key Terms

Clayton Act   475
Concerted activities   483
Conglomerate merger   499
Cost justification defense   496
Exclusive dealing   498
Federal Trade Commission Act   475
Full-line forcing   497
Geographic extension merger   497
Good-faith meeting-of-competition defense   496
Herfindahl-Hirschman Index (HHI)   499
Horizontal merger   499

Horizontal price fixing   478
Horizontal restraints 476
Horizontal territorial agreement   482
Market extension merger   499
Merger   499
Monopoly   486
Noerr-Pennington doctrine   493
Per se illegality   477
Predatory pricing   487
Premerger notification   499
Price fixing   475
Product extension merger   499
Reciprocal dealing   498

Requirements contract   498
Resale price maintenance   481
Restraint of trade   475
Robinson-Patman amendment   495
Rule of reason   477
Sherman Act   474
State action exemption   493
Triple damages   491
Tying contract   497
Vertical merger   499
Vertical price fixing   481
Vertical restraints   476
Vertical territorial agreement   483

Review Questions and Problems

1. *Historical Development*
   (a) The Sherman Act, as amended by the Clayton Act, seeks to preserve competition by declaring two types of anticompetitive behavior to be illegal. Describe these two behaviors.
   (b) Through what agencies does the federal government enforce the antitrust laws?
   (c) What role do state attorneys generally play in antitrust enforcement?
   (d) Can individuals or business organizations enforce antitrust laws?

The Sherman Act

2. *Restraint of Trade*

   All of the orthodontists in your community at their annual holiday party agreed to charge the parents of each child patient a nonrefundable fee of $200 prior to beginning any treatment. They also agreed that the charge for an orthodontia procedure would not be less than $2,000. Are these agreements in violation of the Sherman Act? Explain.

3. *Analysis in Antitrust Law*
   (a) Why is it important for courts to use the rule of reason analysis when considering actions allegedly in violation of the Sherman Act?

(b) What is the significance of the per se analysis under the rule of reason?

Types of Cases

4. *Horizontal Price Fixing*

   The members of a real estate brokers' multiple listing service voted to raise their commission rate from 6% to 7%. The bylaws of the association provided for expulsion of any member charging less than the agreed-upon commission. If broker Hillary continues to charge 6 percent, can she be expelled legally? Why or why not?

5. *Vertical Price Fixing*

   (a) Describe the situations when a supplier can legally fix the minimum price that a customer must charge to its buyers.

   (b) What analysis do courts use when judging the legality of a vertical price-fixing plan? Why is this legal analysis the appropriate one to use?

6. *Indirect Price Fixing*

   Assume that all manufacturers of computer chips entered into an agreement whereby each agreed to exchange information as to the most recent price charged or quoted to a consumer. Is this agreement a violation of the Sherman Act? Why or why not?

7. *Territorial Agreements*

   (a) Are franchise agreements which allocate an exclusive territory to the franchisee always illegal? Explain.

   (b) Give an example of a product where intrabrand competition is as important as interbrand competition.

8. *Concerted Activities*

   In response to public pressure, all of the manufacturers of chewing tobacco agree not to advertise on radio or television. The resulting savings are used to reduce the price of the product to consumers. Furthermore, the use of chewing tobacco by teenagers is reduced dramatically. Is the agreement legal? Explain.

9. *Monopoly*

   The Justice Department filed a civil suit claiming Grinnell Corporation had a monopoly in the operation of central station hazard-detecting devices. These security devices are used to prevent burglary and to detect fires.

   They involve electronic notification of the police and fire departments at a central location. Grinnell, through three separate subsidiaries, controlled 87% of that business. It argues that it faces competition from other modes of protection from burglary, and therefore it does not have monopoly power. What argument does the Justice Department have to make to prove its claim that Grinnell is operating an illegal monopoly?

10. *Sanctions*

    (a) Name the four sanctions used to enforce the Sherman Act.

    (b) What is the relationship between the criminal sanction and suits for triple damages?

    (c) What is the impact of the *nolo contendere* plea?

11. *Exemptions*

    The operators of adult bookstores got together and each agreed to contribute $1,000 to a fund for use in lobbying the city council to repeal an ordinance which made the sale of sexually explicit publications a crime. If the operators are charged with violating the antitrust laws, what will be the likely defense? Explain.

The Clayton Act

12. *Introduction*

    (a) Name the sanctions that can be imposed against a violator of the Clayton Act.

    (b) What is the significance of the word *incipiency* in Clayton Act enforcement?

13. *Price Discrimination*

You are the sales representative for a manufacturer of insulation. A customer that accounts for approximately one-third of your sales suddenly asks for a discount because of the volume of its purchases. You are politely told that a refusal will cause the customer to take its business to another manufacturer. Your income is solely from commissions on sales, which are calculated on gross profit margins.

(a) If you agree to a discount, have you broken any law?

(b) If you have violated a law, what are the potential consequences?

(c) If you give the same discount to all customers, would your actions be illegal? Explain.

14. *Special Arrangements*

(a) An ice-cream franchiser requires its franchisees to purchase all ice cream, cones, and syrups from the franchiser. Does this contract violate the antitrust laws? Why or why not?

(b) Would your answer be the same if the contract also required the franchisees to purchase all of its paper products and cleaning supplies, such as napkins, from the franchiser? Explain.

15. *Mergers and Acquisitions*

The government challenged the acquisition by Procter & Gamble (P&G) of Clorox. Clorox was the leading manufacturer of liquid bleach at the time of the acquisition, accounting for 48% of the national sales. It was the only firm selling nationally, and the top two firms accounted for 65% of national sales. P&G is a large, diversified manufacturer of household products, with its primary activity being in the area of soaps, detergents, and cleaners. P&G accounted for 54% of all packaged detergent sales, and the top three firms accounted for 50% of the market. P&G is among the nation's leading advertisers. What is the basis for the government's challenge to this acquisition? Explain.

The Federal Trade Commission Act—Unfair Competition

16. *Enforcement*

A group of lawyers in private practices who regularly acted as court-appointed counsel for indigent defendants in District of Columbia criminal cases agreed at a meeting of the Superior Court Trial Lawyers Association (SCTLA) to stop providing such representation until the District increased group members' compensation. The boycott had a severe impact on the District's criminal justice system, and the District government capitulated to the lawyers' demands. After the lawyers returned to work, the FTC filed a complaint against SCTLA and four of its officers, alleging that they had entered into a conspiracy to fix prices and to conduct a boycott that constituted unfair methods of competition in violation of Section 5 of the FTC Act. Does the FTC have the authority to bring a Section 5 case against these lawyers? Explain.

17. *Prevention*

(a) The FTC has responsibility for preventing unfair methods of competition and unfair and deceptive business practices. Describe three examples of business activities that could be declared unlawful by the FTC pursuant to these powers.

(b) Does the FTC have to prove that these examples involve violations of the Sherman or Clayton Acts to be successful in establishing an unfair method of competition or an unfair or deceptive business practice? Explain.

International Antitrust Enforcement

18. *In some cases, U.S. antitrust authorities have approved mergers that were rejected by European antitrust authorities. How might such inconsistencies create problems for multinational corporations and what are some possible solutions?*

business *discussions*

You are feeling very good about your life. This positive feeling is due in large part to your recent promotion to national sales manager of Ever-Present Technologies Inc. Your company offers full-service consulting and computer sales to manufacturers, especially those in the consumer products areas.

Two weeks into your new responsibilities, you are beginning to lose your good feelings. This change of spirit results from hearing about various activities among your sales personnel. First, you learn one of your new sales representatives has been visiting with a competitor's salesperson about each focusing on particular customers while agreeing not to call on the other's customers. Second, a district manager reports that a large, extremely valuable customer is asking for a pricing structure that is more favorable than prices offered to any other customer. The district manager expressed concern that your company may lose this customer's business.

What legal worries do you have about each of these situations?

What type of information should a training/education program for your sales force include?

What are the ramifications if you decide to ignore these situations as you try to return to your "happy" state of mind?

17 Financial and Securities Regulations

Learning Objectives

In this chapter you will learn:

17-1. To understand the meaning of the term *securities* and to apply the broad scope of the securities laws and regulations.

17-2. To analyze the differences between a public offering and subsequent securities transactions.

17-3. To apply ways in which the laws cover these differences.

17-4. To evaluate when and why private individuals and organizations make claims to enforce securities laws.

17-5. To evaluate how state regulations add to the requirements of proper securities transactions.

17-6. To understand why the Sarbanes-Oxley Act was passed and evaluate its effectiveness.

17-7. To remember the complexity of the Dodd-Frank Wall Street Reform and Consumer Protection Act.

Chapter 14 examines how business activity can be organized. That chapter relates to the creation and management of business organizations. One way to view this chapter is as a continuation of those topics. The phrase corporate governance as used in this chapter relates to government regulation of the ownership of business organizations. Indeed, of all the topics covered in this text, enforcement and revisions of securities regulations are the principal means used by the federal and state government to create and restore investor confidence following scandals involving Enron, WorldCom, Tyco, Adelphia, HealthSouth, and other major corporations in 2000 and 2001. Financial reforms also followed the economic collapse in 2008, which was caused by the failure or near-failure of Lehman Brothers, Merrill Lynch, AIG, JPMorgan Chase, Bank of America, Wachovia, and other financial institutions.

Your reading and study of this chapter will expose you to numerous examples as to how businesspeople are required to manage their organizations. This chapter also acquaints you, as a potential investor, with the laws protecting you and your fellow investors.

As you study this chapter, remember that the regulation of securities began as part of the program to help the United States overcome the great depression of the early 1930s. You should also realize that these securities laws are designed to give potential investors sufficient information so that they can make intelligent investment decisions based on factual information rather than on other less certain criteria. Although federal securities laws are over 80 years old, their application is at the heart of corporate governance during the first years of the twenty-first century. Table 17.1 provides a chronological summary of various securities laws covered in this chapter.

table 17.1 Laws Regulating Securities Transactions

Statute	Summary of Major Provisions
Securities Act of 1933	• Disclosure law governing initial sale of securities to public
	• Defines the term *security*
	• Creates liability for false or misleading registration statement (Section 11)
	• Creates liability for failure to file a registration statement (Section 12[1])
	• Creates liability for false or misleading prospectus (Section 12[2])
	• Creates liability for fraudulent communications used in the offer of sales of securities (Section 17[a])
Securities Exchange Act of 1934	• Created Securities and Exchange Commission
	• Governs exchanges of securities beyond the initial sale
	• Creates liability for fraudulent manipulation of securities' value (Section 10[b])
	• Creates liability for short-swing profits made by insiders (Section 16)
	• Creates liability for false or misleading filings with the SEC (Section 18)
	• Creates liability for fraudulent transactions related to tender offers (Section 14[e])
Insider Trading and Securities Fraud Enforcement Act of 1988	• Provides for recovery of triple damages in civil actions against user of nonpublic information
	• Increases criminal sanctions for use of nonpublic information
Securities Enforcement Remedies Act of 1990	• Increases civil fines for violations of securities laws
	• Prohibits an individual's service as an officer or director
Private Securities Litigation Reform Act of 1995	• Clarifies that individuals and organizations can sue primary parties, but not secondary parties, for securities violations
	• Requires pleading of specific allegations of wrongdoing

table 17.1 Laws Regulating Securities Transactions—*(Continued)*

Statute	Summary of Major Provisions
State blue sky laws	• Impose another level of securities regulations beyond federal laws • Govern intrastate securities transactions not regulated by federal laws
Sarbanes-Oxley Act of 2002	• Increases budgetary support to Securities and Exchange Commission • Creates Public Company Accounting Oversight Board • Changes membership requirements of corporate audit committees • Requires CEOs to certify financial statements • Protects whistleblowers who reveal fraud
Dodd-Frank Wall Street Reform and Consumer Protection Act of 2010	• Enhances consumer protection • Ends "Too Big to Fail" bailouts • Reforms Federal Reserve • Creates mortgage reforms • Regulates various financial instruments and organizations • Reforms SEC and investor protection • Creates several new administrative oversight agencies
Jumpstart Our Business Startups (JOBS) Act of 2012	• Relaxes some of the regulatory burden for investments in smaller businesses or start-ups • Permits small businesses to advertise for investment • Companies can raise a maximum $1 million through online crowdfunding in a 12-month period

Before we examine any of the laws in depth, the next two sections present introductory materials on the meaning of the term *security* and the role of the federal Securities and Exchange Commission.

WHAT IS A SECURITY?

LO 17-1

Because the objective of securities laws is to protect uninformed people from investing their money without sufficient information, the term **security** has a very broad definition. Indeed, the federal securities laws provide the following definition:

"Security" means any note, stock, treasury stock, bond, debenture, evidence of indebtedness, certificate of interest or participation in any profit-sharing agreement, collateral-trust certificate, preorganization certificate or subscription, transferable share, investment contract, voting-trust certificate, certificate of deposit for a security, fractional undivided interest in oil, gas, or other mineral rights, or in general, any interest or instrument commonly known as a "security," or any certificate of interest or participation in, temporary or interim certificate for receipt for, guarantee of, or warrant or right to subscribe to or purchase, any of the foregoing.[1]

[1]*15 U.S.C.A. §77b(1). This definition is a part of the 1933 Securities Act. It is virtually identical to the definition of security found in the 1934 Securities Exchange Act.*

As this definition indicates, the word *security* includes much more than corporation stock. Historically, the Supreme Court has held that a security exists when one person invests money and looks to others to manage the money for profit. On the basis of this statement, courts seek positive answers to the following three questions when determining whether a person has purchased a security:

1. Is the investment in a common business activity?
2. Is the investment based on a reasonable expectation of profits?
3. Will these profits be earned through the efforts of someone other than the investor?

This three-prong analysis permits courts to find the sale of oil-well interests, the syndication of racehorses, and shares of limited partnerships are securities. The *Howey* case involved the sale of orange trees in a Florida orchard. The Howey-in-the-Hills Services Company offered buyers of trees a management service contract whereby Howey provided care for the trees and harvesting of the fruit. When the investors did not receive the return they expected, Howey was held liable for failing to comply with securities laws.[2]

SECURITIES AND EXCHANGE COMMISSION

The **Securities and Exchange Commission (SEC)** is an administrative agency created in 1934 that is responsible for administering the federal securities laws. The SEC consists of five commissioners appointed by the president for five-year terms. In addition to these commissioners, the SEC employs staff personnel such as lawyers, accountants, security analysts, security examiners, and others.

The SEC has both quasi-legislative and quasi-judicial powers. Under its quasi-legislative power, it has adopted rules and regulations relating to financial and other information that must be furnished to the Commission. Other rules prescribe information that must be given to potential investors. The SEC also regulates the various stock exchanges, utility holding companies, investment trusts, and investment advisers. Under its quasi-judicial power, the SEC also is involved in a variety of investigations.

LO 17-2   The Securities Act of 1933: Going Public

The **Securities Act of 1933** is a disclosure law with respect to the initial sale of securities to the public. This law makes it illegal to use the mails or any other means of interstate communication or transportation to sell securities without disclosing certain financial information to potential investors. The following sections discuss several aspects of the act in detail, including who is regulated, what documents are required, when criminal and civil liability exist, and what defenses are available. As you read, remember that this law applies only to the initial sale of the security. Subsequent transfers of securities are governed by the Securities Exchange Act of 1934, discussed later in this chapter.

In essence, the 1933 Securities Act requires the disclosure of information to the potential investor or other interested party. The information given must

[2]*SEC v. W. J. Howey Co.*, 66 S. Ct. 1100 (1946).

not be untrue or even misleading. If this information is not accurate, liability is imposed upon those responsible.

The act recognizes three sanctions for violations:

- Criminal punishment.
- Civil liability, which may be imposed in favor of injured parties in certain cases.
- Equitable remedy of an injunction.

Proof of an intentional violation usually is required before criminal or civil sanctions are imposed. Proof of negligence will, however, support an injunction.

PARTIES REGULATED

The Securities Act of 1933 regulates anyone who is involved with or who promotes the initial sale of securities. Typically, these parties who must comply with the disclosure requirements of the 1933 Act fall into one or more of four roles.

An **issuer** is the individual or business organization offering a security for sale to the public. An **underwriter** is anyone who participates in the original distribution of securities by selling such securities for the issuer or by guaranteeing their sale. Often securities brokerage firms or investment bankers act as underwriters with respect to a particular transaction. A **controlling person** is one who controls or is controlled by the issuer, such as a major stockholder of a corporation. Finally, a **seller** is anyone who contracts with a purchaser or who is a motivating influence that causes the purchase transaction to occur.

Whenever you operate a business, you and your co-owners must understand the requirements of the 1933 Securities Act. Your organization clearly is an issuer. You and your co-owner clearly are controlling persons. Whether you also are an underwriter or seller or both will depend on the factual situation and relationships you create with other individuals or firms to promote and sell stock in your organization. Regardless of whether you occupy one or more of these roles, you must comply with the 1993 Act or face significant liability.

> Parties subject to the 1933 act include issuers, underwriters, controlling persons, and sellers.

DOCUMENTS INVOLVED

In regulating the initial sales of securities, the Securities Act of 1933 is viewed as a disclosure law. In essence, this law requires that securities subject to its provisions be registered prior to any sale and that a prospectus be furnished to any potential investor prior to any sale being consummated. Thus, an issuer of securities who complies with the federal law must prepare:

- A registration statement
- A prospectus

Registration Statement In an attempt to accomplish its purpose of disclosure, the Securities Act of 1933 contains detailed provisions relating to the registration of securities. These provisions require that a **registration statement** be filed with the SEC. The statement includes a detailed disclosure of financial information about the issuer and the controlling individuals involved in the offering of securities for sale to the public.

With respect to the filing of the registration statement, the law describes selling activities permitted at the various stages of the registration process. This procedure

> Three time periods involved in the registration process are the prefiling period, the waiting period, and the posteffective period.

and its time frame are a primary reason why you and your co-owner described in the Business Discussions cannot begin business immediately.

During the **prefiling period,** it is legal for the issuer of a security to engage in preliminary negotiations and agreements with underwriters. It is illegal to sell a covered security during this period. Offers to sell and offers to buy securities also are prohibited during this prefiling period.

After the registration statement is filed, a **waiting period** commences. This period typically lasts 20 days. During this time, the SEC staff investigates the accuracy of the registration statement to determine whether the sale of the securities should be permitted. During the waiting period, it is still illegal to sell a security subject to the act. However, it is not illegal to solicit a buyer or receive offers to buy. Since contracts to sell are still illegal, offers cannot be accepted during the waiting period. However, during these waiting periods, sellers may solicit offers for later acceptance.

Many solicitations during the waiting period are made in advertisements called **tombstone ads.** These ads are brief announcements identifying the security and stating its price, by whom orders will be executed, and from whom a prospectus may be obtained. Solicitations may also be made during the waiting period by use of a statistical summary, a summary prospectus, or a preliminary prospectus. These techniques allow dissemination of the facts that are to be ultimately disclosed in the formal prospectus.

A registration becomes effective at the expiration of the waiting period, 20 days after it is filed, unless the SEC gives notice that it is not in proper form or unless the SEC accelerates the effective date. Any amendment filed without the commission's consent starts the 20-day period running again. The end of the waiting period is the beginning of the **posteffective period.** During this period, contracts to buy and sell securities are finalized.

Prospectus   During the posteffective period, securities may be sold. A **prospectus** must be furnished to any interested investor, and it must conform to the statutory requirements. Like the registration statement, the prospectus contains financial information related to the issuer and controlling persons. Indeed, the prospectus contains the same essential information contained in the registration statement. The prospectus supplies the investor with sufficient facts (including financial information) so that he or she can make an intelligent investment decision. The SEC has adopted rules relating to the detailed requirements of the prospectus. The major requirements are detailed facts about the issuer and financial statements, including balance sheets and statements of operations of the issuer.

Don't rely on the prospectus as assurance the investment will make money.

Theoretically, any security may be sold under the act, provided the issuer and others follow the law and the rules and regulations enacted under it are followed. The law does not prohibit the sale of worthless securities. An investor may "foolishly" invest his or her money, and a person may legally sell the blue sky if the statutory requirements are met. In fact, the prospectus must contain the following in capital letters and boldface type:

THESE SECURITIES HAVE NOT BEEN APPROVED OR DISAPPROVED BY THE SECURITIES AND EXCHANGE COMMISSION NOR HAS THE COMMISSION PASSED UPON THE ACCURACY OR ADEQUACY OF THIS PROSPECTUS. ANY REPRESENTATION TO THE CONTRARY IS A CRIMINAL OFFENSE.

The SEC has alternative processes to this formal registration process for companies that sell securities to institutional investors. Rule 144A is an example of an SEC-approved regulation allowing sale of securities to investors such as pension funds. Under this Rule, the securities are labeled as restricted. All other provisions of the securities law, such as those related to any fraudulent transactions, remain applicable to transactions involving these restricted securities.

LIABILITY

Under the federal Securities Act of 1933, both criminal and civil liability may be imposed for violations. Criminal liability results from a willful violation of the act or fraud in *any* offer or sale of securities. Fraud occurs when any material fact is omitted, causing a statement to be misleading. The penalty is a fine of up to $10,000 or five years in prison or both.

Civil liability under the 1933 Act usually involves a buyer of securities suing for a refund of the investment. This liability on the issuer, controlling person, underwriter, and seller is significant because the investors' money typically is lost at the time of these civil claims.

Three sections of the Securities Act of 1933 directly apply to civil liability of parties involved in issuing securities:

- Section 11 deals with registration statements.
- Section 12 relates to prospectuses and oral and written communication.
- Section 17 concerns fraudulent interstate transactions.

Section 11: Registration Statement The civil liability provision dealing with registration statements imposes liability on the following persons in favor of purchasers of securities:

1. Every person who signed the registration statement.
2. Every director of the corporation or partner in the partnership issuing the security.
3. Every person who, with his or her consent, is named in the registration statement as about to become a director or partner.
4. Every accountant, engineer, or appraiser who assists in the preparation of the registration statement or its certification.
5. Every underwriter.

These persons are liable if the registration statement:

- Contains untrue statements of material facts.
- Omits material facts required by statute or regulation.
- Omits information that if not given makes the facts stated misleading.

This last situation describes the factual situation of a statement containing a half-truth, which has the net effect of being misleading. The test of accuracy and materiality is as of the date the registration statement becomes effective.

> "In 2006, for example, for the first time, more equity financing was raised in private transactions under the SEC's Rule 144A ($162 billion) than was raised in IPOs on the NYSE, Nasdaq, and the Amex combined ($154 billion)."
>
> **—Peter J. Wallison, "Capital Complaints,"** *The Wall Street Journal,* **March 20, 2007**

The issuer and experts assisting must make sure the registration materials are truthful and not misleading.

A plaintiff-purchaser need not prove reliance on the registration statement in order to recover the amount of an investment. All the plaintiff has to show is omitted or misleading information in the registration statement. A defendant can defend the suit by proving actual knowledge of the falsity by the purchaser. Knowledge of the falsity by a defendant need not be proved. However, a defendant's reliance on an expert such as an accountant is a defense. For example, a director may defend a suit on the basis of a false financial statement by showing reliance on a certified public accountant. This reliance exception logically does not apply to the issuer. Because the issuer provides information to the expert, the issuer should not be allowed to rely on the expert's use of the inaccurate information.

Section 12: Prospectus and Other Communications   This section of the 1933 Act is divided into two parts. The first subsection of Section 12 imposes liability on those who offer or sell securities that are not registered with the SEC. This liability exists regardless of the intent or conduct of those who fail to comply with the registration requirements. Thus, liability traditionally has been imposed against violators even though they lacked any wrongful intent. The Supreme Court has held that a defendant is free from liability if the plaintiff is equally responsible for the failure to file the registration statement.

> Plaintiffs can recover for harm done by false or misleading information in a prospectus even if the prospectus is not read or reviewed.

The second subsection of Section 12 imposes liability on sellers who use a prospectus or make communications (by mail, telephone, or other instrumentalities of interstate commerce) that contain an untrue statement of material facts required to be stated or necessary to make statements not misleading. As under Section 11, the plaintiff does not have to prove reliance on the false or misleading prospectus or communication. Nor does the plaintiff have to establish that the defendant intended the deception.

Purchasers of such securities may sue for their actual damages. If the purchaser still owns the securities and he or she can prove a direct contractual relationship with the seller, the remedy of rescission and a refund of the purchase price is also available.

Section 17: Fraudulent Transactions   This provision concerning fraudulent interstate transactions prohibits the use of any instrument of interstate communication in the offer or sale of any securities when the result is:

1. To defraud.
2. To obtain money or property by means of an untrue or misleading statement.
3. To engage in a business transaction or practice that may operate to defraud or deceive a purchaser.

The requirement that a defendant-seller must act with the intent (**scienter**) to deceive or mislead in order to prove a Section 17 violation has caused much controversy over the years. The Supreme Court has resolved this issue by holding that a plaintiff must prove the defendant's intent to violate 1. However, no proof of the defendant's intent is required to find a violation of 2 or 3. The Court's decision is limited to when the plaintiff is seeking an injunction, because Section 17 does not explicitly provide for the private remedy of monetary damages.

DEFENSES

The Securities Act of 1933 recognized several defenses that may be used to avoid civil liability. Among the most important defenses are:

- Materiality.
- The statute of limitations.
- Due diligence.

Materiality A defendant in a case involving the 1933 Act might argue that the false or misleading information is not *material* and thus should not have had an impact on the purchaser's decision-making process. Determining whether or not a particular fact is material depends on the facts and the parties involved.

The SEC and the courts have attempted to define materiality. The term *material* describes the kinds of information that an average prudent investor would want to have so that he or she can make an intelligent, informed decision whether or not to buy the security. A material fact is one that if correctly stated or disclosed would have deterred or tended to deter the average prudent investor from purchasing the securities in question. The term does not cover minor inaccuracies or errors in matters of no interest to investors. Facts that tend to deter a person from purchasing a security are those that have an important bearing upon the nature or condition of the issuing corporation or its business.

Statute of Limitations The statute of limitations is a defense for both civil and criminal liability. The basic period is one year. The one year does not start to run until the discovery of the untrue statement or omission. Or it does not start to run until the time such discovery would have been made with reasonable diligence. In no event may a suit be brought more than three years after the sale.

> Sarbanes-Oxley does not increase the statute of limitations under the 1933 Act.

A defense similar to the statute of limitations is also provided. The 1933 Act provides that if the person acquiring the security does so after the issuer has made generally available an earnings statement covering at least 12 months after the effective date of the registration statement, then this person must prove actual reliance on the registration statement.

Due Diligence A very important defense for experts such as accountants is the **due diligence defense.**

To establish this defense, the expert must prove that a reasonable investigation of the financial statements of the issuer and controlling persons was conducted. As the result of this investigation, an expert exercising due diligence must prove that there was no reason to believe any of the information in the registration statement or prospectus was false or misleading.

In determining whether or not an expert, such as an accountant, has made a reasonable investigation, the law provides that the standard of *reasonableness* is that required of a prudent person in the management of his or her own property. The burden of proof of this defense is on the expert, and the test is as of the time the registration statement became effective. The due diligence defense, in effect, requires proof that a party was not guilty of fraud or negligence.

concept *summary*

Liability under the Securities Act of 1933

SECTION 11

Purpose: Creates liability for false or misleading registration statements.

Plaintiff's case: Not required to prove defendant's intent to deceive or plaintiff's reliance on documents.

Defendant's defenses: Proof of no false or misleading information; proof that plaintiff knew of false or misleading nature of information; except for issuers, proof of reliance on an expert (attorney or accountant).

SECTION 12

Purpose: (1) Creates liability for failing to file a required registration statement; (2) creates liability for false or misleading prospectus.

Plaintiff's case: Not required to prove defendant's intent to deceive or plaintiff's reliance on documents.

Defendant's defenses: For (1), plaintiff equally at fault for failing to file a registration statement; for (2), same as Section 11 defenses.

SECTION 17

Purpose: In an interstate transaction, it is unlawful to

(1) employ any device, scheme, or artifice of fraud;

(2) obtain money or property by untrue statement or omission of material fact;

(3) engage in events that operate or would operate as fraud or deceit.

Plaintiff's case: For (1), required to prove defendant's intent to deceive; for (2) and (3), not required to prove intent to deceive.

Defendant's defenses: For (1), proof of no intent to deceive and proof of good faith; for (2), proof of no material misstatement or omission; for (3), proof of no involvement in unlawful activities.

CRIMINAL LIABILITY

$10,000 fine or 5 years in prison or both.

LO 17-3

Securities Exchange Act of 1934: Being Public

Whereas the Securities Act of 1933 deals with original offerings of securities, the **Securities Exchange Act of 1934** regulates transfers of securities after the initial sale. The 1934 Act, which created the Securities and Exchange Commission, also deals with regulation of securities exchanges, brokers, and dealers in securities.

The Securities Exchange Act makes it illegal to sell a security on a national exchange unless a registration is effective for the security. Registration under the 1934 Act differs from registration under the 1933 Act. Registration under the 1934 Act requires filing prescribed forms with the applicable stock exchange and the SEC.

Provisions relating to stockbrokers and dealers prohibit the use of the mails or any other instrumentality of interstate commerce to sell securities unless the broker or the dealer is registered. The language is sufficiently broad to cover attempted sales as well as actual sales. Brokers and dealers must keep detailed records of their activities and file annual reports with the SEC.

The SEC requires that issuers of registered securities file periodic reports as well as report significant developments that would affect the value of the security. For example, the SEC requires companies to disclose foreign payoffs or bribes to obtain or retain foreign business operations. Businesses must disclose their minority hiring practices and other social data that may be of public concern. Business has been forced by the SEC to submit certain shareholder proposals to all shareholders as a part of proxy solicitation. When a new pension law was enacted, the SEC required that financial reports disclose the law's impact on the reporting business. The SEC requires more complete disclosure of executive compensation packages.

The SEC's activity concerning information corporations must furnish to the investing public is almost limitless. With the actions of the PCAOB, SEC regulations are of paramount significance to all persons concerned with the financial aspects of business. This area of regulation directly affects the accounting profession. Since the SEC regulates financial statements, it frequently decides issues of proper accounting and auditing theory and practices.

Sarbanes-Oxley, through the PCAOB and SEC regulations, impacts the accounting and audit practices.

The following sections examine how the Securities Exchange Act of 1934 affects the businessperson, the accountant, the lawyer, the broker, and the investor. These sections cover some fundamental concepts of this law, such as civil liability in general and insider transactions in particular, as well as criminal violations and penalties under the 1934 Act.

SECTION 10(b) AND RULE 10b-5

Most of the litigation under the Securities and Exchange Act of 1934 is brought under Section 10(b) of the act and Rule 10b-5 promulgated by the SEC pursuant to the act. Section 10(b) and Rule 10b-5 declare that it is unlawful to use the mails or any instrumentality of interstate commerce or any national securities exchange to defraud *any person* in connection with the *purchase or sale* of any security. Sidebar 17.1 contains the actual language of this section and rule.

---

sidebar 17.1

Language of Section 10(b) of the 1934 Act and SEC's Rule 10b-5

Section 10(b) states:

It shall be unlawful for any person, directly or indirectly, by the use of any means or instrumentality of interstate commerce or of the mails, or of any facility of any national securities exchange—

(b) To use or employ, in connection with the purchase or sale of any security registered on a national securities exchange or any security not so registered, any manipulative or deceptive device or contrivance in contravention of such rules and regulations as the [SEC] may prescribe.

Rule 10b-5, adopted by the SEC in 1942, states:

It shall be unlawful for any person, directly or indirectly, by the use of any means or instrumentality of interstate commerce, or of the mails or of any facility of any national securities exchange,

(a) To employ any device, scheme, or artifice to defraud,

(b) To make any untrue statement of a material fact or to omit to state a material fact necessary in order to make the statements made, in the light of the circumstances under which they were made, not misleading, or

(c) To engage in any act, practice, or course of business which operates or would operate as a fraud or deceit upon any person, in connection with the purchase or sale of any security.

Common issues regarding litigation under Section 10(b) and Rule 10b-5 include the following:

- Who is liable?
- What can be recovered by the plaintiff, and does the defendant have the right to seek contribution from third parties?
- When is information material to the transaction?
- Where does the law apply?

LO 17-4

Liability   The Supreme Court used Case 17.1 as a means to emphasize there is a limited answer to the question who is liable. While many cases clarify that parties directly connected to the sale of securities are liable, the following case focuses on the liability of third parties.

---

case **17.1**

STONERIDGE INVESTMENT PARTNERS, LLC, PETITIONER v. SCIENTIFIC-ATLANTA, INC., ET AL.
128 S. Ct. 761 **(2008)**

Charter Communications operates cable companies throughout the United States. Both Scientific-Atlanta and Motorola supply Charter with digital cable converter boxes that Charter provides to its customers. In 2000, Charter became concerned that it would not meet cash flow projections causing it to miss the financial estimates Wall Street established. To remedy this shortfall, Charter arranged to overpay Scientific-Atlanta and Motorola by the amount of $20 for each converter box. This deal was conditioned on these companies purchasing advertising from Charter in the amount equal to the overpayment. While these transactions had no economic impact, Charter recorded the advertisement purchases as revenue and capitalized the purchases of the converter boxes. This scheme allowed Charter to fool its auditor and to create financial statements that appeared to meet expectations by increasing its cash flow by about $17 million.

Purchasers of Charter stock, upon discovering this fraud, sued Charter, Scientific-Atlanta, and Motorola under the 1934 Securities Exchange Act. The latter two companies asked the District Judge to dismiss these claims since the companies were not parties to any securities fraud and are not subject to a private cause of action under the securities laws. The District Court and the Eighth Circuit Court of Appeals ruled

in favor of Scientific-Atlanta and Motorola finding there was not a private right of action against these third parties since they did not make a public misstatement and did not fail to disclose required information. The Supreme Court granted certiorari to address the conflict among the appellate courts concerning when third parties are liable under the 1934 Securities Exchange Act.

KENNEDY, J.: . . . Though the text of the Securities Exchange Act does not provide for a private cause of action for §10(b) violations, the Court has found a right of action implied in the words of the statute and its implementing regulation. In a typical §10(b) private action a plaintiff must prove (1) a material misrepresentation or omission by the defendant; (2) scienter; (3) a connection between the misrepresentation or omission and the purchase or sale of a security; (4) reliance upon the misrepresentation or omission; (5) economic loss; and (6) loss causation.

. . . [I]n §104 of the Private Securities Litigation Reform Act of 1995 (PSLRA), [Congress] directed prosecution of aiders and abettors by the SEC.

The §10(b) implied private right of action does not extend to aiders and abettors. The conduct of a secondary actor must satisfy each of the elements or preconditions for liability; and we consider whether the allegations here are sufficient to do so.

The Court of Appeals concluded petitioner had not alleged that respondents engaged in a deceptive act within the reach of the §10(b) private right of action, noting that only misstatements, omissions by one who has a duty to disclose, and manipulative trading practices . . . are deceptive within the meaning of the rule. . . . Conduct itself can be deceptive, as respondents concede. In this case, moreover, respondents' course of conduct included both oral and written statements, such as the backdated contracts agreed to by Charter and respondents.

A different interpretation of the holding from the Court of Appeals opinion is that the court was stating only that any deceptive statement or act respondents made was not actionable because it did not have the requisite proximate relation to the investors' harm. That conclusion is consistent with our own determination that respondents' acts or statements were not relied upon by the investors and that, as a result, liability cannot be imposed upon respondents.

Reliance by the plaintiff upon the defendant's deceptive acts is an essential element of the §10(b) private cause of action. It ensures that, for liability to arise, the requisite causal connection between a defendant's misrepresentation and a plaintiff's injury exists. . . . We have found a rebuttable presumption of reliance in two different circumstances. First, if there is an omission of a material fact by one with a duty to disclose, the investor to whom the duty was owed need not provide specific proof of reliance. Second, under the fraud-on-the-market doctrine, reliance is presumed when the statements at issue become public. The public information is reflected in the market price of the security. Then it can be assumed that an investor who buys or sells stock at the market price relies upon the statement.

Neither presumption applies here. Respondents had no duty to disclose; and their deceptive acts were not communicated to the public. No member of the investing public had knowledge, either actual or presumed, of respondents' deceptive acts during the relevant times. Petitioner, as a result, cannot show reliance upon any of respondents' actions except in an indirect chain that we find too remote for liability.

Invoking what some courts call "scheme liability," petitioner nonetheless seeks to impose liability on respondents even absent a public statement. In our view this approach does not answer the objection that petitioner did not in fact rely upon respondents' own deceptive conduct.

. . . It was Charter, not respondents, that misled its auditor and filed fraudulent financial statements; nothing respondents did made it necessary or inevitable for Charter to record the transactions as it did. . . .

Were we to adopt this construction of §10(b), it would revive in substance the implied cause of action against all aiders and abettors except those who committed no deceptive act in the process of facilitating the fraud; and we would undermine Congress' determination that this class of defendants should be pursued by the SEC and not by private litigants. . . .

The §10(b) private cause of action is a judicial construct that Congress did not enact in the text of the relevant statutes. Though the rule once may have been otherwise, it is settled that there is an implied cause of action only if the underlying statute can be interpreted to disclose the intent to create one. . . .

Concerns with the judicial creation of a private cause of action caution against its expansion. The decision to extend the cause of action is for Congress, not for us. Though it remains the law, the §10(b) private right should not be extended beyond its present boundaries. . . .

Secondary actors are subject to criminal penalties and civil enforcement by the SEC. The enforcement power is not toothless. Since September 30, 2002, SEC enforcement actions have collected over $10 billion in disgorgement and penalties, much of it for distribution to injured investors. And in this case both parties agree that criminal penalties are a strong deterrent. In addition some state securities laws permit state authorities to seek fines and restitution from aiders and abettors. All secondary actors, furthermore, are not necessarily immune from private suit. The securities statutes provide an express private right of action against accountants and underwriters in certain circumstances, and the implied right of action in §10(b) continues to cover secondary actors who commit primary violations.

Here respondents were acting in concert with Charter in the ordinary course as suppliers and, as matters then evolved in the not so ordinary course, as customers. Unconventional as the arrangement was, it took place in the marketplace for goods and services, not in the investment sphere. Charter was free to do as it chose in preparing its books, conferring with its auditor, and preparing and then issuing its financial statements. In these circumstances the investors cannot be said to have relied upon any of respondents' deceptive acts in the decision to purchase or sell securities; and as the requisite reliance cannot be shown, respondents have no liability to petitioner under the implied right of action. This conclusion is consistent with the narrow dimensions we must give to a right of action Congress did not authorize when it first enacted the statute and did not expand when it revisited the law.

Affirmed.

[continued]

KEY POINTS

- Scientific-Atlanta and Motorola both supplied Charter Communications with digital converter boxes, a transaction that was fraudulently manipulated to show an increase in cash flow on Charter's financial statements, when in reality there was no economic impact.
- When sued under Section 10(b), Scientific-Atlanta and Motorola contended that neither entity's deceptive statements or acts were relied upon by Charter's investors to constitute a violation under the Section 10(b) private right of action.
- The Supreme Court held that Charter was responsible for misleading financial statements and that its suppliers did not have a duty to Charter's investors to disclose the deception and their involvement was not directly related to the harm suffered by Charter's investors.
- This ruling does not mean that businesses or actors assisting others in Section 10(b) violations are not held responsible through other enforcement actions, including state securities laws, but that Congress has not extended this provision of the 1934 Securities Exchange Act to hold these aiders and abettors accountable.

This decision appears to restrict plaintiffs' ability to recover against auditors, banks, and other parties associated with major scandals. Prior to this ruling, there have been significant settlements reached with auditors involved in some of the largest corporate scandals in history.

Damages A plaintiff in a suit under Rule 10b-5 must prove damages. The damages of a defrauded purchaser are actual out-of-pocket losses or the excess of what was paid over the value of what was received. Courts in a few cases have used the *benefit of the bargain* measure of damages and awarded the buyer the difference between what he or she paid and what the security was represented to be worth. A buyer's damages are measured at the time of purchase.

As Sidebar 17.2 illustrates, a buyer must allege specific damages due to the seller's fraud. An allegation of fraud and a drop in stock price is not enough to prove the case.

Computation of a defrauded seller's damages is more difficult. A defrauding purchaser usually benefits from an increase in the value of the securities, while the plaintiff seller loses this increase. Courts do not allow defrauding buyers to keep these increases in value. Therefore, the measure of the seller's damages is the difference between the fair value of all that the seller received and the fair value of what he or she would have received had there been no fraud. A fraudulent buyer loses all profits flowing from the wrongful conduct.

Plaintiffs under Rule 10b-5 are also entitled to consequential damages. These include lost dividends, brokerage fees, and taxes. In addition, courts may order payment of interest on the funds. Punitive damages are not permitted as they are in cases of common law fraud based on state laws. This distinction results from the language of the 1934 Act, which limits recoveries to actual damages.

The issue of whether a defendant who is liable under Section 10(b) can seek contribution from third parties was not resolved until 1993. In Sidebar 17.3, the Supreme Court concludes that a right of contribution does exist in Section 10(b) private actions.

sidebar 17.2

Proof of Loss Due to Fraud

Shareholders of Dura Pharmaceuticals Inc. sued the company and its directors and officers for violations of the 1934 Securities Exchange Act. These plaintiffs claim they paid an artificially high price for the stock because Dura executives misrepresented that the Food and Drug Administration (FDA) would approve Dura's application to sell a new asthmatic spray. During the time in question, Dura's stock declined in price rapidly when it announced its sales projection would not be met. Later, when Dura announced that the FDA would not approve its new asthmatic spray, the stock declined again. However, within a week, Dura stock had regained much of that lost value.

The shareholder plaintiffs simply alleged they had lost money due to the inflated price of the stock and the misrepresentation by the Dura executives. The Supreme Court held that these simple allegations were not enough to establish the loss of value due to the fraud. More specific proof of the loss caused by the fraud is required.

Source: *Dura Pharmaceuticals, Inc. v. Broudo*, 125 S. Ct. 1627 (2005).

sidebar 17.3

Right to Contribution from Others

To settle a securities lawsuit by its shareholders, Wausau Insurance agreed to pay $13.5 million. Following this settlement, Wausau filed a lawsuit against the attorneys and accountants involved in the public offering. These defendants sought dismissal of this complaint on the grounds that there is no right of contribution under §10(b). The Supreme Court concludes that there is a private right of contribution in §10(b) of the 1934 Act and in Rule 10b-5. Those charged with liability in a §10b-5 action have a right of contribution against other parties who have joint responsibility for the violation.

Source: *Musick, Peeler & Garrett v. Wausau Ins.*, 113 S. Ct. 2085 (1993).

Materiality Section 10(b) and Rule 10b-5 are usually referred to as the *antifraud provisions* of the act. A plaintiff seeking damages under the provisions must establish the existence of a material misrepresentation or omission made in connection with the purchase or sale of a security and the culpable state of mind of the defendant. Materiality under the 1934 Act is the same as materiality under the 1933 Act. However, liability under Rule 10b-5 requires proof of the defendant's intent to deceive. Proof of the defendant's simple negligence is not enough to establish liability. The plaintiff also must establish that the defendant's practice is manipulative and not merely corporate mismanagement.

The concept of fraud under Section 10(b) encompasses not only untrue statements of material facts but also the failure to state material facts necessary to prevent statements actually made from being misleading. In other words, a half-truth that misleads is fraudulent. Finally, failure to correct a misleading impression left by statements already made, or silence where there is a duty to speak, gives rise to a violation of Rule 10b-5 because it is a form of aiding and abetting the deception.

sidebar 17.4

Statute of Limitations for Fraud Claims

Merck & Co. manufactured and marketed the drug Vioxx, a painkiller used to reduce arthritis pain. In 1999, the Food and Drug Administration approved Vioxx as a prescription drug. Shortly after Vioxx was introduced, reports arose questioning whether taking Vioxx increased the risk of heart attack. Merck officials issued many statements and reports that promoted the virtues of Vioxx and downplayed any negative side effects. On October 9, 2001, *The New York Times* reported that Merck "had reexamined its own data and found no evidence that Vioxx increased the risks of heart attacks."

Despite these reassurances, Merck stock price rose and fell depending on the nature (good or bad) of news reported about Vioxx. Finally, on September 30, 2004, Merck withdrew Vioxx from the market.

Based on the uncertainty surrounding Vioxx, many lawsuits were filed against Merck. Included in these cases was one filed on November 6, 2003. A group of shareholders sued Merck, alleging that company officials had engaged in securities fraud under §10(b) by falsely and deceptively denying the risks associated with Vioxx. The defendants sought to

have this case dismissed as being filed too late under the applicable statute of limitations.

Upon its review, the Supreme Court concludes that the applicable statute of limitations, in this case, is two years. The Court also finds the limitations period "begins to run once the plaintiff did discover or a reasonable diligent plaintiff would have discovered the facts constituting the violation—whichever comes first." The Court also concludes the element of scienter (intention to defraud) by the defendant may be considered when determining whether the plaintiff knew or should known the fraud occurred. The element of scienter typically will delay the beginning of the statute of limitations running since the defendant is attempting to hide the fraud.

Based on the facts presented, the Court decides that statute of limitations has not run out since the plaintiffs could not have reasonably known before November 6, 2001 (two years prior to the lawsuit being filed) that Merck officials engaged in the alleged fraud.

Source: *Merck & Co. v. Reynolds*, 130 S. Ct. 1784 (2010).

Another issue impacting materiality relates to when the plaintiff brings the complaint. The Supreme Court looks at when the potentially misleading statements are made and whether the plaintiff did know or should have known the statements were misleading. This examination is further described in Sidebar 17.4.

One of the most difficult issues concerning materiality arises in preliminary merger negotiations. How should management respond when asked about merger possibilities? Should management reveal information about merger possibilities even when the likelihood of an actual merger is very slight? The Supreme Court uses an objective-person case-by-case analysis to determine whether information about potential mergers is material and thus required to be disclosed. The Court said, "materiality depends on the significance the reasonable investor would place on the withheld or misrepresented information."

International Application The application of §10(b) and Rule 10b-5 to international securities transaction appears to depend on the nationality of the purchaser and seller of the securities as well as the location of the actual sales transaction. Case 17.2 discusses the factual situation involving international sellers and buyers on foreign exchanges.

MORRISON v. NATIONAL AUSTRALIA BANK LTD.
130 S. Ct. 2869 (2010)

The National Australia Bank Limited (National or Bank) is the largest bank in Australia. Its common shares are traded on the Australian Stock Exchange and other foreign securities exchanges, but this stock is not listed for sale on any exchange in the United States. What is listed on the New York Stock Exchange is National's American Depositary Receipts (ADRs). An ADR represents the right to receive specified shares of a foreign stock.

In February 1998, National purchased a Florida corporation known as HomeSide Lending Inc. In essence, HomeSide earned profits by collecting mortgage payments. Any early payment of mortgages reduced HomeSide's profits as it reduced its income stream.

National announced it was writing down the value of HomeSide's assests by $450 million in July 2001 and by another $1.75 billion in September 2001. The reason for these adjustments was low interest rates causing many borrowers to refinance existing mortgages. The early payoff due to the refinanced mortgages hurt HomeSide's income.

A group of Australian investors filed a complaint in the United States District Court for the Southern District of New York alleging that the officers of National and HomeSide violated §10(b) of the 1934 Securities Exchange Act. The basis of this complaint is that the officers misrepresented the calculation of HomeSide's value by not considering the reduced income from early payoff.

The District Court found it lacked jurisdiction to hear the case. The plaintiffs argued that HomeSide was a Florida corporation and investors had purchased National ADRs via the New York Stock Exchange. The District Judge found there was no jurisdiction because the acts in the United States were "at most, a link in the chain of an alleged overall securities fraud scheme that culminated abroad." On appeal, the Second Circuit affirmed the dismissal of the complaint. Certiorari was granted.

SCALIA, J.: We decide whether §10(b) of the Securities Exchange Act of 1934 provides a cause of action to foreign plaintiffs suing foreign and American defendants for misconduct in connection with securities traded on foreign exchanges. . . .

Rule 10b–5, the regulation under which petitioners have brought suit, was promulgated under §10(b), and does not extend beyond conduct encompassed by §10(b)'s prohibition. Therefore, if §10(b) is not extraterritorial, neither is Rule 10b–5. . . .

Petitioners and the Solicitor General contend, however, that three things indicate that §10(b) or the Exchange Act in general has at least some extraterritorial application. First, they point to the definition of "interstate commerce," a term used in §10(b), which includes "trade, commerce, transportation, or communication . . . between any foreign country and any State." But we have repeatedly held that even statutes that contain broad language in their definitions of "commerce" that expressly refer to "*foreign* commerce" do not apply abroad. The general reference to foreign commerce in the definition of "interstate commerce" does not defeat the presumption against extraterritoriality.

Petitioners and the Solicitor General next point out that Congress, in describing the purposes of the Exchange Act, observed that the prices established and offered in such transactions are generally disseminated and quoted throughout the United States and foreign countries. The antecedent of such transactions, however, is found in the first sentence of the section, which declares that "transactions in securities as commonly conducted upon securities exchanges and over-the counter markets are affected with a national public interest." Nothing suggests that this *national* public interest pertains to transactions conducted upon *foreign* exchanges and markets. The fleeting reference to the dissemination and quotation abroad of the prices of securities traded in domestic exchanges and markets cannot overcome the presumption against extraterritoriality.

Finally, there is §30(b) of the Exchange Act, which *does* mention the Act's extraterritorial application: "The provisions of [the Exchange Act] or of any rule or regulation thereunder shall not apply to any person insofar as he transacts a business in securities without the jurisdiction of the United States," unless he does so in violation of regulations promulgated by the Securities and Exchange Commission "to prevent . . . evasion of [the Act]." (The parties have pointed us to no regulation promulgated pursuant to §30(b).) The Solicitor General argues that this exemption would have no function if the Act did not apply in the first instance to securities transactions that occur abroad.

We are not convinced. In the first place, it would be odd for Congress to indicate the extraterritorial application of the whole Exchange Act by means of a provision imposing a condition precedent to its application abroad. And if the whole Act applied abroad, why would the Commission's enabling regulations be limited to those preventing "evasion" of the Act, rather than all those preventing "violation"? The provision seems to us directed at actions abroad that might conceal a domestic violation, or might cause what would otherwise be a domestic violation to escape on a technicality. At most, the Solicitor General's proposed inference is possible; but possible interpretations of statutory language do not override the presumption against extraterritoriality. . . .

In short, there is no affirmative indication in the Exchange Act that §10(b) applies extraterritorially, and we therefore conclude that it does not.

Petitioners argue that the conclusion that §10(b) does not apply extraterritorially does not resolve this case. They contend that they seek no more than domestic application anyway, since Florida is where HomeSide and its senior executives engaged in the deceptive conduct of manipulating HomeSide's financial models. . . . This is less an answer to the presumption against extraterritorial application than it is an assertion—a quite valid assertion—that that presumption here (as often) is not self-evidently dispositive, but its application requires further analysis. For it is a rare case of prohibited extraterritorial application that lacks *all* contact with the territory of the United States. But the presumption against extraterritorial application would be a craven watchdog indeed if it retreated to its kennel whenever *some* domestic activity is involved in the case. . . .

We think that the focus of the Exchange Act is not upon the place where the deception originated, but upon purchases and sales of securities in the United States. Section 10(b) does not punish deceptive conduct, but only deceptive conduct "in connection with the purchase or sale of any security registered on a national securities exchange or any security not so registered." Those purchase-and-sale transactions are the objects of the statute's solicitude. It is those transactions that the statute seeks to regulate; it is parties or prospective parties to those transactions that the statute seeks to protect. And it is in our view only transactions in securities listed on domestic exchanges, and domestic transactions in other securities, to which §10(b) applies. . . .

Finally, we reject the notion that the Exchange Act reaches conduct in this country affecting exchanges or transactions abroad. . . . Like the United States, foreign countries regulate their domestic securities exchanges and securities transactions occurring within their territorial jurisdiction. And the regulation of other countries often differs from ours as to what constitutes fraud, what disclosures must be made, what damages are recoverable, what discovery is available in litigation, what individual actions may be joined in a single suit, what attorney's fees are recoverable, and many other matters. . . .

Section 10(b) reaches the use of a manipulative or deceptive device or contrivance only in connection with the purchase or sale of a security listed on an American stock exchange, and the purchase or sale of any other security in the United States. This case involves no securities listed on a domestic exchange, and all aspects of the purchases complained of by those petitioners who still have live claims occurred outside the United States. Petitioners have therefore failed to state a claim on which relief can be granted. We affirm the dismissal of petitioners' complaint on this ground.

Affirmed.

KEY POINTS

- The Court addresses whether Australian investors can utilize Section 10(b) to sue an Australian bank that owns a Florida corporation.
- The Court concludes that Section 10(b) does not include extraterritorial application in light of the limited provision for such jurisdiction in the Exchange Act.
- The investors' contention that they were misled by financial models HomeSlide's officers created in their Florida offices is not sufficient to establish jurisdiction for a cause of action under Section 10(b).
- Section 10(b) seeks to regulate deceptive securities transactions, and not all conduct relates closely to these transactions.

As the result of this *Morrison* decision, an interesting situation would involve an American investor who buys a foreign stock on a foreign exchange. Would §10(b) of the Securities Exchange Act of 1934 protect this investor? While this question is not specifically addressed, it can be argued that *Morrison's* transactional test would seem to deny this American investor a basis for a claim.

INSIDER TRANSACTIONS

Section 16, one of the most important provisions of the Securities Exchange Act of 1934, concerns insider transactions. An **insider** is any person who:

- Owns more than 10% of any security.
- Is a director or an officer of the issuer of the security.

The SEC defines an officer for insider trading purposes as the executive officers, accounting officers, chief financial officers, and controllers. The SEC also examines the individual investor's function within the company rather than the title of the position held.

Section 16 and SEC regulations require that insiders file, at the time of the registration or within 10 days after becoming an insider, a statement of the amount of such issues of which they are the owners. The regulations also require filing within 10 days after the close of each calendar month thereafter if there has been any change in such ownership during such month (indicating the change). Sarbanes-Oxley shortens the time period for filing information about insider transactions. Now, these filings with the SEC must be made electronically within two business days of the insider's transaction.

The reason for prohibiting insiders from trading for profit is to prevent the use of information that is available to an insider but not to the general public. Because the SEC cannot determine for certain when nonpublic information is improperly used, Section 16 creates a presumption that any profit made within a six-month time period is illegal. These profits are referred to as **short-swing profits.** Thus, if a director, officer, or principal owner realizes profits on the purchase and sale of a security within a six-month period, the profits legally belong to the company or to the investor who purchased it from or sold it to an insider, resulting in the insider's profit and the investor's loss. The order of the purchase and sale is immaterial. The profit is calculated on the lowest price in and highest price out during any six-month period. Unlike the required proof of intent to deceive under Section 10(b), the short-swing profits rule of Section 16 does not depend on any misuse of information. In other words, short-swing profits by insiders, regardless of the insiders' states of mind, are absolutely prohibited.

While the SEC enforces the requirements of Section 16 that insiders file certain documents, the SEC does not enforce the provision that prohibits insiders from engaging in short-swing profits. This provision of Section 16 is enforced by civil actions filed by the issuer of the security or by a person who owns a security of the issuer.

NONPUBLIC INFORMATION

The SEC's concern for trading based on nonpublic information goes beyond the Section 16 ban on short-swing profits. Indeed, a person who is not technically an insider but who trades securities without disclosing nonpublic information may violate Section 10(b) and Rule 10b-5. The SEC takes the position that the profit obtained as the result of a trader's silence concerning information that is not freely available to everyone is a manipulation or deception prohibited by Section 10(b) and Rule 10b-5. In essence, the users of nonpublic information are treated like insiders if they can be classified as tippees.

A **tippee** is a person who learns of nonpublic information from an insider. In essence, a tippee is viewed as a temporary insider. A tippee is liable for the use of nonpublic information because an insider should not be allowed to do indirectly what he or she cannot do directly. In other words, a tippee is liable for trading or passing on information that is nonpublic.

The use of nonpublic information for financial gain has not been prohibited entirely. For example, in one case, a financial printer had been hired to print corporate takeover bids. An employee of the printer was able to deduce the identities of both the acquiring companies and the companies targeted for takeover. Without disclosing the knowledge about the prospective takeover bids, the employee purchased stock in the target companies and then sold it for a profit immediately after the takeover attempts were made public. He was indicted and convicted for having violated Section 10(b) and Rule 10b-5. The Supreme Court reversed, holding that the defendant had no duty to reveal the nonpublic information, since he was not in a fiduciary position with respect to either the acquiring or the acquired company.

In another case the U.S. Supreme Court further narrowed a tippee's liability. The Court ruled that a tippee becomes liable under Section 10(b) only if the tipper breaches a fiduciary duty to the business organization or fellow shareholders. Therefore, if the tipper communicated nonpublic information for reasons other than personal gain, neither the tipper nor the tippee could be liable for a securities violation.

These two Supreme Court cases have made it more difficult for the SEC to control the use of nonpublic information. However, the SEC has successfully argued that a person should be considered to be a temporary insider if that person conveys nonpublic information that was to have been kept confidential. This philosophy has become known as the **misappropriation theory** of insider trading. Case 17.3 approves the misappropriation theory.

 case **17.3**

UNITED STATES v. O'HAGAN
117 S. Ct. 2199 (1997)

GINSBURG, J.: . . . Respondent James Herman O'Hagan was a partner in the law firm of Dorsey & Whitney in Minneapolis, Minnesota. In July 1988, Grand Metropolitan PLC (Grand Met), a company based in London, England, retained Dorsey & Whitney as local counsel to represent Grand Met regarding a potential tender offer for the common stock of the Pillsbury Company, headquartered in Minneapolis. Both Grand Met and Dorsey & Whitney took precautions to protect the confidentiality of Grand Met's tender offer plans. O'Hagan did no work on the Grand Met representation. Dorsey & Whitney withdrew from representing Grand Met on September 9, 1988. Less than a month later, on October 4, 1988, Grand Met publicly announced its tender offer for Pillsbury stock.

[continued]

On August 18, 1988, while Dorsey & Whitney was still representing Grand Met, O'Hagan began purchasing call options for Pillsbury stock. Each option gave him the right to purchase 100 shares of Pillsbury stock by a specified date in September 1988. Later in August and in September, O'Hagan made additional purchases of Pillsbury call options. By the end of September, he owned 2,500 unexpired Pillsbury options. . . . O'Hagan also purchased, in September 1988, some 5,000 shares of Pillsbury common stock, at a price just under $39 per share. When Grand Met announced its tender offer in October, the price of Pillsbury stock rose to nearly $60 per share. O'Hagan then sold his Pillsbury call options and common stock, making a profit of more than $4.3 million.

The Securities and Exchange Commission (SEC or Commission) initiated an investigation into O'Hagan's transactions, culminating in a 57-count indictment. The indictment alleged that O'Hagan defrauded his law firm and its client, Grand Met, by using for his own trading purposes material, nonpublic information regarding Grand Met's planned tender offer. . . .

A divided panel of the Court of Appeals for the Eighth Circuit reversed all of O'Hagan's convictions. Liability under §10(b) and Rule 10b-5, the Eighth Circuit held, may not be grounded on the "misappropriation theory" of securities fraud on which the prosecution relied. . . .

Decisions of the Courts of Appeals are in conflict on the propriety of the misappropriation theory under §10(b) and Rule 10b-5. . . . We granted certiorari and now reverse the Eighth Circuit's judgment. . . .

Under the "traditional" or "classical theory" of insider trading liability, §10(b) and Rule 10b-5 are violated when a corporate insider trades in the securities of his corporation on the basis of material, nonpublic information. . . .

The "misappropriation theory" holds that a person commits fraud "in connection with" a securities transaction, and thereby violates §10(b) and Rule 10b-5, when he misappropriates confidential information for securities trading purposes, in breach of a duty owed to the source of the information. Under this theory, a fiduciary's undisclosed, self-serving use of a principal's information to purchase or sell securities, in breach of a duty of loyalty and confidentiality, defrauds the principal of the exclusive use of that information. In lieu of premising liability on a fiduciary relationship between company insider and purchaser or seller of the company's stock, the misappropriation theory premises liability on a fiduciary-turned-trader's deception of those who entrusted him with access to confidential information.

The two theories are complementary, each addressing efforts to capitalize on nonpublic information through the purchase or sale of securities. The classical theory targets a corporate insider's breach of duty to shareholders with whom the insider transacts; the misappropriation theory outlaws trading on the basis of non-public information by a corporate "outsider" in breach of a duty owed not to a trading party, but to the source of the information. The misappropriation theory is thus designed to protect the integrity of the securities markets against abuses by outsiders to a corporation who have access to confidential information that will affect the corporation's security price when revealed, but who owe no fiduciary or other duty to that corporation's shareholders.

In this case, the indictment alleged that O'Hagan, in breach of a duty of trust and confidence he owed to his law firm, Dorsey & Whitney, and to its client, Grand Met, traded on the basis of nonpublic information regarding Grand Met's planned tender offer for Pillsbury common stock. This conduct, the Government charged, constituted a fraudulent device in connection with the purchase and sale of securities.

We agree with the Government that misappropriation, as just defined, satisfies §10(b)'s requirement that chargeable conduct involve a "deceptive device or contrivance" used "in connection with" the purchase or sale of securities. We observe, first, that misappropriators, as the Government describes them, deal in deception. A fiduciary who "[pretends] loyalty to the principal while secretly converting the principal's information for personal gain," "dupes" or defrauds the principal. . . .

Deception through nondisclosure is central to the theory of liability for which the Government seeks recognition. As counsel for the Government stated in explanation of the theory at oral argument: "To satisfy the common law rule that a trustee may not use the property that [has] been entrusted [to] him, there would have to be consent. To satisfy the requirement of the Securities Act that there be no deception, there would only have to be disclosure." . . .

[F]ull disclosure forecloses liability under the misappropriation theory: Because the deception essential to the misappropriation theory involves feigning fidelity to the source of information, if the fiduciary discloses to the source that he plans to trade on the nonpublic information, there is no "deceptive device" and thus no §10(b) violation—although the fiduciary-turned-trader may remain liable under state law for breach of a duty of loyalty.

We turn next to the §10(b) requirement that the misappropriator's deceptive use of information be "in connection with the purchase or sale of [a] security." This element is satisfied because the fiduciary's fraud is consummated, not when the fiduciary gains the confidential information, but when, without disclosure to his principal, he uses the information to purchase or sell securities. The securities transaction and the breach of duty thus coincide. This is so even though the person or entity defrauded is not the other party to the trade; but is, instead, the source of the nonpublic information. A misappropriator who trades on the basis of material, nonpublic information, in short, gains his advantageous market position through deception; he deceives the source of the information and simultaneously harms members of the investing public.

The misappropriation theory targets information of a sort that misappropriators ordinarily capitalize upon to gain no-risk profits through the purchase or sale of securities. . . .

The misappropriation theory comports with §10(b)'s language, which requires deception "in connection with the purchase or sale of any security," not deception of an identifiable purchaser or seller. The theory is also well-turned to an animating purpose of the Exchange Act: to insure honest securities markets and thereby promote investor confidence. Although informational disparity is inevitable in the securities markets, investors likely would hesitate to venture their capital in a market where trading based on misappropriated nonpublic information is unchecked by law. An investor's informational disadvantage vis-à-vis a misappropriator with material, nonpublic information stems from contrivance, not luck; it is a disadvantage that cannot be overcome with research or skill.

In sum, considering the inhibiting impact on market participation of trading on misappropriated information, and the congressional purposes underlying §10(b), it makes scant sense to hold a lawyer like O'Hagan a §10(b) violator if he works for a law firm representing the target of a tender offer, but not if he works for a law firm representing the bidder. The text of the statute requires no such result. The misappropriation at issue here was properly made the subject of a §10(b) charge because it meets the statutory requirement that there be "deceptive" conduct "in connection with" securities transactions. . . .

. . . [T]he misappropriation theory, as we have examined and explained it in this opinion, is both consistent with the statute and with our precedent. Vital to our decision that criminal liability may be sustained under the misappropriation theory, we emphasize, are two sturdy safeguards Congress has provided regarding scienter. To establish a criminal violation of Rule 10b-5, the Government must prove that a person "willfully" violated the provision. Furthermore, a defendant may not be imprisoned for violating Rule 10b-5 if he proves that he had no knowledge of the rule. . . .

The Eighth Circuit erred in holding that the misappropriation theory is inconsistent with §10(b). The Court of Appeals may address on remand O'Hagan's other challenges to his convictions under §10(b) and Rule 10b-5. . . .

Reversed and remanded.

KEY POINTS

- The "traditional" or "classical theory" of insider trading is complemented by the "misappropriation theory" because each targets different sources that undermine the integrity of the purchase or sale of securities.
- The misappropriation theory is focused on the deception of a person with nonpublic information obtained from others using that information to his or her own benefit.
- Liability is based on secretly using the information. The trader must offer full disclosure of his or her intention to no longer keep the information confidential.
- Those who misappropriate nonpublic information to gain an advantage in trading over other traders undermine participation in securities markets.

The SEC continues to focus its enforcement efforts on the misuse of nonpublic information at all levels of transactions. The SEC's efforts are aided by the fact that the civil penalty for gaining illegal profits with nonpublic information is three times the profits gained. In addition, controlling persons who fail to prevent these violations by employees may be civilly liable for the greater amount of triple damages or $1,000,000.

The penalties were increased to their current levels by the Insider Trading and Securities Fraud Enforcement Act of 1988. This law also provides that suits alleging the illegal use of nonpublic information may be filed within a five-year period after the wrongful transaction. This period, being substantially longer than the one year/three years limitation periods for other federal securities violations, illustrates the emphasis Congress has placed on preventing trading on nonpublic information.

Don't be tempted to take advantage of nonpublic information if you are an insider within your company.

ADDITIONAL CIVIL LIABILITY

In 1990, Congress expressed its concern for enforcement of the securities laws. In that year, the Securities Enforcement Remedies Act became law. This legislation provides that civil fines of up to $500,000 per organization and $100,000 per individual may be imposed and collected by the courts. In addition, an individual found to have violated the securities laws may be prohibited by the court from serving as an officer or director of a business organization. These fines and this prohibition from service can be utilized, at the judge's discretion, when a party in a civil case is found to have violated the securities laws. There does not have to be any proof of a criminal violation for these fines to be imposed.

Furthermore, Section 18 of the Securities Exchange Act of 1934 imposes liability on a theory of fraud on any person who shall make or cause to be made any false and misleading statements of material fact in any application, report, or document filed under the act. This liability favors both purchasers and sellers. A plaintiff must prove that the defendant knowingly made a false statement, that plaintiff relied on the false or misleading statement, and that plaintiff suffered damage.

Two distinctions between this section of the 1934 Act and Sections 11 and 12 of the 1933 Act are noteworthy. First, the requirement that an intent to deceive be proven under Section 18 means that the defendant's good faith is a defense. Good faith exists when a person acts without knowledge that the statement is false and misleading. In other words, freedom from fraud is a defense under an action based on Section 18. There is no liability under this section for simple negligence. Second, the plaintiff in a Section 18 case must prove reliance on the false or misleading filing. The simple fact that the filing is inaccurate is not sufficient. In a Section 11 or 12 case under the 1933 Act, the plaintiff does not have to establish reliance.

"Securities fraud class-actions settlements in the U.S. rose 39 percent to more than $3.8 billion in 2009."

–Margaret Cronin Fisk, *Bloomberg.com,* **March 24, 2010**

The Sarbanes-Oxley Act extends the statute of limitations for civil actions under the 1934 Act. Lawsuits must be filed within two years of the time the wrong was discovered (or should have been) and at least within five years of the wrongful act. The expansion of civil liability under the 1934 Act encourages settlement in many cases. Although the number of class-action securities

table 17.2 Largest Securities Class-Action Settlements (2005–2007)		
Dollar Amount of Settlement	**Company**	**Year**
$7.2 billion	Enron	2006
$6.2 billion	WorldCom	2005
$3.2 billion	Tyco	2007

cases increased due to the 2008 market decline, the largest settlements come from the accounting scandals uncovered in 2000 and 2001. Table 17.2 summarizes some of these larger civil settlements.

CRIMINAL LIABILITY

The 1934 Act provides for criminal sanctions for willful violations of its provisions or the rules adopted under it. Liability is imposed for false material statements in applications, reports, documents, and registration statements. In response to the corporate scandals occurring during the beginning of the twenty-first century, Congress in 2002 increased the criminal penalties for violating the Securities Exchange Act of 1934. An individual found guilty of filing false or misleading documents with the SEC may be fined up to $5,000,000 and imprisoned for up to 20 years. A business organization found guilty of filing with the SEC false or misleading documents may be subject to a fine up to $25,000,000. An individual guilty of securities fraud may face a prison sentence of up to 25 years. These increased sanctions emphasize the seriousness with which all businesspeople must treat compliance with securities regulations.

The penalties are not theoretical. Sixteen officials from Enron have pled guilty and face a variety of prison terms. The CEO of WorldCom has been convicted and sentenced to 25 years in prison. The names of other former executives became commonly known because serious prison sentences get the public's attention. Whether these examples serve as deterrents for future fraudulent behavior remains to be seen.

Criminal liability is an important consideration for officers and directors as well as for accountants. Accountants have been found guilty of a crime for failure to disclose important facts to shareholder-investors. Compliance with generally accepted accounting principles is not an absolute defense. The critical issue in such cases is whether the financial statements as a whole fairly present the financial condition of the company and whether they accurately report operations for the covered periods. If they do not, the second issue is whether the accountant acted in good faith. Compliance with generally accepted accounting principles is evidence of good faith, but such evidence is not necessarily conclusive. Lack of criminal intent is the defense usually asserted by accountants charged with a crime. They usually admit mistakes or even negligence but deny any criminal wrongdoing. Proof of motive is not required.

As with issues of civil liability, most cases involving potential criminal liability are litigated under Section 10(b) and Rule 10b-5.

concept *summary*

Securities Exchange Act of 1934

SECTION 10(B)

Purpose: Creates liability for use of mail or any instrumentality of interstate commerce to defraud any person in connection with the purchase or sale of any security.

Plaintiff's case: Proof of defendant's intent to deceive through use of false information or nondisclosure of truthful information; plaintiff's reliance on fraudulent documents; and damages.

Defendant's defenses: No actual fraud was involved; only aided or abetted fraud; information was not material.

Civil liability: Person in violation of §10(b) is liable for actual damages, court costs, and reasonable attorney fees.

SECTION 16(B)

Purpose: Creates strict liability for any insider making a profit on issuer's securities during any six-month period.

Plaintiff's case: Proof of the short-swing nature of the profitable transaction.

Defendant's defenses: Proof of no short-swing transaction; good faith (lack of intent) is no defense.

Civil fines: Up to three times the illegal profits; ban from service as director or officer.

SECTION 18

Purpose: Imposes liability for fraudulently filing false or misleading documents with the SEC or any exchange.

Plaintiff's case: Proof of defendant's intent to make false or misleading documents filed; plaintiff's reliance on documents filed; and damages.

Defendant's defenses: Freedom from fraud; good faith—no intent to defraud; no reliance by plaintiff on documents filed.

CRIMINAL LIABILITY

For securities fraud: Up to 25 years in prison.

For false or misleading documents filed: $5,000,000 fine or 20 years in prison or both per individual; $25,000,000 fine per organization.

For trading on nonpublic information: $1 million fine or 10 years in prison or both per individual; $10 million fine per organization.

Other Considerations

In addition to understanding the historical nature of securities laws, every businessperson and investor should be familiar with two additional topics. First, in the next section, we present materials related to private parties suing to enforce the federal securities laws. Second, in the last section of this chapter, you should gain an understanding of how states also regulate the issuance and sale of securities.

PRIVATE SECURITIES LITIGATION REFORM ACT OF 1995

In 1994, the Supreme Court held that liability under Section 10(b) and Rule 10b-5 did not extend to parties aiding and abetting the primary violator.[3] The following year, Congress passed and President Clinton signed the **Private Securities Litigation Reform Act (PSLRA).** The law made it clear the Court's decision would not be expanded and set up other hurdles to limit the number

"Congress amended the securities laws in 1995 to allow the Securities and Exchange Commission to bring actions against secondary violators that aid and abet securities fraud. Congress wisely declined to extend that right to private parties, out of concern of abusive securities litigation."

–Paul S. Atkins, "Stoneridge and the Rule of Law," *The Wall Street Journal,* **January 25, 2008**

[3]*Central Bank of Denver, N.A. v. First Interstate Bank of Denver, N.A., 114 S.Ct. 1439 (1994).*

table 17.3 Number of Federal Securities Fraud Class Actions (filed each year)

Year	Number of Cases
2002	224
2003	192
2004	228
2005	182
2006	119
2007	177
2008	223
2009	168
2010	176
2011	188
2012	152
2013	166

Source: Stanford Law School Securities Class Action Clearinghouse in cooperation with Cornerstone Research. Retrieved from http://securities.stanford.edu/clearinghouse.research/2010_YIR/Cornerstone_Research_Filing_2010_YIR.pdf.

of class-action claims under federal securities law. Indeed, the PSLRA clarified that only the SEC can pursue claims against third parties not directly responsible for the securities law violation. This part of the law helps form the basis for the decision in Case 17.1.

The PSLRA requires any private plaintiff to allege with specificity the scienter, or intent, of a company or its executives when filing a claim under Section 10(b) and Rule 10b-5. A plaintiff "must plead facts rendering an inference of scienter at least as likely as any plausible opposing inference."[4]

Congress fortified the PSLRA by passing the Securities Litigation Uniform Standards Act of 1998 (SLUSA). SLUSA supported the aims of curbing abusive securities fraud litigation by not allowing plaintiffs to file claims in state courts that PSLRA prevented in federal courts. However, Congress did not choose to eliminate the fraud-on-the-market presumption when it enacted PSLRA. Fraud-on-the-market theory, described by the Supreme Court in *Basic Inc. v. Levinson*,[5] substitutes for proof of direct reliance by each member of a class so that class certification is easier. Recently, the Supreme Court revisited fraud-on-the-market theory in Case 17.4.

Congress, through the PSLRA, limits the amount of damages private plaintiffs can recover and restricts attorney fees. This law also provides requirements for the appointment of lead plaintiffs in securities class-action cases. Even with these restrictions, there are many securities class-actions filed each year. Table 17.3 details the number of these cases during this century. While it appears the number of securities litigation is declining, new scandals and crises provide opportunities for more cases.

[4]*Tellabs, Inc. v. Mabor Issues & Rights, Ltd.*, 127 S.Ct. 2499 (2007).
[5]*Basic, Inc. v. Levinson*, 485 U.S. 224 (1988).

HALLIBURTON CO. v. ERICA P. JOHN FUND, INC.
134 S.Ct. 2398 (2014)

ROBERTS, C.J.: Investors can recover damages in a private securities fraud action only if they prove that they relied on the defendant's misrepresentation in deciding to buy or sell a company's stock. In *Basic Inc. v. Levinson*, 485 U. S. 224 (1988), we held that investors could satisfy this reliance requirement by invoking a presumption that the price of stock traded in an efficient market reflects all public, material information—including material misstatements. In such a case, we concluded, anyone who buys or sells the stock at the market price may be considered to have relied on those misstatements.

We also held, however, that a defendant could rebut this presumption in a number of ways, including by showing that the alleged misrepresentation did not actually affect the stock's price—that is, that the misrepresentation had no "price impact." The questions presented are whether we should overrule or modify *Basic's* presumption of reliance and, if not, whether defendants should nonetheless be afforded an opportunity in securities class action cases to rebut the presumption at the class certification stage, by showing a lack of price impact.

Respondent Erica P. John Fund, Inc. (EPJ Fund), is the lead plaintiff in a putative class action against Halliburton and one of its executives (collectively Halliburton) alleging violations of Section 10(b) of the Securities Exchange Act of 1934, and Securities and Exchange Commission Rule 10b-5. According to EPJ Fund, between June 3, 1999, and December 7, 2001, Halliburton made a series of misrepresentations regarding its potential liability in asbestos litigation, its expected revenue from certain construction contracts, and the anticipated benefits of its merger with another company—all in an attempt to inflate the price of its stock. Halliburton subsequently made a number of corrective disclosures, which, EPJ Fund contends, caused the company's stock price to drop and investors to lose money. . . .

Halliburton urges us to overrule *Basic's* presumption of reliance and to instead require every securities fraud plaintiff to prove that he actually relied on the defendant's misrepresentation in deciding to buy or sell a company's stock. Before overturning a long-settled precedent, however, we require "special justification," not just an argument that the precedent was wrongly decided. . . . Halliburton has failed to make that showing.

Section 10(b) of the Securities Exchange Act of 1934 and the Securities and Exchange Commission's Rule 10b-5 prohibit making any material misstatement or omission in connection with the purchase or sale of any security. Although Section 10(b) does not create an express private cause of action, we have long recognized an implied private cause of action to enforce the provision and its implementing regulation. See *Blue Chip Stamps v. Manor Drug Stores*, 421 U.S. 723 (1975). To recover damages for violations of section 10(b) and Rule 10b-5, a plaintiff must prove "(1) a material misrepresentation or omission by the defendant; (2) scienter; (3) a connection between the misrepresentation or omission and the purchase or sale of a security; (4) reliance upon the misrepresentation or omission; (5) economic loss; and (6) loss causation." *Amgen Inc. v. Connecticut Retirement Plans and Trust Funds*, 133 S. Ct. 1184 (2013)

The reliance element "ensures that there is a proper connection between a defendant's misrepresentation and a plaintiff's injury." "The traditional (and most direct) way a plaintiff can demonstrate reliance is by showing that he was aware of a company's statement and engaged in a relevant transaction—e.g., purchasing common stock—based on that specific misrepresentation."

In *Basic*, however, we recognized that requiring such direct proof of reliance "would place an unnecessarily unrealistic evidentiary burden on the Rule 10b-5 plaintiff who has traded on an impersonal market." That is because, even assuming an investor could prove that he was aware of the misrepresentation, he would still have to "show a speculative state of facts, i.e., how he would have acted . . . if the misrepresentation had not been made."

We also noted that "[r]equiring proof of individualized reliance" from every securities fraud plaintiff "effectively would . . . prevent[ ] [plaintiffs] from proceeding with a class action" in Rule 10b-5 suits. If every plaintiff had to prove direct reliance on the defendant's misrepresentation, "individual issues then would . . . overwhelm[ ] the common ones," making certification under Rule 23(b)(3) inappropriate.

To address these concerns, *Basic* held that securities fraud plaintiffs can in certain circumstances satisfy the reliance element of a Rule 10b-5 action by invoking a rebuttable presumption of reliance, rather than proving direct reliance on a misrepresentation. The

Court based that presumption on what is known as the "fraud-on-the-market" theory, which holds that "the market price of shares traded on well-developed markets reflects all publicly available information, and, hence, any material misrepresentations." The Court also noted that, rather than scrutinize every piece of public information about a company for himself, the typical "investor who buys or sells stock at the price set by the market does so in reliance on the integrity of that price"—the belief that it reflects all public, material information. As a result, whenever the investor buys or sells stock at the market price, his "reliance on any public material misrepresentations . . . may be presumed for purposes of a Rule 10b-5 action."

Based on this theory, a plaintiff must make the following showings to demonstrate that the presumption of reliance applies in a given case: (1) that the alleged misrepresentations were publicly known, (2) that they were material, (3) that the stock traded in an efficient market, and (4) that the plaintiff traded the stock between the time the misrepresentations were made and when the truth was revealed.

At the same time, *Basic* emphasized that the presumption of reliance was rebuttable rather than conclusive. Specifically, "[a]ny showing that severs the link between the alleged misrepresentation and either the price received (or paid) by the plaintiff, or his decision to trade at a fair market price, will be sufficient to rebut the presumption of reliance." So for example, if a defendant could show that the alleged misrepresentation did not, for whatever reason, actually affect the market price, or that a plaintiff would have bought or sold the stock even had he been aware that the stock's price was tainted by fraud, then the presumption of reliance would not apply. In either of those cases, a plaintiff would have to prove that he directly relied on the defendant's misrepresentation in buying or selling the stock. . . .

Even if plaintiffs need not directly prove price impact to invoke the *Basic* presumption, Halliburton contends that defendants should at least be allowed to defeat the presumption at the class certification stage through evidence that the misrepresentation did not in fact affect the stock price. We agree.

There is no dispute that defendants may introduce such evidence at the merits stage to rebut the *Basic* presumption. *Basic* itself "made clear that the presumption was just that, and could be rebutted by appropriate evidence," including evidence that the asserted misrepresentation (or its correction) did not affect the market price of the defendant's stock.

Nor is there any dispute that defendants may introduce price impact evidence at the class certification stage, so long as it is for the purpose of countering a plaintiff's showing of market efficiency, rather than directly rebutting the presumption. As EPJ Fund acknowledges, "[o]f course . . . defendants can introduce evidence at class certification of lack of price impact as some evidence that the market is not efficient. . . ."

. . . As we explained in *Basic*, [a]ny showing that severs the link between the alleged misrepresentation and . . . the price received (or paid) by the plaintiff . . . will be sufficient to rebut the presumption of reliance" because "the basis for finding that the fraud had been transmitted through market price would be gone." And without the presumption of reliance, a Rule 10b-5 suit cannot proceed as a class action: Each plaintiff would have to prove reliance individually, so common issues would not "predominate" over individual ones, as required by Rule 23(b)(3). Price impact is thus an essential precondition for any Rule 10b-5 class action. While *Basic* allows plaintiffs to establish that precondition indirectly, it does not require courts to ignore a defendant's direct, more salient evidence showing that the alleged misrepresentation did not actually affect the stock's market price and, consequently, that the *Basic* presumption does not apply. . . .

More than 25 years ago, we held that plaintiffs could satisfy the reliance element of the Rule 10b-5 cause of action by invoking a presumption that a public, material misrepresentation will distort the price of stock traded in an efficient market, and that anyone who purchases the stock at the market price may be considered to have done so in reliance on the misrepresentation. We adhere to that decision and decline to modify the prerequisites for invoking the presumption of reliance. But to maintain the consistency of the presumption with the class certification requirements of Federal Rule of Civil Procedure 23, defendants must be afforded an opportunity before class certification to defeat the presumption through evidence that an alleged misrepresentation did not actually affect the market price of the stock.

Because the courts below denied Halliburton that opportunity, we vacate the judgment of the Court of Appeals for the Fifth Circuit and remand the case for further proceedings consistent with this opinion.

It is so ordered.

KEY POINTS

- The "fraud-on-the-market" theory holds that the price of shares that are traded on developed markets reflect all publicly available information about the corporation, including any material misrepresentations made by the corporation.
- The *Basic Inc. v. Levinson* decision permitted plaintiffs to utilize the "fraud-on-the-market" theory to show a link between a misrepresentation by a corporation and the required reliance on that misrepresentation to bring a Rule 10b-5 action.
- The *Basic* presumption makes it easier for plaintiffs to address a potential Rule 10b-5 violation as a class action.
- The *Halliburton* decision maintains the use of the *Basic* presumption of reliance on material misrepresentations. However, it clarifies that defendants should have an opportunity to present evidence that the misrepresentation did not affect the market price of the stock. Defeating the presumption, if successful, would make it difficult for plaintiffs to obtain class-action certification.

STATE BLUE SKY LAWS

LO 17-5

Throughout their history, state regulations regarding securities laws commonly have been referred to as **blue sky laws**—probably because they were intended to protect the potential investor from buying "a piece of the attractive blue sky" (worthless or risky securities) without financial and other information about what was being purchased. The blue sky laws can apply to securities subject to federal laws as well as to those securities exempt from the federal statutes. It is clearly established that the federal laws do not preempt the existence of state blue sky laws. Due to their broad application, any person associated with issuing or thereafter transferring securities should survey the blue sky laws passed by the various states.

Although the existence of federal securities laws has influenced state legislatures, enactment of blue sky laws has not been uniform. Indeed, states typically have enacted laws that contain provisions similar to the antifraud provisions, the registration of securities provisions, the registration of securities brokers and dealers provisions, or a combination of these provisions of the federal laws. To bring some similarity to the various blue sky laws, the Uniform Securities Act was proposed for adoption by all states beginning in 1956. Since that time, the Uniform Securities Act has been the model for blue sky laws. A majority of states have used the uniform proposal as a guideline when enacting or amending their blue sky laws.

Registration Requirements Despite the trend toward uniformity, state laws still vary a great deal in their methods of regulating both the distribution of securities and the practices of the securities industry within each state. For example, state regulations concerning the requirements of registering securities vary widely. Some states require *registration by notification,* other states require *registration by qualification.* Registration by notification allows issuers to offer securities for sale automatically after a stated time period expires unless the administrative agency takes action to prevent the offering. This is very similar to the registration process under the Securities Act of 1933. Registration by qualification usually requires a more detailed disclosure by the issuer. Under this type of regulation, a security cannot be offered for sale until the administrative agency grants the issuer a license or certificate to sell securities.

In an attempt to resolve some of this conflict over the registration procedure, the drafters of the Uniform Securities Act may have compounded the problem. This act adopts the registration by notification process for an issuer who has demonstrated stability and performance. Registration by qualification is required by those issuers who do not have a proven record and who are not subject to the Securities Act of 1933. In addition, the Uniform Securities Act created a third procedure—*registration by coordination.* For those issuers of securities who must register with the SEC, duplicate documents are filed with the state's administrative agency. Unless a state official objects, the state registration becomes effective automatically when the federal registration statement is deemed effective.

Exemptions   To further compound the confusion about blue sky laws, various exemptions of the securities or transactions have been adopted by the states. Four basic exemptions from blue sky laws have been identified. Every state likely has enacted at least one and perhaps a combination of these exemptions. Among these common four are the exemptions:

1. For an isolated transaction.
2. For an offer or sale to a limited number of offerees or purchasers within a stated time period.
3. For a private offering.
4. For a sale if the number of holders after the sale does not exceed a specified number.

The second type of exemption probably is the most common exemption, because it is part of the Uniform Securities Act. Nevertheless, states vary on whether the exemption applies to offerees or to purchasers. There also is great variation on the maximum number of such offerees or purchasers involved. That number likely ranges between 5 and 35, depending on the applicable blue sky law. The time period for the offers or purchases, as the case may be, also may vary; however, 12 months seems to be the most common period.

Usually the applicable time limitation is worded to read, for example, "*any* 12-month time period." In essence, this language means that each day starts a new time period running. For example, assume a security is exempt from blue sky registration requirements if the issuer sells (or offers to sell) securities to no more than 35 investors during any 12-month period. Furthermore, assume the following transactions occur, with each investor being a different person or entity:

- On February 1, 2013, issuer sells to five investors.
- On June 1, 2013, issuer sells to ten investors.
- On September 1, 2013, issuer sells to ten investors.
- On December 1, 2013, issuer sells to five investors.
- On March 1, 2014, issuer sells to five investors.
- On May 1, 2014, issuer sells to ten investors.

Only 30 investors are involved during the 12-month period following February 1, 2013. However, 40 investors are purchasers during the 12 months following June 1, 2013. Therefore, this security and the transactions involved are not exempt from the blue sky law. Civil as well as criminal liability may result for failure to comply with applicable legal regulations.

Although blue sky laws may cause confusion because of their variation, ignorance of the state legal requirements is no defense. This confusion is aggravated when the businessperson considers the further applicability of federal securities laws. To diminish this confusion, any person involved in the issuance or subsequent transfer of securities should consult with lawyers and accountants as well as other experts who have a working knowledge of securities regulations.

Sarbanes-Oxley Act of 2002

LO 17-6

When the collapse of Enron was followed by the even larger accounting fraud and bankruptcy of WorldCom, congressional response was passage of the **Sarbanes-Oxley Act of 2002.** This law is named for its sponsors—Senator Paul Sarbanes, a Democrat from Maryland, and Representative Michael Oxley, an Ohio Republican. The Sarbanes-Oxley Act receives mixed reviews; however, most businesspeople agree it has overwhelming positive impacts on the way business is conducted and audited. The act applies to all public companies in the United States and can apply to international companies if they are registered with the SEC. All accounting firms that have auditing work with these companies also are affected by the Sarbanes-Oxley Act rules.

Sarbanes-Oxley is "the most significant change to securities law since they were put into effect in the mid-1930s"

—Dennis M. Nalley Chairman of Price-waterhouse Coopers

REVITALIZATION OF SEC

Through the Sarbanes-Oxley Act of 2002 and in response to the corporate scandals of the first few years of this century, Congress increased the authority it delegated to the SEC. A primary way of accomplishing this reinvigoration of a 70-year-old agency was to increase its budget. Because the budget is not controlled solely by Congress, there initially was some controversy with the Bush Administration as to the amount of the increase. The proposed increase of more than 75 percent of the SEC budget was not accomplished in one year; however, the SEC's increased budget has led to a more active SEC.

Sarbanes-Oxley (SOX) increases the SEC's power over many of the governance issues discussed in this chapter. In addition, Congress empowered the SEC to increase corporate accountability. The SEC instituted rules for internal checks and balances and various levels of sign-off to encourage financial disclosure.

"Our goal is to effectively balance the goal of providing shareholders with timely disclosure of accurate and complete compensation information with the need to prevent strategic company information from being revealed to competitors and damaging a company."

—John J. Castellani President of Business Roundtable

ACCOUNTING REFORMS

Sarbanes-Oxley creates the Public Company Accounting Oversight Board (PCAOB). This Board consists of five members appointed by the SEC commissioners. The PCAOB reports to the commissioners. Congress viewed accounting firms as a major contributor to the corporate scandals involving Enron, WorldCom, HealthSouth, Tyco, and others. This view is based, in part, on the role that the Arthur Andersen accounting firm played with Enron and WorldCom.

See Case 15.1 clarifying the appointment and removal process of PCAOB members.

The PCAOB is given oversight of accounting firms that audit public companies. One of the first steps required of accounting firms was the separation of the auditing and consulting functions. The belief is that firms tainted their independence in the auditing function because they made so much more money consulting with these same corporate clients. This separation of the auditing and consulting functions is the reason why Arthur Andersen consultants formed a separate organization, which is now called Accenture. The management consulting services of PricewaterhouseCoopers (PWC) were sold to IBM, so that PWC can concentrate on its tax and audit practices.

The PCAOB requires that auditing firms refrain from conducting a variety of nonauditing services. These services include bookkeeping, system designs and implementation, appraisals and valuations, actuarial services, human resources functions, and investment banking.

The effectiveness of the role of PCAOB is still being determined. Some critics question the Sarbanes-Oxley Act for not making this Board truly an independent agency. Others believe that having the Board report within the SEC strengthens the new and existing administrative structure. In the years ahead, it will be interesting to observe the PCAOB's role in governing the effectiveness of public accounting firms.

CORPORATE GOVERNANCE

Over time, this area of regulation may be the major contribution of the Sarbanes-Oxley Act. Although other parts of the law get more attention because of the financial impact, restructuring how corporations govern themselves and the governance requirements required by the SEC and the PCAOB are of critical importance. Under this heading, several items relate to the audit of public companies.

Sarbanes-Oxley focuses on increasing the independence of the auditors. Congress seeks to ensure that auditors maintain the trust of the public and the corporate shareholders and not the loyalty of the corporate officers and directors. This effort principally is oriented to the public company's audit committee. Each member of this committee must be independent from the control of the company. No longer may a public company place its finance officer or other employee on the audit committee.

These legal requirements allow the audit firm to do what it historically did—review the company's finances and ensure accuracy.

Further, at least one member of the audit committee has to be a financial expert. To qualify as a financial expert, it must be shown that through experience or education this person has an understanding of generally accepted accounting practices (GAAP), financial statements, audits of public companies, internal audit controls, and the functions of an audit committee.

Sarbanes-Oxley requires that the auditor report to this independent audit committee. The auditor should not have a close working relationship with the company's CFO, accounting staff, and other company officials. In addition, the audit partner of the auditing firm must rotate off the engagement every five years. Auditors also must preserve audit records for seven years.

Similar to the audit-related changes, many of which seek to reduce conflicts of interest or personal connections that could interfere with objective evaluation, board qualifications focus on independent directors. Except for controlled companies, the majority of directors on a public company board must be independent, and the definition for who qualifies as an independent director is stricter under new rules. Public companies must have audit, compensation, and nominating committees that include only independent directors. These changes in board composition encourage unbiased reviews for the long-term benefit of the companies and their investors.

FINANCIAL STATEMENTS AND CONTROLS

These requirements of the Sarbanes-Oxley Act have been the most controversial. One of the major reasons for the controversy is the cost associated with complying with these provisions. Section 302 of the law requires CEOs and CFOs to certify the accuracy of the quarterly and annual financial statements filed with the SEC. These officials also must certify the existence of internal financial controls. These controls are subject to an independent auditor's review, in the same manner that the financial statements must be audited. The certification of internal financial controls is mandated by Section 404 of Sarbanes-Oxley.

Because the compliance costs issue creates political debate, the SEC extended the beginning date of compliance for smaller companies to 2008. The SEC also offered guidelines to reduce the burden on larger companies in certifying internal reporting controls. These actions and the repetitive nature of complying with Section 404 seem to bring down the compliance costs. Each year since 2004, larger companies find efficiencies related to Section 404 certification.

Other evidence that Sarbanes-Oxley is having a positive impact is found in the number of restatements of financial reports. During 2007, there were fewer restatements than in 2006. This was the first year to show a decline since Sarbanes-Oxley was enacted. Other good news was that the amount or severity of the average restatement also declined. These trends indicate that the impact of Sarbanes-Oxley is positive.

An additional provision of Sarbanes-Oxley emphasizes the importance of accurate financial records. Despite the fact that corporate scandals caused shareholders to lose billions of dollars, corporate executives received millions in bonuses and incentive payments. Sarbanes-Oxley provides that whenever there is a restatement of the company's financial condition, executives must return any bonuses paid as a result of the incorrect financial statements. The law also prohibits personal loans from the company to its executives.

> The requirements of Section 404 "offered us an opportunity to look at our processes and in many cases improve them. We found our people really benefited from understanding the processes. It has made Staples a better company."
>
> **—John J. Mahoney CFO of Staples**

WHISTLEBLOWER PROTECTION

Finally, Sarbanes-Oxley provides protections for whistleblowers so that individuals are more willing to report the corruption that can lead to major scandals. Audit committees are required to adopt procedures ensuring that whistle-blowers' reports are taken seriously. Whistleblowers that suffer retaliation are able to recover civil damages and can be reinstated if terminated improperly. Recently, the Supreme Court ruled that Sarbanes-Oxley's provision for whistleblower protection includes not just employees but also outside lawyers and accountants who work as contractors for public companies and reveal fraud to their supervisors. Sidebar 17.5 discusses the decision. Whistleblower protection also is an important feature of the Dodd-Frank Act, described in the following section.

sidebar 17.5

Extending Whistleblower Protection

On March 4, 2014, in *Lawson v. FMR*, 134 S.Ct. 1158 (2014), the U.S. Supreme Court extended whistleblower protections of the Sarbanes-Oxley Act to private contractors of public companies. In reaching this decision, Justice Ruth Bader Ginsburg, writing for the majority, noted one of the financial scandals that led to Congress enacting Sarbanes-Oxley: Enron and its close relationship with accounting firm Arthur Andersen.

In Lawson, both plaintiffs were employees of privately held companies that provide advisory and management services to mutual funds. It is typical for mutual funds to have no employees but to rely on contractors for day-to-day operations. Each plaintiff raised concerns with supervisors about inaccurate financial documents and alleged retaliation based on raising such concerns. The mutual fund parent company maintained the plaintiffs were not covered by Sarbanes-Oxley because the law provides that companies may not "discharge, demote, suspend, threaten, harass or in any other manner discriminate against an employee" who reports wrongdoing.

Denying whistleblower protection to contractors of public companies would leave a "huge hole" in the law, the Court noted, and it is not reasonable to believe this was what Congress intended. Congress learned during hearings following the Enron scandal that led to Arthur Andersen's demise that both employees of Enron and contractors from Arthur Andersen attempted to report fraud and suffered retaliation as a result. Congress included whistleblower protection in Sarbanes-Oxley Act because, in complex securities transactions, "employees are often the only firsthand witnesses to the fraud." Now, whistleblower protection includes contractors of public companies as well as employees.

concept *summary*

Sarbanes-Oxley Act of 2002

INCREASED AUTHORITY TO SEC

- Mandates budgetary increases for SEC.
- Increases power of SEC over many of governance matters.
- Since 2002, SEC enforcement much more active.

ACCOUNTING REFORMS

- Creates Public Company Accounting Oversight Board.
- Oversight of auditing of public companies.
- Requires separation of auditing and consulting functions within accounting firms.

CORPORATE GOVERNANCE

- Increases independence of auditors.
- Requires audit committees to be independent with at least one member being a financial expert.
- Audit partner must rotate off engagement after five years.
- Auditors must preserve audit records for seven years.

- Majority of directors must meet the definition of independent.
- Audit, compensation, and nominating committees are comprised of independent directors only.

FINANCIAL STATEMENTS AND CONTROLS

- CEO and CFO must certify accuracy of financial statements.
- Also must certify existence of internal financial controls.
- Internal financial controls are subject to audit, just like financial statements.
- When restatement is made, executives must return any bonuses paid on incorrect financial statements.

WHISTLEBLOWER PROTECTION

- Audit committees must adopt procedures for whistle-blowing.
- Whistleblowers can recover damages for retaliation and request reinstatement.
- Whistleblowers include contractors as well as employees.

Dodd-Frank Wall Street Reform and Consumer Protection Act of 2010

Following the near collapse of the United States economy in the autumn of 2008 and the lingering adverse impact throughout 2009, Congress passed financial reforms in 2010. President Obama signed what has been called the most extensive reforms since the New Deal, and this massive bill became law on July 21, 2010. The changes in this law are summarized in Table 17.4. While it will take several years to see the full impact of the Dodd-Frank Act, this list demonstrates the extensive nature of these reforms.

There are numerous examples, in our history, when Congress created an administrative agency to ensure that the details contained in the legislation would be carried out. Chapter 15 discusses the principles of this form of government regulation, and we see the specifics of this policy in Chapter 16 (FTC and antitrust laws), this chapter (SEC and securities regulations), Chapter 18 (various agencies and consumer protection), Chapter 20 (EEOC and employment discrimination), Chapter 21 (various agencies and employment laws), and Chapter 22 (NLRB and labor laws).

What is striking about the Dodd-Frank Act is the way it addresses so many issues of reform. To accomplish its broad goals, Congress authorizes

---

table 17.4 Major Provisions of Dodd-Frank Wall Street Reform and Consumer Protection Act

- Enhances consumer protection
- Ends policy on "Too Big to Fail" bailouts
- Reforms Federal Reserve
- Creates mortgage reforms
- Regulates trading of derivatives
- Regulates hedge funds
- Regulates credit rating agencies
- Controls executive compensation and corporate governance
- Reforms regulations of banks and thrifts
- Regulates insurance industry
- Limits credit card interchange fees
- Reforms SEC and investor protections
- Regulates securitizations
- Regulates municipal securities
- Provides financial assistance to overcome mortgage crisis
- Disclosures to SEC of payments to U.S. or foreign governments related to commercial development of oil, natural gas, or minerals
- Disclosures to SEC concerning manufacturing of products derived from minerals from the Congo
- Limits U.S. loans to foreign governments unlikely to repay

Source: http://banking.senate.gov/public/_files/070110_Dodd_Frank_Wall_Street_Reform_comprehensive_summary_Final.pdf.

the creation of many new administrative organizations. Many of these new entities are housed within existing organizations. The following list highlights some of the new agencies:

- Consumer Financial Protection Board—CFPB (independent within Federal Reserve)
- Financial Stability Oversight Council—FSOC (independent)
- Federal Insurance Office—FIO (Treasury)
- Office of Financial Research—OFR (FSOC)
- Offices of Minority and Women Inclusion (within Bank and Securities Regulators)
- Office of Housing Counseling (HUD)
- Office of Credit Ratings (SEC)
- Investment Advisory Committee (SEC)
- Office of Investor Advocate (SEC)

What is most important to remember about these financial reforms is that Congress feels responsibility to react or respond to crises when they arise. The effectiveness of these reforms remains unknown since the full implementation of the Dodd-Frank Act has progressed slowly. History tells us that despite Congress's response to the 2008 financial recession with all these proposed reforms, another crisis will likely lead to more regulation.

One example of how this complex law is being implemented in stages concerns the whistleblower provisions. In 2011, the SEC approved final regulations allowing whistleblowers to report violations directly to the SEC. Businesses argued that the SEC should require employees to use a company's internal reporting systems to have protection under the Dodd-Frank Act. The SEC did not adopt this approach, and now the courts are divided about whether employees who do not report wrongdoing directly to the SEC qualify as whistleblowers under the act. The statute itself contains a conflict in the language. To resolve the debate might require an amendment to the statute or a ruling by the Supreme Court.

Jumpstart Our Business Startups (JOBS) Act of 2012

On April 5, 2012, President Obama signed into law a provision meant to help smaller businesses find the necessary capital to grow. The stated goals of the **JOBS Act** are to ease burdensome federal regulations and allow individuals to invest in start-ups through relaxed rules for some initial public offerings.

The most controversial aspects of the JOBS Act still are not fully implemented, so whether the relaxed regulation creates pathways or financial perils is not yet clear. One closely watched provision encourages new businesses to raise small amounts of investment dollars from many people, using the Internet to spread the investment opportunity, also known as *crowdfunding*. Of course, crowdfunding is not a new concept as charitable organizations and even some celebrities encouraging support for new movies have used small investments promoted through social media to generate a large pool of capital. It is unique, however, to see Congress and the SEC encourage such investment activity.

Title II of the JOBS Act allows companies to advertise or share publicly that they are seeking investments. Title III will allow a company to raise up to $1 million from investors by selling securities through crowdfunding intermediaries in a 12-month period. Similar crowdfunding mechanisms are permitted under some state laws.

Key Terms

Blue sky laws 535
Controlling person 511
Due diligence defense 515
Insider 525
Issuer 511
JOBS Act 542
Misappropriation
   theory 526
Posteffective period 512
Prefiling period 512

Private Securities Litigation
   Reform Act (PSLRA) 531
Prospectus 512
Registration statement 511
Sarbanes-Oxley Act of
   2002 537
Scienter 514
Securities Act of 1933 510
Securities and Exchange
   Commission (SEC) 510

Securities Exchange Act of
   1934 516
Security 509
Seller 511
Short-swing profits 525
Tippee 526
Tombstone ad 512
Underwriter 511
Waiting period 512

Review Questions and Problems

1. *What Is a Security?*

   W.J. Howey Company and Howey-in-the-Hills Service Inc. are Florida corporations under common control and management. Howey Company offers to sell to the public its orange grove, tree by tree. Howey-in-the-Hills Service Inc. offers these buyers a contract wherein the appropriate care, harvesting, and marketing of the oranges would be provided. Most of the buyers who sign the service contracts are nonresidents of Florida who have very little knowledge or skill needed to care for and harvest the oranges. These buyers are attracted by the expectation of profits. Is a sale of orange trees by the Howey Company and a sale of services by Howey-in-the-Hills Service Inc. a sale of a security? Why or why not?

2. *Securities and Exchange Commission*

   (a) When was this administrative agency created?

   (b) What types of regulatory authorities does the SEC have at its disposal?

The Securities Act of 1933: Going Public

3. *Parties Regulated*

   Who are the four types of parties governed by the 1933 Securities Act?

4. *Documents Involved*

   (a) What are the two important documents required by the Securities Act of 1933?

   (b) Under the provisions of the federal Securities Act of 1933, there are three important time periods concerning when securities may be sold or offered for sale. Name and describe these three time periods.

5. *Liability*

   To secure a loan, Rubin pledges stock that he represents as being marketable and worth approximately $1.7 million. In fact, the stock is nonmarketable and practically worthless. He is charged with violating the Securities Act of 1933. He claims that because no sale occurred, he is not guilty. Is he correct? Why or why not?

6. *Defenses*

   What are three defenses that might be used by a party charged with violating the Securities Act of 1933?

Securities Exchange Act of 1934: Being Public

7. *Section 10(b) and Rule 10b-5*

   (a) Section 10(b) of the Securities Exchange Act of 1934 and Rule 10b-5 are of fundamental importance in the law of securities regulations. What is the main purpose of this section and rule?

   (b) Do you suppose that an oral promise made and not performed can be the basis of arguing a party is guilty of defrauding another under §10(b) and Rule 10b-5?

8. *Insider Transactions*

   Donna, a corporate director, sold 100 shares of stock in her corporation on June 1, 2007. The selling price was $10.50 a share. Two months later, after the corporation had announced substantial losses for the second quarter of the year, Donna purchased 100 shares of the corporation's stock for $7.25 a share. Are there any problems with Donna's sale and purchase? Explain.

9. *Nonpublic Information*

   Eric Ethan, president of Inside-Outside Sports Equipment Company, has access to information which is not available to the general investor. What standard should Eric Ethan apply in deciding whether this information is so material as to prevent him from investing in his company prior to the information's public release?

10. *Additional Civil Liability*

    What is the purpose of Section 18 of the Securities Exchange Act of 1934?

11. *Criminal Liability*

    What are the dollar amounts related to fines and what are the number of years related to prison terms for those that violate the Securities Act of 1934?

Other Considerations

12. *Private Securities Litigation Reform Act of 1995*

    (a) What is the purpose of the PSLRA?

    (b) List four ways Congress accomplishes this purpose.

13. *State Blue Sky Laws*

    Why is it important for businesspeople to understand the role of state blue sky laws in addition to federal securities regulations?

Sarbanes-Oxley Act of 2002

14. *Revitalization of SEC*

    What was the primary way the Sarbanes-Oxley Act increased the authority and capabilities of the SEC?

15. *Accounting Reforms*

    List and describe two major developments designed to allow auditors to focus on their review of, and not service to, public companies.

16. *Corporate Governance*

    Some commentators state that the concept of independence is the most important aspect of Sarbanes-Oxley. How is independence required and why is it critical to corporate governance?

17. *Financial Statements and Controls*

    Describe the Sarbanes-Oxley provisions that require certification of financial statements and internal financial controls.

18. *Whistleblower Protections*

    In what three ways did the Sarbanes-Oxley Act strengthen the enforcement of securities fraud?

business *discussions*

1. Two former roommates from college contact you about an opportunity to make big money. Their idea is to start a business to market a new video game system (the computer science major developed the software, the engineer created the hardware). They estimate it will take $5 million to $10 million to begin production, and they want to raise money by selling shares in the company to investors. They think their product is superior, and they are aware of the time factor. They want to get started as soon as possible. Your field of expertise is securities marketing.

Can the three of you just begin advertising for investors?
What steps must be followed to comply with the law?
How much time is needed before potential investors can be approached legally?

2. You and a former classmate started a computer software company five years ago. Originally, the two of you were the owners and only employees. The foundation of your company was your combined expertise in creating custom-designed applications addressing the human resource needs of your clients. As your company grew, you added programmers that now allow your business to provide a greater array of computer applications. You and your co-owner decide to raise capital by making a public offering of stock. In preparation for going public, you visit with several of your most valuable clients about investing in your company.

What concerns should you have regarding these conversations?
Is there anything about your expectations of the company's future performance you must or must not share?

3. You and two partners operate a graphics design and printing company. The success of this business relates to the high-quality service and products you provide to your clients. To move to the next level requires a considerable financial investment in computer software and hardware. You and your partners are considering forming a corporation and offering to sell stock to the public. You anticipate raising at least $40 million in new capital. As you ponder these moves, you seek answers to the following questions:

What requirements of the Sarbanes-Oxley Act will you have to meet?
What is involved in offering a new company's stock for sale to the public?
Are there aspects of doing business as a publicly traded company that are different from operating as a partnership?

18

Regulations Protecting Consumer Purchases, Privacy, and Financial Activities

Learning Objectives

In this chapter you will learn:

18-1. To analyze the Federal Trade Commission's consumer protection mission and why politics influence it.

18-2. To understand the power of federal and state governments to enforce laws against false and deceptive advertising.

18-3. To understand the general framework of consumer privacy protection in the United States and evaluate how the law protects consumers in particular contexts.

18-4. To evaluate the provisions of various consumer and financial protection laws concerning lending, credit reporting protection, debt collection, and bankruptcy.

Consumer protection laws ensure the operation of an efficient marketplace. They are a type of regulation on business. Most consumer protection laws give consumers a type of private property regarding how goods and services are transferred by sellers through contract law. This private property produces greater safety and security for consumers in their purchases and their "privacy," ensuring that sellers do not defraud or take undue advantage. But at the same time, since it limits what is privately proper to sellers, consumer protection laws may result in higher prices and fewer goods and services being easily available.

The exclusive legal fence (or boundary) of property protects us in various ways, principally in the possession, use, and transfer of what we own. Yet we cannot use or transfer what we owns without limits. We must respect the equal property right of others and not interfere with the exclusive legal fence that protects what belongs to them. For example, the doctrine of nuisance (Chapter 7) prevents us from using our land in a way that interferes unreasonably with the use and enjoyment (really, *possession*) of another's land. We cannot injure what others own. Likewise, in transferring ownership of something we own, we cannot sell it through fraud, sometimes called *intentional misrepresentation* or *deception* (see Chapter 10).

It is a mistake, however, to think that the placement of this fence of law is always clearly understood. In the property system, owners often just assume they can do whatever they want with what they own. Property seems open-ended that way. But what one owner does affects other owners, and property also protects the right of other owners not to have what belongs to them injured or to be defrauded out of what they own by what another owner does. The exact definition of what constitutes "injury" and "fraud" is often uncertain, and this means that it may not always be obvious to owners where the limits are regarding what they can do with what they own and how they can affect other owners.

The Federal Trade Commission

The Federal Trade Commission (FTC) is the primary federal agency that protects consumers. Although the Federal Trade Commission Act protects businesses as well as consumers, the consumer protection mission of the FTC is promoted by a special bureau called the Bureau of Consumer Protection. This body within the FTC is the regulatory center for federal consumer protection. The next sections examine activities of the FTC and the Bureau of Consumer Protection.

LO 18-1

THE FTC AND TRADE PRACTICE REGULATION

Created in 1914, the FTC is an "independent" regulatory agency charged with keeping competition free and fair, and with protecting consumers. Independent agencies are less directly controlled by the executive branch, with controlling members (commissioners or board members) representing more than one political party and appointed for staggered terms. The FTC obeys its mandate to promote competition through enforcement of the antitrust laws. It achieves its consumer protection goal by trade practice regulation under that section of the FTC Act which prohibits using "unfair methods of competition" or "unfair or deceptive acts or practices in commerce." It also administers more than 70 other consumer protection acts, some of which are covered in this chapter (see Table 18.1). In the final analysis, promoting competition and protecting consumers overlap considerably. A highly competitive economy produces better goods and services at lower prices, while **trade practice regulation** ensures fair competition by preventing those who would deceive consumers from diverting trade from those who compete honestly.

The FTC furthers consumer protection through trade practice regulation in several ways. For instance, it advises firms that request it as to whether a proposed practice is unfair or deceptive. Although not legally binding, an **advisory opinion** furnishes a good idea about how the FTC views the legality

table 18.1 Consumer Protection Laws the FTC Administers

Laws	Duties
FTC Act	To regulate unfair or deceptive acts or practices
Fair Packaging and Labeling Act	To prohibit deceptive labeling of certain consumer products and require disclosure of certain important information
Equal Credit Opportunity Act	To prevent discrimination in credit extension based on sex, age, race, religion, national origin, marital status, and receipt of welfare payments
Truth-in-Lending Act	To require that suppliers of consumer credit fully disclose all credit terms before an account is opened or a loan made
Fair Credit Reporting Act	To regulate the consumer credit reporting industry
Magnuson-Moss Warranty Act	To require the FTC to issue rules concerning consumer product warranties
Fair Debt Collection Practices Act	To prevent debt-collection agencies from using abusive or deceptive collection practices

of a given trade practice. The FTC also issues **industry guides,** which specify the agency's view of the legality of a particular industry's trade practices. Like advisory opinions, industry guides are informal and not legally binding. The Bureau of Consumer Protection plays the major role in issuing advisory opinions and industry guides on trade regulation issues.

In its function of protecting consumers, however, the FTC goes far beyond merely advising businesses about the legality of trade practices. It also prosecutes them for committing unfair or deceptive trade practices. Such prosecutions arise in one of two related ways. First, the Bureau of Consumer Protection may allege that an individual or company, called a **respondent,** has violated **Section 5** of the FTC Act, which prohibits **unfair or deceptive acts or practices.** Over the years, the FTC's administrative law judges and the commissioners who review decisions of the judges have derived a body of quasi-judicial interpretations as to what constitutes unfair and deceptive acts. FTC inquiries may begin as a result of consumer complaints. Consumers may even file complaints electronically.

Enforcement actions may also arise from allegations under Section 5 that a respondent's actions violate a trade regulation rule of the FTC. At the recommendation of the Bureau of Consumer Protection, the five-member Commission adopts trade regulation rules in exercising its quasi-legislative power. These rules are formal interpretations of what the FTC regards as unfair or deceptive, and they have the force and effect of law. The rules usually deal with a single practice in a single industry, and they cover all firms in the affected industry. Examples of trade regulation rules include required disclosures of

The FTC received 5.7 million consumer complaints in 2013.

–FTC Performance and Accountability Report, December 2013

A deceptive act, or *deception,* usually involves a misrepresentation or omission similar to common-law fraud.

the "R" value for siding and installation and the familiar telemarketing sales rule that established the national "Do Not Call" list.

Alleged trade practice violations may come to the attention of the Bureau of Consumer Protection in a variety of ways. A business executive may complain about another's acts that injure competition, or a consumer may direct the attention of the Bureau to unfair or deceptive acts of a business. Such complaints are filed informally, and the identity of the complainant is not disclosed. A letter signed by a complaining party provides a basis for proceedings if it identifies the offending party, contains all the evidence which is the basis for the complaint, and states the relief desired. Of course, other government agencies, Congress, or the FTC itself may discover business conduct alleged to be illegal.

Don't forget that a cease and desist order from an administrative law judge is very similar to an injunction from a trial court.

The chief legal tools of the Bureau are the consent order and the cease and desist order. Under the consent-order procedure, a party "consents" to sign an order which restrains the promotional activity deemed offensive and agrees to whatever remedy, if any, the Bureau imposes. Most cases brought by the Bureau are settled by this procedure.

If a party will not accept a consent order, it will be prosecuted before an administrative law judge. If the party is found guilty, the judge issues a cease and desist order prohibiting future violations. Parties may appeal cease and desist orders to the full five-member commission and from there to the court of appeals if legal basis for further appeal is present.

FTC PENALTIES AND REMEDIES

Civil Fines   The basic penalty for trade practice violations under the FTC Act is a civil fine of not more than $16,000 per violation. The punishment function of finding violators is only an incidental one, as the FTC's main purpose is to prevent and deter trade practice violations.

To obtain fines, either the FTC or the Justice Department must ask the federal court to assess them. The exception is when companies agree to fines as part of a consent order. Fines may be assessed in three distinct situations: (1) for a violation of a consent or cease and desist order, (2) for a violation of a trade regulation rule, and (3) for a knowing violation of prior FTC orders against others.

The FTC Act provides that "each separate violation of . . . an order [or rule] shall be a separate offense." It also states that in the case of a violation through continuing failure to obey an order, each day the violation continues is a separate offense. Because of these provisions, the total fine against a violator may be considerably more than $16,000. See Sidebar 18.1.

Note that the FTC has not used corrective advertising much when a majority of the five commissioners is politically conservative.

Other Remedies   In addition to assessing penalty fines, the FTC has broad powers to fashion appropriate remedies to protect consumers in trade regulation cases. One remedy the FTC has used in the past to accompany some of its orders is **corrective advertising.**

When a company has advertised deceptively, the FTC can require it to run ads that admit the prior errors and correct the erroneous information. The correction applies to a specific dollar volume of future advertising. The theory is that the future advertising, however truthful itself, will continue to

sidebar 18.1

Keeping Promises

Google is the developer of the world's most popular search engine. The company brings in a tremendous amount of revenue through advertising, and its clients are extremely interested in the browsing and purchasing habits of Google users. However, Google realizes that its users are sensitive about the use of tracking code like "cookies" that can reveal browsing behavior. To allay concerns, Google promised that users of Apple's Safari browser would be able to avoid tracking cookies through Safari's default setting that block third-party cookies.

According to the FTC, Google broke its promise in 2011 and 2012. The company allegedly circumvented Safari's settings to include tracking cookies without the user's knowledge. This resulted in a loss of consumer privacy.

The FTC filed a complaint against Google demanding a change in practices and requesting a civil penalty based on the maximum $16,000 per offence. In August 2012, Google settled. The company agreed to pay $22.5 million, the FTC's largest civil penalty to date. A federal court approved Google's settlement with the FTC in November 2012.

Source: *United States of America v. Google*, CV 12-04177 SI (N.D. Cal, Nov. 16, 2012).

be deceptive unless the correction is made because it will remind consumers of the prior deceptive ads. Corrective ads have forced admissions that a mouthwash does not reduce cold symptoms or prevent sore throats, that an oil-treatment product cannot decrease gasoline consumption, and that an aspirin-based drug cannot relieve tension.

Other remedies the FTC may use in its orders, or may seek to impose by court action under certain circumstances, include (1) recission of contracts (each party must return what has been obtained from the other), (2) refund of money or return of property, (3) payment of damages to consumers, and (4) public notification of trade practice violations. When it is in the public interest, and when harm from an illegal practice is substantial and likely to continue, the FTC may ask the federal court to grant temporary or even permanent injunctions to restrain violators.

Appreciate that traditional frauds that substantially impact interstate commerce not only violate the FTC Act but also may violate federal and state criminal laws, as well as give consumers injured by the fraud a common-law right to sue for actual and punitive damages.

POLITICS, ECONOMICS, AND THE LAW: THE FTC TODAY

The FTC's consumer protection mission and enforcement of Section 5 varies according to the economic orientation of the president and of Congress. The president appoints the FTC commissioners for four-year terms and Congress annually must approve a budget for the FTC. Although the FTC is an *independent regulatory agency,* it is understandable that the FTC commissioners often reflect the views of the president who appointed them. Additionally, Congress can always cut the FTC's budget if it disapproves of the rules made and the cases brought by the FTC.

According to the majority views of the five commissioners who absolutely run the FTC, in some years the FTC is very laissez-faire, meaning that it leaves alone or does not regulate most advertising. The FTC allows the market to regulate advertising under the theory that consumers will not buy again from a seller if they are unhappy with what they

DO note that the Bureau of Consumer Protection may urge that a case be brought, but a majority of the five commissioners is necessary officially to authorize FTC action by the Bureau of Consumer Protection.

bought the first time. In such times, only traditional frauds tend to be regulated. In other years, when politics and the FTC commissioners are more consumer-oriented, the FTC will increase the number of deceptive cases filed and the number of new rules regulating trade practices that are not only deceptive but also "unfair" in the minds of the commissioners. They may allow the Bureau of Consumer Protection to impose new legal remedies like corrective advertising

The FTC has great discretion in deciding what is deceptive or unfair and whether or not to make new rules and bring new cases. Politics, economics, and discretion combine to determine the consumer protection mission of the FTC.

LO 18-2   False Advertising

False or deceptive advertising is one of the most important areas of consumer protection. The government's power to address the claims of multiple consumers at once is one important reason. For example, if a firm makes a false claim about an inexpensive home good, it may not be worthwhile for a customer to sue for fraud. A consumer protection agency, on the other hand, can bring a claim on behalf of all of those defrauded. In addition, false and deceptive advertising statutes may provide more flexibility in bringing a claim than one would have under common law. The necessary elements are commonly reduced (see Table 18.2).

Because the Federal Trade Commission has a national focus, it is the most significant enforcer of false and deceptive advertising laws. The agency's power to regulate advertising is derived from Section 5 of the FTC Act prohibiting deceptive trade practices. To determine deception, the FTC looks at the ad from the point of view of the "reasonable consumer," the typical person looking at the ad. Rather than focusing on certain words, the agency considers the ad in context—words, phrases, and pictures—to determine what it conveys to consumers. The FTC looks at both "express" and "implied" claims. An express claim is a statement that literally appears in the ad. For example, "ABC Mouthwash prevents colds" is an express claim that the product will prevent colds. An implied claim is one made indirectly or by inference. "ABC Mouthwash kills the germs that cause colds" contains an implied claim that the product will prevent colds. Although the ad doesn't literally say that the product prevents

table 18.2 Comparison of Common Law Fraud and False Advertising Elements

	Common Law Fraud	State or Federal False Advertising
Misrepresentation of fact	Required	Required
Scienter	Required	Generally not required
Justified reliance	Required	Misrepresentation must be material
Injury	Required	Generally not required

table 18.3 Typical FTC Deception Cases	
Company	**Order**
Sensa, L'Occitane, HCG Diet Direct, and LeanSpa	Barred from making weight-loss claims about dietary supplements, foods, or drugs unless adequate and well-controlled human clinical studies exist; pay $34 million in consumer redress.
Snapchat	Refrain from misrepresenting privacy, security, or confidentiality of user information, including false promises of disappearing messages; submit independent privacy monitoring for next 20 years.
AJM Packaging Corporation	Barred from making unsubstantiated claims that a product or package is biodegradable, compostable, recyclable, or offers an environmental benefit; disclose information needed to qualify certain green claims to avoid deception; pay $450,000 civil penalty for violating previous FTC order.

colds, it would be reasonable for a consumer to conclude from the statement "kills the germs that cause colds" that the product will prevent colds. Under the law, advertisers must have proof to back up express and implied claims that consumers take from an ad.

Additionally, the FTC looks at what the ad does not say—that is, if the failure to include information leaves consumers with a misimpression about the product. For example, if a company advertised a collection of books, the ad would be deceptive if it did not disclose that consumers actually would receive abridged versions of the books (see Table 18.3).

An important issue in a Section 5 deceptive advertising case is whether the claim would be "material"—that is, important to a consumer's decision to buy or use the product. Examples of material claims are representations about a product's performance, features, safety, price, or effectiveness.

The FTC Act is not the only statute governing false and deceptive advertising. States have enacted false advertising laws as well. Often referred to as "little FTC Acts," these state laws cover similar harms and may look to federal law for guidance. Significantly, state law may allow for private lawsuits in addition to government enforcement, which is an option not available under the FTC Act.

Consumer Privacy

LO 18-3

Consumer privacy has become a much-discussed topic in recent years, rising to the top of the enforcement and legislative agenda. It is clear that consumers expect to have some basic control over their private information. On the other hand, consumers enjoy the benefits that open information provides.

Firms can make advertising more relevant, personalize web searches, and help connect social and work groups by using personal information. The fact that there is conflict in satisfying both privacy and convenience goals is perhaps inevitable. Consumers look to the law to provide clear rules.

Privacy protection in the United States is, in most cases, less robust than many believe. Some essential protections exist against government intrusions. However, protections against intrusions by private actors are often limited to particular business contexts or certain forms of communications. As you will see from the following discussion, in many cases, consumers are left to rely on industry self-regulation or hope for future legislative initiatives.

LIMITATIONS ON GOVERNMENT INTRUSIONS

Many consider privacy to be a fundamental right. The natural place to look for such rights protection is the U.S. Constitution. However, the Constitution does not explicitly mention privacy. Courts have instead found aspects of privacy to be protected by various amendments, particularly in the Bill of Rights. These protections are important, but note that they generally limit *only the government*; limitations on private actors must be found elsewhere. For example, the Fourth Amendment right against "unreasonable searches and seizures" prevents the government from collecting much private information without a search warrant. In a recent case, *Riley v. California*, 134 S.Ct. 2473 (2014), the Supreme Court ruled that the police must generally first obtain a warrant in order to search a cell phone seized from a person who has been arrested. The First Amendment protecting freedom of speech and the free exercise of religion may also prevent intrusions on privacy. Additionally, the due process clause of the Fourteenth Amendment protects a right to liberty that has been extended to marital privacy.

In addition to the limited areas of privacy protection in the Constitution, more substantial privacy rights against the government are provided by statute. The Privacy Act of 1974 places constraints on the collection of certain kinds of information by the federal government and limits the release of such information. It also provides a tort cause of action against those who violate the act. A second statute, the Right to Financial Privacy Act of 1978, requires all government agencies seeking depositor records from banks and other financial institutions to notify depositors of this fact. The individual depositor then has 14 days to challenge an agency's legal basis for seeking the records. Depositors are allowed to sue the government agencies or financial institutions that fail to comply with the statute for actual and punitive damages, plus attorney's fees.

TRADITIONAL BUSINESS PRIVACY

Because limitations on government intrusions generally do not affect private actors, a consumer wishing to assert a right of privacy against a business must base it on another source of law. Many of the basic tenets of our concept of privacy come from the common law. As detailed in Chapter 10, they can be quite effective in preventing the most egregious intrusions into one's personal life. However, in the consumer context, common law privacy protections provide only limited success in protecting information.

Two basic common-law privacy torts arise in consumer transactions. The tort of intrusion on seclusion prevents one from invading another's private affairs if it would be highly offensive to the reasonable person. To be actionable, one must have a reasonable expectation of privacy that was infringed. In general, the expectation of privacy is difficult to establish in a business context, where communications with another in a public setting are the norm. Another potentially useful common law tort is public disclosure of private facts. The disclosure must be highly offensive to the reasonable person, which implies that the disclosed fact must concern a very sensitive issue. This tort could be used to prevent a business from disclosing embarrassing facts about a customer. However, a business that simply collects sensitive, private information is unlikely to be liable.

In a narrower context, the **Health Insurance Portability and Accountability Act (HIPAA)** of 1996 provides for privacy of medical records. Enacted to standardize health care privacy, HIPAA protects individually identifiable health information by limiting how it can be used and disclosed by health plans, health care providers, and health care clearinghouses. Patients ultimately have control over their personal health care information and can authorize disclosures. HIPAA applies to both electronic and physical records.

Another specific instance of legislated privacy related to a specific consumer transaction is the Video Privacy Protection Act (VPPA) of 1988. The act prevents the disclosure of personally identifiable information concerning video rentals and includes a right of civil action with a minimum $2,500 liquidated damages provision. Enacted during a time of videocassette rentals, the law's application to streaming services like Netflix was unclear. In particular, the requirement that consumers provide "written consent" before information is disclosed appeared to preclude sharing viewing preferences over social networking services like Facebook. Therefore, Congress amended the law in 2012 to permit consumers to convey electronic consent.

Several of the consumer financial protection laws discussed later in this chapter contain privacy protection provisions. Under the Fair Credit Reporting Act, for example, a potential employer, insurer, or creditor must inform the consumer that an investigative report is being obtained on him or her. This notice allows the consumer to terminate the contemplated transaction, thus ending the legitimate business reason for the report and preventing the report from being obtained legally. Under the Fair Debt Collection Practices Act, a debt collector may not call a consumer at the workplace in most instances or after 9:00 P.M. or before 8:00 A.M. Both the FDCPA and the Fair Credit Reporting Act recognize the privacy of a consumer in certain circumstances.

ELECTRONIC AND ONLINE PRIVACY PROTECTION

Although some laws like HIPAA apply in both the physical and electronic worlds, we understand that electronic communication and the Internet present special challenges. Laws exist to prevent some kinds of intrusions. But the protections are nevertheless limited, and many believe that additional protections are required.

In 1986, Congress passed the **Electronic Communications Privacy Act (ECPA)** as an update to the Wiretap Act. The law limited government action by extending protections against telephone wiretaps without a search warrant to computer communications. But it also extended the protections against private intrusions on electronic communications, and this has become an important law for modern businesses to understand. The ECPA prevents the interception of electronic or wire communications, including email, by another without authorization. Another provision, called the Stored Communications Act (SCA) was enacted as part of the ECPA in 1986 and protects the privacy of communications stored on a server. The SCA prevents unauthorized access or disclosure of stored communications. Of course, not everything transmitted electronically is a communication. Case 18.1 addresses the question of whether login IDs and personal webpage addresses should be protected as communication content in the same way that e-mail text and voice are.

 case **18.1**

IN RE: ZYNGA & IN RE: FACEBOOK PRIVACY LITIGATIONS
750 F.3d 1098 (9th Cir. 2014)

The plaintiffs represent a group of Facebook and Zynga game users who claim that the companies disclosed their confidential information to third parties without authorization. Specifically, when Facebook users clicked on advertising links or links to Zynga games, the webpage would send an "HTTP request" with a "referral header." The referral header contained the user's Facebook ID and the address of their Facebook page. According to the plaintiffs, this private information was shared with advertisers. The plaintiffs sued Facebook and Zynga, alleging that the disclosure violated the Electronic Communications Privacy Act (ECPA) and Stored Communications Act (SCA). The court was compelled to determine whether the shared information was a protected communication under the law.

IKUTA, Circuit Judge:

Title I of ECPA amended the existing Wiretap Act. As relevant here, the amended Wiretap Act provides that (with certain exceptions), "a person or entity" (1) "providing an electronic communication service to the public" (2) "shall not intentionally divulge the contents of any communication (other than one to such person or entity, or an agent thereof)" (3) "while in transmission on that service" (4) "to any person or entity other than an addressee or intended recipient of such communication or an agent of such addressee or intended recipient." . . . The "contents" of a communication are defined as "any information concerning the substance, purport, or meaning of that communication." . . . Even if a disclosure

is otherwise prohibited by [the law], an electronic communications service provider can reveal the contents of communications transmitted on its service "with the lawful consent of the originator or any addressee or intended recipient of such communication." . . .

Title II of ECPA, termed the Stored Communications Act, covers access to electronic information stored in third party computers. . . . The relevant provision here imposes requirements on providers of remote computing services that are similar to the requirements of the Wiretap Act discussed above. Under the Stored Communications Act, "a person or entity" (1) "providing remote computing service to the public" (2) "shall not knowingly divulge to any person or entity the contents of any communication" (3) "which is carried or maintained on that service . . . on behalf of, and received by means of electronic transmission from (or created by means of computer processing of communications received by means of electronic transmission from), a subscriber or customer of such service" (4) "solely for the purpose of providing storage or computer processing services to such subscriber or customer," unless the provider is authorized to access the contents of any such communications to provide other services. . . . Also, like the Wiretap Act, the Stored Communications Act allows a provider of covered services to "divulge the contents of a communication" to "an addressee or intended recipient of such communication," or "with the lawful consent of the originator or an addressee or intended recipient of such communication, or the subscriber in the case of remote computing service." . . .

The Stored Communications Act incorporates the Wiretap Act's definition of "contents." . . . It also differentiates between contents and record information. Section 2702(c)(6) permits an electronic communications service or remote computing service to "divulge a record or other information pertaining to a subscriber to or customer of such service (not including the contents of communications covered by [the law]) . . . to any person other than a governmental entity." In other words, the Stored Communications Act generally precludes a covered entity from disclosing the contents of a communication, but permits disclosure of record information like the name, address, or client ID number of the entity's customers in certain circumstances. . . .

Because the plaintiffs alleged that Facebook and Zynga violated ECPA by disclosing the HTTP referer information to third parties, we must determine whether such information is the "contents" of a communication for purposes of 18 U.S.C. §§ 2511(3)(a) and 2702(a)(2).

To answer this question, we first must determine Congress's intended meaning of the word "contents." . . . For purposes of §§ 2511(3)(a) and 2702(a), the word "contents" is defined as "any information concerning the substance, purport, or meaning of [a] communication." . . . Because the words "substance, purport, or meaning" are not further defined, we consider the ordinary meaning of these terms, including their dictionary definition. . . . A dictionary in wide circulation during the relevant time frame provides the following definitions: (1) "substance" means "the characteristic and essential part," *Webster's Third New International Dictionary* 2279 (1981); (2) "purport" means the "meaning conveyed, professed, or implied," *id.* at 1847; and (3) "meaning" refers to "the thing one intends to convey . . . by language," *id.* at 1399. These definitions indicate that Congress intended the word "contents" to mean a person's intended message to another (i.e., the "essential part" of the communication, the "meaning conveyed," and the "thing one intends to convey"). . . .

This conclusion is confirmed by ECPA's amendments to the Wiretap Act enacted in 1968. Before ECPA, the Wiretap Act defined "contents" as including "the identity of the parties to such communication or the existence, substance, purport, or meaning of that communication." . . . When it enacted ECPA, Congress amended the definition of "contents" to eliminate the words "identity of the parties to such communication,"

indicating its intent to exclude such record information from its definition of "contents." . . .

Accordingly, we hold that under ECPA, the term "contents" refers to the intended message conveyed by the communication, and does not include record information regarding the characteristics of the message that is generated in the course of the communication. . . .

We must next determine whether the plaintiffs plausibly alleged that the referer header information at issue here constituted the "contents of any communication," . . .

The referer header information that Facebook and Zynga transmitted to third parties included the user's Facebook ID and the address of the webpage from which the user's HTTP request to view another webpage was sent. This information does not meet the definition of "contents," because these pieces of information are not the "substance, purport, or meaning" of a communication. A Facebook ID identifies a Facebook user and so functions as a "name" or a "subscriber number or identity." . . . Similarly, the webpage address identifies the location of a webpage a user is viewing on the internet, and therefore functions like an "address." . . . Congress excluded this sort of record information from the definition of "contents." . . .

The plaintiffs argue that the referer header discloses content information, because when the referer header provides the advertiser with a Facebook ID (which, at the election of the user, may have been changed to a user name) along with the address of the Facebook page the user was previously viewing, an enterprising advertiser could uncover the user's profile page and any personal information made available to the public on that page. But the statutes at issue in these cases do not preclude the disclosure of personally identifiable information; indeed, they expressly allow it. . . . There is no language in ECPA equating "contents" with personally identifiable information. Thus, an allegation that Facebook and Zynga disclosed personally identifiable information is not equivalent to an allegation that they disclosed the contents of a communication.

The plaintiffs also argue that record information can become content if the record is the subject of a communication, as in an email message saying "here's my Facebook ID number," or "you have to check out this website." . . . But the complaints here do not plausibly allege that Facebook and Zynga divulged a user's communications to a website; rather, they allege that Facebook and Zynga divulged identification and address information contained in a referer header automatically generated by the web browser. . . . [T]he information allegedly disclosed by Facebook and Zynga is record information about a user's communication, not the communication itself. ECPA does not apply to such disclosures. . . .

In order for the plaintiffs to state a claim under the Wiretap Act and Stored Communications Act, they must plausibly allege that Facebook and Zynga divulged the "contents" of a communication. Because information disclosed in the referer headers at issue here is not the contents of a communication as defined in ECPA, the plaintiffs cannot state a claim under those statutes. Accordingly, we affirm the district court's dismissal with prejudice.

Affirmed.

KEY POINTS

- The ECPA and SCA do not protect all personally identifiable information. They are limited to the content of communications.
- Although Facebook and Zynga did not violate the ECPA and SCA through their transfer of consumer information to advertisers, they may have violated privacy agreements with consumers. Breach of contract may be a more viable case.
- Consider how other interactions on a social networking page, such as clicking a "like" button, may fit with the court's definition of communication content.

Both the ECPA and SCA have significant limitations. For example, the ECPA allows for interception of business communications on an employer's equipment. More importantly, for both the ECPA and SCA, one can obtain a standing authorization. Therefore, many employers avoid issues with the ECPA and SCA by establishing the right to incept and access employee communications.

Another limitation permits the interception of broadcast radio communications. A recent case considered whether unsecured wi-fi, which is broadcast using radio waves, falls within this exception. In *Joffe v. Google,* 746 F.3d 920 (9th Cir. 2013), the court determined that the meaning of "radio communication" in 1986 could not be extended to include data transmission over radio through wi-fi today. This case demonstrates how the arcane language of the ECPA and SCA can make it difficult to apply the rules to modern technology. The statutes have been referred to as "dial-up law in a broadband world." Figure 18.1 is a flow chart that may assist you in determining when a violation has occurred. Its complexity is evidence of the awkward structure of the law.

Children require special protection in the online world. For that reason, in 1998, Congress passed the Children's Online Privacy Protection Act (COPPA). The law is enforced by the FTC and prohibits the online collection of information on children under the age of 13 without a parent's consent. It also requires firms that collect such information to provide a privacy policy and to secure the information and avoid third-party disclosures. COPPA applies to any company that knowingly collects information from children under the age of 13, even if that is not the primary purpose of the Internet site. That scope means that common Internet shopping sites may inadvertently violate COPPA. For example, in 2009, Iconix Brand Group, which owns youth-oriented apparel brands such as Candie's, OP, Mudd, and Bongo, paid a civil penalty of $250,000 for violating COPPA by collecting personal

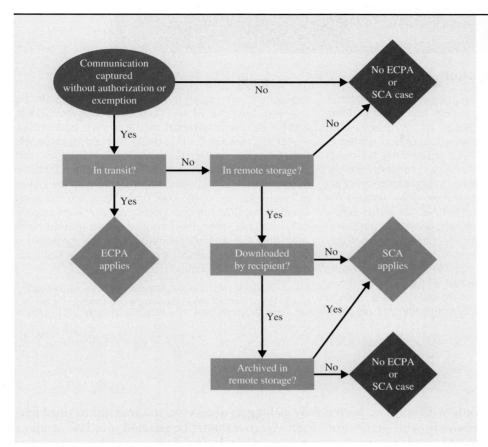

Figure 18.1 *Legal analysis of private-party capture of electronic communications.*

information from children. In 2012, the FTC updated its rules related to COPPA to include social networks and apps in its scope and ensure that protected information included pictures, geographic location, and online behavior.

Due to the limited nature of general privacy rights, the FTC has stepped into the void to provide additional protection. The FTC's main tactic is to scrutinize companies that make affirmative promises about privacy. For example, promises about protecting information may be explicitly communicated in an advertisement, on a webpage, or in a privacy policy. If a company fails to keep a promise, it has engaged in false or deceptive advertising in violation of Section 5 of the FTC Act (see Sidebar 18.1). In addition to enforcing promises, the FTC releases recommendations about best privacy practices to permit firms to self-regulate in an effective manner.

INTERNATIONAL PRIVACY PROTECTION

Many other countries have a deep concern about privacy, particularly on the Internet. One of the strongest forces on the global stage is the European Union. In 1995, the European Parliament passed the **Data Protection Directive**, which mandates that companies may collect personal information

sidebar 18.2

The Right to Be Forgotten

In 2010, a Spanish lawyer named Mario Costeja González filed a complaint with the Spanish Data Protection Agency about Google search results. The results were from a Spanish newspaper and related to legal notices dating from 1998 concerning his debts and forced property sales. According to González, the debt issues had been resolved years earlier, but they still appeared in current searches. This violated his rights under EU data protection rules. When the Spanish agency ordered Google to remove links to the newspaper, Google appealed, and the case was eventually referred to the European Court of Justice (ECJ).

The ECJ determined that Google search results were a type of data collection that fell within the directive. Additionally, it determined that González had a "right to be forgotten" under the directive, meaning that he could request that information that is irrelevant or outdated be removed. The result of the ECJ decision was that Google was forced to remove links to the 1998 newspaper results.

Going forward, the ECJ decision means that Google (and other search engines that operate in Europe) must provide the same options to EU citizens. The right to be forgotten means that some information must be lost or at least less retrievable over time. Many are debating whether the ECJ ruling is good policy or even realistically possible given the flexibility of the Internet. It is very likely that such a policy would be unenforceable in the United States due to the protections of the Constitution's First Amendment.

Sources: *Google Spain SL v. Agencia Española de Protección de Datos*, Case C-131/12 (May 13, 2014); David Streitfeld, "European Court Lets Users Erase Records on Web," New York Times, May 13, 2014, p. A1.

only with consent, keep it only as long as necessary, and transfer to third parties only with permission. Such directives must be enacted into law in all of the EU member states. Companies in the United States quickly realized that the Data Protection Directive could prove a significant hurdle to operating in Europe (particularly if information was to be transferred back to the United States). To make things easier and streamline compliance, the EU and United States agreed to a "safe harbor" framework in which companies self-certify that they comply with seven privacy principles, including notice about data collection, the option to opt-out, security of data, and transfer only to other companies that also comply with the safe harbor framework. Companies provide their certifications to the U.S. Department of Commerce. Any deception about the facts in the certification is subject to FTC penalties for false and deceptive trade practices as discussed earlier.

The European Union is considering updates to the Data Protection Directive, which may further strengthen privacy protection in Europe. Additionally, interpretations of the Directive may be expanding. Sidebar 18.2 details a recent decision from the European Court of Justice.

A robust debate continues about which kinds of information about online behavior should be protected as private and which kinds of information should be freely available to businesses wishing to use it for marketing purposes. Issues raised by these questions are related to the legal fence of private property (see Chapter 7) and are similar to the information issues raised by trade secrets (see Chapter 11).

Federal Credit Regulations

In addition to the FTC Act, the FTC administers several other consumer protection statutes. This means that the FTC can bring enforcement actions against those who violate the statutes. Several of these statutes concern credit regulation because the extension of credit is such an important economic reality of our consumer society. Enforcement of these statutes by other government agencies such as the Department of Justice and the Consumer Financial Protection Bureau may be possible depending on the circumstances.

Considering the importance of credit buying to the consumer and business, you should not be surprised that a number of laws regulating credit extension have been passed. The laws discussed in the following sections cover nondiscrimination in credit extension, the collection of information for credit reports, and the standardized disclosure of credit charges.

THE EQUAL CREDIT OPPORTUNITY ACT

LO 18-4

In 1975, Congress passed the Equal Credit Opportunity Act (ECOA). The ECOA's purpose is to prevent discrimination in credit extension. In an economy in which credit availability is so important, the ECOA is a logical extension in a vital consumer area of the antidiscrimination laws found in the employment field.

ECOA Prohibitions   This act prohibits discrimination based on sex, marital status, race, color, age, religion, national origin, or receipt of welfare in any aspect of a consumer credit transaction. Although the ECOA forbids discrimination on the basis of all these different categories, it is aimed especially at preventing sex discrimination.

The law prohibits one to whom the act applies from discouraging a consumer from seeking credit based on sex, marital status, or any other of the enumerated categories. A married woman, for example, cannot be denied the right to open a credit account separate from her husband's or in her maiden name. Unless the husband will be using the account or the consumer is relying on her husband's credit, it is illegal even to ask if the consumer is married. It is also illegal to ask about birth-control practices or childbearing plans or to assign negative values on a credit checklist to the fact that a woman is of childbearing age.

The ECOA applies to all businesses which regularly extend credit, including financial institutions, retail stores, and credit-card issuers. It also affects automobile dealers, real estate brokers, and others who steer consumers to lenders. Many courts are also ruling that ECOA covers consumer leasing situations, which may substitute in place of credit-based sales.

Responsibilities of the Credit Extender   In basing a credit decision on the applicant's income, the credit extender must consider alimony, child support, and maintenance payments as income, although the likelihood of these payments being actually made may be considered as well. The credit extender must also tell an applicant that she need not disclose income from these sources unless she will be relying on that income to obtain credit. In calculating total income, those subject to the law must include income from regular part-time jobs and public assistance programs.

Information on accounts used by both spouses must be reported to third parties, such as credit reporting agencies, in the names of both spouses. This provision of the law helps women establish a credit history and enables a woman who separates from her husband to obtain credit in her own right.

> A business that denies a consumer credit must give *specific* reasons for the denial to the consumer.

To date, much of the litigation surrounding the ECOA concerns the requirement that *specific* reasons be given a consumer who is denied credit. Several cases have imposed liability upon credit extenders who have failed to provide any reasons for credit denial or who merely informed the consumer that she had failed to achieve a minimum score on a credit rating system. Other cases have dealt with age and race discrimination. It has also been established that the practice of **redlining,** that is, refusing to make loans at all in certain areas where property values are low, can discriminate on the basis of race in granting mortgage credit.

> The FTC determined that using zip codes as a factor in denying credit amounted to racial discrimination under the circumstances. The company should have decided each credit application on its own merits.

ECOA Remedies and Penalties   Private remedies for violation of the ECOA are recovery of actual damages, punitive damages up to $10,000, and attorney's fees and legal costs. Actual damages can include recovery for embarrassment and mental distress. Punitive damages can be recovered even in the absence of actual damages. In addition to private remedies, the government may bring suit to enjoin violations of the ECOA and to assess civil penalties. In one case, the FTC assessed a $200,000 civil penalty against a major national oil company. The FTC charged that the company practiced race and sex discrimination by using zip codes as a factor in deciding whether to extend credit and by failing to consider women's alimony and child support income.

Note that the ECOA has both private remedies that consumers can pursue as well as public enforcement by such agencies as the Federal Trade Commission the Department of Justice, the Department of Housing and Urban Development, and the Consumer Financial Protection Bureau. For this reason, consumers do not need to depend on the government to ensure they have equal opportunities for credit. If there are violations of the ECOA, affected consumers can sue.

THE FAIR CREDIT REPORTING ACT

Every year in the United States the credit reporting industry issues twice as many credit reports as there are people in the country. Examples of the entities that compile such reports include Equifax, Experian, and Trans Union. These reports cover not only consumers seeking credit but also persons seeking jobs or insurance. Although most of the information contained in such reports is accurate, the harm caused by occasionally inaccurate information and the potential for undue invasion of privacy led Congress to pass the Fair Credit Reporting Act (FCRA). FCRA applies to anyone who prepares or uses a credit report in connection with (1) extending credit, (2) selling insurance, or (3) hiring or firing an employee. The law regulates credit reports on consumers but not those on businesses.

Consumer Rights under FCRA The law gives individual consumers certain rights whenever they are rejected for credit, insurance, or employment because of an adverse credit report. These rights include (1) the right to be told the name of the agency making the report, (2) the right to require the agency to reveal the information given in the report, and (3) the right to correct the information or at least give the consumer's version of the facts in dispute.

This law does have one important limitation. It provides that a report containing information solely as to transactions or experiences between the consumer and the person making the report is not a "consumer report" covered by the act. To illustrate this limitation, assume that a bank is asked for information about its credit experience with one of its customers. If it reports only as to its own experiences, the report is not covered by the act. The act is designed to cover credit reporting agencies which obtain information from several sources, compile it, and furnish it to potential creditors. If the bank passed along any information it had received from an outside source, then its credit report would be subject to the provision of the act. Also, if the bank gave its opinion as to the creditworthiness of the customer in question, it would come under the act. The limitation is restricted to information relating to transactions or experiences, and the information furnished must be of a factual nature if the exception in the law is to be applicable.

Many businesses can avoid the pitfalls of being a credit reporting agency, but most businesses will be subject to the "user" provisions of this law. The "user" provision requires that consumers who are seeking credit for personal, family, or household purposes be informed if their application is denied because of an adverse credit report. They must also be informed of the source of the report and the fact that they are entitled to make a written request within 60 days as to the nature of the information received. If they request the information in the report, they are entitled to receive it so that they may challenge the accuracy of the negative aspects of its contents.

Investigative Consumer Reports The act also contains a provision on **investigative consumer reports.** These are reports on a consumer's character, general reputation, mode of living, and so on, obtained by personal interviews in the consumer's community. No one may obtain such a report unless at least three days' advance notice is given the consumer that such a report will be sought. The consumer has the right to be informed of the nature and scope of any such personal investigation. Reports which are intended to be covered by this act are those usually conducted for insurance companies and employment agencies.

Observing Reasonable Procedures In making investigations and collecting information, credit reporting agencies must observe *reasonable procedures*, or they will be liable to consumers. For example, when a consumer investigative report contained false information about a consumer's character—including rumored drug use, participation in demonstrations, and eviction from prior residences—a court found liability against the credit reporting agency. The agency's investigator had obtained the information

A 2012 FTC study of 1,001 consumer credit reports found that "one in 20 of the study participants had an error on his or her credit report that lowered the credit score to a degree that the error likely made getting credit more expensive."

–Senate testimony of Maneesha Mithal, Associate Director for the Division of Privacy and Identity Protection at the FTC, May 7, 2013

Don't ignore the difference between a "consumer report" and an "investigative consumer report."

from a single source, a person with a strong bias against the consumer, and he failed to double-check it. However, if an agency follows reasonable procedures, it is not liable to a consumer, even if it reports false information. Furthermore, several courts have ruled that the FCRA preempts state law. This prevents consumers from filing libel actions against agencies which report false information.

FCRA Penalties and Remedies   The Federal Trade Commission can enforce the FCRA. In addition, anyone who violates the provisions of the act is civilly liable to an injured consumer. The consumer may recover actual damages, attorney's fees, and in some instances punitive damages. Consider in Case 18.2 what the court says about punitive damages under the FCRA.

case **18.2**

SAFECO INSURANCE CO. v. BURR
551 U.S. 47 (2007)

Safeco Insurance Company and GEICO General Insurance Company issued automobile insurance policies to three applicants without telling them that the companies had obtained credit reports on the applicants. One applicant filed a lawsuit against Safeco and two applicants sued GEICO under the Fair Credit Reporting Act. The cases reached the Supreme Court and were consolidated for decision.

SOUTER, J.: . . . The Fair Credit Reporting Act requires notice to any consumer subjected to "adverse action . . . based in whole or in part on any information contained in a consumer credit report." Anyone who "willfully fails" to provide notice is civilly liable to the consumer. The questions in these consolidated cases are whether willful failure covers a violation committed in reckless disregard of the notice violation, and, if so, whether petitioners Safeco and GEICO committed reckless violations. We hold that reckless action is covered, that GEICO did not violate the statute, and that while Safeco might have, it did not act recklessly.

Congress enacted the Act in 1970 to ensure fair and accurate credit reporting, promote efficiency in the banking system, and protect consumer privacy. The Act requires among other things, that "any person who takes any adverse action with respect to any consumer that is based in whole or in part on any information contained in a consumer report" must notify the affected consumer. The notice must point out the adverse action, explain how to reach the agency that

reported on the consumer's credit, and tell the consumer that he can get a free copy of the report and dispute its accuracy with the agency. As it applies to an insurance company, "adverse action" is "a denial or cancellation of, an increase in any charge for, or a reduction or other adverse or unfavorable change in the terms of coverage or amount of, any insurance, existing or applied for."

In GEICO's case, the initial rate offered to Edo [one of the applicants] was the one he would have received if his credit score had not been taken into account, and GEICO owed him no adverse action notice under the Act.

Safeco did not give Burr and Massey (the other applicants) any notice because it thought the Act did not apply to an initial application, a mistake that left the company in violation of the statute if Burr and Massey received higher rates "based in whole or in part" on their credit reports; if they did, Safeco would be liable to them on a showing of reckless conduct (or worse). The first issue we can forget, however, for although the record does not reliably indicate what rights they would have obtained if their credit reports had not been considered, it is clear enough that if Safeco did violate the statute, the company was not reckless in falling down in its duty.

While "the term recklessness is not self-defining," the common law has generally understood it in this sphere of civil liability as conduct violating an objective standard: action entailing "an unjustifiably high risk of harm that is either known or so obvious that it should be known."

There being no indication that Congress had something different in mind, we have no reason to deviate from the common law understanding in applying the statute. Thus, a company subject to the Act does not act in reckless disregard of it unless the action is not only a violation under a reasonable reading of the statute's terms, but shows that the company ran a risk of violating the law substantially greater than the risk associated with a reading that was merely careless. Here, there is no need to pinpoint the negligence/recklessness line, for Safeco's reading of the statute, albeit erroneous, was not objectively unreasonable.

The Court of Appeals correctly held that reckless disregard of a requirement of the Act would qualify as a willful violation within the meaning of the Act. But there was no need for that court to remand the cases for factual development. Geico's decision to issue no adverse action notice to Edo was not a violation of the Act, and Safeco's misreading of the statute was not reckless. The judgments of the Court of Appeals are therefore reversed in both cases, which are remanded for further proceedings consistent with this opinion.

It is so ordered.

KEY POINTS

- The Court expands the interpretation of "willfulness" to include reckless disregard of the notice requirements. This ensures that one cannot avoid the law's penalties by acting out of complete ignorance.
- There must be a "but for" relationship between the use of the credit report and the adverse action. The failure to demonstrate GEICO changed its rate based on the report is why the company escaped liability.
- In assessing Safeco's liability, the Court indicates that misunderstanding the law is different from reckless disregard.

Fair and Accurate Credit Transactions Act Amendments The FCRA was amended in 2003 by the Fair and Accurate Credit Transactions Act (FACT). The FACT Act provides for the right to dispute information on credit reports with the information furnisher and permits consumers to place fraud alerts on the report to notify creditors of identity theft. In addition, the FACT Act allows consumers to obtain a free credit report each year from the national consumer reporting agencies (Experian, Trans Union, Equifax). Notably, the free credit report is not required to contain a credit *score*, which is a proprietary number calculated by the reporting agency. But consumers must be allowed to purchase the score under the FACT Act.

THE TRUTH-IN-LENDING ACT

The Truth-in-Lending Act authorized the Federal Reserve Board to adopt regulations "to assure a meaningful disclosure of credit terms so that the consumer will be able to compare more readily the various credit terms available to him and avoid the uninformed use of credit." That rulemaking authority has now been assumed by the Consumer Financial Protection Bureau. As previously mentioned, the FTC enforces these regulations.

Truth-in-Lending Coverage

The Truth-in-Lending Act covers all transactions in which (1) the lender is in the business of extending credit in connection with a loan of money, a sale of property, or the furnishing of services; (2) the debtor is a natural person, as distinguished from a corporation or business entity; (3) a finance charge may be imposed; and (4) the credit is obtained primarily for personal, family, household, or agricultural purposes. It covers loans secured by real estate, such as mortgages, as well as unsecured loans and loans secured by personal property. Disclosure is necessary whenever a buyer pays in four installments or more.

Truth-in-Lending imposes a duty on all persons regularly extending credit to private individuals to inform them fully of the cost of the credit. It does not regulate the charges which are imposed.

The finance charge is the total cost of the money to the consumer or farmer.

Finance Charge and Annual Percentage Rate

The Truth-in-Lending philosophy of full disclosure is accomplished through two concepts, namely, the **finance charge** and the **annual percentage rate (APR)**. The borrower uses these two concepts to determine the amount he or she must pay for credit and what the annual cost of borrowing will be in relation to the amount of credit received. Theoretically, a debtor armed with this information will be better able to bargain for credit and choose one creditor over the other.

The finance charge is the sum of all charges payable directly or indirectly by the debtor or someone else to the creditor as a condition of the extension of credit. Included in the finance charge are interest, service charges, loan fees, points, finder's fees, fees for appraisals, credit reports or investigations, and life and health insurance required as a condition of the loan.

Among the costs frequently paid by debtors which are not included in the finance charge are recording fees and taxes, such as a sales tax, which are not usually included in the listed selling price. These are items of a fixed nature, the proceeds of which do not go to the creditor. Other items of cost not included are title insurance or abstract fees, notary fees, and attorney's fees for preparing deeds.

The law requires that the lender disclose the finance charge, expressing it as an annual percentage rate, and specifies the methods for making this computation. The purpose is to ensure that all credit extenders calculate their charges in a uniform fashion. This enables consumers to make informed decisions about the cost of credit.

The financing statement is a disclosure document only. It does not regulate the interest charged.

Financing Statement

The finance charge and annual percentage rate are made known to borrowers by use of a financing statement. This statement must be given to the borrower before credit is extended and must contain, in addition to the finance charge and the annual percentage rate, the following information:

1. Any default or delinquency charges that may result from a late payment.
2. Description of any property used as security.
3. The total amount to be financed, including a separation of the original debt from finance charges.

Penalties and Remedies under Truth-in-Lending There are both civil and criminal penalties for violation of Truth-in-Lending. The civil liability provisions make creditors liable to debtors for actual damages and an amount equal to twice the finance charge, but not less than $400 nor more than $4,000 for a closed-end real estate transaction, not less than $500 nor more than $5,000 for an open-ended, non–real estate transaction, plus the costs and attorney's fees required to collect it. Creditors may avoid liability in the event they make an error, provided they notify the debtor within 60 days after discovering the error and also correct the error. In this connection, the law allows for corrections in favor of the debtor only. Creditors cannot collect finance charges in excess of those actually disclosed.

The Truth-in-Lending Act gives debtors the right to rescind or cancel certain transactions for a period of three business days from the date of the transactions or from the date they are given the notice of their right to rescind, whichever is later. For example, consumers may generally cancel transactions in which they give a security interest on their principal residence if they do so within the three-day period. If the transaction is rescinded, the borrower has no liability for any finance charge, and the security which he or she has given is void. The act also allows consumer-borrowers to rescind their mortgage agreements altogether if lenders have failed to comply with important disclosure provisions. For an interesting application of this, see Sidebar 18.3.

sidebar 18.3

Truth-in-Lending and the Subprime Mortgage Mess

Subprime mortgages refer to mortgages securing loans for consumers who do not qualify for ordinary market rates of interest because of lack of credit worthiness. Generally, this means that their income is not high enough or certain enough to qualify under ordinary circumstances. But during the 1990s and early 2000s house prices nationally kept going up and up, and many banks and other financial institutions—encouraged by the government—became willing to loan money to consumers who ordinarily would not qualify for particular loans, because rising house prices made the mortgage securities quite sound. If consumers became unable to pay monthly loan rates, they found it easy to renegotiate lower rates because of the soundness of the mortgages and the equity provided by rising house values.

When the housing bubble burst and, in many parts of the country, house values stopped rising, disaster struck the subprime market, which by 2007 was estimated to be at least $1.3 trillion. Many consumers became unable to pay back their loans and lenders were unwilling to lower monthly repayments because house prices were no longer rising. Foreclosure filings zoomed. Consumers with adjustable rate mortgages

were hardest hit as interest rates began to rise and their monthly house payments did also. The economic effects began to ripple through the economy, which went into recession. Financial institutions collapsed, credit dried up, joblessness rose, and the government passed emergency legislation to bail out financial institutions to help them extend credit required by businesses. Some homeowners were also assisted to help them repay their mortgages.

Lawyers representing consumers with mortgages in foreclosure sometimes turned to the Truth-in-Lending Act, and sued lenders who had not complied with all of the complicated provisions of the Act, especially with provisions relating to how prominently various disclosures of key terms had to be made. In some instances, class-action lawsuits were filed. In other instances, consumers used the threat of lawsuits to pressure banks into renegotiating loan rates downward. Failure to comply with truth-in-lending requirements could even allow consumers to rescind (take back) their mortgage agreements, and cause lenders to lose their security altogether, making them only general creditors unlikely to be able to recover the debt for the large loans.

Truth-in-Lending Trends

In 1980, Congress passed the Truth-in-Lending Simplification Act. Two changes from the original act stand out. First, the law eliminates statutory penalties based on purely technical violations of the act. It restricts such penalties to failures to disclose credit terms that are of *material* importance in credit comparisons. Second, the Simplification Act requires the government to issue model disclosure forms. These are now issued by the Consumer Financial Protection Bureau. The disclosure forms are particularly important to small businesses that cannot afford legal counsel to help prepare such forms. Proper use of the forms proves compliance with the Simplification Act.

Studies conducted by the FTC show that many of those involved in credit extension, such as home builders and realtors, fail to make required Truth-in-Lending disclosures in their advertising. In several instances, the FTC has successfully undertaken programs to educate these businesses about their disclosure obligations under Truth-in-Lending.

Debt Collection and Consumer Protection

In a consumer-credit-oriented economy, the collection of bad debts is very important. At present, there are thousands of collection agencies in the United States engaged in collecting unpaid accounts, judgments, and other bad debts. Thousands of attorneys also collect debts. Annually, creditors turn over bills totaling many billions of dollars for collection. The following sections examine the federal laws of debt collection and consumer protection, which the FTC enforces.

THE FAIR DEBT COLLECTION PRACTICES ACT

Due to complaints that some debt-collection agencies used techniques of harassment, deception, and personal abuse to collect debts, Congress in 1978 passed the Fair Debt Collection Practices Act (FDCPA). The act covers only *consumer* debt collections. It applies to agencies and individuals whose primary business is the collection of consumer debts for others. It also applies to the Internal Revenue Service and attorneys who collect consumer debts on behalf of their clients. Creditor collection efforts are exempt from the act. In the following case, the Supreme Court examines whether attorneys who are litigating a case are subject to the FDCPA.

One of the first actions of a debt collector will usually be to locate the debtor. This action, known as "skip-tracing," may require that the collector contact third parties who know of the debtor's whereabouts. The FDCPA permits the collector to contact third parties, such as neighbors or employers, but it limits the way in which this contact may be carried out. The collector may not state that the consumer owes a debt nor contact any given third party more than once, except in very limited circumstances. When the collector knows that an attorney represents the debtor, the collector may not contact any third parties, except the attorney, unless the attorney fails to respond to the collector's communication.

Having located the debtor, the collector will next seek to get payment on the overdue account. However, the FDCPA restricts methods that can be used in the collection process. Table 18.4 outlines these restrictions.

table 18.4 FDCPA'S Restrictions on Collection Methods of Collection Agencies

The collector cannot:

1. Physically threaten the debtor
2. Use obscene language
3. Represent himself or herself as an attorney unless it is true
4. Threaten debtor with arrest or garnishment unless the collector can legally take such action and intends to do so
5. Fail to disclose his or her identity as a collector
6. Telephone before 8:00 A.M. or after 9:00 P.M. in most instances
7. Telephone repeatedly with intent to annoy
8. Place collect calls to the debtor
9. Use any "unfair or unconscionable means" to collect the debt

FDCPA Remedies and Enforcement If the consumer debtor desires to stop the debt collector from repeatedly contacting him or her about payment, the debtor need only notify the collector in writing of this wish. Any further contact by the collector following such notification violates the act. The collector's sole remedy now is to sue the debtor. Violations of the FDCPA entitle the debtor to sue the debt collector for actual damages, including damages for invasion of privacy and infliction of mental distress, plus court costs and attorney's fees. In the absence of actual damages, the court may still order the collector to pay the debtor up to $1,000 for violations. Class-action suits, as well as individual ones, are permitted under the act. Note, however, that the debt collector can also recover costs if it prevails in the lawsuit. In *Marx v. General Revenue Corp.*, 133 S.Ct. 1166 (2013), the Supreme Court ruled that a district court may award the debt collector costs even if the debtor did not bring the case in bad faith.

In the following case, the Supreme Court decides whether a debt collector may be liable even when it did not intend to violate FDCPA because of a legal mistake about the act's requirements.

 case 18.3

 JERMAN v. CARLISLE, McNELLIE, RINI, KRAMER & ULRICH LPA
559 U.S. 573 (2010)

SOTOMAYOR, J. . . .The Fair Debt Collection Practices Act (FDCPA or Act) imposes civil liability on "debt collector[s]" for certain prohibited debt collection practices. Section 813(c) of the Act, provides that a debt collector is not liable in an action brought under the Act if she can show "the violation was not intentional and resulted from a bona fide error notwithstanding the maintenance of procedures reasonably adapted to avoid any such error." This case presents the question whether the "bona fide error" defense in Section 813(c) applies to a violation resulting from a debt collector's mistaken interpretation of the legal requirements of the FDCPA. We conclude it does not.

Congress enacted the FDCPA in 1977 to eliminate abusive debt collection practices, to ensure that debt collectors who abstain from such practices are not competitively disadvantaged, and to promote consistent state action to protect consumers. . . . Among other things, the Act prohibits debt collectors from making false representations as to a debt's character, amount, or legal status, communicating with consumers at an "unusual time or place" likely to be inconvenient to the consumer, or using obscene or profane language or violence or the threat thereof.

The FDCPA also provides that "any debt collector who fails to comply with any provision of th[e] [Act] with respect to any person is liable to such person." Successful plaintiffs are entitled to "actual damage[s]," plus costs and "a reasonable attorney's fee as determined by the court." A court may also award "additional damages," subject to a statutory cap of $1,000 for individual actions, or, for class actions, "the lesser of $500,000 or 1 per centum of the net worth of the debt collector. In awarding additional damages, the court must consider "the frequency and persistence of [the debt collector's] noncompliance," "the nature of such noncompliance," and "the extent to which such noncompliance was intentional. The Act contains an exception to provisions imposing liability on debt collectors providing that:

"[a] debt collector may not be held liable in any action brought under [the FDCPA] if the debt collector shows by a preponderance of evidence that the violation was not intentional and resulted from a bona fide error notwithstanding the maintenance of procedures reasonably adapted to avoid any such error."

Respondents in this case are a law firm, Carlisle, McNellie, Rini, Kramer & Ulrich, and one of its attorneys, Adrienne S. Foster. In April 2006, Carlisle filed a complaint in Ohio state court on behalf of a client, Countrywide Home Loans, Inc. Carlisle sought foreclosure of a mortgage held by Countrywide in real property owned by petitioner Karen L. Jerman. The complaint included a "Notice," later served on Jerman, stating that the mortgage debt would be assumed to be valid unless Jerman disputed it in writing. Jerman's lawyer sent a letter disputing the debt, and Carlisle sought verification from Countrywide. When Countrywide acknowledged that Jerman had, in fact, already paid the debt in full, Carlisle withdrew the foreclosure lawsuit.

Jerman then filed her own lawsuit seeking class certification and damages under the FDCPA, contending that Carlisle violated the Act by stating that her debt would be assumed valid unless she disputed it in writing. While acknowledging that Carlisle had violated the Act by requiring Jerman to dispute the debt in writing, district court concluded that Section 813(c) shielded it from liability because the violation was not intentional, resulted from a bona fide error, and occurred despite the maintenance of procedures reasonably adapted to avoid any such error. The Court of Appeals for the Sixth Circuit affirmed.

The parties disagree about whether a "violation" resulting from a debt collector's misinterpretation of the legal requirements of the FDCPA can ever be "not intentional" under Section 813(c). Jerman contends that when a debt collector intentionally commits the act giving rise to the violation (here, sending a notice that included the "in writing" language), a misunderstanding about what the Act requires cannot render the violation "not intentional," given the general rule that mistake or ignorance of law is no defense. Carlisle and the dissent, in contrast, argue that nothing in the statutory text excludes legal errors from the category of "bona fide error[s]" covered by the Act.

We have long recognized the "common maxim, familiar to all minds, that ignorance of the law will not excuse any person, either civilly or criminally. Our law is therefore no stranger to the possibility that an act may be "intentional" for purposes of civil liability, even if the actor lacked actual knowledge that her conduct violated the law"

Likely for this reason, when Congress has intended to provide a mistake-of-law defense to civil liability, it has often done so more explicitly than here. Congress also did not confine liability under the FDCPA to "willful" violations, a term more often understood in the civil context to excuse mistakes of law. . . .

We draw additional support for the conclusion that bona fide errors in Section 813(c) do not include mistaken interpretations of the FDCPA, from the requirement that a debt collector maintain "procedures reasonably adapted to avoid any such error." The dictionary defines "procedure" as "a series of steps followed in a regular orderly definite way. In that light, the statutory phrase is more naturally read to apply to processes that have mechanical or other such "regular orderly" steps to avoid mistakes—for instance, the kind of internal controls a debt collector might adopt to ensure its employees do not communicate with consumers at the wrong time of day, or make false representations as to the amount of a debt. For this reason, we find force in the suggestion by the Government that the broad statutory requirement of procedures reasonably designed to avoid "any" bona fide error indicates that the relevant procedures are ones that help to avoid errors like clerical or factual mistakes. Such procedures are more likely to avoid error than those applicable to legal reasoning. . . .

Any remaining doubt about the proper interpretation of Section 813(c) is dispelled by evidence of the meaning attached to the language Congress copied into the FDCPA's bona fide error defense from a parallel provision in an existing statute, the Truth in Lending Act (TILA). As enacted in 1968, the Truth in Lending Act provided a defense that was in pertinent part identical to the provision Congress later enacted into the FDCPA. During the 9-year period between the enactment of TILA and passage of the FDCPA, the three Federal Courts of Appeals to consider the question interpreted TILA's bona fide error defense as referring to clerical errors; no such court interpreted TILA to extend to violations resulting from a mistaken legal interpretation of that Act. We have often observed when "judicial interpretations have settled the meaning of an existing statutory provision, repetition of the same language in a new statute indicates, as a general matter, the intent to incorporate its . . . judicial interpretations as well." This close textual correspondence supports a conclusion that Congress understood the statutory formula it chose for the FDCPA consistent with Federal Court of Appeals interpretations of TILA. . . .

The suggestion that our reading of Section 813(c) will create unworkable consequences is also undermined by the existence of numerous state consumer protection and debt collection statutes that contain bona fide error defenses that are either silent as to, or expressly exclude, legal errors. Several States have enacted debt collection statutes that contain neither an exemption for attorney debt collectors nor any bona fide error defense at all.

For the reasons discussed earlier, the judgment of the United States Court of Appeals for the Sixth Circuit is reversed, and the case is remanded for further proceedings consistent with this opinion.

KEY POINTS

- The Court found Carlisle in violation of the FDCPA for sending a letter to the debtor, Jerman, requiring her to dispute the debt in writing or it would be deemed valid.
- According to the Court, Carlisle's violation of the FDCPA will not be excused because of a misunderstanding of the law. Note that this standard is stricter than the willfulness requirement for violating the FCRA, as discussed in case 18.2.
- The Court notes that the stringent requirements for claiming an unintentional violation are not more burdensome than requirements that exist in similar state statutes.

State Laws Regulating Debt Collection Congress specified that the FDCPA does not preempt state laws regulating debt collections so long as they are more strict than FDCPA standards. Some of these laws apply to debt collections by *creditors* as well as by collection agencies.

CONSUMER FINANCIAL PROTECTION ACT

At the height of the recession in 2010, Congress passed the Consumer Financial Protection Act. The act created the **Consumer Financial Protection Bureau (CFPB).** The CFPB has broad authority over federal financial consumer law. Its authority overlaps that of the **Federal Trade Commission (FTC)** in administering consumer laws such as the Equal Credit Opportunity Act, the Fair Credit Reporting Act, the Truth-in-Lending Act, and the Fair Debt Collection Practices Act, along with several others. The CFPB can also make and enforce rules regulating unfair, deceptive, or abusive acts or practices toward consumers.

Don't forget that state debt collection laws may be stricter than the FDCPA and may apply to the creditor as well as to the debt collection agency.

The CFPB's authority applies to any "covered person" offering or providing a consumer financial product or service and to any business associated with that person. It applies to banks and other financial businesses that extend credit or service loans, provide real estate settlement or appraisal services, take deposits, transmit funds, cash or guarantees checks, provide financial data processing services, provide consumer report information such as credit bureaus, and collect debts. The CFPB does not apply to insurance companies, Internet service providers, real estate agents and brokers, lawyers, car dealers, or persons and businesses regulated by the Securities and Exchange Commission.

BANKRUPTCY

The Federal Trade Commission does not administer all consumer protection laws. For instance, the bankruptcy laws are not subject to regulatory enforcement at all. These laws establish a procedure by which the "honest debtor" can get rid of debts by having them "discharged." The bankruptcy laws are not subject to regulatory interpretation and depend upon assertion by private debtors, both in their capacity as consumers and in business. However, as discussed here, the bankruptcy laws help explain one important consumer protection outcome of our consumer credit society: inability to repay debts.

Bankruptcy Proceedings   **Bankruptcy** proceedings begin upon the filing of either a voluntary or involuntary petition to the court. A *voluntary petition* is one filed by the debtor; an *involuntary petition* is filed by one or more creditors of the debtor. The creditors who sign the involuntary petition must be owed at least $2,300. If the court finds in an involuntary proceeding that the debtor is on the table to pay his or her debts as they mature, the court will order relief against the debtor. Relief may be also ordered if someone has been appointed to control the debtor's property for the purpose of satisfying a judgment or other lien.

Two alternatives are possible in a bankruptcy proceeding against an individual. The individual's property either will be **liquidated** under Chapter 7 of the bankruptcy law and the debts discharged, or the debts will be **adjusted** under Chapter 13. Under Chapter 13, individuals who have secured debts (mortgages, security interests against personal property, and so on) of less than $1,081,400 and unsecured debts of less than $360,475 (these amounts change periodically) can have their debts adjusted by the court for repayment. Time periods for repayment are also adjusted, and the debtor repays the creditors the adjusted debts over a three- to five-year period.

Congress amended the bankruptcy law in 2005 to force above median income earners to repay their adjusted debts under Chapter 13 rather than have them liquidated under Chapter 7. When this happened, bankruptcy filings, which had risen to over two million in 2005, dropped to 827,000 in 2006 but were back to over one million in 2007.

Trustee in Bankruptcy   The **trustee** in bankruptcy is an important person in the bankruptcy proceeding. The trustee is someone elected by the creditors to represent the debtor's estate in taking possession of and liquidating (selling off) the debtor's property. Broad powers are granted to the trustee.

Consumers sometimes get credit that they cannot repay, and consequently they end up going bankrupt.

Do make sure you know the difference between liquidation under Chapter 7 and adjustment of debts under Chapter 13.

The trustee may void gifts and other transfers of assets made for inadequate consideration by a bankruptcy that diminishes the assets the creditors can claim against.

The trustee can (1) affirm or disaffirm contracts with the debtor which are yet to be performed; (2) set aside fraudulent conveyances, that is, transfers of the debtor's property for inadequate consideration or for the purpose of defrauding creditors; (3) void certain transfers of property by the debtor to creditors which prefer some creditors over others; (4) sue those who owe the debtor some obligation; and (5) set aside statutory liens against the debtor's property which take effect upon the beginning of bankruptcy proceedings.

Creditor Priority   Under bankruptcy laws, certain creditors receive priority over others in the distribution of a debtor's assets. The law divides creditors into priority classes, as set forth in Table 18.5. The amounts owing to each creditor class must be satisfied fully before the next lower class of priority can receive anything. Note that secured creditors who hold mortgages or Article 9 security interests in the debtor's property usually have priority over the bankruptcy creditor classes.

Discharge   From the debtor's point of view, the purpose of bankruptcy is to secure a **discharge** of further obligation to the creditor. Certain debts, however, cannot be discharged in bankruptcy. They include those arising from taxes, alimony and child support, intentional torts (including fraud), breach of fiduciary duty, liabilities arising from drunken driving, government fines, and debts not submitted to the trustee because the creditor has lacked knowledge of the proceedings. Education loans which become due within five years of the filing of the bankruptcy petition are also nondischargeable.

In addition to having certain debts denied discharge, the debtor may fail to receive a discharge from *any* of his or her debts if the courts find that the

Courts may deny bankruptcy discharge when they believe the debtor will be able to pay off the debt in the next few years, often because the debtor has a good job.

table 18.5 Priority of Bankruptcy Creditors

1. Spouse, former spouse, child, or guardian with claims for domestic support
2. Creditors with claims that arise from the costs of preserving and administering the debtor's estate (such as the fee of an accountant who performs as audit of the debtor's books for the trustee)
3. Creditors with claims that occur in the ordinary course of the debtor's business after a bankruptcy petition has been filed
4. Employees who are owed wages earned within 180 days of the bankruptcy petition (limited to $12,475 per employee)
5. Employee benefit plans that require contributions based on services rendered within 180 days of the bankruptcy petition (limited to $12,475 per employee)
6. Grain producers or fisherman who have supplied goods
7. Consumers who have paid deposits or prepayments for undelivered goods or services (limited to $2,775 per consumer)
8. Government (for tax claims)
9. Federal depository institution regulatory agency (such as the FDIC) for commitments to maintain capital
10. One who is injured from a motor vehicle operated by the debtor while intoxicated

Source: 11 U.S.C. §507.

debtor has concealed property, falsified or concealed books of record, refused to obey court orders, failed to explain satisfactorily any losses of assets, or been discharged in bankruptcy within the prior six years. Courts may deny this discharge of debts altogether when relief would amount to a "substantial abuse" of the bankruptcy process, meaning usually that the consumer will have the income in the next several years to repay the debts owed.

ADDITIONAL CONSUMER PROTECTION

Additional statutes protect consumers. This section mentions some of the key laws not otherwise covered by this chapter. Some are enforced by the Federal Trade Commission or other regulatory agency, and many give consumers private remedies and rights of enforcement. What follows are just brief summaries of key consumer protection provisions.

- *Fair Credit Billing Act*—administered by the Federal Trade Commission, this act limits liability on lost, stolen, or misused credit cards to $50. Establishes rules for resolving billing disputes with the credit card issuer. Enables consumers who follow certain procedures to assert any defense against the credit card issuer that could have been asserted against a merchant who has sold shoddy merchandise, given bad service, or failed to perform as promised. Basically, the act allows consumers to require credit card issuers to recredit accounts in such a situation. Applies only to amounts over $50 within the consumer's home state or within 100 mile radius of the consumer's home.

The Fair Credit Billing Act applies to credit cards. The Electronic Fund Transfer Act applies to automatic teller machine transactions and point-of-purchase debit transactions. Note the greater amount that the consumer can be responsible for under the latter act.

- *Electronic Fund Transfer Act*—administered by the Consumer Financial Protection Bureau, this act limits liability on lost, stolen, or misused automatic teller and check cards (debit cards) to $50 if reported within two business days of consumers' learning of a misuse. After two business days consumers responsibility is up to $500, except that after 60 days without reporting, responsibility becomes unlimited. The act also establishes procedures that banks and other financial institutions must follow when consumers dispute amounts billed by the bank.

- *Consumer Product Safety Act*—administered by the Consumer Product Safety Commission. The act requires the commission to protect consumers against "unreasonable risk" of harm and applies to thousands of consumer products. The commission protects consumers against unreasonable risk of injury by developing mandatory and voluntary standards, banning harmful consumer products, issuing recalls of products, and researching potential product hazards. The law was amended in 2008 by the Consumer Product Safety Improvement Act, which provided the CPSC with new regulatory and enforcement tools.

- *Magnuson-Moss Warranty Act*—administered by the Federal Trade Commission. Applies to all product warranties on consumer products costing more than $15. These warranties must be identified as "full" or "limited." Under full warranties a warrantor must repair or replace a defective product within a reasonable time and at no charge, including no shipping costs. Implied warranties may not be limited in full warranties, and other limitations must be disclosed fully and conspicuously in readily understood language. All other warranties must be described as "limited warranties," and their limitations must also be described conspicuously and in plain English. Failure to comply with the act enables consumers to sue for damages and reasonable attorney fees.

- *Federal Food, Drug and Cosmetic Act*—administered by the Food and Drug Administration, this act and the rules established under it by the FDA establish that prescription drugs must be proven effective and safe by extensive testing before they can be sold. Medical devices are likewise regulated. The act also empowers the FDA to protect consumers against unsafe and adulterated foods.

- *Various labeling laws*—administered by various federal and state agencies, these laws require informative labels and warnings to be given on various products. Some labels identify the country of clothing manufacture. Other labels specify nutritional amounts for packaged foods. Still other labels, like the surgeon general's warning on cigarette packages, disclose potential dangers of products.

- *State consumer protection*—administered by the states, consumer protection agencies similar to the Federal Trade Commission exist in many states. The states also have other consumer protection laws ranging from the application of warranties under state commercial codes to various antifraud statutes.

Key Terms

Review Questions and Problems

The Federal Trade Commission

1. *The FTC and Trade Practice Regulation*

   (a) Explain the difference between a cease and desist order and a consent order. Which type of order is used most frequently at the FTC for consumer protection? Why do you suppose this type of order is most often used?

   (b) What is a trade regulation rule?

2. *FTC Penalties and Remedies*

   Reader's Digest sent out some 17 million sweepstakes promotions to consumers that featured "travel checks" and "cash convertible bonds" that the FTC claimed were deceptive and violated a previous consent order as well. What potential fine did the *Digest* face?

3. *False and Deceptive Advertising*

   The Mosquito No Company claims that its electronic mosquito device will "eliminate all mosquito problems within a one-half acre area." Actually, the device will only work if there is no standing water on the half acre. Explain how the FTC will evaluate this advertising for deception.

Consumer Privacy

4. *Limitations on Government*

   Explain how the U.S. Constitution limits government privacy intrusions. Why is this not an effective limitation on private businesses?

5. *Traditional Business Privacy*

   If a grocery store records video of a customer as he shops for cereal, will that customer have a case based on intrusion on seclusion?

6. *Electronic and Online Privacy*

   BigCo records all of the phone calls its employees make on BigCo's land-line phones. Is BigCo liable under the Electronic Communications Privacy Act?

7. An online backpack store sells many products that are popular with elementary school children. The store knows some children under 10 subscribe to the store's coupon service. Is the store subject to the Children's Online Privacy Protection Act?

8. Should what people say and do on computers be protected by a legal fence, or should these activities be freely available to businesses wishing to use the information they provide for marketing purposes?

Federal Credit Regulations

9. *The Equal Credit Opportunity Act*

   Jane Thomas applies for automobile financing at Kenwood Cars Inc., a used-car dealership. The dealership obtains a credit report on her. On the basis of this report, the dealership denies her credit. The manager informs her that she will have to get her husband to cosign her application if she wants dealership financing. She refuses, and sues Kenwood under the ECOA. What was the result and why?

10. *The Fair Credit Reporting Act*

    The ABC department store refuses credit to Mary Jane. Mary Jane has a good job and no debts. She cannot understand the refusal. What would you suggest Mary Jane do? Explain.

11. *The Truth-in-Lending Act*

    Under the Truth-in-Lending Act, what is a finance charge? What charges are and are not included as finance charges?

Debt Collection and Consumer Protection

12. *The Fair Debt Collection Practices Act*

    The Zenith Credit Bureau telephones Dan and his family almost daily about payment of a $3,500 debt. The phone calls are causing stress for Dan's family. Dan cannot afford to pay the debt at present, and he needs a listed telephone number for his business. Is there anything Dan can do legally to stop the calls from Zenith?

13. *Consumer Financial Protection Act*

    Why do you think Congress passed the Consumer Financial Protection Act when the FTC already had authority to regulate many acts over which the CFPB also has authority?

14. *Bankruptcy*

    Discuss the concept of "discharge" as used in bankruptcy law. What types of debts are not dischargeable? Explain.

15. *Additional Consumer Protection*

Janet buys a year's membership in a new spa and exercise gym that has just opened. She pays $500 with her credit card. Less than one month later the business closes its doors, leaving 450 members without a place to work out. The owner, who has vanished, also failed to pay his employees, rent on the building, and payments on his leased equipment. Everyone suspects fraud. According to consumer protection laws, what recourse might Janet have under the circumstances?

business *discussions*

1. The regulation of deceptive trade practices under Section 5 of the FTC Act, the disclosures required by the Truth-in-Lending Act, and the provisions of many other consumer protection laws aimed at helping consumers by preventing business activities that might violate what common-law and statutory tort found in Chapter 10? Explain.

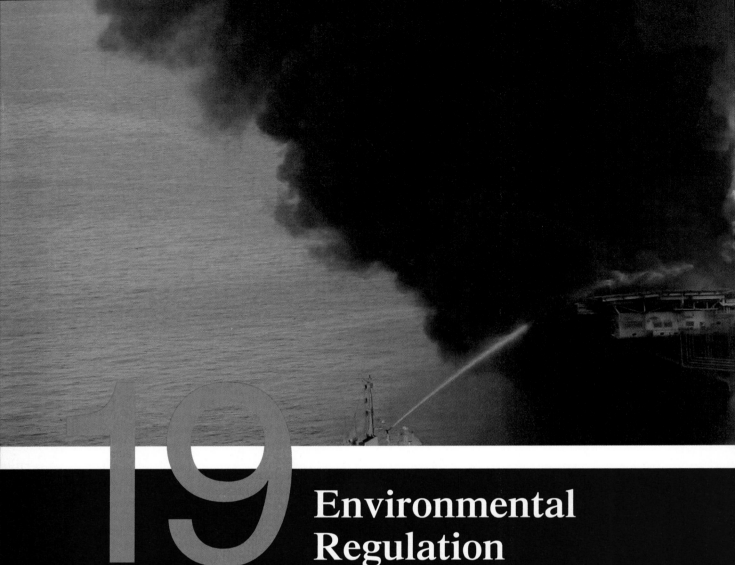

19

Environmental Regulation

▮ Learning Objectives

In this chapter, you will learn:

19-1. To analyze how the government itself regulates its own impact on the environment at both the federal and state levels.

19-2. To understand the laws regulating business uses that have an impact on our shared resources of air and water.

19-3. To explain how public and private laws are used to address harmful substances and the damage to the environment caused by them

19-4. To evaluate why environment will be one of the most important challenges and opportunities for business during the twenty-first century.

Much economic activity causes pollution. This chapter introduces you to the boundaries that the law creates to regulate the environmental pollution created in modern business life.

Private property is the most productive system known for producing the goods and services people want and need. When people have the exclusive use of their resources for productive purposes, it maximizes the wealth of nations, but it can also cause harmful pollution. It can harm public resources like the nation's air and water and the private resources of individual health and wellbeing. It's difficult to have environmental laws that balance commercial production of goods and services with harmful effects to air, water, and human health.

Common law litigation works well in resolving disputes and awarding compensation in cases involving individuals and their problems with each other. Judges and courts, however, do not work as effectively when problems involve immensely complex technical issues of environmental pollution that may affect others over great distances and long periods of time and arise both from business activity and government action. The rules that set the boundaries for what and how much it is proper to pollute do not come from the common law. They come from legislated public policy and the legal authority of large federal and state regulatory agencies. The implementation of environmental law is highly political, and as unemployment and economic woes complicate the expense of pollution regulation, the politics become more heated.

As you read this chapter, keep in mind the wide discretion that regulators have to act or not to act in regulating environmental pollution. It is inevitable that politics become involved in environmental law.

Environmental and pollution-control laws govern regulation on three levels:

- Government's regulation of itself
- Government's regulation of business
- Suits by private individuals

Sidebar 19.1 illustrates this breakdown.

---

sidebar 19.1

Categories of Environmental and Pollution-Control Laws

GOVERNMENT'S REGULATION OF ITSELF

National Environmental Policy Act.
State environmental policy acts.

GOVERNMENT'S REGULATION OF BUSINESS

Clean Air Act.
Clean Water Act.
Pesticide Control Acts.
Solid Waste Disposal Act.
Toxic Substances Control Act.

Resource Conservation and Recovery Act.
Other federal, state, and local statutes.

SUITS BY PRIVATE INDIVIDUALS

Citizen enforcement provisions of various statutes.
Public and private nuisance.
Trespass.
Negligence.
Strict liability for ultrahazardous activity.

This chapter examines environmental and pollution-control laws by looking first at federal environmental policy and then at specific laws aimed at reducing specific kinds of pollution. The emphasis is on the compliance these laws force on business and industry. The final section of this chapter looks at the rights and liabilities of private individuals under environmental law.

Administering environmental laws at the federal level is the Environmental Protection Agency (EPA). Since many of the laws provide for joint federal-state enforcement, the states also have strong environmental agencies. Policies are set at the federal level, and the states devise plans to implement them. States, and even local governments, also enforce their own laws that affect the environment and control pollution.

Government's Regulation of Itself

The modern environmental movement began in the 1960s. As it gained momentum, it generated political pressure that forced government to reassess its role in environmental issues.

THE NATIONAL ENVIRONMENTAL POLICY ACT

LO 19-1

The way the government considers the environmental impact of its decision making greatly interests the business community. For instance, the federal government pays private enterprise almost $100 billion annually to conduct studies, prepare reports, and carry out projects. In addition, the federal government is by far the nation's largest landholder, controlling one-third of the entire area of the United States. Private enterprise must rely on governmental agencies to issue permits and licenses to explore and mine for minerals, graze cattle, cut timber, or conduct other business activities on government property. Thus, any congressional legislation that influences the decision-making concerning federal funding or license granting also affects business. Such legislation is the **National Environmental Policy Act (NEPA).**

NEPA Basics NEPA took effect in 1970. It establishes a "national policy [to] encourage productive and enjoyable harmony" with nature and promotes "the understanding of the ecological systems and natural resources" important to the United States. It imposes specific "action forcing" requirements on federal agencies. The most important requirement demands that all federal agencies prepare an **environmental impact statement (EIS)** prior to taking certain actions. An EIS must be included "in every recommendation or report on proposals for legislation and other major federal actions significantly affecting the quality of the human environment." This EIS is a "detailed statement" that estimates the environmental impact of the proposed action. Any discussion of such action and its impact must contain information on adverse environmental effects that cannot be avoided, any irreversible use of resources necessary, and available alternatives to the action (see Figure 19.1).

There have been hundreds of cases that interpret the EIS requirements. In the following case, the Supreme Court decides whether psychological fear caused by the risk of accident at a nuclear power plant is an "environmental effect."

Several regulatory guidelines have made the EIS more useful. One guideline directs federal agencies to engage in **scoping.** Scoping requires that even

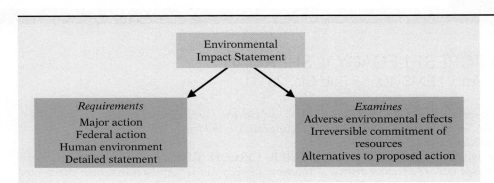

Figure 19.1
Components of the environmental impact statement.

In *Department of Transportation v. Public Citizen,* the Supreme Court upheld a CEQ regulation permitting agencies to prepare an environmental assessment (EA) that is less detailed than an EIS when it is not clear that the law requires an EIS.124 S. Ct. 2204 (2004)

before preparing an EIS, agencies must designate which environmental issues of a contemplated action are most significant. It encourages impact statements to focus on more substantial environmental concerns and reduce the attention devoted to trivial issues. It also allows other agencies and interested parties to participate in the scoping process. Scoping helps ensure that formal impact statements will address matters regarded as most important.

Another guideline directs that EISs be "clear, to the point, and written in plain English." This requirement deters the use of technical jargon and helps those reading impact statements to understand them. The Council on Environmental Quality (CEQ) has also limited the length of impact statements, which once ran to more than 1,000 pages, to 150 pages, except in unusual circumstances.

EVALUATION OF ENVIRONMENTAL IMPACT STATEMENTS

Importantly, NEPA does not require that federal agencies follow the conclusions of an EIS. However, as a practical political matter, agencies are not likely to proceed with a project when an EIS concludes that the environmental costs outweigh the benefits. EISs have been responsible for the abandonment or delay of many federal projects.

Some critics point out that the present process fails to consider the economic injury caused by abandoning or delaying projects. They also contend that those preparing EISs are forced to consider far too many alternatives to proposed federal action without regard to their economic reasonableness. Other critics maintain that most impact statements are too descriptive and not sufficiently analytical. They fear that the EIS is "a document of compliance rather than a decision-making tool." A final general criticism of the EIS process notes the limits of its usefulness. As follow-ups on some EISs have shown, environmental factors are often so complex that projections concerning environmental effects amount to little more than guesswork.

In Case 19.1, note the complexity of the scientific issues and consider whether it would have been possible for the judge to come to the opposite conclusion than he did and to require additional information in the EIS. Such is often the situation in NEPA cases.

 case **19.1**

SIERRA FOREST LEGACY V. SHERMAN
2011 U.S. App. LEXIS 10655 (9th Cir., 2011)

The Sierra Forest Legacy and other plaintiffs challenged the National Forest Service's plan for allowing additional timbering activities in the Sierra Nevada Forest, claiming that the environmental impact statement under NEPA was inadequate. The federal district *court upheld the Forest Service's plan, and the plaintiffs appealed to the federal court of appeals.*

FISHER, CIRCUIT JUDGE: . . . The National Environmental Policy Act is "our basic national charter for protection of the environment." NEPA requires that all agencies of the Federal Government shall include in every recommendation or report on proposals for legislation and other major Federal actions significantly affecting the quality of the human environment, a detailed statement by the responsible official on (1) the environmental impact of the proposed action, (2) any adverse environmental effects which cannot be avoided should the proposal be implemented, (3) alternatives to the proposed action, (4) the relationship between local short-term uses of man's environment and the maintenance and enhancement of long-term productivity, and (5) any irreversible and irretrievable commitments of resources which would be involved in the proposed action should it be implemented.

Agencies must also "study, develop, and describe appropriate alternatives to recommended courses of action in any proposal which involves unresolved conflicts concerning alternative uses of available resources." When an agency produces an environmental impact statement (EIS), it must "provide full and fair discussion of significant environmental impacts and shall inform decisionmakers and the public of the reasonable alternatives which would avoid or minimize adverse impacts or enhance the quality of the human environment."

"NEPA . . . does not impose any substantive requirements on federal agencies—it 'exists to ensure a process.'" So long as "the adverse environmental effects of the proposed action are adequately identified and evaluated, the agency is not constrained by NEPA from deciding that other values outweigh the environmental costs."

The Sierra Forest Legacy and other plaintiffs argue that the Forest Service violated NEPA when approving the 2004 Plan by failing to disclose and to respond to the views of experts opposed to intensified management. "In preparing the final EIS, the agency must discuss at appropriate points . . . any responsible opposing view which was not adequately discussed in the draft statement and [must] indicate the agency's response to the issue raised." . . . The mere presence of expert disagreement does not violate NEPA because "experts in every scientific field routinely disagree." NEPA also does not require an agency to publish "every comment . . . in the final EIS. Nor must an agency set forth at full length the views with which it disagrees."

Sierra Forest and others presented an array of experts who submitted comments to the 2004 draft EIS. As a general matter, the final SEIS incorporates a science consistency review that raises conflicting perspectives. It also acknowledges and responds to general critiques concerning the use of science. Plaintiffs' experts' more specific criticisms can be broken down into five categories.

Most critiques concerned the California spotted owl. The final EIS, however, expressed uncertainty concerning California spotted owl analysis, noted submission of concerns "about the reliability of habitat projections" for the California spotted owl and disclosed "conflicting science about the effects of canopy cover reductions from fuel treatments." Most importantly, the EIS dedicates nearly 12 pages to airing concerns about California spotted owl management and providing agency responses.

Second, the experts expressed concerns regarding the uncertainty inherent in long-term modeling. The final EIS acknowledges that "concerns have been expressed about the reliability of habitat projections used in this analysis and the deterministic nature of the models underlying those projections" but explains the importance and inherent flaws of modeling. The SEIS also includes modeling appendices, which describe modeling assumptions and "sensitivity analysis to address questions about uncertainty in modeling outcomes." Moreover, the Regional Forester acknowledged the validity of some critiques and chose not to rely on 120-year projections when deciding to adopt the 2004 Framework.

Third, the experts argued that the 2004 Framework will lead to further decline of fisher and marten populations. The final EIS acknowledges uncertainty concerning marten and fisher habitat use and the effect of management on persistence in the Sierra Nevada. It also recognizes that concerns have been expressed "that treatments . . . may increase fragmentation and create barriers to fisher movement," that reductions to canopy that will harm fisher habitat and about "effects . . . on marten in eastside pine habitats." The EIS also airs and responds to three pages of additional concerns regarding fisher and marten management.

Fourth, the experts raised concerns regarding meadow species, such as the willow flycatcher and Yosemite toad. The final EIS acknowledges uncertainty concerning the effects of grazing on these species and accepts one of the willow flycatcher working group's suggestions concerning development of a conservation strategy. More importantly, the SEIS raises and addresses a host of public concerns regarding both meadow species in the volume dedicated to responding to public comments.

Fifth, the experts critique the fire ecology underpinning the core management analysis. The final EIS notes uncertainty "whether unaltered wildfires would have a greater or lesser impact . . . on ecosystem integrity and habitat" compared to fires in treated areas. Again, the EIS acknowledges and responds to a substantial number of critics addressing fire and fuels management, including critiques of the scope and methods of treatment.

[continued]

The plaintiffs specifically argue that "the agency did not bring attention to . . . critical expert comments but rather mixed them into the stack of all public comments . . . ." Similarly, they contend that the "SEIS does not disclose that these 'other' viewpoints were expressed by the country's leading spotted owl experts, including the retired Forest Service owl expert . . . and the agency's own wildlife office." However, NEPA does not require that a final EIS prioritize the concern of scientific experts or disclose their identities among public critiques. The practical concerns of individual landholders or hikers may be just as important—and just

as trenchant—as the formal submissions of academic experts. So long as an EIS addresses the substance of public comments, it need not single out the authors.

In sum, the EIS dedicates over 120 pages to raising and meaningfully responding to public critiques. That is all NEPA requires. The plaintiffs do not argue that the Forest Service's decision not to adopt critiques was arbitrary, capricious or contrary to law. Therefore, the Forest Service did not violate NEPA by failing to disclose conflicting scientific opinion.

Affirmed.

KEY POINTS

- NEPA requires agencies to carefully consider environmental impact and, in that way, requires a process but does not determine the decisions.
- NEPA does not require agencies to prioritize scientific experts or give special consideration to particular experts.
- The EIS included a thorough review of project critiques and responded to them adequately. It met the standard imposed by NEPA.

Don't forget that many states have laws similar to NEPA which require environmental impact statements.

Although the NEPA applies only to federal actions, many states have enacted similar legislation to assist their decision making. Many interpretive problems found on the national level are also encountered at the state level. In addition, as the states frequently lack the resources and expertise of the federal government, state EISs are often even less helpful in evaluating complex environmental factors than are those prepared by federal agencies.

NEPA Trends Currently, NEPA is being applied to some of the most significant issues of the day. For instance, those who object to the building of a fence between the United States and Mexico have called for environmental impact statements because of the effect of the fence on wildlife and other environmental aspects. The director of Homeland Security has exercised authority to create exceptions to the NEPA requirement for the fence building. However, in another instance, federal agencies have begun to include the effect of federal actions on greenhouse gases that cause global warming in environmental impact statement preparation. NEPA remains a potentially powerful tool for administrative agency action concerning environmental concerns.

LO 19-2 Government's Regulation of Business

In the past 25 years, the federal government has enacted a series of laws regulating the impact of private enterprise on the environment. More and more companies are hiring environmental managers to deal with environmental compliance issues. This trend reflects the continuing importance of government regulation in this area. Congress may fine-tune environmental acts, but the national commitment to a cleaner environment is here to stay. As the CEO of a large chemical company observed about environmental concern, "Sometimes you find that the public has spoken, and you get on with it."

THE ENVIRONMENTAL PROTECTION AGENCY

One of the first steps taken at the federal level in response to concerns about the environment was the establishment of the **Environmental Protection Agency (EPA)** in 1970. At the federal level, the EPA coordinates public control of private action as it affects the environment.

Today, the EPA is a large agency with a number of major responsibilities (see Sidebar 19.2). Most important, it administers federal laws that concern pollution of the air and water, solid waste and toxic substance disposal, pesticide regulation, and radiation. The following sections examine these laws.

---

sidebar 19.2

Responsibilities of the EPA

- Conducts research on the harmful impact of pollution.
- Gathers information about present pollution problems.
- Assists states and local governments in controlling pollution through grants, technical advice, and other means.

- Advises the CEQ about new policies needed for protection of the environment.
- Administers federal pollution laws.

AIR POLLUTION

In 1257, Queen Eleanor of England was driven from Nottingham Castle because of harsh smoke from the numerous coal fires in London. Coal had come into widespread use in England during this time, following the cutting of forests for fuel and agricultural purposes. By 1307, a royal order prohibited coal burning in London's kilns under punishment of "grievous ransoms." This early attempt at controlling air pollution does not appear, however, to have been very effective. As recently as the London smog of 1952, four thousand people died of air pollution-related causes, including coal smoke.

In the United States, the key federal legislation for controlling air pollution is the Clean Air Act.

Clean Air Act and Amendments The **Clean Air Act** directs the EPA administrator to establish air quality standards and to see that these standards are achieved according to a definite timetable. The administrator has set primary and secondary air quality standards for particulates, carbon monoxide, sulfur dioxide, nitrogen dioxide, hydrocarbons, and lead. **Primary air quality standards** are those necessary to protect public health. **Secondary air**

quality standards guard the public from other adverse air pollution effects such as injury to property, vegetation, and climate and damage to aesthetic values. In most instances, primary and secondary air quality standards are identical.

Government regulation of private action under the Clean Air Act is a joint federal and state effort. The EPA sets national ambient (outside) air quality standards, and the states devise implementation plans, which the EPA must approve, to carry them out. The states thus bear principal responsibility for enforcing the Clean Air Act, with the EPA providing standard setting, coordinating, and supervisory functions. However, the EPA may also participate in enforcement. The administrator can require the operator of any air pollution source to keep such records and perform such monitoring or sampling as the EPA thinks appropriate. In addition, the EPA has the right to inspect these records and data. Various criminal and civil penalties and fines back up the Clean Air Act. In addition, industries that do not obey cleanup orders face payment to the EPA; payment amounts to the economic savings they realize from their failure to install and operate proper antipollution equipment.

In setting air quality standards, does the EPA have to consider the costs to business? In *Whitman v. American Trucking*, the Supreme Court ruled that the Clean Air Act "unambiguously bars cost considerations" from the air quality standards-setting process.

In 1990, Congress passed significant amendments to the Clean Air Act. These amendments have added billions of dollars annually to the cost of complying with environmental regulations. In cities that did not meet clean air standards, businesses were required to install new pollution control equipment, and tail-pipe emissions for cars and trucks were reduced. A pilot program in California has introduced alternative fuel cars, and cleaner gasoline blends are now sold in specific cities with the worst pollution problems.

Since many cities currently do not meet existing Clean Air Act standards, the amendments force businesses in these areas to install new pollution-control equipment to cut emissions. Tailpipe emissions for cars and trucks must be reduced, and companies must phase in alternative fuel vehicles for their fleets of vehicles. A pilot program for California will introduce up to 300,000 alternative fuel cars. The amendments also required sale of cleaner gasoline blends in cities with the worst pollution problems. The goal of all these requirements is to cut pollution by 3% per year until air quality standards are met. The states have prepared blueprints for meeting these goals.

Expressing concern about airborne toxic chemicals, the 1990 amendments require industry to use the "best available technology" on plants to reduce emissions of 189 toxics by 90%. Significantly, the plants covered include bakeries and dry cleaning businesses as well as chemical companies. The EPA must also study how to reduce toxic emissions from vehicles and fuels.

Clean Air Act Enforcement   Civil and criminal penalties enforce the Clean Air Act. Criminal sanctions include fines of individuals up to $250,000 and up to 15 years' imprisonment. Corporations can be fined up to $1 million for knowingly endangering people with emissions and up to $500,000 per incident of negligent emissions. Civil settlements between the EPA and businesses are very common.

Air Pollution Sources   For control purposes, the Clean Air Act amendments divide air pollution sources into two categories: *stationary source* and

The Clean Air Act requires the EPA to set air quality standards without regard to their costs to business.

"Acid rain" is seldom front-page news anymore because of the Clean Air Act's success in controlling sulfur dioxide emissions.

In 2005, DaimlerChrysler agreed to a $94 million settlement with the EPA to pay a civil fine and improve emissions controls on certain Jeep and Dodge models.

mobile source (transportation). Under the state implementation plans, major stationary polluters, such as steel mills and utilities, must reduce their emissions to a level sufficient to bring down air pollution to meet primary and secondary standards. Polluters must follow timetables and schedules in complying with these requirements. To achieve designated standards, they must install a variety of control devices, including wet collectors (scrubbers), filter collectors, tall stacks, electrostatic precipitators, and afterburners. New stationary pollution sources, or modified ones, must install the best system of emission reduction that has been adequately demonstrated. Under the act's provision, citizens are granted standing to enforce compliance with these standards.

The act requires both stationary and mobile sources to meet a timetable of air pollution standards for which control technology may not exist at the time. This *technology-forcing* aspect of the act is unique to the history of governmental regulation of business, yet it has been upheld by the Supreme Court. In large part due to technology forcing, new automobiles today emit less than 1% as much pollution per mile as cars of 25 years ago.

Technology forcing does not always succeed. It is neither always possible nor always feasible to force new technological developments. In recognizing this fact, the Clean Air Act allows the EPA in many instances to grant *compliance waivers* and *variances* from its standards.

CLEAN AIR ACT TODAY

As originally implemented, the Clean Air Act did not try to promote efficient pollution. For instance, if an area's air could tolerate a million tons of pollution per year, the authorities made no attempt to identify those who could make the best productive use of air pollution. Likewise, when a business was permitted to pollute a certain annual amount, the act specified the allowable pollution from each smokestack or other polluting source within the business instead of letting the business arrange its total allowable pollution in the most efficient way.

In the past few years, the EPA has moved to make its regulatory practices more economically efficient. All new pollution-control rules are now subjected to cost-benefit analysis. The EPA has also developed specific policies to achieve air pollution control in an economically efficient manner.

Traditionally, the EPA has regulated each individual pollution emission **point source** (such as a smokestack) within an industrial plant or complex. Increasingly, however, the EPA is encouraging the states, through their implementation plans, to adopt an approach called the **bubble concept.** Under the bubble concept, each plant complex is treated as if it were encased in a bubble. Instead of each pollution point source being licensed for a limited amount of pollution emission, the pollution of the plant complex as a whole is the focus of regulation. Businesses may suggest their own plans for cleaning up multiple sources of pollution within the entire complex as long as the total pollution emitted does not exceed certain limits. This approach permits flexibility in curtailing pollution and provides businesses with economic incentives to discover new methods of control. The Supreme Court has upheld the EPA's authority to approve the bubble concept even in states where pollution exceeds air quality standards.

Emissions Reduction Banking   A number of states have developed EPA-approved plans for **emissions reduction banking.** Under such plans, businesses can cut pollution beyond what the law requires and "bank" these

The bubble concept, emissions reduction, banking, and cap and trade all give incentives to businesses to limit emissions, rather than relying on "command and control," that is, on rules simply requiring attainment of air quality standards.

reductions for their own future use or to sell to other companies as emission offsets. Eventually, we may be headed for a *marketable rights* approach to pollution control, under which the right to discharge a certain pollutant would be auctioned off to the highest bidder. This approach would promote efficiency by offering to those who have the greatest need for pollution rights the opportunity to obtain them by bidding highest for them. Under the 1990 Clean Air Act amendments, Congress specifically allows utility companies to engage in emissions reduction banking and trading. Since 1992, the Chicago Board of Trade has run an auction in pollution credits given by the EPA to the nation's 110 most polluting utility plants.

According to the EPA, emissions trading accounts significantly for the fact that electric utilities today emit a quarter fewer tons of sulfur dioxide than they did in 1980 while producing 41% more electricity. The General Accounting Office figures that emissions trading saves the utility industry $3 billion a year over previous pollution-enforcement approaches. The EPA estimates that for every $1 billion of sulfur dioxide reduction there is a $50 billion saving in health costs. As Sidebar 19.3 discusses, emissions reduction banking and trading is rapidly growing and extending beyond the Clean Air Act.

Prevention of Significant Deterioration   Another important policy of the Clean Air Act is the **prevention of significant deterioration**. Under this policy, pollution emission is controlled, even in areas where the air is cleaner than prevailing primary and secondary air quality standards require. In some of these areas, the EPA permits construction of new pollution emission sources according to a strictly limited scheme. In other areas, it allows no new pollution emission at all. Critics of this policy argue that it prevents industry from moving into southern and western states, where air quality is cleaner than standards require.

The Permitting Process   One of the most controversial issues involving the Clean Air Act concerns the delay and red tape caused by the *permitting process*. Before a business can construct new pollution emission sources, it must obtain the necessary environmental permits from the appropriate

sidebar 19.3

Beyond the Clean Air Act

In 2003, the Chicago Climate Exchange began operation. This program for trading marks the first time that major U.S. companies have begun to take voluntary property-based market steps to cut emissions, called greenhouse gasses (GHGs), linked to global warming.

The European Union already takes a market approach to limiting GHC. These markets are based on the principle of **cap and trade.** The government issues a limited number of pollution permits, effectively capping total GHG pollution. Companies then trade

the permits. Whoever can reduce emissions can sell the unused amount of a permit. The government may slowly reduce the number of outstanding permits.

However, Congress has refused to pass national cap and trade legislation, and the Regional Greenhouse Gas Initiative, a cooperative cap and trade effort to reduce emissions from utilities sources in 10 mid-Atlantic and New England states has lost several members. A similar organization, the Western Climate Initiative, began with seven states and now is also losing members.

state agency. Today, the estimated time needed to acquire the necessary permits to build a coal-fired electric-generating plant is five to ten years. This is nearly twice the length of time it took in the early 1970s. The formalities of the permitting process, the lack of flexibility in state implementation plans, and the requirement that even minor variations in state implementation plans be approved by the EPA—all these factors contribute to delay. Both the EPA and Congress are considering ways to streamline the permitting process.

The EPA is experimenting with allowing states to issue "smart permits" to air polluters. Under these permits, polluters can engage in "a family of alternative operating scenarios" (i.e., engage in new operations) without the expensive delay of obtaining new permits as the EPA previously required. Some environmental groups oppose smart permitting as failing to allow communities a time period to determine if new operations really meet clean air standards.

Indoor Pollution The EPA has also grown increasingly concerned about indoor air pollution. Paints, cleaning products, furniture polishes, gas furnaces, and stoves all emit pollutants that can be harmful to human health. Radioactive radon seeping into homes and buildings from the ground has now been recognized as a major health hazard. Some studies have found that indoor levels of certain pollutants far exceed outdoor levels, whether at work or at home. Although the Clean Air Act does not currently apply to indoor pollution, its application may be extended in the future.

Significantly, the EPA does not regulate indoor air pollution under the Clean Air Act although OSHA could regulate it as to the workplace. Numerous major businesses already ban workplace smoking. Many local governments also regulate or prohibit indoor smoking in public buildings.

Conclusion In spite of the controversy generated by the Clean Air Act, evidence indicates that the overall air quality in the United States is steadily improving. The 16,000 quarts of air we each breathe daily are cleaner and healthier in most places than they were a decade ago. Yet an estimated 80 million persons in the United States still breathe air that violates one or more primary air quality standards. Case 19.2 considers the EPA's efforts to protect air quality generated by upwind sources that affect downwind states.

 case **19.2**

ENVIRONMENTAL PROTECTION AGENCY V. EME HOMER CITY GENERATION L.P.
134 S.Ct. 1584 (2014)

A group of state and local governments, joined by industry and labor groups, sought a review of EPA's Cross-State Air Pollution Rule (known as the Transport Rule). The D.C. Circuit Court vacated the rule in its entirety. The Supreme Court granted certiorari.
GINSBURG, J.: Air pollution is transient, heedless of state boundaries. Pollutants generated by upwind sources are often transported by air currents, sometimes over hundreds of miles, to downwind States. As the pollution travels out of state, upwind States are relieved of the associated costs. Those costs are borne instead by the downwind States, whose ability to achieve and maintain satisfactory air quality is hampered by the steady stream of infiltrating pollution.

For several reasons, curtailing interstate air pollution poses a complex challenge for environmental regulators. First, identifying the upwind origin of downwind air pollution is no easy endeavor. Most upwind States propel pollutants to more than one downwind State, many downwind States receive pollution from multiple upwind States, and some States qualify as both upwind and downwind. The overlapping and interwoven linkages between upwind and downwind States with which EPA had to contend number in the thousands. . . .

Over the past 50 years, Congress has addressed interstate air pollution several times and with increasing rigor. In 1963, Congress directed federal authorities to "encourage cooperative activities by the States and local governments for the prevention and control of air pollution." In 1970, Congress made this instruction more concrete, introducing features still key to the Act. For the first time, Congress directed EPA to establish national ambient air quality standards (NAAQS) for pollutants at levels that will protect public health. Once EPA settles on an NAAQS, the Act requires the Agency to designate "nonattainment" areas, i.e., locations where the concentration of a regulated pollutant exceeds the NAAQS.

The Act then shifts the burden to States to propose plans adequate for compliance with the NAAQS. Each State must submit a State Implementation Plan (SIP) to EPA within three years of any new or revised NAAQS. If EPA determines that a State has failed to submit an adequate SIP . . . the Act requires the Agency to promulgate a Federal Implementation Plan (FIP).

[SIP] has come to be called the Good Neighbor Provision. . . . The statute requires States to eliminate those "amounts" of pollution that "contribute significantly to nonattainment" in downwind States. Thus, EPA's task is to reduce upwind pollution, but only in "amounts" that push a downwind State's pollution concentrations above the relevant NAAQS. As noted earlier, however, the nonattainment of downwind States results from the collective and interwoven contributions of multiple upwind States. The statute therefore calls upon the Agency to address a thorny causation problem: How should EPA allocate among multiple contributing upwind States responsibility for a downwind State's excess pollution?

As EPA interprets the statute, upwind emissions rank as "amounts [that] . . . contribute significantly to nonattainment" if they (1) constitute 1% or more of a relevant NAAQS in a nonattaining downwind State and (2) can be eliminated under the cost threshold set by the Agency. In other words, to identify which emissions were to be eliminated, EPA considered both the magnitude of upwind States' contributions and the cost associated with eliminating them.

The Industry respondents argue that, however EPA ultimately divides responsibility among upwind States, the final calculation cannot rely on costs. . . . Because the Transport Rule considers costs, respondents argue, "States that contribute identical 'amounts' . . . may be deemed [by EPA] to have [made] substantially different" contributions. But, as just explained, the Agency cannot avoid the task of choosing which among equal "amounts" to eliminate. The Agency has chosen, sensibly in our view, to reduce the amount easier, i.e., less costly, to eradicate, and nothing in the text of the Good Neighbor Provision precludes that choice.

Using costs in the Transport Rule calculus, we agree with EPA, also makes good sense. Eliminating those amounts that can cost-effectively be reduced is an efficient and equitable solution to the allocation problem the Good Neighbor Provision requires the Agency to address. Efficient because EPA can achieve the levels of attainment, i.e., of emission reductions, the proportional approach aims to achieve, but at a much lower overall cost. Equitable because, by imposing uniform cost thresholds on regulated States, EPA's rule subjects to stricter regulation those States that have done relatively less in the past to control their pollution. Upwind States that have not yet implemented pollution controls of the same stringency as their neighbors will be stopped from free riding on their neighbors' efforts to reduce pollution. They will have to bring down their emissions by installing devices of the kind in which neighboring States have already invested.

Suppose, for example, that the industries of upwind State A have expended considerable resources installing modern pollution-control devices on their plants. Factories in upwind State B, by contrast, continue to run old, dirty plants. Yet, perhaps because State A is more populous and therefore generates a larger sum of pollution overall, the two States' emissions have equal effects on downwind attainment. If State A and State B are required to eliminate emissions proportionally (i.e., equally), sources in State A will be compelled to spend far more per ton of reductions because they have already utilized lower cost pollution controls. State A's sources will also have to achieve greater reductions than would have been required had they not made the cost-effective reductions in the first place. State A, in other words, will be tolled for having done more to reduce pollution in the past. EPA's cost-based allocation avoids these anomalies. . . .

We further conclude that the Good Neighbor Provision does not require EPA to disregard costs and consider exclusively each upwind State's physically proportionate responsibility for each downwind air quality problem. EPA's cost-effective allocation of emission reductions among upwind States, we hold, is a permissible, workable, and equitable interpretation of the Good Neighbor Provision.

It is so ordered.

KEY POINTS

- Under the Clean Air Act, EPA must determine what upwind states contribute to air pollution to downwind states and work to reduce it.
- The determination is a complex task that establishes air quality standards (NAAQS), identifies states that have not complied with the standards, and implements a plan for reaching the standards (the Good Neighbor Provision).
- The state and local governments and industry groups objected to the EPA prioritizing the pollution that was least costly to eliminate instead of the proportional amounts of pollution contributed by upwind states to the pollution downwind.
- Using costs in the calculation of preventing cross-state pollution makes sense and is both efficient and effective, the Court held.

table 19.1 World's Worst Air Pollution by City

	Comment
1. Beijing, China	World's highest levels of sulfur dioxide concentration
1. New Delhi, India (tie)	40% of residents suffer from respiratory illness
3. Santiago, Chile	Some days reach eight times the danger level for particulate matter
4. Mexico City, Mexico	World's highest levels of ozone
5. Ulaanbaatar, Mongolia	At times, daytime visibility requires cars to use headlights
6. Cairo, Egypt	A WHO report says living there equals smoking a pack a day of cigarettes
7. Chongqing, China	Nearly 5% of children suffer from asthma
8. Guangzhou, China	Sulfur dioxide levels second to Beijing
9. Hong Kong	Government has warned people against outdoor activities
10. Kabul, Afghanistan	Infrastructure designed for 500,000 residents now supports five million

Source: Wall St. 24/7 (2010).

Note, also, that air pollution is an international problem and that not all countries of the world have, or can afford, our air quality standards. Air pollution is especially severe in developing nations of the world, which are striving to reach our standard of living. See Table 19.1.

Air pollution reaches across international borders. Recently, President Obama proposed regulation to reduce greenhouse gases by 30% from their 2005 level by 2030. Many view this as a necessary demonstration of the United States' leadership to press for a reduction in air pollution on a global scale.

WATER POLLUTION

Business enterprise is a major source of water pollution in the United States. Almost one-half of all water used in this country is for cooling and condensing purposes in connection with industrial activities. The resulting discharge into our rivers and lakes sometimes takes the form of heated water, called *thermal effluents.* In addition to thermal effluents, industry also discharges chemical and other effluents into the nation's waterways.

The principal federal law regulating water pollution is the **Clean Water Act,** passed by Congress in 1972. As with the Clean Air Act, the Clean Water Act is administered primarily by the states in accordance with EPA standards. If the states do not fulfill their responsibilities, however, the federal government, through the EPA, can step in and enforce the law. The Clean Water Act applies to all navigable waterways, intrastate as well as interstate. Although the term *navigable* is much broader than merely meaning being able to get a boat down, in *Solid Waste Agency v. United States Army Corps of Engineers,* 531 U.S. 159 (2001), the Supreme Court ruled that mere small ponds that do not empty into streams or rivers are not "navigable" under the Clean Water Act.

The Supreme Court determined in *South Florida Water Management District v. Miccosukee Tribe of Indians* (2004) that a point source did not itself have to generate pollution. It could be merely a pumping station that moved pollution from one site to another. 124 S. Ct. 1537 (2004)

Goals and Enforcement The Clean Water Act sets goals to eliminate water pollution. Principally, these goals are to make the nation's waterways safe for swimming and other recreational use and clean enough for the protection of fish, shellfish, and wildlife. The law sets strict deadlines and strong enforcement provisions, which must be followed by industry, municipalities, and other water polluters. Enforcement of the Clean Water Act revolves around its permit discharge system. Without being subject to criminal penalties, no polluter can discharge pollutants from any *point source* (such as a pipe) without a permit, and municipal as well as industrial dischargers must obtain permits. The EPA has issued guidelines for state permit programs and has approved those programs that meet the guidelines.

Since the Clean Water Act applies to "navigable waterways," the criminal penalties of the act cover only the unpermitted point-source pollution of navigable waterways. However, the penalties under the Clean Water Act can still be substantial. Koch Industries agreed to pay a $30 million fine to settle lawsuits involving oil spills from its pipelines and oil facilities in six states.

Under the Clean Water Act, industries adopt a two-step sequence for cleanup of industrial wastes discharged into rivers and streams. The first step requires polluters to install *best practicable technology (BPT).* The second demands installation of *best available technology (BAT).* Various timetables apply in achieving these steps, according to the type of pollutant being discharged. In 1984, the EPA announced application of the bubble concept to water pollution in the steel industry.

In addition to the Clean Water Act, the EPA administers two other acts related to water pollution control. One, the Marine Protection, Research, and Sanctuaries Act of 1972, requires a permit system for the discharge or dumping of various material into the seas. The other is the Safe Drinking Water Act of 1974, which has forced the EPA to set maximum drinking water contaminant levels for certain organic and inorganic chemicals, pesticides, and microbiological pollutants.

The Clean Water Act and other current statutes do not reach one important type of water pollution: *non–point source pollution,* which comes from runoffs into streams and rivers. These runoffs often contain agricultural fertilizers and pesticides as well as oil and lead compounds from streets and highways. Congress has authorized $400 million for the National Non–Point Source Pollution Program to study the problem. Addressing non-point source pollution, the EPA has issued a rule requiring the states to impose antipollution standards for about 20,000 bodies of water. The rule requires states to set standards for the total "maximum daily load" of pollutants in a body of water. This standard, which went into effect in 2014, would apply to pollutants from non-point sources as well as point sources.

ENDANGERED SPECIES ACT

Every day entire species of animals and plants die off. As with the dinosaurs, sometimes great catastrophes like comet impacts cause species to become extinct. Gradual climate changes and competition from other species also can kill off animals and plants. However, in modern times, human activity has caused the vast majority of species extinctions. Air and water pollution, the clearing of land for agriculture, the development of water resources, hunting and fishing, and a growing human population all potentially threaten other species.

In 1973, Congress passed the Endangered Species Act (ESA), the world's toughest law protecting animals and plants, and, perhaps, the country's most controversial environmental standard. Under the act, the Secretary of the Interior can list any species as "endangered," that is, "in danger of extinction throughout all or a significant portion of its range," except for certain insect pests. ("Threatened" species are also protected.) In determining the factors of endangerment, the secretary must consider the destruction of habitat, disease or predation, commercial and recreational activity, and "other natural or manmade factors." Within a year of listing an endangered species, the secretary is required to define the "critical habitat" of the species which is the area with the biological or physical features necessary to species survival. The Fish and Wildlife Services and the National Marine Fisheries Services administer the ESA for the Department of Interior.

> An endangered species is one determined by the Secretary of the Interior to be "in danger of extinction throughout all or a significant portion of its range."

As of 2014, approximately 2,000 species of animals and plants are listed as endangered or threatened. The act also requires that recovery plans be drawn up for the listed species, and in 2014, there were such plans for approximately 1,200 of the species. Recovery plans may involve breeding of the species.

Application of the ESA Although no federal agency can authorize, fund, or carry out any action that is likely to jeopardize an endangered species, the ESA's application to private business activity has caused the greater debate in recent years. Section 9 of the act prohibits any person from transporting or trading in any endangered species of fish or wildlife (a separate section applies to plants) or from "taking any such species within the United States" or "upon the high seas." *Taking* a species is defined as "harass, harm, pursue, hunt, shoot, wound, kill, trap, capture, or collect or attempt to engage in any such conduct."

The Secretary of the Interior has further defined the "harm" of taking to mean any act that actually kills or injures wildlife, including harming habitat or essential behavior patterns. Thus, neither private businesses nor individuals can harm the habitats of endangered species. In *Babbit v. Sweet Home Chapter* (1995), the Supreme Court ruled that "the Secretary reasonably constructed the intent of Congress when he defined 'harm' to include 'significant habitat modification or degradation that actually kills or injures wildlife.'"

Note that the ESA does not permit courts or regulators to take economic factors into consideration in applying its provisions. There has been much criticism of the act, and amendments to it have been proposed to Congress. Congress has established a review board that can grant exemptions to the ESA for certain important federal projects. However, the exemptions do not apply to private activities.

The ESA requires recovery plans for the species it protects. Question: If pollution causes or contributes to global warming, and global warming endangers species like polar bears by changing their habitat, does the law require that automobile or plant emissions be regulated to diminish global warming? For now, no courts have addressed this issue.

LO 19-3 PESTICIDE CONTROL

Pests, especially insects and mice, destroy over 10% of all crops grown in the United States, causing several billion dollars of damage annually. In many underdeveloped countries, however, a much greater percentage of total crop production is lost to pests, as high as 40–50% in countries such as India. Perhaps the principal reason for our lower rate of crop loss is that the United States uses more pesticides per acre than any other country.

The widespread, continual application of pesticides creates environmental problems, however. Not only is it dangerous to wildlife, particularly birds and fish, but it is also harmful to humans and may eventually threaten our agricultural capacity itself. Rapidly breeding pests gradually become immune to the application of pesticides, and researchers may not always be able to invent new poisons to kill them.

Nationwide, nearly half of the farmers responding to one poll expressed increasing concern about their own safety when using pesticides. A National Cancer Institute report concluded that farm families suffer from elevated rates of seven types of cancer, including leukemia, with pesticides suspected as a leading cause.

The Federal Pesticide Acts Federal regulation of pesticides is accomplished primarily through two statutes: the **Federal Insecticide, Fungicide, and Rodenticide Act of 1947,** as amended, and the **Federal Environmental Pesticide Control Act of 1972 (FEPCA).** Both statutes require the registration and labeling of agricultural pesticides, although FEPCA coverage extends to the application of pesticides as well.

Under the acts, the administrator of the EPA is directed to register those pesticides that are properly labeled, meet the claims made as to their effectiveness, and will not have *unreasonable adverse effects on the environment,* which is defined as "any unreasonable risk to man or the environment, taking into account the economic, social, and environmental costs and benefits of the use of any pesticide." In addition to its authority to request registration of pesticides, the EPA classifies pesticides for either general use or restricted use. In the latter category, the EPA may impose further restrictions that require application only by a trained applicator or with the approval of a trained consultant. Today, the EPA requires that employers train agricultural workers in pesticide safety, post safety information, and place warning signs to keep workers out of freshly sprayed fields.

The EPA must register pesticides for use unless they have unreasonable adverse effects on the environment.

Enforcement The EPA has a variety of enforcement powers to ensure that pesticide goals are met, including the power to deny or suspend registration. In the 1980s, the EPA used this power and banned several pesticides suspected of causing cancer. In 2000, the EPA used its authority to halt the manufacture of household products containing the pesticide chlorpyrifos sold under the trade names Dursban and Lorsban. The EPA determined that the pesticide was more harmful to humans, particularly children, than had been thought previously.

The EPA also defines what a pesticide can and cannot be used for and may seek penalties against violators. For example, the EPA sought criminal charges against several quail-hunting clubs in Florida and Georgia that improperly used the pesticide Furadan to kill predators that ate quail eggs.

Pesticide control has been attacked by both affected businesses and the environmental movement itself. Pesticide manufacturers complain that the lengthy, expensive testing procedures required by the FEPCA registration process delay useful pesticides from reaching the market and inhibit new research. On the other hand, many in the environmental movement contend that our country's pesticide control policy is hypocritical in that the FEPCA does not apply to pesticides U.S. manufacturers ship to foreign countries. Companies can sell overseas what they cannot sell in this country.

SOLID WASTE

Pollution problems cannot always be neatly categorized. For instance, solid waste disposal processes often create pollution in several environmentally related forms. When solid waste is burned, it can cause air pollution and violate the Clean Air Act. When dumped into rivers, streams, and lakes, solid waste can pollute the water beyond amounts permitted under the Clean Water Act. Machinery used in solid waste disposal can also be subject to the regulation of the Noise Control Act.

By all accounts, solid waste pollution problems during the last 25 years have grown as pollution has risen and the country has become more affluent and productive. Currently, total solid wastes produced yearly in the United States exceed 5 billion tons, or almost 25 tons for every individual. Half this amount is agricultural waste, another third is mineral waste, and the remainder is industrial, institutional, and residential waste. Some wastes are toxic and hazardous, while others stink or attract pests. All present disposal problems of significant proportion.

Don't forget that total solid waste created in the United States divided by the U.S. population yields some 25 tons of waste for every person.

Landfills represent the primary disposal sites for most household and much business solid wastes. Figure 19.2 illustrates the composition of solid wastes in the typical landfill. According to Bill Rathje, professor of anthropology at the University of Arizona, paper is the biggest solid waste category in landfills. And paper, which in 1970 constituted 35% of landfill volume, today constitutes 50%. By contrast, disposable diapers take up less than 1% of landfill volume. Polystyrene foam, such as thermal cups, also takes up less than 1% of landfill volume. For additional figures on composition of landfill waste, see Figure 19.2.

The Solid Waste Disposal Act The **Solid Waste Disposal Act** passed in 1965 represents the primary federal effort in solid waste control. Congress recognized in this act that the main responsibility for nontoxic waste

The federal government sets no standards for and enforces no rules about general solid waste disposal.

Figure 19.2 *Composition of a typical landfill by volume.*

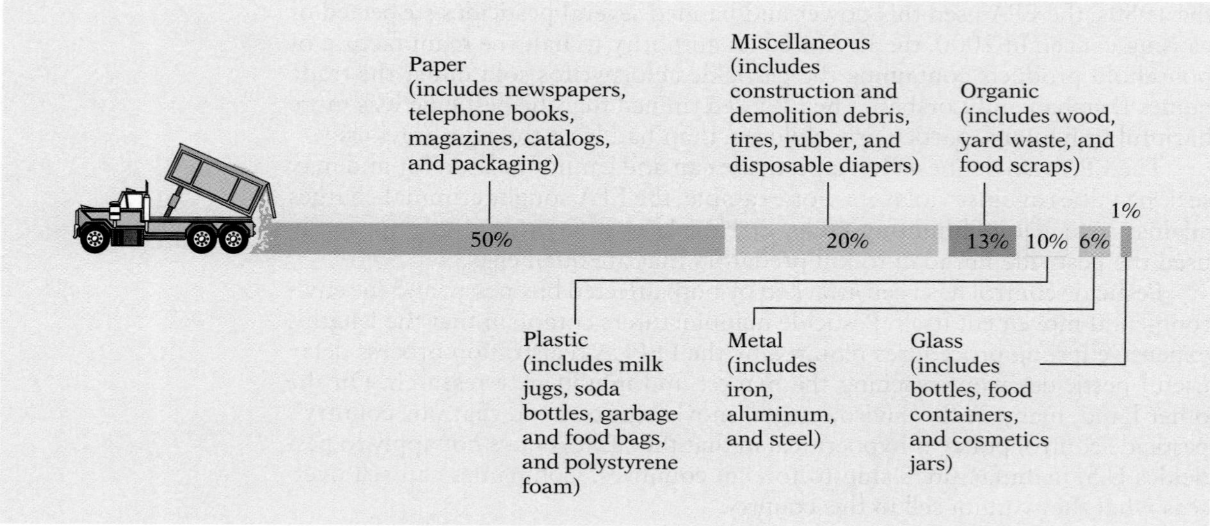

management rests with regional, state, and local management and limited the federal role in this area. Under this act, the federal role in nontoxic waste management is limited mainly to promoting research and providing technical and financial assistance to the states.

In responding to solid waste disposal problems, state and local governments have taken a variety of approaches. These include developing sanitary landfills, requiring that solid waste be separated into categories that facilitate disposal and recycling, and granting tax breaks for industries using recycled materials. A report by the Council of State Governments noted that thousands of cities and towns recycle solid wastes, usually in the form of household trash-separation requirements.

One recycling success story involves tires. The Scrap Tire Management Council estimates that two-thirds of the nearly 300 million tires discarded annually end up in dozens of retail and industrial products. Companies use recycled tires in indoor flooring, fuel alternatives, playground surfaces, and automobile parts. General Motors, for example, uses recycled rubber in 35 parts along the production line.

TOXIC AND HAZARDOUS SUBSTANCES

Legislation divides the regulation of toxic and hazardous substances into their (1) use, (2) disposal, and (3) cleanup.

According to the opinion research organization Yankelovich, Skelly, and White, the control of toxic and hazardous chemicals "ranks first" on the public's list of where the government's regulation of industry is needed. In the last several years, regulation of such chemicals has been expanding rapidly. We can divide public control of private action in this area into three categories:

- Regulation of the use of toxic chemicals.
- Regulation of toxic and hazardous waste disposal.
- Regulation of toxic and hazardous waste cleanup.

The Problem   Even as the Clean Air and Clean Water Acts are slowly beginning to diminish many types of air and water pollution, attention is being drawn to another environmental problem that is potentially the most serious of all: toxic substances. Hardly a day passes without the news media reporting some new instance of alleged threat to human health and well-being from one or another of the chemical substances so important to manufacturing, farming, mining, and other aspects of modern life.

Threats to human welfare from toxic substances are not new to history. Some scholars have suggested that poisoning from lead water pipes and drinking vessels may have depleted the ranks of the ruling class of ancient Rome and thus contributed to the downfall of the Roman Empire. More recently, some think that the "mad hatters" of the nineteenth-century fur and felt trades likely suffered brain disorders from inhaling the vapors of mercury used in their crafts. Today, however, the problem of toxic substances in the environment is more widespread. More than 70,000 industrial and agricultural chemical compounds are in commercial use, and new chemicals, a significant percentage of which are toxic, are being introduced into the marketplace at the rate of more than 1,000 substances annually.

Toxic Substances Control Act   To meet the special environmental problems posed by the use of toxic chemicals, Congress in 1976 enacted the **Toxic Substances Control Act (TSCA).** Prior to passage of the TSCA, there was no coordinated effort to evaluate effects of these chemical compounds. Some of these compounds are beneficial to society and present no threat to the environment. Some, however, are both toxic and nondegradable, a fact that in the past has been uncovered only after these compounds were introduced into wide use and became important to manufacturing and farming. The primary purpose of the TSCA is to force an early evaluation of suspect chemicals before they become economically important.

The EPA collects information under TSCA sections that require manufacturers and distributors to report to the EPA any information they possess that indicates a chemical substance presents a *substantial risk* of injury to health or to the environment. The TSCA further demands that the EPA be given advance notice before the manufacture of new chemical substances or the processing of any substance for a significant new use. Based on the results of its review, the EPA can take action to stop or limit introduction of new chemicals if they threaten human health or the environment with unreasonable risks.

The law also authorizes the EPA to require manufacturers to test their chemicals for possible harmful effects. Since not all the 70,000 chemicals in commerce can be tested all at once, the EPA has developed a priority scheme for selecting substances for testing based on whether or not the chemicals cause cancer, birth defects, or gene mutations. Today, only a small fraction of the total chemicals in production use have been safety tested.

In view of the beneficial role that many chemical substances play in all aspects of production and consumption, Congress directed the EPA through the TSCA to consider the economic and social impact, as well as the environmental one, of its decisions. In this respect, the TSCA is unlike the Clean Air Act, which requires that certain pollution standards be met without regard for economic factors.

Don't forget that the TSCA requires that businesses report to the EPA any information they possess indicating that a chemical presents a *substantial risk* of injury to human health or the environment.

Resource Conservation and Recovery Act

The congressional Office of Technology Assessment reports that more than a ton of hazardous waste per citizen is dumped annually into the nation's environment. A major environmental problem has been how to ensure that the generators of toxic wastes dispose of them safely. In the past, there have been instances where even some otherwise responsible companies have placed highly toxic wastes in the hands of less-than-reputable disposal contractors.

To help ensure proper handling and disposal of hazardous and toxic wastes, Congress in 1976 amended the Solid Waste Disposal Act by the **Resource Conservation and Recovery Act (RCRA).** Under the RCRA, a generator of wastes has two primary obligations:

- To determine whether its wastes qualify as hazardous under RCRA.
- To see that such wastes are properly transported to a disposal facility that has an EPA permit or license.

Do remember how the RCRA regulates the disposal of hazardous and toxic wastes by the manifest system.

The EPA lists a number of hazardous wastes, and a generator can determine if a nonlisted waste is hazardous in terms of several chemical characteristics specified by the EPA. The RCRA accomplishes proper disposal of hazardous wastes through the **manifest system.** This system requires a generator to prepare a manifest document that designates a licensed facility for disposal purposes. The generator then gives copies of the manifest to the transporter of the waste. After receiving hazardous wastes, the disposal facility must return a copy of the manifest to the generator. In this fashion, the generator knows the waste has received proper disposal.

In a recent seven-year-period, the Department of Justice at the request of the EPA brought criminal charges against 253 individuals and corporations under the RCRA.

Failure to receive this manifest copy from the disposal facility within certain time limits requires the generator to notify the EPA. Under RCRA, the EPA has various investigatory powers. The act also prescribes various record-keeping requirements and assesses penalties for failure to comply with its provisions. The penalties include criminal fines and imprisonment.

As amended, the RCRA is moving the handling of toxic wastes away from burial on land to treatments that destroy or permanently detoxify wastes. Today, RCRA requirements cost business an estimated $20 billion annually.

The Superfund

After passage of the TSCA and RCRA in 1976, regulation of toxic and hazardous substances was still incomplete. These acts did not deal with problems of the cleanup costs of unsafe hazardous waste dumps or spills, which are often substantial. Many abandoned dump sites date back as far as the nineteenth century. Even current owners of unsafe dump sites are frequently financially incapable of cleaning up hazardous wastes. Nor are transporters and others who cause spills or unauthorized discharges of hazardous wastes.

In 1980, Congress created the **Comprehensive Environmental Response, Compensation, and Liability Act (CERCLA)** to address these problems. Known as the **Superfund,** this act has allotted billions of dollars for environmental cleanup of dangerous hazardous wastes.

The act requires anyone who releases unauthorized amounts of hazardous substances into the environment to notify the government. Whether it is notified or not, the government has the power to order those responsible to clean up such releases. Refusal to obey can lead to a suit for reimbursement for any cleanup monies spent from the Superfund plus punitive damages of up to triple the cleanup costs. The government can also recover damages for injury done to natural resources. To date, the biggest Superfund case involved Shell Oil and the U.S. Army. These parties agreed to clean up a site outside Denver. Total costs may exceed $1 billion. In 2007, the EPA received private business commitments of $698 million for superfund site cleanups.

Liability under Superfund The Superfund imposes strict liability on those responsible for unauthorized discharges of hazardous wastes. No negligence need be proved. Responsible parties have liability when there is a release or threatened release of a hazardous substance that causes response costs. Responsible parties include (1) those who currently or formerly operate or own waste disposal sites, (2) those who arrange for disposal of wastes, and (3) those who transport wastes. Liability includes the costs of **remediation,** which are basically the costs of restoring land to its previous condition.

Many times, more than one business may have liability for a toxic cleanup. In such an instance, each business may have liability to repay the government for the entire cost of the cleanup unless responsibility can be clearly separated. In the case that follows, the Supreme Court determines who is an "arranger" under CERCLA and whether or not each business is liable for the entire amount. Remember from the torts chapter (Chapter 10) that when more than one defendant is responsible for the entire liability, it is called "joint and several liability."

Superfund provisions also allow a purchaser of land forced by a state or federal agency to clean up hazardous substances to recover contribution from former owners, that is, to make them pay some of the cleanup costs.

> Under the Superfund, those responsible for unauthorized discharges of hazardous and toxic wastes are strictly liable to the government for cleanup costs and damages. Negligence need not be proved.

> Before buying land, purchasers may wish to hire consultants to evaluate the land for hazardous and toxic substances in order to show *due diligence.*

case **19.3**

BURLINGTON NORTHERN AND SANTA FE RAILWAY CO. v. UNITED STATES
129 S. Ct. 1870 (2009)

In 1960, Brown & Bryant Inc. (B&B), began operating an agricultural chemical distribution business, purchasing pesticides and other chemical products from suppliers such as Shell Oil Company (Shell). B&B opened its business on a 3.8 acre parcel of former farmland in Arvin, California, and in 1975, expanded operations onto an adjacent .9 acre parcel of land owned jointly by the Atchison, Topeka & Santa Fe Railway Company, and . . . the Burlington Northern and Santa Fe Railway Company (Railroads). . . . During its years of operation, B&B stored and distributed various hazardous chemicals on its property. Among these were the herbicide dinoseb, sold by Dow Chemicals, and the pesticides D-D and Nemagon, both sold

by Shell. The toxic chemicals leaked, the Government was forced to clean it up and sued all potentially liable parties (PLPs), including Shell and the Railroads. The issues that reach the Supreme Court concluded whether Shell was an "arranger" under CERCLA and whether the railroads were jointly and severally liable.

STEVENS, J: . . . In 1980, Congress enacted the Comprehensive Environmental Response, Compensation, and Liability Act (CERCLA) in response to the serious environmental and health risks posed by industrial pollution. The Act was designed to promote the "timely cleanup of hazardous waste sites" and to ensure that the costs of such cleanup efforts were borne by those responsible for the contamination. . . . CERCLA imposes strict liability for environmental contamination upon four broad classes of PRPs:

(1) the owner and operator of a vessel or a facility,

(2) any person who at the time of disposal of any hazardous substance owned or operated any facility at which such hazardous substances were disposed of,

(3) any person who by contract, agreement, or otherwise arranged for disposal or treatment, or arranged with a transporter for transport for disposal or treatment, of hazardous substances owned or possessed by such person, by any other party or entity, at any facility or incineration vessel owned or operated by another party or entity and containing such hazardous substances, and

(4) any person who accepts or accepted any hazardous substances for transport to disposal or treatment facilities, incineration vessels or sites selected by such person, from which there is a release, or a threatened release which causes the incurrence of response costs, of a hazardous substance. . . .

Once an entity is identified as a PRP, it may be compelled to clean up a contaminated area or reimburse the Government for its past and future response costs.

In these cases, it is undisputed that the Railroads qualify as PRPs under CERCLA because they owned the land leased by B&B at the time of the contamination and continue to own it now. The more difficult question is whether Shell also qualifies as a PRP by virtue of the circumstances surrounding its sales to B&B.

To determine whether Shell may be held liable as an arranger, we begin with the language of the statute. As relevant here CERCLA applies to an entity that "arrange[s] for disposal . . . of hazardous substances." It is plain from the language of the statute that CERCLA liability would attach if an entity were to enter into a transaction for the sole purpose of discarding a used and no longer useful hazardous substance. It is similarly clear that an entity could not be held liable as an arranger merely for selling a new and useful product if the purchaser of that product later, and unbeknownst to the seller, disposed of the product in a way that led to contamination. Less clear is the liability attaching to the many permutations of "arrangements" that fall between these two extremes—cases in which the seller has some knowledge of the buyers' planned disposal or whose motives for the "sale" of a hazardous substance are less than clear. In such cases, courts have concluded that the determination whether an entity is an arranger requires a fact-intensive inquiry that looks beyond the parties' characterization of the transaction as a "disposal" or a "sale" and seeks to discern whether the arrangement

was one Congress intended to fall within the scope of CERCLA's strict-liability provisions.

Although we agree that the question whether liability attaches is fact intensive and case specific, such liability may not extend beyond the limits of the statute itself. Because CERCLA does not specifically define what it means to "arrange for" disposal of a hazardous substance. In common language, the word "arrange" implies action directed to a specific purpose. Consequently, under the plain language of the statute, an entity may qualify as a PRP when it takes intentional steps to dispose of a hazardous substance.

The Government does not deny that the statute requires an entity to "arrange for" disposal; however, they interpret that phrase by reference to the statutory term "disposal," which the Act broadly defines as "the discharge, deposit, injection, dumping, spilling, leaking, or placing of any solid waste or hazardous waste into or on any land or water." The Governments assert that by including unintentional acts such as "spilling" and "leaking" in the definition of disposal, Congress intended to impose liability on entities not only when they directly dispose of waste products but also when they engage in legitimate sales of hazardous substances knowing that some disposal may occur as a collateral consequence of the sale itself. Applying that reading of the statute, the Governments contend that Shell arranged for the disposal of D-D by shipping D-D to B&B under conditions it knew would result in the spilling of a portion of the hazardous substance by the purchaser or common carrier. Because these spills resulted in wasted D-D, a result Shell anticipated, the Governments insist that Shell was properly found to have arranged for the disposal of D-D. . . .

Although the evidence at trial showed that Shell was aware that minor, accidental spills occurred during the transfer of D-D from the common carrier to B&B's bulk storage tanks after the product had arrived at the Arvin facility and had come under B&B's stewardship, the evidence does not support that Shell intended such spills to occur. To the contrary, the evidence revealed that Shell took numerous steps to encourage its distributors to *reduce* the likelihood of such spills, providing them with detailed safety manuals, requiring them to maintain adequate storage facilities, and providing discounts for those that took safety precautions. Although Shell's efforts were less than wholly successful, given these facts, Shell's mere knowledge that spills and leaks continued to occur is insufficient grounds for concluding that Shell "arranged for" the disposal of D-D. Accordingly, we conclude that Shell was not liable as an arranger for the contamination that occurred at B&B's Arvin facility. . . .

We must now determine whether the Railroads were properly held jointly and severally liable for the full cost of the Governments' response efforts.

The seminal opinion on the subject of apportionment in CERCLA actions was written in 1983 by Chief Judge Carl Rubin of the U.S. District Court for the Southern District of Ohio. After reviewing CERCLA's history, Chief Judge Rubin concluded although the Act imposed a "strict liability standard," it did not mandate "joint and several" liability in every case. Rather, Congress intended the scope of liability to "be determined from traditional and evolving principles of common law."

Following *Chem-Dyne,* the courts of appeals have acknowledged that "the universal starting point for divisibility of harm analyses in CERCLA cases" is Section 433A of the Restatement (Second) of Torts: "When two or more persons acting independently cause a distinct or single harm for which there is a reasonable basis for division according to the contribution of each, each is subject to liability only for the portion of the total harm that he has himself caused . . . . But where two or more persons cause a single and indivisible harm, each is subject to liability for the entire harm." In other words, apportionment is proper when "there is a reasonable basis for determining the contribution of each cause to a single harm." . . .

The District Court calculated the Railroads' liability based on three figures. First, the court noted that the Railroad parcel constituted only 19% of the surface area of the Arvin site. Second, the court observed that the Railroads had leased their parcel to B&B for 13 years, which was only 45% of the time B&B operated the Arvin facility. Finally, the court found that the volume of hazardous-substance-releasing activities on the B&B property was at least ten times greater than the releases that occurred on the Railroad parcel . . . . "Allowing for calculation errors up to 50%," the court concluded that the Railroads could be held responsible for 9% of the total CERCLA response cost for the Arvin site.

We conclude that the facts contained in the record reasonably supported the apportionment of liability. The District Court's detailed findings make it abundantly clear that the primary pollution at the Arvin facility was contained in the southeastern portion of the facility most distant from the Railroads' parcel and that the spills of hazardous chemicals that occurred on the Railroad parcel contributed to no more than 10% of the total site contamination, some of which did not require remediation. With those background facts in mind, we are persuaded that it was reasonable for the court to use the size of the leased parcel and the duration of the lease as the starting point for its analysis.

Because the District Court's ultimate allocation of liability is supported by the evidence and comports with the apportionment principles outlined above, we reverse the Court of Appeals' conclusion that the Railroads are subject to joint and several liability for all response costs arising out of the contamination of the Arvin facility.

We conclude that the Court of Appeals erred by holding Shell liable as an arranger under CERCLA for the costs of remediating environmental contamination at the Arvin, California facility. Furthermore, we conclude that the District Court reasonably apportioned the Railroads' share of the site remediation costs at 9%. The judgment is reversed, and the cases are remanded for further proceedings consistent with this opinion.

It is so ordered.

KEY POINTS

- CERCLA imposes strict liability for contamination, but not all actors involved in contamination are "joint and severally" liable. Liability is based on the facts of each case.
- Shell engaged in specific and reasonable efforts to limit minor, accidental spills at the facility. Despite continued spills, these facts do not support that Shell is an "arranger" for disposal of its product that resulted in contamination.
- The contamination was such that the district court could apportion responsibility based on the actions of the railroads. Although the railroads have a portion of responsibility, CERCLA does not demand holding the railroads liable for the entire harm at the toxic site.

For this reason, Superfund law has caused land purchasers to be very careful in buying land that may contain hazardous wastes. The law makes current as well as former landowners liable for hazardous wastes. The purchaser may escape liability by proving that it is innocent of knowledge of the wastes and has used *due diligence* in checking the land for toxic hazards. But exercising due diligence can be both costly and difficult to prove. Fortunately, the Superfund permits a land purchaser to sue a land seller if the purchaser incurs response costs due to hazardous wastes left by the seller.

Banks and other lenders who take out a security interest (such as a mortgage) in land that turns out to be contaminated and subject to the Superfund are not liable responsible parties. However, if a lender exerts control over a borrower's contaminated land, or assumes ownership of it, the lender will become a responsible party. Many lenders have become very wary about loaning money to borrowers who wish to put up as security land that may be contaminated.

As responsible parties engage in Superfund-required cleanup, they try to pass on the costs to others, often their insurers. In the future, insurers may specifically refuse to cover pollution risks in their policies. Some courts, however, have interpreted existing policies to cover waste-cleanup costs as insured-against *damages* arising from an *occurrence,* which includes an *accidental* discharge of pollutants.

Reforms to Superfund   The business community has proposed various reforms to the Superfund law. Possible reforms include:

- Prorating liability for companies in Superfund litigation that agree to pay their share of cleanup costs.
- Exempting companies from liability when they have contributed very small amounts of waste at a dump site.
- Permitting dump site cleanups that meet health and safety standards, rather than requiring that the land be returned to a pristine state.

Finally, take note that both the Clean Air Act and the Clean Water Act also contain provisions related to government suits to recover costs for the cleanup of toxic chemicals. Suits under the Superfund and other acts may be a major area of litigation in coming years. The U.S. Office of Technology Assessment estimates that it will require as much as $500 billion during the next 50 years to clean up the nation's hazardous waste sites. However, since 2000, the pace of cleanups has begun to decline while the number of sites identified to be cleaned has more than doubled. By 2011, one in four Americans lived within three miles of the cleanup site.

Radiation   In 1979, the nuclear power plant accident at the Three Mile Island installation in Pennsylvania and subsequent evacuation of thousands of nearby residents focused the nation's attention on the potential hazards of radiation pollution. Although no single piece of legislation comprehensively controls radiation pollution and no one agency is responsible for administering legislation in this technologically complex area, overall responsibility for such control rests with the Nuclear Regulatory Commission. The EPA, however, does have general authority to conduct testing and provide technical assistance in the area of radiation pollution control. In addition, the Clean Air Act and the Clean Water Act also contain sections applicable to radiation discharges into the air and water.

Overall control of radioactive materials, their use, disposal, and cleanup, rests with the Nuclear Regulatory Commission.

Suits by Private Individuals

Achieving environmental goals requires coordinated strategy and implementation. As private citizens, individuals and groups of individuals lack both the power and foresight necessary to control pollution on a broad scale. There is a role, however, for the private control of private action in two principal areas:

- Citizen enforcement provisions.
- Tort law.

The following sections examine suits by private individuals that relate to environmental concerns.

concept *summary*

An Environmental Alphabet

Environmental and pollution control legislation seems especially given to acronyms. Here's a key.

BAT: best available technology.
BPT: best practicable technology.
CEQ: Council on Environmental Quality.
CERCLA: Comprehensive Environmental Response, Compensation, and Liability Act.

EIS: environmental impact statement.
EPA: Environmental Protection Agency.
FEPCA: Federal Environmental Pesticide Control Act.
NEPA: National Environmental Policy Act.
RCRA: Resource Conservation and Recovery Act.
TSCA: Toxic Substances Control Act.

CITIZEN ENFORCEMENT

Most of the environmental laws, such as the Clean Air and Water Acts, contain *citizen enforcement* provisions, which grant private citizens and groups the standing to sue to challenge failures to comply with the environmental laws. In many instances, private citizens can sue polluters directly to force them to cease violating the law. Private citizens also have standing to sue public agencies (for example, the EPA) to require them to adopt regulations or implement enforcement against private polluters that the environmental laws require.

Private citizens have standing to sue the government or businesses to enforce rules under environmental statutes like the Clean Air Act and the Clean Water Act.

TORT THEORIES

A second area of private control of private action lies in tort law and its state codifications. When pollution directly injures private citizens, they may sue offending polluters under various theories of tort law. Thus, the traditional deterrence of tort law contributes to private control of private action. This section further develops tort law's role in pollution control.

Examination of tort law and pollution control reveals little understanding of the interdependence between ourselves and our environment. Instead, tort theories, as they have been applied to environmental problems, focus on the action of one person (or business) as it injures what legally belongs to another. In other words, tort law attacks the pollution problem by using the established theories of nuisance, trespass, negligence, and strict liability.

Nuisance

Nuisance   The principal tort theory used in pollution control has been that of **nuisance**. The law relating to nuisance is somewhat vague, but in most jurisdictions, the common law has been put into statutory form. Several common elements exist in the law of nuisance in most states. To begin with, there are two types of nuisances: public and private. (See Chapter 7.)

A *public nuisance*
arises from an act that
causes inconvenience
or damage to the
public in the exercise
of rights common to
everyone.

A *public nuisance* arises from an act that causes inconvenience or damage to the public in the exercise of rights common to everyone. In the environmental area, air, water, and noise pollution can all constitute a public nuisance if they affect common rights. More specifically, industrial waste discharge that kills the fish in a stream may be held a public nuisance, since fishing rights are commonly possessed by the public. Public nuisance actions may be brought only by a public official, not private individuals, unless the latter have suffered some special damage to their persons or property as a result of the public nuisance.

Any use of one's land
that unreasonably
interferes with the
use of enjoyment
of another's land
constitutes a *private
nuisance.*

Any use of one's land that unreasonably interferes with the use or enjoyment of another's land establishes a common law *private nuisance*. Courts measure the unreasonableness of the interference by balancing the character, extent, and duration of harm to the plaintiff against the social utility of the defendant's activity and its appropriateness to its location. Since society needs industrial activity as well as natural tranquillity, people must put up with a certain amount of smoke, dust, noise, and polluted water if they live in concentrated areas of industry. But what may be an appropriate industrial use of land in a congested urban area may be a private nuisance if it occurs in a rural or residential location.

Note that the proving of nuisance does not demand that a property owner be found negligent. An unreasonable *use* of one's land does not mean that one's *conduct* is unreasonable.

Other Tort Doctrines

Other Tort Doctrines   Private plaintiffs in pollution cases frequently allege the applicability of tort doctrines other than that of nuisance. These doctrines, however, do overlap that of nuisance, which is really a field of tort liability rather than a type of conduct.

One such doctrine is that of *trespass*. A defendant is liable for trespass if, without right, he or she intentionally enters land in possession of another or causes something to do so. The entrance is considered intentional if the defendant knew that it was substantially certain to result from his or her conduct. Thus, airborne particles that fall on a plaintiff's property can constitute a trespass. In recent years, many courts have merged the theories of nuisance and trespass to such an extent that before plaintiffs can recover for a particle trespass, they must prove that the harm done to them exceeds the social utility of the defendant's enterprise.

Negligence doctrine is sometimes used by private plaintiffs in environmental pollution cases. The basis for the negligence tort lies in the defendant's breach of his or her duty to use ordinary and reasonable care toward the plaintiff, which *proximately* (foreseeably) causes the plaintiff injury. A factory's failure to use available pollution-control equipment may be evidence of its failure to employ *reasonable care*.

Finally, some courts recognize the applicability in pollution cases of *strict liability* tort doctrine. This tort liability arises when the defendant injures the plaintiff's person or property by voluntarily engaging in ultrahazardous activity that necessarily involves a risk of serious harm that cannot be eliminated through the exercise of the utmost care. No finding of *fault,* or *failure of reasonable care,* on the defendant's part is necessary. This doctrine has been employed in situations involving the use of poisons, such as in crop dusting and certain industrial work, the storage and use of explosives, and the storage of water in large quantities in a dangerous place.

In suing for damages, private plaintiffs (as opposed to the government) often base their lawsuits on tort doctrines of (1) trespass, (2) negligence, or (3) strict liability for ultrahazardous activity.

Increasing numbers of private plaintiffs are suing companies for pollution-related harm. In one case, residents in northeast Denver, Colorado, sued Asarco Inc. for environmental property damage caused by its smelter. Asarco settled the suit for $35 million. Not all pollution, however, comes from smokestacks. In agricultural states like Iowa and North Carolina, tort suits arise because of pollution from agricultural production. For example, plaintiffs have sued because of brain damage alleged to be caused by hydrogen sulfide, a by-product of waste from pork production.

Trends in Environmental Regulation

A *Wall Street Journal*/NBC News survey suggests strong nationwide support for environment cleanup. A 61% majority favored more government regulation of the environment. Only 6% thought that there should be less environmental regulation.

Public and business awareness of environmental issues has significantly increased. At the World Economic Forum, 650 business and government leaders ranked the environment as the greatest challenge facing business. Yet, in a recent poll, only 36% of Americans responded that business is doing an adequate job of keeping the environment clean.

AREAS OF ENVIRONMENTAL CONCERN

Researchers almost daily report new instances of how industry and technology affect life on our planet. For every allegation of pollution-caused environmental harm, however, countertheories maintain that the harm is not as significant as alleged or argue that the harm arises from causes unrelated to industrial pollution. Lack of unanimous scientific opinion on many environmental issues underscores their great complexity. It also reveals a key controversy at the heart of environmental regulation: *How much certainty of harm is required to justify regulatory intervention?*

Don't forget that the environment is extremely complex and our understanding of the impacts of pollution on the environment is only partial.

Loss of Natural Ecosystems A report signed by 1,575 scientists, including 100 Nobel Prize winners, warned of the effects of worldwide destruction to natural ecosystems, the cutting of rainforests being the most widely publicized destruction. The report concluded: "If not checked, many of our current practices put at serious risk the future that we wish for human society and the plant and animal kingdoms and may so alter the living world that it will be unable to sustain life in the manner that we know." At risk in the next 30 years are up to 20% of the planet's species of animals and plants.

Ozone   In 1990, 59 countries agreed to stop producing certain chemicals that destroy the Earth's protective *ozone layer* of the atmosphere. The agreement required participating countries to stop production of certain chlorofluorocarbons and halons by the year 2000. Destruction of the ozone layer could lead to hundreds of thousands of cases of cataracts and skin cancer in humans plus unknown serious damage to animals and plants.

As of 2008, these forms of ozone-destroying chemicals are no longer in production. However, a new threat to the ozone has emerged. Air conditioning that uses chemicals that reduce ozone is increasing rapidly in the developing world, especially in India and China, which together have a third of the world's population. New air conditioning installations in India and China are growing at the rate of 25–30% annually.

Greenhouse Effect   Overshadowing even ozone destruction as a future pollution concern are increasing atmospheric concentrations of carbon dioxide. The National Academy of Sciences notes that global carbon dioxide levels have increased 6% since 1960. The increase is due largely to the burning of fossil fuels such as oil and coal.

Higher carbon dioxide levels will likely lead to warmer global temperatures, the so-called *greenhouse effect*. The last decade has had many of the warmest years on record, and atmospheric scientists believe that the rise in global carbon dioxide levels was the cause. Changing climatic patterns and rising sea levels are possible results. The Artic ice cap has shrunk by nearly half in the last 50 years. Carbon dioxide in the atmosphere has reached its highest concentration in the atmosphere in the last 650,000 years.

> The overwhelming scientific evidence confirms that the earth is warming and that humans are the cause. A consequence of this continued warming in the twenty-first century is that our poorest citizens will be the most adversely affected by the ensuing hardships, such as increasing droughts, rising sea levels, and falling agricultural yields.
>
> **Jason Smerdon, Lamont-Doherty Earth Observatory of Columbia University (2011)**

sidebar 19.4

Mass Extinction and Its Consequences

Human alterations of the environment are causing a mass extinction of 30,000–50,000 animal and plant species per year. In the past, most large extinction events have occurred after meteorites or comets smashed into the earth, but the present extinction arises from our own making, mostly from destroying habitats.

Every week we clear an area of tropical rain forest the size of Rhode Island for lumber, cattle raising, and agricultural uses, including large-scale agriculture that involves companies from the developed economies of Europe and the United States. Annually, an area twice the size of Florida vanishes.

Tropical rain forests are an important part of the natural life support system of the planet, removing carbon dioxide from the atmosphere and generating a large portion of the oxygen that we breathe. In addition, by destroying entire unique species of animals and plants found in profusion in the rain forests, we lose the genetic information they possess to produce compounds that are useful to people. At least 25% of all medicines contain ingredients from the rain forests, and 70% of plants known to have anti-cancer properties (1,430 species) are found in the rain forests. There are likely many more such species. Because a cataloging of rainforest species is not complete, we do not even know the full amount of patentable genetic information that we are destroying. By the mass extinction of animals and plants through the destruction of rain forests, we lose an irreplaceable library of information with potentially significant benefit to human health and life.

Source: Contributed by Adam J. Sulkowski, University of Massachusetts Dartmouth.

In 1997, delegates from 150 nations reached a treaty to reduce emission of various greenhouse gases such as carbon dioxide. Under the Kyoto Protocol industrialized nations, including the United States, would lower greenhouse gas emission below 1990 levels. However, the United States had not ratified the Kyoto Protocol as of 2008, and the Bush Administration observed that the developing countries of the world did not have to lower their emissions under the protocol, which would place production in the United States at a disadvantage in global markets by having to compete with nations that did not have to observe emission limitations. The reduction in the burning of fossil fuels—coal and oil—necessary to lower greenhouse gas levels might seriously impact the economy. Business production might also relocate in developing countries like China and India, which the Kyoto Protocol does not require to reduce greenhouse gas emission.

Almost everyone advocates international economic growth as a way of lifting the world's poor from poverty. Yet high-income countries use four to five times as much energy (mostly from polluting fossil fuels like coal and oil) as developing countries. According to the International Energy Agency, in 2005, the United States produced per person nearly two and one-half times the greenhouse gases of the European Union, but 5 times that of the Chinese, and nearly 20 times that of Indians.

Fifteen percent of the world's population uses more than half of its polluting energy. If all nations in the world consume polluting energy at the same rate as high-income nations, what will be the impact on global warning? One thing seems likely. In the words of Nobel laureate economist Thomas Schelling: "In the 21st century, greenhouse gas emissions, global warming, and climate change is going to be the biggest diplomatic issue there is."

> Without ratification of the Kyoto Protocol, global temperature will rise about one degree Celsius by 2050. Even after ratification, the temperature may still rise .94 degree.
>
> **Source: United Nations Intergovernmental Panel on Climate Change.**

Population Growth The world's population continues to grow. According to a Johns Hopkins University study, if human fertility rates do not drop to roughly two children per woman—merely replacing people who die—the world's population will rise to eight billion by 2025 from its current level of around seven billion. Concerns about pollution, climate change, and even food production are magnified by population growth, yet birth control raises controversial cultural and religious issues. As a business student, you must be aware of and appreciate the significance of population growth because during your career the social and environmental problems associated with such growth will rise.

CORPORATE GOVERNANCE AND THE ENVIRONMENT

Concerned about the environment, some investors are turning to corporate governance as a way to make polluting industries more environmentally sensitive. Boards of directors legally control the activities of corporations, but shareholders who own these businesses elect the boards of directors. Increasingly, shareholders are presenting resolutions at the annual meetings of corporations to encourage or require the directors and managers of major polluting industries to analyze and report on certain environmental issues.

In 2011, shareholders filed 66 global warming shareholder resolutions. Pension funds, labor organizations, various foundations, and religious and environmental groups were behind most of the resolutions. Many of the

> "Without substantial participation by developing economies, greenhouse gas emissions will continue to rise rapidly over the next 50 years even if the U.S. and other developed economies cut emissions to zero."
>
> **—James L. Connaughton, Chair, White House Council on Environmental Quality, 2008**

sidebar 19.5

Sustainability Reporting

Thousands of companies, including 80% of the largest 250 companies in the world, annually report on their societal, economic, and environmental impacts. Several terms are used to describe this practice, including sustainability reporting, corporate social responsibility (CSR) reporting, citizenship reporting, triple bottom line (TBL) reporting, and environmental, social, and governance (ESG) reporting.

The most common standard among corporations is the G3 standard of the Global Reporting Initiative (GRI, www.globalreporting.org). An increasing number of reports are audited every year and externally verified, just as financial reports are. A few countries are beginning to make such reports mandatory.

Research indicates that there are several motivations and benefits for disclosing more non-financial data, even when it is not required. Better communication with shareholders and customers and improved brand image are two of the drivers. However, "winning the war for talent"—that is, recruiting, retaining, and motivating the best employees—is also a top motivation, along with inspiring innovation. Other research shows a very strong causal relationship between a company's "green" reputation—which is affected by such reporting—and employee satisfaction.

Some see voluntary sustainability reporting as a kind of "soft law" approach to regulation. Some argue that current SEC reporting rules, correctly interpreted, already require such disclosures because they are material to investment decisions. Regardless, sustainability reporting has become a mainstream annual practice of thousands of companies worldwide.

Source: Contributed by Adam J. Sulkowski, University of Massachusetts Dartmouth.

investors belong to the Institutional Network on Climate Risk that controls more than $5 trillion in assets. Each year, a substantial number of these shareholder resolutions are withdrawn when businesses agree to make environmentally friendly changes in their operations.

Corporate governance concerns have also led to increasing awareness of businesses on the environmental impacts they have; for instance, in annual summaries frequently referred to as sustainability reporting (see Sidebar 19.5).

LO 19-4   PRIVATE PROPERTY AND THE ENVIRONMENT

Considering the human impact on the natural world, does the existence of exclusive private ownership of resources help or hurt the environment? Theory and practice suggest that improper use of common resources causes more environmental problems than does improper use of private resources. Garrett Hardin called this the "tragedy of the commons." People tend to misuse and waste resources that are common to all, like air, water, and public land. They are more careful with their own private resources. Destruction of the world's rain forests is occurring mainly on public or unowned lands. Overall, then, private ownership contributes to a wiser, less wasteful use of resources than do other ways of using resources.

However, exceptions to the general rule do occur. For instance, species of plants and animals that have little immediate market value suffer even on private land. And some companies dump toxic substances that will be hazardous for generations even on their own land. Some landowners have challenged environmental regulation and zoning as a governmental "taking" of private property without "just compensation," which the Fifth Amendment expressly prohibits. The Supreme Court has ruled that land regulation is not a taking that must be compensated as long as an owner is allowed a "reasonable" use of the land. If a law like the Endangered Species Act is applied to prohibit any building on a piece of land, has there been a "taking"? What do you think?

Remember that "property" includes the concept of the equal right of others. In a strong property system, owners cannot use their land or other resources in ways that harm the resources of others, including the resource that others have in their health. The problem is how does the law define "the equal right of others"? Traditional tort law simply does not deal well with pollution harms that occur over long distances or across many years. It is too difficult to prove that the pollution caused the harm. So the government steps in and sets pollution limits that are themselves controversial.

Note that the emissions trading approach to pollution management is a property approach. Granting private owners an exclusive right to sell a quantity of pollution emission to a buyer is the essence of the exclusionary right of property. The world is heading toward increased emissions trading. Imagine in the future that an international treaty sets acceptable emission levels for greenhouse gases and companies worldwide bid for permits to engage in such pollution. What if everyone on earth were considered to own an equal right to engage in greenhouse pollution and proceeds from the emissions auction were distributed to the countries of the world on a population proportional basis?

Key Terms

Bubble concept 587
Cap and trade 588
Clean Air Act 585
Clean Water Act 592
Comprehensive Environmental Response, Compensation, and Liability Act (CERCLA) 598
Emissions reduction banking 587
Environmental impact statement (EIS) 581
Environmental Protection Agency (EPA) 585

Federal Environmental Pesticide Control Act of 1972 (FEPCA) 594
Federal Insecticide, Fungicide, and Rodenticide Act of 1947 594
Manifest system 598
National Environmental Policy Act (NEPA) 581
Nuisance 604
Point source 587
Prevention of significant deterioration 588

Primary air quality standards 585
Remediation 599
Resource Conservation and Recovery Act (RCRA) 598
Scoping 581
Secondary air quality standards 585
Solid Waste Disposal Act 595
Superfund 598
Toxic Substances Control Act (TSCA) 597

Review Questions and Problems

Government's Regulations of Itself

1. *The National Environmental Policy Act*

    (a) Your firm has been hired to build a large government facility near a residential neighborhood. A committee of residents has been formed to oppose the building. You have been asked to assist in writing the EIS. What factors must your EIS take into consideration?

    (b) The Avila Timber Company has asked for and been granted permission by the Department of the Interior to cut 40 acres of timber from the 10,000-acre Oconee National Forest. Prior to the actual logging, a local environmental group files suit in federal district court, contending that the Department of the Interior has not filed an EIS. Can the group challenge the department's action? Analyze whether an EIS should be filed in light of the facts given.

2. *Evaluation of Environmental Impact Statements*

    Outline criticisms of the EIS process. Why are state EISs often less helpful in evaluating complex environmental factors than are those prepared by federal agencies?

Government's Regulation of Business

3. *The Environmental Protection Agency*

    Explain the function of the EPA.

4. *Air Pollution*

    The Akins Corporation wishes to build a new smelting facility in Owens County, an area where air pollution exceeds primary air quality standards.

    (a) What legal difficulties may Akins face?

    (b) What solutions might you suggest for these difficulties?

5. *Clean Air Act Today*

    (a) What is the difference between an individual point-source approach and a bubble-policy approach to dealing with factory pollution?

    (b) For the factory owner, what are the advantages of employing the bubble concept?

6. *Water Pollution*

    Explain the concept of "navigable waterway" and how it is related to the Clean Water Act.

7. *Endangered Species Act*

    How does the ESA apply to private businesses? Explain.

8. *Pesticide Control*

    Before beginning the manufacture of a new pesticide, what process must a company follow under the pesticide-control acts?

9. *Solid Waste*

    (a) Who has the primary responsibility for nontoxic solid waste disposal?

    (b) Describe the role of the Solid Waste Disposal Act in waste disposal.

10. *Toxic and Hazardous Substances*

    (a) As a manufacturer of paints, you need to dispose of certain production by-products that are highly toxic. Discuss the process the law requires you to follow in disposing of these products.

    (b) An abandoned radioactive waste site is discovered by local authorities. The waste came from a company that manufactured radium watch faces and is now out of business. Who will pay to clean up these radioactive wastes? Discuss.

Suits by Private Individuals

11. *Citizen Enforcement*

    Explain the standing to sue doctrine as it applies to the citizen enforcement of federal pollution laws.

12. *Tort Theories*

    Several years ago, the Spul Chemical Corporation built a new plant near your neighborhood. About once a month, clouds of odorous mist have passed across your property, your children have complained of skin rashes, and you have heard that the water table has been contaminated with toxic chemicals. You and your neighbors are fearful of health hazards from the plant, and the neighborhood property values have dropped significantly. Explain possible tort causes of action you may have against the chemical company.

Trends in Environmental Regulation

13. *Areas of Environmental Concern*

    Give examples of why a key controversy at the heart of environmental regulation concerns how much certainty of harm is required to justify regulatory intervention.

14. *Corporate Governance and the Environment*

    How have shareholder groups tried to make environmental concerns relevant to corporate governance?

15. *Private Property and the Environment*

    Explain what it means to say that "emissions trading has propertitized pollution."

business *discussions*

1. You are senior project manager for Superior Paper, Inc., a paper processing company with plants in several states. Recently, you have been given responsibility for overseeing the construction of a new plant in High Top, Tennessee, on the edge of the Talladega National Forest. You must also secure a lease from the U.S. Department of the Interior to harvest timber on federal land. Although many residents welcome the new jobs your company will create, others have moved into the area for its natural beauty and are mounting a campaign to keep out new development.

  What environmental laws will apply to the new plant construction?
  What environmental law will have to be followed as you seek to get the national forest lease?
  What steps should you take to maintain good community relations?

2. International Paint Company wants to sell a large tract of land with several facilities on it to U.S. Parts Inc. As acquisitions manager for U.S. Parts, what do you need to know before buying this land, other than that International Paint has good ownership, that your company needs the site, and that the price is right?

  Why might you need to know the environmental condition of the land?
  What steps might you want to take before buying the land?

Part FOUR

The Employer–Employee Relationship

Employment and labor laws reflect the constant need for balance between the rights and responsibilities of employers and employees and the drive toward production of a company's bottom line. This final section discusses the complexity of those relationships. As you study these chapters, consider the historical development of the law, including how it must continually evolve to address technology developments, changing social values and economic issues affecting the workplace.

The United States enjoys a diverse population, which makes it important to ensure that workers are not discriminated against in hiring, promoting, and firing, as well as in the terms and conditions of employment. Chapter 20 details federal laws prohibiting workplace discrimination, specifically discussing the prohibitions on employment discrimination based on race, sex, national origin, color, pregnancy, age, religion, and disabilities. This chapter focuses on what constitutes illegal discrimination in the workplace, including employment practices—even those that may seem well intentioned on their face—that may be challenged as discriminatory. In addition to federal protections, this chapter notes that state laws may offer additional protection against workplace discrimination. Taken together, these laws provide the framework for fair competition in a workplace free of unlawful discrimination.

Chapter 21 describes other major employment laws, including rules regarding minimum wage and overtime, mass layoffs, family and medical leave, workplace safety and workers' compensation, as well as the limits of employee privacy at work. All of these laws provide important protections for workers and further define the employer–employee relationship. The scope of the employment-at-will doctrine is also presented, along with ways an employer can protect itself from an unjustified lawsuit.

The final chapter in the text, Chapter 22, focuses on labor laws that permit employees to organize their labor through unions. Although they have been met with challenges in the twenty-first century, unions continue to play an important role in the U.S. labor market. The development of labor law in the U.S. illustrates a long history of organized labor and the effort to protect workers. This chapter presents the major labor laws and helps students identify unfair labor practices by management and unions. This chapter also incorporates current issues important to unions. Many unions maintain active political agendas on behalf of their members, including high-profile advocacy during political elections and on labor-related topics such as international trade. Labor advocates are vocal about the kinds of provisions that could be incorporated into trade agreements to allow U.S. workers to compete on a level playing field. For example, a number of free trade agreements discussed in Chapter 12, such as NAFTA, DR-CAFTA, and trade agreements with Korea, Colombia, and Panama, faced vocal opposition from some labor unions. •

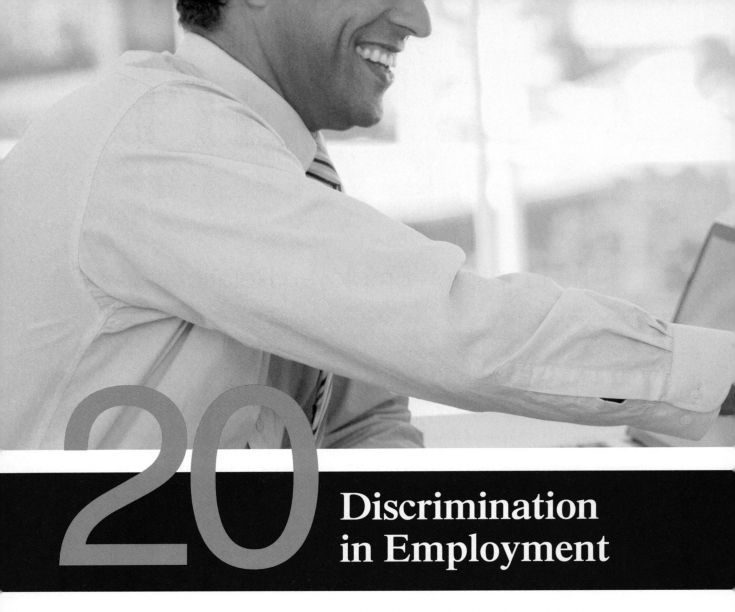

20

Discrimination in Employment

Learning Objectives

In this chapter you will learn:

20-1. To discuss the general provisions of Title VII, enforcement procedures, and the differences between disparate treatment and disparate impact.

20-2. To understand the specific kinds of discrimination prohibited by Title VII.

20-3. To discuss employment practices that may be challenged.

20-4. To apply other federal statutes protecting against employment discrimination.

20-5. To realize that state laws may offer additional protection against workplace discrimination.

Laws prohibiting discrimination exist at both the federal and state levels. The opening sections of the chapter focus on antidiscrimination laws at the federal level. Title VII of the Civil Rights Act of 1964 (including its amendments) is the principal such law. It prohibits certain discrimination based on race, sex, color, religion, and national origin. Next, employment practices that may be challenged as discriminatory are considered. Other antidiscrimination laws covered are the Civil Rights Act of 1866 (42 U.S.C. Section 1981), the Age Discrimination in Employment Act, Americans with Disabilities Act, and the Genetic Information Nondiscrimination Act. The chapter concludes with a discussion of trends in employment discrimination litigation and a discussion about ensuring against employment discrimination claims.

The Civil Rights Act of 1964

"That all men are created equal" was one of the "self-evident" truths recognized by the Founding Fathers in the Declaration of Independence. However, equality among all our citizens clearly has been an ideal rather than a fact. The Constitution itself recognizes slavery by saying that slaves should count as "three fifths of all other Persons" for determining population in House of Representatives elections. And of course, that all *men* are created equal says nothing about women, who did not even get a constitutionally guaranteed right to vote until 1920.

Nowhere have effects of inequality and discrimination been felt more acutely than in the area of job opportunity. Historically, common law permitted employers to hire and fire virtually at will, unless restrained by contract or statute. Under this system, white males came to dominate the job market in their ability to gain employment and their salaries and wages.

Although the Civil Rights Act of 1866 originally protected against race discrimination in the making and enforcement of contracts, its early effectiveness was limited. Passage of labor law in the 1920s and 1930s marks the first significant federal constraint on a relatively unrestricted right of employers to hire and fire. Then, in connection with the war effort, President Franklin D. Roosevelt issued executive orders in 1941 and 1943 requiring a clause prohibiting racial discrimination in all federal contracts with private contractors. Subsequent executive orders in the 1950s established committees to investigate complaints of racial discrimination against such contractors. Affirmative action requirements on federal contracts followed from executive orders of the 1960s.

The most important statute eliminating discriminatory employment practices, however, is the federal Civil Rights Act of 1964, as amended by the Equal Employment Opportunity Act of 1972, the Pregnancy Discrimination Act of 1978, and the Civil Rights Act of 1991.

> Historically, common law permitted employers to hire and fire at will. At-will employment still applies today unless modified by legislation or contract.

GENERAL PROVISIONS

The provisions of Title VII of the Civil Rights Act of 1964 apply to employers with 15 or more employees, labor unions, and certain other employers. The major purpose of these laws is to eliminate job discrimination based on race, color, religion, sex, or national origin. Discrimination for any of these reasons is a violation of the law, except that employers, employment agencies, and labor unions can discriminate on the basis of religion, sex, or national origin where these are **bona fide occupational qualifications (BFOQs)** reasonably necessary to normal business operations. Title VII also does not sanction discrimination if it results unintentionally from a seniority or merit system.

The types of employer action in which discrimination is prohibited include:

- Discharge.
- Refusal to hire.
- Compensation.
- Promotion.
- Terms, conditions, or privileges of employment.

Employment *agencies* are prohibited from either *failing to refer* or from *actually referring* an individual for employment on the basis of race,

> **Don't** forget that a defense to intentional discrimination is that such discrimination is a BFOQ.

> According to the Seventh Circuit Court of Appeals, denial of overtime can constitute an adverse employment action sufficient to trigger Title VII.

color, religion, sex, or national origin. This prohibition differs from the law binding *employers,* where it is unlawful only to fail or refuse to hire on discriminatory grounds—the affirmative act of hiring for a discriminatory reason is apparently not illegal. For example, assume that a contractor with a government contract seeks a qualified African American engineer and requests an employment agency to refer one. The agency complies with the request. Unless a white applicant was discriminated against, the employer likely did not break the law; but the employment agency, by referring on the basis of color, unquestionably *did* violate Title VII. Presumably, however, all non–African American job applicants would have a discrimination claim.

Employers, unions, and employment agencies are also prohibited from discriminating against an employee, applicant, or union member because he or she has made a charge, testified, or participated in an investigation or hearing under the act or otherwise opposed any practice made unlawful by Title VII. These are the statute's antiretaliation provisions.

Note that regarding general hiring, referrals, advertising, and admissions to training or apprenticeship programs, Title VII allows discrimination only on the basis of religion, sex, or national origin and only where these considerations are bona fide occupational qualifications. For example, it is legal for a Baptist church to refuse to engage a Lutheran minister. EEOC guidelines on sex discrimination consider sex to be a bona fide occupational qualification, for example, where it is necessary for authenticity or genuineness in hiring an actor or actress. The omission of *race* and *color* from this exception means that Congress was unwilling to make either of these two factors a bona fide occupational qualification.

> Discriminating in employment on the basis of race or color can almost never be a BFOQ.

Additional exemptions exist with respect to laws creating preferential treatment for veterans and hiring based on professionally developed ability tests that are not designed or intended to be used to discriminate. Such tests must bear a relationship to the job for which they are administered, however.

ENFORCEMENT PROCEDURES

The Civil Rights Act of 1964 created the Equal Employment Opportunity Commission (EEOC). This agency has the primary responsibility of enforcing the provisions of the act. The EEOC is composed of five members, not more than three of whom may be members of the same political party. They are appointed by the president, with the advice and consent of the Senate, and serve a five-year term. In the course of its investigations, the EEOC has broad authority to hold hearings, obtain evidence, and subpoena and examine witnesses under oath.

Under the Equal Employment Opportunity Act of 1972, the EEOC can file a civil suit in federal district court and represent a person or class of persons charging a violation of the act. However, it must first exhaust efforts to settle the claim. Remedies that may be obtained in such an action include reinstatement with back pay or other actions that will make the victim of illegal discrimination whole, including injunctions against future violations of the act by the defendant. See Figure 20.1 for a breakdown of charges received by the EEOC.

> "[M]ajor American businesses have made clear that the skills needed in today's increasingly global marketplace can only be developed through exposure to widely diverse people, cultures, ideas, and viewpoints."
>
> **—Justice Sandra Day O'Connor,** *Grutter v. Bollinger,* **539 U.S. 306, 330 (2003)**

Figure 20.1 *What kinds of claims are being filed with the EEOC?*

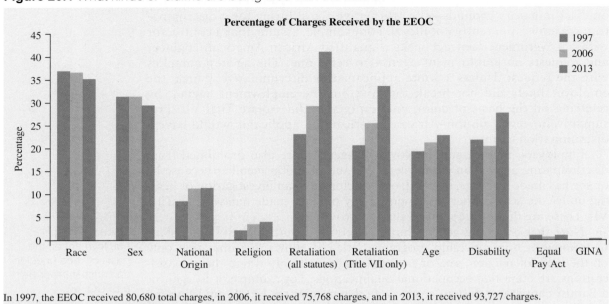

In 1997, the EEOC received 80,680 total charges, in 2006, it received 75,768 charges, and in 2013, it received 93,727 charges.

Source: EEOC Charge Statistics FY1997–2013, http://eeoc.gov/eeoc/statistics/enforcement/charges.cfm.

Under Title VII, a plaintiff can recover up to $300,000 in punitive and compensatory damages for *intentional* discrimination. Back pay or front pay damages can further add to that amount.

The 1991 Amendments   In 1991 Congress amended the Civil Rights Act to allow the recovery of compensatory and punitive damages of up to $300,000 per person depending on the size of the employer. These damages are in addition to other remedies such as job reinstatement and back pay or front pay. Compensatory damages include damages for the pain and suffering of discrimination. Punitive damages are appropriate whenever discrimination occurs with "malice or with reckless or callous indifference to the federally protected rights of others."

In enacting Title VII of the Civil Rights Act of 1964, Congress made it clear that it did not intend to preempt states' fair employment laws. Where state agencies begin discrimination proceedings, the EEOC must wait 60 days before it starts action. Furthermore, if a state law provides relief to a discrimination charge, the EEOC must notify the appropriate state officials and wait 60 days before continuing action.

An employee must file charges of illegal discrimination with the EEOC within 180 days after notice of the unlawful practice. If the employee first filed in a timely fashion with a state fair employment practices commission, the law extends the time for filing with the EEOC to 300 days.

Do remember that the three types of cases permitted under Title VII are for (1) disparate treatment, (2) disparate impact, and (3) retaliation.

Winning a Title VII Civil Action   To win a Title VII civil action, a plaintiff must initially show that steps taken by the employer likely had an illegally discriminatory basis, such as race. Generally, the plaintiff must prove either disparate (unequal) treatment or disparate impact. In proving **disparate treatment,** the plaintiff must convince the court that the employer *intentionally* discriminated against the plaintiff and that any alleged legitimate reasons for such treatment are a mere pretext for discrimination. If discrimination is a substantial or motivating factor, an employer's practice is illegal even though other factors (such as customer preference) also contributed. Even if the plaintiff proves disparate treatment, the defendant can still win by showing that all or substantially all members of the plaintiff's class *cannot* perform the duties of the job. This defense is the BFOQ defense mentioned earlier in this chapter.

In a **disparate impact** case the plaintiff must prove that the employer's practices or policies had a discriminatory effect on a group protected by Title VII. The employer can defeat the plaintiff's claim by proving the **business necessity defense**. This defense requires that the employer prove that the practices or policies used are job related and consistent with a business necessity. However, the plaintiff can still establish a violation by showing that other policies would serve the legitimate interests of business necessity without having undesirable discriminatory effects.

A third type of discrimination case concerns **retaliation**. It is illegal for employers to retaliate against employees for opposing discrimination, filing a charge of discrimination, giving testimony in a discrimination case, or in any way participating in a discrimination investigation. Such retaliation discrimination involves employers taking employment actions against employees that would dissuade a reasonable person from engaging in such an act of protest.

What are ways a company can avoid retaliation claims? As illustrated in Figure 20.1, retaliation claims are on the rise. There are a number of steps an employer can take to address allegations of discrimination without triggering a retaliation claim:

- Comply with all posting requirements.
- Have a written policy prohibiting discrimination and specifying reporting procedures.
- Treat complaints seriously as soon as they are made.
- Investigate the complaint.
- Be sure managers and other employees know and follow the company's policies on discrimination, including harassment.
- Follow-up with the complainant, including explaining how the company will address the problem.
- Create an atmosphere in which the complainant and others with information feel comfortable coming forward with information or other complaints.
- Never retaliate against a complainant or witnesses, based on information obtained in the investigation.

These straightforward steps go a long way to create an atmosphere of fairness and head off additional claims based on retaliation.

Before the 1991 Civil Rights Act amendments, employees or the EEOC sometimes claimed that proving racial or gender statistical imbalances in a workforce established illegal discrimination. They claimed that such imbalances showed illegal discrimination, much like disparate impact discrimination, even in the absence of proof of an employer's discriminatory intent. However, the 1991 amendments state that the showing of a statistically imbalanced workforce is not enough *in itself* to establish a violation of Title VII.

If an employee who complains about discrimination is transferred to the night shift, even without a loss of pay, he may have a claim for retaliation under Title VII. *Burlington Northern and Santa Fe Railroad Co. v. White,* 548 U.S. 53 (2007).

THOMPSON v. NORTH AMERICAN STAINLESS, LP
562 U.S. __ (2011)

After petitioner Eric Thompson's fiancée, Miriam Regalado, filed a sex discrimination charge with the Equal Employment Opportunity Commission (EEOC) against their employer, respondent North American Stainless (NAS), NAS fired Thompson. He filed his own charge and a subsequent suit under Title VII of the Civil Rights Act, claiming that NAS fired him to retaliate against Regalado for filing her charge. The District Court granted NAS summary judgment on the ground that third-party retaliation claims were not permitted by Title VII, which prohibits discrimination against an employee "because he has made a [Title VII] charge." The en banc Sixth Circuit affirmed, reasoning that Thompson was not entitled to sue NAS for retaliation because he had not engaged in any activity protected by the statute. By a vote of 8-0, the Supreme Court overturned the Court of Appeals. (Justice Kagan took no part in the consideration of the case.)

SCALIA, J.: Until 2003, both petitioner Eric Thompson and his fiancée, Miriam Regalado, were employees of respondent North American Stainless (NAS). In February 2003, the Equal Employment Opportunity Commission (EEOC) notified NAS that Regalado had filed a charge alleging sex discrimination. Three weeks later, NAS fired Thompson.

Thompson then filed a charge with the EEOC. After conciliation efforts proved unsuccessful, he sued NAS in the United States District Court for the Eastern District of Kentucky under Title VII of the Civil Rights Act of 1964, 78 Stat. 253, 42 U. S. C. §2000e *et seq.,* claiming that NAS had fired him in order to retaliate against Regalado for filing her charge with the EEOC. The District Court granted summary judgment to NAS, concluding that Title VII "does not permit third party retaliation claims." 435 F. Supp. 2d 633, 639 (ED Ky. 2006). After a panel of the Sixth Circuit reversed the District Court, the Sixth Circuit granted rehearing en banc and affirmed by a 10-to-6 vote. 567 F. 3d 804 (2009). The court reasoned that because Thompson did not "engag[e] in any statutorily protected activity, either on his own behalf or on behalf of Miriam Regalado," he "is not included in the class of persons for whom Congress created a retaliation cause of action." . . .

Title VII provides that "[i]t shall be an unlawful employment practice for an employer to discriminate against any of his employees . . . because he has made a charge" under Title VII. 42 U. S. C. §2000e–3(a). The statute permits "a person claiming to be aggrieved" to

file a charge with the EEOC alleging that the employer committed an unlawful employment practice, and, if the EEOC declines to sue the employer, it permits a civil action to "be brought . . . by the person claiming to be aggrieved . . . by the alleged unlawful employment practice." §2000e–5(b), (f)(1). It is undisputed that Regalado's filing of a charge with the EEOC was protected conduct under Title VII. In the procedural posture of this case, we are also required to assume that NAS fired Thompson in order to retaliate against Regalado for filing a charge of discrimination. This case therefore presents two questions: First, did NAS's firing of Thompson constitute unlawful retaliation? And second, if it did, does Title VII grant Thompson a cause of action?

With regard to the first question, we have little difficulty concluding that if the facts alleged by Thompson are true, then NAS's firing of Thompson violated Title VII. In *Burlington N. & S. F. R. Co. v. White*, 548 U. S. 53 (2006), we held that Title VII's antiretaliation provision must be construed to cover a broad range of employer conduct. We reached that conclusion by contrasting the text of Title VII's antiretaliation provision with its substantive antidiscrimination provision. . . . Title VII's antiretaliation provision prohibits any employer action that "well might have dissuaded a reasonable worker from making or supporting a charge of discrimination." *Id.,* at 68 (internal quotation marks omitted). We think it obvious that a reasonable worker might be dissuaded from engaging in protected activity if she knew that her fiancé would be fired. Indeed, NAS does not dispute that Thompson's firing meets the standard set forth in *Burlington*. Tr. of Oral Arg. 30. NAS raises the concern, however, that prohibiting reprisals against third parties will lead to difficult line-drawing problems concerning the types of relationships entitled to protection. Perhaps retaliating against an employee by firing his fiancée would dissuade the employee from engaging in protected activity, but what about firing an employee's girlfriend, close friend, or trusted co-worker? . . .

Although we acknowledge the force of this point, we do not think it justifies a categorical rule that third-party reprisals do not violate Title VII. . . .

The more difficult question in this case is whether Thompson may sue NAS for its alleged violation of Title VII. The statute provides that "a civil action may be brought . . . by the person claiming to be aggrieved." ". . . to be aggrieved" to bring "a civil action." It is arguable that the aggrievement referred to is nothing more than the minimal Article III standing, which consists of injury in fact caused by the defendant and remediable by the court. See *Lujan v. Defenders of Wildlife*, 504 U. S. 555, 560–561 (1992). But Thompson's claim undoubtedly meets those requirements, so if that is indeed all that aggrievement consists of, he may sue. . . .

We hold that the term "aggrieved" in Title VII incorporates this test, enabling suit by any plaintiff with an interest "arguably [sought] to be protected by the statutes," *National Credit Union Admin. v. First Nat. Bank & Trust Co.*, 522 U.S. 479, 495 (1998) (internal quotation marks omitted), while excluding plaintiffs who might technically be injured in an Article III sense but whose interests are unrelated to the statutory prohibitions in Title VII. Applying that test here, we conclude that Thompson falls within the zone of interests protected by Title VII. Thompson was an employee of NAS, and the purpose of Title VII is to protect employees from their employers' unlawful actions. Moreover, accepting the facts as alleged, Thompson is not an accidental victim of the retaliation—collateral damage, so to speak, of the employer's unlawful act. To the contrary, injuring him was the employer's intended means of harming Regalado. Hurting him was the unlawful act by which the employer punished her. In those circumstances, we think Thompson well within the zone of interests sought to be protected by Title VII. He is a person aggrieved with standing to sue.

Reversed and remanded.

KEY POINTS

- Eric Thompson and his fiancé Miriam Regalado worked for the same employer, NAS. After Regalado filed a Title VII claim with the EEOC, NAS fired Thompson.
- The Supreme Court was asked to determine if firing Thompson constituted unlawful retaliation and, if so, whether he had a cause of action under Title VII.
- The Court held that as an employee of NAS, Thompson was within the zone of interests of Title VII and, as such, the statute's antiretaliation provisions protected him. As such, he has standing to bring a claim against NAS.

DISCRIMINATION ON THE BASIS OF RACE OR COLOR   LO 20-2

The integration of African Americans into the mainstream of American society is the primary objective of the Civil Rights Act of 1964. Title VII, which deals with employment practices, is the key legal regulation for achieving this goal. Without equal employment opportunities, African Americans can hardly enjoy other guaranteed rights, such as access to public accommodations.

Title VII prohibits discriminatory employment practices based on race or color that involve *recruiting, hiring, promotion, discharge,* or *application* of the terms and conditions of employment. Of course, intentional discrimination in these matters is illegal, but, as previously stated, policies with disparate impact are also forbidden. Such discrimination arises from an employer's policies or practices that apply equally to everyone but that discriminate in greater proportion against minorities and have no relation to job qualification.

Examples of disparate impact on race include:

- Using personnel tests that have no substantial relation to job qualification, which have the effect of screening out minorities.
- Denying employment to unwed mothers, when minorities have a higher rate of illegitimate births than whites.
- Refusing to hire people because of a poor credit rating, when minorities are disproportionately affected.

Lockheed Martin settled a race discrimination and retaliation lawsuit for $2.5 million in 2008. The case alleged a racially hostile work environment at several job sites, including threats of lynching and the use of the "N-word."

- Giving hiring priority to relatives of present employees, when minorities are underrepresented in the workforce.

- Excluding applicants for employment based on conviction records when irrelevant to the job and statistics show racial imbalance in conviction rates.

Often at issue in disparate impact cases is whether a discriminatory policy or practice relates to job qualification. Courts require proof, not mere assertion, of job relatedness before upholding an employer's discriminatory personnel test or other practice.

The law also prohibits discrimination in *employment conditions* and *benefits*. EEOC decisions have found such practices as the following to be violations:

- Permitting racial insults in the work situation.
- Maintaining all-white or all-black crews for no demonstrable reasons.
- Providing better housing for whites than blacks.
- Granting higher average Christmas bonuses to whites than blacks for reasons that are not persuasive.

Researchers at the University of Chicago and MIT revealed racial bias in hiring based on an applicant's name. The study tracked response rates to resumes sent to 1,300 help-wanted ads. The authors found that white-sounding names (such as Anne, Emily, Allison, Neil, Todd, and Matthew) are

---

sidebar 20.1

Hithon v. Tyson Foods, Inc.: The Use of the Word "Boy"

John Hithon and Anthony Ash, African American men, worked at a Tyson Foods plant in Alabama. When two supervisor positions opened up, they were passed over for promotion and two white men from other plants were hired. Believing that the failure to be promoted resulted from racial prejudice, Hithon and Ash filed an employment discrimination claim against their employer.

As part of their case, the plaintiffs produced evidence that their white boss used the term "boy" when referring to them. Is the use of the term *boy* racially discriminatory?

In 2002, an Alabama jury awarded Hithon and Ash $250,000 each in compensatory damages and $1.5 million in punitive damages. After a magistrate overruled the jury's verdict, Hilton and Ash appealed. On appeal, the 11th Circuit determined that an adult African American man being called "boy" alone was not discriminatory unless it was preceded by "black" or "white."

The U.S. Supreme Court unanimously reversed the 11th Circuit's decision, stating:

Although it is true that the disputed word will not always be evidence of racial animus, it does not follow that the term, standing alone, is always benign . . . The speaker's meaning may depend on various factors including context, inflection, tone of voice, local custom and historical usage. Ash v. Tyson Foods, 546 U.S. 454 (2006)

Thereafter, in 2007, another Alabama jury found in favor of Hithon, awarding him $35,000 in back pay, $300,000 in compensatory damages for his mental anguish, and $1 million in punitives. The District Court vacated the punitive damage award. Both sides appealed. On appeal, the 11th Circuit voted 2–1 entering a judgment in favor of Tyson Foods. The majority said that the evidence did not support Hithon's argument. A number of civil rights leaders and others interested groups then filed amicus briefs in support of Hithon's petition for en banc rehearing. In 2011, the 11th Circuit panel reversed its prior ruling and reinstated the 2007 verdict.

50 percent more likely to get called for an initial interview than applicants with African American–sounding names (such as Tamika, Latoya, Latonya, Tyrone, Tremayne, and Rasheed). Additionally, race affects the degree to which applicants benefit from having more experience and credentials. The study showed that white applicants with higher-quality resumes received 30 percent more callbacks than whites with lower-quality resumes. By contract, African American applicants experienced only 9 percent more callbacks for the same improvement in credentials.[1]

It is important to appreciate that Title VII prohibits employment discrimination against members of all races. In one recent case, a federal court jury awarded a white senior air traffic official $500,000 in damages against the Federal Aviation Administration. The official charged the FAA had demoted him and replaced him with an African American following complaints that blacks were underrepresented in senior management levels. Note that this case did not involve affirmative action.

> The State of New York has outlawed the display of a noose as a threat, punishable by up to four years in prison.

[1]*Bill Leonard, "Study Suggests Bias Against 'Black' Names on Resumes,"* HR Magazine *(2003).*

---

case **20.2**

RICCI v. DESTEFANO
557 U.S.__ (2009)

New Haven, Conn. (City), uses objective examinations to identify those firefighters best qualified for promotion. When the results of such an exam to fill vacant lieutenant and captain positions showed that white candidates had outperformed minority candidates, a rancorous public debate ensued. Confronted with arguments both for and against certifying the test results—and threats of a lawsuit either way—the City threw out the results based on the statistical racial disparity. Petitioners, white and Hispanic firefighters who passed the exams but were denied a chance at promotions by the City's refusal to certify the test results, sued the City and respondent officials, alleging that discarding the test results discriminated against them based on their race in violation of, inter alia, Title VII of the Civil Rights Act of 1964. The defendants responded that had they certified the test results, they could have faced Title VII liability for adopting a practice having a disparate impact on minority firefighters. The District Court granted summary judgment for the defendants, and the Second Circuit affirmed. Justice Sotomayor was on the Second Circuit at the time of that decision. Justice Kennedy wrote the majority opinion in which Chief Justice Roberts, and Justices Scalia, Thomas and Alito joined.

Justice Ginsburg filed a dissenting opinion in which Justices Stevens, Souter and Breyer joined. In her dissent, Justice Ginsburg notes that firefighting is "a profession in which the legacy of racial discrimination casts an especially long shadow" and that the facts of this case should be assessed "against this backdrop of entrenched inequality."

KENNEDY, J.: In the fire department of New Haven, Connecticut—as in emergency-service agencies throughout the Nation—firefighters prize their promotion to and within the officer ranks. An agency's officers command respect within the department and in the whole community; and, of course, added responsibilities command increased salary and benefits. Aware of the intense competition for promotions, New Haven, like many cities, relies on objective examinations to identify the best-qualified candidates. In 2003, 118 New Haven firefighters took examinations to qualify for promotion to the rank of lieutenant or captain. Promotion examinations in New Haven (or City) were infrequent, so the stakes were high. The results would determine which firefighters would be considered for promotions during the next two years, and the order in which they would be considered. Many firefighters studied for months, at considerable personal and financial cost.

When the examination results showed that white candidates had outperformed minority candidates, the mayor and other local politicians opened a public debate that turned rancorous. Some firefighters argued the tests should be discarded because the results showed the tests to be discriminatory. They threatened a discrimination lawsuit if the City made promotions based on the tests. Other firefighters said the exams were neutral and fair. And they, in turn, threatened a discrimination lawsuit if the City, relying on the statistical racial disparity, ignored the test results and denied promotions to the candidates who had performed well. In the end the City took the side of those who protested the test results. It threw out the examinations.

Certain white and Hispanic firefighters who likely would have been promoted based on their good test performance sued the City and some of its officials. Theirs is the suit now before us. The suit alleges that, by discarding the test results, the City and the named officials discriminated against the plaintiffs based on their race, in violation of both Title VII of the Civil Rights Act of 1964, 78 Stat. 253, as amended, 42 U. S. C. §2000e *et seq.*, and the Equal Protection Clause of the Fourteenth Amendment. The City and the officials defended their actions, arguing that if they had certified the results, they could have faced liability under Title VII for adopting a practice that had a disparate impact on the minority firefighters. The District Court granted summary judgment for the defendants, and the Court of Appeals affirmed.

We conclude that race-based action like the City's in this case is impermissible under Title VII unless the employer can demonstrate a strong basis in evidence that, had it not taken the action, it would have been liable under the disparate-impact statute. The respondents, we further determine, cannot meet that threshold standard. As a result, the City's action in discarding the tests was a violation of Title VII. . . .

Title VII of the Civil Rights Act of 1964, 42 U. S. C. §2000e *et seq.*, as amended, prohibits employment discrimination on the basis of race, color, religion, sex, or national origin. Title VII prohibits both intentional discrimination (known as "disparate treatment") as well as, in some cases, practices that are not intended to discriminate but in fact have a disproportionately adverse effect on minorities (known as "disparate impact"). . . . The Civil Rights Act of 1964 did not include an express prohibition on policies or practices that produce a disparate impact. But in *Griggs v. Duke Power Co.,* 401 U. S. 424 (1971), the Court interpreted the Act to prohibit, in some cases, employers' facially

neutral practices that, in fact, are "discriminatory in operation." *Id.,* at 431. . . . Twenty years after *Griggs,* the Civil Rights Act of 1991, 105 Stat. 1071, was enacted. The Act included a provision codifying the prohibition on disparate-impact discrimination. That provision is now in force along with the disparate-treatment section already noted. Under the disparate-impact statute, a plaintiff establishes a prima facie violation by showing that an employer uses "a particular employment practice that causes a disparate impact on the basis of race, color, religion, sex, or national origin." 42 U. S. C. §2000e–2(k)(1)(A)(i). An employer may defend against liability by demonstrating that the practice is "job related for the position in question and consistent with business necessity." *Ibid.* Even if the employer meets that burden, however, a plaintiff may still succeed by showing that the employer refuses to adopt an available alternative employment practice that has less disparate impact and serves the employer's legitimate needs. . . . Petitioners allege that when the CSB refused to certify the captain and lieutenant exam results based on the race of the successful candidates, it discriminated against them in violation of Title VII's disparate-treatment provision. The City counters that its decision was permissible because the tests "appear[ed] to violate Title VII's disparate impact provisions." . . .

The racial adverse impact here was significant, and petitioners do not dispute that the City was faced with a prima facie case of disparate-impact liability. On the captain exam, the pass rate for white candidates was 64 percent but was 37.5 percent for both black and Hispanic candidates. On the lieutenant exam, the pass rate for white candidates was 58.1 percent; for black candidates, 31.6 percent; and for Hispanic candidates, 20 percent. The pass rates of minorities, which were approximately one half the pass rates for white candidates, fall well below the 80-percent standard set by the EEOC to implement the disparate-impact provision of Title VII. . . .

There is no genuine dispute that the examinations were job-related and consistent with business necessity. . . . On the record before us, there is no genuine dispute that the City lacked a strong basis in evidence to believe it would face disparate-impact liability if it certified the examination results. In other words, there is no evidence—let alone the required strong basis in evidence—that the tests were flawed because they were not job-related or because other, equally valid and less discriminatory tests were available to the City. Fear of litigation alone cannot justify an employer's reliance on race to the detriment of individuals who passed the examinations and qualified for promotions. The City's discarding the test

[continued]

results was impermissible under Title VII, and summary judgment is appropriate for petitioners on their disparate-treatment claim. . . . Many of the candidates had studied for months, at considerable personal and financial expense, and thus the injury caused by the City's reliance on raw racial statistics at the end of the process was all the more severe. Confronted with arguments both for and against certifying the test results—and threats of a lawsuit either way—the City was required to make a difficult inquiry. But its hearings produced no strong evidence of a disparate-impact violation, and the City was not entitled to disregard the tests based solely on the racial disparity in the results.

Reversed.

KEY POINTS

- New Haven, Connecticut (City), administered a test to firefighters to determine who qualified for promotion. The results showed that white and Hispanic candidates outperformed minority candidates.
- Some minority firefighters argued that the test should be disregarded as discriminatory and that it had a disparate impact on minority firefighters.
- Firefighters who passed the test argued that the City's failure to certify the test resulted in disparate-treatment discrimination.
- As a practical matter, the City of New Haven believed that, based on the arguments from both sides, it would be sued if it did or if it did not certify the test results.
- The Supreme Court held that because the examinations were job related and consistent with business necessity, and there was no strong evidence of a disparate-impact violation, the City should have certified the test results.

sidebar 20.2

Abercrombie & Fitch's $40 Million Diversity Lesson

In 2005, Abercrombie & Fitch (A&F) settled a discrimination lawsuit with over 10,000 class members. The suit alleged hiring discrimination against Latino, African American, and Asian American applicants. The checks ranged from several hundred to several thousand dollars each, totaling $40 million. The settlement agreement also requires A&F to:

- Set "benchmarks" (*not* quotas) for hiring and promotion of women, Latinos, African Americans, and Asian Americans.
- Stop targeting fraternities, sororities, or specific colleges for recruitment.
- Hire 25 recruiters who will focus on seeking women and minority employees.
- Implement a new internal complaint procedure.
- Create marketing materials reflecting diversity.

Following the lawsuit, Mike Jeffries, A&F's then Chairman and CEO said, "Diversity and inclusion are key to our organization's success."

A&F, however, is currently litigating a case in which a Muslim teen claims that she was not hired because her hajib was inconsistent with A&F's dress code policy. The U.S. Supreme Court will hear the case in 2015. For more information about the case, see EEOC v. Abercrombie & Fitch Stores, Inc., http://www.scotusblog.com/case-files/cases/equal-employment-opportunity-commission-v-abercrombie-fitch-stores-inc/.

DISCRIMINATION ON THE BASIS OF NATIONAL ORIGIN

Title VII's prohibition against national origin discrimination protects various ethnic groups in the workplace. In a recent case, the court ruled that Title VII had been violated when a bakery employee of Iranian descent was called "Ayatollah" in the workplace by the assistant manager and other employees. After he complained, he was fired.

Don't forget that a policy requiring employees to speak English will violate Title VII as disparate impact unless it is justified by *business necessity*.

Discrimination concerning the speaking of a native language frequently causes national-origin lawsuits under Title VII. For instance, courts have ruled illegal an employer's rule against speaking Spanish during work hours when the employer could not show a business need to understand all conversations between Hispanic employees. On the other hand, some courts have held that if jobs require contact with the public, a requirement that employees speak some English may be a business necessity.

Direct foreign investment in the United States has doubled and redoubled in recent years. This increasing investment has presented some unusual issues of employment discrimination law. For instance, many commercial treaties with foreign countries give foreign companies operating in the United States the right to hire executive-level employees "of their choice." Does this mean that foreign companies in the United States can discriminate as to their managerial employees on a basis forbidden under Title VII? The Supreme Court has partially resolved this issue by ruling that the civil rights law applied to a Japanese company that did business through a subsidiary incorporated in this country.

sidebar 20.3

National Origin Discrimination: Problematic Ethnic Slurs

  The EEOC brought a lawsuit on behalf of Mexican immigrant workers at Sam's Club who claimed they were harassed about their national origin *by a co-worker who is Mexican American.* Among the allegations:

- At least nine female workers of Mexican descent and one woman married to a Mexican were subjected to ethnic slurs and derogatory remarks.
- The insults were made on a "near daily" basis, including being called "f----n' wetbacks" and references to Mexicans only being good to clean the harasser's home.

- The harasser also threatened to report three of the victims to immigration authorities, despite their legal status.
- The victims complained about the hostile work environment but this "only intensified the harassment and led to intimidation."

Wal-Mart Stores agreed to pay $440,000 to settle this case.

Source: EEOC Press Release, Wal-Mart to Pay $440,000 to Settle EEOC Suit for Harassment of Latinos, April 14, 2011, www.eeoc.gov/eeoc/newsroom/release/4-14-11.cfm.

DISCRIMINATION ON THE BASIS OF RELIGION

Note that religious corporations, associations, or societies can discriminate in all their employment practices on the basis of religion, but not on the basis of race, color, sex, or national origin. Other employers cannot discriminate on the basis of religion in employment practices, and they must make reasonable accommodation to the religious needs of their employees if it does not result in undue hardship to them.

In one case, the Supreme Court let stand a lower court ruling that employees cannot be required to pay union dues if they have religious objections to unions. The case determined that a union violated Title VII by forcing a company to fire a Seventh Day Adventist who did not comply with a collective bargaining agreement term that all employees must pay union dues. The union argued unsuccessfully that it had made reasonable accommodation to the worker's religious beliefs by offering to give any dues paid by him to charity. However, in another case the Supreme Court ruled that a company rightfully fired an employee who refused to work on Saturdays due to religious belief. The Court said that the company did not have to burden other employees by making them work Saturdays.

A growing source of religious discrimination lawsuits concerns employees who for religious reasons refuse to perform some task required by the employer. For example, in one case a vegetarian bus driver refused to distribute hamburger coupons on his bus, asserting religious beliefs. When his employer fired him, he sued. The parties settled the case for $50,000. Note that even if an employer wins such a lawsuit, it can be extremely expensive to defend.

Over the last decade, there has been a rise in religious discrimination against Muslims. In 2003, the EEOC settled a complaint by four Muslim machine operators against Stockton Steel of California for $1.1 million. The four operators claimed they were given the worst jobs, ridiculed during their prayers, and called names like "camel jockey" and "raghead."

> In the case of employees of Arab descent, note the close connection between national origin discrimination and religious discrimination.

sidebar 20.4

Workplace Discrimination Against Muslims

The EEOC continues to receive complaints involving religious discrimination against Muslims and national origin discrimination against Muslims. Complaints include:

- Somali immigrants working at a meatpacking company who were cursed for being Muslim; had blood, meat, and bones thrown at them; and were interrupted during prayer breaks.
- Dress policies forbidding headwear, prohibiting Muslim women from wearing headscarves, also called hijabs.
- Name-calling, including "terrorist," "Osama," "camel jockey," and "towel head."

What steps should employers take to accommodate Muslims in the workplace? If it will not cause undue hardship, employers should consider allowing the following kinds of accommodations:

- Prayer breaks with the understanding that Muslims pray five times a day for approximately 5 to 15 minutes.
- Headscarves for women if they do not create a safety issue.
- Facial hair for men.
- Vacation days for religious holidays such as *Eid al-Fitr* and *Eid al-Adha*.

Overall, as is the case with any form of illegal discrimination, employers should be vigilant and take action to ensure that the workplace is free from discriminatory animus.

DISCRIMINATION ON THE BASIS OF SEX

Historically, states have enacted many laws designed supposedly to protect women. For example, many states by statute have prohibited the employment of women in certain occupations such as those that require lifting heavy objects. Others have barred women from working during the night or more than a given number of hours per week or day. A federal district court held that a California state law that required rest periods for women only was in violation of Title VII. Some statutes prohibit employing women for a specified time after childbirth. Under EEOC guidelines, such statutes are not a defense to a charge of illegal sex discrimination and do not provide an employer with a bona fide occupational qualification in hiring standards. Other EEOC guidelines forbid employers:

- To classify jobs as male or female.
- To advertise in help-wanted columns that are designated male or female, unless sex is a bona fide job qualification.

Query: Could Victoria's Secret stores legally hire only women for certain positions?

Similarly, employers may not have separate male and female seniority lists.

Whether sex is a bona fide occupational qualification (and discrimination is thus legal) has been raised in several cases. The courts have tended to consider this exception narrowly. In the following instances involving hiring policy, *no* bona fide occupational qualification was found to exist:

- A rule requiring airline stewardesses, but not stewards, to be single.
- A policy of hiring only females as flight cabin attendants.
- A rule against hiring females with preschool-age children, but not against hiring males with such children.
- A telephone company policy against hiring females as switchers because of the alleged heavy lifting involved on the job.

In the telephone company case, the court held that for a bona fide occupational qualification to exist, there must be "reasonable cause to believe, that is, a factual basis for believing, that all or substantially all women would be unable to perform safely and efficiently the duties of the job involved." The Supreme Court has indicated that for such a qualification to exist, sex must be provably relevant to job performance.

Other examples of illegal sex discrimination include:

- Refusing to hire a female newscaster because "news coming from a woman sounds like gossip."
- Allowing women to retire at age 50, but requiring men to wait until age 55.
- Failing to promote women to overseas positions because foreign clients were reluctant to do business with women.

The much-talked about Hooters restaurant case involved a lawsuit filed by men in Illinois and Maryland who were denied jobs. Hooters paid $3.75 million to settle the lawsuit. The settlement allows Hooters to continue employing voluptuous and scantily clad female "Hooters Girls," but they must create and fill a few other support jobs, like bartenders and hosts, without regard to gender.

The largest gender discrimination case was brought as a class action against Wal-Mart and Sam's Club. In 2011, the U.S. Supreme Court refused to certify the class. For more information about this case, see Case 4.2 in Chapter 4.

sidebar 20.5

Women in Business: A Tough Go for Many

A study by Strategy& (formerly Booz & Co.) of the 2,500 largest public companies by market value revealed that over the past ten years, fewer than three in ten male chief executives were fired, yet almost two in five female bosses were pressured to leave.* The study cited two main reasons: (1) "benefit of the doubt factor" (the strong desire to appoint a female candidate can lead to making a bolder choice with a higher change of going wrong) and (2) boardroom culture remains overwhelmingly male, which can create a difficult working environment. Here are some examples of gender bias cases brought by women against major U.S. firms:

- **Novartis Pharmaceuticals Corp.**—After finding discrimination against women employees in pay, promotion and pregnancy policies, a New York jury awarded the plaintiffs $3,367,250 in compensatory damages and $250 million in punitive damages. In his closing argument, the plaintiffs' lawyer told the jury that the evidence proved that Novartis "tolerated a culture of sexism, a boys' club atmosphere."

Novartis subsequently settled the remaining gender bias claims, agreeing to a settlement of approximately $152.5 million to current and former female sales representatives.

- **Morgan Stanley**—In 2004, the firm agreed to pay $54 million to settle a gender discrimination suit brought by a former bond saleswoman.
- **Goldman Sachs Group Inc.**—Three former female employees sued Goldman Sachs in 2010, alleging "systemic" violations of female employees' rights, including allegations of excluding women from golf outings and other work-related social events, push-up contests, and retaliation after complaining about being groped by a male colleague after an outing at a topless bar. The suit alleges that the decentralized structure gives managers "unchecked discretion" in assigning pay and responsibilities.

* "The 2013 Chief Executive Study: Women CEOs of the Last 10 Years," *Strategy&*, April 29, 2014.

Sexual Harassment A common type of illegal sex discrimination in the workplace is **sexual harassment.** The typical sexual harassment case involves a plaintiff who has been promised benefits or threatened with loss if she or he does not give sexual favors to an employment supervisor. Such a case is also called a *quid pro quo* (this for that) case. Under Title VII and agency law, an employer is liable for this sex discrimination.

Another type of sexual harassment is the **hostile work environment,** one in which co-workers make offensive sexual comments or propositions, engage in suggestive touching, show nude pictures, or draw sexual graffiti. The Supreme Court in *Meritor Savings Bank v. Vinson* ruled that Title VII prohibits "an offensive or hostile working environment," even when no economic loss occurs. By so ruling, the Court acknowledged that the work environment itself is a condition of employment covered by Title VII.

The Supreme Court also addressed the hostile work environment issue in *Harris v. Forklift Systems, Inc.* Specifically, the Court was asked to determine whether, before a person could sue under Title VII, a hostile work environment had "to seriously affect [his or her] psychological well-being" or "cause injury." The Court ruled that illegal sexual harassment goes beyond that which causes "injury." It includes any harassment reasonably perceived as "hostile or abusive."

Is all sexually offensive conduct between employees illegal? The answer is no, although an employee's company may choose to forbid and punish all

> It may be helpful to think of sexual harassment discrimination in terms of (1) quid pro quo cases and (2) hostile work environment cases.

> Well-known talk show hosts Maury Povich and Bill O'Reilly both have been accused of sexual harassment in multimillion-dollar lawsuits. O'Reilly settled the case for an undisclosed amount.

such conduct. In 2005, the Supreme Court in *Clarke County School District v. Breeden* summarized when offensive sexual conduct becomes illegal:

> [S]exual harassment is actionable under Title VII only if it is so severe or pervasive as to alter the conditions of the victim's employment and create an abusive working environment.

The Court continued:

> Workplace conduct is not measured in isolation; instead, whether an environment is sufficiently hostile or abusive must be judged by looking at all the circumstances, including the frequency of the discriminatory conduct; its severity; whether it is physically threatening or humiliating, or a mere offensive utterance; and whether it unreasonably interferes with an employee's work performance.

It is not uncommon for a discrimination lawsuit to involve multiple kinds of claims. A good example of this is a recent case against Cracker Barrel, in which the restaurant agreed to pay $2 million to settle a lawsuit alleging sexual harassment, racial harassment, and retaliation by 51 current or former employees. On behalf of the workers, the EEOC alleged that male co-workers and managers subjected female workers to unwelcome and offensive sexual comments and touching. According to the EEOC, "Black employees said that they experienced racially charged language in the workplace, including 'spear chucking porch monkey,' 'you people,' and the 'n-word.'" In addition to the monetary settlement, Cracker Barrel must train all employees in its stores about harassment.

Employer's Defense to Hostile Environment   Is an employer always liable when fellow employees create a hostile environment based on gender? The answer is that the employer is not always legally responsible for a hostile environment. The employer may have a defense. Courts have ruled that an employer is liable to a plaintiff employee for a hostile working environment created by

17.6% of all sexual harassment claims were filed by men with the EEOC in 2013.

---

sidebar 20.6

Vulgar Workplace Language & Sexual Harassment

Can vulgar language, *even if it is not specifically directed at an individual,* be actionable as sexual harassment under Title VII? Yes—according to the 11th Circuit Court of Appeals. The plaintiff, Ingrid Reeves, worked at a sales company, C.H. Robinson. Reeves alleged that she was subjected to hearing her male co-workers call other women names such as "b***h," "wh**e," and "c**t" on a daily basis. She also claimed that there were repeated vulgar discussions about female body parts and a pornographic image of a woman in the office. Reeves complained to her co-workers, her supervisor, and top company executives, but the offensive conduct was "accepted and tolerated."

According to the 11th Circuit, "if Reeves's account is to be believed, C.H. Robinson's workplace was more than a rough environment—indiscriminately vulgar, profane, and sexual. Instead, a just reasonably could find that it was a workplace that exposed Reeves to disadvantageous terms or conditions of employment to which members of the other sex were not exposed." Moreover, the court stated that it was no defense to assert "that the workplace may have been vulgar and sexually degrading before Reeves arrived."

For more information, see, *Reeves v. C.H. Robinson Worldwide, Inc.,* 07-10270 (11th Cir. Jan. 20, 2010), available at www.ca11.uscourts.gov/opinions/ops/200710270op2.pdf.

fellow employees only when the employer knows of the problem and fails to take prompt and reasonable steps to correct it, such as by moving the harassers away from the plaintiff employee. The employer can defend itself by proving that it exercised reasonable care to prevent and correct promptly any sexually harassing behavior, *and* the plaintiff employee unreasonably failed to take advantage of any preventive or corrective opportunities provided by the employer.

Remember Title VII requires an employee to file a complaint concerning a discriminatory practice with the EEOC within 180 days of their happening (within 300 days if the employee has first filed with a state fair employment practices commission). Employers are liable for acts that occurred before 180 days of the EEOC filing if they are part of a single hostile environment that continued within the 180-day period.

Pregnancy Discrimination Act The Pregnancy Discrimination Act amended the Civil Rights Act in 1978. Under it, employers can no longer discriminate against women workers who become pregnant or give birth. Thus, employers with health or disability plans must cover pregnancy, childbirth, and related medical conditions in the same manner as other conditions are covered. The law covers unmarried as well as married pregnant women. It also states that an employer cannot force a pregnant woman to stop working until her baby is born, provided she is still capable of performing her duties properly. An employer is also prohibited from specifying how long a leave of absence must be taken after childbirth. Coverage for abortion is not required by the statute unless an employee carries to term and her life is endangered or she develops medical complications because of an abortion. If a woman undergoes an abortion, though, all other benefits provided for employees, such as sick leave, must be provided to her.

Note that sex discrimination applies to discrimination against men as well as women. For example, under the Pregnancy Discrimination Act the

Don't forget that employers are liable if plaintiffs prove quid pro quo harassment. But employers may have a defense to hostile environment harassment.

Men as well as women may be subject to illegal sex discrimination.

sidebar 20.7

Pregnancy Discrimination: Claims on the Rise

The EEOC reports that pregnancy-related claims are consistently increasing:

YEAR	CLAIMS RECEIVED
1997	3977
2000	4160
2003	4649
2007	5587
2011	5797

What does a woman need to bring a successful claim? She must prove that her pregnancy or her status as a mother motivated the employer's adverse action.

The U.S. Supreme Court is currently considering a pregnancy discrimination case against UPS. Peggy Young claims that she had to take unpaid leave after her doctor recommended that she not lift heavy items. She claims that UPS did not offer her alternative work. The question before the court: Whether, and under what circumstances the Pregnancy Discrimination Act requires an employer that provides work accommodations to non-pregnant employees with work limitations to provide work accommodations to pregnant employees who are "similar in their ability or inability to work." The decision is expected in 2015.

For more information, see www.eeoc.gov/types/pregnancy.html.

Supreme Court ruled unlawful an employer's health insurance plan that covered the pregnancies of female employees but did not cover the pregnancies of male employees' wives.

Equal Pay Act   Historically, employers have paid female employees less than males, even when they held the same jobs. In 1964, women earned only 59 cents for every dollar earned by males. By 2008, female employees earned just 77 cents for every dollar earned by males.

According to the census statistics, women earned 77 cents on the male dollar in 2014. April 20th is now Equal Pay Day in the United States to highlight awareness of this ongoing discrepancy.

Federal legislation prohibits sex discrimination in employment compensation under both Title VII and the Equal Pay Act of 1963. Administered by the EEOC, the Equal Pay Act prohibits an employer from discriminating on the basis of sex in the payment of wages for performing substantially the same work under similar working conditions and in the same establishment. For jobs to be equal, they must require "equal skill, effort, and responsibility." Discrimination is allowed if it arises from a seniority system, a merit system, or any factor other than sex.

The focus of Equal Pay Act cases is whether the male and female jobs being compared involve "equal" work. Courts have recognized that *equal* does not mean *identical*; it means *substantially* equal. Thus, courts have ruled "equal" the work of male barbers and female beauticians and of male tailors and female seamstresses. Differences in male and female job descriptions will not totally protect employers against charges of equal-pay infractions. The courts have held that "substantially equal" work done on different machines would require the employer to compensate male and female employees equally. The question of what is "equal pay" is also a common focus. Equal pay includes all payments, including fringe benefits such as stock options, incentive bonuses, and other benefits such as vacation or holiday pay, reimbursement for travel, and retirement benefits.

One court ruled that an employer could pay male physician assistants more than female nurses because the physician assistants had administrative duties that nurses did not have to perform.

The Supreme Court has ruled that discriminatory male and female pay differences can also be illegal under Title VII. In *County of Washington v. Gunther,* the Court decided that plaintiffs can use evidence of such pay differences to help prove intentional sex discrimination, even when the work performed is not substantially equal. Relying on the *Gunther* case, at least one lower court has held that women must be paid equally with men who perform comparable work. A federal district court ruled that the state of Washington discriminated against secretaries (mostly women) by paying them less than maintenance and other personnel (mostly men). However, the **comparable worth** theory is highly controversial, and other courts have not agreed with the theory. Equal Pay Act cases tend to rely heavily on statistical analysis of disparities.

In a landmark Title VII decision, *Ledbetter v. Goodyear Tire & Rubber Co., Inc.* (2007), a sharply divided Supreme Court rejected the pro-employee paycheck-accrual theory of pay discrimination previously accepted by many courts. This decision was negated by Congress with the passage of the Lilly Ledbetter Equal Pay Act. Simply stated, each paycheck is not a separate violation and employees have a claim with each violation; however, employees must still file an EEOC charge within 180 or 300 days (depending on their state) after each discriminatory pay decision or forever lose their claim. For more details about the controversial *Ledbetter* case, see Sidebar 20.8.

Examples of successful Equal Pay Act cases include one against Wal-Mart and another against the New York Corrections Department. In the first case,

sidebar 20.8

Did the Supreme Court Get It Wrong? Legislative Action Post-*Ledbetter*

Lilly Ledbetter worked for Goodyear for nearly 20 years. During that time, Ledbetter and other salaried employees received or were denied raises based on their supervisors' evaluation of their performance. Near the end of her tenure at Goodyear, Ledbetter discovered that her pay was significantly less—as much as 40 percent less—than her male counterparts. Ledbetter then filed a charge with the EEOC.

PROCEDURAL HISTORY

The district court allowed Ledbetter to present evidence of her entire 19-year career at Goodyear. A jury found in her favor, awarding both compensatory and punitive damages. The Eleventh Circuit reversed and the Supreme Court (5–4) affirmed the decision that a Title VII pay discrimination claim cannot be based on any pay decision that occurred outside of the EEOC charging period.

DISSENTING VIEWS

Justice Ruth Bader Ginsberg wrote a spirited dissent (joined by Justices Stevens, Souter, and Breyer) arguing that "[p]ay disparities often occur . . . in small increments" and "cause to suspect that discrimination is at work develops only over time." She continued, asserting that discriminatory disparities in pay, like hostile work environment claims, rest not on "one particular paycheck, but on 'the cumulative effect of individual acts.'" Incensed about the majority opinion, Justice Ginsberg read her dissent aloud from the bench.

LEGISLATIVE RESPONSE

The first piece of legislation President Obama signed into law was the Lilly Ledbetter Fair Pay Act of 2009. The Ledbetter Act extends the time for employees to bring gender discrimination claims challenging pay or promotion decision.

a pharmacist who claimed Wal-Mart fired her after asking to be paid the same as her male colleagues won nearly a $2 million award against Wal-Mart. Wal-Mart argued that it fired the pharmacist for leaving the pharmacy unattended and allowing a technician to use her computer security code to issue prescriptions, including a fraudulent prescription for a painkiller. Countering this argument, the pharmacist argued that the prescription incident took place 18 months before her termination and more severe infractions by her male counterparts were unpunished. In the second case, the EEOC settled an Equal Pay Act suit against the New York Department of Corrections for nearly $1 million. The EEOC alleged that female employees were receiving less benefits than their male counterparts.

Sexual Orientation Discrimination   Title VII does not prohibit discrimination against employees based on their sexual orientation, or whether they are gay, lesbian, bisexual, transgendered, or heterosexual. The word *sex* in Title VII refers only to gender, whether someone is female or male. That said, because the focus is on gender, discrimination cases are brought based on illegal gender stereotypes. For instance, discrimination on account of a person's gender identity that offends traditional notions can be a violation of Title VII. A quarter of the states, however, and numerous cities do forbid discrimination based on sexual orientation, and Congress could amend Title VII to protect employees from such discrimination. Already, thousands of companies ranging from American Express, Coca-Cola, and JPMorgan Chase to Ford, General Motors, and Chrysler, offer domestic partner benefits to all employees without regard to sexual orientation.

sidebar 20.9

Sexual Orientation Discrimination: State and Local Laws

Although there is no federal protection prohibiting sexual orientation in the workplace based on sexual orientation, many private employers—especially those who operate in many states—have company policies prohibiting sexual orientation discrimination. Consider these facts and legal developments:

- The majority of Fortune 500 companies provide health insurance for domestic partners of their employees.
- According to Human Rights Campaign, a gay political group, more than 7,000 employers offer domestic partner benefits.
- *State laws.* Twenty-one states and the District of Columbia have laws that currently prohibit sexual orientation discrimination in private employment: California,

Colorado, Connecticut, Delaware, Hawaii, Illinois, Iowa, Maine, Maryland, Massachusetts, Minnesota, Nevada, New Hampshire, New Jersey, New Mexico, New York, Oregon, Rhode Island, Vermont, Washington, and Wisconsin. Most of these states also specifically prohibit discrimination based on gender identity.

- *Local laws.* More than 185 cities and counties nationwide prohibit sexual orientation discrimination in at least some workplaces.

For more information and a state-by-state list of antidiscrimination laws, including city and county ordinances, see the American Civil Liberties Union, Non-Discrimination Laws: State by State Information, aclu.org, and the Lambda Legal Defense and Education Fund website at www.lambdalegal.org.

Although there have been efforts to pass federal legislation, such as the Employment Non-Discrimination Act (ENDA), banning employment discrimination on the basis of sexual orientation, it has not yet become federal law. See Sidebar 20.9 for other developments in sexual orientation laws and protections.

 Employment Practices That May Be Challenged

In studying the Civil Rights Act, we can usefully consider several specific employment practices that employees or job applicants may challenge as discriminatory. These practices include:

- Setting testing and educational requirements.
- Having height and weight requirements for physical labor.
- Maintaining appearance requirements.
- Practicing affirmative action.
- Using seniority systems.

The following sections take a close look at these practices.

QUESTIONNAIRES, INTERVIEWS, TESTING, AND EDUCATIONAL REQUIREMENTS

Employers have used a number of tools to help them find the right person for the right job. Among these tools are questionnaires, interviews, references, minimum educational requirements (such as a high school diploma), and personnel tests. However, employers must be extremely careful not to use tools that illegally discriminate. For example, Rent-A-Center, a Dallas-based appliance-rental company, agreed to pay more than $2 million in damages to more than 1,200 job applicants and employees who were asked questions about their sex lives and religious views in a 500-item true-false questionnaire. Plaintiffs claimed the questionnaire discriminated illegally on the basis of gender and religion and that it violated their privacy.

Interviews can also discriminate illegally, and personnel interviewers must be well trained. One study indicated that interviewers can be biased even if they are not aware of it. The study showed that the interviewers tended to select males over females for sales positions because the interviewers *subconsciously* related sales success with height, and males are on the average taller than females. References may not be so reliable, either. A previous employer's letter may reflect personal biases against an applicant that were not related to job performance.

At the other extreme, an employer may give a poor employee a top recommendation because of sympathy or fear of a lawsuit in case the letter is somehow obtained by the employee. Advocates of personnel tests in the selection process feel they are very valuable in weeding out the wrong persons for a job and picking the right ones. They believe reliance on test results eliminates biases that interviewers or former employers who give references may have.

Tests, however, can have a *disparate impact* on job applicants, discriminating on the basis of race, sex, color, religion, or national origin. Setting educational standards such as requiring a high school diploma for employment can also have a disparate impact. To avoid discrimination challenges, employers must make sure that all testing and educational requirements are job related and necessary for the business.

In the past, some employers have "race normed" employment tests. *Race norming* is the practice of setting two different cutoff test scores for employment based on race or one of the other Title VII categories. For example, on a race-normed test, the minimum score for employment of white job applicants might be set at 75 out of 100. For minority applicants, the minimum score might be set at 65. *The Civil Rights Act amendments of 1991 specifically prohibit the race norming of employment tests.*

> Most employment practices that discriminate illegally do so because of their disparate impact.

> **Don't** forget that for employers to race-norm employment tests violates Title VII.

HEIGHT AND WEIGHT REQUIREMENTS

Minimum or maximum height or weight job requirements apply equally to all job applicants, but if they have the effect of screening out applicants on the basis of race, national origin, or sex, the employer must demonstrate that such requirements are validly related to the ability to perform the work in question. For example, maximum size standards would be permissible, even if they favored women over men, if the available work space were too small to permit large persons to perform the duties of the job properly. Most size requirements have dictated minimum heights or weights, often based on a stereotyped assumption that a certain amount of strength that smaller persons might not have probably was necessary for the work. In one case, a 5-foot, 5-inch, 130-pound Hispanic won a suit against a police department on the basis that the department's 5-foot, 8-inch minimum height requirement discriminated against Hispanics, who often are shorter than that standard. He was later hired when he passed the department's physical agility examination, which included dragging a 150-pound body 75 feet and scaling a 6-foot wall.

APPEARANCE REQUIREMENTS

Walt Disney World has detailed instructions for employees on "The Disney Look," including eyewear, body piercing, earlobe expansion, facial hair, fingernails, hair length, and sideburns. The goal is to look "friendly, approachable, and knowledgeable."

Employers often have set grooming standards for their employees. Those regulating hair length of males or prohibiting beards or mustaches have been among the most common. Undoubtedly, motivation for these rules stems from the feeling of the employer that the image it projects to the public through its employees will be adversely affected if their appearance is not "proper." It is unclear whether appearance requirements are legal or illegal, since there have been rulings both ways. However, in 2000 the EEOC filed a lawsuit in Atlanta against FedEx Corporation for firing a bearded delivery driver who refused to shave in violation of a company policy that permitted beards only when medically necessary. The driver's Islamic beliefs required males to wear beards, and the lawsuit alleged that FedEx's policy constituted religious discrimination. FedEx entered into a consent decree to modify its appearance policy to allow beards or particular hairstyles is an employee's sincerely held religious belief is at issue. FedEx also agreed to pay back pay and compensatory damages.

The burden of proof in a disparate impact case requires the employer to prove that appearance is a business necessity.

In another case, a black employee argued that he was wrongfully fired for breaking a company rule prohibiting beards. Dermatologists testified that the plaintiff had a condition called "razor bumps" (which occurs when the tightly curled facial hairs of black men become ingrown from shaving) and that the only known cure was for him not to shave. Although the federal appeals court found that the plaintiff was prejudiced by the employer's regulation, it held in favor of the company, ruling that its *slight racial impact* was justified by the *business necessity* it served. A conflicting opinion in still another case upheld an employee's right to wear a beard because of razor bumps.

AFFIRMATIVE ACTION PROGRAMS AND REVERSE DISCRIMINATION

It is not unusual for an employment ad to state that the company is an "affirmative action/equal opportunity employer." Some ads also state: "Women and underrepresented minorities are encouraged to apply."

Since the 1940s, a series of presidential executive orders have promoted non-discrimination and **affirmative action** by employers who contract with the federal government. The authority for these orders rests with the president's executive power to control the granting of federal contracts. As a condition to obtaining such contracts, employers must agree contractually to take affirmative action to avoid unlawful discrimination in recruitment, employment, promotion, training, rate of compensation, and layoff of workers.

The affirmative action requirement means that federally contracting employers must actively recruit members of minority groups being underused in the workforce. That is, employers must hire members of these groups when there are fewer minority workers in a given job category than one could reasonably expect, considering their availability. In many instances, employers must develop written affirmative action plans and set goals and timetables for bringing minority (or female) workforces up to their percentages in the available labor pool.

The Labor Department administers executive orders through its Office of Federal Contract Compliance Programs (OFCCP). The OFCCP can terminate federal contracts with employers who do not comply with its guidelines and can make them ineligible for any future federal business. For instance, it required Uniroyal Inc. to give its female employees an estimated $18 million in back pay to compensate for past employment discrimination. The alternative was elimination of $36 million of existing federal contracts and ineligibility for future federal business.

Private Employer Affirmative Action Not all affirmative action programs arise under federal contracting rules. Courts also impose affirmative action on private employers to overcome a history of prior discrimination. Sometimes private employers voluntarily adopt affirmative action or agree to it with unions. These affirmative action programs can give rise to claims of **reverse discrimination** when minorities or women with lower qualifications or less seniority than white males are given preference in employment or training. Even though such programs are intended to remedy the effects of present or past discrimination or other barriers to equal employment opportunity, white males have argued that the law does not permit employers to discriminate against *them* on the basis of race or sex any more than it allows discrimination against minorities or women.

In *United Steelworkers of America v. Weber*, the Supreme Court ruled legal under Title VII a voluntary affirmative action plan between an employer and a union. The plan required that at least 50 percent of certain new work trainees be black. The Court noted that the plan did not require that white employees be fired or excluded altogether from advancement. It was only a temporary measure to eliminate actual racial imbalance in the workforce.

Note the difference between taking affirmative action and setting a "quota." Affirmative action is taken to help correct historic workforce imbalances and usually has target goals that are pursued for a limited time. On the other hand, quotas set rigid standards for various groups, such as that 50 percent of the workforce must be female. The 1991 Civil Rights Act amendments prohibit the setting of quotas in employment.

The EEOC has issued guidelines intended to protect employers who set up affirmative action plans. These guidelines indicate that Title VII is not violated if an employer determines that there is a reasonable basis for concluding that such a plan is appropriate and the employer takes *reasonable* affirmative action. For example, if an employer discovers that it has a job category where one might expect to find more women and minorities employed than are actually in its workforce, the employer has a reasonable basis for affirmative action.

In *Adarand Constructors, Inc. v. Pena,* the Supreme Court emphasized that government-imposed affirmative action plans are subject to *strict judicial scrutiny* under equal protection guarantees of the Fifth and Fourteenth Amendments. To be constitutional, such plans must now be supported by a *compelling interest.* The *Adarand* decision will make it constitutionally difficult to justify some government-imposed affirmative action plans. Much litigation has followed that tests the constitutionality of various plans.

In California voters approved the controversial Proposition 209. In relevant part it says that "the state shall not discriminate against, or grant preferential treatment to, any individual or group on the basis of race, sex, color, ethnicity, or national origin in the operation of public employment, public education, or public contracting." The Supreme Court refused to hear an appeal from a lower court decision that upheld Proposition 209 against

Do remember that the justification for affirmative action is the historic discrimination against protected groups.

In 2005, a federal jury found that the New Orleans district attorney discriminated against 43 white employees by firing them and replacing them with African Americans.

Voluntary affirmative action plans by private employers *may* violate Title VII but do *not* violate constitutional equal protection because they are not "state action."

constitutional challenge and the assertion it violated federal civil rights law. Although Proposition 209 *does not* affect private employer affirmative action plans required by federal law, it does illustrate the current opposition that many Americans have to affirmative action. Polls show that almost three-fourths of the general population disapproves of affirmative action. Nearly 50 percent of African Americans also oppose it.

SENIORITY SYSTEMS

Title VII specifically allows employers to adopt seniority systems even when they may operate to discriminate against protected groups.

Seniority systems give priority to those employees who have worked longer for a particular employer or in a particular line of employment of the employer. Employers may institute seniority systems on their own, but in a union shop they are usually the result of collective bargaining. Their terms are spelled out in the agreement between the company and the union. Seniority systems often determine the calculation of vacation, pension, and other fringe benefits. They also control many employment decisions such as the order in which employees may choose shifts or qualify for promotions or transfers to different jobs. They also are used to select the persons to be laid off when an employer is reducing its labor force. As a result of seniority, the last hired are usually the first fired. Decisions based on seniority have been challenged in recent years as violating the laws relating to equal employment opportunity. Challenges often arose when recently hired members of minority groups were laid off during periods of economic downturn. Firms with successful affirmative action programs often lost most of their minority employees.

Section 703(h) of the Civil Rights Act of 1964 provides that, in spite of other provisions in the act, it is not an unlawful employment practice for an employer to apply different employment standards under a bona fide (good-faith) seniority system if the differences are not the result of an *intention* to discriminate. In *Memphis Fire Dept. v. Stotts* the Supreme Court ruled that discrimination resulting from application of a seniority system was lawful even when it affected minorities hired or promoted by affirmative action.

LO 20-4
Other Statutes and Discrimination in Employment

Although the Civil Rights Act of 1964 is the most widely used antidiscrimination statute, there are other important antidiscrimination laws. They include the Civil Rights Act of 1866, the Age Discrimination in Employment Act, the Americans with Disabilities Act, and various state and local laws. The following sections examine these laws.

CIVIL RIGHTS ACT OF 1866

Denny's restaurants have been repeatedly sued for black customers claiming Denny's violated their civil rights. Denny's has paid more than $54 million to settle the lawsuits.

An important federal law that complements Title VII of the 1964 Civil Rights Act is the Civil Rights Act of 1866. One provision of that act, known as **Section 1981** (referring to its U.S. Code designation, 42 U.S.C. §1981), provides that "all persons . . . shall have the same right to make and enforce contracts . . . as enjoyed by white citizens." Since union memberships and employment relationships involve contracts, Section 1981 bans racial discrimination in these areas.

The courts have interpreted Section 1981 as giving a private plaintiff most of the same protections against racial discrimination that the 1964 Civil Rights Act provides. In addition, there are at least two advantages to the plaintiff who files a suit based on Section 1981. First, there are no procedural requirements for bringing such a suit, whereas there are a number of fairly complex requirements plaintiffs must follow before bringing a private suit under Title VII. For instance, before a plaintiff can file a lawsuit against an employer, the plaintiff must file charges of discrimination with the EEOC and obtain a notice of right to sue from the agency. By using Section 1981, a plaintiff alleging race discrimination can immediately sue an employer in federal court without first going through the EEOC.

Unlimited Damages A second advantage to Section 1981 is that under it the courts can award unlimited compensatory and punitive damages. There are no capped limits as there are under Title VII. As a practical matter, parties alleging racial discrimination usually sue under both Section 1981 and Title VII.

Don't forget that Section 1981 is why racial discrimination is subject to damages far in excess of the $300,000 limit imposed on individuals under Title VII.

Note that Section 1981 does not cover discrimination based on sex, religion, national origin, age, or handicap. As interpreted by the courts, this section applies only to *racial* discrimination. However, what is race? The Supreme Court has held that being of Arabic or Jewish ancestry constitutes "race" as protected by Section 1981. The Court stated that when the law was passed in the nineteenth century, the concept of race was much broader than it is today. Race then included the descendants of a particular "family, tribe, people, or nation." Today, Section 1981 protects persons of all races from discrimination.

In *Patterson v. McLean,* the Supreme Court interpreted Section 1981 to apply only to the actual hiring or firing of employees based on race. Under this interpretation, Section 1981 did not offer protection against discrimination such as a hostile working environment. But the Civil Rights Act amendments of 1991 redefined Section 1981 to include protection against discrimination in "enjoyment of all benefits, privileges, terms and conditions of the contractual relationship." Thus Section 1981 now also protects against hostile environment discrimination. In 2008, the Supreme Court also extended Section 1981 to claims of retaliation for complaining about race discrimination.

Under Section 1981, "race" includes ethnic or national groups.

DISCRIMINATION ON THE BASIS OF AGE

The American workforce is "graying." According to a 2014 report from the Bureau of Labor Statistics, there are record numbers of workers among 55- to 64-year-olds, and the numbers are expected to increase over the next seven years. As percentages of older workers rise in coming years, so will the increase in complaints about age discrimination.

The Civil Rights Act does not protect against discrimination based on age. However, the Age Discrimination in Employment Act (ADEA) does. It prohibits employment discrimination against employees ages 40 and older, and it prohibits the mandatory retirement of these employees. Only certain

"Age bias is still a persistent problem in the 21st century workplace."
—Spencer H. Lewis, EEOC district director

executives and high policymakers of private companies can be forced into early retirement. Specifically, "bona fide" executives and high-level policy makers age 65 and older who are entitled to receive annual retirement benefits of at least $44,000 a year are subject to mandatory retirement policies. The ADEA applies to employers with 20 or more employees. The ADEA also invalidates retirement plans and labor contracts that violate the law.

Types of Age Discrimination

The ADEA recognizes both disparate treatment and disparate impact discrimination for employers with 20 or more employees. The Supreme Court has upheld a jury's finding of disparate treatment in an age discrimination case. The employer had said the employee "was so old [he] must have come over on the Mayflower" and that he "was too damn old to do his job." When the employer later fired the employee, the jury found for the employee in spite of the employer's assertion that it had fired the employee for reasons other than age.

The Supreme Court has also stated that the ADEA recognizes disparate impact in age discrimination cases. The city of Jackson, Mississippi, had awarded pay raises to junior ranks of police officers that were substantially higher than the pay raises given to more senior ranks. These raises had the impact of discriminating on the basis of age. Older officers received lower pay raises because they were mostly in senior ranks.

However, the Supreme Court stated that disparate impact alone did not prove illegality under the ADEA. The city of Jackson was merely attempting to match the salaries offered to junior officers in nearby cities, which was a "reasonable factor other than age." See Sidebar 20.10 for an example of illegal mandatory retirement policy.

Employer Defenses in ADEA Cases

The employer defenses to age discrimination, disparate treatment, and disparate impact differ slightly from the defense in Title VII cases.

For instance, under the ADEA age is seldom recognized as the basis for a bona fide occupational qualification. It is recognized that as people grow older, their physical strength, agility, reflexes, hearing, and vision tend to diminish in quality. However, this generally provides no legal reason for discriminating against older persons as a class. Although courts will uphold job-related physical requirements if they apply on a case-by-case basis, they frequently find as illegal those policies that prohibit the hiring of persons beyond a maximum age or that establish a maximum age beyond which employees are forced to retire for physical reasons. Thus, one court ruled that a mandatory retirement age of 65 was illegally discriminatory as applied to the job of district fire chief. In an exception to the general rule, one court has ruled that age can be a BFOQ in a case where the airlines imposed a maximum age for hiring new pilots. The court observed that the Federal Aviation Administration mandated a retirement age for pilots.

The ADEA also does not require the employer to prove a "business necessity" in order to successfully defend an age discrimination case of disparate impact. All the employer need do is establish that a "reasonable factor other than age" accounted for the discriminatory impact. Further, unlike under Title VII, the employer's defense of a reasonable factor other than age cannot be defeated by the employee's showing of a less discriminatory way of achieving the employer's purpose.

Willful violations of the ADEA allow courts to impose double damage awards against employers.

> *sidebar* 20.10
>
> ### Did You Read the Law? A Law Firm Runs Afoul of the ADEA
>
> The EEOC filed a lawsuit against Sidley Austin Brown & Wood ("Sidley Austin"), a major Chicago-based international law firm, alleging that it violated the ADEA when it selected 32 "partners" for expulsion from the firm on account of their age or forced them to retire.
>
> After over two years of litigation, Sidley Austin agreed to pay $27.5 million to the former partners. The firm also agreed to refrain from "terminating, expelling, retiring, reducing the compensation of, or otherwise adversely changing the partnership status of any partner because of age" or "maintaining any formal or informal policy or practice requiring retirement as a partner or requiring permission to continue as a partner once the partner has reached a certain age."
>
> Source: EEOC Press Releases.

Remedies under the ADEA The ADEA provides for back pay and recovery of attorney fees. Note that *willful* violations of the act permit discrimination victims to be awarded *double damages*.

Note an important exception to this general rule about remedies against state actors under the ADEA. In accordance with the Supreme Court case *Kimel v. Florida Board of Regents* (2000), a plaintiff cannot recover money damages against a state entity. State law and state courts, however, may offer remedies for age discrimination perpetrated by a state. This Eleventh Amendment immunity for states in federal court has been extended to other employment laws, including the Americans with Disabilities Act and the Family Medical Leave Act.

DISCRIMINATION ON THE BASIS OF DISABILITIES

According to a Harris poll, two-thirds of all disabled Americans between the ages of 16 and 64 are not working, even though most of them want to work. To help those with disabilities obtain work, Congress in 1990 passed the Americans with Disabilities Act (ADA). Thereafter, the U.S. Supreme Court rendered a number of employer–friendly decisions restricting the scope of the ADA's protection. Responding to criticism that the U.S. Supreme Court unreasonably restricted the ADA's scope, Congress passed the ADA Amendments Act of 2008, effective January 1, 2009 and, in 2011, the EEOC released its final regulations. The ADA is now expanded to protect a broader group of individuals.

> It is now easier to establish a "disability" within the definition of the ADA and employers need to be prepared to make reasonable accommodations.

To prevent disability discrimination, the ADA prohibits employers from requiring a preemployment medical examination or asking questions about the job applicant's medical history. Only after a job offer has been extended can the employer condition employment on the employee's responses to job-related medical questions.

The ADA prohibits employer discrimination against job applicants or employees based on (1) their having a disability, (2) their having a disability in the past, or (3) their being *regarded as* having a disability. The ADA defines **disability** as "any physical or mental impairment that substantially limits one or more of an individual's major life activities." "Substantially limits" now requires a lower degree of limitation than was previously applied by the courts.

> The concept of "disability" includes mental disabilities and diseases as well as physical impairment.

"Physical and mental impairment" includes physical disorders and conditions, disease, disfigurement, amputation affecting a vital body system, psychological disorders, mental retardation, mental illness, and learning disabilities. An individual can demonstrate that he or she is "regarded as" having a disability by establishing that he or she has been subjected to an action prohibited by the ADA "because of an actual or perceived physical or mental impairment whether or not the impairment limits or is perceived to limit a major life activity."

Impairments, such as cancer, that are substantially limiting when active remain so despite being in remission.

"Major life activities" include such activities as "caring for oneself, performing manual tasks, seeing, hearing, eating, sleeping, walking, standing, lifting, bending, speaking, breathing, learning, reading, concentrating, thinking, communicating, and working." The definition also includes the operation of any major body function, including functions of the immune system, normal cell growth, and digestive, bowel, bladder, neurological, brain, respiratory, circulatory, endocrine, and reproductive functions. The determination of whether an impairment substantially limits a major life activity must be made without regard to the "ameliorative effects of mitigating measures"—that is, individuals who use medications, artificial limbs, or hearing aids qualify for protection under the ADA, even though those measures may overcome the limiting effects of an impairment. (Ordinary eyeglasses and contact lenses are specifically excluded from this list by the amendments to the ADA.) The ADA also states that an individual with an impairment that is "transitory and minor," defined as having an actual or expected duration of six months or less, does not fall under the ADA. However, individuals with impairments that are episodic or in remission, such as epilepsy, diabetes, or cancer are not barred from coverage under the ADA.

Not included by the ADA as protected disabilities are homosexuality, sexual behavior disorders, compulsive gambling, kleptomania, and disorders resulting from *current* drug or alcohol use. The emphasis on current drug or alcohol use means that employees who have successfully recovered or are successfully recovering from drug or alcohol disabilities are protected from employment discrimination.

Individuals with HIV or AIDS are protected by the ADA. Persons who are discriminated against because they are regarded as being HIV-positive are also protected.

The ADA prohibits employers of 15 or more employees (also unions with 15 or more members and employment agencies) from discriminating against the qualified disabled with respect to hiring, advancement, termination, compensation, training, or other terms, conditions, or privileges of employment. **Qualified disabled** are defined as those with a disability who, with or without reasonable accommodation, can perform the essential functions of a particular job position. Employers must make reasonable accommodation only for the *qualified* disabled.

Reasonable Accommodation under the ADA The ADA does not require employers to hire the unqualified disabled, but they must make reasonable accommodation so qualified disabled employees can succeed in the workplace. **Reasonable accommodation** is the process of adjusting a job or work environment to fit the needs of disabled employees. It may include:

- Making the work facilities accessible and usable to disabled employees.
- Restructuring jobs or modifying work schedules.

- Purchasing or modifying necessary equipment for use by the disabled.
- Providing appropriate training materials or assistance modified to fit the needs of disabled employees.

Note that an employer need make only reasonable accommodation for disabled employees. The employer can plead *undue hardship,* defined as "an action requiring significant difficulty or expense," as a reason for not accommodating the needs of disabled employees. The ADA specifies that in evaluating undue hardship, the cost of the accommodation, the resources of the employer, the size of the employer, and the nature of the employer's business be considered.

Businesses must reasonably accommodate not only *employees* for their disabilities under the ADA but also customers and others who use public facilities such as hotels, restaurants, theaters, schools (even private ones), most places of entertainment, offices providing services, and other establishments doing business with the public. The Supreme Court ruled that the Professional Golf Association had to accommodate golfer Casey Martin, who suffered a walking disability because of a circulatory disorder, by allowing him to use a golf cart in PGA tournaments. The Court held (1) that PGA tournaments were open to any member of the public who paid a qualifying fee and participated successfully in a qualifying tournament and (2) that accommodating Casey Martin by allowing him to use a golf cart while other golfers walked a tournament course did not "fundamentally alter the nature" of PGA tournament events.

---

sidebar 20.11

Chipotle Mexican Grill: Must Accommodate Disabled Patrons

 The ADA prohibits discrimination in employment and in public accommodations. Maurizio Antoninetti, a patron of the Chipotle Mexican Grill, complained that a 45-inch barrier at Chipotle restaurants blocked his view of the counter, preventing him from inspecting each dish, choosing his order, and watching it be prepared.

Chipotle argued that it accommodated the needs of customers in wheelchairs by bringing them spoonfuls of their preferred dish for inspection before ordering.

This fell short of being adequate. The Ninth Circuit Court of Appeals held that the barrier "subjects disabled customers to a disadvantage that non-disabled customers do not suffer." The U.S. Supreme Court denied certiorari. Chipotle is retrofitting restaurants affected by the ruling and incorporating new designs into newly built restaurants and remodeled restaurants in the United States.

Remedies under the ADA Remedies under the ADA are basically the same remedies available under the Civil Rights Act, including hiring, reinstatement, back pay, front pay, injunctive relief, and compensatory and punitive damages. As with the Civil Rights Act, a plaintiff must first seek administration remedies with the EEOC. Compensatory and punitive damages are not available for policies that merely have disparate impact. They are available for intentional discrimination and for other employer actions such as failing to make reasonable accommodation for known job applicant or employee disabilities.

> The remedies under the ADA are basically the same remedies available under Title VII.

The ADA replaces the Rehabilitation Act of 1973 as the primary federal law protecting the disabled in private sector employment. The Rehabilitation Act, which applies only to employers doing business with the government under a federal contract for $2,500 or more, still requires that such employers have a qualified affirmative action program for hiring and promoting the disabled.

GENETIC DISCRIMINATION

The **Genetic Information Nondiscrimination Act (GINA)**, effective November 2009, prohibits covered employers from firing, refusing to hire, or otherwise discriminating against individuals on the basis of their genetic information, and from discriminating against employees and applicants on the basis of a family member's genetic information. Genetic information includes information about an individual's genetic tests; genetic information about genetic tests of an individual's family members; information about the manifestation of a disease or disorder in an individual's family history; request for or receipt of genetic services; and genetic information of a fetus and the genetic information of any embryo held by the individual or a family member.

"Covered employers" is defined as all employers subject to Title VII. The act further prohibits the limitation, segregation, or classification of employees in such a way "that would deprive or tend to deprive any employee of employment opportunities or otherwise adversely affect the status of the employee as an employee, because of genetic information with respect to the employee."

Under GINA, it is unlawful for an employer to "request, require, or purchase genetic information with respect to an employee or the family member of an employee," with limited exceptions.

GINA also has ramifications for group health plans and health insurance companies. Although many states have already enacted similar legislation, GINA establishes a federal baseline for protection against employment discrimination based on genetic information.

In November 2010, the EEOC published final regulations implementing Title II of GINA, which protects applicants for employment, current employees, former employees, apprentices, trainees and labor organization members against discrimination based on their genetic information. The EEOC regulations, which became effective on January 11, 2011, are intended to:

- Prohibit the use of genetic information in employment decisions.
- Restrict employers from requesting, requiring, or purchasing genetic information.
- Require that genetic information be maintained as a confidential medical records and place strict limits on the disclosure of genetic information.
- Provide remedies for individuals whose genetic information is acquired, used, or disclosed in violation of GINA.

Tests that are considered to be "genetic tests" under GINA include:

- Tests that might determine if a person is genetically disposed to breast cancer, colon cancer, or Huntington's Disease.
- Amniocentesis and newborn screening.

- Carrier screening for cystic fibrosis, sickle cell anemia, spinal muscular dystrophy, and fragile X syndrome.
- DNA testing to detect genetic markers associated with ancestry information.

---

sidebar 20.12

Protecting against Inadvertent Acquisition of Medical Information in Violation of GINA

Employers should consider incorporating the following language into FMLA and other forms to help establish a defense to any claim that it wrongfully obtained genetic information in response to an otherwise lawful request for medical information:

> The Genetic Information Nondiscrimination Act of 2008 (GINA) prohibits employers and other entities covered by GINA Title II from requesting or requiring genetic information of an individual or family member of the individual, except as specifically allowed by this law. To comply with this law, we are asking that you not provide any genetic information when responding to this request for medical information. "Genetic information" as defined by GINA, includes an individual's family medical history, the results of an individual's or family member's genetic tests, the fact that an individual or an individual's family member sought or received genetic services, and genetic information of a fetus carried by an individual or an individual's family member or an embryo lawfully held by an individual or family member receiving assistive reproductive services.

DISCRIMINATION IN GETTING AND KEEPING HEALTH INSURANCE

Group health plans and health insurance issuers are prohibited from discriminating against employees based on certain factors. The Health Insurance Portability and Accountability Act (HIPAA) forbids group plans and issuers from excluding an employee from insurance coverage or requiring different premiums based on the employee's health status, medical condition or history, genetic information, or disability.

The act primarily prevents discrimination against individual employees in small businesses. Before the act, individual employees with an illness like cancer or a genetic condition like sickle cell anemia were sometimes denied coverage in a new health plan. The small size of the plan deterred insurers from covering individual employees whose medical condition might produce large claims. The act denies insurers the right to discriminate on this basis. It also guarantees that insured employees who leave their old employer and join a new employer are not denied health insurance.

In addition to HIPAA, the Affordable Care Act prohibits insurance companies from refusing to sell coverage to renew policies because of an individual's preexisting conditions.

OTHER FEDERAL LEGISLATION

Other federal legislation dealing with employment discrimination includes the National Labor Relations Act of 1936. The National Labor Relations Board has ruled that appeals to racial prejudice in a collective bargaining representation election constitute an unfair labor practice. The NLRB has also revoked the certification of unions that practice discriminatory admission or representation policies. Additionally, employers have an obligation to bargain with certified unions over matters of employment discrimination. Such matters are considered "terms and conditions of employment" and are thus mandatory bargaining issues.

Finally, various other federal agencies may prohibit discriminatory employment practices under their authorizing statutes. The Federal Communications Commission, for example, has prohibited employment discrimination by its licensees (radio and TV stations) and has required the submission of affirmative action plans as a condition of license renewal.

LO 20-5 | STATE ANTIDISCRIMINATION LAWS

Federal laws concerning equal employment opportunity specifically permit state laws imposing additional duties and liabilities. In recent years, fair employment practices legislation has been introduced and passed by many state legislatures. When the federal Equal Employment Opportunity Act became effective, 40 states had such laws, but their provisions varied considerably. A typical state act makes it an unfair employment practice for any employer to refuse to hire or otherwise discriminate against any individual because of his or her race, color, religion, national origin, or ancestry. If employment agencies or labor organizations discriminate against an individual in any way because of one of these reasons, they are also guilty of an unfair employment practice. State acts usually set up administrative bodies with the power to make rules and regulations and hear and decide charges of violations filed by complainants.

State antidiscrimination laws sometimes protect categories of persons not protected by federal law. For example, some protect persons from employment discrimination based on weight. As discussed earlier, state and local law may prohibit sexual orientation discrimination in the workplace (see Sidebar 20.9). Other state and local laws prohibit employment discrimination based on weight (e.g., Michigan; Santa Cruz and San Francisco, California; and Washington DC). Michigan's antidiscrimination discrimination law also includes height and weight.

State law may also supplement Title VII, offering remedies to victims of sexual harassment. In New York, for example, former Knicks team executive Anucha Browne Sanders sued the owner of the New York Knicks and Madison Square Garden for discrimination using Title VII, as well as New York State Human Rights Law, New York Executive Law §296, and the Administrative Code of the City of New York §8-107, which prohibit unlawful discriminatory practices. After hearing testimony about crude racial and sexual insults and unwanted advances from coach Isiah Thomas, a jury awarded Sanders $11.6 million.

As indicated in Chapter 10 on torts, discrimination plaintiffs can also sue employers under various state common law causes of action, like negligence, assault, battery, intentional infliction of mental distress, invasion of privacy, and defamation. Under common law, plaintiffs may be able to receive unlimited compensatory and punitive damages, and greater numbers of plaintiffs seem to be suing under common law.

State antidiscrimination laws may permit discrimination lawsuits against employers of fewer than 15 employees, the minimum number for a lawsuit under federal Title VII.

According to a study by the Rudd Center at Yale University, discrimination against overweight people, particularly women, is as common as racial discrimination.

Do remember that discrimination lawsuits can be based on multiple causes of action, including common law ones.

TRENDS IN EMPLOYMENT DISCRIMINATION AND LITIGATION

Several current trends in employment discrimination and litigation will require close attention from managers in the coming years. These trends highlight the fact that the workforce is increasingly diverse and that new managers must be alert to the full impact of antidiscrimination laws. They also show the effects of new technology.

Surge in Private Lawsuits Private lawsuits alleging discrimination in employment surged in recent years. Several factors account for the rapid increase. The 1991 revision of the Civil Rights Act to support punitive and compensatory damages has encouraged employees to sue their employers. The passage of and amendments to the Americans with Disabilities Act has led to a new area of discrimination lawsuits, and some 50 million Americans, according to a conservative estimate, may legally qualify as disabled. Finally, as the large generation of baby boomers ages in the workforce, more lawsuits arise under the Age Discrimination in Employment Act. In the new century, these trends continue, making it ever more important for business managers to understand the law prohibiting discrimination in employment. See Sidebar 20.13 for an interesting study about female CEOs.

Arbitration in Employment Discrimination Disputes Arbitration is usually cheaper, quicker, and less public than litigation. Accustomed to using arbitration clauses in contracts with customers and suppliers, many employers also have begun placing arbitration clauses in employment contracts and personnel handbooks. These clauses require arbitration in employment discrimination disputes and with other employment controversies.

sidebar 20.13

Is It Important to Investors If the CEO Is a Man or a Woman?

The clear answer is, unfortunately, "Yes" according to a study by Lyda Bigelow and Judi McLean Parks at the Olin School of Business, Washington University in St. Louis.

Bigelow and McLean Parks created a prospectus for a fictitious company about to go public, along with a set of qualifications for the company's CEO. To determine if gender played a role in the decision, they gave half of the potential investors information with a female CEO and the other half a male CEO—the qualifications, however, were the same. Only the name and gender were different. They then asked individuals with a background in finance to consider investing in the company.

The researchers found that the CEO's gender clearly affected potential investors. For example, the study showed that the participants were inclined to invest up to three times more with the company with the male CEO. Executive compensation was also an issue. The participants in the study indicated that they would pay the female CEO 14 percent less than her male counterpart.

Perhaps even more disturbing, female CEOs were evaluated more harshly in other very subjective categories. Although the only difference given in the study was gender, participants deemed female CEOs as less competent leaders in a variety of realms, including handling a crisis and dealing with the company's board of directors.

Overall, the study showed that participants viewed male CEOs as more favorable representatives of the company in the public eye.

Source: *U.S. News and World Report,* www.usnews.com/usnews/biztech/articles/060508/8investment_bias.htm.

The Federal Arbitration Act (see Chapter 5) prefers arbitration over litigation, but that act may not apply to certain employment contracts. The EEOC has issued a policy statement concluding that "agreements that mandate binding arbitration of discrimination claims as a condition of employment are contrary to the fundamental principles" of antidiscrimination laws.

However, without specifically discussing the EEOC's policy statement, the Supreme Court has upheld arbitration clauses in certain employment discrimination cases. In *Circuit City Stores, Inc. v. Adams,* 532 U.S. 105 (2001), the Supreme Court decided that the Federal Arbitration Act did not prohibit enforceability of the following arbitration provision, which an employee had signed in his job application:

> I agree that I will settle any and all previously unasserted claims, disputes or controversies arising out of or relating to my application or candidacy for employment, employment and/or cessation of employment with Circuit City, *exclusively* by final and binding *arbitration* before a neutral arbitrator. By way of example only, such claims include claims under federal, state, and local statutory or common law, such as the Age Discrimination in Employment Act, Title VII of the Civil Rights Act of 1964, as amended, including the amendments of the Civil Rights Act of 1991, the Americans with Disabilities Act, the law of contract and the law of tort.

Congress may ultimately decide whether binding arbitration as a condition of working for an employer is an acceptable part of the employment contract. In the meantime, employers who wish to have employment disputes, including discrimination disputes, arbitrated should consider the following:

- Ensuring that arbitration agreements allow for the same range of remedies contained in the antidiscrimination laws.
- Allowing limited discovery in arbitration, which traditionally has no discovery process.
- Permitting employees to participate in selecting neutral, knowledgeable professional arbitrators instead of using an industry arbitration panel.
- Not requiring the employee to pay arbitration fees and costs.

These steps should go far toward eliminating many of the objections to the arbitration of employment discrimination disputes.

Proper arbitration agreements should continue to be considered as a business response to litigation of employment disputes. Interestingly, at least one study has found that employees alleging discrimination win more often before arbitration panels than before juries but only two-thirds of the time.

Insuring against Employment Discrimination Claims
Employers commonly insure against many potential liabilities. However, the general liability policies carried by many businesses, which cover bodily injury and property damage, often do not insure against intentional torts. Intent is a key element in many employment discrimination claims. In addition, general policies may not cover the back pay or damages for mental anguish that many discrimination plaintiffs seek. As a result, employers are beginning to ask for and get employment practices liability insurance, a type of insurance aimed specifically at discrimination claims.

Even with the availability of the new insurance, not all types of employment discrimination can be insured against in every state. States like New York and California do not permit companies to insure against "intentional

Insurance policies are more likely to insure against disparate impact claims rather than disparate treatment claims. Do you understand why?

acts." Disparate treatment discrimination is an example of such an act. Similarly, some states do not permit companies to insure against punitive damages that can arise in intentional violations of Title VII. Managers should also be aware that what the new policies cover and what they exclude vary widely.

---

concept *summary*

Illegal Employment Practices

Unless bona fide occupational qualifications or business necessity can be proved, federal law prohibits recruiting, hiring, promoting, and other employment practices that involve disparate treatment or produce a disparate impact on the basis of:

Race or color.

National origin.

Religion.

Sex.

Age.

Disabilities.

Pregnancy.

Genetic discrimination.

Key Terms

Affirmative action 636
Bona fide occupational
    qualifications (BFOQs) 616
Business necessity defense 619
Comparable worth 632
Disability 641
Disparate impact 619

Disparate treatment 618
Genetic Information
    Nondiscrimination Act
    (GINA) 644
Hostile work environment 629
Qualified disabled 642

Reasonable
    accommodation 642
Retaliation 619
Reverse discrimination 637
Section 1981 638
Seniority system 638
Sexual harassment 629

Review Questions and Problems

The Civil Rights Act of 1964

1. *General Provisions*

   Martel, a competent male secretary to the president of ICU, was fired because the new president of the company believed it is more appropriate to have a female secretary.

   (a) Has a violation of the law occurred?

   (b) Assume that a violation of the law has occurred and Martel decided to take an extended vacation after he was fired. Upon his return seven months later, Martel filed suit in federal district court against ICU, charging illegal discrimination under the Civil Rights Act of 1964. What remedies will be available to him under the act?

2. *Enforcement Procedures*

   Muscles-Are-You Inc. a bodybuilding spa targeted primarily toward male bodybuilders, refused to hire a woman for the position of executive director. The spa's management stated that the executive director must have a "macho" image to relate well with the spa's customers. Discuss whether it is likely that the spa has violated Title VII.

3. *Discrimination on the Basis of Race or Color*

   Does Title VII prohibit employment discrimination against members of all races? Explain.

4. *Discrimination on the Basis of National Origin*

   Ace Tennis Co. hires only employees who speak English. Does this policy illegally discriminate against Hispanic job applicants who speak only Spanish? Discuss.

5. *Discrimination on the Basis of Religion*

   Ortega, an employee of ABC Inc. recently joined a church that forbids working on Saturdays, Sundays, and Mondays. Ortega requested that his employer change his work schedule from eight-hour days, Monday through Friday, to ten-hour days, Tuesday through Friday. Ortega's request was refused because the employer is in operation only eight hours per day, five days a week. After a month during which Ortega failed to work on Mondays, he was fired. The employer stated that "only a full-time employee would be acceptable" for Ortega's position. What are Ortega's legal rights, if any?

6. *Discrimination on the Basis of Sex*

   A male supervisor at Star Company made repeated offensive sexual remarks to female employees. The employees complained to higher management, which ignored the complaints. If the company does not discharge or otherwise penalize the employee, has it violated Title VII? Discuss.

Employment Practices That May Be Challenged

7. *Questionnaires, Interviews, Testing, and Educational Requirements*

   Jennings Company, which manufactures sophisticated electronic equipment, hires its assembly employees on the basis of applicants' scores on a standardized mathematics aptitude test. It has been shown that those who score higher on the test almost always perform better on the job. However, it has also been demonstrated that the use of the test in hiring employees has the effect of excluding African Americans and other minority groups. Is this practice of the Jennings Company prohibited by the Civil Rights Act of 1964?

8. *Height and Weight Requirements*

   (a) An employer hires job applicants to wait tables in the Executive Heights Restaurant only if they are over 6 feet tall. Does this policy likely violate Title VII? Explain.

   (b) If a class of job applicants under 6 feet sues the employer, will it likely get compensatory and punitive damages? Explain.

9. *Appearance Requirements*

   Silicon Products requires all male employees to wear their hair "off the collar." Does this policy violate Title VII? Discuss.

10. *Affirmative Action Programs and Reverse Discrimination*

    Kartel Inc. found that historically African Americans had been significantly underrepresented in its workforce. It decided to remedy the situation and place African Americans in 50 percent of all new job openings. Discuss the legality of Kartel's action.

11. *Seniority Systems*

    Are seniority systems in the workplace legal under Title VII if in fact they discriminate on the basis of gender or race? Explain.

Other Statutes and Discrimination in Employment

12. *Civil Rights Act of 1866*

    When is it an advantage for a plaintiff to use Section 1981 as the basis for discrimination litigation as contrasted with using Title VII?

13. *Discrimination on the Basis of Age*

    Cantrell, the controller of Xylec's Inc. was forced to retire at age 58 due to a general company policy. Although Cantrell has a company pension of $50,000 per year, she believes that her lifestyle will soon be hampered due to inflation, since the pension provides for no cost-of-living increases. What are Cantrell's rights, if any?

14. *Discrimination on the Basis of Disabilities*

   Ralph is a systems analyst for the Silicon Corporation, a major defense contractor. When Ralph's co-workers learn that he has AIDS, six of them quit work immediately. Fearing that additional resignations will delay production, the company discharges Ralph. Discuss whether or not the company acted legally.

15. *Genetic Discrimination*

   Amy learns that she has the "breast cancer gene." Devastated, she shares the news with her supervisor. A few days later, Amy receives a harsh employment evaluation—the first of her career—criticizing her handling of a client matter. Two weeks later, Amy is fired. Amy cannot understand how she went from being a model employee with strong performance reviews to unemployed in such a short time. Does she have any claim against her employer?

16. *Discrimination in Getting and Keeping Health Insurance*

   Why does Title VII not apply to preventing discrimination in the getting and keeping of health insurance?

17. *Other Federal Legislation*

   Do employers have an obligation to negotiate with groups of employees over issues of discrimination? Explain.

18. *State Antidiscrimination Laws*

   Explain how state antidiscrimination laws protect workers in situations where federal laws do not.

19. *Trends in Employment Discrimination and Litigation*

   Can arbitration agreements be used to keep employees from litigating discrimination issues? Discuss.

business *discussions*

1. When Maria Suarez got her new job, she was happy. As an oil rigger, she would make enough money to support herself and her two children. But after a week of working with a primarily male crew, her happiness was gone. Her co-workers were the reason. At first the men made unwelcome comments about her body. Then sexual graffiti mentioning her name appeared. When she came to work one morning a nude female picture was pinned to one of the rigs. Her name had been scrawled across the bottom. Maria complained to the crew foreman, who referred her to the site manager. "Let's ignore it for a while," he told Maria. "It's just good fun. The men are testing you. You've got to fit in."

   What are Maria's legal rights in this situation?
   What would you do if you were the site manager?
   Do you think Maria should just try to "fit in"?

2. Delivery Quik Inc. delivers packages to small retail stores from a central distribution point in a major metropolitan area. Drivers both load and unload their packages, some of which weigh close to 100 pounds. Although equipment helps the drivers in their tasks, there is still considerable lifting necessary. Delivery Quik has a policy that drivers must stand at least 6 feet tall and weigh no less than 180 pounds. All drivers must retire at age 45 and have at least a high school education.

   Does the height, weight, age, and education policy discriminate illegally?
   How would you change the policy?
   If your customers prefer male drivers, does their preference mean that the company can hire only males as drivers?

Employment Laws

21

Learning Objectives

In this chapter you will learn:

21-1. To identify major employment laws and their significance for employers and employees.

21-2. To explain the scope and limits of the employment-at-will doctrine.

21-3. To understand the limits of privacy in the workplace and the role of workers' compensation laws.

21-4. To describe the authority of agents to act on behalf of a principal in contracts and beyond.

21-5. To discuss ways an employer should document employee performance in anticipation of potential employee litigation.

In addition to the employment discrimination laws detailed in Chapter 20, there are many other employment laws pertaining to the employer–employee relationship. This chapter surveys a number of important employment laws. As you read, consider how these laws contribute to the employment law framework in the United States. Most of the laws discussed are federal laws. However, it is important to understand that states and local governments may also have employment laws.

One major example of this is workers' compensation laws. Each state has its own laws addressing accidental workplace injuries. This chapter also helps you understand the essential principles of agency law and how business organizations act through their agents. Lastly, in light of the practical reality of defending against employee lawsuits, this chapter suggests ways that employers should document employee performance, so that they are prepared for potential litigation by current and former employees.

PART 4 The Employer–Employee Relationship

Fair Labor Standards Act: To Pay or Not to Pay Overtime?

The number of FLSA (Fair Labor Standards Act) cases is on the rise. Here are points to consider regarding overtime pay to be in compliance with the law:

- **Hourly or Salaried?** It is not uncommon for an employer to pay a salary to an employee who should be paid hourly. "Executive employees" may be paid a salary of at least $455 per week *if* (1) the employee's primary duty is managing the enterprise, or managing a customarily recognized department or subdivision of the enterprise; (2) the employee customarily and regularly directs the work of at least two or more other full-time employees or their equivalent; (3) the employee has the authority to hire or fire other employees, or the employee's suggestions and recommendations as to the hiring, firing, advancement, promotion, or

any other change of status of other employees is given particular weight.

- **Employee or Independent Contractor?** Because the FLSA requires employers to pay non-exempt employees overtime compensation for hours worked in excess of 40 hours per week, employers are sometimes tempted to classify these workers as "independent contractors" to avoid overtime pay.

Although each individual's damages may not be substantial, an employer may face a FLSA collective action involving many workers who are misclassified. Workers are increasingly aware of their rights under wage and hour laws, especially when it comes to overtime pay.

For more information see the U.S. Department of Labor, Wage and Hour Division, *FairPay Overtime Initiative*, available at www.dol.gov/whd/regs/compliance/fairpay/.

LO 21-1 Employment Laws

A complete review of all laws and regulations that impact how employers and employees interact is beyond our scope. The following sections address some of these laws and examine some current issues arising in many companies. Table 21.1 provides a list of some of the major employment laws and the purpose of each. Chapter 20 focused on the first category of laws, those addressing discrimination. This chapter discusses a range of employment laws from the Fair Labor Standards Act to retirement and pension laws. Chapter 22 then details labor laws, the last category in the table.

Employment laws are among the most emotionally and politically charged topics. The reason tempers flare and even violence happens is that these laws go to the heart of how business makes a profit and how people make a living.

MINIMUM WAGES AND MAXIMUM HOURS

The federal government regulates wages and hours through the **Fair Labor Standards Act (FLSA)**. Originally enacted in 1938, the FLSA establishes a minimum wage, overtime pay, record-keeping requirements, and child labor standards. The FLSA has been repeatedly amended to keep it up to date. For example, effective May 25, 2007, the FLSA was amended to increase the federal minimum wage in three steps:

- To $5.85 per hour effective July 24, 2007.
- To $6.55 per hour effective July 24, 2008.
- To $7.25 per hour effective July 24, 2009.

There is currently a bill pending in Congress to raise the federal minimum wage to $10.10 by late 2016.

table 21.1 Summary of Major Federal Employment Laws

Law	Purpose
Civil Rights Acts, Pregnancy Discrimination Act, Americans with Disabilities Act, Age Discrimination in Employment Act, and Genetic Nondiscrimination Act	• Provide national policy governing employment discrimination.
Fair Labor Standards Act (FLSA)	• Provides hourly minimum wage and maximum number of hours before overtime is owed. • Provides restrictions on child labor.
Worker Adjustment and Retraining Notification Act (WARN Act)	• Provides restrictions on plant closings and mass layoffs.
Family Medical Leave Act (FMLA)	• Provides unpaid leave to care for a newborn child, an adopted child, to care for a family member, or for serious health conditions.
Uniformed Services Employment and Reemployment Rights Act (USERRA)	• Provides reemployment rights after performing uniformed service. • Provides those serving in the military the right to be free from discrimination and retaliation based on uniformed service.
Occupational Safety and Health Act (OSHA)	• Provides standards for a safe and healthy working environment.
Social Security Act	• Provides unemployment compensation. • Provides disability benefits.
Employment Retirement Income Security Act (ERISA)	• Provides requirements for private pension plans.
Electronic Communications Privacy Act	• Provides standards to protect privacy.
Railway Labor Act, Norris-LaGuardia Act, Wagner Act, Taft-Hartley Act, and Landrum-Griffin Act	• Provide national policy for governing the union–management relationship.

Additionally, overtime pay at a rate of not less than one and one-half times the employee's regular rate of pay is required after 40 hours of work in a workweek. For example, if an employee earns $8 an hour, the overtime pay must be at least $12 per hour. Employers of "tipped employees" must pay a cash wage of at least $2.13 per hour if they claim a tip credit against their minimum wage obligation. If the employee's tips combined with the cash wage do not meet the minimum hourly wage, the employer must make up the difference (with certain conditions). Many states provide for minimum wages higher than the federal rate. Employers are legally required to pay whichever minimum wage is higher. The FLSA does not require breaks or meal periods to be given to workers. Some states, however, may require breaks or meal periods.

Although a minimum wage and a maximum workweek of 40 hours before overtime is owed seems straightforward, there are many exceptions and

The highest state minimum wages: Washington at $9.32; Connecticut's minimum wage is $8.70, and it passed legislation in 2014 to raise the minimum wage to $10.10 by 2017. Maryland, Hawaii, and Vermont have passed similar laws.

Employers should use care to properly classify workers as either "employees" or "independent contractors."

sidebar 21.2

Internship Programs under the FLSA

Individuals who participate in "for-profit" private sector internships or training programs may do so without compensation. Under what circumstances should interns be paid? According to the Department of Labor, six criteria must be applied when making the determination:

1. The internship, even though it includes actual operation of the facilities of the employer, is similar to training which would be given in an educational environment.
2. The internship experience is for the benefit of the intern.
3. The intern does not displace regular employees, but works under close supervision of existing staff.
4. The employer that provides the training derives no immediate advantage from the activities of the intern; and on occasion its operations may actually be impeded.
5. The intern is not necessarily entitled to a job at the conclusion of the internship.
6. The employer and the intern understand that the intern is not entitled to wages for the time spent in the internship.

If all of the factors listed above are met, an employment relationship *does not exist* under the FLSA, and the minimum wage and overtime provisions *do not apply* to the intern.

Source: U.S. Department of Labor, Wage and Hour Division, *Fact Sheet #71: Internship Programs under the Fair Labor Standards Act*, April 2010, available at www.dol.gov/whd/regs/compliance/whdfs71.pdf.

factual situations complicating the general rules. Some of the general exceptions include pay for workers in executive administrative or professional job positions. These exceptions are commonly referred to as the "white-collar" exemptions to overtime. In Case 21.1, the Supreme Court addresses the legal issue of how an employer is to count work hours.

case 21.1

SANDIFER v. UNITED STATES STEEL CORP.
571 U.S. ___ (2014)

Petitioner Sandifer and others filed a putative collective action under the Fair Labor Standards Act of 1938, seeking back pay for time spent donning and doffing pieces of protective gear that they assert respondent United States Steel Corporation (U.S. Steel) required workers to wear because of hazards at steel plants. U.S. Steel contended that this donning-and-doffing time, which would otherwise be compensable under the Fair Labor Standards Act, is noncompensable under a provision of its collective bargaining agreement with petitioners' union.

The district court granted U.S. Steel summary judgment in pertinent part, holding that petitioners' donning and doffing constituted "changing clothes." It also assumed that any time spent donning and doffing items that were not "clothes" was "de minimis" and hence noncompensable. The Circuit affirmed.

SCALIA, J.: The question us is the meaning of the phrase "changing clothes" as it appears in the Fair Labor Standards Act (Act). . . . [Petitioners] seek backpay for time spent donning and doffing various pieces of protective gear . . . a flame-retardant jacket, a pair of pants, and hood; a hardhat; a "snood"; "wristlets"; work gloves; leggings' "metatarsal" boots; safety glasses; earplugs; and a respirator. At bottom, petitioners want to be paid for the time they have spent putting on and taking off these objects. In the aggregate, the amount of time—and money—involved is likely to be quite large. Because the donning-and-doffing time would otherwise be compensable under the Act, U.S. Steel's contention of non-compensability stands or falls upon the validity of a provision of its collective bargaining agreement with petitioners' union, which says that this time is noncompensable. The validity of that provision depends, in turn, upon the applicability of 29 U.S.C. §203(o) to the time at issue. That subsection allows parties to decide, as part of a collective bargaining agreement, that "time spent in changing clothes . . . at the beginning or end of each workday" is noncompensable. . . .

We begin by examining the meaning of "clothes." . . . The Oxford English Dictionary defines "clothes" as a "[c]overing for the person; wearing apparel; dress; railment, vesture." That is what we hold to be the meaning of the word as used in §203(o). . . . Petitioners argue that the word "clothes" is too indeterminate to be ascribed any general meaning but that, whatever it *includes*, it necessarily *excludes* items designed to be used to protect against workplace hazards. . . . We see no basis for the proposition that the unmodified term "clothes" somehow omits protective clothing. . . .

Having settled upon the meaning of "clothes," we must now consider the meaning of "changing." . . . Petitioners conclude that items of protective gear that are put on over the employee's street clothes are nor covered by §203(o). We disagree . . . We think that despite the usual meaning of "changing clothes," the broader statutory context makes it plain that "time spent in changing clothes" includes time spent altering dress. . . .

Applying the foregoing principles to the facts of this case, we hold that petitioners' donning and doffing of the protective gear at issue qualifies as "changing clothes" within the meaning of §203(o). Petitioners have pointed to 12 particular items. . . . The first nine clearly fit within the interpretation of "clothes." . . . The remaining three items [glasses, earplugs, and a respirator], by contract, do not satisfy our standard. . . . The question is whether the time devoted to the putting on and off of these items must be deducted from the noncompensable time. If so, federal judges must be assigned the task of separating the minutes spent clothes-changing and washing from the minutes devoted to other activities during the period in question. . . .

[I]it is most unlikely that Congress meant §203(o) to convert federal judges into time-study professionals. . . . In the present case, the District Court stated that "the time expended by each employee donning and doffing" safety glasses "is minimal," a conclusion with which the Seventh Circuit agreed. As for the respirators, the District Court [determined that they were outside of the scope of §203(o)]. The Seventh Circuit did not address the respirators at all, and we are not inclined to disturb the District Court's factual conclusion.

The judgment of the Court of Appeals is affirmed.

KEY POINTS

- The Supreme Court held that the time spent donning and doffing their protective gear is not compensable by operation of 29 U.S.C. §203(o) of the FLSA.
- Where employees are donning and doffing items considered to be "clothes," employers should make their practices clear in collective bargaining agreements to avoid legal challenges.
- Although this decision addresses employers with unionized workforces, nonunionized employers should be compensating employees for donning and doffing. As such, they should review any requirements, including the time spent donning and doffing, to determine if the employees are being compensated appropriately.

The FLSA also sets wage, hours worked, and safety requirements for minors (individuals under age 18). The rules vary depending upon the particular age of the minor and the particular job involved. As a general rule, the FLSA sets 14 years of age as the minimum age for employment, and limits the number of hours worked by minors under the age of 16. In 2008, the FLSA was amended to increase penalties against employers who violate child labor laws. The penalties increased from $11,000 to $50,000 for each FLSA violation leading to the serious injury or death of a child worker. The increased fines are subject to doubling for repeated or willful violations.

---

sidebar 21.3

Break Time for Nursing Moms

The FLSA now requires break time for nursing mothers. Employers are required to provide "reasonable break time for an employee to express breast milk for her nursing child for 1 year after the child's birth each time such employee has need to express the milk."

Employers are also required to provide a functional space for expressing breast milk that is "shielded from view and free from intrusion from co-workers and the public." A bathroom, even a private one, is not a permissible location under the FLSA.

Employers with fewer than 50 employees are not subject to the FLSA break time requirement *if*

compliance with the provision would impose an undue hardship.

Employers are not required to compensate nursing mothers for breaks taken for the purpose of expressing milk. However, if the employer already provides compensated breaks, an employee who uses that break time to express milk must be compensated in the same way that other employees are compensated for break time.

Source: U.S. Department of Labor, Wage and Hour Division, *Fact Sheet #73 Break Time for Nursing Mothers under the FLSA*, December 2010, available at www.dol.gov/whd/regs/compliance/whdfs73.htm.

---

 case 21.2

KASTEN v. SAINT-GOBAIN PERFORMANCE PLASTICS CORP.
53 U.S. ___ (2011)

Petitioner Kasten brought an antiretaliation suit against his former employer, respondent (Saint-Gobain), under the Fair Labor Standards Act of 1938 (Act), which provides minimum wage, maximum hour, and overtime pay rules; and which forbids employers "to discharge . . . any employee because such employee has filed any complaint" alleging a violation of the Act, 29 U. S. C. §215(a)(3). In a related suit, the District Court found that Saint-Gobain violated the Act by placing timeclocks in a location that prevented workers from receiving credit for the time they spent donning and doffing work related protective gear.

In this suit Kasten claims that he was discharged because he orally complained to company officials about the timeclocks. The District Court granted Saint-Gobain summary judgment, concluding that the Act's antiretaliation provision did not cover oral complaints. The Seventh Circuit affirmed. Justice Breyer delivered

the opinion of the Court in which Chief Justice Roberts, and Justices Kennedy, Ginsburg, Alito and Sotomayor joined. Justice Scalia filed a dissenting opinion in which Justice Thomas joined in part. Justice Kagan took no part in the consideration or decision of the case.

BREYER, J.: The Fair Labor Standards Act of 1938 (Act) sets forth employment rules concerning minimum wages, maximum hours, and overtime pay. 52 Stat. 1060, 29 U. S. C. §201 *et seq.* The Act contains an antiretaliation provision that forbids employers

> "to discharge or in any other manner discriminate against any employee because such employee has *filed any complaint* or instituted or caused to be instituted any proceeding under or related to [the Act], or has testified or is about to testify in such proceeding, or has served or is about to serve on an industry committee." §215(a)(3) (emphasis added).

We must decide whether the statutory term "filed any complaint" includes oral as well as written complaints within its scope. We conclude that it does.

I The petitioner, Kevin Kasten, brought this anti-retaliation lawsuit against his former employer, Saint-Gobain Performance Plastics Corporation. Kasten says that Saint-Gobain located its timeclocks between the area where Kasten and other workers put on (and take off) their work-related protective gear and the area where they carry out their assigned tasks. That location prevented workers from receiving credit for the time they spent putting on and taking off their work clothes—contrary to the Act's requirements. In a related suit the District Court agreed with Kasten, finding that Saint-Gobain's "practice of not compensating . . . for time spent donning and doffing certain required protective gear and walking to work areas" violated the Act. *Kasten v. Saint-Gobain Performance Plastics Corp.,* 556 F. Supp. 2d 941, 954 (WD Wis. 2008). In this suit Kasten claims unlawful retaliation. He says that Saint-Gobain discharged him because he orally complained to Saint-Gobain officials about the timeclocks.

In particular, Kasten says that he repeatedly called the unlawful timeclock location to Saint-Gobain's attention— in accordance with Saint-Gobain's internal grievance resolution procedure. See Brief for Petitioner 4 (quoting Saint-Gobain's Code of Ethics and Business Conduct as imposing upon every employee "the responsibility to report . . . suspected violations of . . . any applicable law of which he or she becomes aware"); *id.,* at 4–5 (quoting Saint-Gobain's Employee Policy Handbook as instructing employees with "questions, complaints, and problems" to "[c]ontact" their "supervisor[s] immediately" and if necessary "take the issue to the next level of management," then to the "local Human Resources Manager," then to "Human Resources" personnel at the "Regional" or "Headquarters" level).

Kasten adds that he "raised a concern" with his shift supervisor that "it was illegal for the time clocks to be where they were" because of Saint-Gobain's exclusion of "the time you come in and start doing stuff"; he told a human resources employee that "if they were to get challenged on" the location in court, "they would lose"; he told his lead operator that the location was illegal and that he "was thinking about starting a lawsuit about the placement of the time clocks"; and he told the human resources manager and the operations manager that he thought the location was illegal and that the company would "lose" in court. Record in No. 3:07–cv–00686–bbc (WD Wis.), Doc.87–3, pp. 31–34 (deposition of Kevin Kasten). This activity, Kasten concludes, led the company to discipline him and, in December 2006, to dismiss him.

Saint-Gobain presents a different version of events. It denies that Kasten made any significant complaint about the timeclock location. And it says that it dismissed Kasten simply because Kasten, after being repeatedly warned, failed to record his comings and goings on the timeclock.

For present purposes we accept Kasten's version of these contested events as valid. See *Scott v. Harris,* 550 U. S. 372, 380 (2007). That is because the District Court entered summary judgment in Saint-Gobain's favor. . . . Kasten sought certiorari. And in light of conflict among the Circuits as to whether an oral complaint is protected, we granted Kasten's petition. . . . The sole question presented is whether "an oral complaint of a violation of the Fair Labor Standards Act" is "protected conduct under the [Act's] anti-retaliation provision." Pet. for Cert. i. The Act protects employees who have "filed any complaint," 29 U. S. C. §215(a)(3), and interpretation of this phrase "depends upon reading the whole statutory text, considering the purpose and context of the statute, and consulting any precedents or authorities that inform the analysis," *Dolan v. Postal Service,* 546 U. S. 481, 486 (2006). This analysis leads us to conclude that the language of the provision, considered in isolation, may be open to competing interpretations. But considering the provision in conjunction with the purpose and context leads us to conclude that only one interpretation is permissible. We begin with the text of the statute. The word "filed" has different relevant meanings in different contexts. . . .The bottom line is that the text, taken alone, cannot provide a conclusive answer to our interpretive question. The phrase "filed any complaint" might, or might not, encompass oral complaints. We must look further. . . .

Why would Congress want to limit the enforcement scheme's effectiveness by inhibiting use of the Act's complaint procedure by those who would find it difficult to reduce their complaints to writing, particularly illiterate, less educated, or overworked workers? . . . In the years prior to the passage of the Act, illiteracy rates were particularly high among the poor. . . . To limit the scope of the antiretaliation provision to the filing of written complaints would also take needed flexibility from those charged with the Act's enforcement. It could prevent Government agencies from using hotlines, interviews, and other oral methods of receiving complaints. . . . To fall within the scope of the antiretaliation provision, a complaint must be sufficiently clear and detailed for a reasonable employer to understand it, in light of both content and context, as an assertion of rights protected by the statute and a call for their protection. This standard can be met, however, by oral complaints, as well as by written ones. . . .

[continued]

Second, given Congress' delegation of enforcement powers to federal administrative agencies, we also give a degree of weight to their views about the meaning of this enforcement language. . . . The Secretary of Labor has consistently held the view that the words "filed any complaint" cover oral, as well as written, complaints. . . . The EEOC has set forth a similar view in its Compliance Manual. . . . These agency views are reasonable. They are consistent with the Act. . . . We conclude that the Seventh Circuit erred in determining that oral complaints cannot fall within the scope of the phrase "filed any complaint" in the Act's antiretaliation provision. We leave it to the lower courts to decide whether Kasten will be able to satisfy the Act's notice requirement. We vacate the Circuit's judgment and remand the case for further proceedings consistent with this opinion.

Reversed and remanded.

KEY POINTS

- This case involves an antiretaliation action against a former employer. This issue was whether an oral complaint was sufficient to make a complaint under the FLSA.
- After analyzing the FLSA statutory language, "filed any complaint," as well as the statutory context and relevant authorities, the Supreme Court concluded that an oral complaint is sufficient to satisfy the notice requirement.

THE WARN ACT

The WARN notice allows impacted employees and communities some time to prepare for the negative impact of a plant closing or mass layoff.

According to the AFL-CIO, "Layoffs continue at a pace of 1.5 million impacted workers every year and almost half a million have been idled by mass layoffs in the first three months" of 2008.

The Worker Adjustment and Retraining Notification (WARN) Act became law in 1989. Known as the **WARN Act,** this law requires employers to provide notice of plant closings and mass layoffs. This notice must be given in writing and be delivered at least 60 days prior to closing a work site or conducting mass layoffs. The WARN notice must be given to employees or their bargaining representatives (such as a union), the state's dislocated worker unit, and the elected chief officer of the local government impacted.

The WARN notice is required of employers with 100 or more employees. Workers who work less than half-time are not counted to determine this threshold level of 100. Employees entitled to receive the WARN notice include those who are hourly, salaried, supervisory, and managerial. In essence all workers, even part-time, are entitled to receive the notice.

The WARN notice covers plant closings and mass layoffs involving loss of employment. Covered plant closings are defined as the shutting of an employment site resulting in a loss of employment of 50 or more employees during any 30-day period. A mass layoff requires the WARN notice if 500 or more employees lose their jobs in a 30-day period. This notice also must be given if between 50 and 499 employees are laid off if the number terminated make up at least 33% of the employer's workforce. Although they are entitled to receive any applicable WARN notice, less than half-time employees are not counted to reach the requirement of 50 for plant closings or the thresholds for mass layoffs. A loss of employment includes (1) termination of employment, (2) layoff exceeding six months, or (3) a reduction in an employee's work time of more than 50% in each month for six months.

The WARN notice must be provided even if the numbers in the preceding paragraph are not satisfied if there are two or more plant closings or mass layoffs in a 90-day period that when taken together satisfy the threshold numbers. The sale of a business may or may not require the WARN notice. Any required notice prior to the sale being completed is the responsibility of the seller. The buyer of the business assumes this responsibility after the closing date.

The penalty for failure to comply with the WARN notice is back pay to employees to cover the required 60-day period. Each day of the 60-day period that an employer fails to provide written notice to the local government can result in a $500 fine.

When an employer is replacing striking employees in large numbers, the WARN notice is not required. Employers may avoid the need to provide 60-day notice if it can show its business is faltering and to give notice of a plant closing would adversely impact its ability to get financing. Also, unforeseen business circumstances may justify a less than 60-day WARN notice for either plant closing or layoffs. Finally, natural disasters, such as storms, floods, and earthquakes, may justify a less than 60-day notice for a plant closing or mass layoff.

THE FAMILY AND MEDICAL LEAVE ACT

On February 5, 1993, Bill Clinton signed his first piece of legislation as president. This was the **Family and Medical Leave Act (FMLA).** While the details of this law have been called burdensome to business, it has provided eligible employees who work for covered employers to take up to 12 weeks of unpaid leave during any 12-month period if one or more of the following events occur:

> "With the Family Medical Leave Act, the United States at last joined more than 150 other countries in guaranteeing workers some time off when a baby is born or a family member is sick."
>
> **—President Bill Clinton in *My Life***

- Birth and care of a newborn child of the employee.

- Placement with employee of a son or daughter for adoption or foster care.

- Care of an immediate family member with a serious health condition.

- Employee is unable to work due to a serious health condition.

The provisions relating to birth, adoption, and foster care apply to both female and male employees. Increasingly, men are opting to take leave to care for children. See Sidebar 21.4 for FMLA facts and statistics. An immediate family member is a spouse, minor child, or parent of the employee. Under the FMLA, the employee's parents in law do not qualify as an immediate family member. And the employee's children who are over 18 years old do not qualify as an immediate family member, unless that child is incapable of self-care due to a mental or physical disability that limits one or more of the major life activities as defined in the Americans with Disabilities Act (ADA). For a more thorough discussion of the ADA, see Chapter 20.

In 2010, the Department of Labor announced that benefits available to parents of newborns and newly adopted children under the FMLA may apply to same-sex couples.

Covered employers are those who employ 50 or more employees for each working day of 20 or more calendar weeks during either the current or preceding year. Eligible employees have worked for their employer for at least 12 months and have worked at least 1,250 hours during the preceding 12 months. The 12-month work period does not have to be consecutive months. An employee satisfies this requirement so long as that employee has worked for the employer at least a total of 12 months. Furthermore, eligible employees must work at a location where at least 50 employees are employed.

To satisfy the requirement that the employer have 50 employees, all persons who work for the employer within 75 miles can be counted.

sidebar 21.4

FMLA: Facts and Statistics

WHO TAKES FMLA LEAVE?

About 60 percent of workers qualify to take leave under the FMLA.

Over 50 million people have taken FMLA leave.

WHY DO PEOPLE TAKE FMLA LEAVE?

To care for their own serious illness: 55 percent.

To care for a seriously ill family member: 18 percent.

To take care of a new child: 21 percent (29 percent women and 23 percent men).

HOW HAS FMLA AFFECTED EMPLOYERS?

98 percent of eligible employees return to work for the same employer after returning from FMLA leave.

91 percent of covered businesses report that the FMLA has a neutral or positive effect on employee morale.

90 percent of covered businesses reported that the FMLA had either a neutral or positive effect on business profitability. Fewer than 2 percent of covered work sites reported confirmed misuse of FMLA.

Sources: U.S. Department of Labor, *Family Medical Leave in 2012: Executive Summary* (September 13, 2013); U.S. Department of Labor, "FMLA Is Working," FMLA Fact Sheet, dol.gov (May 2014); U.S. *Department of Labor's 2000 Report Balancing the Needs of Families and Employers: Family and Medical Leave Surveys 2000 Update;* Nicole Casta's "Highlights of the 2000 U.S. Department of Labor Report: Balancing the Needs of Families and Employers: Family and Medical Leave Surveys," and the National Partnership for Women & Families' 2005 Report, "Facts about the FMLA: What Does It Do, Who Uses It, and How."

sidebar 21.5

EEOC: Best Practices Recommendations on Work/Family Balance

As part of an ongoing attempt to avoid discrimination against workers with caregiving responsibilities, sometimes called "family responsibilities discrimination," the EEOC issued a document on best practices. Those recommendations include the following:

- Be aware of and train managers about the legal obligations that may impact decisions about the treatment of workers with caregiving responsibilities.
- Develop, disseminate, and enforce a strong EEO policy that clearly addresses the types of conduct that might constitute unlawful discrimination.
- Ensure that managers at all levels are aware of and comply with the organization's work-life policies.
- Respond to complaints of caregiver discrimination efficiently and effectively.
- Protect against retaliation.

The document also encourages employers to develop "flexible work policies," which studies have

demonstrated have a "positive impact on employee engagement organizational productivity and profitability."

Case to Consider: *Chadwick v. Wellpoint, Inc.* (1st Cir. 2009), in which the court held that "unlawful sex discrimination occurs when an employer takes an adverse job action on the assumption that a woman, because she is a woman, will neglect her job responsibilities in favor of her presumed childcare responsibilities." The plaintiff in *Chadwick* was the mother of young triplets. She was passed over for promotion and the position was given to a woman with two older children. The First Circuit held that the district court erred in granting summary judgment in favor of the employer and, accordingly reversed and remanded the case for further proceedings.

Source: EEOC, *Employer Best Practices for Workers with Caregiving Responsibilities,* 2009, available at www.eeoc.gov/policy/docs/caregiver-best-practices.html.

The FMLA places a number of responsibilities on the employer. These responsibilities include notifying the employees that they are eligible for family medical leave and designating in writing when the employee has requested such leave. The employer may request a medical certification that a qualifying event has occurred in the employee's life, but the employer is not entitled to review the actual medical records of the employee.

Once family medical leave is granted, the employer must keep the employee's job available for when the leave is up and the employee returns to work. In essence, the employee who qualifies for family medical leave is not supposed to be disadvantaged by the fact that the leave was taken. For example, if the employer gives a bonus for perfect attendance, the employee on family medical leave should be awarded this bonus, assuming perfect attendance other than the leave period. If a bonus is based on the amount of sales, the FMLA does not require the employer to award sales that the employee would have made if not on family medical leave.

Employees who believe they have been denied their rights under the FMLA can sue the employer in federal district court for equitable relief and back pay damages. Such an employee may sue for reinstatement or may seek damages or both.

---

sidebar 21.6

States Are Immune from FMLA Self-Care Claims

COLEMAN V. MARYLAND, COURT OF APPEALS 132 S. CT. 1327 (2012)

Key Facts: Daniel Coleman was an employee of the Maryland Court of Appeals for six years. In August 2007, he sent a letter requesting sick leave for a documented medical condition. The request was denied and Mr. Coleman was given an ultimatum: resign or be terminated. In this complaint, Mr. Coleman claimed that his FMLA leave was denied in retaliation for his complaints of wrongdoing in the office.

Procedural History: The District Court granted defendants' motion to dismiss, including plaintiffs'

FMLA claims, holding that "the FMLA's self-care provisions did not validly abrogate Eleventh Amendment immunity." The Fourth Circuit affirmed.

Explanation by the Supreme Court: The Eleventh Amendment of the U.S. Constitution bars claims in federal court against an unconsenting state and any governmental units that are arms of the state unless Congress has abrogated immunity. To do so, Congress must make clear its intent to abrogate and must act in accordance with a valid exercise of power.

Supreme Court: Affirmed, holding suits against the states under the self-care provision of the FMLA are barred by sovereign immunity.

FMLA and Military Families In 2010, the National Defense Authorization Act (FY 2010 NDAA) broadened coverage under the FMLA to expand the availability of military caregiver leave and qualifying exigency leave. The FY 2010 NDAA extended military caregiver leave to eligible employees whose family members are recent veterans with serious injuries or illnesses, including conditions that do not arise until after the veteran has left the military. The FY 2010 NDAA also expanded the definition of a serious injury or illness for both current service members and veterans to include serious injuries or illnesses that result from a condition that existed before the service member's active duty service *and* was aggravated by service in the line of duty on active duty.

Additionally, the FY 2010 NDAA expanded qualifying exigency leave to eligible employees with family members serving in the Regular Armed Forces, in addition to the National Guard and Reserves. The FY 2010 NDAA also added the requirement that for all qualifying exigency leave, the military member (National Guard, Reserves, Regular Armed Forces) must be deployed to a foreign country.

Military caregiver leave entitles an eligible employee who is the spouse, parent, son, daughter, or next of kin of a covered service member with a serious illness or injury to take up to a total of 26 workweeks of unpaid, job-protected leave during any single 12-month period to care for the service member. Before the FY 2010 NDAA was enacted, military caregiver leave was limited to eligible employees who were the family members of current service members with a serious injury or illness incurred in the line of duty on active duty.[1]

UNIFORMED SERVICES EMPLOYMENT AND REEMPLOYMENT RIGHTS ACT

The **Uniformed Services Employment and Reemployment Rights Act (USERRA)** protects the rights of individuals who voluntarily or involuntarily leave employment positions to undertake military service or certain types of service in the National Disaster Medical System. Specifically, USERRA provides reemployment rights following a period of service if:

- The individual held a civilian job.
- The employee informed the employer that he/she was leaving the job for service in the uniformed services.
- The period of service did not exceed five years (with exceptions).
- The release from service was under "honorable conditions."
- The individual reports back to the civilian employer in a timely manner or submits a timely application for reemployment.

Those eligible to be reemployed must be restored to the job and receive benefits that would have been attained had there not been an absence due to military service. USERRA protects those performing uniformed service from discrimination in:

- Initial employment.
- Reemployment.
- Retention in employment.
- Promotion.
- Any benefit of employment.

Employers may not retaliate against anyone asserting his or her rights or assisting in the enforcement of USERRA rights, even if that person has no service connection.

An international survey of 173 countries revealed that the United States is only one of four countries that does not guarantee any paid leave for new mothers. The other countries are Liberia, Papua New Guinea, and Swaziland. Source: Project on Global Working Families' 2007 Report "Work, Family, and Equity Index."

---

[1]For more information, see U.S. Department of Labor, *How Did the FY 2010 NDAA Change the Military Leave Entitlements?* www.dol.gov/whd/fmla/2013rule/militaryFR_FAQs.htm#2.

USERRA also contains health insurance provisions. Covered individuals who leave a job to perform military service have the right to elect to continue existing employer-based health plan coverage for up to 24 months. For those who do not elect to continue coverage, they have the right to be reinstated in the employer's health plan when reemployed, generally without any waiting periods or exclusions (except for service-connected illnesses or injuries). Federal law required employers to notify employees of their rights under USERRA, including by displaying government notices.

---

sidebar 21.7

Rand Study: Invisible Wounds of War

Rand, a non-profit global think tank, conducted a study of U.S troops to determine the effects of their service. Since October 2001, approximately 1.64 million U.S. troops have been deployed for operations in Iraq and Afghanistan. The study assessed the post-deployment health-related needs. Major findings:

- About 19 percent of returning veterans report symptoms consistent with a diagnosis of post-traumatic stress disorder (PTSD) or depression.

- About 20 percent reported having suffered a probably traumatic brain injury while deployed.

- Only about half of those who need treatment for PTSD and depression actually seek it, and slightly more than half of those who receive treatment get care that meets minimal clinical standards.

- Concerns about confidentiality and career issues were major reasons why many veterans did not seek treatment.

- Removing such barriers to care and delivering treatment supported by scientific evidence can improve recovery rates and reduce societal costs.

Taking into consideration these issues, the U.S. Department of Labor issued *Hiring Veterans: A Step-by-Step Toolkit for Employers* to help employers working with transitioning service members. The guide includes information about available resources and developing effective strategies to hire veterans.

Source: Rand, *Invisible Wounds of War: Psychological and Cognitive Injuries, Their Consequences, and Services to Assist Recovery*, 2008, available at www.rand.org/health/feature/forty/invisible_wounds.html.

---

 case **21.3**

STAUB v. PROCTOR HOSPITAL
562 U.S. ___ (2011)

This case contains a reference to the Seventeenth Century fable, "The Monkey and the Cat" by French poet Jean de La Fontine. In that fable, a monkey persuades an unsuspecting cat to extract some chestnuts from a fire. The monkey absconds with the nuts, leaving the cat with only a burnt paw. Under the cat's paw theory of liability, an employer may be held liable when a biased non-decision maker (the monkey) influences an unbiased decision maker (the cat) to take action he or she would not otherwise take.

While employed as an angiography technician by respondent Proctor Hospital, petitioner Staub was a member of the United States Army Reserve. Both his immediate supervisor (Mulally) and Mulally's supervisor (Korenchuk) were hostile to his military obligations. Mulally gave Staub disciplinary warning, which included a directive requiring Staub to report to her or Korenchuk when his cases were completed. After receiving a report from Korenchuk that Staub had violated the Corrective Action, Proctor's vice president of human resources (Buck) reviewed Staub's personnel file and decided to fire him. Staub filed a grievance, claiming that Mulally had fabricated the allegation underlying the warning out of hostility toward his military obligations, but Buck adhered to her decision. Staub sued Proctor under the Uniformed Services Employment and Reemployment Rights Act of 1994 (USERRA). He contended not that Buck was motivated by hostility to his military obligations, but that Mulally and Korenchuk were, and that their actions influenced Buck's decision. A jury found Proctor liable and awarded Staub damages, but the Seventh Circuit reversed, holding that Proctor was entitled to judgment as a matter of law because the decision maker had relied on more than Mulally's and Korenchuk's advice in making her decision. The U.S. Supreme Court unanimously reversed. Justice Kagan did not take part in the decision.

SCALIA, J.: We consider the circumstances under which an employer may be held liable for employment discrimination based on the discriminatory animus of an employee who influenced, but did not make, the ultimate employment decision.

Petitioner Vincent Staub worked as an angiography technician for respondent Proctor Hospital until 2004, when he was fired. Staub and Proctor hotly dispute the facts surrounding the firing, but because a jury found for Staub in his claim of employment discrimination against Proctor, we describe the facts viewed in the light most favorable to him. While employed by Proctor, Staub was a member of the U.S Army Reserve, which required him to attend drill one weekend per month and to train full time for two to three weeks a year. . . .

On April 2, 2004, Angie Day, Staub's co-worker, complained to Linda Buck, Proctor's vice president of human resources, and Garrett McGowan, Proctor's chief operating officer, about Staub's frequent unavailability and abruptness. McGowan directed Korenchuk and Buck to create a plan that would solve Staub's "availability' problems." But three weeks later, before they had time to do so, Korenchuk informed Buck that Staub had left his desk without informing a supervisor, in violation of the January Corrective Action. Staub now contends this accusation was false: he had left Korenchuk a voicemail notification that he was leaving his desk. Buck relied on Korenchuk's accusation, however, and after reviewing Staub's personnel file, she decided to fire him. The termination notice stated that Staub had ignored the directive issued in the January 2004 Corrective Action.

Staub challenged his firing through Proctor's grievance process, claiming that Mulally had fabricated the allegation underlying the Corrective Action out of hostility toward his military obligations. Buck did not follow up with Mulally about this claim. After discussing the matter with another personnel officer, Buck adhered to her decision.

Staub sued Proctor under the Uniformed Services Employment and Reemployment Rights Act of 1994, 38 U. S. C. §4301 *et seq.*, claiming that his discharge was motivated by hostility to his obligations as a military reservist. His contention was not that Buck had any such hostility but that Mulally and Korenchuk did, and that their actions influenced Buck's ultimate employment decision. A jury found that Staub's "military status was a motivating factor in [Proctor's] decision to discharge him," App. 68a, and awarded $57,640 in damages.

The Seventh Circuit reversed, holding that Proctor was entitled to judgment as a matter of law. 560 F. 3d 647. The court observed that Staub had brought a "'cat's paw' case," meaning that he sought to hold his employer liable for the animus of a supervisor who was not charged with making the ultimate employment decision. . . . Here, however, Staub is seeking to hold liable not Mulally and Korenchuk, but their employer. Perhaps, therefore, the discriminatory motive of one of the employer's agents (Mulally or Korenchuk) can be aggregated with the act of another agent (Buck) to impose liability on Proctor. . . . The employer is at fault because one of its agents committed an action based on discriminatory animus that was intended to cause, and did in fact cause, an adverse employment decision. . . . motivated by antimilitary animus that is *intended* by the supervisor to cause an adverse employment action, and if that act is a proximate cause of the ultimate employment action, then the employer is liable under USERRA . . . Applying our analysis to the facts of this case, it is clear that the Seventh Circuit's judgment must be reversed. Both Mulally and Korenchuk were acting within the scope of their employment when they took the actions that allegedly caused Buck to fire Staub. . . . As the Seventh Circuit recognized, there was evidence that Mulally's and Korenchuk's actions were motivated by hostility toward Staub's military obligations. There was also evidence that Mulally's and Korenchuk's actions were causal factors underlying Buck's decision to fire Staub. Buck's termination notice expressly stated that Staub was terminated because he had "ignored" the directive in the Corrective Action. Finally, there was evidence that both Mulally and Korenchuk had the specific intent to cause Staub to be terminated. Mulally stated she was trying to "get rid of" Staub, and Korenchuk was aware that Mulally was "out to get" Staub. Moreover, Korenchuk informed Buck, Proctor's

666

personnel officer responsible for terminating employ-ees, of Staub's alleged noncompliance with Mulally's Corrective Action, and Buck fired Staub immediately thereafter; a reasonable jury could infer that Koren-chuk intended that Staub be fired. The Seventh Circuit therefore erred in holding that Proctor was entitled to judgment as a matter of law.

It is less clear whether the jury's verdict should be reinstated or whether Proctor is entitled to a new trial.

The jury instruction did not hew precisely to the rule we adopt today; it required only that the jury find that "military status was a motivating factor in [Proctor's] decision to discharge him." App. 68a. Whether the vari-ance between the instruction and our rule was harm-less error or should mandate a new trial is a matter the Seventh Circuit may consider in the first instance.

Reversed and Remanded.

KEY POINTS

- This case pertains to the situation in which an employer may be held liable when a biased, non-decision maker influences an unbiased decision maker to take action that he or she would not otherwise take. This is referred to as the "cat's paw theory of liability."
- The Supreme Court held that an employer can be at fault when one of its agents commits an action based on discriminatory animus that is intended to cause and does cause an adverse employment action. Discriminatory animus is discrimina-tory intent, motive, or state of mind.
- This case arose in connection with a USERRA claim. The same theory, however, could be used to find liability in Title VII and other discrimination cases.

OCCUPATIONAL SAFETY AND HEALTH ADMINISTRATION

Occupational Safety and Health Administration (OSHA) has jurisdiction over complaints about hazardous conditions in the workplace. Employers are required to comply with OSHA standards to furnish a workplace free from recognized hazards. Employees have the right to request an OSHA inspection if they believe that there are unsafe and unhealthful conditions in the workplace. If employees who make complaints are then subjected to retaliation or discrimination by their employers they may also file a com-plaint with OSHA. There is no private cause of action under OSHA, which means that an employee cannot sue an employer for damages based on an OSHA violation.

OSHA investigates a wide variety of workplace hazards. For example, following the deaths of 20 workers in 2008 in construction accidents in New York City, OSHA is sending inspectors there in an effort to increase safety and improve working conditions. OSHA inspectors will examine cranes and high-rise construction sites. In addition to the inspections, OSHA sent notices to employers' insurance and workers' compensation carriers. Cita-tions involving training violations at unionized sites will also be sent to the unions representing workers and to their training funds. The U.S. House Education and Labor Committee is reviewing the sufficiency of OSHA's construction enforcement. OSHA is also investigating The Atlanta Ballet

sidebar 21.8

New OSHA Crowd Management Safety Guidelines

In 2008, a temporary maintenance worker was pushed to the ground and suffocated to death after approximately 2,000 holiday shoppers broke through Wal-mart's glass doors. The shoppers were racing to buy sharply discounted televisions, computers and other gifts. OSHA filed a citation against Wal-mart's, alleging that it did not furnish a workplace "free from recognizable hazard" that were likely to cause death or serious physical harm to an employee due to "crowd crush." Wal-mart's was fined $7,000 and was required to take steps to correct the hazard. Although the fine is *de minimus* for Wal-mart's, concerned about the ramifications for future crowd-attracting events, the retailer appealed. The fine was upheld on appeal.

As a result of this incident, OSHA issued *Crowd Control Guidelines* in November 2010. The detailed guidelines address steps to be taken during planning, pre-event setup, the sales event and in emergency situations. Considerations include staffing plans, emergency contacts, training workers in crowd management, using barricades or ropes with adequate breaks or turns, using wristbands, tickets or an Internet lottery for "hot items," and ensuring adequate communication between employees, customers, and emergency personnel.

Specific measures implemented by Wal-mart's include issuing tickets for hot items, placing employees on platforms to direct customers, using steel barriers in zig-zag patters in front to the store to guide customers into the store in an orderly fashion—avoiding a shoving and crushing mass trying to enter the store.

Source: For more about OSHA's new rules, see *Crowd Control Guidelines* at www.osha.gov/OshDoc/data_General_Facts/Crowd_Control.pdf.

following the fall of a 17-year-old dancer wearing a panda costume during a performance of "The Nutcracker" at the Fox Theater in Atlanta. The dancer, who fell about 12 feet into the empty orchestra pit, suffered serious injuries, requiring spinal surgery. OSHA conducted over 38,000 inspections in 2006.

sidebar 21.9

OSHA's Severe Violator Enforcement Program

Under the Obama administration, OSHA is increasing its focus on enforcing safe workplaces. One significant step was releasing the Severe Violator Enforcement Program (SVEP) draft directive to concentrate resources on "inspecting employers who have demonstrated indifference" to their OSHA obligations "by willful, repeated, or failure-to-abate violations." If an employer engages in this behavior in one of the following four areas, it is at risk for being placed in the SVEP:

1. Fatality and/or catastrophic situations, such as three or more hospitalizations or the death of an employee;
2. Non-fatality and/or catastrophic situations in which the employer has exposed the employee to one of the most severe workplace hazards, including "high gravity serious violations" such as fall hazards, combustible dust hazards and lead hazards;
3. Hazards due to the potential release of a highly hazardous chemical; or
4. Any violation that is deemed "egregious" under current OSHA regulations.

The SVEP casts a wide enforcement net, applying to employers of all sizes.

Source: OSHA, Severe Violator Enforcement Program Directive, available at www.osha.gov/dep/svep-directive.pdf.

PENSION PLANS

In 1974, Congress passed and President Nixon signed the Employee Retirement Income Security Act (ERISA). This law attempts to protect employees whose employers have voluntary pension plans. These protections include disclosure of information about the management of and fiduciary relationships within the plan. Since ERISA, the federal government has enacted a number of other laws directed at protecting employees' health care. Among these laws are Consolidated Omnibus Budget Reconciliation Act (COBRA), which was passed in 1986, and provides that employees can continue to purchase health insurance even after their employment is terminated. The Health Insurance Portability and Accountability Act (HIPAA) became law in 1996 and protects employees who have preexisting health conditions when they change jobs.

During the early part of this century, we have seen a new crisis arising. This involves businesses that are changing their defined-benefit retirement plans to private individual accounts, such as 401(k) plans. A number of companies have gone into bankruptcy and have sought permission to cancel retirement plans. It appears a very real competitive advantage is to be a new company that is not burdened by large pension plans obligations. For example, many of the legacy airlines, such as Delta, United, and Northwest, have gone into and come out of bankruptcy in the hope that they will be competitive with newer airlines, which do not have the large obligation of paying the pensions of thousands of retirees.

For more details about these laws, visit www .dol.gov/dol/topic/ health-plans/erisa .htm#content.

HEALTH CARE

The Patient Protection Affordable Care Act (Affordable Care Act) was signed into law on March 23, 2010. The goals of the Affordable Care Act include increasing the quality and affordability of health insurance. The act mandates most Americans to purchase health insurance, offering subsidized coverage for qualifying individuals. As you read in Case 3.1, *National Federation of Independent Business v. Sebelius,* the law was met with a number of legal challenges. Key features of the Affordable Care Act include a number of consumer protection features, including:

- Providing the Patient's Bill of Rights.
- Prohibiting denying coverage for children based on preexisting conditions.
- Prohibiting insurance companies from rescinding coverage.
- Eliminating lifetime limits on insurance coverage.
- Providing small businesses with health insurance tax credits.
- Offering seniors on Medicare better prescription drug benefits.
- Expanding coverage to young adults and early retirees.
- Expanding free preventive care.

Note that many of these features apply to health plans beginning on or after September 23, 2010.[2]

---

[2]For more information and elaboration, see U.S. Department of Health and Human Services, *Key Features of the Affordable Care Act by Year,* www.hhs.gov/healthcare/facts/timeline/timeline-text.html.

sidebar 21.10

Business Size and the Affordable Care Act

The Affordable Care Act has varying requirements based on the size of a business. Pursuant to the act, different provisions apply if you are:

Self-employed.

Employers with fewer than 25 employees.

Employers with Up to 50 employees.

Employers with 50 or more employees.

The Small Business Administration sets forth detailed information about the key provisions of the Affordable Care Act by business size. For more information, see U.S. Small Business Administration, Health Care, www.sba.gov/healthcare.

Although implementation of the Affordable Care Act is an ongoing process, see Sidebar 21.10 for an overall sense of how the act applies to employers. By May 2014, more than seven million Americans signed up for health care in connection with the Affordable Care Act.

LO 21-2

LIMITATIONS ON EMPLOYMENT AT WILL

Historically, unless employees contracted for a definite period of employment (such as for one year), employers were able to discharge them without cause at any time. This is called the **employment-at-will doctrine.**

During the 1930s, employers began to lose this absolute right to discharge employees whenever they desired. The Labor–Management Relations Act prohibited employers from firing employees for union activities. Now, many federal laws limit employers in their right to terminate employees. Table 21.2 provides a listing of some of these laws. Some states also prohibit employers by statute from discharging employees for certain reasons, such as for refusing to take lie detector examinations.

Courts, too, have begun limiting the at-will doctrine. Under contract theory, several courts have stated that at-will employment contracts (which are not written and are little more than an agreement to pay for work performed) contain an implied promise of good faith and fair dealing by the employer.

Do understand that any commitments stated in an employee handbook are viewed by courts as a contractual promise by the employer.

Other courts have ruled that the employer's publication of an employee handbook can change the nature of at-will employment. They have held the employer liable for breach of contract for discharging an employee in violation of statements made in the handbook about discharge procedures.

Many contract and tort exceptions to employment at will have involved one of three types of employer behavior:

- Discharge of employee for performance of an important public obligation, such as jury duty.
- Discharge of employee for reporting employer's alleged violations of law (whistle-blowing). The recent financial reform legislation, Dodd-Frank, includes financial incentives to blow the whistle for a broad range of wrongdoing from securities and accounting fraud to bribery allegations. (See Sidebar 21.11 for information about IRS whistleblowers.)
- Discharge of employee for exercising statutory rights.

table 21.2 Federal Statutes Limiting Employment-at-Will Doctrine

Statute	Limitation on Employee Discharge
Labor-Management Relations Act	Prohibits discharge for union activity or for filing charges under the act.
Fair Labor Standards Act	Forbids discharge for exercising rights guaranteed by minimum-wage and overtime provisions of the act.
Occupational Safety and Health Act	Prohibits discharge for exercising rights under the act.
Civil Rights Act	Makes illegal discharge based on race, sex, color, religion, or national origin.
Age Discrimination in Employment Act	Forbids age-based discharge of employees over age 40.
Employee Retirement Income Security Act	Prohibits discharge to prevent employees from getting vested pension rights.
Clean Air Act	Prevents discharge of employees who cooperate in proceedings against an employer for violation of the act.
Clean Water Act	Prevents discharge of employees who cooperate in proceedings against an employer for violation of the act.
Consumer Credit Protection Act	Prohibits discharge of employees due to garnishment of wages for any one indebtedness.
Judiciary and Judicial Procedure Act	Forbids discharge of employees for service on federal grand or petit juries.

sidebar 21.11

IRS Whistleblowers Rewards Program

In 2006, the IRS amended its whistleblower statute to encourage the reporting of tax fraud perpetrated by individuals and corporations. Pursuant to 26 U.S.C. §7623, whistleblowers have an enforceable right to a reward when they report significant tax violations. A person who provides information regarding tax law violations under the IRS Whistleblower Law is known as a whistleblower. To be eligible to recover compensation from the IRS, a person must bring information to the Internal Revenue Service's attention. The whistleblower may receive compensation only from monies actually collected based on the information provided.

Under the IRS Whistleblower Reform Law, a person can receive a reward of between 15 percent and 30 percent of the total collected proceeds (including penalties, interest, additions to tax, and additional amounts). If the IRS moves forward with an administrative or judicial action based on information brought by a whistleblower, the whistleblower is eligible to receive at least 15 percent and up to a cap of 30 percent of the recovery, depending on the whistleblower's contribution to the prosecution of the action. The IRS may give awards of lesser amounts under certain circumstances (i.e., when the fraud has already been publicly disclosed and the whistleblower is not an original source).

WHAT ARE THE MOST COMMON TAX FRAUD SCHEMES?

- Failing to report income earned in a foreign stock exchange.
- Participating in bogus income tax shelters.
- Hiding or transferring assets or income out of the United States.
- Overstating deductions.
- Making false entries in books and records.
- Claiming personal expenses as business expenses.
- Claiming false deductions.
- Underreporting tip income.
- Paying employees in cash.
- Keeping two sets of books.

Most of the cases that limit at-will employment state that the employer has violated *public policy*. What does it mean to say that an employer has violated public policy? Is it a court's way of saying that most people no longer support the employer's right to do what it did?

Limitations on discrimination and employment at will evidence a growing concern for the rights of employees in their jobs and may suggest a trend that could lead to some type of broad, legally guaranteed job security. In recent years, unions have also increasingly focused on job-security issues in their bargaining with employers.

---

sidebar 21.12

Privacy, Technology and Social Media

Technology and social media are raising ongoing issues about privacy in the workplace. Both employers and employees are dealing with how to navigate these issues. Here are a few examples:

- The U.S. Supreme Court unanimously found that notwithstanding a city policy officer's reasonable expectation of privacy in text messages received on a pager provided by the City, the City did not violate his privacy rights under the Fourth Amendment by reviewing transcripts of those text messages. In this case, many of the messages were not work related and were sexually explicit (*City of Ontario v. Quon*, 560 U.S. __ (2010)).

- Employers may review an applicant's Facebook, MySpace, or LinkedIn pages to learn more about potential employees during the recruitment and hiring process.

- Many employers now have documented policies pertaining to their employees' use of social media sites while on the job.

- When using social media sites, employers must use care not to base a decision on something learned that cannot legally be used to make an employment decision.

- At least a dozen states prohibit employers from asking employees and prospective employees for passwords to their social media accounts.

- A study revealed that 36% of employers block access to social media sites and 70% of the responding employers reported disciplinary action for social media misuse in the workplace. (See Proskauer Rose LLP, *2013/14 Survey Social Media in the Workplace and World 3.0,* 2014, www.proskauer.com/files/uploads/social-media-in-the-workplace-2014.pdf.)

LO 21-3

WORKERS' PRIVACY

Don't rely on an expectation of privacy in the workplace; employers may monitor e-mail systems they provide.

Individual privacy is such an important part of individual freedom that both legal and ethical questions regarding privacy are bound to multiply in the computer age. While debate continues concerning the need for further federal privacy legislation, many states have passed their own privacy-related statutes. Several states guarantee workers access to their job personnel files and restrict disclosure of personal information to third parties.

Concerns for individual privacy also contributed to passage of the Electronic Communications Privacy Act of 1986 and the 1988 Employee Polygraph Protection Act. Under this latter federal law, private employers generally are forbidden from using lie detector tests while screening job applicants. Current employees may not be tested randomly but may be tested as a result of a specific incident or activity that causes economic injury or loss to an employer's business. The act permits private security companies to test job applicants and allows companies that manufacture or sell controlled substances to test both job applicants and current employees. The Labor Department may seek fines of up to $10,000 against employers who violate the act. Employees are also authorized to sue employers for violating the act.

Another important privacy concern involves drug testing. At present there is no uniform law regarding the drug testing of employees. Many private companies conduct such testing. However, some states have placed some limits on a private company's right to test for drugs.

Public employees are protected from some drug testing by the Fourth Amendment's prohibition against *unreasonable* searches. However, exactly when drug tests are unreasonable is subject to much debate in the courts. In general, public employees may be tested when there is a proper suspicion that employees are using illegal drugs that impair working ability or violate employment rules. Courts have also upheld drug testing as part of required annual medical exams.

> Unlike the U.S., workers in other jurisdictions, such as the European Union, enjoy a much higher expectation of privacy in the workplace.

---

sidebar 21.13

Is There Any Reasonable Expectation of Privacy in the Workplace?

There is very little expectation of privacy in the American workplace. For example, of the employers surveyed:

- 73 percent monitored e-mail messages.
- 66 percent monitored Web surfing.
- 48 percent monitored with video surveillance.
- 45 percent monitored keystrokes and keyboard time.
- 43 percent monitored computer files.

Of those employers, a number reported firing employees for violating policies regarding use of the Internet (30 percent), e-mail (28 percent), or phones (6 percent).

Source: 2007 Electronic Monitoring & Surveillance Survey (released February 2008) by the American Management Association and the ePolicy Institute.

WORKERS' COMPENSATION ACTS

In Chapter 10, you learned about torts. What happens, however, if a worker is injured at work? Around the turn of the century, the tort system was largely replaced in the workplace by a series of workers' compensation acts. These statutes were enacted at both the state and federal level, and they imposed a type of strict liability on employers for accidental workplace injuries suffered by their employees. The clear purpose of these statues was to remove financial losses of injury from workers and redistribute them onto employers and ultimately onto society.

> Even if an employee's contributory negligence or assumption of risk leads to an accidental injury, the employee still receives workers' compensation.

History **Workers' compensation** laws are state statutes designed to protect employees and their families from the risks of accidental injury, death, or disease resulting from their employment. They were passed because the common law did not give adequate protection to employees from the hazards of their work. At common law, anyone was liable in tort for damages resulting from injuries caused

> Remember workers' compensation is a form of insurance required by the states.

If you are injured at work, report the accident immediately.

to another as a proximate result of negligence. If an employer acted unreasonably and his or her carelessness was the proximate cause of physical injury suffered by an employee, the latter could sue and recover damages from the employer. However, the common law also provided the employer with the means of escaping this tort liability in most cases through the following three defenses:

- Assumption of the risk
- Contributory negligence
- The fellow-servant rule

For example, assume that the employer knowingly instructed workers to operate dangerous machinery not equipped with any safety devices, even though it realized injury to them was likely. A worker had his arm mangled when it was caught in the gears of one of these machines. Even though the employer was negligent in permitting this hazardous condition to persist, if the worker was aware of the dangers that existed, he would be unable to recover damages because he knowingly *assumed the risk* of his injury. In addition, if the injury were caused by *contributory negligence* of the employee as well as the negligence of the employer, the action was defeated. And, if the injury occurred because of the negligence of another employee, the negligent employee, rather than the employer, was liable because of the *fellow-servant rule*.

The English Parliament passed a workers' compensation statute in 1897. Today all states have such legislation, modeled to a greater or lesser degree on the English act. These laws vary a great deal from state to state as to the industries subject to them, the employees they cover, the nature of the injuries or diseases that are compensable, the rates of compensation, and the means of administration. In spite of wide variances in the laws of the states in this area, certain general observations can be made about them.

The System   State workers' compensation statutes provide a system to pay workers or their families if the worker is accidentally killed or injured or incurs an occupational disease while employed. To be compensable, the death, illness, or injury must arise out of and in the course of the employment. Under these acts, the negligence or fault of the employer in causing an on-the-job injury is not an issue. Instead, these laws recognize the fact of life that a certain number of injuries, deaths, and diseases are bound to occur in a modern industrial society as a result of the attempts of businesses and their employees to provide the goods and services demanded by the consuming public. This view leads to the conclusion that it is fairer for the consuming public to bear the cost of such mishaps rather than to impose it on injured workers.

Workers' compensation laws create strict liability for employers of accidentally injured workers. Liability exists regardless of lack of negligence or fault, provided the necessary association between the injuries and the business of the employer is present. The three defenses the employer had at common law are eliminated. The employers, treating the costs of these injuries as part of the costs of production, pass them on to the consumers who created the demand for the product or service being furnished.

Workers' compensation acts give covered employees the right to certain cash payments for their loss of income due to accidental, on-the-job injuries. In the event of a married employee's death, benefits are provided for the surviving spouse and minor children. The amount of such awards usually is subject to a stated maximum and is calculated by using a percentage of the wages of the employee. If the employee suffers permanent, partial disability, most states provide compensation both for injuries that are scheduled in the statute and those that are nonscheduled. As an example of the former, a worker who loses a hand might be awarded 100 weeks of compensation at $95 per week. Besides scheduling specific compensation for certain specific injuries, most acts also provide compensation for nonscheduled ones based upon the earning power the employee lost due to his or her injury. In addition to the above payments, all statutes provide for medical benefits.

In some states, employers have a choice of covering their workers' compensation risk with insurance or of being self-insured (that is, paying all claims directly) if they can demonstrate their capability to do so. Approximately 20% of compensation benefits are paid by self-insurers. In other states, employers pay into a state fund used to compensate workers entitled to benefits. In these states, the amounts of the payments are based on the size of the payroll and the experience of the employer in having claims filed against the system by its employees. Workers' compensation laws are usually administered exclusively by an administrative agency called the industrial commission or board, which has quasi-judicial powers. Of course, the ruling of such boards is subject to review by the courts of the jurisdiction in the same manner as the actions of other administrative agencies.

Tests for Determining Compensation

The tests for determining whether an employer must pay workers' compensation to an employee are simply:

1. Was the injury accidental?
2. Did the injury arise out of and in the course of employment?

Because workers' compensation laws benefit workers, courts interpret them liberally to favor workers. In recent years, cases have tended to expand employers' liability. For instance, courts have held that heart attacks (as well as other common ailments in which the employee has had either a preexisting disease or a physical condition likely to lead to the disease) are compensable as "accidental injuries." One ruling approved an award to a purchasing agent who became mentally ill because she was exposed to unusual work, stresses, and strains.

Her "nerve-racking" job involved a business whose sales grew over sixfold in ten years. Factors contributing to her "accidental injury" included harsh criticism by her supervisor and long hours of work. Likewise, the courts have been liberal in upholding awards that have been challenged on the grounds that the injury did not arise "out of and in the course of employment." Courts routinely support compensation awards for almost any accidental injury that employees suffer while traveling for their employers. A Minnesota Supreme Court decision upheld a lower court award of compensation to a bus driver. On a layover during a trip, the driver had been shot accidentally in a tavern parking lot following a night on the town.

Exclusive Remedy Rule   Recently, some courts have been liberal in their interpretations of the **exclusive remedy rule.** This rule, which is written into all compensation statutes, states that an employee's sole remedy against an employer for workplace injury or illness shall be workers' compensation. In the past few years, courts in several important jurisdictions have created exceptions to this rule. Note that these exceptions recognize in part that workers' compensation laws do not adequately compensate badly injured workers.

Since workers' compensation laws apply only to accidentally injured workers, the exclusive remedy rule does not protect employers who intentionally injure workers. But the issue arises as to how "intentional" such an injury has to be. What if an employer knowingly exposes employees to a chemical that may cause illness in some employees over a long term?

The Future of State Workers' Compensation   Currently, many problems confront the state workers' compensation system. Fifty separate non-uniform acts make up the system. Many acts exclude from coverage groups such as farmworkers, government employees, and employees of small businesses. Many state legislatures have enacted changes in their compensation laws. However, states that have broadened coverage and increased benefits have greatly boosted the cost of doing business within their borders. This discourages new businesses from locating within these states and encourages those already there to move out.

In the last decade, workers' compensation payments have tripled. Many workers exaggerate their injuries to get compensation. At the same time, compensation payments to seriously injured workers are often inadequate, and this has led to attempts to get around the exclusive remedy rule.

As our national economy moves from a manufacturing to a service emphasis, the nature of injuries suffered under workers' compensation programs begins to change. In particular, the number of mental stress claims rises. The National Council on Compensation Insurance states that these claims have increased fivefold in the past few years. Problems of proving (or disproving) mental stress claims bring new concerns for the workers' compensation system.

A major problem concerns slowly developing occupational diseases. Many toxic chemicals cause cancer and other diseases only after workers have been exposed to them over many years. Often it is difficult or impossible for workers or their survivors to recover workers' compensation for such diseases. One solution to the problems confronting the workers' compensation system would be federal reform. Those advocating such reform have put forth several plans, but Congress has shown little inclination so far to adopt a uniform federal act.

EMPLOYMENT ELIGIBILITY VERIFICATION

In accordance with the federal Immigration Reform and Control Act of 1986 ("IRCA"), all U.S. employers must complete and retain Form I-9 **Employment Eligibility Verification** forms for each individual they hire in the United States. Both citizens and noncitizens must complete the form. The employer is required to examine the employment eligibility and identify document(s) an employee presents to determine whether the document(s) reasonably appear to be "genuine." Acceptable documents that establish both identity and employment authorization include:

- U.S. Passport or U.S. Passport Card.
- Permanent Resident Card or Alien Registration Receipt Card.
- Foreign passport that contains a temporary I-551 stamp or temporary I-551 printed notation on a machine-readable visa.
- An Employment Authorization document that contains a photograph.

If none of these documents are available, a worker may use a combination of documents specified by federal law. Employers must use care to determine that the documents appear genuine, but not to go overboard and be liable for "document abuse" or discriminatory practices related to verification. The U.S. Citizen and Immigration Services broadly categorizes document abuse into four categories:

1. Improperly requesting that employees produce more documents than are required by Form I-9 to establish the employee's identity and employment authorization.
2. Improperly requesting that employees present a particular document, such as a "green card," to establish identity and/or employment authorization.
3. Improperly rejecting documents that reasonably appear to be genuine and to relate to the employee presenting them.
4. Improperly treating groups of applicants differently when completing Form I-9, such as requiring certain groups of employees who look or sound "foreign" to present particular documents to the employer.

The completed forms must be retained by the employer either for three years after the date of hire or for one year after employment is terminated, whichever is later.

sidebar 21.14

Arizona Law on Hiring Foreign Workers Is Upheld

By a 5–3 vote, the U.S. Supreme Court ruled in *Chamber of Commerce v. Whiting,* 563 U.S. ___ (2011) that the federal Immigration Reform and Control Act (IRCA) law does *not* pre-empt the Arizona statute that penalizes employers who knowingly hire unauthorized foreign workers. The Legal Arizona Workers Act provides that the licenses of state employers that knowingly or intentionally employ unauthorized aliens may be, and in certain circumstances must be, suspended or revoked. The law also requires all Arizona employers to use E-Verify, an Internet-based system that provides instant verification of work authorization.

The U.S. Chamber of Commerce, along with various business and civil rights organizations, challenged the Arizona law. The Court reasoned that Arizona's licensing law falls well within the confines of the authority Congress chose to leave to the States and therefore is not expressly preempted.

LO 21-4

Agency Law in Contracts and Other Contexts

Business organizations cannot accomplish anything without the assistance of individuals. An accounting firm does nothing as an organization. The work of the firm is done through the accountants and other employees. Likewise, a local restaurant provides food through the work of servers, cooks, managers, and other employees. In both cases, those employees undertake acts that implicate contract, tort, or criminal law.

The people who get the work done are called *agents,* and the principles presented below are referred to as *agency law.* The actions of agents can have significant consequences to business organizations. The concepts presented in the next four sections form the fundamentals of agency relationships in the transaction of everyday business.

TERMINOLOGY

The application of agency law involves the interaction among three parties. Although individuals usually are these parties, agency relationships can involve business organizations. Figure 21.1 illustrates a three-step approach to understanding how the law views the purpose of agency relationship.

Organizations deal with third parties through the actions of agents.

First, a **principal** interacts with someone (or some organization) for the purpose of obtaining that second party's assistance. This second party is the **agent.** Principals hire agents to do tasks and represent them in transactions. All employees are agents of the employer/principal, but not all agents are employees. For example, a principal may hire an **independent contractor** to perform a task. Principals do not directly control independent contractors and independent contractors generally work for more than one principal. Examples of independent contractors include attorneys (other than in-house counsel), outside accountants and subcontractors hired to perform construction projects. The nature of their relationship with the principal determines whether employees or independent contractors have authority to contractually bind the principal.

Next, the agent (on behalf of the principal) interacts with a **third party.** Third, the usual legal purpose of the agent is to create a binding relationship between the principal and third party. Typically, the agent wants Step 3 to involve the understanding that any liability created by Steps 1 and 2 is replaced by the new principal–third party relationship. To accomplish this substitution, the agent must remember to comply with the following duties owed to the principal:

- A duty of loyalty to act for the principal's advantage and not to act to benefit the agent at the principal's expense.
- A duty to keep the principal fully informed.
- A duty to obey instructions.
- A duty to account to the principal for monies handled.

In studying the law of agency, keep in mind that the employer/business organization is the principal and the employee is the agent. Whether employee conduct creates liability for the employer is the usual agency issue facing businesses. Such issues may involve either contracts or torts.

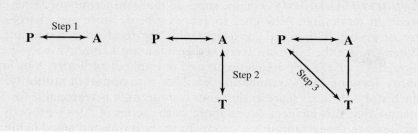

Figure 21.1
Illustration of the agency relationship.

CONTRACTUAL LIABILITY FROM AN AGENT'S ACTS

How is a company bound in a contract? For an employee to bind the employer to a contract negotiated with a third party, the employer must have authorized the employee's actions. Contractual authority can take the following forms:

- Actual authority
- Expressed, written authority
- Implied authority
- Apparent authority

Only when one of these types of authority is present will the principal and the third party become contractually bound.

Actual Authority A simple example helps illustrate the concept of actual authority. Suppose, as an owner of a restaurant, you hire Alex to be an evening manager. You discover that the restaurant is running low on coffee. You write a note to your friend, Terry, the manager of the local grocery store. In this note, you ask Terry to allow Alex to charge $100 worth of coffee to your restaurant's account at the grocery store. You give this note to Alex with instructions to purchase the coffee and deliver the note to Terry. If Terry allows Alex to charge $100 worth of coffee, is your restaurant liable to pay $100 to the grocery store? The answer is yes, because Alex had **actual authority,** which was expressed in writing.

> Specific instructions, whether spoken or written, given by an employer to an employee create actual authority.

Now suppose a week later, you send Alex to the same grocery store to buy pound cake and yogurt. This time you call Terry on the phone and ask that Alex be allowed to charge the cost of the cake and yogurt. Once again, your restaurant is contractually liable to pay for this purchase since Alex was actually authorized to contract through your expressed oral statement to Terry.

Implied Authority What if, sometime later, you and your co-owner are out of town and Alex is in charge of the restaurant for the evening. Alex, realizing that the tuna salad is in short supply, goes to Terry's grocery store and charges to the restaurant $60 worth of tuna fish. Upon your return, you find a bill from Terry for this purchase. Legally, do you have to pay it? Yes. This time Alex's actions contractually bind the restaurant to Terry since Alex had **implied authority** to do what was necessary for the restaurant's benefit. This implied authority arises from the position Alex holds as evening manager and by the history of the express authority situations.

> Implied authority can be inferred from the acts of an agent who holds a position of authority or who had actual authority in previous situations.

Remember to notify third parties if an agent no longer works for you; this notice is essential to cut off apparent authority.

Apparent Authority   Finally, suppose that you terminate Alex's employment. In retaliation, Alex goes to Terry's grocery store and charges a variety of groceries that are consistent with the food your restaurant serves. When you get the bill from Terry, is the restaurant liable? Answer—yes. Even though Alex lacks any actual (expressed or implied) authority, your failure to notify Terry of Alex's termination left Alex with **apparent authority.** Due to the history of Alex's representing your restaurant, it is reasonable for Terry to assume that this incident is one more in the series of Alex's properly charging items to the restaurant's account. To prevent this unwanted liability from occurring, you should have let Terry know that Alex is no longer employed. This notice destroys the existence of apparent authority.

It should be noted that in this last scenario, involving the existence of apparent authority, you would have a claim against Alex for the monies you had to pay Terry. Alex's liability to you arises because Alex breached the duty of loyalty owed to the restaurant.

The basic concepts of agency law apply to the operation of business organizations. Sometimes the law provides technical rules, such as those applicable to how partners can bind their partnership. One such special rule is worthy of mention. A partner in a **trading partnership,** that is, one engaged in the business of buying and selling commodities, has the implied authority to borrow money in the usual course of business and to pledge the credit of the firm. A partner in a **nontrading partnership,** such as an accounting or other service firm, has no implied power to borrow money. In the latter case, such authority must be actual before the firm will be bound.

Ratification   What happens when an agent enters into a contract without proper authority? Although the agent does not have the power to bind the principal, the contract may become binding if ratified. **Ratification** occurs when a principal voluntarily decides to honor an agreement, which otherwise would not be binding due to an agent's lack of authority. Returning to the example of the restaurant's evening manager Alex, suppose Alex enters into a contract on behalf of the restaurant to purchase $100,000 worth of kitchen equipment. If Alex had no authority to bind the restaurant, yet you realize that this is a great deal, you could ratify the contract, and follow through with the transaction.

TORT LIABILITY FROM AN AGENT'S ACTS

The legal elements of a tort are discussed in Chapter 10. For the purpose of this discussion, remember that a tort is a breach of a duty that causes injury to a person or their property. If you drive your car onto the sidewalk and hit a pedestrian, you are personally liable for the tort of negligence due to your poor driving. Now, suppose the driver was your employee delivering items from your business. Can the injured victim collect damage from you and your business? The answer is found in agency law.

An agent who causes harm to a third party may create legal liability owed by the principal to the third party. The legal test for imposing this "vicarious liability" depends on whether the agent was acting within the scope of employment when the tort occurred. Any time an employee is

Do know when agents are and are not acting within the scope of employment.

liable for tortious acts in the *scope of employment,* the employer is also liable. This is because of the tort doctrine of **respondeat superior** ("let the master reply").

The reason for *respondeat superior* is that the employee is advancing the interests of the employer when the tortious act occurs. If the employee is not doing the work, the employer would have to do it. Therefore, the employer is just as liable as the employee when the employee acts tortiously in carrying out the work. In a sense, the employer has set the employee in motion and is responsible for the employee's acts.

Most *respondeat superior* cases involve employee negligence. Note, however, that the employer is strictly liable once the employee's fault is established. And it does not matter that the employer warned the employee against the tortious behavior.

Some *respondeat superior* cases involve an employee's intentional tort. If a store's service representative strikes a customer during an argument over the return of merchandise, the store will be liable under *respondeat superior.* But if the argument concerns football instead of the return of merchandise, the store will not be liable. The difference is that the argument over football is not within the scope of employment.

Usually, the only defense the employer has to the strict liability of *respondeat superior* is that the employee was outside the scope of employment. Sometimes this defense is made using the language **frolic and detour.** An employee who is on a frolic or detour is no longer acting for the employer. If, for example, an employee is driving to see a friend when an accident occurs, the employer is not liable.

An employer who must pay for an employee's tort under *respondeat superior* may legally sue the employee for reimbursement. In practice, this seldom happens because the employer carries insurance. Occasionally, an insurer who has paid a *respondeat superior* claim will sue the employee who caused the claim.

The type of business organization in existence determines the extent of responsibility for agents' torts. In essence, partners are liable for all transactions entered into by any partner in the scope of the partnership business and are similarly liable for any partner's torts committed while she or he is acting in the course of the firm's business. Each partner is in effect both an agent of the partnership and a principal, being capable of creating both contract and tort liability for the firm and for copartners and likewise being responsible for acts of copartners. Generally, shareholders of corporations and members of LLCs are protected from tort liability that exceeds the amount of their investment.

An agent on a frolic and detour leaves the scope of employment, and the principal is not liable for the agent's actions.

CRIMINAL LIABILITY

As with torts and contracts, agents can impose criminal liability on business organizations. There are a variety of ways businesspeople and their organizations can be found criminally responsible. The issue of holding businesses criminally liable has been emphasized by the scandals in the beginning of this century. The repercussions of Enron, WorldCom, Tyco, and others are still being felt. And recent cases like the one involving the Galleon Group demonstrate that the emphasis continues.

EMPLOYEE LAWSUITS

LO 21-5

Despite the presence of many examples of the employer's violating an employment law, most employers strive to obey the law. They still risk lawsuits, however, including many brought by unsatisfactory employees who have been disciplined, denied promotion, or discharged. How can employers protect themselves from unjustified employee lawsuits?

One important protection against unjustified employee lawsuits is an established system of adequate documentation. Sometimes called the **paper fortress,** this documentation consists of job descriptions, personnel manuals, and employee personnel files.

Before handing anyone an employment application, the employer should insist that the potential candidate carefully study a job description. A well-written job description will help potential applicants eliminate themselves from job situations for which they lack interest or qualification, thus preventing employers from having to dismiss them later and risking lawsuits.

Once a new employee is hired, the employer should give the employee a personnel manual. This manual should include information about employee benefits and should also outline work rules and job requirements. The employer should go over the manual with the employee and answer any questions. Clear identification of employer expectations and policies helps provide a defense against employee lawsuits if subsequent discipline or discharge of the employee becomes necessary. The employer should ask that the employee sign a form indicating receipt of the manual and an understanding of the employer's explanation of its contents.

The employer should enter this form, with all other documentation relevant to an employee's work history, into the employee's personnel file. Regular written evaluations of employee performance should also be entered into the personnel file. A chronological record of unsatisfactory work performance is a very useful defense against unjustified lawsuits following discipline, denial of promotion, or discharge.

Another piece of documentation that helps justify employer decisions is the written warning. Anytime an employee breaks a work rule or performs unsatisfactorily, the employer should issue the employee a written warning and place a duplicate in the personnel file. The warning should explain specifically what work rule the employee violated. In addition, employers should either have an employee sign that he or she has received a written warning or else note in the personnel file that the employee has received a copy of it. The employer should also give the employee the opportunity to place a letter of explanation in the personnel file.

Laws discussed in this chapter and the next one should not prevent employers from discharging unsatisfactory employees. In an actual termination conversation, however, the employer should provide the employee with specific reasons for discharge, taken from the personnel file. Detailed documentation is vital in successfully responding to unjustified employee lawsuits. Even better is to prevent them in the first place through the development, enforcement, and review of company policies that promote legal compliance.

See Sidebar 21.15 for practical suggestions for employers to prevent employee lawsuits.

Taking any disciplinary action without documentation fails to build the record for increased sanctions in the future.

sidebar 21.15

What Can Employers Do to Avoid Employment Litigation?

There are a number of steps that employers can take to avoid employment litigation, including:

- Implementing workplace policies and procedures, and training employees to understand the rules and apply them consistently. The policies should cover how to prevent sexual harassment and other forms of discrimination and how to report the same.
- Conducting regular candid performance evaluations, with clear feedback to employees.
- Investigating all complaints thoroughly, never taking any adverse action against persons making honest complaint.

- Documenting all employee incidents, including disciplinary issues and other problems, in each employee's personnel file.
- Being fair and objective when dealing with employees. Being upfront and honest about action taken in the workplace, including termination, helps employees understand the rationale for the action.

Keep these practical suggestions in mind as you study discrimination in Chapter 20, and realize how many workers could potentially assert one or more discrimination claims against their employer.

Key Terms

Actual authority 679
Agent 678
Apparent authority 680
Employment Eligibility
   Verification 676
Employment-at-will doctrine 670
Exclusive remedy rule 676
Fair Labor Standards Act
   (FLSA) 654
Family and Medical Leave Act
   (FMLA) 661

Frolic and detour 681
Implied authority 679
Independent contractor 678
Nontrading partner 680
Occupational Safety and
   Health Administration
   (OSHA) 667
Paper fortress 682
principal 678
Ratification 680
Respondeat superior 681

Third party 678
Trading partnership 680
Uniformed Services
   Employment and
   Reemployment Rights Act
   (USERRA) 664
WARN Act 660
Workers' Compensation 673

Review Questions and Problems

Employment Laws

1. *Minimum Wages and Maximum Hours*
   (a) What federal law establishes the minimum wage and the hours in a workweek?
   (b) What is the minimum wage and what is considered the maximum workweek?
   (c) What is required regarding overtime compensation or time off?
2. *The WARN Act*
   To show your understanding of the WARN notice, answer these questions:
   (a) Who are the covered employers?
   (b) What format is required for a WARN notice?

(c) When must the WARN notice be given?

(d) To whom must the WARN notice be delivered?

3. *The Family and Medical Leave Act*

In the sixth month of her pregnancy, Suzanne was advised by her doctors to slow down the hectic pace of her consulting career. Upon this advice, Suzanne requested and was granted by her employer 12 weeks of medical leave. During the tenth week of this leave, Suzanne had a healthy baby. How much family leave is Suzanne entitled to take under the FMLA to care for her newborn?

4. *Uniformed Services Employment and Reemployment Rights Act*

Robert left his position as commercial airline pilot to undertake his duties in the Marine Reserves for a tour of duty in Iraq. When he returns home a year later, his employer apologetically tells him that they filled his position during his absence and they "will call" when something comes available. They also express concern about his ability to fly commercial jets because he has not flown in the last year. What legal recourse does Robert have, if any?

5. *Occupational Safety and Health Administration*

Larry, a machine operator, is concerned that the cardboard baler he is working on should have a safety shield to protect his arms from the moving parts. He is also worried that if he reports his concerns, he will be put on the night shift. What should he do? Does he have any protection if he reports the issue?

6. *Pension Plans and Health Care*

Why has the aging of the "baby boom" generation put so much pressure on the financial stability of historically successful companies?

7. *Limitations on Employment at Will*

Terry was hired as an assistant manager by the Assurance Manufacturing Company. There was no specific time period related to Terry's employment. During Terry's first day at work, the personnel director of Assurance gave Terry a copy of the employee's handbook. In this handbook, Assurance stated that no employee would be terminated without a justifiable explanation. Five months after beginning work at Assurance, Terry was notified that after an additional two weeks there would be no further job for Terry at Assurance. When Terry asked why this termination was occurring, the personnel director told Terry, "Under state law no reason for termination has to be given. In essence, you are an employee only for as long as Assurance desires." What is the best argument Terry can make that the employment-at-will doctrine is not applicable in this situation? Explain.

8. *Workers' Privacy*

John Hancock Life Insurance Company instructed its employees to create passwords to protect their e-mail accounts. Employees also were told to create personal folders for messages they send and receive. After a company investigation, Nancy and Joanne were terminated as John Hancock employees for using their e-mail accounts to send sexually explicit messages. These employees sued John Hancock for wrongful discharge on the basis that the company's investigation had violated their rights of privacy. Was John Hancock entitled to examine these employees' e-mail accounts?

9. *Workers' Compensation Acts*

If Sam fails to wear a hard hat, as required by Super Construction Inc., his employer, and is injured by a falling hammer, can he recover workers' compensation from Super Construction Inc.? Your answer should explain the basis for recovering workers' compensation.

10. *Employment Eligibility Verification*

Sophia's Glam Designs needs to hire 100 new workers to manufacture a new line of back-to-school outfits. The company received hundreds of applications for the positions. Simone, Sophia's

Glam Designs Human Resources Manager, requires all new hires to complete an I-9 and to produce a valid passport or green card to prove employment eligibility. When one worker attempts to use a combination of a Georgia driver's license and a social security card, Simone refuses to accept the documents. Because of the large amount of workers hired, she wants to use documents she feels comfortable verifying and streamline the documentation process. Is this permissible?

Agency Law

11. *Terminology*

    (a) What are the names given to the three parties typically involved in an agency relationship?

    (b) Describe the general purpose of the agency relationship.

12. *Contractual Liability*

    For several years, Albert acted as a collection agent for Paulette. Recently, Paulette revoked Albert's authority to collect payments from customers. However, neither Paulette nor Albert told any customers of Albert's termination. Yesterday, Theresa, one of Paulette's customers, paid Albert the money owed to Paulette. Albert never gave this money to Paulette. Is Theresa liable to pay Paulette? Why or why not?

13. *Tort Liability from an Agent's Acts*

    Tammy was shopping in Save-a-Lot Grocery Store when Stewart, an employee, brushed Tammy's ankle with a grocery cart. A short time later, while still shopping, Tammy told Stewart that he should say "Excuse me," and then people would get out of his way. Stewart then punched Tammy in the face, knocking her to the floor. If Tammy sues Save-a-Lot, what legal issue must be addressed to determine whether Save-a-Lot is liable?

14. *Criminal Liability*

    Describe how business organizations can be found criminally responsible for their actions. What is the way such organizations are punished?

15. *Employee Lawsuits*

    (a) What is meant by the phrase "paper fortress"?

    (b) How does maintaining a paper fortress aid the employer when the employee claims unfair treatment?

business *discussions*

1. You just had one of those days—exciting and overwhelming. As your company's director of human relations, you have dealt with an employee asking how much leave he can take when his wife has their first baby next month. A phone call from the company's CFO involved discussions of potential layoffs in order to "make the budget." A group of employees came to meet with you, and they indicated they were talking with union organizers as a way to combat the company's policy of monitoring phone calls and e-mail messages. Another group of employees expressed their feelings that they were not being paid for all the time they worked.

Before heading home, you take a few minutes to reflect and ask yourself the following questions:

How is the workday calculated?
What legal requirements have to be met before layoffs can occur?
What is the company's responsibility to educate employees about their rights under the FMLA?
Can your company properly monitor its employees' phone calls and e-mail messages?

22

Labor–Management Relationship

Learning Objectives

In this chapter you will learn:

22-1. To understand the role unions play in the U.S. labor market.

22-2. To describe the development of early labor law, focusing on the Clayton Act, the Railway Labor Act, and the Norris-LaGuardia Act.

22-3. To appreciate the significance of the Wagner Act, including the creation of the National Labor Relations Board and unfair labor practices by management.

22-4. To recognize how the Taft-Hartley Act amended labor law to balance the power between labor and management, including the recognition of unfair labor practices by unions.

Chapters 20 and 21 pertain to "employment law," the area of the law that controls how employers must treat applicants for employment, employees, and former employees. As you know, employment law encompasses a wide variety of employer–employee workplace issues. This chapter focuses on *labor laws*, the area of the law designed to equalize the bargaining power between employers and employees. Specifically, labor law prohibits employers and unions from engaging in specified "unfair labor practices" and establishes an obligation of both parties to engage in good-faith collective bargaining. Labor laws pertain to the relationships between employers and unions, granting employees the right to unionize and allowing employers and employees to engage in certain activities (such as strikes, picketing, seeking injunctions, lockouts). These laws regulating labor–management relations are largely a product of the New Deal era of the 1930s.

Although union membership is not as large as it once was in the United States, unions are alive and well with active agendas on behalf of their members. They are also high-profile advocates during political elections and on labor-related topics such as international trade. A number of free trade agreements discussed in Chapter 12, faced vocal opposition from labor unions. Despite their smaller numbers, labor unions continue to be formidable in the United States.

LO 22-1   Labor Laws

The National Education Association is the largest union with 2.7 million members.

"The basic principle that brings us here today is that American workers cannot win a better life unless more workers belong to unions."

–Statement of five union presidents announcing the Change to Win Coalition

"Forming this coalition is a step in the wrong direction because it's the first step toward a truly divided labor movement. Splitting the AFL-CIO will mean less power for workers."

–Gerald W. McEntee, president of the American Federation of State, County and Municipal Employees

What is your reaction to the word *union?* Do your thoughts have a mostly positive or negative connotation? Society's reaction and the government's response to the union movement have varied over time. Thus, your reaction is not right or wrong; it is likely formed by where you were raised and what your parents did to support you. Children of business managers probably have a very different perspective of unions, than children of workers whose wages were increased and job security strengthened through the efforts of union bargaining agents.

A union is basically workers organizing their collective voices to increase their ability to communicate with their employer. As a concept, a union is neither good nor bad. How the concept is utilized makes all the difference in one's view of unions.

Does such a viewpoint really matter today? Haven't unions outlived their usefulness? These questions and other similar ones are very much in today's public debate. Interestingly, this debate is occurring among union leaders as well. The statistics tell a varied story. Often cited is the declining percentage of the workforce that is unionized. However, Table 22.1 illustrates that story is more complex due to the decline in private employees being offset by the growth of public employees who are union members.

The largest unions in the United States represent teachers, government employees, and service workers. The focus on how much time and money are dedicated to recruiting new members through intensive organizing campaigns at the work site versus through political efforts caused a split in the AFL-CIO, labor's longtime unified voice. Five of the larger unions formed a group called Change to Win. See Sidebar 22.1 for union statistics.

The goal of labor laws is successful **collective bargaining**, the process by which labor and management negotiate and reach agreements on matters of importance to both. Such matters include wages to be paid to workers, hours to be worked, and other terms and conditions of employment. Collective

table 22.1 Statistics on Union Membership

Year	Private		Public		Total Membership	
1953	35.7%*	15,540,000	11.6%	770,000	32.5%*	16,310,000
1975	26.3	16,397,000	39.6	5,810,000	28.9	22,207,000*
2004	7.9	8,205,000	36.6	8,131,000*	12.5	15,472,000
2013	6.7	7,300,000	35.3	7,200,000		14,500,000

*Record highs

Source: www.lraonline.org/econ_stats.org; Bureau of Labor Statistics, Union Members—2013 (January 24, 2014).

sidebar 22.1

2013 Statistics on Union Membership

According to the Department of Labor:

- Union members accounted for 11.3 percent of all employed wage and salary workers. (In 1983, the first year data was available, union membership was 20.1 percent.)
- Education, training, and library occupations had the highest unionization rate among all occupations (35.3 percent).

- Among demographic groups, the union membership rate was highest for black men and lowest for Hispanic women.
- Union membership varies substantially by state. For example, New York had the highest union membership rate (24.4 percent) and North Carolina had the lowest (3.0 percent).

Source: Bureau of Labor Statistics (January 24, 2014), www.bls.gov/news.

bargaining can be successful only if the bargaining power of the parties is equal. Most laws regulating labor–management relations seek to equalize this bargaining power. As a result, some laws add to the bargaining position of labor and others add to that of management.

These laws have been passed when Congress perceived that one side's bargaining power was excessive. As in any balancing process, it is very difficult to hit the right middle point. Thus, as you read the following sections understand that the labor–management relationship is a delicate one involving many nuances. Table 22.2 lists the major federal labor laws.

LAWS BEFORE 1935

LO 22-2

Until 1935, Congress viewed management as having greater bargaining power in the labor–management relationship. This view certainly was justified since the union movement historically was met with strong and swift reprisals by employers. It was not uncommon in the 1800s and early 1900s for workers who tried to unionize to be fired or, worse, beaten, even killed. This treatment of workers engaged in unacceptable behavior, from the employers' viewpoint, certainly kept management in a strong bargaining position and prevented unions from growing. In a series of "prolabor" laws, Congress took action to correct the inequalities. It did so by passing the following:

- The Clayton Act
- The Railway Labor Act
- The Norris-LaGuardia Act

The Clayton Act The first federal statute of any importance to the labor movement is the **Clayton Act** of 1914, which was passed principally to strengthen the antitrust laws. Between 1890 (when the Sherman Antitrust Act was passed) and 1914, labor unions were weak in their ability to represent employees. At least one reason for the relative strength enjoyed by management was the fact that it could and did argue that employees acting together were restraining trade illegally under the Sherman Act.

"With all their faults, trade unions have done more for humanity than any other organization of men that ever existed. They have done more for decency, for honesty, for education, for the betterment of the race, for the developing of character in men, than any other association of men."

–Clarence Darrow,
***The Railroad Trainman* (1909)**

table 22.2 Federal Laws Governing Labor–Management Relations

Year	Statute	Major Provisions
1914	Clayton Act	1. Exempted union activity from the antitrust laws.
1926	Railway Labor Act	1. Governs collective bargaining for railroads and airlines.
		2. Created the National Mediation Board to conduct union elections and mediate differences between employers and unions.
1932	Norris-LaGuardia Act	1. Outlawed yellow-dog contracts.
		2. Prohibited federal courts from enjoining lawful union activities, including picketing and strikes.
1935	Wagner Act (National Labor Relations Act)	1. Created the National Labor Relations Board (NLRB).
		2. Authorized the NLRB to conduct union certification elections.
		3. Outlawed certain conduct by management as unfair to labor (five unfair labor practices).
		4. Authorized the NLRB to hold hearings on unfair labor practices and correct wrongs resulting from them.
1947	Taft-Hartley Act (Labor–Management Relations Act)	1. Outlawed certain conduct by unions as six unfair labor practices.
		2. Provided for an 80-day cooling-off period in strikes that imperil national health or safety.
		3. Allowed states to enact right-to-work laws.
		4. Created the Federal Mediation and Conciliation Service to assist in settlement of labor disputes.
1959	Landrum-Griffin Act (Labor–Management Reporting and Disclosure Act, LMRDA)	1. Created a Bill of Rights for union members.
		2. Requires reports to the secretary of labor.
		3. Added to the list of unfair labor practices.

Do recall that the Clayton Act is considered an antitrust law (see Chapter 16). Congress can use one law to impact various legal areas.

The Clayton Act stated that antitrust laws regulating anticompetitive contracts did not apply to labor unions or their members in lawfully carrying out their legitimate activities. This exemption covered only *legitimate* union practices. Although the Clayton Act exempted employees from the claim that they were restraining trade through unionization, this law did not expressly grant employees the protected right to join a union. Therefore, the Clayton Act did not balance the bargaining power between labor and management. The latter group remained the stronger one.

The Railway Labor Act

Among the first industries to unionize were the railroads. In 1926, Congress enacted the **Railway Labor Act** to encourage collective bargaining in the railroad industry. The goal was to resolve labor disputes that might otherwise disrupt transportation and result in violence. The act was later extended to airlines; today it applies to both air and rail transportation. It established the three-member **National Mediation Board,** which must designate the bargaining representative for any given bargaining unit of employees in the railway or air transport industries. The board generally does this by holding representation elections. Specifically, when the parties to a dispute over proposed contract terms in the transportation industry cannot reach an agreement concerning rates of pay or working conditions, the National Mediation Board must attempt mediation of their differences. If mediation does not resolve their differences, the board encourages voluntary arbitration. If the parties refuse arbitration and the dispute is likely to disrupt interstate commerce substantially, the board informs the president, who then appoints a special emergency board. This emergency board lacks judicial power, but it encourages the parties to reach an agreement by investigating the dispute and publishing its findings of fact and recommendations for settlement. During the investigation, which lasts 30 days, and for an additional 30 days after the report is issued, business is conducted without interruption. The parties, however, have no duty to comply with the special board's proposals. Thus, if no new collective bargaining agreement is reached after the 60-day period, lockouts by management and strikes by workers become legal.

The Railway Labor Act has played a vitally important role in balancing the labor–management relationship in the transportation industries. However, due to this act's limited application, the management of businesses outside the transportation industry generally continued to have superior bargaining power following 1926.

The Norris-LaGuardia Act

Because of management's superior bargaining power, prior to 1932 management often made it a condition of employment that employees agree not to join a labor union. Such agreements became known as **yellow-dog contracts** because any employee who would forsake the right to join fellow employees in unionization was considered a cowardly scoundrel (yellow dog). Passed in 1932, the **Norris-LaGuardia Act** made yellow-dog contracts illegal. In essence, management no longer could explicitly deny an employee the right to unionize.

Seeking injunctions to stop concerted activities had remained an important tool of management in fighting the growth of labor unions. The Norris-LaGuardia Act listed specific acts of persons and organizations participating in labor disputes that were not subject to federal court injunctions. Federal courts cannot enjoin:

- Striking or quitting work.
- Belonging to a labor organization.
- Paying strike or unemployment benefits to participants in a labor dispute.
- Publicizing the existence of a labor dispute or the facts related to it (including picketing).
- Assembling peaceably to promote interests in a labor dispute.
- Agreeing with others or advising or causing them to do any of the above acts without fraud or violence.

Although the Norris-LaGuardia Act greatly restricts the use of injunctions in labor disputes, it does not prohibit them altogether. An injunction may be issued to enjoin illegal strikes, such as ones by public employees. In addition, a party seeking an injunction in a labor dispute must meet the test of a stringent, clean-hands rule. No restraining order will be granted to any

> "It is one of the characteristics of a free and democratic nation that it has free and independent labor unions."
>
> **–Franklin Delano Roosevelt**

The timing of the law (1932) likely limited its impact on helping unions. During the Depression, people were more concerned about finding a job than they were about joining a union.

person who fails to comply with any obligation imposed by law or who fails to make every reasonable effort to settle the dispute.

The Norris-LaGuardia Act restricts the use of federal court injunctions in labor disputes; it does not limit the jurisdiction of state courts in issuing them. The Supreme Court has upheld the jurisdiction of a state court to enjoin a union's work stoppage and picketing in violation of a no-strike clause in its collective bargaining agreement.

sidebar 22.2

Three Pro-Union Executive Orders

During his first month in office, President Obama signed three Executive Orders aimed at reversing Bush-era rules viewed as "anti-union." The Executive Orders:

- Prevent federal contractors from being reimbursed for expenses for their activities undertaken to influence workers deciding whether to unionize and engage in collective bargaining.
- Require successor federal contractors, and their subcontractors, to offer jobs to current workers when contractors change.

- Reverse a Bush order requiring federal contractors to notify workers that they can limit their financial support of unions that are serving as their exclusive bargaining representatives.

Unions are very supportive of these measures. From a management perspective, these Executive Orders take a very different approach to government contracts, with a much greater emphasis on the interest of organized labor.

LO 22-3   The Wagner Act

The labor movement received its greatest stimulus for growth with the enactment in 1935 of the National Labor Relations Act, known as the **Wagner Act.** Perhaps most significantly, Congress explicitly affirmed labor's right to organize and to bargain collectively. Recognizing that a major cause of industrial strife was the inequality of bargaining power between employees and employers, Section 7 of the act states:

> Employees shall have the right to self-organization, to form, join, or assist labor organizations, to bargain collectively through representatives of their own choosing, and to engage in concerted activities for the purpose of collective bargaining or other mutual aid or protection.

In addition to this Section 7 right to unionize, the Wagner Act contains several other key provisions:

- Creating the National Labor Relations Board (NLRB) to administer the act.
- Providing employees the right to select a union to act as their collective bargaining agent.
- Outlawing certain conduct by employers that generally has the effect of either preventing the organization of employees or emasculating their unions where they do exist; these forbidden acts are called *unfair labor practices.*

"Long ago we stated the reason for labor organizations. We said that they were organized out of the necessities of the situation . . . that [a] union was essential to give laborers opportunity to deal on an equality with their employer."

–NLRB v. Jones & Laughlin Steel Corp., 301 U.S. 1 (1937)

- Authorizing the NLRB to conduct hearings on unfair labor practice allegations and, if unfair practices are found to exist, to take corrective action including issuing cease and desist orders and awarding dollar damages to unions and employees.

THE NATIONAL LABOR RELATIONS BOARD

Established by the Wagner Act, the **National Labor Relations Board (NLRB)** operates as an independent agency of the U.S. government. This section discusses the organizational structure of the NLRB, its jurisdiction, and its quasi-judicial function. A later section of this chapter examines the NLRB's authority to certify unions as the collective bargaining representative of employees. After this introduction to the NLRB, the remainder of the chapter will illustrate the significant role this agency plays in balancing the labor–management relationship.

NLRB Organization The NLRB consists of five members, appointed by the president with the advice and consent of the Senate, who serve staggered terms of five years each. In addition, there is a general counsel of the board who supervises board investigations and serves as prosecutor in cases before the board. The general counsel supervises operations of the NLRB so that the board itself may perform its quasi-judicial function of deciding unfair labor practice cases free of bias. Administrative law judges are responsible for the initial conduct of hearings in unfair labor practice cases.

The general counsel also is responsible for conducting representation elections. In addition, the general counsel is responsible for seeking court orders requiring compliance with the board's orders and represents the board in miscellaneous litigation. The board determines policy questions, such as what types of employers and groups of employees are covered by the labor law.

Jurisdiction Congress gave the NLRB jurisdiction over any business "affecting commerce." However, the following personnel are exempt from the NLRB's authority:

- Governmental employees
- Persons covered by the Railway Labor Act
- Independent contractors
- Agricultural laborers
- Household, domestic workers
- Employees who work for their spouse or parents

In FY2010, the NLRB processed more unfair labor practices, levied more fines and processed more petitions for certification and decertification than it did the previous year.

The NLRB cannot exercise its powers over all businesses because it has a limited budget and time constraints. As a result of these self-imposed restrictions, however, federal labor laws do not apply to many small businesses. The management of these businesses may still need to know what state labor laws require of them. See Case 22.1 for an example of an important NLRB decision on social media and the workplace.

> "If capitalism is fair then unionism must be. If men have a right to capitalize their ideas and the resources of their country, then that implies the right of men to capitalize their labor."
>
> **—Frank Lloyd Wright**

sidebar 22.3

Are College Football Players Employees?

If the final answer is "yes," it could change the land-scape of college sports. In 2014, Peter Sung Ohr, NLRB Regional Director in Chicago, considered whether football players receiving grant-in-aid scholarships from Northwestern University are "employees" within the meaning of the National Labor Relations Act and, therefore, entitled to choose whether or not to be rep-resented for the purposes of collective bargaining. Ohr concluded that the players are employees, and he ordered that an election be conducted under the appropriate Regional Director.

Thereafter, 76 active Northwestern players voted on whether to certify a players' union. Northwestern University appealed and the NLRB granted its request

for review. The result of the vote will not be known until the appeal is decided.

The decision likely provided incentive for the NCAA to discuss a restructuring plan involving the Atlantic Coast, Big Ten, Big 12, Pacific-12, and Southeastern Conferences regarding the ability to provide athletes with additional benefits. Although Ohr's decision is con-troversial, it has sparked a much-needed discussion about the treatment of college athletes and proposals for better treatment.

Sources: Northwestern University and College Athletes Players Associa-tion (CAPA), NLRB Case 13-RC-121359 (2014); Ben Strauss and Steve Eder, "Labor Board to Review Northwestern Football Case," *The New York Times* (April 24, 2014).

 Case **22.1**

HISPANICS UNITED OF BUFFALO, INC. AND CARLOS ORTIZ
Case 03-CA-027872 (2012)

CHAIRMAN PEARCE AND MEMBERS HAYES, GRIFFIN, AND BLOCK

. . . At issue in this case is whether the Respon-dent violated Section 8(a)(1) of the Act by discharging five employees for Facebook comments they wrote in response to a coworker's criticisms of their job per-formance. Although the employees' mode of commu-nicating their workplace concerns might be novel, we agree with the judge that the appropriate analytical framework for resolving their discharge allegations has long been settled under Meyers Industries and its progeny. Applying Meyers, we agree with the judge that the Respondent violated 8(a)(1) by discharging the five employees. The relevant facts are as follows. Marianna Cole-Rivera and Lydia Cruz-Moore were cowork-ers employed by the Respondent to assist victims of domestic violence. The two employees frequently com-municated with each other by phone and text message during the workday and after hours. According to Cole-Rivera's credited testimony, Cruz-Moore often criti-cized other employees during these communications, particularly housing department employees who, Cruz-Moore asserted, did not provide timely and adequate

assistance to clients. Other employees similarly testified that Cruz-Moore spoke critically to them about their work habits and those of other employees. This "criti-cism" issue escalated on Saturday, October 9, 2010, a nonworkday, when Cole-Rivera received a text message from Cruz-Moore stating that the latter intended to discuss her concerns regarding employee performance with Executive Director Lourdes Iglesias. Cole-Rivera sent Cruz-Moore a responsive text questioning whether she really "wanted Lourdes to know . . . how u feel we don't do our job. . . ." From her home, and using her own personal computer, Cole-Rivera then posted the following message on her Facebook page:

> Lydia Cruz, a coworker feels that we don't help our clients enough at [Respondent]. I about had it! My fellow coworkers how do u feel?

Four off-duty employees—Damicela Rodriguez, Ludimar Rodriguez, Yaritza Campos, and Carlos Ortiz—responded by posting messages, via their personal com-puters, on Cole-Rivera's Facebook page; the employees' responses generally objected to the assertion that their work performance was substandard. Cruz-Moore also responded, demanding that Cole-Rivera "stop with ur lies about me." She then complained to Iglesias about the Facebook comments, stating that she had been slandered and defamed. At Iglesias' request, Cruz-Moore printed all the Facebook comments and had the printout delivered to Iglesias. On October 12, the first workday after the Facebook postings, Iglesias discharged Cole-Rivera and her four coworkers, stating that their remarks constituted "bullying and harassment" of a coworker and violated the Respondent's "zero tolerance" policy prohibiting such conduct.

In *Meyers I*, the Board held that the discipline or discharge of an employee violates Section 8(a)(1) if the following four elements are established: (1) the activity engaged in by the employee was "concerted" within the meaning of Section 7 of the Act; (2) the employer knew of the concerted nature of the employee's activity; (3) the concerted activity was protected by the Act; and (4) the discipline or discharge was motivated by the employee's protected, concerted activity. . . .

[T]here should be no question that the activity engaged in by the five employees was concerted for the "purpose of mutual aid or protection" as required by Section 7. As set forth in her initial Facebook post, Cole-Rivera alerted fellow employees of another employee's complaint that they "don't help our clients enough," stated that she "about had it" with the complaints, and solicited her coworkers' views about this criticism. By responding to this solicitation with comments of protest, Cole-Rivera's four coworkers made common cause with her, and, together, their actions were concerted within the definition of *Meyers I*, because they were undertaken "with . . . other employees." 268 NLRB at 497. The actions of the five employees were also concerted under the expanded definition of *Meyers II*, because, as the judge found, they "were taking a first step towards taking group action to defend themselves against the accusations they could reasonably believe Cruz-Moore was going to make to management." . . .

In sum, because we have found that the Facebook postings were concerted and protected, and because it is undisputed that the Respondent discharged the five employees based solely on their postings, we conclude that the discharges violated Section 8(a)(1).

KEY POINTS

- The Board found that it was unlawful for a non-profit organization to fire five employees who participated in Facebook postings about a co-worker who intended to complain to management about their work performance.
- The Board majority found that the Facebook conversation was concerted activity and was protected by the National Labor Relations Act.

Quasi-Judicial Authority Throughout this chapter, you will study the various unfair labor practices. Congress granted the NLRB the authority to conduct the quasi-judicial hearings that are required to investigate and to enforce sanctions if these unfair labor practices occur.

This authority is extensive in that NLRB has discretion to order whatever action is necessary to correct the unlawful practice. However, as Sidebar 22.4 illustrates, there are limits to the NLRB's authority to order remedial actions.

CERTIFICATION OF UNIONS

An employer may voluntarily recognize that its workers want to have a certain labor union represent them. The employer is free to agree to bargain with the union as the collective bargaining representative of the employees. In actuality, such voluntary recognition occurs in relatively few situations.

sidebar 22.4

Limitation of NLRB's Remedies

After presenting documents that verified his legal status to work in the United States, Jose Castro was hired by Hoffman Plastic Compounds, Inc. Castro participated in a union-organizing campaign at the Hoffman facility where he worked. Hoffman laid off Castro and others engaged in this organizing effort. When it was presented with this factual situation, the National Labor Relations Board (NLRB) ordered Hoffman to reinstate Castro (and the other employees) with back pay. During a compliance hearing before an NLRB administrative law judge (ALJ), Castro acknowledged that he did not have the proper paperwork to be a legal alien eligible to work. In essence, Castro admitted that he has used another person's birth certificate to get a driver's license and social

security number. Because of these admissions, the ALJ concluded that the NLRB could not award Castro reinstatement and back pay. Castro appealed to the full board, which reversed the ALJ and awarded back pay. Hoffman sought review by the Court of Appeals for the D.C. Circuit. This court upheld the NLRB's award of back pay.

Upon further review, the U.S. Supreme Court reversed the NLRB's decision. It concluded that back pay awarded to illegal aliens would "encourage the successful evasion of apprehension by immigration authorities, condone prior violations of the immigration laws, and encourage future violations."

Source: *Hoffman Plastic Compounds, Inc. v. NLRB*, 535 U.S. 137 (2002).

More common is the NLRB's certification of a union as the bargaining agent for a group of employees. This certification process is the result of an election or occurs through authorization cards. These certification processes are discussed in the next two subsections.

Despite the declining percentage of the workforce that is unionized, unions are winning a greater percentage of the certification elections being held.

Certification Elections   Elections are by secret ballot and are supervised by the NLRB. The board decides what unit of employees is appropriate for purposes of collective bargaining and therefore which employees are entitled to vote in the election. It may select the total employer unit, craft unit, plant unit, or any subdivision of the plant.

Obviously, how the board exercises its discretion in this regard may be crucial to the outcome of a given election. If all 100 workers at one plant operated by an employer desire to organize but 400 out of 500 at another of the employer's plants do not, designation of the total employees as the one appropriate bargaining unit would ensure that both plants would remain nonunion.

The NLRB conducts elections upon receipt of a petition signed by at least 30% of the employees. In addition, an employer may file a petition for selection of an initial representative. An employer may also file a petition for an election to invalidate certification of an incumbent union. It must show that it doubts, in good faith, the continued support of the union by a majority of the employees. Votes to certify a union or to rescind a union's authority also take place by petition.

After a NLRB election, another is not permitted for one year, regardless of whether the union wins or loses the certification vote. Within the term of a collective bargaining agreement or three years after it has been signed, whichever period is shorter, no elections may take place.

Certification through Cards   A union seeking to represent employees may solicit cards from them indicating their willingness for the union to

represent them. An employer may then recognize the union as the bargaining agent for its employees if the cards are signed by a majority of the employees. Employers do not need to recognize the union based on a majority card showing and always have the option to insist on an election. But once an employer recognizes the union—no matter how informally—the employer is bound by the recognition and loses the right to seek an election.

Cards also may substitute for an election if certain conditions are met. The NLRB may issue a bargaining order based on such cards if the cards are unequivocal and clearly indicate that the employee signing the card is authorizing the union to represent him or her. The general counsel of the NLRB does not need to prove that the employees read or understood the cards. If a card states on its face that it authorizes collective bargaining, it will be counted for that purpose unless there is clear proof that the employee was told that it would not be used for that purpose.

sidebar 22.5

Unfair Labor Practice? *The NLRB v. Boeing*

In April 2011, the NLRB filed a complaint against Boeing Co., claiming that Boeing illegally punished the union by building an assembly line for its 787 Dreamliner jet in South Carolina instead of Washington state. The NLRB seeks to compel Boeing to move the work to Boeing's unionized plant in Washington, away from its new $1 billion nonunion plant in South Carolina.

The complaint is drawing criticism from business groups who see the NLRB action as overreaching. Since 1995, three strikes shut down Boeing's facilities near Seattle. In 2008, the work stoppage lasted for eight weeks costing Boeing $2 billion. In connection with the decision, Boeing's Jim McNerney commented on "the negative financial impacts" to Boeing of "strikes happening every three or four years in Puget Sound." The NLRB claims that Boeing engaged in an illegal act of retaliation against strikers in Washington, aimed at intimidating them not to strike in the future.

Consider: Did Boeing engage in an unfair labor practice?

UNFAIR LABOR PRACTICES BY MANAGEMENT

Remember that Congress desired to strengthen the bargaining power of labor unions when it passed the Wagner Act in 1935. A principal means of accomplishing this goal was through the creation of five unfair labor practices by management. These practices are summarized as follows:

- Interfering with union activities
- Dominating a labor organization
- Discriminating based on union affiliation
- Discriminating as a result of NLRB proceedings
- Refusing to bargain in good faith

Conduct may be, and often is, a violation of more than one of the listed unfair labor practices. Indeed, most violations constitute interference with the right to engage in concerted activity (the first category). For example, retaliation against a union leader for filing charges would constitute a violation of both the first and fourth categories.

Interfering with Unionization The first unfair labor practice has two distinct parts. First, it is unfair for an employer to interfere with the efforts of employees to form, join, or assist labor organizations. The second part covers interfering with "concerted activities for mutual aid or protection." This violation does not have to involve a union; the act protects any group of employees acting for their mutual aid and protection.

The first part of this unfair labor practice by management is a catchall intended to guarantee the right of employees to organize and join unions. It clearly prohibits "scare" tactics such as threats by employers to fire those involved in organizing employees or threats to cut back on employee benefits if employees succeed in unionizing. In addition, less obvious activities are outlawed, such as requiring job applicants to state on a questionnaire whether they would cross a picket line in a strike. An employer cannot engage in any conduct calculated to erode employee support for the union.

Interference with unionization may take the form of a carrot as well as a stick. The conferring of benefits by an employer may be an unfair labor practice. In one case, the employer reminded its employees two weeks before a representation election that the company had just instituted a "floating holiday" that employees could take on their birthdays. The union lost the election, but the NLRB set it aside. It was an unfair labor practice for the employer to engage in conduct immediately favorable to employees. The conduct interfered with the freedom of choice for or against unionization.

Interfering with Concerted Activities The term **concerted activity** is given a liberal interpretation in order to create a climate that encourages unionization, collective bargaining, and all that may flow from such activity. For example, some employees refused to work after a heated grievance meeting. They followed their supervisors onto the workroom floor and continued to argue loudly until they were ordered a second time to resume work. The employer issued letters of reprimand alleging insubordination. This was an unfair labor practice. The protection of employee conduct at grievance meetings is extended to a brief cooling-off period following an employer's termination of such a meeting. Protection of employees' participation in the meetings themselves would be seriously threatened if the employer could at any point call an immediate halt to the operation of the law simply by declaring the meeting ended.

The concerted-activity concept is quite extensive. In one case, an employer was investigating theft by employees. One employee asked that a union representative be present during her interview. She was refused. The Supreme Court held that the employee had a right to representation when there was a perceived threat to her employment security. The presence of a representative assures other employees in the bargaining unit that they, too, can obtain aid and protection if they wish when there appears to be a threat to their job security. Refusing the assistance at the interview was an unfair labor practice.

In addition, the right to engage in concerted activity has been expanded to cover the actions of a sole employee under certain circumstances. If an employee has a grievance that may affect other workers, that employee has rights protected by the concerted-activity language of this unfair labor practice, even though no other worker participates in the activity.

Dominating a Labor Organization The second unfair labor practice prohibits the domination of a labor organization by employers or their contribution of financial or other support to any union. Under the Wagner Act, any organization of employees must be completely independent of their employers. In the case of a controversy between competing unions, employers must remain strictly neutral. It is an unfair labor practice for the employer to support a union by giving it a meeting place; providing refreshments for union meetings; permitting the union to use the employer's telephone, secretary, or copying machine; or allowing the union to keep cafeteria or vending-machine profits.

Discriminating Based on Union Affiliation

Under the third unfair labor practice, an employer may neither discharge nor refuse to hire an employee to either encourage or discourage membership in any labor organization. Nor may the employer discriminate regarding any term or condition of employment for such purposes. The law does not oblige an employer to favor union members in hiring employees. It also does not restrict him or her in the normal exercise of any employer's right to select or discharge employees. However, the employer may not abuse that right by discriminatory action based on union membership or activities that encourage or discourage membership in a labor organization.

A company may not go partially out of business because some of its employees have organized, nor may it temporarily close that portion of its business that has unionized. If a company closes one plant because a union is voted in, such action discourages union activity at other plants. Partial closings to "chill" unionism are unfair labor practices.

The Supreme Court has held that an employer who reports the possible existence of illegal aliens to the Immigration and Naturalization Service engages in an unfair labor practice when that report is closely associated with the employees' approval of a labor union as their bargaining agent.

Discriminating as a Result of NLRB Proceedings

The fourth unfair labor practice prohibits discharge or other reprisals by their employers because they are enforcing their rights under the Wagner Act by filing charges or giving testimony in NLRB proceedings. This protection prevents the NLRB's channels of information from evaporating by employer intimidation of complainants and witnesses. An employer cannot refuse to hire a prospective employee because charges have been filed by him or her.

The main defense of any employer accused of reprisal is that he or she discharged or discriminated against the employee for some reason other than filing charges or giving testimony. Most often such cases boil down to trying to prove what motivated the company in pursuing its course of action. If the company can convince the NLRB that the employee was discharged because of misconduct, low production, personnel cutbacks necessitated by economic conditions, or other legitimate considerations, the company will be exonerated. Otherwise, it will be found guilty of this unfair labor practice.

Refusing to Bargain in Good Faith

The fifth unfair labor practice occurs when management refuses to bargain with the collective bargaining representative of its employees. The Wagner Act did not define the phrase "to bargain collectively." Judicial decisions have added the concept of *good faith* to bargaining. To comply with the requirement that they bargain collectively in good faith, employers must approach the bargaining table with fair and open minds and a sincere intent to find a basis of agreement.

Take-it-or-leave-it demands in a negotiation are considered bad-faith bargaining.

The employer's duty to bargain collectively includes a duty to provide relevant information needed by a union for the proper performance of its duties as the employees' bargaining representative. For example, data about job related safety and health must be furnished so that the union can safeguard its members' health and safety.

sidebar 22.6

This Was No Joke: The Writers Guild of America Strike

In November 2007, more than 12,000 film, television, and radio writers joined together in the Writers Guild of America strike against the Alliance of Motion Picture and Television Producers, a trade organization representing nearly 400 American film and television producers.

WHAT WAS AT ISSUE?

The most contentious issues at stake: DVD residuals, union jurisdiction over animation and reality program writers, and compensation for "new media," content written for or distributed through emerging digital technology, including the Internet.

HOW MUCH DID THE STRIKE COST?

According to an NPR report, the strike cost the economy of Los Angeles an estimated $1.5 billion.

The "Big Four" networks (ABC, CBS, FOX, and NBC) suffered ad shortfalls and declines in prime time ratings.

WHAT WAS THE OUTCOME OF THE DISPUTE?

On February 12, 2008, the strike concluded after the parties reached an agreement creating formulas for revenue-based residuals in new media, providing access to deals and financial data to help writers evaluate and enforce the formulas, and establishing the principle for the writers "When they get paid, we get paid." Another outcome was the solidarity that developed throughout the group from the most successful writers to those fighting to get into the business.

For more information about the agreement, see http://unitedhollywood.blogspot.com/.

Refusing to meet at reasonable times with representatives of the other party, refusing to reduce agreements to writing, and designating persons with no authority to negotiate as representatives at meetings are examples of this unfair labor practice.

The 73,000 United Automobile Workers went on strike at General Motors in 2007, seeking job security during restructuring of the company. GM is seeking to lower its cost structure and to have a more flexible workforce to compete with other automakers such as Toyota and Honda.

A more fundamental issue inherent in the requirement that parties bargain collectively is: "About what?" Must the employer bargain with the union about all subjects and all management decisions in which the union or the employees are interested? Are there subjects and issues upon which management is allowed to act alone? See Sidebar 22.6 for a discussion about the "Writers Strike."

In answering these questions, the law divides issues into two categories—**compulsory bargaining issues** and **voluntary bargaining issues**. Compulsory, or mandatory, bargaining issues are those concerned with wages, hours, and other terms and conditions of employment. Although the parties may voluntarily consider other issues, the refusal by either to bargain in good faith on such other permissive matters is not an unfair labor practice.

Classifying an issue as *compulsory* or *voluntary* is done on a case-by-case basis. For example, questions relating to fringe benefits are compulsory bargaining issues because they are "wages." The NLRB and the courts are called on to decide whether management and labor must bargain with each other on a multitude of issues. A good example of a case in which bargaining was required is *Ford Motor Co. v. NLRB* (441 U.S. 488).

Employees of the Ford Motor Company belong to the United Auto Workers. Ford provides in-plant cafeterias and vending machines as two ways to ensure its employees with food services. An independent caterer managed both the cafeterias and vending machines. This caterer informed Ford that the increased costs associated with these food services required food prices to go up. When Ford notified the union representative of these food cost increases, the union requested bargaining be held over the food prices and services.

Ford refused to bargain, and the union filed a charge with the NLRB alleging Ford's refusal to bargain in good faith, which is an unfair labor practice. The NLRB concluded that in-plant food and related services are "other terms and conditions of employment." Therefore, Ford must negotiate with the union over this compulsory bargaining issue. The Supreme Court's review of these facts results in the NLRB's ruling being affirmed.

A party to labor negotiations may present a demand to bargain about a voluntary issue as long as this issue does not have to be resolved before the parties can resolve compulsory bargaining issues. Tying a voluntary bargaining issue to a compulsory bargaining issue results in a failure to bargain in good faith and is in effect an unfair labor practice.

Courts tend to defer to the special expertise of the NLRB in classifying collective bargaining subjects, especially in the area of "terms or conditions of employment." Examples of board rulings holding that issues such as union dues checkoff; health and accident insurance; safety rules; merit pay increases; incentive pay plans; Christmas and other bonuses; stock purchase plans; pensions; paid vacations and holidays; the privilege of hunting on a reserved portion of a paper company's forest preserve; proposals for effective arbitration and grievance procedures; and no-strike and no-lockout clauses are compulsory bargaining issues.

Remember that neither the employer nor the union must make concessions to the other concerning a mandatory subject of bargaining. The law only demands that each negotiate such matters in good faith with the other before making a decision and taking unilateral action. If the parties fail to reach an agreement after discussing these problems, each may take steps that are against the wishes and best interests of the other party. For example, the employer may refuse to grant a wage increase requested by the union, and the union is free to strike.

---

sidebar 22.7

Fired! Venting About the Boss on Facebook

Can you imagine calling your supervisor a "scumbag" or comparing him to a psychiatric patient? Dawnmarie Souza, an employee of American Medical Response of Connecticut Inc. (AMR), criticized her supervisor on her Facebook page. Souza was terminated for violating AMR's policy, which states: "Employees are prohibited from making disparaging, discriminatory or defamatory comments when discussing the Company or the employee's supervisors, co-workers and/or competitors." The policy also prohibits "Rude or discourteous behavior to a client or co-worker."

The NLRB issued a complaint claiming that AMR's firing was an unfair labor practice. The NLRB also alleged that AMR's Internet policies were overly broad and interfere with an employee's right to engage in protected activities under the NLRA.

The NLRB settled the case, requiring AMR to "revise its Internet policy to allow workers to discuss wages, hours and working conditions with co-workers outside of the workplace; and refrain from disciplining or discharging employees for engaging in those discussions." AMR reached a separate, private settlement with Souza.

The NLRB's complaint is available at www.employmentlawalert.com/uploads/file/PDFComplaint.pdf.

The Taft-Hartley Act

In its attempt to balance the bargaining power between labor unions and management, the Taft-Hartley Act:

- Provides for an *80-day cooling-off period* in strikes that imperil the nation's health or safety.
- Reinforces the employer's freedom of speech in labor–management relations.
- Outlaws the *closed-shop* concept but permits *union shops* in the absence of a state *right-to-know* law.
- Permits suits by union members for breach of contract against unions.
- Creates six unfair labor practices by unions.

President George W. Bush used this provision to end the longshoremen's strike on the West Coast in 2002.

The Wagner Act opened the door for the rapid growth of the union movement. From 1935 to the end of World War II, the strength and influence of unions grew substantially. Where, prior to the Wagner Act, employers had the greater advantage in bargaining power, by 1946 many persons felt the pendulum had shifted and that unions, with their ability to call nationwide, crippling strikes, had the better bargaining position. To balance the scale, the Labor–Management Relations Act (the **Taft-Hartley Act**) was enacted in 1947 to amend the Wagner Act.

The purposes of the Taft-Hartley Act are to ensure the free flow of commerce by eliminating union practices that burden commerce and to provide procedures for avoiding disputes that jeopardize the public health, safety, or interest. It recognizes that both parties to collective bargaining need protection from wrongful interference by the other and that employees sometimes need protection from the union itself. Finally, it sought to protect the public interest in major labor disputes. Congress authorized the creation of the Federal Mediation and Conciliation Service to help achieve the goals of the Taft-Hartley Act. Members of this service are available to assist the parties in settling labor disputes.

EIGHTY-DAY COOLING-OFF PERIOD

Somewhat like the 60-day period provided under the Railway Labor Act, the Taft-Hartley Act provides for an *80-day cooling-off period* following certain procedures. This provision's intent is to limit the adverse impact of the nationwide strikes by steelworkers, mineworkers, autoworkers, and longshoremen that can paralyze the economy. When a threatened or actual strike or lockout affecting an entire industry or substantial part thereof will, if permitted to occur or to continue, imperil the national health or safety, the 80-day period may be enforced. The procedure starts with the president recognizing the emergency and appointing a board of inquiry to obtain facts about the threatened or actual strike or lockout. The board studies the situation and reports back to the president. If the board finds that the national health or safety is indeed affected by the strike, then the president, through the attorney general, goes to the federal court for an injunction ordering the union to suspend the strike (or the company to suspend the lockout) for 80 days.

During the 80-day period, the Federal Mediation and Conciliation Service works with the labor–management parties to try to achieve an agreement. If during this time the reconciliation effort fails, the presidential board holds new hearings and receives the company's final offer. The union members are then allowed to vote on this final proposal by the company. If they vote for the new proposal, the dispute is over and work continues as usual. If they vote against the proposal, the workers may again be called out on strike. At this point, the strike may continue indefinitely until the disagreement causing it is resolved by collective bargaining or unless there is additional legislation by Congress to solve the problem.

Experience has shown that disputes are often settled during the 80-day period. The injunction provided for in the Taft-Hartley Act may not be used for all strikes and lockouts. This injunction is limited to *national emergency* strikes and lockouts, those that involve national defense or key industries or have a substantial effect on the economy.

sidebar 22.8

Tweeting His Way to Termination

The *Arizona Daily Star* fired one of its public safety reporters for inappropriate and unprofessional tweets, including the following:

- "You stay homicidal, Tucson. See Star Net for the bloody deets."
- "What?!?!? No overnight homicide? WTF? You're slacking Tucson."
- "Suggestion for new Tucson-area theme song: Droening [sic] pool's 'let the bodies hit the floor'."
- "I'd root for daily death if it always happened in close proximity to Gus Balon's."
- "Hope everyone's having a good Homicide Friday, as one Tucson police officer called it."
- "My discovery of the Red Zone channel is like an adolescent boy's discovery of h . . . let's just hope I don't end up going blind."

Even after Human Resources encouraged the reporter to discuss concerns with colleagues instead of Twitter and his managing editor told him that he should not make comments on social media that could damage the paper's reputation, the reporter continued to tweet. The *Arizona Daily Star* did not have a written policy about using Twitter.

The reporter was fired. What was the position of the NLRB? In a memorandum, the NLRB stated "The charging party's conduct was not protected and concerted: It did not relate to the terms and conditions of his employment or seek to involve other employees in issues related to employment."

Source: NLRB Advice Memorandum, Lee Enterprises, Inc. d/b/a *Arizona Daily Star,* Case 28-CA-23267 (April 21, 2011).

FREE SPEECH

Employers complained that the Wagner Act violated their right of free speech. Statements by management formed the basis of unfair labor practices claims. To meet this objection, Congress, in Taft-Hartley, added the following provision:

> 8(c) The expressing of any views, argument, or opinion, or the dissemination thereof, whether in written, printed, graphic, or visual form, shall not constitute or be evidence of an unfair labor practice under any of the provisions of this Act, if such expression contains no threat of reprisal or force or promise of benefit.

This provision gives employers limited free speech, at best. It is difficult to make statements that cannot be construed as a threat or a promise. For example, if an employer predicts dire economic events as a result of unionization, such may be an illegal threat if the employer has it within his or her power to make the prediction come true. Whether particular language is coercive or not often depends on the analysis of the total background of facts and circumstances in which it was uttered. To be forbidden, the statements of an employer need not be proved to have been coercive in fact but only to have had a reasonable tendency to intimidate employees under the circumstances.

An employer's threats to withdraw existing benefits if employees unionize is not speech protected by Section 8(c). However, mere predictions and prophecies are protected. For example, in one case an employer's speeches and handbills during the union's organizational campaign stated its intention to fight the union in every legal way possible and to "deal hard" with the union at arm's length if it were voted in. The employer also warned that employees could be permanently replaced if the union called an economic strike. This language was held to fall within the protection of Section 8(c). The right of free speech guaranteed by the Taft-Hartley Act applies to labor

sidebar 22.9

Restricting Workplace Speech: Setting the Parameters

These NLRB cases shed light on the kinds of speech restrictions that are permissible—or not—in the workplace. Section 7 of the National Labor Relations Act (NLRA) guarantees that *all* employees (regardless of union status) have the right to engage in "concerted activities for the purpose of . . . mutual aid or protection."

The Policy: Employees are prohibited from discussing work conditions, wages, benefits, and discipline.

NLRB Decision: This policy is illegally broad and violates the NLRA by promulgating a confidentiality rule prohibiting employees from discussing disciplinary information, grievances and complaints, performance evaluations, or salary information with any persons outside the company or with fellow employees.

See *Double Eagle Hotel & Casino,* 341 NLRB No. 17 (January 20, 2004), upheld by the 10th Cir (2005); see also *Longs Drug Stores California, Inc.,* 347 NLRB No 45 (2006).

The Policy: Maintenance of work rules prohibit the use of "abusive and profane language," "verbal, mental, and physical abuse," and "harassment . . . in any way."

NLRB Decision: The rule is lawful and could not reasonably be understood as interfering with employees' Section 7 rights. The rule is lawful because it is based on the employer's legitimate right to establish a "civil and decent" workplace to protect itself from liability for workplace harassment. *Lutheran Heritage Village-Livonia,* 343 NLRB No. 75 (2004).

---

unions as well as employers. However, there is a rule prohibiting either side from making election speeches on company time to massed assemblies of employees within 24 hours before an election.

UNION SHOP—MEMBERSHIPS AND FEES

The Wagner Act's strong support of unionization gave unintended bargaining power to unions with respect to an employer's hiring practices. In many bargaining situations, the union became so strong that it successfully insisted on management's hiring only union members. In essence, to apply for a prospective job, a person would have to join the union. These situations became known as **closed shops.**

One of the major changes brought about by the Taft-Hartley Act was outlawing of the closed shop. This act still permitted the **union shop.** In a union shop contract, also known as a **union security clause,** the employer agrees that after an employee is hired that employee must join the union as a condition of continued employment. The Taft-Hartley Act prohibits such a requirement until the thirtieth day after employment begins.

Through a series of cases, the Supreme Court clarified the limited mandatory relationship created by the inclusion of the union security clause in a contract. This type of relationship requires that the union members pay reasonable membership fees and dues. In turn, the union can use these fees and dues only for collective bargaining, contract administration, and grievance activities. Unions are not allowed to use members' dues to support political activities.

One of the sections of the Taft-Hartley Act most distasteful to unions is 14(b), which outlaws the union shop in states that have adopted a right-to-work law. **Right-to-work laws** prohibit agreements requiring membership in a labor organization as a condition of continued employment of a person who was not in the union when hired. Approximately 20 states have right-to-work laws today. Workers in these states who do not belong to a union may not be required

Right-to-work laws are mostly in the South and Southwest, areas that historically have been antiunion.

to pay representation fees to the union that represents the employees. However, such workers are subject to the terms of the collective bargaining agreement, and the union must handle their grievances, if any, with management.

SUITS AGAINST UNIONS

Section 301 of the Taft-Hartley Act provides that suits for breach of a contract between an employer and a labor organization can be filed in the federal district courts without regard to the amount in question. A labor organization is responsible for the acts of its agents and may sue or be sued. Any money judgment against it is enforceable only against its assets and not against any individual member. Moreover, individuals cannot be sued for actions such as violating no-strike provisions of a collective bargaining contract.

Many suits against unions are by members alleging a breach of the duty of fair representation.

In addition, members may sue their union and recover the money damages they suffer because of an illegal strike. If a union activity is both an unfair labor practice and a breach of a collective bargaining agreement, the NLRB's authority is not exclusive and does not destroy the jurisdiction of courts under Section 301 of the Taft-Hartley Act.

Since workers cannot bargain individually when represented by a union, the union has an implied duty of fair representation to act reasonably, with honesty of purpose, and in good faith. The union must represent all the employees in the bargaining unit, including those who are nonunion, impartially and without hostile discrimination. Failure to do so may give rise to a lawsuit.

The duty of fair representation applies not only to the *negotiation* of a collective bargaining agreement but also to the *administration* of the agreement. Unions must fairly represent employers in disputes with the employer regarding the *interpretation* and *application* of the terms of an existing contract.

An employee may file suit against the union and its representatives for damages resulting from breach of their duty of fair representation in processing his or her grievance against the employer. A union may not process a grievance in an arbitrary, indifferent, or careless manner.

Finally, a union member may sue a local union for failing to enforce the international union's constitution and bylaws. Thus, Section 301 of the Taft-Hartley Act authorizes an employer to sue a union for breach of contract as well as employees to sue to enforce either the union–management collective bargaining agreement or a union contract with a member.

sidebar 22.10

Making a Point: Union Protests with Giant Inflatable Rats

 Over the last two decades, giant inflatable rats—as tall as 25 feet—have gained popularity as symbols of anti-union activity. The rats make a graphic visual statement in connection with union protests against companies that hire nonunion workers or do not pay union wages.

In one such protest, the Sheet Metal Workers International Association Local 15 staged a mock funeral in front of a Florida hospital along with a giant rat. That case involved using a staffing agency that employed nonunion workers.

The NLRB ruled that the rats are legally permissible, that the tactic does not violate labor law and is protected speech. Ironically, the manufacturer of the balloons is allegedly a nonunion company. See Sheet Metal Workers Local 15, 356 NLRB No. 162 (2011).

UNFAIR LABOR PRACTICES BY UNIONS

Perhaps more than with any other provision of the Taft-Hartley Act, Congress attempted to balance the bargaining power in the labor–management relationship by enacting six unfair labor practices by unions. These balance the unfair labor practices by management in the Wagner Act, as discussed earlier in the chapter. Six unfair labor practices by unions are:

- Restraining or coercing an employee to join a union or an employer in selecting representatives to bargain with the union.
- Causing or attempting to cause the employer to discriminate against an employee who is not a union member unless there is a legal union shop agreement in effect.
- Refusing to bargain with the employer if it is the NLRB-designated representative of the employees.
- Striking, picketing, or engaging in secondary boycotts for illegal purposes.
- Charging new members excessive or discriminatory initiation fees when there is a union shop agreement.
- Causing an employer to pay for work not performed (featherbedding).

Three of these illegal practices can be presented in a summary fashion due to the preceding discussions in this chapter or because they have very little impact today. The third unfair labor practice by unions is complementary to the fifth unfair labor practice by management. In essence, Congress requires unions to bargain in good faith as is required of management. The fifth unfair labor practice by unions simply means that unions cannot take advantage of the union shop agreement by charging unreasonable dues or fees when members and nonmembers are obligated to pay them. Today, the sixth unfair labor practice, involving *featherbedding,* or payment for work not actually performed, is of less importance than when it was enacted in 1947.

The other unfair labor practices by unions are presented in the following subsections.

Restraining or Coercing an Employee into Joining a Union

This unfair labor practice includes misconduct by unions directed toward employees. The law makes it illegal for a union to restrain or coerce employees in the exercise of their rights to bargain collectively, just as it is an unfair labor practice by employers to interfere with the same rights. Employees also are guaranteed the right to *refrain* from union activities unless they are required to join the union by a legal union shop agreement.

Causing an Employer to Discriminate against a Nonunion Member

If a legal union shop agreement is in effect, a labor organization may insist that the employer observe its terms. But even when a legal union shop contract is in effect, the law prohibits a union from attempting to cause an employer to discriminate against an employee who has been denied membership or had his or her membership terminated for some reason other than failure to pay the dues and initiation fees uniformly required of all members. And even if an employee is a member, the union may not cause the employer to discriminate against him or her for not following union rules. This prohibition prevents the use of the union shop as a means of intimidating employees who were at odds with union officials over their policies.

Striking or Picketing for Illegal Purposes or Engaging in Secondary Boycotts

Jurisdictional strikes are unfair labor practices. A **jurisdictional strike** is used to force an employer to assign work to employees in one craft union rather than another. Since the dispute is between the two unions and not with the employer, the law requires that such disputes be submitted to the NLRB by the unions.

It is also an unfair labor practice for a union to threaten or to coerce by picketing, for example, an employer to recognize or bargain with one union if another one has been certified as the representative of its employees.

It is an unfair labor practice for a union to threaten, coerce, or restrain a third person not party to a labor dispute for the purpose of causing that third person to exert pressure on the company involved in the labor dispute. This law requires that strikes and picketing be directed at the employer with which the union actually has a labor dispute.

An example of illegal secondary activity occurs when a union induces the employees of an employer to strike or engage in a concerted refusal to use, handle, or work on any goods or to perform any service to force the employer to stop doing business with some third person. For example, assume that a supplier (like a bakery) has a workforce that is nonunionized. A customer (i.e., a grocery store) has employees who belong to a union. This union would like to be the bargaining representative for the supplier's employees. It would be an illegal secondary boycott for this union to have its members either strike or picket the grocery store on the basis of it selling nonunionized baked goods from the bakery in the hope that the grocery store would discontinue its buying from this bakery. The union must deal directly with the bakery.

AMENDMENTS

Congressional hearings in the 1950s uncovered widespread corruption, violence, and lack of democratic procedures in some labor unions. As a result, Congress passed the **Landrum-Griffin Act**, or Labor–Management Reporting and Disclosure Act (LMRDA), in 1959. Its provisions constitute a "bill of rights" for union members and provide for union reform. Also in this act, Congress included some amendments to the unfair labor practices by management and unions.

In essence, in its continuing attempt to balance the bargaining power in the labor–management relationship, Congress added one unfair labor practice by management and two by unions.

Agreeing to Engage in a Secondary Boycott

You should recall from your reading in the preceding section that unions cannot engage in secondary boycotts. Technically, nothing in that unfair labor practice, as enacted in the Taft-Hartley Act, prohibited a union and an employer from agreeing to engage in a secondary boycott. The original restriction applied only to the unilateral acts of the union. The Landrum-Griffin Act clarified the concern over secondary boycotts by prohibiting a union–management agreement that would adversely impact a neutral third party.

It is also an unfair labor practice for both the employer involved and the union to enter into a **hot-cargo contract.** A hot-cargo contract is one in which an employer voluntarily agrees with a union that the employees should not be required by their employer to handle or work on goods or materials going to or coming from an employer designated by the union as "unfair." Such goods are said to be hot cargo. These clauses were common in trucking and construction labor contracts. The law thus forbids an employer and a labor organization to make an agreement under which the employer agrees to stop doing business with any other employer.

Picketing When Not Certified   In certain cases it is illegal for unions to force an employer to recognize or bargain with the union if it is not currently certified as the duly authorized collective bargaining representative. The purpose is to reinforce the effectiveness of the election procedures employed by the NLRB by outlawing certain tactics used by unions backed by only a minority of the employees of a particular employer. Thus, picketing to force an employer to recognize an uncertified union is an unfair labor practice in the following cases:

1. When the employer has lawfully recognized another union as the collective bargaining representative of its employees.
2. When a valid representation election has been conducted by the NLRB within the past 12 months.
3. When picketing has been conducted for an unreasonable time, in excess of 30 days, without a petition for a representation election being filed with the NLRB.

Including these amendments by the Landrum-Griffin Act, the law on unfair labor practices is summarized in the following concept summary. Remember, as you review these materials, Congress used three laws to create these lists. The first five items on management's side were enacted in 1935. The first six on the union side came in 1947. The sixth item on the left side and the last two items on the right side were added in 1959.

concept *summary*

Unfair Labor Practices

BY MANAGEMENT	BY UNIONS
1. Interfering with unionization and concerted activities by employees.	1. Restraining or coercing an employee to join a union.
2. Dominating a union or contributing to it, financially or otherwise.	2. Causing an employer to discriminate against a nonunion member.
3. Discriminating in hiring or tenure of employees on the basis of union affiliation.	3. Refusing to bargain collectively in good faith.
4. Discriminating against employees who seek to enforce their Wagner Act rights.	4. Striking, picketing, or engaging in secondary boycotts for illegal purposes.
5. Refusing to bargain collectively in good faith.	5. Charging excessive or discriminatory fees.
6. Agreeing with a labor organization to engage in a secondary boycott.	6. Causing an employer to pay for work not performed.
	7. Picketing to force an employer to recognize or bargain with an uncertified union.
	8. Agreeing with an employer to engage in a secondary boycott.

Key Terms

Clayton Act 689
Closed shops 704
Collective bargaining 688
Compulsory bargaining
  issues 700
Concerted activity 698
Hot-cargo contract 707
Jurisdictional strike 707

Landrum-Griffin Act 707
National Labor Relations
  Board (NLRB) 693
National Mediation
  Board 690
Norris-LaGuardia Act 691
Railway Labor Act 690
Right-to-work laws 704

Taft-Hartley Act 702
Union security clause 704
Union shop 704
Voluntary bargaining
  issues 700
Wagner Act 692
Yellow-dog contract 691

Review Questions and Problems

Labor Laws

1. *Law before 1935*

    (a) What is the specific purpose of (1) the Clayton Act, (2) the Railway Labor Act, and (3) the Norris-LaGuardia Act?

    (b) Why did these laws not increase laborers' bargaining power to the degree that is considered equal to management's bargaining power?

The Wagner Act

2. *National Labor Relations Board*

    Describe the nature and limitations of the NLRB's jurisdiction.

3. *Certification of Unions*

    The NLRB conducted a certification election, and the union won by a vote of 22–20. Management refused to bargain with this union.

    The reason for this refusal to recognize the union as the employees' bargaining agent was that the union had used "recognition slips" as a means of indicating the employees' support for the union. Several employees testified that they signed these slips to avoid the payment of the initiation fee. Further, at least a few employees indicated that they thought they had to vote for the union since they had signed a recognition slip. Should the NLRB set aside this election of the union? Explain.

4. *Unfair Labor Practices by Management*

    (a) List the five unfair labor practices created by the Wagner Act.

    (b) Describe a situation for each of these unfair labor practices.

The Taft-Hartley Act

5. *Eighty-Day Cooling-Off Period*

    (a) Under what circumstances is the president authorized to order parties in a labor dispute back to work for 80 days?

    (b) Describe the procedures that must be followed to invoke this cooling-off period.

6. *Free Speech*

    The personnel director of your company has been asked to talk with the employees about the benefits and detriments of voting for or against the union in an upcoming certification election. What should this director keep in mind about the Free Speech Clause in the Taft-Hartley Act? Explain.

7. *Union Shop—Memberships and Fees*

    Pat lives in a state that has enacted a right-to-work law. The company that employs her has recognized the United Clerical Workers (UCW) as the bargaining representative of its workers.

The union has sought to collect union dues or their equivalent from Pat. Is she required to pay them? Why or why not?

8. *Suits against Unions*

Ed is discharged for allegedly stealing property from his employer. He asks his union to have him reinstated because his discharge violates the collective bargaining agreement in force. However, the union does not investigate the incident until it is too late to file a request for arbitration under the collective bargaining agreement. Assuming that Ed is innocent of the charges, does he have any rights against the union? Explain.

9. *Unfair Labor Practices by Unions*

(a) List the six unfair labor practices created by the Taft-Hartley Act.

(b) Describe a situation for each of these unfair labor practices.

10. *Amendments*

(a) What were the two basic purposes for Congress's passing the Landrum-Griffin Act?

(b) What are the additional unfair labor practices added by this law?

business *discussions*

1. For years, your small electronics company has given all its employees one week's pay and a turkey each Christmas. But now a recession is eroding profitability and the company is operating at a significant loss, so you consider canceling the Christmas presents for this year. The employees have just voted for union representation, and the extra pay and turkeys are not mentioned in the collective bargaining agreement.

> Is a Christmas gift still purely a management decision?
> Are you in trouble if you cancel the turkeys?
> What is the union's role in the decision?

2. Sarah works at a small accounting firm. The firm's handbook contains the following policy:

> Employees are prohibited from discussing their salary, bonuses, or any other forms of compensation, including benefits and vacation time.

Sarah is very careful not to violate the policy but, after she becomes married to her co-worker Bill, Sarah realizes that her salary is 20% less than Bill's salary. Bill and Sarah were hired at the same time and at the same position level. Sarah is even more upset when she learns that Bill started at the higher salary on his first day on the job. When Sarah asks her boss about the difference, she is terminated.

> What potential claims could Sarah assert against her employer?
> What defenses should the employer raise?

Case Briefing and Legal Study Tips

To gain the most from this textbook, you should learn how to study written material effectively. You can achieve effective study through use of the SQ3R method, a method widely taught by study-skills psychologists for learning textual material.

SQ3R stands for **survey, question, read, recite,** and **review.** As a study method, it has dramatically improved the grade-point averages of most students who have practiced it. It is based upon the concept that active study of written material improves memory and comprehension of information far better than passive reading. Unfortunately, many students have not recognized the difference between active study and mere passive reading.

Students often read a textbook chapter exactly as they would read a novel or a magazine article. They begin with the first sentence of the chapter and read straight through the material, pausing only to underline occasionally. This way of reading may be suitable for a novel, but it is quite inappropriate for a textbook. Psychologists insist that an active study method must begin with a **survey** of the material to be read. If you plan to spend two hours studying a 30-page chapter, take three to five minutes in the beginning and survey the chapter. First, read the bold-type section headings (each chapter of this book is divided into numbered sections). Second, read a sentence or two from the text of each section. The purpose of this survey is to familiarize you with the topics covered in the chapter. Fight the tendency to stop your surveying process in order to comprehend all of the concepts you are surveying. Comprehension is not the goal of surveying.

Following the survey of all the sections, go back to the beginning of the chapter: Ask yourself a **question** before reading each section. Ask it aloud, if possible, but silently if circumstances demand. The important thing is actually to "talk to yourself." Normally, each section heading can easily be turned into a question. If the section heading reads *Stare Decisis,* ask yourself the question, "What does *stare decisis* mean?"

Only after asking a question are you finally ready to **read** a chapter section. In reading keep your question in mind. By so doing you will be reading for a purpose: To discover the answer to your question.

Upon finishing each section, stop and **recite** the answer to your question. As an example, at the end of the section on *stare decisis* say to yourself, "*Stare*

decisis refers to the legal tradition that a judge in a given case will follow the precedent established in similar cases decided by courts in the jurisdiction." According to psychologists, to recite this way greatly aids memory. Recitation also lets you know whether or not you have understood the material just read.

The last step of the SQ3R method is **review.** When devoting two hours to the study of a chapter, take the final 15 minutes of the time to review the material. Review the questions taken from the headings of each chapter section and recite the answers to them, rereading material if necessary to answer accurately.

A CASE BRIEFING SYSTEM

Although the SQ3R method may be used effectively to study any subject, the **case briefing system** is uniquely designed to aid in the study of court decisions. In studying law, students frequently write up case briefs of each decision they read. Whether you are required to write up every decision is up to your individual instructor. However, the case briefing system provides an excellent framework for comprehending complicated judicial reasoning processes, and you should brief cases whether required to do so or not.

To avoid getting lost in a maze of judicial terminology, you should ask yourself a standard set of questions about each case decision and read to discover the answers to these questions. These standard questions lie at the heart of the case briefing system. They are as follows:

1. Who is the plaintiff and who is the defendant?
2. What are the facts of the case? (Who did what to whom? What is the behavior complained of?)
3. Did the plaintiff or the defendant win in the lower court(s), and which party is appealing? (All decisions in this textbook come from appellate courts.)
4. What was the legal issue or issues appealed?
5. Does the plaintiff or the defendant win on the appeal?
6. What rules of law and reasoning does the appellate court use in deciding the issue?

Here is an illustration of a written case brief. It is a brief of the first case in the textbook, which you can find in Chapter 3 Case 3.1. Before looking at the brief, you should now read that case. An important part of law requires you to learn new vocabulary. To understand the case you read, you need to know several new terms. You can find the terms in the glossary of this textbook, but to make it easier, we will define several new terms for you:

appellant The losing party at the district court level.

appellee The prevailing party in the district court who is responding to the appellant.

appeal To ask a higher court to decide whether an inferior court (e.g., trial court) made a legal mistake in its decision; also to ask a higher court to review (decide) the case.

dissent To disagree with both the result and the legal reasoning of the majority opinion.

opinion The court's decision in a case.

petitioner The losing party in the court of appeals who asks (i.e., "petitions") the Supreme Court to decide whether the lower court made a mistake.

respondent The prevailing party in the court of appeals who is responding to the petitioner.

reversed What an appeals court says when it disagrees with the court beneath it. If it agrees with the lower court, it says "affirmed."

CASE BRIEF

National Federation of Independent Business v. Sebelius, 567 U.S. __, 132 S. Ct. 2566 (2012)
How do i read this citation?

- "National Federation of Independent Business" refers to the petitioner.
- "v" means versus or against.
- "Sebelius" refers to the respondent.
- 567 is the volume number of the official U.S. Supreme Court Reporter, and __ refers to the page number where the case begins (once it is assigned a page number). The date, 2012, is the year when the case was decided.

Facts Twenty-six states, several individuals, and the National Federation of Independent Business (plaintiffs) brought this action against the federal Health and Human Services, Treasury, and Labor departments and their Secretaries (defendants), in federal district court, challenging the constitutionality of two aspects of the Affordable Care Act: the individual mandate and the expansion to Medicaid.

Procedural History This case was brought in the U.S. District Court for the Northern District of Florida. The District Court granted summary judgment to the defendants on the claim that the Affordable Care Act's expansion of Medicaid was unconstitutional. Because the court concluded that the individual mandate provision exceeded congressional authority and was not severable, it declared the entire Affordable Care Act invalid.

On appeal to the Eleventh Circuit, the circuit judges agreed that the individual mandate was unconstitutional, affirmed as to the constitutionality of the Medicaid expansion, but reversed the determination about severability.

The case was then appealed to the U.S. Supreme Court.

Issues Appealed The key issues on appeal were:

1. Whether the individual mandate, imposing a minimum essential coverage requirement, is within Congress's power under the Commerce Clause of the U.S. Constitution.
2. Whether the provision giving the federal government the authority to penalize states that chose not to participate in the expansion of the Medicaid program exceeded Congress's power under the Spending Clause.

Who Wins and Why?

1. Although the Supreme Court found that the individual mandate exceeded Congress's power under the Commerce Clause, it was upheld as a "tax" pursuant to Congress's taxing powers.
2. The statutory provision giving the federal government the authority to penalize states that chose not to participate in the expansion of Medicaid exceeded Congress's authority under the Spending Clause.

What Does This Mean? Overall, this case was seen as a victory for the proponents of the Affordable Care Act. The individual mandate requiring nonexempt individuals to purchase and maintain minimum essential health care coverage was upheld. Although the Supreme Court found that the statutory provision giving the federal government the authority to penalize states that chose not to participate in the expansion of the Medicaid program exceeded Congress's authority, it also held that this penalization provision was severable. As such, only the provision is unenforceable. In all other respects, the Affordable Care Act was left intact. Although the law and its implementation continue to face challenges, health care exchanges opened in the fall of 2013 to facilitate the purchase of health insurance in every state.

Sample Complaint

IN THE SUPERIOR COURT OF CLARKE
COUNTY, STATE OF GEORGIA

JOHN DOE,

      Plaintiff,

v.

                                        CIVIL ACTION FILE
                                        NO: 2011

RELIANT MOTOR COMPANY, INC.,

      Defendant.

COMPLAINT FOR DAMAGES

COMES NOW Plaintiff John Doe, by and through counsel, and hereby files his Complaint, showing as follows:

PARTIES, JURISDICTION, AND VENUE

1.

This Court has subject matter jurisdiction over this matter and venue is proper in this judicial district pursuant to Ga. Const. Art. VI, Sec. II, Para. VI and O.C.G.A. §14-2-510(b) because the defendant conducts business, its registered agent is located and the cause of action originated in this judicial district.

2.

Plaintiff, John Doe, is a citizen of the State of Georgia and a resident of Athens, Clarke County, Georgia, and submits himself to the jurisdiction of this Court.

3.

Defendant "Reliant" Motor Company is a Georgia Corporation conducting business as an automobile dealer in Athens, Clarke County, Georgia. James Smith is the Registered Agent for Reliant Motor Company on whom service is proper. James Smith may be served at Terry Drive, Athens, Georgia, subjecting Reliant Motor Company to the jurisdiction of this Court.

<u>Statement of Facts</u>

4.

On or about February 1, 2011, John Doe purchased a 2010 Ford Explorer, Serial Number PJSJWMMAP 2010, from Defendant automobile dealership.

5.

The vehicle was identified as having undergone a 50 point inspection, and as having attained a "Platinum Check Quality Assurance." Among the items listed as passed "inspection" were all components of the front-end.

6.

The vehicle was sold with a 90 day/3000 mile warranty that covered all major component parts, including, but not limited to, engine, transmission, drive axle, brakes, steering, and electrical.

7.

While test driving the vehicle, Plaintiff noticed excessive road noise and informed Defendant of the problem. Defendant assured Plaintiff that vehicle had been inspected and was mechanically sound. Defendant said that excessive noise was from worn tires and offered to replace tires.

8.

Relying on Defendant's explanation and offer to replace tires, Plaintiff entered into a sales contract to buy the vehicle from Defendant. After Plaintiff purchased vehicle and had the tires replaced, the excessive road noise continued unabated. While Plaintiff returned the vehicle to Defendant several times to have the problem corrected, Defendant was unable to eliminate the excessive road noise. The vehicle became inoperative when the front-end locked up.

9.

Through an independent mechanic, Plaintiff learned that the entire problem with the vehicle was the "front-end" assembly. Component parts of the front-end were worn and damaged which caused the excessive road noise. Failure to fix the problem resulted in the front-end locking up. The independent mechanic also stated that the front-end had not been properly inspected.

10.

The fraudulent misrepresentations by Defendant that the vehicle had passed a thorough inspection induced Plaintiff to purchase the vehicle.

11.

Defendant refused to honor the warranty on the vehicle, make necessary repairs, or properly diagnose problem with the vehicle.

12.

As a result of these willful and wanton acts by Defendant, Plaintiff has been harmed by purchasing an inoperable vehicle for a sum exceeding $20,000. Plaintiff also has suffered other expenses, including the purchasing of another automobile for transportation and expenses in attempting to repair the vehicle at issue.

COUNT I
Fraud in the Inducement

13.

Plaintiff incorporates by reference the allegations in paragraphs 1 through 12 of his Complaint as if fully restated herein.

14.

Defendant, by its actions, intentionally concealed from the plaintiff the damage to the vehicle.

15.

The intentional concealments, misrepresentations and omissions set out herein were made by defendant in order to deceive plaintiff and induce him to purchase the vehicle.

16.

Plaintiff, in fact, reasonably relied on defendant's misrepresentations, which did, in fact, induce him to purchase the vehicle and to incur damages for repair and replacement of the vehicle as well as other foreseeable and consequential damages.

17.

Defendant's fraudulent concealments, misrepresentations and omissions showed willful misconduct malice, wantonness, and oppression and were conducted with specific intent to cause harm thereby entitling plaintiff to punitive damages.

COUNT II
Breach of Warranty

18.

Plaintiff incorporates by reference the allegations in paragraphs 1 through 17 of his Complaint as if fully restated herein.

19.

Defendant's actions breached the express warranty made to plaintiff in connection with his purchase of the vehicle, thereby entitling plaintiff to compensatory damages.

<u>Prayer for Relief</u>

WHEREFORE, Plaintiff respectfully prays that this Court:

1. Grant to Plaintiff judgment in this action and against Defendant under Counts One and Two of this complaint;

2. Grant to Plaintiff compensatory damages in an amount reasonable and commensurate with the losses imposed upon him by Defendant's unlawful acts, including his pain and emotional distress;

3. Grant to Plaintiff punitive damages in an amount reasonable and commensurate with the harm done and calculated to be sufficient to deter such conduct in the future;

4. Grant to Plaintiff his costs in this action and reasonable attorneys' fees as provided by OCGA §13-6-11; and

5. Grant to Plaintiff a jury trial on all issues so triable;

6. Grant such additional relief as the Court deems proper and just.

Respectfully submitted this _____ day of, _____ 2011,

_____

Lawyer
Ga. State Bar #000000

Attorneys for Plaintiff

The Constitution of the United States of America

We, the People of the United States, in Order to form a more perfect Union, establish Justice, insure domestic Tranquility, provide for the common defense, promote the general Welfare, and secure the Blessings of Liberty to ourselves and our Posterity, do ordain and establish this Constitution for the United States of America.

Article I

Section 1. All legislative Powers herein granted shall be vested in a Congress of the United States, which shall consist of a Senate and House of Representatives.

Section 2. The House of Representatives shall be composed of Members chosen every second Year by the People of the several States, and the Electors in each State shall have the Qualifications requisite for Electors of the most numerous Branch of the State Legislature.

No Person shall be a Representative who shall not have attained the Age of twenty five Years, and been seven Years a Citizen of the United States, and who shall not, when elected, be an Inhabitant of that State in which he shall be chosen.

Representatives and direct Taxes shall be apportioned among the several States which may be included within this Union, according to their respective Numbers, which shall be determined by adding the whole Number of free Persons, including those bound to Service for a Term of Years, and excluding Indians not taxed, three-fifths of all other Persons. The actual Enumeration shall be made within three Years after the first Meeting of the Congress of the United States, and within every subsequent Term of ten Years, in such Manner as they shall by Law direct. The Number of Representatives shall not exceed one for every thirty Thousand, but each State shall have at Least one Representative; and until such enumeration shall be made, the State of New Hampshire shall be entitled to chuse three, Massachusetts eight, Rhode Island and Providence Plantations one, Connecticut five, New-York six, New Jersey four, Pennsylvania eight, Delaware one, Maryland six, Virginia ten, North Carolina five, South Carolina five, and Georgia three.

When vacancies happen in the Representation from any State, the Executive Authority thereof shall issue Writs of Election to fill such Vacancies.

The House of Representatives shall chuse their Speaker and other Officers; and shall have the sole Power of Impeachment.

Section 3. The Senate of the United States shall be composed of two Senators from each State, chosen by the Legislature thereof, for six Years; and each Senator shall have one Vote.

Immediately after they shall be assembled in Consequence of the Election, they shall be divided as equally as may be into three Classes. The Seats of the Senators of the first Class shall be vacated at the Expiration of the second Year, of the second Class at the Expiration of the fourth Year, and of the third Class at the Expiration of the sixth Year, so that one third may be chosen every second Year; and if Vacancies happen by Resignation, or otherwise, during the Recess of the Legislature of any State, the Executive thereof may make temporary Appointments until the next Meeting of the Legislature, which shall then fill such Vacancies.

No Person shall be a Senator who shall not have attained to the Age of thirty Years, and been nine Years a Citizen of the United States, and who shall not, when elected, be an Inhabitant of that State for which he shall be chosen.

The Vice President of the United States shall be President of the Senate, but shall have no Vote, unless they be equally divided.

The Senate shall chuse their other Officers, and also a President pro tempore, in the Absence of the Vice President, or when he shall exercise the Office of the President of the United States.

The Senate shall have the sole Power to try all Impeachments. When sitting for that Purpose, they shall be on Oath or Affirmation. When the President of the United States is tried, the Chief Justice shall preside: and no Person shall be convicted without the Concurrence of two-thirds of the Members present.

Judgment in Cases of Impeachment shall not extend further than to removal from Office, and disqualification to hold and enjoy any Office of honor, Trust or Profit under the United States: but the Party convicted shall nevertheless be liable and subject to Indictment, Trial, Judgment and Punishment, according to Law.

Section 4. The Times, Places and Manner of holding Elections for Senators and Representatives, shall be prescribed in each State by the Legislature thereof: but the Congress may at any time by Law make or alter such Regulations, except as to the Places of chusing Senators.

The Congress shall assemble at least once in every Year, and such Meeting shall be on the first Monday in December, unless they shall by Law appoint a different Day.

Section 5.   Each House shall be the Judge of the Elections, Returns and Qualifications of its own Members, and a Majority of each shall constitute a Quorum to do Business; but a smaller Number may adjourn from day to day, and may be authorized to compel the Attendance of absent Members, in such Manner, and under such Penalties as each House may provide.

Each House may determine the Rules of its Proceedings, punish its Members for disorderly Behaviour, and, with the concurrence of two thirds, expel a Member.

Each House shall keep a Journal of its Proceedings, and from time to time publish the same, excepting such Parts as may in their Judgment require Secrecy; and the Yeas and Nays of the Members of either House on any question shall, at the Desire of one-fifth of those Present, be entered on the Journal.

Neither House, during the Session of Congress, shall, without the Consent of the other, adjourn for more than three days, nor to any other Place than that in which the two Houses shall be sitting.

Section 6.   The Senators and Representatives shall receive a Compensation for their Services, to be ascertained by Law, and paid out of the Treasury of the United States. They shall in all Cases, except Treason, Felony and Breach of the Peace, be privileged from Arrest during their Attendance at the Session of their respective Houses, and in going to and returning from the same; and for any Speech or Debate in either House, they shall not be questioned in any other Place.

No Senator or Representative shall, during the Time for which he was elected, be appointed to any civil Office under the Authority of the United States, which shall have been created, or the Emoluments whereof shall have been increased during such time; and no Person holding any Office under the United States, shall be a Member of either House during his Continuance in Office.

Section 7.   All Bills for raising Revenue shall originate in the House of Representatives; but the Senate may propose or concur with Amendments as on other Bills.

Every Bill which shall have passed the House of Representatives and the Senate, shall, before it become a Law, be presented to the President of the United States; If he approve, he shall sign it, but if not he shall return it, with his Objections to that house in which it shall have originated, who shall enter the Objections at large on their Journal, and proceed to reconsider it. If after such Reconsideration two thirds of that House shall agree to pass the Bill, it shall be sent, together with the Objections, to the other House, by which it shall likewise be reconsidered, and if approved by two thirds of that House, it shall become a Law. But in all such Cases the Votes of both Houses shall be determined by Yeas and Nays, and the Names of the Persons voting for and against the Bill shall be entered on the Journal of each House respectively. If any Bill shall not be returned by the President within ten Days (Sundays excepted) after it shall have been presented to him, the Same shall be a Law, in like Manner as if he had signed it, unless the Congress by their Adjournment prevent its Return, in which Case it shall not be a Law.

Every Order, Resolution, or Vote to which the Concurrence of the Senate and House of Representatives may be necessary (except on a question of Adjournment) shall be presented to the President of the United States; and before the Same shall take Effect, shall be approved by him, or being disapproved by him, shall be repassed by two thirds of the Senate and House of Representatives, according to the Rules and Limitations prescribed in the Case of a Bill.

Section 8.   The Congress shall have the Power to lay and collect Taxes, Duties, Imposts and Excises, to pay the Debts and provide for the common Defence and general Welfare of the United States; but all Duties, Imposts and Excises shall be uniform throughout the United States;

To borrow Money on the credit of the United States;

To regulate Commerce with foreign Nations, and among the several States, and with the Indian Tribes;

To establish an uniform Rule of Naturalization, and uniform Laws on the subject of Bankruptcies throughout the United States;

To coin Money, regulate the Value thereof, and of foreign Coin, and fix the Standard of Weights and Measures;

To provide for the Punishment of counterfeiting the Securities and current Coin of the United States;

To establish Post Offices and post Roads;

To promote the Progress of Science and useful Arts, by securing for limited Times to Authors and Inventors the exclusive Right to their respective Writings and Discoveries;

To constitute Tribunals inferior to the supreme Court;

To define and punish Piracies and Felonies committed on the high Seas, and Offenses against the Law of Nations;

To declare War, grant Letters of Marque and Reprisal, and make rules concerning Captures on Land and Water;

To raise and support Armies, but no Appropriation of Money to that use shall be for a longer Term than two Years;

To provide and maintain a Navy;

To make Rules for the Government and Regulation of the land and naval Forces;

To provide for calling forth the Militia to execute the Laws of the Union, suppress Insurrections and repel Invasions;

To provide for organizing, arming and disciplining, the Militia, and for governing such Part of them as may be employed in the Service of the United States, reserving to the States respectively, the Appointment of the Officers, and the Authority of training the Militia according to the discipline prescribed by Congress;

To exercise exclusive Legislation in all Cases whatsoever, over such District (not exceeding ten Miles square) as may, by Cession of particular States, and the acceptance of Congress, become the Seat of the Government of the United States, and to exercise like Authority over all Places purchased by the Consent of the Legislature of the State in which the Same shall be, for the Erection of Forts, Magazines, Arsenals, dock Yards, and other needful buildings;—And

To make all Laws which shall be necessary and proper for carrying into Execution the foregoing Powers, and all other Powers vested by the Constitution in the Government of the United States, or in any Department or Officer thereof.

Section 9.   The Migration or Importation of such Persons as any of the States now existing shall think proper to admit, shall not be prohibited by the Congress prior to the Year one thousand eight hundred and eight, but a Tax or Duty may be imposed on such Importation, not exceeding ten dollars for each Person.

The Privilege of the Writ of Habeas Corpus shall not be suspended, unless when in Cases of Rebellion or Invasion the public Safety may require it.

No Bill of Attainder or ex post facto Law shall be passed.

No Capitation, or other direct, Tax shall be laid, unless in Proportion to the Census or Enumeration herein before directed to be taken.

No Tax or Duty shall be laid on Articles exported from any State.

No Preference shall be given by any Regulation of Commerce or Revenue to the Ports of one State over those of another: nor shall Vessels bound to, or from, one State, be obliged to enter, clear, or pay Duties in another.

No Money shall be drawn from the Treasury, but in Consequence of Appropriations made by Law; and a regular Statement and Account of the Receipts and Expenditures of all public Money shall be published from time to time.

No Title of Nobility shall be granted by the United States: And no Person holding any Office or Profit or Trust under them, shall, without the Consent of the Congress, accept of any present, Emolument, Office, or Title, of any kind whatever, from any King, Prince, or foreign State.

Section 10.   No State shall enter into any Treaty, Alliance, or Confederation; grant Letters of Marque and Reprisal; coin Money; emit Bills of Credit; make any Thing but gold and silver Coin a Tender in Payment of Debts; pass any Bill of Attainder, ex post facto Law, or Law impairing the Obligation of Contracts, or grant any Title of Nobility.

No State shall, without the Consent of the Congress, lay any Imposts or Duties on Imports or Exports, except what may be absolutely necessary for executing its inspection Laws: and the net Produce of all Duties and Imposts, laid by any State on Imports or Exports, shall be for the Use of the Treasury of the United States; and all such Laws shall be subject to the Revision and Control of the Congress.

No State shall, without the Consent of Congress, lay any Duty of Tonnage, keep Troops, or Ships of War in time of Peace, enter into any Agreement or Compact with another State, or with a foreign Power, or engage in War, unless actually invaded, or in such imminent Danger as will not admit of delay.

Article II

Section 1.   The executive Power shall be vested in a President of the United States of America. He shall hold Office during the Term of four Years, and, together with the Vice President, chosen for the same Term, be elected as follows:

Each State shall appoint, in such Manner as the Legislature thereof may direct, a Number of Electors, equal to the whole Number of Senators and Representatives to which the State may be entitled in the Congress: but no Senator or Representative, or Person holding an Office or Trust or Profit under the United States, shall be appointed an Elector.

The Electors shall meet in their respective States, and vote by Ballot for two Persons, of whom one at least shall not be an Inhabitant of the same State with Themselves. And they shall make a List of all the Persons voted for, and of the Number of Votes for each; which List they shall sign and certify, and transmit sealed to the Seat of the Government of the United States, directed to the President of the Senate. The President of the Senate shall, in the Presence of the Senate and House of Representatives, open all the Certificates, and the Votes shall then be counted. The Person having the greatest Number of Votes shall be the President, if such Number be a Majority of the whole Number of Electors appointed; and if there be more than one who have such Majority, and have an equal Number of Votes, then the House of Representatives shall immediately chuse by Ballot one of them for President; and if no Person have a Majority, then from the five highest on the List the said House shall in like Manner chuse the President. But in chusing the President, the Votes shall be taken by States, the Representation from each State having one Vote; a quorum for this Purpose shall consist of a Member or Members from two thirds of the States, and a Majority of all the States shall be necessary to a Choice. In every Case, after the Choice of the President, the Person having the greatest Number of Votes of the Electors shall be the Vice President. But if there should remain two or more who have equal Votes, the Senate shall chuse from them by Ballot the Vice President.

The Congress may determine the Time of chusing the Electors, and the Day on which they shall give their Votes; which Day shall be the same throughout the United States.

No Person except a natural born Citizen, or a Citizen of the United States, at the time of the Adoption of this Constitution, shall be eligible to the Office of President; neither shall any Person be eligible to that Office who shall not have attained to the Age of thirty five Years, and been fourteen Years a Resident within the United States.

In Case of the Removal of the President from Office, or of his Death, Resignation, or Inability to discharge the Powers and Duties of the said Office, the Same shall devolve on the Vice President, and the Congress may by Law provide for the Case of Removal, Death, Resignation, or Inability, both of the President and Vice President, declaring what Officer shall then act as President, and such Officer shall act accordingly, until the Disability be removed, or a President shall be elected.

The President shall, at stated Times, receive for his Services, a Compensation, which shall neither be increased nor diminished during the Period for which he shall have been elected, and he shall not receive within that Period any other Emolument from the United States, or any of them.

Before he enter on the Execution of his Office, he shall take the following Oath or Affirmation:—"I do solemnly swear (or affirm) that I will faithfully execute the Office of President of the United States, and will to the best of my Ability, preserve, protect and defend the Constitution of the United States."

Section 2. The President shall be Commander in Chief of the Army and Navy of the United States, and of the Militia of the several States, when called into the actual Service of the United States; he may require the Opinion, in writing, of the principal Officer in each of the executive Departments, upon any Subject relating to the Duties of their respective Offices, and he shall have Power to grant Reprieves and Pardons for Offenses against the United States, except in Cases of Impeachment.

He shall have Power, by and with the Advice and Consent of the Senate, to make Treaties, providing two thirds of the Senators present concur; and he shall nominate, and by and with the advice and consent of the Senate, shall appoint Ambassadors, other public Ministers and Consuls, Judges of the supreme Court, and all other Officers of the United States, whose Appointments are not herein otherwise provided for, and which shall be established by Law: but the Congress may by Law vest the Appointment of such inferior Officers, as they think proper, in the President alone, in the Courts of Law, or in the Heads of Departments.

The President shall have the Power to fill up all Vacancies that may happen during the Recess of the Senate, by granting Commissions which shall expire at the End of their next Session.

Section 3. He shall from time to time give to the Congress Information of the State of the Union, and recommend to their Consideration such Measures as he shall judge necessary and expedient; he may, on extraordinary Occasions, convene both Houses, or either of them, and in Case of Disagreement between them, with Respect to the Time of Adjournment, he may adjourn them to such Time as he shall think proper; he shall receive Ambassadors and other public Ministers; he shall take Care that the Laws be faithfully executed, and shall Commission all the Officers of the United States.

Section 4. The President, Vice President, and all civil Officers of the United States, shall be removed from Office on Impeachment for, and Conviction of, Treason, Bribery, or other high Crimes and Misdemeanors.

Article III

Section 1. The judicial Power of the United States, shall be vested in one supreme Court, and in such inferior Courts as the Congress may from time to time ordain and establish. The Judges, both of the supreme and inferior Courts, shall hold their Offices during good Behaviour, and shall, at stated Times, receive for their Services, a Compensation, which shall not be diminished during their Continuance in Office.

Section 2.   The judicial Power shall extend to all Cases, in Law and Equity, arising under this Constitution, the Laws of the United States, and Treaties made, or which shall be made, under their Authority;—to all Cases affecting Ambassadors, other public Ministers and Consuls;—to all Cases of admiralty and maritime Jurisdiction;—to Controversies to which the United States shall be a Party;—to Controversies between two or more States;—between a State and Citizens of another State;—between Citizens of different States;—between Citizens of the same State claiming Lands under Grants of different States, and between a State, or the Citizens thereof, and foreign States, Citizens or Subjects.

In all Cases affecting Ambassadors, other public Ministers and Consuls, and those in which a State shall be Party, the supreme Court shall have original Jurisdiction. In all the other Cases before mentioned, the supreme Court shall have appellate Jurisdiction, both as to Law and Fact, with such Exceptions, and under such Regulations as the Congress shall make.

The Trial of all Crimes, except in Cases of Impeachment, shall be by Jury; and such Trial shall be held in the State where the said Crimes shall have been committed; but when not committed within any State, the Trial shall be at such Place or Places as the Congress may by Law have directed.

Section 3.   Treason against the United States, shall consist only in levying War against them, or in adhering to their Enemies, giving them Aid and Comfort. No Person shall be convicted of Treason unless on the Testimony of two Witnesses to the same overt Act, or on Confession in open Court.

The Congress shall have Power to declare the Punishment of Treason, but no Attainder of Treason shall work Corruption of Blood, or Forfeiture except during the Life of the Person attainted.

Article IV

Section 1.   Full Faith and Credit shall be given in each State to the public Acts, Records, and judicial Proceedings of every other State. And the Congress may by general Laws prescribe the Manner in which such Acts, Records and Proceedings shall be proved, and the Effect thereof.

Section 2.   The Citizens of each State shall be entitled to all Privileges and Immunities of Citizens in the several states.

A person charged in any State with Treason, Felony, or other Crime, who shall flee Justice, and be found in another State, shall on Demand of the executive Authority of the State from which he fled, be delivered up, to be removed to the state having Jurisdiction of the Crime.

No Person held to Service or Labour in one State, under the Laws thereof, escaping into another, shall, in Consequence of any Law or Regulation therein, be discharged from such Service or Labour, but shall be delivered up on Claim of the Party to whom such Service or Labour may be due.

Section 3.   New States may be admitted by the Congress into this Union; but no new State shall be formed or erected within the Jurisdiction of any other State, nor any State be formed by the Junction of two or more States, or Parts of States, without the Consent of the Legislatures of the States concerned, as well as of the Congress.

The Congress shall have Power to dispose of and make all needful Rules and Regulations respecting the Territory or other Property belonging to the United States; and nothing in this Constitution shall be so construed as to Prejudice any Claims of the United States, or of any particular State.

Section 4.   The United States shall guarantee to every State in this Union a Republican form of Government, and shall protect each of them against Invasion; and on Application of the Legislature, or of the Executive (when the Legislature cannot be convened) against domestic Violence.

Article V.   The Congress, whenever two thirds of both Houses shall deem it necessary, shall propose Amendments to this Constitution, or, on the Application of the Legislatures of two thirds of the several States, shall call a Convention for proposing Amendments, which, in either Case, shall be valid to all Intents and Purposes, as Part of this Constitution, when ratified by the Legislatures of three fourths of the several States, or by Conventions in three fourths thereof, as the one or the other Mode of Ratification may be proposed by the Congress; Provided that no Amendment which may be made prior to the Year One thousand eight hundred and eight shall in any Manner affect the first and fourth Clauses in the Ninth Section of the first Article; and that no State, without its Consent, shall be deprived of its equal Suffrage in the Senate.

Article VI.   All Debts contracted and Engagements entered into, before the Adoption of this Constitution, shall be as valid against the United States under this Constitution, as under the Confederation.

This Constitution, and the Laws of the United States which shall be made in Pursuance thereof; and all Treaties made, or which shall be made, under the Authority of the United States, shall be the supreme Law of the Land; and the Judges in every State shall be bound thereby, any Thing in the Constitution or Laws of any State to the Contrary notwithstanding.

The Senators and Representatives before mentioned, and the Members of the several State Legislatures, and all executive and judicial Officers, both of the United States and of the several States, shall be bound by Oath or Affirmation, to support this Constitution; but no religious Test shall ever be required as a Qualification to any Office or public Trust under the United States.

Article VII.   The Ratification of the Conventions of nine States, shall be sufficient for the Establishment of this Constitution between the States so ratifying the Same.

Amendment I [1791].   Congress shall make no law respecting an establishment of religion, or prohibiting the free exercise thereof; or abridging the freedom of speech, or of the press; or the right of the people peaceably to assemble, and to petition the Government for a redress of grievances.

Amendment II [1791].   A well regulated Militia, being necessary to the security for a free State, the right of the people to keep and bear Arms, shall not be infringed.

Amendment III [1791].   No Soldier shall, in time of peace be quartered in any house, without the consent of the Owner, nor in time of war, but in a manner to be prescribed by law.

Amendment IV [1791].   The right of the people to be secure in their persons, houses, papers, and effects, against unreasonable searches and seizures, shall not be violated, and no Warrants shall issue, but upon probable cause, supported by Oath or affirmation, and particularly describing the place to be searched, and the persons or things to be seized.

Amendment V [1791].   No person shall be held to answer for a capital, or otherwise infamous crime, unless on a presentment or indictment of a Grand Jury, except in cases arising in the land or naval forces, or in the Militia, when in actual service in time of War or public danger; nor shall any person be subject for the same offense to be twice put in jeopardy of life or limb; nor shall be compelled in any criminal case to be a witness against himself, nor be deprived of life, liberty, or property, without due process of law; nor shall private property be taken for public use without just compensation.

Amendment VI [1791].   In all criminal prosecutions, the accused shall enjoy the right to a speedy and public trial, by an impartial jury of the State and district wherein the crime shall have been committed, which district shall have been previously ascertained by law, and to be informed of the nature and cause of the accusation; to be confronted with the Witnesses against him; to have compulsory process for obtaining witnesses in his favor, and to have the Assistance of counsel for his defense.

Amendment VII [1791].   In suits at common law, where the value in controversy shall exceed twenty dollars, the right of trial by jury shall be preserved, and no fact tried by a jury, shall be otherwise re-examined in any Court of the United States, than according to the rules of the common law.

Amendment VIII [1791].   Excessive bail shall not be required, nor excessive fines imposed, nor cruel and unusual punishments inflicted.

Amendment IX [1791].   The enumeration in the Constitution, of certain rights, shall not be construed to deny or disparage others retained by the people.

Amendment X [1791].   The powers not delegated to the United States by the Constitution, nor prohibited by it to the States, are reserved to the States respectively, or to the people.

Amendment XI [1798].   The Judicial power of the United States shall not be construed to extend to any suit in law or equity, commenced or prosecuted against one of the United States by Citizens of another State, or by Citizens or Subjects of any Foreign State.

Amendment XII [1804].   The Electors shall meet in their respective states and vote by ballot for President and Vice-President, one of whom, at least, shall not be an inhabitant of the same state with themselves; they shall name in their ballots the person voted for as President, and in distinct ballots the person voted for as Vice-President, and they shall make distinct lists of all persons voted for as President, and of all persons voted for as Vice-President, and of the number of votes for each, which lists they shall sign and certify, and transmit sealed to the seat of the government of the United States, directed to the President of the Senate;—The President of the Senate shall, in the presence of the Senate and House of Representatives, open all the certificates and the votes shall then be counted;—The person having the greatest number of votes for President, shall be the President, if such number be a majority of the whole number of Electors appointed; and if no person have such majority, then from the persons having the highest numbers not exceeding three on the list of those voted for as President, the House of Representatives shall choose immediately, by ballot, the President. But in choosing the President, the votes shall be taken by states, the representation from each state having one vote; a quorum for this purpose shall consist of a member or members from two-thirds of the states, and a majority of all the states shall be necessary to a choice. And if the House of Representatives shall not choose a President whenever the right of choice shall devolve upon them, before the fourth day of March next following, then the Vice-President shall act as President. The person having the greatest number of votes as Vice-President, shall be the Vice-President, if such number be a majority of the whole number of electors appointed, and if no person have a majority, then from the two highest numbers on the list, the Senate shall choose the Vice-President; a quorum for the purpose shall consist of two-thirds of the whole number of Senators, and a majority of the whole number shall be necessary to a choice. But no person constitutionally ineligible to the office of President shall be eligible to that of the Vice-President of the United States.

Amendment XIII [1865]

Section 1.   Neither slavery nor involuntary servitude, except as a punishment for crime whereof the party shall have been duly convicted, shall exist within the United States, or any place subject to their jurisdiction.

Section 2.   Congress shall have power to enforce this article by appropriate legislation.

Amendment XIV [1868]

Section 1.   All persons born or naturalized in the United States, and subject to the jurisdiction thereof, are citizens of the United States and of the State wherein they reside. No State shall make or enforce any law which shall abridge the privileges or immunities of citizens of the United States; nor shall any State deprive any person of life, liberty, or property, without due process of law; nor deny to any person within its jurisdiction the equal protection of the laws.

Section 2.   Representatives shall be appointed among the several States according to their respective numbers, counting the whole number of persons in each State, excluding Indians not taxed. But when the right to vote at any election for the choice of electors for President and Vice President of the United States, Representatives in Congress, the executive and judicial officers of a State, or the members of the Legislature thereof, is denied to any of the male inhabitants of such State, being twenty-one years of age, and citizens of the United States, or in any way abridged, except for participation in rebellion, or other crime, the basis of representation therein shall be reduced in the proportion which the number of such male citizens shall bear to the whole number of male citizens twenty-one years of age in such State.

Section 3.   No person shall be a Senator or Representative in Congress, or elector of President and Vice President, or hold any office, civil or military, under the United States, or under any State, who, having previously taken an oath, as a member of Congress, or as an officer of the United States, or as a member of any State legislature, or as an executive or judicial officer of any State, to support the Constitution of the United States, shall have engaged in insurrection or rebellion against the same, or given aid or comfort to the enemies thereof. But Congress may by a vote of two-thirds of each House, remove such disability.

Section 4.   The validity of the public debt of the United States, authorized by law, including debts incurred for payment of pensions and bounties for services in suppressing insurrection or rebellion, shall not be questioned. But neither the United States nor any State shall assume or pay any debt or obligation incurred in aid of insurrection or rebellion against the United States, or any claim for the loss or emancipation of any slave; but all such debts, obligations and claims shall be held illegal and void.

Section 5.   The Congress shall have the power to enforce, by appropriate legislation, the provisions of this article.

Amendment XV [1870]

Section 1.   The right of citizens of the United States to vote shall not be denied or abridged by the United States or by any State on account of race, color, or previous condition of servitude.

Section 2.   The Congress shall have power to enforce this article by appropriate legislation.

Amendment XVI [1913].   The Congress
shall have power to lay and collect taxes on incomes, from whatever sources derived, without apportionment among the several States, and without regard to any census or enumeration.

Amendment XVII [1913]. The Senate of the United States shall be composed of two Senators from each State, elected by the people thereof, for six years; and each Senator shall have one vote. The electors in each State shall have the qualifications requisite for electors of the most numerous branch of the State legislatures.

When vacancies happen in the representation of any State in the Senate, the executive authority of such State shall issue writs of election to fill such vacancies: *Provided,* That the legislature of any State may empower the executive thereof to make temporary appointments until the people fill the vacancies by election as the legislature may direct.

This amendment shall not be so construed as to affect the election or term of any Senator chosen before it becomes valid as part of the Constitution.

Amendment XVIII [1919]

Section 1. After one year from the ratification of this article the manufacture, sale, or transportation of intoxicating liquors within, the importation thereof into, or the exportation thereof from the United States and all territory subject to the jurisdiction thereof for beverage purposes is hereby prohibited.

Section 2. The Congress and the several States shall have concurrent power to enforce this article by appropriate legislation.

Section 3. This article shall be inoperative unless it shall have been ratified as an amendment to the Constitution by the legislatures of the several States, as provided in the Constitution, within seven years from the date of the submission hereof to the States by the Congress.

Amendment XIX [1920].

The right of citizens of the United States to vote shall not be denied or abridged by the United States or by any State on account of sex.

Congress shall have power to enforce this article by appropriate legislation.

Amendment XX [1933]

Section 1. The terms of the President and the Vice President shall end at noon on the 20th day of January, and the terms of Senators and Representatives at noon on the 3rd day of January, of the years in which such terms would have ended if this article had not been ratified; and the terms of their successors shall then begin.

Section 2. The Congress shall assemble at least once in every year, and such meeting shall begin at noon on the 3rd day of January, unless they shall by law appoint a different day.

Section 3. If, at the time fixed for the beginning of the term of the President, the President elect shall have died, the Vice President elect shall become President. If a President shall not have been chosen before the time fixed for the beginning of his term, or if the President elect shall have failed to qualify, then the Vice President elect shall act as President until a President shall have qualified; and the Congress may by law provide for the case wherein neither a President elect nor a Vice President shall have qualified, declaring who shall then act as President, or the manner in which one who is to act shall be selected, and such person shall act accordingly until a President or Vice President shall have qualified.

Section 4. The Congress may by law provide for the case of the death of any of the persons from whom the House of Representatives may choose a President whenever the right of choice shall have devolved upon them, and for the case of the death of any of the persons from whom the Senate may choose a Vice President whenever the right of choice shall have devolved upon them.

Section 5. Sections 1 and 2 shall take effect on the 15th day of October following the ratification of this article.

Section 6. This article shall be inoperative unless it shall have been ratified as an amendment to the Constitution by the legislatures of three-fourths of the several States within seven years from the date of its submission.

Amendment XXI [1933]

Section 1. The eighteenth article of amendment to the Constitution of the United States is hereby repealed.

Section 2. The transportation or importation into any State, Territory, or possession of the United States for delivery or use therein of intoxicating liquors, in violation of the laws thereof, is hereby prohibited.

Section 3. This article shall be inoperative unless it shall have been ratified as an amendment to the Constitution by conventions in the several States, as provided in the Constitution, within seven years from the date of the submission hereof to the States by the Congress.

Amendment XXII [1951]

Section 1. No person shall be elected to the office of the President more than twice, and no person who has held the office of President, or acted as President, for more than two years of a term to which some other person was elected President shall be elected to the office of President more than once. But this Article shall not apply to any person holding the office of President when this Article was proposed by the Congress, and shall not prevent any person who may be holding the office of President, or acting as President, during the term within which this Article becomes operative from holding the office of President or acting as President during the remainder of such term.

Section 2. This article shall be inoperative unless it shall have been ratified as an amendment to the Constitution by the legislatures of three-fourths of the several States within seven years from the date of its submission to the States by the Congress.

Amendment XXIII [1961]

Section 1. The District constituting the seat of Government of the United States shall appoint in such manner as the Congress may direct:

A number of electors of President and Vice President equal to the whole number of Senators and Representatives in Congress to which the District would be entitled if it were a State, but in no event more than the least populous State; they shall be in addition to those appointed by the States, but they shall be considered, for the purposes of the election of President and Vice President, to be electors appointed by a State; and they shall meet in the District and perform such duties as provided by the twelfth article of amendment.

Section 2. The Congress shall have power to enforce this article by appropriate legislation.

Amendment XXIV [1964]

Section 1. The right of citizens of the United States to vote in any primary or other election for President or Vice President, for electors for President or Vice President, or for Senator or Representative in Congress, shall not be denied or abridged by the United States or any State by reason of failure to pay poll tax or any other tax.

Section 2. The Congress shall have power to enforce this article by appropriate legislation.

Amendment XXV [1967]

Section 1. In case of the removal of the President from office or of his death or resignation, the Vice President shall become President.

Section 2. Whenever there is a vacancy in the office of the Vice President, the President shall nominate a Vice President who shall take the office upon confirmation by a majority vote of both Houses of Congress.

Section 3. Whenever the President transmits to the President pro tempore of the Senate and the Speaker of the House of Representatives his written declaration that he is unable to discharge the powers and duties of his office, and until he transmits to them a written declaration to the contrary, such powers and duties shall be discharged by the Vice President as Acting President.

Section 4. Whenever the Vice President and a majority of either the principal officers of the executive departments or of such other body as Congress may by law provide, transmit to the President pro tempore of the Senate and the Speaker of the House of Representatives their written declaration that the President is unable to discharge the powers and duties of his office, the Vice President shall immediately assume the powers and duties of the office as Acting President.

Thereafter, when the President transmits to the President pro tempore of the Senate and the Speaker of the House of Representatives his written declaration that no inability exists, he shall resume the powers and duties of his office unless the Vice President and a majority of either the principal officers of the executive departments or of such other body as Congress may by law provide, transmit within four days to the President pro tempore of the Senate and the Speaker of the House of Representatives their written declaration that the President is unable to discharge the powers and duties of his office. Thereupon Congress shall decide the issue, assembling within forty-eight hours for that purpose if not in session. If the Congress, within twenty-one days after receipt of the latter written declaration, or, if Congress is not in session, within twenty-one days after Congress is required to assemble, determines by two-thirds vote of both houses that the President is unable to discharge the powers and duties of his office, the Vice President shall continue to discharge the same as Acting President; otherwise, the President shall resume the powers and duties of his office.

Amendment XXVI [1971]

Section 1. The right of citizens of the United States, who are eighteen years of age or older, to vote shall not be denied or abridged by the United States or any State on account of age.

Section 2. The Congress shall have power to enforce this article by appropriate legislation.

Amendment XXVII [1992]. No law, varying the compensation for the services of the Senators and Representatives shall take effect, until an election of Representatives shall have intervened.

appendix IV

Selected Sections of Article 2 of Uniform Commercial Code

§2-104. Definitions: "Merchant"; "Between Merchants"; "Financing Agency."

(1) "Merchant" means a person who deals in goods of the kind or otherwise by his occupation holds himself out as having knowledge or skill peculiar to the practices or goods involved in the transaction or to whom such knowledge or skill may be attributed by his employment of an agent or broker or other intermediary who by his occupation holds himself out as having such knowledge or skill.

(3) "Between Merchants" means in any transaction with respect to which both parties are chargeable with the knowledge or skill of merchants.

§2-201. Formal Requirements; Statute of Frauds.

(1) Except as otherwise provided in this section a contract for the sale of goods for the price of $500 or more is not enforceable by way of action or defense unless there is some writing sufficient to indicate that a contract for sale has been made between the parties and signed by the party against whom enforcement is sought or by his authorized agent or broker. A writing is not insufficient because it omits or incorrectly states a term agreed upon but the contract is not enforceable under this paragraph beyond the quantity of goods shown in such writing.

(2) Between merchants if within a reasonable time a writing in confirmation of the contract and sufficient against the sender is received and the party receiving it has reason to know its contents, it satisfies the requirements of subsection (1) against such party unless written notice of objection to its contents is given within 10 days after it is received.

(3) A contract which does not satisfy the requirements of subsection (1) but which is valid in other respects is enforceable

(a) if the goods are to be specially manufactured for the buyer and are not suitable for sale to others in the ordinary course of the seller's business and the seller, before notice of repudiation is received and under circumstances which reasonably indicate that the goods are for the buyer, has made either a substantial beginning of their manufacture or commitments for their procurement; or

(b) if the party against whom enforcement is sought admits in his pleading, testimony or otherwise in court that a contract for sale was made, but the contract is not enforceable under this provision beyond the quantity of goods admitted; or

(c) with respect to goods for which payment has been made and accepted or which have been received and accepted (Section. 2-606).

§2-205. Firm Offers.
An offer by a merchant to buy or sell goods in a signed writing which by its terms gives assurance that it will be held open is not revocable, for lack of consideration, during the time stated or if no time is stated for a reasonable time, but in no event may such period of irrevocability exceed three months; but any such term of assurance on a form supplied by the offeree must be separately signed by the offeror.

§2-206. Offer and Acceptance in Formation of Contract.

(1) Unless otherwise unambiguously indicated by the language or circumstances

(a) an offer to make a contract shall be construed as inviting acceptance in any manner and by any medium reasonable in the circumstances;

(b) an order or other offer to buy goods for prompt or current shipment shall be construed as inviting acceptance either by a prompt promise to ship or by the prompt or current shipment of conforming or non-conforming goods, but such a shipment of non-conforming goods does not constitute an acceptance if the seller seasonably notifies the buyer that the shipment is offered only as an accommodation to the buyer.

(2) Where the beginning of a requested performance is a reasonable mode of acceptance an offeror who is not notified of acceptance within a reasonable time may treat the offer as having lapsed before acceptance.

§2-207. *Additional Terms in Acceptance or Confirmation.*

(1) A definite and seasonable expression of acceptance or a written confirmation which is sent within a reasonable time operates as an acceptance even though it states terms additional to or different from those offered or agreed upon, unless acceptance is expressly made conditional on assent to the additional or different terms.

(2) The additional terms are to be construed as proposals for addition to the contract. Between merchants such terms become part of the contract unless:

(a) the offer expressly limits acceptance to the terms of the offer;

(b) they materially alter it; or

(c) notification of objection to them has already been given or is given within a reasonable time after notice of them is received.

(3) Conduct by both parties which recognizes the existence of a contract is sufficient to establish a contract for sale although the writings of the parties do not otherwise establish a contract. In such case the terms of the particular contract consist of those terms on which the writings of the parties agree, together with any supplementary terms incorporated under any other provisions of this Act.

§2-209. *Modification,   Rescission and Waiver.*

(1) An agreement modifying a contract within this Article needs no consideration to be binding.

(2) A signed agreement which excludes modification or rescission except by a signed writing cannot be otherwise modified or rescinded, but except as between merchants such a requirement on a form supplied by the merchant must be separately signed by the other party.

(3) The requirements of the statute of frauds section of this Article (Section 2-201) must be satisfied if the contract as modified is within its provisions.

(4) Although an attempt at modification or rescission does not satisfy the requirements of subsection (2) or (3) it can operate as a waiver.

(5) A party who has made a waiver affecting an executory portion of the contract may retract the waiver by reasonable notification received by the other party that strict performance will be required of any term waived, unless the retraction would be unjust in view of a material change of position in reliance on the waiver.

§2-210. *Delegation of Performance; Assignment of Rights.*

(1) A party may perform his duty through a delegate unless otherwise agreed or unless the other party has a substantial interest in having his original promisor perform or control the acts required by the contract. No delegation of performance relieves the party delegating of any duty to perform or any liability for breach.

(2) Unless otherwise agreed all rights of either seller or buyer can be assigned except where the assignment would materially change the duty of the other party, or increase materially the burden or risk imposed on him by his contract, or impair materially his chance of obtaining return performance. A right to damages for breach of the whole contract or a right arising out of the assignor's due performance of his entire obligation can be assigned despite agreement otherwise.

(3) Unless the circumstances indicate the contrary a prohibition of assignment of "the contract" is to be construed as barring only the delegation to the assignee of the assignor's performance.

(4) An assignment of "the contract" or of "all my rights under the contract" or an assignment in similar general terms is an assignment of rights and unless the language or the circumstances (as in an assignment for security) indicate the contrary, it is a delegation of performance of the duties of the assignor and its acceptance by the assignee constitutes a promise by him to perform those duties.

This promise is enforceable by either the assignor or the other party to the original contract.

(5) The other party may treat any assignment which delegates performance as creating reasonable grounds for insecurity and may without prejudice to his rights against the assignor demand assurances from the assignee (Section 2-609).

§2-301. *General   Obligations   of Parties.*   The obligation of the seller is to transfer and deliver and that of the buyer is to accept and pay in accordance with the contract.

§2-302. *Unconscionable   contract   or Clause.*

(1) If the court as a matter of law finds the contract or any clause of the contract to have been unconscionable at the time it was made the court may refuse to enforce the contract, or it may enforce the remainder of the contract without

the unconscionable clause, or it may so limit the application of any unconscionable clause as to avoid any unconscionable result.

(2) When it is claimed or appears to the court that the contract or any clause thereof may be unconscionable the parties shall be afforded a reasonable opportunity to present evidence as to its commercial setting, purpose and effect to aid the court in making the determination.

§2-305. *Open Price Term.*

(1) The parties if they so intend can conclude a contract for sale even though the price is not settled. In such a case the price is a reasonable price at the time for delivery if

(a) nothing is said as to price; or

(b) the price is left to be agreed by the parties and they fail to agree; or

(c) the price is to be fixed in terms of some agreed market or other standard as set or recorded by a third person or agency and it is not so set or recorded.

(2) A price to be fixed by the seller or by the buyer means a price for him to fix in good faith.

(3) When a price left to be fixed otherwise than by agreement of the parties fails to be fixed through fault of one party the other may at his option treat the contract as cancelled or himself fix a reasonable price.

(4) Where, however, the parties intend not to be bound unless the price be fixed or agreed and it is not fixed or agreed there is no contract. In such a case the buyer must return any goods already received or if unable so to do must pay their reasonable value at the time of delivery and the seller must return any portion of the price paid on account.

§2-306. *Output, Requirements and Exclusive Dealings.*

(1) A term which measures the quantity by the output of the seller or the requirements of the buyer means such actual output or requirements as may occur in good faith, except that no quantity unreasonably disproportionate to any stated estimate or in the absence of a stated estimate to any normal or otherwise comparable prior output or requirements may be tendered or demanded.

(2) A lawful agreement by either the seller or the buyer for exclusive dealing in the kind of goods concerned imposes unless otherwise agreed an obligation by the seller to use best efforts to supply the goods and by the buyer to use best efforts to promote their sale.

§2-307. *Delivery in Single Lot or Several Lots.* Unless otherwise agreed all goods called for by a contract for sale must be tendered in a single delivery and payment is due only on such tender but where the circumstances give either party the right to make or demand delivery in lots the price if it can be apportioned may be demanded for each lot.

§2-308. *Absence of Specified Place for Delivery.* Unless otherwise agreed

(a) the place for delivery of goods is the seller's place of business or if he has none his residence; but

(b) in a contract for sale of identified goods which to the knowledge of the parties at the time of contracting are in some other place, that place is the place for their delivery; and

(c) documents of title may be delivered through customary banking channels.

§2-310. *Open Time for Payment or Running of Credit; Authority to Ship Under Reservation.* Unless otherwise agreed

(a) payment is due at the time and place at which the buyer is to receive the goods even though the place of shipment is the place of delivery; and

(b) if the seller is authorized to send the goods he may ship them under reservation, and may tender the documents of title, but the buyer may inspect the goods after their arrival before payment is due unless such inspection is inconsistent with the terms of the contract (Section 2-513); and

(c) if delivery is authorized and made by way of documents of title otherwise than by subsection (b) then payment is due at the time and place at which the buyer is to receive the documents regardless of where the goods are to be received; and

(d) where the seller is required or authorized to ship the goods on credit the credit period runs from the time of shipment but post-dating the invoice or delaying its dispatch will correspondingly delay the starting of the credit period.

§2-503. *Manner of Seller's Tender of Delivery.*

(1) Tender of delivery requires that the seller put and hold conforming goods at the buyer's disposition and give the buyer any notification reasonably necessary to enable him to take delivery. The manner, time and place for

tender are determined by the agreement and this Article, and in particular

(a) tender must be at a reasonable hour, and if it is of goods they must be kept available for the period reasonably necessary to enable the buyer to take possession; but

(b) unless otherwise agreed the buyer must furnish facilities reasonably suited to the receipt of the goods.

(2) Where the case is within the next section respecting shipment tender requires that the seller comply with its provisions.

(3) Where the seller is required to deliver at a particular destination tender requires that he comply with subsection (1) and also in any appropriate case tender documents as described in subsections (4) and (5) of this section.

(4) Where goods are in the possession of a bailee and are to be delivered without being moved

(a) tender requires that the seller either tender a negotiable document of title covering such goods or procure acknowledgment by the bailee of the buyer's right to possession of the goods; but

(b) tender to the buyer of a non-negotiable document of title or of a written direction to the bailee to deliver is sufficient tender unless the buyer seasonably objects, and receipt by the bailee of notification of the buyer's rights fixes those rights as against the bailee and all third persons; but risk of loss of the goods and of any failure by the bailee to honor the non-negotiable document of title or to obey the direction remains on the seller until the buyer has had a reasonable time to present the document or direction, and a refusal by the bailee to honor the document or to obey the direction defeats the tender.

(5) Where the contract requires the seller to deliver documents

(a) he must tender all such documents in correct form, except as provided in this Article with respect to bills of lading in a set (subsection (2) of Section 2-323); and

(b) tender through customary banking channels is sufficient and dishonor of a draft accompanying the documents constitutes non-acceptance or rejection.

§2-504. *Shipment by Seller.*

Where the seller is required or authorized to send the goods to the buyer and the contract does not require him to deliver them at a particular destination, then unless otherwise agreed he must

(a) put the goods in the possession of such a carrier and make such a contract for their transportation

as may be reasonable having regard to the nature of the goods and other circumstances of the case; and

(b) obtain and promptly deliver or tender in due form any document necessary to enable the buyer to obtain possession of the goods or otherwise required by the agreement or by usage of trade; and

(c) promptly notify the buyer of the shipment.

Failure to notify the buyer under paragraph (c) or to make a proper contract under paragraph (a) is a ground for rejection only if material delay or loss ensues.

§2-507. *Effect of Seller's Tender; Delivery on Condition.*

(1) Tender of delivery is a condition to the buyer's duty to accept the goods and, unless otherwise agreed, to his duty to pay for them. Tender entitles the seller to acceptance of the goods and to payment according to the contract.

(2) Where payment is due and demanded on the delivery to the buyer of goods or documents of title, his right as against the seller to retain or dispose of them is conditional upon his making the payment due.

§2-509. *Risk of Loss in the Absence of Breach.*

(1) Where the contract requires or authorizes the seller to ship the goods by carrier

(a) if it does not require him to deliver them at a particular destination, the risk of loss passes to the buyer when the goods are duly delivered to the carrier even though the shipment is under reservation (Section 2-505); but

(b) if it does require him to deliver them at a particular destination and the goods are there duly tendered while in the possession of the carrier, the risk of loss passes to the buyer when the goods are there duly so tendered as to enable the buyer to take delivery.

(2) Where the goods are held by a bailee to be delivered without being moved, the risk of loss passes to the buyer

(a) on his receipt of a negotiable document of title covering the goods; or

(b) on acknowledgment by the bailee of the buyer's right to possession of the goods; or

(c) after his receipt of a non-negotiable document of title or other written direction to deliver, as provided in subsection (4)(b) of Section 2-503.

(3) In any case not within subsection (1) or (2), the risk of loss passes to the buyer on his receipt of the goods if the seller is a merchant; otherwise the risk passes to the buyer on tender of delivery.

(4) The provisions of this section are subject to contrary agreement of the parties and to the provisions of this Article on sale on approval (Section 2-327) and on effect of breach on risk of loss (Section 2-510).

§2-510. Effect of Breach on Risk of Loss.

(1) Where a tender or delivery of goods so fails to conform to the contract as to give a right of rejection the risk of their loss remains on the seller until cure or acceptance.

(2) Where the buyer rightfully revokes acceptance he may to the extent of any deficiency in his effective insurance coverage treat the risk of loss as having rested on the seller from the beginning.

(3) Where the buyer as to conforming goods already identified to the contract for sale repudiates or is otherwise in breach before risk of their loss has passed to him, the seller may to the extent of any deficiency in his effective insurance coverage treat the risk of loss as resting on the buyer for a commercially reasonable time.

§2-511. Tender of Payment by Buyer; Payment by Check.

(1) Unless otherwise agreed tender of payment is a condition to the seller's duty to tender and complete any delivery.

(2) Tender of payment is sufficient when made by any means or in any manner current in the ordinary course of business unless the seller demands payment in legal tender and gives any extension of time reasonably necessary to procure it.

(3) Subject to the provisions of this Act on the effect of an instrument on an obligation (Section 3-802), payment by check is conditional and is defeated as between the parties by dishonor of the check on due presentment.

§2-615. Excuse by Failure of Presupposed Conditions. Except so far as a seller may have assumed a greater obligation and subject to the preceding section on substituted performance:

(a) Delay in delivery or non-delivery in whole or in part by a seller who complies with paragraphs (b) and (c) is not a breach of his duty under a contract for sale if performance as agreed has been made impracticable by the occurrence of a contingency the non-occurrence of which was a basic assumption on which the contract was made or by compliance in good faith with any applicable foreign or domestic governmental regulation or order whether or not it later proves to be invalid.

(b) Where the causes mentioned in paragraph (a) affect only a part of the seller's capacity to perform, he must allocate production and deliveries among his customers but may at his option include regular customers not then under contract as well as his own requirements for further manufacture. He may so allocate in any manner which is fair and reasonable.

(c) The seller must notify the buyer seasonably that there will be delay or non-delivery and, when allocation is required under paragraph (b), of the estimated quota thus made available for the buyer.

§2-703. Seller's Remedies in General.
Where the buyer wrongfully rejects or revokes acceptance of goods or fails to make a payment due on or before delivery or repudiates with respect to a part or the whole, then with respect to any goods directly affected and; if the breach is of the whole contract (Section 2-612), then also with respect to the whole undelivered balance, the aggrieved seller may

(a) withhold delivery of such goods;

(b) stop delivery by any bailee as hereafter provided (Section 2-705);

(c) proceed under the next section respecting goods still unidentified to the contract;

(d) resell and recover damages as hereafter provided (Section 2-706);

(e) recover damages for non-acceptance (Section 2-708) or in a proper case the price (Section 2-709);

(f) cancel.

§2-711. Buyer's Remedies in General; Buyer's Security Interest in Rejected Goods.

(1) Where the seller fails to make delivery or repudiates or the buyer rightfully rejects or justifiably revokes acceptance then with respect to any goods involved, and with respect to the whole if the breach goes to the whole contract (Section 2-612), the buyer may cancel and whether or not he has done so may in addition to recovering so much of the price as has been paid

(a) "cover" and have damages under the next section as to all the goods affected whether or not they have been identified to the contract; or

(b) recover damages for non-delivery as provided in this Article (Section 2-713).

(2) Where the seller fails to deliver or repudiates the buyer may also

(a) if the goods have been identified recover them as provided in this Article (Section 2-502); or

(b) in a proper case obtain specific performance or replevy the goods as provided in this Article (Section 2-716).

(3) On rightful rejection or justifiable revocation of acceptance a buyer has a security interest in goods in his possession or control for any payments made on their price and any expenses reasonably incurred in their inspection, receipt, transportation, care and custody and may hold such goods and resell them in like manner as an aggrieved seller (Section 2-706).

§2-725. *Statute of Limitations in Contracts for Sale.*

(1) An action for breach of any contract for sale must be commenced within four years after the cause of action has accrued. By the original agreement the parties may reduce the period of limitation to not less than one year but may not extend it.

(2) A cause of action accrues when the breach occurs, regardless of the aggrieved party's lack of knowledge of the breach. A breach of warranty occurs when tender of delivery is made, except that where a warranty explicitly extends to future performance of the goods and discovery of the breach must await the time of such performance the cause of action accrues when the breach is or should have been discovered.

(3) Where an action commenced within the time limited by subsection (1) is so terminated as to leave available a remedy by another action for the same breach such other action may be commenced after the expiration of the time limited and within six months after the termination of the first action unless the termination resulted from voluntary discontinuance or from dismissal for failure or neglect to prosecute.

(4) This section does not alter the law on tolling of the statute of limitations nor does it apply to causes of action which have accrued before this Act becomes effective.

Selected Sections of the Sarbanes-Oxley Act of 2002

TITLE I—PUBLIC COMPANY ACCOUNTING OVERSIGHT BOARD

Sec. 101. Establishment; Administrative Provisions.

(a) Establishment of Board.—There is established the Public Company Accounting Oversight Board, to oversee the audit of public companies that are subject to the securities laws, and related matters, in order to protect the interests of investors and further the public interest in the preparation of informative, accurate, and independent audit reports for companies the securities of which are sold to, and held by and for, public investors. The Board shall be a body corporate, operate as a nonprofit corporation, and have succession until dissolved by an Act of Congress.

(c) Duties of the Board.—The Board shall, subject to action by the Commission under section 107, and once a determination is made by the Commission under subsection (d) of this section—

(1) register public accounting firms that prepare audit reports for issuers, in accordance with section 102;

(2) establish or adopt, or both, by rule, auditing, quality control, ethics, independence, and other standards relating to the preparation of audit reports for issuers, in accordance with section 103;

(3) conduct inspections of registered public accounting firms, in accordance with section 104 and the rules of the Board;

(4) conduct investigations and disciplinary proceedings concerning and impose appropriate sanctions where justified upon, registered public accounting firms and associated persons of such firms, in accordance with section 105;

(5) perform such other duties or functions as the Board (or the Commission, by rule or order) determines are necessary or appropriate to promote high professional standards among, and improve the quality of audit services offered by, registered public accounting firms and associated persons thereof, or otherwise to carry out this Act, in order to protect investors, or to further the public interest;

(6) enforce compliance with this Act, the rules of the Board, professional standards, and the securities laws relating to the preparation and issuance of audit reports and the obligations and liabilities of accountants with respect thereto, by registered public accounting firms and associated persons thereof; and

(7) set the budget and manage the operations of the Board and the staff of the Board.

(h) Annual Report to the Commission.—The Board shall submit an annual report (including its audited financial statements) to the Commission, and the Commission shall transmit a copy of that report to the Committee on Banking, Housing, and Urban Affairs of the Senate, and the Committee on Financial Services of the House of Representatives, not later than 30 days after the date of receipt of that report by the Commission.

Sec. 107. Commission Oversight of The Board.

(a) General Oversight Responsibility.—The Commission shall have oversight and enforcement authority over the Board, as provided in this Act. . . .

TITLE II—AUDITOR INDEPENDENCE

Sec. 203. Audit Partner Rotation.

(j) Audit Partner Rotation.—It shall be unlawful for a registered public accounting firm to provide audit services to an issuer if the lead (or coordinating) audit partner (having primary responsibility for the audit), or the audit partner responsible for reviewing the audit, has performed audit services for that issuer in each of the 5 previous fiscal years of that issuer.

Sec. 204. Auditor Reports to Audit Committees.

(k) Reports to Audit Committees.—Each registered public accounting firm that performs for any issuer any audit required by this title shall timely report to the audit committee of the issuer—

(1) all critical accounting policies and practices to be used;

(2) all alternative treatments of financial information within generally accepted accounting principles that have been discussed with management officials of the

issuer, ramifications of the use of such alternative disclosures and treatments, and the treatment preferred by the registered public accounting firm; and

(3) other material written communications between the registered public accounting firm and the management of the issuer, such as any management letter or schedule of unadjusted differences.

TITLE III—CORPORATE RESPONSIBILITY

Sec. 302. Corporate Responsibility for Financial Reports.

(a) Regulations Required.—The Commission shall, by rule, require, for each company filing periodic reports under section 13(a) or 15(d) of the Securities Exchange Act of 1934, that the principal executive officer or officers and the principal financial officer or officers, or persons performing similar functions, certify in each annual or quarterly report filed or submitted under either such section of such Act that—

(1) the signing officer has reviewed the report;

(2) based on the officer's knowledge, the report does not contain any untrue statement of a material fact or omit to state a material fact necessary in order to make the statements made, in light of the circumstances under which such statements were made, not misleading;

(3) based on such officer's knowledge, the financial statements, and other financial information included in the report, fairly present in all material respects the financial condition and results of operations of the issuer as of, and for, the periods presented in the report;

(4) the signing officers—

(A) are responsible for establishing and maintaining internal controls;

(B) have designed such internal controls to ensure that material information relating to the issuer and its consolidated subsidiaries is made known to such officers by others within those entities, particularly during the period in which the periodic reports are being prepared;

(C) have evaluated the effectiveness of the issuer's internal controls as of a date within 90 days prior to the report; and

(D) have presented in the report their conclusions about the effectiveness of their internal controls based on their evaluation as of that date;

(5) the signing officers have disclosed to the issuer's auditors and the audit committee of the board of directors (or persons fulfilling the equivalent function)—

(A) all significant deficiencies in the design or operation of internal controls which could adversely affect the issuer's ability to record, process, summarize, and report financial data and have identified for the issuer's auditors any material weaknesses in internal controls; and

(B) any fraud, whether or not material, that involves management or other employees who have a significant role in the issuer's internal controls; and

(6) the signing officers have indicated in the report whether or not there were significant changes in internal controls or in other factors that could significantly affect internal controls subsequent to the date of their evaluation, including any corrective actions with regard to significant deficiencies and material weaknesses.

(b) Foreign Reincorporations Have No Effect.—Nothing in this section 302 shall be interpreted or applied in any way to allow any issuer to lessen the legal force of the statement required under this section 302, by an issuer having reincorporated or having engaged in any other transaction that resulted in the transfer of the corporate domicile or offices of the issuer from inside the United States to outside of the United States.

(c) Deadline.—The rules required by subsection (a) shall be effective not later than 30 days after the date of enactment of this Act.

Sec. 303. Improper Influence on Conduct of Audits.

(a) Rules To Prohibit.—It shall be unlawful, in contravention of such rules or regulations as the Commission shall prescribe as necessary and appropriate in the public interest or for the protection of investors, for any officer or director of an issuer, or any other person acting under the direction thereof, to take any action to fraudulently influence, coerce, manipulate, or mislead any independent public or certified accountant engaged in the performance of an audit of the financial statements of that issuer for the purpose of rendering such financial statements materially misleading.

Sec. 304. Forfeiture of Certain Bonuses and Profits.

(a) Additional Compensation Prior to Noncompliance With Commission Financial Reporting Requirements.—If an issuer is required to prepare an accounting restatement due to the material noncompliance of the issuer, as a result of misconduct, with

any financial reporting requirement under the securities laws, the chief executive officer and chief financial officer of the issuer shall reimburse the issuer for—

(1) any bonus or other incentive-based or equity-based compensation received by that person from the issuer during the 12-month period following the first public issuance or filing with the Commission (whichever first occurs) of the financial document embodying such financial reporting requirement; and (2) any profits realized from the sale of securities of the issuer during that 12-month period.

Sec. 306. Insider Trades During Pension Fund Blackout Periods.

(a) Prohibition of Insider Trading During Pension Fund Blackout Periods.—

(1) IN GENERAL.—Except to the extent otherwise provided by rule of the Commission pursuant to paragraph (3), it shall be unlawful for any director or executive officer of an issuer of any equity security (other than an exempted security), directly or indirectly, to purchase, sell, or otherwise acquire or transfer any equity security of the issuer (other than an exempted security) during any blackout period with respect to such equity security if such director or officer acquires such equity security in connection with his or her service or employment as a director or executive officer.

(2) REMEDY.—

(A) IN GENERAL.—Any profit realized by a director or executive officer referred to in paragraph (1) from any purchase, sale, or other acquisition or transfer in violation of this subsection shall inure to and be recoverable by the issuer, irrespective of any intention on the part of such director or executive officer in entering into the transaction.

(B) ACTIONS TO RECOVER PROFITS.—An action to recover profits in accordance with this subsection may be instituted at law or in equity in any court of competent jurisdiction by the issuer, or by the owner of any security of the issuer in the name and in behalf of the issuer if the issuer fails or refuses to bring such action within 60 days after the date of request, or fails diligently to prosecute the action thereafter, except that no such suit shall be brought more than 2 years after the date on which such profit was realized.

(3) CIVIL PENALTIES FOR FAILURE TO PROVIDE NOTICE.—
(7) The Secretary may assess a civil penalty against a plan administrator of up to $100 a day from the date of the plan administrator's failure or refusal to provide notice to participants and beneficiaries in accordance

with section 101(i). For purposes of this paragraph, each violation with respect to any single participant or beneficiary shall be treated as a separate violation.

TITLE IV—ENHANCED FINANCIAL DISCLOSURES

Sec. 404. Management Assessment of Internal Controls.

(a) Rules Required.—The Commission shall prescribe rules requiring each annual report required by section 13(a) or 15(d) of the Securities Exchange Act of 1934 to contain an internal control report, which shall—

(1) state the responsibility of management for establishing and maintaining an adequate internal control structure and procedures for financial reporting; and
(2) contain an assessment, as of the end of the most recent fiscal year of the issuer, of the effectiveness of the internal control structure and procedures of the issuer for financial reporting.

(b) Internal Control Evaluation and Reporting. —With respect to the internal control assessment required by subsection (a), each registered public accounting firm that prepares or issues the audit report for the issuer shall attest to, and report on, the assessment made by the management of the issuer. An attestation made under this subsection shall be made in accordance with standards for attestation engagements issued or adopted by the Board. Any such attestation shall not be the subject of a separate engagement.

Sec. 407. Disclosure of Audit Committee Financial Expert.

(a) Rules Defining "Financial Expert".—The Commission shall issue rules, as necessary or appropriate in the public interest and consistent with the protection of investors, to require each issuer, together with periodic reports required pursuant to sections 13(a) and 15(d) of the Securities Exchange Act of 1934, to disclose whether or not, and if not, the reasons therefor, the audit committee of that issuer is composed of at least 1 member who is a financial expert, as such term is defined by the Commission.

(b) Considerations.—In defining the term "financial expert" for purposes of subsection (a), the Commission shall consider whether a person has, through education and experience as a public accountant or auditor or a principal financial officer, comptroller, or

principal accounting officer of an issuer, or from a position involving the performance of similar functions—

(1) an understanding of generally accepted accounting principles and financial statements;

(2) experience in—

(A) the preparation or auditing of financial statements of generally comparable issuers; and

(B) the application of such principles in connection with the accounting for estimates, accruals, and reserves;

(3) experience with internal accounting controls; and

(4) an understanding of audit committee functions.

TITLE VIII—CORPORATE AND CRIMINAL FRAUD ACCOUNTABILITY

Sec. 801. Short Title. This title may be cited as the "Corporate and Criminal Fraud Accountability Act of 2002."

Sec. 804. Statute of Limitations for Securities Fraud. . . . [A] private right of action that involves a claim of fraud, deceit, manipulation, or contrivance in contravention of a regulatory requirement concerning the securities laws . . . may be brought not later than the earlier of—

(1) 2 years after the discovery of the facts constituting the violation; or

(2) 5 years after such violation.

Sec. 806. Protection for Employees of Publicly Traded Companies Who Provide Evidence of Fraud.

(a) Whistleblower Protection for Employees of Publicly Traded Companies.—No company with a class of securities registered under section 12 of the Securities Exchange Act of 1934 or that is required to file reports under . . . the Securities Exchange Act of 1934 or any officer, employee, contractor, subcontractor, or agent of such company, may discharge, demote, suspend, threaten, harass, or in any other manner discriminate against an employee in the terms and conditions of employment because of any lawful act done by the employee—

(1) to provide information, cause information to be provided, or otherwise assist in an investigation regarding any conduct which the employee reasonably believes constitutes a violation of . . . any rule or regulation of the Securities and Exchange Commission, or

any provision of Federal law relating to fraud against shareholders, when the information or assistance is provided to or the investigation is conducted by—

(A) a Federal regulatory or law enforcement agency;

(B) any Member of Congress or any committee of Congress; or

(C) a person with supervisory authority over the employee (or such other person working for the employer who has the authority to investigate, discover, or terminate misconduct); or

(2) to file, cause to be filed, testify, participate in, or otherwise assist in a proceeding filed or about to be filed (with any knowledge of the employer) relating to an alleged violation of . . . any rule or regulation of the Securities and Exchange Commission, or any provision of Federal law relating to fraud against shareholders.

Sec. 807. Criminal Penalties for Defrauding Shareholders of Publicly Traded Companies.

(a) In General—Chapter 63 of title 18, United States Code, is amended by adding at the end the following:

"§1348. Securities fraud

"Whoever knowingly executes, or attempts to execute. a scheme or artifice—

"(1) to defraud any person in connection with any security of an issuer with a class of securities registered under section 12 of the Securities Exchange Act of 1934 or that is required to file reports under section 15(d) of the Securities Exchange Act of 1934; or

"(2) to obtain, by means of false or fraudulent pretenses, representations, or promises, any money or property in connection with the purchase or sale of any security of an issuer with a class of securities registered under section 12 of the Securities Exchange Act of 1934 or that is required to file reports under section 15(d) of the Securities Exchange Act of 1934 shall be fined under this title, or imprisoned not more than 25 years, or both."

TITLE IX—WHITE-COLLAR CRIME PENALTY ENHANCEMENTS

Sec. 903. Criminal Penalties for Mail and Wire Fraud.

(a) Mail Fraud.—Section 1341 of title 18, United States Code, is amended by striking "five" and inserting "20."

(b) Wire Fraud.—Section 1343 of title 18, United States Code, is amended by striking "five" and inserting "20."

TITLE XI—CORPORATE FRAUD ACCOUNTABILITY

Sec. 1106. Increased Criminal Penalties Under Securities Exchange Act of 1934.
Section 32(a) of the Securities Exchange Act of 1934 is amended—

(1) by striking "$1,000,000, or imprisoned not more than 10 years" and inserting "$5,000,000, or imprisoned not more than 20 years"; and

(2) by striking "$2,500,000" and inserting "$25,000,000."

Sec. 1107. Retaliation Against Informants.

(a) In General.—Section 1513 of title 18, United States Code, is amended by adding at the end the following:

"(e) Whoever knowingly, with the intent to retaliate, takes any action harmful to any person, including interference with the lawful employment or livelihood of any person, for providing to a law enforcement officer any truthful information relating to the commission or possible commission of any Federal offense, shall be fined under this title or imprisoned not more than 10 years, or both."

Selected Sections of Securities Act of 1933

Section 6—Registration of Securities and Signing of Registration Statement

a. Any security may be registered with the Commission under the terms and conditions hereinafter provided, by filing a registration statement in triplicate, at least one of which shall be signed by each issuer, its principal executive officer or officers, its principal financial officer, its comptroller or principal accounting officer, and the majority of its board of directors or persons performing similar functions (or, if there is no board of directors or persons performing similar functions, by the majority of the persons or board having the power of management of the issuer) . . .

Section 11—Civil Liabilities on Account of False Registration Statement

a. In case any part of the registration statement, when such part became effective, contained an untrue statement of a material fact or omitted to state a material fact required to be stated therein or necessary to make the statements therein not misleading, any person acquiring such security (unless it is proved that at the time of such acquisition he knew of such untruth or omission) may, either at law or in equity, in any court of competent jurisdiction, sue—

1. every person who signed the registration statement;
2. every person who was a director of (or person performing similar functions) or partner in the issuer at the time of the filing of the part of the registration statement with respect to which his liability is asserted;
3. every person who, with his consent, is named in the registration statement as being or about to become a director, person performing similar functions, or partner;
4. every accountant, engineer, or appraiser, or any person whose profession gives authority to a statement made by him, who has with his consent been named as having prepared or certified any part of the registration statement, or as having prepared or certified any report or valuation which is used in connection with the registration statement, with respect to the statement in such registration statement, report, or valuation, which purports to have been prepared or certified by him;
5. every underwriter with respect to such security.

Section 12—Civil Liabilities Arising in Connection with Prospectuses and Communications

a. **In General.** Any person who—

1. offers or sells a security in violation of section 5, or
2. offers or sells a security . . . by the use of any means or instruments of transportation or communication in interstate commerce or of the mails, by means of a prospectus or oral communication, which includes an untrue statement of a material fact or omits to state a material fact necessary in order to make the statements, in the light of the circumstances under which they were made, not misleading (the purchaser not knowing of such untruth or omission), and who shall not sustain the burden of proof that he did not know, and in the exercise of reasonable care could not have known, of such untruth or omission, shall be liable, subject to subsection (b), to the person purchasing such security from him, who may sue either at law or in equity in any court of competent jurisdiction, to recover the consideration paid for such security with interest thereon, less the amount of any income received thereon, upon the tender of such security, or for damages if he no longer owns the security.

b. **Loss Causation.** In an action described in subsection (a)(2), if the person who offered or sold such security proves that any portion or all of the amount recoverable under subsection (a)(2) represents other than the depreciation in value of the subject security resulting from such part of the prospectus or oral communication, with respect to which the liability of that person is asserted, not being true or omitting to state a material fact required to be stated therein or necessary to make the statement not misleading, then such portion or amount, as the case may be, shall not be recoverable.

Section 17—Fraudulent Interstate Transactions

a. It shall be unlawful for any person in the offer or sale of any securities by the use of any means or instruments of transportation or communication in interstate commerce or by the use of the mails, directly or indirectly—

1. to employ any device, scheme, or artifice to defraud, or

2. to obtain money or property by means of any untrue statement of a material fact or any omission to state a material fact necessary in order to make the statements made, in the light of the circumstances under which they were made, not misleading, or

3. to engage in any transaction, practice, or course of business which operates or would operate as a fraud or deceit upon the purchaser.

b. It shall be unlawful for any person, by the use of any means or instruments of transportation or communication in interstate commerce or by the use of the mails, to publish, give publicity to, or circulate any notice, circular, advertisement, newspaper, article, letter, investment service, or communication which, though not purporting to offer a security for sale, describes such security for a consideration received or to be received, directly or indirectly, from an issuer, underwriter, or dealer, without fully disclosing the receipt, whether past or prospective, of such consideration and the amount thereof.

Section 24—Penalties

Any person who willfully violates any of the provisions of this title, or the rules and regulations promulgated by the Commission under authority thereof, or any person who willfully, in a registration statement filed under this title, makes any untrue statement of a material fact or omits to state any material fact required to be stated therein or necessary to make the statements therein not misleading, shall upon conviction be fined not more than $10,000 or imprisoned not more than five years, or both.

Selected Sections of Securities Exchange Act of 1934

Section 4—Securities and Exchange Commission

1. There is hereby established a Securities and Exchange Commission (hereinafter referred to as the "Commission") to be composed of five commissioners to be appointed by the President by and with the advice and consent of the Senate. Not more than three of such commissioners shall be members of the same political party, and in making appointments members of different political parties shall be appointed alternately as nearly as may be practicable. No commissioner shall engage in any other business, vocation, or employment than that of serving as commissioner, nor shall any commissioner participate, directly or indirectly, in any stock-market operations or transactions of a character subject to regulation by the Commission pursuant to this title. Each commissioner shall hold office for a term of five years and until his successor is appointed and has qualified . . .

Section 10—Regulation of the Use of Manipulative and Deceptive Devices

It shall be unlawful for any person, directly or indirectly, by the use of any means or instrumentality of interstate commerce or of the mails, or of any facility of any national securities exchange—

b. To use or employ, in connection with the purchase or sale of any security registered on a national securities exchange or any security not so registered, any manipulative or deceptive device or any securities-based swap agreement . . ., or contrivance in contravention of such rules and regulations as the Commission may prescribe as necessary or appropriate in the public interest or for the protection of investors.

Section 16—Directors, Officers, and Principal Stockholders

a. DISCLOSURES REQUIRED.—

(1) *Directors, officers, and principal stockholders required to file.*—Every person who is directly or indirectly the beneficial owner of more than 10 percent of any class of any equity security (other than an exempted security) which is registered pursuant to section 12, or who is a director or an officer of the issuer of such security, shall file the statements required by this subsection with the Commission (and, if such security is registered on a national securities exchange, also with the exchange).

(2) TIME OF FILING.—The statements required by this subsection shall be filed—

(A) at the time of the registration of such security on a national securities exchange or by the effective date of a registration statement filed pursuant to section 12(g);

(B) within 10 days after he or she becomes such beneficial owner, director, or officer;

(C) if there has been a change in such ownership, or if such person shall have purchased or sold a security- based swap agreement . . . involving such equity security, before the end of the second business day following the day on which the subject transaction has been executed, or at such other time as the Commission shall establish, by rule, in any case in which the Commission determines that such 2-day period is not feasible.

(3) CONTENTS OF STATEMENTS.—A statement filed—

(A) under subparagraph (A) or (B) of paragraph (2) shall contain a statement of the amount of all equity securities of such issuer of which the filing person is the beneficial owner; and

(B) under subparagraph (C) of such paragraph shall indicate ownership by the filing person at the date of filing, any such changes in such ownership, and such purchases and sales of the security-based swap agreements as have occurred since the most recent such filing under such subparagraph.

(4) ELECTRONIC FILING AND AVAILABILITY. — Beginning not later than 1 year after the date of enactment of the Sarbanes-Oxley Act of 2002—

(A) a statement filed under subparagraph (C) of paragraph (2) shall be filed electronically;

(B) the Commission shall provide each such statement on a publicly accessible Internet site not later than the end of the business day following that filing; and

(C) the issuer (if the issuer maintains a corporate website) shall provide that statement on that corporate website, not later than the end of the business day following that filing.

Section 18—Liability for Misleading Statements

a. Any person who shall make or cause to be made any statement in any application, report, or document filed pursuant to this title or any rule or regulation thereunder or any undertaking contained in a registration statement . . ., which statement was at the time and in the light of the circumstances under which it was made false or misleading with respect to any material fact, shall be liable to any person (not knowing that such statement was false or misleading) who, in reliance upon such statement, shall have purchased or sold a security at a price which was affected by such statement, for damages caused by such reliance, unless the person sued shall prove that he acted in good faith and had no knowledge that such statement was false or misleading. A person seeking to enforce such liability may sue at law or in equity in any court of competent jurisdiction. In any such suit the court may, in its discretion, require an undertaking for the payment of the costs of such suit, and assess reasonable costs, including reasonable attorneys' fees, against either party litigant.

b. Every person who becomes liable to make payment under this section may recover contribution as in cases of contract from any person who, if joined in the original suit, would have been liable to make the same payment.

c. No action shall be maintained to enforce any liability created under this section unless brought within one year after the discovery of the facts constituting the cause of action and within three years after such cause of action accrued.

Section 32—Penalties

a. Any person who willfully violates any provision of this chapter . . . or any rule or regulation thereunder the violation of which is made unlawful or the observance of which is required under the terms of this chapter, or any person who willfully and knowingly makes, or causes to be made, any statement in any application, report, or document required to be filed under this chapter or any rule or regulation thereunder or any undertaking contained in a registration statement . . . or by any self-regulatory organization in connection with an application for membership or participation therein or to become associated with a member thereof, which statement was false or misleading with respect to any material fact, shall upon conviction be fined not more than $5,000,000, or imprisoned not more than 20 years, or both, except that when such person is a person other than a natural person, a fine not exceeding $25,000,000 may be imposed; but no person shall be subject to imprisonment under this section for the violation of any rule or regulation if he proves that he had no knowledge of such rule or regulation.

glossary

A fortiori   Even more clearly; said of a conclusion that follows with even greater logical necessity from another that is already included in the argument.

Abatement   Decrease, reduction, or diminution.

Acceptance   The contractual communication of agreeing to another's offer. The acceptance of an offer creates a *contract.*

Accession   Property acquired by adding something to an owned object.

Accessory   A term used at the state level that is similar to "aiding and abetting." Accessory to a crime generally is either before the criminal act or after it.

Accord and satisfaction   Payment of money, or other thing of value, usually less than the amount demanded, in exchange for cancellation of a debt that is uncertain in amount.

Act   Legislation proposed by a legislative body such as the U.S. Congress. When enacted, it has a meaning identical to "law," or "statute."

Actual authority   The authority a principal expressly or implicitly gives to an agent in an agency relationship. This authority may be written, spoken, or derived from the circumstances of the relationship.

Ad infinitum   Without limit; endlessly.

Ad substantiation program   A program of the Federal Trade Commission under which the FTC demands that an advertiser substantiate any claims made in advertising. Even if the claims are not provably untrue, they are considered deceptive if they cannot be substantiated.

Ad valorem   According to value.

Adverse possession   Property ownership acquired through open, notorious, actual, exclusive, continuous, and wrongful possession of land for a statutorily prescribed period of time.

Adjudication   The judicial determination of a legal proceeding.

Adjustment   Under the Bankruptcy Act the procedure followed when a debtor's debts are partly reduced and partly rearranged for repayment.

Administrative agency   An organization, usually a part of the executive branch of government, that is created to serve a specific purpose as authorized by the legislative branch. An agency's function usually is characterized as quasi-legislative or quasi-judicial.

Administrative law   The legal principles involved in the workings of administrative agencies within the regulatory process.

Administrative law judge   The individual employed by an administrative agency who is in charge of hearing the initial presentations in a quasi-judicial case.

ADRs   An abbreviation for alternative dispute resolution systems that may be used in lieu of litigation.

Advisory opinion   A formal opinion by a judge, court, regulatory agency, or law officer upon a question of law.

Affidavit   A sworn written statement made before an officer authorized by law to administer oaths.

Affirmative action   Positive steps taken in order to alleviate conditions resulting from past discrimination or from violations of a law.

Affirmative action program   A program designed to promote actively the position of minority workers with regard to hiring and advancement.

Affirmative defenses   Defenses that must be raised and proved by the defendant.

Agent   The person who on behalf of a principal deals with a third party.

Agreement on Trade-Related Aspects of Intellectual Property Rights (TRIPS)   The WTO agreement that discusses the applicability of GATT principles and intellectual property agreements in the international sphere.

Aiding and abetting   A criminal action that arises from association with and from assistance rendered to a person guilty of another criminal act.

Alien corporation   A corporation created under the authority of a foreign country.

Alien Tort Claims Statute (ATCS)   The federal law that grants jurisdiction to U.S. federal district courts over any civil action by an alien for a tort only, committed in violation of the law of nations or a treaty of the United States.

Alter-ego theory   One method used by courts to pierce the corporate veil when a shareholder fails to treat the corporate organization as a separate legal entity.

Amicus curiae   A friend of the court who participates in litigation though not a party to the lawsuit.

Annual percentage rate (APR)   A rate of interest that commercial lenders charge persons who borrow money. This rate is calculated in a standardized fashion required by the Truth-in-Lending Act.

Annuity   A contract by which the insured pays a lump sum to the insurer and later receives fixed annual payments.

Answer   The responsive pleading filed by a defendant.

Apparent authority   The authority that a third party in an agency relationship perceives to exist between the principal and the agent. In fact, no actual authority does exist. Sometimes also called *ostensible authority.*

Appeal   The right of the litigation parties to have the legal decisions of the trial judge reviewed by an appellate court.

Appellant   The party seeking review of a lower court decision.

Appellate court   A court that decides whether a trial judge has made a mistake of law.

Appellee   The party responding to an appeal; the winner in the trial court.

Arbitration   Submission of a dispute to an extrajudicial authority for decision.

Arbitrator   The individual or panel members authorized by disputing parties to resolve a dispute through the arbitration process.

Arguendo   For the sake of argument.

Articles of incorporation   The legal document that forms the application for a state charter of incorporation.

Articles of organization   The document used to create a limited liability company. Its purpose corresponds to the purpose of the articles of partnership and the articles of incorporation.

Articles of partnership   Another name for a formally drafted partnership agreement.

Artisan's lien   The lien that arises in favor of one who has expended labor upon, or added value to, another person's personal property. The lien allows the person to possess the property as security until reimbursed for the value of labor or materials. If the person is not reimbursed, the property may be sold to satisfy the claim.

Assault   The intentional creation of immediate apprehension of injury or lack of physical safety.

Assignee   A third party, who is not an original contracting party, to whom contractual rights or duties or both are transferred. This party may enforce the original contract.

Assignment   A transfer of contractual rights.

Assignor   An original contracting party who assigns or transfers contractual rights or duties or both to a third party.

Assumed-name statute   A state law that requires partners to make a public filing of their identities if their partnership operates under a name that does not reveal the partners' identities.

Assumption of risk   Negligence doctrine that bars the recovery of damages by an injured party on the ground that such a party acted with actual or constructive knowledge of the hazard causing the injury.

Attachment   The term *attachment* has three meanings. First, attachment is a method of acquiring in rem jurisdiction of a nonresident defendant who is not subject to the service of process to commence a lawsuit. By "attaching" property of the nonresident defendant, the court acquires jurisdiction over the defendant to the extent of the value of the property attached. Second, attachment is a procedure used to collect a judgment. A plaintiff may have the property of a defendant seized, pending the outcome of a lawsuit, if the plaintiff has reason to fear that the defendant will dispose of the property before the court renders its decision. Third, attachment is the event that creates an enforceable security interest under the Uniform Commercial Code (UCC). In order that a security interest attach, there must be a signed, written security agreement, or possession of the collateral by the secured party; the secured party must give value to the debtor; and the debtor must maintain rights in the collateral.

Award   The decision announced by an arbitrator.

Bailee   In a bailment, the person who takes possession of an object owned by another and must return it or otherwise dispose of it.

Bailment   An owner's placement of an object into the intentional possession of another person with the understanding that the other person must return the object at some point or otherwise dispose of it.

Bailor   In a bailment, the person who transfers possession of tangible, personal property to another person with the understanding that the other person must return the object at some point or otherwise dispose of it.

Bait-and-switch promotion   An illegal promotional practice in which a seller attracts consumer interest by promoting one product, the "bait," then once interest has been attracted switches it to a second, higher-priced product by making the "bait" unavailable or unattractive.

Balance of trade   The difference between the amount of exports and imports of goods by a nation. A favorable balance would indicate more exports than imports. The United States has run an unfavorable balance of trade for several years.

Bankruptcy   Traditionally, the financial condition where debts exceed assets and one is unable to pay debts as they mature.

Bankruptcy crime   An action involving the falsification of documents filed in a bankruptcy case.

Bargained for   A term used in conjunction with the requirement of contractual consideration to represent the exchange of benefits and burdens between the contracting parties.

Battery   The cause of action for physical contact that is not consented to and is offensive.

Benefit corporation   A corporate form that requires directors to ensure that the corporation meets explicit social goals (i.e., confers a public benefit) in addition to producing shareholder profits.

Best evidence rule   A principle requiring that the original of a document be submitted to the court as proof of the document's contents.

Beyond a reasonable doubt   The burden of proof required in a criminal case. The prosecution in a criminal case has the burden of proving the defendant is guilty, and the jury must have no reasonable doubt about the defendant's guilt. See also *Burden of proof.*

Bilateral contract   An agreement that contains mutual promises, with each party being both a promisor and a promisee.

Bill of lading   A document issued by a carrier indicating that goods to be shipped have been received by the carrier.

Bill of particulars   In legal practice, a written statement furnished by one party to a lawsuit to another, describing in detail the elements upon which the claim of the first party is based.

Biodegradable   Capable of being decomposed by organic action.

Blue sky laws   Securities law enacted by States.

Blurring   A type of trade mark dilution that occurs when the distinctiveness of a mark is reduced by another's use of the same mark in a different context

Bona fide   In good faith; innocently; without fraud or deceit.

Bona fide occupational qualification (BFOQ)
A qualification that permits discriminatory practices in employment if a person's religion, sex, or national origin is reasonably related to the normal operation of a particular business.

Brand   A marketing device that distinguishes one firm's products and services from another's. In general, brands are synonymous with trademarks under the law. See *Trademark.*

Breach of contract   A party's failure to perform some contracted-for or agreed-upon act, or failure to comply with a duty imposed by law.

Bribery   The offering, receiving, or soliciting of something of value for the purpose of influencing the action of an official in the discharge of his or her public or legal duties.

Brief   A written document produced by a party for a reviewing court that contains the facts, propositions of law, and argument of a party. It is in this document that the party argues the desired application of the law and any contentions as to the rulings of the lower court.

Browse-wrap agreement   An agreement proposed on a website that may be accepted by an explicit act, such as clicking an agreement button or simply using the service. Related forms are known as "click-wrap" and "shrink-wrap" agreements.

Bubble concept   A procedure by which the Environmental Protection Agency (EPA) allows a business to treat its entire plant complex as though encased in a bubble. The business suggests its own methods of cleanup, provided the total pollution does not exceed certain limits.

Bulk transfer   A transfer made outside the ordinary course of the transferor's business involving a major part of the business's inventory. Bulk transfers are subject to Article 6 of the Uniform Commercial Code (UCC).

Burden of proof   The term *burden of proof* has two meanings. It may describe the party at a trial with the burden of coming forward with evidence to establish a fact. The term also describes the party with the burden of persuasion. This party must convince the judge or jury of the disputed facts in issue or else lose that issue. There are various degrees of proof. See also *Beyond a reasonable doubt, Preponderance of evidence,* and *Clear and convincing proof.*

Burglary   Theft by breaking and entering.

Business judgment rule   A legal principle used by the courts to uphold the decisions of corporate directors and officers who have exercised good faith and due care in their business practices.

Business necessity defense   An affirmative defense under Title VII of the Civil Rights Act. It is raised to disparate impact claims and asserts that a facially neutral but discriminatory policy is job related.

Buy and sell agreement   A contract, usually among partners, but perhaps among shareholders, wherein one party agrees to buy the ownership interest held by another party or the first party agrees to sell such an interest to the other party. These contractual provisions help provide for a transition of owners without harming the business of the organization.

Buyer in the ordinary course of business   A buyer who buys from someone who ordinarily sells such goods in his or her business.

Cap and trade   A pollution policy that caps allowable pollution at a certain amount, distributes the rights to engage in that pollution, then allows the owners of the rights to trade them.

Capacity   Mental ability to make a rational decision that includes the ability to perceive and appreciate all relevant facts. A required element of a contract.

Case law   The legal principles that are developed by appellate judges through their written opinions. See *Common law.*

Categorical imperative   A concept by the philosopher Kant that a person should never act in a certain way unless he or she is willing to have everyone else act in the same way.

Caucus   The name used for a private meeting between a mediator and one of the parties involved in a mediation.

Cause in fact   The actual cause of an event; the instrument that is the responsible force for the occurrence of a certain event. A required element of a tort.

Cause of action   This phrase has several meanings, but it is commonly used to describe the existence of facts giving rise to a judicially enforceable claim.

Caveat emptor   Let the buyer beware; rule imposing on a purchaser the duty to inform him- or herself as to defects in the property being sold.

Caveat venditor   Let the seller beware; it is the seller's duty to do what the ordinary person would do in a similar situation.

Cease and desist order   The sanction that may be issued by an administrative agency to prevent a party from violating the law.

Celler-Kefauver amendment   Passed in 1950 to amend the Clayton Act by broadening the scope of Section 7 on mergers and acquisitions.

Central America-Dominican Republic Free Trade Agreement (CAFTA-DR)   An agreement between the United States, Costa Rica, El Salvador, Guatemala, Honduras, Nicaragua, and the Dominican Republic designed to eliminate trade barriers.

Certification mark   A mark used by someone other than its owner to certify the quality, point of origin, or other characteristic of goods or services. The Good Housekeeping "Seal of Approval" is an example.

Certiorari   A Latin word that means "to be informed of." This is the name of a writ that a higher court grants permitting the review of a lower court's ruling.

Changing conditions defense   A defense to a price discrimination (Section 2 of the Clayton Act) case wherein the defendant seeks to justify charging different customers different prices due to a change in the conditions of the product or marketplace.

Charter   The legal document issued by a state when creating a new corporation.

Circuit court   This term frequently is used to describe two distinct courts. First, the appellate courts in the federal court system often are called circuit courts of appeals. Second, the trial courts of general subject matter jurisdiction in some state court systems also are referred to as circuit courts.

Citation   The reference identifying how to find a case.

Civil law   The area of law governing the rights and duties between private parties as compared with the criminal law. This term also describes the system of codifying law in many countries as compared with the judicial orientation of the common law system.

Civil rights   The area of law designed to protect an individual's right to freedom from discrimination. In employment, this area of law prohibits unequal treatment based on race, color, national origin, religion, and sex.

Class-action suit   A method of litigation that allows one or more plaintiffs to file a lawsuit on behalf of a much larger group of persons, all of whom have a common interest in the claims being litigated.

Clayton Act   Legislation passed in 1914 that exempts labor unions from the Sherman Act. This law expanded the national antitrust policy to cover price discrimination, exclusive dealings, tying contracts, mergers, and interlocking directors.

Clean Air Act   The principal federal law regulating air pollution.

Clean Water Act   The principal federal law regulating water pollution.

Clean-hands doctrine   An equitable principle that requires a party seeking an equitable remedy to be free from wrongdoing.

Clear and convincing proof   A burden of proof that requires the party with the burden to establish clearly the existence of the alleged facts. This burden requires more proof than merely having a preponderance of evidence on one's side.

Closed shop   A contractual agreement between an employer and a union that all applicants for a job with the employer will have to join the union. This type of agreement was outlawed by the Taft-Hartley Act.

Closely held   An organization that is owned by only a few people.

Code   A compilation of legislation enacted by a federal, state, or local government.

Colgate doctrine   The legal principle that allows a form of vertical price fixing in that manufacturers may maintain the resale price of their products by announcing their pricing policy and refusing to deal with customers who fail to comply with the policy.

Collateral The valuable thing put up by someone to secure a loan or credit.

Collective bargaining The process used by an employer and a union representing employees to discuss and resolve differences so that the parties can agree to a binding contract.

Collective mark A mark representing membership in a certain organization or association. The "union label" is an example.

Commerce clause A provision in Article I, Section 8, of the U.S. Constitution that grants the federal government the power to regulate business transactions.

Commercial impracticability A Uniform Commercial Code (UCC) defense to contractual nonperformance based on happenings that greatly increase the difficulty of performance and that violate the parties' reasonable commercial expectations.

Commercial speech Speech that has a business-oriented purpose. This speech is protected under the First Amendment, but this protection is not as great as that afforded to noncommercial speech.

Common law That body of law deriving from judicial decisions as opposed to legislatively enacted statutes and administrative regulations.

Comparable worth Jobs that, although different, produce substantially equal value for the employer.

Comparative negligence A doctrine that compares the plaintiff's contributory fault with the defendant's fault and allows the jury to reduce the plaintiff's verdict by the percentage of the plaintiff's fault.

Comparative responsibility A doctrine that compares the plaintiff's contributory fault with the defendant's fault and allows the jury to reduce the plaintiff's verdict by the percentage of the plaintiff's fault. Also called *comparative negligence.*

Compensatory damages Usually awarded in breach-of-contract cases to pay for a party's losses that are a direct and foreseeable result of the other party's breach. The award of these damages is designed to place the non-breaching party in the same position as if the contract had been performed.

Complaint In legal practice, the first written statement of the plaintiff's position and allegations, which initiates the lawsuit.

Complete performance Degree of performance recognizing that each contracting party has performed every duty required by the contract.

Comprehensive Environmental Response, Compensation, and Liability Act (CERCLA) This legislation, also known as the Superfund, addresses the environmental cleanup of hazardous wastes from property.

Compulsory bargaining issue Mandatory bargaining issue regarding wages, hours, or other terms or conditions of employment. Refusal to engage in good-faith bargaining with regard to these issues is an unfair labor practice.

Concealment An intentional misrepresentation of a material fact occurring through the silence of a party.

Concerted activities Those activities involving an agreement, contract, or conspiracy to restrain trade that may be illegal under the Sherman Antitrust Act.

Concurrent conditions Mutual conditions under which each party's contractual performance is triggered by the other party's tendering (offering) performance.

Condition precedent An event in the law of contracts that must occur before a duty of immediate performance of the promise arises. Contracts often provide that one party must perform before there is a right to performance by the other party. For example, completion of a job is often a condition precedent to payment for that job. One contracting party's failure to perform a condition precedent permits the other party to refuse to perform, cancel the contract, and sue for damages.

Condition subsequent A fact that will extinguish a duty to make compensation for breach of contract after the breach has occurred.

Conduct Under the Uniform Commercial Code (UCC) the conduct of contracting parties (i.e., their actions) is important in determining the meaning of a sales contract.

Confiscation The seizure of property without adequate compensation.

Conflict The common occurrence in life when two or more points of view exist.

Conflict of law Rules of law the courts use to determine that substantive law applies when there is an inconsistency between laws of different states or countries.

Confusion Property ownership that arises when identical masses of objects, such as grain, are mixed together.

Conglomerate merger The merger resulting when merging companies have neither the relationship of competitors nor that of supplier and customer.

Consent order   Any court or regulatory order to which the opposing party agrees; a contract of the parties entered upon the record with the approval and sanction of a court.

Consequential damages   The amount of money awarded in a breach-of-contract case to the non-breaching party to pay for the special damages that exceed the normal compensatory damages. Lost opportunities may create consequential damages if the breaching party was aware of the special nature of the contract.

Consequentialism   An ethical system that concerns itself with the moral consequences of actions. Also called *teleology.*

Consideration   An essential element in the creation of a contract obligation that creates a detriment to the promisee or a benefit to the promisor.

Consolidation   The process by which two or more corporations are joined to create a new corporation.

Conspiracy   A combination or agreement between two or more persons for the commission of a criminal act.

Constitution   When capitalized, the term refers to the U.S. federal Constitution, which sets out the basic framework for federal government and, as amended, for individual rights.

Constitutional law   The legal issues that arise from interpreting the U.S. Constitution or a state constitution.

Constitutional relativity   The idea that constitutional interpretation is relative to the time in which the Constitution is being interpreted.

Constructive discharge   The event of an employee resigning because the employer has made working conditions too uncomfortable for continued employment.

Consumer Financial Protection Bureau (CFPB)   A federal regulatory agency established by the Consumer Financial Protection Act of 2010. The CFPB has authority over federal financial consumer law.

Consumer investigative report   A report on a consumer's character, general reputation, mode of living, etc., obtained by personal interviews in the community where the consumer works or lives.

Contempt of court   An order by a judge to punish wrongdoing with respect to the court's authority.

Contingency fee   An arrangement whereby an attorney is compensated for services in a lawsuit according to an agreed percentage of the amount of money recovered.

Contract   A legally enforceable promise.

Contract clause   The constitutional provision that prohibits states from enacting laws that interfere with existing contracts. The Supreme Court has refused to interpret this clause in an absolute manner.

Contract law   The law of legally enforceable promises.

Contribution   The right of one who has discharged a common liability to recover from another also liable the proportionate share of the common liability.

Contributory negligence   A failure to use reasonable care by the plaintiff in a negligence suit.

Controlling person   The person who has the control of, or is controlled by, the issuer of securities in securities laws.

Convention on the International Sale of Goods (CISG)   The agreement that sets forth standard international practices for the sale of goods.

Conversion   An unlawful exercise of dominion and control over another's property that substantially interferes with property rights.

Cooling-off period   A time provided by the Taft-Hartley Act during which labor and management must suspend the work stoppage (strike or lockout) and continue their working relationship while negotiating a resolution of the dispute. This period is for 80 days.

Copyright   A statutorily created property right in creative expression that protects authors.

Corporate codes of conduct   Policy statements adopted by companies to define ethical standards for their conduct.

Corporate governance   A term that has at least two meanings. One relates to how business organizations are created and managed. A second concerns how the various levels of government regulate business organizations as they transact business.

Corporation   An artificial, but legal, person created by state law. As a business organization, the corporation's separation of owners and managers gives it a high level of flexibility.

Corrective advertising   A Federal Trade Commission (FTC) remedy that requires companies that have advertised deceptively to run ads that admit the prior errors and correct the erroneous information.

Cost justification defense   A defense to a price discrimination (Section 2 of the Clayton Act) case wherein the defendant seeks to justify charging different customers different prices due to that defendant's costs varying because of the differing quantities purchased by the customers.

Counterclaim   Any claim filed by the defendant in a lawsuit against the plaintiff in the same suit.

Counterdefendant   The party involved in litigation against whom a counterclaim is filed. This party is the original plaintiff.

Counteroffer An offer made in response to another's offer. Usually made in place of an acceptance. A counteroffer usually terminates an offer.

Counterplaintiff The party involved in litigation who files a counterclaim. This party is the original defendant who is making a claim against the original plaintiff.

Course of dealing The way parties to a contract have done business in the past. Important in helping to determine the meaning of a contract for the sale of goods.

Courts of appeal A court that reviews decisions by lower courts.

Covenant An agreement or promise in writing by which a party pledges that something has been done or is being done. The term is often used in connection with real estate to describe the promises of the grantor of the property.

Covenant not to compete An agreement in which one party agrees not to compete directly with the business of the other party; may be limited by geography or length of time.

Criminal law That area of law dealing with wrongs against the state as representative of the community at large, to be distinguished from civil law, which hears cases of wrongs against persons.

Cross-examination The process of questioning a witness by the lawyer who did not call the witness to testify on behalf of that lawyer's client.

Cruel and unusual punishment Protection against such punishment is provided by the Eighth Amendment of the U.S. Constitution. To be cruel and unusual, the punishment must be disproportionately harsh when compared to the offense committed.

Damages Monetary compensation recoverable in a court of law.

Data Protection Directive A directive adopted by the European Union in 1995 that requires all member states to regulate the collection and processing of personal data by private firms. U.S. companies operating in the EU may certify compliance through a "safe harbor" framework.

D.B.A. Doing business as.

De novo judicial review A proceeding wherein the judge or hearing officer hears the case as if it had not been heard before.

Decree The decision of a court of equity.

Deed A document representing the title or ownership of land.

Deeds of trust A type of document to secure an extension of credit through an interest in the land.

Defamation The publication of anything injurious to the good name or reputation of another.

Default The failure of a defendant to answer a plaintiff's complaint within the time period allowed by the court. Upon the defendant's default, a judgment is entered in the plaintiff's favor.

Defect Something that makes a product not reasonably safe for a use that can be reasonably anticipated.

Defendant The party involved in a lawsuit that is sued; the party required to respond to the plaintiff's complaint.

Deficiency In a land-based security interest, the amount of the loan which remains unpaid after the land has been sold.

Defined benefit plan A money-purchase plan that guarantees a certain retirement income based on the employee's service and salary under the Employee Retirement Income Security Act. The benefits are fixed, and the contributions vary.

Defined contribution plan A money-purchase plan that allows employers to budget pension costs in advance under the Employee Retirement Income Security Act. The contribution is fixed, and the benefits vary.

Delivery The physical transfer of something. In sale-of-goods transactions, delivery is the transfer of goods from the seller to the buyer.

Demurrer A formal statement by the defendant that the facts alleged by the plaintiff are insufficient to support a claim for legal relief in common law pleading.

Deontology An ethical system that affirms an absolute morality. Also called *formalism*.

Deposited acceptance rule The contractual doctrine that a binding acceptance of an offer occurs when a mailed acceptance is irrevocably placed with the postal service.

Deposition A discovery process outside the court's supervision that involves the sworn questioning of a potential witness. This oral questioning is reduced to a written form so that a record is established.

Derivative action A lawsuit filed by a shareholder of a corporation on behalf of the corporation. This action is filed to protect the corporation from the mismanagement of its officers and directors.

Derivative suit A lawsuit filed by one or more shareholders of a corporation against that organization's management. This suit is brought to benefit the corporation directly and its shareholders indirectly.

Design defect A defect arising when a product does not meet society's expectation for a safely designed product.

Design patent A property right awarded for a new, original, and ornamental design for an article of manufacture.

Dicta   Statements made in a judicial opinion that are not essential to the decision of the case.

Digital Millennium Copyright Act   A law passed by Congress in 1998 that makes circumvention of copyright protections illegal and requires Internet Service Providers to remove infringing material when notified.

Direct examination   The process of questioning a witness conducted by the lawyer who called the witness to testify on behalf of that lawyer's client.

Directed verdict   A motion for a directed verdict requests that the judge direct the jury to bring in a particular verdict if reasonable minds could not differ on the correct outcome of the lawsuit. In deciding the motion, the judge will view in the light most favorable to the nonmoving party, and if different inferences may be drawn by reasonable people, then the court cannot direct a verdict. In essence, a directed verdict removes the jury's discretion.

Directors   Those individuals who are elected by the shareholders to decide the goals and objectives for the corporate organization.

Disability   Any physical or mental impairment that substantially limits a major life activity.

Disaffirm   To void. Used to describe a minor's power to get out of a contract because of age.

Discharge   In bankruptcy the forgiving of an honest debtor's debts. In contract law an act that forgives further performance of a contractual obligation.

Discovery   Procedures by which one party to a lawsuit may obtain information relevant to the case from the other party or from third persons.

Discretionary function exception   An exception to the waiver of the doctrine of sovereign immunity. Officials of administrative agencies are exempt from personal liability if their performance or lack thereof is based on a discretionary function.

Discrimination in effect   The discriminatory result of policies that appear to be neutral.

Disparate impact   A term of employment litigation that refers to the disproportionate impact of a policy neutral on its face on some protected class (e.g., race or sex).

Disparate treatment   A term of employment litigation that refers to the illegal discriminatory treatment of an individual in some protected class (e.g., race or sex).

Dispute   The circumstance when a party in conflict claims the right to do or have something and the other party denies, rejects, or ignores the claim.

Dissolution   The cancellation of an agreement, thereby rescinding its binding force. A partnership is dissolved anytime there is a change in partners. A corporation's dissolution occurs when that business entity ceases to exist.

Diversity of citizenship   The plaintiffs filing a lawsuit must be from states different from those of the defendants. This requirement, along with over $75,000 at stake, is one method a federal court gains jurisdiction over the subject matter of a lawsuit.

Divestiture   The antitrust remedy that forces a company to get rid of assets acquired through illegal mergers or monopolistic practices.

Docket   A book containing a brief summary of all acts done in court in the conduct of each case.

Doctrine of abstention   A principle used by federal courts to refuse to hear a case. When used by the federal courts, the lawsuit involved is sent to the state court system.

Domestic corporation   A business organization created by the issuance of a state charter that operates in the state that issued the charter.

Domicile   That place that a person intends as his or her fixed and permanent legal residence; place of permanent abode, as contrasted with a residence, which may be temporary; a person can have a number of residences but only one domicile; the state of incorporation of a corporation.

Donee beneficiary   A noncontracting third party who receives as a gift the benefits of a contract made between two other parties. This third party is empowered to enforce the contract to ensure the receipt of the contract's benefits.

Double jeopardy   A constitutional doctrine that prohibits an individual from being prosecuted twice by the same governing body based on the same factual situation.

Double tax   A disadvantage of a corporate form of organization in that the corporation must pay a tax on the money earned and the shareholder pays a second tax on the dividends distributed.

Dram shop acts   Statutes adopted in many states that impose strict liability upon tavern owners for injuries to third parties caused by their intoxicated patrons.

Due diligence defense   A defense that experts may assert in a 1933 Securities Act case involving the failure to register securities or the failure to provide accurate documents. The expert utilizing this defense attempts to prove his or her reasonable investigation into all available information.

Due process   Fundamental fairness. As applied to judicial proceedings, adequate notice of a hearing and an opportunity to appear and defend in an orderly tribunal.

Due process clause   A provision found in the Fifth and Fourteenth Amendments of the U.S. Constitution. This clause assures all citizens of fundamental fairness in their relationship with the government.

Dumping   The practice of selling foreign goods in one country at less than the comparable price in the country where the goods originated.

Duress   Action by a person that compels another to do what he or she would not otherwise do. It is a recognized defense to any act that must be voluntary in order to create liability in the actor.

Duty   A legal obligation imposed by the law.

Duty of performance   In contract law the legal obligation of a party to a contract.

Duty of reasonable care   The legal duty owed under negligence doctrine.

Easement   The right of one other than the owner of land to some use of that land.

Economic boycott   Used in three basic forms (primary, secondary, and tertiary), a practice aimed at cutting off trade opportunities for enemy countries.

Economic Espionage Act   A federal law that creates criminal liability for trade secret misappropriation. Penalties are enhanced for misappropriation intended to benefit a foreign government.

Eighty-day cooling-off period   A provision in the Taft-Hartley Act that allows the president to require that laborers continue working and that the laborers' representatives and management continue bargaining for at least 80 days during which it is intended that federal mediation will resolve the dispute. This provision can be utilized by the president only when there is a determination that the work stoppage is adversely affecting the national health and safety.

Ejusdem generis   Of the same kind or class; a doctrine of legislative interpretation.

Electronic Communications Privacy Act (ECPA)   A federal law that prevents interception of and unauthorized access to electronic communications such as email.

Embezzlement   The fraudulent appropriation by one person, acting in a fiduciary capacity, of the money or property of another.

Eminent domain   The government's constitutional power to take private property for public use upon the payment of just compensation.

Emissions reduction banking   The policy stating that businesses that lower pollution beyond the requirements of the law may use the additional reductions in the future.

Employment at will   A hiring for an indefinite period of time.

En banc   Proceedings by or before the court as a whole rather than any single judge.

Endangerment of workers   A criminal act that involves placing employees at risk with respect to their health and safety in the work environment.

Enforceable contract   A contract that can be enforced in court.

Enjoin   To require performance of, or abstention from, some act through issuance of an injunction.

Environmental impact statement (EIS)   A filing of documents required by the National Environmental Policy Act that forces governmental agencies to consider the environmental consequences of their actions.

Environmental Protection Agency (EPA)   An administrative agency established in 1970 to enforce federal laws concerning the environment.

Equal protection clause   A provision in the Fourteenth Amendment of the U.S. Constitution that requires all citizens to be treated in a similar manner by the government unless there is a sufficient justification for the unequal treatment.

Escrow   A deed, bond, or deposit that one party delivers for safekeeping by a second party who is obligated to deliver it to a third party upon the fulfillment of some condition.

Establishment clause   A provision in the First Amendment of the U.S. Constitution that prohibits the federal government from establishing any government-supported religion or church.

Estate   The bundle of rights and powers of real property ownership.

Estoppel   The legal principle that one may not assert facts inconsistent with one's own prior actions.

Ethics   A systematic statement of right and wrong together with a philosophical system that both justifies and necessitates rules of conduct.

European Union (EU)   Created by the Treaty of Rome, an organization that seeks to facilitate the free movement of goods, services, labor, professions, transportation, and capital among European countries.

Exclusive dealing   A buyer agrees to purchase a certain product exclusively from the seller or the seller agrees to sell all of his or her production to the buyer.

Exclusive remedy rule   The rule that limits an injured employee's claim against the employer to workers' compensation.

Exculpatory clause   A provision in a contract whereby one of the parties attempts to relieve itself of liability for breach of a legal duty.

Exculpatory contract   A contract that excuses one from accepting responsibility or blame. For example, a contract that excuses one from having to accept liability for one's negligence or another's injury or loss.

Exculpatory no   The doctrine that merely denying guilt is not a criminal lie in response to a question from an agency of the federal government. This doctrine is no longer valid.

Executed contract   A contract that is fully accomplished or performed, leaving nothing unfulfilled.

Execution   To carry out some action to completion. With respect to enforcing a court's judgment, an execution involves the seizure of the debtor's property, a sale of the property, and the payment of proceeds to the creditor.

Executory contract   An agreement that is not completed. Until the performance required in a contract is completed, it is executory.

Exemplary damages   Punitive damages. Monetary compensation in excess of direct losses suffered by the plaintiff that may be awarded in intentional tort cases where the defendant's conduct deserves punishment.

Exhaustion of remedies   A concept used in administrative law that requires any party to an administrative proceeding to give the administrative agency every opportunity to resolve the dispute before appealing to the court system.

Expectation of privacy   The expectation that one will not be observed by the state.

Experience rating system   A system of sliding taxation under which employers are charged less unemployment compensation tax as they lay off fewer workers due to economic conditions.

Export controls   Action taken on a national and multilateral basis to prevent the exportation of controlled goods and technology to certain destinations.

Express authority   Actual authority that arises from specific statements made by the principal to the agent.

Express conditions   Conditions that are explicitly set out in a contract.

Express contract   A contract in which parties show their agreement in words.

Express warranty   Any statement of fact or promise about the performance of a product made by a seller.

Expropriation   A foreign government's seizure of privately owned property.

Extortionate picketing   Picketing by employees in an attempt to force an employer to pay money to union officials or other individuals when these payments provide personal benefit to the officials or individuals instead of benefiting the union membership generally.

Extradition   The process that one state uses to have another state transfer to the jurisdiction of the first state a person accused of criminal activities.

Failing-company doctrine   A merger between a failing company and a competitor may be allowed, although such a merger would be illegal if both companies were viable competitors.

Fair Labor Standards Act (FLSA)   Originally passed in 1938, this law provides basic protections for employees, including the minimum wage and maximum number of hours before overtime must be paid.

Fair use   A statutorily permitted use of another's copyright for criticism, comment, news reporting, teaching, scholarship, or research.

False advertising   Untrue and fraudulent statements and representations made by way of advertising a product or a service.

False imprisonment   The tort of an intentional, unjustified confinement of a nonconsenting person who knows of the confinement.

Family and Medical Leave Act (FMLA)   This law, which became effective in 1993, allows eligible workers up to 12 weeks of unpaid leave in any 12-month period to care for a newborn baby, to care for a child placed for adoption or foster care, to care for an immediate family member with a serious health condition, or when the employee is unable to work because of a serious health condition.

Family resemblance test   A legal principle used to determine whether or not promissory notes or other similar investment opportunities are securities.

Featherbedding   A term used in the labor laws to describe workers who are paid although they do not perform any work. Under the Taft-Hartley Act, featherbedding is an unfair labor practice by unions.

Federal Environmental Pesticide Control Act of 1972 (FEPCA)   This law requires registration and labeling of agriculture pesticides and regulates the application of pesticides.

Federal Insecticide, Fungicide, and Rodenticide Act of 1947   A law that requires registration and labeling of pesticides.

Federal question cases   Litigation involving the application or interpretation of the federal Constitution, federal statutes, federal treaties, or federal administrative agencies. The federal court system has subject matter jurisdiction over these issues.

Federal Rules of Civil Procedure   A law passed by Congress that provides the procedural steps to be followed by the federal courts when handling civil litigation.

Federal Trade Commission (FTC)   The federal regulatory agency that enforces the Federal Trade Commission Act of 1914 and various antitrust and consumer protection laws.

Federal Trade Commission Act   Passed in 1914, this legislation created the Federal Trade Commission (FTC) and authorized it to protect society against unfair methods of competition. The law was amended in

1938 (by the Wheeler-Lea amendment) to provide the FTC with authority to regulate unfair or deceptive trade practices.

Federalism A term used to describe the vertical aspect of the separation of powers. The coexistence of a federal government and the various state governments, with each having responsibilities and authorities that are distinct but overlap, is called federalism.

Fee schedule A plan, usually adopted by an association, that establishes minimum or maximum charges for a service or product.

Fee simple The maximum bundle of rights, or estate, permitted by law.

Fellow-servant doctrine The doctrine that precludes an injured employee from recovering damages from his employer when the injury resulted from the negligent act of another employee.

Felony A criminal offense of a serious nature, generally punishable by death or imprisonment in a penitentiary; to be distinguished from a misdemeanor.

Fiduciary One having a duty to act for another's benefit in the highest good faith.

Finance charge Any charge for an extension of credit, which specifically includes interest, service charges, and other charges.

Financing statement An established form that a secured party files with a public officer, such as a state official or local court clerk, to perfect a security interest under the Uniform Commercial Code (UCC). It is a simple form that contains basic information such as a description of the collateral, names, and addresses. It is designed to give notice that the debtor and the secured party have entered into a security agreement.

Firm offer An offer in signed writing by a merchant to buy or sell goods; it gives assurances that the offer will be held open for acceptance under the Uniform Commercial Code (UCC).

Focus group A group acting as a mock jury; attorneys present cases to such a group to get the members' feedback on the merits of the various arguments presented.

Foreclosure If a mortgagor fails to perform his or her obligations as agreed, the mortgagee may declare the whole debt due and payable, and she or he may foreclose on the mortgaged property to pay the debt secured by the mortgage. The usual method of foreclosure authorizes the sale of the mortgaged property at a public auction. The proceeds of the sale are applied to the debt.

Foreign corporation A business organization, created by the issuance of a state charter, that operates in states other than the one issuing the charter.

Foreign Corrupt Practices Act (FCPA) A U.S. law that seeks to ban the payment of bribes to foreign officials in order to obtain business.

Foreign Sovereign Immunities Act (FISA) A federal law passed in 1976 that codifies the restrictive theory of *sovereign immunity* and rejects immunity for commercial acts carried on in the United States or having direct effects in this country.

Foreign subsidiary A practice common in a multinational corporation that conducts part of its business operations in a foreign country.

Formalism An ethical system that affirms an absolute morality. Also called *deontology.*

Forum non conveniens The doctrine under which a court may dismiss a lawsuit in which it appears that for the convenience of the parties and in the interest of justice the action should have been brought in another court.

Franchise A marketing technique whereby one party (the franchisor) grants a second party (the franchisee) the right to manufacture, distribute, or sell a product using the name or trademark of the franchisor.

Fraud A false representation of fact made with the intent to deceive another that is justifiably relied upon to the injury of that person.

Free exercise clause A provision in the First Amendment of the U.S. Constitution that allows all citizens the freedom to follow or believe any religious teaching.

Frolic and detour The activity of an agent or an employee who has departed from the scope of the agency and is not, therefore, a representative of his or her employer.

Full faith and credit clause A provision in the U.S. Constitution that requires a state to recognize the laws and judicial decisions of all other states.

Full-line forcing An arrangement in which a manufacturer refuses to supply any portion of the product line unless the retailer agrees to accept the entire line.

Functional discount A reduction in price as the result of the buyer's performing some service that usually is provided by the seller.

Garnishment A legal proceeding whereby a creditor may collect directly from a third party who is obligated to the debtor.

General Agreement on Tariffs and Trade (GATT) An international treaty that requires member countries to abide by the principles of open and free trade.

General counsel An individual who is responsible for coordinating all law-related issues, such as the quasijudicial hearings in administrative agencies. This term is also used to describe the principal lawyer of a company.

General partner   The owner of a limited partnership that enjoys the control of the partnership's operation. This type of partner is personally liable for the debts of the limited partnership.

General partnership   A business organization wherein all owners (partners) share profits and losses and all are jointly and severally liable for the organization's debts.

Generic   To lose distinctiveness in reference to the source of goods and thus to lose trademark protection.

Genetic Information Nondiscrimination Act (GINA)   Prohibits covered employers from firing, refusing to hire, or otherwise discriminating against individuals on the basis of their genetic information or a family member's genetic information.

Geographic extension merger   A combining of companies involved with the same product or service that do not compete in the same geographical regions or markets.

Geographic market   The relevant section of the country affected by a merger.

Gift   Transfer of ownership by intent and the delivery of the object gifted.

Going bare   A professional practicing (in her or his field of expertise) without liability insurance.

Good, the   In philosophy the moral goals and objectives that people choose to pursue.

Good faith   Honesty in dealing; innocence; without fraud or deceit.

Good-faith meeting-of-competition defense
A bona fide business practice that is a defense to a charge of violation of the Robinson-Patman Act. The Robinson-Patman Act is an amendment to the Clayton Act, which outlaws price discrimination that might substantially lessen competition or tends to create a monopoly. This exception allows a seller in good faith to meet the equally low price, service, or facility of a competitor. The good-faith exception cannot be established if the purpose of the price discrimination has been to eliminate competition.

Goods   Tangible (touchable), movable personal property.

Greenmail   Forcing a corporation to buy back some of its own stock at an inflated price to avoid a takeover.

Guardian   One charged with the duty of care and maintenance of another person such as a minor or incompetent under the law.

Guardian *ad litem*   A guardian appointed to prosecute or defend a lawsuit on behalf of an incompetent or a minor.

Guidelines   A result of an administrative agency's quasi-legislative function that assists parties being regulated to understand the agency's functions and intentions. Guidelines do not have the force of the law, but they can be helpful in anticipating the application of an agency's regulations.

Habeas corpus   The name of a writ that orders one holding custody of another to produce that individual before the court for the purpose of determining whether such custody is proper.

Health Insurance Portability and Accountability Act (HIPAA)   Federal law protecting personal health care information and limiting its disclosure and use by health plans and health care providers and clearinghouses.

Hearsay evidence   Evidence of statements made or actions performed out of court that is offered to prove the truth thereof.

Hearsay rule   The exclusion, with certain exceptions, of hearsay evidence because of the lack of opportunity to cross-examine the original source of the evidence.

Herfindahl-Hirschman Index (HHI)   A measure of market concentration commonly used in merger analysis. It is calculated by squaring the market shares of competing firms and summing the results.

Holding   The precise legal response in an opinion by an appellate court on an issue of law raised on appeal.

Holder in due course   One who has acquired possession of a negotiable instrument through proper negotiation for value, in good faith, and without notice of any defenses to it. Such a holder is not subject to personal defenses that would otherwise defeat the obligation embodied in the instrument.

Horizontal merger   Merger of corporations that were competitors prior to the merger.

Horizontal price fixing   A per se illegal agreement among competitors as to the price all of them will charge for their similar products.

Horizontal restraint   An agreement between direct competitors that restricts their rivalry, particularly related to the goods or services they offer.

Horizontal territorial agreement   An arrangement between competitors with respect to geographical areas in which each will conduct its business to the exclusion of the others. This type of agreement is illegal per se under the Sherman Act.

Hostile work environment   Under Title VII an environment where co-workers make offensive sexual comments or propositions, engage in suggestive touching, show nude pictures, or draw sexual graffiti.

Hot-cargo contract   An agreement whereby an employer agrees to refrain from handling, using, selling, transporting, or otherwise dealing in the products of another employer or to cease doing business with any other person.

Illegal search and seizure   The area covered by the Fourth Amendment that protects individuals and organizations from unreasonable intrusion without a court-issued warrant.

Immunity   Status of exemption from lawsuits or other legal obligations.

Implied authority   Actual authority that is incidental to express authority.

Implied conditions   Conditions to a contract that are implied by law rather than by contractual agreement.

Implied contract   A legally enforceable agreement inferred from the circumstances and conduct of the parties. Also called an *implied-in-fact contract.*

Implied-in-fact contract   A legally enforceable agreement inferred from the circumstances and conduct of the parties.

Implied-in-law contract   A quasi-contract.

Implied warranty   A warranty implied by law rather than by express agreement of the parties to a contract.

Implied warranty of fitness for a particular purpose   An implied Uniform Commercial Code (UCC) warranty that arises when a buyer specifies a purpose for a product, then relies on the seller's skill and judgment to select the product.

Implied warranty of habitability   A warranty implied by law in a number of states that guarantees the quality of new home construction.

Implied warranty of merchantability   A warranty (implied) that the goods are reasonably fit for the general purpose for which they are sold.

Impossibility of performance   A defense to contractual nonperformance based on special circumstances that render the performance illegal, physically impossible, or so difficult as to violate every reasonable expectation the parties have regarding performance.

In pari materia   Concerning the same subject matter. A rule of statutory construction that two such statutes will be construed together.

In personam   The jurisdiction of a court to affect the rights and duties of a specific individual.

In rem   The jurisdiction of a court to affect property rights with respect to a specific thing.

Incidental beneficiary   A person who may incidentally benefit from the creation of a contract. Such a person cannot enforce any right to incidental benefit.

Incorporators   Those individuals who are responsible for bringing a corporation into being.

Indefiniteness   When the terms of an agreement are not sufficiently specific, the agreement does not rise to the level of a contract because of the doctrine of indefiniteness.

Independent contractor   A person who contracts to do work for another person or entity, who is not considered to be an employee.

Indictment   A document issued by a grand jury formally charging a person with a felony.

Individual retirement account   A retirement account for persons who can make either tax deductible contributions, which are taxed on withdrawal, or contributions that are taxed, which produce tax-free withdrawals. This latter type of account is known as a Roth IRA.

Industry guide   An issue of the Federal Trade Commission (FTC) defining the agency's view of the legality of an industry's trade practice.

Infliction of mental distress   An intentional tort of the emotions that causes both mental distress and physical symptoms as a result of the defendant's outrageous behavior.

Information   A written accusation by the prosecutor presented in court charging an accused person with a crime.

Infringement   The tort establishing violation of intellectual property rights.

Injunction   A court order directing a party to do or to refrain from doing some act.

Injurious falsehood   A statement of untruth that causes injury or damage to the party against whom it is made.

Insider   A person who owns 10% or more of a company or who is a director or officer of the company; a term used in securities law. This term is also used to describe a person possessing nonpublic information.

Intangible personal property   Something that represents value but has no physical attributes, such as a copyright, patent, or franchise right.

Intellectual property   A type of property in information and its application or expression. Patents and copyrights are examples.

Intent   A legal doctrine indicating that parties meant to do what they did.

Intent to defraud   Applies to an individual who knowingly and willfully makes a misrepresentation of a material fact that is relied on and thereby causes injury or harm.

Intentional interference with contractual relations   The tort of causing another to break a contract.

Intentional tort   Noncontractual legal wrong caused by one who desires to cause the wrong or where the wrong is substantially likely to occur from the behavior.

Inter se   Between themselves.

Interference with contractual relations   A business tort in which persons are induced to breach binding agreements.

International Court of Justice (ICJ)   The judicial branch of the United Nations, which sits at The Hague in the Netherlands and consists of 15 judges representing the world's major legal systems.

International Monetary Fund (IMF)   An international economic organization.

Interpleader   A legal procedure by which one holding a single fund subject to conflicting claims of two or more persons may require the conflicting claimants to come into court and litigate the matter between themselves.

Interrogatory   A written question submitted by one party to another in a lawsuit; a type of discovery procedure.

Intestate   A person who dies without a will.

Invasion of privacy   A tort based on misappropriation of name or likeness, intrusion upon physical solitude, or public disclosure of objectionable, private information.

Investigative consumer report   A consumer report under the Fair Credit Reporting Act that arises when a credit reporting agency goes beyond reporting financial transactions and also reports the habits and practices of someone seeking credit or a job.

Involuntary petition   The document filed by a creditor to initiate bankruptcy proceedings against a debtor.

Irrevocable letter of credit   Reduces the risk to parties in cases where business is extended across national borders between strangers by providing guarantees of payment and delivery of goods.

Issuer   The term in securities law for an individual or business organization offering a security for sale to the public.

JOBS Act Jumpstart Our Business Startups (JOBS)   Act of 2012 eases federal regulations of initial public offerings to promote investment in startup companies.

Joint tenancy   A property ownership that is undivided (common) and equal between two or more owners. Permits survivorship.

Joint venture   Two or more persons or business organizations agreeing to do business for a specific and limited purpose.

Jointly and severally liable   The legal principle that makes two or more people, usually partners, liable for an entire debt as individuals or in any proportional combination.

Judgment   Official adjudication of a court of law.

Judgment notwithstanding the verdict   The decision of a court that sets aside the verdict of a jury and reaches the opposite result.

Judgment on the pleadings   A principle of litigation, in the form of a motion, whereby one party tests the validity of the allegations contained in the complaint and answer. Upon this motion a judge might determine that the pleadings contain no issues of fact or law and thus grant a judgment prior to a trial.

Judicial activism   An activist judge tends to abide by the following judicial philosophies: (1) The political process cannot adequately handle society's difficult issues; (2) the courts can correct society's ills through the decision-making process; (3) following precedent is not crucial; and (4) "judge-made law" is often necessary to carry out the legislative intent of the law. See also *Judicial restraint*.

Judicial admission   An exception under the statute of frauds allowing courts to enforce oral contracts when a party acknowledges the oral promise in a formal judicial/court environment.

Judicial restraint   A judge who abides by the judicial restraint philosophy (1) believes that the political process, and not the courts, should correct society's ills; (2) decides an issue on a narrow basis, if possible; (3) follows precedent whenever possible; and (4) does not engage in "judge-made law" but interprets the letter of the law. See also *Judicial activism*.

Judicial review   The power of courts to declare laws enacted by legislative bodies and actions by the executive branch to be unconstitutional.

Jurisdiction   The power and authority of a court or other governmental agency to adjudicate controversies and otherwise deal with matters brought before it.

Jurisdictional strike   A stoppage of work that arises from a dispute between two or more unions as to what work should be assigned to the employees belonging to the disputing unions. This work stoppage is an unfair labor practice. This dispute between the unions should be resolved by the NLRB.

Jurisprudence   The science of the law; the practical science of giving a wise interpretation of the law.

Jury instruction   A statement made by the judge to the jury informing them of the law applicable to the case the jury is bound to accept and apply.

Kickbacks   Payments made to a person who has facilitated a transaction.

Knowingly　Intentionally.

Laches　Defense to an equitable action based on the plaintiff's unreasonable delay in bringing the action.

Land sales contract　A type of document to secure an extension of credit through an interest in the land purchased.

Landrum-Griffin Act　The federal law passed in 1959 that provides union members with a "Bill of Rights" and requires union officers to file reports with the Department of Labor. This law, which is known as the Labor-Management Reporting and Disclosure Act, also added unfair labor practices by unions.

Larceny　The unlawful taking of personal property with the intent to deprive the right owner of this property.

Law　The rules of the state backed up by enforcement.

Law of agency　That body of law concerning one's dealing with another on behalf of a principal.

Law of nations　The law embodied in international agreements, treaties, and conventions.

Leading question　A question that indicates the appropriate answer because of the way or manner in which it is asked. Typically, such questions are allowed during the cross-examination of a witness but not during the direct examination.

Leashold estate　The property granted to tenants (lessees) by a landlord (lessor).

Legacy　A gift of money under a will. It is a type of bequest, which is a gift of personal property. The word *devise* is used in connection with real property distributed by will.

Legal capacity　The ability of a business organization to sue and be sued in its own name rather than having to sue or be sued in the name of its owners.

Legal clinic　A term referring to a law firm that specializes in low-cost, generally routine legal procedures.

Legislation　Laws passed by an elected body such as Congress, a state legislation, or local council/commission. Those laws enacted at the federal and state levels are called statutes. At the local level, such laws are often referred to as ordinances.

Legislative history　A technique used by courts in interpreting statutes. Courts often examine the record of the legislators' debate in an attempt to determine what was intended by the legislation.

Letter of credit　A document commonly used in international transactions to ensure payment and delivery of goods.

Libel　A defamatory written statement communicated to a third party.

License　A common method of controlling product or technology transfers across national borders.

Lien　A claim to an interest in property in satisfaction of a debt or claim.

Life estate　A property that grants land ownership for the lifetime of a specified person.

Likelihood of confusion　Standard employed in trademark law to determine if the use of a mark by two companies is too similar.

Limited liability　This term is used to describe the exposure of business owners to pay the debts of their businesses when such exposure does not exceed the owner's investment in the business.

Limited liability company (LLC)　A type of business organization that has characteristics of both a partnership and a corporation. The owners of an LLC are called members, and their personal liability is limited to their capital contributions. The LLC, as an organization, is not a taxable entity.

Limited liability partnership　A hybrid business partnership.

Limited partners　Those owners of a limited partnership who forgo control of the organization's operation in return for their liability being limited to the amount of their investment.

Limited partnership　A partnership in which one or more individuals are general partners and one or more individuals are limited partners. The limited partners contribute assets to the partnership without taking part in the conduct of the business. Such individuals are liable for the debts of the partnership only to the extent of their contributions.

Limited personal liability　See *Limited liability*.

Liquidated damages clause　A contractual provision that specifies a predetermined amount of damages or a formula for such a determination to be utilized if a breach of contract occurs.

Liquidation　The process of winding up the affairs of a business for the purpose of paying debts and disposing of assets. May be voluntary or under court order.

Litigation　The process of utilizing the court system to resolve a legal dispute.

Long-arm statute　A state statute that gives extraterritorial effect to process (summon) in specified cases. It allows state courts to obtain jurisdiction in civil actions over defendants who are beyond the border of the state provided the defendants have minimum contact with the state sufficient to satisfy due process.

Mailbox rule　The rule that an acceptance is effective once it is sent. See *Deposited acceptance rule*.

Mail fraud   The use of the U.S. Postal Service or any interstate carrier to conduct fraudulent activities with the intent to deprive an owner of property.

Malfeasance   Doing of some wrongful act.

Malice   The state of mind that accompanies the intentional doing of a wrongful act without justification or excuse.

Malicious prosecution   An action for recovery of damages that have resulted to person, property, or reputation from previous unsuccessful civil or criminal proceedings that were prosecuted without probable cause and with malice.

Manager   A person designated and charged with day-to-day operations of a limited liability company.

Mandamus   A court order directing the holder of an office to perform his or her legal duty.

Mandatory arbitration   A form of resolving a dispute, as an alternative to litigation, that is required by a statute.

Manifest system   A documentary system required by the Resource Conservation and Recovery Act. Used in the disposal of toxic chemicals.

Market extension merger   An acquisition in which the acquiring company increases its market through product extension or geographical extension.

Master   The term used in an agency relationship to describe the principal (employer) of a servant (employee) who is involved in a tort.

Material breach   A level of performance below what is reasonably acceptable. A substantial failure, without excuse, to perform a promise that constitutes the whole or part of a contract. A party who has materially breached cannot sue the other party for performance and is liable for damages.

Mayhem   Unlawfully depriving a human being of a member of his or her body.

Mechanic's lien   A lien on real estate that is created by statute to assist suppliers and laborers in collecting their accounts and wages. Its purpose is to subject the owner's land to a lien for material and labor expended in the construction of buildings and other improvements.

Med-Arb   An abbreviation for an alternative dispute resolution system that involves parties going through mediation and agreeing to resolve as many issues as possible. These parties agree that any matters not resolved in the mediation process will then be arbitrated.

Mediation   An alternative to litigation whereby a third party attempts to assist the disputing parties in reaching a settlement. The third-party mediator lacks authority to impose on the parties a binding solution to the dispute.

Mediator   An individual who assists disputing parties in their efforts to resolve their differences. Mediators must rely on their persuasive abilities since they have no authority to settle the dispute.

Members   The individuals or business entities that belong to a limited liability company.

Merger   The extinguishment of a corporate entity by the transfer of its assets and liabilities to another corporation that continues in existence.

Minimum rationality   A legal test used by courts to test the validity of governmental action, such as legislation, under the equal protection clause of the U.S. Constitution. To satisfy this test, the government needs to demonstrate that there is a good reason for the government's action.

Minimum wage   Minimum hourly wages, established by Congress under the Fair Labor Standards Act, to maintain the health, efficiency, and general well-being of workers.

Ministerial duty   An example of a definite duty regarding that nothing be left to discretion or judgment.

Minitrial   An alternative dispute resolution system that involves lawyers presenting both sides of a business dispute to the executives of the organizations involved.

Mirror image rule   The common law rule that the terms of an acceptance offer must mirror exactly the terms of the offer. Any variation of terms would make the attempted acceptance a counteroffer.

Misappropriation   A term referring to the wrongful taking of what belongs to an owner. Often used in intellectual property law.

Misappropriation theory   The legal doctrine supported by the Securities and Exchange Commission (SEC) and the courts that any person who shares nonpublic information with another party or who trades on the information violates the securities laws if that information was intended to be kept confidential.

Misdemeanor   A criminal offense of less serious nature than a felony, generally punishable by fine or jail sentence other than in a penitentiary.

Misfeasance   A misdeed or trespass.

Misrepresentation   An untrue manifestation of fact by word or conduct; it may be unintentional.

Mitigate   To lessen the consequences of. Usually used to refer to the contractual duty to lessen damages following breach of contract.

Mock trial   An alternative dispute resolution system that involves lawyers presenting their clients' cases to a group of citizens who render their opinion about the relative merits of the parties' positions.

Monopoly   Exclusive control of a market by a business entity.

Morality   The values of right and wrong.

Mortgage   1. A transfer of an interest in property for the purpose of creating a security for a debt. 2. A type of security interest in land, usually securing an extension of credit.

Mortgagee   The creditor in a mortgage agreement.

Mortgagor   The owner of land who places a mortgage on it.

Motion   The process by which the parties make written or oral requests that the judge issue an order or ruling.

Mutual assent   A contractual doctrine requiring that the minds of the contracting parties must meet before there exists a binding contract.

Mutual mistake   A situation in which parties to a contract reach a bargain on the basis of an incorrect assumption common to both parties.

National Environmental Policy Act (NEPA)   Legislation that imposes specific requirements on federal agencies to protect the environment, including the preparation of an environmental impact statement (EIS) prior to taking certain actions.

National Labor Relations Board (NLRB)   The federal administrative agency created in 1935 to conduct certification/decertification elections of unions and to conduct quasi-judicial hearings arising from the labor–management relationship.

National Mediation Board   Created by the Railway Labor Act, this federal agency is to help the parties resolve labor–management disputes arising in transportation industries.

Nationalization   A claim made by a foreign government that it owns expropriated property.

Natural law   A philosophy of law that says certain legal rules can be reasoned out from nature itself and always hold true.

Necessaries of life   Food, clothing, shelter, medical care, and, in some states, education. A minor is legally responsible to pay a reasonable value for purchased necessaries of life.

Negligence   A person's failure to exercise reasonable care that foreseeably causes another injury.

Negotiable instrument or document   A special type of written promise to pay money (instrument) or deliver goods (document). Personal defenses do not apply against the holder in due course of a negotiable instrument or document.

Negotiated settlement   A voluntary but binding agreement that settles a legal dispute, such as one involving a contractual breach or a tort lawsuit.

Negotiation   The process used to persuade or coerce someone to do or to stop doing something.

NLRB   National Labor Relations Board.

Noerr-Pennington doctrine   This doctrine exempts from the antitrust laws concerted efforts to lobby government officials regardless of the anticompetitive purposes. It is based on the First Amendment freedom of speech.

No-fault laws   Laws barring tort actions by injured persons against third-party tortfeasors and requiring such persons to obtain recovery from their own insurers.

Nolo contendere   A plea entered by the defendant in a criminal case that neither admits nor denies the crime allegedly committed but, if accepted by the court, permits the judge to treat the defendant as guilty.

Non-profit corporation   A corporation that must return all profits to the organization for use in future operations. Such corporations are often exempt from federal income tax.

Nontrading partnership   A business organization made up of two or more partners engaged in buying and selling goods.

Norris-LaGuardia Act   The federal legislation adopted in 1932 that attempted to increase union membership by prohibiting the use of injunctions issued by federal courts against certain union activities and by outlawing yellow-dog contracts.

North American Free Trade Agreement (NAFTA)   An agreement reached in 1993 among the United States, Mexico, and Canada to increase economic growth through mutual trade.

Noscitur a sociis   The principle that the scope of general words is defined by specific accompanying words; a doctrine of legislative interpretation.

Notary public   A public officer authorized to administer oaths and certify certain documents.

Notice   Communication sufficient to charge a reasonable person with knowledge of some fact.

Novation   The substitution of a new contract in place of an old one.

Nuisance   A physical condition constituting an unreasonable and substantial interference with the rights of individuals or the public at large.

Obligee   One who is entitled to receive a payment or performance under a contract.

Obligor   One who is obligated to pay or perform under a contract.

Obscenity   A category of speech not protected by the First Amendment.

Obstruction of justice   A criminal act involving the interference of the administration of the laws during the investigations and conduct of trials.

Occupational Safety and Health Administration (OSHA)   The organization that has jurisdiction over complaints about hazardous conditions in the workplace.

Offer   A contractual communication that contains a specific promise and a specific demand. The offer initiates the process of making a contract.

Officers   Those individuals appointed by directors of a corporation to conduct the daily operations of the corporate organization.

Oligopoly   Control of the supply and price of a commodity or service in a given market by a small number of companies or suppliers.

Opinion   The decision of a judge, usually issued in a written form.

Option   A contractual arrangement under which one party has for a specified time the right to buy certain property from or sell certain property to the other party. It is essentially a contract to not revoke an offer.

Oral argument   Attorneys appear in person before the appellate court to explain orally to the court their position in the case and answer the court's questions about the case.

Ordinance   The legislative enactment of a city, county, or other municipal corporation.

Organizers   The parties responsible for bringing a limited liability company into existence. These parties correspond to the functions of incorporators with respect to corporations.

Originalism   Stands for the idea that courts should interpret the Constitution according to the intentions of those who wrote it.

Overbreadth doctrine   A principle used by courts to invalidate legislation that is broader in scope than is necessary to regulate an activity. This doctrine may be utilized to protect constitutional rights, such as freedom of speech, against a wide sweep of some governmental action.

Overt act   An essential element of a crime. Without this action by a party, the intent to engage in criminal activity is not wrongful.

Ownership   The term refers to the exclusive legal right to possess, transfer, and use resources. It is a synonym for "property."

Paper fortress   A term referring to the documentation an employer should keep about an employee's performance.

Parker v. Brown doctrine   The name given to the state action exemption to the Sherman Act. See also *State action exemption.*

Parol evidence   Legal proof based on oral statements; with regard to a document, any evidence extrinsic to the document itself.

Parol evidence rule   Parol evidence is extrinsic evidence. In contracts, the parol evidence rule excludes the introduction of evidence of prior written or oral agreements that may vary, contradict, alter, or supplement the present written agreement. There are several exceptions to this rule. For example, when the parties to an agreement do not intend for that agreement to be final and complete, then parol evidence is admissible.

Part performance   The contractual doctrine that says when a buyer of land has made valuable improvements in it or has paid part or all of the purchase price, the statute of frauds does not apply to prevent an oral land sales contract from being enforceable.

Partnership   A business organization involving two or more persons agreeing to conduct a commercial venture while sharing its profits and losses.

Patent   A statutorily created property right in inventions and discoveries. See *Utility patent, Design patent,* and *Plant patent.*

Patent Troll   A firm or individual that produces no products or services and owns patents only to obtain licensing fees from other firms.

Pattern of racketeering   Under RICO, two or more similar acts of organized crime in a ten-year period.

Pay-for-play   A term referencing the need for one to have to pay to get performed a duty that an official, frequently a government official, is already obligated to perform, for example, an appointment by the official. Pay-for-play usually indicates official corruption.

Per capita   By or for each individual.

Per curiam   By the court; said of an opinion expressing the view of the court as a whole as opposed to an opinion authored by any single member of the court.

Per se   In itself.

Per se illegality   Under the Sherman Act, agreements and practices are illegal only if they are unreasonable. The practices that are conclusively presumed to be unreasonable are per se illegal. If an activity is per se illegal, only proof of the activity is required, and it is not necessary to prove an anticompetitive effect. For example, price fixing is per se illegal. See also *Rule of reason.*

Peremptory challenge The power granted each party to reject a limited number of potential jurors during voir dire examination. No reason for the rejection need be given.

Perfection The status ascribed to security interests after certain events have occurred or certain prescribed steps have been taken, for example, the filing of a financing statement.

Perjury The giving of false testimony under oath.

Personal jurisdiction The power of a court over the parties involved in the litigation process.

Personal property All property that does not involve land and interests in land.

Petit jury The fact-finding body during a trial. Also called a trial or traverse jury.

Petitioner The party filing either a case in equity or a petition for a writ of *certiorari* before a supreme court.

Petty offenses Criminal acts that are viewed as minor and thus are typically punished by a fine only.

Piercing the corporate veil The legal doctrine used by courts to disregard the existence of a corporation, thereby holding the shareholders personally liable for the organization's debts.

Piracy Traditionally a form of theft on the high seas, but also applied to criminal misappropriation of intellectual property, particularly copyrighted media.

Plaintiff The person who initiates a lawsuit.

Plan termination insurance The insurance required by federal law on regulated pension plans. It protects against plan termination that leaves pension benefits underfunded.

Plant patent A property right awarded for a new variety of plant that can be produced asexually. Note that inventions involving plants may be protected as utility patents. See *Utility patent.*

Pleadings The system for defining and narrowing the issues by parties who file formal documents stating their respective positions in a lawsuit.

Plenary Entire; complete in all respects.

Point source Any source of air pollution that must be licensed under the Clean Air Act.

Positional bargaining A method of negotiation that focuses on the parties exchanging offers, with concessions being made so that parties find a middle ground. The seller refers to the last offer made as its bottom line, and the buyer refers to the last offer made as its top dollar.

Possession Dominion and control over property; the holding or detention of property in one's own power or command.

Postdispute arbitration clause Can be applicable to arbitration, mediation, or other methods of ADR; such a clause is signed by parties that are already in dispute.

Posteffective period As it relates to an initial public offering of securities, this is the period during which the securities may be sold. This period usually follows a 20-day waiting period.

Precedent A prior judicial decision relied upon as an example of a rule of law.

Predatory pricing A policy of lowering the price charged to customers for the purpose of driving competitors out of business. Typically, this policy involves prices that are below the seller's costs of the products sold with resulting losses to the seller.

Predispute arbitration clause Applicable to ADR systems agreed to by contracting parties prior to a dispute arising; usually this clause is a part of the original contract between the parties.

Preemption A condition when a federal statute or administrative rule governs an issue to the extent that a state or local government is prohibited from regulating that area of law.

Preemptive right A corporation's shareholder's right to maintain the same percentage ownership of the organization whenever newly authorized stock is sold.

Preferred stock A type of stock issued by a corporation that entitles the owner to receive a dividend before owners of common stock.

Prefiling period As it relates to an initial public offering of securities, this is that period of time prior to the filing of a registration statement with the SEC.

Prejudicial error An error in judicial proceedings that may have affected the result in the case.

Premerger notification Requirement under the federal Hart-Scott-Rodino Act that requires firms involved in large mergers and acquisitions to notify the FTC and DOJ before they occur.

Preponderance of evidence In the judgment of the jurors, evidence that has greater weight and overcomes the opposing evidence and presumptions.

Presumption of innocence The basis of requiring the government to prove a criminal defendant's guilt beyond a reasonable doubt.

Prevention of significant deterioration A rule implemented under the Clean Air Act that prohibits the degradation of air quality in regions where air quality is better than required by primary air quality standards.

Price discrimination   A seller charging different purchasers different prices for the same goods at the same time.

Price fixing   An agreement or combination by which the conspirators set the market price, whether high or low, of a product or service whether being sold or purchased.

Prima facie   On the face of it; thus, presumed to be true unless proved otherwise.

Primary air quality standards   The standards necessary to protect human health. Secondary air quality standards are stricter standards necessary to protect various environmental amenities.

Primary jurisdiction   A doctrine used by reviewing courts to determine whether a case is properly before the courts or whether it should be heard by an administrative agency first since such an agency might have expertise superior to the courts'.

Principal   The person who gives an agent authority.

Principled, interest-based, negotiations   A method of negotiation that focuses on the parties' interests as opposed to positions. The language used to describe this bargaining includes options, alternatives, objective criteria, and relationships.

Prior consideration   Service or gift from the past that presently induces one to make a promise. Prior consideration does not enable that promise to bind one. It is not legal consideration.

Prior restraint   A principle applicable under the freedom of press and speech clauses of the First Amendment of the U.S. Constitution. The courts have announced decisions that encourage governments to allow the publication or expression of thoughts rather than to restrain such thoughts in advance of their publication or expression.

Private international law   A body of rules that deal with controversies between private persons, such as those created by commercial transactions.

Private law   A classification of legal subject matters that deals most directly with relationships between legal entities. The law of contracts and the law of property are two examples of this classification.

Private nuisance   An unreasonable use of one's land so as to cause substantial interference with the enjoyment or use of another's land.

Private Securities Litigation Reform Act (PSLRA)   A 1995 federal statute that limits the recovery for securities violations against third parties who are not directly responsible for the violation. For example, only the Securities and Exchange Commission can pursue these claims. This law also requires lead plaintiffs in class-action securities suits and restricts recovery of damages and attorneys' fees.

Privilege   A special advantage accorded by law to some individual or group; an exemption from a duty or obligation generally imposed by law.

Privileged communication   A rule of evidence that protects conversations that society deems to be confidential. For example, a witness cannot be required to disclose communications between an attorney and a client.

Privileges and immunities clause   A provision found in Article IV and the Fourteenth Amendment of the U.S. Constitution that prevents a state government from discriminating in favor of its citizens and against citizens from another state. This clause, while not interpreted to be absolute, has emphasized national rather than state citizenship.

Privity   Interest derived from successive relationship with another party; a contractual connection.

Probable cause   The reasonable basis on which law enforcement officials convince a judge that criminal activity has occurred. This is the basis that must be satisfied before a judge will issue a criminal search warrant.

Procedural due process   The process or procedure ensuring fundamental fairness that all citizens are entitled to under the U.S. Constitution.

Procedural law   The body of rules governing the manner in which legal claims are enforced.

Product extension merger   A merger that extends the products of the acquiring company into a similar or related product but one that is not directly in competition with existing products.

Product liability   The liability that sellers have for the goods they sell.

Production defect   A defect arising when a product does not meet its manufacturer's own standards.

Promise   A commitment or willingness to be bound to a contract obligation.

Promissory estoppel   Court enforcement of an otherwise unbinding promise if injustice can be avoided only by enforcement of the promise. A substitute for consideration.

Property   A bundle of private, exclusive rights in people to acquire, possess, use, and transfer scarce resources.

Property law   The law of the legal fence that establishes exclusive right in someone called an owner.

Proportionality review   The process that appellate courts use to determine the appropriateness of a criminal sentence.

Prospectus   The legal document required by the 1933 Securities Act to be made available to potential purchasers of securities.

Pro tanto   So far as it goes.

Protestant ethic   A set of beliefs urging that human desire and indulgence be bent to God's will through hard work, self-denial, and rational planning.

Proximate causation   The doctrine that limits an actor's liability to consequences that could reasonably be foreseen to have resulted from the act.

Proximate cause   In tort law and legal requirement that an act foreseeably causes an injury.

Proxy   The legal document whereby a shareholder appoints an agent to vote the stock at a corporation's shareholders' meeting.

Public international law   A body of rules that examines relationships among nations and seeks to bind them to common principles in the international community.

Public law   A classification of legal subject matters that regulates the relationship of individuals and organizations to society.

Public nuisance   An owner's use of land that causes damage or inconvenience to the general public.

Public policy   Accepted standards of behavior. For instance, a contract is illegal if it violates public policy.

Publicly held   A business organization that has hundreds, if not thousands, of owners who can exchange their ownership interests on public exchanges.

Punitive damages   Monetary damages in excess of a compensatory award, usually granted only in intentional tort cases where defendant's conduct involved some element deserving punishment. Also called *exemplary damages*.

Purchase money security interest (PMSI)   A security interest given to the party that loans the debtor the money that enables the debtor to buy the collateral.

Qualified disabled   A disabled person who can perform the duties of a job.

Qualified pension plan   A private retirement plan that gains favorable income tax treatment from the Internal Revenue Service (IRS). A qualified pension plan allows for the deduction of contributions made to fund the plan. Also, earnings from fund investments are not taxable, and employees defer personal income tax liability until payments are received after retirement. To qualify, the plan must cover a high percentage of workers (usually 70%) or cover classifications of employees that do not discriminate in favor of management or shareholders.

Quantity discount   The practice of giving a lower per unit price to businesses that buy a product in volume than to their competitors that do not.

Quasi-contract   A quasi-contract, often referred to as an implied-in-law contract, is not a true contract. It is a legal fiction that the courts use to prevent unjust enrichment and wrongdoing. Courts permit the person who conferred a benefit to recover the reasonable value of that benefit. Nonetheless, the elements of a true contract are not present.

Quasi-judicial   Administrative actions involving factual determinations and the discretionary application of rules and regulations.

Quasi-legislative   This term describes the rule-making functions of administrative agencies.

Quasi-strict scrutiny   A legal test used by courts to test the validity of governmental action, such as legislation, under the equal protection clause of the U.S. Constitution. To satisfy this test, the government needs to demonstrate that the purpose of the action is substantially related to an important governmental objective.

Quick-look analysis   A process of review used by courts in antitrust cases to determine the legality of an anticompetitive act. This analysis is something greater than the per se determination of illegality and less than the full consideration of the rule of reason analysis.

Quid pro quo   The exchange of one thing of value for another.

Quitclaim deed   The transfer by deed of all the grantor's rights, title, and interest in property.

Quo warranto   An action brought about by the government to test the validity of some franchise, such as the privilege of doing business as a corporation.

Racketeering   A crime under RICO involving a pattern of actions that are indictable under state or federal laws.

Railway Labor Act   The federal law passed in 1926 to encourage collective bargaining in the railroad industry. The law also created the National Mediation Board.

Ratification   What occurs when a principal voluntarily decides to honor an agreement.

Ratio decidendi   Logical basis of judicial decision.

Real property   Property in land and interests in land.

Reasonable accommodation   The actions that an employer must take under Title VII of the Civil Rights Act and under the Americans with Disabilities Act to adapt employment conditions to an employee's religious belief or disability.

Reciprocal dealing   A contract in which two parties agree to mutual actions so that each party can act as both a buyer and a seller. The agreement violates the Clayton Act if it results in a substantial lessening of competition.

Redlining   An act or refusal to act that results in a discriminatory practice. For example, refusing to make loans in low-income areas can discriminate against minorities in granting credit.

Reformation   A contractual remedy exercised by a court to correct a mistake of drafting or some other nonessential mistake. After reformation the parties remain bound to the contract.

Registration statement   The legal document required to be filed with the Securities and Exchange Commission (SEC) prior to securities being offered for sale to the public.

Reimbursement   Restoration; to pay back or repay that expended; the act of making one whole.

Rejection   The refusal of an offer. A rejection terminates an offer.

Release   The relinquishment of a right or claim against another party.

Remand   The return of a case by an appellate court for further action by the lower court.

Remedial statute   Legislation designed to provide a benefit or relief to a victim of a violation of law.

Remediation   Restoring land to its previous condition.

Remedy   The action or procedure that is followed in order to enforce a right or to obtain damages for injury to a right; the means by which a right is enforced or the violation of a right is prevented, redressed, or compensated.

Reorganization   The legal process of forming a new corporation after bankruptcy or foreclosure.

Replevin   An action for the recovery of goods wrongfully taken or kept.

Representational standing   The requirements that must be satisfied for an organization to have the right to file a lawsuit on behalf of its members.

Request for an admission   A method of discovery used to narrow the issues to be litigated by having a party request that the other party admit the facts that are not in dispute.

Request for production of documents   A method of discovery whereby one party asks the other to provide documents for the requesting party's review.

Requirements contract   A contract under which the buyer agrees to buy a certain item only from the seller.

Res   A thing, object, or status.

Res ipsa loquitur   The thing speaks for itself. A rule of evidence whereby negligence of the alleged wrongdoer may be inferred from the mere fact that the injury occurred.

Res judicata   The doctrine that deems a former adjudication conclusive and prevents a retrial of matters decided in the earlier lawsuit.

Resale price maintenance   Manufacturer control of a brand- or trade-name product's minimum resale price.

Rescind   To cancel or annul a contract and return the parties to their original positions.

Rescission   A contractual remedy that cancels the agreement and returns the consideration exchanged to each party.

Respondeat superior   The doctrine imposing liability on one for torts committed by another person who is in his or her employ and subject to his or her control.

Respondent   The party answering a petition for a writ of *certiorari* in the Supreme Court.

Restitution   A contractual remedy involving one party returning to another the value previously received.

Restraint of trade   Monopolies, combinations, and contracts that impede free competition.

Restrictive covenants   Private agreements that restrict land use.

Retaliation   Striking back against someone for what they did to you. Used in labor law, employment discrimination cases, and whistle-blowing as part of a doctrine prohibiting an employer from firing or taking other adverse actions against employees for reporting the employer to federal agencies for violating various laws.

Retaliatory trade practices   Actions by aggrieved nations responding to tariffs and other unfair trade restrictions imposed by foreign governments.

Reverse   Overturn or vacate the judgment of a court.

Reverse discrimination   The advancement and recruitment of minority workers ahead of similarly qualified nonminority workers.

Revocation   The contractual communication of withdrawing an offer.

RICO   The Racketeer Influenced and Corrupt Organizations Act.

Right of redemption   The right to buy back. A debtor may buy back or redeem his or her mortgaged property when he or she pays the debt.

Right-to-work law   A state statute that outlaws a union shop contract—one by which an employer agrees to require membership in the union sometime after an employee has been hired as a condition of continued employment.

Robbery   Illegally taking something by force.

Robinson-Patman Act   The amendment to Section 2 of the Clayton Act covering price discrimination. As originally adopted, the Robinson-Patman Act outlawed price discrimination in interstate commerce that might substantially lessen competition or tends to create a monopoly.

Rule against perpetuities   The rule that prohibits an owner from controlling what he or she owns beyond a life in being at the owner's death, plus 21 years.

Rule of first possession   The rule that says one becomes an owner by reducing to possession previously unowned objects or abandoned objects.

Rule of law   The general and equal application of laws, even to lawmakers.

Rule of reason   Under the Sherman Act, contracts or conspiracies are illegal only if they constitute an unreasonable restraint of trade or attempt to monopolize. An activity is unreasonable if it adversely affects competition. An act is reasonable if it promotes competition. The rule of reason requires that an anticompetitive effect be shown. See also *Per se illegality*.

Rules of evidence   The laws governing the admission of evidence, such as testimony and documents, during the trial of a case.

S corporation   A business organization that is formed as a corporation but, by a shareholders' election, is treated as a partnership for taxation purposes.

Sale of business doctrine   The legal principle in securities law that might be used to remove the sale of corporate stock from the securities laws' protection if the purchaser of such stock is to operate the business instead of relying on others to do so.

Sanctions   Penalties imposed for violation of a law.

Sarbanes-Oxley Act of 2002   The law enacted to correct inadequacies in the law that existed and allowed numerous examples of corporate fraud. In essence, through increased criminal sanctions and specific requirements, this law attempts to make corporate CEOs more responsible.

Scheme to defraud   A plan to misrepresent a material fact in order to obtain something, usually money, from another.

Scienter   With knowledge; particularly, guilty knowledge.

Scoping   A regulatory step required of a federal agency by the Council on Environmental Quality. Before preparing an environmental impact statement, an agency must designate which environmental issues of a proposed action are most significant.

Search warrant   A court order required by the Fourth Amendment of the U.S. Constitution to be obtained from government officials prior to private property being searched or seized.

Secondary air quality standards   Clean Air Act standards designed to protect environmental quality other than human health.

Secondary boycott   Conspiracy or combination to cause the customers or suppliers of an employer to cease doing business with that employer.

Section 1981   That provision of the Civil Rights Act of 1866 that forbids racial discrimination in the making of contracts.

Section 402A   That section of the Second Restatement of Torts that imposes strict liability on product sellers who sell a product in a "defective condition unreasonably dangerous to the user or consumer or his property."

Section 5   Section of the Federal Trade Commission act which authorizes the commission to regulate unfair or deceptive acts or practices in trade.

Secured transactions   Any credit transaction creating a security interest; an interest in personal property that secures the payment of an obligation.

Securities Act of 1933   The federal law that regulates (through disclosure requirements) the initial sale of securities to the public.

Securities and Exchange Commission (SEC)   The federal administrative agency that regulates the securities industry.

Securities Exchange Act of 1934   The federal law that regulates sales (other than the initial sale) of securities. This law governs the resale of securities whether by individuals or through brokers and exchanges.

Security   Under the securities law, an investment in which the investor does not participate in management.

Security interests   An application of property that gives someone an interest in what belongs to another, usually to secure an extension of credit.

Self-regulation   An entire industry's regulation of itself, as opposed to government regulation of the businesses in the industry.

Seller   In commercial law, a person who sells or contracts to sell goods.

Seniority system   A plan giving priority to employees based on the length of time an employee has worked for an employer. An employer may apply different standards pursuant to a good-faith seniority system if the differences are not the result of an intention to discriminate.

Sentencing guidelines   Adopted by the U.S. Sentencing Commission as a means of standardizing the sentences given to similar criminals committing similar crimes.

Separation of powers   The doctrine that holds that the legislative, executive, and judicial branches of government function independently of one another and that each branch serves as a check on the others.

Servant   The person hired to act on behalf of a principal in an agency relationship.

Service mark   Any mark, word, picture, or design that attaches to a service and indicates its source.

Set-off   A counterclaim by a defendant against a plaintiff that grows from an independent cause of action and diminishes the plaintiff's potential recovery.

Sexual harassment   Under Title VII, for an employer or workplace supervisor to promise benefits or threaten loss if an employee does not give sexual favors.

Shareholders   The owners of corporations. Typically these owners vote on major decisions impacting their corporations, most commonly the election of a board of directors.

Shark repellent   Corporate action to make a threatened acquisition unattractive to the acquiring company.

Shelf registration   The process in securities law under Securities and Exchange Commission (SEC) Rule 415 that allows an issuer to satisfy the registration statement requirements, thereby allowing the issuer immediately to offer securities for sale.

Sherman Act   An 1890 congressional enactment designed to regulate anticompetitive behavior in interstate commerce.

Short-swing profits   The proceeds gained by an insider buying and selling, or vice versa, securities within a six-month time period. Such profits are considered to be illegal.

Simplified employee pension   A type of pension permitted by the Revenue Act of 1978. Under this pension type, employers contribute up to a specified amount to employee individual retirement accounts.

Slander   An oral defamatory statement communicated to a third person.

Small-claims court   A court of limited jurisdiction, usually able to adjudicate claims up to a certain amount, such as $3,000, depending on the state.

Social contract theory   A theory by John Rawls that proposes a way for constructing a just society.

Sole proprietorship   The simplest form of business organization, created and controlled by one owner.

Solid Waste Disposal Act

Sovereign immunity   A doctrine of state and international law that permits a foreign government to claim immunity from suit in the courts of other nations.

Sovereignty   The supreme, absolute, and uncontrollable power by which any state is governed.

Specific performance   Equitable remedy that requires defendants in certain circumstances to do what they have contracted to do.

Stakeholder theory   Ethical theory which asserts that in order to be ethical a business must take into consideration not only the making of a profit but the impacts of the business on all interests that are affected by the business.

Standing   The doctrine that requires the plaintiff in a lawsuit to have a sufficient legal interest in the subject matter of the case.

Standing to sue   The requirement that a plaintiff must satisfy by demonstrating a personal interest in the outcome of litigation or an administrative hearing.

Stare decisis   The doctrine that traditionally indicates that a court should follow prior decisions in all cases based on substantially similar facts.

State action exemption   The Sherman Act exemption of the sovereign action of a state that replaces competition with regulation if the state actively supervises the anticompetitive conduct.

State-of-the-art defense   A defense that the defendant's product or practice was compatible with the current state of technology available at the time of the event in question.

States' relations article   Article IV of the U.S. Constitution. Among its purposes, this article prevents a state from favoring its citizens over the citizens of another state, thereby making the United States one nation as opposed to 50 subgroups.

Status quo   The conditions or state of affairs at a given time.

Statute   A legislative enactment.

Statute of frauds   Legislation that states that certain contracts will not be enforced unless there is a signed writing evidencing the agreement.

Statute of limitations   A statute that sets a date after which a lawsuit may not be brought. The statute begins running after the happening of a certain event, such as the occurrence of an injury or the breach of a contract.

Statute of repose   A statute that applies to product liability cases. It prohibits initiation of litigation involving products more than a certain number of years (e.g., 25) following their manufacture.

Statutory construction   The rules courts use in interpreting the meaning of legislation.

Strict liability   The doctrine under which a party may be required to respond in tort damages without regard to such party's use of due care.

Strict products liability   The cause of action under which commercial sellers of defective products are held liable without negligence.

Strict scrutiny   A legal test used by courts to test the validity of governmental action, such as legislation, under the equal protection clause of the U.S. Constitution. To satisfy this test, the government needs to demonstrate that there is a compelling state interest justifying the government's action.

Structured settlement   A periodic payment of damages, usually taking the form of a guaranteed annuity.

Subject matter jurisdiction   The authority of a court to hear cases involving specific issues of law.

Submission   The act or process of referring an issue to arbitration.

Subpoena   A court order directing a witness to appear or to produce documents in his or her possession.

Substantial performance   Degree of performance recognizing that a contracting party has honestly attempted to perform but has fallen short. One who has substantially performed is entitled to the price promised by the other less that party's damages.

Substantive due process   The use of the due process provision of the U.S. Constitution to make certain that the application of a law does not unfairly deprive persons of property rights.

Substantive law   A body of rules defining the nature and extent of legal rights.

Summary judgment   A judicial determination that no genuine factual dispute exists and that one party to the lawsuit is entitled to judgment as a matter of law.

Summons   An official notice to a person that a lawsuit has been commenced against him or her and that he or she must appear in court to answer the charges.

Superfund   The Comprehensive Environmental Response, Compensation, and Liability Act of 1980.

Supremacy clause   Article VI of the U.S. Constitution, which states that the Constitution, laws, and treaties of the United States shall be the "supreme law of the land" and shall take precedence over conflicting state laws.

Supreme Court   The highest appellate court.

Surety   One who incurs a liability for the benefit of another. One who undertakes to pay money in the event that his or her principal is unable to pay.

Symbolic speech   Nonverbal expression.

Taft-Hartley Act   The federal law enacted in 1947 to increase the bargaining power of management by creating unfair labor practices by unions, by outlawing the closed shop, by creating an 80-day cooling-off period, by permitting states to adopt right-to-work laws, and by creating the Federal Mediation and Conciliation Service.

Tangible personal property   Physical property.

Tarnishment   A type of trademark dilution that occurs when a mark's reputation is harmed by another's use of the same mark in a different context.

Teleology   An ethical system that concerns itself with the moral consequences of actions. Also called *consequentialism.*

Tenancy in common   A property ownership that is undivided (common) but not necessarily equal between two or more owners.

Tender offer   An invited public offer by a company or organization to buy shares from existing shareholders of another public corporation under specified terms.

Tender performance   The offer by one contracting party to perform a promise; usually associated with the offer to pay for or to ship items under the contract.

Testator   One who has made a will.

Third party   One who enters into a relationship with a principal by way of interacting with the principal's agent.

Third-party beneficiaries   Persons who are recognized as having enforceable rights created for them by a contract to which they are not parties and for which they have given no consideration.

Third-party defendant   A party who is not a party (plaintiff or defendant) to the original litigation. Typically, a defendant might file a claim against a third party stating that if the defendant is liable to the plaintiff, then this third party will be liable to the defendant.

Tippee   A person who learns of nonpublic information about a security from an insider.

Title   A synonym for ownership. Sometimes represented as a document.

Tombstone ad   An advertisement announcing the public offering of securities; these usually run during the waiting period.

Tort   A civil wrong other than a breach of contract.

Toxic Substances Control Act   A law passed by Congress in 1967 to meet the special environmental problems posed by the use of toxic chemicals.

Trade disparagement   The publication of untrue statements that disparage the plaintiff's ownership of property or its quality.

Trade dress   A legal doctrine giving someone ownership of a distinctive overall appearance or look and feel of a product or service.

Trade practice regulation   A term generally referring to laws that regulate competitive practices.

Trade secret   Any formula, pattern, machine, or process of manufacturing used in one's business that may give the user an opportunity to obtain an advantage over its competitors. Trade secrets are legally protectable.

Trade-Related Aspects of Intellectual Property Agreement (TRIPS)   International agreement requiring members to enact basic intellectual property protections.

Trade usage   Refers to the particular use of a word in business that may differ from its common use.

Trademark   A statutorily created property in a mark, word, picture, or design that attaches to goods and indicates their source.

Trademark dilution   Using someone's trademark in such a way so as to reduce the value of the trademark's significance, reputation, and goodwill, even if the public is not confused by the use.

Trading partnership   A business organization made up of two or more partners engaged in providing services.

Treason   Breach of allegiance to one's government, specifically by levying war against such government or by giving aid and comfort to the enemy.

Treaty of Rome   A historic agreement reached by six European countries in 1957 to achieve economic unity in the European Community. The latter is now known as the European Union, and its membership has grown to 15 nations.

Treble damages   See *Triple damages*.

Trespass   An act done in an unlawful manner so as to cause injury to another; an unauthorized entry upon another's land.

Trial court   The level of any court system that initially resolves the dispute of litigants. Frequently, but not always, a jury serves as a fact-finding body while the judge issues rulings on the applicable law.

Triple damages (or treble damages)   An award of damages allowable under some statutes equal to three times the amount found by the jury to be a single recovery.

Trustee   One who holds legal title to property for the benefit of another.

Truth in lending   A federal law that requires the disclosure of total finance charges and the annual percentage rate for credit in order that borrowers may be able to shop for credit.

Tying contract   A contract that ties the sale of one piece of property (real or personal) to the sale or lease of another item of property.

Ultra vires   Beyond the scope of corporate powers granted in the charter.

Unconscionable   In the law of contracts, provisions that are oppressive, overreaching, or shocking to the conscience.

Underwriter   The party that, in securities law, guarantees the issuer that the securities offered for sale will be sold.

Undue burden   Under the Civil Rights Act of 1964 and the Americans with Disabilities Act an employer need not take action that is excessively costly or creates excessive inefficiency in order to accommodate an employee's religious beliefs or disability. This is the concept of undue burden.

Unenforceable contract   A contract that cannot be enforced in court.

Unfair competition   A group of statutory torts that include misappropriation of trademarks, patent violations, and copyright breaches. One aspect of the Federal Trade Commission's authority. Section 5 of the FTC Act makes unfair methods of competition illegal.

Unfair labor practices   Activities by management or labor unions that have been declared to be inappropriate by the Wagner Act and Taft-Hartley Act, respectively.

Uniform Commercial Code (UCC)   The most successful attempt to have states adopt a uniform law. This code's purpose is to simplify, clarify, and modernize the laws governing commercial transactions.

Uniformed Services Employment and Reemployment Rights Act (USERRA)   The act which protects the rights of individuals who voluntarily or involuntarily leave employment positions to undertake military service.

Unilateral contract   A contract in which the promisor does not receive a promise as consideration; an agreement whereby one makes a promise to do, or refrain from doing, something in return for a performance, not a promise.

Unilateral mistake   Arises when only one of the parties to a contract is wrong about a material fact. It is not usually a basis for rescinding a contract.

Union security clause   The contractual provision that creates a union shop agreement. This clause requires any person hired as an employee to join the union representing the employees.

Union shop   This term applies, in labor law, to an agreement by management and labor that all employees of a business will be or become union members. Union shops are not allowed in states with right-to-work laws.

United Nations   The principal political organization of the world.

Unreasonable search and seizure   A violation of the Fourth Amendment of the U.S. Constitution that occurs when a valid search warrant is not obtained or when the scope of a valid warrant is exceeded.

Usury   A loan of money at interest above the legal rate.

Utilitarianism   A form of consequentialist ethics.

Utility patent   A property right awarded for a new and non-obvious process, machine, or composition of matter that has a useful function.

Valid contract   A contract that contains all of the proper elements of a contract.

Venue   The geographical area over which a court presides. Venue designates the court in which the case should be tried. Change of venue means moving to another court.

Verdict   Findings of fact by the jury.

Vertical merger   A merger of corporations where one corporation is the supplier of the other.

Vertical price fixing   An agreement between a seller and a buyer (for example, between a manufacturer and a retailer) to fix the resale price at which the buyer will sell goods.

Vertical restraint   An restrictive agreement between parties in the supply or distribution chain, such as between a manufacturer and retailer.

Vertical territorial agreement   Arrangement between a supplier and its customers with respect to the geographical area in which each customer will be allowed to sell that supplier's products. This type of agreement is analyzed under the rule of reason to determine whether it violates the Sherman Act. Limitations on intrabrand competition may be permitted if there is a corresponding increase in interbrand competition.

Vested rights   Rights that have become so fixed that they are not subject to being taken away without the consent of the owner.

Void contract   A contract that is empty, having no legal force; ineffectual, unenforceable.

Voidable contract   Capable of being declared a nullity, though otherwise valid.

Voir dire   The preliminary examination of prospective jurors for the purpose of ascertaining bias or interest in the lawsuit.

Voluntary arbitration   A method of resolving a dispute, as an alternative to litigation, that the parties agree to utilize. This agreement may be made before or after a dispute arises.

Voluntary bargaining issue   Either party may refuse to bargain in good faith regarding matters other than wages, hours, and other terms and conditions of employment. This refusal does not constitute an unfair labor practice. An issue over which parties may bargain if they choose to do so.

Voluntary petition   The document filed by a debtor to initiate bankruptcy proceedings.

Wagner Act   The federal law passed in 1935 that recognizes employees' rights to organize. This law also created the National Labor Relations Board and defined unfair labor practices by management. It is formally known as the National Labor Relations Act.

Waiting period   As it relates to an initial public offering of securities, this is the period of time that follows the filing of documents with the SEC and that precedes when the securities can be sold. Unless the SEC objects and extends this period of time, the waiting period lasts only 20 days.

Waiver   An express or implied relinquishment of a right.

WARN Act   The Worker Adjustment and Retraining Notification Act of 1989; this law requires employers to give notice of plant closings and mass layoffs.

Warrant   A judicial authorization for the performance of some act.

Warranty of authority   An agent's implied guarantee that he or she has the authority to enter into a contract. The agent is liable for breaching the warranty if he or she lacks proper authority.

Warranty of merchantability   A promise implied in a sale of goods by merchants that the goods are reasonably fit for the general purpose for which they are sold.

White-collar crime   Violations of the law by business organizations or by individuals in a business-related capacity.

White knight   A slang term that describes the inducement of a voluntary acquisition when an involuntary acquisition is threatened. The voluntary acquisition group is a white knight since it saves the corporation from an unfriendly takeover.

Willful and wanton negligence   Extremely unreasonable behavior that causes injury.

Willfully   With intent to defraud or deceive.

Wire fraud   The use of radio, television, telephone, Internet, or other wired forms of communication to conduct fraudulent activities with the intent to deprive an owner of property.

Work rules   A company's regulations governing the workplace, the application of which often becomes an issue in the ability of employees to organize for their mutual benefit and protection.

Workers' compensation   A plan for the compensation for occupational diseases, accidental injuries, and deaths of employees that arise out of employment. Compensation includes medical expenses and burial costs and lost earnings based on the size of the family and the wage rate of the employee.

World Bank   The world's principal financial institution.

World Intellectual Property Organization   A specialized agency of the United Nations that administers certain intellectual property treaties and provides related educational resources.

World Trade Organization (WTO)   Mechanism for enforcing the General Agreement on Tariffs and Trade that allows GATT member countries to bring complaints and seek redress.

Wright-Line doctrine   Establishes procedures for determining the burden of proof in cases involving mixed motivation for discharge.

Writ of certiorari   A discretionary proceeding by which an appellate court may review the ruling of an inferior tribunal.

Writ of habeas corpus   A court order to one holding custody of another to produce that individual before the court for the purpose of determining whether such custody is proper.

Yellow-dog contract   An agreement in which a worker agrees not to join a union and that discharge will result from a breach of the contract.

Zoning ordinance   Laws that limit land use based usually on residential, commercial, or industrial designations.

CHAPTER 1

Opener: © C. Lee/PhotoLink/Getty Images RF.

CHAPTER 2

Opener: © Michael H/Getty Images RF.

CHAPTER 3

Opener: © Library of Congress Prints and Photographs Division [LC-DIG-highsm-25855]; p.82: © Collection of the Supreme Court of the United States, Photographer: Steve Petteway; p.82 (Antonin Scalia & Anthony Kennedy): © Collection of the Supreme Court of the United States; p.80: © Collection of the Supreme Court of the United States, Photographer: Steve Petteway.

CHAPTER 4

Opener: © Westend61 GmbH/Alamy; p.93: © AP Images/Paul Sakuma; p.102: © Purestock/Getty Images RF; p.103 (Left): © Denis Doyle/Bloomberg via Getty Images; p.103 (Right) © AP Images/Craig Ruttle; p.105: © Collection of the Supreme Court of the United States.

CHAPTER 5

Opener: © Exactostock/SuperStock RF; p.132: © Collection of the Supreme Court of the United States; p.135: © Collection of the Supreme Court of the United States, Photographer: Steve Petteway.

CHAPTER 6

Opener: © Library of Congress, Prints and Photographs Division [LC-DIG-highsm-12945]; p.161: © Jerome Wilson/Alamy; p.163: © AP Images; p.164: © Collection of the Supreme Court of the United States, Photographer: Steve Petteway; p.167: © Collection of the Supreme Court of the United States; p.172: © Collection of the Supreme Court of the United States, Photographer: Steve Petteway.

CHAPTER 7

Opener: © amygdala_imagery/Getty Images RF.

CHAPTER 8

Opener: © eccolo74/Getty Images RF.

CHAPTER 9

Opener: © Robert Daly/Getty Images RF.

CHAPTER 10

Opener: © Nico Hermann/Getty Images RF.

CHAPTER 11

Opener: © John Foxx/Getty Images RF; p.342: © Collection of the Supreme Court of the United States.

CHAPTER 12

Opener: © Damien Te Whiu/Getty Images; p.353 (Left): © simple stock shots/Age fotostock; p.353 (Right): © i studio/Alamy ; p.353 (Bottom): © AP Photo/Frank Franklin II; p.356: © AP Images/dycj–Imaginechina; p.359: © HO/Reuters/Corbis; p.370: © Ulrich Baumgarten/Getty Images; p.371: © Collection of the Supreme Court of the United States, Photographer: Steve Petteway; p.374 (Top): © AP Images/Paul Sakuma; p.374 (Center): © James Leynse/Corbis; p.374 (Bottom): © Wendell Teodoro/WireImage/Getty Images.

CHAPTER 13

Opener: © Ivan Bliznetsov/ E+/Getty Images RF; p.381 (Left): © Bloomberg/Getty Images; p.381 (Right): © Bloomberg/Getty Images; p.381 (Bottom): © Spencer Platt/ Getty Images News/Getty Images; p.383: © James Leynse/Corbis News/Corbis; p.386: © Collection of the Supreme Court of the United States, Photographer: Steve Petteway; p.393: © Collection of the Supreme Court of the United States, Photographer: Steve Petteway; p.398 (Top Right): © Jeff Mitchell/ Reuters/Corbis; p.398 (Center Left): © Reuters/Corbis; p.398 (Center Right): © Dave Einsel/Getty Images News/Getty Images; p.399: © Stephen Lovekin/Getty Images Entertainment/ Getty Images; p.399 (Bottom Left): © MANDEL NGAN/AFP/Getty Images; p.399 (Bottom Right): © Justin Sullivan/Getty Images News/Getty Images.

CHAPTER 14

Opener: © XiXinXing/Getty Images RF; p.436: © Collection of the Supreme Court of the United States, Photographer: Steve Petteway.

CHAPTER 15

Opener: © Chris Ryan/AGE Fotostock RF; p.451: © Collection of the Supreme Court of the United States, Photographer: Steve Petteway; p.459: © Library of Congress Prints and Photographs Division/Sven Manguard.

CHAPTER 16

Opener: © Library of Congress Prints and Photographs Division [LC-DIG-highsm-09920]; p.483: © Collection of the Supreme Court of the United States, Photographer: Steve Petteway.

CHAPTER 17

Opener: © vichie81/iStock/360/Getty Images RF; p.518: © Collection of the Supreme Court of the United States; p.523: © Collection of the Supreme Court of the United States; p.526: © Collection of the Supreme Court of the United States, Photographer: Steve Petteway; p.533: © Collection of the Supreme Court of the United States, Photographer: Steve Petteway.

CHAPTER 18

Opener: © TARIK KIZILKAYA/iStock/360/Getty Images RF; p.564 © Collection of the Supreme Court of the United States; p.569 © Collection of the Supreme Court of the United States, Photographer: Steve Petteway.

CHAPTER 19

Opener: © U.S. Coast Guard; p.582: © AP Photos; p.589: © Collection of the Supreme Court of the United States, Photographer: Steve Petteway. p.599: © Collection of the Supreme Court of the United States, Photographer: Steve Petteway

CHAPTER 20

Opener: © Wavebreakmedia Ltd/Getty Images RF; p.620: © Collection of the Supreme Court of the United States; p.623: © Collection of the Supreme Court of the United States; p.626 (left): © Justin Sullivan/Getty Images News/Getty Images; p.643 (Right): © Scott Olson/Getty Images News/Getty Images; p.643: © Lucy Nicholson/Reuters.

CHAPTER 21

Opener: © DNY59/Getty Images; p.656: © Collection of the Supreme Court of the United States; p.658: © Collection of the Supreme Court of the United States, Photographer: Steve Petteway; p.665: © Collection of the Supreme Court of the United States.

CHAPTER 22

Opener: © Susan See; p.705: AP Images/Bebeto Matthews.

index

O

P

Q